Contents

Chapter 17

THE EMERGENCE OF THE EUROPEAN STATE SYSTEM 479

Chapter 18

THE WEALTH OF NATIONS 515

Chapter 19

THE AGE OF ENLIGHTENMENT 541

VOLUME II:
SINCE THE SIXTEENTH CENTURY

THE WESTERN EXPERIENCE

Tenth Edition

MORTIMER CHAMBERS
University of California, Los Angeles

BARBARA HANAWALT
The Ohio State University

THEODORE K. RABB
Princeton University

ISSER WOLOCH
Columbia University

LISA TIERSTEN
Barnard College

Mc Graw Hill

Connect
Learn
Succeed™

Published by McGraw-Hill, an imprint of The McGraw-Hill Companies, Inc., 1221 Avenue of the Americas, New York, NY 10020. Copyright © 2010, 2007, 2003, 1999, 1995, 1991, 1987, 1983, 1979, 1974. All rights reserved. No part of this publication may be reproduced or distributed in any form or by any means, or stored in a database or retrieval system, without the prior written consent of The McGraw-Hill Companies, Inc., including, but not limited to, in any network or other electronic storage or transmission, or broadcast for distance learning.

This book is printed on acid-free paper.

1 2 3 4 5 6 7 8 9 0 DOW/DOW 0 9

ISBN: 978-0-07-729116-7
MHID: 0-07-729116-6

Vice President, Editorial: *Michael Ryan*
Publisher: *Christopher Freitag*
Sponsoring Editor: *Matthew Busbridge*
Managing Editor: *Nicole Bridge*
Marketing Manager: *Pamela Cooper*
Developmental Editor: *Denise Wright*
Production Editor: *Regina Ernst*
Manuscript Editor: *Barbara Hacha*
Design Manager: *Allister Fein*
Photo Research Coordinator: *Alexandra Ambrose*
Photo Researchers: *Deborah Bull & Jullie Chung*
Production Supervisor: *Louis Swaim*
Composition: *9.5/12 Trump Mediaeval by Aptara®, Inc.*
Printing: *45# New Era Matte Thin Bulk, R. R. Donnelley & Sons*

Cover: © The Palma Collection/Photodisc/Getty Images

Credits: The credits section for this book begins on page C-1 and is considered an extension of the copyright page.

Library of Congress Cataloging-in-Publication Data

The Western experience/Mortimer Chambers ... [et al.].—10th ed.
 p. cm.
 Includes bibliographical references and index.
 ISBN-13: 978-0-07-729116-7 (acid-free paper)
 ISBN-10: 0-07-729116-6 (alk. paper)
 1. Civilization—History. 2. Civilization, Western—History. I. Chambers, Mortimer.
CB59.W38 2009
909′.09821—dc22

                2009034534

The Internet addresses listed in the text were accurate at the time of publication. The inclusion of a Web site does not indicate an endorsement by the authors or McGraw-Hill, and McGraw-Hill does not guarantee the accuracy of the information presented at these sites.

www.mhhe.com

About the Authors

Mortimer Chambers is Professor of History at the University of California at Los Angeles. He was a Rhodes Scholar from 1949 to 1952 and received an M.A. from Wadham College, Oxford, in 1955 after obtaining his doctorate from Harvard University in 1954. He has taught at Harvard University (1954–1955) and the University of Chicago (1955–1958). He was Visiting Professor at the University of British Columbia in 1958, the State University of New York at Buffalo in 1971, the University of Freiburg (Germany) in 1974, and Vassar College in 1988. A specialist in Greek and Roman history, he is coauthor of *Aristotle's History of Athenian Democracy* (1962), editor of a series of essays entitled *The Fall of Rome* (1963), and author of *Georg Busolt: His Career in His Letters* (1990) and of *Staat der Athener*, a German translation and commentary to Aristotle's *Constitution of the Athenians* (1990). He has edited Greek texts of the latter work (1986) and of the *Hellenica Oxyrhynchia* (1993). He has contributed articles to the *American Historical Review* and *Classical Philology* as well as to other journals, both in America and in Europe. He is also an editor of *Historia*, the international journal of ancient history.

Barbara Hanawalt holds the King George III Chair of British History at The Ohio State University and is the author of numerous books and articles on the social and cultural history of the Middle Ages. Her publications include *The Middle Ages: An Illustrated History* (1999), *'Of Good and Ill Repute': Gender and Social Control in Medieval England* (1998), *Growing Up in Medieval London: The Experience of Childhood in History* (1993), *The Ties That Bound: Peasant Life in Medieval England* (1986), and *Crime and Conflict in English Communities, 1300–1348* (1979). She received her M.A. in 1964 and her Ph.D. in 1970, both from the University of Michigan. She has served as president of the Social Science History Association and the Medieval Academy of America and has been on the Council of the American Historical Association and the Medieval Academy of America. She was a fellow of the Netherlands Institute for Advanced Study (2005–2006), a fellow of the Guggenheim Foundation (1998–1999), an ACLS Fellow in 1975–1976, a fellow at the National Humanities Center (1997–1998), a fellow at the Wissenschaftskolleg in Berlin (1990–1991), a member of the School of Historical Research at the Institute for Advanced Study, and a senior research fellow at the Newberry Library in 1979–1980.

Theodore K. Rabb is Emeritus Professor of History at Princeton University. He received his Ph.D. from Princeton in 1961 and subsequently taught at Stanford, Northwestern, Harvard, and Johns Hopkins universities. He is the author of numerous articles and reviews in journals such as *The New York Times* and the *Times Literary Supplement*, and he has been editor of *The Journal of Interdisciplinary History* since its foundation. Among his books are *The Struggle for Stability in Early Modern Europe* (1975), *Renaissance Lives* (1993), *Jacobean Gentleman* (1999), and *The Last Days of the Renaissance & the March to Modernity* (2006). He has won awards from the Guggenheim Foundation, the National Endowment for the Humanities, the American Historical Association, and the National Council for History Education. He was the principal historian for the PBS series *Renaissance*, which was nominated for an Emmy.

Isser Woloch is Moore Collegiate Professor of History at Columbia University. He received his Ph.D. (1965) from Princeton University in the field of eighteenth- and nineteenth-century European history. He has taught at Indiana University and at the University of California at Los Angeles, where, in 1967, he received a Distinguished Teaching Citation. He has been a fellow of the ACLS, the National Endowment for the Humanities, the Guggenheim Foundation, and the Institute for Advanced Study at Princeton. His publications include *Jacobin Legacy: The Democratic Movement under the Directory* (1970), *The Peasantry in the Old Regime: Conditions and Protests* (1970), *The French Veteran from the Revolution to the Restoration* (1979), *Eighteenth-Century Europe: Tradition and Progress, 1715–1789* (1982), *The New Regime: Transformations of the French Civic Order, 1789–1820s* (1994), *Revolution and the Meanings of Freedom in the Nineteenth Century* (1996), and *Napoleon and His Collaborators: The Making of a Dictatorship* (2001).

Lisa Tiersten is Professor of History at Barnard College, Columbia University. She received her Ph.D. (1992) at Yale University and has taught at Wellesley College and Barnard College. She has been the recipient of a Chateaubriand Fellowship, a French Historical Studies Society Fellowship, and a Getty Fellowship. She also received the Emily Gregory Teaching Award at Barnard College in 1996. Her publications include *Marianne in the Market: Envisioning Consumer Society in Fin-de-Siècle Francé* (Berkeley: University of California Press, 2001).

She is currently at work on a history of bankruptcy and credit in modern France, entitled *Sentimental Modernity: Business Culture in Nineteenth-Century France;* is coauthoring a comparative history of children's rights, entitled *The Child, the Family, and the State in Sweden, France, and the U.S.;* and is working on an edited volume on the comparative history of children's rights in twentieth-century Europe. Her research interests include modern France, gender, consumer culture, empire, and the comparative culture of capitalism.

This book is dedicated to the memory of David Herlihy, whose erudition and judgment were central to its creation and whose friendship and example continue to inspire his coauthors.

Brief Contents

Chapter 23

STAGES AND NATIONS IN THE NINETEENTH CENTURY, 1830–1870 663

Chapter 24

PROGRESS AND ITS DISCONTENTS 697

Chapter 25

NINETEENTH-CENTURY EMPIRES 731

Chapter 29

EUROPE IN THE POSTWAR ERA 885

Chapter 30

EUROPE IN THE GLOBAL ERA 913

Maps

Boxes

Primary Source Boxes

Historical Issues Boxes

Chronological Boxes

Global Moment Boxes

Preface

When *The Western Experience* was originally conceived, we sought to write a textbook that would introduce students to the growing field of social history and exciting new ways of thinking about history. We wanted the textbook not merely to set forth information but to serve as an example of historical writing. That means we cared a lot about the quality of the writing itself and also that we wanted the chapters to be examples of a historical essay that set up a historical problem and developed arguments about that problem using historical evidence. We also recognized that for American students the Western Civilization textbook needed to provide an overview of that civilization, giving students an introduction to the major achievements in Western thought, art, and science as well as the social, political, and economic context for understanding them. And lastly, we were determined that our book would treat all these various aspects of history in an integrated way. Too many books, we felt, dealt with cultural or social change entirely separately, even in separate chapters, and we sought to demonstrate and exemplify the connections. To that end, *The Western Experience* is designed to provide an analytical and reasonably comprehensive account of the contexts within which, and the processes by which, European society and civilization evolved.

Now in its tenth edition, *The Western Experience* has continued its evolution. Throughout, this edition has incorporated new scholarship while maintaining its thematic approach. The ninth edition's Chapters 22, 23, and 24 have now been compressed and reorganized into new Chapters 22 and 23. These new chapters describe the early nineteenth century, with a special focus on industrialization and its effects, in a more streamlined fashion. New Chapter 28, which covers World War II, has been reorganized to meet that same goal. New Chapter 29, devoted to Europe in the postwar era, expands the ninth edition's discussion of the topic to include a crucial examination of Americanization and decolonization. An entirely new Chapter 30, "Europe in the Global Era," addresses contemporary issues, including transnational and unity trends, postcolonial immigration issues, and economic globalization.

EXPERIENCING HISTORY

Everyone uses history. We use it to define who we are and to connect our personal experience to the collective memory of the groups to which we belong, including a particular region, nation, and culture. We invoke the past to explain our hopes and ambitions and to justify our fears and conflicts. The Charter of the United Nations, like the American Declaration of Independence, is based on a view of history. When workers strike or armies march, they cite the lessons of their history. Because history is so important to us psychologically and intellectually, historical understanding is always shifting and often controversial.

Historical knowledge is cumulative. Historians may ask many of the same questions about different periods of history or raise new questions or issues; they integrate the answers, and historical knowledge grows. The study of history cannot be a subjective exercise in which all opinions are equally valid. Regardless of the impetus for a particular historical question, the answer to it stands until overturned by better evidence. We now know more about the past than ever before, and we understand it as the people we study could not. Unlike them, we know the outcome of their history; we can apply methods they did not have, and often we have evidence they never saw.

Humans have always found pleasure in the reciting and reading of history. The poems about the fall of Troy or the histories of Herodotus and Thucydides entertained the ancient Greeks. The biographies of great men and women, dramatic accounts of important events, colorful tales of earlier times can be fascinating in themselves. Through these encounters with history we experience the common concerns of all people; and through the study of European history, we come to appreciate the ideals and conflicts, the failures and accidents, the social needs and human choices that formed the Western world in which we live. Knowing the historical context also enriches our appreciation for the achievements of European culture, enabling us to see its art, science, ideas, and politics in relationship to real people, specific interests, and burning issues.

We think of Europe's history as the history of Western civilization because the Greeks gave the names east and west to the points on the horizon at which the sun rises and sets. Because the Persian Empire and India lay to their east, the Greeks labeled their own continent, which they called Europe, the west. However, we need to be cautious about the view that Western civilization is a united whole, entirely distinct from other civilizations, except perhaps in its cultural development. We will see many occasions when a larger context is appropriate.

The Western Experience thus gives primary attention to a small part of the world and honors a particular cultural tradition. Yet the concentration on Europe does allow us to explore contrasts of worldwide significance: between city and rural life; among empires and monarchies and republics; in life before and after industrialization; among societies that organized labor through markets, serfdom, and slavery; between cultures little concerned with science and those that used changing scientific knowledge; among different ways of creating and experiencing forms of literature and the arts; and among Christian and non-Christian religions and all the major forms of Christianity.

A college course alone cannot create an educated citizen. Moreover, Western history is not the only history a person should know, and an introductory survey is not necessarily the best way to learn it. Yet, as readers consider and then challenge interpretations offered in this text, they will exercise critical and analytical skills. They can begin to overcome the parochialism that attributes importance only to the present. To learn to think critically about historical evidence and know how to formulate an argument on the bases of this evidence is to experience the study of history as one of the vital intellectual activities by which we come to know who and where we are.

A Balanced, Interpretive, and Flexible Approach

At the same time, we recognize that the professional scholar's preference for new perspectives over familiar ones makes a distinction that students may not share. For them, the latest interpretations need to be integrated with established understandings and controversies, with the history of people and events that are part of our cultural lore. We recognize that a textbook should provide a coherent presentation of the basic information from which students can begin to form their historical understanding. We believe this information must be part of an interpretive history but also that its readers—teachers, students, and general readers—should

be free to use it in many ways and in conjunction with their own areas of special knowledge and their own interests and curiosity.

Use of Themes

Throughout this book, from the treatment of the earliest civilizations to the discussion of the present, we pursue certain key themes. These seven themes constitute a set of categories by which societies and historical change can be analyzed.

Social Structure In early chapters, social structure involves how the land was settled, divided among its inhabitants, and put to use. Later discussions of how property is held must include corporate, communal, and individual ownership, then investment banking and companies that sell shares. Similarly, in each era we treat the division of labor, noting whether workers are slave or free, male or female, and when there are recognized specialists in fighting or crafts or trade. The chapters covering the ancient world, the Middle Ages, and the early modern period explore social hierarchies that include nobles, clergy, commoners, and slaves or serfs; the treatments of the French Revolution, the Industrial Revolution, and twentieth-century societies analyze modern social classes.

The Body Politic Another theme we analyze throughout this book is what used to be called the body politic. Each era contains discussions of how political power is acquired and used and of the political structures that result. Students learn about the role of law from ancient codes to the present, as well as problems of order, and the formation of governments, including why government functions have increased and political participation of the population has changed.

Technology From cultivation in the plains of the Tigris and Euphrates to the global economy, we follow changes in the organization of production and in the impact of technology. We note how goods are distributed, and we observe patterns of trade as avenues of cultural exchange in addition to wealth. We look at the changing economic role of governments and the impact of economic theories.

Gender Roles and Family The evolution of the family and changing gender roles are topics fundamental to every historical period. Families give form to daily life and kinship structures. The history of demography, migration, and work is also a history of the family. The family has always been a central focus of social organization and religion, as well as the principal instrument by which societies assign specific practices, roles, and values to women and men. Gender roles have changed from era to era, differing according to social class and between rural and urban societies. Observing gender roles across time, the student discovers that social, political, economic, and cultural history are always interrelated; that the present is related to the past; and that social change brings gains and losses rather than evolution in a straight line—three lessons all history courses teach.

War   No history of Europe could fail to pay attention to war, which, for most polities, has been their most demanding activity. Warfare has strained whatever resources were available from ancient times to the present, leading governments to invent new ways to extract wealth and mobilize support. War has built and undermined states, stimulated science and consumed technology, made heroes, and restructured nobility, schooling, and social services. Glorified in European culture and often condemned, war in every era has affected the lives of all its peoples. This historical significance, more than specific battles, is one of the themes of *The Western Experience*.

Religion   Religion has been basic to the human experience, and our textbook explores the different religious institutions and experiences that societies developed. Religion affects and is affected by all the themes we address, creating community and causing conflict, shaping intellectual and daily life, providing the experiences that bind individual lives and society within a common system of meaning.

Cultural Expression   For authors of a general history, no decision is more difficult than the space devoted to cultural expression. In this respect, as elsewhere, we have striven for a balance between high and popular culture. We present as clearly and concisely as possible the most important formal ideas, philosophies, and ideologies of each era. We emphasize concepts of recognized importance in the general history of ideas and those concepts that illuminate behavior and discourse in a given period. We pay particular attention to developments in science that we believe are related to important intellectual, economic, and social trends. Popular culture appears both in specific sections and throughout the book. We want to place popular culture within its social and historical context but not make the gulf too wide between popular and high or formal culture. Finally, we write about many of the great works of literature, art, architecture, and music. Because of the difficulties of selection, we have tried to emphasize works that are cultural expressions of their time but that

also have been influential over the ages and around the globe.

Attention to these seven themes occasions problems of organization and selection. We could have structured this book around a series of topical essays, perhaps repeating the series of themes for each of the standard chronological divisions of European history. Instead, we chose to preserve a narrative flow that emphasizes interrelationships and historical context. We wanted each chapter to stand as an interpretive historical essay, with a beginning and conclusion. As a result, the themes emerge repeatedly within discussions of a significant event, an influential institution, an individual life, or a whole period of time. Or they may intersect in a single institution or historical trend. Nevertheless, readers can follow any one of these themes across time and use that theme as a measure of change and a way to assess the differences and similarities between societies.

CHANGES TO THE TENTH EDITION

For us the greatest pleasure in a revision lies in the challenge of absorbing and then incorporating the latest developments in historical understanding. From its first edition, this book included more of the results of quantitative and social history than most general textbooks of European history, an obvious reflection of our own research. Each subsequent edition provided an occasion to incorporate current methods and new knowledge, such as the rise of gender studies: a challenge that required reconsidering paragraphs, sections, and whole chapters in the light of new theories and new research, sometimes literally reconceptualizing part of the past.

New Chapter 22: "Foundations of Nineteenth Century Europe" and Chapter 23: "States and Nations in the Nineteenth Century, 1830–1870"

From the previous edition, Chapters 22, 23, and 24 have been compressed into new Chapters 22 and 23. These new condensed chapters have made the discussion of the early nineteenth-century more thematically coherent, especially in regard to industrialization and its effects.

New Chapter 28: "The Nightmare: World War II" and Chapter 29: "Europe in the Postwar Era"

In the tenth edition, Chapter 28 has been streamlined for better understanding and emphasis. In new Chapter 29, we have expanded the previous ninth edition discussion of postwar Europe while incorporating critical new scholarship to provide a comprehensive treatment of the period. This revision addresses the postwar Americanization of Europe and adds a completely new and much-amplified section on decolonization.

New Chapter 30: "Europe in the Global Era"

This timely new chapter takes on the issues in contemporary history, including such topics as transnational and unity trends in Europe, postcolonial immigration issues in Europe, and Europe and economic globalization. By increasing the amount of scholarship on contemporary Europe included in *The Western Experience*, the tenth edition contains original and hard-hitting material on the global dimensions of European history.

PEDAGOGICAL FEATURES

Each generation of students brings different experiences, interests, and training into the classroom—changes that are important to the teaching-learning process. The students we teach have taught us what engages or confuses them, what impression of European history they bring to college, and what they can be expected to take from a survey course. Current political, social, and cultural events also shape what we teach and how we teach. Our experience as teachers and the helpful comments of scores of other teachers have led to revisions and new additions throughout the book as we have sought to make it clearer and more accessible without sacrificing our initial goal of writing a reasonably sophisticated, interpretive, and analytic history.

Primary Source Boxes

These excerpts from primary sources are designed to illustrate or supplement points made in the text, to provide some flavor of the issues under discussion, and to allow beginning students some of that independence of judgment that comes from a careful reading of historical sources.

Historical Issues Boxes

These boxes explain major controversies over historical interpretations so that students can see how historical understanding is constructed. They encourage students to participate in these debates and formulate their own positions.

Global Moment Boxes

These boxes focus on particularly vivid occasions when Europeans encountered other world civilizations, in order to suggest the broader context within which Western history unfolded.

Chapter-Opening Timelines

Each chapter opens with a new timeline. These timelines are meant to offer students a visual aid with which to track simultaneous developments and important dates to remember. Ultimately, we hope that they will help give readers a grounded sense of chronology.

Chapter-Opening Outlines

Each chapter opens with a short outline to give students a sense of what's to come in each chapter.

Glossary and Key Terms

Glossary words are bolded in each chapter and compiled in the end-of-book glossary.

The Art

The tenth edition of *The Western Experience* continues the precedent of earlier editions, with more than four hundred full-color reproductions of paintings and photographs and over one hundred clearly focused maps.

The Maps

The maps in *The Western Experience* are already much admired by instructors. Each carries an explanatory caption that enhances the text coverage to help students tackle the content without sacrificing subtlety of interpretation or trying to escape the fact that history is complex. Each caption is enhanced with a thought question.

Questions for Further Thought

To encourage students to move beyond rote learning of historical "facts" and to think broadly about history, the authors have added "Questions for Further Thought" at the end of each chapter. These are too broad to be exam questions; instead, they are meant to be questions that stimulate the students to think about history and social, political, and economic forces. Some are comparative, some require students to draw on knowledge of a previous chapter, some ask about the role of great leaders in politics, and some ask about how the less famous people living at the time perceived the events surrounding them.

Heading Levels

We have given particular attention to descriptive content guides, such as the consistent use of three levels of headings. We believe these will help students identify specific topics for purposes of study and review as well as give a clear outline of a chapter's argument.

Chronological Charts

Nearly every chapter employs charts and chronological tables that outline the unfolding of major events and social processes and serve as a convenient reference for students.

AVAILABLE FORMATS

To provide an alternative to the full-length hardcover edition, *The Western Experience*, tenth edition, is available in a two-volume edition.

- Volume I includes chapters 1–17 and covers material through the eighteenth century.
- Volume II includes chapters 15–30 and covers material since the sixteenth century.

SUPPLEMENTARY INSTRUCTIONAL MATERIALS

McGraw-Hill offers instructors and students a variety of ancillary materials to accompany *The Western Experience*. Please contact your local McGraw-Hill representative for details concerning policies, prices, and availability.

Online Learning Center for Instructors   At www.mhhe.com/chambers10. At this home page for the text-specific Web site, instructors will find a series of online tools to meet a wide range of classroom needs. The Instructor's Manual, PowerPoint presentations, and blank maps can be downloaded by instructors, but are password protected to prevent tampering. Instructors can also create an interactive course syllabus using McGraw-Hill's *PageOut* (www.mhhe.com/pageout).

McGraw-Hill's Primary Source Investigator (PSI) Now online at www.mhhe.com/psi, PSI is designed to support and enrich the text discussion in *The Western Experience*. It gives instructors and students access to hundreds of primary and secondary sources, including documents, images, maps, and videos, keyed to each chapter of *The Western Experience*. Students can use these resources to formulate and defend their arguments and as a study tool to further their understanding of the topics discussed in each chapter. All assets are also indexed by type, subject place, and time period, allowing students and instructors to locate resources quickly and easily.

The Online Learning Center   At www.mhhe.com/chambers10. The Online Learning Center is a fully interactive, book-specific Web site featuring numerous student study tools such as multiple-choice practice quizzes, interactive maps, an essay quiz, problems for analysis, chapter outlines, and chapter overviews.

ACKNOWLEDGMENTS

Manuscript Reviewers, Tenth Edition

Lars R. Jones, Florida Institute of Technology; Mark Micale, University of Illinois; Shannon O'Bryan, Greenville Technical College; Geraldine Ryder, Ocean County College; Linda Wilke Heil, Central Community College.

Manuscript Reviewers, Ninth Edition

Robert Bast, University of Tennessee; Stephen Blumm, Montgomery County Community College; Nathan Brooks, New Mexico State University; Susan Carrafiello, Wright State University; Steven Fanning, University of Illinois at Chicago; Betsy Hertzler, Mesa Community College; Paul Hughes, Sussex County Community College; Mary Kelly, Franklin Pierce College; Paul Lockhart, Wright State University; Eileen Moore, University of Alabama at Birmingham; Penne Prigge, Rockingham Community College; William Roberts, Fairleigh Dickinson University; Steven Ross, Louisiana State University; Charles Sullivan, University of Dallas; Robert Thurston, Miami University.

THE WESTERN
EXPERIENCE

Francois Dubois

THE MASSACRE OF ST. BARTHOLOMEW'S DAY

Although it makes no attempt to depict the massacre realistically, this painting by a Protestant does convey the horrors of religious war. As the victims are hanged, disemboweled, decapitated, tossed from windows, bludgeoned, shot, or drowned, their bodies and homes are looted. Dubois may have intended the figure dressed in widow's black and pointing at a pile of corpses near the river at the back to be a portrait of Catherine de Medici, who many thought inspired the massacre.

Musée Cantonal des Beaux-Arts, Lausanne

Chapter Fifteen

WAR AND CRISIS

RIVALRY AND WAR IN THE AGE OF PHILIP II • FROM UNBOUNDED WAR TO
INTERNATIONAL CRISIS • THE MILITARY REVOLUTION • REVOLUTION IN ENGLAND •
REVOLTS IN FRANCE AND SPAIN • POLITICAL CHANGE IN AN AGE OF CRISIS

In the wake of the rapid and bewildering changes of the early sixteenth century—the Reformation, the rises in population and prices, the overseas discoveries, and the dislocations caused by the activities of the new monarchs—Europe entered a period of fierce upheaval. So many radical alterations were taking place that conflict became inevitable. There were revolts against monarchs, often led by nobles who saw their power dwindling. The poor launched hopeless rebellions against their social superiors. And the two religious camps struggled relentlessly to destroy each other. From Scotland to Russia, the century following the Reformation, from about 1560 to 1660, was dominated by warfare; and the constant military activity had widespread effects on politics, economics, society, and thought. The fighting, in fact, helped bring to an end the long process

whereby Europe came to terms with the revolutions that had begun about 1500. As we will see, two distinct periods of ever more destructive warfare—the age of Philip II from the 1550s to the 1590s, and the age of the Thirty Years' War from the 1610s to the 1640s, with a decade of uneasy peace in between—led to a vast crisis of authority throughout Europe in the mid-1600s. From the struggles of that crisis there emerged fundamental economic, political, social, and religious changes, as troubled Europeans at last found ways to accept their altered circumstances. Interestingly, there were peasant revolts in Russia and China at the same time as those in western Europe in the mid-seventeenth century, and they, too, reflected unease with state power, which was growing in Russia, but declining in China as the Ming Dynasty came to an end.

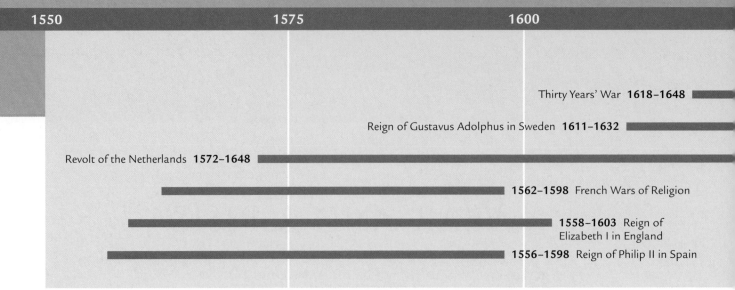

Thirty Years' War **1618–1648**

Reign of Gustavus Adolphus in Sweden **1611–1632**

Revolt of the Netherlands **1572–1648**

1562–1598 French Wars of Religion

1558–1603 Reign of
Elizabeth I in England

1556–1598 Reign of Philip II in Spain

RIVALRY AND WAR IN THE AGE OF PHILIP II

The wars that plagued Europe from the 1560s to the 1650s involved many issues, but religion was the burning motivation, the one that inspired fanatical devotion and the most vicious hatred. A deep conviction that heresy was dangerous to society and hateful to God made Protestants and Catholics treat one another brutally. Even the dead were not spared: Corpses were sometimes mutilated to emphasize how dreadful their sins had been. These emotions, which shaped politics in this period, especially the decades dominated by Philip II, gave the fighting a brutality unprecedented in European history.

Philip II of Spain

During the second half of the sixteenth century, international warfare was ignited by the leader of the Catholics, Philip II of Spain (r. 1556–1598), the most powerful monarch in Europe. A stern defender of the Catholic faith, who is looked back on by Spaniards as a model of prudence, self-discipline, and devotion, he was also a tireless administrator, building up and supervising a vast and complex bureaucracy. It was needed, he felt, because of the far-spreading territories he ruled: the Iberian Peninsula, much of Italy, the Netherlands, and a huge overseas empire. Yet his main concern was to overcome the two enemies of his church, the Muslims and the Protestants.

Against the Muslims in the Mediterranean area, Philip's campaigns seemed to justify the financial strains they caused. In particular, his naval victory over the Ottomans at Lepanto, off the Greek coast, in 1571 made him a Christian hero at the same time that it reduced Muslim power. Although the Ottomans remained a considerable force in the eastern half of the Mediterranean, and indeed were able to besiege Vienna again in 1683, Philip was unchallenged in the west. He dominated the rich Italian peninsula; in 1580 he inherited the kingdom of Portugal; and his overseas wealth, passing through Seville, made this the fastest-growing city in Europe. The sixteenth century was the last age in which the Mediterranean was the heart of the European economy, but its prosperity was still the chief pillar of Philip's power.

Farther north, Philip fared less well. He tried to prevent a Protestant, Henry IV, from inheriting the French crown and continued the fighting even though Henry converted to Catholicism. Philip's policy toward England and the Netherlands was similarly ineffective. After the Protestant Queen Elizabeth I came to the English throne in 1558, Philip remained uneasily cordial toward her for about ten years. But relations deteriorated as England's sailors and explorers threatened Philip's wealthy New World possessions. Worse, in 1585 Elizabeth began to help the Protestant Dutch, who were rebelling against Spanish rule. Though their countries were smaller than Spain, the English and Dutch were able to inflict on Philip the two chief setbacks of his reign; and in the years after his death they were to wrest the leadership of Europe's economy away from the Mediterranean.

Elizabeth I of England

In a struggle with Spain, England may have seemed an unlikely victor: a relatively poor kingdom that had lost its continental possessions and for some time had played a secondary role in European affairs. Yet its

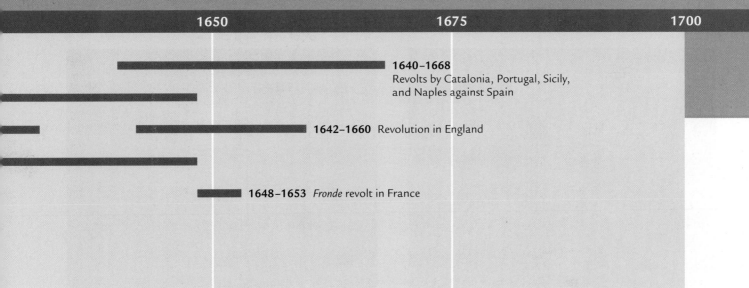

1640–1668
Revolts by Catalonia, Portugal, Sicily, and Naples against Spain

1642–1660 Revolution in England

1648–1653 *Fronde* revolt in France

people were united by such common bonds as the institution of Parliament and a commitment to the international Protestant cause that was carefully promoted by Queen Elizabeth I (r. 1558–1603).

Elizabeth is an appealing figure because she combined shrewd hardheadedness with a disarming appearance of frailty. Her qualities were many: her dedication to the task of government; her astute choice of advisers; her civilizing influence at court, where she encouraged elegant manners and the arts; her tolerance of religious dissent as long as it posed no political threat; and her ability to feel the mood of her people, to catch their spirit, to inspire their enthusiasm. Although social, legal, and economic practices usually subordinated women to men in this age, inheritance was respected; thus, a determined woman with a recognized claim to authority could win complete acceptance. Elizabeth was the most widely admired and most successful queen of her time, but she was by no means alone; female rulers also shaped the histories of France, Sweden, and the southern Netherlands in the sixteenth and seventeenth centuries.

Royal Policy Elizabeth could be indecisive, notably where the succession was concerned. Her refusal to marry caused serious uncertainties, and it was only the shrewd planning of her chief minister, Robert Cecil, that enabled the king of Scotland, James Stuart, to succeed her without incident in 1603. Similar dangers arose from her indecisive treatment of England's remaining Catholics. They hoped that Mary Queen of Scots, a Catholic, would inherit the throne; and since she was next in line, they were not above plotting against Elizabeth's life. Eventually, in 1587, Elizabeth had Mary executed and the plots died away. Despite her reluctance to take firm positions, Elizabeth showed great

skill in balancing policy alternatives, and her adroit maneuvering assured her of her ministers' loyalty at all times. She also inspired the devotion of her subjects by traveling throughout England to make public appearances; by delivering brilliant speeches (see "Queen Elizabeth's Armada Speech," p. 423); and by shaping her own image, even regulating how she was to be depicted in portraits. She thus retained her subjects' allegiance despite the profound social changes that were eroding traditional patterns of deference and order. England's nobility, for instance, no longer dominated the military and the government; nearly all Elizabeth's ministers were new in national life; and the House of Commons was beginning to exert more political influence within Parliament than the House of Lords. All groups in English society, however, shared a resentment of Spanish power, and Elizabeth cultivated this sentiment astutely as a patriotic and Protestant cause.

The Dutch Revolt

The same cause united the people living in the provinces in the Netherlands that Philip inherited from his father, the Emperor Charles V. Here his single-minded promotion of Catholicism and royal power provoked a fierce reaction that grew into a successful struggle for independence: the first major victory in western Europe by subjects resisting royal authority.

Causes of Revolt The original focus of opposition was Philip's reorganization of the ecclesiastical structure so as to gain control over the country's Catholic Church, a change that deprived the aristocracy of important patronage. At the same time, the **billeting** of troops aroused the resentment of ordinary citizens. In this situation, the local nobles, led by William of Orange,

El Greco
THE DREAM OF PHILIP II, 1578
Characteristic of the mystical vision of El Greco is this portrayal of the devout, black-clad figure of Philip II. Kneeling alongside the doge of Venice and the pope, his allies in the victory of Lepanto over the Turks, Philip adores the blazing name of Jesus that is surrounded by angels in heaven, and he turns his back on the gaping mouth to hell.
By courtesy of the Trustees, © The National Gallery, London (NG6260)/Art Resource, NY

William Segar (attrib.)
PORTRAIT OF ELIZABETH I, 1585
Elizabeth I was strongly aware of the power of propaganda, and she used it to foster a dazzling public image. Legends about her arose in literature. And in art she had herself portrayed in the most elaborate finery imaginable. Here, she is every inch the queen, with her magnificent dress, the trappings of monarchy, and the symbol of virginity, the ermine.
By courtesy of The Marquess of Salisbury

warned of mass disorder, but Philip kept up the pressure: He put the Inquisition to work against the Calvinists, who had begun to appear in the Netherlands, and also summoned the Jesuits to combat the heretics. These moves were disastrous because they further undermined local autonomy and made the Protestants bitter enemies of the king.

Philip's aggressiveness provoked violence in 1566. Although the Protestants were still a tiny minority, they formed mobs in a number of cities, assaulted Catholics, and sacked churches. In response, Philip tightened the pressure, appointing as governor the ruthless duke of Alba, who used his Spanish troops to suppress opposition. Protestants were hanged in public, rebel groups were hunted down, and two nobles who had been guilty of nothing worse than demanding that Philip change his policy were executed.

Full-Scale Rebellion Organized revolt broke out in 1572, when a small group of Dutch sailors flying the flag of William of Orange seized the fishing village of Brill, on the North Sea. The success of these "sea beggars," as the Spaniards called them, stimulated uprisings in towns throughout the Low Countries. The banner of William of Orange became the symbol of resistance, and under his leadership full-scale rebellion erupted. By 1576, when Philip's troops mutinied and rioted in Antwerp, sixteen

QUEEN ELIZABETH'S ARMADA SPEECH

Elizabeth's ability to move her subjects was exemplified by the speech she gave to her troops as they awaited the fight with the Spanish Armada. She understood that they might have doubts about a woman leading them in war, but she turned that issue to her own advantage in a stirring cry to battle that enhanced her popularity at the time and her legendary image thereafter.

"My loving People: We have been persuaded by some that are careful of our safety, to take heed how we commit ourselves to armed multitudes, for fear of treachery; but I assure you, I do not desire to live to distrust my faithful and loving people.

"Let tyrants fear; I have always so behaved myself, that, under God, I have placed my chiefest strength and safeguard in the loyal hearts and good will of my subjects, and therefore I am come amongst you, as you see, at this time, not for my recreation . . . but being resolved in the midst and heat of the battle, to live or die amongst you all, to lay down for my God, and for my kingdoms, and for my people, my honour and my blood, even in the dust.

"I know I have the body of a weak and feeble woman; but I have the heart and stomach of a king, and of a king of England too; and think foul scorn that . . . Spain, or any prince of Europe should dare to invade the borders of my realm; to which rather than any dishonour shall grow by me, I myself will take up arms, I myself will be your general, judge, and rewarder of every one of your virtues in the field. . . . By your concord in the camp, and your valour in the field, we shall shortly have a famous victory over those enemies of my God, of my kingdoms, and of my people."

Walter Scott (ed.), *A Collection of Scarce and Valuable Tracts, on the Most Interesting and Entertaining Subjects: But Chiefly Such as Relate to the History and Constitution of These Kingdoms*, Vol. 1, London, 1809, pp. 429–430.

Anonymous
ENGRAVING OF THE SPANIARDS IN HAARLEM
This engraving was published to arouse horror at Spanish atrocities during the Dutch revolt. As the caption indicates, after the Spanish troops (on the right) captured the city of Haarlem, there was a great bloodbath (*ein gross bluit batt*). Blessed by priests, the Haarlemites were decapitated or hung, and then tossed in a river so that the city would be cleansed of them. The caption states that even women and children were not spared.
New York Public Library

of the seventeen provinces in the Netherlands had united behind William. The next year, however, Philip offered a compromise to the Catholic nobles, and the ten southern provinces returned to Spanish rule.

The United Provinces   In 1579 the remaining seven provinces formed the independent United Provinces. Despite the assassination of William in 1584, they managed to resist Spain's army for decades, mainly because they could open dikes, flood their country, and thus drive the invaders back. Moreover, Philip was often diverted by other wars and, in any case, never placed total confidence in his commanders. The Calvinists formed the heart of the resistance; though still a minority, they had the most to lose, because they sought freedom for their religion as well as their country. William never showed strong religious commitments, but his son, Maurice of Nassau, a brilliant military commander who won a series of victories in the 1590s, embraced Calvinism and helped make it the country's official religion. Unable to make any progress, the Spaniards agreed to a twelve-year truce in 1609, but they did not recognize the independence of the United Provinces until the Peace of Westphalia in 1648.

The Armada   In 1588 Philip tried to end his troubles in northern Europe with one mighty blow. Furious that the English were interfering with his New World empire (their traders and raiders had been intruding into Spain's American colonies for decades) and that Elizabeth was helping Dutch Protestants, he sent a mammoth fleet—the Armada—to the Low Countries. Its task was to pick up a Spanish army, invade England, and thus undermine Protestant resistance. By this time, however, English mariners were among the best in the world, and their ships had greater maneuverability and firepower than did the Spaniards'. After several skirmishes in the Channel, the English set fire to a few of their own vessels with loaded cannons aboard and sent them drifting toward the Spanish ships, anchored off Calais. The Spaniards had to raise anchor in a hurry, and some of the fleet was lost. The next day the remaining Spanish ships retreated up the North Sea. The only way home was around Ireland; and wind, storms, and the pursuing English ensured that less than half the fleet returned safely to Spain. This shattering reversal was comparable in scale and unexpectedness only to Xerxes' disaster at Salamis more than two thousand years earlier. More than any other single event, it doomed Philip's ambitions in England, the Netherlands, and France and signaled a northward shift in power in Europe.

Civil War in France

The other major power of western Europe, France, was torn apart by religious war in this period, but it too felt

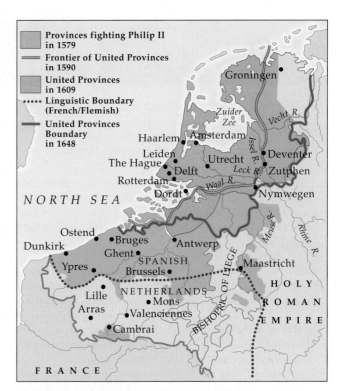

MAP 15.1 THE NETHERLANDS, 1579–1609
The seventeen provinces making up the Netherlands, or the Low Countries, were detached from the Holy Roman Empire when Charles V abdicated in 1556. As the map indicates, their subsequent division into two states was determined not by the linguistic differences between French-speaking people of the south and Dutch-speaking people of the north but rather by geography. The great river systems at the mouth of the Rhine eventually proved to be the barrier beyond which the Spaniards could not penetrate. Notice the shifting boundaries. Did the United Provinces gain more between 1590 and 1648 than they lost after 1579?

the effects of the Armada's defeat. By the 1550s Calvinism was gaining strength among French peasants and in the towns of the south and southwest, and its leaders had virtually created a small semi-independent state. To meet this threat, a great noble family, the Guises, assumed the leadership of the Catholics; in response, the Bourbons, another noble family, championed the Calvinists, about a twelfth of the population. Their struggle split the country apart.

It was ominous that in 1559—the year that Henry II, France's last strong king for a generation, died—the Calvinists (known in France as Huguenots) organized their first national synod, an indication of impressive strength. During the next thirty years, the throne was occupied by Henry's three ineffectual sons. The power behind the crown was Henry's widow, Catherine de Medici (see "The Kings of France in the Sixteenth Century," p. 425), who tried desperately to preserve royal

Anonymous
THE ARMADA
This depiction suggests the sheer splendor of the scene as Philip II's fleet sailed through the Channel on its way to invading England. The opposing ships were never this close, but the colorful flags (red cross English, yellow cross Spanish) and the elaborate coats of arms must have been dazzling. The firing cannon and the sinking ship remind us that, amidst the display, there was also death and destruction.
National Maritime Museum, Greenwich, London

THE KINGS OF FRANCE IN THE SIXTEENTH CENTURY

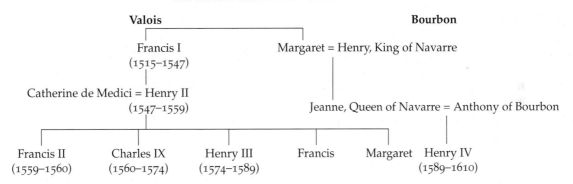

Valois   **Bourbon**

Francis I   Margaret = Henry, King of Navarre
(1515–1547)

Catherine de Medici = Henry II
(1547–1559)   Jeanne, Queen of Navarre = Anthony of Bourbon

Francis II   Charles IX   Henry III   Francis   Margaret   Henry IV
(1559–1560)   (1560–1574)   (1574–1589)   (1589–1610)

authority. But she was often helpless because the religious conflict intensified the factional struggle for power between the Guises and the Bourbons, both of whom were closely related to the monarchy and hoped one day to inherit the throne.

The Wars Fighting started in 1562 and lasted for thirty-six years, interrupted only by short-lived peace agreements. Catherine switched sides whenever one party became too powerful; and she may have approved the notorious massacre of St. Bartholomew's Day—August 24, 1572—which started in Paris, spread through France, and destroyed the Huguenots' leadership. Henry of Navarre, a Bourbon, was the only major figure who escaped. When Catherine switched sides again and made

peace with the Huguenots in 1576, the Guises formed the Catholic League, which for several years dominated the eastern half of the country. In 1584 the league allied with Spain's Philip II to attack heresy in France and deny the Bourbon Henry's legal right to inherit the throne.

The defeat of the Armada in 1588 proved to be the turning point in the French civil wars, for Spain could not continue helping the duke of Guise, who was soon assassinated, and within a few months Henry of Navarre inherited the throne as Henry IV (r. 1589–1610). He had few advantages as he began to reassert royal authority, because the Huguenots and Catholics ran almost independent governments in large sections of France. In addition, the royal administration was in a sorry state because the crown's oldest rivals, the great nobles,

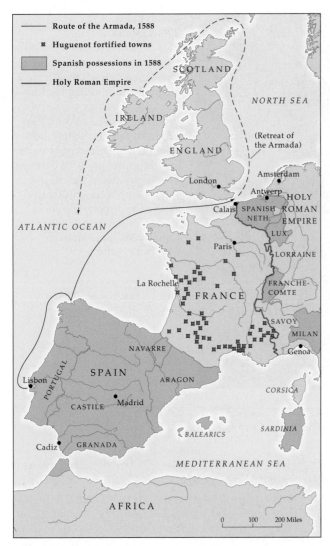

- — Route of the Armada, 1588
- ⊠ Huguenot fortified towns
- ▭ Spanish possessions in 1588
- — Holy Roman Empire

MAP 15.2 CATHOLIC AND PROTESTANT POWERS IN THE LATE SIXTEENTH CENTURY
The heart of the Catholic cause in the wars of religion was the Spain of Philip II. Spanish territories surrounded France and provided the route to the Netherlands, where the Protestant Dutch had rebelled against the Spaniards (see map 15.1). The Armada was launched to help that cause by crushing the ally of the Dutch, Protestant England. In the meantime, the surrounded French had problems of their own with the Huguenots, who protected their Protestantism in a network of fortified towns. Why did the Armada follow the route shown on the map?

could now resist all outside interference in their domains.

Peace Restored Yet largely because of the assassination of the duke of Guise, Henry IV was able to restore order. The duke had been a forceful leader and a serious contender for the throne. His replacement was a Spanish candidate for the crown who had little chance of success. The distaste for a possible foreign ruler, combined

with war weariness, destroyed much of the support for the Catholic League, which finally collapsed as a result of revolts against it in eastern France in the 1590s. These uprisings, founded on a demand for peace, increased in frequency and intensity after Henry IV renounced Protestantism in 1593 in order to win acceptance by his Catholic subjects. The following year Henry had himself officially crowned, and all of France rallied to the king as he beat back a Spanish invasion—Spain's final, rather weak, attempt to put its own candidate on the throne.

When Spain finally withdrew and signed a peace treaty in 1598, the fighting came to an end. To complete the reconciliation, Henry issued (also in 1598) the Edict of Nantes, which granted limited toleration to the Huguenots. Although it did not create complete religious liberty, the edict made Calvinist worship legal, protected the rights of the minority, and opened public office to Huguenots.

FROM UNBOUNDED WAR TO INTERNATIONAL CRISIS

During the half century after Philip II's death, warfare spread throughout Europe. There was a brief lull in the early 1600s, but then the slaughter and the devastations began to multiply. For a while it seemed that nothing could bring the fighting to an end, and a feeling of irresolvable crisis descended on international affairs. Not until an entirely new form of peacemaking was devised, in the 1640s, was the fighting brought under control.

The Thirty Years' War

The new arena in which the warfare erupted was the Holy Roman Empire. Here religious hatreds were especially disruptive because the empire lacked a central authority and unifying institutions. Small-scale fighting broke out repeatedly after the 1550s, always inspired by religion. Although elsewhere the first years of the seventeenth century were a time of relative peace that seemed to signal a decline of conflict over faith, in the empire the stage was being set for the bloodiest of all the wars fired by religion.

Known as the Thirty Years' War, this ferocious struggle began in the Kingdom of Bohemia in 1618 and continued until 1648. The principal battleground, the empire, was ravaged by the fighting, which eventually involved every major ruler in Europe. At first it was a renewed struggle between local Protestants and Catholics, but eventually it became a fight among political rivals who were eager to take advantage of the fragmentation of the empire to advance their own ambitions. As the devastation spread, international relations seemed to be sinking into total chaos; but the

"THE HANGING TREE," ENGRAVING FROM JACQUES CALLOT'S MISERIES OF WAR, 1633
An indication of the growing dismay over the brutality of the Thirty Years' War was the collection of sixteen prints produced by the French engraver Callot depicting the life of the soldier and the effects of armies on civilian populations. His soldiers destroy, loot, and rape, and only a few of them receive the punishments they deserve, like this mass hanging.
Anne S. K. Brown Military Collection, Brown University Library

"HEADS OF THE BOHEMIAN REBELS," ENGRAVING FROM MATHAUS MERIAN, THEATRUM EUROPAEUM, CA. 1630
Since the scene had not changed when the engraving was made, this illustration is probably a fairly accurate representation of the punishment in 1621 of the leaders of the Bohemian rebellion. Twenty-four rebels were executed, and the heads of twelve of them were displayed on long poles at the top of the tower (still standing today) on the bridge over Prague's river. The heads were kept there for ten years.

chief victims were the Germans, who, like the Italians in the sixteenth century, found themselves at the mercy of well-organized states that used another country as a place to settle their quarrels.

The First Phase, 1618–1621 The immediate problem was typical of the situation in the empire. In 1609 the Habsburg Emperor Rudolf II promised toleration for Protestants in Bohemia. When his cousin Ferdinand, a pious Catholic, succeeded to the Bohemian throne in 1617, he refused to honor Rudolf's promise, and the Bohemians rebelled in 1618. They declared Ferdinand deposed, replacing him with the leading Calvinist of the empire, Frederick II of the Palatinate. Frederick accepted the crown, an act of defiance whose only possible outcome was war.

The first decade or so of the war was a time of victories for the Catholics. When Ferdinand became emperor (r. 1619–1637), the powerful Catholic Maximilian of Bavaria put an army at his disposal. Within a year, the imperial troops won a stunning victory over the Bohemians. Ferdinand II confiscated all of Frederick's lands. Maximilian received half as a reward for his army, and the remainder went to the Spaniards, who occupied it as a valuable base for their struggle with the Dutch. In this first round, the Catholic and imperial cause had triumphed.

The Second Phase, 1621–1630 When the truce between the Spaniards and the Dutch expired in 1621 and warfare resumed in Germany as well as in the Netherlands, the Protestants made no progress for ten years. A new imperial army was raised by Albrecht von

Gerard Terborch
The Peace of Westphalia, **1648**
The artist was an eyewitness to this scene, the formal signing of peace between the United Provinces and Spain in Münster on May 15, 1648. The two leaders of the Spanish delegation on the right put their hands on a Bible as they swear to uphold the terms of the treaty, and the Dutch on the left all raise their hands as they declare "So help me God." Terborch himself, dressed in brown, is looking out at the viewer on the far left.
By courtesy of the Trustees, © The National Gallery, London (NG896)/Art Resource, NY

Wallenstein, a minor Bohemian nobleman and remarkable opportunist who had become one of the richest men in the empire. By 1627 Wallenstein's army had begun to conquer the northern region of the empire, the last major center of Protestant strength. To emphasize his supremacy, Ferdinand issued the Edict of Restitution in 1629, ordering the restoration to Catholics of all the territories they had lost to Protestants since 1552.

But these Habsburg successes were more apparent than real, because it was only the extreme disorganization of the empire that permitted a mercenary captain like Wallenstein to achieve such immense military power. Once the princes realized the danger he posed to their independence, they united (Catholic as well as Protestant) against the Habsburgs, and in 1630 they forced the dismissal of Wallenstein by threatening to keep Ferdinand's son from the imperial succession. This concession proved fatal to the emperor's cause, for Sweden and France were preparing to unleash new aggressions against the Habsburgs, and Wallenstein was the one military leader who might have been able to resist the onslaught.

The Third Phase, 1630–1632 The year 1630 marked the beginning of a change in fortune for the Protestants and also a drift toward the purely political aim (of resisting the Habsburgs) that was coming to dominate the war. Although France's king was a Catholic, he was

ready to join with Protestants against other Catholics so as to undermine Habsburg power. In 1631, the French allied with Gustavus Adolphus of Sweden, who, dismayed by Ferdinand's treatment of Protestants and fearing a Habsburg threat to Swedish lands around the Baltic Sea, had invaded the empire in 1630. The following year Gustavus destroyed an imperial army in a decisive battle that turned the tide against the Habsburgs.

Ferdinand hastily recalled Wallenstein, whose troops met the Swedes in battle at Lützen in 1632. Although Gustavus' soldiers won the day, he himself was killed, and his death saved the Habsburg Dynasty. Nothing, however, could restore Ferdinand's former position. The emperor was forced by the princes to turn against Wallenstein once more; a few months later Ferdinand had Wallenstein assassinated. The removal of the great general marked the end of an era, because Wallenstein was the last leader for more than two centuries who was capable of establishing unified authority in what is now Germany.

The Fourth Phase, 1632–1648 Gustavus' success opened the final phase of the war, as political ambitions—the quest of the empire's princes for independence and the struggle between the Habsburgs and their enemies—almost completely replaced religious aims. The Protestant princes began to raise new armies, and by 1635 Ferdinand had to make peace with them. In return for their promise of assistance in driving out the Swedes, Ferdinand agreed to suspend the Edict of Restitution and to grant amnesty to all but Frederick of the Palatinate and a few Bohemian rebels. Ferdinand was renouncing most of his ambitions, and it seemed that peace might return at last.

But the French could not let matters rest. In 1635 they finally declared war on Ferdinand. For the next thirteen years, the French and Swedes rained unmitigated disaster on Germany. Peace negotiations began in 1641, but not until 1648 did the combatants sign the treaties of Westphalia. Even thereafter the war between France and Spain, pursued mainly in the Spanish Netherlands, continued for another eleven years; and hostilities around the Baltic among Sweden, Denmark, Poland, and Russia, which had started in 1611, did not end until 1661.

The Effect of War   The wars and their effects (such as the diseases spread by armies) killed off more than a third of Germany's population. The conflict caused serious economic dislocation because a number of princes—already in serious financial straits—sharply debased their coinage. Their actions worsened the continent-wide trade depression that had begun around 1620 and had brought the great sixteenth-century boom to an end, causing the first drop in prices since 1500. Few contemporaries perceived the connection between war and economic trouble, but nobody could ignore the drain on men and resources, the crisis in international relations, or the widespread destruction caused by the conflict.

The Peace of Westphalia

By the 1630s it was becoming apparent that the fighting was getting out of hand and that it would not be easy to bring the conflicts to an end. There had never been such widespread or devastating warfare, and many diplomats felt that the settlement had to be of far greater scope than any negotiated before. And they were right. When at last the treaties were signed in 1648, after seven years of negotiation in the German province of Westphalia, a landmark in international relations was passed—remarkable not only because it brought an anarchic situation under control but because it created a new system for dealing with wars.

The most important innovation was the gathering at the peace conference of all the participants in the Thirty Years' War, rather than the usual practice of bringing only two or three belligerents together. The presence of delegations from 109 interested parties made possible, for the first time in European history, a series of all-embracing treaties that dealt with nearly every major international issue at one stroke. Visible at the meetings was the emergence of a state system.

These independent states recognized that they were creating a mechanism for controlling their relations with one another. Although some fighting continued, the Peace of Westphalia in 1648 became the first comprehensive rearrangement of the map of Europe in modern times.

Peace Terms   The principal beneficiaries were France and Sweden, the chief aggressors during the last decade of the war. France gained the provinces of Alsace and Lorraine, and Sweden obtained extensive territories in the Holy Roman Empire. The main loser was the House of Habsburg, since both the United Provinces and the Swiss Confederation were recognized as independent states; and the German princes, who agreed not to join an alliance against the emperor, were otherwise given almost complete independence.

The princes' autonomy was formally established in 1657, when they elected as emperor Leopold I, the head of the House of Habsburg, in return for two promises. First, Leopold would give no help to his cousins, the rulers of Spain; and second, the empire would be a state of princes, in which each ruler would be free from imperial interference. This freedom permitted the rise of Brandenburg-Prussia and the growth of absolutism—the belief that the political authority of the ruler was unlimited—within the major principalities. Moreover, the Habsburgs' capitulation prepared the way for their reorientation toward the east along the Danube River—the beginnings of the Austro-Hungarian Empire.

The Effects of Westphalia   For more than a century, the settlement reached at Westphalia was regarded as the basis for all international negotiations. Even major new accords, such as the one that ended yet another series of wars in 1713, were seen mainly as adjustments of the decisions of 1648. In practice, of course, multinational conferences were no more effective than brief, limited negotiations in reducing tensions among states. Wars continued to break out, and armies grew in size and skill. But diplomats did believe that international affairs were under better control and that the chaos of the Thirty Years' War had been replaced by something more stable and more clearly defined.

This confidence was reinforced as it became clear after 1648 that armies were trying to improve discipline and avoid the excesses of the previous thirty years. As religious passions waned, combat became less vicious and the treatment of civilians became more orderly. On battlefields, better discipline reduced the casualty rate from one death per three soldiers in the 1630s to one death in seven, or even one in twenty, during the early 1700s. The aims of war also changed significantly.

MAP 15.3 TERRITORIAL CHANGES, 1648–1661
This map shows the territorial changes that took place after the Thirty Years' War. The treaties of Westphalia (1648) and the Pyrenees (1659) arranged the principal transfers, but the settlements in the Baltic were not confirmed until the treaties of Copenhagen, Oliva (both 1660), and Kardis (1661). Who were the main winners and losers in the territorial changes of this period?

Changed International Relations　The most obvious differences after the Peace of Westphalia were that France replaced Spain as the continent's dominant power and that northern countries—especially England and the Netherlands, where growth in population and in commerce resumed more quickly than elsewhere—took over Europe's economic leadership. But behind this outward shift a more fundamental transformation was taking place. What had become apparent in the later stages of the Thirty Years' War was that Europe's

states were prepared to fight only for economic, territorial, or political advantages. Dynastic aims were still important, but supranational goals like religious causes could no longer determine a state's foreign policy.

The Thirty Years' War was the last major international conflict in Europe in which two religious camps organized their forces as blocs. After 1648 such connections gave way to purely national interests; it is no surprise that the papacy denounced the peace vehemently. For this shift marked the decisive stage of a process that had been under way since the Late Middle Ages: the emergence of the state as the basic unit and object of loyalty in Western civilization. That it had taken a major crisis, a descent into international anarchy, to bring about so momentous a change is an indication of how profoundly the upheavals of the mid-seventeenth century, this age of crisis, affected European history.

THE MILITARY REVOLUTION

The constant warfare of the sixteenth and seventeenth centuries brought about dramatic changes in the ways that battles were fought and armies were organized.

Weapons and Tactics

The Use of Gunpowder   Though it had been known since the 1330s, gunpowder became central to warfare only around 1500. The result was the creation of a new type of industry, cannon and gun manufacture, and also a transformation of tactics. Individual castles could no longer be defended against explosives; even towns had to build heavy and elaborate fortifications if they were to resist the new firepower. Sieges became expensive, complex operations whose purpose was to bring explosives right up to a town wall so that it could be blown up. This process required an intricate system of trenches, because walls were built in star shapes so as to multiply angles of fire and make any approach dangerous. Although they became increasingly costly, sieges remained essential to the strategy of warfare until the eighteenth century.

New Tactics   In open battles, the effects of gunpowder were equally expensive. The new tactics that appeared around 1500, perfected by the Spaniards, relied on massed ranks of infantry, organized in huge squares, that made the traditional cavalry charge obsolete. Interspersed with the gunners were soldiers carrying pikes. They fended off horses or opposing infantry while the men with guns tried to mow the enemy down. The squares with the best discipline usually won, and for more than a century after the reign of Ferdinand of Aragon, the Spaniards had the best army in Europe. Each square had about three thousand troops, and to maintain enough squares to fight all of Spain's battles required an army numbering approximately forty thousand. The cost of keeping that many men clothed, fed, and housed, let alone equipped and paid, was enormous. But worse was to come: New tactics emerged in the early seventeenth century that required even more soldiers.

Since nobody could outdo the Spaniards at their own methods, a different approach was developed by their rivals. The first advance was made by Maurice of Nassau, in the Dutch revolt against Spain. He relied

Anonymous
***WAFFENHANDLUNG*, ENGRAVING AFTER JACQUES DE GHEYN**
The expansion of armies and the professionalization of war in the seventeenth century were reflected in the founding of military academies and in the growing acceptance of the notion that warfare was a science. There was now a market for published manuals, especially if they had illustrations like this one, which shows how a pikeman was supposed to crouch and hold his weapons (stabilizing his pike against his foot) when facing a cavalry charge.
Deutsches Historisches Museum, Berlin, Germany

not on sheer weight and power but on flexibility and mobility. Then Sweden's Gustavus Adolphus, one of the geniuses of the history of warfare, found a way to achieve mobility on the field without losing power. His main invention was the salvo: Instead of having his musketeers fire one row at a time, like the Spaniards, he had them all fire at once. What he lost in continuity of shot he gained in a fearsome blast that, if properly timed, could shatter enemy ranks. Huge, slow-moving squares were simply no match for smaller, faster units that riddled them with well-coordinated salvos.

The Organization and Support of Armies

These tactical changes brought about steady increases in the size of armies, because the more units there were, the better they could be placed on the battlefield. Although the Spanish army hardly grew between 1560 and 1640, remaining at 40,000 to 60,000 men, the Swedes had 150,000 by 1632; and at the end of the century, Louis XIV considered a force of 400,000 essential to maintain his dominant position in Europe.

This growth had far-reaching consequences. One was the need for **conscription,** which Gustavus introduced in the late 1620s. At least half his army consisted of his own subjects, who were easier to control than foreign mercenaries. Because it also made sense not to disband such huge forces each autumn, when the campaigning season ended, most armies were kept permanently ready. To strengthen discipline, new mechanisms were developed: drilling, combat training, uniforms, and the various officer ranks we still have. And the need to maintain so many soldiers the year round caused a rapid expansion of supporting administrative personnel. Taxation mushroomed. All levels of society felt the impact, but especially the lower classes, who paid the bulk of the taxes and provided most of the recruits.

The Life of the Soldier

Some soldiers genuinely wanted to join up. They had heard stories of adventure, booty, and comradeship, and they were tempted by free food and clothing. But many "volunteers" did not want to go, for they had also heard of the hardship and danger. Unfortunately for them, recruiting officers had quotas, and villages had to provide the numbers. Community pressure, bribery, enlistment of drunken men, and even outright kidnapping helped fill the ranks.

Joining an army did not necessarily mean cutting oneself off from friends or family. Men from a particular area enlisted together and, in some cases, wives and even children came along. There were dozens of jobs to do aside from fighting, because soldiers needed cooks, launderers, peddlers, and other tradespeople. An army in the field often needed five people for every soldier. Few barracks were built, and therefore, unless they were on the march or out in the open on a battlefield, troops were housed (or billeted) with ordinary citizens. Since soldiers almost never received their wages on time—delays could be as long as a year or more—they rarely could pay for their food and housing. Local civilians, therefore, had to supply their needs or risk the thievery that was universal. It was no wonder that the approach of an army was a terrifying event.

Sebastian Vrancx
A MILITARY CAMP
Vrancx was himself a soldier, and the many military scenes he painted during the Thirty Years' War give us a sense of the life of the soldier during the long months when there were no campaigns or battles. Conditions could be grim, but there were many hours during which a soldier could simply nap, chat, or play dice.
Hamburg/Hamburger Kunsthalle/The Bridgeman Art Library

Discomforts of Military Life   Military life was not easy. Soldiers suffered constant discomfort. A garrison might be able to settle into a town in reasonable conditions for a long stretch, but if it was besieged, it became hungry, fearful, and vulnerable. Days spent on the march could be grim, exhausting, and uncertain; even in camps soldiers were often filthy and wet. Real danger was not common, though it was intense during battles and occasionally during sieges. Even a simple wound could be fatal, because medical care was generally appalling. Despite traditional recreations—drink, gambling, and the brawls common among soldiers—the attractions of army service were limited; most military men had few regrets when they returned to civilian life.

REVOLUTION IN ENGLAND

In the 1640s and 1650s the growing burdens of war and taxation, and the mounting assertiveness of governments, sparked upheavals throughout Europe that were the equivalent in domestic politics of the crisis in international relations. In country after country, people rose up in vain attempts to restore the individual and regional autonomies that were being eroded by powerful central governments. Only in England, however, did the revolt become a revolution—an attempt to overturn the social and political system and create a new structure for society.

Pressures for Change

The Gentry   The central figures in the drama were the gentry, a social group immediately below the nobles at the head of society. They ranged from people considered great in a parish or other small locality to courtiers considered great throughout the land. Although in Elizabeth's reign there were never more than sixty nobles, the gentry numbered close to twenty thousand. Most of the gentry were doing well economically, profiting from agricultural holdings and crown offices. A number also became involved in industrial activity, and hundreds invested in new overseas trading and colonial ventures. The gentry's participation in commerce made them unique among the landed classes of Europe, whose members were traditionally contemptuous of business affairs, and it testified to the enterprise and vigor of England's social leaders. Long important in local administration, they flocked to the House of Commons to express their views on public matters. Their ambitions eventually posed a serious threat to the monarchy, especially when linked with the effects of rapid economic change.

Economic Advance   In Elizabeth's reign, thanks to a general boom in trade, England's merchants, aided by leading courtiers, had begun to transform the country's economy. They opened commercial links throughout Europe and parts of Asia and promoted significant industrial development at home. Mining and manufacture developed rapidly, and shipbuilding became a major industry. The production of coal increased fourteen-fold between 1540 and 1680, creating fortunes and an expertise in industrial techniques that took England far ahead of its neighbors.

The economic vigor and growth that ensued gave the classes that benefited most—gentry and merchants—a cohesion and a sense of purpose that made it dangerous to oppose them when they felt their rights infringed. They were coming to see themselves as leaders of the nation, almost alongside the nobility. They wanted respect for their wishes, and they bitterly resented the economic interference and political high-handedness of Elizabeth's successors.

The Puritans   Heightening this unease was the sympathy that many of the gentry felt toward a small but vociferous group of religious reformers, the **Puritans.** Puritans believed that the Protestant Anglican Church established by Elizabeth was still too close to Roman Catholicism, and they wanted further reductions in ritual and hierarchy. Elizabeth refused, and although she tried to avoid a confrontation, in the last years of her reign she had to silence the most outspoken of her critics. As a result, the Puritans became a disgruntled minority. By the 1630s, when the government tried to repress religious dissent more vigorously, many people in England, non-Puritan as well as Puritan, felt that the monarchy was leading the country astray and was ignoring the wishes of its subjects. Leading parliamentarians in particular soon came to believe that major changes were needed to restore good government in England.

Parliament and the Law

The place where the gentry made their views known was Parliament, the nation's supreme legislative body. Three-quarters of the House of Commons consisted of gentry. They were better educated than ever before, and nearly half of them had legal training. Since the Commons had to approve all taxation, the gentry had the leverage to pursue their grievances.

The monarchy was still the dominant force in the country when Elizabeth died in 1603, but Parliament's demand to be heard was gathering momentum. Although the queen had been careful with money, in the last twenty years of her reign her resources had been overtaxed by war with Spain and an economic depression. Thus, she bequeathed to her successor, Scotland's James Stuart, a huge debt—£400,000, the equal of a year's royal revenue; his struggle to pay it off gave the Commons the means to seek changes in royal policy.

James I's Difficulties

James I's Difficulties Trouble began during the reign of James I (r. 1603–1625), who had a far more exalted view of his own powers than Elizabeth and who did not hesitate to tell his subjects that he considered his authority almost unlimited. In response, gentry opposed to royal policies dominated parliamentary proceedings, and they engaged in a running battle with the king. They blocked the union of England with Scotland that James sought. They drew up an "Apology" explaining his mistakes and his ignorance, as a Scotsman, of English traditions. They forced two of his ministers to resign in disgrace. And they wrung repeated concessions from him, including the unprecedented right for Parliament to discuss foreign policy.

Conflict over the Law The Commons used the law to justify their resistance to royal power. The basic legal system of the country was the common law—justice administered on the basis of precedents and parliamentary statutes and relying on the opinions of juries. This system stood in contrast to Roman law, prevalent on the Continent, where royal edicts could make law and decisions were reached by judges without juries. Such practices existed in England only in a few royal courts of law, such as Star Chamber, which, because it was directly under the crown, came to be seen as an instrument of repression.

The common lawyers, whose leaders were also prominent in the Commons, resented the growing business of the royal courts and attacked them in Parliament. Both James and his successor were accused of pressuring judges, particularly after they won a series of famous cases involving a subject's right to criticize the monarch. Thus, the crown could be portrayed as disregarding not only the desires of the people but the law itself. The king still had broad powers, but when he exercised them contrary to Parliament's wishes, his actions seemed to many to be taking on the appearance of tyranny.

Rising Antagonisms

The confrontation between Parliament and king grew worse during the 1620s, especially in the reign of James's son, Charles I (r. 1625–1649). At the Parliament of 1628–1629, the open challenge to the crown reached a climax in the Petition of Right, which has become a landmark in constitutional history. The petition demanded an end to imprisonment without cause shown, to taxation without the consent of Parliament, to martial law in peacetime, and to the billeting of troops among civilians. Charles agreed, in the hope of gaining much-needed subsidies, but then broke his word. To many, this betrayal seemed to threaten Parliament's essential role in government alongside the king. Seeking to end discussion of these issues in the Commons, Charles ordered Parliament dissolved.

Resentful subjects were clearly on the brink of openly defying their king. Puritans, common lawyers, and disenchanted country gentry had taken over the House of Commons; Charles avoided further trouble only by refusing to call another session of Parliament. This he managed to do for eleven years, all the while increasing the repression of Puritanism and using extraordinary measures (such as reviving crown rights to special taxes that had not been demanded for a long time) to raise revenues that did not require parliamentary consent. But in 1639, the Calvinist Scots took up arms rather than accept the Anglican prayer book, and the parliamentarians had their chance. To pay for an army to fight the Scots, Charles had to turn to Parliament, which demanded that he first redress its grievances. When he resisted, civil war followed.

Civil War

By the summer of 1640, the Scots occupied most of northern England, and Charles, after quarreling with and dismissing one assembly, was forced to summon a new Parliament. This sat for thirteen years, earning the appropriate name of the Long Parliament.

In its first year, the House of Commons abolished the royal courts, such as Star Chamber, and made mandatory the writ of habeas corpus (which prevented imprisonment without cause shown); it declared taxation without parliamentary consent illegal; and it ruled that Parliament had to meet at least once every three years. Meanwhile, the Puritans in the Commons prepared to reform the church. Oliver Cromwell, one of their leaders, demanded abolition of the Anglican Book of Common Prayer and strongly attacked the authority and very existence of bishops. The climactic vote came the next year, when the Commons passed a Grand Remonstrance, which outlined for the king all the legislation they had passed and asked that bishops be deprived of votes in the House of Lords.

The Two Sides This demand was the prelude to a more revolutionary Puritan assault on the structure of the church, but in fact the Grand Remonstrance passed by only eleven votes. A moderate group was detaching itself from the Puritans, and it was to become the nucleus of a royalist party. The nation's chief grievances had been redressed, and there was no longer a uniform desire for change. Still, Charles misjudged the situation and tried to arrest five leaders of the Commons,

Anonymous
ENGRAVING OF THE EXECUTION OF CHARLES I
This contemporary Dutch engraving of the execution of Charles I shows the scaffold in front of the Banqueting House in Whitehall—a building that still can be seen in London. On the far right of the scaffold, the executioner displays the severed head for the crowd.
The Granger Collection, New York

supposedly for plotting treason with the Scots. But Parliament resisted, and the citizens of London, openly hostile to Charles, sheltered the five. England now began to split in two. By late 1642 both the royalists and the antiroyalists had assembled armies, and the Civil War was under way.

What made so many people overcome their habitual loyalty to the monarchy? We know that the royalists in Parliament were considerably younger than their opponents, which suggests that it was long experience with the Stuarts and nostalgia for Elizabeth that created revolutionaries. Another clear divide was regional. The south and east of England were primarily antiroyalist, while the north and west were mostly royalist. These divisions indicated that the more cosmopolitan areas, closer to the Continent and also centers of Puritanism, were largely on Parliament's side. The decision was often a personal matter: A prominent family and its locality chose one side because its rival, a nearby family, had chosen the other. The Puritans were certainly antiroyalist, but they were a minority in the country and influential in the House of Commons only because they were so vocal and determined. Like all revolutions, this one was animated by a small group of radicals (in this case, Puritans) who alone kept the momentum going.

Independents and Presbyterians

As the fighting began, a group among the Puritans known as Independents urged that the Anglican Church be replaced by a congregational system in which each local congregation, free of all central authority, would decide its own form of worship. The most important leader of the Independents in Parliament was Oliver Cromwell.

Opposed to them, but also considered Puritans, were the Presbyterians, who wanted to establish a strictly organized Calvinist system, like the one in Scotland in which local congregations were subject to centralized authority. Since both the Scots, whose alliance was vital in the war, and a majority of the Puritans in the Commons were Presbyterians, Cromwell agreed to give way, but only for the moment. The two sides also quarreled over the goals of the war. The Independents were in general more determined to force Charles into total submission, and eventually they had their way.

As the fighting continued, Cromwell persuaded the Commons to allow him to reorganize the antiroyalist troops. His New Model Army—whipped to fervor by sermons, prayers, and the singing of psalms—became unbeatable. At Naseby in 1645, it won a major victory, and a year later Charles surrendered. The next two years were chaotic. The Presbyterians and Independents quarreled over what to do with the king, and finally civil war resumed. This time the Presbyterians and Scots backed Charles against the Independents. But even with this alliance the royalists were no match for the New Model Army; Cromwell soon defeated his opponents and captured the king.

The King's Fate

At the same time, in 1647, the Independents abolished the House of Lords and removed all Presbyterians from the House of Commons. This "Rump" Parliament tried to negotiate with Charles but discovered that he continued to plot a return to power. With Cromwell's approval, the Commons decided that their monarch, untrustworthy and a troublemaker, would have to die. A trial of dubious legality was held, and though many of the participants refused to sign the death warrant, the "holy, anointed" king was executed by his subjects in January 1649, to the horror of all Europe and most of England.

England under Cromwell

Oliver Cromwell was now master of England. The republic established after Charles's execution was officially ruled by the Rump Parliament, but a Council of State led by Cromwell controlled policy with the backing of the army. And they had to contend with a ferment of political and social ideas. One group, known as the Levellers, demanded the vote for nearly all adult males and parliamentary elections every other year. The men of property among the Puritans, notably Cromwell himself, were disturbed by the egalitarianism of these proposals and insisted that only men with an "interest" in England—that is, land—should be qualified to vote.

Radical Ideas   Even more radical were the Diggers, a communistic sect that sought to implement the spirit of primitive Christianity by abolishing personal property; the Society of Friends, which stressed personal inspiration as the source of faith and all action; and the Fifth Monarchists, a messianic group who believed that the "saints"—themselves—should rule because the Day of Judgment was at hand. People of great ability, such as the famous poet John Milton, contributed to the fantastic flood of pamphlets and suggestions for reform that poured forth in these years, and their ideas inspired future revolutionaries. But at the time, they merely put Cromwell on the defensive, forcing him to maintain control at all costs.

Cromwell's Aims   Cromwell himself fought for two overriding causes: religious freedom (except for the Anglican and Catholic churches) and constitutional government. But he achieved neither, and he grew increasingly unhappy at the Rump Parliament's refusal to enact reforms. He dissolved the assembly in 1653 (the final end of the Long Parliament), and during the remaining five years of his life he tried desperately to lay down a new constitutional structure for his government.

Cromwell was driven by noble aspirations, but in the end he had to rule by military dictatorship. From 1653 on he was called lord protector and ruled through eleven major generals, each responsible for a different district of England and supported by a tax on the estates of royalists. To quell dissent, he banned newspapers; to prevent disorder, he took such measures as enlisting innkeepers as government spies. Cromwell was always a reluctant

revolutionary; he hated power and sought only limited ends. Some revolutionaries, like Lenin, have a good idea of where they would like to be carried by events; others, like Cromwell, move painfully, hesitantly, and uncertainly to the extremes they finally reach. It was because he sought England's benefit so urgently and because he considered the nation too precious to abandon to irreligion or tyranny that Cromwell remained determinedly in command to the end of his life.

The End of the Revolution   Gradually, more traditional political forms reappeared. The Parliament of 1656 offered Cromwell the crown, and, though he refused, he took the title of "His Highness" and ensured that the succession would go to his son. Cromwell was monarch in all but name, yet only his presence ensured stability (see "Oliver Cromwell's Aims," p. 437). After he died, his quiet, retiring son Richard proved no match for the scheming generals of the army, who created political turmoil. To bring an end to the uncertainty, General George Monck, the commander of a well-disciplined force in Scotland, marched south in 1660, assumed control, and invited the son of Charles I, Charles II, to return from exile and restore the monarchy.

Results of the Revolution   Only the actions taken during the first months of the Long Parliament—the abolition of royal courts, the prohibition of taxation without parliamentary consent, and the establishment of the writ of habeas corpus—persisted beyond the revolution. Otherwise, everything seemed much the same as before: Bishops and lords were reinstated, religious dissent was again repressed, and Parliament was called and dissolved by the monarch. But the tone and balance of political relations had changed for good.

Henceforth, the gentry could no longer be denied a decisive voice in politics. In essence, this had been their revolution, and they had succeeded. When in the 1680s a king again tried to impose his wishes on the country without reference to Parliament, there was no need for another major upheaval. A quiet, bloodless coup reaffirmed the new role of the gentry and Parliament. The crisis of authority that had arisen from a long period of growing unease and open conflict had been resolved, and the English could settle into a system of rule that with only gradual modification remained in force for some two centuries.

REVOLTS IN FRANCE AND SPAIN

The fact that political upheaval took place not only in England but in much of Europe in the 1640s and 1650s is the main reason that historians have come to speak of

OLIVER CROMWELL'S AIMS

When Parliament in late 1656 offered to make Oliver Cromwell the king of England as a way of restoring political stability, he hesitated before replying. When he finally came to Parliament with his response on April 13, 1657, he turned down the offer of a crown and explained in a long speech—from which a passage follows—why he felt it would be wrong to reestablish a monarchy in England.

"I do think you ought to attend to the settling of the peace and liberties of this Nation. Otherwise the Nation will fall in pieces. And in that, so far as I can, I am ready to serve not as a King, but as a Constable. For truly I have, before God, often thought that I could not tell what my business was, save comparing myself to a good Constable set to keep the peace of the parish. And truly this hath been my content and satisfaction in the troubles I have undergone . . . I was a person who, from my first employment, was suddenly lifted up from lesser trusts to greater. . . . The Providence of God hath laid aside this Title of King; and that not by sudden humor, but by issue of ten or twelve years Civil War, wherein much blood hath been shed. I will not dispute the justice of it when it was done. But God in His severity hath eradicated a whole Family, and thrust them out of the land. And God hath seemed providential not only in striking at the family but at the Name [of king]. It is blotted out. God blasted the very Title. I will not seek to set up that which Providence hath destroyed, and laid in the dust: I would not build Jericho again."

From Thomas Carlyle (ed.), *Oliver Cromwell's Letters and Speeches,* Vol. 3, London, 1908, pp. 230, 231, and 235.

Anonymous
THE SEINE FROM THE PONT NEUF, CA. 1635
Henry IV of France, celebrated in the equestrian statue overlooking the Seine that stands in Paris to this day, saw the physical reshaping of his capital as part of the effort to restore order after decades of civil war. He laid out the first squares in any European city, and under the shadow of his palace, the Louvre, he built the Pont Neuf (on the right)—the first open bridge (without houses on it) across the Seine.
Giraudon/Art Resource, NY

a "general crisis" during this period. Political institutions and political authority were being challenged in many countries, and although only England went through a revolution, the disruptions and conflicts were also significant in the two other major states of the age, France and Spain.

The France of Henry IV

In the 1590s Henry IV resumed the strengthening of royal power, which had been interrupted by the civil wars that had begun in the 1560s. He mollified the traditional landed aristocracy, known as the nobility of the sword, with places on his Council of Affairs and with large financial settlements. The principal bureaucrats, known as the nobility of the robe, controlled the country's administration, and Henry made sure to turn their interests to his benefit. Because all crown offices had to be bought, he used the system both to raise revenues and to guarantee the loyalty of the bureaucrats. He not only accelerated the sales of offices but also invented a new device, an annual fee known as the *paulette,* which ensured that an officeholder's job would remain in his family when he died. This increased royal profits and also reduced the flow of newcomers, thus strengthening the commitment of existing officeholders to the crown.

By 1610 Henry had imposed his will throughout France, and he was secure enough to plan an invasion of the Holy Roman Empire. Although he was assassinated before he could join his army, and the invasion was called off, his heritage, especially in economic affairs, long outlived him. France's rich agriculture may have had one unfortunate effect—successful merchants abandoned commerce as soon as they could afford to move to the country and buy a title of nobility (and thus gain exemption from taxes)—but it did ensure a solid basis for the French economy. Indeed, agriculture suffered little during the civil wars, though the violence and the rising taxes did cause uprisings of peasants (the main victims of the tax system) almost every year from the 1590s to the 1670s.

Mercantilism By restoring political stability, Henry ended the worst economic disruptions, but his main legacy was the notion that his increasingly powerful government was responsible for the health of the country's economy. This view was justified by a theory developed mainly in France: **mercantilism,** which became an essential ingredient of absolutism. Mercantilism was more a set of attitudes than a systematic economic theory. Its basic premise—an erroneous one—was that the world contained a fixed amount of wealth and that each nation could enrich itself only at the expense of others. To some thinkers, this theory meant hoarding bullion (gold and silver); to others, it required a favorable bal-

ance of trade—more exports than imports. All mercantilists, however, agreed that state regulation of economic affairs was necessary for the welfare of a country. Only a strong, centralized government could encourage native industries, control production, set quality standards, allocate resources, establish tariffs, and take other measures to promote prosperity and improve trade. Thus, mercantilism was as much about politics as economics and fit perfectly with Henry's restoration of royal power. In line with their advocacy of activist policies, the mercantilists also approved of war. Even economic advance was linked to warfare in this violent age.

Louis XIII

Unrest reappeared when Henry's death left the throne to his nine-year-old son, Louis XIII (r. 1610–1643). The widowed queen, Marie de Medici, served as regent and soon faced revolts by Calvinists and disgruntled nobles. In the face of these troubles, Marie summoned the Estates General in 1614. This was their last meeting for 175 years, until the eve of the French Revolution; and the weakness they displayed, as various groups within the Estates fought one another over plans for political reform, demonstrated that the monarchy was the only institution that could unite the nation. The session revealed the impotence of those who opposed royal policies, and Marie brought criticism to an end by declaring her son to be of age and the regency dissolved. In this absolutist state, further protest could be defined as treason.

Richelieu For a decade, the monarchy lacked energetic direction; but in 1624, one of Marie's favorites, Armand du Plessis de Richelieu, a churchman who rose to be a cardinal through her favor, became chief minister and took control of the government. Over the next eighteen years, this ambitious and determined leader resumed Henry IV's assertion of royal authority (see "Richelieu on Diplomacy," p. 439).

The monarchy had to manage a number of vested interests as it concentrated its power, and Richelieu's achievement was that he kept them under control. The strongest was the bureaucracy, whose ranks had been swollen by the sale of offices. Richelieu always paid close attention to the views of the bureaucrats, and one reason he had such influence over the king was that he acted as the head and representative of this army of royal servants. He also reduced the independence of traditional nobles by giving them positions in the regime as diplomats, soldiers, and officials without significant administrative responsibility. Finally, he took on the Huguenots in a military campaign. After he defeated them, he abolished most of the guarantees in the Edict of Nantes and ended the Huguenots' political independence.

RICHELIEU ON DIPLOMACY

The following passages are taken from a collection of the writings of Cardinal Richelieu that was put together after his death and published in 1688 under the title Political Testament. *The book is presented as a work of advice to the king and summarizes what Richelieu learned of politics and diplomacy as one of Europe's leading statesmen during the Thirty Years' War.*

"One cannot imagine how many advantages States gain from continued negotiations, if conducted wisely, unless one has experienced it oneself. I admit I did not realize this truth for five or six years after first being employed in the management of policy. But I am now so sure of it that I say boldly that to negotiate everywhere without cease, openly and secretly, even though one makes no immediate gains and future gains seem unlikely, is absolutely necessary for the good of the State. . . . He who negotiates all the time will find at last the right moment to achieve his aims, and even if he does not find it, at least it is true that he can lose nothing, and that through his negotiations he knows what is happening in the world, which is of no small consequence for the good of the State. . . . Important negotiations must not be interrupted for a moment. . . . One must not be disheartened by an unfortunate turn of events, because sometimes it happens that what is undertaken with good reason is achieved with little good fortune. . . . It is difficult to fight often and always win. . . . It is often because negotiations are so innocent that one can gain great advantages from them without ever faring badly. . . . In matters of State one must find an advantage in everything; that which can be useful must never be neglected."

From Louis Andrè (ed.), *Testament Politique* (Editions Robert Laffont, 1947), pp. 347–348 and 352; translated by T. K. Rabb.

Royal Administration Under Richelieu the sale of offices broke all bounds: By 1633 it accounted for approximately one-half of royal revenues. Ten years later more than three-quarters of the crown's direct taxation was needed to pay the salaries of the officeholders. It was a vicious circle, and the only solution was to increase the taxes on the lower classes. As this financial burden grew, Richelieu had to improve the government's control over the realm to obtain the revenue he needed. He increased the power of the **intendants,** the government's chief agents in the localities, and established them (instead of the nobles) as the principal representatives of the monarchy in each province of France. Unlike the nobles, the *intendants* depended entirely on royal favor for their position; consequently, they enthusiastically recruited for the army, arranged billeting, supervised the raising of taxes, and enforced the king's decrees. They soon came to be hated figures, both because of the rising taxes and because they threatened the power of the nobles. The result was a succession of peasant uprisings, often led by local notables who resented the rise of the *intendants* and of royal power.

Political and Social Crisis

France's foreign wars made the discontent worse, and it was clear that eventually the opponents of the central government would reassert themselves. But the centralization of power by the crown had been so successful that when trouble erupted, in a series of revolts known as the *Fronde* (or "sling," the simple weapon of the rebels), there was no serious effort to reshape the social order or the political system. The principal actors in the Fronde came from the upper levels of society: nobles, townsmen, and members of the regional courts and legislatures known as parlements. Only rarely were these groups joined by peasants, who may have been resentful of taxes and other government demands and vulnerable to starvation when harvests failed, but the Fronde never raised issues that connected with the peasants' uprisings. These focused on issues like food scarcities, which often brought women into prominent roles, especially since soldiers were reluctant to shoot them. But without noble support, such disorders remained fairly low-scale; they never reached the level of disruption that was to overtake France in the Revolution.

Mazarin The death of Louis XIII in 1643, followed by a regency because Louis XIV was only five years old, offered an opportunity to those who wanted to reverse the rise of absolutism. Louis XIII's widow, Anne of Austria, took over the government and placed all the power in the hands of an Italian, Cardinal Giulio Mazarin. He used his position to amass a huge fortune, and he was therefore a perfect target for the anger caused by the encroachment of central government on local authority.

Early in 1648 Mazarin sought to gain a respite from the monarch's perennial financial trouble by withholding payment of the salaries of some royal officials for four years. In response, the members of various institutions in Paris, including the Parlement, drew up a charter of demands. They wanted the office of *intendant* abolished, no new offices created, power to approve taxes, and enactment of a habeas corpus law.

The Fronde   Mazarin reacted by arresting the Paris Parlement's leaders, thus sparking a popular rebellion in the city that forced him and the royal family to flee from the capital—an experience the young Louis XIV never forgot. In 1649 Mazarin promised to redress the *parlementaires'* grievances, and he was allowed to return to Paris. But the trouble was far from over; during that summer, uprisings spread throughout France, particularly among peasants and in the old Huguenot stronghold, the southwest.

The next three years were marked by political chaos, mainly as a result of intrigues and shifting alliances among the nobility. As it became clear that the perpetual unrest was producing no results, Mazarin was able to take advantage of disillusionment among nobles and *parlementaires* to reassert the position of the monarchy. He used military force and threats of force to subdue Paris and most of the rebels in the countryside, and he brought the regency to an end by declaring the fourteen-year-old Louis of age in 1652. Although the nobles were not finally subdued until the following year, and peasants continued their occasional regional uprisings for many years to come, the crown now established its authority as the basis for order in the realm. As surely as England, France had surmounted its crisis and found a stable solution for long-standing conflicts.

Sources of Discontent in Spain

For Spain the crisis that swept much of Europe in the mid-seventeenth century—with revolt in England and France and war in the empire—meant the end of the

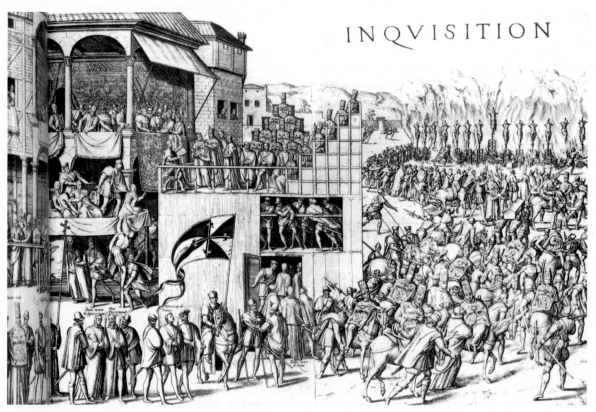

Anonymous
ENGRAVING OF THE SPANISH INQUISITION, 1560
The burning of heretics was a major public event in sixteenth-century Spain. Aimed mainly at people who practiced Judaism or Islam secretly and in a few cases at Protestants, the Inquisition's investigations usually led to imprisonment or lesser punishments. The occasional executions of those who determinedly refused to accept Catholic teachings, even after torture, were carried out by secular authorities, and they attracted huge crowds.
Bibliothèque Nationale de France, Paris

country's international power. Yet the difficulties the monarchy faced had their roots in the sixteenth century. Philip II had already found it difficult to hold his sprawling empire together despite his elaborate bureaucracy. Obsessively suspicious, he maintained close control over all administrative decisions, and government action was, therefore, agonizingly slow. Moreover, the bureaucracy was run by Castilian nobles, who were resented as outsiders in other regions of the empire. And the standing army, though essential to royal power, was a terrible financial drain.

Philip did gain wide admiration in Spain for his devoutness. His commitment to religion undoubtedly promoted political cohesion, but the economic strains caused by relentless religious warfare eventually undermined Spanish power.

Economic Difficulties Spain was a rich country in Philip's reign, but the most profitable activities were monopolized by limited groups. Because royal policy valued convenience above social benefit, the city of Seville (dominated by foreign bankers) received a monopoly over shipping to and from the New World; other lucrative pursuits, such as wool and wine production, were also controlled by a small coterie of insiders. The only important economic activities that involved large numbers of Spaniards were shipping and the prosperous Mediterranean trade, centered in Barcelona, which brought wealth to much of Catalonia. Thus, the influx of silver into Spain was not profitably invested within the country. Drastically overextended in foreign commitments, Philip had to declare himself bankrupt three times. For a while it seemed that the problems might ease because there was peace during the reign of Philip's son, Philip III (r. 1598–1621). But in fact, Philip III's government was incompetent and corrupt, capable neither of dealing with the serious consequences of the spending on war nor of broadening the country's exports beyond wool and wine. And when the flow of treasure from the New World began to dwindle after 1600, the crown was deprived of a major source of income that it was unable to replace (see "Imports of Treasure to Spain. . .," above). The decline was caused partly by a growing use of precious metals in the New World colonies but also by depletion of the mines.

In the meantime, tax returns at home were shrinking. The most significant cause of this decrease was a series of severe plagues, which reduced the population of Castile and Aragon from 10 million in 1590 to 6 million in 1700. No other country in Europe suffered a demographic reversal of this proportion during the seventeenth century. In addition, sheep farming took over huge tracts of arable land, and Spain had to rely increasingly on imports of expensive foodstuffs

IMPORTS OF TREASURE TO SPAIN FROM THE NEW WORLD, 1591–1660	
Decade	Total Value*
1591–1600	85,536,000
1601–1610	66,970,000
1611–1620	65,568,000
1621–1630	62,358,000
1631–1640	40,110,000
1641–1650	30,651,000
1651–1660	12,785,000

* In ducats.
Adapted from J. H. Elliott, *Imperial Spain, 1469–1716*, Edward Arnold, Hodder Neadling PLC Group, 1964, p. 175.

to feed its people. When Spain resumed large-scale fighting against the Dutch and French under Philip IV (r. 1621–1665), the burdens became too much to bear. The effort to maintain the commitment to war despite totally inadequate finances was to bring the greatest state in Europe to its knees.

Revolt and Secession

The final crisis was brought about by the policies of Philip IV's chief minister, the count of Olivares. His aim was to unite the realm so that all the territories shared equally the burden of maintaining Spanish power. Although Castile would no longer dominate the government, it would also not have to provide the bulk of the taxes and army. Olivares' program was called the Union of Arms, and while it seemed eminently reasonable, it caused a series of revolts in the 1640s that split Spain apart.

The reason was that Castile's dominance had made the other provinces feel that local independence was being undermined by a centralized regime. They saw the Union of Arms, imposed by Olivares, as the last straw. Moreover, the plan appeared at a time when Spain's military and economic fortunes were in decline. France had declared war on the Habsburgs in 1635, the funds to support an army were becoming harder to raise, and in desperation Olivares pressed more vigorously for the Union of Arms. But all he accomplished was to provoke revolts against Castile in the 1640s by Catalonia, Portugal, Naples, and Sicily. By 1641 Catalonia and Portugal had declared themselves independent republics and placed themselves under French protection. Plots began to appear against Olivares, and Philip dismissed the one minister who had understood Spain's problems but who, in trying to solve them, had made them worse.

The Revolts The Catalonian rebellion continued for another eleven years, and it was thwarted in the end only because the peasants and town mobs transformed the resistance to the central government into an attack on the privileged and wealthy classes. When this happened, the Catalan nobility abandoned the cause and joined the government side. About the same time, the Fronde forced the withdrawal of French troops from Catalonia. When the last major holdout, Barcelona, fell to a royal army in 1652, the Catalan nobles could regain their rights and powers, and the revolt was over.

The Portuguese had no social upheaval; as a result, though not officially granted independence from Spain until 1668, they defended their autonomy easily and even invaded Castile in the 1640s. But the revolts that the people of Sicily and Naples directed at their Castilian rulers in 1647 took on social overtones. In Naples the unrest developed into a tremendous mob uprising led by a local fisherman. The poor turned against all representatives of government and wealth they could find, and chaos ensued until the leader of the revolt was killed. The violence in Sicily, the result of soaring taxes, was aimed primarily at government officials. But in both Naples and Sicily the government was able to reassert its authority by force within a few months.

Consequences The effect of this unrest was to end the Spanish government's international ambitions and, thus, the worst of its economic difficulties. Like England and France, Spain found a new way of life after its crisis: It became a stable second-level state, heavily agricultural, run by its nobility.

POLITICAL CHANGE IN AN AGE OF CRISIS

Although the level of violence was highest in England and Spain, almost all of Europe's countries experienced the political upheavals of this era of "general crisis." In some cases—for instance, Sweden—the conflict was minor and did little to disturb the peace of the land. But everywhere the basic issue—Who should hold political authority?—caused some degree of strife. And each state had to find its own solutions to the competing demands of governments and their subjects.

The United Provinces

The Dutch did not escape the struggles against the power of centralized governments that created an atmosphere of crisis in much of Europe during the middle decades of the seventeenth century. Despite the remarkable fluidity of their society, the Dutch, too, became embroiled in a confrontation between a ruling family seeking to extend its authority and citizens defending the autonomy of their local regions. The

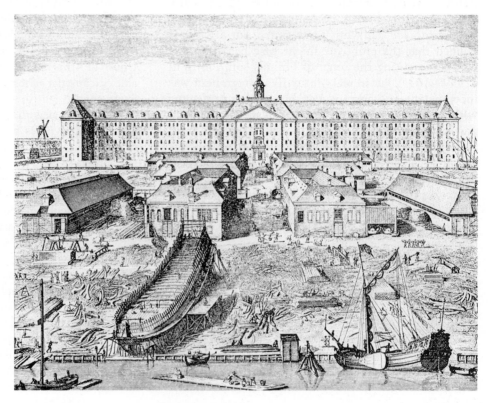

Anonymous
ENGRAVING OF A DUTCH SHIPYARD
The Dutch became the best shipbuilders in Europe in the seventeenth century; the efficiency of their ships, which could be manned by fewer sailors than those of other countries, was a major reason for their successes in trade and commerce.
The Granger Collection, New York

outcome determined the structure of their government for more than a century.

The United Provinces were unique in a number of ways. Other republics existed in Europe, but they were controlled by small oligarchies; the Dutch, who had a long tradition of a strong representative assembly, the Estates General, had created a nation in which many citizens participated in government through elected delegates. Although powerful merchants and a few aristocrats close to the House of Orange did create a small elite, the social differentiation was less than elsewhere in Europe. The resulting openness and homogeneity underlay the economic mastery and cultural brilliance of the United Provinces.

Commerce and Tolerance   The most striking accomplishment of the Dutch was their rise to supremacy in the world of commerce. Amsterdam displaced Antwerp as the Continent's financial capital and gained control of the trade of the world's richest markets. In addition, the Dutch rapidly emerged as the cheapest international shippers. As a result, by the middle of the seventeenth century they had become the chief carriers of European commerce.

The openness of Dutch society permitted the freest exchange of ideas of the time. The new state gave refuge to believers of all kinds, whether extreme Protestant radicals or Catholics who wore their faith lightly, and Amsterdam became the center of a brilliant Jewish community. This freedom attracted some of the greatest minds in Europe and fostered remarkable artistic creativity. The energy that produced this outpouring reflected the pride of a tiny nation that was winning its independence from Spain.

Two Political Parties   There was, however, a basic split within the United Provinces. The two most urbanized and commercial provinces, Holland and Zeeland, dominated the Estates General because they supplied a majority of its taxes. Their representatives formed a mercantile party, which advocated peace abroad so that their trade could flourish unhampered, government by the Estates General so that they could make their influence felt, and religious toleration so that their cities could attract enterprising people of all faiths. In opposition to this mercantile interest was the House of Orange: the descendants of William of Orange, who sought to establish their family's leadership of the Dutch. They were supported by the more rural provinces and stood for war because their authority and popularity derived from their command of the army, for centralized power to enhance the position of the family, and for the strict Calvinism that was upheld in the rural provinces.

The differences between the two factions led Maurice of Nassau to use religion as a pretext to execute his chief opponent, Jan van Oldenbarneveldt, the representative of the province of Holland, in 1618. Oldenbarneveldt was against war with Spain, and his removal left the House of Orange in control of the country. Maurice resumed the war in 1621, and for more than twenty years, his family remained in command, unassailable because it led the army in wartime. Not until 1648—when a new leader, William II, tried to prolong the fighting—did the mercantile party reassert itself by insisting on peace. As a result, the Dutch signed the Treaty of Westphalia, which recognized the independence of the United Provinces. It now seemed that Holland and Zeeland had gained the upper hand. But their struggle with the House of Orange continued

CHRONOLOGY
An Age of Crisis
1618–1660

1618	Revolt in Bohemia, beginning of Thirty Years' War.
1621	Resumption of war between Spanish and Dutch.
1629	Edict of Restitution—high point of Habsburg power.
1630	Sweden enters war against Habsburgs.
1635	France declares war on Habsburgs.
1639	Scots invade England.
1640	Revolts in Catalonia and Portugal against Spanish government.
1642	Civil War in England.
1647	Revolts in Sicily and Naples against Spanish government.
1648	Peace of Westphalia ends Thirty Years' War. Outbreak of *Fronde* in France. Coup by nobles in Denmark. Revolt of Ukraine against Poland. Riots in Russian cities.
1650	Constitutional crisis in Sweden. Confrontation between William of Orange and Amsterdam in Netherlands.
1652	End of Catalan revolt.
1653	End of *Fronde*.
1655	War in Baltic region.
1659	Peace of the Pyrenees between France and Spain.
1660	End of English revolution. Treaties end war in Baltic.

(there was even a threat by Orange troops to besiege Amsterdam) until William II suddenly died in 1650, leaving as his successor a baby son, William III.

Jan De Witt   The mercantile interest now assumed full power, and Jan De Witt, the representative of the province of Holland, took over the government in 1653. De Witt's aims were to leave as much authority as possible in the hands of the provinces, particularly Holland; to weaken the executive and prevent a revival of the House of Orange; to pursue trading advantage; and to maintain peace so that the economic supremacy of the Dutch would not be endangered. For nearly twenty years he guided the country in its golden age. But in 1672 French armies overran the southern provinces, and De Witt lacked the military instinct to fight a dangerous enemy. The Dutch at once turned to the family that had led them to independence; a mob murdered De Witt; and the House of Orange, under William III, resumed the centralization that henceforth was to characterize the political structure of the United Provinces. The country had not experienced a midcentury upheaval as severe as those of its neighbors, but it had nevertheless been forced to endure unrest and violence before the form of its government was securely established.

Sweden

The Swedes, too, settled their political system in the mid-seventeenth century. In 1600 Sweden, a Lutheran country of a million people, was one of the backwaters of Europe. A feudal nobility dominated the countryside, a barter economy made money almost unknown, and both trade and towns were virtually nonexistent. Moreover, the country lacked a capital, central institutions, and government machinery. The royal administration consisted of the king and a few courtiers; other officials were appointed only to deal with specific problems as they arose.

Gustavus Adolphus (r. 1611–1632) transformed this situation. He won over the nobles by giving them dominant positions in a newly expanded bureaucracy, and he reorganized his army. Thus equipped both to govern and to fight, Gustavus embarked on a remarkable series of conquests abroad. By 1629 he had made Sweden the most powerful state in the Baltic area. He then entered the Thirty Years' War, advancing victoriously through the Holy Roman Empire until his death, in 1632, during the showdown battle with Wallenstein. Without their great general, the Swedes could do little more than hang on to their gains, but they were now a force to be reckoned with in international affairs.

Government and Economy   The highly efficient system of government established by Gustavus and his chief adviser, Axel Oxenstierna, was to be the envy of other countries until the twentieth century. At the heart of the system were five administrative departments, each led by a nobleman, with the most important—the Chancellery, for diplomacy and internal affairs—run by Oxenstierna. An administrative center emerged in Stockholm, and the new bureaucracy proved that it could run the nation, supply the army, and implement policy even during the last twelve years of Gustavus' reign, when the king himself was almost always abroad.

A major cause of Sweden's amazing rise was the development of the domestic economy, stimulated by the opening up of copper mines and the development of a major iron industry. The country's traditional tar and timber exports were also stepped up, and a fleet was built. By 1700 Stockholm had become an important trading and financial center, growing in the course of the century from fewer than five thousand to more than fifty thousand inhabitants.

The Nobles   The one source of tension amidst this remarkable progress was the position of the nobles. After Gustavus died, they openly challenged the monarchy for control of government and society. Between 1611 and 1652 they more than doubled the proportion of land they owned in Sweden, and much of this growth was at the expense of the crown, which granted away or sold lands to help the war effort abroad. Both peasants and townspeople viewed these developments with alarm, because the nobility usually pursued its own, rather than public, interests. The concern intensified when, in 1648, the nobles in neighboring Denmark took advantage of the death of a strong king to gain control of their government. Two years later the showdown came in Sweden.

Political Confrontation   The monarch now was Gustavus' daughter Christina, an able but erratic young queen who usually allowed Oxenstierna to run the government. For some time, she had hoped to abdicate her throne, become a Catholic, and leave Sweden—an ambition she fulfilled in 1654. She wanted her cousin Charles recognized as her successor, but the nobles threatened to create a republic if she abdicated. The queen, therefore, summoned the Riksdag, Sweden's usually weak representative assembly, in 1650; she encouraged the townspeople and peasants to raise their grievances and allowed them to attack the aristocracy. Soon these groups were demanding the return of nobles' lands to the crown, freedom of speech, and real power; under this pressure, the nobility gave way and recognized Charles X as successor to the throne.

The political upheaval of 1650 was short-lived. Once Christina had her way, she turned against the Riksdag and rejected the lower estates' demands. Only gradually did power shift away from the great nobles toward a broader elite of lesser nobles and bureaucrats, but the turning point in Sweden, as elsewhere, was during the crisis years of the mid-seventeenth century.

Eastern Europe and the Crisis

In eastern Europe, too, long-term patterns became clear in this period. The limits of Ottoman rule were reconfirmed when an attack on Vienna failed in 1683. Although the Ottomans' control of the Balkans did not immediately waver, their government was increasingly beset by internal problems, and their retreat from Hungary was under way by 1700. Further north, Poland's weak central government lost all claim to real authority in 1648 when it proved unable to stop a group of nobles in the rich province of the Ukraine from switching allegiance from the king of Poland to the tsar in Moscow. And in Russia, following a period of disorder known as the Time of Troubles (1584–1613), the new Romanov

Dynasty began consolidating its power. The nobility was won over; the last possibilities for escaping serfdom were closed; the legal system was codified; the church came under the tsar's control; and the revolts that erupted against these changes between 1648 and 1672—involving peasants and Cossacks (marauding horsemen, mainly from the South), and often looking like rural revolts in the West, especially France—were brutally suppressed. As elsewhere in Europe, long-standing conflicts between centralizing regimes and their opponents were resolved, and a new political system, supported by the government's military power, was established for centuries to come. Further east, the Ming Dynasty of China was overthrown by the new Ch'ing Dynasty in 1644, a shift that was also accompanied by peasant revolts. That parallel suggests that this was a time of upheaval throughout much of the world, possibly because of a cooling in climate that affected food crops. But everywhere the outcome was a return to stability: crisis there may have been, but the restoration of order was a worldwide phenomenon, too.

Summary

Because these struggles were so widespread, historians have called the midcentury period an age of "general crisis." In country after country, people tried to resist the growing ambitions of central governments. These confrontations reached crisis proportions in almost all cases during the 1640s and 1650s and then subsided at the very time that the anarchy of warfare and international relations was resolved by the Peace of Westphalia. As a result, the sense of settlement after 1660 contrasted sharply with the turmoil of the preceding decades. Moreover, the progression in politics from turbulence to calm had its analogs in the cultural and social developments of the sixteenth and seventeenth centuries.

QUESTIONS FOR FURTHER THOUGHT

1. Are the social benefits of warfare so minimal, compared to its destructive effects, that one can dismiss them as unimportant?

2. Why are there differences in the ways warfare changes domestic politics?

RECOMMENDED READING

Sources

Kossmann, E. H., and A. E. Mellink. *Texts Concerning the Revolt of the Netherlands*. 1974. A collection of Spanish and Dutch documents that reveal the different political and religious goals of the two sides.

Studies

Aston, Trevor (ed.). *Crisis in Europe, 1560–1660: Essays from Past and Present*. 1965. This is a collection of the essays in which the "general crisis" interpretation was initially put forward and discussed.

Braudel, Fernand. *The Mediterranean and the Mediterranean World in the Age of Philip II.* S. Reynolds (tr.). 2 vols. 1972 and 1973. A pioneering and far-ranging work of social history.

Coward, Barry. *The Cromwellian Protectorate.* 2002.

Duplessis, Robert R. *Transitions to Capitalism in Early Modern Europe.* 1997.

Elliott, J. H. *Richelieu and Olivares.* 1984. A comparative study of the two statesmen who dominated Europe in the 1620s and 1630s; also analyzes the changing nature of political authority.

Hale, J. R. *War and Society in Renaissance Europe, 1450–1620.* 1985. A vivid account of what it meant to be a soldier.

Kishlansky, Mark A. *A Monarchy Transformed: Britain, 1603–1714.* 1997.

MacCaffrey, Wallace. *Elizabeth I.* 1994.

Mattingly, Garrett. *The Armada.* 1959. This beautifully written book, which was a best seller when it first appeared, is a gripping account of a major international crisis.

Moote, A. Lloyd. *The Revolt of the Judges: The Parlement of Paris and the Fronde, 1643–1652.* 1971. The most detailed account of the causes of the Fronde and its failures.

*Munck, Thomas. *Seventeenth-Century Europe: State, Conflict and the Social Order in Europe, 1598–1700.* 2005.

Parker, Geoffrey. *The Army of Flanders and the Spanish Road, 1567–1659: The Logistics of Spanish Victory and Defeat in the Low Countries' Wars.* 2004.

———. *The Dutch Revolt.* 1977. This brief book gives a good introduction to the revolt of the Netherlands and the nature of Dutch society in the seventeenth century.

———. *The Thirty Years' War.* 1984. The most up-to-date history of the war.

Parker, Geoffrey, and Lesley M. Smith (eds.). *The General Crisis of the Seventeenth Century.* 1997.

Pierson, Peter. *Philip II of Spain.* 1975. A clear and lively biography of the dominant figure of the second half of the sixteenth century.

Rabb, Theodore K. *The Struggle for Stability in Early Modern Europe.* 1975. An assessment of the "crisis" interpretation, including extensive bibliographic references.

Rogers, Clifford, J. *The Military Revolution Debate: Readings on the Military Transformation of Early Modern Europe.* 1995.

*Available in paperback.

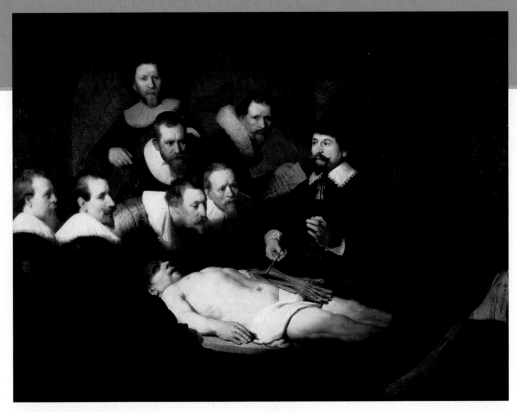

Rembrandt van Rijn
THE ANATOMY LESSON OF DR. NICOLAAS TULP, 1632
Among the many representations of the public anatomy lessons so popular in seventeenth-century Holland, the most famous is one of Rembrandt's greatest paintings, *The Anatomy Lesson of Dr. Nicolaas Tulp.* Here art reflects the new fascination with science.
Mauritshuis, The Hague

Chapter Sixteen

CULTURE AND SOCIETY IN THE AGE OF THE SCIENTIFIC REVOLUTION

SCIENTIFIC ADVANCE FROM COPERNICUS TO NEWTON • THE EFFECTS OF THE DISCOVERIES • THE ARTS AND LITERATURE • SOCIAL PATTERNS AND POPULAR CULTURE

Of all the many changes of the sixteenth and seventeenth centuries, none had a more far-reaching impact than the scientific revolution. By creating a new way of understanding how nature worked—and by solving long-standing problems in physics, astronomy, and anatomy—the theorists and experimenters of this period gave Europeans a new sense of confidence and certainty. They also began to set their civilization apart from the rest of the world, where the outlook of the scientist did not take hold for centuries. Although the revolution began with disturbing questions, but few clear answers, about the physical world, it ended by offering a promise of knowledge and truth that was eagerly embraced by a society racked by decades of religious and political turmoil and uncertainty. Indeed, it is remarkable how closely intellectual and cultural patterns paralleled the progression from struggle and doubt to stable resolution that marked the political developments of these years. In the mid-seventeenth century, just as Europe's states were able to create more settled conditions following a major crisis, so in the realms of philosophy and the study of nature a long period of searching, anxiety, and dispute was resolved by scientists whose discoveries and self-assurance helped restore a sense of order in intellectual life. And in literature, the arts, and social relations, a time of insecurity and doubt also gave way to an atmosphere of confidence and calm.

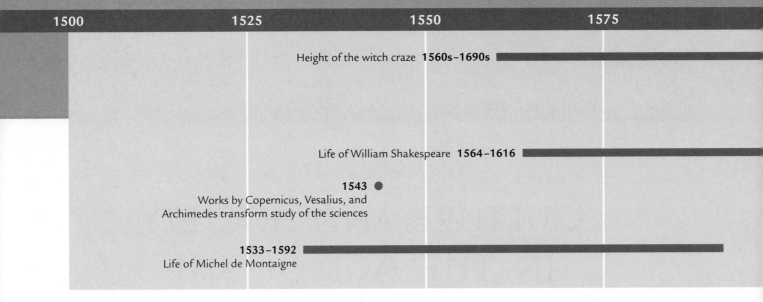

Height of the witch craze **1560s–1690s**

Life of William Shakespeare **1564–1616**

1543 ●
Works by Copernicus, Vesalius, and
Archimedes transform study of the sciences

1533–1592
Life of Michel de Montaigne

SCIENTIFIC ADVANCE FROM COPERNICUS TO NEWTON

Fundamental to the transformation of Europe in the seventeenth century were advances in the knowledge of how nature worked. At first the new discoveries added to the uncertainties of the age, but eventually the scientists were seen as models of orderly thought, who had at last solved ancient problems in convincing fashion.

Origins of the Scientific Revolution

The Importance of Antiquity   Until the sixteenth century, the study of nature in Europe was inspired by the ancient Greeks. Their work shaped subsequent research in three main fields: Aristotle in physics, Ptolemy in astronomy, and Galen in medicine. The most dramatic advances during the **scientific revolution** came in these fields, to some extent because it was becoming evident that the ancient theories could not account for new observations without highly complicated adjustments. For instance, Ptolemy's picture of the heavens, in which all motion was circular around a central earth, did not readily explain the peculiar motion that observers noticed in some planets, which at times seemed to be moving backward. Similarly, dissections often showed Galen's anatomical theories to be wrong.

Despite these problems, scientists (who in the sixteenth and seventeenth centuries were still known as "natural philosophers," or seekers of wisdom about nature) preferred making adjustments rather than beginning anew. And it is unlikely they would have abandoned their cherished theories if it had not been for other influences at work in this period. One such stimulus to rethinking was the Humanists' rediscovery of a number of previously unknown ancient scientists, who had not always agreed with the theories of Aristotle or Ptolemy. A particularly important rediscovery was the work of Archimedes, whose writings on dynamics helped inspire new ideas in physics.

The Influence of "Magical" Beliefs   Another influence was a growing interest in what we now dismiss as "magic," but which at the time was regarded as a serious intellectual enterprise. There were various avenues of magical inquiry, many of which had been pursued in other civilizations, as well as Europe, for centuries. Alchemy was the belief that matter could be understood and transformed by mixing substances and using secret formulas. A famous sixteenth-century alchemist, Paracelsus, suggested that metals as well as plants might have medicinal properties, and he helped demonstrate that mercury (if carefully used) could cure syphilis. Another favorite study was astrology, which claimed that natural phenomena could be predicted if planetary movements were properly interpreted.

What linked these "magical" beliefs was the conviction that the world could be understood through simple, comprehensive keys to nature. The theories of Neoplatonism—an influential school of thought during the Renaissance, based on Plato's belief that truth lay in essential but hidden "forms"—supported this conviction, as did some of the mystical ideas that attracted attention at this time. One of the latter, derived from a system of Jewish thought known as *cabala*, suggested that the universe might be built around magical arrangements of numbers. The ancient Greek mathematician Pythagoras had also suggested that numerical patterns might connect all of nature, and his ideas now gained new attention. For all its irrational elements, it

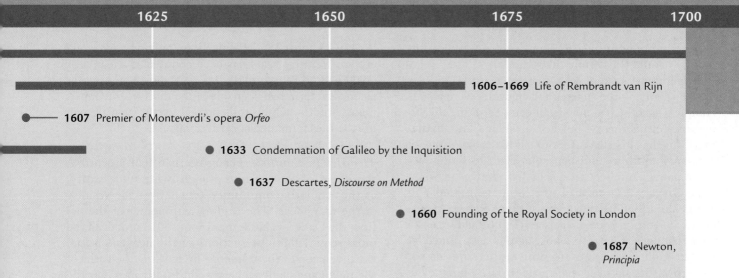

1625   1650   1675   1700

1606–1669 Life of Rembrandt van Rijn

1607 Premier of Monteverdi's opera *Orfeo*

1633 Condemnation of Galileo by the Inquisition

1637 Descartes, *Discourse on Method*

1660 Founding of the Royal Society in London

1687 Newton, *Principia*

was precisely this interest in new and simple solutions for long-standing problems that made natural philosophers capable, for the first time, of discarding the honored theories they had inherited from antiquity, trying different ones, paying greater attention to mathematics, and eventually creating an intellectual revolution.

Observations, Experiments, and Instruments Two other influences deserve mention. The first was Europe's fascination with technological invention. The architects, navigators, engineers, and weapons experts of the Renaissance were important pioneers of a new reliance on measurement and observation that affected not only how domes were built or heavy cannons were moved but also how problems in physics were addressed. A second, and related, influence was the growing interest in experiment among anatomists. In particular, the medical school at the University of Padua became famous for its dissections and direct observations of nature; many leading figures in the scientific revolution were trained there.

It was not too surprising, therefore, that during the sixteenth and seventeenth centuries important new instruments were invented, which helped make scientific discovery possible: the telescope, the vacuum pump, the thermometer, the barometer, and the microscope. These instruments encouraged the development of a scientific approach that was entirely new in the seventeenth century: It did not go back to the ancients, to the practitioners of magic, or to the engineers. This approach rested on the belief that in order to make nature reveal its secrets, it had to be made to do things it did not do normally. What this meant was that one did not simply observe phenomena that occurred normally in nature—for instance, the way a stick seems to bend when it is placed in a glass of water—but created

conditions that were not normal. With the telescope, one saw secrets hidden to the naked eye; with the vacuum pump, one could understand the properties of air.

The Breakthroughs

Vesalius The earliest scientific advances came in anatomy and astronomy, and by coincidence they were announced in two books published in 1543, which was also the year when the earliest printed edition of Archimedes appeared. The first book, *The Structure of the Human Body* by Andreas Vesalius (1514–1564), a member of the Padua faculty, pointed out errors in the work of Galen, the chief authority in medical practice for over a thousand years. Using dissections, Vesalius produced anatomical descriptions that opened a new era of careful observation and experimentation in studies of the body.

Copernicus The second book, *On the Revolutions of the Heavenly Spheres* by Nicolaus Copernicus (1473–1543), a Polish cleric who had studied at Padua, had far greater consequences. A first-rate mathematician, Copernicus believed that the calculations of planetary movements under Ptolemy's system had grown too complex. In Ptolemaic astronomy, the planets and the sun, attached to transparent, crystalline spheres, revolved around the earth. All motion was circular, and irregularities were accounted for by **epicycles**—movement around small revolving spheres that were attached to the larger spheres. Influenced by Neoplatonic ideas, Copernicus believed that a simpler picture would reflect more accurately the true structure of the universe. In sound Neoplatonic fashion, he argued that the sun, as the most splendid of celestial bodies, ought rightfully to be at the center of an orderly

451

and harmonious universe. The earth, no longer immobile, would thus circle the sun.

Copernicus' system was, in fact, scarcely simpler than Ptolemy's—the spheres and epicycles were just as complex—and he had no way of demonstrating the superiority of his theory. But he was such a fine mathematician that his successors found his calculations of planetary motions indispensable. His ideas thus became part of intellectual discussion, drawn on when Pope Gregory XIII decided to reform the calendar in 1582. The Julian calendar, in use since Roman times, counted century years as leap years, thus adding extra days that caused Easter—whose date is determined by the position of the sun—to drift farther and farther away from its normal occurrence in late March. The reform produced the Gregorian calendar, which we still use. Ten days were simply dropped: October 5, 1582,

became October 15; and since then only one out of every four century years has been counted as a leap year (1900 had no February 29, but 2000 did). The need for calendar reform had been one of the motives for Copernicus' studies, which thus proved useful even though his theories remained controversial.

Theories in Conflict   For more than half a century, the effect of *Revolutions* was growing uncertainty, as the scholarly community argued over the validity of the new ideas. The leading astronomer of the period, the Dane Tycho Brahe (1546–1601), produced the most remarkable observations of the heavens before the invention of the telescope by plotting the paths of the moon and planets every night for decades. But the only theory he could come up with was an uneasy compromise between the Ptolemaic and Copernican systems. There was similar indecision among anatomists, who admired Vesalius but were not ready to discard Galen.

Kepler and Galileo Address the Uncertainties

As late as 1600, it seemed that scientists were creating more problems than solutions. But then two brilliant discoverers—the German Johannes Kepler (1571–1630) and Galileo Galilei, an Italian professor of mathematics—made major advances on the work of Copernicus and helped resolve the uncertainties in the field of astronomy.

Kepler and the Laws of Planetary Motion   Like Copernicus, Kepler believed that only the language of mathematics could describe the movements of the heavens. He was a famous astrologer and an advocate of magical theories, but he was also convinced that Copernicus was right. He threw himself into the task of confirming the sun-centered (heliocentric) theory, and by studying Brahe's observations, he discovered three laws of planetary motion (published in 1609 and 1619) that opened a new era in astronomy. Kepler was able to prove that the orbits of the planets are ellipses and that there is a regularity, based on their distance from the sun, which determines the movements of all planets. So revolutionary were these laws that few astronomers accepted them until Isaac Newton used them fifty years later as the basis for a new system of the heavens.

Galileo and a New Physics   A contemporary of Kepler's, the Italian Galileo Galilei (1564–1642), made further advances when he became the first to perceive the connection between planetary motion and motion on

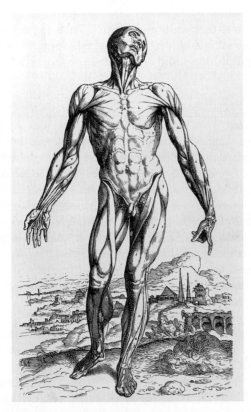

Titian (attrib.)
ENGRAVING ILLUSTRATING THE STRUCTURE OF THE HUMAN BODY BY ANDREAS VESALIUS, 1543
Almost as remarkable as the findings themselves were these illustrations of the results of Vesalius' dissections. Traditionally, professors of anatomy read from textbooks to their students while lowly barber-surgeons cut up a cadaver and displayed the parts being discussed. Vesalius did his dissections himself and thus could observe directly such structures as the musculature. Here his illustrator displays the muscles on a gesturing figure and places it in a stretch of countryside near Padua, where Vesalius taught.

CHRONOLOGY
The Scientific Revolution

adapting a Dutch lens maker's invention, he built a primitive telescope that was essential to his studies of the heavens; and his seemingly mundane experiments, such as swinging a pendulum or rolling balls down inclined planes, were crucial means of testing his theories. Indeed, it was by moving from observations to abstraction that Galileo arrived at the first wholly new way of understanding motion since Aristotle: the principle of inertia.

This breakthrough could not have been made by observation alone, for the discovery of inertia depended on mathematical abstraction, the ability to imagine a situation that cannot be created experimentally: the motion of a perfectly smooth ball across a perfectly smooth plane, free of any outside forces, such as friction. Galileo's conclusion was that "any velocity once imparted to a moving body will be rigidly maintained as long as external causes of acceleration and retardation are removed. . . . If the velocity is uniform, it will not be diminished or slackened, much less destroyed." This insight overturned the Aristotelian view. Galileo had demonstrated that only mathematical language could describe the underlying principles of nature.

A New Astronomy   Galileo's most celebrated work was in astronomy. He first became famous in 1610,

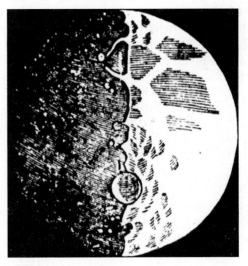

Galileo Galilei
THE MOON, 1610
This sketch of the moon's surface appeared in Galileo's *Starry Messenger* (1610). It shows what he had observed through the telescope and had interpreted as proof that the moon had a rugged surface because the lighted area within the dark section had to be mountains. These caught the light of the setting sun longer than surrounding lower terrain and revealed, for example, a large cavity in the lower center of the sketch.
New York Public Library

earth. His studies revealed the importance to astronomy not only of observation and mathematics but also of physics. Moreover, Galileo's self-consciousness about technique, argument, and evidence marks him as one of the first investigators of nature to approach his work in essentially the same way as a modern scientist.

The study of motion inspired Galileo's most fundamental scientific contributions. When he began his investigations, the Aristotelian view that a body is naturally at rest and needs to be pushed constantly to keep moving dominated the study of dynamics. Galileo broke with this tradition, developing instead a new type of physical explanation that was perfected by Isaac Newton half a century later. Much of Galileo's work was based on observation. From watching how workers at the Arsenal in Venice used pulleys and other devices to lift huge weights, he gained insights into physics;

GALILEO AND KEPLER ON COPERNICUS

In 1597 Kepler sent Galileo a copy of his New Astronomy, *which argued for the Copernican theory of the heavens, and asked the Italian for his opinion. The exchange of letters that followed, with Galileo cautious and Kepler urging him on, reflects an age when the new ideas were not yet proved and also gives a hint, in Kepler's last comments, of the troubles that lay ahead.*

Galileo to Kepler: "Like you, I accepted the Copernican position several years ago. I have written up many reasons on the subject, but have not dared until now to bring them into the open. I would dare publish my thoughts if there were many like you; but, since there are not, I shall forbear."

Kepler's Reply: "I could only have wished that you, who have so profound an insight, would choose another way. You advise us to retreat before the general ignorance and not to expose ourselves to the violent attacks of the mob of scholars. But after a tremendous task has been begun in our time, first by Copernicus and then by many very learned mathematicians, and when the assertion that the Earth moves can no longer be considered something new, would it not be much better to pull the wagon to its goal by our joint efforts, now that we have got it under way, and gradually, with powerful voices, to shout down the common herd? Be of good cheer, Galileo, and come out publicly! If I judge correctly, there are only a few of the distinguished mathematicians of Europe who would part company with us, so great is the power of truth. If Italy seems a less favorable place for your publication, perhaps Germany will allow us this freedom."

From Giorgio de Santillana, *The Crime of Galileo*, Chicago: University of Chicago Press, 1955, pp. 11, 14–15.

---

when he published his discoveries, made with the telescope, that Jupiter has satellites and the moon has mountains. Both these revelations were further blows to traditional beliefs, which held that the earth is changing and imperfect while the heavens are immutable and unblemished. Now, however, it seemed that other planets had satellites, just like the earth, and that these satellites might have the same rough surface as the earth. This was startling enough, but Galileo also argued that the principles of terrestrial physics could be used to explain phenomena in the heavens. He calculated the height of the mountains on the moon by using the geometric techniques of surveyors, and he described the moon's secondary light—seen while it is a crescent—as a reflection of sunlight from the earth. Galileo was treating his own planet simply as one part of a uniform universe. Every physical law, he was saying, is equally applicable on earth and in the heavens, including the laws of motion. As early as 1597 Galileo had admitted that some of his discoveries in physics could be explained only if the earth were moving, and during the next thirty years he became the most famous advocate of Copernicanism in Europe (see "Galileo and Kepler on Copernicus," above).

Galileo made a powerful case. Why, he asked, was it necessary to say that the entire universe revolved around the earth when all celestial motions could be explained by the rotation of a single planet, the earth?

When academic and religious critics argued that we would feel the earth moving or pointed out that the Bible said Joshua made the sun stand still, he reacted with scorn. In response to religious objections, he asserted that "in discussions of physical problems we ought to begin not from the authority of scriptural passages, but from sense experience and necessary demonstrations."

Conflict with the Church   For all the brilliance of his arguments, Galileo was now on dangerous ground. Although traditionally the Catholic Church had not concerned itself with investigations of nature, in the early seventeenth century the situation was changing. The Church was deep in the struggle with Protestantism, and it responded to the challenge to its authority by trying to control potentially questionable views. And Galileo's biting sarcasm toward other scientists antagonized Jesuit and Dominican astronomers. These two orders were the chief upholders of orthodoxy in the Church. They referred Galileo's views to the Inquisition and then guided the attack on Copernicanism by seeking to condemn the brilliant advocate who had made the theory famous throughout Europe.

The Book and the Trial   In 1616 the Inquisition forbade Galileo, within certain limits, to teach the heretical doctrine that the earth moves. When one of his friends was elected pope in 1623, however, Galileo thought he would be safe in writing a major work on astronomy. The result was his *Dialogue on the Two Great World Systems,* published in 1632 (with the approval, probably accidental, of the Church). A marvelously witty, elegant book, the *Dialogue* is one of the few monuments in the history of science that the layperson can read with pleasure. And so it was intended. Galileo wrote it in Italian, not the Latin that had always been used for scholarly works, because he wanted to reach the widest possible audience.

In April 1633 he was brought before the Inquisition for having defied the order not to teach Copernicanism. In a trial that has caused controversy ever since, the aged astronomer, fearing excommunication, abjured the "errors and heresies" of believing that the earth moved. But he did not remain docile for the remainder of his life, though he was kept under house arrest and progressively lost his eyesight. Many of his letters ridiculed his opponents, and in 1638 he published (in tolerant Holland) his principal work on physics, the *Two New Sciences.*

Galileo's Legacy   The condemnation of Galileo discouraged further scientific activity by his compatriots. Italy had been a leader of the new investigations, but now major further advances were made by the English, Dutch, and French. Yet this shift showed merely that the rise of science, once begun, could not be halted for long. By the late 1630s, no self-respecting astronomer could deny the correctness of the Copernican theory.

Assurance Spreads   The new studies of nature may have caused tremendous bewilderment at first, as scientists struggled with the ideas of pioneers like Copernicus and Vesalius. But in the end these investigations created a renewed sense of certainty about the physical world, which was to have a far-reaching influence. This was true not only in physics and astronomy but also in anatomy, where, in 1628, another genius of the scientific revolution, the English doctor William Harvey, revolutionized the understanding of the human body when he identified the function of the heart and proved that the blood circulates.

The Climax of the Scientific Revolution: Isaac Newton

The culmination of the scientific revolution was the work of Isaac Newton (1642–1727), who made decisive contributions to mathematics, physics, astronomy, and optics and brought to a climax the changes that had begun with Copernicus. He united physics and astronomy into a single system to explain all motion, he helped transform mathematics by developing the calculus, and he established some of the basic laws of modern physics.

Part of the explanation of his versatility lies in the workings of the scientific community at the time. Newton was a retiring man who nevertheless got into fierce arguments with prominent contemporaries, such as the learned German scholar and scientist Wilhelm von Leibniz, who was working on the calculus. If not for his active participation in meetings of scientists at the recently founded Royal Society of London (see p. 459), Newton might never have pursued his researches to their conclusion. He disliked the give-and-take of these discussions, but he felt forced, in order to prove that he had solved various problems, to prepare some of his most important papers for the Royal Society. Such institutions were now being established throughout Europe to promote the advance of science, and their creation indicates how far the scientific community had come since the days of Copernicus, who had worked largely in isolation.

The Principia   Newton's masterpiece, *The Mathematical Principles of Natural Philosophy* (1687)—usually referred to by the first word of its Latin title, the *Principia*—claimed that everything he said was proved by experiment or by mathematics.

The most dramatic of Newton's findings was the solution to the ancient problem of motion. Building on Galileo's advances and overturning Aristotle's theories once and for all, Newton defined his system in three laws: first, in the absence of force, motion continues in a straight line; second, the rate of change of the motion is determined by the forces acting on it (such as friction); and third, action and reaction between two bodies are equal and opposite. To arrive at these laws, he defined the concepts of mass, inertia, and force in relation to velocity and acceleration as we know them today.

Newton extended these principles to the entire universe by demonstrating that his laws govern the motions of the moon and planets too. Using the concept of gravity, he provided the explanation of the movement of objects in space that is the foundation for current space travel. There is a balance, he said, between the earth's pull on the moon and the forward motion of the satellite, which would continue in a straight line were it not for the earth's gravity. Consequently, the moon moves in an elliptical orbit in which neither gravity nor inertia gains control. The same pattern is followed by the planets around the sun (as Kepler had shown).

The Influence of Newton   The general philosophical implication of the uniformity that Newton described—that the world was stable and orderly—was as important as his specific discoveries in making him one of the idols of his own and the next centuries. The educated applauded Newton's achievements, and he was the first scientist to receive a knighthood in England. Only a few decades after the appearance of the *Principia,* the poet Alexander Pope summed up the public feeling:

Nature and nature's law lay hid in night;
God said, "Let Newton be!" and all was light.

So overpowering was Newton's stature that in physics and astronomy the remarkable advances of 150 years slowed down for more than half a century after the publication of the *Principia.* There was a general impression that somehow Newton had done it all, that no important problems remained. There were other reasons for the slowdown—changing patterns in education, an inevitable lessening of momentum—but none was so powerful as the reverence for Newton, who became the intellectual symbol of his own and succeeding ages.

THE EFFECTS OF THE DISCOVERIES

The scientists' discoveries about the physical universe made them famous. But it was the *way* they proved their case that made them so influential. The success of their reasoning encouraged a new level of confidence in human powers that helped end the doubts and uncertainties of the previous age.

A New Epistemology

Galileo had stressed that his discoveries rested on a way of thinking that had an independent value, and he refused to allow traditional considerations, such as common sense or theological teachings, to interfere with his conclusions. Scientists were now moving toward a new **epistemology,** a new theory of how to obtain and verify knowledge. They stressed experience, reason, and doubt; they rejected all unsubstantiated authority; and they developed a revolutionary way of determining what was a true description of physical reality.

Scientific Method   The process the scientists said they followed, after they had formulated a hypothesis, consisted of three parts: first, observations; second, a generalization induced from the observations; and third, tests of the generalization by experiments whose outcome could be predicted by the generalization. A generalization remained valid only as long as it was not contradicted by experiments specifically designed to

test it. The scientist used no data except the results of strict observation—such as the time it took balls to roll down Galileo's inclined planes—and scientific reasoning uncovered the laws, principles, or patterns that emerged from the observations. Since measurement was the key to the data, the observations had a numerical, not a subjective, value. Thus, the language of science came to be mathematics.

In fact, scientists rarely reach conclusions in the exact way this idealized scheme suggests. Galileo's perfectly smooth balls and planes, for instance, did not exist, but Galileo understood the relevant physical theory so well that he knew what would happen if one rolled across the other, and he used this "experiment" to demonstrate the principle of inertia. In other words, experiments as well as hypotheses can occur in the mind; the essence of scientific method is a special way of looking at and understanding nature.

The Wider Influence of Scientific Thought

The principles of scientific inquiry received attention throughout the intellectual community only gradually; it took time for the power of the scientists' method to be recognized. If the new methods were to be accepted, their effectiveness would have to be demonstrated to more than a few specialists. This wider understanding was eventually achieved by midcentury, as much through the efforts of ardent propagandizers as through the writings of the great innovators themselves. Gradually, they convinced a broad, educated public that science, after first causing doubts by challenging ancient truths, now offered a promise of certainty that was not to be found anywhere else in an age of general crisis.

Bacon and Descartes

Bacon's Vision of Science   Although he was not an important scientist himself, Francis Bacon was the greatest of science's propagandists, and he inspired a whole generation with his vision of what it could accomplish for humanity. His description of an ideal society in the *New Atlantis*—published in 1627, the year after his death—is a vision of science as the savior of the human race. It predicts a time when those doing research at the highest levels will be regarded as the most important people in the state and will work on vast government-supported projects to gather all known facts about the physical universe. By a process of gradual **induction,** this information will lead to universal laws that, in turn, will enable people to improve their lot on earth. Bacon's view of research as a collective enterprise inspired a number of later scientists, and by the mid-seventeenth century, his ideas had entered the mainstream of European thought.

Descartes and the Principle of Doubt   The Frenchman René Descartes (1596–1650) made the first concentrated attempt to apply the new methods of science to theories of knowledge, and, in so doing, he laid the foundations for modern philosophy. The impulse behind his work was his realization that, for all the importance of observation and experiment, people can be deceived by their senses. In order to find some solid truth, therefore, he decided to apply to all knowledge the principle of doubt—the refusal to accept any authority without strict verification. He began with the assumption that he could know unquestionably only one thing: that he was doubting. This assumption allowed him to proceed to the observation "I think, therefore I am," because the act of doubting proved he was thinking, and thinking, in turn, demonstrated his existence.

From the proof of his own existence he derived a crucial statement: That whatever is clearly and distinctly thought must be true. This assertion in turn enabled him to construct a proof of God's existence. We cannot fail to realize that we are imperfect, he argued, and we must therefore have an idea of perfection against which we may be measured. If we have a clear idea of what perfection is, then it must exist; hence, there must be a God.

The Discourse on Method   Descartes' proof may have served primarily to show that the principle of doubt did not contradict religious belief, but it also reflected the emphasis on the power of the mind in his major work, *Discourse on the Method of Rightly Conducting the Reason and Seeking Truth in the Sciences* (1637). Thought is a pure and unmistakable guide, he said, and only by relying on its operations can people hope to advance their understanding of the world. Descartes developed this view into a fundamental proposition about the nature of the world—a proposition that philosophers have been wrestling with ever since. He stated that there is an essential divide between thought and extension (tangible objects) or, put another way, between spirit and matter. Bacon and Galileo had insisted that science, the study of nature, is separate from and unaffected by faith. But Descartes turned this distinction into a far-reaching principle, dividing not only science from faith but even the reality of the world from our perception of that reality. There is a difference, in other words, between a chair and how we think of it as a chair.

The Influence of Descartes   Descartes' emphasis on the operations of the mind gave a new direction to epistemological discussions. A hypothesis gained credibility not so much from external proofs as from the logical tightness of the arguments used to support it. Descartes thus applied what he considered the methods of science to all of knowledge. Not only the phenomena of nature but all truth had to be investigated according to the methods of the scientist.

Descartes' contributions to scientific research were theoretical rather than experimental. In physics, he was the first to perceive the distinction between mass and weight; and in mathematics, he was the first to apply algebraic notations and methods to geometry, thus founding analytic geometry. Above all, his emphasis on the principle of doubt undermined forever traditional assumptions such as the belief in the hierarchical organization of the universe.

Pascal's Protest Against the New Science

At midcentury only one important voice still protested against the new science and, in particular, against the philosophy of Descartes. It belonged to a Frenchman, Blaise Pascal (1623–1662), a brilliant mathematician and experimenter. Pascal's investigations of probability in games of chance produced the theorem that still bears his name, and his research in conic sections helped lay the foundations for integral calculus. He also helped discover barometric pressure and invented a calculating machine. In his late twenties, however, Pascal became increasingly dissatisfied with scientific research, and he began to wonder whether his life was being properly spent. Moved by a growing concern with faith, Pascal had a mystical experience in November 1654 that made him resolve to devote his life to the salvation of his soul.

The Pensées   During the few remaining years of his life, Pascal wrote a collection of reflections—some only a few words long, some many pages—that were gathered together after his death and published as the *Pensées* (or "Reflections"). These writings revealed not only the beliefs of a deeply religious man but also the anxieties of a scientist who feared the growing influence of science. He did not want to put an end to research; he merely wanted people to realize that the truths uncovered by science were limited and not as important as the truths perceived by faith. As he put it in one of his more memorable *pensées*, "The heart has its reasons that reason cannot know."

Pascal's protest was unique, but the fact that it was put forward at all indicates how high the status of the scientist and his methods had risen by the 1650s. Just a quarter-century earlier, such a dramatic change in fortune would have been hard to predict. But now the new epistemology, after its initial disturbing assault on ancient views, was offering one of the few promises of certainty in an age of upheaval and general crisis. In intellectual matters as in politics, turmoil was gradually giving way to assurance.

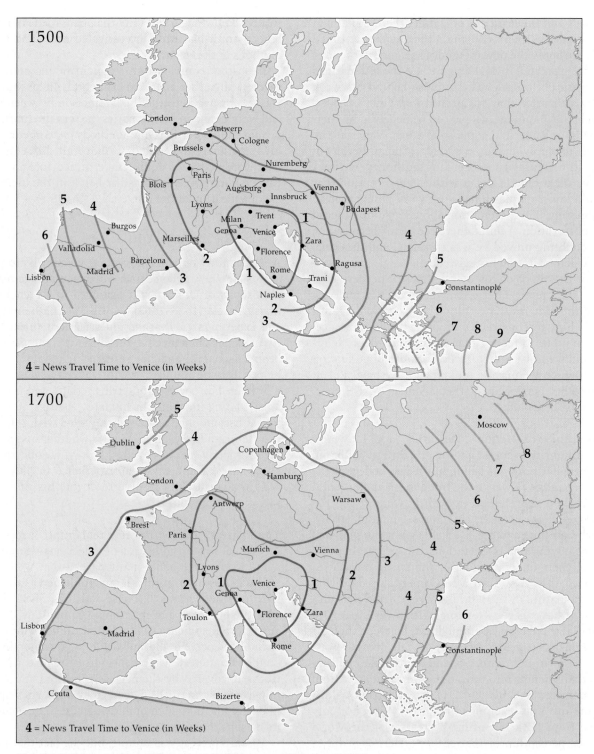

MAP 16.1 SPEED OF NEWS TRAVELING TO VENICE IN 1500 AND 1700
Although the dramatic advances in communications lay in the future, by 1700 improved roads and canals and more efficient shipping did bring about significant advances in the distance news could travel in two or three weeks. How much faster could news get from Madrid to Venice in 1700 than in 1500? What about from Constantinople to Venice? Why might communication across western Europe have speeded up more than across eastern Europe?

Science Institutionalized

Many besides Bacon realized that scientific work should be a cooperative endeavor and that information should be exchanged among all its practitioners. A scientific society founded in Rome in 1603 made the first major effort to apply this view, and it was soon followed up in France, where in the early seventeenth century a friar named Marin Mersenne became the center of an international network of correspondents interested in scientific work. He also spread news by bringing scientists together for discussions and experiments. Contacts that were developed at these meetings led eventually to a more permanent and systematic organization of scientific activity.

The Royal Society   In England, the first steps toward such organization were taken at Oxford during the Civil War in the 1640s, when the revolutionaries captured the city and replaced those at the university who taught traditional natural philosophy. A few of the newcomers formed what they called the Invisible College, a group that met to exchange information and discuss each other's work. The group included only one first-class scientist, the chemist Robert Boyle; but in 1660 he and eleven others formed an official organization, the Royal Society of London for Improving Natural Knowledge, with headquarters in the capital. In 1662 it was granted a charter by Charles II—the first sign of a link with political authority that not only boosted science but also indicated the growing presence of central governments in all areas of society.

The Royal Society's purposes were openly Baconian. Its aim for a few years—until everyone realized it was impossible—was to gather all knowledge about nature, particularly if it had practical uses. For a long time the members offered their services for the public good, helping in one instance to develop for the government the science of social statistics ("political arithmetic," as it was called). Soon, however, it became clear that the society's principal function was to serve as a headquarters and clearing center for research. Its secretaries

L'ACADEMIE DES SCIENCES   ET DES BEAUX ARTS
DEDIEE   AU ROY

Charles-Nicolas Cochin
THE ACADÈMIE ROYALE DES SCIENCES, PARIS, ENGRAVING, 1698
This celebration of the work done by one of the first scientific societies suggests the variety of research that these organizations promoted. In contrast to the students of theology, who merely read books (as we see through the arch on the right), the geographers, engineers, astronomers, physicists, and anatomists of the scientific academy examine the real world.
© British Museum, Department of Prints and Drawings ([C292] Neg # N/N R8–85)

maintained an enormous correspondence to encourage English and foreign scholars to send in news of their discoveries. And in 1665 the society began the regular publication of *Philosophical Transactions,* the first professional scientific journal.

Other Scientific Societies Imitators soon followed. In 1666 Louis XIV gave his blessing to the founding of a French Royal Academy of Sciences, and similar organizations were established in Naples and Berlin by 1700. Membership in these societies was limited and highly prized, a sign of the glamour that was beginning to attach itself to the new studies. By the 1660s there could be no doubt that science, secure in royal patronage, had become a model for all thought. Its practitioners were extravagantly admired, and throughout intellectual and high social circles, there was a scramble to apply its methods to almost every conceivable activity.

The Wider Appeal of Science Descartes had applied the ideas of science to philosophy in general; Bacon had said they must be useful. And the applications soon were widespread. Formal gardens were designed to show the order, harmony, and reason that science had made such prized qualities. Methods of fortification and warfare were affected by the new emphasis on accurate measurement. As the scientists' activities became more popular and fashionable, even aristocrats began to spend time playing at science. Herbariums and small observatories were added to country estates, and parties featured an evening of star gazing. Science also fascinated the general populace. Among the most eagerly anticipated occasions in seventeenth-century Holland was the public anatomy lesson. The body of a criminal would be brought to an enormous hall that was packed with students and a fascinated public. A famous surgeon would dissect the cadaver, announcing and displaying each organ as he removed it.

On the whole, the reverence for science and its methods did not develop from an understanding of its actual accomplishments or its potential consequences. Rather, it was caused by the fame of the spectacular discoveries that had offered new and convincing solutions to centuries-old problems in astronomy, physics, and anatomy. Here was a promise of certainty and order in a world that otherwise was bedeviled by conflict and doubt. As a result, the protests of Pascal could be ignored, and the new discipline could be given unblemished admiration. The entire world was coming to be viewed through the scientist's eyes—a striking achievement for a recently minor member of the intellectual community—and the qualities of regularity and harmony associated with science began to appear in the work of artists and writers.

THE ARTS AND LITERATURE

We have seen that in the mid-seventeenth century a more settled Europe emerged from the political turbulence and crisis of the late 1500s and early 1600s. And we have seen that the development of science followed a similar pattern—with decades of uncertainty as old truths were challenged, and then a new sense of assurance in the mid-seventeenth century. Not surprisingly, so, too, did the concerns of the arts and literature.

Unsettling Art

Mannerism One response that was provoked by the upheavals of the sixteenth century was the attempt to escape reality, an effort that was echoed by some of the painters of the age, known as *Mannerists.* The Mannerists and their patrons reacted against the serenity and idealization of the High Renaissance by cultivating artificial and esoteric images of the world; they undermined perspective, distorted human figures, and devised unnatural colors and lighting to create startling effects.

El Greco Mannerism was embodied in El Greco (1541–1614), a Greek who was trained in Italy and settled in Spain. His compelling and almost mystic canvases created an otherworldly alternative to the troubles of his time. El Greco's cool colors, eerie lighting, and elongated and often agonized human beings make him one of the most distinctive painters in the history of art (see p. 422). After 1600, though, painters increasingly rejected the Mannerists' flight from reality; eventually the arts, too, reflected the sense of settlement that descended over European civilization in the mid-seventeenth century.

Unsettling Writers

Michel de Montaigne In the world of literature, the concerns of the age were most vividly expressed by the Frenchman Michel de Montaigne (1533–1592). Obsessed by the death he saw all around him and determined to overcome his fears, he retired in 1570 to his country home in order to "essay," or test, his innermost feelings by writing short pieces of prose even about subjects he did not fully comprehend. In the process he created a new literary form, the essay, that also helped shape the modern French language. But his chief influence was philosophical: He has inspired the search for self-knowledge ever since.

At first Montaigne's anxieties led him to radical doubt about the possibility of finding truth; known as **skepticism,** this preoccupation inspired the total uncertainty of his motto, "Que sais-je?" ("What do I know?"). Eventually, however, Montaigne struggled toward a more confident view, taking as his model the ancient saying "Know thyself." By looking into one's own person, one can find values that hold true at least for oneself, and these will reflect the values of all humanity. Montaigne came close to a morality without theology, because good and self-determination were more important to him than doctrine, and he saw everywhere religious people committing inhuman acts. Trying to be an angel is wrong, he said; being good is enough.

Montaigne was also one of the first writers to use non-Western models to criticize Europeans. He met a cannibal who had been brought to France, and he suggested that those who kill for food were more moral than those who kill for other purposes, such as religious beliefs.

Neostoicism   A more general approach to morality was a theory known as **Neostoicism,** inspired by the ancient Stoics' emphasis on self-knowledge and a calm acceptance of the world. The most influential of the Neostoics, a Dutch writer named Justus Lipsius, argued that public leaders ought to be guided by profound self-examination. Lipsius urged rulers to be restrained and self-disciplined, and he was much admired by the kings and royal ministers of the seventeenth century.

Cervantes   In Spain the disillusionment that accompanied the political and economic decline of Europe's most powerful state was perfectly captured by Miguel de Cervantes (1547–1616). Cervantes saw the wide gap between the hopes and the realities of his day—in religion, in social institutions, in human behavior—and made the dichotomy the basis of scathing social satire in his novel *Don Quixote.*

At one level, Cervantes was ridiculing the excessive chivalry of the Spanish nobility in his portrayal of a knight who was ready to tilt at windmills, though he obviously admired the sincerity of his well-meaning hero and sympathized with him as a perennial loser. On another level, the author brought to life the Europe of the time—the ordinary people and their hypocrisies and intolerances—with a liveliness rarely matched in literature. Cervantes avoided politics, but he was clearly directing many of his sharpest barbs at the brutality and disregard for human values that were characteristic of his fanatical times. And in England another towering figure was grappling with similar problems.

Shakespeare   For the English-speaking world, the most brilliant writer of this and all other periods was William Shakespeare (1564–1616), whose characters bring to life almost every conceivable mood: searing grief, airy romance, rousing nationalism, uproarious humor. Despite his modest education, his imagery shows a familiarity with subjects ranging from astronomy to seamanship, from alchemy to warfare. During most of his writing career, Shakespeare was involved with a theatrical company, where he often had to produce plays on short notice. He thus had the best of all possible tests—audience reactions—as he gained mastery of theatrical techniques.

Shakespeare's plays made timeless statements about human behavior: love, hatred, violence, sin. Of particular interest to the historian, however, is what he tells us about attitudes that belong especially to his own era. Again and again, legality and stability are shown as fundamental virtues amidst turbulent times. Shakespeare's expressions of patriotism are particularly intense; when in *Richard II* the king's uncle, John of Gaunt, lies dying, he pours out his love for his country in words that have moved the English ever since:

> This royal throne of kings, this scepter'd isle,
> This earth of majesty, this seat of Mars,
> This other Eden, demi-paradise, . . .
> This happy breed of men, this little world,
> This precious stone set in the silver sea, . . .
> This blessed plot, this earth,
> This realm, this England.
>
> *Richard II*, act 2, scene 1

As in so much of the art and writing of the time, instability is a central concern of Shakespeare's plays. His four most famous tragedies—*Hamlet, King Lear, Macbeth,* and *Othello*—end in disillusionment: The heroes are ruined by irresoluteness, pride, ambition, and jealousy. Shakespeare was exploring a theme that had absorbed playwrights since Euripides—the fatal flaws that destroy the great—and producing dramas of revenge that were popular in his day; but the plays also demonstrate his deep understanding of human nature. Whatever one's hopes, one cannot forget human weakness, the inevitability of decay, and the constant threat of disaster. The contrast appears with compelling clarity in a speech delivered by Hamlet:

> What a piece of work is man! How noble in reason!
> how infinite in faculties! in form and moving how
> express and admirable! in action how like an angel!
> in apprehension how like a god! the beauty of the
> world, the paragon of animals! And yet to me what
> is this quintessence of dust? Man delights not me.
>
> *Hamlet*, act 2, scene 2

Despite such pessimism, despite the deep sense of human inadequacy, the basic impression Shakespeare gives is of immense vigor, of a restlessness and confidence that recall the many achievements of the sixteenth century. Yet a sense of decay is never far absent. Repeatedly, people seem utterly helpless, overtaken by events they cannot control. Nothing remains constant or dependable, and everything that seems solid or reassuring, be it the love of a daughter or the crown of England, is challenged. In this atmosphere of ceaseless change, where landmarks easily disappear, Shakespeare conveys the tensions of his time.

The Return of Assurance in the Arts

The Baroque   After 1600, the arts began to move toward the assurance and sense of settlement that was descending over other areas of European civilization. A new style, the **Baroque,** sought to drown the uneasiness of Mannerism in a blaze of grandeur. Passion, drama, mystery, and awe were the qualities of the Baroque: Every art form—from music to literature, from architecture to opera—had to involve, arouse, and uplift its audience.

The Baroque style was closely associated with the Counter-Reformation's emphasis on gorgeous display in Catholic ritual. The patronage of leading Church figures made Rome a magnet for the major painters of the period. Elsewhere, the Baroque flourished primarily at the leading Catholic courts of the seventeenth century,

most notably the Habsburg courts in Madrid, Prague, and Brussels, and remained influential well into the eighteenth century in such Catholic areas as the Spanish Empire. Few styles have conveyed so strong a sense of grandeur, theatricality, and ornateness.

Caravaggio   The artist who first shaped the new aesthetic, Caravaggio (1571–1610), lived most of his life in Rome. Although he received commissions from high Church figures and spent time in a cardinal's household, he was equally at home among the beggars and petty criminals of Rome's dark back streets. These ordinary people served as Caravaggio's models, which shocked those who believed it inappropriate for such humble characters to represent the holy figures of biblical scenes. Yet the power of Caravaggio's paintings—their depiction of highly emotional moments, and the drama created by their sharp contrasts of light and dark—made his work much prized. He had to flee Rome after he killed someone

Caravaggio
THE SUPPER AT EMMAUS, CA. **1597**
By choosing moments of high drama and using sharp contrasts of light, Caravaggio created an immediacy that came to be one of the hallmarks of Baroque painting. Here he shows the moment during the supper at Emmaus when his disciples suddenly recognized the resurrected Christ. The force of their emotions and their almost theatrical gestures convey the intensity of the moment, but many at the time objected to the craggy, tattered appearance of the disciples. These were not idealized figures, as was expected, but ordinary people at a humble table.
By courtesy of the Trustees, © The National Gallery, London (NG172)/Art Resource, NY

Artemisia Gentileschi
JUDITH SLAYING HOLOFERNES, CA. 1620
Female artists were rare in the seventeenth century
because they were not allowed to become apprentices.
But Artemisia (1593–1652) was the daughter of a painter
who happened to be a friend of Caravaggio, and she had
the opportunity to become a gifted exponent of Baroque
style. Known throughout Europe for her vivid portrayals
of dramatic scenes (she painted the murder of Holofernes
by the biblical heroine Judith at least five times), she
practiced her chosen profession with considerable
success, despite the trauma of being raped at age
seventeen by a friend of her father's—an act of violence
that may be reflected (and avenged) in this painting.
Uffizi, Florence, Italy. Scala/Art Resource, NY

Peter Paul Rubens
DESCENT FROM THE CROSS, 1612
This huge altarpiece was one of the first pictures Rubens painted
upon returning to his native Antwerp after spending most of his
twenties developing his art in Italy. The ambitious scale, the
strong emotions, the vivid lighting, and the dramatic action
showed the artist's commitment to the Baroque style that had
recently evolved in Italy. The powerful impact of the altarpiece
helped make him one of the most sought-after painters of the day.
Center panel. Scala/Art Resource, NY

in a brawl, but he left behind an outpouring of work that influenced an entire generation of painters.

Rubens Among those who came to Rome to study Caravaggio's art was Peter Paul Rubens (1577–1640), the principal ornament of the brilliant Habsburg court at Brussels. His major themes typified the grandeur that came to be the hallmark of Baroque style: glorifications of great rulers and also of the ceremony and mystery of Catholicism. Rubens' secular paintings convey enormous strength; his religious works overwhelm the viewer with the majesty of the Church and excite the believer's piety by stressing the power of the faith.

Velázquez Other artists glorified rulers through idealized portraiture. The greatest court painter of the age was Diego Velázquez (1599–1660). His portraits of members of the Spanish court depict rulers and their surroundings in the stately atmosphere appropriate to the theme. Yet occasionally Velázquez hinted at the weakness of an ineffective monarch in his rendering of the face, even though the basic purpose of his work was always to exalt royal power. And his celebration of a notable Habsburg victory, *The Surrender of Breda,* managed to suggest the sadness and emptiness as much as the glory of war.

Bernini GianLorenzo Bernini (1598–1680) brought to sculpture and architecture the qualities that Rubens brought to painting, and like Rubens he was closely associated with the Counter-Reformation. Pope Urban VIII commissioned him in 1629 to complete both the inside

Diego Velázquez
THE SURRENDER OF BREDA, 1635
The contrasting postures of victory and defeat are masterfully captured by Diego Velázquez in *The Surrender of Breda.* The Dutch soldiers droop their heads and lances, but the victorious Spaniards hardly show triumph, and the gesture of the victorious general, Ambrogio Spinola, is one of consolation and understanding.
Oroñoz

GianLorenzo Bernini
ST. PETER'S SQUARE AND CHURCH, ROME
The magnificent circular double colonnade that Bernini created in front of St. Peter's is one of the triumphs of
Baroque architecture. The church itself was already the largest in Christendom (markers in the floor still indicate
how far other famous churches would reach if placed inside St. Peter's), and it was topped by the huge dome
Michelangelo had designed. The vast enclosed space that Bernini built reinforced the grandeur of a church that
was the pope's own.
Corbis

and the outer setting of the basilica of St. Peter's in
Rome. For the interior, Bernini designed a splendid
papal throne that seems to float on clouds beneath a
burst of sunlight. For the exterior, he created an
enormous plaza, surrounded by a double colonnade, that
is the largest such plaza in Europe. Similarly, his dramatic religious works reflect the desire of the Counter-
Reformation popes to electrify the faithful. The sensual
and overpowering altarpiece dedicated to the Spanish
mystic St. Teresa makes a direct appeal to the emotions
of the beholder that is the epitome of the excitement and
confidence of the Baroque.

New Dimensions in Music   The seventeenth century
was significant, too, as a decisive time in the history of
music. New instruments, notably in the keyboard and
string families, enabled composers to create richer effects than had been possible before. Particularly in
Italy, which in the sixteenth and seventeenth centuries
was the chief center of new ideas in music, musicians
began to explore the potential of a form that first
emerged in these years: the opera. Drawing on the resources of the theater, painting, architecture, music,
and dance, an operatic production could achieve splendors that were beyond the reach of any one of these arts
on its own. The form was perfectly attuned to the
courtly culture of the age, to the love of display among
the princes of Europe, and to the Baroque determination to overwhelm one's audience.

The dominant figure in seventeenth-century music
was the Italian Claudio Monteverdi (1567–1643), one of
the most innovative composers of all time. He has been
called with some justification the creator of both the
operatic form and the orchestra. His masterpiece, *Orfeo*
(1607), was a tremendous success, and in the course of
the next century operas gained in richness and complexity, attracting composers, as well as audiences, in
ever-increasing numbers.

GianLorenzo Bernini
THE ECSTASY OF ST. TERESA, **1652**
Bernini's sculpture is as dramatic an example of Baroque art as the paintings of Caravaggio. The moment that St. Teresa described in her autobiography at which she attained mystic ecstasy, as an angel repeatedly pierced her heart with a dart, became in Bernini's hands the centerpiece of a theatrical tableau. He placed the patrons who had commissioned the work on two walls of the chapel that houses this altarpiece, sitting in what seem to be boxes and looking at the stage on which the drama unfolds.
Scala/Art Resource, NY

Stability and Restraint in the Arts

Classicism **Classicism,** the other major style of the seventeenth century, attempted to recapture (though on a much larger scale than Renaissance imitations of antiquity) the aesthetic values and the strict forms that had been favored in ancient Greece and Rome. Like the Baroque, Classicism aimed for grandiose effects, but unlike the Baroque, it achieved them through restraint and discipline within a formal structure. The gradual rise of the Classical style in the seventeenth century echoed the trend toward stability that was taking place in other areas of intellectual life and in politics. In the arts, the age of striving and unrest was coming to an end.

Poussin The epitome of disciplined expression and conscious imitation of Classical antiquity was Nicolas Poussin (1594–1665), a French artist who spent much of his career in Rome. Poussin was no less interested than his contemporaries in momentous and dramatic subjects, but the atmosphere is always more subdued than in the work of Velázquez or Rubens. The colors are muted, the figures are restrained, and the settings are serene. Peaceful landscapes, men and women in togas, and ruins of Classical buildings are features of his art.

The Dutch Style In the United Provinces different forces were at work, and they led to a style that was much more intimate than the grandiose outpourings of a Rubens or a Velázquez. Two aspects of Dutch society, Protestantism and republicanism, had a particular influence on its painters. The Reformed Church frowned on religious art, which reduced the demand for paintings of biblical scenes. Religious works, therefore, tended to express personal faith. And the absence of a court meant that the chief patrons of art were sober merchants, who were far more interested in precise, dignified portraits than in ornate displays. The result, notably in the profound and moving works of Rembrandt, was a compelling art whose beauty lies in its calmness and restraint.

Rembrandt

Rembrandt van Rijn (1606–1669) explored an amazing range of themes, but he was particularly fascinated by human character, emotion, and self-revelation. Whether children or old people, simple servant girls or rich burghers, his subjects are presented without elaboration or idealization; always the personality speaks for itself. Rembrandt's most remarkable achievement in portraiture—and one of the most moving series of canvases in the history of art—is his depiction of the changes in his own face over his lifetime. The brash youth turns into the confident, successful, middle-aged man, one of the most sought-after painters in Holland. But in his late thirties the sorrows mounted: He lost his beloved wife, and commissions began to diminish. Sadness fills the eyes in these pictures. The

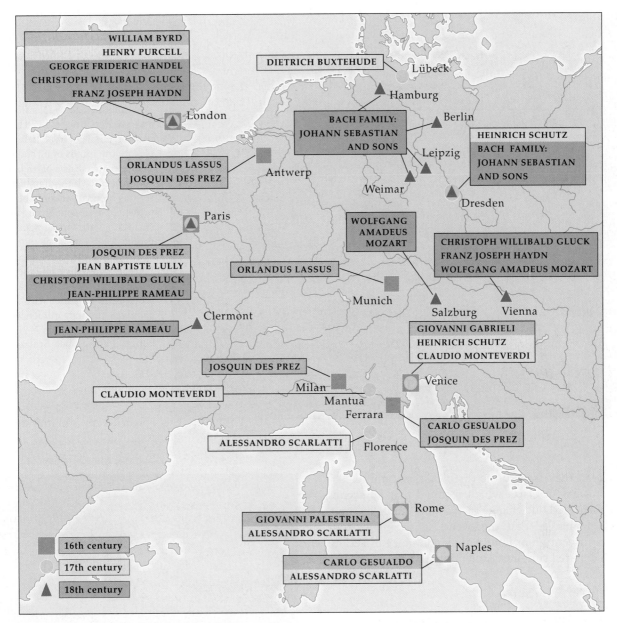

MAP 16.2 CENTERS OF MUSIC, 1500–1800
This map indicates the shifting centers of new ideas in music from Flanders and Italy in the sixteenth century, to Italy in the seventeenth, and on to Germany in the eighteenth. Where, outside of Germany, were other key centers of creativity in music in the eighteenth century?

last portraits move from despair to a final, quiet resignation as his sight slowly failed. Taken together, these paintings bear comparison with Montaigne's essays as monuments to the exploration of one's own spirit—a searching appraisal that brings all who see it to a deeper understanding of human nature.

Like the advocates of Classicism, Rembrandt in his restraint seems to anticipate the art of the next generation. After his death in 1669, serenity, calm, and elegance became the watchwords of European painting. An age of repose and grace was succeeding a time of upheaval as surely in the arts as in other spheres of life.

Classicism in Drama

By the middle of the seventeenth century, the formalism of the Classical style was also being extended to literature, especially drama. This change was most noticeable in France, but it soon moved through western Europe, as leading critics insisted that new plays conform to the structure laid down by the ancients. In

Nicolas Poussin
THE INSPIRATION OF THE POET,
CA. 1628
Whereas Baroque art emphasized emotion, the Classical style sought to embody reason. Poussin, the leading Classical artist of his time, believed that painting, like poetry, had to elevate the minds of its audience. The poet was thus a particularly apt subject for him—a noble and serious theme that could be presented as a scene from antiquity, with formal figures, muted colors, and ancient symbols like the laurel wreath. Poussin's views became the official doctrine of the academy of art founded in France with royal approval, and they influenced generations of painters.
Louvre, Paris, France. Scala/Art Resource, NY

particular, they wanted the three Classical unities observed: unity of place, which required that all scenes take place without change of location; unity of time, which demanded that the events in the play occur within a twenty-four-hour period; and unity of action, which dictated simplicity and purity of plot.

Corneille

The work of Pierre Corneille (1606–1684), the dominant figure in the French theater during the midcentury years, reflects the rise of Classicism. His early plays were complex and involved, and even after he came into

Rembrandt van Rijn
SELF-PORTRAIT WITH PALETTE, 1660
More than sixty self-portraits by Rembrandt have survived; though all are penetrating explorations of human character, those from his last years are especially moving. We see him here in his mid-fifties with the tools of his trade. Adapting Caravaggio's interest in light, he uses different shades of brown and the illumination of the face to create a somber and reflective mood. The very act of thinking is captured in this canvas, not to mention the full life that is etched in Rembrandt's wrinkles.
Louvre, Paris, France. Scala/Art Resource, NY

contact with the Classical tradition, he did not accept its rules easily. His masterpiece, *Le Cid* (1636), based on the legends of a medieval Spanish hero, technically observed the three unities, but only by compressing an entire tragic love affair, a military campaign, and many other events into one day. The play won immediate popular success, but the critics, urged on by the royal minister Cardinal Richelieu, who admired the regularity and order of Classical style, condemned Corneille for imperfect observance of the three unities. Thereafter, he adhered to the Classical forms, though he was never entirely at ease with their restraints.

Passion was not absent from the Classical play; the works of Jean Racine (1639–1699), the model Classical dramatist, generate some of the most intense emotion ever seen on the stage. But the exuberance of earlier drama was disappearing. Nobody summed up the values of Classicism better than Racine in his eulogy of Corneille:

> You know in what a condition the stage was when he began to write. . . . All the rules of art, and even those of decency and decorum, broken everywhere. . . . Corneille, after having for some time sought the right path and struggled against the bad taste of his day, inspired by extraordinary genius and helped by the study of the ancients, at last brought reason upon the stage.
>
> Paul Mesnard (ed.), *Oeuvres de J. Racine*, Vol. 4, 1886, p. 366, trans. T. K. Rabb.

This was exactly the progression—from turbulence to calm—that was apparent throughout European culture in this period.

SOCIAL PATTERNS AND POPULAR CULTURE

The new sense of orderliness, of upheaval subdued, was visible throughout European society in the last years of the seventeenth century. After decades of political and religious conflict, of expressions of uneasiness in philosophy, literature, and the arts, stability and confidence were on the rise. Similarly, the end of population decline, the restoration of social order, and the suppression of disruptive forces like witchcraft indicated that the tensions were easing at all levels of society.

Population Trends

The sixteenth-century rise in Europe's population was succeeded by a period of decline that in most areas lasted long after the political and intellectual upheavals subsided. The rise had been fragile, because throughout these centuries only one child in two reached adulthood. Each couple had to give birth to four children merely to replace themselves, and since they had to wait until they were financially independent to marry—usually in their mid-twenties—they rarely had the chance to produce a big family. Before improvements in nutrition in the nineteenth century, women could bear children only until their late thirties; on average, therefore, a woman had some twelve years in which to give birth to four children to maintain the population. Because lactation delayed ovulation, the mean interval between births was almost two and a half years, which meant that most couples were capable of raising only two children to adulthood. As soon as there was outside pressure—such as plague, famine, or war—population growth became impossible.

The worst of these outside pressures in the seventeenth century was the Thirty Years' War, which alone caused the death of more than five million people. It also helped plunge Europe into a debilitating economic depression, which, in turn, decreased the means of relieving the regular famines that afflicted all areas. Disasters like these were not easily absorbed, despite government efforts to distribute food and take other measures to combat natural calamities. Only when better times returned could population increase resume. Because England and the Netherlands led the economic recovery, they experienced a demographic revival long before their neighbors; indeed, the rise in their numbers, which began in the 1660s, accounted for most of the slight population increase the whole of

EUROPE'S POPULATION, 1600–1700, BY REGIONS			
Region	*1600**	*1700*	*Percentage Change*
Spain, Portugal, Italy	23.6	22.7	−4
France, Switzerland, Germany	35.0	36.2	+3
British Isles, Low Countries, Scandinavia	12.0	16.1	+34
Total	70.6	75.0	+6

* All figures are in millions.

From Jan de Vries, *The Economy of Europe in an Age of Crisis, 1600–1750*, Cambridge, 1976, p. 5.

Europe was able to achieve in this difficult century. By 1700, though, prosperity and population were again on the rise—both a reflection and a cause of Europe's new-found assurance and stability.

Social Status

The determinants of status in modern times—wealth, education, and family background—were viewed rather differently in the seventeenth century. Wealth was significant chiefly to merchants, education was important mainly among professionals, and background was vital primarily to the nobility. But in this period the significance of these three social indicators began to shift. Wealth became a more general source of status, as ever-larger numbers of successful merchants bought offices, lands, and titles that allowed them to enter the nobility. Education was also becoming more highly prized; throughout Europe attendance at institutions of higher learning soared after 1550, bringing to universities the sons of artisans as well as nobles. And although background was being scrutinized ever more defensively by old-line nobles, who regarded family lineage as the only criterion for acceptance into their ranks, their resistance to change was futile as the "new" aristocrats multiplied.

In general, it was assumed that everyone occupied a fixed place in the social hierarchy and that it was against the order of nature for someone to move to another level. The growing social importance of wealth and education, however, indicates that mobility was possible. Thanks to the expansion of bureaucracies, it became easier to move to new levels, either by winning favor at court or by buying an office.

Contradictions in the Status of Women At each level of society, women were usually treated as subordinate by the legal system: In many countries, even the widows of aristocrats could not inherit their husbands' estates; an abbess could never become prominent in church government; and the few women allowed to practice a trade were excluded from the leadership of their guild. Yet there were notable businesswomen and female artists, writers, and even scientists among the growing numbers of successful self-made people in this period. Widows often inherited their husbands' businesses and pursued thriving careers in their own right, from publishing to innkeeping. One of Caravaggio's most distinguished disciples was Artemisia Gentileschi; the Englishwoman Aphra Behn was a widely known playwright; and some of the leading patrons of intellectual life were the female aristocrats who ran literary circles, particularly in Paris. In fiction and drama, female characters often appeared as the equals

of males, despite the legal restrictions of the time and the warnings against such equality in sermons and moral treatises.

Mobility and Crime

The Peasants' Plight The remarkable economic advances of the sixteenth century helped change attitudes toward wealth, but they brought few benefits to the lower levels of society. Peasants throughout Europe were, in fact, entering a time of increasing difficulty at the end of the sixteenth century. Their taxes were rising rapidly, but the prices they got for the food they grew were stabilizing. Moreover, landowners were starting what has been called the "seigneurial reaction"—making additional demands on their tenants, raising rents, and squeezing as much as they could out of the lands they owned. The effects of famine and war were also more severe at this level of society. The only escapes were to cities or armies, both of which grew rapidly in the seventeenth century. Many of those who fled their villages, however, remained on the road, part of the huge bodies of vagrants and beggars who were a common sight throughout Europe.

A few of those who settled in a town or city improved their lot, but for the large majority, poverty in cities was even more miserable and hungry than poverty on the land. Few could become apprentices, and day laborers were poorly paid and usually out of work. As for military careers, armies were carriers of disease, frequently ill fed, and subject to constant hardship.

Crime and Punishment For many, therefore, the only alternative to starvation was crime. One area of London in the seventeenth century was totally controlled by the underworld. It offered refuge to fugitives and was never entered by respectable citizens. Robbery and violence—committed equally by desperate men, women, and even children—were common in most cities. As a result, social events like dinners and outings, or visits to the theater, took place during the daytime because the streets were unsafe at night.

If caught, Europe's criminals were treated harshly. In an age before regular police forces, however, catching them was difficult. Crime was usually the responsibility of local authorities, who depended on part-time officials (known in England as constables) for law enforcement. Only in response to major outbreaks, such as a gang of robbers preying on travelers, would the authorities recruit a more substantial armed band (rather like a posse in the American West) to pursue criminals. If such efforts succeeded in bringing offenders to justice, the defendants found they had few rights, especially if they were poor, and punishments were severe. Torture was a common means of extracting confessions; various forms of maiming, such as chopping off a hand or an ear, were considered acceptable penalties; and repeated thefts could lead to execution. Society's hierarchical instincts were apparent even in civil disputes, where nobles were usually immune from prosecution and women often could not start a case. If a woman was raped, for example, she had to find a man to bring suit.

Change in the Villages and Cities

Loss of Village Cohesiveness   Over three-quarters of Europe's population still lived in small village communities, but their structure was changing. In Eastern Europe, peasants were being reduced to serfdom; in the West—our principal concern—familiar relationships and institutions were changing.

The essence of the traditional village had been its isolation. Cut off from frequent contact with the world beyond its immediate region, it had been self-sufficient and closely knit. Everyone knew everyone else, and mutual help was vital for survival. There might be distinctions among villagers—some more prosperous, others less so—but the sense of cohesiveness was powerful. It extended even to the main "outsiders" in the village, the priest and the local lord. The priest was often indistinguishable from his parishioners: almost as poor and sometimes hardly more literate. He adapted to local customs and beliefs, frequently taking part in semipagan rituals so as to keep his authority with his flock. The lord could be exploitative and demanding; but he considered the village his livelihood, and he therefore kept in close touch with its affairs and did all he could to ensure its safety, orderliness, and well-being.

Forces of Change   The main intrusions onto this scene were economic and demographic. As a result of the boom in agricultural prices during the sixteenth century, followed by the economic difficulties of the seventeenth, differences in the wealth of the villagers became more marked. The richer peasants began to set themselves apart from their poorer neighbors, and the feeling of village unity began to break down. These divisions were exacerbated by the rise in population during the sixteenth century—which strained resources and forced the less fortunate to leave in search of better opportunities in cities—and by the pressures of taxation, exploitation, plague, and famine during the more difficult times of the seventeenth century.

Another intrusion that undermined the traditional cohesion of the community was the increased presence of royal officials. For centuries, elected councils, drawn from every part of the population, had run village affairs throughout Europe. In the late seventeenth century, however, these councils began to disappear as outside forces—in some cases a nearby lord, but more often government officials—asserted their control over the localities. Tax gatherers and army recruiters were now familiar figures throughout Europe. Although they were often the target of peasant rebellions, they were also welcomed when, for example, they distributed food during a famine. Their long-term influence, however, was the creation of a new layer of outside authority in the village, which was another cause of the division and fragmentation that led many to flee to the city.

As these outside intrusions multiplied, the interests of the local lord, who traditionally had defended the village's autonomy and had offered help in times of need, also changed. Nobles were beginning to look more and more to royal courts and capital cities, rather than to their local holdings, for position and power. The natural corollary was the "seigneurial reaction," with lords treating the villages they dominated as sources of income and increasingly distancing themselves from the inhabitants. Their commitment to charitable works declined, and they tended more and more to leave the welfare of the local population to church or government officials.

City Life   As village life changed, the inhabitants who felt forced to leave headed for the city—an impersonal place where, instead of joining a cohesive population, they found themselves part of a mingling of peoples. The growing cities needed ever wider regions to provide them with food and goods, and they attracted the many who could not make ends meet in the countryside. Long-distance communications became more common, especially as localities were linked into national market and trade networks, and in the cities the new immigrants met others from distant villages.

A city was a far more chaotic place than a rural community. Urban society in general was fragmentary and disorganized, even if an individual area, such as a parish, seemed distinct and cohesive—some parishes, for example, were associated with a single trade. A city's craft guilds gave structure to artisans and shopkeepers, regulating their lives and providing welfare, but less than half the population could join a guild. The rest did odd jobs or turned to crime. The chief attraction of cities was the wide variety of economic opportunity: for women, in such areas as selling goods and processing food; for men, in construction, on the docks, and in delivery services. But employment was unpredictable, and citizens did not have community support to fall back on in hard times as they did in the

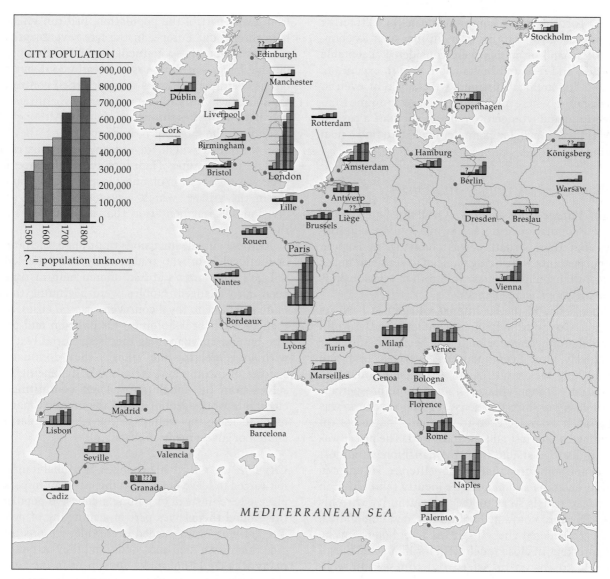

MAP 16.3 THE GROWTH OF CITIES, 1500–1800
In addition to the remarkable rise in the population of Europe's cities, particularly after 1550, this map reveals the northward shift in the distribution of the largest cities: in 1500, three of the four largest were in Italy; in 1700, only one. When did London overtake Paris as the largest city in Europe?

village. Even forms of recreation and enjoyment were different in the city.

Popular Culture in the City One major difference between country and town was the level of literacy. Only in urban areas were there significant numbers of people who could read: It has been estimated that in cities perhaps a third of adult males were literate by 1700. Not only was reading necessary for commerce but it had been strongly encouraged by the Reformation, with its insistence that the faithful read the Bible for themselves. This stimulus ensured that literacy also rose among women, who increasingly became pupils at

the growing number of schools in Europe (although they were still not admitted to universities). As many as 25 percent of the adult women in cities may have been able to read.

These changes had a notable effect on urban life. There was now a readership for newspapers, which became common by the mid-seventeenth century, as did the coffeehouses in which they were often read. Although newspaper stories were regularly inaccurate or untrue, and their writers (relying on informants at courts) could find themselves prosecuted for showing the authorities in a bad light, they were avidly consumed, and they made politics for the first time a

Der Kramer mit der newe zeittung.

Ihr liebe gütte fromme Herzen,
Die ihr hört Neuwe zeitung gern,
Hie bring ich euch ein gantzen hauffen.
Die wil ich euch al bar verkauffen.
Ist alles war vnd nichts erlogen,
Wir de euwer kramer nit betrogen.
Groß wunder sagt euch meine Zeittung.
Von der arm ababrücter seitten.
Auß Frauckrich vnd auß Engellandt.
Geb ich bericht euch aller handt.

Ich crag nicht brieff wie andre botten,
Die euch verieren vnd euwer spotten.
Was ich hab ist nach allem lust.
Drey tag er logen vor der vist.
Dieß muß ihr alles glauben frey.
Weill alles noch ist frisch vnd new.
Auch geb ich euch es wolfel hin.
Weil ich des gelas bedrötiget bin.
Mein wam rest ist sehr boß vnd schwach.
Ist zeit das ich ein anders mach.

Auff das ab geht die Neuwe mehr.
Von der Hertzog von gursen sehr.
Hab ich mit gantzen fleiß gethan.
Dar auch frantzösch hossen an.
Vnd das ir wist, so wil ich's ich.
Die bleiben sehn, lang seinen mich.
Drumb sorach mein fuchs schwantz gesell.
Kaufft ihn, das ist luß euwer gell.
An sedern ist der augen schein.
Was ich mich für ein vogel sein.

Anonymous
THE NEWSVENDOR, WOODCUT
The ancestor of the regularly published newspaper was the occasional single sheet describing the latest news or rumors. Printers would produce a few hundred copies and have them sold by street vendors whenever they had an event of some importance to describe: a battle, the death of a ruler, or some fantastic occurrence like the birth of a baby with two heads. As cities and the potential readership grew, the news sheets expanded; by the seventeenth century they had distinctive names and began to appear every week.
Bibliothèque Nationale de France, Paris

subject of wide interest and discussion. Theater and opera also became popular entertainments, with women for the first time taking stage roles and obtaining performances for plays they had written. Sales of books surged, often because they had a popular audience, and they gave broad circulation to traditional favorites, such as travel stories and lives of saints, as well as to the latest ideas of science.

Belief in Magic and Rituals

Although in the countryside cultural patterns looked different—with lower literacy, simpler recreations, and more visible religiosity—there was one area of popular culture in which the outlook of the city and the village was remarkably similar: the belief in magic. The townspeople may have seemed more sophisticated, but the basic assumption they shared with their country cousins was that mysterious forces controlled nature and their own lives and that there was little they could do to ensure their own well-being. The world was full of spirits, and all one could do was encourage the good, defend oneself against the evil, and hope that the good would win. Nothing that happened—a calf dying, lightning striking a house—was accidental. Everything had a purpose. Any unusual event was an omen, part of a larger plan, or the action of some unseen force.

Charivari

To strengthen themselves against trouble, people used whatever help they could find. They organized special processions and holidays to celebrate good times such as harvests, to lament misfortunes, to complain about oppression, or to poke fun at scandalous behavior. These occasions, known as "rough music" in England and *charivari* in France, often used the theme of "the world turned upside down" to make their point. In the set pieces in a procession, a fool might be dressed up as a king, a woman might be shown beating her husband, or a tax collector might appear hanging from a tree. Whether ridiculing a dominating wife or lamenting the lack of bread, the community was expressing its solidarity in the face of difficulty or distasteful behavior through these rituals. They were a form of public opinion, enabling people to let off steam and express themselves.

The potential for violence was always present at such gatherings, especially when religious or social differences became entangled with other resentments. The viciousness of ordinary Protestants and Catholics toward one another revealed a frustration and aggressiveness that was not far below the surface. When food was scarce or new impositions had been ordered by their rulers, peasants and townspeople needed little excuse to show their anger openly. Women often took the lead, not only because they had firsthand experience of the difficulty of feeding a family but also because troops were more reluctant to attack them.

Magical Remedies

Ordinary people also had other outlets for their frustrations. Recognizing their powerlessness in the face of outside forces, they resorted to their version of the magic that the literate were finding so fashionable at this very time. Whereas the sophisticated patronized astrologers, paying handsomely for horoscopes and advice about how to live their lives, the peasants and the poor consulted popular almanacs or sought out "cunning men" and wise women for secret spells, potions, and other remedies for their anxieties. Even religious ceremonies were thought of as being related to the rituals of the magical world, in which so-called white witches—the friendly kind—gave

assistance when a ring was lost or when the butter would not form out of the milk.

Witches and Witch-Hunts

Misfortunes were never just plain bad luck; rather, there was intent behind everything that happened. Events were willed, and if they turned out badly, they must have been willed by the good witch's opposite, the evil witch. Such beliefs often led to cruel persecutions of innocent victims—usually helpless old women, able to do nothing but mutter curses when taunted by neighbors, and easy targets if someone had to be blamed for unfortunate happenings.

This quest for scapegoats naturally focused on the most vulnerable members of society, such as Jews or, in the case of witches, women. Accusations were often directed at a woman who was old and alone, with nobody to defend her. She was feared because she seemed to be an outsider or not sufficiently deferential to her supposed betters. It was believed that witches read strange books and knew magic spells, an indication of what many regarded as inappropriate and dangerous levels of literacy for a woman.

In the sixteenth and seventeenth centuries, the hunt for witches intensified to levels never previously reached. This period has been called the era of the "great witch craze," and for good reason. There were outbursts in every part of Europe, and tens of thousands of the accused were executed. Dozens of men, most of them clerics, made witch-hunting a full-time profession and persuaded civic and other government authorities to devote their resources to stamping out this threat to social and religious stability. Suspects were almost always tortured, and it is not too surprising that they usually "confessed" and implicated others as servants of the devil. The practices that were uncovered varied—in some areas witches were said to dance with the devil, in others to fly on broomsticks, in others to be possessed by evil spirits who could induce dreadful (and possibly psychosomatic) symptoms—but the punishment was usually the same: burning at the stake. And the hysteria was infectious. One accusation could trigger dozens more until entire regions were swept with fear and hatred.

Forces of Restraint

By the middle of the seventeenth century, the wave of assaults on witches was beginning to recede (see "A Witness Analyzes the Witch Craze," p. 476). Social and political leaders came to realize that the campaigns against witches could endanger authority, especially when accusations were turned against the rich and privileged classes. Increasingly, therefore, cases were

Hans Baldung Grien
WITCHES, WOODCUT
This woodcut by the German artist Grien shows the popular image of witches in early modern Europe. One carries a potion while flying on a goat. The others put together the ingredients for a magic potion in a jar inscribed with mystical symbols. The fact that witches were thought to be learned women who could understand magic was another reason they were feared by a Europe that expected women to be uneducated.

not brought to trial, and when they were, lawyers and doctors (who treated the subject less emotionally than the clergy) cast doubt on the validity of the testimony. Gradually, excesses were restrained and control was reestablished; by 1700 there was only a trickle of new incidents.

The decline in accusations of witchcraft reflected not only the more general quieting down of conflict and upheaval in the late seventeenth century but also the growing proportion of Europe's population that was living in cities. Here, less reliant on the luck of good weather, people could feel themselves more in control of their own fates. If there were unexpected fires, there were fire brigades; if a house burned down, there might even be insurance—a new protection for individuals that was spreading in the late 1600s. A process that has been called the "disenchantment" of the world—growing skepticism about spirits and mysterious forces, and greater self-reliance—was under way.

A WITNESS ANALYZES THE WITCH CRAZE

Although for most Europeans around 1600 witchcraft was real—a religious problem caused by the devil—there were a few observers who were beginning to think more analytically about the reasons for the rapid spread of accusations. One such observer was a clergyman named Linden, who was attached to the cathedral of the great city of Trier in western Germany. His description of a witch-hunt in the Trier region ignored the standard religious explanations.

"Inasmuch as it was popularly believed that the continued sterility of many years was caused by witches, the whole area rose to exterminate the witches. This movement was promoted by many in office, who hoped to gain wealth from the persecution. And so special accusers, inquisitors, notaries, judges, and constables dragged to trial and torture human beings of both sexes and burned them in great numbers. Scarcely any of those who were accused escaped punishment. So far did the madness of the furious populace and the courts go in this thirst for blood and booty that there was scarcely anybody who was not smirched by some suspicion of this crime. Meanwhile, notaries, copyists and innkeepers grew rich. The executioner rode a fine horse, like a noble of the court, and dressed in gold and silver; his wife competed with noble dames in the richness of her array. A direr pestilence or a more ruthless invader could hardly have ravaged the territory than this inquisition and persecution without bounds. Many were the reasons for doubting that all were really guilty. At last, though the flames were still unsated, the people grew poor, rules were made and enforced restricting the fees and costs of examinations, and suddenly, as when in war funds fail, the zeal of the persecutors died out."

From George L. Burr (ed.), "The Witch Persecutions," *Translations and Reprints from the Original Sources of European History*, Vol. 3, Philadelphia: University of Pennsylvania, 1902, pp. 13–14.

Religious Discipline The churches played an important part in suppressing the traditional reliance on magic. In Catholic countries the Counter-Reformation produced better-educated priests who were trained to impose official doctrine instead of tolerating unusual local customs. Among Protestants, ministers were similarly well educated and denounced magical practices as idolatrous or superstitious. And both camps treated passion and enthusiasm with suspicion. Habits did not change overnight, but gradually ordinary people were being persuaded to abandon old fears and beliefs. There were still major scares in midcentury. An eclipse in 1654 prompted panic throughout Europe; comets still inspired prophecies of the end of the world; and in the 1660s a self-proclaimed messiah named Shabtai Zvi attracted a massive following among the Jews of Europe and the Middle East. Increasingly, though, such visions of doom or the end of time were becoming fringe beliefs, dismissed by authorities and most elements of society. Eclipses and comets now had scientific explanations, and the messiah came to be regarded as a spiritual, not an immediate, promise.

Summary

Even at the level of popular culture, therefore, Europeans had reason to feel, by the late seventeenth century, that a time of upheaval and uncertainty was over. A sense of confidence and orderliness was returning, and in intellectual circles the optimism seemed justified by the achievements of science. In fact, there arose a scholarly dispute around 1700, known as the "battle of the books," in which one side claimed, for the first time, that the "moderns" had outshone the "ancients." Using the scientists as their chief example, the advocates of the "moderns" argued—in a remarkable break with the reverence for the past that had dominated medieval and Renaissance culture—that advances in thought were possible and that one did not always have to accept the superiority of antiquity. Such self-confidence made it clear that, in the world of ideas as surely as in the world of politics, a period of turbulence had given way to an era of renewed assurance and stability.

QUESTIONS FOR FURTHER THOUGHT

1. Are there similarities in the creativity that marks the scientist and the artist?

2. Is it fair to ask whether popular beliefs and rituals do more harm than good?

RECOMMENDED READING

Sources

Drake, Stillman (tr. and ed.). *Discoveries and Opinions of Galileo.* 1957. The complete texts of some of Galileo's most important works.

Hall, Marie Boas (ed.). *Nature and Nature's Laws: Documents of the Scientific Revolution.* 1970. A good collection of documents by and about the pioneers of modern science.

Studies

Biagioli, Mario. *Galileo, Courtier: The Practice of Science in the Culture of Absolutism.* 1993. A fascinating study of the political forces at work in Galileo's career.

Braudel, Fernand. *Capitalism and Material Life, 1400–1800.* Translated by Miriam Kochan. 1973. A classic, pioneering study of the structure of daily life in early modern Europe.

Burke, Peter. *Popular Culture in Early Modern Europe.* 1978. A lively introduction to the many forms of expression and belief among the ordinary people of Europe.

Fara, Patricia. *Newton: The Making of a Genius.* 2002.

Gutmann, Myron P. *Toward the Modern Economy: Early Industry in Europe, 1500–1800.* 1988. A clear survey of recent work on economic development in this period.

Ladurie, Emmanuel Le Roy. *The Peasants of Languedoc.* Translated by John Day. 1966. A brilliant evocation of peasant life in France in the sixteenth and seventeenth centuries.

Levack, Brian P. *The Witch-Hunt in Early Modern Europe.* 1987. An excellent survey of the belief in witchcraft and its consequences.

Rabb, Theodore K. *Renaissance Lives.* 1993. Brief biographies of fifteen people, both famous and obscure, who lived just before and during this period.

———. *The Last Days of the Renaissance: & the March to Modernity.* 2006

Shapin, S. *The Scientific Revolution.* 1996.

Shearman, John. *Mannerism.* 1968. The best short introduction to a difficult artistic style.

Thomas, Keith. *Religion and the Decline of Magic.* 1976. The most thorough account of popular culture yet published, this enormous book, while dealing mainly with England, treats at length such subjects as witchcraft, astrology, and ghosts in a most readable style.

Wiesner, Merry E. *Women and Gender in Early Modern Europe.* 1993.

Nicolas de Largilliére
LOUIS XIV AND HIS FAMILY

Louis XIV (seated) is shown here in full regal splendor surrounded by three of his heirs. On his right is his eldest son, on his left is his eldest grandson, and reaching out his hand is his eldest great-grandson, held by his governess. All three of these heirs died before Louis, and thus they never became kings of France.

Chapter Seventeen

THE EMERGENCE OF THE EUROPEAN STATE SYSTEM

ABSOLUTISM IN FRANCE • OTHER PATTERNS OF ABSOLUTISM • ALTERNATIVES TO
ABSOLUTISM • THE INTERNATIONAL SYSTEM

The acceptance of strong central governments that emerged out of the crisis of the mid-seventeenth century was a victory not merely for kings but for an entire way of organizing society. As a result of huge increases in the scale of warfare and taxation, bureaucracies had mushroomed, and their presence was felt throughout Europe. Yet no central administration, however powerful, could function without the support of the nobles who ruled the countryside. Regional loyalties had dominated European society for centuries, and only a regime that drew on those loyalties could hope to maintain the support of its subjects. The political structures that developed during the century following the 1650s were,

therefore, the work not only of ambitious princes but also of a nobility long accustomed to exercising authority and now prepared to find new ways of exerting its influence. To the leaders of society during the century following the crisis of the 1640s and 1650s, it was clear that state building and the imposition of their power on the rest of the world were now ever more central to rulers' ambitions, and required a common effort to establish stronger political, social, military, financial, and religious structures that would support effective government. The institutions and practices they created have remained essential to the modern state ever since.

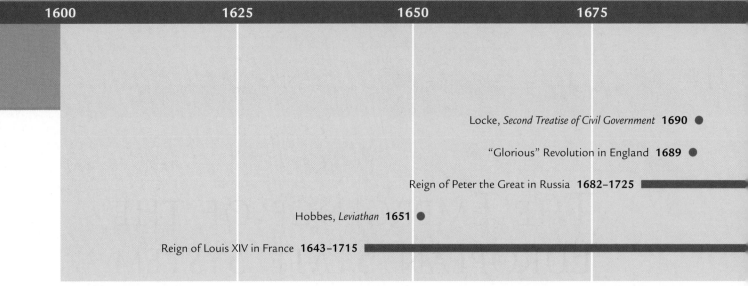

| 1600 | 1625 | 1650 | 1675 |

Locke, *Second Treatise of Civil Government* **1690** ●

"Glorious" Revolution in England **1689** ●

Reign of Peter the Great in Russia **1682–1725** ▬

Hobbes, *Leviathan* **1651** ●

Reign of Louis XIV in France **1643–1715** ▬

ABSOLUTISM IN FRANCE

One way of creating a strong, centralized state was the political system known as **absolutism:** the belief that power emanated from the monarch's unlimited authority. Absolutism was based on a theory known as the **divine right of kings,** derived from the fact that kings were anointed with holy oil at their coronations; it asserted that the monarch was God's representative on earth.

The Rule of Louis XIV

The most famous absolutist state was the Kingdom of France, which became the most powerful regime in Europe. Taken to an extreme, as it was by Louis XIV (1643–1715), absolutism justified unlimited power and treated treason as blasphemy. The leading advocate of the theory, Bishop Bossuet, called Louis God's lieutenant and argued that the Bible itself endorsed absolutism. In reality, the king worked in close partnership with the nobles to maintain order, and he often (though not always) felt obliged to defend their local authority as a reinforcement of his own power. Nevertheless, the very notion that the king not only was supreme but could assert his will with armies and bureaucracies of unprecedented size gave absolutism both an image and a reality that set it apart from previous systems of monarchical rule. Here at last was a force that could hold together and control the increasingly complex interactions of regions and interest groups that made up a state.

Versailles The setting in which a central government operated often reflected its power and its methods. Philip II in the late 1500s had created, at the Escorial outside Madrid, the first isolated palace that controlled a large realm. A hundred years later, Louis XIV created at Versailles, near Paris, a far more elaborate court as the center of an even larger and more intrusive bureaucracy than Philip's. The isolation of government and the exercise of vast personal power seemed to go hand in hand.

The king moved the court in the 1680s to Versailles, twelve miles from Paris, where, at a cost of half a year's royal income, he transformed a small chateau his father had built into the largest building in Europe. There, far from Parisian mobs, he enjoyed the splendor and the ceremonies, centered on himself, which exalted his majesty. Every French nobleman of any significance spent time each year at Versailles, not only to maintain access to royal patronage and governmental affairs but also to demonstrate the wide support for Louis' system of rule. Historians have called this process the domestication of the aristocracy, as great lords who had once drawn their status from their lineage or lands came to regard service to the throne as the best route to power. But the benefits cut both ways. The king gained the services of influential administrators, and they gained privileges and rewards without the uncertainties that had accompanied their traditional resistance to central control.

Court Life The visible symbol of Louis' absolutism was Versailles. Here the leaders of France assembled, and around them swirled the most envied social circles of the time. From the court emanated the policies and directives that increasingly affected the lives of the king's subjects and also determined France's relations with other states.

At Versailles, too, French culture was shaped by the king's patronage of those artists and writers who appealed to the royal taste. For serious drama and history,

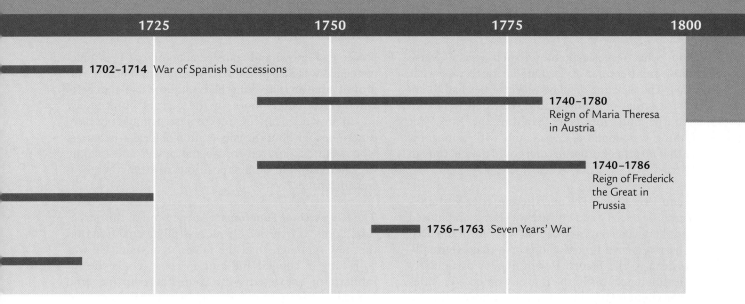

| 1725 | 1750 | 1775 | 1800 |

1702–1714 War of Spanish Successions

1740–1780
Reign of Maria Theresa
in Austria

1740–1786
Reign of Frederick
the Great in
Prussia

1756–1763 Seven Years' War

Louis turned to the playwright and writer Racine (1639–1699); for comedy, to the theatrical producer and playwright Molière (1622–1673); and for opera and the first performances of what we now call ballet, to the composer Lully (1632–1687). Moreover, all artistic expression, from poetry to painting, was regulated by royal academies that were founded in the 1600s; backed by the king's authority, these academies laid down

PERSPECTIVE VIEW OF VERSAILLES FROM THE PLACE D'ARMES, 1698
This painting shows Versailles not long before Louis decided to move there; he was soon to begin an enormous expansion into the gardens at the back that more than doubled the size of the buildings. In this scene, the royal coach, with its entourage, is just about to enter the château.
Giraudon/Art Resource, NY

481

rules for what was acceptable in such areas as verse forms or architectural style. Official taste was what counted. The dazzling displays at Versailles had to observe strict rules of dignity and gravity that were considered the only means of exalting the king. Yet everything was done on a scale and with a magnificence that no other European ruler could match, though many tried.

Paris and Versailles   The one alternative to Versailles as a center of society and culture was Paris, and indeed the split between court and capital was one of the divisions between government and people that eventually was to lead to the French Revolution. A particularly notable difference was in the role of women. Versailles was overwhelmingly a male society. Women achieved prominence only as royal mistresses in Louis' early years or as the creators of a rigidly pious atmosphere in his last years. They were also essential to the highly elaborate rituals of civility and manners that developed at Versailles. But they were allowed no independent initiative in social or cultural matters.

In Paris, by contrast, women established and dominated the gatherings known as **salons** that promoted easy conversation, a mixture of social backgrounds, and forms of expression—political discussion and ribald humor, for example—that were not acceptable at the staid and sober court. Yet the contrasts were not merely between the formal palace and the relaxed salon. Even before Louis moved to Versailles, he banned as improper one of Molière's comedies, *Tartuffe*, which mocked excessive religious devoutness. It took five years of reworking by Molière before Louis allowed the play to be performed (1669), and it then became a major hit in Paris, but it was never a favorite at court.

Government

Absolutism was more than a device to satisfy royal whims, for Louis was a gifted administrator and politician who used his power for state building. By creating and reorganizing government institutions, he strengthened his authority at home and increased his ascendancy over his neighbors. The longest-lasting result of his absolutism was that the French state won control over three crucial activities: the use of armed force, the formulation and execution of laws, and the collection and expenditure of revenue. These functions, in turn, depended on a centrally controlled bureaucracy responsive to royal orders and efficient enough to carry them out in distant provinces over the objections of local groups.

Nobody could suppress all vested interests and local loyalties, but the bureaucracy was supposed to be insulated from outside pressure by the absolute monarch's power to remove and transfer appointees. This independence was also promoted by training programs, improved administrative methods, and the use of experts wherever possible—both in the central bureaucracy and in provincial offices. Yet the system could not have functioned without the cooperation of local aristocrats, who were encouraged to use the power and income they derived from official positions to strengthen central authority.

The King's Dual Functions   At the head of this structure, Louis XIV carried off successfully a dual function that few monarchs had the talent to sustain: He was both king in council and king in court. Louis the administrator coexisted with Louis the courtier, who hunted, cultivated the arts, and indulged in huge banquets. Among his many imitators, however, the easier side of absolutism, court life, consumed an excessive share of a state's resources and became an end in itself. The effect was to give prestige to the leisure pursuits of the upper classes while sapping the energies of influential figures. Louis was one of the few who avoided sacrificing affairs of state to regal pomp.

Like court life, government policy under Louis XIV was tailored to the aim of state building. As he was to discover, the resources and powers at his disposal were not endless. But until the last years of his reign, they served his many purposes extremely well (see "Louis XIV on Kingship," p. 483). Moreover, Louis had superb support at the highest levels of his administration—ministers whose viewpoints differed but whose skills were carefully blended by their ruler.

Competing Ministers   Until the late 1680s, the king's two leading advisers were Jean-Baptiste Colbert and the marquis of Louvois. Colbert was a financial wizard who gathered detailed information about the kingdom and advocated a mercantilist policy. He believed that the government should give priority to increasing France's wealth. As a result, he believed that the chief danger to the country's well-being was the United Provinces, Europe's great trader state, and that royal resources should be poured into the navy, manufacturing, and shipping. By contrast, Louvois, the son of a military administrator, consistently emphasized the army as the foundation of France's power. He believed that the country was threatened primarily by land—by the Holy Roman Empire on its flat, vulnerable northeast frontier—and thus that resources should be allocated to the army and to border fortifications.

Foreign Policy

Louis tried to balance these goals within his overall aims—to expand France's frontiers and to assert his

LOUIS XIV ON KINGSHIP

From time to time, Louis XIV put on paper brief accounts of his actions: For example, he wrote some brief memoirs in the late 1660s. These reflections about his role as king were intended as a guide for his son and indicate both his high view of kingship and the seriousness with which he approached his duties. The following are extracts from his memoirs and other writings.

"Homage is due to kings, and they do whatever they like. It certainly must be agreed that, however bad a prince may be, it is always a heinous crime for his subjects to rebel against him. He who gave men kings willed that they should be respected as His lieutenants, and reserved to Himself the right to question their conduct. It is His will that everyone who is born a subject should obey without qualification. This law, as clear as it is universal, was not made only for the sake of princes: it is also for the good of the people themselves. It is therefore the duty of kings to sustain by their own example the religion upon which they rely; and they must realize that, if their subjects see them plunged in vice or violence, they can hardly render to their person the respect due to their office, or recognize in them the living image of Him who is all-holy as well as almighty.

"It is a fine thing, a noble and enjoyable thing, to be a king. But it is not without its pains, its fatigues, and its troubles. One must work hard to reign. In working for the state, a king is working for himself. The good of the one is the glory of the other. When the state is prosperous, famous, and powerful, the king who is the cause of it is glorious; and he ought in consequence to have a larger share than others do of all that is most agreeable in life."

From J. M. Thompson, *Lectures on Foreign History, 1494–1789*, Oxford: Blackwell, 1956, pp. 172–174.

Antoine Watteau
FÊTE IN THE PARK, 1718
The luxurious life of the nobility during the eighteenth century is captured in this scene of men and women in fine silks, enjoying a picnic in a lovely park setting.
© By kind permission of the Trustees of the Wallace Collection, London

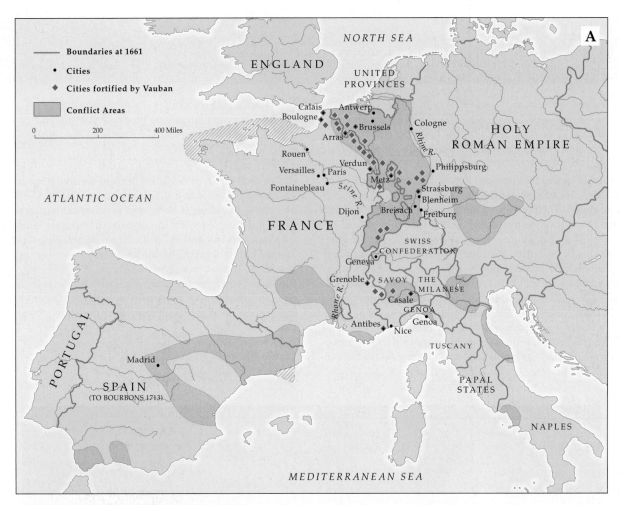

MAP 17.1A THE WARS OF LOUIS XIV
Louis XIV's aggressive aims took his troops to many areas of Europe.

superiority over other European states. Like the magnificence of his court, his power on the international scene served to demonstrate *la gloire* (the glory) of France. But his effort to expand that power prompted his neighbors to form coalitions and alliances of common defense, designed to keep him in check. From this response was to emerge the concept of a state system and the notion of a **balance of power** among the states of Europe.

In his early years Louis relied heavily on Colbert, who moved gradually toward war with the Dutch when he was unable to undermine their control of French maritime trade. But the war (1672–1678) was a failure, and so the pendulum swung toward Louvois' priorities. In the early 1680s Louis adopted the marquis's aims and claimed a succession of territories on France's northeast border. No one claim seemed large enough to provoke his neighbors to fight, especially since the Holy Roman Emperor, Leopold I, was distracted by a resumption in 1682 of war with the Turks in the east.

The result was that France was able to annex large segments of territory until, in 1686, a league of other European states was formed to restrain Louis' growing power (see maps 17.1A and 17.1B).

Louis versus Europe The leaders of the league were William III of the United Provinces and Emperor Leopold. Leopold was prepared to join the struggle because his war with the Turks turned in his favor after 1683, when his troops broke a Turkish siege of Vienna. And six years later William became a far more formidable foe when he gained the English throne. In 1688 the league finally went to war to put an end to French expansion. When Louis began to lose the territories he had gained in the 1680s, he decided to seek peace though the war did not end until 1697. But the respite did not last long. Four years later France became involved in a bitter war that brought famine, wretched poverty, and humiliation. This was a war to gain the Spanish throne for Louis' family, regardless of the

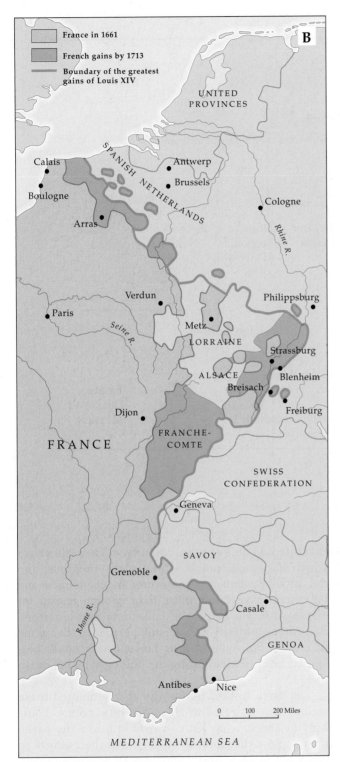

MAP 17.1B
THE WARS OF LOUIS XIV
The main conflict was on France's eastern border, where Louis made small but significant gains. Why was there so much conflict along this border?

devastating consequences of the fighting. This final, ruinous enterprise revealed both the new power of France and its limits. By launching an all-out attempt to establish his supremacy in Europe, Louis showed that he felt capable of taking on the whole of the continent; but by then he no longer had the economic and military base at home or the weak opposition abroad to ensure success.

Economic strains had begun to appear in the 1690s, when shattering famines throughout France reduced tax revenues and the size of the workforce, even as enemies began to unite abroad. Louis had the most formidable army in Europe—400,000 men by the end of his reign—but both William and Leopold believed he could be defeated by a combined assault, and they led the attack in the final showdown when the Habsburg king of Spain, Charles II, died without an heir in 1700.

The War of Spanish Succession There were various claimants to the Spanish throne, but Charles's choice was Philip, Louis XIV's grandson (see "The Spanish Succession, 1700," p. 486). Had Louis been willing to agree not to unite the thrones of France and Spain and to allow the Spanish empire to be opened (for the first time) to foreign traders, Charles's wish might have been respected. But Louis refused to compromise, and in 1701 William and Leopold created the so-called Grand Alliance, which declared war on France the following year. The French now had to fight virtually all of Europe in a war over the Spanish succession, not only at home but also overseas, in India, Canada, and the Caribbean.

Led by two brilliant generals—the Englishman John Churchill, duke of Marlborough, and the Austrian Prince Eugène—the Grand Alliance won a series of smashing victories. France's hardships were increased by a terrible famine in 1709. Although the criticism of his policies became fierce and dangerous rebellions erupted, the Sun King retained his hold over his subjects. Despite military disaster, he was able to keep his nation's borders intact and the Spanish throne for his grandson (though he had to give up the possibility of union with France and end the restrictions on trade in the Spanish empire) when peace treaties were signed at Utrecht in 1713 and 1714. When it was all over, Louis' great task of state building, both at home and abroad, had withstood the severest of tests: defeat on the battlefield.

Domestic Policy

Control and Reform The assertion of royal supremacy at home was almost complete by the time Louis came to power, but he extended centralized control to religion and social institutions. Both the Protestant

THE SPANISH SUCCESSION, 1700

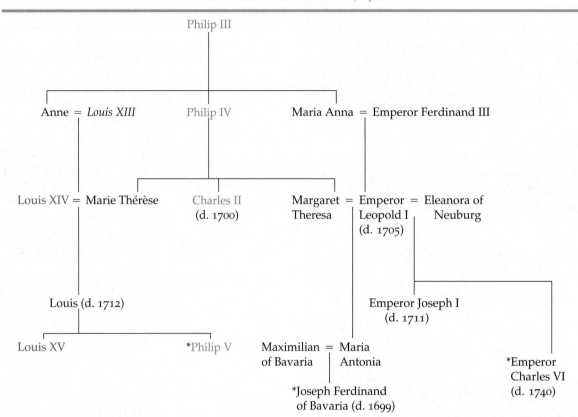

Note: Names in blue = kings of Spain; names in red = kings of France.
*People designated at various times as heirs of Charles II.

Huguenots and the Catholic Jansenists interfered with the religious uniformity that Louis considered essential in an absolutist state. As a result, pressures against these groups mounted steadily. In 1685 Louis revoked the Edict of Nantes, now almost a century old, which had granted Protestants limited toleration, and he forced France's one million Huguenots either to leave the country (four-fifths did) or to convert to Catholicism. This was a political rather than a religious step, taken to promote unity despite the economic consequences that followed the departure of a vigorous, productive, and entrepreneurial minority.

Jansenism was more elusive. It had far fewer followers, and it was a movement that emphasized spiritual values within Catholicism. But the very fact that it challenged the official church emphasis on ritual and was condemned by Rome made it a source of unrest. Even more unsettling was its success in gaining support among the magistrate class—the royal officers in the parlements, who had to register all royal edicts before they became law. The Parlement of Paris was the only governmental institution that offered Louis any real resistance. The issues over which it caused trouble were usually religious, and the link between *parlementaire* independence and Jansenism gave Louis more than enough reason for displeasure. He razed the Jansenists' headquarters, the Abbey of Port-Royal, and persuaded the pope to issue a bull condemning Jansenism. He was prevented from implementing the bull only by his death in 1715.

The drive toward uniformity that prompted these actions was reflected in all of domestic policy. Louis kept in check what little protest arose in the parlements and either forbade or overruled their efforts to block his decrees; major uprisings by peasants in central France in the 1690s and 1700s were ruthlessly suppressed; Parisian publishers came under bureaucratic supervision; and the *intendants*, the government's chief provincial officers, were given increased authority, especially to supply the ever-growing money and recruitment needs of the army.

At the outset of his rule, Louis also used his power to improve France's economy. In these early years, under Colbert's ministry, major efforts were made to stimulate manufacturing, agriculture, and home and foreign trade. Some industries, notably those involving luxuries, like the silk production of Lyons, received considerable help and owed their prosperity to royal patronage. Colbert also tried, not entirely effectively, to reduce the crippling effects of France's countless internal tolls. These were usually nobles' perquisites, and they could multiply the cost of shipped goods. The government divided the country into a number of districts, within which shipments were to be toll-free, but the system never removed the worst abuses. Louis also hoped to boost foreign trade, at first by financing new overseas trading companies and later by founding new port cities as naval and commercial centers. He achieved notable success only in the West Indies, where sugar plantations became a source of great wealth.

The End of an Era

Louis' success in state building was remarkable, and France became the envy of Europe. Yet ever since the Sun King's reign, historians have recalled the famines and wars of his last years and have contrasted his glittering court with the misery of most French people. Taxes and rents rose remorselessly, and in many regions the hardships were made worse by significant declines in the population. Particularly after the famines of the 1690s and 1709, many contemporaries remarked on the dreadful condition of France's peasants.

The reign of Louis XIV can thus be regarded as the end of an era in the life of the lower classes. By pushing his need for resources to its limits, he inflicted a level of suffering that was not to recur, because governments increasingly came to realize that state building depended on the welfare and support of their people. In the eighteenth century, although there was still much suffering to come, the terrible subsistence crises, with their cycles of famine and plague, came to an end, largely because of official efforts to distribute food in starving areas and to isolate and suppress outbreaks of plague. Thus, although the hand of the central government was heavier in 1715 than a hundred years before, it was becoming more obviously a beneficent as well as a burdensome force. The Church also had a more salutary influence as religious struggles died away, for it brought into local parishes better-educated and more dedicated priests who, as part of their new commitment to service, exerted themselves to calm the outbreaks of witchcraft and irrational fear that had swept the countryside for centuries. Despite the strains Louis had caused, therefore, his absolutist authority was now firmly in place and

could ensure a dominant European role for a united and powerful France.

France after Louis XIV

The Sun King had created a model for absolutism in partnership with his nobility, but the traditional ambitions of the nobles reasserted themselves after he died in 1715, leaving a child as his heir. The duke of Orlèans, Louis XIV's nephew, who became regent until 1723, sought to restore the aristocrats' authority. He also gave the parlements political power and replaced royal bureaucrats with councils composed of leading members of the nobility. The councils were unable to govern effectively, but the parlements would never again surrender their power to veto royal legislation. They became a rallying point for those who opposed centralization and wished to limit the king's powers.

Finance was also a serious problem for the government, because of the debts left by Louis XIV's wars. A brilliant Scottish financier, John Law, suggested an answer: a government-sponsored central bank that would issue paper notes, expand credit, and encourage investment in a new trading company for the French colonies. By tying the bank to this company, the Company of the Occident, a venture that promised subscribers vast profits from the Louisiana territory in North America, Law set off an investment boom. But the public's greed soon pushed prices for the company's stock to insanely high levels. A bust was inevitable, and when it came, in 1720, the entire scheme of bank notes and credit collapsed.

Louis XV and Fleury   Political and financial problems were to plague France throughout the eighteenth century, until the leaders of the French Revolution sought radical ways to solve them in the 1790s. Yet the uncertainties of the regency did give way to a long period of stability after 1726, when Louis XV gave almost unlimited authority to his aging tutor and adviser, Cardinal Fleury. Cautious, dedicated to the monarchy, and surrounded by talented subordinates, Fleury made absolutism function quietly and effectively and enabled France to recover from the setbacks that had marked the end of Louis XIV's reign. Fleury's tenure coincided with abundant harvests, slowly rising population, and increased commercial activity.

Political Problems   Fleury contained the ambitions of the governing class, but when he died in 1743 at the age of 90, the pressures exploded. War hawks plunged France into the first of several unsuccessful wars with its neighbors that strained French credit to the breaking point. At home royal authority also deteriorated.

HISTORICAL ISSUES: TWO VIEWS OF LOUIS XIV

Implicit in any assessment of the reign of Louis XIV in France is a judgment about the nature of absolutism and the kind of government the continental European monarchies created in the late seventeenth and eighteenth centuries. From the perspective of Frenchman Albert Sorel, a historian of the French Revolution writing at the end of the nineteenth century, the Revolution had been necessary to save France from Louis' heritage. For the American John Rule, a historian who concerned himself primarily with the development of political institutions during the seventeenth century, the marks of Louis XIV's rule were caution, bureaucracy, and order.

Sorel: "The edifice of the state enjoyed incomparable brilliance and splendor, but it resembled a Gothic cathedral in which the height of the nave and the arches had been pushed beyond all reason, weakening the walls as they were raised ever higher. Louis XIV carried the principle of monarchy to its utmost limit, and abused it in all respects to the point of excess. He left the nation crushed by war, mutilated by banishments, and impatient of the yoke which it felt to be ruinous. Men were worn-out, the treasury empty, all relationships strained by the violence of tension, and in the immense framework of the state there remained no institution except the accidental appearance of genius. Things had reached a point where, if a great king did not appear, there would be a great revolution."

From Albert Sorel, *L'Europe et la rèvolution française*, 3rd ed., Vol. 1, Paris, 1893, p. 199, as translated in William F. Church (ed.), *The Greatness of Louis XIV: Myth or Reality?*, Boston: D. C. Heath, 1959, p. 63.

Rule: "As Louis XIV himself said of the tasks of kingship, they were at once great, noble, and delightful. Yet Louis' enjoyment of his craft was tempered by political prudence. At an early age he learned to listen attentively to his advisers, to speak when spoken to, to ponder evidence, to avoid confrontations, to dissemble, to wait. He believed that time and tact would conquer. Despite all the evidence provided him by his ministers and his servants, Louis often hesitated before making a decision; he brooded, and in some instances put off decisions altogether. As he grew older, the king tended to hide his person and his office. Even his officials seldom saw the king for more than a brief interview. And as decision-making became centralized in the hands of the ministers, [so] the municipalities, the judges, the local estates, the guilds and at times the peasantry contested royal encroachments on their rights. Yet to many in the kingdom, Louis represented a modern king, an agent of stability whose struggle was their struggle and whose goal was to contain the crises of the age."

From John C. Rule, "Louis XIV, *Roi-Bureaucrate*," in Rule (ed.), *Louis XIV and the Craft of Kingship*, Columbus: Ohio State University Press, 1969, pp. 91–92.

Having no one to replace Fleury as chief minister, Louis XV put his confidence in a succession of advisers, some capable, some mediocre. But he did not back them when attacks arose from court factions. Uninterested in government, he avoided confrontation, neglected affairs of state, and devoted himself instead to hunting and to court ceremony.

Although Louis XV provided weak leadership, France's difficulties were structural as well as personal. The main problems—special privileges and finance—posed almost impossible challenges. Governments that levy new taxes arbitrarily seem despotic, even if the need for them is clear and the distribution equitable. One of France's soundest taxes was the *vingtième*, or twentieth, which was supposed to tap the income of all parts of French society roughly equally. But the nobility and clergy evaded most of the tax. Naturally, aggressive royal ministers wanted to remedy that situation. In the 1750s, for example, an effort was made to put teeth into the *vingtième*'s bite on the clergy's huge wealth. But the effort failed. The clergy resisted furiously; and the parlements denounced the "despotism" of a crown that taxed its subjects arbitrarily. Thus, the privileged groups not only blocked reforms but also made the monarch's position more difficult by their opposition and rhetoric of liberty.

The Long Term   Despite these special interests, the 1700s were a time of notable advance for Europe's most populous and wealthy state. France enjoyed remarkable expansion in population, in the rural economy, in commerce, and in empire building. No one knew at the time that the failures of reforming royal ministers in the mid-1700s foretold a stalemate that would help bring the old regime crashing down.

OTHER PATTERNS OF ABSOLUTISM

Four other monarchies pursued state building through absolutist regimes in this period, often in imitation of the French model. The governments they created in Vienna, Berlin, Madrid, and St. Petersburg differed in strengths and weaknesses, but all were attempts to centralize power around a formidable ruler.

The Habsburgs at Vienna

The closest imitation of Versailles was the court of the Habsburg Leopold I, the Holy Roman emperor (1658–1705). Heir to a reduced inheritance that gave him control over only Bohemia, Austria, and a small part of Hungary, Leopold still maintained a splendid establishment. His plans for a new palace, Schönbrunn, that was supposed to outshine Versailles were modified only because of a lack of funds. And his promotion of the court as the center of all political and social life turned Vienna into what it had never been before: a city for nobles as well as small-time traders.

Nevertheless, Leopold did not display the pretensions of the Sun King. He was a younger son and had come to the throne only because of the death of his brother. Indecisive, retiring, and deeply religious, he had no fondness for the bravado Louis XIV enjoyed. He was a composer of some talent, and his patronage laid the foundation for the great musical culture that was to be one of Vienna's chief glories. But he did inherit considerable royal authority, which he sought to expand—though unlike Louis XIV he relied on a small group of leading nobles to devise policy and run his government.

Government Policy The Thirty Years' War that ended in 1648 had revealed that the elected head of the Holy Roman Empire could no longer control the princes who nominally owed him allegiance. In his own domains, however, he could maintain his control with the cooperation of his nobility. The Privy Council, which in effect ran Leopold's government, was filled largely with members of aristocratic families, and his chief advisers were always prominent nobles. To make policy, he consulted each of his ministers and then, even when all agreed, came to decisions with agonizing slowness.

Unlike the other courts of Europe, Schönbrunn did not favor only native-born aristocrats. The leader of Austria's armies during the Turks' siege of Vienna in 1683 was Charles, duke of Lorraine, whose duchy had been taken over by the French. His predecessor as field marshal had been an Italian, and his successor was to be one of the most brilliant soldiers of the age, Prince Eugène of Savoy. They became members of the Austrian nobility only when Leopold gave them titles within his own dominions, but they all fitted easily into the aristocratic circles that controlled the government and the army.

Eugène and Austria's Military Success Prince Eugène (1663–1736) was a spectacular symbol of the aristocracy's continuing dominance of politics and society. A member of one of Europe's most distinguished families, he had been raised in France but found himself passed over when Louis XIV awarded army commissions, perhaps because he had been intended for the Church. Yet he was determined to have a military career, and he volunteered to serve the Austrians in the war with the Turks that, following the siege of Vienna, was to expand Habsburg territory in the Balkans by the time peace was signed in 1699 (see map 17.2). Eugène's talents quickly became evident: He was field marshal of Austria's troops by the time he was 30. Over the next forty years, as intermittent war with the Turks continued, he became a decisive influence in Habsburg affairs. Though foreign-born, he was the minister primarily responsible for the transformation of Vienna's policies from defensive to aggressive.

Until the siege of Vienna by the Turks in 1683, Leopold's cautiousness kept Austria simply holding the line, both against Louis XIV and against the Turks. In the 1690s, however, at Eugène's urging, he tried a bolder course and in the process laid the foundations for a new Habsburg empire along the Danube River: Austria-Hungary. He helped create the coalition that defeated Louis in the 1700s, he intervened in Italy so that his landlocked domains could gain an outlet to the sea, and he began the long process of pushing the Turks out of the Balkans. Although Leopold did not live to see the advance completed, by the time of Eugène's death, the Austrians' progress against the Turks had brought them within a hundred miles of the Black Sea.

The Power of the Nobility Yet the local power of the nobility tempered the centralization of Leopold's dominions. Unlike Louis XIV, who supported his nobles only if they worked for him, Leopold gave them influence in the government without first establishing control over all his lands. The nobles did not cause the Habsburgs as much trouble as they had during the Thirty Years' War, but Leopold had to limit his centralization outside Austria. Moreover, as Austrians came increasingly to dominate the court, the nobles of Hungary and Bohemia reacted by clinging stubbornly to their local rights. Thus, compared to France, Leopold's was an absolutism under which the nobility retained far more autonomous power.

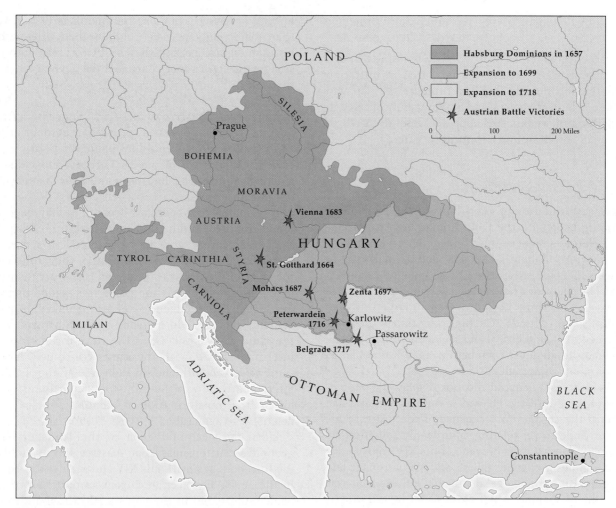

MAP 17.2 THE AUSTRIAN EMPIRE, 1657–1718
The steady advance of the Habsburgs into the Balkans was marked by a succession of victories; their gains were confirmed by treaties with the Turks at Karlowitz (1699) and Passarowitz (1718). How much bigger were Habsburg dominions in 1718 than they were in 1657?

The Hohenzollerns at Berlin

The one new power that emerged to prominence during the age of Louis XIV was Brandenburg-Prussia, and here again state building was made possible by a close alliance between a powerful ruler and his nobles. Frederick William of Hohenzollern (r. 1640–1688), known as the "great elector," ruled scattered territories that stretched seven hundred miles from Cleves, on the Rhine, to a part of Prussia on the Baltic. That so fragmented and disconnected a set of lands could be shaped into a major European power was a testimony to the political abilities of the Hohenzollerns. The process began when, taking advantage of the uncertainties that followed the Thirty Years' War, Frederick William made his territories the dominant principality in northern Germany and at the same time strengthened his power over his subjects.

Foreign Policy His first task was in foreign affairs, because when he became elector, the troops of the various states that were fighting the Thirty Years' War swarmed over his possessions. Frederick William realized that even a minor prince could emerge from these disasters in a good position if he had an army. With some military force at his disposal, he could become a useful ally for the big powers, who could then help him against his neighbors; while at home he would have the strength to crush his opponents.

By 1648 Frederick William had eight thousand troops, and he was backed by both the Dutch and the French in the Westphalia negotiations that year as a possible restraint on Sweden in northern Europe. Without having done much to earn new territory, he did very well in the peace settlement, and he then took advantage of wars around the Baltic in the 1650s to confirm his gains by switching sides at crucial moments. In the process, his army grew to twenty-two thousand men, and he began to use it to impose his will on his own lands. The fact that the army was essential to Frederick William's success—at home and abroad—was to influence much of Prussia's and thus also Germany's subsequent history.

Domestic Policy The role of the military in establishing the elector's supremacy was apparent throughout Brandenburg-Prussia's society. In 1653 the Diet of Brandenburg met for the last time, sealing its own fate by giving Frederick William the right to raise taxes without its consent. The War Chest, the office in charge of financing the army, took over the functions of a treasury department and collected government revenue even when the state was at peace. The implementation of policies in the localities was placed in the hands of war commissars—who originally were responsible for military recruitment, billeting, and supply but now became the principal agents of all government departments.

Apart from the representative assemblies, Frederick William faced real resistance only from the long-independent cities of his realm. Accustomed to going their own way because authority had been fragmented in the empire for centuries, and especially during the Thirty Years' War, city leaders were dismayed when the elector began to intervene in their affairs. Yet once again sheer intimidation overcame opposition. The last determined effort to dispute his authority arose in the rich city of Königsberg, which allied with the Estates General of Prussia to refuse to pay taxes. But this resistance was crushed in 1662, when Frederick William marched into the city with a few thousand troops. Similar pressure brought the towns of Cleves into submission after centuries of proud independence.

The Junkers The main supporters and beneficiaries of the elector's state building were the Prussian nobles, known as **Junkers** (from the German for "young lord," *jung herr*). In fact, it was an alliance between the nobility and Frederick William that undermined the Diet, the cities, and the representative assemblies. The leading Junker families saw their best opportunities for the future in cooperation with the central government, and both in the representative assemblies and in the localities, they worked to establish absolutist power—that is, to remove all restraints on the elector. The most significant indicator of the Junkers' success was that by the end of the century, two tax rates had been devised, one for cities and one for the countryside, to the great advantage of the latter.

As the nobles staffed the upper levels of the elector's army and bureaucracy, they also won new prosperity for themselves. Particularly in Prussia, the support of the elector enabled them to reimpose serfdom and consolidate their land holdings into vast, highly profitable estates. This area was a major grain producer, and the Junkers maximized their profits by growing and distributing their produce themselves, thus eliminating middlemen. Efficiency became their hallmark, and their wealth was soon famous throughout the Holy Roman Empire. These Prussian entrepreneurs were probably the most successful group of European aristocrats in pursuing economic and political power.

Frederick III Unlike Louis in France, Frederick William had little interest in court life. The Berlin court became the focus of society only under his son, Elector Frederick III, who ruled from 1688. The great elector had begun the development of his capital, Berlin, into a cultural center—he founded what was to become one of the finest libraries in the world, the Prussian State Library—but this was never among his prime concerns. His son, by contrast, had little interest in state building, but he did enjoy princely pomp and encouraged the arts with enthusiasm.

Frederick III lacked only one attribute of royalty: a crown. When Emperor Leopold I, who still had the right to confer titles in the empire, needed Prussia's troops during the War of the Spanish Succession, he gave Frederick, in return, the right to call himself "king in Prussia"; the title soon became "king of Prussia." At a splendid coronation in 1701, Elector Frederick III of Brandenburg was crowned King Frederick I, and thereafter his court felt itself the equal of the other monarchical centers of Europe.

Frederick determinedly promoted social and cultural glitter. He made his palace a focus of art and polite society that competed, he hoped, with Versailles. A construction program beautified Berlin with new churches and huge public buildings. He also established an Academy of Sciences and persuaded the most famous German scientist and philosopher of the day, Gottfried Wilhelm von Leibniz, to become its first president. All these activities obtained generous support from state revenues, as did the universities of Brandenburg and Prussia. By the end of his reign in 1713, Frederick had given his realm a throne, celebrated artistic and intellectual activity, and an elegant aristocracy at the head of social and political life.

Rivalry and State Building

Europe's increasingly self-confident states were in constant rivalry with their neighbors during the eighteenth century. The competition intensified their state building, because the conflicts forced rulers to expand their

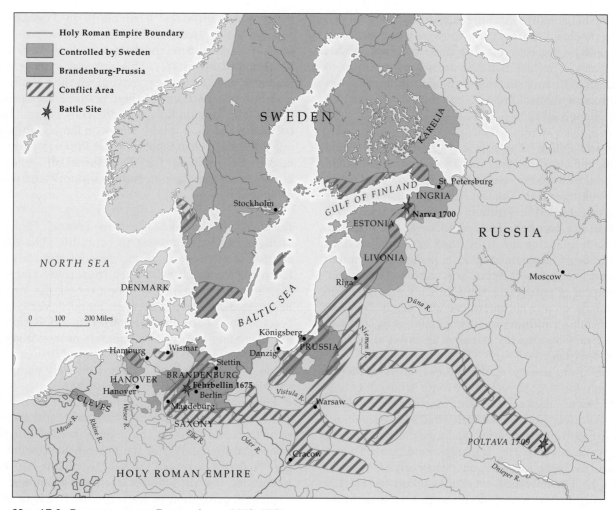

MAP 17.3 CONFLICT IN THE BALTIC AREA, 1660–1721
The fighting around the Baltic eventually destroyed Sweden's power in northern Europe; the new powers were to be Brandenburg-Prussia and Russia. At what point did Sweden no longer dominate the Baltic?

revenues, armies, and bureaucracies. The counterexample was Poland, which failed to centralize and was partitioned three times by Russia, Austria, and Prussia, until in 1795 it ceased to exist as a sovereign state. Political consolidation, by putting a premium on military and economic power, shaped both the map of modern Europe and the centralization of the major states.

The relationship between international rivalry and internal development is well illustrated by Prussia and Austria. In the mid-eighteenth century these two powers sought to dominate central Europe, and they launched reforms to wage their struggle more effectively. Their absolute rulers built their states by increasing the size of their armies, collecting larger revenues, and developing bureaucracies for the war effort. Whether the ruler was a modern pragmatist like Frederick II of Prussia or a pious traditionalist like Maria Theresa of Austria, both understood the demands of the state system.

The Prussia of Frederick William I

Prussia's Frederick William I (r. 1713–1740) relentlessly pursued a strengthened absolutism at home and Europe-wide influence abroad. Strikingly different from his refined father, this spartan ruler approached affairs of state as all business and little pleasure. He disdained court life, dismissed numerous courtiers, and cut the salaries of those who remained. Uncluttered by royal ceremonies, his days were strictly regulated as he attempted to supervise all government activities personally.

Emphasis on the Military   It has been said that Frederick William I organized his state to serve his military power. During his reign the army grew from 38,000 to 83,000, making it the fourth largest in Europe, behind France, Russia, and Austria. And all his soldiers had to undergo intensive drilling and wear standardized uniforms. Determined to build an effective force, he forbade his subjects to serve in foreign armies and compelled the sons of nobles to attend cadet schools to learn martial skills and attitudes. But Frederick William did not intend to die in battle. For all his involvement with military life, he avoided committing his army to battle and was able to pass it on intact to his son.

Centralization kept pace with the growth of the army. In 1723 the General Directory of Finance, War, and Domains took over all government functions except justice, education, and religion. A super-agency, it collected revenues and oversaw expenditures (mostly military) and local administration. Even education was seen merely as a way to encourage people to serve the state. Frederick made education compulsory for all children, ordering local communities to set up schools where there were none, though he never enforced these decrees. Uninterested in intellectual pursuits for their own sake, the king allowed the universities to decline; they did not fit his relentless vision of how to build his state.

Frederick the Great

Frederick William I's most notable triumph, perhaps, was the grooming of his successor. This was no mean task. Frederick II (r. 1740–1786) seemed opposite in temperament to his father and little inclined to follow in his footsteps. The father was a God-fearing German Protestant. The son disdained German culture and was a deist (see p. 544). Sentimental and artistically inclined, Frederick II was a composer of music who played the flute, wrote poetry, and greatly admired French culture. He even wrote philosophical treatises and corresponded with leading European intellectuals.

But the young prince was not exempt from the effort to draw all Prussians into the task of state building. On the contrary: His father forced him to work at all levels of the state apparatus so as to experience them directly, from shoveling hay on a royal farm to marching with the troops. The father trained his son for kingship, reshaping his personality, giving him a sense of duty, and toughening him for leadership. Despite Frederick's resistance, this hard apprenticeship succeeded.

Frederick's Absolutism   When he assumed the throne in 1740, Frederick II was prepared to lead Prussia in a ruthless struggle for power and territory. While his intellectual turn of mind caused him to agonize over moral issues and the nature of his role, he never flinched from exercising power. But he did try to justify absolutism at home and aggression abroad. He claimed undivided power for the ruler, not because the dynasty had a divine mission but because only absolute rule could bring results. The king, he said, was the first servant of the state, and in the long run an enlightened monarch might lead his people to a more rational and moral existence. Some of his objectives, such as religious toleration and judicial reform, he could reach at once, and by putting them into effect Frederick gained a reputation as an **"enlightened" absolutist.**

But these were minor matters. The paramount issue, security, provided the best justification for absolutism. Success here required Prussia to improve its vulnerable geographic position by acquiring more territory, stronger borders, and the power to face other European states as an equal. Until that was achieved, Frederick would not consider the domestic reforms that might disrupt the flow of taxes or men into the army, or provoke his nobility. The capture of territory was his most singular contribution to the rise of Prussia and what earned him his title of Frederick the Great. As it happened, a suitable task for his army presented itself in the year Frederick II came to the throne, 1740—an attack on the province of Silesia, which the Habsburgs controlled but were unable to defend. Prussia had no claim to the province; it was simply a wealthy neighboring domain that would expand Prussia's territory. Yet the conquest of Silesia brought to a new level the state building that the great elector had begun in 1648; the reaction also shaped state building in the Habsburg Empire.

The Habsburg Empire

The Habsburg Empire was like a dynastic holding company of diverse territories under one crown: Austria, Bohemia, Hungary, and other possessions such as the Austrian Netherlands, Lombardy, and Tuscany. The emperors hoped to integrate Austria, Bohemia, and Hungary into a Catholic, centralized, German-speaking super-state. But the traditional representative assemblies in these provinces resisted such centralization.

International Rivalry   In the reign of Leopold's successor, Charles VI (r. 1711–1740), yet another problem complicated the destiny of this multinational empire, for his only heir was his daughter, Maria Theresa. In 1713 Charles drafted a document known as the Pragmatic Sanction, declaring that all Habsburg dominions would pass intact to the eldest heir, male or female; and for the next twenty-five years he sought recognition of the Pragmatic Sanction from the European powers. By making all kinds of concessions and promises, he won this recognition on paper. But when he died in 1740, his daughter found that the commitments were worthless: The succession was challenged by force from several sides. Concentrating on diplomacy alone, Charles had neglected the work of state building, leaving an empty treasury, an inadequately trained army, and an ineffective bureaucracy.

In contrast to Austria, Prussia had a full treasury, a powerful army, and a confident ruler, Frederick II, who seized the Habsburg province of Silesia without qualm. His justification was simply **"reasons of state,"** combined with the Habsburgs' faltering fortunes. And Maria Theresa had her hands more than full, because the French declared war on her to support their ally Bavaria's claim to the Habsburg throne. Meanwhile, Spain hoped to win back control of Austria's Italian possessions. Worse yet, Maria Theresa faced a rebellion by the Czech nobles in Bohemia. Her position would probably have been hopeless if Hungary's Magyar nobles had followed suit. But Maria Theresa promised them autonomy within the Habsburg Empire, and they offered her the troops she needed to resist the invaders.

The War of Austrian Succession In the War of Austrian Succession (1740–1748) that followed, Maria Theresa learned the elements of state building. With her Hungarian troops and with financial help from her one ally, Britain, she fought her opponents to a stalemate. Frederick's conquest of Silesia proved to be the only significant territorial change produced by the war. Even for England and France, who fought the war mainly in overseas colonies, it was a standoff. But Maria Theresa was now determined to recover Silesia and humiliate Prussia, and this required a determined effort of state building.

Maria Theresa The woman whose authority was established not by her father's negotiations but by force of arms was a marked contrast to her archenemy, Frederick. The Prussian king was practical and irreligious; Maria Theresa was moralistic and pious. Her personality and her ruling style were deceptively traditional, however, for she was a shrewd innovator in the business of building and reasserting the power of her state.

E. F. Cunningham
The Return of Frederick II from a Maneuvre, 1787
Were it not for the richly embroidered saddle cover and the fine white horse, Frederick the Great would be hard to spot among his officers. Nor is there anything to indicate that the two men on the black and brown horses behind him are his nephew and grandnephew. This sober evocation of a king as a professional soldier contrasts strikingly with earlier glorifications (see painting, p. 408).
Staatliche Museen Preussischer Kulturbesitz Nationalgalerie/BPK Berlin

Unlike Frederick, Maria Theresa had a strong regard for her dynasty. In this respect, being a woman made no difference to the policies or government of the empire. She believed in the divine mission of the Habsburgs and conscientiously attended to the practical needs of her realm.

Reform in Church and State   It was because she put the state's interests first that this most pious of Catholic sovereigns—who disdained religious toleration and loathed atheists—felt obliged to reform the Church. Responding to waste and self-interest in her monasteries, she forbade the founding of new establishments. She

Martin van Meytens
MARIA THERESA AND HER FAMILY, 1750
Although the setting is just as splendid, the portrayal of Maria Theresa with her husband and thirteen of her sixteen children suggests a domesticity that is absent from Louis XIV's family portrait of half a century before (see painting, p. 478).
Galleria Palatina, Palazzo Pitti, Florence, Italy. Scala/Art Resource, NY

also abolished the clergy's exemptions from taxes, something the French king found impossible to do.

A new bureaucratic apparatus was constructed on the models of French and Prussian absolutism. In Vienna, reorganized central ministries recruited staffs of experts. In the provinces, new agents were appointed who were largely free of local interests, though some concession did have to be made to the regional traditions of the Habsburg realm. The core domains (excluding Hungary and the Italian possessions) were reorganized into ten provinces, each subdivided into districts directed by royal officials. With the help of these officials, the central government could wrest new taxes from the local diets. Meanwhile, Maria Theresa brought important nobles from all her domains to Vienna to participate in its social and administrative life. She also reformed the military, improving the training of troops and establishing academies to produce a more professional officer corps. Thus did international needs help shape domestic political reforms.

Habsburgs and Bourbons at Madrid

In Spain the Habsburgs had little success in state building either at home or abroad. The king who followed Philip IV, Charles II (r. 1665–1700), was a sickly man, incapable of having children; and the War of the Spanish Succession seriously reduced the inheritance he left. Both the southern Netherlands and most of Italy passed to the Austrian Habsburgs, and Spain's overseas possessions often paid little notice to the homeland.

The Spanish nobility was even more successful than the Austrian in turning absolutism to its advantage. In 1650 the crown had been able to recapture Catalonia's loyalty only by granting the province's aristocracy virtual autonomy, and this pattern recurred throughout Spain's territories. Parasitic, unproductive nobles controlled the regime, often for personal gain. The country fell into economic and cultural stagnation, subservient to a group of powerful families, with its former glory visible mainly in its strong navy.

Bourbon Spain Yet Spain and its vast overseas possessions remained a force in eighteenth-century affairs. When the Bourbons gained the crown, following the War of Spanish Succession, they ended the traditional independence of Aragon, Catalonia, and Valencia and integrated these provinces into the kind of united Spain Olivares had sought eighty years earlier. They imported the position of *intendant* from France to administer the provinces, and although the nobles remained far more independent, the Bourbons did begin to impose uniform procedures on the country. In midcentury the ideas of enlightened absolutism that were visible elsewhere in Europe had their effect, largely because of a liberal reformer, Count Pedro de Campomanes. The most remarkable change concerned the religious order that had been identified with Spain since the days of its founder, Loyola: the Jesuits. They had become too powerful and too opposed to reform, and so they were expelled from Spanish territory in 1767.

In a sense, though, the Jesuits were to have their revenge. Spain's colonies in America were flourishing in the eighteenth century: Their trade with Europe was booming; they were attracting new settlers; and by 1800 they had over 14 million inhabitants. But they were still subject to the same absolutist control as the homeland. It was largely under the inspiration of disgruntled Jesuits that the idea of breaking free from Spain took hold in the empire, an idea that led to the independence movements of the 1800s.

Peter the Great at St. Petersburg

One of the reasons the new absolutist regimes of the late seventeenth and eighteenth centuries seemed so different from their predecessors was that many of them consciously created new settings for themselves. Versailles, Schönbrunn, and Berlin were all either new or totally transformed sites for royal courts. But only one of the autocrats of the period went so far as to build an entirely new capital: Tsar Peter I (the Great) of Russia (1682–1725), who named the new city St. Petersburg after his patron saint.

Peter's Fierce Absolutism None of the state-building rulers of the period had Peter's terrifying energy or ruthless determination to exercise absolute control. He was only nine when he was chosen tsar, and in his early years, when his sister and his mother were the effective rulers, he witnessed ghastly massacres of members of his family and their associates by soldiers in Moscow. Like little Louis XIV, endangered by Paris mobs during the Fronde, Peter determined to leave his capital city. Soon after he assumed full powers in 1696, therefore, he shifted his court to St. Petersburg, despite thousands of deaths among the peasants who were forced to build the city in a cold and inhospitable swamp. Well over six feet tall—a giant by the standards of the time—Peter terrorized those around him, especially during his many drunken rages. His only son, Alexis, a weak and retiring figure, became the focus of opposition to the tsar, and Peter had him put in prison, where Alexis mysteriously died. Peter refused even to attend his funeral.

Western Models Early in his reign, Peter suffered a humiliating military defeat at the hands of the Swedes. This merely confirmed his view that, in order to compete with Europe's powers, he had to bring to Russia

PETER THE GREAT AT ST. PETERSBURG
In the eighteenth century Peter the Great of Russia outstripped the grandeur of other monarchs of the period by erecting an entirely new city for his capital. St. Petersburg was built by forced labor of the peasants under Peter's orders; they are shown here laying the foundations for the city.
Tass/Sovfoto

some of the advances the Western nations had recently made. To observe these achievements firsthand, Peter traveled incognito through France, England, and the Netherlands in 1697 and 1698, paying special attention to economic, administrative, and military practices (such as the functioning of a Dutch shipyard). Many of his initiatives were to derive from this journey, including his importation of Western court rituals, his founding of an Academy of Sciences in 1725, and his encouragement of the first Russian newspaper.

Italian artists were brought to Russia, along with Scandinavian army officers, German engineers, and Dutch shipbuilders, not only to apply their skills but also to teach them to the Russians. St. Petersburg, the finest eighteenth-century city built in Classical style, is mainly the work of Italians. But gradually Russians took over their own institutions—military academies produced native officers, for example—and by the end of Peter's reign they had little need of foreign experts.

Bureaucratization

In ruling Russia, Peter virtually ignored the Duma, the traditional advisory council, and concentrated instead on his bureaucracy. He carried out countless changes until he had created an administrative apparatus much larger than the one he had inherited. Here again he copied Western models—notably Prussia, where nobles ran the bureaucracy and the army, and Sweden, where a complex system of government departments had been created. Peter organized his administration into similar departments: Each had either a specialized function, such as finance, or responsibility for a geographic area, such as Siberia. The result was an elaborate but unified hierarchy of author-

ity, rising from local agents of the government through provincial officials up to the staffs and governors of eleven large administrative units and finally to the leaders of the regime in the capital. Peter began the saturating bureaucratization that characterized Russia from that time on.

The Imposition of Social Order

The tsar's policies laid the foundations for a two-class society that persisted until the twentieth century. Previously, a number of ranks had existed within both the nobility and the peasantry, and a group in the middle was seen sometimes as the lowest nobles and sometimes as the highest peasants. Under Peter such mingling disappeared. All peasants were reduced to one level, subject to a new poll tax, military conscription, and forced public work, such as the building of St. Petersburg. Below them were serfs, whose numbers were increased by legislation restricting their movement. Peasants had a few advantages over serfs, such as the freedom to move, but their living conditions were often equally dreadful. Serfdom itself spread throughout all areas of Peter's dominions and became essential to his state building because, on royal lands as well as the estates of the nobles, serfs worked and ran the agricultural enterprise that was Russia's economic base.

At the same time, Peter created a single class of nobles by substituting status within the bureaucracy for status within the traditional hierarchy of titles. In 1722 he issued a table of bureaucratic ranks that gave everyone a place according to the office he held. Differentiations still existed, but they were no longer unbridgeable, as they had been when family was the decisive determinant of status. The result was a more controlled social order and greater uniformity than in France or Brandenburg-Prussia. The Russian aristocracy was the bureaucracy, and the bureaucracy the aristocracy.

The Subjugation of the Nobility This was not a voluntary alliance between nobles and government, such as existed in the West; in return for his support and his total subjection of the peasantry, Peter required the nobles to provide officials for his bureaucracy and officers for his army. When he began the construction of St. Petersburg, he also demanded that the leading families build splendid mansions in his new capital. In effect, the tsar offered privilege and wealth in exchange for conscription into public service. Thus, there was hardly any sense of partnership between nobility and throne: The tsar often had to use coercion to ensure that his wishes were followed. On the other hand, Peter helped build up the nobles' fortunes and their control of the countryside. It has been estimated that by 1710 he had put under the supervision of great landowners more than forty thousand peasant and serf households that had formerly been under the crown.

Control of the Church Peter's determination to stamp his authority on Russia was also apparent in his destruction of ecclesiastical independence. He accomplished this with one blow: He simply did not replace the patriarch of the Russian Church who died in 1700. Peter took over the monasteries and their vast income for his own purposes and appointed a procurator (at first an army officer) to supervise religious affairs. The Church was, in effect, made a branch of government.

Military Expansion The purpose of all these radical changes was to assert the tsar's power both at home and abroad. Peter established a huge standing army, more than three hundred thousand strong by the 1720s, and imported the latest military techniques from the West. One of Peter's most cherished projects, the creation of a navy, had limited success, but there could be no doubt that he transformed Russia's capacity for war and its position among European states. He extended Russia's frontier to the south and west, and, at the battle of Poltava in 1709, reversed his early defeat by the Swedes. This victory began the dismantling of Sweden's empire, for it was followed by more than a decade of Russian advance into Estonia, Livonia, and Poland. The very vastness of his realm justified Peter's drive for absolute control, and by the time of his death he had made Russia the dominant power in the Baltic and a major influence in European affairs.

ALTERNATIVES TO ABSOLUTISM

The absolutist regimes offered one model of political and social organization, but an alternative model—equally committed to uniformity, order, and state building—was also created in the late seventeenth century: governments dominated by aristocrats or merchants. The contrast between the two was noted by contemporary political theorists, especially opponents of absolutism, who preferred **constitutionalism.** And yet the differences were often less sharp than the theorists suggested, mainly because the position of the aristocracy was similar throughout Europe.

Aristocracy in the United Provinces, Sweden, and Poland

In the Dutch republic, the succession of William III to the office of Stadholder in 1672 seemed to be a move toward absolutism. As he led the successful resistance to Louis XIV in war (1672–1678), he increasingly concentrated government in his own hands. Soon, however, the power of merchants and provincial leaders in the Estates General reasserted itself. William did not want to sign a peace treaty with Louis when the French invasion failed. He wanted instead to take the war into France and reinforce his own authority by keeping the position of commander in chief. But the Estates General, led by the province of Holland, ended the war.

A decade later William sought the English crown, but he did so only with the approval of the Estates General, and he had to leave separate the representative assemblies that governed the two countries. When William died without an heir, his policies were continued by his close friend Antonius Heinsius, who held the same position of grand pensionary of Holland that Jan de Witt had once occupied; but the government was in effect controlled by the Estates General. This representative assembly now had to preside over the decline of a great power. In finance and trade, the Dutch were gradually overtaken by the English, while in the war against Louis XIV, they had to support the crippling burden of maintaining a land force, only to hand over command to England.

Dutch Society The aristocrats of the United Provinces differed from the usual European pattern. Instead of ancient families and bureaucratic dynasties, they boasted merchants and mayors. The prominent citizens of the leading cities were the backbone of the Dutch upper classes. Moreover, social distinctions were less prominent than in any other country of Europe. The elite was composed of hard-working financiers and traders, richer and more powerful but not essentially more privileged or leisured than those

MAP 17.4 THE EXPANSION OF RUSSIA AND THE PARTITION OF POLAND
All three of the powers in Eastern Europe—Prussia, Russia, and Austria—gained territory from the dismemberment
of Poland. Which country was the chief beneficiary of the partition? In addition to the territory it gained from
Poland, where else was Russia expanding in the period 1721–1795?

farther down the social ladder. The inequality described in much eighteenth-century political writing—the special place nobles had, often including some immunity from the law—was far less noticeable in the United Provinces. There was no glittering court, and although here as elsewhere a small group controlled the country, it did so for largely economic ends and in different style.

Sweden   The Swedes created yet another nonabsolutist model of state building. After a long struggle with the king, the nobles emerged as the country's domi-

nant political force. During the reign of Charles XI (1660–1697), the monarchy was able to force the great lords to return to the state the huge tracts of land they had received as rewards for loyalty earlier in the century. Since Charles stayed out of Europe's wars, he was able to conserve his resources and avoid relying on the nobility as he strengthened the smoothly running bureaucracy he had inherited from Gustavus Adolphus.

His successor, Charles XII (r. 1697–1718), however, revived Sweden's tradition of military conquest. He won land from Peter the Great, but then made the fatal decision to invade Russia. Defeated at the battle of

Poltava in 1709, Charles had to retreat and watch helplessly as the Swedish Empire was dismembered. By the time he was killed in battle nine years later, his neighbors had begun to overrun his lands, and, in treaties signed from 1719 to 1721, Sweden reverted to roughly the territory it had had a century before.

Naturally, the nobles took advantage of Charles XII's frequent absences to reassert their authority. They ran Sweden's highly efficient government while he was campaigning and forced his successor, Queen Ulrika, to accept a constitution that gave the Riksdag effective control over the country. The new structure, modeled on England's political system, gave the nobility the role of the English gentry—leaders of society and the shapers of its politics. A splendid court arose, and Stockholm became one of the more elegant and cultured aristocratic centers in Europe.

Poland Warsaw fared less well. In fact, the strongest contrast to the French political and social model in the late seventeenth century was Poland. The sheer chaos and disunity that plagued Poland until it ceased to exist as a state in the late eighteenth century were the direct result of continued dominance by the old landed aristocracy, which blocked all attempts to centralize the government. There were highly capable kings in this period—notably John III, who achieved Europe-wide fame by relieving Vienna from the Turkish siege in 1683. These monarchs could quite easily gather an army to fight, and fight well, against Poland's many foes: Germans, Swedes, Russians, and Turks. But once a battle was over, the ruler could exercise no more than nominal leadership. Each king was elected by the assembly of nobles and had to agree not to interfere with the independence of the great lords, who were growing rich from serf labor on fertile lands. The crown had neither revenue nor bureaucracy to speak of, and so the country continued to resemble a feudal kingdom, where power remained in the localities.

The Triumph of the Gentry in England

The model for a nonabsolutist regime was England, even though King Charles II (r. 1660–1685) seemed to have powers similar to those of his ill-fated father, Charles I. He still summoned and dissolved Parliament, made all appointments in the bureaucracy, and signed every law. But he no longer had prerogative courts like Star Chamber, he could not arrest a member of Parliament, and he could not create a new seat in the Commons. Even two ancient prerogatives, the king's right to dispense with an act of Parliament for a specific individual or group and his right to suspend an act completely, proved empty when Charles II tried to exercise them. Nor could he raise money without Parliament;

instead, he was given a fixed annual income, financed by a tax on beer.

The Gentry and Parliament The real control of the country's affairs had by this time passed to the group of substantial landowners known as the gentry. In a country of some five million people, perhaps fifteen to twenty thousand families were considered gentry—local leaders throughout England, despite having neither titles of nobility nor special privileges. Amounting to 2 percent of the population, they probably represented about the same proportion as the titled nobles in other states. Yet the gentry differed from these other nobles in that they had won the right to determine national policy through Parliament. Whereas nobles elsewhere depended on monarchs for power, the English revolution had made the gentry an independent force. Their authority was now hallowed by custom, upheld by law, and maintained by the House of Commons.

ENGRAVING FROM *THE WESTMINSTER MAGAZINE*, 1774
Political cartoons were standard fare in eighteenth-century newspapers and magazines. This one shows a weeping king of Poland and an angry Turk (who made no gains) after Poland was carved up in 1772 by Frederick the Great, the Austrian emperor, and the Russian empress. Louis XV sits by without helping his ally Poland, and all are urged on by the devil under the table.

Not all the gentry took a continuing interest in affairs of state, and only a few of their number sat in the roughly five-hundred-member House of Commons. Even the Commons did not exercise a constant influence over the government; nevertheless, the ministers of the king had to be prominent representatives of the gentry, and they had to be able to win the support of a majority of the members of the Commons. Policy was still set by the king and his ministers, but the Commons had to be persuaded that the policies were correct; without parliamentary approval, a minister could not long survive.

The Succession   Despite occasional conflicts, this structure worked relatively smoothly throughout Charles II's reign. But the gentry feared that Charles's brother, James, next in line for the succession and an open Catholic, might try to restore Catholicism in England. To prevent this, they attempted in 1680 to force Charles to exclude James from the throne. But in the end the traditional respect for legitimacy, combined with some shrewd maneuvering by Charles, ensured that there would be no tampering with the succession.

Soon, however, the reign of James II (r. 1685–1688) turned into a disaster. Elated by his acceptance as king,

James rashly offered Catholics the very encouragement the gentry feared. This was a direct challenge to the gentry's newly won power, and in 1688 seven of their leaders, including members of England's most prominent families, invited the Protestant ruler of the United Provinces, William III, to invade and take over the throne. Though William landed with an army half the size of the king's, James, uncertain of his support, decided not to risk battle and fled to exile in France. Because the transfer of the monarchy was bloodless and confirmed the supremacy of Parliament, it came to be called the Glorious Revolution.

William and Mary   The new king gained what little title he had to the crown through his wife, Mary (see the genealogical table below), and Parliament proclaimed the couple joint monarchs early in 1689. The Dutch ruler took the throne primarily to bring England into his relentless struggles against Louis XIV, and he willingly accepted a settlement that confirmed the essential role of Parliament in the government. A **Bill of Rights** determined the succession to the throne, defined Parliament's powers, and established basic civil rights. An Act of Toleration put an end to all religious persecution, though members of the official Church of

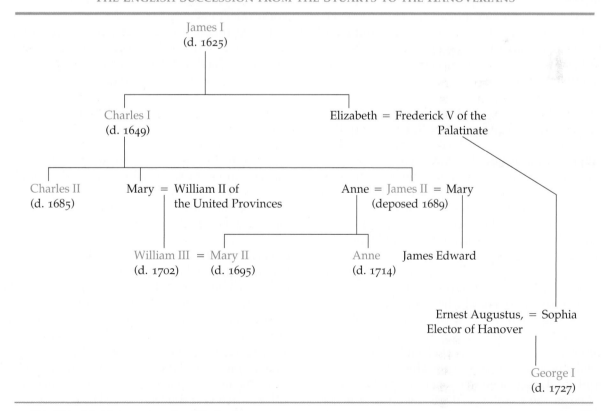

THE ENGLISH SUCCESSION FROM THE STUARTS TO THE HANOVERIANS

Note: Names in blue = monarchs of England.

England were still the only people allowed to vote, sit in Parliament, hold a government office, or attend a university. In 1694 a statute declared that Parliament had to meet and new elections had to be held at least once every three years.

Despite the restrictions on his authority, William exercised strong leadership. He guided England into an aggressive foreign policy, picked ministers favorable to his aims, and never let Parliament sit when he was out of the country to pursue the war or to oversee Dutch affairs. In his reign, too, the central government grew considerably, gaining new powers and positions, and thus new opportunities for political patronage. But unlike James, William recognized his limits. He tried to have the Bill of Rights reversed and a standing army established, but he gave up when these efforts provoked major opposition. By and large, therefore, the gentry were content to let the king rule as he saw fit, for they had shown by their intervention in 1688 that ultimately they controlled the country.

Politics and Prosperity

The political system in England now reflected the social system: A small elite controlled both the country's policy and its institutions. This group was far from united, however, as was apparent when a party system began to appear in Parliament during Charles II's reign. On one side was the **Whig** party, which opposed royal prerogatives and Catholicism and was largely responsible for the attempt to exclude James II from the throne. The rival **Tory** party stood for the independence and authority of the crown and favored a ceremonial and traditional Anglicanism.

Party Conflict Because the Whigs had been the main advocates of the removal of James II, they controlled the government for most of William III's reign. They supported his war against Louis XIV (1689–1697), because France harbored both James and his followers (the romantic but ill-fated Jacobites, who kept trying to restore James's line to the throne). This was a fairly nonpartisan issue, but the Tories and Whigs still competed fiercely for voters. Because the qualification for voting—owning land worth forty shillings a year in rent—had become less restrictive as a result of inflation (which made forty shillings a fairly modest sum) and was not to be raised to a higher minimum until the late 1700s, England now had what would be its largest electorate before the 1860s. Almost 5 percent of the population (more than 15 percent of adult males) could vote, and although results were usually determined by powerful local magnates, fierce politicking was common. And in the election of 1700 there was a major upset: The Tories won by opposing renewal of war with Louis XIV, who had seemed restrained since the end of the previous war in 1697.

Within two years, however, and despite William's death in 1702, England was again at war with France, this time over the Spanish succession; and soon the Whigs were again in control of the government. The identification of the parties with their attitude toward war continued until 1710, when weariness over the fighting brought the Tories back into power. They persuaded Queen Anne, William's successor, to make peace with France at Utrecht in 1713; and they lost power only because they made the mistake of negotiating with the rebel Jacobites after Anne died in 1714 without an heir. Anne's successor was a German prince, the elector of Hanover, who founded the new Hanoverian Dynasty as George I (1714–1727). Because they firmly supported his succession, the Whigs regained control of the government when George came to the throne. They then entrenched themselves for almost a century.

The Sea and the Economy At the same time, England was winning for itself unprecedented prosperity and laying the foundations of its world power. The English navy was the premier force on the sea, the decisive victor over France during the worldwide struggle of the early eighteenth century. Overseas, England founded new colonies and steadily expanded the empire. When England and Scotland joined into one kingdom in 1707, the union created a Great Britain ready to exercise a worldwide influence.

The economic advances were equally remarkable. A notable achievement was the establishment of the Bank of England in 1694. The bank gained permission to raise money from the public and then lend it to the government at a favorable 8 percent interest. Within twelve days its founders raised more than a million pounds, demonstrating not only the financial stability of England's government but also the commitment of the elite to the country's political structure. London was becoming the financial capital of the world, with her merchants gaining control of maritime trade from east Asia to North America. And the benefits of the boom also helped the lower levels of society.

English Society With the possible exception of the Dutch, ordinary English people were better off than their equivalents elsewhere in Europe. Compared with the sixteenth century, there was little starvation. The system of poor relief may often have been inhumane in forcing the unfortunate to work in horrifying workhouses, but it did provide them with the shelter and food they had long lacked. It is true that thousands still found themselves unable to make a living in their home villages each year and were forced by poverty to take to the roads. And the many who ended up in London

William Hogarth
THE POLLING, **1754**
Despite the high reputation of the polling day as the central moment in the system of representative government, Hogarth's depiction of it in this scene suggests how corrupt and disheveled the process of voting was. The sick and the foolish are among the mob of voters; the central figure looks bewildered as he is told what to do; on the right a bloated official cannot decide whether a voter should be allowed to take his oath on the Bible with a wooden hand; and all ignore the distress of Britannia, the symbol of Britain, in her coach on the left.
By courtesy of the Trustees of Sir John Soane's Museum, London

hardly improved their situation. The stream of immigrants was driving the capital's population toward half a million, and the city contained frightful slums and miserable crime-ridden sections. Even a terrible fire in London in 1666 did little to improve the appallingly crowded living conditions, because the city was rebuilt much as before, the only notable additions being a series of splendid churches. But the grimness should not be overdrawn.

After more than a century of inflation, the laborer could once again make a decent living, and artisans were enjoying a growing demand for their work. Higher in the social scale, more men had a say in the political process than before, and more found opportunities for advancement in the rising economy—in trade overseas, in the bureaucracy, or in the expanding market for luxury

goods. It has been estimated that in 1730 there were about sixty thousand adult males in what we would call the professions. England also had better roads than any other European country and a more impartial judicial system. Yet none of these gains could compare with those that the gentry made. In fact, many of the improvements, such as fair administration of justice, were indirect results of what the upper classes had won for themselves. The fruits of progress clearly belonged primarily to the gentry.

The Growth of Stability

Like the absolutist regimes, the British government in the 1700s was able to advance state building—to expand its authority and its international power. This

***New Gallows at the Old Bailey,* Engraving**
It was an indication of the severity of English criminal justice that the gallows erected near the chief court in London, the Old Bailey, in the mid-eighteenth century was specially constructed so that ten condemned criminals, both men and women, could be executed at once.
The British Library, London

was the work not so much of a monarch as of the "political nation": the landowners and leading townsmen who elected almost all the members of Parliament. Their control of the nation was visible in the distribution of the 558 seats in the House of Commons, which bore little relation to the size of constituencies. In 1793, for example, fifty-one English and Welsh boroughs, with fewer than fifteen hundred voters, elected one hundred members of Parliament, nearly a fifth of the Commons. Many districts were safely in the pocket of a prominent local family; and elsewhere elections were often determined by bribery, influence, and intimidation. On the national level, loose party alignments pitted Whigs, who wanted a strong Parliament and usually preferred commercial to agricultural interests, against Tories, who tended to support the king and policies that favored large landholders. But the realities of politics were shaped by small factions within these larger groups, and alliances revolved around the control of patronage and office.

War and Taxes As the financial and military needs and capabilities of the government expanded, Parliament now created a thoroughly bureaucratized state. Britain had always prided itself on having a smaller government and lower taxes than its neighbors, largely

because, as an island, it had avoided the need for a standing army. All that now came to an end. Starting with the struggle against Louis XIV, wars required constant increases in resources, troops, and administrators. A steadily expanding navy had to be supported, as did an army that reached almost two hundred thousand men by the 1770s. Before the 1690s, public expenditures rarely amounted to two million pounds a year; by the 1770s, they were almost thirty million pounds, and most of that was spent on the military. In this period, as a result, Britain's fiscal bureaucracy more than tripled in size. The recruiting officer became a regular sight, and so too did the treasury men who were imposing increasingly heavy tax burdens.

Unlike their counterparts on the Continent, however, the wealthier classes in Britain paid considerable taxes to support this state building, and they maintained more fluid relations with other classes. The landed gentry and the commercial class, in particular, were often linked by marriage and by financial or political associations. Even great aristocrats sometimes had close ties with the business leaders of London. The lower levels of society, however, found the barriers as high as they had ever been. For all of Britain's prosperity, the lower third of society remained poor and often desperate. As a result, despite a severe system of justice and frequent

Samuel Scott
The Building of Westminster Bridge
The elegance, but not the squalor, of city life in the eighteenth century is suggested by this view of Westminster. The Metropolitan Museum of Art, Purchase, Charles B. Curtis Fund and Joseph Pulitzer Bequest, 1944. (44.56) Photograph © 1993 The Metropolitan Museum of Art/Art Resource, NY

capital punishment, crime was endemic in both country and town. The eighteenth century was the heyday of that romantic but violent figure, the highwayman.

The Age of Walpole   The first two rulers of the Hanoverian Dynasty, George I (r. 1714–1727) and George II (r. 1727–1760), could not speak English fluently. The language barrier and their concern for their German territory of Hanover left them often uninterested in British politics, and this helped Parliament grow in authority. Its dominant figure for over twenty years was Sir Robert Walpole, who rose to prominence because of his skillful handling of fiscal policy during the panic following the collapse of an overseas trading company in 1720. This crash, known as the South Sea Bubble, resembled the failure of John Law's similar scheme in France, but it had less effect on government finances. Thereafter, Walpole controlled British politics until 1742, mainly by dispensing patronage liberally and staying at peace.

Many historians have called Walpole the first prime minister, though the title was not official. He insisted that all ministers inform and consult with the House of Commons as well as with the king, and he continued to sit in Parliament in order to recruit support for his decisions. Not until the next century was it accepted that the Commons could force a minister to resign. But Walpole took a first step toward ministerial responsibility, and to the notion that the ministers as a body or "cabinet" had a common task, and he thus shaped the future structure of British government.

Commercial Interests   In Great Britain as in France, the economic expansion of the eighteenth century increased the wealth and the social and political weight of the commercial and financial middle class. Although Londoners remained around 11 percent of the population, the proportion of the English who lived in other sizable towns doubled in the 1700s; and by 1800 some 30 percent of the country's inhabitants were urbanized. Walpole's policy of peace pleased the large landlords but angered this growing body of merchants and businesspeople, who feared the growth of French commerce and colonial settlements. They found their champion in William Pitt, later earl of Chatham, the grandson of a man who had made a fortune in India. Eloquent, self-confident, and infused with a vision of Britain's imperial destiny, Pitt began his parliamentary career in 1738 by attacking the government's timid policies and demanding that France be driven from the seas. Though Walpole's policies continued even after his resignation in 1742, Pitt's moment finally came in 1758, when Britain became involved in a European war that was to confirm its importance in continental affairs (see pp. 510–511).

Contrasts in Political Thought

The intensive development of both absolutist and antiabsolutist forms in the seventeenth century stimulated an outpouring of ideas about the nature and purposes of government. Two Englishmen, in particular, developed theories about the basis of political authority that have been influential ever since.

Hobbes   Thomas Hobbes, a brilliant scholar from a poor family who earned his livelihood as the tutor to aristocrats' sons, determined to use the strictly logical methods of the scientist to analyze political behavior. And the almost scientific reasoning is the essence of his masterpiece, *Leviathan* (1651), which began with a few premises about human nature from which Hobbes deduced major conclusions about political forms.

LOCKE ON THE ORIGINS OF GOVERNMENT

The heart of John Locke's Second Treatise of Civil Government, *written in the mid-1680s before England's Glorious Revolution but published in 1690, is its optimism about human nature—as opposed to Hobbes's pessimism. In this passage Locke explains why, in his view, people create political systems.*

"If man in the state of nature be so free, if he be absolute lord of his own person and possessions, equal to the greatest, and subject to nobody, why will he part with his freedom, and subject himself to the dominion and control of any other power? To which it is obvious to answer, that though in the state of nature he hath such a right, yet the enjoyment of it is very uncertain, and constantly exposed to the invasions of others. This makes him willing to quit this condition, which, however free, is full of fears and continual dangers; and it is not without reason that he seeks out and is willing to join in society with others, who have a mind to unite, for the mutual preservation of their lives, liberties, and estates, which I call by the general name, property. The great and chief end, therefore, of men's putting themselves under government, is the preservation of their property.

"But though men when they enter into society give up the equality, liberty, and power they had in the state of nature into the hands of society; yet it being only with an intention in every one the better to preserve himself, his liberty, and property, the power of the society can never be supposed to extend further than the common good. And all this to be directed to no other end but the peace, safety, and public good of the people."

From John Locke, *Second Treatise of Civil Government,* Thomas P. Peardon (ed.), Indianapolis: Bobbs-Merrill, 1952, chapter 9, pp. 70–73.

Leviathan Hobbes's premises, drawn from his observation of the strife-ridden Europe of the 1640s and 1650s, were stark and uncompromising. People, he asserted, are selfish and ambitious; consequently, unless restrained, they fight a perpetual war with their fellows. The weak are more cunning and the strong more stupid. Given these unsavory characteristics, the **state of nature**—which precedes the existence of society—is a state of war, in which life is "solitary, poor, nasty, brutish, and short." Hobbes concluded that the only way to restrain this instinctive aggressiveness is to erect an absolute and sovereign power that will maintain peace. Everyone should submit to the sovereign because the alternative is the anarchy of the state of nature. The moment of submission is the moment of the birth of orderly society.

In a startling innovation, Hobbes suggested that the transition from nature to society is accomplished by a contract that is implicitly accepted by all who want to end the chaos. The unprecedented feature of the contract is that it is not between ruler and ruled; it is binding only on the ruled. They agree among themselves to submit to the sovereign; the sovereign is thus not a party to the contract and is not limited in any way. A government that is totally free to do whatever it wants is best equipped to keep the peace, and peace is always better than the previous turmoil. The power of Hobbes's logic, and the endorsement he seemed to give to absolutism, made his views enormously influential. But his

approach also aroused hostility. Although later political theorists were deeply affected by his ideas, many of Hobbes's successors denounced him as godless, immoral, cynical, and unfeeling. It was dislike of his message, not weaknesses in his analysis, that made many people unwilling to accept his views.

Locke John Locke, a quiet Oxford professor who admired Hobbes but sought to soften his conclusions, based his political analysis on a general theory of knowledge. Locke believed that at birth a person's mind is a *tabula rasa,* a clean slate; nothing, he said, is inborn or preordained. As human beings grow, they observe and experience the world. Once they have gathered enough data through their senses, their minds begin to work on the data. Then, with the help of reason, they perceive patterns, discovering the order and harmony that permeate the universe. Locke was convinced that this underlying order exists and that every person, regardless of individual experiences, must reach the same conclusions about its nature and structure.

When Locke turned his attention to political thought, he put into systematic form the views of the English gentry and other antiabsolutists throughout Europe. The *Second Treatise of Civil Government,* published in 1690, was deeply influenced by Hobbes. From his great predecessor, Locke took the notions that a state of nature is a state of war and that only a contract among the people can end the anarchy that precedes the establishment of civil society. But his conclusions were decidedly different.

Of Civil Government Using the principles of his theory of knowledge, Locke asserted that, applying reason to politics, one can prove the inalienability of three rights of an individual: life, liberty, and property. Like Hobbes, he believed that there must be a sovereign power, but he argued that it has no power over these three natural rights of its subjects without their consent. And this consent—for taxes, for example—must come from a representative assembly of men of property, such as Parliament. The affirmation of property as one of the three natural rights (it became "the pursuit of happiness" in the more egalitarian American Declaration of Independence) is significant. Here Locke revealed himself as the voice of the gentry. Only those with a tangible stake in their country have a right to control its destiny, and that stake must be protected as surely as their life and liberty. The concept of liberty remained vague, but it was taken to imply the sorts of

freedom, such as freedom from arbitrary arrest, that appeared in the English Bill of Rights. Hobbes allowed a person to protect only his or her life. Locke permitted the overthrow of the sovereign power if it infringed on the subjects' rights—a course the English followed with James II and the Americans with George III.

Locke's prime concern was to defend the individual against the state, a concern that has remained essential to liberal thought ever since (see "Locke on the Origins of Government," p. 506). But it is important to realize that his emphasis on property served the elite better than the mass of society. With Locke to reassure them, the upper classes put their stamp on eighteenth-century European civilization.

THE INTERNATIONAL SYSTEM

While rulers built up their states by enlarging bureaucracies, strengthening governmental institutions, and expanding resources, they also had to consider how

Louis Nicolas Blarenberghe
THE BATTLE OF FONTENOY, 1745
This panorama shows the English and Dutch assaulting the French position in a battle in present-day Belgium. The French lines form a huge semicircle from the distant town to the wood on the left. The main attacking force in the center, surrounded by gunfire, eventually retreated, and news of the victory was brought to Louis XV, in red on the right, by a horseman in blue who is doffing his hat.
Photo: Gérard Blot. Château de Versailles et de Trianon, Versailles, France. Réunion des Musées Nationaux/Art Resource, NY. Giraudon/Art Resource, NY

best to deal with their neighbors. In an age that emphasized reasoned and practical solutions to problems, there was hope that an orderly system could be devised for international relations. If the reality fell short of the ideal, there were nevertheless many who thought they were creating a more systematic and organized structure for diplomacy and warfare.

Diplomacy and Warfare

One obstacle to the creation of impersonal international relations was the continuing influence of traditional dynastic interests. Princes and their ministers tried to preserve a family's succession, and they arranged marriages to gain new titles or alliances. Part of the reason that those perennial rivals, Britain and France, remained at peace for nearly thirty years until 1740 was that the rulers in both countries felt insecure on their thrones and thus had personal motives for not wanting to risk aggressive foreign policies.

Gradually, however, dynastic interests gave way to policies based on a more impersonal conception of the state. Leaders like Frederick II of Prussia and William Pitt of Britain tried to shape their diplomacy to what they considered the needs of their states. "Reasons of state" centered on security, which could be guaranteed only by force. Thus, the search for defensible borders and the weakening of rivals became obvious goals. Eighteenth-century leaders believed that the end (security and prosperity) justified the means (the use of power). Chasing the impossible goal of complete invulnerability, leaders felt justified in using the crudest tactics in dealing with their neighbors.

"Balance of Power" and the Diplomatic System If there was any broad, commonly accepted principle at work, it was that hegemony, or domination by one state, had to be resisted because it threatened international security. The concern aroused by Louis XIV's ambitions showed the principle at work, when those whom he sought to dominate joined together to frustrate his designs. The aim was to establish equilibrium in Europe by a balance of power, with no single state achieving hegemony.

ENGRAVING OF A MILITARY ACADEMY, FROM H. F. VON FLEMING, *VOLKOMMENE TEUTSCHE SOLDAT*, 1726
This scene, of young men studying fortifications and tactics in a German academy, would have been familiar to the sons of nobles throughout Europe who trained for a military career in the eighteenth century.

The diplomats, guided by reasons of state and the balance of power, knew there were times when they had to spy and deceive. Yet diplomacy also could stabilize: In the eighteenth century it grew as a serious profession, paralleling the rationalization of the state itself. Foreign ministries were staffed with experts and clerks, who kept extensive archives, while the heads of the diplomatic machine, the ambassadors, were stationed in permanent embassies abroad. This routinized management of foreign relations helped foster a sense of collective identity among Europe's states despite their endless struggles. French was now the common language of diplomacy; by 1774 even a treaty between Turks and Russians was drafted in that language. And socially the diplomats were cosmopolitan aristocrats who saw themselves as members of the same fraternity, even if the great powers dominated international agreements, usually at the expense of the smaller states. Resolving disputes by negotiation could be as amoral as war.

Armies and Navies

Despite the settlement of some conflicts by diplomacy, others led to war. Whereas Britain emphasized its navy, on the Continent the focus of bureaucratic innovation and monetary expenditure was the standing army, whose growth was striking. France set the pace. After 1680 the size of its forces never fell below 200,000. In Prussia the army increased in size from 39,000 to 200,000 men between 1713 and 1786. But the cost, technology, and tactics of armies and navies served to limit the devastation of eighteenth-century warfare. The expenses led rulers to conserve men, equipment,

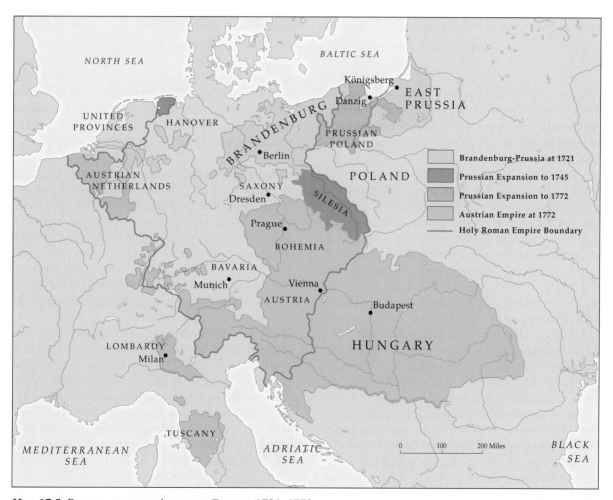

MAP 17.5 PRUSSIA AND THE AUSTRIAN EMPIRE, 1721–1772
The steady territorial advances of Prussia had created a major power in northern and eastern Europe, alongside the Austrian Empire, by the time of the first partition of Poland in 1772. Which was the most extensive of Prussia's gains between 1721 and 1772?

Maria Theresa in a Vehement Mood

The animosities and ambitions that shaped international relations in the eighteenth century were exemplified by the Empress Maria Theresa. Her furious reaction to the event that destroyed Europe's old diplomatic system— England's signing of the Convention of Westminster with Maria Theresa's archenemy, Frederick the Great—suggests how deep were the feelings that brought about the midcentury conflagration. After learning the news and deciding (in response) to ally herself with France, she told the British ambassador on May 13, 1756, exactly where she stood.

"I have not abandoned the old system, but Great Britain has abandoned me and the system, by concluding the Prussian treaty, the first intelligence of which struck me like a fit of apoplexy. I and the king of Prussia are incompatible; and no consideration on earth will ever induce me to enter into any engagement to which he is a party. Why should you be surprised if, following your example in concluding a treaty with Prussia, I should now enter into an engagement with France?

"I am far from being French in my disposition, and do not deny that the court of Versailles has been my bitterest enemy; but I have little to fear from France, and I have no other recourse than to form such arrangements as will secure what remains to me. My principal aim is to secure my hereditary possessions. I have truly but two enemies whom I really dread, the king of Prussia and the Turks; and while I and Russia continue on the same good terms as now exist between us, we shall, I trust, be able to convince Europe, that we are in a condition to defend ourselves against those adversaries, however formidable."

From William Coxe, *History of the House of Austria*, Vol. 3, London: Bohn, 1847, pp. 363–364.

and ships carefully. Princes were quick to declare war but slow to commit armies or navies to battle. Casualties also became less numerous as discipline improved and the ferocity that had been caused by religious passions died away.

Tactics and Discipline   On land, the building and besieging of fortresses continued to preoccupy military planners, even though the impregnable defenses built by the French engineer Sebastian Vauban to protect France's northeastern border were simply bypassed by the English general Marlborough when he pursued the French army in the War of the Spanish Succession. The decisive encounter was still the battle between armies, where the majority of the troops—the infantry—used their training to maneuver and fire in carefully controlled line formations. The aim of strategy was not to annihilate but to nudge an opposing army into abandoning a position in the face of superior maneuvers. Improved organization also reduced brutality. Better supplied by a system of magazines and more tightly disciplined by constant drilling, troops were less likely to desert or plunder than they had been during the Thirty Years' War. At sea, the British achieved superiority by maneuvering carefully controlled lines of ships and seeking to outnumber or outflank the enemy.

As these practices took hold, some encounters were fought as if they were taking place on a parade ground or in a naval strategy room. Pitched battles were increasingly avoided, for even important victories might be nullified if a winning army or navy returned to its home bases for the winter. And no victor ever demanded unconditional surrender; in almost all cases, a commander would hesitate to pursue a defeated company or squadron.

Officers   The officer corps were generally the preserve of Europe's nobility, though they also served as channels of upward social mobility for wealthy sons of middle-class families who purchased commissions. In either case, the officer ranks tended to be filled by men who lacked the professional training for effective leadership. The branches of service that showed the most progress were the artillery and the engineers, in which competent middle-class officers played an unusually large role.

Weak Alliances   A final limit on the scale of war in the eighteenth century was the inherent weakness of coalitions, which formed whenever a general war erupted. On paper these alliances looked formidable. On battlefields, however, they were hampered by primitive communications and lack of mobility even at the peak of cooperation. Moreover, the partnerships rarely lasted very long. The competitiveness of the state system bred distrust among allies as well as enemies.

The Seven Years' War

The pressures created by the competition of states and dynasties finally exploded in a major war, the Seven Years' War (1756–1763). Its roots lay in a realignment of diplomatic alliances prompted by Austria. Previously, the Bourbon-Habsburg rivalry had been the cornerstone of European diplomacy. But by the 1750s two other antagonisms had taken over: French competition with the British in the New World and Austria's vendetta against Prussia over Silesia. For Austria, the rivalry with Bourbon France was no longer important. Its position in the Holy Roman Empire depended now on humbling Prussia. French hostility toward Austria had also lessened, and thus Austria was free to lead a turnabout in alliances—a diplomatic revolution—so as to forge an anti-Prussian coalition with France and Russia. Russia was crucial. The pious Empress Elizabeth of Russia loathed Frederick II and saw him as an obstacle to Russian ambitions in Eastern Europe. Geographical vulnerability also made Prussia an inviting target, and so the stage was set for war.

Prussia tried to compensate for its vulnerability. But its countermoves only alienated the other powers. Frederick sought to stay out of the Anglo-French rivalry by coming to terms with both these states. He had been France's ally in the past, but he now sought a treaty with England, and in January 1756 the English, hoping to protect the royal territory of Hanover, signed a neutrality accord with Prussia, the Convention of Westminster. The French, who had not been informed of the negotiations in advance, saw the Convention as an insult, if not a betrayal: the act of an untrustworthy ally. France overreacted, turned against Prussia, and thus fell into Austria's design (see "Maria Theresa in a Vehement Mood," p. 510). Russia too considered the Convention of Westminster a betrayal by its supposed ally England. English bribes and diplomacy were unable to keep Russia from actively joining Austria to plan Prussia's dismemberment.

The Course of War

Fearing encirclement, Frederick gambled on a preventive war through Saxony in 1756. Although he conquered the duchy, his plan backfired, for it activated the coalition that he dreaded. Russia and France met their commitments to Austria, and the three began a combined offensive against Prussia. For a time Frederick's genius as a general brought him success. Skillful tactics and daring surprise movements brought some victories, but strategically the Prussian position was shaky. Frederick had to dash in all directions across his provinces to repel invading armies whose combined strength far exceeded his own. Disaster was avoided mainly because the Russian army returned east for winter quarters regardless of its gains, but even so, the Russians occupied Berlin.

On the verge of exhaustion, Prussia at best seemed to face a stalemate with a considerable loss of territory; at worst, the war would continue and bring about a total Prussian collapse. But the other powers were also war-weary, and Frederick's enemies were becoming increasingly distrustful of one another. In the end, Prussia was saved by one of those sudden changes of reign that could cause dramatic reversals of policy in Europe. In January 1762 Empress Elizabeth died and was replaced temporarily by Tsar Peter III, a passionate admirer of Frederick. He quickly pulled Russia out of the war and returned Frederick's conquered eastern domains of Prussia and Pomerania. In Britain, meanwhile, William Pitt was replaced by the more pacific earl of Bute, who brought about a reconciliation with France; both countries then ended their insistence on punishing Prussia. Austria's coalition collapsed.

Peace

The terms of the Peace of Hubertusburg (1763), settling the continental phase of the Seven Years' War, were therefore surprisingly favorable to Prussia. Prussia returned Saxony to Austria but paid no compensation for the devastation of the duchy, and the Austrians recognized Silesia as Prussian. In short, the status quo was restored. Frederick could return to Berlin, his dominion preserved partly by his army but mainly by luck and the continuing fragility of international alliances.

Summary

If, amidst the state building of the eighteenth century, Europe's regimes were ready to sustain a major war even if it brought about few territorial changes, that was not simply because of the expansion of government and the disciplining of armies. It was also the result of remarkable economic advances and the availability of new resources that were flowing into Europe from the development of overseas empires. In politics, this was primarily an age of consolidation; in economics, it was a time of profound transformation.

QUESTIONS FOR FURTHER THOUGHT

1. Although Americans naturally prefer regimes that provide for representation and citizen participation in government, are there times when it is advantageous for a state to have an authoritarian or absolutist regime?

2. How important is the development of a capital city or a center of government in the process of state building?

RECOMMENDED READING

Sources

Hobbes, Thomas. *Leviathan.* 1651. Any modern edition.

Locke, John. *Second Treatise of Civil Government.* 1690. Any modern edition.

Luvvas, J. (ed.). *Frederick the Great on the Art of War.* 1966.

Studies

Behrens, C. B. A. *Society, Government, and the Enlightenment: The Experience of Eighteenth-Century France and Prussia.* 1985.

Brewer, John. *The Sinews of Power: War, Money, and the English State, 1688–1783.* 1989. The work that demonstrated the importance of the military and the growth of bureaucracy in eighteenth-century England.

Hatton, R. N. *Europe in the Age of Louis XIV.* 1969. A beautifully illustrated and vividly interpretive history of the period that Louis dominated.

Holmes, Geoffrey. *The Making of a Great Power: Late Stuart and Early Georgian Britain, 1660–1722; and The Age of Oligarchy: Pre-industrial Britain, 1722–1783.* 1993. The best detailed survey.

Hughes, Lindsey. *Peter the Great: A Biography.* 2002.

Lossky, Andrew. *Louis XIV and the French Monarchy.* 1994.

Mettam, Roger. *Power and Faction in Louis XIV's France.* 1988. An analysis of government and power under absolutist rule.

Oresko, Robert, G. C. Gibbs, and H. M. Scott (eds.). *Royal and Republican Sovereignty in Early Modern Europe.* 1997.

Plumb, J. H. *The Growth of Political Stability in England, 1675–1725.* 1969. A brief, lucid survey of the development of parliamentary democracy.

Raeff, Marc. *The Well-Ordered Police State: Social and Institutional Change through Law in the Germanies and Russia, 1600–1800.* 1983.

Tuck, Richard. *Hobbes.* 1989. A clear introduction to Hobbes's thought.

Weigley, R. F. *The Age of Battles: The Quest for Decisive Warfare from Breitenfeld to Waterloo.* 1991. The best military history of the age.

Philip van Dijk
BRISTOL DOCKS AND QUAY, CA. **1780**
Commerce increased dramatically in the Atlantic ports of England and France as ships embarked for Africa, the Caribbean, North America, and Spanish America as well as other parts of Europe. Shown here, the port of Bristol in England.
Bristol City Museum and Art Gallery, UK/Bridgeman Art Library

Chapter Eighteen

THE WEALTH OF NATIONS

DEMOGRAPHIC AND ECONOMIC GROWTH • THE NEW SHAPE OF INDUSTRY •
INNOVATION AND TRADITION IN AGRICULTURE • EIGHTEENTH-CENTURY EMPIRES

In the early eighteenth century the great majority of Europe's people still lived directly off the land. With a few regional exceptions, the agrarian economy remained immobile: It seemed to have no capacity for dramatic growth. Technology, social arrangements, and management techniques offered little prospect of improvement in production. Several new developments, however, were about to touch off a remarkable surge of economic advance. The first sign, and a growing stimulus for this new situation, was the sustained growth of Europe's population. This depended in turn on an expanding and surer food supply. While changes in agrarian output on the Continent were modest but significant, in England innovations in the control and use of land dramatically increased food production and changed the very structure of rural society.

The exploitation of overseas colonies provided another critical stimulus for European economic growth. Colonial trade in slaves and in sugar, tobacco, and other raw materials radiated from port cities like London and Bristol in England and Bordeaux and Nantes in France. An infrastructure of supportive trades and processing facilities developed around these ports and fed trade networks for the reexport across Europe of finished colonial products. The colonies, in turn, offered new markets for goods manufactured in Europe, such as cotton fabrics. The Atlantic slave trade and plantation slavery in the New World underpinned most of this commerce.

In one small corner of the economy, the growing demand for cotton cloth at home and abroad touched off a quest among English textile merchants for changes in the organization and technology of production. Dramatic structural change in English cotton manufacturing heralded the remarkable economic transformation known as industrialization. By the early nineteenth century, fundamental changes in the methods of raising food and producing goods were under way in Britain and were spreading to the Continent. This chapter explores the character of economic development; the impediments to that process; the nature of eighteenth-century innovations in agriculture, manufacturing, and trade; and some of the social consequences of these economic transformations.

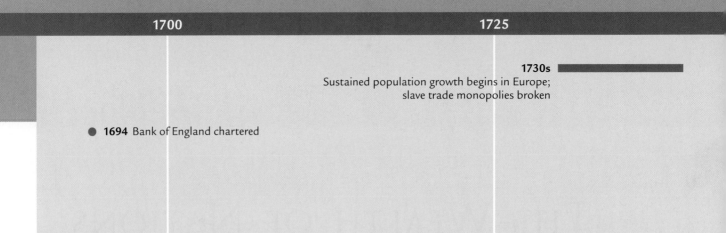

1730s
Sustained population growth begins in Europe;
slave trade monopolies broken

● **1694** Bank of England chartered

DEMOGRAPHIC AND ECONOMIC GROWTH

Perhaps the most basic, long-term historical variable is the movement of population. Historical demographers deal with the migrations of existing populations, from country to city, across national borders or even oceans. More fundamentally, they study the trends over time within populations and chart death rates, birthrates, and the growth or decline of population. Similarly, economic historians analyze macroeconomic trends in production and prices, which in turn can reinforce population growth or deter it. In this section we will consider certain trends in the demography and economy of eighteenth-century Europe that combined to support economic growth.

A New Demographic Era

In the relationship between people and the land, between demography and agriculture, European life before the eighteenth century showed little change. Levels of population seemed to flow like the tides, in cyclical or wavelike patterns. Population might increase substantially over several generations, but eventually crop failures or the ravages of plague and other contagious diseases would drive the level of population down again. In extreme cases, a lack of able-bodied workers led to the abandonment of land, and entire villages disappeared altogether. Such dramatic population losses had last occurred in seventeenth-century Germany, Poland, and Mediterranean Europe (the southern parts of Italy, Spain, and France).

For centuries Europe's population had been vulnerable to subsistence crises. Successions of poor harvests or crop failures might leave the population without adequate food and would drive up the price of grain and flour beyond what the poorest people could afford. If actual starvation did not carry them off, undernourishment made people more vulnerable than usual to disease. Such crises could also set off a chain of side effects, from unemployment to pessimism, that made people postpone marriage and childbearing. Thus, subsistence crises could drive down the birthrate as well as drive up the death rate, causing in combination a substantial loss in population.

Population Growth Although barely perceived by most Europeans at the time, a new era in Europe's demography began around 1730, and by 1800 Europe's population had grown by at least 50 percent. (Because the first censuses were not taken until the early nineteenth century, all population figures prior to that time are only estimates.) Europe's estimated population jumped from about 120 million to about 180 or 190 million. Europe had probably never before experienced so rapid and substantial an increase in the number of its people. Prussia and Sweden may have doubled their populations, while Spain's grew from 7.5 million to about 11.5 million. High growth rates in England and Wales raised the population there from an estimated 5 million people in 1700 to more than 9 million in 1801, the date of the first British census. The French, according to the best estimates, numbered about 19 million at the death of Louis XIV in 1715 and probably about 26 million in 1789. France was the most densely populated large nation in Europe in the late eighteenth century and, with the exception of the vast Russian Empire, the most populous state.

Europe's population growth of the eighteenth century continued and indeed accelerated during the nineteenth century, thus breaking once and for all the tidelike cycles and immobility of Europe's demography.

1750s Enclosure movement begins in England

● **1757** Battle of Plassey in Bengal

● **1763** Peace of Paris settles Great War for Empire

● **1776** Smith, *Wealth of Nations*; Watt develops steam engine

Arkwright opens Cromford cotton-spinning factory **1780s**

India Act begins the British raj **1784** ●

Radischev's exposé of Russian serfdom **1790** ●

Baptisms and Burials at Auneuil (1660–1790)

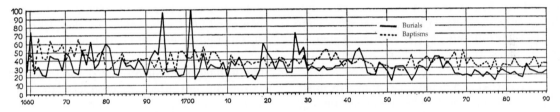

Baptisms and Burials at Saint-Lambert des Levées (1600–1790)

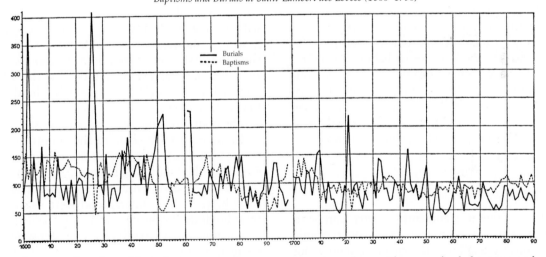

In these two French parishes, the seventeenth century came to a close with severe food shortages and sharp surges of mortality. In a more favorable economic climate, by contrast, the later eighteenth century brought an almost consistent annual surplus of births over deaths.

What caused this fundamental transformation in the underlying structure of European history?

Falling Death Rates There are two possible explanations for rapid population growth: a fall in death rates or a rise in birthrates. The consensus among historians is that a decline in mortality rates, rather than a rise in birthrates, accounts for most of the population growth in the eighteenth century, although England seems to have been an exception. Declines in the death rate did not occur because of improvements in medical science or hygiene, which became important factors in driving down mortality only in the later nineteenth century. Instead, Europe was beginning to enjoy a stabler and better food supply, perhaps owing to a mild improvement in average climate compared with that of the seventeenth century, which some historians regard as a "little ice age" of unusually cold and wet weather. The opening of new agricultural land in Poland, Hungary, and Russia helped increase Europe's food supplies, as did incremental advances in transportation networks and agrarian changes in England (to be discussed later in this chapter).

Europe's population remained extremely vulnerable to disease. Endemic diseases such as tuberculosis, typhoid, and malaria still ravaged the populations of many regions. Periodic epidemics of dysentery (which attacked the digestive system), influenza (lethal to the respiratory systems of the elderly), typhus (a lice-borne disease that flourished in the conditions of poverty), and smallpox (which assaulted rich and poor alike) continued to take their toll. But a better-nourished population could perhaps stand up to those assaults with greater success.

With the exception of England, birthrates in most regions of Europe do not seem to have increased in the eighteenth century. A high average age at marriage, with women typically well into their twenties and men in their mid to late twenties, served to check population growth. Because the birth of illegitimate children remained relatively rare, late marriages kept women from becoming pregnant during some of their most fecund years; they therefore had fewer babies altogether. In England, however, where greater geographic mobility and economic opportunities may have encouraged young couples to start families earlier, the average age at marriage came down and birthrates increased, helping to explain Britain's explosive population growth.

Profit Inflation: The Movement of Prices

The population grew in eighteenth-century Europe in tandem with an increasing pace and scale of economic activity. Europe's overall wealth expanded, though not steadily and consistently. While the economy experienced periods of fluctuation, of growth and decline, the long-term, or secular, trend was positive, compared with the stagnation and economic difficulty that prevailed (outside of England) during the "long seventeenth century," until roughly 1730. Scholars have made particularly rigorous studies of the economic cycles in France as revealed through the history of prices, and there is reason to believe that economies elsewhere in Europe behaved comparably to France's.

During the first decades of the eighteenth century, prices generally remained stable, perpetuating the long depression of the seventeenth century and no doubt reflecting the exhaustion of the European states from the War of the Spanish Succession. As with Europe's demographic growth, significant economic growth began around 1730 and lasted up until the peace settlements that followed the Napoleonic wars in 1815. Gradual inflation in prices dominated the era. Because French money was kept stable after 1726, the upward movement of prices must be attributed to other causes. Primarily, the rise in prices reflected the stimulus and pressures of a growing population in France and a growing demand for food, land, goods, and employment.

Gently rising prices and gradual, mild inflation usually stimulate the economy—unlike sharp spikes of inflation that create hard times. This nearly century-long cycle of "profit inflation" generated economic growth. There were, of course, periodic reversals or countercyclical trends. In France, for example, prosperity leveled off around 1770, ushering in two decades of falling profits, unemployment, and hard times.

The Impact of Inflation   Over the long term, the inflation did not affect all products, all sectors of the economy, or all segments of society equally. Prices in France between 1726 and 1789 increased by an average of about 65 percent. The cost of grains, the basic food for the poor, rose slightly more than the average and considerably more than other agricultural products, such as wine and meat. Rents rose sharply, suggesting a shortage of available land. Real wages, on the other hand, increased by a meager 22 percent in the same period, which points to a glut of workers competing for employment and to hard times for many wage earners.

These differentials had important social and economic effects. High rents in the countryside and low wages in the city took wealth from the poor and delivered it to the landlord and employer. Inflation helped drive many tenants from the soil, to the advantage of their better-off neighbors, who were eager to expand their holdings. In the city, inflation enabled merchants and manufacturers to sell goods for more and pay workers relatively less.

Protoindustrialization

Agriculture alone could not ensure economic growth in a heavily populated country like England, France, or the Netherlands. The excess of people to land in such countries meant that many rural people could not actually earn their livelihood in agriculture. One solution for needy families was domestic manufacturing. Traditionally, artisans in urban guilds manufactured the

In contrast to textile work, common artisanal trades such as shoemaking, tailoring, dressmaking, furniture making, and food services would continue to be conducted in small workshops down through the nineteenth century. Bulloz/© Photo RMN/Art Resource, NY

cloth fabrics used by Europeans. But textiles could also be produced through the putting-out system, whereby merchants distributed raw materials like wool or flax to rural households. Men and women would spin the raw material into yarn on hand-powered spinning machines; rural weavers working on looms in their cottages would then weave the yarn into cloth.

Protoindustrialization is the name historians give to a type of economic development that occurred before the rise of the factory system in the late eighteenth century. In this phase, the volume of rural manufacturing increased under the putting-out system, as more rural families devoted more time to industrial work—primarily spinning, weaving, or finishing textiles. This trend was particularly noticeable in certain regions of the Netherlands, Belgium, the Rhineland, France, and England, where the towns remained sources of capital, materials, and marketing services but where merchants employed labor in the countryside.

Protoindustrialization had important economic, social, and demographic repercussions. Economically, it

strengthened marketing networks, spurred capital accumulation that could be reinvested in production, generated additional revenue for needy rural families, and thereby increased their demand for products and services. Socially, it familiarized rural inhabitants with industrial processes and cash relationships. Demographically, it may have loosened restraints on marriages and births, which in turn might have led to increased migration into the cities and thus to urban growth. On the other hand, protoindustrialization did not lead to significant technological improvements or to marked advances in productivity.

THE NEW SHAPE OF INDUSTRY

While most economic activity continued in traditional fashion, dramatic change began during the late eighteenth century in a few corners of the English economy, especially in the manufacture of cotton cloth. Structural economic transformation hinged on increasing the productivity of labor, through two kinds of innovation: the development of more efficient tools and machines and the exploitation of new sources of energy to drive those machines. These innovations in turn led to a reorganization of labor in a new kind of site called the factory.

Such changes in production, however, did not arise out of thin air. They were rooted in a host of favorable preconditions in English society. The legal system regulating property rights, efficient financial institutions, market structures, growing consumer demand, even a new mode of economic analysis—the free-market doctrines of Adam Smith—provided a favorable environment for the innovations in textile manufacturing toward the end of the century. As such changes spread and visibly changed the landscape, critics would later describe them as an "industrial revolution." That term no doubt overstates the case—since it took decades for such changes to take hold more widely—but it is safe to say that the European economy would never be the same.

Toward a New Economic Order

In analyzing any economic system—traditional or modern, capitalist or socialist—economists distinguish between performance and structure. *Performance* is measured by output: the total, or gross, product and the amount produced per individual in the community. This per capita productivity is generally the best measure of an economy's performance. A distinctive feature of an industrial economy is its capacity for sustained growth in per capita production. *Structure* refers to all those characteristics of a society that support or affect performance. Economic, legal, and political institutions; tax policies; technology; demographic movements; even culture and ideology all make up the structure underlying the economy.

Industrialization required innovations in technology, which dramatically raised per capita productivity, but these innovations alone do not entirely explain the advent of industrialism. Social structure itself influences technological development in any age. To ask why dramatic change occurred in industry is thus to pose two deeper questions: What were the structural obstacles to technological innovation and entrepreneurship in traditional European society? And what changes in that society, from the late eighteenth century onward, promoted and rewarded innovation?

Impediments to Economic Innovation   One major obstacle to innovation was the small size of most European markets, which were cut off from one another by physical barriers, political frontiers, tariff walls, and different laws, moneys, and units of measurement.

Small markets slowed the growth of specialized manufacture and limited the mobility of capital and labor. Similarly, the highly skewed distribution of wealth typical of many European communities distorted the structure of demand. In many countries, a narrow aristocracy absorbed most disposable income, and the economy organized itself largely to serve the wealthy few. Catering to the desires of the rich, the economy produced expensive luxury goods, often exquisite in quality and workmanship but always in relatively small quantities. Such small markets and skewed demand dampened the incentive to manufacture an abundance of relatively inexpensive goods.

Also crucial to the industrializing process was the question of property rights and privileges—whether they would encourage a high rate of return on innovation or impede it. In the towns, the guilds presented a major obstacle to economic innovation. Guild regulations, or government regulation of the economy enforced by the guilds, prescribed the techniques to be used in production and often dictated the terms and conditions under which goods could be sold, apprentices taken on, or workers hired. Out of simple self-interest, given their stake in existing arrangements, the guilds favored traditional technology and managerial techniques.

Governments, too, helped sustain these restrictive practices, principally by exploiting them for their own fiscal benefit. The French government, for example, collected substantial fees from guilds and could turn to them for loans as well. Governments also restricted economic activity by licensing monopoly companies with exclusive rights to trade in certain regions, such as the East Indies, or to manufacture certain products, such as fine porcelain. With ensured markets and profits, these companies were not likely to assume the risks of new ventures, and they blocked others from doing so. Cultural attitudes may also have discouraged entrepreneurial efforts. Many persons, particularly in the aristocratic classes, still regarded money made in trade or manufacture as somehow tainted. The highest aspiration of successful French business families seems often to have been the purchase of a noble title.

Adam Smith   Although these institutions and attitudes still marked European life in the eighteenth century, they were subject to ever sharper criticisms. From midcentury on, certain French social thinkers denounced guild control of production in the towns and economic privilege and monopoly in all forms. But the seminal work in this new school of economic thought was *An Inquiry into the Nature and Causes of the Wealth of Nations* (1776) by the Scottish philosopher Adam Smith. Smith argued that money in and of itself did not constitute wealth but was merely its marker. Wealth derived from the added value in manufactured

LAISSEZ-FAIRE IDEOLOGY

At the heart of Adam Smith's laissez-faire ideology was a belief that individual self-interest is the motor of economic progress, a notion epitomized in this selection by Smith's reference to the "invisible hand." By the same token, each region or country should pursue what it does best, an argument against protective tariffs for domestic industry.

"Every individual is continually exerting himself to find out the most advantageous employment for whatever capital he can command. . . . But it is only for the sake of profit that any man employs a capital in the support of industry; and he will always, therefore, endeavor to employ it in the support of that industry of which the produce is likely to be of the greatest value, or to exchange for the greatest quantity either of money or of other goods. . . . [In so doing] he generally neither intends to promote the public interest, nor knows how much he is promoting it. . . . he intends only his own security; and by directing that industry in such a manner as its produce may be of the greatest value, he intends only his own gain. [But] he is in this, as in many other cases, led by an invisible hand to promote an end which was not part of his intention. By pursuing his own interest he frequently promotes that of the society more effectually than when he really intends to promote it.

"What is the species of domestic industry which his capital can employ, and of which the produce is likely to be of the greatest value, every individual, it is evident, can, in his local situation, judge much better than any statesman or lawgiver can do for him. . . .

"To give the monopoly of the home market to the produce of domestic industry, in any particular art or manufacture, is in some measure to direct private people in what manner they ought to employ their capitals, and must, in almost all cases, be either a useless or hurtful regulation. If the produce of domestic can be brought there as cheaply as that of foreign industry, the regulation is evidently useless. If it cannot, it must generally be hurtful. . . . If a foreign country can supply us with a commodity cheaper than we ourselves can make it, better buy it from them with some part of the produce of our own industry."

A. Smith, *An Inquiry into the Nature and Causes of the Wealth of Nations*, 1776, book 4, ch. 2.

items produced by the combination of invested capital and labor. Smith believed that economic progress required that each individual be allowed to pursue his or her own self-interest freely, without restriction by guilds, the state, or tradition. He argued that on all levels of economic activity—from manufacturing to the flow of international trade—a natural division of labor should be encouraged. High tariffs, guild restrictions, and mercantilist restraints on free trade all artificially obstructed economic activity. Smith became a founding father of **laissez-faire** economic theory, meaning, in effect: Let individuals freely pursue their own economic interests. In the aggregate, free individual enterprise would create more wealth than any artificial regulation could encourage (see "Laissez-Faire Ideology," above).

Laissez-faire became a battle cry taken up by British businesspeople and factory owners in the early nineteenth century. Such arguments slowly affected policy. In 1786 France and Britain signed a free-trade treaty, lowering protective tariffs on imported textiles. Guilds were already growing weaker in most towns and were relatively powerless in towns of recent growth, like Manchester and Birmingham in England, where new industries such as cotton manufacturing escaped guild supervision altogether. This trend reached its culmination when the government of revolutionary France permanently dissolved all guilds and restrictive trade associations in 1791. Similarly, the British Parliament revoked the laws regulating apprenticeships in the 1790s. Legally and socially, the entrepreneur was winning greater freedom.

The Roots of Economic Transformation in England

Of all the nations of Europe, England was the first to develop a social structure that strongly supported innovation and economic growth. England's advantages were many, some of them deeply rooted in geography and history. This comparatively small realm contained an excellent balance of resources. The plain to the south and east, where traditional centers of English settlement concentrated, was fertile and productive. The uplands to the north and west possessed rich deposits of coal and iron, and their streams had powered flour mills since the Middle Ages.

Proximity to the sea was another natural advantage. No part of the island kingdom was distant from the coast. At a time when water transport offered the sole economical means for moving bulky commodities, the sea brought coal close to iron, raw materials close to factories, and products close to markets. Above all, the sea gave Britain's merchants access to the much wider world beyond their shores.

Efficiency of transport was critical in setting the size of markets. During the eighteenth century, Britain witnessed a boom in the building of canals and turnpikes by private individuals or syndicates. By 1815 the country possessed some 2,600 miles of canals linking rivers, ports, and other towns. In addition, few institutional obstructions to the movement of goods existed. United under a strong monarchy, Britain was free of internal tariff barriers, unlike prerevolutionary France, Germany, or Italy. Merchants everywhere counted in the same money, measured their goods by the same standards, and conducted their affairs under the protection of the common law. By contrast, in France differences in provincial legal codes and in weights and measures complicated and slowed exchange. As the writer Voltaire sarcastically remarked, the traveler crossing France by coach changed laws as frequently as horses.

The English probably had the highest standard of living in Europe and generated strong consumer demand for manufactured goods. English society was less stratified than that on the Continent, the aristocracy powerful but much smaller. Primogeniture (with the family's land going to the eldest son) was the rule among both the peers (the titled members of the House of Lords) and the country gentlemen or squires. Left without lands, younger sons had to seek careers in other walks of life, and some turned toward commerce. They frequently recruited capital for their ventures from their landed fathers and elder brothers. English religious dissenters, chiefly Calvinists and Quakers, formed another pool of potential entrepreneurs; denied careers in government because of their religion, many turned their energies to business enterprises.

British Financial Management A high rate of reinvestment is critical to industrialization; reinvestment, in turn, depends on the skillful management of money by both individuals and public institutions. Here again, Britain enjoyed advantages. Early industrial enterprises could rely on Britain's growing banking system to meet their capital needs. In the seventeenth century, the goldsmiths of London had assumed the functions of bankers. They accepted and guarded deposits, extended loans, transferred upon request credits from one account to another, and changed money. In the eighteenth century, banking services became available beyond London; the number of country banks rose from three hundred in 1780 to more than seven hundred by 1810. English businesspeople were familiar with banknotes and other forms of commercial papers,

and their confidence in paper facilitated the recruitment and flow of capital.

The founding of the Bank of England in 1694 marked an epoch in the history of European finance. The bank took responsibility for managing England's public debt, sold shares to the public, and faithfully met the interest payments due to the shareholders, with the help of government revenue (such as the customs duties efficiently collected on Britain's extensive foreign trade). When the government needed to borrow, it could turn to the Bank of England for assistance. This stability in government finances ensured a measure of stability for the entire money market and, most important, held down interest rates in both the public and private sectors. In general, since the Glorious Revolution of 1688, England's government had been sensitive to the interests of the business classes, who in turn had confidence in the government. Such close ties between money and power facilitated economic investment.

In contrast, France lacked a sound central bank, and extensive government borrowing drove up interest rates in the private sector as well. On balance, although limited capital and conservative management held back French business enterprises, they dampened but did not suppress the expansion of the economy. France remained a leader in producing wool and linen cloth as well as iron, but it seemed more inclined to produce luxury items or very cheap, low-quality goods. On the other hand, England (with its higher standard of living and strong domestic demand) seemed more adept at producing standardized products of reasonably good quality.

Cotton: The Beginning of Industrialization

The process of early industrialization in England was extremely complex and remains difficult to explain. What seems certain is that a strong demand for cheap goods was growing at home and abroad in the eighteenth century, and a small but important segment of the English community sensed this opportunity and responded to it.

Specifically, the market for cotton goods became the most propulsive force for change in industrial production. Thanks to slave labor in plantation colonies, the supply of raw cotton was rising dramatically. On the demand side, lightweight cotton goods were durable, washable, versatile, and cheaper than woolen or linen cloth. Cotton, therefore, had a bright future as an item of mass consumption. But traditional textile manufacturing centers in England (the regions of protoindustrialization such as East Anglia and the Yorkshire districts) could not satisfy the growing demand. The organization and technology of the putting-out system had reached its limits. For one thing, the merchant was

RICHARD ARKWRIGHT'S ACHIEVEMENT

This celebration of British industrialization, the factory system, and entrepreneurship begins by extolling Richard Arkwright's accomplishments in the 1780s.

"When the first water frames for spinning cotton were erected at Cromford, about sixty years ago, mankind were little aware of the mighty revolution which the new system of labour was destined by Providence to achieve, not only in the structure of British society, but in the fortunes of the world at large. Arkwright alone had the sagacity to discern, and the boldness to predict in glowing language, how vastly productive human industry would become, when no longer proportioned in its results to muscular effort, which is by its nature fitful and capricious, but when made to consist in the task of guiding the work of mechanical fingers and arms, regularly impelled with great velocity by some indefatigable physical power [such as a steam engine].

"The main difficulty did not lie so much in the invention of a proper self-acting mechanism for drawing out and twisting cotton into a continuous thread, as in the distribution of different members of the apparatus into one cooperative body . . . and above all, in training human beings to renounce their desultory habits of work, and to identify themselves with the unvarying regularity of the complex automaton. To devise and administer a successful code of factory discipline, suited to the necessities of factory diligence, was the Herculean enterprise, the noble achievement of Arkwright. . . . It required, in fact, a man of Napoleonic nerve and ambition to subdue the refractory tempers of work-people accustomed to irregular paroxysms of diligence, and to urge on his multifarious and intricate constructions in the face of prejudice, passion, and envy."

Andrew Ure, *The Philosophy of Manufactures*, 1835.

Richard Arkwright not only invented this power-driven machine to spin cotton yarn but also proved to be a highly successful entrepreneur with the factory he constructed at Cromford in the Lancashire region.
The Science Museum, London

limited to the labor supply in his own district; the farther he went to find cottage workers, the longer it took and the more cumbersome it became to pass the materials back and forth. Second, he could not adequately control his workers. Clothiers were bedeviled with embezzlement of raw materials, poor workmanship, and lateness in finishing assigned work. English clothiers were therefore on the lookout for technological or organizational innovations to help them meet a growing demand for textiles.

Machine and Factories   Weavers could turn out large amounts of cloth thanks to the invention of the fly shuttle in the 1730s, which permitted the construction of larger and faster handlooms. But traditional methods of spinning the yarn caused a bottleneck in the production process. Responding to this problem, inventors built new kinds of spinning machines that could be grouped in large factories or mills. Richard Arkwright's water frame drew cotton fibers through rollers and twisted them into thread. Not simply an inventor but an entrepreneur (one who combined the various factors of production into a profitable enterprise), Arkwright initially housed his machines in a large factory sited near a river so that his machines could be propelled by waterpower.

At around the same time, James Watt had been perfecting the technology of steam engines—machinery originally used to power suction pumps that would evacuate water from the pits of coal mines. The earliest steam engine had produced a simple up-and-down motion. Watt not only redesigned it to make it far more efficient and powerful but also developed a system of gears to harness the engine's energy into rotary motion that could drive other types of machines. In 1785 Arkwright became one of Watt's first customers when he switched from waterpower to steam engines as the means of driving the spinning machines in his new cotton factory at Cromford. With Arkwright (who became a millionaire) and Watt, the modern factory system was launched (see "Richard Arkwright's Achievement," p. 523).

Spinning factories, however, disrupted the equilibrium between spinning and weaving in the other direction: Yarn was now abundant, but hand-loom weavers could not keep up with the pace. This disequilibrium created a brief golden age for the weavers, but merchants were eager to break the new bottleneck. In 1784 Edmund Cartwright designed a power-driven loom. Small technical flaws and the violent opposition of hand-loom weavers retarded the widescale adoption of power looms until the early nineteenth century, but then both spinning and weaving were totally transformed. Power-driven machinery boosted the output of yarn and cloth astronomically, while merchants could assemble their workers in factories and scrutinize their every move to maximize production. In a factory, one small boy could watch over two mechanized looms whose output was fifteen times greater than that of a skilled hand-loom weaver.

Innovation and Tradition in Agriculture

In England around 1700, an estimated 80 percent of the population lived directly from agriculture; a century later that proportion had fallen to approximately 40 percent. This shift of labor from agriculture would have been inconceivable had English farming not become far more productive during that period. English farmers introduced significant improvements in their methods of cultivation, including the techniques of convertible husbandry and the enclosure of large compact farms. These enabled English agriculture to supply the growing towns with food as well as excess labor and capital. On the Continent, however, whether bound to the land as serfs in eastern Europe or legally free in the west, peasants generally clung to traditional agrarian ways. Time-worn survival strategies provided the best hope for security but also ensured a climate hostile to untested innovations.

Convertible Husbandry

A central problem in any agricultural system is that repeated harvests on the same land eventually rob the soil of its fertility. Since the Early Middle Ages, the usual method of restoring a field's fertility involved letting the land lie fallow for a season (that is, resting it by planting nothing) every second or third year. This fallowing allowed bacteria in the soil to take needed nitrogen from the air. A quicker and better method, heavy manuring, could not be used widely because most farmers were unable to support sufficient livestock to produce the manure. Feeding farm animals, particularly with fodder during the winter, was beyond the means of most peasants.

But fallowing was an extremely inefficient and wasteful method of restoring the soil's fertility. One key to improving agricultural productivity, therefore, lay in eliminating the fallow periods, which in turn required that more animals be raised to provide fertilizer. In a given year, instead of being taken out of cultivation, a field could be planted not with grain but with turnips or with nitrogen-fixing grasses that could supply fodder for livestock. The grazing livestock would in turn deposit abundant quantities of manure on those fields. Thus, by the end of that season the soil's fertility

Livestock and people could range freely over the land in open-field villages after the crops were harvested. The regrouping of scattered parcels and the enclosure of those consolidated properties would put an end to an entire rural way of life.

would be greater, and next year's grain crop was likely to produce a higher yield than if the field had simply been left fallow the year before.

One of the first British landlords to adopt this approach on a broad scale was Jethro Tull, an agriculturist and inventor. Tull's zeal in advocating new farming methods proved infectious. By the late eighteenth century, Norfolk, in the east of England, had achieved particular prominence for such techniques, known as convertible husbandry.

Improving Landlords With convertible husbandry, innovative (or "improving") landlords never let their land lie fallow but always put it to some productive use. They also experimented with techniques designed to enhance the texture of the soil. If soil was normally too thin to retain water effectively, farmers added clays or marl to help bind the soil. In those regions in which the soil had the opposite problem of clumping too rigidly after rainfalls, they lightened the soil by adding chalk and lime to inhibit the clotting.

Eighteenth-century agrarian innovators also experimented with the selective breeding of animals. Some improved the quality of pigs, while others developed new breeds of sheep and dramatically increased the weight of marketed cattle. Soil management and livestock breeding did not depend on any high-tech knowledge or machinery but simply on a willingness to experiment in land management and to invest capital to achieve higher yields.

The Enclosure Movement in Britain

To make use of new agricultural methods, farmers had to be free to manage the land as they saw fit. This land management was all but impossible under the **open-field system** that had dominated the countryside in Europe since the Middle Ages. Under the open-field system, even the largest landlords usually held their property in numerous elongated strips that were mixed in with and open to the land of their neighbors. Owners of contiguous strips had to follow the same routines of cultivation. One farmer could not plant grasses to graze cattle when another was raising wheat or leaving the land fallow. The village as a whole determined what routines should be followed. The village also decided such matters as how many cattle each member could graze on common meadows and how much wood each could take from the forest. The open-field system froze the technology of cultivation at the levels of the Middle Ages.

Landowners who wished to form compact farms and apply new methods could do so only by enclosing their own properties. Both common law and cost considerations, however, worked against fencing the numerous narrow strips unless the property of the entire village could be rearranged, which required the agreement of all the community. Such voluntary **enclosures** were nearly impossible to organize. In England, however, there was an alternative: An act of Parliament, usually passed in response to a petition by large landowners, could order the enclosure of all agrarian property in a village even against the opposition of some of its inhabitants. Then large landowners could fence in their land and manage it at their discretion.

Enclosing properties in a village was expensive. The lands of the village had to be surveyed and redistributed, in compact blocks, among the members in proportion to their former holdings. But over the course of the eighteenth century, the high rents and returns that could be earned with the new farming methods made enclosures very desirable investments. Numerous acts authorizing enclosure in a village had been passed by Parliament in earlier periods, but a new wave of such acts began to mount around the middle of the eighteenth century. Parliament passed 156 individual acts of enclosure in the decade of the 1750s; from 1800 to 1810 it passed 906 acts. Cumulatively, the enclosure movement all but eradicated the traditional open-field village from the British countryside.

The Impact of Enclosure While enclosure was clearly rational from an economic standpoint, it brought much human misery in its wake. The redistribution of the land deprived the poor of their traditional rights to the village's common land (which was usually divided among the villagers as well) and often left them with tiny, unprofitable plots. Frequently, they were forced to sell their holdings to their richer neighbors and seek employment as laborers or urban workers. However, no massive rural depopulation occurred in the wake of enclosures. For one thing, the actual work of fencing the fields required a good deal of labor, and some of the new husbandry techniques were also labor-intensive.

The enclosure movement transformed the English countryside physically and socially, giving it the appearance it retains today of large verdant fields, neatly defined by hedges and fences. Enclosures in Britain led to the domination of rural society by great landlords and their prosperous tenant farmers, who usually held their farms under long leases. Conversely, enclosures resulted in the near disappearance in England of the small peasant-type cultivators still typical of western Europe. If enclosures did not abruptly push people to the towns, neither did they encourage growth in rural settlements. Enclosures were, therefore, a major factor in the steady shift of Britain's population from countryside to city and in the emergence of the first urban, industrial economy in the nineteenth century.

MAP 18.1 An Open-Field Village in France
The land in this northern French village, originally blocked out in large fields, was subsequently subdivided into small strips owned by individual landowners or peasants. What do you notice about the holdings of the two landowners Vanier and LeFebvre? What might have been the challenges to managing such holdings in an open-field system? How would consolidating and enclosing their properties affect the ability of these landowners to manage and cultivate the land? How would such changes affect peasants and other villagers who once had access to the open fields?

Serfs and Peasants on the Continent

On the Continent, peasants continued to work their small plots of land—whether owned or rented—in the village of their ancestors. In eastern Europe, however, the peasants' status was still defined by a system of **serfdom** similar to that which prevailed in western Europe during the Middle Ages.

Lords and Serfs in Eastern Europe   In most of central and eastern Europe, nobles retained a near monopoly on the ownership of land and peasants remained serfs, their personal freedom severely limited by the lord's supervision. Serfs could not marry, move away, or enter a trade without their lord's permission. This personal servitude ensured that peasants would be available to provide the labor that the lord required. In return the peasants received access to plots of land (which they did not actually own) and perhaps some rudimentary

capital, such as seed for their crops. Much of their time, however, was spent in providing unpaid labor on their lord's domain, the amount of labor service determined by custom rather than by law. Labor service often took up three days a week, and even more during harvest time. In Russia it was said that the peasants worked half the year for their master and only half for themselves (see "The Condition of the Serfs in Russia," p. 527).

The degree of exploitation in European serfdom naturally varied. In Russia, Poland, Hungary, and certain small German states, the status of the serf scarcely differed from that of a slave. Russian and Polish serfs were in effect chattels who could be sold or traded at their lords' discretion, independent of the land they lived on or their family ties. In Russia the state itself owned many peasants and could assign them to work in the mines and factories of the Ural Mountains. Russian and Polish lords could inflict severe corporal punishment on their serfs, up to forty lashes or six months in prison.

THE CONDITION OF THE SERFS IN RUSSIA

For publishing this unprecedented critique of the miseries and injustices of serfdom, the author was imprisoned by Catherine II.

"A certain man left the capital, acquired a small village of one or two hundred souls [i.e., serfs], and determined to make his living by agriculture. . . . To this end he thought it the surest method to make his peasants resemble tools that have neither will nor impulse; and to a certain extent he actually made them like the soldiers of the present time who are commanded in a mass, who move to battle in a mass, and who count for nothing when acting singly. To attain this end he took away from his peasants the small allotment of plough land and the hay meadows which noblemen usually give them for their bare maintenance, as a recompense for all the forced labor which they demand from them. In a word, this nobleman forced all his peasants and their wives and children to work every day of the year for him. Lest they should starve, he doled out to them a definite quantity of bread. . . . If there was any real meat, it was only in Easter Week.

"These serfs also received clothing befitting their condition. . . . Naturally these serfs had no cows, horses, ewes, or rams. Their master did not withhold from these serfs the permission, but rather the means to have them. Whoever was a little better off and ate sparingly, kept a few chickens, which the master sometimes took for himself, paying for them as he pleased.

"In a short time he added to his two hundred souls another two hundred as victims of his greed, and proceeding with them just as with the first, he increased his holdings year after year, thus multiplying the number of those groaning in his fields. Now he counts them by the thousands and is praised as a famous agriculturalist.

"Barbarian! What good does it do the country that every year a few thousand more bushels of grain are grown, if those who produce it are valued on a par with the ox whose job it is to break the heavy furrow? Or do we think our citizens happy because our granaries are full and their stomachs empty?"

Alexander Radischev, *A Journey from St. Petersburg to Moscow,* 1790.

In Poland and Russia rural lords had direct control over their serfs without intervention by the state. Their powers included the right to inflict corporal punishment.
Bettmann/Corbis

Peasants had no right of appeal to the state against such punishments.

Serfdom was not as severe in Prussia or the Habsburg monarchy, and the state did assure peasants of certain basic legal rights. In theory, peasants could not be expelled from their plots so long as they paid all their dues and rendered all the services they owed, although in practice the lords could usually remove them if they wished to. Since it was increasingly profitable for the lords to farm large domains directly, many felt an incentive to oust peasants from their tenures or to increase peasant labor services beyond customary limits.

Lords and Peasants in Western Europe In western Europe, by contrast, serfdom had waned. Most peasants were personally free and were free to buy land if they could afford it. Peasants were not necessarily secure or prosperous, however. There was not enough land to satisfy the needs of all peasant families, and lack of real independence was the rule. Moreover, most French, German, Spanish, and Italian peasants still lived under the authority of a local noble in a system called **seigneurialism.** The peasants owed these lords various dues and obligations on their land, even if the peasants otherwise owned it. Seigneurial fees and charges (for example, a proportion of the harvest, somewhere between 5 and 15 percent) could be a considerable source of income for the lord and an oppressive burden to the already hard-pressed peasant. In addition, the lords administered petty justice in both civil and criminal matters; enjoyed the exclusive privilege of hunting rights across the lands of the village, no matter who owned them; and profited from monopolies on food-processing operations such as flour mills, bread ovens, and wine presses.

Concerned as they were with securing their basic livelihood, few peasants worried about trying to increase productivity with new farming methods. Satisfied with time-tested methods of cultivation, they could not risk the hazards of novel techniques. Along with growing grain for their own consumption, peasant households had to meet several obligations as well: royal taxes, rents, seigneurial dues, the tithe to the local church, and interest payments on their debts. In short, most peasant households in western Europe were extremely insecure and relied on custom and tradition as their surest guides.

Peasant Survival Strategies Every peasant household in western Europe hoped to control enough land to ensure its subsistence and meet its obligations. Ideally, it would own this land. But most peasants did not own as much land as they needed and were obliged to rent additional plots or enter into sharecropping arrangements.

Peasants therefore hated to see the consolidation of small plots into large farms, for this meant that the small plots that they might one day afford to buy or lease were becoming scarcer. The lords and the most prosperous peasants, on the other hand, were interested in extending their holdings, just like the "improving" landlords across the English Channel.

When the land that small peasants owned and rented did not meet their needs, they employed other survival strategies. Peasants could hire out as laborers on larger farms or migrate for a few months to other regions to help with grain or wine harvests. They might practice a simple rural handicraft or weave cloth for merchants on the putting-out system. Some peasants engaged in illegal activities such as poaching game on restricted land or smuggling salt in avoidance of royal taxes. When all else failed, a destitute peasant family might be forced to take to the road as beggars.

The Family Economy In their precarious situation, peasants depended on strong family bonds. A peasant holding was a partnership between husband and wife, who usually waited until they had accumulated enough resources, including the bride's dowry, to establish their own household. Men looked for physical vigor and domestic skills in their prospective brides. ("When a girl knows how to knead and bake bread, she is fit to wed," went a French proverb.) In peasant households the wife's domain was inside the cottage, where she cooked, repaired clothing, and perhaps spent her evenings spinning yarn. Wives were also responsible for the small vegetable gardens or the precious hens and chickens that peasants maintained to raise cash for their obligations. The husband's work was outside: gathering fuel, caring for draft animals (if the family owned any), plowing the land, planting the fields, and nurturing the crops. But at harvest time everyone worked in the fields.

Peasants also drew strength from community solidarity. Many villages possessed common lands open to all residents. Poorer peasants could forage there for fuel and building materials, and could inexpensively graze whatever livestock they owned. Since villagers generally planted the same crops at the same times, after the harvest livestock was allowed to roam over the arable fields and graze on the stubble of the open fields, a practice known as vacant pasture. All in all, insecurity and the scarcity of land in continental villages made it risky and improbable that peasants would adopt innovative methods or agree to the division of common land.

The Limits of Agrarian Change on the Continent Change, therefore, came more slowly to the continental countryside than it did to England. The Netherlands, the Paris basin and the northeast of France, the

Nicolas-Bernard Lépicié
COUR DE FERME
While changes in agricultural practices transformed the rural population of England and Russia, the small-holding peasant remained the most typical social type in France. In the peasant "family economy," husband and wife each made vital contributions to the household's productivity.
Musée du Louvre, Photo © R.M.N./ Art Resource, NY

Rhineland in Germany, and the Po Valley of Italy experienced the most active development—all areas of dense settlement in which high food prices encouraged landlords with large farms to invest in agricultural improvements and to adopt innovative methods.

Like their English counterparts, innovating continental farmers waged a battle for managerial freedom, though the changes they sought were not as sweeping as the English enclosure movement. Most French villages worked the land under an open-field system in which peasants followed the same rhythms and routines of cultivation as their neighbors, with the village also determining the rights of its members on common lands. From the middle of the century on, the governing institutions of several provinces banned obligatory vacant pasture and allowed individual owners to enclose their land; some authorized the division of communal lands as well. But the French monarchy did not adopt enclosure as national policy, and after the 1760s provincial authorities proved reluctant to enforce enclosure ordinances against the vigorous opposition of peasants. Traces of the medieval village thus lasted longer in France and western Europe than in England.

In France in 1789, on the eve of the Revolution, probably 35 percent of the land was owned by the peasants who worked it. In this regard, the French peasants were more favored than those of most other European countries. But this society of small peasant farms was vulnerable to population pressures and was threatened by sharp movements in prices—two major characteristics of eighteenth-century economic history, as we have seen.

In the regions close to the Mediterranean Sea, such as southern Italy, difficult geographical and climatic conditions—the often rugged terrain, thin soil, and dearth of summer rain—did not readily allow the introduction of new techniques either, although many peasants improved their income by planting market crops such as grapes for wine or olives for oil instead of grains for their own consumption. Still, most peasants continued to work their lands much as they had in the Late Middle Ages and for the same poor reward. Fertile areas near the Baltic Sea, such as east Prussia, benefited from the growing demand for grains in western countries, but on the whole, eastern Europe did not experience structural agrarian change until the next century.

EIGHTEENTH-CENTURY EMPIRES

The economic dynamism of the eighteenth century derived not simply from growing population and consumer demand, or from English innovations in agriculture and textile manufacturing. Europe's favorable position as a generator of wealth owed as much to its mercantile empires across the seas. Colonial trade became an engine of economic growth in Britain and France. Plantation economies in the Atlantic world, fueled by the West African slave trade, provided sugar, tobacco, and cotton for an ever-expanding consumer demand. In the East spices, fine cloths, tea, and luxury goods similarly enriched European merchants. But behind the merchants and trading companies stood the military and naval muscle of the British and French states. Their rivalry finally erupted in a "Great War for Empire"—the global dimension of the Seven Years' War on the Continent. Here British victories came not only in North America and the Caribbean, but also in South Asia, where they ousted the French from their foothold in India. This left the British free to extend their sway in the nineteenth century over India, which became "the jewel in the crown" of British imperial dominion.

Mercantile and Naval Competition

After 1715 a new era began in the saga of European colonial development. The three pioneers in overseas expansion had by now grown passive, content to defend domains already conquered. Portugal, whose dominion over Brazil was recognized at the Peace of Utrecht in 1715, retired from active contention. Likewise, the Dutch could scarcely compete for new footholds overseas and now protected their interests through cautious neutrality. Although Spain continued its efforts to exclude outsiders from trade with its vast empire in the New World, it did not pose much of a threat to others. The stage of active competition was left to the two other Atlantic powers, France and Britain.

The Decline of the Dutch   The case of Dutch decline is an instructive counterexample to the rise of French and British fortunes. In the seventeenth century the United Provinces, or Dutch Netherlands, had been Europe's greatest maritime power. But this federated state emerged from the wars of Louis XIV in a much weakened position. The country had survived intact, but it now suffered from demographic and political stagnation. The population of 2.5 million failed to rise much during the eighteenth century, thus setting the Dutch apart from their French and British rivals. As a federation of loosely joined provinces, whose seven provincial oligarchies rarely acted in concert, the Netherlands could barely ensure the common defense of the realm.

The Dutch economy suffered when French and English merchants sought to eliminate them as the middlemen of maritime commerce and when their industry failed to compete effectively. Heavy taxes on manufactured goods and the high wages demanded by Dutch artisans forced up the price of Dutch products. What kept the nation from slipping completely out of Europe's economic life was its financial institutions. Dutch merchants shifted their activity away from actual trading ventures into the safer, lucrative areas of credit and finance. Their country was the first to perfect the uses of paper currency, a stock market, and a central bank. Amsterdam's merchant-bankers loaned large amounts of money to private borrowers and foreign governments, as the Dutch became financial brokers instead of traders.

The British and French Commercial Empires   Great Britain, a nation that had barely been able to hold its own against the Dutch in the seventeenth century, now began its rise to domination of the seas. Its one serious competitor was France, the only state in Europe to maintain both a large army and a large navy. Their rivalry played itself out in four regions. The West Indies, where both France and Britain had colonized several sugar-producing islands, constituted the fulcrum of both empires. The West Indian plantation economy, in turn, depended on slave-producing West Africa. The third area of colonial expansion was the North American continent, where Britain's thirteen colonies became centers of settlement whereas New France remained primarily a trading area. Finally, both nations sponsored powerful companies for trade with India and other Asian lands. These companies were supposed to compete for markets without establishing colonies.

The two colonial systems had obvious differences and important similarities. French absolutism fostered a centralized structure of control for its colonies, with intendants and military governors ruling across the seas as they did in the provinces at home. Britain's North American colonies, by contrast, remained independent from each other and to a degree escaped direct control from the home government, although Crown and Parliament both claimed jurisdiction over them. British colonies each had a royal governor but also a local assembly of sorts, and most developed traditions of self-government. Nonetheless, the French and British faced similar problems and achieved generally similar results. Both applied mercantilist principles to the regulation of colonial trade, and both strengthened their navies to protect it.

Mercantilism   Mercantilist doctrine supported the regulation of trade by the state in order to increase the state's power against its neighbors (see chapter 15). **Mercantilism** was not limited to the Atlantic colonial powers. Prussia was guided by mercantilism as much as were Britain and France, for all regarded the economic activities of their subjects as subordinate to the interests of the state.

Mercantilist theory advocated a favorable balance of trade as signified by a net inflow of gold and silver, and it assumed that a state's share of bullion could increase only at its neighbor's expense. (Adam Smith would attack this doctrine in 1776, as we have seen.) Colonies could promote a favorable balance of trade by producing valuable raw materials or staple crops for the parent country and by providing protected markets for the parent country's manufactured goods. Foreign states were to be excluded from these benefits as much as possible. By tariffs, elaborate regulations, bounties, or prohibitions, each government sought to channel trade between its colonies and itself. Spain, for example, restricted trade with its New World colonies exclusively to Spanish merchant vessels, although smugglers and pirates made a mockery of this policy.

Europe's governments sought to exploit overseas colonies for the benefit of the parent country and not simply for the profit of those who invested or settled abroad. But most of the parties to this commerce prospered. The large West Indian planters made fortunes, as did the most successful merchants, manufacturers, and shipowners at home who were involved in colonial trade. Illicit trade also brought rewards to colonial merchants; John Hancock took the risk of smuggling food supplies from Boston to French West Indian planters in exchange for handsome profits.

"Empire" generally meant "trade," but this seaborne commerce depended on naval power: Merchant ships had to be protected, trading rivals excluded, and regulations enforced. This reciprocal relationship between the expansion of trade and the deployment of naval forces added to the competitive nature of colonial expansion. Naval vessels needed stopping places for re-provisioning and refitting, which meant that ports had to be secured in strategic locations such as Africa, India, and the Caribbean and denied to rivals whenever possible.

The Profits of Global Commerce

The call of colonial markets invigorated European economic life. Colonial commerce provided new products, like sugar, and stimulated new consumer demand, which in turn created an impetus for manufacturing at home. It is estimated that the value of French commerce quadrupled during the eighteenth century. By the 1770s commerce with their colonies accounted for almost one-third of the total volume of both British and French foreign trade. The West Indies trade (mainly in sugar) bulked the largest, and its expansion was truly spectacular. The value of French imports from the West Indies increased more than tenfold between 1716 and 1788, from 16 million to 185 million livres.

The West Indies seemed to be ideal colonies. By virtue of their tropical climate and isolation from European society, which made slavery possible, the islands

THE GROWTH OF ENGLAND'S FOREIGN TRADE IN THE EIGHTEENTH CENTURY

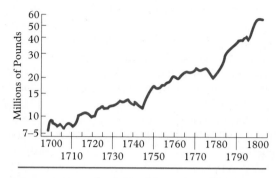

Three-year averages of combined imports and exports
Adapted from Phyllis Dean and W. A. Cole, *British Economic Growth, 1688–1959*, Cambridge University Press, 1964, p. 49.

produced valuable crops difficult to raise elsewhere: tobacco, cotton, indigo, and especially sugar, a luxury that popular European taste soon turned into a necessity. Moreover, the islands could produce little else and therefore depended on exports from Europe. They could not raise an adequate supply of food animals or grain to feed the vast slave population, they could not cut enough lumber for building, and they certainly could not manufacture the luxury goods demanded by the planter class.

Triangular Trade Numerous variations of **triangular trade** (between the home country and two overseas areas) revolved around the West Indies. One pattern began with a ship departing from a British port with a cargo of manufactured products—paper, knives, pots, blankets, and the like—destined for the shopkeepers of North America. Landing at Marblehead, Massachusetts, or Philadelphia, the ship might exchange its goods for New England fish oil, fish, beef, and timber. These products would then be transported to Jamaica or Barbados to be traded for sugar that would be turned over to British refineries many months later. Another variation might see a ship set out from Newport, Rhode Island (the chief slaving port in North America), with a cargo of New England rum. Landing in West Africa, the ship would acquire slaves in exchange for the rum and then sail to the Indies to sell the slaves for bills of exchange or for molasses, from which more rum could be distilled. French and British manufacturers in the port cities made fortunes by refining or finishing colonial products such as sugar, indigo, tobacco, and furs and reexporting them to other European markets. Colonial commerce was superimposed on a complex pattern of European trade in which the Atlantic states carried off the lion's share of the profits.

MAGNITUDE OF THE SLAVE TRADE

The following figures represent the best current estimate of the number of persons removed from Africa and transported as slaves to the New World during the entire period of the Atlantic slave trade.

British Caribbean	1,665,000
British North America (to 1786)	275,000
United States (after 1786)	124,000
French Caribbean	1,600,000
Dutch Caribbean	500,000
Brazil	3,646,000
Spanish America	1,552,000

From Philip D. Curtain, *The Atlantic Slave Trade: A Census*, University of Wisconsin Press, 1969.

Slavery, the Foundation of Empire

Much of this dynamic global trade rested on slavery. Endless, backbreaking labor transformed a favorable climate and the investment of speculators into harvested plantation crops (see "A British Defense of Slavery and the Plantation Economy," p. 533). A publication of the chamber of commerce of Nantes, France's chief slaving port, publicly argued that without slavery there would be no French colonial commerce at all. At the height of the Atlantic slave traffic, about 88,000 blacks were removed from Africa annually—half in British ships, a quarter in French, and the rest in Dutch, Portuguese, Danish, and American ships (see "Magnitude of the Slave Trade"). More than 600,000 slaves were imported into the island of Jamaica in the eighteenth century. The population of Saint-Domingue around 1790 comprised about half a million slaves, compared with 35,000 whites of all nationalities and 28,000 mulattoes and free blacks.

Trafficking in slaves was competitive and risky but highly profitable. The demand for slaves in the West Indies, Brazil, Venezuela, and the southern colonies of North America kept rising, pushing up prices. In both Britain and France, chartered companies holding exclusive rights from the Crown originally monopolized the slave trade. They did not actually colonize or conquer African territory but instead established forts, or "factories," on the West African coast for the coordination and defense of their slaving expeditions. Gradually, the monopolies were challenged by other merchants and investors who combined to launch their own ships on slaving voyages. The West Indian planters, who needed more slaves, welcomed all additional sources. The independent traders clustered in port cities like Bristol and Liverpool in England, and by the 1730s they had broken the monopoly on the slave trade.

The Ordeal of Enslavement Europeans alone did not condemn black Africans to slavery. In this period, Europeans scarcely penetrated the interior of the continent; the forbidding topography and the resistance of the natives confined them to coastal areas. The actual enslavement took place in the interior at the hands of aggressive local groups whose chiefs became the intermediaries of this commerce. The competition among European traders for the slaves tended to drive up the prices that African middlemen could command in hardware, cloth, liquor, or guns. In response, some traders ventured into new areas in which the Africans might be more eager to come to terms. Increasing demand, rising prices, and competitiveness spread the slave trade and further blighted the future of West African society.

Many blacks failed to survive the process of enslavement at all. Some perished on the forced marches from the interior to the coast or on the nightmarish **Middle Passage** across the Atlantic, which has been compared to the transit in freight cars of Jewish prisoners to Nazi extermination camps in World War II. Because the risks of slaving ventures were high and the time lag between investment and return somewhere from one to two years, the traders sought to maximize their profits by jamming as many captives as possible onto the ships. Medium-sized ships carried as many as five hundred slaves on a voyage, all packed below deck in only enough space for each person to lie at full length pressed against neighboring bodies, and with only enough headroom to crawl, not to stand. Food and provisions were held to a minimum. The mortality rate that resulted from these conditions was a staggering 10 percent or more on average, and in extreme cases exceeded 50 percent.

Agitation against slavery by Quakers and other reformers in Britain and France focused initially on the practices of the slave trade rather than on slavery itself. After the 1780s, participation in the Atlantic slave trade tapered off, and the supply of slaves was replenished mainly from children born to slaves already in the New World. A dismal chapter in Europe's relations with the outside world dwindled to an end, although the final suppression of slaving voyages did not come for several more decades.

Mounting Colonial Conflicts

In the New World, the population of Britain's North American colonies reached about 1.5 million by midcentury. Some colonists pushed the frontier westward, while others clustered around the original settlements, a few of which—like Boston, New York, and Philadelphia—could now be called cities. The westward extension of the frontier and the growth of towns gave a vitality to the

A British Defense of Slavery and the Plantation Economy

"The most approved judges of the commercial interests of these Kingdoms have ever been of the opinion that our West Indies and African Trades are the most nationally beneficial of any we carry on. It is also allowed on all hands that the Trade to Africa is the branch which renders our American Colonies and Plantations so advantageous to Great Britain; that traffic only affording our plantations a constant supply of Negroe servants [slaves] for the culture of their lands in the produce of *sugars, tobacco, rice, rum, cotton, pimento,* and all others our plantations produce. So that the extensive employment of our shipping in, to, and from America, the great brood of seamen consequent thereupon, and the daily bread of the most considerable part of our British Manufacturers, are owing primarily to the labor of Negroes; who, as they were the first happy instrument of raising our Plantations, so their labor only can support and preserve them, and render them still more and more profitable to their Mother Kingdom.

"The Negroe Trade therefore, and the natural consequences resulting from it, may be justly esteemed an inexhaustible fund of Wealth and Naval Power to this Nation. And by the overplus of Negroes above what have served our own Plantations, we have drawn likewise no inconsiderable quantities of treasure from the Spaniards. . . . What renders the Negroe Trade still more estimable and important is that near nine tenths of those Negroes are paid for in Africa with British produce and manufactures only. We send no specie of bullion to pay for the products of Africa. . . . And it may be worth consideration, that while our Plantations depend only on planting by Negroes, they will neither depopulate our own Country, become independent of her Dominion, or any way interfere [i.e., compete] with the interests of the British Manufacturer, Merchant, or Landed Gentleman."

Malachy Postlethwayt, *The National and Private Advantages of the African Trade Considered*, London, 1746.

This image conveys the horror of the trans-Atlantic slaving voyages, known as the Middle Passage.
Historicus

British colonial world that New France appeared to lack. Since there was little enthusiasm among the French for emigration to the Louisiana Territory or Canada, the French remained thinly spread in their vast dominions. Yet France's colonies were well organized and profitable.

As French fishermen and fur traders prospered in Canada, French soldiers established a series of strongholds to support them, including the bastion of Fort Louisbourg at the entrance to the Gulf of St. Lawrence and a string of forts near the Great Lakes (see map 18.2), which served as bridgeheads for French fur traders and as a security buffer for Quebec province. In Louisiana, at the other end of the continent, New Orleans guarded the terminus of the Mississippi River. On their side, the British established their first large military base in North America at Halifax, Nova Scotia, contesting French penetration of the fishing grounds and waterways of the St. Lawrence Gulf.

Conflict on the Frontier The unsettled Ohio Valley was a second focus of colonial rivalry in North America. Pushing south from their Great Lakes trading forts and north from their posts on the Mississippi, the French began to assume control over that wilderness. A new string of forts formed pivots for potential French domination of the whole area between the Appalachian Mountains and the Mississippi—territory claimed and coveted by British subjects in the thirteen colonies.

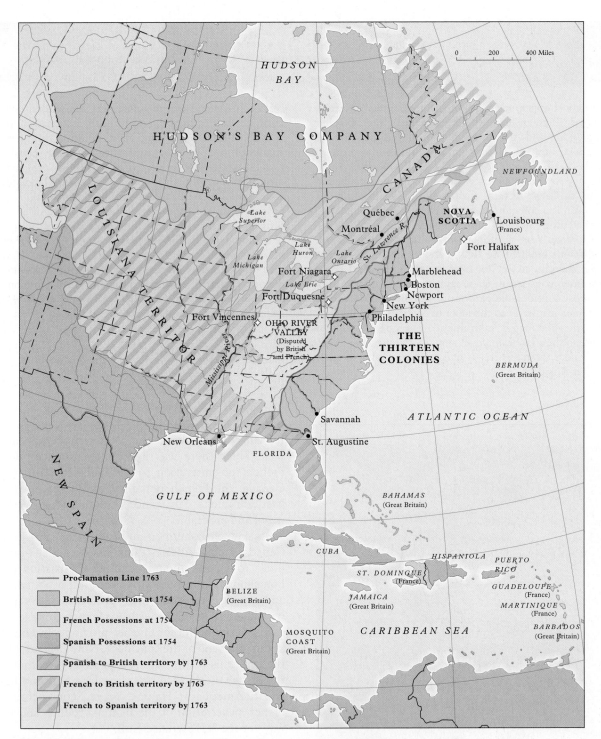

MAP 18.2 ANGLO-FRENCH RIVALRY IN NORTH AMERICA AND THE CARIBBEAN AS OF 1756
Notice the French and British possessions in North America in 1754. Is it clear from this map why the French and British struggled for control of the Ohio River Valley? Who appears to have had the advantage?

The threat grew that the French might completely cut off the westward expansion of these colonies. On their side, the French feared that British penetration of the Ohio Valley would lead to encroachments on their Canadian territory.

In jockeying for position, both sides sought the allegiance of the American Indians, and in this respect the French gradually gained the upper hand. Because they were traders only, not settlers, the French did not force the Native Americans from their traditional hunting grounds as the British had done repeatedly. Hence, the American Indians were willing to cooperate with the French in sealing off the Ohio Valley. A large land investment company, the Ohio Company of Virginia, faced ruin with that prospect, and in 1745 it attempted to break the French and Indian hold on the Ohio Valley by sending an expedition against Fort Duquesne. Led by a young militiaman named George Washington, the raid failed.

Contrary to a British tradition of letting settled colonies pay for themselves, the home government eventually shouldered the burden of colonial defense. An expedition of British army regulars was sent to do the job that the colonial militia could not accomplish. Limited skirmishes were about to give way to a full-scale war as each side began to reinforce its garrisons and naval squadrons. In May 1756, after several years of unofficial hostilities, Britain and France formally declared war.

The Great War for Empire

The pressures created by the competition of states, dynasties, and colonial empires in the eighteenth century exploded in midcentury in Europe's last large-scale war before the French Revolution. Its continental phase, known as the Seven Years' War, centered on the bitter rivalry between Austria and Prussia, but enmeshed Russia, France, and Britain as well. As we saw in chapter 17, this protracted war ended in 1763 with a peace treaty that essentially restored the status quo. The other phase of this midcentury conflagration revolved around Anglo-French competition for empire in North America, the West Indies, and India. Historians call it the Great War for Empire, and its North American sector is known as the French and Indian War. It was this great global confrontation that produced the most striking changes when the smoke cleared.

The Great War for Empire was one of Britain's high moments in history, the stuff of patriotic legends. The conflict started, however, in quite another fashion. Jumping to the initiative on several fronts, the better-coordinated French struck the first blows. Several key British forts on the Great Lakes fell to the French. At the same time, Britain's expeditionary force to the Continent, fighting in alliance with Prussia, suffered humiliating defeats. Yet the French had disadvantages that would show in the long run. Spread so thinly in

BRITAIN'S GLORY, CA. 1758
British naval power is shown here laying siege to the French stronghold of Louisbourg in July 1758.
New Brunswick Museum, Saint John, N.B.

North America, they would be hard put to follow their early success in the French and Indian War. More important, France depended on naval support to reinforce, supply, and move its troops; unfortunately for France, a fairly even naval matchup in the 1740s had turned into clear British naval superiority by the 1750s. British ships of the line outnumbered French ships almost two to one.

Pitt's Strategy　When William Pitt became Britain's prime minister in 1758, the tide was about to turn in the Great War for Empire. Pitt, later the Earl of Chatham, was the grandson of a man who had made a fortune in India. Eloquent, supremely self-confident, and infused with a vision of Britain's imperial destiny, Pitt had begun his career in Parliament in 1738 by denouncing the timid policies of the government and demanding that France be driven from the seas. Now he had his chance to lead Britain in the battle against its archrival. Pitt brought single-mindedness and vigor to his task. Although he honored Britain's commitment to Prussia, he attached highest priority to defeating France in the colonial world. His strategy involved an immediate series of offensives and an imaginative use of the British navy. He assigned the largest segment of the British fleet to cover the French home fleet, and he waited.

The French hoped to invade the British Isles as the surest method of bringing the enemy to the peace table, and the French fleet was ordered to prepare the way. In 1759 major battles were joined between French squadrons from Brest and Toulon and the British ships assigned to cover them. The British decimated the French fleet in these naval battles and thus decided the fate of colonial empires. Henceforth, the British had an almost free hand at sea and could prevent France from deploying its superior military forces in the colonial world. Unable to transport men and supplies to its colonies, France could no longer reinforce its garrisons or repel amphibious landings by the British. In every theater of the war, French colonial possessions fell to the British, thanks to Britain's naval supremacy.

In the French and Indian War, for example, Britain's forces defeated France in the battle of Quebec in September 1759. Had the French been able to reinforce Montreal, which they still held, they could have launched a counterattack against Britain's overextended lines. But Pitt's successful naval strategy had made it impossible for the French to reinforce their overseas garrisons. By September 1760 this last outpost of French power in North America capitulated to the British, who had already ousted the French from the Ohio Valley and the Great Lakes area. In the West Indies the long duel between the two powers also turned into a rout. One by one Britain seized the French islands.

The Treaty of Paris　In the peace negotiations that followed (concluded by the **Treaty of Paris** in 1763), Britain did not insist on retaining all its conquests. A war-weary British government was prepared to return certain colonies to France in exchange for an end to the fighting. Since British West Indian planters feared competition from the inclusion of the French islands in the British trading system, the British government returned several of those sugar-producing islands. But France did surrender Canada, which Britain chose to retain, perhaps unwisely; the British occupation of Canada removed the threat of French power, which had helped keep the restive colonists of North America loyal to Britain. (On that front, France would soon have its revenge when it came to the aid of the rebellious thirteen colonies in the War for American Independence.) In the long run, a relatively minor matter in the Treaty of Paris, which excluded French troops from India, proved to be supremely important.

The British Foothold in India

A Decaying Empire　Like England and France in the Late Middle Ages or like fifteenth-century Italy, the Indian subcontinent was in a state of political disintegration by the eighteenth century. The decline of the once mighty Mughal Empire stemmed from ethnic strife, dynastic instability, and factionalism, greed, and incompetence in the ruling circles. As yet the decline had little to do with European incursions. In 1739, for example, it was a Persian army that fought its way to Delhi and sacked that ancient capital of the Mughal Empire.

Trading for the spices, tea, and textiles produced in India, British and French merchants had quietly prospered on the fringes of the subcontinent. Britain administered its political and commercial interests in India through the London **East India Company**—a private corporation established in the seventeenth century to compete with the Dutch in the Far East. The company's commercial depots in India formed a tripod pattern at Bombay, Calcutta, and Madras. Initially, neither the English nor the French sought to establish colonies in India. They used small armed forces merely to defend their commercial interests and property and depended on the good will of the native *nawabs* (provincial governors), who encouraged European traders in order to fill their own coffers with tribute payments.

As their struggle for supremacy around the globe heated up, however, the French and British began to maneuver more aggressively by force and diplomacy among native groups in India, much as they were doing in the Ohio Valley and the Great Lakes regions of North America. While the French initially got the better of this game, taking Madras from the British briefly in the

1740s, the British were learning fast how to maximize their military and diplomatic assets to outmaneuver both the French and any natives who rose to challenge them. When the *nawab* of Bengal tilted toward the French in 1756 and decided to teach the British a lesson after they had fortified their positions without his permission, he set in motion a catastrophic change in the subcontinent's balance of power.

From Trade to Conquest   Young Robert Clive, who had sailed to India as a lowly and ill-paid clerk of the East India Company in the 1740s, was by now in charge of the nine hundred Europeans and fifteen hundred *sepoys*, or native soldiers, employed by the company. The company directed Clive to oust the French and to suppress any native opposition to British influence in the huge and populous province of Bengal. Clive faced an army of almost 50,000 men fielded by the *nawab*, but he subverted it by bribing a general who coveted the

nawab's position for himself. After the decisive battle of Plassey (June 1757), as the body of the *nawab* floated downriver, Clive escorted his successor to the throne.

After Plassey the *nawabs* became figureheads. Real power lay in the East India Company's hands, in an arrangement known as "dual government." The East India Company exercised the most oppressive kind of domination in Bengal: unchecked power without responsibility. The company collected taxes, controlled trade, and increased its military control. Greedy company officials siphoned off much of the treasure into their own pockets. Men like Clive who had sailed to India poor later returned with fortunes to England, where they were known as "nabobs" (a sarcastic play on the term *nawab*).

Britain thus won primacy in Bengal, the economic heartland of India, by exploiting Indian rivalries in the

MAP 18.3 THE BEGINNINGS OF THE BRITISH RAJ IN INDIA
Britain's interests in India were initially commercial, with the London East India Company's merchants setting up depots to trade for such key Indian goods as spices, tea, and textiles. Eventually, trade interest turned to conquest.

Thomas Hickey
COLONEL KIRKPATRIC WITH ATTENDANTS
This painting depicts a British district officer in 1799 in Madras, one of the regions of the Indian subcontinent in which the British began to exercise control after they ousted the French and defeated native forces that challenged them. The official's main function was to supervise the collection of taxes, which he did with the cooperation of local Indian princes and merchants.
© The National Gallery of Ireland. Photographer: Roy Hewson

chaos of the tottering Mughal Empire, at first ruling indirectly through native puppets. A number of civil wars made it easier for the British to dominate much of India. The company's muskets, cannons, and discipline defeated the last serious attack mounted against it in 1764. In the process the British ousted the French from any influence in the subcontinent, as agreed in the Treaty of Paris. Thus, on the verge of losing one empire in North America, the British were laying the foundations for another in South Asia.

When Parliament passed the India Act of 1784, the British government effectively replaced the company as the ultimate authority and named a new ruling official, the governor-general of India. Ironically, the first to fill that office was Lord Cornwallis, who had brought the American War of Independence to a close by surrendering to the rebels at Yorktown in 1781.

The British Raj To create a class loyal to British rule, or **raj,** Cornwallis turned India's rural gentry into landlords by giving them title deeds. Traditionally, the gentry had collected rents from their peasants, but could not remove them from the land. Now, as owners in the new Western sense, they could evict the peasants and do with the land whatever they wished. The governor-general reserved the highest positions in the army and civil bureaucracy for whites, however. In each district he appointed two British magistrates, one combining the functions of police superintendent and tax collector and the other responsible for administering justice. They were assisted by a horde of Indian clerks, runners, and translators. In addition the British monopolized the commerce in salt and opium. The salt monopoly extracted money from the Indian population, while opium was exported to China in exchange for Chinese tea to satisfy consumer demand back in Britain.

Later in the nineteenth century, behind the British soldiers, tax collectors, and magistrates, came educators and reformers with a novel sense of mission. As one of them put it, "we hope to create a class of persons Indian in blood and color, but English in taste, in opinion, in morals and intellect." By the 1830s, in other words, the British were not simply extracting wealth or strategic advantage from India but considered India as their own dominion in which they were duty bound to impose their own values on the Indian people.

Summary

French and English merchants capitalized aggressively on the commercial opportunities afforded by overseas colonies, plantation economies, and slavery, but these traders required backing by their states in the form of naval power. The growth of the British and French empires thus reflected the dynamics of the competitive European state system. Those empires propelled the growth of a global maritime economy and thus became major factors in the economic dynamism of the eighteenth century. It is well to remember, however, that two totally disenfranchised groups supported the entire structure of state power and mercantile profit: the slaves in the colonies and the serfs, peasants, or agricultural laborers in Europe. Their toil produced the food supplies, staple commodities, and revenues that sustained the merchants, landowners, rulers, armies, and navies of the great powers. The economic future, however, lay not with plantation slavery, serfdom, or seigneurialism but with innovations in agriculture and industrial production that would yield sustained economic growth and whose roots in England we have sketched. Along with the intellectual and cultural transformations to be discussed in the next chapter, these agricultural and industrial innovations heralded the dawn of the modern era.

QUESTIONS FOR FURTHER THOUGHT

1. In what ways can demographic trends affect economic and social development?
2. How can one best understand the economic transformations observable in late eighteenth-century England? What particular advantages did English society have in fostering innovation?
3. What are the principal characteristics of a traditional peasant society? How significant were the differences between peasant society in eastern and western Europe, and what accounts for the differences?
4. How did the imperial rivalry of France and Britain play out across the globe in the eighteenth century?

RECOMMENDED READING

Sources

Forster, Robert, and Elborg Forster (eds.). *European Society in the Eighteenth Century.* 1969. A varied and suggestive anthology.

Radischev, Alexander. *A Journey from St. Petersburg to Moscow* [1790]. 1958. The first major exposé of the miseries of Russian serfdom.

Smith, Adam. *An Inquiry into the Nature and Causes of the Wealth of Nations* [1776]. 1961. The seminal work in the liberal economic tradition.

Young, Arthur. *Travels in France during the Years 1787, 1788, 1789.* 1972. A critical view of French agriculture by an English expert.

Studies

Ashton, T. S. *The Industrial Revolution, 1760–1830.* 1968. A brief, classic account of early industrialization in Britain.

Berg, Maxine. *The Age of Manufactures: Industry, Innovation, and Work in Britain, 1700–1820.* 1986. An important revisionist view, emphasizing the persistence of domestic and workshop manufacturing alongside the new factory system.

Blum, Jerome. *The End of the Old Order in Rural Europe.* 1976. A valuable trove of information on rural conditions, particularly in the regions of serfdom.

Brewer, John, N. McKendrick, and J. H. Plumb. *Birth of a Consumer Society: The Commercialization of Eighteenth Century England.* 1982. A pioneering book on the development of consumer demand.

Chambers, J. D., and G. E. Mingay. *The Agricultural Revolution, 1750–1880.* 1966. A reliable overview and interpretation.

Craton, Michael. *Sinews of Empire: A Short History of British Slavery.* 1974. An excellent synthesis.

Davis, David B. *The Problem of Slavery in Western Culture.* 1966. And *The Problem of Slavery in the Age of Revolutions.* 1975. A comparative history of Western attitudes toward slavery from ancient times to the nineteenth century.

De Vries, Jan. *The Economy of Europe in an Age of Crisis, 1600–1750.* 1976. A reliable survey of the European economy before the industrial revolution.

Flinn, M. W. *The European Demographic System, 1500–1820.* 1981. A concise overview of the historical demography of early modern Europe.

Gutmann, Myron. *Toward the Modern Economy: Early Industry in Europe.* 1988. Another fine synthesis illustrating the complexity of the European economy.

Hufton, Olwen. *The Poor of Eighteenth-Century France.* 1974. A luminous study of the survival strategies of the indigent and of the institutions that aided or repressed them.

Klein, Herbert S. *The Atlantic Slave Trade.* 1999. A wide-ranging comparative synthesis.

LeRoy Ladurie, Emmanuel. *The Ancien Regime: A History of France, 1610–1774.* 1996. A synthesis by a leading French social and cultural historian.

Mathias, Peter. *The First Industrial Nation: An Economic History of Britain, 1700–1914.* 2d ed. 1976. A reliable survey combining quantitative and descriptive analysis.

North, Douglass C. *Structure and Change in Economic History.* 1981. Stresses the importance of supportive legal institutions in the coming of industrialism.

Parry, J. H. *Trade and Dominion: The European Overseas Empires in the Eighteenth Century.* 1971. A panoramic overview.

Post, John D. *Food Shortage, Climatic Variability, and Epidemic Disease in Pre-industrial Europe: The Mortality Peak in the Early 1740s.* 1985.

Rediker, Marcus. *The Slave Ship: A Human History.* 2007. A vivid account of Trans-Atlantic slaving voyages and their brutality.

Reiley, James. *International Government Finance and the Amsterdam Capital Market, 1740–1815.* 1980. The Dutch success in shifting from commerce to finance.

Rothschild, Emma. *Economic Sentiments: Adam Smith, Condorcet and the Enlightenment.* 2001. A provocative study of the rise of political economy.

Sheridan, Richard. *Sugar and Slavery: An Economic History of the British West Indies, 1623–1755.* 1974.

Uglow, Jennifer. *The Lunar Men: Five Friends Whose Curiosity Changed the World.* 2002. Lively study of the engineers, entrepreneurs, and scientists of the Lunar Society of Birmingham whose innovations in technology spurred industrialization.

Valenze, Deborah. *The First Industrial Woman.* 1995. A rich synthesis on women workers before and during early industrialization in Britain.

Woloch, Isser. *Eighteenth-Century Europe: Tradition and Progress, 1715–1789.* 1982.

Wrigley, E. A. *Population and History.* 1969. A fascinating introduction to the field of historical demography.

Pietro Longhi
THE GEOGRAPHY LESSON
This painting of *The Geography Lesson* evokes the interest in exotic places among Europe's educated elites, male and female, during the eighteenth centruy.
Cameraphoto/Art Resource, NY

Chapter Nineteen

The Age of Enlightenment

The Enlightenment • Eighteenth-Century Elite Culture • Popular Culture

Sharp breaks have been rare in Europe's intellectual and religious life—two of the defining themes in the Western experience—but we are about to witness one. During the eighteenth century, the great scientific and philosophical innovations of the previous century evolved into a naturalistic worldview divorced from religion. Scientific knowledge and religious skepticism, previously the concerns of an extremely narrow group of learned people, entered the consciousness of Europe's elites in a way that would have startled Descartes or Newton. Displacing the authority of religion with that of reason, the new outlook offered an optimistic vision of future progress in human affairs. Known as the Enlightenment, this movement formed the intellectual foundation for a new sense of modernity.

Never since pagan times, certainly not during the Renaissance, was religious belief so directly challenged. Many important eighteenth-century intellectuals no longer believed in Christianity and wished to reduce its influence in society. They argued that there was no divine standard of morality, no afterlife to divert humanity from worldly concerns. These writers developed a strong, sometimes arrogant, sense of their own capacity to ignore traditional authority and guide society toward change.

The evolution of cultural institutions and the media of the day gave these writers an increasingly wide forum. While aristocratic patronage and classical culture remained influential, a new kind of middle-class culture was developing alongside a much wider reading public and an expanding sphere of public discussion.

Yet, as we turn to consider the Enlightenment within the varied cultural environments of the eighteenth century, we should not exaggerate. Although they were critics of their society, most eighteenth-century intellectuals lived comfortably amid Europe's high culture. They had scant interest in or understanding of the vibrant popular culture around them. On the contrary, their growing belief in "public opinion" referred solely to the educated elites of the aristocracy and the middle classes.

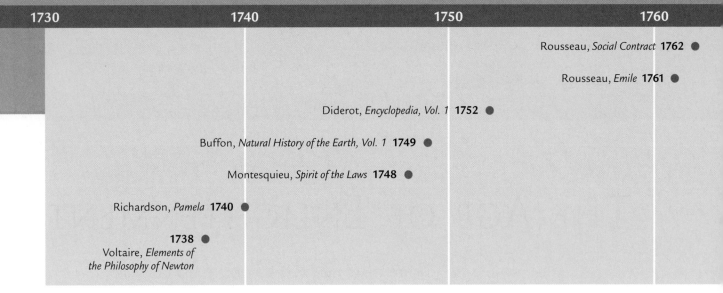

Rousseau, *Social Contract* **1762** ●

Rousseau, *Emile* **1761** ●

Diderot, *Encyclopedia, Vol. 1* **1752** ●

Buffon, *Natural History of the Earth, Vol. 1* **1749** ●

Montesquieu, *Spirit of the Laws* **1748** ●

Richardson, *Pamela* **1740** ●

1738 ●
Voltaire, *Elements of
the Philosophy of Newton*

THE ENLIGHTENMENT

Building on seventeenth-century science, skepticism in matters of religion, and a heightened appreciation for the culture of classical antiquity, eighteenth-century intellectuals approached their calling in a new spirit. They believed that human behavior and institutions could be studied rationally, like Newton's universe, and that their faults could be corrected. They saw themselves as participants in a movement—which they called the Enlightenment—that could make educated men and women more rational, tolerant, and virtuous. Although the Enlightenment had creative adherents across the Western world, its capital was undoubtedly in Paris, where an ideology of progress and freedom gradually took shape. Renowned writers such as Voltaire, Diderot, and Rousseau produced a steady flow of remarkable works across a wide range of subjects, which governmental censorship could not suppress, try as it might.

The Broadening Reverberations of Science

It is hard to think of two men less revolutionary in temperament than the seventeenth century's René Descartes and Isaac Newton. Both were conservative on matters outside the confines of science, had relatively little concern for social institutions, remained practicing Christians, and wrote only for small learned audiences. Yet their legacy of insight into the world of nature produced in succeeding generations what has been described as "a permanent intellectual insurrection," which unfolded in a spirit undreamed of by either man.

The Popularization of Science While eighteenth-century scientists pondered the cosmologies of Descartes and Newton, nonscientists in England and on the Continent applied the methodologies of Descartes, Newton, and the philosopher John Locke to other realms of human thought. They fused the notion of methodical doubt and naturalistic explanations of phenomena into a scientific or mathematical spirit, which at bottom simply meant confidence in reason and a skeptical attitude toward accepted dogmas. They attempted to popularize scientific method, with the aim of transforming the values of Western civilization. Writers translated the discoveries of scientists into clear and even amusing general reading. The literary talents of these enthusiasts helped make household words of Newton and Descartes among educated Europeans.

A more calculating and ambitious propagandist of the scientific spirit was the Frenchman François-Marie Arouet, who wrote under the pen name of Voltaire and is virtually synonymous with the Enlightenment. Although his chief talents lay in literature and criticism, Voltaire also spent some time studying Newton's work. In 1738, in collaboration with his friend Madame du Châtelet, he published a widely read popularization called *Elements of the Philosophy of Newton*. However dry the study of physics, Voltaire argued, it frees the mind from dogma, and its experimental methods provide a model for the liberation of human thought. Moreover, Voltaire related Newton's achievement to the environment of a liberal England that also produced Francis Bacon and John Locke, the three of whom Voltaire adopted as his personal Trinity. In his *Philosophical Letters on the English* (1734)—a celebration of English toleration and an indirect attack on religious bigotry, censorship, and social snobbery in France—Voltaire had already noted the respect enjoyed in England by its writers and scientists.

Popularizations of scientific method stimulated public interest in science, as mathematicians, cartographers,

1764 Voltaire, *Philosophical Dictionary*

● **1772** Completion of Diderot's *Encyclopedia*

● **1774** Goethe, *Sorrows of Young Werther; Habsburg School Ordinance*

● **1778** Death of Voltaire

● **1781** Joseph II's Edict of Toleration

1780s Jacques-Louis David's neoclassical masterpieces

Wollstonecraft, *Vindication of the Rights of Woman* **1792** ●

French chemist Lavoisier conducts an experiment in his laboratory to study the composition of air during the process of respiration. Bettmann/Corbis

and astronomers made notable advances in their fields. But further scientific progress was far from automatic. In chemistry, for example, the traditions of alchemy persisted, and phenomena such as fire long escaped objective analysis. At the end of the century, however, a major breakthrough occurred when the Englishman Joseph Priestley isolated oxygen and the Frenchman Antoine Lavoisier analyzed the components of air and water and came close to explaining the process of combustion.

The vogue for science also had a dubious side, apparent, for example, in the great popularity of mesmerism. This pseudoscience of magnetic fields purported to offer its wealthy devotees relief from a variety of ailments by the use of special "electrical" baths and treatments. Although repeatedly condemned by the Academy of Sciences in Paris, mesmerism continued to attract educated followers.

Natural History The most widely followed scientific enterprise in the eighteenth century was **natural history,** the science of the earth's development—a combination of geology, zoology, and botany. This field of study was easy for the nonscientist to appreciate. Its foremost practitioner was G. L. Buffon, keeper of the French Botanical Gardens—a patronage position that allowed him to produce a multivolume *Natural History of the Earth* between 1749 and 1778. Drawing on a vast knowledge of phenomena such as fossils, Buffon went beyond previous attempts to classify the data of nature and provided both a description and a theory of the earth's development.

Although he was a nonbeliever, Buffon did not explicitly attack religious versions of such events as the Creation; he simply ignored them, an omission of obvious significance to his readers. Similarly, while he did not specifically contend that human beings have evolved from beasts, he implied it. "It is possible," he wrote, "to descend by almost insensible degrees from the most perfect creature to the most formless matter." Buffon's earth did not derive from a singular act of divine creation that would explain the origins of human beings. The readers of his *Natural History* or its numerous popularizations in several languages thus encountered a universe that had developed through evolution.

Beyond Christianity

The erosion of biblical revelation as a source of authority is one hallmark of the Enlightenment. This shift derived some of its impetus from seventeenth-century scientists and liberal theologians who were themselves believing Christians but who opposed religious superstition or "enthusiasm," as they called it. They had hoped to accommodate religion to new philosophical standards and scientific formulations by eliminating the superstitious imagery that could make religion seem ridiculous and by treating the world of nature as a form of revelation in which God's majesty could be seen. The devil, for example, could be considered as a category of moral evil rather than as a specific horned creature with a pitchfork. They hoped to bolster the Christian religion by deemphasizing miracles and focusing on reverence for the Creator and on the moral teachings of the Bible. Their approach did indeed help educated people adhere to Christianity during the eighteenth century. In the final analysis, however, this kind of thinking diminished the authority of religion in society.

Toleration One current of thought that encouraged a more secular outlook was the idea of toleration, as propounded by the respected French critic Pierre Bayle. Consciously applying methodical doubt to subjects that Descartes had excluded from such treatment, Bayle's *Critical and Historical Dictionary* (1697) put the claims of religion to the test of critical reason. Certain Christian traditions emerged from this scrutiny as the equivalent of myth and fairy tale, and the history of Christianity appeared as a record of fanaticism and persecution. Bayle's chief target was Christianity's attempts to impose orthodoxy at any cost (for example, the Spanish Inquisition and Louis XIV's revocation of the Edict of Nantes and persecution of French Protestants). Though a devout Calvinist himself, Bayle advocated complete toleration, which would allow any person to practice any religion or none at all. An individual's moral behavior rather than his or her creed is what mattered, according to Bayle.

The most striking success of the eighteenth-century campaign for toleration came with the Edict of Toleration issued by the Habsburg emperor Joseph II on his ascendancy to the throne in 1781. For the first time, a

In 1745 the Habsburg monarchy expelled an estimated seventy thousand Jews from Prague to appease anti-Semitic sentiment.

JOSEPH II ON RELIGIOUS TOLERATION

Between 1765 and 1781 Joseph II was joint ruler of the Habsburg Empire with his pious mother, Empress Maria Theresa. Joseph advocated a utilitarian approach to religious toleration (Document 1) but made little headway against Maria Theresa's traditional insistence that the state must actively combat religious dissent. Soon after Maria Theresa's death, Joseph promulgated a series of decrees on religion, including a landmark Toleration Edict for Protestants (Document 2) and even a special, if somewhat less sweeping, edict of toleration for the Jews of his domains.

1. LETTER TO MARIA THERESA, JULY 1777

"The word toleration has caused misunderstanding.... God preserve me from thinking it a matter of indifference whether the citizens turn Protestant or remain Catholics.... I would give all I possess if all the Protestants of your States would go over to Catholicism. The word *toleration* as I understand it, means only that I would employ any persons, without distinction of religion, in purely temporal matters, allow them to own property, practice trades, be citizens if they were qualified and if this would be of advantage to the State and its industry.... The undisturbed practice of their religion makes them far better subjects and causes them to avoid irreligion, which is a far greater danger to our Catholics."

2. TOLERATION EDICT OF OCTOBER 1781

"We have found Ourselves moved to grant to the adherents of the Lutheran and Calvinist religions, and also to the non-Uniat Greek religion, everywhere, the appropriate private practice of their faith.... The Catholic religion alone shall continue to enjoy the prerogative of the public practice of its faith.... Non-Catholics are in future admitted under dispensation to buy houses and real property, to acquire municipal domicile and practice as master craftsmen, to take up academic appointments and posts in the public service, and are not to be required to take the oath in any form contrary to their religious tenets.... In all choices or appointments to official posts ... difference of religion is to be disregarded."

From C. A. Macartney (ed.), *The Habsburg and Hohenzollern Dynasties in the 17th and 18th Centuries,* HarperCollins, 1970, pp. 151, 155–157.

Catholic Habsburg ruler recognized the right of Protestants and Jews in his realm to worship freely and to hold property and public office (see "Joseph II on Religious Toleration," above). Joseph also tried to reduce the influence of the Catholic Church by ordering the dissolution of numerous monasteries on the grounds that they were useless and corrupt. Part of their confiscated wealth was used to support the medical school at the University of Vienna.

Deism Voltaire became the Enlightenment's most vigorous antireligious polemicist. This prolific writer was one of the century's most brilliant literary stylists, historians, and poets. Those talents alone would have ensured his fame. But Voltaire was also a dedicated antagonist of Christianity. For tactical reasons, much of his attack against *l'infame* ("the infamous thing"), as he called Christianity, targeted such practices as monasticism or the behavior of priests. His ultimate target, though, was Christianity itself, which, he declared, "every sensible man, every honorable man must hold in horror."

Voltaire's masterpiece, a best seller called *The Philosophical Dictionary* (1764), had to be published anonymously and was burned by the authorities in Switzerland, France, and the Netherlands. Modeled after Bayle's dictionary, it was far more blunt. Of theology, he wrote, "We find man's insanity in all its plenitude." Organized religion is not simply false but pernicious, he argued. Voltaire believed that religious superstition inevitably bred fanaticism and predictably resulted in bloody episodes like the Saint Bartholomew's Day Massacre.

Voltaire hoped that educated Europeans would abandon Christianity in favor of **deism,** a belief that recognized God as the Creator but held that the world, once created, functions according to natural laws without interference by God. Humanity thus lives essentially on its own in an ordered universe, without hope or fear of divine intervention and without the threat of damnation or the hope of eternal salvation. For deists, religion should be a matter of private contemplation rather than public worship and mythic creeds. Although certain figures in the Enlightenment went beyond deism to a philosophical atheism, which rejected any concept of God as unprovable, Voltaire's mild deism remained a characteristic view of eighteenth-century writers. At bottom, however, this form of spirituality was essentially secular. Broad-minded clergy could accept many of the arguments of eighteenth-century science and philosophy, but they could not accept deism.

The Philosophes

Science and secularism became the rallying points of a group of French intellectuals known as the **philosophes.** Their traditionalist opponents employed this term to mock the group's pretensions, but the philosophes themselves used that label with pride. They saw themselves as a vanguard, the men who raised the Enlightenment to the status of a self-conscious movement. The leaders of this influential coterie of writers were Voltaire and Denis Diderot. Its ranks included mathematicians Jean d'Alembert and the Marquis de Condorcet, the magistrate Baron de Montesquieu, the government official Jacques Turgot, and the atheist philosopher Baron d'Holbach. Thus, the French philosophes came from both the aristocracy and the middle class. Outside of France their kinship extended to a group of brilliant Scottish philosophers, including David Hume and Adam Smith; to the German playwright Gotthold Lessing and the philosopher Immanuel Kant; to the Italian economist and penal reformer the Marquis of Beccaria; and to such founders of the American Philosophical Society as Benjamin Franklin and Thomas Jefferson.

Intellectual Freedom   The philosophes shared above all else a critical spirit, the desire to reexamine the assumptions and institutions of their societies and expose them to the tests of reason, experience, and utility. Today this might sound banal, but it was not so at a time when almost everywhere religion permeated society. Asserting the primacy of reason meant turning away from faith, the essence of religion. It meant a decisive break with the Christian worldview, which placed religious doctrine at the center of society's values. The philosophes invoked the paganism of ancient Greece and Rome, where the spirit of rational inquiry prevailed among educated people. They ridiculed the Middle Ages as the "Dark Ages" and contrasted the religious spirit of that era to their own sense of liberation and modernity. In *The Decline and Fall of the Roman Empire* (1776–1788), the historian Edward Gibbon declared that Christianity had eclipsed a Roman civilization that had sought to live according to reason rather than myths.

The inspiration of antiquity was matched by the stimulus of modern science and philosophy. The philosophes laid claim to Newton, who made the universe intelligible without the aid of revelation, and Locke, who uncovered the workings of the human mind. From Locke they went on to argue that human personality is malleable: Its nature is not fixed, let alone corrupted by original sin. People are, therefore, ultimately responsible to themselves for what they do with their lives. Existing arrangements are no more nor less sacred than experience has proved them to be. As the humanists had several centuries before, the philosophes placed human beings at the center of thought. Unlike most humanists, however, philosophes placed thought in the service of change and launched a noisy public movement.

Persecution and Triumph   Philosophes appeared clamorous to their contemporaries because they had to battle entrenched authority. Religious traditionalists and the apparatus of censorship in almost all countries threatened the intellectual freedom demanded by the philosophes. They often had to publish their works clandestinely and anonymously. Sometimes they were pressured into withholding manuscripts from publication altogether or into making humiliating public apologies for controversial books. Even with such caution, almost all philosophes saw some of their publications confiscated and burned. A few were forced into exile or sent to jail: Voltaire spent several decades across the French border in Switzerland, and Voltaire and Diderot both spent time in prison. Although the notoriety produced by these persecutions stimulated the sale of their works, the anxiety took its toll.

By the 1770s, however, the philosophes had survived their running war with the authorities. Some of them lived to see their ideas widely accepted and their works acclaimed. In 1778, the last year of his life, Voltaire returned triumphantly to Paris. When he attended a performance of one of his plays at the national theater, the audience greeted him with tumultuous enthusiasm. Even if the philosophes had contributed little else to the Western experience, their struggle for freedom of expression would merit them a significant place in its history.

Pioneering in the Social Sciences   But the philosophes achieved far more. In their scholarly and polemical writings, they investigated a wide range of subjects and pioneered in several new disciplines. Some philosophes—Voltaire, for example—were pathbreaking historians. Moving beyond traditional chronicles of battles and rulers' biographies, they studied culture, social institutions, and government structures in an effort to understand past societies as well as describe major events. Practically inventing the notion of social science, they investigated the theoretical foundations of social organization (sociology) and the workings of the human mind (psychology). On a more practical level, they proposed fundamental reforms in such areas as the penal system and education.

The philosophes embedded their study of social science in questions of morality and the study of ethics.

WHAT IS ENLIGHTENMENT?

The most concise formulation of the Enlightenment's spirit is conveyed in an essay of the 1780s by the German philosopher Immanuel Kant. As Kant makes clear, intellectual freedom and the role of public opinion refer not so much to the average person in the street as to the educated classes—serious writers (whom he calls "scholars") and their public. Note that in drawing the distinction between the public realm (where freedom is vital) and the private realm (where obedience is rightly expected), Kant reverses the labels that we would likely assign to the two realms today.

"Enlightenment is man's emergence from his self-imposed nonage. Nonage is the inability to use one's own understanding without another's guidance. This nonage is self-imposed if its cause lies not in lack of understanding but in indecision and lack of courage to use one's own mind without another's guidance. Dare to know. (*Sapere aude*). 'Have the courage to use your own understanding,' is therefore the motto of the Enlightenment.

"Laziness and cowardice are the reasons why such a large part of mankind gladly remain minors all their lives, long after nature has freed them from external guidance. They are the reasons why it is so easy for others to set themselves up as guardians. It is so comfortable to be a minor. If I have a book that thinks for me, a pastor who acts as my conscience, then I have no need to exert myself. . . .

"This enlightenment requires nothing but freedom: freedom to make public use of one's reason in all matters. . . . On the other hand, the private use of reason may frequently be narrowly restricted without especially hindering the progress of enlightenment. By 'public use of reason' I mean that use which man, as a scholar, makes of it before the reading public. I call 'private use' that use which a man makes of his reason in a civic post that has been entrusted to him . . . and where arguing is not permitted: one must obey. . . . Thus it would be very unfortunate if an officer on duty and under orders from his superiors should want to criticize the appropriateness or utility of his orders. He must obey. But as a scholar he could not rightfully be prevented from taking notice of the mistakes in the military service and from submitting his views to his public for its judgement."

Enlightenment ethics were generally utilitarian. Such philosophers as David Hume tried to define good and evil in pragmatic terms; they argued that social utility should become the standard for public morality. This approach to moral philosophy in turn raised the question of whether any human values were absolute and eternal. Among the philosophers who grappled with this challenge, Kant tried to harmonize the notion of absolute moral values with practical reason.

Political Liberty   The most influential work of social science produced by the Enlightenment was probably *The Spirit of the Laws* (1748) by the French magistrate Montesquieu. The book offered a comparative study of governments and societies. On the one hand, Montesquieu introduced the perspective of relativism: He tried to analyze the institutions of government in relation to the special customs, climate, religion, and commerce of various countries. He thus argued that no single, ideal model of government existed. On the other hand, he deeply admired his own idealized version of the British system of government; he thereby implied that all societies could learn from the British about liberty.

Montesquieu's sections on liberty won a wide readership in Europe and in America, where the book was influential among the drafters of the U.S. Constitution. Political liberty, said Montesquieu, requires checks on those who hold power in a state, whether that power is exercised by a king, an aristocracy, or the people. Liberty can thrive only with a balance of powers, preferably by the separation of the executive, the legislative, and the judicial branches of government. Montesquieu ascribed a central role to aristocracies as checks on royal despotism. Indeed, many eighteenth-century writers on politics considered strong privileged groups, independent from both the crown and the people, as the only effective bulwarks against tyranny. To put it another way, Montesquieu's followers thought that the price for a society free from despotism was privilege for some of its members.

Liberal Economics   French and British thinkers of the Enlightenment transformed economic theory with attacks against mercantilism and government regulation. We noted in chapter 18 Adam Smith's critique of artificial restraints on individual economic initiative. In France, the Physiocrats similarly argued that economic progress depended on freeing agriculture and trade from restrictions. Since in their view (unlike Adam Smith's) land was the only real source of wealth, they also called for reforms in the tax structure, with a uniform and

An English engraving entitled "Voltaire's Staircase" suggests how the great writer stood at the center of Europe's literary and intellectual life. The fifth figure from the right at the top, Voltaire is bidding good-bye to d'Alembert, coeditor of the *Encyclopedia.*
Bettmann/Corbis

equitable land tax. In opposition to a traditional popular insistence on government intervention to maintain supplies of grain and flour at fair prices, the Physiocrats advocated freedom for the grain trade to operate according to the dictates of supply and demand. The incentive of higher prices would encourage growers to expand productivity, they believed, and in this way the grain shortages that plagued Europe could eventually be eliminated, although at the cost of temporary hardship for most consumers.

Diderot and the Encyclopedia

The Enlightenment thus produced not only a new intellectual spirit but also a wide range of critical writings on various subjects. In addition, the French philosophes collectively generated a single work that exemplified their notion of how knowledge could be useful: Diderot's *Encyclopédie* (*Encyclopedia*).

Within a few years of arriving in Paris as a young man, Denis Diderot had published novels, plays, treatises on mathematics and moral philosophy, and critical essays on religion. His most original writings examined the role of passion in human personality and in any system of values derived from an understanding of human nature. Specifically, Diderot affirmed the role of sexuality, arguing against artificial taboos and repression. As an advocate of what was sometimes called "the natural man," Diderot belies the charge leveled against the philosophes that they overemphasized reason to the neglect of feeling.

Diderot's unusual boldness in getting his works published brought him a considerable reputation but also some real trouble. Two of his books were condemned by the authorities as contrary to religion, the state, and morals. In 1749 he spent one hundred days in prison and was released only after making a humiliating apology. At about that time, Diderot was approached by a publisher to translate a British encyclopedic reference work into French. After a number of false starts, he persuaded the publisher to sponsor instead an entirely new and more comprehensive work that would reflect the interests of the philosophes.

The Encyclopedia The *Encyclopedia, or Classified Dictionary of the Sciences, Arts, and Occupations,* an inventory of all fields of knowledge from the most theoretical to the most mundane, constituted an arsenal of critical concepts. As the preface stated: "Our Encyclopedia is a work that could only be carried out in a philosophic century. . . . All things must be examined without sparing anyone's sensibilities. . . . The arts and sciences must regain their freedom." The ultimate purpose of the *Encyclopedia,* wrote its editors, was "to change the general way of thinking." Written in this spirit by an array of talented collaborators, the expensive twenty-eight-volume *Encyclopedia* (1752–1772) fulfilled the fondest hopes of its editors and four thousand initial subscribers.

In such a work, religion could scarcely be ignored, but neither could it be openly attacked. Instead, the editors treated religion with artful satire or else relegated it to a philosophical or historical plane. Demystified and subordinated, religion was probed and questioned like any other subject, much to the discomfort of learned but orthodox critics.

Science stood at the core of the *Encyclopedia,* but the editors emphasized the technological or practical side of science with numerous articles and plates illustrating machines, tools, and manufacturing processes. They praised the roles of mechanics, engineers, and artisans in society and stressed the benefits of efficient production in the advance of civilization. Such emphasis implied that technology and artisanal skills constituted valuable realms of knowledge comparable to theoretical sciences such as physics and mathematics.

On economic topics the encyclopedists tended to echo the Physiocratic crusade against restrictions on trade and agriculture. On questions of government, the authors generally endorsed absolute monarchy, provided it was reasonably efficient and just. The major political concerns of the editors were civil rights, freedom of expression, and the rule of law.

The Encyclopedia's Impact In retrospect, after the French Revolution, the *Encyclopedia* does not seem very revolutionary. Yet in the context of the times, it assuredly was. The revolution that Diderot sought was intellectual. As he wrote in a letter to a friend, the encyclopedists were promoting "a revolution in the minds of men to free them from prejudice." Judging by the reaction of religious and government authorities, they were eminently successful. "Up till now," commented one French bishop, "hell has vomited its venom drop by drop." Now, he concluded, it could be found assembled between the *Encyclopedia's* covers.

After allowing the first three volumes to appear, the French government banned the *Encyclopedia* in 1759 and revoked the bookseller's license to issue the remaining volumes. As the attorney general of France put it: "There is a project formed, a society organized to propagate materialism, to destroy religion, to inspire a spirit of independence, and to nourish the corruption of morals." Most of the *Encyclopedia's* contributors prudently withdrew from the project, but Diderot went underground and continued the herculean task until the subscribers received every promised volume, including eleven magnificent folios of illustrations. By the time these appeared, the persecutions had receded. Indeed, the *Encyclopedia* was reprinted in cheaper editions (both legal and pirated) that sold out rapidly, earning fortunes for their publishers. This turn of events ensured the status of Diderot's project as the landmark of its age.

Jean-Jacques Rousseau

Arguably the most original and influential eighteenth-century thinker, Jean-Jacques Rousseau stood close to but self-consciously outside the coterie of the philosophes, for Rousseau provided in his life and writing a critique not only of the status quo but of the Enlightenment itself. Obsessed with the issue of moral freedom, Rousseau found society far more oppressive than most philosophes would admit, and he considered the philosophes themselves to be part of the problem.

Young Rousseau won instant fame when he submitted a prize-winning essay in a contest sponsored by a provincial academy on the topic, "Has the restoration of the arts and sciences had a purifying effect upon morals?" Unlike most respondents, Rousseau answered that it had not. He argued that the lustrous cultural and scientific achievements of recent decades were producing pretension, conformity, and useless luxury. Most scientific pursuits, he wrote, "are the effect of idleness which generate idleness in their turn." The system of rewards in the arts produces "a servile and deceptive conformity . . . the dissolution of morals . . . and the corruption of taste." Against the decadence of high culture, he advocated a return "to the simplicity which prevailed in earliest times"—manly physical pastimes, self-reliance, independent citizens instead of fawning courtiers.

Rousseau's Moral Vision Rousseau had no wish to return to a state of nature, a condition of anarchy in which force ruled and people were slaves of appetite. But the basis of morality, he argued, was conscience, not reason. "Virtue, sublime science of simple minds: are not your principles graven on every heart?" This became one of his basic themes in two popular works of fiction, *Julie, or the New Héloise* (1761), and *Emile, or Treatise on Education* (1762).

In the first novel, Julie is educated in virtue by her tutor St. Preux but allows herself to fall in love with and be seduced by him. In the second half of the novel, Julie breaks away from St. Preux and marries Monsieur de Wolmar, her father's wealthy friend. She maintains a distant friendship with her old lover and rears her children in exemplary fashion, overseeing their education. In the end she overcomes her past moral lapse and sacrifices her own life to save one of her children. Wolmar then brings in the chastened St. Preux to continue the children's education. This tale of love, virtue, and motherhood won an adoring audience of male and female readers who identified with the characters, shed tears over their moral dilemmas, and applauded Rousseau for this superb lesson in the new sensibility.

Emile recounts the story of a young boy raised to be a moral adult by a tutor who emphasized experience over book learning and who considered education a matter of individual self-development. This new kind of man of course required a comparably sensitive wife, attuned to practical matters and without vain aristocratic pretenses. Sophie, the girl in question, received a very different type of education, however, one concerned with virtue but far more limited in its scope. Rousseau depicted men and women liberating themselves from stultifying traditional values, yet in the new relationships he portrayed in these novels, women held a decidedly subordinate position. Their virtues were to be exclusively domestic in character, while the men would be prepared for public roles—a distinction that deeply troubled feminist thinkers in the future (see "Mary Wollstonecraft on the Education of Women," p. 551).

Nicolas Henri Jeaurat de Bertry
ALLEGORY OF THE REVOLUTION WITH A PORTRAIT
MEDALLION OF J. J. ROUSSEAU
The French revolutionaries acclaimed both Voltaire and
Rousseau and transferred their remains to a new Pantheon.
But Rousseau was the man considered by many French
people to be the Revolution's spiritual father, as suggested
by his position in this allegorical painting of 1793, filled
with the new symbolism of liberty and equality.
Musée de la Ville de Paris, Musée Carnavalet, Paris, France.
Giraudon/Art Resource, NY

The Rebel as Cultural Hero   Rousseau himself was by
no means a saint. His personal weaknesses—including
the illegitimate child that he fathered and abandoned—
doubtless contributed to his preoccupation with morality and conscience. Nonetheless, his rebellious life as
well as his writings greatly impressed the generation of
readers and writers coming of age in the 1770s and
1780s. Not only did he quarrel with the repressive authorities of church and state—who repeatedly banned
his books—but he also attacked the pretensions of his
fellow philosophes, whom he considered arrogant, cynical, and lacking in spirituality.

By the 1770s the commanding figures of the Enlightenment, such as Voltaire and Diderot, had won their
battles and had become masters of the most prestigious
academies and channels of patronage. In a sense, they
had themselves become the establishment. For younger
writers frustrated by the existing distribution of influence and patronage, Rousseau became the inspiration.

Rousseau's Concept of Freedom   What proved to be
Rousseau's most enduring work, *The Social Contract*,
published in 1762, became famous only after the French
Revolution dramatized the issues that the book had
raised. (The Revolution, it could be said, did more for
the book than Rousseau did for the Revolution, which
he neither prophesied nor advocated.) *The Social Contract* was not meant as a blueprint for revolution but
rather as an ideal standard against which readers might
measure their own society. Rousseau did not expect
that this standard could be achieved in practice, because existing states were too large and complex to allow the kind of participation that he considered
essential.

For Rousseau, a government distinct from the individuals over whom it claims to exercise authority has
no validity. Rousseau denied the almost universal idea
that some people are meant to govern and others to
obey. In the ideal polity, Rousseau said, individuals
have a role in making the law to which they submit. By
obeying it, they are thus obeying themselves as well as
their fellow citizens. For this reason, they are free from
arbitrary power. To found such an ideal society, each
citizen would have to take part in creating a social contract laying out the society's ground rules. By doing so,
these citizens would establish themselves as "the sovereign." This sovereign—the people—then creates a
government that will carry on the day-to-day business
of applying the laws.

Rousseau was not advocating simple majority rule
but rather a quest for consensus as to the best interests
of all citizens. Even if it *appears* contrary to the welfare of some or even many citizens, Rousseau believed,
the best interest of the community must be every individual's best interest as well, since that individual is a
member of the community. Rousseau called this difficult concept the **"general will."** Deferring to the general will means that an individual ultimately must do
what one *ought*, not simply what one *wants*. This
commitment derives from conscience, which must do
battle within the individual against passion, appetite,
and mere self-interest. Under the social contract, to
use Rousseau's most striking phrase, the individual
"will be forced to be free" (see "Rousseau's Concept of
the General Will," p. 552). Thus, for Rousseau, individual freedom depends on a political framework involving consent and participation as well as
subordination of individual self-interest to the com-
monweal. More than any of the philosophes, Rousseau

MARY WOLLSTONECRAFT ON THE EDUCATION OF WOMEN

The sharpest challenge to Rousseau's widely shared attitude toward women came only in 1792, with the publication of Mary Wollstonecraft's A Vindication of the Rights of Woman. *Inspired by the French Revolution's doctrine of natural rights, this spirited writer deplored the fact that society kept women (in her words) frivolous, artificial, weak, and in a perpetual state of childhood. While men praised women for their beauty and grace, they hypocritically condemned them for a concern with vanity, fashion, and trivial matters, yet refused to treat them as rational human beings who could contribute to society as much as men. Her book emphasized the need for educational reform that would allow women to develop agile bodies and strong minds. Along the way Wollstonecraft took particular aim at Rousseau's* Emile.

"The conduct and manners of women, in fact, evidently prove that their minds are not in a healthy state; for, like the flowers which are planted in too rich a soil, strength and usefulness are sacrificed to beauty. . . . One cause of this barren blooming I attribute to a false system of education, gathered from the books written on this subject by men who, considering females rather as women than human creatures, have been more anxious to make them alluring mistresses than affectionate wives and rational mothers. The understanding of the sex has been so bubbled by this specious homage, that the civilized women of the present century, with a few exceptions, are only anxious to inspire love, when they ought to cherish a nobler ambition, and by their abilities and virtues exact respect.

"[T]he most perfect education, in my opinion, is such an exercise of the understanding as is best calculated to strengthen the body and form the heart. Or, in other words, to enable the individual to attain such habits of virtue as will render it independent. In fact, it is a farce to call any being virtuous whose virtues do not result from the exercise of its own reason. This was Rousseau's opinion respecting men: I extend it to women, and confidently assert that they have been drawn out of their sphere by false refinement, and not by an endeavor to acquire masculine qualities. Still the regal homage which they receive is so intoxicating, that till the manners of the times are changed, and formed on more reasonable principles, it may be impossible to convince them that the illegitimate power, which they obtain by degrading themselves, is a curse, and that they must return to nature and equality."

From Sandra M. Gilbert and Susan Gubar (eds.), *The Norton Anthology of Literature by Women: The Tradition in English,* W. W. Norton Co, 1985.

argued that individual freedom depends on the arrangements governing the collectivity.

EIGHTEENTH-CENTURY ELITE CULTURE

The Enlightenment was merely one dimension of Europe's vibrant cultural life in the eighteenth century. An explosive increase in publishing activity, legal and underground, served diverse audiences. New cultural forums and institutions, such as salons and freemasons lodges, combined with new media to create a **"public sphere"** for the uninhibited exchange of ideas. Meanwhile, the realm of literature saw remarkable innovation, including the rise of the novel. Royal courts and aristocracies still dominated most activity in music and the fine arts through their patronage, but here too the presence of a growing middle-class audience made itself felt and offered new opportunities of recognition for composers and artists.

Cosmopolitan High Culture

As the expansive, cosmopolitan aspects of European high culture are described here, it must be remembered that the mass of Europe's peasants and workers remained virtually untouched by these developments, insulated within their local environments and traditions. But the educated and wealthy, the numerically small and influential elites, enjoyed a sense of belonging to a common European civilization. French was the international language of this culture; even King Frederick II of Prussia favored French over German. Whatever the effects of Frederick's attitude might have been—the German dramatist Lessing, for one, considered it a deplorable cultural prejudice—the widespread knowledge of French meant that ideas and literature could circulate easily past language barriers.

The Appeal of Travel Europeans sharpened their sense of common identity through travel literature and by their appetite for visiting foreign places. Although

ROUSSEAU'S CONCEPT OF THE GENERAL WILL

"The essence of the social compact reduces itself to the following terms: Each of us puts his person and all his power in common under the supreme direction of the general will, and, in our collective capacity, we receive each member as an indivisible part of the whole. . . .

"In fact, each individual, as a man, may have a particular will contrary or dissimilar to the general will which he has as a citizen. His particular interest may speak to him quite differently from the common interest: his absolute and naturally independent existence may make him look upon what he owes to the common cause as a gratuitous contribution, the loss of which will do less harm to others than the payment of it is burdensome to himself. . . . He may wish to enjoy the rights of citizenship without being ready to fulfill the duties of a subject. The continuance of

such an injustice could not but prove the undoing of the body politic.

"In order then that the social compact may not be an empty formula, it tacitly includes the undertaking, which alone can give force to the rest, that whoever refuses to obey the general will shall be compelled to do so by the whole body. This means nothing less than that he will be forced to be free; for this is the condition which, by giving each citizen to his country, secures him against all personal dependence. In this lies the key to the working of the political machine."

From Jean-Jacques Rousseau, *The Social Contract*, Book 1, David Campbell Publishers.

transportation was slow and uncomfortable, many embarked on a "grand tour," whose highlights included visits to Europe's large cities (such as London, Paris, Rome, and Vienna) and to the ruins of antiquity—to the glories of the modern and the ancient worlds.

Kings, princes, and municipal authorities were embellishing their towns with plazas, public gardens, theaters, and opera houses. Toward the end of the century, amenities such as street lighting and public transportation began to appear in a few cities, with London leading the way. From the private sector came two notable additions to the urban scene: the coffeehouse and the storefront window display. Coffeehouses, where customers could chat or read, and enticing shop windows, which added to the pleasures of city walking (and stimulated consumer demand), enhanced the rhythms of urban life for tourists and residents alike. When a man is tired of London, Samuel Johnson remarked, he is tired of life.

Travelers on tour invariably passed from the attractions of bustling city life to the silent monuments of antiquity. As the philosophes recalled the virtues of pagan philosophers like Cicero, interest grew in surviving examples of Greek and Roman architecture and sculpture. Many would have agreed with the German art historian Johann Winckelmann that Greek sculpture was the most worthy standard of aesthetic beauty in all the world.

The Republic of Letters Among writers, intellectuals, and scientists, the sense of a cosmopolitan European culture devolved into the concept of a "republic of

letters." The phrase, introduced by sixteenth-century French humanists, was popularized by Pierre Bayle (noted earlier as a proponent of religious toleration), who published a critical journal that he called *News of the Republic of Letters*. The title implied that the realm of culture and ideas stretched across Europe's political borders. In one sense, it was an exclusive republic, limited to the educated; but it was also an open society to which people of talent could belong regardless of their social origins.

Aside from the medium of the printed word, the republic of letters was organized around the salons and the academies. Both institutions encouraged social interchange by bringing together socially prominent men and women with talented writers. The philosophes themselves exemplified this social mixture, for their "family" was composed in almost equal measures of nobles (Montesquieu, Holbach, Condorcet) and commoners (Voltaire, Diderot, d'Alembert). Voltaire, while insisting that he was as good as any aristocrat, had no desire to topple the aristocracy from its position; rather, he sought amalgamation. As d'Alembert put it, talent on the one hand and birth and eminence on the other both deserve recognition.

The Salons and Masonic Lodges Usually organized and led by women of wealthy bourgeois or noble families, the **salons** sought to bring together important writers with the influential persons they needed for favors and patronage. The salon of Madame Tencin, for example, helped launch Montesquieu's *Spirit of the Laws* in the 1740s, while the salon of Madame du Deffand in

Anicet Charles G. Lemonnier
READING OF VOLTAIRE'S TRAGEDY "L'ORPHELIN DE LA CHINE" AT THE SALON OF MADAME GEOFFRIN, **1755**
This 1814 painting of Mme. Geoffrin's Salon in 1755 reflects the artist Lemonnier's imagination rather than historical reality. His canvas depicts an assemblage of all the major philosophes and their patrons that never actually took place. Yet it does accurately convey the social atmosphere and serious purpose of the Parisian salons. At the center is a bust of Voltaire, who lived in exile at the time.
Giraudon/Art Resource, NY

the 1760s became a forum in which the philosophes could test their ideas (see figure, above). The salons also helped to enlarge the audience and contacts of the philosophes by introducing them to a flow of foreign visitors, ranging from German princes to Benjamin Franklin. Private newsletters kept interested foreigners and provincials abreast of activities in the Parisian salons when they could not attend personally, but salons also operated in Vienna, London, and Berlin.

The salons placed a premium on elegant conversation and wit. The women who ran them insisted that intellectuals make their ideas lucid and comprehensible, which increased the likelihood that their thought and writings would have some impact. The salons were also a forum in which men learned to take women seriously, and they constituted a unique cultural space for women between the domestic and public spheres. But the salons' emphasis on style over substance led Rousseau to denounce them as artificial

rituals that prevented the display of genuine feeling and sincerity.

Throughout Europe, freemasonry was another important form of cultural sociability that often crossed the lines of class and (less commonly) of gender. Operating in an aura of secretiveness and symbolism, the masonic lodges fostered a curious mixture of spirituality and rationalism. Originating as clubs or fraternities dedicated to humane values, they attracted a wide range of educated nobles, commoners, and liberal clergy, while some lodges accepted women as well. But toward the end of the century, freemasonry was torn by sectarian controversies, and its influence seemed to be diminishing.

The Learned Academies   As important for the dissemination of ideas in the eighteenth century as the salons were the learned academies. These ranged from the Lunar Society in Birmingham, a forum for innovative

British industrialists and engineers, to state-sponsored academies in almost every capital of southern and central Europe, which served as conduits for advanced scientific and philosophical ideas coming from western Europe. In France, moreover, academies were established in more than thirty provincial cities, most of which became strongholds of advanced thinking outside the capital.

These provincial academies were founded after the death of Louis XIV in 1715, as if in testimony to the liberating effect of his demise. Most began as literary institutes, concerned with upholding the purity of literary style. A few academies adhered to such goals well into midcentury, but most gradually shifted their interests from literary matters to scientific and practical questions in such areas as commerce, agriculture, and local administration. They became offshoots, so to speak, of the *Encyclopedia*'s spirit. Indeed, when a Jesuit launched an attack against the *Encyclopedia* in the Lyons Academy, many members threatened to resign unless he retracted his remarks.

By the 1770s the essay contests sponsored by the provincial academies and the papers published by their members had turned to such topics as population growth, capital punishment and penology, education, poverty and welfare, the grain trade, the guilds, and the origins of sovereignty. A parallel shift in membership occurred. The local academies began as privileged corporations, dominated by the nobility of the region. Associate membership was extended to commoners from the ranks of civil servants, doctors, and professionals. Gradually, the distinction between regular and associate participants crumbled. The academies admitted more commoners to full membership, and a fragile social fusion took place.

Publishing and Reading

The eighteenth century saw a notable rise in publishing geared to several kinds of readers. Traveling circulating libraries originated in England around 1740 and opened untapped markets for reading material; by the end of the century almost one thousand traveling libraries had been established. "Booksellers," or publishers—the intermediary between author and reader—combined the functions of a modern editor, printer, salesperson, and (if need be) smuggler. Their judgment and marketing techniques helped create as well as fill the demand for books, since they conceived and financed a variety of works. The *Encyclopedia* originated as a bookseller's project; so, too, did such enduring masterpieces as Samuel Johnson's *Dictionary*, a monumental lexicon that helped purify and standardize the English language. Booksellers commissioned talented stylists to write popular versions of serious scientific, historical, and philosophical works. Recognizing a specialized demand among women readers, they increased the output of fictional romances and fashion magazines and also began to publish more fiction and poetry by women.

Journals and Newspapers　The eighteenth century saw a proliferation of periodicals. In England, which pioneered in this domain, the number of periodicals increased from 25 to 158 between 1700 and 1780. In one successful model, Addison and Steele's *Spectator* (1711), each issue consisted of a single essay that sought in elegant but clear prose to raise the reader's standards of morality and taste. Their goal was "to enliven Morality with Wit, and to temper Wit with Morality. . . . To bring Philosophy . . . to dwell in clubs and assemblies, at tea-tables and coffeehouses." Eliza Haywood adapted this format in her journal, *The Female Spectator* (1744–1756), in which she advocated improvement in the treatment of women and greater "opportunities of enlarging our minds." Another type of journal published extracts and summaries of books and covered current events and entertainment; one such journal, the *Gentleman's Magazine*, reached the impressive circulation of fifteen thousand in 1740. More learned periodicals specialized in book reviews and serious articles on science and philosophy.

Most important for the future of reading habits in Europe was the daily newspaper, which originated in England. Papers like the *London Chronicle* at first provided family entertainment and then took on classified advertisements (thereby spurring consumerism and the notion of fashion). English newspapers of course published news of current events, but only after strenuous battles for permission from a reluctant government did they win the right to report directly on parliamentary debates. In France, a handful of major Parisian newspapers enjoyed privileged monopolies in exchange for full compliance with government censorship. This arrangement severely restricted their ability to discuss government and politics, although other periodicals published outside France's borders helped satisfy the demand for such coverage in France.

"Bad Books"　The demand for books and the dynamism of the publishing industry created new employment opportunities for men and women. Although the number of would-be writers swelled, relatively few could achieve financial independence without patronage. Many remained poverty-stricken and frustrated.

Publishers thus could hire legions of otherwise unemployed writers to turn out the kinds of books for which they sensed a great demand: potboilers, romances, salacious pamphlets, and gossip sheets, which pandered to low tastes. Paid for quantity and speed rather than quality, these hack writers led a precarious,

A

DICTIONARY

OF THE

ENGLISH LANGUAGE:

IN WHICH

The WORDS are deduced from their ORIGINALS,

AND

ILLUSTRATED in their DIFFERENT SIGNIFICATIONS

BY

EXAMPLES from the beſt WRITERS.

TO WHICH ARE PREFIXED,

A HISTORY of the LANGUAGE,

AND

AN ENGLISH GRAMMAR.

BY SAMUEL JOHNSON, A.M.

IN TWO VOLUMES.

VOL. I.

Cum tabulis animum cenforis fumet honeſti :
Audebit quæcunque parum ſplendoris habebunt,
Et fine pondere erunt, et honore indigna ferentur.
Verba movere loco ; quamvis invita recedant,
Et verſentur adhuc intra penetralia Veſtæ :
Obſcurata diu populo bonus eruet, atque
Proferet in lucem ſpecioſa vocabula rerum,
Quæ priſcis memorata Catonibus atque Cethegis,
Nunc ſitus informis premit et deſerta vetuſtas.   HOR.

—

LONDON

Printed by W. STRAHAN,

For J. and P. KNAPTON ; T. and T. LONGMAN ; C. HITCH and L. HAWES ;
A. MILLAR· and R. and J. DODSLEY.

MDCCLV.

The title page of Samuel Johnson's pioneering *Dictionary of the English Language* (1755 edition), one of the masterpieces of eighteenth-century literature. The Mary Evans Picture Library

humiliating existence. Booksellers and desperate writers saw money to be made in sensational pamphlets assailing the character of notorious aristocrats; in partisan pamphlets attacking a particular faction in court politics; and in pornography. Sometimes they combined character assassination and pornography in pamphlets dwelling on the alleged perversions of rulers or courtiers. For all its wild exaggeration, such material helped "desacralize" monarchy and created a vivid image of a decadent aristocracy.

To satisfy the public's demand for gossip, character assassination, and pornography in violation of laws regulating the book trade in France, publishers located just across the French border marketed such books and pamphlets clandestinely. They smuggled this material into France, along with banned books by writers like Voltaire and Rousseau, using networks of couriers and distributors. In their sales lists of what they called Philosophic Books, the clandestine publishers lumped together banned books by serious writers along with such illicit publications as *The Scandalous Chronicles, The Private Life of Louis XV,* and *Venus in the Cloister* (a pornographic account of the alleged perversions of the clergy). The police made the same judgment. In attempting to stop the flow of "bad books," they scarcely distinguished between a banned work by Voltaire assaulting religious bigotry and a libelous pamphlet depicting the queen as a corrupt pervert.

Literature, Music, and Art

Unlike the artistic style of the seventeenth century, generally classified as baroque, the artistic style of the eighteenth century cannot be given a single stylistic label. The nature of the audience and the sources of support for writers and composers also varied considerably. But several trends proved to be of lasting importance: the rise of the novel in England, the birth of Romantic poetry, the development of the symphony in Austria, and the changing social context of French painting late in the century.

The Rise of the Novel   The modern novel had its strongest development in England, where writers and booksellers cultivated a growing middle-class reading public. The acknowledged pioneer of this new genre was Samuel Richardson. With a series of letters telling the story, Richardson's *Pamela, or Virtue Rewarded* (1740) recounted the trials and tribulations of an honest if somewhat hypocritical servant girl. Pamela's sexual virtue is repeatedly challenged but never conquered by her wealthy employer, Mr. B., who finally agrees to marry her. An instant success, this melodrama broke from the standard forms and heroic subjects of most narrative fiction. Richardson dealt with recognizable types of people.

Pamela's apparent hypocrisy, however, prompted a playwright and lawyer named Henry Fielding to pen a short satire called *Shamela*, which he followed with his own novel *Joseph Andrews*. Here comedy and adventure replaced melodrama; Fielding prefaced *Joseph Andrews* with a manifesto claiming that the novel was to be "a comic epic in prose." Fielding realized the full potential of his bold experimentation with literary forms in *Tom Jones* (1749), a colorful, robust, comic panorama of English society featuring a gallery of brilliantly developed characters and vivid depictions of varied social environments.

The novel was thus emerging as a form of fiction that told its story and treated the development of personality in a realistic social context. It seemed to mirror its times better than other forms of fiction. Like the dramas that filled the stage in the second half of the century, most novels focused on family life and everyday problems of love, marriage, and social relations. Novelists could use broad comedy, or they could be totally serious; they could experiment endlessly with forms and techniques and could deal with a wide range of social settings.

In *Evelina, or A Young Lady's Entrance into the World* (1778), the writer Fanny Burney used the flexibility of the novel to give a woman's perspective on eighteenth-century English social life. In the form of letters, like *Pamela* and Rousseau's *Julie, Evelina* traces a provincial girl's adventures in London as she discovers her true father and finds a suitable husband. While falling back on conventional melodrama, in which marriage is the only happy ending for a young woman, Burney also uses social satire to suggest how society restricts, and even endangers, an independent woman's life. If Burney was ambivalent about the possibilities for female independence in the social world, her own writing, together with that of other women writers of the period, demonstrated the opportunities for female artistic achievement.

The Birth of Romantic Poetry   During most of this century of innovation in prose fiction, poetry retained its traditional qualities. Still the most prized form of literary expression, poetry followed unchanging rules on what made good literature. Each poetic form had its particular essence and rules, but in all types of poems diction was supposed to be elegant and the sentiments refined. Poets were expected to transform the raw materials of emotion into delicate language and references that only the highly educated could appreciate. In this neoclassical tradition, art was meant to echo eternal standards of truth and beauty. Poets were not permitted to unburden their souls or hold forth on their own experiences. The audience for poetry was the narrowest segment of the reading public—"the wealthy few," in the phrase of William Wordsworth, who criticized eighteenth-century poets for pandering exclusively to that group.

By the end of the century, however, the restraints of **Neoclassicism** finally provoked rebellion in the ranks of English and German poets. Men like Friedrich von Schiller and Wordsworth defiantly raised the celebration of individual feeling and inner passion to the level of a creed, which came to be known as **Romanticism.** These young poets generally prized Rousseau's writings, seeing the Genevan rebel as someone who had forged a personal idiom of expression and who valued inner feeling, moral passion, and the wonders of nature. Hoping to appeal to a much broader audience, these poets decisively changed the nature of poetic composition and made this literary form, like the novel, a flexible vehicle of artistic expression.

Goethe   The writer who came to embody the new ambitions of poets, novelists, and dramatists was Johann von Goethe, whose long life (1749–1832) spanned the beginnings and the high point of the Romantic movement. A friend of Schiller and many of the German writers and philosophers of the day, he soon came to tower over all of them. Goethe first inspired a literary movement known as **Sturm und Drang** (Storm and Stress), which emphasized strong artistic emotions and gave early intimations of the Romantic temperament. The best-known work of Sturm und Drang was Goethe's *The Sorrows of Young Werther* (1774), a novel about a young man driven to despair and suicide by an impossible love.

Courted by many of the princes and monarchs of Germany, Goethe soon joined the circle of the duke who ruled the small city-state of Weimar, where he remained for the rest of his life. There flowed from his pen an astonishing stream of works—lyrical love poetry, powerful dramas, art and literary criticism, translations, philosophic reflections, an account of his travels in Italy, and studies of optics, botany, anatomy, and mathematics. Even though he held official posts in the duke's court, Goethe's literary output never flagged. His masterpiece, *Faust*, occupied him for nearly fifty years and revealed the progress of his art. The first part (published in 1808) imbued with romantic longing the story of a man who yearns to master all of knowledge and who makes a pact with the devil to achieve his goal. But the second part (1831) emphasized the determination that came to be Goethe's credo. The final lines are:

> He only earns his freedom and existence
> Who daily conquers them anew.

What had begun in the youthful exuberance and energy of Romanticism ended in an almost classical mood of discipline. No wonder that Goethe seemed to his contemporaries to be the last "universal man," the embodiment of conflicting cultural values and Western civilization's struggle to resolve them.

The Symphony   For Europe's elites, music offered the supreme form of entertainment, and the development of the symphony in music paralleled the rise of the novel in literature. For much of the century, composers still served under royal, ecclesiastical, or aristocratic patronage. They were bound by rigid formulas of composition and by prevailing tastes tyrannically insistent on conventions. Most listeners wanted little more than pleasant melodies in familiar forms; instrumental music was often commissioned as background fare for balls or other social occasions.

The heartland of Europe's music tradition shifted during the eighteenth century from Italy and France to Austria. Here a trio of geniuses transformed the routines of eighteenth-century composition into original and enduring masterpieces. True, the early symphonies of Franz Joseph Haydn and young Wolfgang Amadeus Mozart were conventional exercises. As light and tuneful as its audience could wish, their early music had little emotional impact. By the end of their careers,

however, these two composers had altered the symphonic form from three to four movements, had achieved extraordinary harmonic virtuosity, and had brought a deep if restrained emotionalism to their music. Haydn and Mozart had changed the symphony radically from the elegant trifles of earlier years.

Beethoven   Ludwig van Beethoven consummated this development and ensured that the symphony, like the novel and Romantic poetry, would be an adaptable vehicle for the expression of creative genius. In each of his nine symphonies, as well as in his five piano concertos, Beethoven progressively modified the standard formulas, enlarged the orchestra, and wrote movements of increasing intricacy. His last symphony burst the bonds of the form altogether. Beethoven introduced a large chorus singing one of Schiller's odes to conclude his *Ninth Symphony* (1824), making it a celebration in music of freedom and human kinship. Laden with passion, the music is nevertheless recognizable as an advanced form of the classical symphony. Thus, it provides a bridge between the music of two periods: eighteenth-century classicism and nineteenth-century Romanticism.

Aristocratic and court patronage remained the surest foundation for a career in music during the eighteenth century. Haydn, for example, worked with mutual satisfaction as the court composer for one prince from 1761 to 1790. At the end of his long life, however, Haydn moved out on his own, having won enough international recognition to sign a lucrative contract with a London music publisher who underwrote performances of his last twelve symphonies. In contrast, Mozart had an unhappy experience trying to earn his living by composing. After a few miserable years as court composer for the Archbishop of Salzburg, Mozart escaped to Vienna but could not find a permanent employer. He was obliged to eke out an inadequate living by teaching, filling private commissions, and giving public concerts. Beethoven did much better at freeing himself from dependence on a single patron through individual commissions and public concerts.

The Social Context of Art   Unlike the situation in literature and music, there were no notable innovations in the field of painting during most of the eighteenth century. With the exception of the Frenchman Jacques-Louis David, eighteenth-century painters were overshadowed by their predecessors. Neoclassicism remained a popular style in the late eighteenth century, with its themes inspired by antiquity and its timeless conceptions of form and beauty, comparable to the rules of Neoclassical poetry.

The social context of painting, however, was changing. Most commissions and patronage still depended on

Jean-Baptiste Greuze
THE FATHER'S CURSE, 1777
Instead of the aristocrats or classical figures that most artists chose for their subjects, Jean-Baptiste Greuze painted ordinary French people. His portraits and dramatic scenes (such as *The Father's Curse*) seemed to echo Rousseau's call for honest, "natural" feeling.
Louvre, Paris, France. Giraudon/ Arts Resource, NY

Élisabeth Vigée-Le Brun
MARIE ANTOINETTE WITH A ROSE
One of the leading French portrait painters, and the most successful female artist of the era anywhere, Élisabeth Vigée-Le Brun enjoyed the patronage of Queen Marie Antoinette. Shown here is one of several portraits that she painted of the French queen.
Giraudon/Art Resource, NY

aristocrats and princes, but the public was beginning to claim a role as the judge of talent in the visual arts. Public opinion found its voice in a new breed of art critics, unaffiliated with official sources of patronage, who reached their new audience through the press in the second half of the century. The Royal Academy of Art in France created the opening for this new voice by sponsoring an annual public exhibition, or "salon," starting in 1737. People could view the canvases chosen by the Academy for these exhibitions and could reach their own judgments about the painters.

David and Greuze   David, a brilliant painter in the Neoclassical style, won the greatest renown in this arena of public opinion during the 1780s. He skillfully celebrated the values of the ancient world in such historical paintings as *The Oath of the Horatii* (see figure, p. 559), *The Death of Socrates*, and *Brutus*. Discarding many of the standard conventions for history painting (and thereby drawing criticism from the Academy), David overwhelmed the public with his vivid imagery and the emotional force of his compositions. His paintings of the 1780s unmistakably conveyed a yearning for civic virtue and patriotism that had yet to find its political outlet in France. Not surprisingly, David became

Jacques-Louis David
THE OATH OF THE HORATII
The greatest innovation in French painting came in reaction to the artificiality of the rococo style and subject matter, with a return to favor of "noble simplicity and calm grandeur." This Neoclassical style found its supreme expression in the work of Jacques-Louis David. Such history paintings as *The Oath of the Horatii* evoked the ideal of civic virtue in ancient Greek and Roman civilization.
Louvre, Paris, France. Erich Lessing/Art Resource, NY

the most engaged and triumphant painter of the French Revolution.

In an entirely different vein, a few eighteenth-century artists chose more mundane and "realistic" subjects or themes for their canvases, parallel in some respects to what novelists and playwrights were doing. Jean-Baptiste Greuze, for example, made a hit in the Parisian exhibitions of the 1770s with his sentimentalized paintings of ordinary people in family settings caught in a dramatic situation, such as the death of a father or the banishment of a disobedient son. William Hogarth, a superb London engraver who worked through the medium of prints and book illustrations, went further down the social pyramid with his remarkable scenes of life among the working classes and the poor.

POPULAR CULTURE

Although the cultural world of aristocratic and middle-class elites has been extensively studied, the culture of artisans, peasants, and the urban poor remains more dimly known. In those sectors of society, culture primarily meant recreation, and it was essentially public and collective. Despite traditions of elementary schooling in certain regions and the spread of literacy among some groups, literacy rates remained generally low. Popular culture did have its written forms, but these were less prevalent than the oral traditions embodied in songs, folktales, and proverbs. Despite the rare firsthand traces of popular culture in the historical record, it is possible to suggest the rich variety of sociability and recreational practice among working people in traditional society.

Popular Literature

Far removed from the markets for Voltaire and the *Gentleman's Magazine* existed a distinct world of popular literature—the reading matter consumed by journeymen and peasants, the poor and the almost poor, those who could barely read and those who could not read at all. From the seventeenth through the early nineteenth century, publishers produced for this audience small booklets written anonymously, printed on cheap paper, costing only a few pennies, and sold by itinerant peddlers who knew the tastes of their customers. Presumably the booklets were often read aloud by those who could read to those who could not.

This popular literature took three major forms. Religious material included devotional tracts, saints' lives, catechisms, manuals of penitence, and Bible stories, all written simply and generously laced with miracles. Readers who were preoccupied with fears of death and damnation sought reassurance in these works that a virtuous life would end in salvation. Almanacs constituted a second type of popular literature,

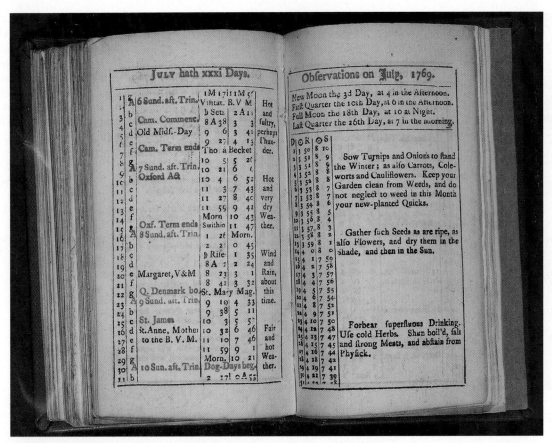

A page from an English almanac of 1769 on the month of July includes saints' days, information about likely weather patterns, and advice about agricultural matters and health care.
New York Public Library, Astor, Lenox, and Tilden Foundations

which appealed to the readers' concern for getting along in this life. Almanacs discussed things like the kinds of potions to take for illnesses, and featured astrology—how to read the stars and other signs for clues about the future. The third type of popular literature provided entertainment: tales and fables, burlesques and crude satires, mixtures of fiction and history in which miraculous events frequently helped bring the story to a satisfactory conclusion.

Although useful information may have trickled down through these booklets, most of them were escapist. The religiosity and supernatural events of popular literature separate it from the growing rationalism and secularism of elite culture. Moreover, it could be argued that by ignoring such problems as food shortages, high taxes, and material insecurity, popular writings fostered submissiveness, a fatalistic acceptance of a dismal status quo. Glimpsing the content of this popular literature helps us understand why Voltaire had no hope of extending his ideas on religion to the masses.

Oral Tradition   **Oral tradition** encompassed folktales told at the fireside on long winter nights, songs passed on from generation to generation, and sayings that embodied the conventional wisdom of the people.

Themes touching on hunger, sex, or oppression were more likely to turn up in songs or oral tales than in booklets. Songs and tales expressed the joyful bawdiness of ordinary men and women but also the everpresent hardships and dangers of daily life: the endless drudgery of work in the fields, the gnawing ache of an empty stomach, the cruelty of parental neglect or mean stepparents, the desperation of beggars on the road. The most fantastic tales evoked a threatening world in which strangers might turn out to be princes or good fairies but might just as well turn into wolves or witches. Oral tradition also celebrated the shrewdness and cunning of ordinary people struggling for survival, in the spirit of the saying: "Better a knave than a fool."

Literacy and Primary Schooling

The wars of religion had spurred the spread of literacy and elementary schooling in Europe. Protestantism explicitly promoted literacy so that Christians could read

Most eighteenth-century elementary school teachers used the extremely inefficient individual method of instruction, in which pupils read to the teacher from whatever book they happened to bring from home, while the other pupils occupied themselves as best they could. Tallandier, Bibliothèque des Arts Décoratifs, Paris. Editions

their Bibles directly; strongly Protestant societies such as Scotland, Switzerland, and Sweden had unusually high rates of literacy by the eighteenth century. The Catholic Church, as well, believed that the spread of literacy would serve its cause in the battle against heresy. While teaching reading, Catholic schoolmasters could provide religious instruction and could socialize children into the beliefs and behavior of a Catholic way of life.

A unique study of literacy in France carried out in the late nineteenth century, based on signatures versus *X*s on parish marriage registers all across the country, indicates a national literacy rate (meaning the ability to read) in 1686 of about 21 percent, which reached 37 percent a century later. These national averages, however, conceal striking regional and social disparities. The south of France had much lower rates than the north/northeast, and rural literacy rates lagged significantly behind those of the towns. While agricultural laborers rarely could read, urban artisans were generally literate. The widest gap of all separated men from women, the rates in 1786 being 47 and 27 percent, respectively. Similarly, estimates for England suggest a male literacy rate of slightly under 60 percent and a female rate of about 40 percent.

Primary Education   Schooling was not intended to transform society or lift the mass of people out of the situations into which they were born. On the contrary, it was supposed to maintain the social order and reinforce the family in promoting piety and decent behavior among the young. Many among the elites (including

Voltaire) were skeptical about the value of education for peasants and laborers. Might it not confuse them, or make it more difficult for them to accept the drudgery to which they seemed destined? Peasant or laboring parents might well have shared such skepticism about educating their young. Education could seem a waste of time when their children could be contributing to the family's livelihood; they might especially begrudge spending the money on tuition that most elementary schooling required.

A village usually hired a schoolmaster in consultation with the pastor or priest; schools usually straddled community and church, since the schoolmaster often served as the pastor's aide. Except in towns that had charitable endowments to support schooling, the parents, the village, or some combination of the two paid the schoolmaster, and for that reason numerous villages did without any schooling. Even a modest tuition could deter impoverished parents from hiring a master, enrolling their children, or keeping them in school for a sufficient time. Since schoolmasters taught reading first and writing separately and later, many pupils, especially girls, were not kept in school long enough to learn how to write anything but their names. Schooling, in other words, was largely demand-driven, the product of a community's level of wealth and interest.

Schooling in Central Europe   Whereas England and France left primary schooling entirely to the chance of local initiative, the Habsburg monarchy seriously promoted primary education and thereby became the first

Catholic realm to do so. The Habsburg General School Ordinance of 1774 authorized state subsidies, in combination with local funds, for the support of a school in almost every parish. Attendance was supposed to be compulsory, though the state had no way to enforce it. The state also intended to train future teachers at institutions called normal schools. A similar two-pronged strategy was adopted in Prussia under Frederick II at about the same time, although little was done to implement it.

In Prussia, as in most of Europe, schoolmasters remained barely competent and poorly paid. Frederick II indeed had a limiting vision of popular education: "It is enough for the country people to learn only a little reading and writing. . . . Instruction must be planned so that they receive only what is most essential for them but which is designed to keep them in the villages and not influence them to leave." As elsewhere in Europe,

the goals of elementary schooling were to inculcate religion and morality, propagate the virtues of hard work, and promote deference to one's superiors.

Sociability and Recreation

If the educated elites had their salons, masonic lodges, and learned academies, the common people also formed organized cultural groups. Many artisans, for example, belonged to secret societies that combined fraternal and trade-union functions. Young unmarried artisans frequently traveled the country, stopping periodically to work with comrades in other towns to hone their skills. Artisans also relied on their associations for camaraderie and ritual celebrations. Married artisans often joined religious confraternities, which honored a patron saint and ensured a dignified funeral when they died, or mutual aid societies to which they contributed

William Hogarth
Gin Lane and Beer Street
In his *Gin Lane* etching of 1750, Hogarth depicted the results of excessive gin drinking by the English common people as death, apathy, and moral decay. A cheerful companion piece called *Beer Street*, however, suggested that drinking in moderation was an acceptable practice.

Hogarth, *Gin Lane.* The Metropolitan Museum of Art, Harris Brisbane Dick Fund, 1932. [32.35 (124)]. Photography, all rights reserved, The Metropolitan Museum of Art/Art Resource, NY

Hogarth, *Beer Street.* The Metropolitan Museum of Art, Harris Brisbane Dick Fund, 1932. [32.35 (123)]. Photography, all rights reserved, The Metropolitan Museum of Art/Art Resource, NY small monthly dues to pay for assistance if illness or accident should strike.

Taverns and Festivals   Corresponding to the coffee-houses of the urban middle classes were the taverns in working-class neighborhoods. These noisy, crowded places catered to a poor clientele, especially on Sunday and on Monday, which workingmen often took as a day off, honoring (as they put it) "Saint Monday." The urban common people were first beginning to consume wine in the eighteenth century, still something of a luxury except in its cheapest watered form. In England gin was the poor person's drink, cheap and plentiful until the government levied a hefty excise tax after realizing that too many people were drinking themselves into disability and death—a concern depicted in Hogarth's etchings, p. 562.

More commonly, drinking was not done in morbid fashion but as part of a healthy and vibrant outdoor life. Popular pastimes followed a calendar of holidays that provided occasions for group merrymaking, eating, drinking, dressing up, contests, and games. Local festivals were particularly comfortable settings for single young men and women to meet each other. The high-light of a country year usually came in early autumn after the summer harvest was in, when most villages held a public feast that lasted several days. In Catholic countries similar festivities were often linked with church rituals. Popular observances included the commemoration of local patron saints, pilgrimages to holy places, and the period of Carnival before Lent. More generally, a growing "commercialization of leisure" in the eighteenth century supported new spectator sports, such as horse racing and boxing matches.

In early modern Europe, gentlefolk and commoners had been accustomed to mixing in recreational and religious settings: fairs and markets, sporting events, village or town festivals, Carnival in Catholic countries. But in the eighteenth century, as aristocrats and bourgeois alike became more concerned with good manners and refinement, these elite groups began to distance themselves from the bawdy and vulgar behavior of ordinary people. With growing intolerance, they censured popular recreational culture in the hope of "reforming" the people into a more sober and orderly lifestyle. Social status was based on birth or wealth, but cultural taste was becoming its behavioral marker.

Summary

The philosophes, celebrated members of Europe's cultural establishment by the 1770s, hoped that their society would gradually reform itself under their inspiration. Although these writers criticized their society, they were not its subverters. Distrustful of the uneducated masses and afraid of popular emotion, superstition, and disorder, the philosophes were anything but democrats. Nonetheless, the Enlightenment challenged basic traditional values of European society: from Voltaire's polemics against Christianity through the sober social science of Diderot's *Encyclopedia* to the impassioned writings of Rousseau. Along with a flood of "bad books"—the pornography and scandal sheets of the clandestine publishers—booksellers, writers, and journalists disseminated critical ideas among Europe's educated men and women. The philosophes challenged the automatic respect for convention and authority, promoted the habit of independent reflection, and implanted the conviction that the reform of institutions was both necessary and possible. They promoted a climate that put the status quo on the defensive and in which revolution—when provoked under particular circumstances—would not be unthinkable.

QUESTIONS FOR FURTHER THOUGHT

1. What were the core values of the Enlightenment and how would you assess their strengths and weaknesses? What might have produced a backlash against Enlightenment values in subsequent periods? How might one defend them today?

2. How does the music, painting, and literature of the eighteenth century compare to the high culture of earlier periods you have studied, such as the Renaissance or the seventeenth century? Has the social or political context of cultural life changed? Were there comparable changes in the realm of popular culture?

3. What do you make of Jean-Jacques Rousseau?

RECOMMENDED READING

Sources

Gay, Peter (ed.). *The Enlightenment: A Comprehensive Anthology.* 1973.

Gendzier, Stephen (ed.). *Denis Diderot: The Encyclopedia: Selections.* 1967.

Jacob, Margaret C. *The Enlightenment: A Brief History with Documents.* 2001.

Mohl, Mary R., and Helene Koon (eds.). *The Female Spectator: English Women Writers Before 1800.* 1977.

Vigée-Le Brun, Marie-Louise . . . Élisabeth. *Memoirs.* S. Evans (ed.). 1989. Memoirs of the most notable female painter in eighteenth-century France.

Studies

Brewer, John. *The Pleasures of the Imagination: English Culture in the Eighteenth Century.* 1997. A lively, panoramic survey of the production and consumption of high culture in all its forms.

Bruford, W. H. *Germany in the Eighteenth Century: The Social Background of the Literary Revival.* 1952. A useful survey.

Buchan, James. *Crowded with Genius: The Scottish Enlightenment: Edinburgh's Moment of the Mind.* 2003. A popular history of the remarkable circle of Scottish philosophes, including Adam Smith and David Hume.

Capp, Bernard. *English Almanacs, 1500–1800: Astrology and the Popular Press.* 1979. A probing study of the most important genre of popular literature.

Chartier, Roger. *The Cultural Origins of the French Revolution.* 1991. A synthesis of recent research on publishing, the public sphere, and the emergence of new political attitudes.

Cranston, Maurice. *Jean-Jacques, The Noble Savage,* and *The Solitary Self.* 1982, 1991, and 1995. A three-volume study of the life and work of Rousseau, critical but sympathetic.

Crow, Thomas. *Painters and Public Life in Eighteenth-Century Paris.* 1985. A pioneering work on the development of a public sphere of critical discourse about art.

Darnton, Robert. *The Forbidden Best Sellers of Pre-Revolutionary France.* 1995. A pathbreaking work on the circulation, content, and impact of banned books.

Gay, Peter. *The Enlightenment: An Interpretation.* 2 vols. 1966 and 1969. A masterly, full-bodied exposition of Enlightenment thought.

Goodman, Dena. *The Republic of Letters: A Cultural History of the French Enlightenment.* 1994. Focuses on the salons and the roles of women in cultural and intellectual life.

Isherwood, Robert. *Farce and Fantasy: Popular Entertainment in Eighteenth-Century Paris.* 1986. A cultural and institutional history of fairs and popular theater.

Malcolmson, R. W. *Popular Recreations in English Society, 1700–1850.* 1973. A good survey of a neglected subject.

May, Gita. *Elisabeth Vigée-Le Brun: The Odyssey of an Artist in an Age of Revolution.* 2005. The public and private life of the period's most prominent female painter.

Maza, Sarah. *Private Lives and Public Affairs: The Causes Célèbres of Pre-Revolutionary France.* 1993. An original analysis of scandals and lawsuits that raised social consciousness in the later eighteenth century.

McClellan, James. *Science Reorganized: Scientific Societies in the Eighteenth Century.* 1985.

Melton, James Van Horn. *Absolutism and the Eighteenth-Century Origins of Compulsory Schooling in Prussia and Austria.* 1988.

————. *The Rise of the Public in Enlightenment Europe.* 2001. An excellent comparative survey of the developing "public sphere" in Europe.

Palmer, Robert R. *Catholics and Unbelievers in Eighteenth-Century France.* 1939. The response of Catholic intellectuals to the century's philosophic thought.

Porter, Roy, and Mikulas Teich (eds.). *The Enlightenment in National Context.* 1981. A comprehensive geographic overview.

Roche, Daniel. *France in the Enlightenment.* 1998. A masterly synthesis, especially on the Enlightenment and French society.

Shovlin, John. *The Political Economy of Virtue: Luxury, Patriotism, and the Origins of the French Revolution.* 2006. Reconstructs French debates over economic activity and moral values.

Spencer, Samia (ed.). *French Women and the Age of Enlightenment.* 1984. A pioneering collection of essays on a variety of literary and historical themes.

Venturi, Franco. *Italy and the Enlightenment.* 1972. Essays on important Italian philosophes by a leading historian.

Watt, Ian. *The Rise of the Novel: Studies of Defoe, Richardson, and Fielding.* 1957. The view from England.

Wilson, Arthur. *Diderot.* 1972. An exhaustive, reliable biography of the consummate French philosophe.

Jean Duplessis-Bertaux
STORMING OF THE TUILERIES, COURS DU CAROUSSEL, AUGUST 10, 1792
The armed assault on the Tuileries Palace of August 10, 1792, brought an end to the monarchy and led directly to the founding of the first French Republic.
Giraudon/Art Resource, NY

Chapter Twenty

THE FRENCH REVOLUTION

REFORM AND POLITICAL CRISIS • 1789: THE FRENCH REVOLUTION •
THE RECONSTRUCTION OF FRANCE • THE SECOND REVOLUTION

Well into the eighteenth century, the long-standing social structures and political institutions of Europe were securely entrenched. Most monarchs still claimed to hold their authority directly from God. In cooperation with their aristocracies, they presided over realms composed of distinct orders of citizens, or *estates* as they were sometimes known. Each order had its particular rights, privileges, and obligations. But pressures for change were building during the century. In France, the force of public opinion grew increasingly potent by the 1780s. A financial or political crisis that could normally be managed by the monarchy threatened to snowball in this new environment. Such vulnerability was less evident in Austria, Prussia, and Russia, however, where strong monarchs instituted reforms to streamline their governments. Similarly, in Britain the political system proved resilient despite explosions of discontent at home and across the Atlantic.

Unquestionably, then, the French Revolution constituted the pivotal event of European history in the late eighteenth century. From its outbreak in 1789, the Revolution transformed the nature of sovereignty and law in France. Under its impetus, civic and social institutions were renewed, from local government and schooling to family relations and assistance for the poor. Soon its ideals of liberty, equality, and fraternity resonated across the borders of other European states, especially after war broke out in 1792 and French armies took the offensive.

The French Revolution's innovations defined the foundations of a liberal society and polity. Both at home and abroad, however, the new regime faced formidable opposition, and its struggle for survival propelled it in unanticipated directions. Some unforeseen turns, such as democracy and republicanism, became precedents for the future even if they soon aborted. Other developments, such as the Reign of Terror, seemed to nullify the original liberal values of 1789. The bloody struggles of the Revolution thus cast a shadow over this transformative event as they dramatized the brutal dilemma of means versus ends.

Civil Constitution of the Clergy **1790** ●

Peasant revolts and August 4 decree **July–August 1789** ●

Storming of the Bastille **July 1789** ●

Estates General become National Assembly **June 1789** ●

Failed Assembly of Notables in France **1787** ●

1780s
Joseph II's authoritarian reforms in Habsburg Empire
● **1776** American Declaration of Independence

REFORM AND POLITICAL CRISIS

To put the French Revolution into perspective, it helps to compare political tensions and conflicts elsewhere in Europe. Strong monarchs with reputations for being "enlightened" reigned in Prussia, Austria, Spain, and even Russia. Their stature seemingly contrasts with the mediocrity of Louis XV and Louis XVI, who ruled in France. Yet the former did not get far in reforming their realms or granting rights and freedom to their subjects. The limits of "enlightened absolutism," therefore, should be kept in mind when considering the crisis that confronted France. Meanwhile, in Britain energetic movements for political reform ran into determined opposition. This rigidity had a particular impact across the Atlantic, where Britain's thirteen colonies in North America were driven to rebellion and a revolutionary war for independence.

Enlightened Absolutism in Central and Eastern Europe

During the late nineteenth century, German historians invented the concept of enlightened absolutism to describe the Prussian and Habsburg monarchies of the eighteenth century. Critical of the ineptitude and weakness of French monarchs in that period, these historians argued that the strength of an enlightened ruler had been the surest basis for progress in early modern Europe. A king who ruled in his subjects' interest, they implied, avoided violent conflicts like those of the French Revolution. Earlier strong monarchs, such as Philip II of Spain and France's Louis XIV (who had once declared: "I am the state"), had been irresponsible; in contrast, these German historians argued, Frederick II of Prussia symbolized the enlightened phase of absolutism with his comment that the ruler is the "first servant of the state."

Previous chapters, however, have demonstrated that monarchs dealt with the same fundamental issues during all stages of absolutism. They always strove to assert their authority over their subjects and to maximize the power of their state in relation to other realms, principally by means of territorial expansion. Any notion that Enlightenment thinking caused monarchs to abandon these efforts is misleading. Still, several eighteenth-century monarchs did initiate reforms and did modify their styles of ruling in order to appear more modern or enlightened. Frederick II of Prussia and Catherine II of Russia, for example, lavished praise on Voltaire and Diderot, and those philosophes returned the compliment. These rulers may simply have been engaging in public relations. Yet the fact that they seemed supportive of such writers suggests that absolutism had indeed adopted a new image.

Catherine the Great (r. 1762–1796) played this game to its limit. In 1767 she announced a new experiment in the direction of representative government—a policy hailed as a landmark by her philosophe admirers, who were too remote from St. Petersburg to see its insincerity. Catherine convened a Legislative Commission, a body of delegates from various strata of Russian society who were invited to present grievances, propose reforms, and then debate the proposals. In the end, however, she sent the delegates home under the pretext of having to turn her attention to a war with Turkey. Little came of the Legislative Commission except some good publicity for Catherine. In fact, she later promulgated a Charter of the Nobility, which, instead of limiting the nobility's privileges, strengthened their corporate status and increased their control over their serfs in exchange for their loyalty to the throne.

● **April 1792** French war against Austria and Prussia

● **August 1792** French monarchy overthrown

● **January 1793** Execution of Louis XVI

● **March 1793** Vendée rebellion begins

● **June 1793** Purge of the Girondins

● **August 1793** *Levée en masse*

● **September–October 1793** Jacobin dictatorship and Reign of Terror begin

● **July 1794** Fall of Robespierre

Conceptions of Enlightened Rule in Germany In justification of absolute monarchy, eighteenth-century German writers depicted the state as a machine and the ruler as its mainspring. Progress came from sound administration, through an enlightened monarch and well-trained officials. In keeping with this notion, German universities began to train government bureaucrats, and professors offered courses in the science of public finance and administration called *cameralism*.

The orders for the bureaucracy came from the monarchs, who were expected to dedicate themselves to the welfare of their subjects in return for their subjects' obedience. The framework for this command-obedience chain was to be a coherent body of public law, fairly administered by state officials. According to its advocates, this system would produce the rule of law without the need for a written constitution or a representative parliament. The ruler and his or her officials, following their sense of public responsibility and rational analysis, would ensure the citizens' rights and well-being.

Joseph II and the Limits of Absolutism

Joseph II, coruler of the Habsburg Empire with his mother, Maria Theresa, from 1765 and sole ruler in the 1780s, vigorously promoted reform from above. Unlike Frederick or Catherine, he did not openly identify with the philosophes, and he maintained his own Catholic faith. But Joseph proved to be the most innovative of the century's major rulers as well as one of its most autocratic personalities. It was a problematic combination.

Sound rule for Emperor Joseph involved far more than the customary administrative and financial reform necessary for survival in the competitive state system. With startling boldness he implemented several reforms long advocated by Enlightenment thinkers: freedom of expression, religious toleration, greater state control over the Catholic Church, and legal reform. A new criminal code, for example, reduced the use of the death penalty, ended judicial torture, and allowed for no class differences in the application of the laws. By greatly reducing royal censorship, Joseph made it possible for Vienna to become a major center of literary activity. And we have already noted Joseph's remarkable Edicts of Religious Toleration for Protestants and for Jews. But Joseph's religious policies did not stop there. To make the Catholic Church serve its parishioners better, Joseph forced the clergy to modernize its rituals and services. Most of his Catholic subjects, however, preferred their traditional ways to Joseph's streamlined brand of Catholicism. These "reforms" proved extremely unpopular.

Agrarian Reform Joseph's most ambitious policies aimed to transform the economic and social position of the peasants. Elsewhere, agrarian reform was generally the weak side of enlightened absolutism, since Frederick II and Catherine II did little to improve the lot of the peasants or serfs in their realms. Joseph, however, set out to eradicate serfdom and to convert Habsburg peasants into free individuals in command of their persons and of the land they cultivated.

By royal decree, Joseph abolished personal servitude and gave peasants the right to move, marry, and enter any trade they wanted. He then promulgated laws to secure peasants' control over the land they worked. Finally and most remarkably, he sought to limit the financial obligations of peasant tenants to their lords and to the state. All land was to be surveyed and subject to a uniform tax. Twelve percent of the land's annual yield would go to the state and a maximum of 18 percent would go to the lord. This tax replaced previous

Joseph II, shown here visiting a peasant's field, actually promulgated his momentous agrarian reform edicts without any significant consultation with the peasants before or after the fact.
Austrian Press & Information Service

seigneurial obligations in which peasants owed service to their lord that could consume more than one hundred days of labor a year.

Joseph ordered these reforms in an authoritarian fashion, with little consultation and no consent from any quarter. Predictably, these reforms provoked fierce opposition among the landowning nobles. But they also perplexed most peasants, who already distrusted the government because of its arbitrary religious policies. Joseph made no effort to build support among the peasants by carefully explaining the reforms, let alone by modifying their details after getting feedback from the grass roots.

His arbitrary manner, however, was not incidental. Joseph acknowledged no other way of doing things, no limitation on his own sovereignty. In reaction to the opposition that his reforms aroused, he moved to suppress dissent in the firmest possible way. Not only did he restore censorship in his last years, but he elevated the police department to the status of an imperial ministry and gave it unprecedented powers. By the time he died, in 1790, Joseph was a disillusioned man. His realm resembled a police state, and his successors quickly restored serfdom.

Upheavals in the British Empire

An aggressive monarch, George III, helped ignite political unrest in Great Britain. He was intent on advancing royal authority, but rather than bypass Parliament altogether, he simply tried, as Whig ministers had before him, to control its members through patronage and influence. The Whig aristocrats saw this operation as a threat to their own traditional power. Not only did they oppose the king and his ministers in Parliament, but they enlisted the support of citizens' groups outside of Parliament as well. These organizations were calling for political reform, including representation in Parliament proportionate to population, stricter laws against political corruption, and greater freedom of the press.

"Wilkes and Liberty" John Wilkes, a member of Parliament and a journalist, became the center of this rising storm. Wilkes viciously attacked the king's prime minister, and by implication the king himself, over the terms of the Treaty of Paris, which ended the Seven Years' War in 1763. The government arrested him for seditious libel on a general warrant. When the courts quashed the indictment, the government then accused Wilkes of having authored a libelous pornographic poem, and this time he fled to France to avoid prison. He stayed in France for four years; but in 1768, still under indictment, he returned to stand once more for Parliament. Three times he was reelected, and three times the House of Commons refused to seat him. With the ardent support of radicals and to the acclaim of crowds in London, who marched to the chant of "Wilkes and Liberty," Wilkes finally took his seat in 1774.

Agitation for parliamentary reform drew support primarily from shopkeepers, artisans, and property owners, who had the franchise in a few districts but were denied it in most others. Thus, even without a right to vote, English citizens could engage in politics and mobilize the power of public opinion, in this case by rallying to Wilkes. Most radicals called only for political reform, not for the overthrow of the British political system. They retained a measure of respect for the nation's political traditions, which ideally guaranteed the rights of "freeborn Englishmen."

The committee that drafted the American Declaration of Independence included John Adams, Thomas Jefferson, and Benjamin Franklin, all shown here standing at the desk.
The Library of Congress

Rebellion in America Great Britain did face revolutionary action in the thirteen North American colonies. George III and his prime minister, Lord North, attempted to force the colonies to pay the costs, past and present, of their own defense. The policy would have meant an increase in taxes and a centralization of authority in the governance of the British Empire. Colonial landowners, merchants, and artisans of the eastern seaboard organized petitions and boycotts in opposition to the proposed fiscal and constitutional changes.

The resistance in North America differed fundamentally from comparable movements in Europe. American political leaders did not appeal to a body of privileges that the actions of the monarchy were allegedly violating. Instead, they appealed to traditional rights supposedly enjoyed by all British subjects, regardless of status, and to theories of popular sovereignty and natural rights advanced by John Locke and other English libertarian writers. When conciliation and compromise with the British government failed,

the American Declaration of Independence in 1776 gave eloquent expression to those concepts. The lack of a rigid system of estates and hereditary privileges in American society, the fluid boundaries that separated the social strata, and the traditions of local government in the colonies—from town meetings in New England to the elected legislatures that had advised colonial governors—blunted the kinds of conflicts between aristocrats and commoners that derailed incipient revolutionary movements in Ireland, Belgium, and the Dutch Netherlands.

These differences help to explain the unique character of the American rebellion, which was simultaneously a war for independence and a political revolution. The theories that supported the rebellion, and the continuing alliance between social strata, made it the most democratic revolution of the eighteenth century before 1789. The American Revolution created the first state governments, and ultimately a national government, in which the exercise of power was grounded not on royal sovereignty or traditional privilege but on the participation and consent of male citizens (apart from the numerous black slaves, whose status did not change). Even more important as a historical precedent, perhaps, it was the first successful rebellion by overseas colonies against their European masters.

1789: The French Revolution

Although the rebellion in America stirred sympathy and interest across the Atlantic, it seemed remote from the realities of Europe. The French Revolution of 1789 proved to be the turning point in European history. Its sheer radicalism, creativity, and claims of universalism made it unique. Its ultimate slogan—"Liberty, Equality, Fraternity"—expressed social and civic ideals that became the foundations of modern Western civilization. In the name of individual liberty, French revolutionaries swept away the institutionalized constraints of the old regime: seigneurial charges upon the land, tax privileges, guild monopolies on commerce, and even (in 1794) black slavery overseas. The revolutionaries held that legitimate governments required written constitutions, elections, and powerful legislatures. They demanded equality before the law for all persons and uniformity of institutions for all regions of the country, denying the claims to special treatment of privileged groups, provinces, towns, or religions. The term *fraternity* expressed a different kind of revolutionary goal. Rousseauist in inspiration, it meant that all citizens, regardless of social class, or region, shared a common fate in society and that the nation's well-being could override the interests of individual citizens.

Origins of the Revolution

Those who made the Revolution believed they were rising against despotic government, in which citizens had no voice, and against inequality and privilege. Yet the government of France at that time was no more tyrannical or unjust than it had been in the past. On the contrary, a process of modest reform had been under way for several decades. What, then, set off the revolutionary upheaval? What had failed in France's long-standing political system?

An easy answer would be to point to the incompetence of King Louis XVI (r. 1774–1792) and his queen, Marie Antoinette. Louis was good-natured but weak and indecisive, a man of limited intelligence who lacked self-confidence and who preferred hunting deer to supervising the business of government. By no stretch of the imagination was he an enlightened absolutist. Worse yet, his young queen, a Habsburg

princess, was frivolous, meddlesome, and tactless. But even the most capable French ruler could not have escaped challenge and unrest in the 1780s.

The Cultural Climate   In eighteenth-century France, as we have seen, intellectual ferment preceded political revolt. For decades the philosophes had questioned accepted political and religious beliefs. They undermined confidence that traditional ways were the best ways. But the philosophes harbored deep-seated fears of the uneducated masses and did not question the notion that educated and propertied elites should rule society; they wished only that the elites should be more enlightened and more open to new ideas. Indeed, the Enlightenment had become respectable by the 1770s, a kind of intellectual establishment. Rousseau damned that establishment and wrote of the need for simplicity, sincerity, and virtue, but the word *revolution* never flowed from his pen either.

More subversive perhaps than the writings of Enlightenment intellectuals were several sensational lawsuits centered on the scandalous doings of high aristocrats. The melodramatic legal briefs published by the lawyers in such cases were eagerly snatched up by the reading public along with prohibited "bad books"—the clandestine gossip sheets, libels, exposés, and pornography—discussed earlier. All this material—indirectly, at least—portrayed the French aristocracy as decadent and the monarchy as a ridiculous despotism. Royal officials and philosophes alike regarded the authors of this material as "the excrement of literature," as Voltaire put it. And writers forced to earn their living by turning out such stuff were no doubt embittered at being stuck on the bottom rung in the world of letters. Their resentment would explode after the Revolution began in 1789, and many became radical journalists either for or against the new regime. In itself, however, the "literary underground" of the old regime did not advocate, foresee, or directly cause the Revolution.

Class Conflict?   Did the structure of French society, then, provoke the Revolution? Karl Marx, and the many historians inspired by him, certainly believed so. Marx saw the French Revolution as the necessary break marking the transition from the aristocratic feudalism of the Middle Ages to the era of middle-class capitalism. In this view, the French bourgeoisie, or middle classes, had been gaining in wealth during the eighteenth century and resented the privileges of the nobility, which created obstacles to their ambition. Though they framed their ideology in universal terms in 1789, the middle classes led the Revolution in order to change the political and social systems in their own interests.

Three decades of research have rendered this theory of the Revolution's origins untenable. Whether a sizable and coherent capitalist middle class actually existed in eighteenth-century France is questionable. In any case, the leaders of the Revolution in 1789 were lawyers, administrators, and liberal nobles, and rarely merchants or industrialists. Moreover, the barrier between the nobility of the Second Estate and the wealthy and educated members of the Third Estate was porous, the lines of social division frequently (though not always) blurred. Many members of the middle class identified themselves on official documents as "living nobly," as substantial property owners who did not work for a living. Conversely, wealthy nobles often invested in mining, overseas trade, and finance—activities usually associated with the middle classes. Even more important, the gap between the nobility and the middle classes was nothing compared with the gulf that separated both from the working people of town and country. In this revisionist historiography, the bourgeoisie did not make the Revolution so much as the Revolution made the bourgeoisie (see "On the Origins of the French Revolution," p. 574).

Yet numerous disruptive pressures were at work in French society. A growing population left large numbers of young people in town and country struggling to attain a stable place in society. New images and attitudes rippled through the media of the day, despite the state's efforts to censor material it deemed subversive. The nobility, long since banished by Louis XIV from an independent role in government, chafed at its exclusion, although it continued to enjoy a near monopoly on positions in the officer corps. The prosperous middle classes too aspired to a more active role in government. The monarchy struggled to contain these forces within the established social and political systems. Until the 1780s it succeeded, but then its troubles began in earnest.

Fiscal Crisis and Political Deadlock

When he took the throne in 1774, Louis XVI tried to conciliate elite opinion by recalling the parlements, or sovereign law courts, that his grandfather had banished in 1770 for opposing his policies. This concession to France's traditional "unwritten constitution" did not suffice to smooth the new sovereign's road. Louis' new controller-general of finances, Jacques Turgot, encountered a storm of opposition from privileged groups to the reforms he proposed.

The Failure of Reform Turgot, an ally of the philosophes and an experienced administrator, hoped to encourage economic growth by a policy of nonintervention, or *laissez-faire*, that would give free play to economic markets and allow individuals maximum freedom to pursue their own economic interests. He proposed to remove all restrictions on commerce in grain and to abolish the guilds. In addition, he tried to cut down on expenses at court and to replace the obligation of peasants to work on the royal roads (the *corvée*) with a small new tax on all landholders. Privately, he also considered establishing elected advisory assemblies of landowners to assist in local administration. Vested interests, however, viewed Turgot as a dangerous innovator. When agitation against him mounted in the king's court at Versailles and in the Paris parlement, Louis took the easy way out and dismissed his contentious minister. With Turgot went perhaps the last hope for significant reform in France under royal leadership.

Deficit Financing The king then turned to Jacques Necker, a banker from Geneva who had a reputation for financial wizardry. Necker had a shrewd sense of public relations. To finance the heavy costs of France's aid to the rebellious British colonies in North America, Necker avoided new taxes and instead floated a series of large loans at exorbitant interest rates as high as 10 percent.

By the 1780s royal finances hovered in a state of permanent crisis. Direct taxes on land, borne mainly by the peasants, were extremely high but were levied inequitably. The great variations in taxation from province to province and the numerous exemptions for privileged groups were regarded by those who benefited from them as traditional liberties. Any attempt to revoke these privileges therefore appeared to be tyrannical. Meanwhile, indirect taxes on commercial activity (customs duties, excise or sales taxes, and royal monopolies on salt and tobacco) hit regressively at consumers, especially in the towns. At the same time, the cycle of borrowing—the alternative to increased taxes—had reached its limits. New loans would only raise the huge interest payments already being paid out. By the 1780s those payments accounted for about half the royal budget and created additional budget deficits each year.

Calonne and the Assembly of Notables When the king's new controller-general, Charles Calonne, pieced all this information together in 1787, he warned that, contrary to Necker's rosy projections, the monarchy was facing outright bankruptcy. Though no way had yet been found to win public confidence and forge a consensus for fiscal reform, the monarchy could no longer rely on old expedients. Calonne accordingly proposed to establish a new tax, called the *territorial subvention*, to be levied on the yield of all landed property without exemptions. At the same time, he proposed to

HISTORICAL ISSUES: ON THE ORIGINS OF THE FRENCH REVOLUTION

A long-held view of the French Revolution's origins attributed the starring role to the middle class, "the rising bourgeoisie." Liberal historians of the nineteenth century regarded the middle class as the carrier of liberal ideals—individual freedom, civil equality, representative government—that finally came to fruition in the French Revolution. Marxists considered the triumph of capitalism to be the pivotal issue in modern history and linked it to the political ascendancy of the middle class in the French Revolution. In a sense, both versions of this "social interpretation" of the French Revolution read its causes back from its results. In his classic synthesis of 1939 embodying the social interpretation, for example, Georges Lefebvre begins with these observations:

"The ultimate cause of the French Revolution of 1789 goes deep into the history of France and of the western world. At the end of the eighteenth century the social structure of France was aristocratic. It showed the traces of having originated at a time when land was almost the only form of wealth, and when the possessors of land were the masters of those who needed it to work and to live. It is true that in the course of age-old struggles the king had been able gradually to deprive the lords of their political powers and subject nobles and clergy to his authority. But he had left them the first place in the social hierarchy.

"Meanwhile the growth of commerce and industry had created, step by step, a new form of wealth, mobile or commercial wealth, and a new class, called in France the bourgeoisie.... In the eighteenth century commerce, industry and finance occupied an increasingly important place in the national economy. It was the bourgeoisie that rescued the royal treasury in moments of crisis.... The role of the nobility had correspondingly declined; and the clergy, as the ideal which it proclaimed lost prestige, found its authority growing weaker. These groups preserved the highest rank in the legal structure of the country, but in reality economic power, personal abilities and confidence in the future had passed largely to the bourgeoisie. Such a discrepancy never lasts forever. The Revolution of 1789 restored the harmony between fact and law."

From Georges Lefebvre, *The Coming of the French Revolution*, R. R. Palmer (trans.), Princeton University Press, 1989.

Since the 1950s, revisionist historians have challenged this "social interpretation" of the French Revolution. In his synthesis, William Doyle summarizes some of their research and arguments.

"Money, not privilege, was the key to pre-revolutionary society in France. Wealth transcended all social barriers and bound great nobles and upper bourgeois together into an upper class unified by money. . . . Eighteenth-century capitalism was far from a bourgeois monopoly. One of its basic features was the heavy involvement of nobles. . . . [On the other hand,] the wealth of all social groups in pre-revolutionary France was overwhelmingly non-capitalist in nature. Capitalism had not become the dominant mode of production in the French economy before 1789. . . . there was between most of the nobility and the proprietary sectors of the middle class, a continuity of investment forms and socioeconomic values that made them, economically, a single group.

"If the nobility and the bourgeoisie had so much in common, why did they become such implacable enemies in 1789? [Since] the Revolution could not be explained in economic terms as a clash of opposed interests. . . . it was time to revert to a political explanation of the Revolution's outbreak. The radical reforms of 1789 were products of a political crisis, and not the outcome of long-maturing social and economic trends. [As historian George Taylor concluded:] 'It was essentially a political revolution with social consequences and not a social revolution with political consequences.' "

From William Doyle, *Origins of the French Revolution*, Oxford University Press, 1988.

convene *provincial assemblies* elected by large landowners to advise royal officials on the collection and allocation of revenues.

Certain that the parlements would reject this scheme, Calonne convinced the king to convene an Assembly of Notables, comprising about 150 influential men, mainly but not exclusively from the aristocracy, who might more easily be persuaded to support the reforms. To Calonne's shock, the Assembly of Notables refused to endorse the proposed decrees. Instead, they denounced the lavish spending of the court and insisted on auditing the monarchy's financial accounts. Moreover, when the government now submitted Calonne's proposals to the parlement, it not only rejected them but demanded that Louis convene the **Estates General,** a body representing the clergy, nobility, and Third Estate, which had not met since 1614. Louis responded by sending the members of the parlements into exile. But a huge outcry in Paris and in the provinces against this arbitrary act forced the king to back down: After all, the whole purpose of Calonne's proposals had been to build public confidence in the government.

Facing bankruptcy and unable to float new loans in this atmosphere, the king recalled the parlements, reappointed Necker, and agreed to convene the Estates General in May 1789. In the opinion of the English writer Arthur Young, who was visiting France, the kingdom was "on the verge of a revolution, but one likely to add to the scale of the nobility and clergy." The aristocracy's determined opposition was putting an end to absolutism in France. But it was not clear what would take its place.

From the Estates General to the National Assembly

The calling of the Estates General in 1789 created extraordinary excitement across the land. The king invited his subjects to express their opinions about this great event, and thousands did so in pamphlet form. Here the "patriot," or liberal, ideology first took shape. Self-styled patriots came from the ranks of the nobility and clergy as well as from the middle classes; they opposed traditionalists, whom they labeled as "aristocrats." Their top priority was the method of voting to be used in the Estates General. While the king accorded the Third Estate twice as many delegates as the two higher orders, he refused to promise that the deputies would all vote together (by head) rather than separately in three chambers (by order). Voting by order would mean that the two upper chambers would outweigh the Third Estate no matter how many deputies it had. Patriots had hoped that the lines dividing the nobility from the middle class would crumble in a common effort by France's elites at reform. Instead, it appeared as if the Estates General might sharpen the lines of separation between the orders.

The Critique of Privilege   It did not matter that the nobility had led the fight against absolutism. Even if they endorsed new constitutional checks on absolutism and accepted equality in the allocation of taxes, nobles would still hold vastly disproportionate powers if the Estates General voted by order. In the most influential pamphlet about the Estates General, Emmanuel Sieyès posed the question, "What is the Third Estate?" and answered flatly, "Everything." "And what has it been until now in the political order?" he asked. Answer: "Nothing." The nobility, he claimed, monopolized all the lucrative positions in society while doing little of its productive work. In the manifestos of Sieyès and other

The Awakening of the Third Estate
Thousands of pamphlets discussed the calling of the Estates General in 1789, but the grievances of the Third Estate translated most readily into vivid imagery and caricature. Roger-Viollet/Bibliothèque Nationale de France, Paris

patriots, the enemy was no longer simply absolutism but privilege as well.

Unlike reformers in England or the American revolutionaries of 1776, the French patriots did not simply claim that the king had violated historic traditions of liberty. Rather, they contemplated a complete break with a discredited past. As a basis for reform, they would substitute reason for tradition. It is this frame of mind that made the French Revolution so radical.

Cahiers and Elections   For the moment, however, patriot spokesmen stood far in advance of opinion at the grass roots. The king had invited all citizens to meet in their local parishes to elect delegates to district electoral assemblies and to draft grievance petitions (**cahiers**) setting forth their views. The great majority of rural cahiers were highly traditional in tone and complained only of particular local ills or high taxes, expressing confidence that the king would redress them. Only a few cahiers from cities like Paris invoked concepts of natural rights and popular sovereignty or demanded that France must have a written constitution, that sovereignty belonged to the nation, or that feudalism and regional privileges should be abolished. It is impossible, in other words, to read in the cahiers the future course of the Revolution. Still, these gatherings of citizens promoted reflection on France's problems and encouraged expectations for change. They thereby raised the nation's political consciousness.

So, too, did the local elections, whose royal ground rules were remarkably democratic. Virtually every

When the king opened the meeting of the Estates General, the deputies for each estate were directed to sit in three separate sections of the hall.
Bulloz/© Photo RMN/Art Resource, NY

adult male taxpayer was eligible to vote for electors, who, in turn, met in district assemblies to choose representatives of the Third Estate to the Estates General. The electoral assemblies were a kind of political seminar, where articulate local leaders emerged to be sent by their fellow citizens as deputies to Versailles. Most of these deputies were lawyers or officials, without a single peasant or artisan among them. In the elections for the First Estate, meanwhile, parish priests rather than church notables formed a majority of the deputies. And in the elections for the Second Estate, about one-third of the deputies could be described as liberal nobles or patriots, the rest traditionalists.

Deadlock and Revolution Popular expectation that the monarchy would provide leadership in reform proved to be ill-founded. When the deputies to the Estates General met on May 5, Necker and Louis XVI spoke to them only in generalities and left unsettled whether the estates would vote by order or by head. The upper two estates proceeded to organize their own chambers, but the deputies of the Third Estate balked. Vainly inviting the others to join them, the Third Estate took a decisive revolutionary step on June 17 by proclaiming that it formed a "National Assembly." A few days later more than a third of the deputies from

the clergy joined them. The king, on the other hand, decided to cast his lot with the nobility and locked the Third Estate out of its meeting hall until he could present his own program. But the deputies moved to an indoor tennis court and swore that they would not separate until they had given France a constitution.

The king ignored this act of defiance and addressed the delegates of all three orders on June 23. He promised equality in taxation, civil liberties, and regular meetings of the Estates General at which, however, voting would be by order. France would be provided with a constitution, he pledged, "but the ancient distinction of the three orders will be conserved in its entirety." He then ordered the three estates to retire to their individual meeting halls, but the Third Estate refused to move. "The assembled nation cannot receive orders," declared its spokesman. Startled by the determination of the patriots, the king backed down. For the time being, he recognized the National Assembly and ordered deputies from all three estates to join it.

Thus, the French Revolution began as a nonviolent, "legal" revolution. By their own will, delegates elected by France's three estates to represent their own districts to the king became instead the representatives of the entire nation. As such, they claimed to be the sovereign power in France—a claim that the king now

Jacques-Louis David
OATH OF THE TENNIS COURT, THE 20TH OF JUNE, 1789
Jacques-Louis David's depiction of the Tennis Court Oath, one of the great historical paintings, captures the
deputies' sense of idealism and purpose.
Giraudon/Art Resource, NY

seemed powerless to contest. In fact, however, he was merely biding his time until he could deploy his army to subdue the capital and overwhelm the deputies at Versailles. The king ordered twenty thousand royal troops into the Paris region, due to arrive sometime in July.

The Convergence of Revolutions

The political struggle at Versailles was not occurring in isolation. The mass of French citizens, politically aroused by elections to the Estates General, was also mobilizing over subsistence issues. The winter and spring of 1788–1789 had brought severe economic difficulties, as crop failures and grain shortages almost doubled the price of flour and bread on which the population depended for subsistence. Unemployed vagrants filled the roads, angry consumers stormed grain convoys and marketplaces, and relations between town and country grew tense. Economic anxieties merged with rage over the obstructive behavior of aristocrats in Versailles. Parisians believed that food shortages and royal troops would be used to intimidate the people

into submission. They feared an "aristocratic plot" against the National Assembly and the patriot cause.

The Fall of the Bastille   When the king dismissed Necker on July 11, Parisians correctly assumed that a counterrevolution was about to begin. They prepared to resist, and most of the king's military units pulled back in the face of determined crowds. On July 14 Parisian crowds searching for weapons and ammunition laid siege to the **Bastille,** an old fortress that had once served as a royal prison and in which gunpowder was stored. The small garrison resisted, and a fierce firefight erupted. Although the troops soon capitulated, dozens of citizens were hit, providing the first martyrs of the Revolution, and the infuriated crowd massacred several soldiers as they left the fortress. Meanwhile, patriot electors ousted royal officials of the Paris city government, replaced them with a revolutionary municipality, and organized a citizens' militia to patrol the city. Similar municipal revolutions occurred in twenty-six of the thirty largest French cities, thus ensuring that the defiance in the capital would not be an isolated act.

THE STORMING OF THE BASTILLE
The fall of the Bastille was understood at the time to be a great turning point in history, and July 14 eventually became the French national holiday. Numerous prints and paintings evoke the daunting qualities of the fortress, the determination of the besieging crowd, and the valor of individuals in that crowd.
Bulloz/© Photo RMN/Art Resource, NY

The Parisian insurrection of July 14 not only saved the National Assembly but altered the Revolution's course by giving it a far more popular dimension. Again the king capitulated. He traveled to Paris on July 17 and, to please the people, donned a ribbon bearing three colors: white for the monarchy and blue and red for the capital. This *tricolor* would become the emblem of the new regime.

Peasant Revolts and the August 4 Decree These events did not pacify the anxious and hungry people of the countryside. Peasants had numerous and long-standing grievances. Population growth and the parceling of holdings reduced the margin of subsistence for many families, while the purchase of land by rich townspeople further shrank their opportunities for economic advancement. Seigneurial dues and church tithes weighed heavily on many peasants. Now, in addition, suspicions were rampant that nobles were

hoarding grain in order to stymie the patriotic cause. In July peasants in several regions sacked the houses of the nobles and burned the documents that recorded their seigneurial obligations.

This peasant insurgency blended into a vast movement known to historians as "the Great Fear." Rumors abounded that the vagrants who swarmed through the countryside were actually "brigands" in the pay of nobles, who were marching on villages to destroy the new harvest and cow the peasants into submission. The fear was baseless, but it stirred up the peasants' hatred and suspicion of the nobles, prompted armed mobilizations in hundreds of villages, and set off new attacks on manor houses.

Peasant revolts worried the deputies of the National Assembly, but they decided to appease the peasants rather than simply denounce their violence. On the night of August 4, therefore, certain deputies of the nobility and clergy dramatically renounced their ancient privileges. This action set the stage for the Assembly to decree "the abolition of feudalism" as well as the end of the church tithe, the sale of royal offices, regional tax privileges, and social privilege of all kinds. Later, it is true, the Assembly clarified the August 4 decree to ensure that property rights were maintained. While personal servitudes such as hunting rights, manorial justice, and labor services were suppressed outright, the Assembly decreed that most seigneurial dues would end only after the peasants had paid compensation to their lords. Peasants resented this onerous requirement, and most simply refused to pay the dues; pressure built until all seigneurial dues were finally abolished without compensation by a more radical government in 1793.

THE RECONSTRUCTION OF FRANCE

The summer of 1789 had seen a remarkable sequence of unprecedented events. A bloodless, juridical revolution from above (engineered by the patriot deputies to the Estates General) combined with popular mobilization from below in town and country made the French Revolution seem irresistible. After the clearing operations of August 4, the National Assembly set out not simply to enact reforms but to reconstruct French institutions on entirely new principles. With sovereignty wrested from the king and vested in the people's deputies, no aspect of France's social or political system was immune to scrutiny, not even slavery in the colonies. First, the Assembly adopted a set of general principles known as the Declaration of the Rights of Man and Citizen. Then it proceeded to draft a constitution, settle the question of voting rights (where the issue of women's citizenship first came up), reorganize the structures of public life, and determine the future of the Catholic clergy. None of this occurred without intense disagreement, especially over the religious issue and the role of the king. Moreover, Austria and Prussia eventually decided on armed intervention against revolutionary France. In 1792 war broke out, which led directly to the fall of the monarchy and to a new, violent turn in the Revolution.

The Declaration of the Rights of Man and Citizen

By sweeping away the old web of privileges, the August 4 decree permitted the Assembly to construct a new regime. Since it would take months to draft a constitution, the Assembly drew up a Declaration of the Rights of Man and Citizen to indicate its intentions (see "Two Views of the Rights of Man," p. 580). The Declaration was the death certificate of the old regime and a rallying point for the future. It affirmed individual liberties but also set forth the basic obligation of citizenship: obedience to legitimate law. The Declaration enumerated **natural rights,** such as freedom of expression and freedom of religious conscience, but (unlike the America Bill of Rights) stipulated that even these rights could be circumscribed by law. It proclaimed the sovereignty of the nation and sketched the basic criteria for a legitimate government, such as representation and the separation of powers. The Declaration's concept of natural rights meant that the new regime would be based on the principles of reason rather than history or tradition.

In his *Reflections on the Revolution in France*, published in 1790, the Anglo-Irish statesman Edmund Burke condemned this attitude, as well as the violence of 1789. In this influential counterrevolutionary tract, Burke argued that France had passed from despotism to anarchy in the name of misguided, abstract principles. Burke distrusted the simplicity of reason that the Assembly celebrated. In his view, the complexity of traditional institutions served the public interest. Burke attacked the belief in natural rights that guided the revolutionaries; something was natural, he believed, only if it resulted from long historical development and habit. Trying to wipe the slate of history clean was a grievous error, he wrote, since society "is a contract between the dead, the living, and the unborn." Society's main right, in Burke's view, was the right to be well-governed by its rulers. Naturally this argument did not go unchallenged, even in England. Mary Wollstonecraft countered with *A Vindication of the Rights of Man*, followed shortly by her seminal *Vindication of the Rights of Woman*, while Thomas Paine published *The Rights of Man* in 1792 to refute Burke.

The New Constitution

Representative Government   From 1789 to 1791, the National Assembly acted as a Constituent Assembly to produce a constitution for France. While proclaiming equal civil rights for all French citizens, it effectively transferred political power from the monarchy and the privileged estates to the body of propertied citizens; in 1790 nobles lost their titles and became indistinguishable from other citizens. The new constitution created a limited monarchy with a clear separation of powers. Sovereignty effectively resided in the representatives of the people, a single-house legislature to be elected by a system of indirect voting. The king was to name and dismiss his ministers, but he was given only a suspensive or delaying veto over legislation; if a bill passed the Assembly in three successive years, it would become law even without royal approval.

TWO VIEWS OF THE RIGHTS OF MAN

The radical theoretical and practical implications of French revolutionary ideology are suggested in a comparison of two essentially contemporaneous documents. The Prussian General Code, a codification initiated by Frederick the Great and issued in its final form in 1791 after his death, reinforced the traditional prerogatives of the nobility under an umbrella of public law. The French National Assembly's Declaration of the Rights of Man and Citizen (1789) established the principle of civil equality alongside the doctrines of national sovereignty, representation, and the rule of law. While the Prussian General Code exemplifies the old order against which French revolutionary ideology took aim, the Declaration became a foundational document of the liberal tradition.

EXCERPTS FROM THE PRUSSIAN GENERAL CODE, 1791

- This general code contains the provisions by which the rights and obligations of inhabitants of the state, so far as they are not determined by particular laws, are to be judged.
- The rights of a man arise from his birth, from his estate, and from actions and arrangements with which the laws have associated a certain determinate effect.
- The general rights of man are grounded on the natural liberty to seek and further his own welfare, without injury to the rights of another.
- Persons to whom, by their birth, destination or principal occupation, equal rights are ascribed in civil society, make up together an *estate* of the state.
- The nobility, as the first estate in the state, most especially bears the obligation, by its distinctive destination, to maintain the defense of the state. . . .
- The nobleman has an especial right to places of honor in the state for which he has made himself fit.
- Only the nobleman has the right to possess noble property.
- Persons of the burgher [middle-class] estate cannot own noble property except by permission of the sovereign.
- Noblemen shall normally engage in no burgher livelihood or occupation.

From R. R. Palmer (trans.), *The Age of Democratic Revolution*, Princeton University Press, 1959, pp. 510–511.

EXCERPTS FROM THE FRENCH DECLARATION OF THE RIGHTS OF MAN AND CITIZEN, 1789

1. Men are born and remain free and equal in rights. Social distinctions may be based only on common utility.
3. The principle of all sovereignty rests essentially in the nation. No body and no individual may exercise authority which does not emanate expressly from the nation.
4. Liberty consists in the ability to do whatever does not harm another; hence the exercise of the natural rights of each man has no limits except those which assure to other members of society the enjoyment of the same rights. These limits can only be determined by law.
6. Law is the expression of the general will. All citizens have the right to take part, in person or by their representatives, in its formation. It must be the same for all whether it protects or penalizes. All citizens being equal in its eyes are equally admissible to all public dignities, offices and employments, according to their capacity, and with no other distinction than that of their virtues and talents.
13. For maintenance of public forces and for expenses of administration common taxation is necessary. It should be apportioned equally among all citizens according to their capacity to pay.
14. All citizens have the right, by themselves or through their representatives, to have demonstrated to them the necessity of public taxes, to consent to them freely, to follow the use made of the proceeds, and to determine the shares to be paid, the means of assessment and collection and the duration.

Under the French Constitution of 1791, every adult male of settled domicile who satisfied minimal tax-paying requirements (roughly two-thirds of all adult males) gained the right to vote, with a higher qualification needed to serve as an elector. Although it favored the propertied, France's new political system was vastly more democratic than Britain's. Still, the National Assembly considered the vote to be a civic function rather than a natural right. "Those who contribute nothing to the public establishment should have no direct influence on government," declared Sieyès. In the same frame of mind the Assembly excluded all women from voting.

Women in the Revolution   That the Assembly even debated political rights for women testifies to the potential universalism of the Revolution's principles. A brief but spirited drive for women's suffrage advanced through pamphlets, petitions, and deputations to the Assembly—most notably the "Declaration of the Rights

In October 1789 Parisian women were furious over the high cost of bread and suspicious of the king and queen. In concert with the National Guard, they set out on an armed march to confront the royal couple in Versailles. To appease the menacing crowd, Louis XVI agreed to return to Paris and to cooperate with revolutionary authorities.
Giraudon/Art Resource, NY

of Women" (1791) drafted by the playwright Olympe de Gouges. But the notion of gender difference and separate spheres, popularized by Rousseau, easily prevailed. The great majority of deputies believed women to be too emotional. Too easily influenced to be independent, they must be excluded from the new public sphere—the more so because of the deputies' belief that elite women had used their sexual powers nefariously behind the scenes during the old regime to influence public policy. Now public life would be virtuous and transparent, uninfluenced by feminine wiles. Instead, women would devote themselves to their crucial nurturing and maternal roles in the domestic sphere.

This type of discourse has prompted some feminist scholars to claim that the revolutionary public sphere "was constructed not merely without women but against them." Balanced against this argument, however, is an offsetting consideration. Male revolutionaries may have distrusted women, and some were overt misogynists, yet their own ideology and political culture created unprecedented public space for women. True, women could not vote or hold office, but otherwise *citoyennes* had extensive opportunity for political participation. Women actively engaged in local conflicts over the Assembly's religious policy

(discussed later in this chapter). In the towns they agitated over food prices, and in October 1789 Parisian women led a mass demonstration to Versailles that forcibly returned the king and queen to Paris. Combining traditional concerns over food scarcities with antiaristocratic revolutionary ideology, women frequently goaded authorities like the national guard into action.

In unprecedented numbers women also took up the pen to publish pamphlets and journals. Their physical presence in public spaces was even more important. Women helped fill the galleries of the Assembly, of the Paris Jacobin Club, and later of the Revolutionary Tribunal—shouting approval or disapproval and in general monitoring their officials. In at least sixty towns women formed auxiliaries to the local Jacobin club, where they read newspapers, debated political issues, and participated in revolutionary festivals.

Nor did Rousseauian antifeminism prevent the revolutionaries from enacting dramatic advances in the civil status of women. Legislation between 1789 and 1794 created a more equitable family life by curbing paternal powers over children, lowering the age of majority, and equalizing the status of husbands and wives in regard to property. Viewing marriage as a contract between a free

MAP 20.1 REDIVIDING THE NATION'S TERRITORY IN 1789
The old regime provinces (left) were replaced by revolutionary departments (right). What advantages did this change bring for the French state?

man and a free woman, the revolutionaries provided the right of divorce to either spouse should the marriage go sour. A remarkably egalitarian inheritance law stipulated that daughters as well as sons were entitled to an equal share of a family's estate. Finally, in the domain of education—central to the feminist vision of Mary Wollstonecraft that the French Revolution had crystalized—an unprecedented system of universal and free primary schooling in 1794 extended to girls as well as boys and provided for state-salaried teachers of both sexes.

Race and Slavery As the Assembly excluded women from voting citizenship without much debate, other groups posed challenges on how to apply "the rights of man" to French society. In eastern France, where most of France's forty thousand Jews resided amid discrimination, public opinion scorned them as an alien race not entitled to citizenship. Eventually, however, the Assembly rejected that argument and extended civil and political equality to Jews. A similar debate raged over the status of the free Negroes and mulattoes in France's Caribbean colonies. White planters, in alliance with the merchants who traded with the islands, were intent on preserving slavery and demanded local control over the islands' racial policy as their best defense. The planters argued that they could not maintain slavery, which was manifestly based on race, unless free people of color were disenfranchised.

When the Assembly accepted this view, the mulattoes rebelled. But their abortive uprising had the unintended consequence of helping ignite a slave rebellion. Led by Toussaint-L'Ouverture, the blacks turned violently on their white masters and proclaimed the independence of the colony, which became known as Haiti. In 1794 the French revolutionary government abolished slavery in all French colonies. (For further discussion see "The Fight for Liberty and Equality in Saint-Domingue," p. 584.)

Unifying the Nation Within France the Assembly obliterated the political identities of the country's historic provinces and instead divided the nation's territory into eighty-three departments of roughly equal size (see map 20.1). Unlike the old provinces, each new department was to have exactly the same institutions. The departments were, in turn, subdivided into districts, cantons, and communes (the common designation for a village or town). On the one hand, this administrative transformation promoted local autonomy: The citizens of each department, district, and commune elected their own local officials, and in that sense political power was decentralized. On the other hand, these local governments were subordinated to the national legislature in Paris and became instruments for promoting national integration and uniformity.

The new administrative map also created the boundaries for a new judicial system. Sweeping away the parlements and law courts of the old regime, the revolutionaries established a justice of the peace in each canton, a civil court in each district, and a criminal court in each department. The judges on all tribunals were to be elected. The Assembly rejected the use of juries in civil cases but decreed that felonies would be tried by juries; also, criminal defendants for the first time gained the right to counsel. In civil law, the Assembly encouraged arbitration and mediation to avoid the time-consuming and expensive processes of formal litigation. In general, the revolutionaries hoped to make the administration of justice faster and more accessible.

Economic Individualism   The Assembly's clearing operations extended to economic institutions as well. Guided by the dogmas of laissez-faire theory and by its uncompromising hostility to privileged corporations, the Assembly sought to open up economic life to individual initiative, much as Turgot had attempted in the 1770s. Besides dismantling internal tariffs and chartered trading monopolies, it abolished merchants' and artisans' guilds and proclaimed the right of every citizen to enter any trade and conduct it freely. The government would no longer concern itself with regulating wages or the quality of goods. The Assembly also insisted that workers bargain in the economic marketplace as individuals, and it therefore banned workers' associations and strikes. The precepts of economic individualism extended to the countryside as well. At least in theory, peasants and landlords were free to cultivate their fields as they saw fit, regardless of traditional collective practices. In fact, those deep-rooted communal restraints proved to be extremely resistant to change.

The Revolution and the Church

To address the state's financial problems, the National Assembly acted in a way that the monarchy had never dared contemplate. Under revolutionary ideology, the French Catholic Church could no longer exist as an independent corporation—as a separate estate within the state. The Assembly, therefore, nationalized Church property (about 10 percent of the land in France), placing it "at the disposition of the nation," and made the state responsible for the upkeep of the Church. It then issued paper notes called *assignats,* which were backed by the value of these "national lands." The property was to be sold by auction at the district capitals to the highest bidders. This plan favored the bourgeois and rich peasants with ready capital and made it difficult for needy peasants to acquire the land, though some pooled their resources to do so.

The sale of Church lands and the issuance of assignats had several consequences. In the short run, they eliminated the need for new borrowing. Second, the hundreds of thousands of purchasers gained a strong vested interest in the Revolution, because a successful counterrevolution was likely to reclaim their properties for the Church. Finally, after war broke out with an Austrian-Prussian coalition in 1792, the government made the assignats a national currency and printed a volume of assignats way beyond their underlying value in land, thereby touching off severe inflation and new political turmoil.

Religious Schism   The issue of Church reform produced the Revolution's first and most fateful crisis. The Assembly intended to rid the Church of inequities that enriched the aristocratic prelates of the old regime. Many Catholics looked forward to such healthy changes that might bring the clergy closer to the people. In the **Civil Constitution of the Clergy** (1790), the Assembly reduced the number of bishops from 130 to 83 and reshaped diocesan boundaries to conform exactly with those of the new departments. Bishops and parish priests were to be chosen by the electoral assemblies in the departments and districts and were to be paid according to a uniform salary scale that favored those currently at the lower end. Like all other public officials, the clergy was to take an oath of loyalty to the constitution.

The clergy generally opposed the Civil Constitution because it had been dictated to them by the National Assembly; they argued that such questions as the selection of bishops and priests should be negotiated either with the Pope or with a National Church Council. But the Assembly asserted that it had the sovereign power to order such reforms, since they affected temporal rather than spiritual matters. In November 1790 the Assembly demanded that all clergy take the loyalty oath forthwith; those who refused would lose their positions and be pensioned off. In all of France only seven bishops and about 54 percent of the parish clergy swore the oath; but in the west of France only 15 percent of the priests complied. A schism tore through French Catholicism because the laity had to take a position as well: Should parishioners remain loyal to their priests who had refused to take the oath (the nonjuring, or refractory, clergy) and thus be at odds with the state? Or should they accept the unfamiliar "constitutional clergy" designated by the districts to replace their own priests?

The Assembly's effort to impose reform in defiance of religious sensibilities and Church autonomy was a grave tactical error. The oath crisis polarized the nation. It seemed to link the Revolution with impiety and the Church with counterrevolution. In local communities,

Global Moment

THE FIGHT FOR LIBERTY AND EQUALITY IN SAINT-DOMINGUE

The French colony Saint-Domingue shared the Caribbean island of Hispaniola with Spain's colony, Santo Domingo (today's Dominican Republic). The crown jewel of France's colonial empire, Saint-Domingue was responsible for about two-fifths of its overseas trade. Worked by about 500,000 slaves from Africa, its 8,000 plantations produced half of all the sugar consumed in continental Europe and the Americas. In the decade before the French Revolution, 30,000 to 40,000 new slaves had to be imported from Africa annually, to compensate for the loss of life from the brutal regimen of slavery on the plantations.

Forty thousand white people (including planters, tradesmen, and soldiers) inhabited this colony alongside the 500,000 black slaves and 30,000 free people of color—freed slaves and their descendants, who often intermarried with whites. Many of these free coloreds managed or possessed estates and slaves of their own. By the 1789s, however, the colony's white authorities were subjecting free people of color to stringent racial laws barring them from the professions and positions in the armed forces, and restricting them to wearing certain types of dress.

The outbreak of the French Revolution in 1789 had a profoundly unsettling effect on the island. While the revolutionaries fought for the principles of liberty, equality, and fraternity in Europe, the members of the National Assembly rebuffed similar demands from delegates of Saint-Domingue's people of color. Racial laws, the Assembly insisted, were a local matter for white planters and merchants, and revolutionary principles did not apply across the color line. In their view, plantation slavery contributed to French economic prosperity, and the maintenance of slavery depended on white supremacy. The Assembly gave in to pressure from the white colonial lobby in the belief that this alone would keep Saint-Domingue under French control.

Thwarted in Paris, the free colored people attempted to achieve liberation by force of arms, which the colony's whites, rich and poor alike, repelled. Neither side realized that a restive slave population was about to seize the initiative itself. In November 1791 thousands of slaves in the north of the colony rose up, setting fire to more than a thousand plantations and massacring hundreds of whites. Still, as the free people of color and whites continued their own battle, each side began to recruit slaves as their foot soldiers. Finally, in April 1792 a more liberal legislature in Paris granted members of the free colored community full French citizenship. Furious at this decision, royalist planters (who soon heard that the king himself had been overthrown) were ready to break free of France, its new Republic, and its new emissary to Saint-Domingue, a man named L.-F. Sonthonax. The son of a French planter, Sonthonax had risen through the ranks of the French Revolution. His main supporters on the island were the free people of color.

To complicate matters, in 1793 Britain and Spain declared war on France, and each sent military forces to wrest Saint-Domingue from the French. Sonthonax now had another fight on his hands. In return for their service as French soldiers, he freed many slaves, and in August 1793 he proclaimed the abolition of slavery in Saint-Domingue. This move then spurred abolitionist sentiment in the National Convention. In a historic decree of February 1794, it abolished slavery in all French colonies—a radical expansion of democratic ideals with enormous implications for the rest of the Atlantic world.

But the story does not end there. If the decrees of the Convention and its commissioner abolished slavery in Saint-Domingue, only the rebellion of the island's slaves and their continued fight for freedom under a forceful leader made emancipation permanent. That leader, Toussaint (1743–1803), was born on the island into slavery and served as a coachman on the Bréda sugar plantation until he was freed sometime in the 1770s. A man with great military aptitude, in 1793 he

Rebellious slaves in pitched battle with French soldiers on Saint-Domingue.
Bettmann/Corbis

joined the Spanish forces and earned the nickname *L'Ouverture* ("the opening") because "he could make an opening anywhere" in the French defenses. But in 1794 he changed sides, organized a new army for the French out of freed slaves, and led his troops into battles that eventually pushed out the Spanish and the British forces. By the time the British left in 1798, Toussaint had eliminated other political rivals to emerge as the supreme authority in the colony. Supporting emancipation, Toussaint proclaimed: "I want liberty and equality to reign in Saint-Domingue." To keep the economy and his army afloat, however, Toussaint reinstated the plantation system of cultivation and used his army to impose forced labor and corporal punishment. In the constitution he promulgated in 1801, he made himself governor for life with the right to choose his successor.

By that time things had changed dramatically in France as well. Napoleon Bonaparte sought to regain full control of the colony. Toussaint L'Ouverture led the fight against the invading French army, but one of his own generals, J.-J. Dessalines, betrayed him. In June 1802 the first black leader in the Western world was handed over to French troops and sent to France, where he soon died in prison. Around that time news arrived that Bonaparte intended to restore slavery. Large numbers of former slaves and free coloreds joined the remnants of Toussaint's army, now led by Dessalines, who exhorted his troops to "burn houses, cut off heads"— brutality that the French returned in kind. Decimated by fever, however, and unable to receive reinforcements or supplies because of an English naval blockade, the remaining French force withdrew in 1804, and Dessalines declared full independence from France. To symbolize this dramatic break, he renamed his country Haiti, a term used on the island before the French had arrived. "I have given the French cannibals blood for blood," Dessalines declared; "I have avenged America."

The repercussions of the Haitian revolution spread throughout the Americas. The loss of life and property

continued

in the Haitian upheaval encouraged plantation societies elsewhere to reinforce their grip on slave labor. Cuba, Brazil, and the southern United States tightened their slave and race codes, making it more difficult to free slaves and restricting free people of color. Napoleonic France restored slavery in Guadeloupe, another French colony in the Caribbean. Scorned or ignored by other governments and commercial interests, Haiti became an isolated backwater until the twentieth century.

But the Haitian slave rebellion also stimulated anti-slavery movements. Abolitionists in Britain and the United States argued that unless their governments moved toward gradual emancipation, similar violence would occur in British colonies and the American South. A reenergized British antislavery movement finally convinced Parliament to abolish the African slave trade in 1807. In the United States, New York and New Jersey passed emancipation laws, although similar legislation had failed in those states in the 1780s.

Despite the bitterness and bloodshed, the events in Haiti shook the rationale for slavery in the Atlantic world. The National Convention's pioneering decree of 1794 established emancipation as a legitimate goal of any democratic society. (It was France's democratic Second Republic of 1848 that definitively abolished slavery in all French colonies.) More fundamentally the Haitian revolution demonstrated the fervent desire of black slaves for freedom. Haiti's independence became irrefutable proof that slavery was not a natural condition for blacks; already in 1791, news of the uprising inspired Jamaican slave songs, and whites throughout the West Indies and North America noticed a growing insolence among the black population. In subsequent insurrections in Havana and Charleston, black militants tried to imitate the actions of Toussaint L'Ouverture and other leaders of the revolt. Haiti provided millions of blacks with a sense of identity apart from that of slave, and a ray of inspiration for their own liberation.

refractory clergy began to preach against the entire Revolution. Local officials fought back by arresting them and demanding repressive laws. Civil strife rocked hundreds of communities.

Counterrevolution, Radicalism, and War

The King's Flight Opposition to the Revolution had actually begun much earlier. After July 14 some of the king's relatives had left the country in disgust, thus becoming the first émigrés, or political exiles, of the Revolution. During the next three years, thousands of nobles, including two-thirds of the royal army's officer corps, joined the emigration. Across the Rhine River in Coblenz, émigrés formed an army that threatened to overthrow the new regime at the first opportunity. The king himself publicly submitted to the Revolution, but privately he smoldered in resentment. Finally, in June 1791, Louis and his family fled in secret from Paris, hoping to cross the Belgian frontier and enlist the aid of Austria. But Louis was stopped at the French village of Varennes and was forcibly returned to Paris.

Moderates hoped that this aborted escape would finally end the king's opposition to the Revolution. The Assembly, after all, needed his cooperation to make its constitutional monarchy viable. It did not want to open the door to a republic or to further unrest. Radicals such as the journalist Jean-Paul Marat, on the other hand, had long thundered against the treachery of the king and the émigrés and against the Assembly itself for not acting vigorously against aristocrats and counterrevolutionaries. But the Assembly was determined to maintain the status quo and adopted the fiction that the king had been kidnapped. The Assembly reaffirmed the king's place in the new regime, but Louis' treasonous flight to Varennes ensured that radical agitation would continue.

The Outbreak of War When the newly elected Legislative Assembly convened on October 1, 1791, the questions of counterrevolution at home and the prospect of war abroad dominated its stormy sessions. Both the right and the left saw advantages to be gained in a war between France and Austria. The king and his court hoped that a military defeat would discredit the new regime and restore full power to the monarchy. Most members of the **Jacobin Club**—the leading radical political club in Paris—wanted war to strike down the foreign supporters of the émigrés along with domestic counterrevolutionaries.

When Francis II ascended the throne of the Habsburg monarchy in March 1792, the stage was set for war. Unlike his father, Leopold, who had rejected intervention in France's affairs, Francis fell under the influence of émigrés and bellicose advisers. He was determined to assist the French queen, his aunt, and he also expected to make territorial gains. With both sides thus eager for battle, France went to war in April 1792 against a coalition of Austria, Prussia, and the émigrés.

Each camp expected rapid victory, but both were deceived. The French offensive quickly faltered, and invading armies soon crossed France's borders. The Legislative Assembly ordered the arrest of refractory clergy and called for a special corps of twenty thousand national guardsmen to protect Paris. Louis vetoed both measures and held to his decisions in spite of demonstrations against them in the capital. For all practical purposes, these vetoes were his last acts as king. The legislature also called for one hundred thousand volunteers to bolster the French army and defend the homeland.

The Fall of the Monarchy   As Prussian forces began a drive toward Paris, their commander, the Duke of Brunswick, rashly threatened to level the city if it resisted or if it harmed the royal family. When Louis XVI published this Brunswick Manifesto, it seemed proof that he was in league with the enemy. Far from intimidating the revolutionaries, the threat drove them forward. Because a divided Legislative Assembly refused to act decisively in the face of royal obstructionism, Parisian militants, spurred on by the Jacobin Club, organized an insurrection.

On August 10, 1792, a crowd of armed Parisians stormed the royal palace at the Tuileries, literally driving the king from the throne. The Assembly then had no choice but to declare Louis XVI suspended. That night more than half the Assembly's members themselves fled Paris, making it clear that the Assembly, too, had lost its legitimacy. The deputies who remained ordered elections for a National Convention to decide the king's fate, to draft a republican constitution, and to govern France during the current emergency. What the events of 1789 in Versailles and Paris had begun, the insurrection of August 10, 1792, completed. The old regime in France had truly been destroyed.

THE SECOND REVOLUTION

By 1792—just three years after the fall of the Bastille—the Revolution had profoundly altered the foundations of government and society in France. The National Assembly introduced constitutional government, legislative representation, and a degree of local self-government. It repudiated absolutism, as well as aristocratic and group privilege; established civil equality and uniform institutions across the country; freed peasants from much of the seigneurial system and religious minorities from persecution. Yet the Revolution was far from over, for these changes had been won only against intense opposition, and the old order was far from vanquished. European monarchs and aristocrats encouraged refractory priests, émigrés, and royalists in France to resist.

The patriots, threatened in 1792 by military defeat and counterrevolution, were themselves divided. Some became radicalized, while others grew alienated from the Revolution's increasingly radical course. But each increment of opposition stiffened the resolve of the Revolution's strongest partisans. The dominant Jacobins forged an alliance with Parisian militants known as the **sans-culottes** (literally, men who wore trousers rather than fashionable knee breeches). Together they propelled France into a second revolution: a democratic republic that espoused a broadening notion of equality. At the same time, however, the Jacobin government instituted an improvised revolutionary dictatorship and a reign of terror against "the enemies of the people." Thus, the second revolution was distorted, as the ideals of equality became confused with the impulse to repress any opposition by the most drastic means.

The National Convention

The insurrection of August 10, 1792, created a vacuum of authority until the election of a National Convention was completed. A revolutionary Paris Commune, or city government, became one power center, but that bastion of radicalism could not control events even within its own domain. As thousands of volunteers left for the battlefront, Parisians nervously eyed the capital's jails, which overflowed with political prisoners and common criminals. Radical journalists like Marat saw these prisoners as a counterrevolutionary striking force and feared a plot to open the prisons. A growing sense of alarm finally exploded early in September. For three days groups of Parisians invaded the prisons, set up "popular tribunals," and slaughtered more than two thousand prisoners. No official dared intervene to stop the carnage, known since as the September massacres.

Beset by invasion jitters and fearing a plot to force open the capital's overcrowded jails, mobs of Parisians invaded the prisons and over the course of three days in September 1792 slaughtered more than two thousand prisoners. Bulloz/© Photo RMN/Art Resource, NY

The sense of panic eased, however, with the success of the French armies. Bolstered by units of volunteers, the army finally halted the invaders at the Battle of Valmy on September 20. Two months later it defeated the allies at Jemappes in the Austrian Netherlands, which the French now occupied. Meanwhile, the Convention convened and promptly declared France a republic.

Settling Louis XVI's fate proved to be extremely contentious. While the deputies unanimously found the former king guilty of treason, they divided sharply over the question of his punishment. Some argued for clemency, while others insisted that his execution was a necessary symbolic gesture as well as a fitting punishment for his betrayal. Finally, by a vote of 387 to 334, the Convention sentenced Louis to death and voted down efforts to reprieve this sentence or delay it for a popular referendum. On January 21, 1793, Louis was guillotined, put to death like an ordinary citizen. The deputies to the Convention had become regicides (king killers) and would make no compromise with counterrevolution.

Factional Conflict   From the Convention's opening day, two bitterly hostile groups of deputies vied for leadership and almost immobilized it with their rancorous conflict. One group became known as the *Girondins*, because several of its spokesmen were elected as deputies from the Gironde department. The Girondins were fiery orators and ambitious politicians who advocated provincial liberty and laissez-faire economics. They

reacted hostilely to the growing radicalism of Paris and broke with or were expelled by the Jacobin Club, to which some had originally belonged. Meanwhile Parisian electors chose as their deputies leading members of the Jacobin Club, such as Danton, Robespierre, and Marat. The Parisian deputation to the Convention became the nucleus of a group known as the *Mountain*, so-called because it occupied the upper benches of the Convention's hall. The Mountain attracted the more militant provincial deputies and attacked the Girondins as treacherous compromisers unwilling to adopt bold measures in the face of crisis. The Girondins, in turn, denounced the Mountain as would-be tyrants and captives of Parisian radicalism and held them responsible for the September prison massacres.

Several hundred deputies stood between these two factions. These centrists (known as the *Plain*) were committed to the Revolution but were uncertain which path to follow. The Plain detested popular agitation, but they were reluctant to turn against the sans-culottes.

The Revolutionary Crisis

By the spring of 1793 the National Convention faced a perilous convergence of invasion, civil war, and economic crises that demanded imaginative responses. Austria and Prussia had mounted a new offensive in 1793, their alliance strengthened by the addition of Spain, Piedmont, and Britain. Between March and

After the National Convention concluded its trial of former King Louis XVI and voted to impose the death penalty without reprieve, "Louis Capet" was guillotined and the leaders of the Republic became regicides, king killers. Bulloz/© Photo RMN/Art Resource, NY

September, military reversals occurred on every front. The Convention reacted by introducing a military draft, which in turn touched off a rebellion in western France by peasants and rural weavers, who had long resented the patriot middle class in the towns for monopolizing local political power and for persecuting their priests. In the isolated towns of the Vendée region, south of the Loire River, the rebels attacked the Republic's supporters. Priests and nobles offered leadership to the insurgents, who first organized into guerrilla bands and finally into a "Catholic and Royalist Army." The Vendée rebels briefly occupied several towns, massacred local patriots, and even threatened the port of Nantes, where British troops could have landed.

Meanwhile, economic troubles were provoking the Parisian sans-culottes. By early 1793 the Revolution's paper money, the assignat, had declined to 50 percent of its face value. Inflation was compounded by a poor harvest, food shortages, hoarding, and profiteering. Municipal authorities fixed the price of bread but could not always secure adequate supplies. Under these conditions the government could not even supply its armies.

The Purge of the Girondins Spokesmen for the sans-culottes demanded that the Convention purge the Girondins and adopt a program of "public safety," including price controls for basic commodities, execution of hoarders and speculators, and forced requisitions of grain. Behind these demands lay the threat of armed insurrection. This pressure from the sans-culottes aided the Mountain in their struggle against the Girondins, but it could easily have degenerated into anarchy. In a sense, all elements of the revolutionary crisis hinged on one problem: the lack of an effective government that would not simply respond to popular pressures but would organize and master them. When the sans-culottes mounted a massive armed demonstration for a purge of the Girondins on June 2, centrist deputies reluctantly agreed to go along. The Convention expelled twenty-three Girondin deputies, who were subsequently tried and executed for treason.

Factionalism in the Convention reflected conflict in the provinces. Moderate republicans in several cities struggled with local Jacobin radicals and sympathized with the Girondin deputies in their campaign against the Parisian sans-culottes. In the south, local Jacobins lost control of Marseilles, Bordeaux, and Lyons to their rivals, who then repudiated the Convention. As in the Vendée revolt, royalists soon took over the resistance in Lyons, France's second largest city. This act was an intolerable challenge to the Convention. Labeling the anti-Jacobin rebels in Lyons and elsewhere as "federalists," the Convention dispatched armed forces to suppress them (see map 20.2). In the eyes of the Jacobins, to defy the Convention's authority was to betray France itself.

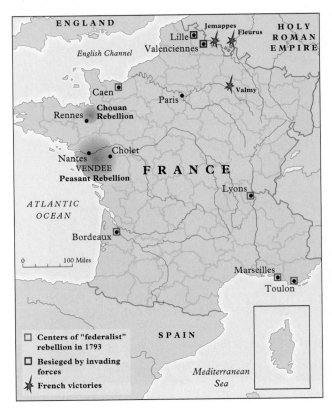

MAP 20.2 CONFLICTS IN REVOLUTIONARY FRANCE
According to this map, what were three types of conflicts challenging revolutionary France?

The Jacobin Dictatorship

Popular radicalism in Paris had helped bring the Mountain to power in the Convention. The question now was: Which side of this coalition between the Mountain and the sans-culottes would dominate the other? The sans-culottes seemed to believe that the sovereign people could dictate their will to the Convention. Popular agitation peaked on September 5, when a mass demonstration in Paris demanded new policies to ensure food supplies. To give force to the law, urged the sans-culottes, "Let terror be placed on the order of the day." The Convention responded with the Law of the Maximum, which imposed general price controls, and with the Law of Suspects, which empowered local revolutionary committees to imprison citizens whose loyalty they suspected.

Revolutionary Government   In June the triumphant Mountain had drafted a new democratic constitution for the French Republic and had submitted it to an unprecedented referendum, in which almost two million citizens had overwhelmingly voted yes. But the Convention formally laid the constitution aside and proclaimed the government "revolutionary until the peace." Elections, local self-government, and guarantees of individual liberty were to be suspended until

the Republic had defeated its enemies within and without. The Convention placed responsibility for military, economic, and political policy, as well as control over local officials, in the hands of a twelve-man **Committee of Public Safety.** Spontaneous popular action was about to give way to revolutionary centralization.

Maximilien Robespierre emerged as the Committee's leading personality and tactician. An austere bachelor in his mid-thirties, Robespierre had been a provincial lawyer before the Revolution. As a deputy to the National Assembly he had ardently advocated greater democracy. His main political forum was the Paris Jacobin Club, which by 1793 he more or less dominated. In the Convention, Robespierre was inflexible and self-righteous in his dedication to the Revolution. He sought to appease the sans-culottes but also to control them, for he placed the Revolution's survival above any one viewpoint (see "Robespierre's Justification of the Terror," p. 591).

Local political clubs (numbering more than five thousand by 1794) formed crucial links in the chain of revolutionary government. The clubs nominated citizens for posts on local revolutionary institutions, exercised surveillance over those officials, and served as "arsenals of public opinion." The clubs fostered the egalitarian ideals of the second revolution and supported the war effort. They also saw it as their civic duty to denounce fellow citizens for unpatriotic behavior and thereby sowed fear and recrimination across the land.

The Jacobins tolerated no serious dissent. The government's demand for unity during the emergency nullified the right to freedom of expression. Among those to fall were a group of ultrarevolutionaries led by Jacques-René Hébert, a leading radical journalist and Paris official. The extremists were accused of a plot against the Republic and were guillotined. In reality, Hébert had questioned what he deemed the Convention's leniency toward "enemies of the people." Next came the so-called indulgents. Headed by Georges-Jacques Danton, a leading member of the Jacobin Club, they publicly argued for a relaxation of rigorous measures. For this dissent they were indicted on trumped-up charges of treason and were sentenced to death by the revolutionary tribunal. This succession of purges, which started with the Girondins and later ended with Robespierre himself, suggested, as one victim put it, that "revolutions devour their own children."

The Reign of Terror   Most of those devoured by the French Revolution, however, were not its own children but a variety of armed rebels, counterrevolutionaries, and unfortunate citizens swept into the vortex of war and internal strife. As an official policy, the Reign of Terror sought to organize repression so as to avoid anarchic violence like the September massacres. It reflected a state of mind that saw threats and plots everywhere

Robespierre's Justification of the Terror

"If the spring of popular government in time of peace is virtue, the springs of popular government in revolution are at once *virtue and terror*: virtue, without which terror is fatal; terror, without which virtue is powerless. Terror is nothing other than justice, prompt, severe, inflexible; it is therefore an emanation of virtue. . . . It is a consequence of the general principle of democracy applied to our country's most urgent needs.

"It has been said that terror is the principle of despotic government. Does your government therefore resemble despotism? Yes, as the sword that gleams in the hands of the heroes of liberty resembles that with which the henchmen of tyranny are armed. Let the despot govern his brutalized subjects by terror; he is right, as a despot. Subdue by terror the enemies of liberty, and you will be right, as founders of the Republic. The government of the revolution is liberty's despotism against tyranny. Is force made only to protect crime?

"Society owes protection only to peaceable citizens; the only citizens in the Republic are the republicans. For it, the royalists, the conspirators are only strangers or, rather, enemies. This terrible war waged by liberty against tyranny—is it not indivisible? Are the enemies within not the allies of the enemies without? The assassins who tear our country apart, the intriguers who buy the consciences that hold the people's mandate; the traitors who sell them; the mercenary pamphleteers hired to dishonor the people's cause, to kill public virtue, to stir up the fire of civil discord, and to prepare political counterrevolution—are all those men less guilty or less dangerous than the tyrants [abroad] whom they serve?

"We try to control revolutions with the quibbles of the courtroom; we treat conspiracies against the Republic like lawsuits between individuals. Tyranny kills, and liberty argues."

From Robespierre's speech to the Convention on "The Moral and Political Principles of Domestic Policy," February 1794.

The Paris Jacobin Club began as a caucus for a group of liberal deputies to the National Assembly. During the Convention it became a bastion of democratic deputies and middle-class Parisian radicals while continuing to serve as a "mother club" for affiliated clubs in the provinces.
Bibliothèque Nationale, Paris, France. Giraudon/Art Resource, NY

(some real, most imagined). The laws of the Terror struck most directly at the people perceived to be enemies of the Revolution: Refractory priests and émigrés, for instance, were banned from the Republic upon pain of death. But the Law of Suspects also led to the incarceration of as many as 300,000 ordinary citizens for their opinions, past behavior, or social status.

The Terror produced its own atrocities: the brutal drowning of imprisoned priests at Nantes; the execution of thousands of noncombatants during the military campaigns of the Vendée; and the summary executions of about two thousand citizens of Lyons, more than two-thirds of them from the wealthy classes. ("Lyons has made war against liberty," declared the Convention,

CHRONOLOGY

Turning Points in the French Revolution

June 17, 1789	Third Estate declares itself a National Assembly.
July 14, 1789	Storming of the Bastille and triumph of the patriots.
August 10, 1792	Storming of the Tuileries and the end of the monarchy (followed by the September prison massacres).
January 21, 1793	Execution of Louis XVI.
March 1793	Vendée rebellion begins.
June 2, 1793	Sans-culottes intimidate the Convention into purging the Girondin deputies. "Federalist" rebellion begins in Lyons.
September 5, 1793	Sans-culottes demonstrate for the enactment of economic controls and Terror.
October 1793	The Jacobin dictatorship and the Terror begin: The Convention declares that "the government is revolutionary until the peace."
9 Thermidor year II (July 27, 1794)	Fall of Robespierre.
1–2 Prairial year III (May 20–21, 1795)	Failed insurrection by Parisian sans-culottes for "Bread and the Constitution of 1793."
18 Brumaire year VIII (November 9, 1799)	Coup d'état by General Bonaparte and the "revisionists."

"thus Lyons no longer exists.") But except in the two zones of intense civil war—western France and the area of "federalist" rebellion in the south (see map 20.2)—the Terror struck by examples, not by mass executions.

The Sans-Culottes: Revolution from Below

The Parisian sans-culottes formed the crowds and demonstrations that produced the Revolution's dramatic turning points, but they also threw themselves into a daily routine of political activism during the second revolution of 1792–1794. The sans-culottes were mainly artisans, shopkeepers, and workers—building contractors, carpenters, shoemakers, wine sellers, clerks, tailors, cafe keepers. Many owned their own businesses; others were wage earners. But they shared a strong sense of local community in the capital's varied neighborhoods.

Popular Attitudes The supply and price of bread obsessed the sans-culottes. As consumers, they faced inflation and scarcities with fear and rage and demanded forceful government intervention to ensure the basic necessities of life. Sans-culotte militants believed in property rights, but they insisted that people did not have the right to misuse property by hoarding food or speculating. As one petition put it, "What is the meaning of freedom, when one class of men can starve another? What is the meaning of equality, when the rich, by their monopolies, can exercise the right of life and death over their equals?" The sans-culotte call for price controls clashed dramatically with the dogma of laissez-faire. By 1793, however, the Jacobins had acknowledged "the right to subsistence" in their new constitution and had instituted price controls under the Law of the Maximum to regulate the economy during the emergency.

Bitterly antiaristocratic, the sans-culottes displayed their social attitudes in everyday behavior. They advocated simplicity in dress and manners and attacked opulence and pretension wherever they found or imagined them to be. Under the sans-culottes' disapproving eye, high society and fancy dress generally disappeared from view. Vices like prostitution and gambling were attributed to aristocrats and were denounced in the virtuous society of the Revolution; drinking, the common people's vice, was tolerated.

The revolutionaries symbolized their break with the past by changing the names of streets and public places to eliminate signs of royalism, religion, or aristocracy. The Palais Royal thus became the Palais d'Egalité (Equality Palace). Some citizens exchanged their Christian names for the names of secular heroes from antiquity, like Brutus. And all citizens were expected to drop honorifics like *monsieur* and *madame* in favor of the simple, uniform designation of citizen. Even the measurement of time changed when the Convention decreed a new republican calendar that renamed the months and replaced the seven-day week with a symmetrical ten-day *décadi*. The year I dated from the establishment of the Republic in 1792.

Popular Politics The Convention believed in representative democracy with an active political life at the grass roots, but during the emergency it decreed a centralized revolutionary dictatorship. The sans-culottes preferred a more decentralized style of participatory democracy. They believed that the local assembly of

A Portrait of the Parisian Sans-Culotte

"A Sans-Culotte is a man who goes everywhere on his own two feet, who has none of the millions you're all after, no mansions, no lackeys to wait on him, and who lives quite simply with his wife and children, if he has any, on the fourth or fifth floor. He is useful, because he knows how to plough a field, handle a forge, a saw, or a file, how to cover a roof or how to make shoes and to shed his blood to the last drop to save the Republic. And since he is a working man, you will never find him in the Cafe de Chartres where they plot and gamble. . . . In the evening, he is at his Section, not powdered and perfumed and all dolled up to catch the eyes of the *citoyennes* in the galleries, but to support sound resolutions with all his power and to pulverize the vile faction [of moderates]. For the rest, a Sans-Culotte always keeps his sword with a sharp edge, to clip the ears of the malevolent. Sometimes he carries his pike and at the first roll of the drum, off he goes to the Vendée, to the Army of the Alps or the Army of the North."

From a pamphlet attributed to the Parisian militant Vingternier: "A Reply to the Impertinent Question: But What Is a Sans-Culotte?" 1794.

Air: Ou Courez vous Mr. L'Abbé.
Ne redoutez plus les Brocards.
Gentes Nonettes beaux trocards

De la Metamorphose
He bien
L'Amour rit et pour cause
Et vous mentendez bien.

On me Raze ce Matin, Je me Marie ce Soir.

At the height of a radical "dechristianization" movement (which lasted for about eight months in 1793–1794), more than eighteen thousand priests renounced their vocations under pressure from militant revolutionaries. About a third also agreed to marry as a way of proving the sincerity of their resignations. (The print's caption states: "They shave me in the morning and have me married by evening.")
Bibliothèque Nationale de France, Paris

citizens was the ultimate sovereign body. At the beginning of the year II (1793–1794), the forty-eight sections of Paris functioned almost as autonomous republics in which local activists ran their own affairs. Political life in Paris and elsewhere had a naive, breathless quality and made thousands of ordinary citizens feel that they held real political power (see "A Portrait of the Parisian Sans-Culotte," above).

Within this upsurge of activism, the Society of Revolutionary-Republican Women, founded in Paris in the spring of 1793, constituted a vanguard of female radicals. The members of this club were undeterred by their exclusion from the vote, which did not much concern them at this point. Even without voting rights, women considered themselves citizens in revolutionary France.

In agitating for severe enforcement of price controls and the compulsory use of republican symbols, however, these women irritated the revolutionary government. Before long the ruling Jacobins perceived them as part of an irresponsible ultra-left opposition, whom they denounced as *enragés*, rabid ones. In October the government arrested the most prominent *enragés*, male and female, closed down the Society of Revolutionary-Republican Women, and forbade the formation of

The radical activists of the Paris sections—the sans-culottes and their female counterparts—made a point of their plebeian forms of dress, their freedom to bear arms, and their egalitarian insignias, such as the red liberty cap.
Bulloz/© Photo RMN/Art Resource, NY

female political clubs in the future. The government's spokesman derided these activists as "denatured women," viragos who neglected their maternal duties. Behind this bitter antifeminist rhetoric lay a sense of anxiety. In the virile and punitive world of radical republicanism (see the illustration of Hercules on p. 595), the Jacobins yearned for an offsetting feminine virtue to soften the severity required in the public sphere.

To Robespierre, in any case, the notion of direct democracy appeared unworkable and akin to anarchy. The Convention watched the sans-culottes with concern, supportive of their democratic egalitarianism but fearful of the unpredictability, disorder, and inefficiency of this popular movement. The Mountain attempted to encourage civic participation yet control it. From the forty-eight sections of Paris, however, came an endless stream of petitions, denunciations, and veiled threats to the government. In the spring of 1794 the Convention finally curbed the power of the sections by drastically restricting their rights and activities. But in forcibly cooling down the ardor of the sans-culottes, the revolutionary government necessarily weakened its own base of support.

The Revolutionary Wars

Ultimately, the Revolution's fate rested in the hands of its armies, although no one had thought in such terms in 1789. France's revolutionary ideology had initially posed no direct threat to the European state system. Indeed, the orators of the National Assembly had argued that the best foreign policy for a free society was peace, neutrality, and isolation from the diplomatic intrigues of monarchs. But peaceful intentions did not imply pacifism. When counterrevolution at home coalesced with threats from abroad, the revolutionaries vigorously confronted both. As in most major wars, however, the initial objectives were soon forgotten. As the war expanded, it brought revolution to other states.

The revolutionary wars involved standard considerations of international relations as well as new and explosive purposes. On the one hand, France pursued the traditional aim of extending and rounding off its frontiers. On the other hand, France now espoused revolutionary principles such as the right of a people to self-determination. As early as September 1791, the National Assembly had declared that "the rights of peoples are not determined by the treaties of princes."

Foreign Revolutionaries and French Armies   Even before 1789 "patriots" in Geneva, the Dutch Netherlands, and the Austrian Netherlands (Belgium) had unsuccessfully challenged the traditional arrangements that governed their societies, and the French Revolution rekindled those rebellious sentiments. Foreign revolutionaries were eager to challenge their governments again, and they looked to revolutionary France for assistance. Refugees from these struggles had fled to France and now formed pressure groups to lobby French leaders for help in liberating their own countries during France's war against Austria and Prussia. Some revolutionaries from areas contiguous to France (Belgium, Savoy, and the Rhineland) hoped that the French Republic might simply annex those territories. Elsewhere—in the Dutch Netherlands, Lombardy, Ireland, and the Swiss Confederation—insurgents hoped that France would help establish independent republics by overthrowing the ruling princes or oligarchies.

Few French leaders were interested in leading a European crusade for liberty, but practical considerations led them to intervene. As the war spilled over into Belgium and the Rhineland, the French sought to establish support abroad by incorporating the principles of the Revolution into their foreign policy. Thus, in December 1792 the Convention decided that feudal practices and hereditary privileges would be abolished wherever French armies prevailed. The people thus liberated, however, would have to pay for their liberation

Amidst elaborate arrays of symbolism, revolutionary iconography generally used the figure of a woman to represent its ideals. Briefly in the period 1793–1794, however, the Jacobins introduced the more aggressive masculine figure of Hercules to represent the Republic.

Attributed to Louis Joseph Watteau
THE DEPARTURE OF THE VOLUNTEERS
To bolster the professional troops of the line army in 1791 and again in 1792 after the war began, the government called for volunteers, one of whom is shown in this sentimental and patriotic portrait bidding farewell to his family. By 1793, the National Convention had to go further and draft all able-bodied young, single men.
Musée Carnavalet, Paris, France/Giraudon/Bridgeman Art Library

with special taxes and requisitions of supplies for French troops. By 1794 France had a permanent foothold in Belgium and soon annexed that territory to the Republic. Yet Robespierre was dubious about foreign entanglements; he believed that liberty had to be secured in France before it could be exported abroad. The Committee of Public Safety thus declined to support a distant Polish revolutionary movement, refused to invade Holland, and attempted to avoid any involvements in Italy.

Citizen-Soldiers The fighting men who defended France and carried its revolution abroad were a far different body from the old royal army. The National Assembly of 1789 retained the notion of a professional army but opened officers' careers to ordinary soldiers, especially after most of the royal officer corps emigrated or resigned. At the same time, the concept of the citizen-soldier was introduced in the newly organized national guard, which had elected officers. When the war against the coalition began in 1792, the government enrolled more than 100,000 volunteers for short-term service at the front. But when the coalition launched its second offensive in 1793, the inadequacy of the French army demanded drastic innovations.

The Convention responded with the mass levy of August 1793 (***levée en masse***). All able-bodied unmarried men between the ages of eighteen and twenty-five were drafted for military service, without the option of buying themselves a replacement. About 300,000 new recruits poured into the armies, while perhaps 200,000 draftees fled to avoid service. By the end of 1794 the French had almost 750,000 men under arms. With elected officers at their head, the citizen-soldiers marched off to the front under banners that read "The French people risen against the tyrants." The Convention merged these recruits with the regulars of the line army so that the professionals could impart their military skills to the new troops.

Revolutionary Warfare Military tactics in the field reflected a combination of revolutionary spirit and pragmatism. The new units did not have the training to be deployed in the well-drilled line formations of old-regime armies. Commanders instead favored mass columns that could move quickly without much drilling. Mass and mobility characterized the armies of the French Revolution. The Committee of Public Safety advised its commanders, "Act offensively and in masses. Use the bayonet at every opportunity. Fight great battles and pursue the enemy until he is destroyed."

The revolutionary government fostered new attitudes toward military life. The military was under civilian control. Discipline applied equally to officers and men, and wounded soldiers received generous veterans benefits. The Convention insisted that generals show not only military talent but the will to win. Many young officers rose quickly to command positions, but some generals fared badly. The commander of the defeated Rhine army in early 1793, for example, was branded a traitor, tried, and guillotined. Meanwhile, economic mobilization at home produced the weapons, ammunition, clothing, and food necessary to support this mass army.

In late 1793 and early 1794 the armies of the Republic won a string of victories, culminating in the Battle of Fleurus in June 1794, which liberated Belgium for the second time. French armies also triumphed at the Péyérnes and the Rhine and forced their enemies one by one to the peace table—first Spain and Prussia, then Piedmont. An army crippled at the outset by treason and desertion, defeat, lack of training and discipline, and collapsing morale had been forged into a potent force in less than two years. Militarily, at least, the revolutionary government had succeeded brilliantly.

Summary

To its most dedicated supporters, the revolutionary government had two major purposes: first, to surmount a crisis and steer the Republic to victory; and second, to democratize France's political and social fabric. Only the first objective, however, won widespread adherence. The National Convention held a polarized nation together, consolidated the Republic, and defeated its foreign enemies, but only at enormous and questionable costs. Moderates and ultrarevolutionaries alike resented the stifling political conformity imposed by the revolutionary government. Wealthy peasants and businesspeople chafed under the economic regimentation, and Catholics bitterly resented local "dechristianization" campaigns. The Jacobins increasingly isolated themselves, making enemies on every side. It is not surprising, then, that the security provided by the military victories of 1793–1794 would permit the Convention to end the Jacobin dictatorship and abandon its rhetoric of radical egalitarianism. But the question remained: What would take its place?

QUESTIONS FOR FURTHER THOUGHT

1. How do you explain the onset of the French Revolution? Was it an accident, so to speak, or did it have long-term causes that made it in some sense inevitable?
2. How do you see the relationship between the liberal phase of the French Revolution (1789–1792) and its radical phase (1792–1794)? Why do revolutions often "devour their own children"?
3. The slogan of the French Revolution eventually became "Liberty, Equality, Fraternity." What was meant by fraternity? Are liberty and equality inherently in tension or are they complementary and mutually reinforcing?

RECOMMENDED READING

Sources

Beik, Paul H. (ed.). *The French Revolution.* 1971. A comprehensive anthology.

Dubois, Laurent, and John Garrigus. *Slave Revolution in the Caribbean 1789–1804. A Brief History with Documents.* 2006. Illuminates the uprisings in Saint-Domingue through a wide range of voices.

Hunt, Lynn (ed.). *The French Revolution and Human Rights: A Brief Documentary History.* 1996. Excerpts from revolutionary debates on the rights of the poor, free blacks and slaves, Jews, and women.

Levy, Darlene, H. Applewhite, and M. Johnson (eds.). *Women in Revolutionary Paris, 1789–1795.* 1979. A documentary history of women activists.

Stewart, J. H. *A Documentary Survey of the French Revolution.* 1951. A compendium of important official documents.

Walzer, Michael (ed.). *Regicide and Revolution: Speeches at the Trial of Louis XVI.* 1992. Documents and penetrating analysis.

Studies

Blanning, T. C. W. *The French Revolutionary Wars, 1787–1802.* 1996. A brief but comprehensive synthesis.

———. *Joseph II and Enlightened Despotism.* 1970. A convenient synthesis on a fundamental subject.

Christie, Ian. *Wars and Revolutions: Britain, 1760–1815.* 1982. Focuses on British government policy in the age of revolutions.

Cobb, Richard. *The French and Their Revolution: Selected Writings.* Edited by D. Gilmour. 1998. An anthology of writings by a great historian of ordinary people caught up in the French Revolution. Should be compared to Soboul's account of the popular movement.

Desan, Suzanne. *The Family on Trial in Revolutionary France.* 2004. Changing law, institutions, and social practice on a variety of gender and family issues.

De Tocqueville, Alexis. *The Old Regime and the French Revolution.* Translated by Stuart Gilbert. 1955. A classic interpretation of the Revolution's genesis, first published in the 1850s.

Doyle, William. *Origins of the French Revolution.* 1999. A reliable synthesis of revisionist historiography.

———. *The Oxford History of the French Revolution.* 1989. A readable, detailed narrative.

Dubois, Laurent. *Avengers of the New World: The Story of the Haitian Revolution.* 2004. The most recent study of Toussaint L'Ouverture and the Saint-Domingue slave revolt during the French Revolution.

Fitzsimmons, Michael. *The Night the Old Regime Ended: August 4, 1789, and the French Revolution.* 2003. Illuminates a major and dramatic leap forward in the Revolution.

Forrest, Alan. *Soldiers of the French Revolution.* 1990. A deft synthesis of recent research.

Furet, Francois, and Mona Ozouf (eds.). *A Critical Dictionary of the French Revolution.* 1989. A collection of essays, some brilliant and some idiosyncratic, on selected events, actors, institutions, ideas, and historians of the French Revolution.

Godineau, Dominique. *The Women of Paris and Their French Revolution.* 1998. The best account of ordinary Parisian women's participation in the French Revolution—a story of citizenship without voting rights.

Hunt, Lynn. *Politics, Culture, and Class in the French Revolution.* 1984. A pioneering analysis of the imagery and sociology of revolutionary politics.

Jones, Peter. *The Peasantry in the French Revolution.* 1988. A comprehensive study of the impact of the Revolution on rural society.

Kennedy, Emmet. *A Cultural History of the French Revolution.* 1989. The Revolution's impact on cultural institutions and artistic activity.

McManners, John. *The French Revolution and the Church.* 1970. A superb synthesis on a major issue.

Middlekauff, Robert. *The Glorious Cause: The American Revolution 1763–1789.* 1982. A comprehensive and balanced synthesis.

Palmer, Robert R. *The Age of the Democratic Revolution: A Political History of Europe and America, 1760–1800.* 2 vols. 1959 and 1962. A magisterial comparative survey of the origins and course of revolutionary movements in the eighteenth century, from America to Poland.

———. *Twelve Who Ruled: The Year of the Terror in the French Revolution.* 1941. A modern classic, by far the best book on the subject.

Popkin, Jeremy. *Revolutionary News: The Press in France 1789–1799.* 1990. An excellent analysis of journalism and the impact of journalists in the revolutionary decade.

Scott, H. M. (ed.). *Enlightened Absolutism: Reforms and Reformers in Later Eighteenth-Century Europe.* 1990. A comprehensive assessment.

Scurr, Ruth. *Fatal Purity: Robespierre and the French Revolution.* 2006. A careful portrait emphasizing Robespierre's self-fashioning as a revolutionary.

Soboul, Albert. *The Parisian Sans-Culottes and the French Revolution.* 1964. An abridgement of a landmark French thesis; should be compared to Cobb's study.

Sutherland, Donald. *France 1789–1815: Revolution and Counter-revolution.* 1985. A fine general history of the period.

Tackett, Timothy. *When the King Took Flight.* 2003. A lively account of the flight to Varennes in 1791 and its explosive aftermath.

Woloch, Isser. *The New Regime: Transformations of the French Civic Order, 1789–1820s.* 1994. A thematic study of new civic institutions and how they fared, from the beginning of the Revolution to the Restoration of the Bourbons.

Jacques-Louis David
NAPOLEON BONAPARTE, SKETCH
General Bonaparte, in an uncompleted portrait by Jacques-Louis David.
Giraudon/Art Resource, NY

Chapter Twenty-One

THE AGE OF NAPOLEON

FROM ROBESPIERRE TO BONAPARTE • THE NAPOLEONIC SETTLEMENT IN FRANCE •
NAPOLEONIC HEGEMONY IN EUROPE • RESISTANCE TO NAPOLEON

The second phase of the French Revolution (1792–1794) left a stark legacy of contradictions. On the one hand, the National Convention moved for the first time since ancient Athens to institute a democratic republic: a government without kings, based on universal male suffrage and affirming such popular rights as the right to subsistence and to education for all. On the other hand, the Convention responded to foreign military threats, internal rebellion, and intense factionalism by establishing a revolutionary dictatorship. Individual liberties disappeared, and terror against "enemies of the people" became the order of the day. With the crisis finally surmounted by repression and military victories in 1794, most members of the Convention wearied of those repressive policies and wanted to terminate the Revolution as quickly as possible.

Ending the Terror while preserving the Revolution's positive gains, however, proved extremely difficult. By 1794 too much blood had been spilled, too much social hatred and recrimination had accumulated. The new regime could not easily be steered toward the safe har-bor of republican liberty in such a polarized atmosphere. In the end, General Napoleon Bonaparte replaced the Republic with a personal dictatorship—an outcome that the men of 1789 (schooled in the history of the Roman Republic) had feared from the start.

Would Bonaparte betray the Revolution or consolidate it, as he transformed the Republic's political institutions and social policies? And, since the struggle for and against revolution had long since spilled across France's borders, what would be the consequences for Europe of Napoleon's ascendancy? After 1800 the public life of both France and Europe hinged to an unparalleled degree on the will of a single man. Gradually his designs became clear: a strong centralized state ruled from the top down in France and an imperial reorganization of Europe totally dominated by France. Undergirding both developments was arguably the most significant priority of Napoleon: the implementation of mass conscription and the consequent militarization of European society. On a vast new scale, war once again became the central motif of the Western experience.

Treaty of Amiens with Britain **1802** ●

Concordat with the Pope **1801** ●

Coup d'etat of 18 Brumaire **1799** ●

War of the Second Coalition begins **1798** ●

Treaty of Campo Formio with Austria **1797** ●

Constitution of the year III (Directory) **1795** ●

Thermidorian reaction **1794–1795** ▬▬

FROM ROBESPIERRE TO BONAPARTE

Relatively secure after the military victories of 1793–1794, the National Convention repudiated the Terror and struck at the leading terrorists in a turnabout known as the Thermidorian reaction. Jacobinism, however, was now a permanent part of French political experience, along with antirevolutionary royalism. The political spectrum of modern European history was beginning to emerge. Most revolutionaries now attempted to establish a moderate or centrist position, but they proved unequal to the task. During the four unsteady years of the Directory regime (1795–1799), meanwhile, French armies helped bring revolution to other parts of Western Europe, only to provoke a second anti-French coalition. This new challenge brought the weaknesses of the Republic to a head and allowed an ambitious general and hero of the Republic to seize power. With the backing of disillusioned civilian politicians, Napoleon Bonaparte emerged as the head of the French state.

The Thermidorian Reaction (1794–1795)

When the military victories over the coalition and the Vendée rebels in the year II (1793–1794) eased the need for patriotic unity, long-standing clashes over personalities and policies exploded in the Convention. Robespierre prepared to denounce yet another group of unspecified intriguers, presumably to send them to the guillotine as he had Hébert and Danton. But his enemies made a preemptive strike and denounced Robespierre to the Convention as a tyrant. The Convention no longer needed Robespierre's uncompromising style of leadership. Moderate deputies now repudiated him along with his policies of terror. The Parisian sans-culottes might have intervened to keep Robespierre in power, but the Jacobins

ROBESPIERRE GUILLOTINING THE EXECUTIONER
With its field of guillotines, this Thermidorian caricature portrays Robespierre as a murderous tyrant who had depopulated France.
Giraudon/Art Resource, NY

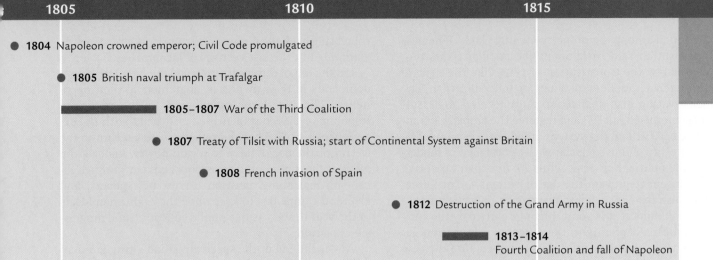

● **1804** Napoleon crowned emperor; Civil Code promulgated

● **1805** British naval triumph at Trafalgar

1805–1807 War of the Third Coalition

● **1807** Treaty of Tilsit with Russia; start of Continental System against Britain

● **1808** French invasion of Spain

● **1812** Destruction of the Grand Army in Russia

1813–1814
Fourth Coalition and fall of Napoleon

had alienated their one-time allies when they curbed the sans-culottes' political activities several months earlier. On July 27, 1794 (9 Thermidor year II in the revolutionary calendar), the Convention declared Robespierre an outlaw; he was guillotined the following day, along with several loyal associates.

Anti-Jacobinism   As the Convention dismantled the apparatus of the Terror, suspects were released from jail, the revolutionary committees were abolished, and some of their members were arrested in turn. The Convention closed the Paris Jacobin Club, once the main forum for Robespierre's influence, while the political clubs in the provinces gradually withered away. The Convention also extended an amnesty to the surviving Girondins and arrested a few leading deputies of the Mountain. Those who had established the Terror in the year II now found themselves under attack. The anti-Jacobin thirst for retribution eventually produced a "white terror" against the Jacobins and the sans-culottes that resulted in arrests, assassinations, and, in the south of France, wholesale massacres.

The **Thermidorian reaction** also released France from the social austerity of the year II. The Jacobins' insistence on public virtue gave way to the toleration of luxury and self-indulgence among the wealthy. The titles *monsieur* and *madame* reappeared, replacing the republican designation of *citizen*. In keeping with laissez-faire ideology, the Thermidorians rescinded economic controls. With the marketplace again ruled by supply and demand, skyrocketing inflation reignited. Worse yet, the harvest of 1795 proved mediocre, and many consumers suffered worse privations than those during the shortages of 1793. In near-famine conditions, mortality rates rose markedly; police reports spoke of little but popular misery.

The Last Revolutionary Uprising   Former militants attempted to spark a political reversal and halt the Thermidorian reaction. In the spring of 1795 sans-culottes began to demonstrate in Paris with the slogan "Bread and the Constitution of 1793." The Thermidorians, however, were moving in the opposite direction. They viewed the Jacobin Constitution of 1793 as far too democratic and looked for an excuse to scrap it altogether. In May sans-culottes launched a poorly organized insurrection (the revolt of Prairial year III). In a grim and desperate gamble, they invaded the Convention's hall, where they won the sympathy of only a handful of deputies. Their hours were numbered. In two days of street fighting, government forces overwhelmed the insurgents. Afterward, thirty-six sans-culottes were executed, and twelve hundred more were imprisoned for their activism during the Terror. This event proved to be the last mobilization of the Parisian revolutionary crowd and the final eclipse of the egalitarian movement.

The Directory (1795–1799)

By the end of 1795, the remaining members of the Convention considered the Revolution over. The extremes had been vanquished, and the time for the "peaceable enjoyment of liberty" seemed at hand. The Thermidorians drafted a new constitution—the constitution of the year III (1795)—proclaimed a general amnesty, and hoped to turn a new page. The revolutionary government, which had replaced the fallen constitutional monarchy in 1793, gave way to a constitutional republic, known as the **Directory** after its five-man executive.

The Directory's proponents declared that the Republic should "be governed by the best citizens, who are found among the property-owning class." The new constitution said little about the popular rights proclaimed by the Constitution of 1793, like the right to subsistence, public assistance, or free education. The constitution also abandoned the universal male suffrage promised in 1793 and restored the propertied franchise of 1791 and the system of indirect elections. The regime's two-house legislature was designed to moderate the political process, while its five-man executive was meant to prevent the rise of a dictator. The Directory also feared a royalist resurgence. Since genuinely free elections at this point might be carried by the anti-republicans of the right, the outgoing Convention decided to co-opt two-thirds of its members into the new legislature, thereby ensuring a substantial degree of political continuity. Government troops led by an officer named Napoleon Bonaparte easily crushed a royalist revolt against this power grab.

The Political Spectrum The Directory wanted to command the center of the political spectrum, which one historian has aptly called "the mirage of the moderates." To maintain themselves in power, however, the directorials violated the liberties pledged in their own constitution. They repeatedly purged elected officials and periodically suppressed political clubs and newspapers on the left and right. In general they refused to acknowledge the legitimacy of organized opposition of any kind. This attitude explains the succession of coups and purges that marked the Directory's four years. Although the repressive measures were mild compared with those of the Terror, they ultimately undermined the regime's viability. In the end many moderate republicans would walk away from their own creation.

For all its repressive qualities, however, the Directory regime was democratic enough to allow most shades of the political spectrum some visibility. The full range of opinions in France, obscured previously by the Terror, was evident during the years of the Directory and would persist with some modifications into the twentieth century. The most important legacy of all, no doubt, was the apathy born of exhaustion or cynicism. Most citizens, especially peasants, had wearied of politics and distrusted all officials, whatever government they served. Participation in the Directory regime's annual elections was extremely low.

Within this context of massive apathy, politically conscious minorities showed fierce partisanship. On the right, ultraroyalists (including émigrés, refractory priests, and armed rebels in western France) hoped to overthrow the Republic altogether. Some worked with the exiled Bourbon princes and with British secret agents. More moderate royalists hoped to win control of the Republic's political institutions lawfully and then bring back the émigrés and refractory priests while stamping out the last vestiges of Jacobinism.

On the left of the spectrum stood the Neo-Jacobins—democrats in their own eyes, anarchists to their opponents. The Neo-Jacobins adhered to the moderate Republic of 1795 but identified positively with the experience of 1793. They did not advocate a return to the Terror or the use of force to regain power. Instead, the Neo-Jacobins promoted grassroots activism through local political clubs, petition drives, newspapers, and electoral campaigns to keep alive the egalitarian ideals of the year II, such as free public education and progressive taxation.

At the far end of the spectrum stood a tiny group of radicals whose significance would loom larger in the next century than it did in 1796. Their leader was François-Noël Babeuf, who had changed his name to Gracchus Babeuf in 1793. The Babeuvists viewed the revolutionary government of the year II as a promising stage that had to be followed by a final revolution in

THE DIRECTORY FALLS BETWEEN TWO STOOLS
This caricature depicts the political dilemma of the Directory, which vainly sought a centrist position between the left and right.
Bulloz/© Photo RMN/Art Resource, NY

the name of the masses. The Babeuvists advocated a vaguely defined material equality, or communism, for all citizens—a "community of goods," as they called it. They also assigned a key role to a small revolutionary vanguard in carrying out this final revolution. Regarding the present Republic as simply a new form of oppression by the elites, they conspired to overthrow it.

The Elusive Center   The Directory's adherents stood somewhere in the center of this broad spectrum, hostile to royalists and Neo-Jacobins alike and ready to shift their ground with any change in the political balance. Thus, although the Neo-Jacobins had spurned Babeuf's calls for insurrection, after Babeuf's plot was exposed the Directory joined forces with the right. But when the first regular elections in the year V (1797) produced a royalist victory, the Directory reversed field. Backed by influential generals, the government purged newly elected royalist deputies, suppressed royalist newspapers, and allowed the Neo-Jacobins to open new clubs.

After a few months, however, the Directory grew fearful of the revived left. During the elections of the year VI (1798), Neo-Jacobins and Directorial moderates vied for influence in what almost amounted to party rivalry. But in the end the Directory would not risk the results of free elections. Again it intervened: It closed down clubs and newspapers, manipulated electoral assemblies, and purged those Neo-Jacobins who were elected anyway. Interestingly, at almost the same moment that France's government was quashing its political rivals, leaders of the American republic were reluctantly coming to accept opposition parties as legitimate. In France, however, the Directory would not tolerate organized opposition, and that rigidity contributed to the Republic's demise.

The Rise of Bonaparte

Meanwhile, the Directory years provided unexpected impetus for revolutionary expansion in Europe, which brought into being a half-dozen **sister republics** (see map 21.1), including the Batavian Republic in the Netherlands and the Helvetic Republic in the Swiss Confederation. Revolutionary change also spread through the entire Italian peninsula, as French commanders in the field began to make their own diplomacy. Among them was a young brigadier general, Napoleon Bonaparte.

Bonaparte personifies the world-historic individual—the rare person whose life decisively dominates the course of historical events. Born in 1769 of an impoverished but noble family on the French-controlled island of Corsica, Napoleon scarcely seemed destined to play such a historic role. His youthful ambitions and fantasies involved little more than leading Corsica to independence from France. Sent to French military academies, he proved a diligent student, adept at mathematics. Aloof from his aristocratic classmates, whose pretensions he resented, self-reliant and energetic, Bonaparte became an expert on artillery.

After 1789 the young officer returned to Corsica, but his ambitions ran up against more conservative forces on the island. Eventually, local factional conflict drove him and his family off Corsica altogether. Bonaparte then moved onto a much larger stage. He rose steadily and rapidly through the military ranks, based in part on the luck of opportunities but equally on his ability to act decisively. While on leave in Paris in 1795, Bonaparte was assigned to the planning bureau of the war ministry. There he advocated a new strategy: opening a front in Italy to strike at Austrian forces from the south, while French armies on the Rhine pushed as usual from the west. The strategy was approved, and Bonaparte gained command of the Army of Italy in 1796.

The Making of a Hero   Austria's forces outnumbered the French in Italy, but Bonaparte moved his troops rapidly to achieve surprise and numerical superiority in specific encounters. The end result was a major victory that brought the French into the Habsburg domain of Lombardy and its capital, Milan. Bonaparte's overall plan almost miscarried because the Army of the Rhine did not advance as planned. But this mishap made his own triumphs all the more important to the Directory. And Bonaparte ensured his popularity with the government by making his campaign self-supporting through organized levies on the Italians.

Bonaparte brought a great sense of excitement and drama to the French occupation of Lombardy. His personal magnetism and his talent in manipulating people attracted many Italians. The general encouraged the Italians to organize their own revolutionary movement; the liberation of northern Italy, he believed, would solidify support for his army and enhance his own reputation. This policy distressed the Directory because it had intended to trade back conquests in Italy in exchange for security on the Rhine frontier. But in the end the Directory endorsed the Treaty of Campo Formio, in which Bonaparte personally negotiated a peace settlement with Austria in October 1797. Austria recognized a new, independent state in northern Italy, the Cisalpine Republic, and left the Rhine question to future negotiations. The Directory regime had found the hero it desperately needed.

The French now focused their patriotic aspirations on defeating the last member of the coalition: the hated British enemy. Bonaparte naturally yearned for the glory of accomplishing this feat, and he was authorized to prepare an invasion force. Previous seaborne landings

MAP 21.1 FRANCE AND ITS SISTER REPUBLICS, 1798
Notice the locations of France's sister republics. Which republics were likely to be the most viable?

directed at Ireland had failed, however, and Bonaparte too finally had to abandon the scheme because of France's insufficient naval force.

Instead, in the spring of 1798, Bonaparte launched an expedition to Egypt intended to strike at Britain's approaches to India. But British naval superiority, in the form of Admiral Horatio Nelson's fleet, turned the expedition into a debacle. The British destroyed the French fleet at the Battle of the Nile, thereby marooning a French army in North Africa. Worse yet, the French were beaten back in several engagements with Turkish forces. Only cynical news management prevented the full story of this defeat from reaching France. Instead, the expedition's exotic details and scientific explorations held the attention of the French public. Bonaparte extricated himself from this mess by slipping off through the British blockade, in effect abandoning his army as he returned to France.

The Brumaire Coup

While Bonaparte floundered in Egypt, the Directory was faltering under political pressures at home. Charges of tyranny and ineptitude accumulated against the directors. Further French expansion into Italy, which produced new sister republics centered in Rome and Naples, precipitated a new coalition against France, consisting of Britain, Russia, and Austria. In June 1799 ill-supplied French forces were driven out of most of Italy and Switzerland.

The legislature ousted four of the five directors and named Sieyès, a respected leader of the patriots in 1789, among the replacements. Sieyès and his supporters secretly wished to alter the constitution itself, for they had lost confidence in the regime's institutions, especially its annual elections. These "revisionists" wanted to redesign the Republic along more oligarchic lines, as opposed to the Neo-Jacobins, who wished to democratize the Republic. The centrist position had virtually disappeared. The revisionists blocked emergency measures proposed by the Neo-Jacobins in reaction to the new war crisis and breathed a sigh of relief as French armies rallied and repulsed Anglo-Russian forces in the Batavian Republic and Switzerland. Most of Italy was lost for the time being, but the threat to France itself had passed. Sieyès and the revisionists moved against the Neo-Jacobins by closing their clubs and newspapers and prepared for a coup.

A General Comes to Power   Although no dire military threat remained to propel the country into the arms of a general, the revisionists wanted to establish a more centralized, oligarchic republic, and they needed a general's support. Generals were the only national heroes in France, and only a general could organize the force necessary to ensure the coup's success. Bonaparte's return to France from Egypt thus seemed most timely. Bonaparte was not the revisionists' first choice, but he proved to be the best available one.

Contrary to the intentions of Sieyès and his fellow conspirators, Bonaparte became the tail that wagged the dog. Once the coup began, he proved to be far more ambitious and energetic than the other conspirators and thrust himself into the most prominent position. Bonaparte addressed the legislature to denounce a mythical Jacobin plot and to demand emergency powers for a new provisional government. Intimidated into submission, a cooperative rump of the legislature approved the new arrangements. Along with Sieyès, Bonaparte was empowered to draft a new constitution. Thus unfolded the coup of 18 Brumaire (November 9, 1799).

The **Brumaire** coup had not been intended to install a dictatorship, but that was its eventual result. In the maneuvering among the revisionists, Bonaparte's ideas and personality prevailed. The plotters agreed to eliminate meaningful elections, which they saw as promoting political instability. They agreed also to enshrine the social ideals of 1789, such as civil equality, and to bury those of the year II, such as popular democracy. The vague notion of popular sovereignty gave way to concentrated authority. The general came out of the coup as the regime's strongman, and Sieyès' elaborate plans for a republican oligarchy ended up in the wastebasket. On one other point, the plotters were particularly deceived. With General Bonaparte's leadership they hoped to achieve durable peace through military victory. Instead, the Napoleonic regime promoted unbounded expansion and endless warfare.

THE NAPOLEONIC SETTLEMENT IN FRANCE

Bonaparte's prime asset in his rapid takeover of France was the apathy of its citizens. Most French people were so weary politically that they saw in Bonaparte what they wished to see.[1] The Committee of Public Safety had won grudging submission through its terroristic policies; Bonaparte achieved the same result almost by default. As a brilliant propagandist for himself and a man of great personal appeal, he soothed a divided France. Ultraroyalists and dedicated Jacobins never warmed to his regime, but most citizens fell between those positions. They relished the prospect of a strong, reliable government, a return to order and stability, a codification of basic revolutionary gains, and settlement of the religious conflict.

The Napoleonic Style

Napoleon Bonaparte was not a royalist or a Jacobin, not a conservative or a liberal, though his attitudes were flavored by a touch of each viewpoint. Authority, not ideology, was his great concern, and he justified his actions by their results. The revolutionaries of 1789 could consider Napoleon one of theirs because of his hostility toward the unjust and ineffective institutions of the old regime. He had little use for seigneurialism, the cumbersome institutions of Bourbon absolutism, or the congealed structures of aristocratic privilege, which the Revolution had destroyed. Napoleon valued the Revolution's commitment to equality of opportunity and continued to espouse that liberal premise. Other rights and liberties of 1789 he curtailed or disdained.

Ten years of upheaval had produced a grim paradox: The French Revolution had proceeded in the name of

---

[1] It is customary to refer to him as Bonaparte until 1804, when the general crowned himself Emperor Napoleon I.

liberty, yet successive forms of repression had been mounted to defend it. Napoleon fit comfortably into this history; unlike the Directory, he made no pretense about it. The social gains of the Revolution would be preserved through political centralization and authoritarian control. Napoleon's field of action was in fact far greater than that of the most powerful eighteenth-century monarch, for no entrenched aristocracy existed to resist him. Thanks to the clearing operations of the Revolution, he could reconstruct at will.

Tragically, however, Napoleon drifted away from his own rational ideals. Increasingly absorbed in his personal power, he began to force domestic and foreign policies on France that were geared to his imperial ambitions. Increasingly he concentrated his government on raising men and money for his armies and turned his back on revolutionary liberties.

Political and Religious Settlements

Centralization   Bonaparte gave France a constitution, approved in a plebiscite, that placed almost unchecked authority in the hands of a First Consul (himself) for ten years. Two later constitutional revisions, also approved overwhelmingly in plebiscites, increased executive power and diminished the legislative branch until it became simply a rubber stamp. The first revision, in 1802, converted the consulship into a lifetime post; the second, in 1804, proclaimed Napoleon hereditary emperor. The task of proposing new laws passed from elected representatives to appointed experts in the Council of State. This new body advised the ruler, drafted legislation under his direction, and monitored public officials. Such government by experts stood as an alternative to meaningful parliamentary democracy for the next century.

The system of local government established by Bonaparte in 1800 came ironically close to the kind of royal centralization that public opinion had roundly condemned in 1789. Bonaparte eliminated the local elections that the Revolution had emphasized. Instead, each department was now administered by a **prefect** appointed by the ruler. The four-hundred-odd subprefects on the district level as well as the forty thousand mayors of France's communes were likewise appointed. With minor changes, the unquestionably efficient prefectorial system survived in France for 150 years, severely limiting local autonomy and self-government.

Police-state methods finished what constitutional change began: the suppression of independent political activity. From the legislature to the grass roots, France was depoliticized. The government permitted no organized opposition, reduced the number of newspapers drastically, and censored the remaining ones. The free journalism born in 1789 gave way to government press releases and news management. In 1811 only four newspapers remained in Paris, all hewing to the official line. Political clubs were prohibited, outspoken dissidents deported, and others placed under police surveillance. All these restrictions silenced liberal intellectuals as well as former political activists.

The Concordat   Napoleon's religious policies promoted tranquillity at home and a good image abroad. Before Brumaire the Republic tolerated Catholic worship in theory but severely restricted it in practice. Continued proscription of the refractory clergy; insistence on the republican calendar, with its ten-day weeks that made Sunday a workday; and a drive to keep religious instruction out of elementary schools curtailed the free and familiar exercise of Catholicism. These policies

Antoine Jean Gros
PORTRAIT OF BONAPARTE AS FIRST CONSUL
Napoleon Bonaparte as First Consul, at the height of his popularity, painted by his admirer J.-B. Gros.
Bulloz/© Photo RMN/Art Resource, NY

The Era of the Notables

With civil equality established and feudalism abolished, Napoleon believed that the Revolution was complete. It remained to encourage an orderly hierarchical society to counteract what he regarded as the excessive individualism of revolutionary social policy. Napoleon intended to reassert the authority of the state, the elites, and, in family life, the father.

In the absence of electoral politics, Napoleon used the state's appointive powers to confer status on prominent local individuals, or **notables,** thus associating them with his regime. These local dignitaries were usually chosen from among the largest taxpayers: prosperous landowners, former nobles, businessmen, and professionals. Those who served the regime with distinction were honored by induction into the Legion of Honor, nine-tenths of whose members were military men. "It is with trinkets that mankind is governed," Napoleon once said. Legion of Honor awards and appointments to prestigious but powerless local bodies were precisely such trinkets.

Napoleon offered more tangible rewards to the country's leading bankers when he chartered a national bank that enjoyed the credit power derived from official ties to the state. In education, Napoleon created elite secondary schools, or *lycées*, to train future government officials, engineers, and officers. The *lycées* embodied the concept of careers open to talent and became part of a highly centralized French academic system called the *University*, which survived into the twentieth century.

The Civil Code   Napoleon's most important legacy was a civil code regulating social relations and property rights. Baptized the Napoleonic Code, it was in some measure a revolutionary law code that progressives throughout Europe embraced. Wherever it was implemented, the **Civil Code** swept away feudal property relations and gave legal sanction to modern contractual notions of property. The code established the right to choose one's occupation, to receive equal treatment under the law, and to enjoy religious freedom. At the same time, it allowed employers to dominate their workers by prohibiting strikes and trade unions. Nor did the code match property rights with popular rights like the right to subsistence.

Revolutionary legislation had emancipated women and children by establishing their civil rights. Napoleon undid most of this by restoring the father's absolute authority in the family. "A wife owes obedience to her husband," said the code, which proceeded to deprive wives of property and juridical rights established during the 1790s. The code curtailed the right to divorce, while establishing a kind of double standard in the dissolution of a marriage (see "Family and Gender Roles under the Napoleonic Civil Code," p. 608). The

CHRONOLOGY
Napoleon's Ascendancy in France

Nov. 1799	Coup d'etat of 18 Brumaire.
Dec. 1799	Bonaparte becomes First Consul.
Feb. 1800	Inauguration of prefectorial system.
July 1801	Concordat with the Church.
May 1802	Legion of Honor founded.
Aug. 1802	Bonaparte becomes Life Consul.
March 1804	Promulgation of Civil Code.
May 1804	Napoleon becomes emperor.
Aug. 1807	Suppression of the Tribunate.
March 1808	Organization of the Imperial Nobility.

provoked wide resentment among the mass of citizens whose commitment to Catholicism remained intact throughout the Revolution.

Though not a believer himself, Napoleon judged that major concessions to Catholic sentiment were in order, provided that the Church remained under the control of the state. In 1801 he negotiated a **Concordat,** or agreement, with Pope Pius VII. It stipulated that Catholicism was the "preferred" religion of France but protected religious freedom for non-Catholics. The Church was again free to operate in full public view and to restore the refractory priests. Primary education would espouse Catholic values and use Catholic texts, as it had before the Revolution, and clerical salaries would be paid by the state. Though nominated by the ruler, bishops would again be consecrated by the pope. But as a major concession to the Revolution, the Concordat stipulated that land confiscated from the Church and sold during the Revolution would be retained by its purchasers. On the other hand, the government dropped the ten-day week and restored the Gregorian calendar.

The balance of church-state relations tilted firmly in the state's favor, for Napoleon intended to use the clergy as a major prop of his regime. The pulpit and the primary school became instruments of social control, to be used, as a new catechism stated, "to bind the religious conscience of the people to the august person of the Emperor." As Napoleon put it, the clergy would be his "moral prefects." Devout Catholics came to resent this subordination of the Church. Eventually Pope Pius renounced the Concordat, to which Napoleon responded by removing the pontiff to France and placing him under house arrest.

FAMILY AND GENDER ROLES UNDER THE NAPOLEONIC CIVIL CODE

"Art. 148. The son who has not attained the full age of 25 years, the daughter who has not attained the full age of 21 years, cannot contract marriage without the consent of their father and mother; in case of disagreement, the consent of the father is sufficient.

"Art. 212. Married persons owe to each other fidelity, succor, assistance.

"Art. 213. The husband owes protection to his wife, the wife obedience to her husband.

"Art. 214. The wife is obliged to live with her husband, and to follow him to every place where he may judge it convenient to reside: the husband is obliged to receive her, and to furnish her with everything necessary for the wants of life, according to his means and station.

"Art. 215. The wife cannot plead [in court] in her own name, without the authority of her husband, even though she should be a public trader . . . or separate in property.

"Art. 217. A wife . . . cannot give, alienate, pledge, or acquire by free or chargeable title, without the concurrence of her husband in the act, or his consent in writing.

"Art. 219. If the husband refuses to authorize his wife to pass an act, the wife may cause her husband to be cited directly before the court of first instance . . . which may give or refuse its authority, after the husband shall have been heard, or duly summoned.

"Art. 229. The husband may demand a divorce on the ground of his wife's adultery.

"Art. 230. The wife may demand divorce on the ground of adultery in her husband, when he shall have brought his concubine into their common residence.

"Art. 231. The married parties may reciprocally demand divorce for outrageous conduct, ill-usage, or grievous injuries, exercised by one of them towards the other."

Nicolas Andre Monsiau
Deputies from the Cisalpine Republic of Italy proclaim Napoleon Bonaparte their president in 1802.
Chateaux de Versailles et de Trianon, Versailles, France. Erich Lessing/Art Resource, NY

code also expanded the husband's options in disposing of his estate, although each child was still guaranteed a portion.

The prefectorial system of local government, the Civil Code, the Concordat, the University, the Legion of Honor, and the local bodies of notables all proved to be durable institutions. They fulfilled Napoleon's desire to create a series of "granite masses" on which to reconstruct French society. His admirers emphasized that these institutions contributed to social stability as skillful compromises between revolutionary liberalism and an older belief in hierarchy and central authority. Detractors point out that these institutions were class oriented and excessively patriarchal. Moreover, they fostered overcentralized, rigid structures that might have sapped the vitality of French institutions in succeeding generations. Whatever their merits or defects, these institutions took root, unlike Napoleon's attempt to dominate all of Europe.

NAPOLEONIC HEGEMONY IN EUROPE

After helping to give France a new government, Bonaparte turned to do battle against the second anti-French coalition in northern Italy. The outcome of his campaign against Austria would either solidify or destroy his regime. Within a few years, in the arena of international relations his ambitions lost all semblance of re-

straint. Bonaparte evolved from a winning general of the Republic to an imperial conqueror. After defeating his continental opponents on the battlefield in a series of ever more murderous campaigns, he still faced an implacable enemy in Britain. Unable to invade Britain, he resorted to economic warfare and blockade, but Britain withstood that assault as well. Meanwhile, the raw militarism of Napoleon's rule became evident in the relentless expansion of military conscription within the empire.

Military Supremacy and the Reorganization of Europe

Bonaparte's strategy in 1800 called for a repeat of the 1797 campaign: He would strike through Italy while the Army of the Rhine pushed eastward against Vienna. Following French victories at Marengo in Lombardy and in Germany, Austria sued for peace. The Treaty of Lunéville (February 1801) essentially restored France to the position it had held after Bonaparte's triumphs in Italy in 1797.

In Britain a war-weary government now stood alone against France and decided to negotiate. The Treaty of Amiens (March 1802) ended hostilities and reshuffled territorial holdings outside Europe, such as the Cape Colony in South Africa, which passed from the Dutch to the British. But this truce proved precarious because it did not settle the future of French influence in Europe or of commercial relations between the two great powers.

Nicholas Pocock
NELSON'S FLAGSHIPS AT ANCHOR, **1807**
Admiral Nelson's heavily armed three-decker ship of the line, which inflicted devastation on the French fleet at Trafalgar. National Maritime Museum, Greenwich, London

Napoleon abided by the letter of the treaty but soon violated its spirit. Britain and Austria alike were dismayed by further expansion of French influence in Italy and Switzerland. Most important, perhaps, France seemed determined to exclude British trade rather than restore normal commercial relations. Historians agree that the Treaty of Amiens failed to keep the peace because neither side was ready to abandon its century-long struggle for predominance.

The Third Coalition   A third anti-French coalition soon took shape, a replay of its predecessors. France ostensibly fought to preserve the new regime at home and its sister republics abroad. The coalition's objectives included the restoration of the Netherlands and Italy to "independence," the limitation of French influence elsewhere, and, if possible, a reduction of France to its prerevolutionary borders. Like most such alliances, the coalition would be dismembered piecemeal.

French hopes of settling the issue directly by invading Britain proved impossible once again. At the Battle of Trafalgar (October 1805), Admiral Nelson's fleet crushed the combined naval forces of France and its ally Spain (see page 609). Nelson, an innovative tactician who broke rule-book procedures on the high seas just as French generals did on land, died of his wounds in the battle but ensured the security of the British Isles for the remainder of the Napoleonic era.

Napoleon, meanwhile, had turned against the Austro-Russian forces. Moving 200,000 French soldiers with unprecedented speed across the Continent, he took his enemies by surprise and won a dazzling succession of victories. After occupying Vienna he proceeded against the coalition's main army in December. Feigning weakness and retreat at the moment of battle, he drew his numerically superior opponents into an exposed position, crushed the center of their lines, and inflicted a decisive defeat. This Battle of Austerlitz was Napoleon's most brilliant tactical achievement, and it forced the Habsburgs to the peace table. The resulting Treaty of Pressburg (December 1805), extremely harsh and humiliating for Austria, imposed a large indemnity and required the Habsburgs to cede their Venetian provinces.

France and Germany   By now the French sphere of influence had increased dramatically to include most of southern Germany, which Napoleon reorganized into the Confederation of the Rhine, a client realm of France (see map 21.2). France had kept Prussia neutral during the war with Austria by skillful diplomacy. Only after Austria made peace did Prussia recognize its error in failing to join with Austria to halt Napoleon. Belatedly, Prussia mobilized its famous but antiquated army; it was rewarded with stinging defeats by France

in a number of encounters culminating in the Battle of Jena (October 1806). With the collapse of Prussian military power, the conquerors settled in Berlin and watched the prestige of the Prussian ruling class crumble. Napoleon was now master of northern Germany as well as the south. For a while it appeared that he might obliterate Prussia entirely, but he restored its sovereignty—after amputating part of its territory and imposing a crushing indemnity.

Napoleon was free to reorganize central Europe as he pleased. After formally proclaiming the end of the Holy Roman Empire in 1806, he liquidated numerous small German states and merged them into two new ones: the Kingdom of Westphalia, with his brother Jérôme on the throne, and the Grand Duchy of Berg, to be ruled by his brother-in-law Joachim Murat. His ally Saxony became a full-scale kingdom, while a new duchy of Warsaw was carved out of Prussian Poland. This "restoration" of Poland had propaganda value; it made the emperor appear as a champion of Polish aspirations, compared to the rulers of Prussia, Russia, and Austria, who had dismembered Poland in a series of partitions between 1772 and 1795. Moreover, Napoleon could now enlist a Polish army and use Polish territory as a base of operations against his remaining continental foe, Russia.

France and Russia   In February 1807 Napoleon confronted the colossus of the east in the Battle of Eylau; the resulting carnage was horrifying but inconclusive. When spring came, only a dramatic victory could preserve his conquests in central Europe and vindicate the extraordinary commitments of the past two years. The Battle of Friedland in June was a French victory that demoralized Russia's Tsar Alexander I and persuaded him to negotiate.

Meeting at Tilsit, the two rulers buried their differences and agreed, in effect, to partition Europe into eastern and western spheres of influence. Each would support the other's conquests and mediate in behalf of the other's interests. The Treaty of Tilsit (July 1807) sanctioned new annexations of territory directly into France and the reorganization of other conquered countries. The creation of new satellite kingdoms became the vehicle for Napoleon's domination of Europe. Like the French Republic, the sister republics became kingdoms between 1805 and 1807. And it happened that Napoleon had a large family of brothers ready to wear those new royal crowns.

The distorted shape of Napoleonic Europe is apparent on maps dating from 1808 to 1810 (see map 21.2). His chief satellites included the Kingdom of Holland, with brother Louis on the throne; the Kingdom of Italy, with Napoleon himself as king and his stepson Eugène de Beauharnais as viceroy; the Confederation of the

Charles Meynier
THE DAY AFTER THE BATTLE OF EYLAU, 9 FEBRUARY 1807
Napoleon amidst the carnage on the battlefield of Eylau, the bloodiest engagement to date of the revolutionary-Napoleonic era, where the French and Russians fought each other to a stalemate in 1807.
Versailles, France. Giraudon/Art Resource, NY

Rhine, including brother Jérôme's Kingdom of Westphalia; the Kingdom of Naples, covering southern Italy, with brother Joseph the ruler until Napoleon transferred him to Spain and installed his brother-in-law Murat; and the Duchy of Warsaw. Belgium, the Rhineland, Tuscany, Piedmont, Genoa, and the Illyrian provinces had been annexed to France. Switzerland did not become a kingdom, but the Helvetic Republic (as it was now called) received a new constitution dictated by France. In 1810, after yet another war with Austria, a marriage was arranged between the house of Bonaparte and the house of Habsburg. Having divorced Joséphine de Beauharnais, Napoleon married princess Marie Louise, daughter of Francis II, who bore him a male heir the following year.

Naval War with Britain

For a time it seemed that Britain alone stood between Napoleon and his dream of hegemony over Europe. Since Britain was invulnerable to invasion, Napoleon hoped to destroy its influence by means of economic warfare. Unable to blockade British ports directly, he could try to close off the Continent: keep Britain from

its markets, stop its exports, and thus ruin its trade and credit. Napoleon reasoned that if Britain had nowhere to sell its manufactured goods, no gold would come into the country and bankruptcy would eventually ensue. Meanwhile, overproduction would cause unemployment and labor unrest, which would turn the British people against their government and force the latter to make peace with France. At the same time, French advantages in continental markets would increase with the elimination of British competition.

The Continental System   Napoleon therefore launched his **Continental System** to prohibit British trade with all French allies. Even neutral ships were banned from European ports if they carried goods coming from the British Isles. Britain responded in 1807 with the Orders in Council, which in effect reversed the blockade: It *required* all neutral ships to stop at British ports to procure trading licenses and pay tariffs. In other words, the British insisted on regulating all trade between neutral states and European ports. Ships that failed to obey would be stopped on the high seas and captured. In an angry response, Napoleon, in turn, threatened to seize any neutral ship that obeyed the Orders in Council by stopping at British ports.

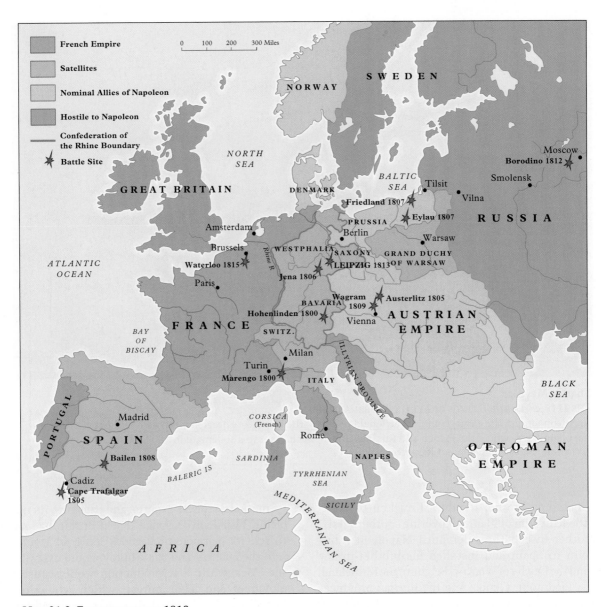

MAP 21.2 EUROPE AROUND 1810
Note the extent of the French Empire as well as its satellite territories and allies. Was it plausible that the Napoleonic Empire could sustain its military power from Madrid to Warsaw?

Thus, a total naval war between France and Britain enveloped all neutral nations. Indeed, neutral immunity virtually disappeared because every ship was obliged to violate one system or the other and thus run afoul of naval patrols or privateers. Although the British captured only about forty French ships a year after 1807 (for few were left afloat), they seized almost three thousand neutral vessels a year, including many from the United States.

The Continental System did hurt British trade. British gold reserves dwindled, and 1811 saw widespread unemployment and rioting. France was affected, in turn, by Britain's counterblockade, which cut it off from certain raw materials necessary for industrial production. But the satellite states, as economic vassals of France, suffered the most. In Amsterdam, for example, shipping volume declined from 1,350 ships entering the port in 1806 to 310 in 1809, and commercial revenues dropped calamitously. Out of loyalty to the people whom he ruled, Holland's King Louis Bonaparte tolerated smuggling. But this action so infuriated Napoleon that he ousted his brother from the throne and annexed the Kingdom of Holland directly to France. Smuggling was, in fact, the weak link in the system, for it created holes in Napoleon's wall of economic sanctions that constantly needed plugging. This problem drove the emperor to ever more drastic actions.

Jean-Auguste-Dominique Ingres
NAPOLEON ON HIS IMPERIAL THRONE, 1806
Emperor Napoleon I on his imperial throne in 1806, by the great portrait painter Ingres. Note the dramatic contrast in appearance with the young, intense military hero of the Republic in David's portrait at the beginning of this chapter. Musée des Beaux-Arts, Rennes, France. Erich Lessing/Art Resource, NY

CHRONOLOGY
Napoleon and Europe

June 1800	Battle of Marengo and defeat of the Second Coalition.
Feb. 1801	Treaty of Lunéville with Austria.
March 1802	Treaty of Amiens with Britain.
Sept. 1802	Annexation of Piedmont.
1805–1806	Third Coalition forms.
Oct. 1805	Battle of Trafalgar and defeat of French fleet.
Dec. 1805	Battle of Austerlitz; defeat of Austria.
1806	Battle of Jena and humiliation of Prussia.
1807	Battles of Eylau and Friedland; stalemate with Russia.
July 1807	Treaty of Tilsit with Russia. Consolidation of satellite kingdoms.
1807	Launching of Continental System against British trade.
Feb. 1808	Invasion of Spain.
July 1809	Battle of Wagram; Austria defeated again.
April 1810	Napoleon weds princess Marie Louise of Austria.
Dec. 1810	Annexation of Holland.
July 1812	Invasion of Russia.
Oct. 1812	Retreat and destruction of Grand Army.
Oct. 1813	Battle of Leipzig and formation of Fourth Coalition.
March 1814	Battle of France and Napoleon's abdication.

The Napoleonic Conscription Machine

One key to Napoleon's unrestrained ambitions in Europe was the creation of an efficient administrative state in France and its annexed territories with the ability to continuously replenish the ranks of the imperial army.

The National Convention's mass levy of August 1793 had drafted all able-bodied unmarried men between the ages of eighteen and twenty-five. But this unprecedented mobilization had been meant as a one-time-only emergency measure, a temporary "requisition." There was no implication that subsequent cohorts of young men would face conscription into the army as part of their civic obligations. When the war resumed in 1798, however, the Directory passed a conscription law that made successive "classes" of young men (that is, those born in a particular year) subject to a military draft should the need arise. The Directory immediately implemented this law and called up three classes, but local officials reported massive draft evasion in most of the departments. Many French youths found the prospect of military service repugnant. From this shaky foundation, however, the Napoleonic regime developed a remarkably successful conscription system.

The Rules of the Game After much trial and error with the details, timetables, and mechanisms, the system began to operate efficiently within a few years.

The government assigned an annual quota of conscripts for each department. Using parish birth registers, the mayor of every community compiled a list of men reaching the age of nineteen that year. These youths were then led by their mayor to the cantonal seat on a specified day for a draft lottery. Panels of doctors at the departmental capitals later verified or rejected claims for medical exemptions. In all, about a third of French youths legally avoided military service because they were physically unfit—too short, lame, or suffering from poor eyesight, chronic diseases, or other infirmities.

In the draft lottery, youths picked numbers out of a box; marriage could no longer be used as an exemption, for obvious reasons. Those with high numbers were spared (for the time being), while those who drew low numbers filled the local induction quota. Two means of avoiding service remained: The wealthy could purchase a replacement, and the poor could flee. True, the regime had a bad conscience about allowing draftees to hire replacements, because the practice made its rhetoric about the duties of citizenship sound hollow. But to placate wealthy notables and peasants with large holdings (who were sometimes desperate to keep their sons on the farm), the government permitted the hiring of a replacement under strict guidelines that made it difficult and expensive but not impossible. The proportion of replacements was somewhere between 5 and 10 percent of all draftees.

Draft Evasion For Napoleon's prefects, conscription levies were always the top priority among their duties, and draft evasion was the number one problem. Dogged persistence, bureaucratic routine, and various forms of coercion gradually overcame this chronic resistance. From time to time, columns of troops swept through areas in which evasion and desertion were most common and arrested culprits by the hundreds. But draft evaders usually hid out in remote places—mountains, forests, marshes—so coercion had to be directed against their families as well. Heavy fines assessed against the parents did little good because most were too poor to pay anything. A better tactic was to billet troops in the draft evaders' homes; if their families could not afford to feed the troops, then the community's wealthy taxpayers were required to do so. All these actions created pressure on the youths to turn themselves in. By 1811 the regime had broken the habit of draft evasion, and conscription was grudgingly becoming accepted as a disagreeable civic obligation, much like taxes. Just as draft calls began to rise sharply, draft evasion fell dramatically.

Napoleon had begun by drafting 60,000 Frenchmen annually, but by 1810 the annual quotas had risen steadily to 120,000, and they continued to climb. Moreover, in 1810 the emperor ordered the first of many

Royalist caricatures often depicted Napoleon as an ogre whose conscription machine devoured the nation's young men. Bibliothèque Nationale de France, Paris

"supplementary levies," calling up men from earlier classes who had drawn high lottery numbers. In January 1813, to look ahead, Napoleon replenished his armies by calling up the class of 1814 a year early and by making repeated supplementary calls on earlier classes.

RESISTANCE TO NAPOLEON

By 1808, with every major European power except Britain vanquished on the battlefield, Napoleon felt that nothing stood in his way. Since Spain and, later, Russia seemed unable or unwilling to stop smuggling from Britain, thus thwarting his strategy of economic warfare, the emperor decided to deal with each by force of arms. His calculations proved utterly mistaken, and in both places he ultimately suffered disastrous defeats. More generally, Napoleon's intrusion into Italy, Germany, Spain, and Russia set in motion various responses and movements of resistance. French expansion sparked new forms of nationalism in some quarters, but also liberalism and reaction. Finally, all his opponents coalesced, defeated Napoleon on the battlefield, and drove him from his throne.

The "Spanish Ulcer"

Spain and France shared a common interest in weakening British power in Europe and the colonial world. But the alliance they formed after making peace with each other in 1795 brought only troubles for Spain, including the loss of its Louisiana Territory in America and (at the Battle of Trafalgar) most of its naval fleet. The Spanish royal household, meanwhile, was mired in scandal. Prime Minister Manuel de Godoy, once a lover of the queen, was a corrupt opportunist and extremely unpopular with the people. Crown Prince Ferdinand despised Godoy and Godoy's protectors, the king and queen, while Ferdinand's parents actively returned their son's hostility.

Napoleon looked on at this farce with irritation. At the zenith of his power, he concluded that he must reorganize Spain himself to bring it solidly into the Continental System. As a pretext for military intervention, he set in motion a plan to invade Portugal, supposedly to partition it with Spain. Once the French army was well inside Spain, however, Napoleon intended to impose his own political solution to Spain's instability.

Napoleon brought the squabbling king and prince to France, where he threatened and bribed one and then the other into abdicating. The emperor then gathered a group of handpicked Spanish notables who followed Napoleon's scenario by petitioning him to provide a new sovereign, preferably his brother Joseph. Joseph was duly proclaimed king of Spain. With 100,000 French troops already positioned around Madrid, Joseph prepared to assume his new throne, eager to rule under a liberal constitution and to believe his brother's statement that "all the better Spanish people are on your side." As he took up the crown, however, an unanticipated drama erupted.

Popular Resistance   Faced with military occupation, the disappearance of their royal family, and the crowning of a Frenchman, the Spanish people rose in rebellion.

Francisco de Goya
***The Third of May*, 1808**
The great Spanish artist Francisco de Goya memorably captured the brutality of French reprisals against the citizens of Madrid who dared to rebel against the Napoleonic occupation on May 2, 1808.
Painted in 1814. Museo del Prado, Madrid, Spain. Erich Lessing/Art Resource, NY

Francisco de Goya
The Disasters of War: Populacho
In a relentlessly bleak series of drawings collectively entitled *The Horrors of War,* Goya went on to record the savagery and atrocities committed by both sides of the struggle in Spain.
The Norton Simon Art Foundation, Pasadena, CA

It began on May 2, 1808, when an angry crowd in Madrid rioted against French troops, who responded with firing squads and brutal reprisals. This bloody incident, known as the Dos de Mayo and captured in Goya's famous paintings, has remained a source of Spanish national pride, for it touched off a sustained uprising against the French. Local notables created committees, or *juntas,* to organize resistance and to coordinate campaigns by regular Spanish troops. These troops were generally ineffective against the French, but they did produce one early victory: A half-starved French army was cut off and forced to surrender at Bailén in July 1808. This defeat broke the aura of Napoleonic invincibility.

The British saw a great opportunity to attack Napoleon in concert with the rebellious Spanish people. Landing an army in Portugal, the British bore the brunt of anti-French military operations in Spain. In what they called the Peninsular War, a grueling war of attrition, their forces drove the French out of Portugal. After five years of fighting and many reversals, they pushed the French back across the Pyrénées in November 1813. The British commander, the Duke of Wellington, grasped the French predicament when he said: "The more ground the French hold down in Spain, the weaker they will be at any given point."

About 30,000 Spanish **guerilla** fighters helped wear down the French and forced the occupiers to struggle for survival in hostile country. The guerillas drew French forces from the main battlefields, inflicted casualties, impeded the French access to food, and pun-

ished Spanish collaborators. Their harassment kept the invaders in a constant state of anxiety, which led the French to adopt harsh measures in reprisal. But these "pacification" tactics only escalated the war's brutality and further enraged the Spanish people.

Together, the Spanish regulars, the guerillas, and the British expeditionary force kept a massive French army of up to 300,000 men pinned down in Spain. Napoleon referred to the war as his "Spanish ulcer," an open sore that would not heal. Though he held the rebel fighters in contempt, other Europeans were inspired by their example of armed resistance to France.

The Spanish Liberals   The war, however, proved a disaster for Spanish liberals. Torn between loyalty to Joseph, who would have liked to be a liberal ruler, and nationalist rebels, liberals faced a difficult dilemma. Those who collaborated with Joseph hoped to spare the people from a brutal war and to institute reform from above in the tradition of Spanish enlightened absolutism. But they found that Joseph could not rule independently; Napoleon gave the orders in Spain and relied on his generals to implement them. The liberals who joined the rebellion organized a provisional government by reviving the ancient Spanish parliament, or Cortes, in the southern town of Cádiz. Like the French National Assembly of 1789, the Cortes of Cádiz drafted a liberal constitution in 1812 (see "Spanish Liberals Draft a Constitution, 1812," p. 617), which pleased the British and was therefore tolerated for the time being by the juntas.

SPANISH LIBERALS DRAFT A CONSTITUTION, 1812

"The general and extraordinary Cortes of the Spanish nation, duly organized . . . in order duly to discharge the lofty objective of furthering the glory, prosperity and welfare of the Nation as a whole, decrees the following political Constitution to assure the well-being and upright administration of the State.

"Art. 1: The Spanish Nation is the union of all Spaniards from both hemispheres.

"Art. 3: Sovereignty resides primarily in the Nation and because of this the right to establish the fundamental laws belongs to it exclusively.

"Art. 4: The Nation is obligated to preserve and protect with wise and just laws civil liberty, property and the other legitimate rights of all the individuals belonging to it.

"Art. 12: The religion of the Spanish Nation is and always will be the Catholic, Apostolic, Roman and only true faith. The Nation protects it with wise and just laws and prohibits the exercise of any other.

"Art. 14: The Government of the Spanish Nation is an hereditary limited Monarchy.

"Art. 15: The power to make laws resides in the Cortes with the King.

"Art. 16: The power to enforce laws resides in the King.

"Art. 27: The Cortes is the union of all the deputies that represent the Nation, named by the citizens.

"Art. 34: To elect deputies to the Cortes, electoral meetings will be held in the parish, the district, and the province.

"Art. 59: The electoral meetings on the district level will be made up of the electors chosen at the parish level who will convene at the seat of every district in order to name the electors who will then converge on the provincial capital to elect the deputies to the Cortes.

"Art. 338: The Cortes will annually establish or confirm all taxes, be they direct or indirect, general, provincial or municipal. . . .

"Art. 339: Taxes will be apportioned among all Spaniards in proportion to their abilities [to pay], without exception to any privilege."

From *Political Constitution of the Spanish Monarchy*, proclaimed in Cádiz, March 19, 1812, James B. Tueller (tr.).

In reality, most nationalist rebels despised the liberals. They were fighting for the Catholic Church, the Spanish monarchy, and the old way of life. When in 1814 Wellington finally drove the French out of Spain and former crown prince Ferdinand VII took the throne, the joy of the Cádiz liberals quickly evaporated. As a royalist mob sacked the Cortes building, Ferdinand tore up the constitution of 1812, reinstated absolutism, restored the monasteries and the Inquisition, revived censorship, and arrested the leading liberals. Nationalist reactionaries emerged as the victors of the Spanish rebellion.

Independence in Spanish America

The Creoles, descendants of Spanish settlers who were born in the New World, also profited from the upheaval in Spain. Spain had been cut off from its vast empire of American colonies in 1805, when the British navy won control of the Atlantic after the Battle of Trafalgar. In 1807 a British force attacked Buenos Aires in Spain's vice-royalty of the Río de la Plata (now Argentina). The Argentines—who raised excellent cattle on the *pampas*, or grassy plains—were eager to trade their beef and hides for British goods, but Spain's rigid mercantilism had always prevented such beneficial commerce. The Argentines welcomed the prospect of free trade, but not the prospect of British conquest. With Spain unable to defend them, the Creoles organized their own militia and drove off the British, pushed aside the Spanish viceroy, and took power into their own hands. The subsequent upheaval in Spain led the Argentines to declare their independence. After Ferdinand regained the Spanish throne in 1814, he sent an army to reclaim the colony, but the Argentines, under General José de San Martín, drove it off, and Argentina made good on its claim to full independence.

Rebellion spread throughout Spanish America, led above all by Simón Bolívar, revered in the hemisphere as "The Liberator." After Napoleon removed the king of Spain in 1808, the Creoles in Spain's vice-royalty of New Granada (encompassing modern-day Venezuela, Colombia, and Ecuador) elected a congress, which declared independence from Spain. An arduous, protracted war with the Spanish garrisons followed, and by 1816 Spain had regained control of the region.

Bolívar resumed the struggle and gradually wore down the Spanish forces; in one campaign his army marched six hundred miles from the torrid Venezuelan lowlands over the snow-capped Andes Mountains to Colombia. Finally in 1819 the Spanish conceded defeat. Bolívar's dream of one unified, conservative republic of

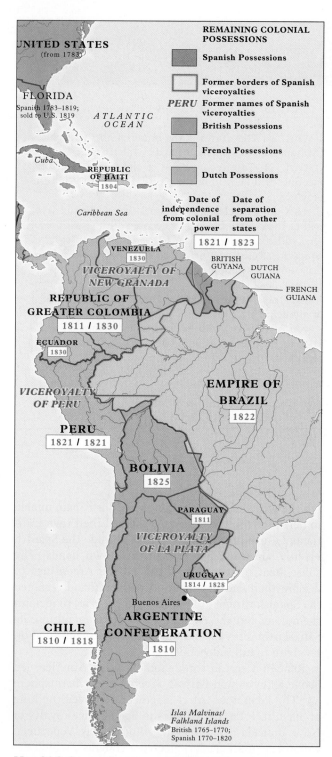

MAP 21.3 SOUTH AMERICA AFTER INDEPENDENCE

The Russian Debacle

Napoleon did not yet realize in 1811 that his entanglement in Spain would drain French military power and encourage resistance in central Europe. On the contrary, never were the emperor's schemes more grandiose. Surveying the crumbling state system of Europe, he imagined that it could be replaced with a vast empire, ruled from Paris and based on the Napoleonic Code. He mistakenly believed that the era of the balance of power among Europe's states was over and that nationalist sentiments need not constrain his actions.

Russia now loomed as the main obstacle to Napoleon's imperial reorganization and domination of Europe. Russia, a restive ally with ambitions of its own in eastern Europe, resented the restrictions on its trade under the Continental System. British diplomats, anti-Napoleonic exiles such as Baron Stein of Prussia, and nationalist reactionaries at court all pressured the tsar to resist Napoleon. Russian court liberals, more concerned with domestic reforms, hoped on the contrary that Alexander would maintain peace with France, but by 1812 their influence on the tsar had waned. For his part, Napoleon wanted to enforce the Continental System and humble Russia. As he bluntly put it: "Let Alexander defeat the Persians, but don't let him meddle in the affairs of Europe."

Napoleon prepared for his most momentous military campaign. His objective was to annihilate Russia's army or, at the least, to conquer Moscow and chase the army to the point of disarray. To this end he marshaled a "Grand Army" of almost 600,000 men (half of them French, the remainder from his satellite states and allies) and moved them steadily by forced marches across central Europe into Russia. The Russians responded by retreating in orderly fashion and avoiding a fight. Many Russian nobles abandoned their estates and burned their crops to the ground, leaving the Grand Army to operate far from its supply bases in territory stripped of food. At Borodino the Russians finally made a stand and sustained a frightful 45,000 casualties, but the remaining Russian troops managed to withdraw in order. Napoleon lost 35,000 men in that battle, but far more men and horses were dying from hunger, thirst, fatigue, and disease in the march across Russia's unending, barren territory. The greatly depleted ranks of the Grand Army staggered into Moscow on September 14, 1812, but the Russian army was still intact and far from demoralized.

The Destruction of the Grand Army In fact, the condition of Moscow demoralized the French. They found the city deserted and bereft of badly needed supplies. The next night Moscow was mysteriously set ablaze, causing such extensive damage as to make it unfit to

Gran Colombia soon disintegrated under regional pressures into several independent states, but not before Bolívar launched one final military campaign and liberated Peru, Spain's remaining colony in South America (see map 21.3).

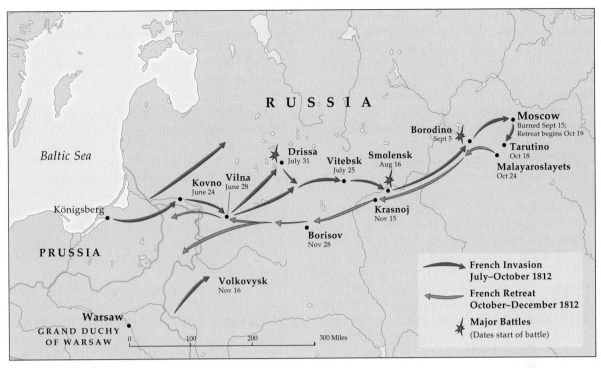

MAP 21.4 THE RUSSIAN CAMPAIGN OF 1812

Just as Goya's drawings captured the unique ferocity of the Spanish campaign, this illustration evokes the particular agonies of climate and logistics in the Russian debacle. Photo Archive, Nationalbibliothek Austria

be the Grand Army's winter quarters. Realistic advisers warned the emperor that his situation was dangerous, while others told him what he wished to hear—that Russian resistance was crumbling. For weeks Napoleon hesitated. Logistically it was imperative that the French begin to retreat immediately, but that would constitute a political defeat. Only on October 19 did Napoleon finally order a retreat, but the order came too late.

The delay forced an utterly unrealistic pace on the bedraggled army as it headed west. Supplies were gone, medical care for the thousands of wounded nonexistent, horses lacking. Food shortages compelled foraging parties to sweep far from the main body of troops, where these men often fell prey to Russian guerillas. And there was the weather—Russia's bitter cold and deep snow, in which no commander would wish to find himself leading a retreat of several hundred miles, laden with wounded and loot but without food, fuel, horses, or proper clothing. Napoleon's poor planning, the harsh weather, and the operation of Russian guerilla bands made the long retreat a nightmare of suffering for the Grand Army (see page 619). No more than 100,000 troops survived the ordeal. Worse yet, the Prussian contingent took the occasion to desert Napoleon, opening the possibility of mass defections and the formation of a new anti-Napoleonic coalition.

German Resistance and the Last Coalition

Napoleon was evidently impervious to the horror around him. On the sleigh ride out of Russia, he was already planning how to raise new armies and set things aright. Other European statesmen, however, were ready to capitalize on Napoleon's defeat in Russia and demolish his empire once and for all. Provocative calls for a national uprising in various German states to throw off the tyrant's yoke reinforced the efforts of diplomats like Prussia's Baron Stein and Austria's Klemens von Metternich to revive the anti-Napoleonic coalition.

Reform from Above in Prussia   In Prussia after the defeat of 1806, the government had introduced reforms intended to improve the quality of the bureaucracy by offering nonnobles more access to high positions and by reducing some of the nobility's privileges. The monarchy hoped thereby to salvage the position of the nobility and the authority of the state. Prussian military reformers adopted new methods of recruitment to build up a trained reserve force that could be rapidly mobilized, along with a corps of reserve officers to take command of these units. Prussia, in other words, hoped to achieve French-style efficiency and military mobilization without resorting to

new concepts of citizenship, constitutions, legislatures, or the abolition of seigneurialism. On the level of propaganda and the symbolic gesture, writers in Prussia and other German states called for a popular war of liberation under the slogan "With God for King and Fatherland."

Against this background of Prussian military preparation and growing nationalist sentiment, the diplomats maneuvered and waited. Finally, in March 1813, King Frederick William III of Prussia signed a treaty with Russia to form an offensive coalition against Napoleon. A great struggle for Germany ensued between the Russo-Prussian forces and Napoleon and his allies. Austria continued to claim neutrality and offered to mediate the dispute, but at a meeting in Prague, Napoleon rejected an offer of peace in exchange for restoring all French conquests since 1802.

In August, as Napoleon learned of new defeats in Spain, Habsburg Emperor Francis finally declared war on his son-in-law. Napoleon called up underage and overage conscripts and was able to field one last army, but his major southern German ally, Bavaria, finally changed sides. A great battle raged around Leipzig for three days in October, and when the smoke cleared, Napoleon was in full retreat. German states were free from Napoleon's domination, but Prussia's rulers were also free from the need to concede further reforms in the political and social order.

The Fall of Napoleon   In the belief that he could rely on his conscription machine, Napoleon had rebuffed offers by the allies to negotiate peace in 1813. In fact, however, he reached the end of the line in November 1813 with a desperate call for 300,000 more men to defend France against the allies. Difficulties were inevitable, wrote one prefect, "when the number of men required exceeds the number available." Another reported: "There is scarcely a family that is not oppressed by conscription." Alongside sizable contingents of Italians, Germans, and other foreigners from the annexed territories and satellite states, nearly 2.5 million Frenchmen had been drafted by Napoleon. At least 1 million of those conscripts never returned.

With Napoleon driven back into France, British troops reinforced the coalition to ensure that it would not disintegrate once central Europe had been liberated. The coalition offered final terms to the emperor: He could retain his throne, but France would be reduced to her "normal frontiers." (The precise meaning of this term was left purposely vague.) Napoleon, still hoping for a dramatic reversal, chose to fight, and with some reluctance the allies invaded France. Napoleon led the remnants of his army skillfully but to no avail. The French had lost confidence in him, conscription had reached its limits, and no popular spirit of resistance to

NAPOLEON JUSTIFIES HIMSELF IN 1815

"I have cleansed the Revolution, ennobled the common people, and restored the authority of kings. I have stirred all men to competition, I have rewarded merit wherever I found it, I have pushed back the boundaries of greatness. Is there any point on which I could be attacked and on which a historian could not take up my defense? My despotism? He can prove that dictatorship was absolutely necessary. Will it be said that I restricted freedom? He will be able to prove that license, anarchy, and general disorder were still on our doorstep. Shall I be accused of having loved war too much? He will show that I was always on the defensive. That I wanted to set up a universal monarchy? He will explain that it was merely the fortuitous result of circumstances and that I was led to it step by step by our very enemies. My ambition? Ah, no doubt he will find that I had ambition, a great deal of it—but the grandest and noblest perhaps, that ever was: the ambition of establishing and consecrating at last the kingdom of reason and the full exercise, the complete enjoyment, of all human capabilities!"

From B. Las Cases (ed.), *Mémorial de Sainte-Hélène.*

invasion developed as it had in 1792. Paris fell in March 1814. The price of this defeat was unconditional surrender and the emperor's abdication. Napoleon was transported to the island of Elba, between Corsica and Italy, over which he was granted sovereignty. After twenty-two years of exile, the Bourbon Dynasty returned to France.

The Napoleonic Legend

For Napoleon, imperial authority—originating with him in France and radiating throughout Europe—represented the principle of rational progress. In his view, the old notion of balance of power among European states merely served as an excuse for the British to pursue their selfish interests. While paying lip service to the notion of Italian, Spanish, and Polish nationhood, Napoleon generally scorned patriotic opposition to his domination as an outmoded, reactionary sentiment— exemplified by the "barbaric" guerillas in Spain fighting for king and religion. Modern-minded Europeans, he believed, would see beyond historic, parochial traditions to the prospect of a new European order. Indeed, Napoleon's credibility with some reformers in Europe was considerable. The Bavarian prime minister, for instance, justified his collaboration with France in 1810 in these words: "The spirit of the new age is one of mobility, destruction, creativity. . . . The wars against France offer the [unfortunate] possibility of bringing back old constitutions, privileges, and property relations."

During his final exile, however, Napoleon came to recognize that nationalism was not necessarily reactionary—as one could plainly see in the nationalistic but liberal Cortes of Cádiz of 1812. Progressive thinking and nationalist aspirations could coexist.

From exile Napoleon rewrote his life story to portray his career as a series of defensive wars against selfish adversaries (especially Britain) and as a battle in behalf of the nations of Europe against reactionary dynasties. In this way, Napoleon brilliantly (if falsely) put himself on the side of the future.

These memoirs and recollections from exile formed the basis of the Napoleonic legend, as potent a force historically, perhaps, as the reality of the Napoleonic experience. The image they projected emphasized how General Bonaparte had consolidated what was best about the French Revolution while pacifying a bitterly divided nation and saving it from chaos. They cast the imperial experience in a deceptively positive light, glossed over the tyranny and unending military slaughter, and aligned Napoleon with reason, efficiency, and modernity (see "Napoleon Justifies Himself in 1815," above).

The Napoleonic legend also evoked a sense of grandeur and glory that moved ordinary people in years to come. Napoleon's dynamism and energy became his ultimate inspirational legacy to succeeding generations. In this way, the Napoleonic legend fed on the Romantic movement in literature and the arts. Many young romantics (including the poet William Wordsworth and the composer Ludwig van Beethoven) saw in the French Revolution a release of creativity and a liberation of the individual spirit. Napoleon's tyranny eventually alienated most such creative people. But the Napoleonic legend, by emphasizing the bold creativity of his career, meshed nicely with the sense of individual possibility that the romantics cultivated. Napoleon's retrospective justifications of his reign may not be convincing, but one can only marvel at the irrepressible audacity of the man.

Summary

In the confrontations between Napoleon and his European adversaries, France still embodied the specter of revolution. Even if the revolutionary legacy in France amounted by that time to little more than Napoleon's contempt for the inefficiency and outmoded institutions of the old regime, France after Brumaire remained a powerful challenge to the status quo. Napoleon intended to abolish feudalism, institute centralized administrations, and implant the French Civil Code in all of France's satellite states. But by 1808 his extravagant international ambitions relied on increasingly tyrannical and militaristic measures. These in turn provoked a range of responses, including nationalist rebellions. Britain and Russia, then Prussia and Austria, joined forces once more to bring the Napoleonic Empire down, to restore the balance of power in Europe, and to reinstall the Bourbons in France. But the clock could not really be set back from Europe's experience of revolution and Napoleonic transformation. The era of modern political and social conflicts had begun.

QUESTIONS FOR FURTHER THOUGHT

1. Apart from Jesus, more books have probably been written about Napoleon than any other historical figure. What accounts for this enduring fascination? Compare Napoleon to dominant leaders of the past whom you have studied (e.g., Alexander the Great, Caesar, Philip II, and Louis XIV).

2. Was Napoleon a revolutionary? Did he consolidate or betray the French Revolution?

3. Using the boxed excerpt in which Napoleon justifies his conduct as a starting point, what is *your* assessment of his reign?

RECOMMENDED READING
(SEE ALSO CHAPTER 20)

Sources

De Caulaincourt, Armand. *With Napoleon in Russia.* 1935. A remarkable account of the diplomacy and warfare of the 1812 debacle by a man at Napoleon's side.

Herold, J. C. (ed.). *The Mind of Napoleon.* 1961.

Thompson, J. M. (ed.). *Napoleon Self-Revealed.* 1934.

Walter, Jakob. *The Diary of a Napoleonic Foot Soldier.* Edited by M. Raeff. 1991. A vivid and appalling account of the Russian campaign.

Studies

Bell, David. *The First Total War: Napoleon's Europe and the Birth of Warfare as We Know It.* 2007. A persuasive account of the period's militarism.

Bergeron, Louis. *France under Napoleon.* 1981. A fresh and insightful evaluation of the Napoleonic settlement in France.

Broers, Michael. *Europe under Napoleon, 1799–1815.* 1996. An incisive and up-to-date synthesis on French expansion in Europe.

Chandler, David. *Napoleon's Marshals.* 1986. By a leading expert on Napoleonic military history.

Connelley, Owen. *Blundering to Glory: Napoleon's Military Campaigns.* 1988. An irreverent but incisive account of Napoleon's military leadership.

———. *Napoleon's Satellite Kingdoms.* 1965. A study of the states conquered by France and ruled by the Bonaparte family.

Dwyer, Philip (ed.). *Napoleon and Europe.* 2001. A well-focused yet wide-ranging collection of essays with a comprehensive bibliography.

Ellis, Geoffrey. *Napoleon.* 1997. A concise profile of the era.

Elting, John. *Swords around a Throne: Napoleon's Grande Armee.* 1988. An eminently readable military history.

Englund, Steven. *Napoleon: A Political Life.* 2004. A recent, and perhaps the best, one-volume biography in English.

Esdaile, Charles. *Fighting Napoleon: Guerrillas, Bandits, and Adventurers in Spain, 1808–1814.* 2004.

———. *Napoleon's Wars: An International History 1803–1815.* 2008. A panoramic survey and interpretation.

Forrest, Alan. *Conscripts and Deserters: The Army and French Society during the Revolution and Empire.* 1988. A study of popular resistance to revolutionary and Napoleonic conscription.

Gates, David. *The Spanish Ulcer: A History of the Peninsular War.* 1986. On the Spanish rebellion, the French response, and Wellington's expeditionary force.

Geyl, Pieter. *Napoleon, For and Against.* 1949. Napoleon and the historians, as reviewed by a Dutch scholar with no illusions.

Hazareesingh, Sudhir. *The Legend of Napoleon.* 2004. A lively and suggestive study of an elusive subject.

Lynch, John. *The Spanish American Revolutions, 1808–1826.* 1986. A comprehensive account of the independence movements in Spanish America and their aftermath.

Lyons, Martyn. *France under the Directory.* 1975. A brief topical survey of the Revolution's later, unheroic phase.

———. *Napoleon Bonaparte and the Legacy of the French Revolution.* 1994. A good recent textbook.

Marcus, G. J. *A Naval History of England, II: The Age of Nelson.* 1971. The standard history of British naval supremacy.

Palmer, Robert R. *The World of the French Revolution.* 1971. Emphasizes the interplay of French power and revolutionary movements outside of France.

Rothenberg, Gunther. *The Art of Warfare in the Age of Napoleon.* 1978. A good analysis of strategy and tactics.

Sheehan, James. *German History, 1770–1866.* 1989. An outstanding overview of this and other periods in German history.

Sutherland, D. M. G. *France, 1789–1815: Revolution and Counter-revolution.* 1985. A fine general history of France in this period.

Tulard, Jean. *Napoleon: The Myth of the Savior.* 1984. A synthesis by the leading French expert on Napoleon.

Woloch, Isser. *Napoleon and His Collaborators: The Making of a Dictatorship.* 2001.

Woolf, Stuart. *A History of Italy, 1700–1860.* 1979. An authoritative general history, with fine chapters on this period.

This painting of a copper foundry in the 1830s evokes the grandeur and ugliness of early industrialization.
The Art Archive/Bibliothéque des Arts Decoratifs. Paris/Dagli Orti

Chapter Twenty-Two

FOUNDATIONS OF NINETEENTH-CENTURY EUROPE

THE POLITICS OF ORDER • THE PROGRESS OF INDUSTRIALIZATION
• SOCIETY IN THE EARLY INDUSTRIAL AGE
• RECONSIDERING SELF AND SOCIETY IN THE EARLY NINETEENTH CENTURY

After twenty-five years of war, the powers that had opposed Napoleon sought to guarantee that no one state would be able to dominate the Continent again. The wars against France had been about more than territory or the balance of power, however. The allies also had fought to safeguard monarchy and social hierarchy and, by so doing, to prevent the outbreak of future revolutions. Their first step was to bring back the dynasties that had been overturned. These restored regimes were nonetheless new, and establishing them raised questions about how power should be organized, what institutions should direct society, and who should participate in deciding policy. The possibility of revolution thus remained a fact of life, dreaded by some and hoped for by others, reinvoked in each country by the uprisings, acts of repression, and major reforms of the next several decades.

European nations faced major economic and social challenges as well as political ones in the aftermath of the revolutionary and Napoleonic wars. In parts of western Europe, industrialization was beginning to transform the very structure of society. Social relations based on custom were giving way to ones seemingly determined by the impersonal rules of economics. As populations grew larger, more people migrated to cities, where they were plunged into harsh material circumstances and faced novel social problems. Industrialization increased production exponentially but also subjected millions to hardships for which neither charity nor government had adequate answers. These changes, experienced more in western than in southern or eastern Europe, opened the way to a new era of passionate social reform and became a central preoccupation of European thought.

● 1798 Coleridge & Wordsworth, *Lyrical Ballads*

1814-15 Congress of Vienna ▬

1815 Napoleon's "Hundred Days" ●

1817 Ricardo, *Principles of Political Economy* ●

1819 Carlsbad Decrees ●

1820-21 Uprising in Italy and Spain ▬

1821 Greek Revolution Begins ●

1824 Charles X crowned King of France ●

THE POLITICS OF ORDER

Allied leaders wanted to design a peace that would impose order across the continent. Once they settled the boundaries between states, they placed conservative kings on hereditary thrones and pressed these monarchs to prevent disorder in their own lands. Internationally, they sought to establish an intricate balance of power that would make war unlikely and ensure that the major powers would join in stamping out any future threat of revolution. But revolutions broke out in 1820–1821 and 1830, an early measure of the limited effectiveness of the experiment in international conservatism.

The Congress of Vienna

To forge these arrangements, the great international conference known as the **Congress of Vienna** met in September 1814, an occasion for serious deliberations and elaborate pomp centered on the monarchs of Austria, Prussia, Russia, and dozens of lesser states. Officials, expert advisers, princesses and countesses, dancers and artists, and the ambitious of every rank flocked to the Austrian capital. Their gaiety and elegance made the Congress a symbol of aristocratic restoration.

The business of the Congress remained the responsibility of the four victorious powers—Austria, Great Britain, Russia, and Prussia—an inner circle to which France was soon admitted. Austria's foreign minister, Prince Klemens von Metternich, had welded the international alliance that defeated Napoleon, and he now conducted the affairs of the Congress with such skill that its provisions can be seen as largely his work. Handsome, elegant, and arrogant, Metternich was the epitome of an aristocrat, fluent in all the major European languages, a dandy who dabbled in science and shone in the ballroom. Metternich was generally supported by Lord Castlereagh, England's able foreign minister. By contrast, Russia's Tsar Alexander I, who acted as his own chief diplomat, was more unpredictable and quixotic, given to mysticism and grandiose ideas that ran counter to the practical calculations by which the Congress reached agreement.

The Peace Terms The most pressing issue these statesmen faced was the future of France. Most favored restoring the monarchy, and the Treaty of Paris, signed in May 1814, had recognized as king Louis XVIII, a brother of the executed Bourbon, Louis XVI. The treaty also restored France to its slightly expanded frontiers of 1792. A settlement covering all the territory affected by the Napoleonic wars would take longer. Those negotiations included Prince Talleyrand, the French representative, a shrewd politician noted for having held high office during the French Revolution and under Napoleon, and who now ably served Louis XVIII in his efforts to reassert French political influence in Europe.

The concerns of these men focused on continental Europe, since only Great Britain among the victors had extensive interests overseas, and no one objected to its claims on South Africa, Ceylon, and Malta. Conflicting interests kept Austria, Prussia, and Russia from dividing up Poland as they had in the eighteenth century, but neither did they want to risk creating an independent Poland. So Russia received most of Poland to be ruled as a separate kingdom, and Prussia took about half of Saxony—a triumph of old regime diplomacy in which each of the powers gained something (see map 22.1). Prussia was also given greatly enlarged territories in the Rhineland, ensuring that formidable Prussian armies would stand along the French border.

● 1833 *Zollverein* in Germany

1846-47 Famine in Ireland ▬

1851 Crystal Palace Exhibition ●

1851 Mill, On *Liberty* ●

The Congress of Vienna is portrayed here as a kind of elegant salon in which the very clothes these statesmen wore mix the styles of the old regime and the new century.
AKG London

The former Austrian Netherlands were absorbed into a new, independent Kingdom of the Netherlands, which created another strong buffer against France and prevented any major power from controlling the Low Countries' strategically located river ports. Austria, in return for ceding the southern Netherlands, acquired Venetia and recovered Lombardy, which greatly strengthened Austrian dominance of northern Italy. The other duchies of northern Italy went to dukes with close Austrian ties.[1]

[1] The Kingdom of Sardinia would have liked Lombardy but got Genoa, the ancient Italian maritime republic. Russia took Finland from Sweden, which in turn got Norway from Denmark.

The terms agreed on at Vienna constituted the most extensive European peace settlement since the Treaty of Westphalia in 1648. Each of the victors gained territory, and France was surrounded by states capable of resisting any future French aggression. The final act was signed in June 1815 by the five great powers, as well as Sweden, Spain, and Portugal, a gracious recognition of their past importance.

Napoleon's Hundred Days

The terrifying news of Napoleon's escape from exile interrupted the deliberations of the Congress in March 1815. He had tried to make the best of ruling the island of Elba and had even showed something of his old flair as he designed uniforms, held receptions, and inquired into the local economy. But the island principality was far too small to contain an emperor's ambition. Landing in the south of France, he was joined by units of the French army as he moved toward Paris. Louis XVIII waited for signs of resistance that did not develop, then climbed into his carriage and headed for the eastern border. Napoleon again became the ruler of France without firing a shot. He then tried to negotiate with the powers allied against him, but they declared him an outlaw and quickly assembled their troops. After several minor battles, allied armies led by Wellington defeated Napoleon for the last time at Waterloo, in Belgium, on June 18. The allies quickly dispatched him, essentially as prisoner, to the tiny, distant island of St. Helena in the South Atlantic. Napoleon's dashing venture lasted only a hundred days, but it permanently altered the terms and spirit of the peace for France: the new Treaty of Paris signed in 1815 required France to pay an indemnity and reduced its boundaries to those of 1789. The Bourbons again returned to the French throne, but the fear of another uprising haunted the regime and gave rise, at least in part, to its repressive policies.

Principles of International Order

The **restorations** of 1815 acknowledged many of the changes of the past twenty-five years. The restored Bourbons now governed France with a constitution, even if it was drafted and proclaimed by themselves alone. In Germany, the Holy Roman Empire and hundreds of minor German principalities, all abolished by Napoleon, were not restored but were consolidated into thirty-nine states, including Prussia and Austria, and joined in a loose confederation. The Congress also set down rules of diplomatic conduct useful to this day, and due in part to the complicated arrangements negotiated at Vienna, the Continent would be free of a general European war for the next hundred years. Yet the Congress was also a reactionary force, emphasizing tradition as the sole source of legitimacy for the restored regimes. One of the great symbols of its conservatism—although one with little practical effect—was the Holy Alliance, Tsar Alexander's vague proposal that European politics be governed by Christian principles. (See "Metternich Analyzes the Threat to Stability.")

Opposition to the Settlement

The new order faced serious challenges almost immediately. In 1820 and 1821, uprisings occurred in both Italy and Spain, led by young army officers influenced by Napoleonic reforms and convinced that individual advancement and efficient government required a constitution. Metternich quickly called for a **"Concert of Europe"** to snuff the flames of revolution by force, but unanimity among the former allies was breaking down. Great Britain did not even attend the conference, which approved Austrian intervention in Naples and called on France to intervene in Spain. French forces met little resistance in Spain, and their royal parade was welcomed by conservatives throughout Europe as evidence of the French monarchy's revived prestige.

Colonial independence movements in Latin America, which had steadily gained ground during the Napoleonic era, also burst forth anew with the 1820 revolution in Spain. But talk of European intervention to quash the revolts brought stern warnings from Britain, and the United States' proclamation of the Monroe Doctrine in 1823 declared the Americas outside the sphere of European power politics. In 1821, the outbreak of the Greek war for independence against Ottoman Turk rule sparked the opposite response from the European powers. Cries for freedom from that home of ancient democracy excited liberals throughout Europe, an early demonstration of the power of nationalist movements. Metternich restrained Russia from rushing to war against the Ottomans, but he could not keep British and French fleets from intervening in 1827, when the Ottoman sultan seemed about to subdue the Greeks. Russia declared war a few months later. Greece was granted independence in 1829 on terms arranged by the European powers, which stipulated that it must have a king who was not a member of the ruling family of a major power. This was done partly in response to public opinion, but also to make sure that the Greek rising would go no further. In the name of Greek freedom, Britain, France, and Russia displayed a willingness to use force and an eagerness to carve up the Ottoman Empire that foreshadowed the practices of imperialism later in the century.

The Pillars of the Restoration: Russia, Austria, Prussia

Even the most reactionary rulers accepted some of the changes brought by revolution, war, and Napoleonic occupation. They understood that to maintain social

MAP 22.1 EUROPE, 1815

Examine the territorial boundaries of Europe after the Congress of Vienna. What do you notice about the extent of the French and Austrian empires in 1815 compared to 1810 (see map 21.1)? Compare the compact nation-states of western Europe to the geographically fragmented areas of Italy and Germany, and to the multinational Habsburg, Ottoman, and Russian empires.

order, their governments had to be better able to sustain large armies and collect taxes, support a trained bureaucracy, dispense justice evenly, and provide services. Because the state thus affected the lives of its subjects more directly, even the conservative governments of Russia, Austria, and Prussia had to be concerned with popular sentiment.

The Russian Empire   By 1820 Tsar Alexander had become Metternich's staunchest ally, imposing harsh censorship, increasing restrictions on universities, and making sure that the constitution granted to the newly

organized Kingdom of Poland was largely ignored. On Alexander's death in 1825, a group of young army officers, the "Decembrists," attempted a coup and called for a constitution to ensure a more efficient and enlightened administration in Russia. Their poorly planned and isolated conspiracy was easily defeated, but it would be remembered by conservatives as an ever-present danger and by revolutionaries as part of Russia's radical tradition.

Alexander's younger brother, Nicholas I, succeeded him, convinced that only a loyal army and his own decisiveness had prevented revolution. He turned Russia

METTERNICH ANALYZES THE THREAT TO STABILITY

On December 15, 1820, Metternich wrote the Habsburg emperor from the international conference he had called to deal with the threat of revolution. Metternich argued that all monarchs must act together against the common threat, which he blamed on the middle class.

"The governments, having lost their balance, are frightened, intimidated, and thrown into confusion by the cries of the intermediary class of society, which, placed between the Kings and their subjects, breaks the scepter of the monarch, and usurps the cry of the people—that class so often disowned by the people, and nevertheless too much listened to. . . .

"We see this intermediary class abandon itself with a blind fury and animosity. . . . applying itself to the task of persuading Kings that their rights are confined to sitting upon a throne, while those of the people are to govern, and to attack all that centuries have bequeathed as holy and worthy of man's respect—denying, in fact, the value of the past, and declaring themselves the masters of the future.

". . . The evil is plain; the means used by the faction which causes these disorders are so blamable in principle, so criminal in their application, and expose the faction itself to so many dangers, that . . . we are convinced that society can no longer be saved without strong and vigorous resolutions on the part of the Governments. . . .

"By this course the monarchs will fulfill the duties imposed upon them by Him who, by entrusting them with power, has charged them to watch the maintenance of justice, and the rights of all, to avoid the paths of error . . . and to show themselves as they are, fathers invested with the authority belonging by right to the heads of families, to prove that, in days of mourning, they know how to be just, wise, and therefore strong. . . .

"The Governments, in establishing the principle of stability, will in no wise exclude the development of what is good, for stability is not immobility. But it is for those who are burdened with the heavy task of government to augment the well-being of their people! It is for Governments to regulate it according to necessity and to suit the times. It is not by concessions, which the factious strive to force from legitimate power, . . . that wise reforms can be carried out. That all the good possible should be done is our most ardent wish; but . . . even real good should be done only by those who unite to the right of authority the means of enforcing it."

From Prince Richard Metternich (ed.), *Memoirs of Prince Metternich, 1815–1829,* Mrs. Alexander Napier (tr.), Scribner's Sons Publishers, 1970.

into Europe's strongest pillar of reaction by his example at home and his willingness to use force abroad. He was also a diligent administrator who built up the Russian army and police force and who established a more effective bureaucracy by making it less attached to the nobility. Despite fears that education bred discontent, his regime also sponsored the building of schools. Nevertheless, petty corruption, the arrogance of local officials, and fear of change continued to undermine the government's capacity to manage a vast land of varied peoples in which communication was poor and few had the means or the will to effect reform.

Most thoughtful people, including the state's highest officials, agreed that serfdom had become a hindrance to Russia's development, but they proposed no solution. Intellectuals who expected Russia to develop along familiar European lines were known as Westernizers. Others, called **Slavophiles,** argued that Russia's Orthodox Christian religion, peasant communes, and traditional culture gave Russia a unique destiny. Yet, in spite of much debate about Russia's place in a changing world and the bitter grievances of Poles and peasants, the authority of the Russian state remained intact. Nicholas would watch with pride in 1848 as his empire escaped the revolutions that swept over most thrones of Europe.

The Habsburg Empire Habsburg rule over German, Italian, and eastern European lands relied on a well-organized bureaucracy. Forged by Maria Theresa and Joseph II in the eighteenth century, that system of government had enabled Austria to survive the Napoleonic wars without dramatic transformation despite repeated military defeat. Metternich and others recognized the need for domestic reform, but projects for stronger local government and for recognition of the empire's diverse nationalities came to nothing. Habsburg rule remained locked in stalemate between an increasingly cautious central bureaucracy and selfish local aristocracies.

Hungary proved particularly troublesome for the Habsburg Empire, for the dominant **Magyar** aristocracy had a strong sense of their historical identity and a good deal of power, although they remained an ethnic minority in their own country. Emperor Francis I grudgingly recognized many of their claims, and by the 1840s Magyar had replaced German as the official language of administration and schooling in Hungary. More demands followed. The campaign for a more representative Diet or parliament and related reforms was led by Lajos Kossuth, a liberal nationalist who became Hungary's leading public figure, reaching much of the nation through newspapers and public meetings.

This widespread Hungarian agitation encouraged other groups subject to Habsburg rule to claim national rights of their own (see map 22.1). Much of Polish Galicia rose in revolt in 1846, but weakened by the bitter antagonism between Polish peasants and their masters, the uprising was soon suppressed. In Croatia and Bohemia, too, angry peasants and nationalists often had different aims. The various national groups opposed to Habsburg rule, often hostile to each other, were also internally divided by class, religion, and language. Although their dissension helped sustain Habsburg control through its divide and rule strategy, nationalist movements sought to overcome these divisions and to give broader appeal to the nationalist cause (see chapter 23).

Prussia and the German Confederation Germans called the later battles against Napoleon (1813–1814) the Wars of Liberation and after that common national experience, talk of "Germany" meant more than it had before. The Congress of Vienna acknowledged this awareness with the creation of the German Confederation. A cautious gesture toward national sentiment, the Confederation still preserved the position of the strongest local rulers while facilitating some coordination among Germany's many states. Any stronger union was prevented by the rivalry of Austria and Prussia, by distaste for reform among restoration regimes, and by the conflicting ambitions of German princes. The Confederation's Diet, a council of ambassadors from member states rather than a representative assembly, was permitted to legislate only on certain limited matters, such as restrictions on the press.

In practice, the German Confederation was important in German politics largely when Metternich wished it to be. He used it, for example, to suppress agitation led by nationalist and reformist student groups in the universities. In 1817 some of these groups organized a celebration of the three hundredth anniversary of Luther's theses with a rally, the Wartburg Festival. Several hundred young people gathered to drink, listen to speeches full of mystical nationalist rhetoric, sing songs, and cheer as a Prussian military manual was tossed into a bonfire. Even such symbolic challenges to military authority alarmed the governments in Berlin and Vienna. When a well-known reactionary writer was assassinated, the Confederation issued the Carlsbad Decrees of 1819, which intensified censorship, proscribed dangerous professors and students, outlawed certain fraternities and political clubs, and required each state to guarantee that its universities would be kept safely conservative. (See "Policing the Universities.")

Despite these fears, there was less agitation within the German Confederation than in most of the rest of Europe. Meanwhile, Prussian influence increased. Its national educational system was capped by the new but prestigious University of Berlin, its administration and its army seemed models of modern efficiency, and its policies included measures that stimulated economic growth. In 1818 Prussia lowered tariffs, allowing raw materials free entry into both its eastern and western Prussian territories. By 1833 most German governments except Austria had joined Prussia's customs union, the **Zollverein**, which proved a further spur to commerce. One of the most important steps toward German unification under Prussia had been taken without clear nationalist intent.

The Test of Restoration: Spain, Italy, and France

The durability of the conservative order that the Congress of Vienna sought to impose would depend less on the autocracies in Russia, Austria, and Prussia than on the new regimes imposed in Spain, Italy, and France. There, the effects of revolution and Bonapartism had been woven into the fabric of public life. Intensely divided over questions of government—its form, powers, and policies—conservatives and liberals alike considered politics central to everything else.

Spain and Italy In Spain the Bourbon king Ferdinand VII regained his throne in 1814 when Napoleon's army was expelled. Strong enough to renounce the constitution he had promised, Ferdinand was too weak to find a solution for his government's inefficiency or the nation's poverty. In Spain's American colonies, the revolts led by José de San Martín and Simón Bolívar gained strength, and in 1820 the army that was assembled in Spain to reconquer the colonies mutinied instead and marched on Madrid. The king was then forced to grant a constitution after all, and for three years the constitutional regime struggled to cope with Spain's enormous problems, weakened by internal dissension and its uncooperative monarch. The regime's restrictions on religious orders raised powerful opposition from the Church, freedom of the press produced more devastating criticism, and the government was unable to reconquer the rebellious colonies. When a French army again crossed into Spain in 1823, this time with the blessing of the Concert of Europe and in the name of order, the Spaniards who had fought French invasion so heroically just ten years earlier were strangely acquiescent. The constitution disappeared again, but the threat of revolution did not.

POLICING UNIVERSITIES—THE CARLSBAD DECREES

The Carlsbad Decrees, drafted by Metternich, were adopted by the Diet of the German Confederation in 1819 to be applied in all its member states. Their spirit is in complete opposition to the ideal of academic freedom.

"1. There shall be appointed for each university a special representative of the ruler of each state, the said representatives to have appropriate instructions and extended powers, and they shall have their place of residence where the university is located. . . .

"This representative shall enforce strictly the existing laws and disciplinary regulations, he shall observe with care the attitude shown by the university instructors in their public lectures and registered courses; and he shall, without directly interfering in scientific matters or in teaching methods, give a beneficial direction to the teaching, keeping in view the future attitude of the students. Finally, he shall give unceasing attention to everything that may promote morality . . . among the students. . . .

"2. The confederated governments mutually pledge themselves to eliminate from the universities or any other public educational institutions all instructors who shall have obviously proved their unfitness for the important work entrusted to them by openly deviating from their duties, or by going beyond the boundaries of their functions, or by abusing their legitimate influence over young minds, or by presenting harmful ideas hostile to public order or subverting existing governmental instructions. . . .

"3. The laws that for some time have been directed against secret and unauthorized societies in the universities shall be strictly enforced. . . . The special representatives of the government are enjoined to exert great care in watching these organizations.

"The governments mutually agree that all individuals who shall be shown to have maintained their membership in secret or unauthorized associations, or shall have taken membership in such associations, shall not be eligible for any public office.

"4. As long as this edict remains in force, no publication which appears daily, or as a serial not exceeding twenty sheets of printed matter, shall be printed in any state of the Confederation without the prior knowledge and approval of the state officials. . . ."

Excerpt from Louis L. Snyder (ed.), *Documents of German History*, Rutgers University Press, 1958, pp. 158–159.

In Italy restoration meant the return to power of the aristocracies ousted by the French and reestablishment of the separate Italian states.[2] Yet the years of Napoleonic rule had established institutions that the new regimes could not ignore. Their insecure rulers at least promised constitutions, enlightened administration, peace, and lower taxes, even though they were hardly prepared to take such initiatives. Cautious, moderately repressive, and conveniently corrupt, these regimes provided the sleepy stability Metternich thought appropriate for Italians. Such an atmosphere bred some conspiracy and rumors of far more. Secret groups, known collectively as the *Carbonari* (charcoal burners), began to meet across Italy. Most were middle class, although their name suggested a life of rural simplicity. Some talked of tyrannicide, some sought equality and justice, and some advocated mild reform; they had in common the excitement of secret meetings, terrifying oaths, and ornate rituals.

By 1820 news of revolution in Spain was enough to prompt revolts in Italy. Young army officers led the demand for a constitution in Naples; but when the Neapolitan army turned to put down a rising in Sicily, an Austrian army was dispatched to Naples to remove the new constitutional regime. A similar revolt erupted in Piedmont, causing the king to abdicate in favor of his son, and Charles Albert, the prince regent, hastily granted a constitution. But when the new monarch arrived, the Austrian army was with him. Piedmont's constitution lasted two weeks. These revolutions, which left Italy's reactionary governments more rigid and Austrian influence more naked, demonstrated the inadequacy of romantic conspiracies but affirmed an Italian radical and patriotic tradition that would continue to grow.

The Bourbons Restored in France More than anything else, Europe's conservative order was meant to prevent France from again becoming the center of military aggression or revolutionary ideas, and the restoration there was an especially complex compromise. France received a constitution called the Charter, presented

---

[2] Italy was divided into three monarchies, four duchies, and a republic. The Kingdom of Sardinia (Sardinia and Piedmont), the Papal States, and the Kingdom of the Two Sicilies were monarchies. The Grand Duchy of Tuscany and the duchies of Lucca, Modena, and Parma were all tied to the Habsburgs, who annexed Lombardy and Venetia. The disappearance of the republics of Genoa (part of Piedmont) and Venice left tiny San Marino, safe on its mountaintop, the oldest republic in the world.

CHRONOLOGY
Challenges to the Vienna Settlement

May 1814	Treaty of Paris.
September 1814–June 1815	Congress of Vienna.
March 1815–June 1815	Napoleon's 100 days.
1817	German students at Wartburg.
1820–1821	Revolts in Spain and Italy.
1821–1829	Greek war of independence.
1825	Decembrist rising in Russia.
1830	Revolution in France and Belgium.

as a gift from Louis XVIII rather than a right. It granted the legislature—a hereditary Chamber of Peers and a Chamber of Deputies chosen by a small, wealthy electorate—more authority than Napoleon had allowed but left the government largely in the hands of the king. The Bourbons willingly retained Napoleon's centralized administration and effective system of taxation.

The regime's supporters, shaken by Napoleon's easy return during the Hundred Days, now determined to crush their enemies. A violent "white terror" broke out in parts of the countryside as those tainted with a revolutionary past were ousted from local office or even killed. Yet Louis XVIII resisted as best he could the more extreme demands of the reactionary ultraroyalists; he did not return land confiscated from the Church and from the émigré aristocracy during the Revolution and allowed most of those who had gained office or wealth since 1789 quietly to live out their lives. From 1816 to 1820 the Bourbons governed in a relatively peaceful and prosperous country, and Paris again became Europe's center of science and the arts.

Meanwhile, the Catholic Church, weakened in the intervening years by the loss of property and a decline in the number of new priests, revived remarkably. Missions of preachers toured the countryside calling for a return to the faith, praising the monarchy, and ceremonially planting crosses of repentance for the sins of revolution. To the surprise of many Catholics, however, Napoleon's 1801 Concordat with the Church remained in effect.

From Opposition to Revolution in France   Despite its achievements, the regime remained insecure and uncertain, satisfying neither Catholics nor anticlericals, neither ultraroyalists nor liberals. The assassination of the duke of Berry, the son of Louis' younger brother, in 1820 reminded everyone how fragile the monarchy was. Louis XVIII reacted to the assassination by naming more conservative ministers, increasing restrictions on the press, and dismissing some leading professors. The air of reaction grew heavier in 1824 when his brother succeeded to the throne as Charles X. A leader of the ultraroyalists, Charles had himself crowned at Reims in medieval splendor, in a ceremony steeped in symbols of the divine right of kings and the alliance of throne and altar.

The new government gave the Church fuller control of education, declared sacrilege a capital crime, and granted a cash indemnity to those who had lost land in the Revolution. In reality, the law against sacrilege was never enforced, and the indemnity, which helped end one of the most dangerous issues left from the Revolution, was a limited one. France still remained freer than most European countries, but Charles's subjects worried about the intentions of an ultraroyalist regime that disliked the compromises on which it rested. Public criticism increased, radical secret societies blossomed, and liberals made gains in the elections of 1827.

By 1829 the king could tolerate no more. While political disputes grew more inflamed, he appointed a cabinet of ultraroyalists only to have the Chamber of Deputies reject them. He called new elections, but instead of regaining seats, the ultraroyalists lost still more. Determined not to show the hesitancy of Louis XVI, Charles X reacted with firmness. In 1830 he and his ministers suddenly issued a set of secretly drafted decrees, the July Ordinances, which dissolved the new Chamber of Deputies even before it met, further restricted suffrage, and muzzled the press. Having shown his fiber, the king went hunting.

A shocked Paris slowly responded. Crowds began to mill about, some barricades went up, and stones were thrown at the house of the prime minister. Newspapers disregarded the ordinances and denounced the violation of the constitution, and the government responded with enough troops to raise tempers but too few to enforce order. Charles began to back down, but people were being killed (nearly seven hundred died in the three days of Paris fighting), some of the soldiers were mingling with the crowds, and liberal leaders were planning for a new regime. Once again, Paris was the scene of a popular uprising, and Charles X, victim of what he most detested, abdicated on August 2. For fifteen years France had been governed largely by its aristocracy, but the restoration had been meant above all to provide political stability. This the Bourbon regime had failed to do.

THE PROGRESS OF INDUSTRIALIZATION

Political instability was one aspect of the larger process of change in the early nineteenth century. Meanwhile, in certain parts of Europe, industrialization was creating a dynamic of economic expansion in which the elements of growth—new inventions, demand for more capital, factory organization, more efficient transportation, and increased consumption—stimulated each other and thus led to further growth.

The Technology to Support Machines

Industrialization required the efficient use of raw materials, beginning with cheap metals, such as iron, which could be formed into machines, and cheap fuel, such as coal. The increased importance of iron and coal gave England an important advantage, for it was well supplied with deposits of coal that lay conveniently close to its iron ore.

Coal and Iron   The English had increasingly turned to the use of coal as their once-great forests were cut down, and miners had begun taking coal from deeper veins, often beneath the water table. Coal in its natural form was not useful in smelting iron, however, because its impurities combined with the iron and resulted in an inferior product. For high-quality wrought iron, ironmasters at the turn of the eighteenth century turned from the traditional but expensive charcoal to coke, a purified form of coal, to produce iron. It was a breakthrough that convinced ironmasters like John Wilkinson that iron would be the building material of a new age. His improved techniques for boring cylinders made it possible to make better cannons and steam engines, and he built the world's first iron bridge over the Severn River in 1779, experimented with iron rails, launched an iron boat, and at his death was buried in an iron coffin.

The Steam Engine   The need for powerful pumps to remove the water in coal mines stimulated experiments to harness steam. The first commercially successful steam engine, based on the use of atmospheric pressure to push a piston through a cylinder, was invented in England by Thomas Savery in 1698. Used as a pump, Savery's engine was woefully inefficient, but a decade later another Englishman, Thomas Newcomen, developed a different design for an atmospheric-pressure piston engine that proved one-third more efficient. Newcomen engines were soon being used to remove water from mines not only in Great Britain but in France, Denmark, Austria, and Hungary.

The crucial resource of industrialization was coal, and coal mining was one of the earliest industrial activities, employing steam engines to pump water and creating large, polluting enterprises in which hundreds of workers labored painfully, as at this English mine in Northumberland.
The Mary Evans Picture Library

The most fundamental step in the development of steam was the work of James Watt, a young mechanic and instrument maker working at the University of Glasgow. In the 1760s, in the process of making improvements to the Newcomen engine, he came up with the idea for a new type of steam engine, one based on the creation of a separate chamber for the condensation of steam, outside of but adjacent to the cylinder. His work took years, for it required new levels of precision in machining cylinders and pistons, new designs for valves, and new knowledge of lubricants and the properties of steam itself. Finally patented in 1782, Watt's first practical model was nearly three times more efficient than the Newcomen engine. After he added a system of gears and cams for converting the piston's reciprocating motion to the rotary motion needed to drive most machines, the steam engine became much more than a pump.

Putting these inventions to use required the business talents of Watt's partner, the Birmingham industrialist Matthew Boulton. He recognized that the demand for cheap power had become more critical with the new inventions in the textile industry (including Arkwright's waterframe, Crompton's spinning mule, and Cartwright's power loom, discussed in chapter 18). From the 1780s on, the steam engine was being used in factories, and some five hundred were built before 1800. Even these early machines represented a remarkable improvement over traditional sources of power. They produced between six and twenty horsepower, comparable to the largest windmills and water mills, and did so more reliably and wherever they were needed. An economy traditionally starved for sources of power had overcome that obstacle.

Railroads New inventions grew into whole industries and were integrated into the economy with dazzling speed. The steam engine's application to rail travel is a classic case. The first successful railway line using a mounted steam engine or locomotive was built in England in 1825. A few years later an improved engine impressed spectators by outracing a horse, and in 1830 the first passenger line took its riders the thirty-two miles from Liverpool to Manchester in an hour and a quarter. Just more than a decade later, there were 2,000 miles of such rail lines in Great Britain; by 1851 there were 7,000.

Railroads constituted a new industry that stimulated further industrialization. They bought huge quantities of coal for their locomotives and iron for rails. They carried food and raw materials to cities, manufactured products to consumers, and heavy building materials and chemical fertilizers to the countryside. They made it easier for the men and women who crowded into railway cars to travel in search of work. Similarly, the telegraph, developed by a generation of scientists working in many countries and quickly adopted as an adjunct of

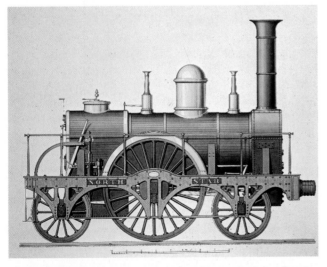

Stephenson's North Star engine of 1837 was meant to be an object of beauty, combining technology and craftsmanship.
Science Museum, London, UK/Bridgeman Art Library

railroading, expanded to other uses, becoming a military necessity and a conveyor of news to the general public.

Yet the leap from new invention to industrialization was not necessarily direct or predictable. Often dozens of subsidiary inventions or improvements were necessary to make a new machine competitive. Everywhere small-scale manufacturing and crafts persisted alongside the new. But the water-driven mills, charcoal-fired smelters, and hand-powered looms that dotted the countryside were gradually displaced, as were hundreds of thousands of skilled artisans and rural families working in their homes to make products in the old ways—a transformation that accounted for much of the human suffering occasioned by industrialization.

Patterns of Industrialization in the Early Nineteenth Century

Although twenty-five years of war had slowed and disrupted Europe's economic growth, the French Revolution and the Napoleonic era had also cleared the way for future industrialization. In France, western Germany, northern Italy, and the Low Countries, land tenure was no longer the most pressing economic and social issue. Less constrained by custom and legal restrictions, landowners, including peasant proprietors, could more easily shift their production to meet the demands of a national market. The abolition of guilds and old commercial restrictions had eliminated some obstacles to the free movement of workers and the establishment of new enterprises.

The Napoleonic Code and French commercial law not only favored free contracts and an open marketplace but also introduced the advantages of uniform and clear commercial regulations. The French government had exported a common and sensible standard of weights and measures based on the metric system, encouraged the establishment of technical schools (the Polytechnic School in Paris long remained the world's best), and honored inventors and inventions, from improved gunpowder to new techniques for raising sugar beets. Under Napoleon, Europe had benefited from improved highways and bridges and a large zone of free trade, while the Bank of France, as restructured in 1800, had become the European model of a bank of issue providing a reliable currency.

The British Model Even during the years of war and revolution, Great Britain's lead over continental countries in goods produced, capital invested, and machinery employed had widened steadily from 1789 to 1815. By the mid-1820s, after a postwar depression, British trade was reviving, and by 1830 its economy was being further transformed. Growth in one economic sector stimulated growth in others. Increased textile production, for example, accelerated the use of chemical dyes; greater iron production required more coal. A few factories in one place encouraged the growth of others in the same region, where they could take advantage of the available workforce and capital. This concentration of production in turn increased the demand for roads, canals, and, later, railways. All this growth required more capital, and on the cycle went. In continuity, range of industries affected, national scope, and rate of increase, Great Britain's industrial growth in the first half of the nineteenth century was the greatest humankind had ever experienced.

The cotton industry dominated the booming British economy. In 1760 Britain imported only 2.5 million pounds of raw cotton; by 1830 it was importing 366 million pounds. Spurred by consumer demand, cotton textiles had become the single most important industrial product in terms of output, capital investment, and number of workers. Its production was almost exclusively organized in factories using power-driven machinery for spinning yarn and weaving cloth. In the process, the price of cotton yarn fell to about one-twentieth of what it had been in the 1760s. Lancashire, with its abundant waterways and coal deposits to fuel steam engines, became the center of a booming cotton cloth industry, and Manchester, its leading city, became the cotton capital of the world.

National Differences In 1815 many regions of the Continent, including such traditional commercial centers as Barcelona and Naples, had seemed ready to follow the British example of industrial growth, but by the 1850s the zone of industrialization had narrowed to include only northeastern France, Belgium and the Netherlands, western Germany, and northern Italy. Industrial change in this zone was uneven but more extensive than outside it. Countries poorly endowed in coal and iron, such as Italy, faced formidable obstacles. Although Saxony in eastern Germany was an early industrial center, most of Germany remained an area of quiet villages in which commerce relied on peddlers and trade fairs, even though by midcentury the German states were crisscrossed by the Continent's largest railway network. Except for pockets of industrial development, eastern Europe remained a world of agricultural estates.

Belgium, which had prospered from its former connections with Holland, built on its tradition of technological skill, its geographical advantages as a trade center accessible by water, and its excellent supplies of coal to become the Continent's first industrialized nation. Belgium extracted more coal than France or Germany and was the first country to complete a railway network. The French railway system, on the other hand, was not finished until after Germany's, because it was slowed by political conflict despite early and ambitious plans. France's production of iron, coal, and

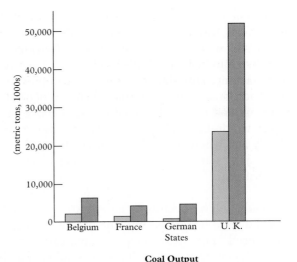

Coal Output

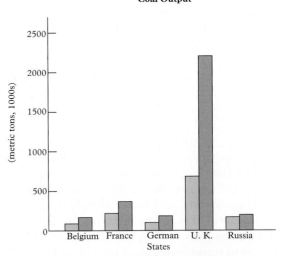

Pig Iron Production

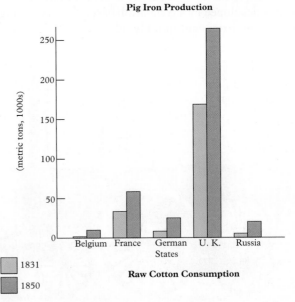

1831
1850

Raw Cotton Consumption

Production in Belgium, France, the German states, and the United Kingdom
From B. R. Mitchel, *European Historical Statistics, 1750–1970,* Columbia University Press, 1975, pp. 360–361, 428–429.

textiles increased several-fold between 1815 and 1848, but Britain's expansion in each of these sectors was much greater. In iron production, for example, the two countries were about equal in 1800, but by 1850 Britain's output was six or seven times greater. Britain outstripped France still more in textiles and coal, producing by midcentury half the world total of these items.

The Role of Government Although many writers argued that the new prosperity followed from natural economic laws that worked best unimpeded by government, by midcentury the state was centrally involved in the process of economic growth even in Britain. Tariffs, the dominant issue in British politics in the 1840s, became a critical question in every country. In 1846, after a wrenching public campaign, Britain abolished the tariff on imported grain, known as the Corn Laws (after the generic British term for grain), which had protected large domestic grain producers from foreign competition. In doing so, the nation expressed confidence in its position as the world's greatest center of manufacture and trade and sided with those who favored a lower price for bread rather than with the landowners who benefited from higher, protected grain prices. Equally important to economic development was the role of government in banking and currency. Just before the middle of the century, Parliament granted the Bank of England a monopoly on issuing money and required companies to register with the government and publish their annual budget as a guide to investors. Similar steps were taken across Europe. But before industries could effectively tap private wealth, investors needed assurance that they risked only the money they invested, without being liable (as in a partnership) for all a firm's debts. In response, many European nations passed new legislation establishing limited liability and encouraging the formation of corporations.

At the same time, the growth of cities and the development of new technology created additional social demands on government. By the 1840s most cities had a public omnibus, some sidewalks, and gas lighting in certain areas. Such services, usually provided by private companies, had to be subsidized, regulated, and given legal protection by the government. As the cost and importance of these services increased, so did the state's participation in them, often extending to full ownership. By the 1840s, the leaders of Britain, France, and Belgium sought to promote economic development in a variety of ways: by subsidizing ports, transportation, and new inventions; by registering patents and sponsoring education; by encouraging investment and enforcing contracts; and by maintaining order and preventing strikes.

The growing role of government was exemplified by the postal service, which most states had provided since the seventeenth and eighteenth centuries. These

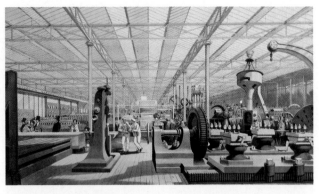

British products dominated the machinery section of the Crystal Palace Exhibition. Here men and women marveled at Joseph Whitworth's lathe for forming railway wheels, a machine for making machines.
Guildhall Library, Corporation of London, UK/Bridgeman Art Library

postal systems proved inadequate for an industrial era. In Britain, demands for improvement led a little-known inventor to propose a solution that captured the thinking of the new age. He called for standard envelopes and payment in advance by means of an adhesive stamp. These innovations would not only eliminate graft and reduce costs, he argued, but the service would pay for itself because lower rates would increase volume. His reforms, denounced as dangerous and impractical, passed nevertheless in 1840, and within twenty years the volume of mail in Britain increased sixfold. By then, money orders, savings accounts, and the telegraph had been added to postal services. In France, mail delivery was extended to rural areas, and by the 1850s every major government was adopting the new system, including the postage stamp.

The Crystal Palace The British celebrated their position as the masters of industrialization in 1851 with the first international industrial exhibition. A specially designed glass and steel pavilion was built in London, a sort of giant greenhouse called the Crystal Palace, which proved to be an architectural milestone. Many governments feared that Britain risked revolution by attracting huge throngs to London, but the admiring crowds proved well behaved. The exhibition provided a significant comparison of the relative economic development of the participating countries. Russia displayed primarily raw materials; Austria, the German *Zollverein*, and the Italian states showed mainly luxury handicrafts. Although unable to fill all the space it had demanded, the United States impressed viewers with collections of fossils, cheap manufactured products for use in the home, mountains of tooth powder and soap, and a series of new inventions, including Colt revolvers, a sewing machine, and McCormick's grain reaper.

EXTERIOR OF THE CRYSTAL PALACE,

London's imposing Crystal Palace was designed to house the first international industrial exhibition, held there in 1851. The building was constructed of cast iron and glass, a significant innovation in architecture. The exhibits held here were organized as a kind of encyclopedia of world industry, with subcategories for different products.
Hulton Archive/Getty Images

French machines, which ranged from a much-admired device for folding envelopes to a submarine, were generally considered the most elegant. But British machines surpassed everyone's in quantity, size, and variety. By 1850 Great Britain was the wealthiest nation in history,[3] and over the next twenty years, it would continue to increase its lead in goods produced.

[3] Although all estimates for this period are uncertain, it seems likely that by 1860 the per capita wealth of the French was about two-thirds and of the Germans about two-fifths that of the British.

SOCIETY IN THE EARLY INDUSTRIAL AGE

Economic growth on such a scale predictably set off far-reaching social change. Even in its early stages, industrialization impinged on much of society, from the state to the family, affecting governmental functions, the nature of work, women's roles, and childhood. Child factory labor, teeming slums, and severe cyclical unemployment required new social policies as the growing prosperity and security of the middle classes contrasted sharply with the destitution of the urban poor.

The Worlds of Industrial Work

The Factory The factory quickly became the symbol of the age. Well before industrialization, there had been workplaces in which hundreds of people labored under one roof; conversely, even in industrialized societies, most wage earners did not work in factories. But the factory symbolized new kinds of power—the power of steam and of technology, the power of capital to assemble machinery and laborers, the power of competition to drive down prices and wages, the power of markets to absorb ever more production and determine what would be produced. Above all, the factory symbolized the capacity of this whole system to change the landscape, to erect or transform cities, and to reshape the lives of masses of men, women, and children.

The factory model was most clearly triumphant in the production of textiles. Spinning and weaving had always been domestic tasks, done in the home and potentially involving the whole family. The most successful weavers often employed other workers, so that the average domestic establishment contained about a half-dozen weavers. Pay and working conditions varied with the region, the season, and the ability of middlemen to control the prices of the yarn they supplied and the cloth they purchased and resold. Textile factories, on the other hand, required an investment in buildings, machinery, and raw materials far beyond the reach of most weavers; and production per worker increased more than a thousand-fold with the factory's specialization of labor, efficient organization, and power-driven machinery. By the 1830s, cotton factories in Manchester, larger than most, averaged nearly three hundred employees.

These factories would slowly drive the older forms of textile production out of business, although the flexibility of domestic production sustained it in some regions and for certain products. The first factories hired less-skilled laborers, especially women and children, to tend power looms, splice thread, or sweep the floor. Children were paid less than women, and women less than men, who did the heaviest work and served as carpenters and mechanics. At first, children usually worked with their parents in the factories, but the increased specialization of labor meant that, like their mothers and fathers, children came to be employed and supervised without regard to family ties.

Factory Life Time clocks, bells, and whistles defined the regimentation and lock step workday of the factory. It usually began at 5:30 or 6:00 in the morning and lasted for twelve hours of work, plus whatever time was allotted for meals and for recesses (when belts were replaced and machinery fixed). The workrooms were stiflingly hot in summer and cold in winter. Textile factories were usually kept damp so the taut thread would break less readily. The pace of production was relentless and the danger of accidents from machinery great.

Employers frequently found their workers to be lethargic and sullen, prone to drunkenness and indifference. To maintain the discipline that efficient production demanded, foremen hit, cursed, and most of all,

Under the foreman's close supervision, women kept the textile looms running.

imposed fines (for lateness, for slacking off, for flawed work, for talking, and sometimes even for singing or whistling). For their part, workers periodically balked at the constant surveillance and brutal work discipline. Their loss of control over their work environment and the process of production became a major cause of labor conflict over the course of the century.

The best employers, and the inspectors subsequently appointed as the result of factory legislation, were shocked by factory conditions and by the behavior of the workers themselves, in whom they discovered foul language, slovenliness, poor health, ignorance, and promiscuity. Most factory owners could see no solution beyond more discipline, however, and nearly all employers opposed measures such as the law finally passed in England in 1847 that limited the workday to ten hours. Even that legislation was primarily an embarrassed response to the evils of child labor, which reformers and writers had long criticized.

Specialization beyond the Factory The increased specialization of labor was not limited to the allocation of work within factories. The spread of specialization among groups and institutions was a characteristic of the nineteenth-century society. Just as factories separated work from family life, so money exchange and legal contracts differentiated economic from personal or social relationships. Business affairs and governmental functions became more specialized, matters determined by calculation or regulation rather than status or social connection. Maintaining the peace, collecting taxes, inspecting factories and schools, and administering poor relief fell to separate agencies. Each nation differed in the pace and manner of institutional differentiation. In Britain, more than Continental states, local government and private groups had great authority; in France the role of the national government increased; and the German states tended to combine centralizing bureaucracies with considerable local autonomy.

The Changing Structure of Society

Political change, population growth, industrialization, and urbanization altered the way people lived and the way in which society was perceived. In the old regime, discussion of the "orders" or "ranks" in society had referred to an imaginary social pyramid rising from the lowliest peasant through all the ranks to the monarch. In this idealized picture, each person had by birth an assigned place in that pyramid, and social relations were governed by elaborate networks of obligations. In the nineteenth century, by contrast, society was most often described in terms of a few broad strata, called classes. A person was said to belong to a given social class less on the basis of connection to others than as

an attribute of his, or her husband's, occupation. The source of income was assumed to imply something of the values held, the style of life led, and later, the political and social interests likely to be favored. Social relations were represented as matters of free contract between individuals, with middle-class mobility the model. Descriptive of an expanding, fluid, unequal, national society, the concept of class gained urgency with the sharpening contrast between the middle class and the urban poor.

The Aristocracies The class most easily identified was the aristocracy. Recognized since the Middle Ages as a special group, it included all nobles (whose rank conferred many privileges) and their immediate relatives, whether they held noble titles or not: members of the upper gentry, large landholders who lived like nobles, and the established and wealthy patrician families of the commercial cities of the Netherlands, northern Germany, and northern Italy.

In the nineteenth century, however, the aristocracy was on the defensive. It had been a principal target of the French Revolution, and its privileges and influence were subsequently challenged by new industrial wealth (which overshadowed the fortunes of all but the largest landholders), wider participation in politics, the growth of the state, and cultural change. The aristocracy's relative decline was so clear, in fact, that its continued importance is easily overlooked. In most countries aristocrats continued to control most of the wealth, were closely allied to an established church, and dominated the upper levels of administration and the military. Aristocrats also stimulated some of the most influential critiques of nineteenth-century society, denouncing the middle classes for selfishness and materialism, proclaiming urban life morally inferior to rural, and lamenting the loss of gentlemanly honor.

In much of Europe, especially the south and east, a tiny aristocracy, constituting only about one percent of the population, held on to tremendous wealth and local power over the peasant masses. In the Kingdom of Naples, for example, the aristocracy had reestablished its authority after Napoleon's defeat and ruled over the three-fifths of the population that lived on their baronial estates. In Russia a fraction of the nobility held one-third of the land and administered much of the land owned by the state. Tyrants on their estates and dominant in local administration, Russia's aristocrats were pillars of tsarist rule.

In countries in which the nobles made up a higher proportion of the population, a different pattern emerged. In Poland, Hungary, and Spain, many nobles were extremely poor and some of them were sympathetic to social and political reform. In Hungary, confident Magyar aristocrats sought to strengthen their influence by cooperating with reformers seeking representative government and the decentralization of power, as did aristocrats in northern Italy and Belgium. They were thus prominent during the revolutions of 1848 in Hungary and northern Italy and in the subsequent nationalist movements in those countries (see chapter 23). In Great Britain, above all, the aristocracy proved willing to accept liberal programs in exchange for keeping their political prominence; perhaps as many as four-fifths of the members of Parliament were large landholders or their representatives. On the other hand, in Britain, younger sons from aristocratic families (who would not inherit estates) were closely associated with the upper-middle class, which lessened the sharpness of social division.

In Prussia, the most influential aristocrats were the Junkers of east Prussia, owners of large estates, some of which included sizable villages. The Junkers maintained their traditional position even when the state became the instrument of dramatic and rapid change. Considered crude and ignorant by most of the aristocracies of Europe—which set great store by polished manners, elegant taste, and excellent French—the Junkers had a proud tradition of service to the state and loyalty to their king. Their manners and values—from fondness for dueling, arrogance, and loyalty—set the tone of Prussian public life. In France, where the old aristocracy was reduced to a minor role in national politics after the revolution of 1830, its members still retained the highest social prestige, along with major influence in the Church, army, officer corps, and foreign service. And even in France, aristocrats maintained a strong voice in local affairs and continued to influence manners.

Peasants   The overwhelming majority of all Europeans were peasants, a social class as firmly tied to the land and to tradition as the aristocracy. The peasantry was deeply divided between those who owned land and those forced to sell their labor. Some of the former, especially in the west, grew relatively prosperous, but most peasants were tenants who received only a portion of the crops they raised, with the rest going to their landlords. Rural laborers were the poorest and most insecure of all, the tinder of violence and the recruits for factory work.

A critical change in peasants' lives occurred with their emancipation from traditional obligations to the lord whose land they worked. These "feudal" obligations typically might have required the peasant to give the lord a number of days of labor or to use the lord's grain mill at rates set by the lord. The French Revolution abolished such requirements, a policy carried by Napoleon to much of western Europe and that spread to most of eastern Europe with the revolutions of 1848.

These changes encouraged peasant producers to enter the commercial market; but they also deprived peasants of such traditional protections against hard times as the use of a common pasture, the right to glean what was left after the first harvest, and the practice of foraging for firewood in forests owned by others. Similarly, the decline of the putting-out system in textiles and of local industries took away critical income, especially during the winter months. Agriculture became more commercial, its production increasingly intended for market rather than for subsistence or local consumption. Profits could increase with the cultivation of one or two cash crops and with the use of improved fertilizers and machinery, but these changes were easier for farmers with more capital and bigger holdings than most peasants enjoyed.

Peasants, however, were not just passive victims of outside forces. Their suspicion of outsiders and tenacious loyalty to their region and its customs made them the despair of reformers. Yet they were not always resistant to change. Shrewd judges of their own best interests, they often cooperated with measures they saw as advantageous. Their land hunger, resentment of taxes and military service, and antipathy toward those above them could also become a major political force. Peasant involvement made a crucial difference in the early days of the French Revolution, in the Spanish resistance to Napoleon, in the wars of German liberation, and in the later strength of nationalism in Germany and Italy. Rulers were kept on edge by eruptions of peasant violence in southern England in the 1820s; Ireland in the 1830s and 1840s; Wales, Silesia, and Galicia in the 1840s; and on a smaller scale in most other countries.

A central problem for nineteenth-century European society was how to integrate the agricultural economy and the masses dependent on it into the developing commercial and industrial economy. By the 1850s the process had gone farthest in France and Great Britain but by opposite means. In Britain the peasantry was largely eliminated as the continuing enclosures of great estates concentrated land ownership in the hands of the wealthy and reduced the rural poor to laborers, hiring out for the season or by the day (see chapter 18). In France, on the other hand, peasants owned approximately one-third of the arable land and many maintained small-scale craft industries as well. Patterns elsewhere lay between these two extremes. Small landholding persisted in western Germany, northern Italy, Switzerland, the Netherlands, Belgium, and Scandinavia, alongside a trend toward the consolidation of larger farms that reduced millions to day laborers. In Germany, emancipation from obligations to the lord usually required peasants to pay for their freedom with part (often the best part) of the land they had previously cultivated.

The clear distinction remained, however, between these western and central regions and eastern Europe, where peasants were more directly subject to the power of the lord, most of all under Russian serfdom. There, landowners' authority over their peasants included claims to their unpaid labor, which in Russia ranged from a month or so of work each year to several days a week. The disadvantages of such a system were many, and the eventual emancipation of Russian serfs in the 1860s proved necessary for economic growth and minimal military and administrative efficiency.

Workers and Artisans   Industrial workers attracted far more attention than did the peasantry, although they were a minority even among paid laborers and were still outnumbered by domestic servants. Factory hands were seen as emblematic of the new age, not least because of their absolute dependence on wages set by employers, who could fire them at will and who determined the tasks performed as well as the conditions of work and the length of the workday. Most factory workers earned too little to sustain a family even when work was steady, making the employment of women and children as necessary to the family's survival as it was advantageous to employers, who appreciated their greater dexterity and the lower wages they would accept. Even so, factory workers were, in income at least, better off than about half of all laborers, and their lot improved a bit as legislation hesitantly restricted hours and set some standards of hygiene and safety.

Industrial workers were set apart not only by the conditions of their labor, but by the slums in which

This Nasmyth steam hammer looms above the men who endured heat and noise to feed it—in every way the symbol of a new era.
The Science Museum, London

they lived, and special restrictions such as the *livret*, or passport, that all French workers were required to present when applying for a job and on which previous employers recorded comments on the worker's conduct and performance. Life was still more precarious for the millions without regular employment, who did such tasks as they could find, hauling or digging for a few pence. Understandably, the powerful worried about the social volcano atop which they lived.

The most independent workers were the artisans. True, they had been stripped of their tight guilds and formal apprenticeships by the legislation of the French Revolution, by a comparable series of laws passed in Britain in the decades before the 1830s, and by a similar process in Germany that was completed by the revolutions of 1848. Nevertheless, artisans continued to ply their crafts in a hierarchy of masters, journeymen, and apprentices working in small workshops or construction sites. These skilled or semiskilled workers—carpenters, tailors, shoemakers, mechanics, stonemasons, and locksmiths—were better paid than the unskilled and often looked down on the latter. Although they could be laid off during frequent economic slumps, in general their real wages tended slowly to increase, and they tended to earn enough to support their families in one or two bare rooms on a simple diet.

Early Labor Movements   Uneducated and exhausted industrial workers, often strangers to one another, for the most part lacked the means necessary for effective concerted action to improve their lot. Their frequent outbursts of resentment and intermittent strikes usually ended in sullen defeat.

Skilled workers, by contrast, held clearer visions of their rights and tended to feel most keenly the threat of economic change. They took the lead in forming labor organizations and agitating for political redress. Although trade unions were banned everywhere except in England in the early nineteenth century, many skilled workers joined local, often secret, organizations for mutual aid. By 1850 more than 1.5 million British workers may have belonged to such groups, called friendly societies in England and confraternities in France. These societies provided burial costs for members or assistance in times of illness. Other organizations, such as artisans' production cooperatives, aimed to increase workers' control over their lives. The hundreds of strikes staged by artisans throughout western Europe in the first half of the century also hinted at what trade unions might accomplish in the future.

The meetings, the torchlight parades and the working-class press, steeped in the rhetoric of natural rights and social justice, all contributed to workers' growing sense of belonging to a distinctive class. So, above all, did the repression by police and courts that usually followed.

By midcentury, millions of workers in Britain, somewhat fewer perhaps in France, and smaller numbers elsewhere shared heroes and rituals, believed they faced a common enemy, and adopted organization as the prime means of defending themselves in a hostile world. In Britain, the national trade unions of skilled workers formed in the 1830s and 1840s (with only some 100,000 members then) steadily increased their size and influence, reaching more than a million members a generation later. The vast majority of the working class, however, remained essentially defenseless, possessing meager skills, dependent on unstable employment, and living in the isolation of poverty.

The Middle Classes   Of all the social classes, the most confident and assertive were the middle classes. At the top stood the great bankers, often connected to the aristocracy and with considerable political influence. Just below them in status were the great industrialists and the wealthiest merchants. The bottom—and largest—segment of the middle class, known as the petite bourgeoisie or lower-middle class, comprised office clerks, schoolteachers, and small shopkeepers, often distinguishable from artisans only by their pretensions. But the middle classes were epitomized by the strata in between, consisting of merchants, managers, bureaucrats, lawyers, doctors, engineers, and professors. Opposed to aristocratic privilege, they saw themselves as the beneficiaries of social changes that allowed talented people to gain security and influence.

Primarily urban, the middle classes were intimately connected with the commerce and politics of city life. In Paris they made up about one-fifth of the population, constituting nearly all those prosperous enough to pay taxes and to employ at least one maid. In other cities their proportion was probably somewhat smaller. Among nations, they were most numerous in Great Britain, a sizable fraction existed in France and Belgium, and a smaller minority elsewhere. The middle class was the only social class from which one could fall, and people established their membership in it by economic self-sufficiency, literacy, and respectability. No matter how favored by birth or fortune, they tended to think of themselves as self-made.

More than any other group, the middle classes of the nineteenth century were associated with an ideology that advocated constitutionalism, legal equality, individual rights, and economic freedom. The conquests of the middle class were measurable by the gradual adoption of values. Being in the middle—between the extremes of aristocratic privilege and power and mass poverty and ignorance—was seen as an advantage, a kind of inherent moderation. Most of Europe's writers, scientists, doctors, lawyers, and businesspeople would have been pleased to find themselves called by a London

paper in 1807 "those persons always counted the most valuable, because the least corrupted, members of society," or hearing John Stuart Mill speak a generation later of "the class which is universally described as the most wise and the most virtuous part of the community, the middle rank." Women, assigned the role of guardians of morality, played a key role in creating this middle-class identity.

Family Life in the Nineteenth Century

To a great many nineteenth-century observers, social change threatened to undermine the family, and moralists of every sort warned that the very institution most central to civilization was in danger. Recent research suggests a different view. The heightened concern for the family was a response to real stress, but it was also an expression of a growing belief in the importance of the family, which would prove to be an extraordinarily adaptable institution.

Traditional Roles   Family life in Europe had always been related to social status. For the aristocracy, family encompassed a wide network of relatives, privilege, and power. Women played a critical but subordinate role as carriers of the dowries that joined estates, as managers of large domestic staffs, and as centers of the social circles in which aristocrats met. Among peasants, the family unit might include grandparents or, where plots were large enough, even in-laws, cousins, and nephews. Particularly in the Mediterranean regions, such extended families often shared housing in the village but worked in different nearby fields. When they could, however, a young couple generally set up a household of their own. In regions where peasants owned land, they had difficulty keeping their holdings viable while still giving something to all their children. Law and custom might require equal division of inheritance (as in France), primogeniture (inheritance by the eldest son, as in England), or other more complicated arrangements. But bitter disputes occurred frequently, for the elderly feared dispossession, and children feared that they would not get their share in time.

The family was the basic economic unit, pooling income from various sources and dividing labor in customary ways. In the villages, women usually handled household chores and the smaller animals, men were responsible for the heavier work, and everyone worked together in critical periods of planting and harvest. Often the women had more access than the men to additional sources of income—piecework from a nearby mill or domestic service for the well-to-do—and they played a central role in marketing produce. Men were more likely to migrate, especially in hard times, to find work on roads or docks or at some landlord's harvest. As population increased, children were more often pushed out to seek employment as domestic servants or in the nearest mills. For artisans as well as peasants, the family was often the unit of production, although even small workshops had long tended to exclude women, at least from the better-paid tasks.

Industrialization and the Working-Class Family

The advent of industrialization presented the family economic unit with new problems, including a lack of decent housing, poor working conditions, and a higher risk of unemployment. Women and children had to supplement the father's income, but were now less likely to work side by side; if taught a trade, children were less likely to learn it from their parents. Adolescents in factory towns, hardened at an early age, often left home when their pay allowed, and urban conditions made it more difficult for the family to support the aged and the sick. Such factors could indeed weaken family ties. Critics pointed to the rise in illegitimate births and the common practice of working men and women living together without being married as signs of trouble. Yet among workers, too, the family survived.

Middle-Class Domesticity

While the breakdown of the traditional household economy loosened family ties among workers, home and family emerged as linchpins of middle-class life and the stay-at-home wife became one of the chief signifiers of middle-class respectability. The life of the middle-class woman thus contrasted greatly with that of her poorer counterparts. Well-to-do women continued to be the organizers, patrons, and ornaments of many of Europe's most cultivated circles, but the middle classes isolated their women from the harsh competition of business and politics. As the contemporary French historian Jules Michelet complained, "By a singular set of circumstances—social, economic, religious—man lives separated from woman." In Victorian England, gentlemen met in their clubs or withdrew from the ladies after dinner for their cigars and weighty talk.

Except for the prosperous who had domestic (female) servants, wives—no matter what their other burdens—were expected to prepare and serve food, wash and mend clothes, and clean the home. Nineteenth-century discourse often made the image of femininity appear to be an idle and pallid creature, encased in corset or bustle, whose tendency to faint was a sign of delicacy. In reality women's roles were far more significant and varied, but the image reflected values widely shared. Allowing a wife to be idle even if her husband worked hard was a kind of conspicuous consumption, a partial imitation of aristocratic elegance. If men must be competitive, hard, and practical, women should be tender,

innocent, and gracious—the weak but pure upholders of morality and taste. The middle-class woman with no estate to manage and few servants to direct was almost literally placed on a pedestal. Neither her needlework nor her piano playing was viewed as serious, but her role in maintaining the protective calm of the home was critical.

Middle-class concern with the family also emphasized the special moral role of women within the home, conceived as a private citadel largely closed to the outside world. The liberal dream of combining individualism and social order found its model in the family, where the patriarchal father, devoted mother, and carefully trained children were meant to live in disciplined harmony. Childhood itself lasted longer in the middle classes, for manners, education, and character required elaborate preparation. The mother was the core of this home; books, newspapers, magazines, and sermons enthusiastically described the talents her role required. Motherhood was treated as an honored occupation, fondly depicted in novels and in the new women's magazines founded, like the Parisian *Journal des Femmes*

The bourgeois family at breakfast: perfect domestic harmony, father looks up from the morning newspaper to enjoy the scene of an angelic child and adoring wife, while a servant tends to them in front of the Chinese screen that sets off the eating space.
Editions Tallandier

of 1832, to make women "skilled in their duties as companions and mothers."

Clearly, these attitudes also underpinned the famous prudery of the age and the distrust of sexual passion. In 1818 Thomas Bowdler produced his *Family Shakespeare*, a "bowdlerized" version "in which those words and phrases are omitted which cannot with propriety be read in a family," a strange sensitivity after two hundred years of admiration for Shakespeare's language. Similarly "the anti-English pollution of the waltz," imported from the Continent, was denounced as degenerate in *The Ladies' Pocket Book of Etiquette* of 1840. The middle classes sought to maintain an orderly world through convention. At a time when prostitution and drunkenness were believed to have reached new heights, prudery was more than repression. It was an effort to bend society to the self-discipline on which morality, a thriving commerce, the advancement of knowledge, and personal fulfillment were thought to rest.

The Changing Population

While Europeans grappled with political, economic, and social changes, they also faced the fact that there were more and more people—more people to feed, more seeking work, and more living in cities.

Demographic Growth The effects of population growth were visible everywhere, particularly in areas in which industrialization was under way. Research attributes the increase to a variety of factors, including a decline in disease-carrying germs, an increase in the food supply, a lowering of the age of marriage, and, after 1870, some improvement in public sanitation. Admittedly spotty data suggest that the world experienced a decline in some common diseases beginning in the eighteenth century. Microbes have cycles, and remissions had undoubtedly occurred many times before. Now, however, better supplies of food allowed the larger number of babies surviving the perilous years of infancy to reach adulthood and form families of their own.

The food supply rose because of better transportation, more effective agricultural techniques, and the potato. Agricultural associations, usually led by enlightened aristocrats, campaigned for more scientific farming, and the potato, a South American import that was easy to cultivate and yielded more calories per acre than any other crop, became a staple of the peasant diet in much of Europe by 1830. While infant mortality remained enormously high by modern standards, even a slight decline in death rates could make a great difference in the total number of people, so close to subsistence did most Europeans live.

The reasons for the trend toward earlier marriage are less clear, but peasants freed from servile obligations apparently tended to marry and form new households at a younger age. Early marriage was facilitated by the spread of cottage industry, which preceded the new factories and enabled families to add to their income by spinning or weaving at home.

The increased number of people in a single generation multiplied in the next generation and led to an enormous increase in the aggregate. As population grew, the proportion in the childbearing years grew still faster, which increased the ratio of births to the total population. The net result was that the 180 to 190 million Europeans of 1800 had become 266 million by 1850 and 295 million by 1870.

Urbanization At the turn of the century, greater London had reached one million in population. No European city since imperial Rome had ever approached this size. Paris, with about half that number, would reach one million a generation later. The third-largest European city, Naples, had 350,000 inhabitants, and in all of Europe only twenty-two cities had populations greater than 100,000. By midcentury there were forty-seven. Great Britain was the leader, with six cities over the 100,000 mark; London's population had surpassed 2.5 million by 1856, Liverpool had grown from 80,000 to almost 400,000, and Manchester and Glasgow each had more than 300,000 people. By the 1850s, half of Britain's population lived in towns or cities, making it the most urbanized society since the Classical era.

On the Continent, most old cities increased by at least 50 percent in the first half of the century, and many a town became a city. The major capitals burgeoned. Paris reached a population of nearly 1.5 million by 1850; Berlin almost trebled, to 500,000; and a similar growth rate pushed Brussels to 250,000. St. Petersburg, Vienna, and Budapest all had populations between 400,000 and 500,000. By the 1860s, the English countryside was actually losing people, as were some sections of France. The tide of urbanization was overwhelming, and nearly all the subsequent increase in European population would end up in cities swelling with new arrivals as rural folk moved to nearby towns, and town dwellers to cities.

Effects of the Population Boom The effects of a larger population were far reaching. More people consumed more food, which necessitated more intensive cultivation and the use of land previously left fallow. An increasing population also meant an expanding market for goods other than food, an element of growth that would have stronger impact later in the century. More people meant a larger potential workforce ready to leave the countryside for industrial jobs. This mobility became a social change of immeasurable importance, for it reduced the isolation of the peasantry and in some regions sparked what would become a vast migration to the Americas. Young people constituted a greater proportion of the population, which may have made for increased restiveness and a larger pool of potential revolutionaries.[4] There was also a distinction in birthrates by social class, which demographers call *differential fertility*. On the whole, affluent people had fewer children, which led some to interpret the lower classes' fertility as a lack of foresight and moral restraint and to worry that they would eventually overwhelm society.

The most influential analysis of population was Thomas R. Malthus's *An Essay on the Principle of Population as It Affects the Future Improvement of Society*, first published in 1798. Malthus argued that human population, unless checked by death (through war, famine, or pestilence) or deliberate sexual continence, increases faster than the supply of food. As a clergyman, he advocated continence, but was pessimistic that most people could exercise restraint. An economist as well, Malthus presented demography as a science closely attached to liberal economic theory, with the convenient corollary that the misery of the poor resulted from their own improvidence.

The Irish Famine Although the periodic famines and subsistence crises of earlier centuries were on the decline, they still occurred occasionally. One of the last great European subsistence crises was the disastrous Irish potato famine of 1845. By winter, the blighted harvest left Irish tenant farmers unable to pay rent for the tiny plots they worked, and hundreds of thousands of families were forced off their land to starve. Hope rested on a good harvest the following year, but when desperate peasants dug up the potato plants, they found only stinking rot. By 1847, a million Irish, about a quarter of the population, had died, and abandoned huts dotted the landscape.

While the famine sparked a good deal of debate about whether the English government should take action, the Irish received little assistance, and officials who tried to organize relief were constrained by the noninterventionist precepts of liberal economics (see "Economic Liberalism," p. 655). Meanwhile, the English absentee landowners of many Irish estates followed market principles and exported most Irish wheat to England, where it fetched a better price. Many viewed

the famine as a natural disaster rather than a failure of policy and blamed Irish laziness for the country's dependence on potatoes, an easy crop to grow. The Irish famine sparked a massive Irish migration to the United States and fanned a longstanding hatred of English rule.

Confronting the Problems of Industrial Society

The new industrial order was burdened by many social problems, including public health and morals, class division, and appalling poverty. As the terrible conditions of modern urban life were uncovered through parliamentary and scholarly inquiries, these issues were debated in hundreds of speeches, pamphlets, and newspaper articles.

Urban Squalor Poverty of the bleakest sort was nothing new to European laborers. What was new was the urban squalor in industrial areas and cities for all but the reasonably prosperous. Narrow alleys were littered with garbage and ordure that gave off an overpowering stench. The water supply in Paris, better than in most large cities, offered access to safe water only at fountains that dotted the city (the affluent paid carriers by the bucket); in London, private water companies allowed it to flow only a few hours a day. In most cities the water supply came from dangerously polluted rivers. Sewage was an even more serious problem. A third of Manchester's houses used privies in the 1830s, and a decade later the ratio of inside toilets to population was 1 to 212. In London, cesspools menaced health only slightly less than still more public means of disposal. In every city the poor lived crowded into dark, filthy, stuffy, unheated rooms; and over the cities, especially manufacturing and mining towns, chemical smog and coal smoke darkened the sky and made tuberculosis widespread among workers. (See "The Housing Crisis in France and Germany" p. 648.)

Not surprisingly, urban poverty generated rampant crime, including prostitution, street crime, and gang activity, and maintaining public order in this setting required new police forces. London's force was established by Sir Robert Peel in 1829, and the Paris Municipal Guard was created under Guizot a few years later. Peel's role led to the nickname "bobbies," by which the police are still referred to in London.

The New Vulnerability of Industrial Workers Workers' demoralizing dependence on their employers was another characteristic feature of the industrial age. Most new factories employed between 150 and 300 men, women, and children whose well-being was largely tied to a single employer. A high proportion of

---

[4] The nationalist organization Young Italy limited membership to those under forty, and probably most of the leaders of the revolutions of 1848 would have met that standard. The relation of youth to revolution is interestingly discussed in Herbert Moller, "Youth as a Force in the Modern World," *Comparative Studies in Society and History*, April 1968.

Gustave Doré
In this famous engraving of London, the rhythmic sameness and cramped efficiency of new housing suggest a machine for living appropriate to the age of the railroad.
New York Public Library

these people, new to the area in which they lived, depended on cash to pay their rent, to purchase rough cotton clothes, to provide the bread that was the staple of their diet, and to buy some candles and coal. For most workers employment was never steady. It was common for a third of the adult males of a town to be without work, especially in the winter, and pauperism was acknowledged to be the social disease of the century, a condition that included some 10 percent of the population in Britain and only slightly less in France.

Workers were the people hit hardest by the periodic economic depressions that baffled even the most optimistic observers. The depression of 1846 was nearly universal, and that of 1857 extended from North America to eastern Europe. When Britain lost access to American cotton during the Civil War of the 1860s, layoffs in the Lancashire cotton industry ran so high that at one point over 250,000 workers, more than half

the total, lived on relief. Recipes for watery soup handed out by the charitable agencies of every city defined the thinness of survival.

The Standard of Living   Although most workers everywhere suffered from the changing conditions of employment, workers in some trades and places were distinctly better off. Overall, real wages—measured by what people could buy—may have begun to increase somewhat even before a general rise in wages occurred in the mid-1840s and notably again in the 1850s. These gains meant less in new factory towns, however, where workers could be forced to buy shoddy goods at high prices in company stores. Alcoholism was so extensive that in many a factory town paydays were staggered in order to reduce the dangerous number of drunks. But technology brought benefits as well. The spread of the use of soap and cotton underwear were boons to health,

THE HOUSING CRISIS IN FRANCE AND GERMANY

The housing crisis was not limited to cities with a lot of new industry, as these two descriptions, expressing the shock of middle-class reformers, show. The first is from André Guépin, Nantes au XIXe siècle (Nantes, 1835); the second, giving Dr. Bluemner's impression of Breslau, is from Alexander Schneer, Über die Zuständer der arbeitenden Klassen in Breslau (Berlin, 1845).

"If you want to know how he [the poorer worker] lives, go—for example—to the Rue des Fumiers which is almost entirely inhabited by this class of worker. Pass through one of the drain-like openings, below street-level, that lead to these filthy dwellings, but remember to stoop as you enter. One must have gone down into these alleys where the atmosphere is as damp and cold as a cellar; one must have known what it is like to feel one's foot slip on the polluted ground and to fear a stumble into the filth: to realise the painful impression that one receives on entering the homes of these unfortunate workers. Below street-level on each side of the passage there is a large gloomy cold room. Foul water oozes out of the walls. Air reaches the room through a sort of semi-circular window which is two feet high at its greatest elevation. Go in—if the fetid smell that assails you does not make you recoil. Take care, for the floor is uneven, unpaved and untiled—or if there are tiles, they are covered with so much dirt that they cannot be seen. And then you will see two or three rickety beds fitted to one side because the cords that bind them to the worm-eaten legs have themselves decayed. Look at the contents of the bed—a mattress; a tattered blanket of rags (seldom washed since there is only one); sheets sometimes; and a pillow sometimes. No wardrobes are needed in these homes. Often a weaver's loom and a spinning wheel complete the furniture. There is no fire in the winter. No

sunlight penetrates [by day], while at night a tallow candle is lit. Here men work for fourteen hours [a day]."

"*Question:* What is the condition of the living quarters of the class of factory workers, day labourers and journeymen?

"*Reply of the City Poor Doctor, Dr. Bluemner:* It is in the highest degree miserable. Many rooms are more like pigsties than quarters for human beings. The apartments in the city are, if possible, even worse than those in the suburbs. The former are, of course, always in the yard, if places in which you can hardly turn round can be called apartments. The so-called staircase is generally completely in the dark. It is also so decrepit that the whole building shakes with every firm footstep; the rooms themselves are small and so low that it is hardly possible to stand upright, the floor is on a slope, since usually part of the house has to be supported by struts. The windows close badly, the stoves are so bad that they hardly give any heat but plenty of smoke in the room. Water runs down the doors and walls. The ground-floor dwellings are usually half underground."

From Sidney Pollard and Colin Holmes (eds.), *Documents of European Economic History*, Vol. 1, St. Martin's Press, 1968, pp. 494–495, 497–498.

and, by midcentury, brick construction and iron pipes had improved housing even for many of the relatively poor. Luxuries such as sugar, tea, and meat were becoming available to the lower-middle class and to the more prosperous artisans.

That the more fortunate workers and the middle classes were unquestionably more prosperous than they had been in the recent past made the contrast with the poverty of those beneath them even more striking. A luxury restaurant in Paris might charge twenty-five or thirty times an average worker's daily wage for a single meal, and even modest restaurants charged twice a worker's daily wage—to a clientele that ate three or four times a day, in contrast to the two meals of many workers. From the top to the bottom of society, the differences between the comfortable minority and the poor majority were striking in every aspect of daily life.

Charity　Responding to the plight of the lower classes, many well-to-do people, especially women, favored charity as the best means of redressing social ills. In Britain, religious revival provided a powerful impetus to philanthropic initiatives, and on the Continent new Catholic religious orders with social reform missions were founded by the hundreds. The Society of St. Vincent de Paul, founded in Paris in 1835 and soon established all over Catholic Europe, dispatched upper-class men to visit the poor regularly with the goal of teaching thrift and inspiring by example. Other charitable organizations sought to help workers help themselves, establishing night schools for workers and sponsoring lectures, although ambitious members of the lower-middle classes were more likely than workers to avail themselves of such opportunities. Still other groups organized wholesome recreation to diminish the draw of

HISTORICAL ISSUES: INDUSTRIALIZATION AND THE STANDARD OF LIVING

These excerpts show the diverse emphases and shifting conclusions in this debate but not the careful reasoning and the extraordinary range of the research that makes this literature still worth reading. The first four excerpts are anthologized in Philip A. M. Taylor (ed.), The Industrial Revolution in Britain: Triumph or Disaster?, *D. C. Heath, 1970.*

JOHN L. AND BARBARA HAMMOND

"The apologies for child labour were precisely the same as the apologies for the slave trade. This was no travesty of their argument. The champions of the slave trade pointed to the £70,000,000 invested in the sugar plantations, to the dependence of our commerce on the slave trade. . . . The argument for child labour followed the same line. . . . Sir James Graham thought that the Ten Hours Bill would ruin the cotton industry and with it the trade of the country. . . . Our population, which had grown rapidly in the Industrial Revolution was no longer able to feed itself; the food it bought was paid for by its manufactures: those manufactures depended on capital: capital depended on profits: profits depended on the labour of the boys and girls who enabled the manufacturer to work his mills long enough at a time to repay the cost of the plant and to compete with foreign rivals. This was the circle in which the nation found its conscience mangled.

". . . Thus England asked for profits and received profits. Everything turned to profit. The towns had their profitable dirt, their profitable smoke, their profitable slums, their profitable disorder, their profitable ignorance, their profitable despair. The curse of Midas was on this society. . . . For the new town was not a home where man could find beauty, happiness, leisure, learning, religion, the influences that civilize outlook and habit, but a bare and desolate place. . . . The new factories and the new furnaces were like the Pyramids, telling of man's enslavement, rather than of his power, casting their long shadow over the society that took such pride in them."

From John L. and Barbara Hammond, *The Rise of Modern Industry*, M. S. G. Haskell House, 1925.

THOMAS S. ASHTON

"Let me confess at the start that I am of those who believe that, all in all, conditions of labour were becoming better, at least after 1820, and that the spread of the factory played a not inconsiderable part in the improvement. . . . One of the merits of the factory system was that it offered, and required, regularity of employment and hence stability of consumption. During the period 1790–1830 factory production increased rapidly. A greater proportion of the people came to benefit both as producers and as consumers. The fall in the price of textiles reduced the price of clothing. Government contracts for uniforms and army boots called into being new industries, and after the war the products of these found a market among the better-paid artisans. Boots began to take the place of clogs and hats replaced shawls, at least for wear on Sundays. Miscellaneous commodities, ranging from clocks to pocket handkerchiefs, began to enter into the scheme of expenditure, and after 1820 such things as tea and coffee and sugar fell in price substantially. The growth of trade-unions, friendly societies, savings banks, popular newspapers and pamphlets, schools, and nonconformist chapels—all give evidence of the existence of a large class raised well above the level of mere subsistence."

From Thomas S. Ashton, "The Standard of Life of the Workers in England, 1790–1830," *Journal of Economic History*, Vol. 9, 1949.

ERIC J. HOBSBAWM

"We may consider three types of evidence in favour of the pessimistic view: those bearing on (a) mortality and health, (b) unemployment and (c) consumption. . . . The rise in mortality rates in the period 1811–41 is clearly of *some* weight for the pessimistic case, all the more as modern work . . . tend[s] to link such rates much more directly to the amount of income and food consumption than to other social conditions.

". . . It is too often forgotten that something like 'technological' unemployment was not confined to those workers who were actually replaced by new machines. It could affect almost all pre-industrial industries and trades. . . . Doubtless the general expansion of the early industrial period (say 1780–1811) tended to diminish unemployment except during crises: doubtless the decades of difficulty and adjustment after the wars tended to make the problem more acute. From the later 1840s, the working classes began to adjust themselves to life under a new set of economic rules . . . but it is highly probable that the period 1811–42 saw abnormal problems and abnormal unemployment. . . . These notes on unemployment are sufficient to throw doubt upon the less critical statements of the optimistic view, but not to establish any alternative view. . . . Per capita consumption can hardly have risen. The discussion of food consumption thus throws considerable doubt on the optimistic view."

From Eric J. Hobsbawm, "The British Standard of Living, 1790–1850," *Economic History Review*, 1957.

continued

RONALD M. HARTWELL

"[I]ncreasing life expectation and increasing consumption are no measures of ultimate well-being, and to say that the standard of living for most workers was rising, is *not* to say that it was high, *nor* that there was no dire poverty, and cyclical fluctuations and technological unemployment of a most distressing character.

"... Thus much misunderstanding has arisen because of assumptions—mainly misconceptions—about England before the Industrial Revolution; assumptions, for example, that rural life was naturally better than town life, that working for oneself was better and more secure than working for an employer, that child and female labour was something new, that the domestic system . . . was preferable to the factory system, that slums and food adulteration were peculiar products of industrialization, and so on. . . . The new attitude to social problems that emerged with the industrial revolution was that ills should be identified, examined, analysed, publicised and remedied, either by voluntary or legislative action. Thus evils that had long existed—child labour, for example—and had long been accepted as inevitable, were regarded as new ills to be remedied rather than as old ills to be endured. It was during the industrial revolution, moreover, and largely because of the economic opportunities it afforded to the working class women, that there was the beginning of the most important and most beneficial of all the social revolutions of the last two centuries, the emancipation of women."

From Ronald M. Hartwell, "The Rising Standard of Living in England, 1800–1850," *Economic History Review*, 1961.

THEODORE S. HAMEROW

"For most [workers] the coming of the industrial revolution made little difference with regard to income, workday, diet, or housing. This was especially true of those employed in agriculture, who still made up the great bulk of the labor force. Yet even those engaged in manufacture experienced only minor changes in their accustomed level of subsistence. The goods and services generated by early industrialization remained largely inaccessible to them. But the new hardships imposed on the working population by the rationalization of production were less the result of a long-term decline in income than of psychological disorientation. Millions of people who had grown up amid the certainties and traditions of the village or small town were suddenly thrown into an alien environment of factories, shops, tenements, and slums, where the values of rural society soon disintegrated before the hard realities of the urban experience. The outcome was a profound demoralization, which primarily reflected not a change in the standard of living but a change in the way of life.

"Such generalizations about the initial effect of the industrial revolution may be open to challenge, but there can be little doubt about what happened subsequently. Within fifty years the standard of living of the lower classes began to rise. The evidence on this point is incontrovertible."

From Theodore S. Hamerow, *The Birth of a New Europe: State and Society in the Nineteenth Century*, University of North Carolina Press, 1983, pp. 140–141.

the pub. They set up trade apprenticeships; provided expectant mothers with a clean sheet and a pamphlet on child care; opened savings banks that accepted even tiny deposits; campaigned for hygiene and temperance; gave away soup and bread; supported homes for abandoned children and fallen women; and ran nurseries, schools, or hostels. Despite these efforts, philanthropy was wholly inadequate to the challenges it faced, and most of Europe's urban masses remained largely untouched by it.

Government Regulation Gradually, and often reluctantly, governments began to take a more active role in meeting the challenges of the industrial order. By the 1830s and 1840s, despite the resistance of industrialists to the expansion of state authority, some governments began to regulate child labor, banning employment of those under ten in British mines, under nine in British textile mills and in Prussian factories, and under eight in French factories. Britain and France included additional requirements that the very young be provided with a couple of hours of schooling

each day, and Britain dispatched teams of factory inspectors to enforce the new regulations. In other parts of Germany, and in Italy and Russia, similar measures were adopted, which limited the workday to eight or nine hours for children under twelve or thirteen years old and to twelve hours for those under sixteen or eighteen.

A key example of expanding government intervention—and the most bitterly controversial welfare measure of the period—was Britain's Poor Law of 1834. The old parish system of paternalistic relief permitted each county to supplement local wages up to a level of subsistence determined by the price of bread. Liberal economists contended that the system was costly and ineffective because easy handouts discouraged workers from seeking jobs. Their campaign for reform led to the Poor Law of 1834, which sought to make unemployment as unattractive as possible. The able-bodied poor requiring aid had to live in workhouses, where discipline was harsh, conditions were kept suitably mean, and the sexes were separated. Workers detested the new Poor Law, dubbing the new workhouses "Bastilles."

J. Leonard
THE DOCTOR FOR THE POOR
Hopelessness dominates J. Leonard's painting of the poor coming to the charitable doctor in an endless stream.
Musée des Beaux-Arts, Valenciennes/Giraudon/Bridgeman Art Library

Public Health Governments gradually took on a more active role in promoting public health as well, but they were often uncertain of the causes of diseases and hesitated over how to respond. Vaccination, invented by Edward Jenner, made smallpox less threatening once it was widely adopted. But serious epidemics of other kinds still broke out in every decade. Typhus, carried by lice, was a constant threat, accounting for one death in nine in Ireland between 1816 and 1819, and infected water spread typhoid fever in city after city. In the 1830s, a deadly cholera epidemic originating in India spread rapidly through East Asia, North Africa, and Europe, killing hundreds of thousands. In France, Germany, and Britain, officials knew little about the disease, but sought to mitigate the epidemic by ordering tenements to be whitewashed by the tens of thousands, foods to be inspected, and streets and sewers to be cleaned.

Over time, however, the collection of statistics and the systematic investigation of living conditions in poor neighborhoods led to better understanding of how disease spread and of the importance of social factors for public health. Gradually, hospitals, too, came under

more direct state supervision as the cost and complexity of medical treatment increased. By midcentury, housing and sanitary codes regulated most urban construction throughout the West, and inspectors were empowered to enforce these rules.

Education Public education also became a matter of national policy over the course of the century. Prussia had declared local schooling compulsory in 1716, and in 1807 created a bureau of education to promote it. In the following decades the government established an efficient system of universal primary instruction, staffed by trained teachers expected to keep the curriculum politically safe, and enlarged a separate network of secondary schools. Similar arrangements in most of the German states established nearly universal elementary education.

In France the Revolution had provided the framework for a national system of free public schools meant as a substitute for the extensive but more informal and largely religious schools of the old regime. On paper, by 1833 every commune was supposed to support a public school, and schooling steadily expanded while the quality of teachers improved and the power of state inspectors over tightfisted local authorities increased. By the Revolution of 1848, three-fourths of France's school-age children were receiving some formal instruction. Although conflict between the Church of England and other Protestant churches prevented the creation of a state-controlled system of elementary schools in Britain, by 1833 Parliament voted to underwrite the construction of private schools and to increase subsidies for education. From Spain to Russia, governments and liberal constituencies supported the establishment of public elementary schools; inadequate and impoverished though they were, few doubted that they could be a major instrument for improving society as well as a force for social peace.

RECONSIDERING SELF AND SOCIETY IN THE EARLY NINETEENTH CENTURY

Political ideas, social theories, and new movements in the arts were all closely interconnected in the early nineteenth century. They altered the way people painted pictures, wrote poetry, collected statistics, analyzed society, studied biology, and understood history. Several elements served to connect this creative diversity and increase its impact. The writers, artists, scientists, and scholars whose works were most influential increasingly saw themselves as having a special place in society because of their talents and knowledge. Primarily male and largely from the middle class, they depended less on patronage than on their connections to established institutions such as academies, universities, publishing houses, magazines, and newspapers. Through exhibitions, public lectures, and publications, they sought to reach others like themselves and then a broader audience. Their need to explain modern society, like their effort to comprehend the French Revolution, produced competing interpretations that were, in fact, debates about the nature of society and the sources of historical change.

Romanticism and the Primacy of the Individual

Romanticism, a movement in philosophy and the arts, cannot be captured in any simple definition. Associated with a great burst of creativity in Germany in the latter part of the eighteenth century and with the ideas of Jean-Jacques Rousseau (see chapter 19), the Romantic movement, initially strongest in Germany and England, rapidly spread across the Continent and to North America. Romanticism affected every aspect of culture and in such a variety of ways that it is best understood as a set of attitudes and aesthetic preferences rather than as a defined doctrine. Although by midcentury other styles and concerns challenged Romanticism, its influence continued into the twentieth century. Certain themes were characteristic: an emphasis on the individual's feelings, emotions, and direct experience more than on universal principles; a preoccupation with erotic love, often unrequited, and mortality; fascination with nature understood as an unconquerable power; a search for the organic relatedness of all life that went beyond the cold analysis of cause and effect; a concern for spirituality, deep and mysterious, that tended to dismiss the hollowness of Enlightenment materialism; and an admiration for imagination and originality that hailed the individual genius who was capable of feelings more profound than those of ordinary mortals. Romantic artists and writers favored flamboyant dress that distinguished them from aristocrats or bourgeois, and presented themselves as pensive and passionate.

Romantic Philosophy and Literature Romantic modes of thought flourished in conjunction with religious revivals, an increased interest in history, and rising nationalism (discussed in the next chapter). Romantic philosophers wrote about aesthetics and the philosophy of nature; writers expressed themselves in poetry, aphorisms, meditations on death, and autobiographical accounts of youthful yearnings for truth. The German scholar and poet August Wilhelm Schlegel and the English poet Samuel Taylor Coleridge (heavily influenced by German philosophy) were among the most influential Romantic thinkers. Coleridge and his closest friend William Wordsworth (see chapter 19) campaigned for a new kind of poetry, direct and emotive. Wordsworth's poems contrasted the beauty of nature with urban corruption and, like the poet William Blake before him, he denounced the materialism of his age. (See "Wordsworth on the Role of the Poet.") Blake, whose drawings and poems were filled with religious mystery, also believed that poets had a special wisdom that society should heed.

In France, where Romanticism developed somewhat later, Madame Anne-Louise de Staël's essays on the German thinkers stimulated a whole generation of philosophers, historians, and novelists. These ranged from the young Victor Hugo, whose plays and novels (*The Hunchback of Notre Dame* and *Les Misérables* are the best known) made him a towering figure of French letters, to the swashbuckling stories of Alexander Dumas' *Three Musketeers*. Novelists and dramatists in Italy and Russia, as well as in England, France, and Germany, often set their tales in the distant past and tended to favor flamboyant description and gothic settings.

WORDSWORTH ON THE ROLE OF THE POET

Wordsworth was one of England's most popular poets, and the success of his Lyrical Ballads *may have encouraged him to write a preface to the second edition, explaining what he was up to. He points out that his poems differ from classical poetry with its greater formality and lofty themes, and he justifies his use of ordinary speech. In making his case, he touches on many of the themes characteristic of the Romantic movement.*

"The principle object of these Poems was to choose incidents and situations from common life, and to relate or describe them, throughout, as far as was possible in a selection of language really used by men, and, at the same time, to throw over them a certain colouring of imagination, whereby ordinary things could be presented to the mind in an unusual aspect. . . . Humble and rustic life was generally chosen because, in that condition, the essential passions of the heart find a better soil in which they can attain their maturity, are less under restraint, and speak a plainer and more emphatic language; because in that condition of life our elementary feelings co-exist in a state of greater simplicity, and, consequently, may be more accurately contemplated and more forcibly communicated; because the manners of rural life germinate from those elementary feelings . . . ; and, lastly, because in that condition the passions of men are incorporated with the beautiful and permanent forms of nature. . . .

" . . . For all good poetry is the spontaneous overflow of powerful feelings: and though this be true, Poems to which any value can be attached were never produced on any variety of subjects but by a man who, being possessed of more than usual organic sensibility, had also thought long and deeply. . . .

"The Man of science seeks truth as a remote and unknown benefactor; he cherishes and loves it in his solitude; the Poet, singing a song in which all human beings join with him, rejoices in the presence of truth as our visible friend and hourly companion. Poetry is the breath and finer spirit of all knowledge; it is the impassioned expression which is the countenance of all Science. Emphatically may it be said of the Poet, as Shakespeare hath said of man, 'that he looks before and after.' He is the rock of defence for human nature; an upholder and preserver, carrying everywhere with him relationship and love . . . ; the Poet binds together by passion and knowledge the vast empire of human society, as it is spread over the whole earth, and over all time."

From William Wordsworth, "Preface to the Second Edition of *Lyrical Ballads*," in *William Wordsworth: Selected Poems and Prefaces*, Jack Stillinger (ed.), Houghton-Mifflin, 1965.

Turning from the Enlightenment veneration for the Renaissance, they preferred the rougher, sprawling picture of human experience in writers like Shakespeare and Cervantes and felt a particular kinship with the spirituality of medieval art and architecture.

The Wider Influence of Romanticism Like romantic literature, romantic art burst beyond classical forms. Romantic painters favored scenes of storms and ruins that evoked unseen powers, as in the landscapes of J. M. W. Turner in England and Caspar David Friedrich in Germany. Others, such as Théodore Géricault in France, emphasized vibrant color and swirling lines without the sharp outlines and balanced composition so important to their predecessors. Like Eugène Delacroix (see his paintings on p. 668), they were drawn to exotic scenes from the past and from North Africa and the Middle East.

Romantic attitudes attained powerful expression in music, admired for its ability to communicate an ineffable understanding deeper than words. The response to the later works of Beethoven had brought a self-conscious seriousness to music. Critics wrote of his symphonies and string quartets in terms of their philosophic profundity, and audiences listened in reverent silence, finding in that shared experience something akin to religion. Subsequent Romantic composers appealed ever more directly to the heart, emphasizing soaring melody and using freer harmonies. When words and music were combined, as in the song cycles of Franz Schubert, or in grand opera (often hailed as the highest of the arts), it was the music that mattered most.

Both conservatives and radicals drew inspiration from the Romantic movement. Conservatives found in Romantic values powerful arguments for rejecting the French Revolution, which they regarded as a lamentable product of Enlightenment rationalism and of a universalism that ignored local tradition. Stability, they argued, was possible only in a society organically connected, held together as it had been in the Middle Ages by respect for custom and religion. Some conservatives contrasted their vision of an organic society with the competition and selfish individualism of modern capitalism.

Joseph Mallord William Turner
Interior of Tintern Abbey, Exhibited 1794
The evocation of nature and time, favorite Romantic themes, made the ruins of Tintern Abbey the subject of a poem by Wordsworth and of this watercolor by Turner. Watercolor. Victoria and Albert Museum, London/Art Resource, NY

Radicals, however, used Romantic themes to argue that freedom required shattering old institutional shackles, much as creativity in the arts fostered the breaking of established forms. Romantic thinkers tended to see folk culture and local language as natural expressions of the nation. For conservatives, this validated rural life and custom; for radicals, the promise of this culture would be realized when the people arose to achieve new freedoms for their nation. Victor Hugo, for example, turned from an early conservatism to become a lifelong advocate of radical change. In its aspirations and tumultuousness, Romanticism expressed the preoccupation with change that marked the age.

Social Thought

Conservatives and Reactionaries Conservatism grew from opposition to the French Revolution to become what today would be called an ideology—a coherent view of human nature, social organization, and political power that generally justified the status quo. This conservatism was not mere nostalgia for the past.

Rather, conservatives advocated changes when designed to strengthen the kind of society they favored. Emphasizing the wisdom of established customs, the value of hierarchy, and the social importance of religion, conservatives mounted a powerful critique not just of radical programs but of modern society itself as perilously inclined toward antisocial individualism, materialism, and immorality.

From the late eighteenth century on, the powerful English prose of Edmund Burke (see discussion on p. 579) provided one of the most influential formulations of the conservative position. Burke posited that social stability derived from continuity over time. By granting special privileges to certain groups, society fulfilled social needs in a way that sustains order, achieving a delicate arrangement in which rank is related to social function and in which differences of status are acceptable to all. According to Burke, this organic, historically rooted society allowed for gradual change. In his view, the abstract plans of radicals for revolutionary transformation were not only unnecessary but unattainable in the sense that no man-made social schemes or written constitutions could ever reconstitute the great interconnecting web of society.

Espousing a more hard-line conservatism than Burke, the French conservatives Joseph de Maistre and Louis de Bonald identified the Church as the linchpin of the social order. Society's first task, they maintained, was self-preservation through the exercise of an authority based on undivided sovereignty, inflexible social hierarchy, the vigilant suppression of dangerous ideas, and close links between church and state. For de Maistre, revolution was divine retribution for false ideas. Terrified of weakening the dikes that held back revolution, this brand of conservatism left little room for compromise and appealed mainly to those who shared its fears. Nevertheless, as a way of understanding change, mobilizing opposition to liberal demands, and criticizing modern life, conservatism would be a profoundly influential strand in modern thought.

Liberalism Like conservatism, liberalism was less a doctrine than a set of attitudes. Whereas conservatives emphasized tradition and hierarchy, liberals espoused ideas of social progress, economic development, and values associated with the middle classes. Confident that their ideas would triumph, they generally welcomed social change.

Influenced by John Locke and the eighteenth-century philosophes, liberals sought to guarantee legal and political freedoms. Consequently, they generally favored a written constitution and representative institutions, freedom of the press and of assembly, an extension of the jury system, separation of church and state, public education, and administrative reform. Most liberals did not favor democracy—political wisdom, they thought, required the advantages of education and leisure and the restraint that came with owning property—but nearly all believed that giving ideas a free hearing and propertied voters a free voice would result in policies beneficial to everyone.

Liberals sought a society that promoted individual freedom and afforded opportunities for individual growth. They believed that the principles of individualism and competition were universally valid and would lead to morality, prosperity, and progress for all. Yet to their perpetual surprise, liberalism proved a creed of limited appeal, subject to frequent attack and internal division. In practice, reconciling liberty with order, or equal rights with private property, proved contentious. Enthusiasm for limited constitutional reform, for example, produced disagreements over just how limited it should be. In each country, moreover, the temper of liberalism differed, shaped by a national history liberals never wholly determined.

Although many liberals advocated a minimalist state to guarantee the freedom of the individual, in some cases the liberal call for reform entailed greater emphasis on the role of the state, as in the **utilitarianism** of the Englishman Jeremy Bentham. Like the philosophes, Bentham believed he could rationally deduce practical programs from universal principles. In contrast to most philosophes, however, he rejected the doctrine of natural rights as a meaningless abstraction. In his system, utility replaced natural rights as the basis of public policy, and he measured utility according to what brought the greatest good to the greatest number. Bentham defined the good as that which avoids pain and gives pleasure—a calculation all people make for themselves anyway and that better education would enable them to make more wisely. It was the state's task to promote the good by penalizing undesirable actions and rewarding socially beneficial behavior.

Bentham's followers, sober intellectuals who called themselves *philosophic radicals*, did not necessarily adopt all his doctrines, but they applied his principles in many spheres. By his death in 1832, they were among the most important British reformers of Parliament, law, prisons, education, and welfare. A special group within a larger liberal movement, the Benthamites shared the tendency of most liberals everywhere to press for humane reforms on grounds of common sense and social harmony.

John Stuart Mill   Liberalism's broader meaning is best exemplified by John Stuart Mill, the most important liberal thinker of the nineteenth century. Mill's father was a leading Benthamite, but the younger Mill gradually came to modify the doctrines taught to him in his youth. Mill was extraordinarily learned—a philosopher, economist, and publicist—and he wrote some of the most influential classics of modern thought. Fearful of the intolerance and oppression of which any social class or political majority was capable, he made freedom of thought a first principle. He advocated universal suffrage as a necessary check on the elite and proportional representation as a means of protecting minorities. Mill acknowledged that institutions, even liberal ones, suited to one stage of historical development might not be appropriate for another.

To counterbalance the influence of the established elites, Mill favored a more open administration, organized interest groups, and workers' cooperatives. Moved by the problems of the industrial poor, he distinguished between the production of goods (which operated best without the interference of the state) and their distribution (in which the state might intervene in behalf of justice), and he came to see that collective action by the workers could enhance freedom rather than restrict it. In later years, under the influence of his wife, Harriet Taylor, Mill courageously advocated the emancipation of women, a cause that seemed radical to most contemporaries. (See "Mill Opposes the Subjection of Women.") His liberalism, thus modified and extended, remained steadfast. His essay *On Liberty* (1859) stands as one of the classic works of European political theory, an insistent declaration that society can have no higher interest than the freedom of each of its members.

Economic Liberalism   Although liberal politics and liberal economic theory were closely related, they were nevertheless separable, and the advocates of one were not always committed to the other. Still, in the case of English liberalism, belief in an unfettered market tended to converge with support for political liberty. Economic liberalism had its roots in the classical economic thought of Adam Smith (see chapter 18). Smith had argued that government-authorized monopolies, high tariffs, and other forms of state restrictions on trade hampered the individual economic pursuits that created wealth. It became a dogma of economic liberalism that if left to themselves, market forces would increase productivity and prosperity.

In his *Principles of Political Economy and Taxation* (1817), the Englishman David Ricardo systematically codified liberal economic theory. The wealth of the community, Ricardo declared, comes from land, capital, and labor. These three "classes" are compensated respectively by rent, profit, and wages. A product's value results primarily from the labor required to make it. This was *the labor theory of value*, which socialists would later invoke for very different

MILL OPPOSES THE SUBJECTION OF WOMEN

John Stuart Mill published his essay The Subjection of Women *in 1869. His arguments were based on familiar ideas about individualism and modern progress, but their extension to women's rights and in such absolute terms went much further than most contemporary discussion.*

"The object of this Essay is to explain, as clearly as I am able, the grounds of an opinion which . . . has been constantly growing stronger by the progress of reflection and the experience of life: That the principle which regulates the existing social relations between the two sexes—the legal subordination of one sex to the other—is wrong in itself, and now one of the chief hindrances to human improvement; and that it ought to be replaced by a principle of perfect equality, admitting no power or privilege on the one side, nor disability on the other.

" . . . The masters of all other slaves rely, for maintaining obedience, on fear; either fear of themselves, or religious fears. The masters of women wanted more than simple obedience, and they turned the whole force of education to effect their purpose. All women are brought up from the very earliest years in the belief that their ideal of character is the very opposite to that of men; not self-will, and government by self-control, but submission, and yielding to the control of others. All the moralities tell them that it is the duty of women, and all the current sentimentalities that it is their nature, to live for others; to make complete abnegation of themselves, and to have no life but in their affections.

" . . . So far as the whole course of human improvement up to this time, the whole stream of modern tendencies, warrants any inference on the subject, it is, that this relic of the past is discordant with the future, and must necessarily disappear.

"For what is the peculiar character of the modern world—the difference which chiefly distinguishes modern institutions, modern social ideas, modern life itself, from those of times long past? It is, that human beings are no longer born to their place in life, and chained down by an inexorable bond to the place they are born to, but are free to employ their faculties, and such favourable chances as offer, to achieve the lot which may appear to them most desirable.

"If this general principle of social and economical sciences is . . . true, we ought to act as if we believed it, and not to ordain that to be born a girl instead of a boy, any more than to be born black instead of white, or a commoner instead of a nobleman, shall decide the person's position through all life. . . .

"At present, in the more improved countries, the disabilities of women are the only case, save one, in which laws and institutions take persons at their birth, and ordain that they shall never in all their lives be allowed to compete for certain things. The one exception is that of royalty.

" . . . The social subordination of women thus stands out an isolated fact in modern social institutions; a solitary breach of what has become their fundamental law; a single relic of an old world of thought and practice exploded in everything else, but retained in the one thing of most universal interest."

From John Stuart Mill, "The Subjection of Women," *Three Essays*, Oxford: Oxford University Press, 1975.

---

purposes. For Ricardo, as for Adam Smith before him, the theory led to an emphasis on labor-saving efficiencies as the route to profit. The value of land or of work was determined by the operation of impersonal economic laws. The rate of pay to workers, for example, is determined by an "iron law of wages," which dictates that when labor is plentiful workers tend to be paid at the lowest possible level. Short-term fluctuations in prices are the natural regulator within this system, pushing people to activities for which demand is high. For Ricardo, both land and labor are commodities, their value quite unaffected by any sentimental talk about the virtues of rural life or artisanship. Society is a collection of competing interests, and legislation cannot hope to raise wages or prevent the marketplace from working in its natural way.

While his opponents referred to it as "the dismal science," Ricardo called his subject *political economy*, and a powerful reform movement developed around it. Landed interests, liberals argued, had misused political power for their own benefit while harming the rest of society. Throughout Europe, liberal economic theory thus added important weight to demands that special privilege be eliminated (as the French Revolution had done), that governments be responsive to their citizens (who best know their own interests), and above all that the state not try to regulate production and trade.

Critics of Capitalism: The Early Socialists

Socialist thought offered a radical alternative to conservative and liberal ideologies and the most thoroughgoing critique of industrial capitalism. Among scores of socialist schemes, those of Saint-Simon, Fourier, and Owen gained particular attention among intellectuals and political leaders. All three men argued that capitalist competition is wasteful and cruel, induces hard-hearted indifference to suffering, misuses wealth, and leads to frequent economic crises. Organizing production and distribution on a different basis, they believed, would create a harmonious, orderly, and truly free society.

Saint-Simon As a young French officer, Comte Claude de Saint-Simon fought alongside George Washington at Yorktown. During the French Revolution, he abandoned his title, made and lost a fortune speculating in land, and then devoted himself to social philosophy and reform. Injustice, social divisions, and inefficiency could be overcome, he believed, in a society governed by experts. Scientists, businessmen, and managers would lead humanity to self-fulfillment through the design of plans to increase productivity and prosperity. In this way, the integrated, organic quality of Greek city-states and of the Middle Ages could be recaptured in the industrial age.

Saint-Simon's theories won a following especially among young engineers at France's Ecole Polytechnique. In their penchant for planning, in their grand economic projects, and in their schemes for social reform, they carried elements of his teaching into the business world and the realm of respectable politics. Important Saint-Simonian movements took shape in several countries, and later socialists would long sustain his respect for industrialization and the power of social planning.

Fourier Charles Fourier had been a traveling salesman before dedicating himself to a theory that he firmly believed would rank among the greatest discoveries ever made. His cantankerous yet shrewd writings on contemporary society were so copious that his manuscripts have still not all been printed, despite the devotion of generations of admirers.

Fourier's central concept was an ideal community, the *phalanstery* (from *phalanx*). A phalanstery should contain some sixteen hundred men, women, and children, representatives of all the types of personality identified in Fourier's elaborate psychology. He proposed to organize the phalanstery in such a way that individuals would accomplish the tasks society required simply by doing what they wanted. Each member would perform a variety of tasks, engaging in no one task for too long, so that pleasure and work would flow together. Largely self-sufficient, a phalanstery would produce some goods for export and pay its members according to the capital, labor, and talent that each contributed. After even one such community was created, the happiness and well-being of its members would inspire the establishment of others until all of society was converted. Although no phalanstery was ever established exactly as Fourier planned, communities founded on Fourierist principles appeared from the United States to Romania. Few of them survived for long, but the vision endured of a society in which cooperation replaced compulsion, and joy transformed drudgery.

Robert Owen Robert Owen was one of the success stories of industrial capitalism: A self-made man, he rose from selling cloth to be the manager and part owner of a large textile mill in New Lanark, Scotland. Owen ran the mill in a way that transformed the whole town, and by the end of the Napoleonic wars, distinguished visitors were traveling from all over Europe to see the miracle he had wrought in New Lanark. He shortened the workday to ten hours. New housing allowed an employee's family several rooms, inspection committees maintained cleanliness, and gardens were planted and sewers installed. In nursery schools with airy, pleasant rooms, children were given exercise, encouraged to sing and dance, taught without corporal punishment, and trained in the useful arts. Most promising of all, the subjects of this paternalistic realm developed a pride in their community. Productivity in the factory rose, and profits increased.

Owen's success in New Lanark encouraged him to establish ideal communities elsewhere, particularly in the United States. Situated rurally, they were to supply most of their own needs. Members would eat meals and enjoy entertainment together, and children would be raised communally. Standardized production would offer goods at lower prices, while higher wages would increase consumption of manufactured products. "It is scarcely to be supposed," he declared in a speech before the U.S. Congress in 1825, "that anyone would continue to live under the miserable, anxious, individual system of [competition], when they could with ease form themselves into, or become members of, one of these associations of union, intelligence, and kind feeling." Even after losing most of his wealth when the community of New Harmony, Indiana, failed, Owen remained the most important figure in the labor movement and in the workers' cooperatives that he helped spread across England in the 1830s and 1840s.

The Socialist Critique Although much in these socialist movements was easily ridiculed, the values they

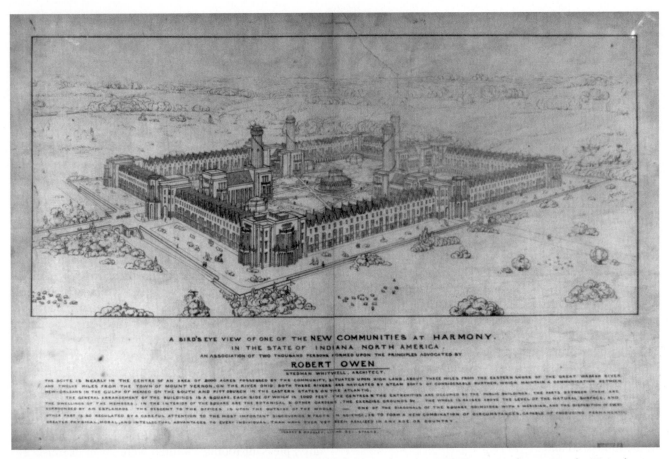

After his ventures in Scotland, Robert Owen funded the establishment of a new, cooperative settlement in the United States. But what actually took shape in New Harmony fell far short of his grandiose vision for this utopian community in Indiana, as conveyed in this model sketch.

stressed echoed those of workers' movements everywhere. These early socialists sought to combine an older sense of community with the possibilities of a society enriched by new inventions and new means of production in which new forms of social organization would foster cooperation and pleasure. Their indictment of capitalism, their insights into the nature of productivity and exchange, and their attention to social planning and education had an impact far beyond their relatively small circles of believers. The dream of fraternity and of fulfilling work echoed through later socialist and anarchist movements, yet nearly everyone ultimately rejected their ideas as impractical and too radical.

The nature of their radicalism, however, deserves a closer look. What most shocked contemporaries were their views on the status of women, sexual mores, and Christianity. Fourier rejected the place assigned to women in bourgeois society, and Owen not only specified that women should share in governing but believed

that their emancipation required lessening their family responsibilities. All wrote of sensual pleasure as good and of its repression as a characteristic European error. The Saint-Simonians publicly advocated free love, and Fourier stipulated that neither young nor old should be deprived of the pleasures of the flesh. Owen was only slightly less outspoken in his contempt for traditional marriage. At the same time, all three stressed spirituality as a source of community feeling, brotherhood, and ethics. As Owen put it, "charity, benevolence and kindness: this is the *universal religion* of human nature." Their systems, therefore, included echoes of Christian ritual and a foggy mysticism that provided an easy target for their opponents. By the end of the nineteenth century, these thinkers would be remembered (and generally dismissed) as "utopian socialists." For by then, socialist thought would center on the more hard-headed and materialistic theories of Karl Marx.

Summary

The reorganization of Europe in 1815 had focused on politics as the key to social order. The system of international relations the victors established proved reasonably effective, but the conservative domestic arrangements they favored were challenged from the start. In trying various combinations of repression and compromise, the restoration regimes acknowledged that they had not achieved the stability hoped for. At the same time, accelerating industrial growth made new demands of government and placed new strains on society. Change, not stability, would be the central reality of the new century. While Europe's leaders chose different means for containing change, millions dealt with it in daily struggles over wages and housing, food and family. Preoccupation with change dominated ideological debate as well, over how to prevent revolutions or achieve them, and of the kind of future that industrialization might bring. In the arts and philosophy, Romanticism pointed nostalgically to the past but also toward the new, hailing individual genius yet yearning for community. Conservatives sustained standards critical of the new age; liberals gained strength from their confidence in the future; and socialists envisioned alternatives to economic competition and capitalist industrialization. In fact, all available ideas, institutions, and policies were challenged by the social changes that accompanied industrialization, factory labor, demographic growth, and urbanization. Living with change had become a definition of modernity. As chapter 23 will show, the explosive mixture in these intellectual, social, and political trends came together in the revolutions that swept across Europe in 1848 and in the increased importance of national states that could demand the supreme loyalty of their citizens.

QUESTIONS FOR FURTHER THOUGHT

1. What kinds of people were most likely to be drawn to liberalism or to reject its appeal? Does that change over time?
2. Urbanization and the rise of the factory system were hallmarks of change in the nineteenth century. What did workers gain and what did they lose when caught up in those trends?
3. Why did John Stuart Mill value individual freedom so highly? How should the limits of individual freedom be established?
4. Middle-class domesticity was based on separate spheres for men and women. To what extent were women constrained or empowered by their ascribed domestic roles?

RECOMMENDED READING

Sources

The published memoirs and correspondence of diplomats are a wonderful source. *The Memoirs of Prince Metternich* (5 vols., published in the United States in the 1890s), *The Memoirs and Correspondence of Viscount Castlereagh* (12 vols.), and the *Memoirs of the Prince of Talleyrand* (5 vols.) give a lively picture of the Congress of Vienna.

Novels are important sources for insight into nineteenth-century society. Elizabeth Gaskell (*Mary Barton* and *North and South*) and Charles Dickens (*Hard Times* and *Oliver Twist*) provided contemporaries with influential pictures of social conditions in England; Honoré de Balzac's *Père Goriot* set the tone for criticisms of the selfishness of the middle classes.

Engels, Friedrich. *The Condition of the Working Class in England*. Written in 1844 and available in many modern editions, this influential work by Karl Marx's friend and coauthor paints a dark picture of the working-class slums of Manchester and conveys the moral outrage radicals felt.

Studies

Bellamy, Richard. *Liberalism and Modern Society: A Historical Argument*. 1992. Treats the changes over time and the national differences in the meanings of liberalism.

Briggs, Asa. *Victorian Cities*. 1970. Colorful studies of the urban politics and social life of individual cities.

Carr, Raymond. *Spain, 1808–1975*. 1982. The most balanced and comprehensive account in any language.

Clark, Geoffrey. *A Farewell to Alms: A Brief Economic History of the World*. 2007. A global economic history, seeking to explain why the industrial revolution occurred in Europe rather than in Asia.

Coffin, Judith G. *The Politics of Women's Work: The Paris Garment Trades, 1750–1915*. 1996. Reveals the long evolution of women in the labor movement and of ideas about gender in this key area of women's work.

Davidoff, Leonore, and Catherine Hall. *Family Fortunes: Men and Women of the English Middle Class, 1780–1850*. 1985. A rich and concrete picture of the aspirations and concerns of middle-class life.

Davies, Norman. *God's Playground: A History of Poland*. Vol. 2: *From 1789 to the Present*. 1981. Effectively studies the development of a nation without a national government.

Dennis, Richard. *English Industrial Cities of the Nineteenth Century*. 1984. A comprehensive study of the special problems of this new kind of city.

Foster, R. F. *Modern Ireland 1600–1972*. 1988. A magisterial, well-written synthesis.

Frader, Laura L., and Sonya O. Rose. *Gender and Class in Modern Europe*. 1996. Essays exploring the relationship between social change and conceptions of gender and class.

Franklin, S. H. *The European Peasantry: The Final Phase*. 1969. These essays on different countries reveal not only the striking differences in peasants' lives but the importance of the peasantry for understanding the general history of European nations.

Gash, Norman. *Aristocracy and People: Britain, 1815–1865*. 1979. An incisive and balanced account of how British politics adapted to social and economic change.

Gideon, Sigfried. *Mechanization Takes Command*. 1948. This provocative analysis of the social and aesthetic implications of the machine age has become a classic.

Goldstein, Jan. *The Post-Revolutionary Self: Politics and Psyche in France 1750–1850*. 2005. On the philosophical sources of bourgeois selfhood in the early nineteenth century.

Hamerow, Theodore S. *The Birth of a New Europe: State and Society in the Nineteenth Century*. 1983. On the major social changes of the nineteenth century, noting their connection to industrialization and the role of the state.

Heilbroner, Robert L. *The Worldly Philosophers*. 1972. A good introduction to the ideas of the economic liberals.

Hilton, Boyd. *A Mad, Bad and Dangerous People? England, 1783–1846*. 2008. A rich interpretive synthesis of English political and social history.

Hobsbawm, E. J. *Industry and Empire*. 1969. A lively account of British economic transformation by an influential Marxist historian.

Hopkins, Eric. *Industrialisation and Society: A Social History, 1830–1951*. 2000. A wide-ranging discussion of the impact of industrialization on British society through the nineteenth century.

Katznelson, Ira, and Artistide R. Zolberg (eds.). *Working-Class Formation: Nineteenth-Century Patterns in Western Europe and the United States*. 1986. Interpretative essays by some leading scholars take a fresh look at how working-class awareness was formed.

Kemp, Tom. *Industrialization in Nineteenth-Century Europe*. 2nd ed. 1985. Comparative analysis of differences and similarities in the process of industrialization as it spread across Europe.

Koditschek, Theodore. *Class Formation and Urban-Industrial Society: Bradford, 1750–1850*. 1990. Analyzes the emergence of the industrial middle classes against the backdrop of Bradford's transformation from village to factory town to industrial city.

Kossman, Ernst H. *The Low Countries, 1780–1940*. 1978. Balanced treatment of a region that was an important participant in all the trends of modern European history.

Lichtheim, George. *A Short History of Socialism*. 1975. Well-constructed treatment of the evolution of socialist ideas in their historical context.

Lindemann, Albert S. *A History of European Socialism*. 1984. Establishes the line of continuity from the early socialists through labor movements and the eventual dominance of Marxism.

Macartney, C. A. *The Habsburg Empire, 1790–1918*. 1968. Detailed and authoritative.

Magraw, Roger. *France, 1815–1914: The Bourgeois Century*. 1986. A clear general account attentive to social change.

Manuel, Frank. *The Prophets of Paris*. 1962. Illuminating chapters on the thought of Saint Simon and Fourier.

Mayer, Arno. *The Persistence of the Old Regime: Europe to the Great War*. 1981. Emphasizes the continued prominence and power of aristocrats in most of Europe.

Maza, Sarah. *The Myth of the French Bourgeoisie, 1750–1850*. 2003. Undermines some of the clichés about the French middle classes before and after the Revolution.

More, Charles. *Understanding the Industrial Revolution*. 2000. Applies modern theory to rethinking the origins, nature, and development of the industrial revolution in Britain.

Nicolson, Harold. *The Congress of Vienna: A Study in Allied Unity, 1812–1822*. 1970. A classic account of the process of peacemaking, written by a British diplomat.

O'Brien, Patrick, and Caglar Keyder. *Economic Growth in Britain and France, 1780–1914*. 1978. A thorough examination of statistical methods and data for the period, focusing in particular on wages and productivity.

Porter, Roy, and Mikul Teich (eds.). *Romanticism in National Context*. 1988. Particularly useful for the student because this volume of interpretive essays includes many on smaller European nations.

Price, Roger. *An Economic History of Modern France, 1730–1914*. 1981. Underlines the importance of modes of communication and transportation in the development of the marketplace.

Rémond, René. *Religion and Society in Modern Europe*. 1999. An impressive overview of a topic too often neglected.

Riasanovsky, Nicholas V. *The Emergence of Romanticism*. 1992. An introduction to the origins of European Romanticism that emphasizes its importance for rising nationalism.

Scally, Robert. *The End of Hidden Ireland: Rebellion, Famine, and Emigration*. 1995. Uses a vivid local study to paint the larger picture.

Schroeder, Paul. *The Transformation of European Politics, 1763–1848*. 1994. An authoritative synthesis on Europe's state system before, during, and after the French Revolution.

Seton-Watson, Hugh. *The Russian Empire, 1801–1917*. 1967. A solid, largely political survey.

Sewell, William H., Jr. *Work and Revolution in France: The Language of Labor from the Old Regime to 1848*. 1980. An important study that shows the radical potential and continuing strength of a preindustrial working-class culture.

Smith, Bonnie G. *Changing Lives: Women in European History since 1700*. 1989. Discussion of the major trends affecting women of all classes; excellent bibliographies.

Sylla, Richard, and Gianni Toniolo. *Patterns of European Industrialization: The Nineteenth Century*. 1991.

Thompson, Edward P. *The Making of the English Working Class*. 1964. A remarkable work of sympathetic insight and exhaustive research that continues to influence studies of the working class in all societies.

Tilly, Louise, and Joan Scott. *Women, Work, and Family*. 1978. Discusses the impact of industrialization on women and on the family economy.

Trebilcock, Clive. *The Industrialization of the Continental Powers, 1780–1914*. 1981. A synthesis that uses modern research to emphasize the political implications of industrialization.

Weiss, John. *Conservatism in Europe, 1770–1945: Traditionalism, Reaction, and Counter-Revolution*. 1977. A valuable survey of the rich variety and social insight in conservative thought and of its political importance.

Woloch, Isser (ed.). *Revolution and the Meanings of Freedom in the Nineteenth Century*. 1996. Ten specialists assess the political culture of different European countries (and Latin America) in an era obsessed with the promise and dangers that revolution might bring.

Anton von Werner
Proclamation of the German Empire on January 18, 1871 at the Hall of Mirrors in Versailles, **1885**
Victory and the birth of a new Germany: The halls of Versailles ring as Prussian officers hail the proclamation of Prussia's King Wilhelm as German Kaiser.
Bildarchiv Preussischer Kulturbesitz/Art Resource, NY

Chapter Twenty-Three

States and Nations in the Nineteenth Century, 1830–1870

The Spread of Liberal Government • The Revolutions of 1848 •
The Politics of Nationalism • Nineteenth-Century Culture

The social and economic transformations and the political arrangements of the early nineteenth century raised explosive issues. In western Europe they led to new liberal regimes that sponsored fundamental reforms. Although these regimes fostered uniform justice, legal equality, individual rights, and broader political participation, liberal reform tended to empower the middle classes while leaving unaddressed many concerns of peasants and workers.

It was their grievances, in part, that set off the wave of revolutions that swept across the continent in the spring of 1848. Popular uprisings transformed Europe from France to Hungary in a few dramatic months. In western Europe, the revolutions revealed the fault lines created by class conflict and proved that the claims of the lower classes to rights of their own could win passionate support. In the autocratic multinational realms of central and eastern Europe, the revolutions of 1848 were fought to establish national states linked to liberal constitutional regimes. Perhaps more than anything, they demonstrated the incalculable appeal of nationalism. Although the revolutions of 1848 failed, two powerful new national states, Italy and Germany, came into being in the next thirty years, and nation-states everywhere took increased responsibility for shaping public life. That included supporting culture that was an expression of national identity and a means of propagating it.

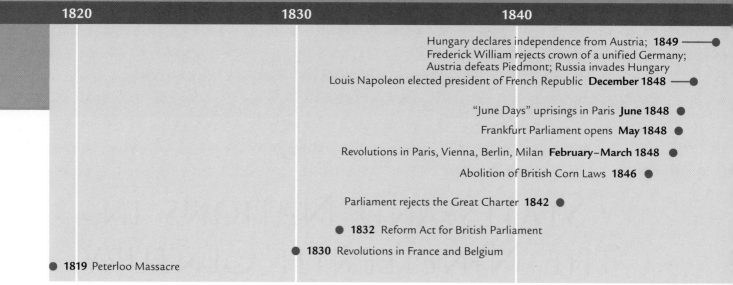

| 1820 | 1830 | 1840 |

Hungary declares independence from Austria; **1849** ●
Frederick William rejects crown of a unified Germany;
Austria defeats Piedmont; Russia invades Hungary
Louis Napoleon elected president of French Republic **December 1848** ●

"June Days" uprisings in Paris **June 1848** ●

Frankfurt Parliament opens **May 1848** ●

Revolutions in Paris, Vienna, Berlin, Milan **February–March 1848** ●

Abolition of British Corn Laws **1846** ●

Parliament rejects the Great Charter **1842** ●

● **1832** Reform Act for British Parliament

● **1830** Revolutions in France and Belgium

● **1819** Peterloo Massacre

THE SPREAD OF LIBERAL GOVERNMENT

The great age of liberalism began in 1830. With England its model, it spread to the Continent with a revolution in France and the revolt that created Belgium. The representative monarchies of the West now stood in sharp contrast to the autocratic states of central and eastern Europe. These liberal constitutional regimes were committed to civil rights and the rule of law and, above all, to the idea of social progress through reform.

Great Britain

By the 1820s Britain had withdrawn from Metternich's Concert of Europe. This move represented more than insular habit; the world's leading example of liberalism, Britain began to favor liberal programs elsewhere and to distance itself from more repressive continental regimes. Nevertheless, the triumph of liberalism at home did not come without serious conflict.

Pressure for Reform Acute pressure for reform emerged out of the turmoil of the postwar years. The demobilization of the army and the collapse of wartime markets created economic distress and the government's economic policies—removal of the wartime income tax and a higher tariff on grains, which made bread more expensive—favored the rich. To change these policies required reform of the political system; agitation for such reform swept the country.

The government at first responded with repression, suspending habeas corpus for the first time in English history in 1817. A mass meeting for reform at St. Peter's Field, Manchester, in 1819, so terrified local magistrates that they called out troops. The ensuing charge wounded hundreds of demonstrators, including women and children, and killed several. With bitter mockery people called it the Peterloo Massacre.

Parliament reacted by passing the repressive Six Acts of 1819, which restricted public meetings, facilitated the prosecution of radicals, and imposed a stamp tax intended to cripple the radical press. Support for the established order continued to ebb, and George IV's scandalous personal life earned public contempt. Old restrictions on Protestant dissenters and Roman Catholics (who could not hold public office, for example) now brought rising criticism of the special privileges accorded the Church of England.

Even an unreformed Parliament had to respond to public opinion, however, and it began to support compromises on some critical issues. The government reduced some tariffs and repealed the Combination Acts that had banned trade unions, although an amendment effectively outlawing strikes was added. As the minister in charge of the Home Office, Sir Robert Peel ceased the prosecution of dissident newspapers and the use of political spies, halved the list of capital crimes, and put domestic order in the hands of civil authority by creating a police force. Tories who opposed such measures looked to the conservative Duke of Wellington, the prestigious victor over Napoleon at Waterloo, to resist further reforms. Yet as prime minister even Wellington saw the need to push through Parliament a measure he himself disliked, allowing Catholics and religious dissenters to vote and to hold public office.

● —— **1851** Louis Napoleon's coup d'etat

● —— **1852** Cavour prime minister of Piedmont

● **1854** Crimean War

● **1859** Piedmont's war on Austria

● **1861** Kingdom of Italy established; emancipation of Russian serfs

● **1862** Bismarck prime minister of Prussia

● **1866** Austro-Prussian War

● **1867** Austro-Hungarian Dual Monarchy

● **1870** Franco-Prussian War

● **1871** German Reich established

CHRONOLOGY
Major Reform Legislation in Britain

1828	Restrictions on non-Anglican Protestants lifted; London police force created.
1829	Catholic emancipation, Catholics allowed in Parliament.
1832	Parliament reformed.
1833	Slavery abolished in British Empire; child labor in factories restricted to nine hours for those more than nine years old.
1834	Poor Law.
1846	Corn Laws repealed.
1847	Ten-hour workday.

These issues—religious freedom, the legitimacy of unions, tariffs, freedom of the press—led to agitation that focused increasingly on the need to reform Parliament itself. Elections in 1830, after the death of King George IV and the accession of William IV, raised the political temperature. In the countryside, disenfranchised laborers set haystacks afire by night; by day, stern magistrates ordered laborers accused of seditious activity transported to Australia.

The Reform Bill of 1832 As public turmoil rose (and British leaders warily watched the revolution of 1830

Joseph Nash
INTERIOR OF THE HOUSE OF COMMONS
The British House of Commons sat in a new building of Gothic splendor that made parliamentary liberty seem ancient and the two-party system inevitable.
Houses of Parliament, Westminster, London, UK/Bridgeman Art Library

665

in France), a new cabinet presented a bill to reform the electoral system. The House of Commons approved the bill but only after a new election; the Lords then rejected it until the king reluctantly threatened to create enough new peers to get it through. Each defeat made the public mood angrier, and the king's intervention came amid demonstrations, the burning of the town hall and bishop's palace in Bristol, and much dark talk about the French example.

The bill itself offered a good deal less than radicals had wanted, but it nonetheless marked a fundamental change in Britain's electoral system. It expanded the suffrage, allowing some 800,000 well-to-do men to vote, based on the property they owned or the rents they paid.[1] More important, the bill eliminated local variation in voting in favor of a uniform national standard that, as many Tories warned, could easily be broadened in the future. Before the Reform Bill, many boroughs that sent representatives to Parliament were depopulated villages (the most notorious, Old Sarum, was by now uninhabited altogether), while the bustling cities of Birmingham and Manchester had had no representatives at all. Perhaps a third of the members of Parliament owed their seats to the influence of some lord. Although restricted suffrage and the custom of open voting guaranteed the continued dominance of the upper classes, now representation was at least crudely related to population, and the votes of the commercial and manufacturing classes would be more numerous.

After 1832, Parliament turned to other reforms. It abolished slavery in Britain's colonies in 1833, a victory for Protestant reformers and humanitarian radicals. The Factory Act, limiting the hours children worked,[2] soon followed, as did the popularly despised Poor Law of 1834 (see chapter 22). A law granting all resident taxpayers the right to vote in municipal elections challenged aristocratic influence even more directly than the Reform Bill of 1832. By the time the young Queen Victoria ascended the throne in 1837, representative government was stronger than ever; during her reign of more than six decades, she would remain subordinate (often against her wishes) to an increasingly flexible political system.

Chartism and the Corn Laws　Two great popular movements helped define the limits of that political system. **Chartism** was a huge, amorphous workers' movement to extend political democracy, as spelled out in "the People's Charter."[3] With articulate leaders and a broad working-class base, Chartists propagandized widely. They held huge demonstrations in 1839, 1840, and 1848 and were accused of causing riots that ended with scores of deaths. Although treated by the state as dangerous revolutionaries, their principal tactic was to present Parliament with petitions containing tens of thousands of signatures (see "The Great Charter," p. 667). Parliament summarily rejected these petitions, however, and by 1842 the movement petered out. Despite its size, it failed to define a program that could mobilize workers struggling for survival or to stir the consciences of those in power. Angry, desperate workers might riot here or there, but they were still too isolated from one another and from other classes to gain their political, let alone their social and economic, goals.

The other great popular movement, against the grain tariff, was victorious. The Anti-Corn Law League grew out of urban resentment over the high cost of bread resulting from grain tariffs—the **Corn Laws**—that benefited the landowning classes. From Manchester the movement spread throughout the country, becoming a kind of crusade against the privileges of the landowning aristocracy in the name of the "productive orders" of society, the middle and working classes. The league's propaganda used the new techniques of popular politics: parades and rallies, songs and speeches, pamphlets and cartoons. Its slogans were printed on trinkets for children, ribbons for women, drinking cups for men. Two manufacturers, Richard Cobden and John Bright, became influential as the spokesmen of the movement, spreading the gospel of free trade across the land. The conservative upper classes deplored these activities, insisting that the nation's greatness was rooted in its landed estates.

Parliament proved responsive, however, to this coalition of the middle and working classes. Twice Sir Robert Peel's government lowered duties on a wide range of items, including grain, but the League demanded more. Finally, in 1846, Peel moved to repeal the Corn Laws outright, reducing the grain tariff to almost nothing and abolishing or lowering nearly all duties. Peel's initiative split his party and ended his ministry. Peel was jeered by angry Tories as a young newcomer, Benjamin Disraeli, rose to decry his treachery to the

---

[1] This electorate was considerably broader than that established in either France or Belgium in 1830, though Belgium, the only country to give elected representatives a salary, had in many respects Europe's most liberal constitution. About 1 Frenchman in 160 could vote in 1830; 1 Briton in 32, after the Reform Bill of 1832. About 1 Belgian in 95 could vote by 1840; and 1 in 20 by 1848. Universal male suffrage permits approximately one-fifth of the total population to go to the polls.

[2] The workweek was limited to 48 hours for children between the ages of six and thirteen and to 69 hours for those between ages fourteen and eighteen.

[3] The six demands of the People's Charter were universal male suffrage, a written ballot, abolition of property qualifications for members of Parliament, payment of the members, constituencies of equal population, and annual elections. All but the last of these points had been adopted by 1918.

THE GREAT CHARTER

The Chartist movement reached its peak in 1842 with the presentation to the House of Commons of the Great Charter. There were more than 3 million signatures on this petition calling for universal male suffrage, annual parliaments, lower taxes, and greater attention to the needs of the poor.

TO THE HONOURABLE THE COMMONS OF GREAT BRITAIN AND IRELAND, IN PARLIAMENT ASSEMBLED.

"The petition of the undersigned people of the United Kingdom. . . .

"That as Government was designed for the benefit and protection of, and must be obeyed and supported by all, therefore all should be equally represented.

"That any form of Government which fails to effect the purposes for which it was designed, and does not fully and completely represent the whole people, who are compelled to pay taxes to its support, and obey the laws resolved upon by it, is unconstitutional, tyrannical, and ought to be amended or resisted.

"That your honourable House, as at present constituted, has not been elected by, and acts irresponsibly of, the people; and hitherto has only represented parties, and benefited the few, regardless of the miseries, grievances, and petitions of the many. Your honourable House has enacted laws contrary to the expressed wishes of the people, and by unconstitutional means enforced obedience to them, thereby creating an unbearable despotism on the one hand, and degrading slavery on the other. . . .

"That the existing state of representation is not only extremely limited and unjust, but unequally divided, and gives preponderating influence to the landed, and monied interests, to the utter ruin of the small-trading and labouring classes.

"That bribery, intimidation, corruption, perjury, and riot, prevail at all parliamentary elections, to an extent best understood by the Members of your honourable House. . . .

"That your petitioners would direct the attention of your honourable House to the great disparity existing between the wages of the producing millions, and the salaries of those whose comparative usefulness ought to be questioned, where riches and luxury prevail amongst the rulers, and poverty and starvation amongst the ruled. . . .

"That your petitioners believe all men have a right to worship God as may appear best to their consciences, and that no legislative enactments should interfere between man and his Creator.

"That your petitioners maintain that it is the inherent, indubitable, and constitutional right, founded upon the ancient practice of the realm of England, and supported by well approved statutes, of every male inhabitant of the United Kingdom, he being of age and of sound mind, non-convict of crime, and not confined under any judicial process, to exercise the elective franchise in the choice of Members to serve in the Commons House of Parliament."

Mass meetings had been one of the Chartists' most effective devices, and this one held on Kensington Common in London, April 10, 1848, was one of the most publicized. With revolution on the Continent and famine in Ireland, radical hopes were as high as conservative fears. The twenty thousand who attended this meeting had passed armed soldiers, policemen, and special constables. The expectation of violence explains the small number of women and children in this photograph. What might have been the beginning of a revolution in England was instead the Chartists' last national demonstration. The Royal Archives © 2009 Her Majesty Queen Elizabeth II

great landlords. Nevertheless, the repeal of the Corn Laws showed that the political system could bend after reform gained widespread support among the liberal middle classes.

The Revolutions of 1830

Uprisings across Europe   The cause of reform in Britain had benefited from fear of violent revolt, following a wave of revolutions on the Continent in 1830. The first of these occurred in France, largely limited to Paris. Minor revolts stimulated by the French example occurred in central Italy, Spain, Portugal, some of the German principalities, and Poland. Austria again extinguished revolt in Italy, and the Russian army crushed Poland's rebels; elsewhere, the results were more lasting.

Belgium   In the southern Netherlands, Catholics and liberals rose against Dutch rule, directly challenging the provisions of the Congress of Vienna. Britain opposed any intervention by the great powers, and (once convinced that France had no designs on that region) led in arranging international guarantees for the independence of the southern Netherlands, henceforth known as Belgium. The British and French then pressured the Dutch to accept this loss of territory.

The Belgian monarchy created in 1830 marked a triumph of liberal constitutionalism. The new state took as its king Leopold I, an uncle of Queen Victoria who had lived in England and who soon married the daughter of France's new king, Louis-Philippe. The constitution went further than France's in guaranteeing civil rights and the primacy of the Chamber of Deputies. Politics revolved around a coalition—rare in Europe— of Catholics and liberals, aristocrats and members of the upper-middle class. Rapidly emerging as the most industrialized nation on the Continent, Belgium became prosperous. The Belgians, building on administrative traditions from earlier Austrian and French rule, proved themselves as adept at constructing railroads, reforming taxes, and establishing schools as they were at the art of political compromise.

France's July Monarchy   In France, Charles X's abdication led not to the succession of his son, as the king had hoped, but to a provisional government. Most of France supported the installation of a liberal monarchy when the Marquis de Lafayette, still a popular national hero, stepped out on the balcony of the Paris town hall to present the candidate for the throne. Louis-Philippe was head of the House of Orleans, the liberal branch of the royal line, whose father had voted with the Jacobins in 1793 for the death of his cousin Louis XVI. France's new monarchy thus neatly combined symbols of revolution and liberal moderation.

Posters proclaimed Louis-Philippe the citizen-king, and the Revolution's tricolor once again replaced the white Bourbon flag. Known as the **July Monarchy,** the

Eugène Delacroix
LIBERTY LEADING THE PEOPLE,
28 JULY 1830
Delacroix's painting presents the revolution of 1830 in France as the heroic rising of the people, poor and middle class together, being led by Liberty into a new era. Louvre, Paris, France/Peter Willi/ Bridgeman Art Library

new regime began with a constitution presented as a contract the king swore to keep, not as a gift he granted. Although similar to the Bourbon charter it replaced, the constitution offered stronger guarantees of political freedom, lowered property requirements for voters (nearly doubling their number to some 170,000, but safely restricting them to men of means), and replaced the hereditary upper house with lifetime peers. Most of the old aristocracy resigned their offices, replaced by professional people and bearers of newer (often Napoleonic) titles. The new government also hastened to assure other European monarchs that this French revolution would not sponsor revolts elsewhere.

The overriding political question of the 1830s in France was the July Monarchy itself, which evoked opposition from both left and right. On the right, *legitimists* (those in favor of the Bourbons) campaigned against Louis-Philippe in the countryside via the conservative press with support from the church. In 1832 the duchess of Berry, whose infant son was now the legitimist claimant to the throne, tried to stage an uprising. On the left, republicans also mobilized against the regime, often in secret groups with provocative names like the Society of the Rights of Man. When the silk workers of Lyons went on strike in 1834, their banners read "Live freely or die." The government viewed the strike as a republican revolt. With bitter class hatred on both sides, the bourgeois national guard of Lyon forcibly suppressed the uprising.

Limited Liberalism in France Despite such turbulence, the July Monarchy presented itself as a center of stability and patriotism. It even laid claim to the cult of Napoleon I by bringing the emperor's remains back from St. Helena and interring them with nationalist pomp in the marble crypt of the Invalides. The government built on the administrative system that had developed under the Revolution and Napoleon to promote public education and industrialization. With time (and restrictions on the press) opposition quieted, and many middle-class notables rallied to a government of cautious moderation committed to progress.

Yet French politics remained divided between those, led by Adolphe Thiers, who wanted further reform and wider suffrage and those, like the king himself and the politician François Guizot, who believed the proper balance between liberty and order had been achieved. From 1840 to 1848 Guizot dominated the government, endorsing liberty, progress, and law in eloquent speeches that made his cautious and rigid practices seem hypocritical to many. In 1848 the whole regime would collapse overnight.

More generally, the two freest and most prosperous of Europe's great nations had developed similarly since 1830. In Britain and France, liberal governments led by able men sought through compromise, the rule of law, and parliamentary politics to unify their nations and to make "progress" compatible with stability. Workers' misery and discontent, however, was viewed primarily as a threat to order. In Britain reform had to be wrung from a powerful aristocracy that, in the end, felt secure enough to cede under pressure. In France the aristocracy counted for little after the revolution of 1830; but the government, fearful of the more radical pressures for democracy and social justice that it excluded, remained uncertain of its popular support.

Spain The victories of French and British liberalism seemed part of a general trend. In Spain the monarchy itself wooed liberals. When the reactionary King

Carefully staged ceremonies marked the return of Napoleon's ashes from St. Helena for internment in Paris on December 15, 1840, as a national, patriotic event.
AKG London

Ferdinand VII died in 1833, he had carefully arranged for his three-year-old daughter, Isabella, to succeed him. But the king's brother, Don Carlos, denounced the arrangement as illegal and staged an uprising that lasted until 1839. The *Carlists*, who favored autocracy and religious traditionalism, found their greatest support in rural areas and regions of the north resentful of rule from Madrid. Despite eventual defeat, Don Carlos won a place in Spanish legend as a dashing and chivalric hero, protector of old Spanish virtues. Carlism would remain a conservative rallying cry in every subsequent Spanish revolution.

To win liberal support, meanwhile, the regency ruling in Isabella's name granted a constitution in 1834. Cautiously modeled on the French constitution of 1814, with narrow suffrage and protection of royal power, it nonetheless established representative institutions as a lasting feature of Spanish politics. Even so modest a step placed Spain in the liberal camp, and Isabella's government relied on support from Britain and France. Internal war brought generals into politics and sparked conflict between moderates (who supported the constitution and admired Guizot's France) and anticlerical progressives (who demanded a more democratic constitution). Only in the 1840s, after a couple of military coups, did moderates manage to establish a regime strong enough to hold power for a decade.

THE REVOLUTIONS OF 1848

Although liberal reforms brought representative government and expanded the power of the middle classes in western Europe, they did not, by and large, take up the social and political claims of the popular classes. In central and eastern Europe, autocratic regimes blocked liberal change entirely. In response, popular movements spread in 1848 in a kind of spontaneous wave of imitation from city to city. Although their causes and ultimate defeat differed in each case, the ensuing revolutions all went through comparable phases in which early victory and euphoria was followed by intensifying social conflict and, ultimately, by the triumph of the forces of order.

Two years of poor harvests and industrial recession in most of Europe preceded these outbreaks, but economic crisis alone does not make for revolution. In Ireland, more than a million people died from starvation during the famine years of the late 1840s, yet that tragedy did nothing to shake British rule. Similarly, liberal reform occurred in Switzerland, Belgium, and the Netherlands without the eruption of a serious revolt. Revolutions took place where governments were distrusted and where the fear and resentment fed by rising food prices and unemployment found a focus in specific political demands.

The Opening Phase

France   In France the Guizot government's stubborn refusal to broaden the plutocratic suffrage led to the fall of the July Monarchy. (If you want to qualify for the vote, he once stated, then "enrich yourself.") The parliamentary opposition to Guizot launched a protest movement that staged large fraternal banquets across the country. When the nervous government, aware of its unpopularity, banned a banquet scheduled for Paris in late February 1848, some members of the Chamber of Deputies announced they would attend anyway. Crowds gathered in the streets, and workers built barricades. When Louis-Philippe's militia, the National Guard, refused to cheer him, he knew his days were numbered. He abdicated in favor of his grandson and left for England, much as Charles X had done just eighteen years before.

A provisional government of men chosen in the offices of two rival opposition newspapers appeared at the Paris city hall and declared France a republic to the cheering of Parisian crowds. Led by the much-admired Romantic poet Alphonse de Lamartine and dominated by moderates, the new cabinet at first cooperated with more radical members, including the socialist Louis Blanc. Under its rule, the republic adopted the radical measure of universal male suffrage, proclaimed the citizen's right to employment, and established a commission to hold public hearings on labor problems.

At the same time, the new regime demonstrated its restraint. It refused to intervene on behalf of revolutions in other countries, kept the familiar tricolor flag in lieu of adopting the red flag of socialism, levied new taxes to balance the budget, and maintained good relations with the Catholic Church. In elections for a constituent assembly that April, nearly 85 percent of the eligible electorate voted and gave moderate republicans an overwhelming majority. The Second Republic seemed solidly established.

Revolution Spreads   As news of the events in France sped across Europe, a conservative nightmare became a reality. In Hungary on March 3 the Diet cheered Lajos Kossuth, the Magyar leader (see chapter 22), as he called for representative government. In the same week, demonstrations with similar demands erupted in the cities of the Rhineland, soon giving way to revolution there, followed by uprisings in Vienna (March 12), Berlin (March 15), Milan (March 18), and Venice (March 22).

Each of these revolutions followed a similar pattern. The news from France attracted excited crowds, and journalists, lawyers, and students congregated in cafés

Felix Philippoteaux
LAMARTINE REJECTS THE RED FLAG, **1848**
Lamartine persuades the crowd to reject the red flag and let the new French republic keep the tricolor.
Musée du Petit Palais, Paris. Giraudon/Bridgeman Art Library

to discuss rumors and newspaper reports. Governments that did not quickly grant constitutions (as they did in Italy) called out troops to maintain order, and inevitably some incident occurred—a shot fired by a soldier insulted once too often, for example—that resulted in violence. Barricades were erected out of paving stones, trees, and furniture. When blood was shed, the revolution had its martyrs. In Paris, revolutionaries carried corpses around on a cart to inspire the crowd. In Berlin, after a round of violent conflict in the streets, the king acceded to the revolutionaries' demands and even paid his respects to those killed by his own troops. When concessions were won, the atmosphere grew festive. New flags flew, often a tricolor echoing the French Revolution, but with colors symbolizing some other nation, and newspapers and pamphlets proliferated (one hundred new newspapers were established in Vienna, nearly five hundred in Paris).

Central Europe   In the Austrian Empire, the Hungarian Diet had by mid-March established a free press and a national guard, abolished feudal obligations (with compensation to the lords), and required nobles to pay taxes. Everyone noticed the parallel to 1789. Reluctantly, Vienna agreed that Hungary could levy its own taxes and direct its own army; but the Hungarian example encouraged students in Vienna to demand representative government for Austria as well,

and crowds soon clashed with troops there. In rapid order Metternich resigned, censorship was abolished, the king promised a constitution, and insurgents seized firearms. When students rejected the proposal that all men except factory workers and servants be allowed to vote, the monarchy conceded universal male suffrage. Hungarian autonomy also brought similar demands from Czechs in Bohemia, Croatians in Croatia, and Romanians in Transylvania (these last two domains under Hungarian rule). The old Habsburg Empire seemed to be collapsing.

When Frederick William IV of Prussia learned the incredible news of an uprising in Vienna and the fall of Metternich, he granted the concessions on which he had stalled, relaxed censorship, and called a meeting of the Landtag. Fighting broke out anyway, and Frederick William then agreed to remove his hated troops from Berlin, used the evocative word Germany in proclamations to "my dear Berliners," and wore the German national colors: black, gold, and red. A constituent assembly was elected in May by universal but indirect male suffrage, and when it met in Berlin, where a civic guard now kept order, revolution seemed to have triumphed in Prussia, too.

Events in the rest of Germany confirmed that victory. In May, 830 delegates elected in the various German states convened the **Frankfurt Parliament** to write a constitution for all of Germany. Mostly liberals, more than half of them were lawyers and professors, but there were also businessmen, members of the liberal gentry, and even nobles. The great majority favored a monarchical German state under a liberal constitution.

The arrangements contrived in 1815 at the Congress of Vienna were under siege in Italy as well, where in the 1820s and 1830s the kingdoms of Piedmont in the north and Naples (including Sicily) in the south had barely weathered earlier revolts, which had also threatened the smaller duchies in between. (See map 22.1.) News of the revolution in Paris led to demands for constitutions in Naples, Tuscany, and Piedmont. Even the Papal States got a constitution, though it awkwardly preserved a veto for the pope and the College of Cardinals. Lombardy and Venetia had been ruled as part of the Habsburg Empire since 1815, but shortly after the revolution in Vienna, a revolt broke out in Milan against the Austrian forces there. The Austrians were forced to retreat, and the "Five Glorious Days of Milan" became part of the heroic legends of 1848. Then Venice rose up to reestablish the Venetian republic of old. The possibility that the Italian peninsula might be freed from all foreign rule stimulated a nationalist fervor that pushed Piedmont into joining the struggle against Austria.

The Fatal Dissensions

Social Class Everywhere, however, the new freedom exposed divisions among the revolutionaries. In France these divisions were primarily social—between Paris and the countryside, between the middle classes and the workers. Workers pinned their hopes on social programs such as the national workshops established by the socialist Louis Blanc, a series of public works projects fixing roads and walls around Paris that hired tens of thousands of unemployed workers. To moderate republicans, the workshops represented a dangerous principle and outrageous waste, and the government disbanded them in June. Artisans and workers in Paris saw this as a symbolic issue for the place of labor in the new republic. They responded by building barricades in the working-class sections of Paris. For three days they desperately fought the Republic's troops, led by General Cavaignac.

More than a thousand people died in these **June Days** and thousands more would be sent to prison or deported as a result of their participation. The uprising remained the very essence of class conflict for socialists and radicals. Granted essentially dictatorial powers, Cavaignac moved to restrict the press, suppress radical societies, and discipline workers. Despite his role in suppressing the June Days, Cavaignac remained a convinced republican, and the assembly continued to write a constitution that maintained universal suffrage and in unprecedented fashion provided for a president

Ernest Meissonier
THE BARRICADE IN RUE MORTELLERIE, PARIS, JUNE 1848
A silent street in Paris after the June Days, its rubble, bodies, and blood—the emblems of revolution defeated.
Louvre, Paris, France. Erich Lessing/Art Resource, NY

directly elected by popular vote. Nevertheless, after June there was something hollow about the Second Republic.

National Ambitions In Germany and Austria, too, revolution uncovered latent conflicts between workers and the middle class and among artisans, peasants, and nobles. The outcomes there, however, were determined more by competing nationalisms and the fact that kings still had control of their armies. The Frankfurt Parliament felt little sympathy for uprisings by other nationalities against German rule in places like Bohemia. Instead of protesting the repression of revolution, it congratulated the Austrian field marshal who bombarded Prague (where Czechs had staged a Pan-Slav conference) on his German victory; and it applauded the Austrian forces that regrouped in northern Italy and fought their way back into Milan. It also called on the Prussian army to put down a Polish uprising in Posen and to fight against insurgent Danes in the province of Schleswig. In September, when riots broke out in Frankfurt itself, the assembly invited

Prussian troops to restore order. Conflicts between nationalities also strengthened the position of the Habsburgs at home, as the emperor mobilized Croatians demanding autonomy from Hungary for use against Kossuth's forces. In parts of the empire, Austrian officials were also able to win peasant support by abolishing serfdom and by playing on their distrust of local upper-class revolutionaries.

The Prussian and Habsburg armies that soon moved on Frankfurt and Vienna confronted resistance that, like the June Days in Paris, revealed popular fury and more radical demands than the risings of February and March. Politics turned more radical in Rome, too, where the pope had resisted Italian nationalism, where economic conditions worsened, and where a government that had promised much accomplished little. When his prime minister was assassinated, Pius IX slipped across the border into the Kingdom of Naples, and a representative assembly gave the eternal city its ancient title of Roman Republic. Venice and France were also republics, and assemblies were still busy drafting constitutions in Vienna, Berlin, and Frankfurt, but there could be no doubt that conservative forces were gaining ground.

The Final Phase

New Leaders   In December 1848, France elected a president, and the candidates prominent in the new

republic finished far behind Louis Napoleon Bonaparte, who won 70 percent of the votes. The ambitious nephew of Napoleon had campaigned as a republican. He had written some pamphlets about social questions and workers' needs. For lack of an alternative, the Catholic Church and the monarchists generally supported him as a man of order. Above all, Louis Napoleon had his name recognition.[4]

Austria, too, found a strong new leader in Prince Felix von Schwarzenberg, who took Metternich's place. In December he persuaded the emperor to abdicate in favor of his eighteen-year-old nephew, Franz Joseph I, who could promise a fresh start. In Prussia the king felt confident enough to dissolve the Landtag and promulgate a constitution of his own. Ten months of turmoil had led back to the arrangements of February.

Military Force   One by one, the remaining revolutionary regimes were subdued. In March 1849, the Frankfurt Assembly, its constitution for a unified Germany completed, chose the Prussian king, Frederick

---

[4] On trial for an attempted coup in 1840, Louis Napoleon had concluded his defense with these words: "I represent before you a principle, a cause, and a defeat: the principle is sovereignty of the people; the cause, that of the Empire; the defeat, Waterloo. The principle you have recognized; the cause you have served; the defeat you want to avenge."

An engraving of the violence in Frankfurt in September 1848 contrasts the fighting styles of troops and the defenders of revolution.
The Granger Collection, New York

THE FRANKFURT CONSTITUTION

The Frankfurt Parliament completed its work on a constitution for Germany in 1849. It was a long and detailed document, carefully proscribing the repressive acts that had been most common in the preceding years. Its proud assertions of German freedom remain significantly vague, however, about the enforcement of its provisions and what the boundaries of the German nation will be.

THE FUNDAMENTAL RIGHTS OF THE GERMAN PEOPLE

Article 1

¶ 131. The German people consists of the citizens of the states, which make up the Reich.

¶ 132. Every German has the right of German Reich's citizenship. He can exercise this right in every German land. Reich's franchise legislation shall provide for the right of the individual to vote for members of the national assembly.

¶ 133. Every German has the right to live or reside in any part of the Reich's territory, to acquire and dispose of property of all kinds, to pursue his livelihood, and to win the right of communal citizenship. . . .

¶ 134. No German state is permitted to make a distinction between its citizens and other Germans in civil, criminal, and litigation rights which relegates the latter to the position of foreigners.

¶ 135. Capital punishment for civil offenses shall not take place, and, in those cases where condemnation has already been made, shall not be carried out, in order not to infringe upon the hereby acquired civil law.

¶ 136. Freedom of emigration shall not be limited by any state; emigration levies shall not be established.

All matters of emigration remain under the protection and care of the Reich.

Article 2

¶ 137. There are no class differences before the law. The rank of nobility is abolished.

All special class privileges are abolished.

All Germans are equal before the law.

All titles, insofar as they are not bound with an office, are abolished and never again shall be introduced.

No citizen shall accept a decoration from a foreign state.

Public office shall be open to all men on the basis of ability.

All citizens are subject equally to military service; there shall be no draft substitutions.

Article 3

¶ 141. The confiscation of letters and papers, except at an arrest or house search, can take place with a legally executed warrant, which must be served on the arrested person at once or within the next twenty-four hours.

¶ 142. The secrecy of letters is inviolable.

Necessary exceptions in cases of criminal investigation and in the event of war shall be established by legislation.

Article 4

¶ 143. Every German shall have the right freely to express his opinion through speech, writing, publication, and illustration.

The freedom of the press shall be suspended under no circumstances through preventive measures, namely, censorship, concessions, security orders, imposts, limitation of publication or bookselling, postal bans, or other restraints.

From Louis L. Snyder (ed.), *The Documents of German History*, Rutgers University Press, 1958.

William, as emperor of Germany, only to have him reject as illegitimate this "crown from the gutter," in contrast to those rightfully conferred by the grace of God. The Frankfurt constitution—which included universal male suffrage and civil rights–would never be implemented (see "The Frankfurt Constitution," above). New revolutions then broke out in the Rhineland, Saxony, and Baden, but all were quashed in June and July with the aid of Prussian troops. Meanwhile, the Habsburgs' multinational armies bombarded the revolutionaries of Vienna into submission and soon turned on Hungary, where a republic had been declared when Schwarzenberg refused to approve Hungary's consti-

tution. Led by Kossuth, who tried to replicate the French Revolution's *levée en masse*, the Hungarians battled for months to a standoff against armies of Austrians, Croatians, and Romanians. Finally Russia intervened in June to doom the Hungarian republic.

In Italy, too, military force was decisive. Austria defeated Piedmont again, leaving it nothing to show for its support of Italian independence except an enormous debt, an unpopular government, a new ruler, a cautious constitution, and the red, white, and green flag of Italian nationalism. The Roman Republic collapsed after a three-month battle with French armies sent by Louis Napoleon to defend the papacy. The

Kingdom of Naples reconquered Sicily in May 1849 only after a bombardment of the city of Messina that gave Ferdinand II the nickname King Bomba. The last of the revolutionary regimes to fall was the Venetian republic, defeated in August 1849 less by the Austrian artillery that lobbed shells three miles from the mainland into the island city than by starvation and cholera. Finally, Prussian troops crushed an insurrection in the South German state of Baden.

The Results A famous liberal historian, G. M. Trevelyan, called 1848 "the turning-point at which modern history failed to turn," and his epigram captures the sense of destiny thwarted that still colors the liberal view of 1848. Current historical analysis of the failures of 1848 generally makes five broad points. First, liberal constitutions and increased civil rights failed to pull strong and lasting support from artisans, peasants, and workers, whose more immediate needs were neither met nor understood. Second, the revolutions of February and March were made primarily by the middle classes, strengthened for the moment by popular discontent, but when radicals sought more than representative government and legal equality, the middle classes worried about order and private property. Isolated from the masses, they were too weak to retain power except in France, and there order came only after repression of the urban artisans and workers in the June Days and the subsequent curtailment of constitutional liberties. Third, the leaders of the revolutions, inexperienced in practical politics, often mistook parliaments for power and left intact the established royal bureaucracies and armies that would soon turn on them. Fourth, nationalism motivated some revolutionaries but divided others and prevented the transnational cooperation essential for durable success. Finally, no major nation was ready to intervene in behalf of change. Britain was sympathetic, France encouraging, and the United States (its consulates centers of republicanism) enthusiastic; but none of that sympathy offset the military assistance Russia gave the Austrian emperor or the formidable armies of Austria and Prussia.

The events of 1848 had significant effects nonetheless. Widespread revolution reflected the failures of restoration and exposed the effects of a generation of profound social change. Many of the gains of that year endured: 1848 emancipated the peasants of eastern Prussia and the Austrian Empire from serfdom and gave new limited constitutions to Piedmont and Prussia. The monarchs triumphant in 1849 punished revolutionaries with execution, prison, and exile, but they also learned the importance of popular support. Political leaders of every hue now recognized the potential force of nationalism.

THE POLITICS OF NATIONALISM

Why **nationalism** assumed such importance in the nineteenth century and has retained it to the present day remains a key question of modern history. As an ideology, it represents itself as a natural, age-old sentiment arising spontaneously; yet nationalism is essentially a modern phenomenon and often seems to require persistent propaganda. Associated with liberalism in the first part of the nineteenth century, nationalism came to be embraced and used by both the left and the right. It affected politics on every level: domestic policies in every sort of government and international relations.

The Elements of Nationalism

Nationalism's deepest roots lie in a shared sense of regional and cultural identity, especially as those roots are expressed in custom, language, and religion. This shared culture had been greatly affected, and often shaped, by the development of the state, whose power and importance had increased since the state building of the seventeenth century. But it was the experience of the French Revolution that established nationalism as a political force capable of mobilizing popular enthusiasm, of reforming society, of creating seemingly irresistible political movements, and ultimately of greatly adding to the power of the state.

Liberation and Modernization Napoleon I had appealed to national feeling in much of Europe, most notably Poland and Italy. Conversely, in Germany the fight against Napoleon was called a national war of liberation, and the Allies had evoked national feeling to recruit opposition to the French in Spain and (less successfully) in Italy. The association of liberation and nationalism had been particularly marked in the New World, where the American Revolution fostered a fervent nationalism and where, as a result of their revolt against Spanish rule, elite groups carved Central and South America into new states and claimed a national identity for each of them (see chapter 21).

Nationalism was also a movement for self-conscious modernization, embraced by people who believed that their societies might attain the industrial wealth of England and acquire political systems as responsive and efficient as those of Britain and France. In the course of the nineteenth century, increased communication, literacy, and mobility further stimulated the sense of belonging to a larger but definable community. Nationalism was thus a response to social and economic change, one that promised to bring middle classes and masses together in support of common goals. Nationalists, like conservatives and socialists, stressed the values of community; like liberals, they tended to believe that change could bring progress.

National Identity As an intellectual movement, nationalism was an international phenomenon, everywhere emphasizing the importance of culture, and often inspired by Romanticism, with its rejection of Enlightenment universalism. Thus, German intellectuals such as Johann Gottlieb Fichte urged their countrymen to put aside values imported from France in favor of a uniquely German culture.

The exploration of ethnic origins took many forms. A group of German scholars made philology (the study of language) a science, and by the 1830s and 1840s an extraordinary revival of national languages had occurred across Europe. Gaelic was hailed as the national tongue of Ireland; in Finland the first public lecture in Finnish marked a break from the dominant Swedish culture; intellectuals in Bohemia began abandoning their customary German to write in Czech. More remarkable still was the number of languages consciously contrived out of local dialects and invented vocabularies. Norwegian became distinct from Danish, Serbian from other Slavic languages, and Slovak from Czech—all literary languages by the 1840s, each the work of a handful of scholars whose task of establishing a national language was actually made easier by widespread illiteracy.

This fascination with folk culture and language was reinforced by an emphasis on history as a popular but scholarly form of knowledge that revealed each nation's historic character. Germans wrote of a special sense of freedom originally embodied in Germanic tribes, expanded by the Reformation, and now extended to the state. French historians wrote eloquently of France's call to carry reason and liberty across Europe, and Italian writers proclaimed that Italy was again destined to lead Europe as it once had as the home of Roman civilization and the center of Christianity. The poet Adam Mickiewicz, lecturing in Paris, inspired Polish nationalists with his descriptions of how Poland's history paralleled the life of Christ and had yet to achieve Resurrection. Francis Palacky stressed the role of the Czechs as leaders of the Slavic peoples. Such visions were echoed in poetry and drama, which now blossomed in the native tongues and justified resistance to alien rule. This cultural nationalism appealed to middle-class people—intellectuals, students, professional people, and journalists—who felt constrained by social hierarchy, rigid bureaucracy, or stagnant economy. For them the dream of nationhood was entwined with liberal visions of progress, of a meritocratic society in which deserving individuals met no obstacles to their success.

Political Goals In places subject to foreign rule, the political goal of nationalist movements was independence. Economic problems often became wedge issues. Campaigns for agricultural improvement, promoted by the liberal aristocracy, became nationalist programs in Hungary and Italy. In Germany Friedrich List, a leading liberal economist, argued that only a united Germany with a national tariff could create an internal sphere of free trade sufficient to promote the industry and the vigorous middle class necessary for economic strength. Nationalist groups also demanded public education, more political freedom, and efficient government. With promises of economic growth and its respect for native traditions, nationalism could mobilize popular enthusiasms. Daniel O'Connell's stirring speeches won thousands to his Young Ireland organization and its call to end the union with Great Britain. In the 1830s and 1840s, he led the largest such protest movement Europe had yet seen.

A New Regime: The Second Empire in France

From Republic to Empire Elections in France had left the Second Republic in the hands of president Louis Napoleon, who would eventually subvert it, a Chamber of Deputies in which a majority seemed to be monarchists who did not want a republic at all, and a minority of social democrats (as they called themselves) who demanded more egalitarian policies. Often at odds with the deputies, Louis Napoleon continued to play to public opinion; in the third year of his four-year term, when the Chamber rejected a constitutional amendment that would have allowed him to run for a second term, he made his move. His coup d'état came on the eve of December 2, 1851—the anniversary of the first Napoleon's coronation as emperor in 1804 and of his victory at Austerlitz in 1805. He arrested potential opponents, including two hundred deputies, and sent troops to occupy the streets and dismantle hastily built barricades. At the same time, he restored universal male suffrage, which the conservative Chamber had recently restricted. Resistance was considerable in many parts of provincial France—hundreds were killed and more than 20,000 people arrested—but brief. Three weeks later, Louis Napoleon's actions were ratified by more than 90 percent of the voters in a national plebiscite. Exactly one year after this first coup, Louis Napoleon transformed the Second Republic into the **Second Empire** and declared himself Emperor Napoleon III, a change overwhelmingly supported in another plebiscite.

The Second Empire thus claimed a democratic mandate but held authoritarian power. It was supported by most businessmen and the Catholic Church, and

Haussmann's rebuilding of Paris began with the demolition of buildings that had stood for centuries and included a ring of spacious boulevards around the city.
Giraudon/Art Resource, NY

accepted by most monarchists, local notables, and peasants. To a degree, Napoleon III was influenced by Saint-Simonian socialism, attracted by liberal nationalism, and obsessed by belief in his own destiny—Napoleon the Little to his opponents, the Emperor to most of the French. Under his rule, the French state sponsored programs for social welfare and fostered economic growth more systematically than any other government in Europe, using tax incentives to stimulate investment, making it easier to form companies with limited liability, and adding its own special investment funds. The French economy boomed in the 1850s.

Among the government's many programs of public works, the rebuilding of Paris topped the agenda. A pioneering venture in city planning, the project typified Napoleon III's imperial ambitions. Plans were reviewed by the emperor himself, who favored symmetry and structures of equal height, and executed by his extraordinarily able prefect of Paris, Georges Haussmann. Haussmann created new parks and cleared slums in the city center, often with painful dislocation for their residents. A ring of wide new boulevards served multiple purposes, providing striking vistas, aiding traffic flow, and, equally important, discouraging the construction

of barricades. The city also received a vast new sewer and water system. Such massive projects stimulated land speculation and profiteering; yet the result was a city healthier and more convenient, envied and imitated throughout the world. The court of Napoleon III and Empress Eugénie was brilliant, and French prestige in the arts and sciences (enhanced by the fame of Louis Pasteur's discoveries in biology) was never higher. The emperor presented himself as the patron of educational and social reform and, in the Napoleonic tradition, rewarded talent with honors and promotions.

The Liberal Empire By the 1860s, however, the empire's fortunes were changing, its policies at home and abroad subject to rising criticism. The coalition of interests that had supported Napoleon III was breaking up, and foreign ventures intended to extend French influence had their political costs. Support of Italian unification (see "A New Nation: The Unification of Italy," p. 680) antagonized French Catholics, and an attempt to gain imperial glory by intervention in Mexico ended in disaster. Steps toward free trade, including a major tariff agreement with Great Britain in 1860, appealed to liberal economists but upset many producers. At the same time, workers wanted more from the government than public works projects and support for mutual-aid societies. Restrictions of political freedom were increasingly resented, and opponents' criticisms became more intense.

Napoleon III responded with a gradual liberalization that in 1860 enlarged the role of the legislature and by 1868 included freedom of the press and of assembly; a full-fledged parliamentary system was in place two years later. The government also encouraged workers' organizations and acknowledged the right to strike. Like the establishment of public secondary schools, which the church opposed, these new measures alienated some old supporters without, however, mollifying an opposition that gained in each election. Republicans held nearly half the lower house in 1869, and a republican was prime minister the following year, which turned out to be the Second Empire's last.

The Second Empire had pioneered a new kind of regime—one which was authoritarian but played to public opinion, which imposed order but fostered social programs and economic growth, and which used national prestige to counter domestic division. Balancing those tensions, however, became increasingly difficult for the emperor.

Nationalism and International Relations

1848 had revealed the political potential of nationalism, a lesson that Prussia, Austria, Britain, Piedmont, and France would all seek to apply domestically. In international relations as well, the politics of patriotism marked the second half of the century.

The Crimean War The pursuit of international influence led France and Great Britain to war against Russia in 1854 over competing claims by Roman Catholic and Greek Orthodox monks to be the guardians of Jerusalem's holy places. France pressed the Ottoman sultan, whose empire included Jerusalem, to grant the Catholic Church specific privileges. Russia, as defender of the Orthodox faith, demanded a protectorate over Orthodox churches within the Ottoman Empire and occupied Wallachia and Moldavia, Danubian lands under Ottoman authority. (See map 23.1.) This Russian expansion, part of a long-term pattern, worried the British, who saw their own empire threatened by the extension of Russian influence in the direction of Persia or Afghanistan. Britain encouraged the Ottoman sultan to resist Russia's demands.

When negotiations broke down, Britain and France sent their fleets into the Aegean Sea, and in October 1853 the sultan exuberantly declared war on Russia. Russian forces destroyed an Ottoman fleet, however, and Britain and France decided in 1854 to fight Russia

directly. The war, which took place on the Crimean peninsula in the Black Sea, was conducted with remarkable incompetence on both sides. Russia could not mobilize or effectively deploy its massive armies, and Britain's supply system proved inadequate for war at such a distance. In 1855 the allies welcomed the aid of little Piedmont and, a full year after invading the Crimea, finally took Sevastopol. Russia sued for peace and agreed to accept terms to be defined at a European congress in Paris.

Congress of Paris The Congress signaled an important shift in the European balance. It met in Paris rather than Vienna and was preoccupied with nationalist issues. In 1856 Russia counted for less than it had in 1815, and the conservative alliance of Austria, Prussia, and Russia that had dominated for a generation had broken up over competing ambitions in the Balkans and Germany. Russia ceded to the demand of the Congress that it surrender claims to any protectorate over Christians in the Ottoman Empire and accept a ban on warships in the Black Sea, but conflicts persisted over national claims. Britain and France did not want to give the Danubian principalities to either Russia or Austria. The issue was postponed because the obvious resolution—uniting the two territories and allowing them autonomy, a procedure that began a few years later—would create the basis for a Romanian national state, and Austria feared nationalism as a threat to the Habsburg Empire. Similar fears thwarted Napoleon III from putting the question of Polish independence on the agenda as he wanted to.

In the Crimean War, almost 500,000 soldiers died, the highest toll of any European conflict between the Napoleonic wars and World War I. Two-thirds of the casualties were Russian, and two-thirds of all losses resulted from sickness and bad care. Yet the outbreak of war produced a surge of enthusiasm no government could ignore. The public diplomacy that led to the war, the parades of magnificently uniformed soldiers, and the heroic stories reported by aggressive journalists underscored its political importance. Under Western pressure, the Ottoman Empire began to adopt the modernizing institutions of the West; and Russia, sobered by defeat, launched an era of fundamental reform unequaled since the days of Peter the Great. In Italy and Germany the way began to open for still more drastic change.

A New Nation: The Unification of Italy

Giuseppe Mazzini Across the Italian peninsula, the revolutions of 1848 had declared an independent nation as a primary goal. In doing so, revolutionaries employed the ideas of Giuseppe Mazzini (see "Mazzini's

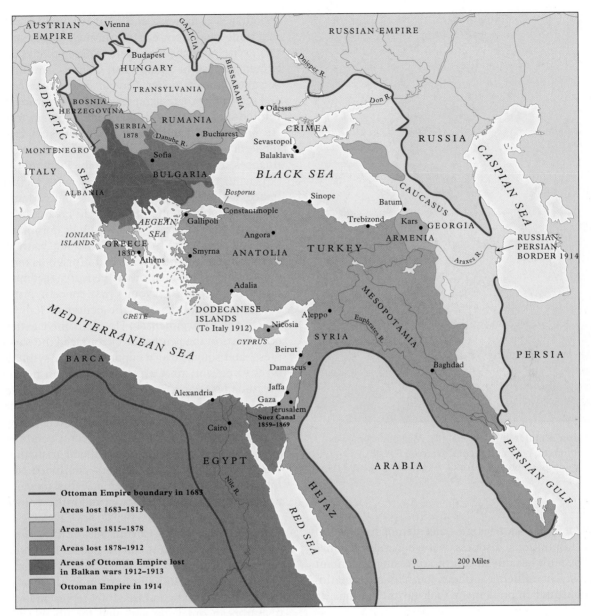

MAP 23.1 THE DECLINE OF THE OTTOMAN EMPIRE, 1683–1914
In the nineteenth century the Russian and Habsburg empires kept up the pressure against a weakening Ottoman Empire in the Caucusus and the Balkans. But it remained a formidable presence in the Arab world and in the Mediterranean region and was thus of great interest to Britain and France. How did the Ottoman Empire's existence affect the balance of power in Europe?

Nationalism," p. 681). For fifteen years, Mazzini had lived in exile, mainly in London, organizing failed conspiracies and writing passionate propaganda in pamphlets and letters. His nationalist movement, Young Italy, stimulated similar efforts in Ireland, Switzerland, and Hungary. Until 1848, the conspiracies he fostered had resulted in tragic failures, but had disseminated the belief that after corrupt regimes were toppled, the people would rise in common cause. Revolutionary and democratic, Mazzini was also a moralist who

criticized the French Revolution for stressing rights over moral duty and who rejected socialism as materialistic. In nationalism he saw the expression of natural communities, the basis for popular democracy and international brotherhood. Italy renewed, he believed, would lead the way.

Mazzini's influence was especially strong in northern Italy where, in the 1830s and 1840s, young lawyers and liberal landowners began to find national implications in nearly everything they did. Annual congresses

In his portraits and in his personal life, Mazzini seemed as much a romantic poet as a revolutionary agitator.
The Granger Collection, New York

of Italian scientists became quiet demonstrations of patriotic aspirations; disputes over where railroad lines should be built became means of expressing discontent with Austrian influence. Literary journals and societies for agricultural improvement took up the nationalist theme.

For Mazzinians, 1848 was the great chance (Mazzini himself was one of the leaders of the Roman Republic), and the defeats that followed dealt them a great blow. As Austria regained dominance of the peninsula, Mazzini returned to exile and Italian nationalists began to look elsewhere for leadership. The papacy, restored by the French army, was no longer sympathetic to Italian unity; Austria ruled Lombardy and Venetia repressively, and all the other Italian regimes except Piedmont seemed to be Austrian dependencies.

The Role of Piedmont Although a small state, Piedmont held some promise for Italian patriots. It had fought Austria, and its young king, Victor Emmanuel II, though no liberal, ruled with a parliament. The kingdom had a tradition of military strength and bureaucratic rectitude. More recently, its government had encouraged commerce and industry, and its efforts to win trade away from Austria through commercial treaties excited Italians elsewhere. These policies acquired firmer purpose in 1852, when Count Camillo Cavour became prime minister. Cavour believed in economic and scientific progress, representative government with limited suffrage, the rule of law, and religious tolerance. He understood nationalism primarily as an avenue to modernization, and he believed that free trade, sound finances, and railroads could remake Piedmont.

Cavour pursued his liberal goals with tactical brilliance, skillfully using newspapers and parliamentary debate to mold public opinion. He created a centrist parliamentary coalition with which he dominated both king and parliament from 1852 until his death in 1861. In that brief time he established himself as one of the outstanding statesmen of the century. Piedmont's internal strength was Cavour's first concern, but he also sought to make his state the center of Italy's resurgence, the **risorgimento**.[5] He welcomed exiles from other parts of the peninsula, encouraged the nationalist press, and sought every opportunity for symbolic gestures of patriotism. Cavour was aided in his goals by the Italian National Society, one of whose founders had been president of the Venetian republic in 1848. The National Society propagandized for Italian unity under Piedmont's king and established secret committees in most Italian cities. Comprising liberal aristocrats, lawyers, and professors, the society combined Mazzini's romantic rhetoric with pragmatic insistence on the need for international alliances and military force.

War against Austria Cavour was best known for his astute foreign policy. He had pushed for Piedmont's participation in the Crimean War and was rewarded with discussion of the Italian question at the Congress of Paris. Arguing that an unfree Italy represented a danger to European order, he appealed for liberal sympathy throughout western Europe and courted Napoleon III in particular. At last, in July 1858, Cavour and Napoleon III met secretly. It was easy to argue that war with Austria was inevitable, given Austria's resentment of Piedmont's growing prominence. If France would support Piedmont against Austria, Cavour promised to accept a complicated set of arrangements designed to benefit France and limit Piedmont's expansion.

Austria, watching young Lombards and Venetians escape conscription by streaming to Piedmont as volunteers, determined to end the nationalist threat

---

[5] Risorgimento, now the historian's label for the whole period of Italian unification, was a term meaning "resurgence," often used by nationalists and the title of a liberal newspaper that Cavour helped to found and edit.

MAZZINI'S NATIONALISM

"On the Duties of Man" is one of Giuseppe Mazzini's most famous essays. It was first written in 1844 for Italian workers living in England; the excerpts here are from the fifth chapter, which was added for a new edition in 1858. Despite the events of the intervening years, Mazzini's romantic faith had changed little. The essay's title was meant to contrast with the French Revolution's "Declaration of the Rights of Man," which Mazzini criticized for encouraging selfishness and materialism.

"Your first duties—first as regards importance—are, as I have already told you, towards Humanity. . . . If you do not embrace the whole human family in your affection, . . . if, wheresoever a fellow-creature suffers, or the dignity of human nature is violated by falsehood or tyranny—you are not ready, if able, to aid the unhappy, and do not feel called upon to combat, if able, for the redemption of the betrayed or oppressed—you violate your law of life, you comprehend not that Religion which will be the guide and blessing of the future.

"But what can each of you, singly, *do* for the moral improvement and progress of Humanity? . . . The watchword of the faith of the future is *Association*, and . . . [the] means was provided for you by God when he gave you a country; when, even as a wise overseer of labour distributes the various branches of employment according to the different capacities of the workmen, he divided Humanity into distinct groups or nuclei upon the face of the earth, thus creating the germ of Nationalities. Evil governments have disfigured the divine design. Nevertheless you may still trace it, distinctly marked out—at least as far as Europe is concerned—by the course of the great rivers, the direction of the higher mountains, and other geographical conditions. They have disfigured it by their conquests, their greed, and their jealousy even of the righteous power of others. . . .

"These governments did not, and do not, recognize any country save their own families or dynasty, the egotism of caste. But the Divine design will infallibly be realized. Natural divisions, and the spontaneous, innate tendencies of the peoples, will take the place of the arbitrary divisions sanctioned by evil governments. The map of Europe will be redrawn. The countries of the Peoples, defined by the vote of free men, will arise upon the ruins of the countries of kings and privileged castes. . . .

"O my brothers, love your Country! Our country is our Home, the house that God has given us, placing therein a numerous family that loves us, and whom we love. . . . Our country is our common workshop, whence the products of our activity are sent forth for the benefit of the whole world. . . . In labouring for our own country on the right principle, we labour for Humanity."

From Giuseppe Mazzini, *On the Duties of Man*, Greenwood Publishing Group.

once and for all. It sent Piedmont an ultimatum so strong that Cavour needed only to reply with cautious dignity in order to have his war. On April 29, 1859, Austria invaded Piedmont, and France went to the rescue of a small state attacked by her giant neighbor. The rapid movement of large French armies was impressive, but thereafter both sides fought with little tactical brilliance. As the Austrians retreated, Napoleon suddenly lost his taste for war and assented to a truce. The French and Austrian emperors agreed that Piedmont should have Lombardy but not Venetia and that the other Italian states should remain as before.

Formation of the Italian Kingdom

Those other Italian states, however, were not immune to the excitement of a national war. Gentle revolutions accompanied the march of Piedmontese troops throughout northern Italy. When local patriots gathered in the streets, the dukes of Modena, Parma, and Tuscany simply fled, to be replaced by provisional governments led by members of the National Society. These governments quickly adopted Piedmontese laws and held elections to representative assemblies. The terms of the truce arranged by France and Austria could not be carried out and, after a few months, the provisional governments held plebiscites on annexation of their states to Piedmont. Northern Italians trooped to the polls with bands playing and flags waving, peasants behind their lords and workers with their guilds. The result: Piedmont's King Victor Emmanuel now ruled from the Alps to Rimini on the Adriatic. To compensate Napoleon III, the Piedmontese province of Savoy and the city of Nice were turned over to France.

Moderate liberals had united half of Italy. Sputtering revolts in Sicily gave more democratic nationalists a chance to lead a different sort of risorgimento. Former Mazzinians, eager to promote a Sicilian uprising,

MAP 23.2 THE UNIFICATION OF ITALY
Dreams of Italian unification began during the French revolutionary era, when "sister republics" were briefly established up and down the peninsula. What were the major obstacles to Italian unification? How was it that the Kingdom of Piedmont became the engine that drove the process to success?

gathered guns in Genoa and planned an expedition that Cavour dared neither support nor oppose. Its leader was Giuseppe Garibaldi, Italy's most popular hero. Exiled for his Mazzinian activity in the 1830s, Garibaldi had spent ten years fighting for democratic causes in South America, returning to Italy in time to take part in the wars of 1848. He had directed the heroic defense of the Roman Republic in 1849 and led the most effective corps of volunteers in 1859. In his greatest exploit of all, he set sail for Sicily one night in May 1860 with a thousand men, mainly middle-class youths from Lombardy, Venetia, and the Romagna.

Garibaldi Goes South

No event in the nineteenth century so captured the popular imagination as that daring venture. The Expedition of the Thousand was like some ancient epic come to life in an industrial age. Untrained men, wearing the red shirts Garibaldi had adopted in South America, fought with bravery and discipline, enthusiastically supported in the Sicilian countryside. Garibaldi's tactics confused and defeated the Neapolitan generals, despite their far larger and better-equipped forces. In two weeks the Red Shirts occupied Palermo and within two months almost all of Sicily. Volunteers flocked from all over Italy to join Garibaldi, and money was raised in his behalf in the towns of northern Italy and from New York to Stockholm.

The epic continued when, against all odds, Garibaldi sailed across the strait and landed on the Italian mainland. He declared his goal to be Rome itself and not just Naples. That worried Cavour, who considered Garibaldi irresponsible and believed that an attack on Rome might lead Austria and France to intervene on behalf of the pope. To prevent that outcome, Cavour encouraged uprisings in the Papal States and then sent Piedmontese troops to preserve order. Carefully skirting the area around Rome, they moved south to meet Garibaldi. On September 18, between lines of tense men, Giuseppe Garibaldi and Victor Emmanuel rode out to shake hands and unite Italy. Garibaldi added to his legend by giving way in the interests of union, and letting the Piedmontese take over. Plebiscites confirmed the union, and in March 1861 the Kingdom of Italy was proclaimed. (See map 23.2.)

United Italy

The Kingdom of Italy included almost all of Italy except for Rome and Venetia. Catholics throughout the world opposed the annexation of Rome, which Napoleon III was pledged to protect, and Austrian troops were massed in Venetia. Italy finally acquired Venetia in 1866 as a consequence of war between Austria and Prussia. Austria offered it in return for Italy's neutrality, and Prussia promised it if Italy helped Prussia defeat Austria. Italy went to war for Prussia and got Venetia following Prussia's rapid victory. Rome was then annexed when French troops withdrew from it during the **Franco-Prussian War** of 1870 (see "The Franco-Prussian War, 1870," p. 685), and the new nation finally had its ancient capital.

Serious problems faced the regime. To many Italians, especially in the south, unification felt like a foreign occupation. Pius IX forbade Catholics to take part in national elections and rejected the indemnity and guarantees of protection the government offered. United Italy was appallingly poor and overwhelmingly agricultural. It had no coal or iron, and three-quarters of the population was illiterate. With liberal conviction, the new government assumed the debts of all the former states and struggled to balance the annual budget. Yet, despite taxes that were among the highest in Europe, Italy continued to lag in schools, railways, and roads. The sale of Church lands failed to benefit peasants as much as hoped, and the lower Piedmontese tariffs brought instant distress to hundreds of small producers in the rest of the peninsula. It took years of sporadic fighting to enforce order in the south. For millions of artisans and peasants, few tangible benefits followed from replacing reactionary dukes with a liberal national state.

A New Nation: The Unification of Germany

German cultural identity had grown throughout the first half of the nineteenth century, from the battles against Napoleon to the vision of the Frankfurt Parliament. It was strengthened by achievements in philosophy, science, literature, and music that were seen as German accomplishments no matter which kingdom, principality, or free city they occurred in. The open question was what the political expression of that identity should be. The German Confederation was ineffectual, none of the unification schemes of 1848 had been adopted, and Austria—eager to reassert Habsburg influence in Germany after the revolution—had blocked Prussian plans for leadership in 1850. The Prussian and Austrian monarchies continued to vie for primacy among the German states, but it was Prussia that created modern Germany.

The Dominance of Prussia

Several factors account for Prussia's dominance, one being economic. The *Zollverein* (see chapter 22), the tariff union Prussia led, continued to prosper with industrialization in the Rhineland and Prussia, and by 1853 every German state except Austria had joined it. Another factor was Austria's multinational preoccupations and its vulnerability to divisive nationalisms, underscored by the unification of Italy. Most important of all was the dynamism of Prussia itself. It was the largest German state, with a powerful army and an efficient administration, and Prussian politics began a new era in 1858 with the rule of William I.

After a long period of reaction, in which the press and public discussion had been repressed, politics became more open and livelier. The Prussian constitution of 1850 allowed universal male suffrage but avoided democracy by dividing voters into three "classes" according to the taxes they paid. Each of the three classes, though extremely unequal in numbers, elected an equal number of representatives, ensuring that those chosen by the two wealthier classes would have a majority. In addition, the king could veto any legislation and appoint ministers of his choice without parliamentary approval.

Although designed to ensure conservative dominance, the three-class system had the effect of magnifying the voice of new industrial wealth, and the majority of the Landtag was now prepared to challenge the monarch. The military budget became their battleground. With William's support, his minister of war and his chief of staff proposed to double the army and add to its equipment. Although the Landtag defeated the proposal, the government went ahead with its plan. Liberals, who distrusted Prussian militarism and an army dominated by Junkers (Prussian noblemen), insisted the government must be responsible to the legislature, and the opposition gained in the elections of 1862. Convinced that royal authority was at stake, William called on God and conscience, threatened abdication, and named **Otto von Bismarck** his chief minister.

Bismarck's Leadership Bismarck was a member of the Junker class, but better educated and more cosmopolitan than many. Liberals resented his pride of caste and reactionary views, whereas many conservatives considered him to be as erratic and dangerous as Napoleon III. Bismarck surprised conservatives with his appeal to nationalism, shrewdly used power wherever he found it, and made success in foreign policy his justification. He lectured the deputies that Germans looked to Prussia because of its powerful army, not because of any liberal institutions, adding, in the most famous statement he ever uttered: "the great questions of the day will not be settled by speeches and majority decisions— that was the mistake of 1848 and 1849—but by blood and iron."

Bismarck dissolved the parliament and used heavy government pressure in the subsequent elections but with little effect. So Bismarck ignored parliament whenever he could and encouraged divisions within the legislature as much as possible. He closed opposition newspapers and manipulated the rest. Promotions in the civil service and judiciary went only to supporters. Once confident of his position, Bismarck spent funds and collected taxes without parliamentary authorization.

In return he offered a remarkable string of foreign triumphs. He used conflict over Schleswig and Holstein (see map 23.3), for example, to assert Prussian leadership in German affairs. When German nationalists were outraged at attempts by the king of Denmark to annex Schleswig and to extend his authority over Holstein, Prussia persuaded Austria to join in war against Denmark in January 1864. Bismarck then foiled international negotiations until the Danes were defeated. Schleswig came under Prussian administration and Holstein, surrounded by Prussian troops, was put under Austrian control in an awkward arrangement sure to breed contention between Austria and Prussia.

The Austro-Prussian War, 1866 Friction with the Habsburg Empire increased almost daily, and Bismarck prepared for war while ensuring Austria's diplomatic isolation. He dangled visions of territory along the Rhine before Napoleon III, won Italy's support by promising it Venetia, and gained Russia's assurance of neutrality. Both Austria and Prussia were already mobilizing when Prussian troops found an excuse to march into Holstein in June 1866. Initially, Austria had the support of most of the German Confederation, but Hanover surrendered to Prussia within two weeks. Three Prussian armies swept into Bohemia, and at the Battle of Sadowa, Austria suffered overwhelming defeat. The Austro-Prussian War lasted just seven weeks. Experts had predicted a long fight, but Prussia, well-equipped and ready, applied the lessons of the American Civil War, using railroads and the telegraph to move with a speed for which Austria was unprepared.

Even Prussian conservatives who had been shocked by Bismarck's treatment of Austria now looked forward to territorial gains. Instead—and against the wishes of his king and generals—Bismarck insisted on leniency. Austria surrendered no territory, but Prussia's gains elsewhere changed the face of Europe. It annexed several states that had sided with Austria, established a confederation of North German states under Prussian leadership (see map 23.3), and pressured the South German states to accept military alliances with Prussia.

The North German Confederation The North German Confederation was a Bismarckian structure that seemed to protect local interests and yet ensured the dominance of Prussia. It left member states free to regulate their local affairs but linked them through a common army under Prussian officers and a bicameral federal parliament. The upper house, the Bundesrat, was composed of forty-three delegates sent in varying numbers from the separate states; Prussia's seventeen seats gave it more than the one-third necessary for a veto. The lower house, the Reichstag, was elected by universal male suffrage, but the King of Prussia appointed the chancellor, who was responsible to no one else.

No German nationalist believed Bismarck's federation to be a satisfactory or permanent solution, and Germany's unification, like Italy's, would be achieved in stages, through war and diplomacy. While northern Germany, Protestant and more industrial than

MAP 23.3 THE UNIFICATION OF GERMANY
This map makes clear the two-step process by which Prussia first unified the many separate states in the north of Germany, and then brought the southern states in as well. Austria was as "German" as Prussia, but still the unified German Reich of 1871 came into being without it. What accounts for this outcome?

the south, offered a sound foundation for the kind of Germany Bismarck envisioned, the largely agricultural and Catholic south had its own cultural traditions and established dynasties. It still looked to Vienna as its traditional center, admired Paris, and remained suspicious of Berlin.

The Franco-Prussian War, 1870 War with France quickly followed. Historians once hotly disputed who was to blame for that war and whether it was inevitable. New research and changing perspectives have

defused the controversy. Bismarck wanted the war but France first declared it. On both sides it resulted more from nationalist impulse than from long-range calculation. The nominal cause of the war derived from competition over influence in Spain. Queen Isabella II had been forced to abdicate in 1868, and the provisional government there, seeking a replacement, picked a Hohenzollern prince. He declined, under heavy French pressure; but a shaky French government, eager to curry popular favor at home, continued to press its case. In a famous interview at the western German spa of Ems, where William I was taking the waters, the French ambassador demanded a public guarantee that the Hohenzollern candidacy would not be put forward again. The king refused and telegraphed a report to Bismarck, who edited the Ems dispatch to make French demands seem more arrogant and the king's refusal more abrupt, then released it to the press. Bismarck correctly assumed that war would follow. The French government responded to the patriotic fury it had helped ignite and declared war on Prussia in July 1870.

France hoped for support from Italy and Austria but had failed to establish formal agreements, and these states remained neutral. The French army, more formidable than Austria's had been, possessed modern equipment in some respects superior to that of the Germans, but the Germans were better prepared and far more decisively led. In rapid movements, German armies pushed through Alsace and encircled the French army at Metz. After heavy losses on both sides, another French force, attempting to relieve Metz, was defeated at Sedan in September. There Napoleon III surrendered and was taken prisoner. Major fighting was over, but French resistance continued. Paris, quickly surrounded by German troops, held out under a long siege, and a provisional French government kept an army in the field. An armistice came only at the end of January 1871, when Paris capitulated.

The brief war had profound effects. A German national state was created in its wake. In France the Second Empire fell and was succeeded by the Third Republic after bitter internal conflict. France was required to pay an indemnity of 5 billion francs and to cede Alsace and Lorraine, harsh terms that established enmity between France and Germany as a central fact of European affairs.

The German Reich
The decision to annex Alsace-Lorraine (where many French citizens still spoke German) was primarily a military one, intended to provide Germany with strong fortifications in case of future conflict with France. But it was also a response to the demands of German nationalists. Well before the final French surrender, Bismarck began difficult negotiations with each of the South German states. They had joined in fighting France with a mixture of enthusiasm and fear, but it took threats, concessions, and secret funds to arrive at terms for a permanent union with North Germany. William I was then crowned German Kaiser (emperor) in the Hall of Mirrors of the French palace of Versailles on January 18, 1871, the anniversary of the founding of the Prussian monarchy.

With modifications, the constitution of the North German Confederation was extended to the new Reich. Although many matters were to be decided locally by its twenty-five states, there could be no doubt of Prussia's dominance in the new nation. The Second Reich[6] was from its inception a powerful nation. Germany in 1871 was already more populous than France, and its rate of demographic growth was the fastest Europe had ever known. Germany's industrial production also increased at an astounding rate. Because it had developed later than Great Britain and France, its industrial equipment was more modern, and the French indemnity added to available capital. The German government made heavy investments in railroads and spurred industrialization with tax benefits, tariffs, and policies encouraging the formation of large combines, the famous German cartels. German universities led all others in the application of scientific methods to various disciplines.

Internal Conflict
Such rapid growth fed tensions between powerful conservative circles, a growing but insecure middle class, and workers increasingly aware of their distinct interests. Bismarck, worried about internal discord in the new nation, chose to demonstrate the supremacy of the state by moving against two potential opponents: first the Catholic Church and then the socialist party.

Rather grandiosely named the *Kulturkampf* ("Struggle for Civilization"), the conflict with the Catholic Church centered on the state's right to approve clerical appointments, restrict religious orders, and supervise seminaries. Some of these measures were common in much of Europe, but there was a harshness in the new state's execution of them and in the rhetoric surrounding them. Intended to ensure the "Germanization" of Alsace and the Polish parts of Prussia (both largely Catholic), the measures accentuated regional and ideological differences. Yet the Kulturkampf was not a success. It made martyrs of many ousted priests and nuns, and Catholics rallied to their Church as a majority of bishops went into exile. The Catholic Center party steadily gained votes, and when the more flexible Leo XIII became pope in 1878, Bismarck sought an understanding with the Vatican. The Kulturkampf subsided as Bismarck turned his sights on the growing socialist movement.

Socialism did not offend Bismarck either in its criticism of laissez-faire economics or in its call for the state to be socially active, and he had gotten on well with the leading German socialist of the 1860s, Ferdinand Lassalle. But as socialists sought a mass following and in 1875 established the Social Democratic party, their attacks on autocracy, the military, and nationalism seemed dangerous. Using as justification two attempts in 1878 to assassinate the kaiser (neither by a socialist),

---

[6] The old Holy Roman Empire was patriotically honored as having been the First Reich.

BISMARCK'S SOCIAL PROGRAM

Between 1883 and 1887 the German parliament passed three laws that created a new model for the role of the state in social legislation. Bismarck introduced the first of these (providing for sickness insurance) in April 1881 in a speech to the parliament that reflects the power of his personality as well as the clarity of his reasoning and of his prejudices.

"For the past fifty years we have been talking about the social question. Since the Socialist Law was passed, I have been repeatedly reminded, in high quarters as well as low, of the promise I then gave that something positive should be done to remove the causes of Socialism. . . . I do not believe that our sons, or even our grandsons, will be able finally to solve the question. Indeed, no political questions can ever be mathematically settled, as books are balanced in business; they crop up, have their time, and give way to other questions propounded by history. Organic development wills that it shall be so. I consider it my duty to take up these questions without party feeling or excitement, because I know not who is to do so, if not the imperial government.

"Deputy Richter has pointed out the responsibility of the state for what it is now doing. Well, Gentlemen, I feel that the state should also be responsible for what it leaves undone. I am not of the opinion that *laissez faire, laissez aller,* 'pure Manchester policy,' 'everybody takes care of himself,' 'the weakest must go the wall,' 'to him who hath shall be given, from him who hath not shall be taken even that which he hath,' can be practiced in a monarchically, patriarchically governed state. . . .

"An appropriate title for our enterprise would be 'practical Christianity,' but we do not want to feed poor people with figures of speech, but with something solid. Death costs nothing; but unless you will put your hands in your pockets and into the state Exchequer, you will not do much good. To saddle our industry with the whole affair—well, I don't know that it could bear the burden."

From Louis L. Snyder (ed.), *The Documents of German History,* New Brunswick: Rutgers University Press, 1958.

Bismarck demanded laws repressing socialism, but the Reichstag refused. The government went ahead anyway and banned most socialist publications and prohibited socialist meetings unless supervised by the police. The Social Democrats were, in effect, forced underground, although they were free to speak in the Reichstag, and their party gained support with every election.

While the campaigns against Catholics and socialists were abandoned by the 1880s, they were part of a larger political realignment. The conservatives and Catholics who first had resisted the new Germany had come to accept it, while liberals, torn between Bismarck's achievements and their principles, had grown weaker. A new coalition, one which gave the conservative state its political base, took shape around the tariff of 1879. A response to economic problems caused by rapid growth and by a European agricultural depression, the tariff's higher duties protected both manufactured and agricultural goods against foreign competition and thus drew together the most powerful interest groups in German society, including Junker landlords, industrialists, the army and navy, and nationalists.

In the 1880s Bismarck also established a system of national insurance to aid workers in times of illness and unemployment and to help provide for pensions upon retirement. Paid for by contributions from employers and workers, these measures became an influential model of modern social policy (see "Bismarck's Social Program," above). At home and abroad, Bismarck had mastered techniques for preserving conservative interests in a dynamic society.

Reshaping the Older Empires

In a Europe of industrial growth and national states, war served as the ultimate test of the state's efficiency. The wars, including those that created Italy and Germany, sparked drastic changes in the losing nations—Russia in 1856, Austria in 1859 and 1866, France in 1870.

Limited Reform in the Russian Empire Of the 74 million people in Russia, some 47 million were serfs. Intellectuals had argued against serfdom for generations, and peasants rebelled in frequent uprisings. Serfdom constricted economic development, and any major political reform required its abolition. Defeat in the Crimean War added urgency to the issue, and Tsar Alexander II, who had assumed the throne in 1855, announced his commitment to modernization. He pressed reluctant nobles to lead the way to emancipation, but most dragged their feet; ultimately, emancipation was imposed in 1861 by the tsar's decree.

More than 22 million serfs gained legal rights and were promised title to the land they worked or its equivalent. If they accepted one-quarter of that, they would owe no payments; otherwise they contracted a long-term debt to the state, which in turn compensated the lord. In practice, the lord usually kept the best land for himself and often received an inflated price for the land he lost. Former serfs on the whole found themselves with less land than they needed to support families and make their payments. They often remained dependent on those nobles for pasture and water rights and for work as wage laborers. A few years later, the government liberated nearly 25 million peasants who worked on state-owned estates on somewhat more favorable terms. Russia's peasants nevertheless remained a caste distinguishable in dress, speech, and customs, with special laws and punishments, including flogging.

The law of 1861 also gave the *mir*, or village commune, new importance. It elected its own officials and its peasants held their land in common; *mir* officials assigned plots to individuals, decided what would be planted, and assessed the taxes owed to the state. Former serfs could not leave the commune or sell their land without permission. The *mir*, which came to be considered a characteristic Slavic institution, thus sustained traditional ways and served as the agent of the state at the same time that it provided peasants with a voice in communal decisions.

Other reforms followed. In 1864 district councils (*zemstvos*, elected through a three-class system like Prussia's) were made responsible for local primary schools, roads, and poor relief. Along with increased schooling, relaxed censorship, and reduced military service,[7] these steps made Russia more like other European nations.

Despite these reforms, much more needed to be done, and Russian leaders remained fearful of revolution. When concessions in Poland were followed by a revolution in 1863, the uprising was harshly quelled and Poland lost its separate status. Repression increased in Russia, too, as censorship and police surveillance increased again. While pan-Slavists stressed Russia's special destiny and disdained liberal parliamentarianism as alien, some intellectuals were drawn to radical ideas, and conspirators plotted more drastic remedies. Yet when a bomb killed Alexander II in 1881, his son smoothly succeeded him as Alexander III. Tsarist Russia could survive an assassination.

Compromise to Preserve the Austro-Hungarian Empire

Following the revolutions of 1848, the Habsburg monarchy under the young Franz Joseph I had sought to create a modern, unitary state. For the first time in its history, almost all regions in the empire were subjected to uniform laws and taxes. But military defeats in Italy and then at the hands of Prussia, along with mounting debts, proved that more change was needed. In 1860 Franz Joseph announced a new federal constitution, giving considerable authority to regional diets. Intended to reduce resentment against high-handed government, it was a failure from the start, opposed by liberals and bureaucrats alike while provoking dangerous arguments among the empire's diverse nationalities. So the emperor reversed himself the next year and established a bicameral parliament for the entire empire. Having stirred visions of local self-government and autonomous nationalities, he now wanted to subordinate local governments to rule from Vienna and to a parliament in which a lower house elected by a four-class system ensured the dominance of the German-speaking middle class.

Hungary in particular objected, led by the liberal nationalist Ferencz Deák, who had campaigned for

In this 1861 photograph a Russian official is reading to peasants on a Moscow estate the "Regulations Concerning the Peasantry," the decree that abolished serfdom.
Novosti/Sovfoto

---

[7] The old military system, which required selected serfs to serve twenty-five years, was changed in 1874 to one of universal service, with generous exemptions and only six years of active duty. Those who completed primary school were liable for only four years of duty; those who finished secondary school, for two years; and those with university education, for just six months.

Hungary's Constitution of 1848. Neither side was strong enough to have its way, and the losing war with Prussia finally brought a compromise. In 1867 Hungary became an autonomous state, joined to Austria through the person of the emperor, Franz Joseph, who became king of Hungary, and through common policies for defense and diplomacy, an arrangement known as the Dual Monarchy. The emperor had kept his authority in foreign policy, which was what he cared about most, by conceding to one nationality what he denied to other ethnic groups in the empire. Within Hungary itself, domestic politics centered on conflict between the dominant Magyars and the non-Magyar majority, and between the diverging interests of Austrian industry and Hungary's great landholders.

Within Austria's imperial parliament, the emperor turned for support first to the German liberals, who offended him by their anticlericalism, and then to the Czechs and Poles, who disturbed him with their nationalist demands. Consensus for more fundamental reform proved elusive. Although ministers were now responsible to parliament, execution of policy rested on a conservative bureaucracy dominated by Germans. An awkward compromise, the Dual Monarchy gave power to wealthy landlords and merchants and ratified the dominance of Magyars (over Romanians, Croatians, and Serbs) and of Germans in cooperation with Czechs and Poles (over Slovenes, Slovaks, and Ruthenians). It lasted for fifty years as one of Europe's great powers, an empire of diversified peoples and cultures, threatened by nationalism, and sustained at its center by the graceful civilization of Vienna.

NINETEENTH-CENTURY CULTURE

Europe's cultural life was as dynamic as its economy and politics. In the nineteenth century the arts, understood to be national and urban, centered less and less on princely courts or aristocratic salons. There were more writers, artists, musicians, and scholars than ever before; and they reached larger audiences through expanding cultural institutions and markets.

The Organization of Culture

Before the nineteenth century, most paintings and musical compositions were commissioned for a particular place or occasion. Now music moved from palaces, churches, and private salons to public concert halls. By midcentury, artists sold their paintings to any purchaser in galleries created for that purpose. Theaters ranged from the new music halls to the great stages and opera houses built (usually by the state) to rank with parliament buildings as monuments of national or

civic pride. Most major cities supported choirs, bands, and symphony orchestras. Conservatories and museums became national public institutions, maintaining official taste and training artists, musicians, and scholars. Whether in palaces once private or in imposing new structures, cultural institutions had the status of civic and national monuments. In Paris the Louvre became the model art museum that provided access to everyone and expressed the era's understanding of culture by displaying works of art by country of origin and in chronological order. This was an urban, bourgeois culture that sought to make the city itself a cultural statement.

Cultural life—associated with the state, tied to a market economy, and promulgating shared values and taste—helped to create national identity and to ratify social status. The intended public was, for the most part, the same middle-class public that was active in politics, the professions, and business. They bought tickets for concerts just as they frequented restaurants with famous chefs, enjoying in both cases pleasures once part of exclusive social circles but now open to all who had the inclination and money. Participation in this exciting culture also distinguished the middle classes from those below them. At the same time, many artists and intellectuals attacked a system that left an artist's fate dependent on what would sell to the public. The tension between creative expression and the market became a lamented hallmark of modernity.

Reaching a Wider Public   Public culture encompassed an expanded range of activities. For those who sought self-improvement, there were public lectures on political economy, the wonders of steam power, or the new art of photography, widely used for portraits.[8] No cultural institution was more important than the press, and the newspaper became a major instrument of culture and politics. By 1830 there were more than two thousand European newspapers, and liberals everywhere fought the censorship, special taxes, and police measures with which governments sought to constrain so awesome a social force. The *Times* of London had a circulation of 5,000 in 1815 and of 50,000 by midcentury; two of the most popular French papers, the *Presse* and *Siècle*, reached circulations of 70,000.

As newspapers came to rely more on advertising than on subscriptions for their revenue, they increased in size, published articles on a wider range of topics (including items on fashion and domestic matters aimed at women), and attracted readers by serializing novels

---

[8] Louis-Jacques-Mandé Daguerre announced his photographic process to the French Academy in 1839, which persuaded the government to purchase his rights and give the new technique to the world, unencumbered by royalties.

Honoré Daumier
FAT BANKER, LE CHARIVRAI, 1835
A typically devastating caricature of a banker by
Honoré Daumier.
Photos12.com

by writers as famous as Honoré de Balzac, Alexandre
Dumas, and Charles Dickens. Technology aided these
changes. Press services such as the Agence Havas and
Reuters quickly adopted the telegraph. The *London
Illustrated News* created the picture magazine in 1842,
which was immediately copied in every large country.
Satirical magazines made the cartoon a powerful political weapon, raised to art by Honoré Daumier's biting
images of fat bankers and complacent bourgeois.

The Cultural Professions   Professionalization affected
the arts as much as other occupations. The violinist
Niccolò Paganini, who transformed violin technique,
commanded huge fees and enormous crowds wherever
he played; soprano Jenny Lind and piano virtuoso and
composer Franz Liszt were the rage of Europe. Many a
young man announced to his family that he was a painter
and proudly went off to starve, if necessary, in Paris if
possible (there were 354 registered artists in Paris in
1789; 2,159 in 1838). A few, such as England's great landscape painter J. M. W. Turner, became wealthy.

The most popular writers—Balzac, Sir Walter Scott,
Victor Hugo, Dickens—were able to live by their pen
alone, among the most honored figures of their age.
Many women also wrote novels. Expected to write
light romances, they generally were not taken seriously, and some adopted masculine pen names to avoid
that fate. The rising prestige of the professional writer
thus enabled some extraordinary women, like George
Eliot (Mary Evans Cross) in England and Georges Sand
(Aurore Dupin) in France, to achieve recognition. Critics became important as professional intellectuals who
guided middle-class tastes much as the popular books
on etiquette and gastronomy taught manners to people
of new means.

The Content of Culture

Varied Forms   The most admired artistic works were
valued for a moral seriousness and formality that distinguished them from popular culture. In painting, great
historical scenes were still favored above genre painting
or portraits. Music was increasingly treated as a kind of
spiritual essay, to be heard reverentially in concerts.
The novel's great popularity derived from its exploration of the conflict between individual feeling (especially romantic love) and social convention as well as
from its presentation of the social panorama. Balzac attempted in his novels to encompass the entire "human
comedy," ranging from the wealthy to the poor and, like
Dickens, used social types to dissect society and challenge the public conscience. Theater and opera often featured historical settings. The dramas of Hugo, Alexander
Pushkin, and Alessandro Manzoni promulgated French,
Russian, and Italian patriotism, respectively, by connecting high ideals to their national pasts.

Conceptions of culture were also strongly gendered.
Women were held to have qualities—including a natural sense of beauty and openness to emotion—that
made them especially responsive to art. Women were
thought to be the principal readers of novels, and novels
presented women's lives in ways that underscored the
inequities of their social subordination and ultimately
enlarged the perception of women's abilities. Women
were especially associated with the intimate side of
middle-class culture; poetry, lithographs, watercolor
paintings, and piano music were all to be savored in the
parlor, with the woman of the house at the center.

Changing Styles   In culture, as in philosophy, there
was also a strong desire for synthesis, for ideas and
forms that would tie everything together. In the arts
this urge gave lyric opera special resonance. Opera was
first of all theater, combining popular appeal with aristocratic elegance. It featured elaborate plots, often in
historical settings, and flowery poetic texts, enriched

by ballet and colorful sets. The two leading operatic composers of the period were Giuseppe Verdi and Richard Wagner. Verdi, an Italian national hero, explored human emotion and character in diverse contexts, often historical ones explicitly about politics. Wagner carried the search for an artistic synthesis still further. He wrote his own texts and used Germanic myths with nationalist intent. His operas linked recurrent musical themes or *leitmotifs* with major ideas and characters to create a total experience comprising voices, instruments, words, and visual effects.

By the 1840s rapidly changing and competing artistic styles had become a characteristic of modern culture, a response to social change and new audiences but also an expression of the creative artist's sense of self. Artists influenced by Romanticism celebrated individual genius and endorsed "art for art's sake," independent of any social purpose. For others, the artist's goal was to capture the essence of "modernity." By midcentury, the **realism** of such writers as Jane Austen, Balzac, and Dickens was carried to new levels of intensity. Novelists and painters used close observation and heightened stylistic virtuosity to portray ordinary people, sometimes with shocking honesty, as in Gustave Flaubert's *Madame Bovary* (1857), an acid account of a young middle-class wife's aimless existence in a small French town, or Gustave Courbet's paintings of rural villages. The direct style and candid subject matter of innovative or *avant-garde* figures like Flaubert sometimes scandalized the middle-class public.

Religious Thought In some respects the nineteenth century was also a very religious age. Protestant and Catholic missions campaigned with an intensity not seen since the seventeenth century. The pious became more militant and turned to social action, preaching temperance, teaching reading, and establishing charities. This focus on the problems of modern society was connected to the fear that religion was losing its social importance. Many intellectuals were bitter anticlericals, seeing the churches as a barrier to progress. Others, such as the Danish philosopher Soren Kierkegaard, upheld the importance of religion as a source of ethical selfhood in the modern world, but criticized current religious practices. Meanwhile, historical research created a sensation across Europe when the Protestant David Strauss published his *Life of Jesus* in 1835, casting doubt on the accuracy of the Gospels and upsetting many with the apparent need to choose between scholarship and Christ.

The Sense of History Nineteenth-century intellectual life emphasized historical thinking. A romantic respect for the past, nationalists' claims, explanations of revolution, economic theory, and preoccupation with change all underscored the importance of history. Its systematic study became an admired profession. In England, France, and Germany, national projects were launched for publishing historical documents and for training scholars to interpret them. Some historians were read as widely as novelists, among them Jules

Jean-François Millet
THE GLEANERS, **1857**
Splendid example of realism in nineteenth-century French painting.
Musée d'Orsay, Paris, France.
Réunion des Musées Nationaux/ Art Resource, NY

Michelet, for whom French history was a dramatic story of the people's fight for freedom, and Thomas B. Macaulay, for whom the history of England was a record of progressive change through moderation and compromise. In each country certain events and themes—in England, the Glorious Revolution of 1688; in France, the Revolution of 1789; in Germany, the rise of Prussia—dominated the search for distinctive national roots, heroes, and patterns of development significant for the present.

Summary

In western Europe, the early nineteenth century was an era of liberal reform. Yet, while constitutional governments propagated civil rights and the rule of law, strengthening the political position of the middle classes, they stopped short of broad democratic reform. In central and eastern Europe, autocratic regimes tended to obstruct change. Then, in 1848 an unprecedented wave of revolutions briefly brought new governments to power everywhere except England. Defeated before they could complete their democratic programs, these revolutionary regimes left important legacies. In the future, radicals would not rely on middle-class support for political reform, whereas liberals would be even more willing to sacrifice democracy for social order. The most effective governments of the 1850s thus were those that adopted parts of the revolutionaries' programs and some of their techniques for reaching a broader public while keeping the forces of order paramount. The 1848 revolutions also unleashed the forces of nationalism. Piedmont and Prussia, as the focus of nationalist movements, won significant followings and triumphed dramatically in creating national states in Italy and Germany. In this Europe of the modern national state, astute political leaders from England to Prussia found ways for their states to assume new social responsibilities, facilitate industrialization, and mobilize a degree of popular support without giving way to full democracy or radical programs. Closely associated with the nation, cultural institutions flourished and supported a dynamic culture that was one of the great achievements of the age. By the 1870s, European nations had unprecedented power and the will to spread their influence around the world. Yet nationalism had undergone a sea change: once tied to ideals of freedom, it lost its liberal and idealist underpinnings. As will be seen in chapters 24 and 25, nationalism became a movement of hardheaded political pragmatism, fomenting chauvinism at home and strident competition in the international arena.

QUESTIONS FOR FURTHER THOUGHT

1. To what extent did the repressive, antiliberal, and antinational political arrangements made at the Congress of Vienna give rise to 1848?
2. What is the historical significance of revolutions in which the revolutionaries are defeated?
3. Why did nationalism become so important in the nineteenth century? What was the nature of the connection between liberalism and nationalism?
4. When you look at art, listen to music, or read works written in the nineteenth century, what characteristics do you identify with the period in which they were created?

RECOMMENDED READING

Sources

Marx, Karl. *The Class Struggles in France, 1848–1850* and *The Eighteenth Brumaire of Louis Napoleon.* Early and polemical applications of Marx's ideas about class conflict to the revolution of 1848 in France and to Napoleon's coup d'état of 1851.

Treitschke, Heinrick. *History of Germany in the Nineteenth Century.* Written shortly after German unification, this vast work exemplifies the importance of history as nationalist propaganda.

Studies

Agulhon, Maurice. *The Republican Experiment, 1848–1852.* Translated by Janet Lloyd. 1983. An authoritative study of politics and society during the Second French Republic, sensitive to popular attitudes and concerns.

Alter, Peter. *Nationalism.* 1989. A valuable introduction to the different kinds of nationalism.

Anderson, Benedict. *Imagined Communities: Reflections on the Origin and Spread of Nationalism.* 1983. A classic analysis of modern nationalism worldwide, stressing its origins in European culture and capitalism.

Beales, Derek. *The Risorgimento and the Unification of Italy.* 1982. Concise, skeptical introduction to the history of Italian unification.

Bellamy, Richard. *Liberalism and Modern Society: A Historical Argument.* 1992. Treats the changes over time and the national differences in the meanings of liberalism.

Berdahl, Robert M. *The Politics of the Prussian Nobility: The Development of a Conservative Ideology.* 1988. Shows how political interests and social structure led to the formation of a conservatism that dominated much of German history.

Brock, Michael. *The Great Reform Act.* 1974. Analyzes the significance of the Reform Bill of 1832 through a close examination of the political and social forces that brought it about.

Chadwick, Owen. *The Secularization of the European Mind.* 1975. Perceptive introduction to changing patterns of thought about religion.

Church, Clive H. *Europe in 1830: Revolution and Political Change.* 1983. Emphasizes the significance of the revolutions of 1830 by noting their transnational connections and impact.

Freifel, Alice. *Nationalism and the Crowd in Liberal Hungary, 1848–1914.* 2000. Demonstrates the unique aspects of Hungarian nationalism.

Gash, Norman. *Aristocracy and People: Britain, 1815–1865.* 1979. An incisive and balanced account of how British politics adapted to social and economic change.

Gellner, Ernest. *Nations and Nationalism.* 1983. An effort to build a theory by analyzing the relation of industrialization to nationalism.

Greenfield, Kent R. *Economics and Liberalism in the Risorgimento: A Study of Nationalism in Lombardy, 1814–1848.* 1965. A classic study of the connection between economic change and nationalism.

Hamerow, Theodore S. *Restoration, Revolution, and Reaction: Economics and Politics in Germany, 1815–1871.* 1958. A complex analysis of the relationship of social classes, economic change, and the state in this revolutionary period.

———. *The Social and Economic Foundations of German Unification, 1858–1871.* 2 vols. 1969 and 1972. The politics and ideas of unification placed in the context of a developing economy.

Harrison, J. F. C. *The Early Victorians, 1832–1851.* 1971. A lively account of the personalities and issues that marked the beginning of a new era.

Hazaree Singh, Sudhir. *From Subject to Citizen: The Second Empire and the Emergence of Modern French Democracy.* 1998. An authoritative reevaluation of Napoleon III's regime.

Hemmings, F. W. J. *Culture and Society in France, 1789–1848.* 1987 and *Culture and Society in France, 1848–1898.* 1971. A literary scholar's provocative analysis of the relationship between cultural styles and social context.

Holmes, Stephen. *Benjamin Constant and the Making of Modern Liberalism.* 1984. The biographical focus offers a valuable insight into the evolution of liberalism on the Continent.

Howard, Michael. *The Franco-Prussian War.* 1969. Exemplary study of how war reflects (and tests) an entire society.

Jelavich, Barbara. *History of the Balkans.* 2 vols. 1983. A thorough survey of society and politics, from the eighteenth century to the present.

Johnson, Douglas. *Guizot: Aspects of French History.* 1963. Essays on the dominant figure of the July Monarchy reveal the tensions between aspirations for a liberal society and conservative fear of disorder.

Lukács, Georg. *The Historical Novel.* Hannah and Stanley Mitchell (trs.). 1962. Insightful study of the social significance of the nineteenth-century novel by one of Europe's leading Marxist scholars.

Mack Smith, Denis. *Cavour.* 1985. An expert and well-written assessment of the personalities and policies that created an Italian nation.

Mosse, George L. *The Nationalization of the Masses: Political Symbolism and Mass Movements in Germany from the Napoleonic Wars through the Third Reich.* 1975. One of the most thorough efforts to find the roots of Nazism in an earlier popular nationalism.

Nipperdey, Thomas. *Germany from Napoleon to Bismarck, 1800–1866.* 1996. An invaluable modern synthesis.

Olsen, Donald J. *The City as a Work of Art: London, Paris, Vienna.* 1986. Combines an analysis of how ordinary people really lived with an appreciation of the aesthetics of the modern city and the economic and political realities behind it.

Perkin, Harold. *The Origin of Modern English Society, 1780–1860.* 1969. Emphasizes the distinct value systems of various sectors of English society and how they adapted to the changes of the period.

Pflanze, Otto. *Bismarck and the Development of Germany: The Period of Unification, 1815–1871.* 1963. Places each of Bismarck's important moves in its larger context.

Pinkney, David. *Napoleon III and the Rebuilding of Paris.* 1958. Studies the political background to one of the most extensive and successful examples of urban transformation.

Plessis, Alain. *The Rise and Fall of the Second Empire, 1852–1871.* Translated by Jonathan Mandelbaum. 1985. A balanced assessment of this important political experiment.

Poovey, Mary. *Making a Social Body: British Cultural Formation, 1830–1864.* 1995. This study of how the public was conceived in literature and politics exposes the ways in which public institutions helped construct categories of gender and class.

Price, Roger. *A Social History of Nineteenth-Century France.* 1987. A clear synthesis of recent research that provides a good introduction.

Reardon, B. M. G. *Religion in the Age of Romanticism: Studies in Early Nineteenth-Century Thought.* 1985. An excellent introduction to the formation of an important intellectual tradition.

Rich, Norman. *Why the Crimean War? A Cautionary Tale.* 1985. A concise synthesis and engaging interpretation of the political and diplomatic problems involving the major powers.

Salvemini, Gaetano. *Mazzini.* 1957. Still the best introduction to Mazzini's thought and its relationship to his revolutionary activities.

Saville, John. 1848: *The British State and the Chartist Movement.* 1987. Why Chartism failed to win its aims.

Sperber, Jonathan. *The European Revolutions, 1848–1851.* 1994. A fresh, thematic synthesis that highlights popular attitudes and symbolic actions as well as political and social conflict.

Stearns, Peter N. 1848: *The Revolutionary Tide in Europe.* 1974. Assesses conflicting interpretations in bringing together accounts of the major revolutions.

Thompson, Dorothy. *The Chartists: Popular Politics in the Industrial Revolution.* 1984. A lively and sympathetic account that relates working-class action to the larger social context.

Walker, Mack. *German Home Towns: Community, State, and General Estate, 1648–1871.* 1971. Sensitive treatment of the response of small-town life to political and social change.

Wandycz, Piotyr S. *The Lands of Partitioned Poland, 1795–1918.* 1974. An excellent overview of the history of divided Poland.

Ernst Ludwig Kirchner
STREET, DRESDEN, 1908
Kirchner's stark painting of Dresden's Königstrasse evokes the sensory barrage of modern urban life. In the midst of the crowd, the individual figures appear anguished and cut off from one another.
Digital Image © The Museum of Modern Art/Licensed by Scala/Art Resource, NY

Chapter Twenty-Four

PROGRESS AND ITS DISCONTENTS

ECONOMIC TRANSFORMATIONS • UNDERSTANDINGS OF NATURE AND SOCIETY •
THE BELLE EPOQUE • ATTACKS ON LIBERAL CIVILIZATION • DOMESTIC POLITICS

In the second half of the nineteenth century, economic growth became an expectation for the first time in history. New technologies, large-scale industry, better communication, and greater capital investment made unprecedented productivity possible and seemingly self-sustaining, and these gains were in turn a triumph of social organization and new knowledge. Large-scale institutions—business corporations, government agencies, political parties, labor unions, national associations, and newspapers—became essential to a new society characterized by rapid economic growth and broader political participation. Most observers hailed this period as an age of progress, marked by a rising standard of living, greater democracy, new opportunities for education and employment, and greater leisure.

Yet as European power reached its peak, the weaknesses inherent in liberalism and capitalism began to show. Although millions shared in Europe's consumer culture, contemporaries worried about rampant materialism and its corrupting effects on moral standards, the erosion of community by widespread urbanization, and the poverty and hopelessness that persisted among the lower classes. Many organized movements, both radical and religious, stepped up their attacks on this confident society, and new intellectual currents questioned the basis for its optimism. Groups that felt most neglected or threatened—women, the lower classes, and those who feared political or economic change—sometimes turned to violence and revolution or encouraged racial hatred for political gain. Just as ominous were rising international tensions. Britain and France, historically the most powerful European nations, found themselves economically eclipsed by American and German industrial growth, and the expansionist ambitions of Germany and Japan threatened Britain's and Russia's global influence. An age that would be remembered for its optimism and peaceful prosperity was also a time of division and conflict.

Meeting of the first Congress of the Rights of Women **1878** ●

Third Republic established **1875** ●

Paris Commune **1871** ●

Second Industrial Revolution begins **1870s** ▬▬▬▬▬▬

Russian chemist Mendeleev publishes periodic table **1869** ●

1867 ●
Electorate doubled in British parliamentary system

● **1864** Meeting of the First International; Pope attacks liberalism in *Quanta Cura*

● **1859** Charles Darwin, *On the Origin of Species*

ECONOMIC TRANSFORMATIONS

The dynamism of Europe's economy in the second half of the nineteenth century was unprecedented. As economic growth accelerated, it reached into sectors previously little affected and spread beyond Europe's industrial heartlands into most of the continent. While Europe's population grew more rapidly than ever before, the value of manufacturing went up three times as fast. Factories, especially those that produced steel and chemicals, coupled large-scale production with new technologies, like those connected to electricity. The impact of these developments was so great that historians often speak of this as the second industrial revolution. Distribution and marketing operated on a larger scale, too, and department stores used new techniques of merchandising to entice a wider public to higher levels of consumption.

The Second Industrial Revolution

New Technologies Exciting new inventions were adapted to commercial uses with striking speed. A whole new industry developed to produce and supply electricity. Thomas Edison's incandescent light bulb, developed in the 1870s, was quickly followed by central power stations to distribute power over a wide area, including public lighting in New York and London in 1882 and in Berlin a few years later. The steam turbine, shown in the 1880s to be more efficient than the steam engine, was soon widely employed in ships and factories, fueled by oil as well as coal. By 1900 the manufacture of generators, cables, and motors, an important new industry in itself, allowed greater and cheaper production in scores of other fields. The telephone, invented in 1876, became a business necessity and an established private convenience within a few

decades. New chemical processes and synthetics led to improved products ranging from dyes, textiles, and paints to fertilizers and explosives.

Inventions now affected people's everyday lives more than ever as the introduction of many new products into the consumer market responded to the growing purchasing power of the masses. Home sewing machines spread rapidly, first in the United States and then across Europe, the most important of many new labor-saving devices that allowed women to increase their contribution to the home economy even

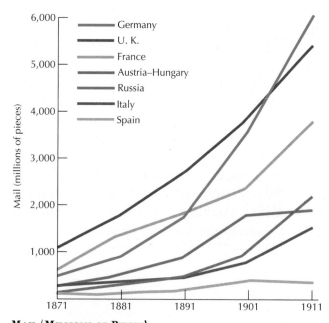

MAIL (MILLIONS OF PIECES)
Scholars use mail volume as an indicator of modernization because it reflects increased literacy, internal communication, and commercial activity. Notice the years in which a general spike in the volume of mail occurs.

1880s–1890s
Anarchists bomb public places and assassinate heads of state

1885 Karl Marx, first volume of *Das Kapital*

Russo-Japanese War **1904** ●

Russian Revolution of 1905; parliamentary institutions created **1905** ●

Georges Sorel, *Reflections on Violence* **1908** ●

Britain grants Ireland home rule **1914** ●

The Bessemer process of removing impurities from molten iron, which revolutionized the industry, was based on English and American patents; but the Krupp steelworks installed these massive converters in 1862 and continued to lead in steel production in both size and efficiency when this photograph was taken in 1880.
Ullstein Bilderdienst/The Granger Collection, New York

when they also worked outside the home. The automobile in the 1890s, the airplane in the 1900s, and the radio a decade later were all greeted with enthusiasm and heightened mass expectations that technological progress would continue to improve everyday life.

699

MAKING THE DEALS THAT CREATED A CARTEL

Cartels, strongest in Germany, existed in other countries too. Here, the general manager of an iron rolling mill that made rails describes how a cartel of rail producers came to be formed in Austria in 1878.

"In 1878 there were in Austria-Hungary nine rail rolling mills with an annual capacity of about 120,000 tons. A large part of these mills had been set up in the years 1869–73, that is to say in a period in which railway building flourished in Austria-Hungary as never before. . . . The picture changed in the course of 1873. The lines that had been started were being finished, but no new ones were being built. . . .

"I was then the general manager of one of these rail rolling mills. . . . If our works did not get an annual minimum quantity of orders of 10,000 tons, it would be faced with the impossibility of employing its work force. We should have had to close and face bankruptcy. . . . My task was therefore a simple one; to get orders at all costs.

"In 1878 . . . on the day when contracts were awarded [by the Kaiser Franz-Joseph Railway], the manager . . . told me: 'Yours was the lowest; but since two other works are also prepared to come down to our price, I shall divide the order into three parts. . . .' I tried to make representations; in vain, the decision stood. After I had left the office of the managing director, I met the managers of the other two

works which had come down to my price. Because of the years of bitter competition, our personal relations had also suffered, but this time we shook hands, and the rail cartel, the first cartel in Austria, the model for other later cartels, also in Germany, was born. At the moment when it became clear that no works could succeed in getting sufficient orders to stay fully employed, each reached the conviction that there was nothing left but at last to attempt to get higher prices. The course of the tendering negotiations with the Franz-Joseph Railway had shown the way. We reached agreement to distribute the total demand according to certain ratios among all the works, and sought then to get the highest prices possible in the light of foreign competition, and the rates of freight and of customs duty."

From Karl Wittgensteing, "Kartelle in Österreich," in Gustav Schmoller (ed.), *Über wirtschaftliche, Kartelle in Deutschland und im Auslande,* Leipzig, 1894; as quoted in Carroll and Embree, *Readings in European History since 1814,* 1930.

By 1890 Europe was producing even more steel than iron. The Bessemer converter developed in the 1860s permitted far higher temperatures in smelter furnaces, and subsequent discoveries made it profitable to use lower-grade ores. British, German, and French maritime shipping, which doubled between 1870 and 1914, depended on faster and larger steamships.

Germany's Economic Growth   The German economy, especially, expanded spectacularly following unification. Already rich in natural resources, Germany acquired more raw materials as well as factories with the annexation of Alsace-Lorraine. Its system of railroads provided excellent communications; its famous educational system produced ample numbers of the administrators and engineers the commercial sector now required. The government, which had played an active role in every facet of industrialization, continued to cooperate with business interests. Military needs stimulated basic industry, and a growing population provided an eager domestic market.

German factories, being newer than those of Britain or France, employed the latest and most efficient equipment, obtaining the necessary capital through a modern banking structure. By 1900 those

plants were far bigger than anyone else's, and firms engaged in the various stages of production often combined in huge **cartels** that dominated an entire sector of industry, from raw material to finished product, as Germany became preeminent in new fields such as chemicals and electricity (see "Making the Deals That Created a Cartel," above). German salespeople appeared all over the world with catalogs in local languages and products suited to local conditions, selling with a drive and confidence British merchants resented as bad manners.

Older Industrial Economies   The older industrial economies of Great Britain, Belgium, and France continued to grow but more slowly. By 1900 France's industrial production, despite the loss of important textile and iron centers in Alsace, had reached the level of Great Britain's a generation earlier, when Britain had led the world. French iron production more than doubled in the first twenty-five years of the Third Republic, and new processes made the nation's ore output second only to that of the United States. In value of production per capita, one measure of a nation's standard of living, France remained ahead of Germany, though behind England.

By the turn of the century, Great Britain, whose industrial superiority had seemed a fact of nature, was clearly being surpassed in some of the critical indices of production by both Germany and the United States. Although the British economy did continue to grow, the fear that it was falling behind became a serious issue in English public life. Several factors explain its relative decline. British plants and equipment were old, and owners hesitated to undertake the cost of modernizing or replacing them. Well-established firms often made it hard for new companies to get a start. Without technical secondary schools like those of Germany and France, English schooling remained weak in technical subjects and provided less opportunity for social mobility than on the Continent. Social attitudes also played a role. British industrialists were slow to appreciate the value of specialization and resistant to new ways. Even so, London remained the financial capital of the world.

The Spread of Industrialization   That world was increasingly industrialized. The industrial potential of the United States was apparent by the time of the Civil War, although few expected subsequent growth to be as dramatic as it was at the turn of the century. Rich in natural resources, America had a continent in which to expand, millions of immigrants eager to supply needed labor, schooling that sustained technological inventiveness, an openness and mobility that encouraged enterprise, and a democracy that pioneered in creating a consumer society.

But other nations were industrializing too, among them Italy and Japan, which had very limited natural resources, and Russia and Sweden, which had appeared rural, poor, and backward compared to industrialized western Europe. Assumptions that related industrial progress to European values, Protestantism, or Anglo-Saxon institutions were belied by the changes in the nature of industrialization itself. It no longer depended so directly on the possession of critical resources like coal and iron ore but could be accomplished with foreign investment and imported technology.

Agriculture   Although greater prosperity and growing populations increased the demand for food, the percentage of the population that made its living in agriculture continued to decline, down to only 8 percent in Britain, 22 percent in Belgium, and 35 percent in Germany toward the end of the century. In France, the

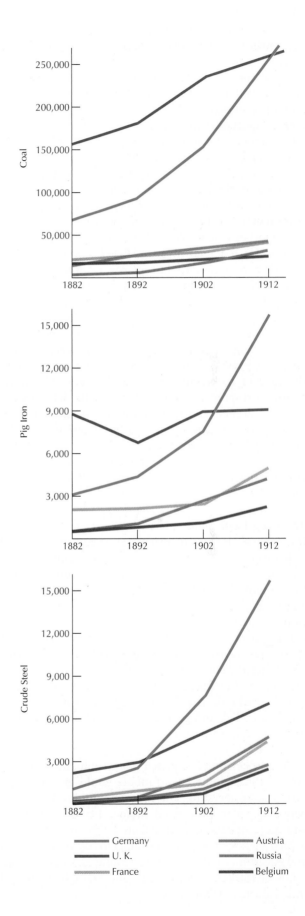

INDUSTRIAL PRODUCTION (THOUSANDS OF METRIC TONS)
Production of coal, pig iron, and crude steel indicates the rise of large-scale manufacturing and infrastructure using new technologies. Compare the industrial development of the United Kingdom and Germany.

Netherlands, and Sweden, by contrast, agriculture continued to play a larger role in the economy. Everywhere, the wider use of machinery and chemical fertilizers increased the capital investment required for farming, and improved transportation intensified international competition. These factors encouraged much greater specialization. A good example is Denmark, where agriculture began to center on a highly capitalized and profitable dairy industry.

Global connections were increasingly important. Civil war in the United States, which cut off Europe's supply of cotton from the southern states, caused unemployment in England's mills and created a boom for Egyptian cotton. After 1865, larger ships and improved railroads allowed cheaper grain from the Americas and eastern Europe, especially Russia, to pour into western Europe, driving prices down at a time when farmers needed cash for the improvements required to make farming profitable. Britain now imported almost all its grain, and Germany, a great deal. More young men abandoned the countryside, and landed interests pressed their governments for help in the face of recurrent agricultural crises. The most common response was protective **tariffs,** which were raised in France, Germany, Austria, Russia, Italy, and Spain. Initially applied primarily to agriculture, the new tariffs were soon extended to manufactured goods as well, reversing the trend toward liberal policies that had favored free trade from the 1830s to the 1870s.

The Long Depression The trade barriers did not stop the general decline in prices. Strangely, the second industrial revolution occurred in one of the longest and most severe periods of deflation in European history. From the 1870s to 1896, prices, interest rates, and profits fell, with far-reaching effects. This situation, in which one part of the economy soared while another declined, was socially disruptive. Handicraft industries, which had survived side by side with mechanized manufacturing throughout Europe, were forced out of business. So were numerous smaller and less efficient industrial firms. The great boom in railroad building ended, and governments had to save socially or politically important lines deserted by bankrupt companies.

As competition sharpened, many industrialists welcomed the support governments could give through tariffs, state spending, and colonial policies. Economic demands became a central theme of politics as more and more of economic life centered on great factories owned by large corporations (and closely tied to banks and government) that employed hundreds or even thousands of workers who, in turn, increasingly organized into industrial labor unions.

Urbanization and Demographic Change

Europe's population continued to grow during the second industrial revolution and did so at an increasing rate. The 295 million Europeans of 1870 had become nearly 450 million by 1914, and the age distribution, or demographic profile, had changed completely.

The Demographic Transition: Declining Rates of Mortality and Fertility Population increased despite the fact that in most of Europe birthrates had begun to decline, and it did so because mortality rates were falling still more rapidly. This pattern of a declining birthrate accompanied by a more rapidly falling mortality rate, which is called the **demographic transition,** continues in our own time and has become one of the hallmarks of modernity.

Death rates initially declined because of lower infant mortality rates, a result of improved sanitation, better diet, and the virtual elimination of diseases such as cholera and typhus. By the turn of the century, improvements in medical care lowered mortality rates

Department stores, like this one in Paris—a combination of theater and commercial display—were the seductive symbols of consumerism and prosperity.
Editions Tallandier

among adults as well. Thus, the population grew despite the declining birthrate.

Lower mortality rates reflected the benefits of industrial prosperity, but the declining birthrates marked a subtler change.[1] The number of children in a family was becoming more a matter of choice with the spread of contraception; where bourgeois values took root and child labor declined, workers followed the upper classes in the trend toward later marriage, fewer births, and smaller families.

UNDERSTANDINGS OF NATURE AND SOCIETY

Knowledge was expanding, too. Scientific discoveries underlay technological innovation far more directly than in the first industrial revolution, and science itself was becoming ever more the province of the expert. The field was increasingly organized into distinctive specialties and pursued by professional researchers (the term *scientist* was first used in the 1830s), freely exchanging ideas across national boundaries and working with precise methods and the logic of mathematics. Research demanded more systematic organization and larger and more expensive laboratories. The success of science stimulated a general expansion of secondary and higher education, and most of the academic disciplines that constitute the modern university achieved their separate identity in the late nineteenth century. The educated public could understand many of the new scientific theories, and scientific ideas were an important part of the general discourse about religion, progress, and ethics. The scientific establishment of the laws of nature rekindled hope that laws of social development might similarly be discovered and beneficially applied.

The Conquests of Science

Biology: The Darwinian Revolution A disturbing theory of human development emerged from Charles Darwin's *On the Origin of Species,* a milestone in the history of science published in 1859. He first formulated his concept of natural selection in 1838, but not until Alfred R. Wallace independently developed a similar theory could Darwin be persuaded to publish his findings.

Although Darwin's presentation was the more fully and carefully developed, the parallel theories of the two

---

[1] *Birthrate* is used here as the more familiar term, but *fertility rate*—the ratio of the number of children born to the number of women of childbearing age—is the more precise term preferred by demographers.

CHRONOLOGY
Scientific and Technological Advances

1830s–1840s	Michael Faraday discovers that changing magnetic fields induce electric currents, enabling creation of the electric generator.
1859	Charles Darwin publishes *On the Origin of Species,* elaborating theory of evolution.
1860s	Bessemer process for removing impurities from iron perfected, leading to more efficient steel production; Louis Pasteur develops pasteurization process as a means of eradicating germs; Gregor Mendel develops the gene-based theory of heredity.
1860–1880s	Internal combustion engine developed.
1869	Dmitry Mendeleev publishes periodic table of elements.
1870s	Thomas Alva Edison invents the light bulb.
1873	James Maxwell publishes a formal theory of electromagnetism.
1876	Alexander Graham Bell invents the telephone.

---

men suggest how much both owed to ideas already current. Darwin established that the variety of species is potentially infinite—rejecting the classical and Christian ideas of immutable forms in nature—and argued that there is an almost constant modification of species, each tested in the universal struggle for existence. He not only presented detailed evidence for **evolution** but described its mechanism: Only those well adapted to their environment survived to reproduce, as their progeny would after them. Over millions of years, through the process of natural selection, more complex or "higher" forms of life emerged, each form proliferating as its environment dictated and as competition for food and survival permitted.

This scientific theory, expressed with caution and supported by massive evidence, almost instantly became the center of controversies that raged throughout Europe for a generation. Evolution, mutable species, survival determined by brute conflict rather than divine will—each of these theories challenged established assumptions in science and theology. Nor did

Darwin hide his belief that the same laws apply to the development of human beings and beasts. This seemed to many a scandalous disregard of divine providence and Christian teaching. Nowadays, most theologians and scientists generally agree that there is no necessary conflict between the concept of evolving species and Christian doctrine, but such tolerance required a differentiation between the study of natural laws and religious tradition that few in the nineteenth century were willing to make.

Medicine   In the medical disciplines, the identification of germs and the realization that they were not spontaneously generated had immediate practical results. In the 1860s the discoveries of Louis Pasteur in France led to the techniques for destroying germs, called pasteurization, which were of crucial importance to the wine, dairy, and silk industries. As a result of his work in immunology, Pasteur also developed a preventive vaccine against rabies. In England, Joseph Lister discovered that germs could be killed by carbolic acid, and the application of that knowledge made surgery a reasonable remedy rather than a desperate gamble. A decade later Robert Koch in Germany showed that different diseases were caused by distinct microbes, discovered the microorganism responsible for tuberculosis, and opened the way to new techniques in bacteriology and in the battle against communicable diseases. Advances such as these not only improved agriculture and medicine but also stimulated the drive to make sanitation and public health into systematic sciences.

Physics and Chemistry   Advances in physics and chemistry gave a greater sense of a controllable and predictable universe. The fundamental generalizations of chemistry are contained in the periodic law and periodic table published by Dmitry Mendeleev in 1869. Mendeleev's table established a marvelous symmetry, so precise that the elements could all be charted by atomic weight, with similar elements occurring at regular intervals. This regularity even allowed for the prediction of unknown elements that would, when discovered, fill the gaps in the table.

Thermodynamics, the study of the relationship between heat and mechanical energy, became the core of nineteenth-century physics. The combined work of scientists in many countries culminated in the mathematical formulation of the two fundamental laws of thermodynamics. One states the principle of the conservation of energy: Energy can be transformed into heat or work but can be neither created nor destroyed, and heat or work can be transformed into energy. The other law declares that any closed physical system tends toward equilibrium, a system in which heat becomes uniformly distributed and which therefore cannot be used to produce work.[2]

The study of magnetism advanced in a similar way from the work of Michael Faraday. He had shown in the 1830s and 1840s that lines of magnetic force are analogous to gravity and that magnetic fields induce electric currents, allowing for creation of the electric generator. In 1873 James Clerk Maxwell published equations that described the behavior of electricity, magnetism, and light in terms of a single, universal system. By the end of the century, physics had established mathematical laws of theoretical beauty and practical power relating the forces of gravity, magnetism, electricity and light, and extending from the universe to the atom. Thermodynamics led to the development of more efficient sources of power. Research on electricity led to the telegraph by midcentury and to electric lights and motors for many uses a generation later.

Social Science and Ideas of Progress

In conjunction with the progress in science, theories of social change emphasized systematic improvement.

Auguste Comte   Philosopher Auguste Comte sought to erect a comprehensive philosophical system that would encompass all human knowledge. He was especially impressed, as were most contemporary intellectuals, by the social role of religion, the conquests of natural science, and the possibilities of human progress. For many years private secretary to Saint-Simon (see p. 657), Comte retained a confidence characteristic of the early socialists that society would soon be reorganized on rational principles.

He systematically elaborated his philosophy, which he called *positivism*, in ten volumes published between 1830 and 1845. These established positivism as an influential international movement.[3] The key to civilization, he argued, is humanity's understanding of the world, which has developed through three historical stages. In the first, the theological stage, humankind interpreted everything in terms of gods who lived in nature. In the second, or metaphysical stage, people learned through Christianity to think in more abstract terms. In the third, or positive stage, now dawning, human understanding was becoming scientific through objective and precise observation followed by

---

[2] The measure of the energy available for work is called *entropy,* a term coined by the physicist Rudolf Clausius in 1865.

[3] Later, the term *positivism* came to refer not so much to Comte's specific theories as to a method he advocated: the construction of logical theories based on facts established through empirical research.

generalization in the form of scientific laws. Every science, he argued, has already passed through the first two stages and into the third—astronomy first, then physics, chemistry, and biology. Now a new science, *sociology* (Comte coined the term), must crown the progression.

While thus honoring the role of established religion, Comte announced its demise, substituting a "religion of humanity" of his own invention. Comte's ideas contributed greatly to widespread acceptance of the view that civilization progresses with increased knowledge discovered through the scientific method and that the great need now was for the scientific study of society and of humankind itself. This creed inspired and shaped much of the rapid development of the social sciences—economics, political science, anthropology, sociology, and psychology—later in the century.

Georg Wilhelm Friedrich Hegel

Even more influential than Comte, Georg Wilhelm Friedrich Hegel set the tone for nineteenth-century intellectuals with a philosophy as comprehensive as that of Thomas Aquinas or Aristotle. He was determined to reconcile contradictions between science and faith, Christianity and the state, the ideal and the real, the eternal and the temporal. The key, he believed, lay in the meaning of history and the nature of the historical process. According to Hegel, that process is dialectical. The dialectical process works as follows: Society in any era constitutes an implicit statement about life and values expressed through social structure and actions, which can be thought of as its thesis. That thesis, however, is never adequate to every need, and its incompleteness generates contrary views, institutions, and practices—the antithesis. Thus, every society gives rise to conflict between thesis and antithesis until a new synthesis is born from that **dialectic.** This synthesis becomes, in turn, another thesis that generates a new antithesis. History moves by this dialectic in a steady unfolding of what Hegel called the World Spirit, toward greater human freedom and self-awareness. Hegel's influence increased after his death in 1831. By midcentury, it was a European habit to approach any question of society, culture, or politics in terms of historical change. Hegel also helped shape the most significant theory of social change in nineteenth- and twentieth-century Europe, for Marxism relied heavily on Hegelian philosophy.

Karl Marx

No theory about society and history has proved more influential than the work of Karl Marx. Trained in German philosophy, abreast of contemporary economics, and in touch with the currents of radical thought, Marx outlined his theory of history in a powerful, apocalyptic tone in the *Communist Manifesto,* written jointly with his friend Friedrich Engels, which was published just before the revolutions of 1848. Little noticed at first, it proved to be one of the greatest pieces of propaganda of all time, a specific program and a general call to action combined with a philosophy of history. Marx devoted the rest of his life—which he spent in poverty-stricken exile in London from 1849 to 1883—to the painstaking elaboration of his ideas in essays, letters, and the comprehensive treatise *Das Kapital.*

Marx's Theory of History

Marx wrote about contemporary affairs, but fundamentally he wanted, like so many thinkers of his time, to build a comprehensive philosophical system. Later in the century his followers would compare him with Darwin as the "discoverer" of the "law" of history: dialectical materialism. The dialectic came from Hegel and his followers. Marx kept the idea of a dialectic as the process of historical change but rejected Hegel's idealism—the view that the dialectic works through ideas that constitute the spirit of the age—and insisted instead that any society

Something of the power of his personality shows through in this photograph of Karl Marx, bourgeois and scholar (with reading glass).
The Granger Collection, New York

rests fundamentally on the organization of its economy, on its mode of production.

Political systems, Marx said, grow from these material underpinnings, and in each system the dominant social class expresses the needs, values, and interests associated with a particular mode of production. The agricultural economy of the Middle Ages required the feudal system with its particular social values and laws, upheld by the landowning aristocracy. That system produced its antithesis in the middle class. But the industrial society of capitalism, dominated by the middle class, was now producing a new antithesis embodied in the rising working class, or *proletariat.* Class conflict is the mechanism of historical progress, and the triumph of the proletariat will bring a new synthesis, a classless society.

By its own inevitable laws, history would thus lead to a new era, one similar to the future envisioned by other socialists. In the classless society, people would no longer be forced into the inequality that capitalist production requires. At present, the primary purpose of the state was to protect property and enforce inequality, but in the new era the state would wither away, unneeded. Revolutions thus mark the arrival to power of a new class. They are, however, more than mere transfers of power. A new class brings changes in law, religion, and customs, which it then maintains in its own interest. The advent of middle-class rule thus represented progress. But capitalism, despite all the ideologies and social institutions designed to shore it up, would fail through its own internal contradictions.

Marx's Analysis of Capitalism

Marx's detailed analysis of capitalism took much from the classical economists. The value of a product, he insisted somewhat obscurely, comes from the value of all the labor required to produce it, all the labor necessary to transform raw materials into manufactured goods. The capitalist makes a profit by keeping part of the value added by all this labor done by others, that is, by exploiting the working class. But capitalists must compete with each other, and to do so, they are forced to lower prices, which in turn reduces profits. This reduction in profits has two effects. First, the capitalist must exploit labor more harshly, cutting wages to the minimum required for subsistence. Second, the smaller producers will fail, which will lead to larger concentrations of capital and force more and more members of the middle class into the proletariat, the class of people who have nothing but their labor to sell. Thus, a shrinking capitalist class suffering from declining profits will face a growing proletariat. Capitalism, therefore, lays the basis for socialism by depriving all but a few of property. The contradictions will be resolved when the whole system fails.

The Appeal of Marxism

Although many of Marx's specific predictions were proven wrong, **Marxism** has deeply affected all modern thought, shaped the policies of all sorts of governments, and provided a core for some of the most powerful political movements of the last hundred years. Such impact requires explanation, and perhaps four points can capture something of the answer.

First, Marxism not only sees society as a whole and explains historical change but demands systematic and detailed analyses of the interrelationship among social values, institutions, politics, and economic conditions. It also suggests methods for conducting such analyses.

Second, Marxism accepts and indeed hails industrialization as inevitable and beneficial, even while accepting most criticism of industrial society. Marx believed that the machine can free human beings from brute labor and that it can, through greater productivity, provide well being for all. Industrialization could be made to provide solutions to the very problems it created. Thus, Marxism has special appeal for societies eager to modernize.

Third, the theory is rich in moral judgments without having to defend any ethical system. Although social values are considered relative, and those of his opponents are denounced as hypocritical, Marx's own rage at injustice rings out in a compelling call to generous sentiments that rejects sentimentality.

Finally, Marxism not only claims the prestige of science but offers the security of determinism. Knowing where destiny leads, Marxists can accept the uneven flow of change, confident that any defeats are temporary. Opponents are to be recognized and fought less for what they say or do than for what they represent—for their "objective" role in the structure of capitalism. Their concessions do not alter their destiny, and the Marxist is free to adopt whatever tactics will further the inevitable movement of history toward the victory of the proletariat. Just as Marx believed that small (quantitative) changes may lead to sudden qualitative ones, so Marxists can favor short-term reforms as well as revolution. The variety inherent in Marx's system has been a source of bitter division as well as strength among socialists, but it helped keep Marxism more vigorous and coherent than any other of the grand theories spawned in the nineteenth century.

Social Darwinism

Just as Marxists claimed scientific objectivity, so too did those who extended Darwin's principles to more current concerns, a tendency that came to be called **social Darwinism.** Social Darwinists tended to ignore the long time span in which Darwinian theory operated and saw the formal concept of species as loosely analogous to groups, classes, nations, or civilizations.

HUXLEY'S SOCIAL DARWINISM

"Evolution and Ethics," a much reprinted lecture that T. H. Huxley gave at Oxford in 1893, was perhaps the most famous statement of what can be called the gentle interpretation of the social implication of Darwin's theories.

"Man, the animal, in fact, has worked his way to the head-ship of the sentient world, and has become the superb animal which he is, in virtue of his success in the struggle for existence. The conditions having been of a certain order, man's organization has adjusted itself to them better than that of his competitors in the cosmic strife. In the case of mankind, the self-assertion, the unscrupulous seizing upon all that can be grasped, the tenacious holding of all that can be kept, which constitute the essence of the struggle for existence, have answered. For his successful progress, throughout the savage state, man has been largely indebted to those qualities which he shares with the ape and the tiger; his exceptional physical organization; his cunning, his sociability, his curiosity, and his imitativeness; his ruthless and ferocious destructiveness when his anger is roused by opposition.

"But, in proportion as men have passed from anarchy to social organization, and in proportion as civilization has grown in worth, these deeply ingrained serviceable qualities have become defects. . . . In fact, civilized man brands all these ape and tiger promptings with the name of sins, he punishes many of the acts which flow from them as crimes; and, in extreme cases, he does his best to put an end to the survival of the fittest of former days by axe and rope.

" . . . The history of civilization details the steps by which men have succeeded in building up an artificial world within the cosmos. Fragile reed as he may be, man, as Pascal says, is a thinking reed: there lies within him a fund of energy operating intelligently and so far akin to that which pervades the universe, that it is competent to influence and modify the cosmic process.

" . . . Moreover, the cosmic nature born with us and, to a large extent, necessary for our maintenance, is the outcome of millions of years of severe training, and it would be folly to imagine that a few centuries will suffice to subdue its masterfulness to purely ethical ends. Ethical nature may count upon having to reckon with a tenacious and powerful enemy as long as the world lasts. But, on the other hand, I see no limit to the extent to which intelligence and will, guided by sound principles of investigation, and organized in common effort, may modify the conditions of existence, for a period longer than that now covered by history. And much may be done to change the nature of man himself."

From Thomas H. Huxley, *Evolution and Ethics and Other Essays*, New York: D. Appleton and Company, 1916.

An invitingly tough-minded way to reason, social Darwinism was used to argue for opposing policies. Thomas Huxley, the greatest intellectual propagandist for Darwin's theories, held social Darwinism to be consonant with the teachings of Indian philosophy, Buddhism, ancient Greece, and Christianity (see "Huxley's Social Darwinism," above). Some writers in Great Britain and the United States used the vocabulary of social Darwinism to argue that better education and social welfare constitute a higher stage of evolution and would help produce a superior species. But Darwinism was more commonly used to justify competition in the marketplace or between nations, as the mechanism of evolution in which the fittest triumph. Such assumptions infiltrated many aspects of late-nineteenth-century social thought. Ideas of biological determinism were widespread. These ideas cropped up in loose talk about national characteristics and were used to rank races as superior or inferior, to discourage the unfit from breeding, to support traditional views of male dominance based on innate differences between men and women, and to identify criminal types by physiognomy.

Herbert Spencer   One of the grandest statements of the laws of progress was the *Synthetic Philosophy* of Herbert Spencer, published in a series of studies that first appeared in the 1850s and continued to 1896. Spencer's ideas were closely tied to those of Comte and Darwin, and his contemporaries (especially in Great Britain and the United States) ranked him among the major philosophers of all time. Spencer's central principle, which made progress "not an accident, but a necessity," was the evolution of all things from simplicity to complexity, from homogeneity to diversity. With great erudition, he traced this process in physics and biology, sociology and psychology, economics and ethics. Such comprehensiveness was part of his appeal, and he applied his theses to physical matter, to human understanding, and to social institutions. While he refused to worry about the metaphysical abstractions of traditional philosophy, Spencer maintained the assumptions of a narrow and rigid liberalism.

He argued that the marketplace is the true test of the fittest and that it must be uninhibited by state intervention even on behalf of welfare or public education. When he died in 1903, much of his work was already outmoded. Strict laissez-faire had been abandoned even by most liberals, and his sort of rationalism had come under heavy attack. His confidence that universal laws of development enshrined the values of middle-class English Protestants would soon seem quaint.

THE BELLE EPOQUE

With a touch of nostalgia, the thirty years or so before 1914 has come to be called the Belle Epoque, a phrase evocative of the Paris of the 1890s, the city of lights where the Eiffel Tower was new, the grand boulevards were crowded with cafés, and great department stores were palaces of consumerism. In all the great cities of Europe, a sense of spectacle and dynamism accompanied the drearier realities of urban life as the industrial age fostered a culture of mass consumption.

The Culture of Capitalism

Mass Culture and the Business of Entertainment Like the sciences, entertainment and sport became professions. Folk songs about work, the life of the soldier or sailor, and young love continued to be sung but more often now by paid singers in pubs or cafés or beer halls that featured singing and dancing. Music halls combined adaptations of opera, theater, and symphony with forms borrowed from the circus and vaudeville. The entertainments available in outdoor gardens (there were more than two hundred such places in London alone) and less expensive theaters also used elements of folk and high culture.

In the late nineteenth century, these entertainments became available to increasingly broader segments of society. First, laws restricting working hours all over western Europe (for example, the adoption of the "English week," with Sundays and half of Saturdays off) provided workers with leisure time to fill. Second, the rise in real wages in the last quarter of the century meant that more people could afford entertainment. Leisure

Jean Béraud
OUTSIDE THE THEATRE DU VAUDEVILLE
The street life and vaudeville of Paris provided an international model, and all Europe's great cities delighted in an urban life that provided attractions for every class.
Christie's Images/Bridgeman Art Library/© 2010 Artists Rights Society (ARS), New York/ADAGP, Paris

thus emerged as an important business, with a clientele that included families from the lower-middle and working classes. Performance designed to appeal to different social classes—revues, operettas, melodramas, and comedy routines (especially popular at the beach resorts now opening up to families from the lower-middle and working classes)—reached an ever larger part of the population. By the turn of the century, silent motion pictures won a still greater audience.

Women of all social classes also took part in the world of mass leisure. They were increasingly visible in a variety of new public venues, as consumers in department stores, spectators in dance and music halls, and cyclists in public parks. Their unprecedented freedom and mobility in the public sphere worried many contemporaries, who saw it as compromising women's ability to perform their primary domestic roles.

The world of sports epitomized the transformation of leisure. Its roughest forms (free-for-alls and animal baiting) had been banned and were replaced by more regulated activities; the Marquis of Queensberry rules for boxing, for instance, date from 1867. Many traditional games faded away, leaving a trace in ball games like cricket, soccer, and rugby. By midcentury, these ball games had become the sports of elite English secondary schools and had earned increasing notice in the press. Then teams formed in cities with players from the working classes, and the best of these teams began to be paid. Leagues were formed, and their matches became important communal events.

Professional soccer teams attracted huge, noisy, paying Sunday crowds, and the game spread across Europe. Most of the European professional teams famous today (like the older American baseball teams) were founded around the turn of the century. Their games became an important part of civic life, and teams depended on their ability to appeal to workers as well as to members of the middle class, while the upper-middle classes took to more individualistic games like golf and tennis.

Britain's elite schools had emphasized athletics, believing they inculcated the "manly virtues" of perseverance, sacrifice for the team, and playing by the rules. Sport, it was said, trained leaders (especially the sort of leaders empire required) and fostered religion, a "muscular Christianity" that was also embraced by schools in the United States, Canada, and Australia. But sports soon demonstrated the capacity to promote communal identity on a much broader civic and national scale. Athletic competition could invoke both individualism and nationalism, as it did in the modern Olympic games, established in 1896 through the efforts of Baron Pierre de Coubertin of France.

The Rise of Mass Media Limited hours of work (and long tram rides home) left employees with time to read newspapers, and the papers quickly discovered ways to increase their circulation. Appealing to a broader public, several newspapers now approached daily sales of a million copies. The most popular of them gave more space to sensational accounts of crime and disasters and sought out colorful human-interest features.

Like the millions of popular novels, such writing candidly sought a wide audience rather than a learned one. For the first time in Western history, in the wealthier nations at least, a majority of the adult population was literate. By the 1880s governments almost everywhere, recognizing the importance of literacy to politics and industry, had made education universal and compulsory and had reduced or eliminated school fees.

In 1850 Prussia was the only major nation in which a majority of the adult population could read and write. By 1900 more than 90 percent of the adult population of Germany, France, and Great Britain was literate, and the proportion elsewhere was climbing rapidly. Mass schooling was usually limited to a few years of the most elementary subjects, and the kind of education received became one of the clearest markers of class status. Nevertheless, the schooling available to everyone would be steadily extended, and access to secondary school, technical school, and university gradually increased.

Artistic Modernism

The creative arts continued to flourish, benefiting from ever larger and more sophisticated audiences. Yet the forms and styles employed grew so diverse that the arts hardly seemed to speak for a single civilization. One reason for the change (and the one most welcomed) was the trend toward national styles. The use of folk elements and distinct traditions gave an instantly recognizable national identity to English or Russian novels and French, German, or Russian music. Another reason for the variety of artistic styles was the tendency of artists to act as social critics, thereby bringing into the realm of aesthetics the issues of politics and values that troubled society. Thus, the tension between the individual and society, between the artist's personal perceptions and the unstable conventions of a world undergoing rapid change, remained a central theme of nineteenth-century art.

Divergent Schools These concerns and then the reaction against them in favor of a "purer" art led to a bewildering variety of competing movements. "Naturalism," the "Pre-Raphaelites," "Impressionism," the "Decadents," "Symbolism"—such self-conscious labels for new artistic movements were frequently proclaimed with angry manifestos against previous art and present culture.

Auguste Renoir
DANCE AT THE MOULIN DE LA GALETTE, **1876**
Renoir's festive scene of the outdoor Sunday dance at *Le Moulin de la Galette,* an outdoor café in Paris that
catered to the working class and lower middle class as well as to artists, is characteristic of the Impressionists'
interest in urban life.
Musée d'Orsay, Paris, France. Erich Lessing/Art Resource, NY

Naturalists claimed that the artist, like a scientist, should present life in objective detail after careful research. This aim was particularly suited to the novel, and Émile Zola, with his precise descriptions of industrial and Parisian life, was a master of the school. Determinism, the view that behavior was determined by social circumstance or blood inheritance, was a favorite theme in this Darwinian age. It proved especially effective on the stage, where the protagonist's destiny inexorably unfolded, and it gradually won new audiences to realistic drama in the plays of Henrik Ibsen of Norway, August Strindberg of Sweden, and Anton Chekhov of Russia.

The realistic painters of midcentury had turned to scenes from ordinary life. Like England's pre-Raphaelites, who took their name from the pious and simpler art of the early Renaissance, however, they tended to believe that much of a painting's importance lay in the message it conveyed and, therefore, in its subject matter. For them, art was supposed to be uplifting.

Toward a More Subjective Art   A new generation of painters called the **Impressionists** broke with this tradition to concentrate on capturing the effects of light and color, making the artist's brilliance in analyzing and re-creating such effects in itself a purpose of painting. Many of them, including Edgar Degas, August Renoir, Claude Monet, and the Postimpressionist Paul Cézanne were recognized in their own lifetimes as ranking among the great artists of Western history. Today their works remain the most reproduced and widely enjoyed of Western art. Yet painters only slightly younger, like Paul Gauguin and Vincent van Gogh, quickly turned to still newer, more challenging, and more personal styles.

Poetry, like painting, became an increasingly private expression, indifferent to conventional morality, and constructed according to complex aesthetic doctrines. Decried as decadent for its fashionable fascination with death, languid despair, and obscure references, the Symbolist movement in poetry interpreted the things one sees and describes as signs of a deeper and more spiritual reality. Art was to be complexly understood on several levels of meaning at once, and individual style became a personal conquest, a private bridge between the artist's identity and external realities.

Architecture, as the most public and functional of the arts, was less able to address the tensions between individual and society. Only at the end of the century were the structural and aesthetic possibilities hidden in railroad sheds, bridges, and exhibit halls developed into a new architectural style that included the skyscraper. Even as that was happening, the international style known as Art Nouveau turned its back on the practical and efficient industrial world of the turn of the century and delighted in applying ornamental arabesques to everything from wrought iron to poster lettering and printed cloth.

Vincent van Gogh
THE CHURCH AT AUVERS, FRANCE, JUNE 1890
Much influenced by the Impressionists, Vincent van Gogh developed a style featuring vigorous strokes that made a dazzling, and often fervently mystical, personal statement. By 1890, when he painted this picture of a village church, Impressionism was being superseded.
Musée d'Orsay, Paris, France. Erich Lessing/Art Resource, NY

ATTACKS ON LIBERAL CIVILIZATION

Although by the end of the century an increasingly prosperous and democratic Europe appeared to be fulfilling much of liberalism's promise, liberal civilization itself came under heavy attack during this period. Women agitated for greater political participation, radicals sought the end of the capitalist system, and conservatives and Christians mounted new attacks on liberal values. These attacks had their intellectual foundations in well-developed systems of thought, but they had their greatest impact in organized movements that clamored for public attention and fought for political power.

Gender Wars in the Fin de Siècle

From the 1860s on, women everywhere had begun to organize on behalf of their own distinctive interests. While they pressed for further change, the existence of these organizations also reflected important changes already taking place in the workplace, in social attitudes, and in the educational opportunities available to women.

Women's Movements Often divided over goals and tactics, women's movements tended to separate themselves into three types. The first and largest were led by middle-class women and often reflected their experience in charitable work and education. The meeting of

Edvard Munch
THE DANCE OF LIFE, 1899–1900
In Norway, Edvard Munch's use of Symbolism pointed the way to German Expressionism, using color and line to convey the anxiety underlying ordinary life, as in this bitter comment on the tragedy of the *Dance of Life.*
Nasjonalgalleriet, Oslo, Norway/Bridgeman Art Library/© 2010 The Munch Museum/The Munch-Ellingsen Group/Artists Rights Society (ARS), New York

the International Congress of the Rights of Women on the occasion of the Paris exposition of 1878 brought together representatives from twelve countries, including the United States. Women's issues were becoming a regular part of the public agenda.

By the 1880s and 1890s, this growing awareness led to a second, politically more radical type of movement, less intent upon protecting women and more explicitly concerned with equal rights. Particularly in Germany, England, and France, these movements realized that their demands required fundamental social change, and they often looked toward the traditional left for support. But they met a mixed response. Working men, who were the strength of Britain's Labour party and the continental socialist parties, feared competition from women, who were traditionally paid less. And many feminist leaders worried that to seek special laws regulating women's work would tend to preserve paternalistic attitudes and close off new opportunities.

A third variant was the growing women's trade union movement, which was concerned primarily with the immediate problems of pay and working conditions. Yet employers' resistance, low pay, the nature of the jobs most working women were permitted, and a lack of sympathy from men's unions made it difficult to establish strong women's unions.

Working Women   The fact remained that in the late nineteenth century most women in industrial nations worked for wages from their early teens until they married and many continued to work afterward, once their children were no longer infants, making an often essential contribution to family income. The proportion of women who worked for pay was highest in France— about 40 percent—but the increase in the number of women workers was especially noticeable in countries in which industrialization was more recent, such as Germany, Italy, and the Scandinavian countries.

Jobs remained tightly tied to gender. More women in England and Germany were employed as domestic servants than in any other field. Many young women newly arrived in the city found jobs in the growing service sector, as laundresses or waitresses. Only about one-fifth were employed in factories and usually assigned tasks associated with domestic skills. In the textile industries the proportion of women workers steadily rose to become the majority everywhere. Women were less numerous in the burgeoning industries of the second industrial revolution than in more stagnant ones in which pay was lower; and far more women than men did piecework, fabricating buttons or cardboard boxes in shops or at home. The garrets of every city were filled with women living in tiny rooms where they worked late into the night making hats, artificial flowers, and lace; a measure establishing a minimum rate for piecework in England was an unusual protection, even in 1910.

New Opportunities   Some significant changes in women's employment were helpful to the women's movement generally. With the spread of elementary schooling, women slowly took over as bookkeepers, office clerks, and secretaries, occupations in which prestige, opportunities for advancement, and pay declined as they came to be women's work. Some professions also opened to women, especially nursing (primarily provided by nuns in Catholic countries) and teaching in elementary school. By the end of the century three-quarters of the elementary school teachers in England were women, as were more than half the teachers in Sweden and France and one-fifth of those in Germany.

The expanding field of social work began to pay women, often the sort of middle-class women whose earlier charitable work had pioneered in creating the field. Small shops and, more slowly, the great department stores also hired women as clerks, preferably women from the lower-middle class who were trained to speak and dress in the ways considered proper by a bourgeois clientele.

Public Policy   These developments, along with the women's movements and the formidable resistance to them, made "the woman question" a persistent topic

Jens Ferdinand Willumsen
IN A FRENCH LAUNDRY, 1889
Middle-class women were the leaders in feminist movements, and efforts to organize women workers concentrated on industrial work; but far more women earned money in menial drudgery, like these women in a French laundry.
Göteborgs Konstmuseum, Sweden. Bridgeman Art Library/ © 2010 Artists Rights Society (ARS), New York/COPY-DAN, Copenhagen

of debate in newspapers, from pulpits, and in learned essays. The very awkwardness of the phrase suggested some embarrassment and confusion. Feminists found themselves combating custom and widespread attitudes as well as the prejudices of supposed experts: doctors who cited women's physical weakness and psychological instability and social Darwinists who declared that civilization required women to concentrate on their biological function. Nevertheless, dominant attitudes did begin to change.

Women's colleges were established at Oxford and Cambridge in the 1870s; and in Italy, where universities had never been closed to women, Marie Montessori's lectures at the end of the century on the "new woman" were widely hailed. Outstanding achievements by individual women in science, medicine, education, literature, art, economics, and social reform challenged stereotypes; it became far less unusual for women to attend school beyond the elementary grades, to take part in demonstrations, and even to speak at public meetings.

As women lived longer and bore fewer children, legal and cultural constraints that assumed their lives would be circumscribed by marriage and motherhood became harder to defend. By 1910 most European nations had passed laws protecting women workers and increasing women's rights to dispose of property, to share in decisions affecting their children, and to take part in civic life. Wherever suffrage was universal for men, demands that women be allowed to vote were becoming louder.

Working-Class Movements

Although Marx had spent much of his career in the library of the British Museum, he and Engels aspired to lead an effective social movement. Their influence grew greatly toward the end of the century.

The First International When in 1864 a group of English labor leaders called a small international conference in London, Marx readily agreed to attend as a representative of German workers. The International Working Men's Association, usually called the First International, was founded at that meeting, and Marx dominated it from the start. He did his best to replace traditional radical rhetoric about truth and justice with the hard language of Marxism. During the eight years the First International lasted, he gradually succeeded in expelling those who disagreed with him.

Socialist Parties and Trade Unions As Marx gained ascendancy over the international workers' movement, socialist parties became an important part of political life in nearly every European country. Except in Great Britain, most socialist parties were at least formally Marxist. As they began to win elections, socialists disagreed over whether to follow a more moderate policy aimed at electoral success or to adhere rigidly to the teachings of Marx. The most common compromise combined moderate policies with flaming rhetoric, and the Second International, formed in 1889 with representatives from parties and unions in every country, sought to maintain doctrinal rigor and socialist unity. The Marxist critique of liberalism and capitalism was spread through print media, parliamentary debates, and election campaigns.

Labor organizations outside Germany were not often consistently Marxist, but trade unions everywhere were class conscious, frequently tempted by violent protest, and suspicious of politics. Their membership soared, with millions of workers paying dues in the industrialized countries, and the strike became the common expression of social protest. Skilled artisans, threatened by new modes of production yet strengthened by their own traditions of cooperation, often continued to be the leaders in militant action; but it was the successful organization of workers in larger factories that led to a great wave of larger, better organized strikes.

This advertisement in a German magazine was typical in selling not just an inexpensive means of transport but the joys of youth, style, and a new freedom for women.
The Mary Evans Picture Library

LA DYNAMITE A LA CHAMBRE
L'EXPLOSION

The nation was shocked when an anarchist bomb exploded in the French Chamber of Deputies in 1893, shown in this illustration in *Le Petit Journal,* France's most popular newspaper.
The Mary Evans Picture Library

Anarchism Most people did not distinguish clearly among the various radical movements, and newspapers were quick to associate socialists and labor leaders with the anarchist "propaganda of the deed," violent acts that made headlines. In the 1880s and 1890s, bombs were thrown into parades, cafés, and theaters in cities all over Europe. Acting on their own, individual **anarchists** assassinated the president of France in 1894, the prime minister of Spain in 1897, the empress of Austria in 1898, the king of Italy in 1900, and the president of the United States in 1901. Such incidents were followed by the arrest of known radicals, spectacular trials, and denunciations of leftists.

But bomb throwers and assassins were only a tiny part of the broad anarchist movement. Anarchism's intellectual tradition was continuous from the time of the French Revolution. The Russian anarchist Mikhail Bakunin had established himself by 1848 as one of Europe's more flamboyant revolutionaries. Bakunin respected Marx, but his enthusiastic support of nationalism and his distrust of what he saw as a dangerous authoritarianism in Marxism led to his expulsion from the First International. Anarchism's most famous figure after Bakunin was Prince Peter Kropotkin, an exiled Russian aristocrat, who advocated for what he called anarcho-communism, but he was unable to unify the movement. Some anarchists stressed individualism, some pacifism, and some the abolition of private property. All rejected imposed authority and denounced the state as a repressive machine serving the interests of wealth.

They won their largest following among the poor who felt crushed by industrialization: immigrants to the United States, peasants in southern Spain, artisans and some industrial workers in Italy and France. Anarchism was an influential element in the opposition to bureaucratic centralization and to militarism. It appealed to artists and writers who shared the anarchists' contempt for bourgeois values, while it contributed heroes and martyrs to the growing mystique of the radical left.

Socialism, anarchism, and trade unions all fostered feelings of brotherhood and addressed the sense of justice and common interest that had developed within working-class life. Expressed in songs and speeches at meetings, demonstrations, and strikes, these shared values had developed over generations to be reinforced now by militant organizations but also by changes that made the conditions of labor in different industries more similar and by housing patterns that created working-class districts. One of the functions of radical movements was to sustain this solidarity by linking the immediate issues of the workplace to broad principles and to national politics. The result was a powerful challenge to the established system. Nevertheless, the left remained far from united. Different interests often divided skilled from unskilled workers, those in established trades from those employed in new industries, male from female workers, and labor unions from political parties.

The Christian Critique

While some Protestants felt a natural affinity for liberalism, it nevertheless was subject to a strong moral critique by the churches of Europe and the United States. Ministers and priests excoriated liberalism's tendency to mistake selfishness for individualism, moral indifference for toleration, and materialism for progress. Theories of evolution, positivism, and biblical criticism put defenders of traditional beliefs on the defensive and made them seem opponents of science. The expanding role of government, especially in matters of education and welfare, made conflicts between church and state a major theme of European life. Churches often found themselves opposing the growing claims of the state, and both Protestants and Catholics denounced the injustices of capitalist society as forcefully as socialists did.

Roman Catholic Opposition   Since the French Revolution, the Roman Catholic Church found itself at odds with many modern trends, and it was particularly hostile to liberalism. In 1864 Pope Pius IX issued the encyclical *Quanta Cura*, which denounced total faith in human reason, the exclusive authority of the state, and attacks on traditional rights of the Church and stated that the pope had the option of opposing "progress, liberalism and modern civilization."

The Vatican Council of 1869–1870, the first council of the Church in three hundred years, confirmed the impression of intransigence, as prelates came from around the world to proclaim the dogma of papal infallibility. This belief had long been a tradition, and its elevation to dogma revealed increased centralization within the Church and affirmed the solidarity of Catholics in the face of new social and political dangers. Throughout Europe, political leaders wondered whether Catholics who now followed an infallible pope could be reliable citizens of a secular state.

As chancellor of the new German state, Bismarck launched and then abandoned attacks on the Catholic Church as his government relied more and more on the Catholic Center party. The conflict between church and state was most open and bitter, however, in Spain, Italy, and France, where it was the central political division of the 1880s and 1890s. Generally, such church-state conflicts subsided somewhat after the turn of the century. Relatively secure states, having established the breadth of their authority, tended to become more tolerant; the churches, too, became more flexible, in the style of Pope Leo XIII (r. 1878–1903), who established an understanding with Bismarck and encouraged French Catholics to accept the Third Republic.

Social Action   At the same time, Christianity displayed renewed vigor. Christian political and social movements learned to mobilize enormous support and became more active in social work (the Protestant Salvation Army was founded in 1865). This engagement in charity, religious missions at home and overseas, education, labor unions, and hundreds of special projects not only strengthened Christian social influence but gave concreteness to religious denunciations of immoral and unjust conditions.

Pope Leo XIII added a powerful voice to the rising cry for social reform. The Catholic Church, he wrote, recognizes the right of workers to their own organizations and to "reasonable and frugal comfort"; but the state, he warned, should not favor any single class, and society must not consider human beings as merely a means to profit.

Strongest in rural areas and with more support among women than men, Christian churches knew a lot about those who had not necessarily benefited from modern social change. The churches now made more effort to reach workers and the middle class, urban groups whose special needs had often been overlooked in the past, and they spoke more readily for those discontented groups that tended not to rely on close ties to the state. By 1910 Christianity was more respectable among intellectuals, more active in society, and more prominent in politics than it had been since the early nineteenth century. Whether of the political left or right, Protestants and Catholics found in Christian teaching a whole arsenal of complaints against liberalism and industrial capitalism.

Beyond Reason

Until World War I, European political thought remained predominantly liberal, but some of its optimism was fading. Liberals themselves worried more about problems of community and social justice, and others questioned the power of human reason and argued for leadership by a small elite.

Georges Sorel and Henri Bergson   The Frenchman Georges Sorel shared the growing suspicion that public opinion owed more to prejudice than to reason. Like many intellectuals, he felt contempt for middle-class society, but he argued that its overthrow would not come in the way predicted by Marx. His most important book, *Reflections on Violence* (1908), postulated that historic changes occur when people are inspired by some great myth beyond the test of reason. As a myth for his times, Sorel proposed the general strike. Sorel thus contributed to the widespread **syndicalist** movement, which called on workers' organizations, or *syndicats*, to bring down bourgeois society. He rejected bourgeois rationalism in favor of violence as an expression of the will that could create powerful political movements, finding the energy for change in humanity's irrationality.[4]

Sorel's countryman, Henri Bergson, the most eloquent and revered philosopher of his day, expounded gentler, more abstract theories; yet he, too, pictured much of human understanding as arising not from reason but intuitively from subjective and unconscious feelings. Bergson was close to contemporary movements in the arts, psychology, and religion; and he believed society needed the new spirit of energy and common endeavor that could be achieved through spontaneity. That concern to translate feeling into action led away from liberalism's emphasis on the importance of law and formal procedures.

---

[4] Vilfredo Pareto and Sorel, both trained as engineers, are usually grouped together with Robert Michels as leading theorists of the new political "realism."

THE ARGUMENT OF ANTI-SEMITISM

Anti-Semitism became more organized and more vocal in most European countries in the 1880s. Despite important variations of tone and tactic in each nation, certain myths and themes were common to most of these movements. In 1883 a German publication calling itself The Journal for the Universal Rally for Combatting Jewdom (Zeitschrift für die Allgemeine Vereinigung zur Bekämpfung des Judentums) *repeated many of these themes. The article was presented in the form of a petition to Chancellor Bismarck, calling for a ban on Jews holding important offices and a restriction on their immigration.*

"Wherever Christian and Jew enter into social relations, we see the Jew as master and the native-born Christian population in a servile position. The Jew takes only a vanishingly small part in the hard work of the great mass of our people; in field and workshop, in mines and on scaffolding, in swamps and canals—everywhere it is only the calloused hand of the Christian that is active. But it is above all the Jew who harvests the fruits of this labor. By far the greatest portion of capital produced by national labor is concentrated in Jewish hands. Jewish real estate keeps pace with the growth of mobile capital. Not only the proudest palaces of our cities belong to the Jewish masters (whose fathers or grandfathers crossed the borders of our fatherland as peddlers and hawkers), but the rural estate—this highly significant and conserving basis of our state structure—is falling into Jewish hands with ever greater frequency.

"Truly, in view of these conditions and because of the massive penetration of the Semitic element into all positions affording power and influence, the following question seems justified on an ethical as well as national standpoint: *what future is left our fatherland if the Semitic element is allowed to make a conquest of our home ground for another generation as it has been allowed to do in the last two decades?* If the concept of 'fatherland' is not to be stripped of its ideal content, if the idea that it was our fathers who tore this land from the wilderness and fertilized it with their blood in a thousand battles is not to be lost, if the inward connection between German custom and morality and the Christian outlook and tradition is to be maintained, then an alien tribe may never, ever rise to rule on German soil. This tribe, to whom our humane legislation extended the rights of hospitality and the rights of the native, stands further from us in thought and feeling than any other people in the entire Aryan world.

"The danger to our national way of life must naturally mount not only when the Jews succeed in not only encroaching upon the national and religious consciousness of our people by means of the *press*, but also when they succeed in obtaining state offices, the bearers of which are obliged to guard over the idealistic goods of our nation. We think above all of the professions of *teacher* and *judge*. Both were inaccessible to Jews until very recently, and both must again be closed if the concept of authority, the feeling for legality and fatherland, are not to become confused and doubted by the nation. Even now the Germanic ideals of honor, loyalty, and genuine piety begin to be displaced to make room for a cosmopolitan pseudoideal."

From Richard S. Levy (tr. and ed.), *Antisemitism in the Modern World*, D. C. Heath, 1991.

Friedrich Nietzsche   The revolutionary challenge that such ideas contained was clearest in the works of Friedrich Nietzsche. He, too, emphasized human will in a philosophy that lashed out at contemporary civilization. His disdain for ideas of equality and democracy was balanced by his hatred of nationalism and militarism; he rejected his society not only for what it was but also for what it meant to be. The only hope for the future was the work of a few, the supermen who would discard the inhibitions of bourgeois society and the "slave morality" of Christianity. A deeply original thinker, Nietzsche would prove vastly influential for twentieth-century thought.

Anti-Semitism   Like Nietzsche's philosophy, **anti-Semitism,** which he detested, was part of the rising current of opposition to liberal society. Anti-Semitism in the 1890s was remarkably widespread. Venomous assertions of Jewish avarice and lack of patriotism were used to discredit the entire republic in France and the opponents of imperial policy in Great Britain. Sixteen deputies from anti-Semitic parties won seats in the German Reichstag in 1893, and Germany's prestigious Conservative party added anti-Semitism to its program (see "The Argument of Anti-Semitism," above). The Lord mayor of Vienna from 1895 to 1910 found anti-Semitism invaluable in his electoral victories, and anti-Semitism was an official policy of the Russian government from the terrible pogroms of 1881 on.

There is no simple explanation for the phenomenon, but scholars note that Jews were often perceived as a symbol of liberal, capitalist society. They first won their civil rights during the French Revolution, lived primarily in urban environments, and excelled in the expanding professions and businesses of the nineteenth century. Since nationalism, especially in Germany, stressed folk culture and race, conservatives attacked Jews as part of the liberal, capitalist world alien to national traditions. Conspiracy theories and racist distortions of Darwinism gave concrete and simple explanations for the baffling pace of social change, offering the hope that by circumscribing specific groups—and especially Jews—society could resist change itself.

Late-nineteenth-century anti-Semitism was no mere continuation of medieval prejudices. Social Darwinists of the era despised Jews not so much on the basis of religion as on their status as a biologically inferior "race." In Germany, Austria, and France, anti-Semitism emerged within a new politics of mass appeal; its prominence in France, where French Jews had long been recognized as equal citizens, was especially shocking. For Theodor Herzl, who became the leading spokesperson of Zionism, the lesson was clear: Jews must have a homeland of their own.

The Revival of the Right   Neither irrationalism nor anti-Semitism belongs inherently to a single political persuasion, but both were used primarily by the political right in the decades preceding World War I. Rightist movements revived notably in these years, building among those social groups that felt most harmed by the changes of the century: aristocrats, rural people, members of the lower-middle class whose status was threatened, and many Christians. A reinvigorated right also voiced concerns about the materialism of middle-class culture and the evils of unchecked capitalism. Rightwingers tried, frequently with success, to use patriotism and national strength as their battle cry, learning to make the effective mass appeal that had often eluded them in the past. Yet as critical as they were of liberal centrists, they saw socialists as their primary foes, declaring socialism the menace of the hour and the natural consequence of liberal error.

Thus, critics from the right and the left gained by addressing the discontents that liberalism tended to ignore and by criticizing the modern changes that most people still labeled progress. So many simultaneous assaults created grave political crises in many states. How those assaults were dealt with in each country reshaped the political system that would guide it through the challenges ahead.

DOMESTIC POLITICS

In many respects political systems were more similar at the end of the nineteenth century than they had been since before the French Revolution, and everywhere they faced many of the same issues. Yet each nation evolved its own distinctive response to the pressures for continuity and change.

Common Problems

There were certain issues that every political system confronted. One was who should participate in political life. The trend was to increase suffrage until every adult male had the right to vote, but extending that right to women became a divisive issue in many countries by the turn of the century. Each political system also found its own ways of constraining democracy, through royal prerogatives, a conservative second chamber, or limits on what legislatures could do.

The state was now a participant in social and economic life, but its precise role was often hotly contested, especially its responsibility for social welfare and its economic policies that affected banks, commerce, and labor unions. Powerful groups, such as the church, the military, or the aristocracy, sought to enlist the state on their side. Sometimes these competing interests could be balanced, but often these conflicts reinforced older ideological divisions that threatened to undermine the political system itself.

Large-Scale Organizations   These tensions emerged as states and social groups throughout Europe were increasingly represented by large bureaucracies. As governments took on increased responsibilities for public health, transportation, communications (the post and telegraph), their bureaucratic organization expanded, as did that of larger business companies. In response, smaller firms organized in associations that could represent their interests in dealings with government and with other lobbying groups.

Workers, too, were increasingly organized in national trade unions that negotiated for particular industries and mobilized major strikes in every industrial country from the 1880s. Political parties also adopted some form of national organization and a permanent staff, especially where universal male suffrage made such efforts worthwhile. The massive Marxist German Social Democratic party was the most impressive example of this.

New professional associations set standards, lobbied governments, and conferred prestige on the physicians, lawyers, engineers, and teachers that belonged to them. Like political parties, associations offered a means whereby scattered groups and new interests could make their presence felt in public life. This institutionalization of society was in many respects a source of stability, providing rapidly expanding occupations with norms, internal discipline, and a means for negotiating conflicts. But the very size of these organizations often promoted the growth of factions within them.

Nearly every country also struggled with the definition of national community and whether some groups—ethnic minorities, foreigners, Catholics, Jews, anarchists, or socialists—should be excluded as alien or of uncertain loyalty. The way each society responded to this challenge became an important test of its political system.

France: The Third Republic

In France political conflict revolved around the form of government following the fall of the Second Empire.

Monarchy or Republic   Shortly after Louis Napoleon surrendered in the Franco-Prussian War of 1870, Parisian crowds cheered the proclamation of a republic, and new leaders sought to mobilize the nation as an earlier republic had done in 1792. German forces quickly surrounded Paris, but French forces, strengthened by newly recruited peasants, still made some gains until, overmatched, they were pushed back in December.

Paris remained under German siege. Refusing to surrender, its citizens held out for four months. They cut down the trees of the boulevards for fuel, slaughtered pets, and emptied the zoo as a starving city continued to resist during a winter as severe as any on record. But heroism and patriotic fervor could not defeat a modern army, and at the end of January Paris capitulated.

France's newly elected assembly met at Versailles and quickly accepted peace on German terms. The assembly, divided between monarchists and republicans, could not agree, however, on the form of government. It compromised by naming Adolphe Thiers, a moderate politician who had been prominent in the July Monarchy thirty years earlier, as chief of the "Executive Power," thereby postponing the issue of whether France was to have a king or a president.

The Paris Commune   Thiers knew that his government must establish control of Paris, which had been cut off from the rest of France. As a first step, he decided to disarm the city's National Guard. When troops from Versailles tried to remove some cannons, however, they were confronted by an angry crowd. Shots were fired; by day's end, two generals lay dead. Faced with insurrection, Thiers withdrew his army, determined first to isolate the revolution and then to crush it. The municipal council of Paris, in another echo of the French Revolution of 1789, declared the city a self-governing commune and prepared to fight. The Paris Commune included moderate and radical republicans, militant socialists, and a few members of the Marxist First International. Its program, favoring democracy and federalism, was not very specific on other matters, and it had little time to experiment.

Scenes of the Paris Commune and the destruction that resulted were in great demand afterward. One dramatic moment was the execution of Generals Clément-Thomas and Lecomte by the communards on March 18, 1871. That scene was reconstructed a few months later in this composite photograph. Created for its commercial possibilities (in books and on postcards, for example), the image echoed traditional scenes of comparable historical episodes.
Roger-Viollet/Getty Images

Civil War   While German armies idly watched, the French engaged in civil war. The conservative assembly in Versailles sent its armies to assault the Paris Commune. The mutual hatred in this civil war was exacerbated by the recent anguish of siege and defeat as well as by the long-standing differences, ideological and social, between rural France and the capital. The two camps fought for competing visions of what the nation should become, and they fought with rising fury. On both sides, hostages were taken and prisoners shot. It took almost two months of bloodshed before government troops broke into the city in May.

Even then the fighting continued, barricade by barricade, into the working-class quarters, where the group commanded by the anarchist Louise Michel was among the last to fall. Among the most famous of hundreds of militant communards, she would later tell her captors, "I belong entirely to the Social Revolution." Solid citizens shuddered at revolutionary excess (and especially at the part played by women), but on the whole, the victors were more brutal. Tens of thousands of Parisians died in the streets, and summary court martials ordered execution, imprisonment, or deportation for tens of thousands more.

Throughout Europe, the Commune raised the specter of revolution. From the first, Marxists hailed it as a proletarian rising, the dawning of a new era, though Marx was indignant with the communard's lack of revolutionary daring and their respect for property and legality. Former communards became the heroes of socialist gatherings for the next generation, and to this day the cemetery where many of them were executed remains a shrine honored by socialists and communists.[5] Historians have been at great pains to show how little socialism, still less Marxism, there was in the Paris Commune (it respectfully left the Bank of Paris intact); yet myth has its historical importance, too. The Commune was indisputably a class conflict, and the rage on both sides was more significant than mere differences of program. After 1871 a proletarian revolution became a credible possibility to radical and conservative alike, and working-class movements across Europe pointed to the martyrs of the Commune as evidence of the cruelty of bourgeois rule.

The Founding of the Third Republic Remarkably, a stable republic gradually emerged from this unpromising beginning. The administrative structure of the French state remained strong, and Thiers used it effectively. The loan needed to pay the indemnity to Germany was soon oversubscribed. As elections produced victories for moderate republicans, monarchists feared that their chance was slipping away. They ousted Thiers, put a monarchist in his place, and looked for a chance to restore the monarchy. They never found it.

The monarchists themselves were divided between the conservative supporters of the grandson of Charles X and those who favored the grandson of Louis-Philippe. Meanwhile, moderate republicans continued to gain in popularity, and in 1875 the assembly passed a law declaring that "the president of the republic" should be elected by the two legislative houses. The Third Republic was thus quietly established as the government that, as Thiers put it, divided Frenchmen least.

There was a Chamber of Deputies, elected by direct universal male suffrage, and a Senate, indirectly elected by local officials. In elections the following year, republicans captured two-thirds of the seats in the Chamber and almost half those in the Senate. The presidency, which had been so strong under Thiers, was still in monarchist hands, but its authority continued to decline. That established a further precedent: The Republic would have a weak executive. Made acceptable by having crushed the Commune and by having a conservative Senate, this republic was a regime of compromise; it would last longer than any French regime since 1789.

Successive republican governments guaranteed political freedom and deferred to the middle class, while France's public institutions preserved the remarkable administrative continuity that had characterized them

since 1800. For twenty years, from 1879 to 1899, the leading politicians were moderates who recognized unions and made elementary education in state schools compulsory but initiated few projects of public works or social welfare. Economic growth, less dramatic than in Great Britain or Germany, was also less disruptive. France found its own balance between the demand for order and the need for change.

Nevertheless, there were threats to the republic's moderate politics in the last years of the nineteenth century. In 1889, France escaped the threat of a coup d'etat by the authoritarian General Georges Boulanger, whose anti-German diatribes and speeches expressing concern for workers attracted public attention and support. Then the republic faced a scandal after companies financing a canal through Panama went bankrupt and investigations uncovered political graft. There followed a stormy campaign against republican politicians, liberal newspapers, and Jewish financiers. Only when the regime seemed close to toppling did its defenders pull together.

The Dreyfus Affair The Third Republic's greatest trial came with the Dreyfus case. In 1894 a court-martial convicted Captain Alfred Dreyfus, a Jew and a member of the General Staff, of providing the German military

CHRONOLOGY
Radicalism and Violent Protest in the Belle Epoque

1864–1872	First International.
1871	Paris Commune.
1887	Assassination of the prime minister of Spain.
1889	Strike of London dockworkers; formation of the Second International.
1894	Assassination of the president of France; Dreyfus affair.
1898	Assassination of the empress of Austria; left-wing riots in Milan.
1901	Assassination of the president of the United States.
1905	Russian Revolution of 1905.
1909	Left-wing riots in Barcelona.
1910–1914	Strikes in London.
1912	Social Democrats gain majority in Reichstag.

Every stage of the Dreyfus affair was the occasion for public demonstrations. *Le Petit Journal,* which had the largest circulation of any Paris newspaper, printed this scene of a crowd of magistrates and ordinary citizens hailing the news in February 1898 that Zola has been convicted of libel.
Edimedia

attaché with secret French documents. Although the sensational press denounced Jewish treachery, the issue only became the center of public attention three years afterward, when evidence appeared implicating another officer as the guilty party.

The army's principal officers, refusing to reopen the case, spoke darkly of honor and state secrets, and the right-wing press hailed their patriotism. The controversy escalated with charges and countercharges in parliament and the press, a series of sensational trials, and huge public demonstrations. The nation was divided. The majority of Catholics, monarchists, and conservatives joined in patriotic indignation against Jews and socialists who were allegedly conspiring to sell out France and weaken a loyal army. The left—intellectuals, socialists, and republicans—came to view Dreyfus as the innocent victim of a plot against republican institutions.

Figures like the novelist Émile Zola, who was twice convicted of libel for his efforts, led in demanding a new trial. The military courts, however, were reluctant to admit past mistakes. A court-martial in 1898 instead acquitted the man who forged the principal evidence against Dreyfus, and a year later it convicted Dreyfus a second time but "with extenuating circumstances," a confusing ruling that led to a presidential pardon. The defenders of Dreyfus narrowly won the battle for public opinion,[6] yet that victory set the tone of subsequent French politics, cementing traditions of republican unity on the left and greatly reducing the political influence of the Church and monarchists.

A Stable Republic   From 1900 until World War I, government was in the hands of firm republicans who called themselves the Radical party. They purged the

[6] A few Dreyfusards continued collecting evidence and finally won acquittal in a civil trial in 1906. Dreyfus was then decorated and promoted to the rank of major.

At a mine entrance in the Ruhr in 1912, striking German mine workers read an official proclamation warning that the police are authorized to shoot.
Ullstein Bilderdienst/The Granger Collection, New York

army of the most outspoken opponents of the republic and passed a law separating church and state in 1905. Yet these so-called radicals also solidified support for the republic through reform and conciliation, reaching out, for example, to small businessmen and peasant farmers, traditionally defenders of the status quo. At the same time, although the trade union movement doubled its membership during this period, frequent strikes never culminated in the revolutionary general strike so much talked about. On the eve of world war, France, prosperous and stable, appeared to have surmounted its most dangerous divisions.

Germany: The Reich

Bismarck had given Germany a constitution that established representative institutions but left power in the hands of a conservative monarchy, and throughout its history the Reich would be haunted by the question of whether this awkward system could hold together or must veer sharply toward autocracy or democracy. Until 1890 Bismarck dominated German public life with an authority few modern figures have equaled. Scornful of criticism, he made many enemies but remained untouchable until William II ascended the throne in 1888 and subsequently forced Bismarck's resignation.

The Army and the Conservative Leagues   Bismarck's policies had allowed for great concentrations of political and economic power in a rapidly expanding society, one in which court, army, bureaucracy, and business were treated as semiautonomous interests. Holding the system together while balancing the demands of parliament and public opinion was a growing challenge, especially as the decline in agriculture threatened the power base of the Junker ruling elite. Bismarck's successors tried to match his dazzling successes in foreign policy and followed him in attending to the army. Yet military appropriations were a constant, intense source of conflict between right and left, and each time the army expanded and government rhetoric grew more nationalistic, German society became increasingly divided.

Germany's conservatives had learned from Bismarck the value of appealing to the public, and they did so through the strident propaganda of political leagues—the Landlords', Peasants', Pan-German, Colonial, and Naval Leagues—organized in the 1890s. Well-financed by Prussian Junkers and some industrialists, these leagues campaigned for high tariffs, overseas empire, and the military, with attacks on socialists, Jews, and foreign enemies. As pressure groups, they won significant victories, including the naval bill of 1898, which proposed to create a fleet that could compete with Britain's. In addition to building railroads, roads, and schools, the government extended the comprehensive social welfare programs begun under Bismarck, and William II was hailed as "the Labor Emperor" for supporting social security, labor arbitration, the regulation of workers' hours, and provisions for their safety.

The Social Democrats   But Bismarck's hope that such measures would weaken the socialists was not realized. The well-organized Social Democrats continued to gain in the 1890s, and they became the largest party in the Reichstag in 1912 (and the strongest socialist party in Europe) despite the distortions of the electoral system. Socialists also dominated Germany's vigorous labor unions, which had 2.5 million members by 1912, and the Social Democratic party sustained an influential subculture that had its own newspapers, libraries, and recreation centers.

In theory, at least, the Social Democrats remained firm revolutionaries, formally rejecting the revisionism of Eduard Bernstein, who in his book *Evolutionary Socialism* (1897), argued for less emphasis on economic determinism or revolution and a greater focus instead on improving working conditions and strengthening democracy. The subject of international debate, Bernstein's criticism of Marx and his alternative theory implied a less militant socialism willing to cooperate with other democratic parties, and it was an important moment in the history of socialism when Germany's powerful Social Democrats chose instead to make a rigorous Marxism their official policy.

The uncompromising stance of the left was matched in vigor and fury by conservatives. The royal court spoke openly of using the army against radicals. As the chancellor still remained responsible to the crown and not to the Reichstag, Germany's experiment with liberal institutions seemed to be coming to an end. Europe's other powers, facing economic competition from Germany, watched with anxiety as in the last years before World War I, its politicians emphasized militarism and risked imperial clashes with foreign powers to avoid facing political problems at home.

Italy: The Liberal Monarchy

Italy's liberal monarchy was committed to modernizing the nation while balancing the budget and steadily sponsoring modest reforms, but the political system in which only the well-to-do could vote and in which the government kept its parliamentary majority by means of political favors made it hard to win broad popular support.

The Crisis of the 1890s　As a hero of Italian unification and a former radical, Francesco Crispi, prime minister in the late 1880s and 1890s, tried to change that. His policies—which included anticlericalism, a trade war with France, and a disastrous imperial adventure in Ethiopia—proved divisive instead.

Domestic unrest increased both in the poverty-stricken agrarian south and in the rapidly industrializing north, where anarchist bombs, socialist demonstrations, and waves of strikes culminated in riots that reached revolutionary scale in Milan in 1898. The government restored order but at the cost of bloodshed, the suppression of scores of newspapers, and a ban on hundreds of socialist, republican, and Catholic organizations. Many conservatives argued for still firmer measures; yet the Chamber of Deputies, although frightened, refused further restriction of civil liberties, a stand supported in the elections of 1900. In Italy, as in France at the same time,

the political campaign of a revitalized right was defeated by parliament and public opinion.

Limited Liberalism　The political system acquired a broader base of support under Giovanni Giolitti, prime minister from 1903 to 1914. He acknowledged the right to strike, nationalized railroads and life insurance, sponsored public health measures, and in 1911 supported universal male suffrage. Giolitti also encouraged Catholics to enter the national politics they had boycotted since 1870. Like Crispi, he pursued imperial ambitions, waging war on the Ottomans for control of some of their Mediterranean holdings, including Tripoli in Libya. But in contrast to Crispi, whose military debacle in Ethiopia forced him from office, Giolitti's successful war earned his government fervent popular support. Although the economic problems of the south remained grave and the discontent of more and more militant workers went largely unappeased, the Italian economy, less developed than that of the great industrial powers, experienced the fastest growth rate in Europe during the decade ending in 1914. Italy appeared firmly set on a liberal, democratic course.

Russia: Defeat and Revolution

In Russia the pressures for political change were held in check for a generation by official policies that centered on a program of "Russification," meant to create a united nation. But defeat in war and the first stages of industrialization produced a revolution.

Reaction　Alexander III had become tsar in 1881 on his father's assassination, an event that he believed resulted from too much talk about further reform following the abolition of serfdom. He sought to achieve stability by using the Orthodox Church and the police to extend an official reactionary ideology through public life, and he gave nobles an increased role in regional councils, the *zemstvos*, and in rural administration. Local governors were authorized to use martial law, to restrict or ban the religions and languages of non-Russian peoples, and to persecute Jews.[7] These policies were continued with equal conviction but less energy by Tsar Nicholas II, who ascended the throne in 1894. As unrest increased in cities and in the countryside, many in the government searched for other ways of achieving the solidarity that repression had failed to create.

---

[7] One of history's famous forgeries, the *Protocols of the Elders of Zion,* was published (and written) by the Russian police in 1903. The protocols purported to be the secret minutes of a Jewish congress that revealed a conspiracy to control the world.

Umberto Boccioni
RIOT IN THE GALLERY, **1910**
Social tension in an era of prosperity: The excitement and uncertainty of a riot contrasts with the stable warmth of an elegant café. Pinacoteca di Brera, Milan, Italy. Scala/Art Resource, NY

The Russo-Japanese War War, and the patriotism it evokes, was thus welcomed in 1904, when Japan suddenly attacked the Russians at Port Arthur on the Yellow Sea. Russia had leased Port Arthur from China in 1898 as part of its expansion into East Asia and Manchuria. For years these moves had troubled the Japanese, and Russia had neither kept its promises to withdraw nor acknowledged Japan's proposals for establishing mutually acceptable spheres of influence. The war was a disaster for Russia. Surprise attack was followed by defeats in Manchuria, the fall of Port Arthur, and then the annihilation of a large Russian fleet. In the peace treaty, Russia ceded most of its recent gains and recognized Japanese interest in Korea.

The Revolution of 1905 So dramatic a defeat increased pressure for major reforms deep within Russian society. Peasant agitation had been on the rise since a terrible famine in 1891. Secret organizations were growing among the non-Russian nationalities, and workers drawn to St. Petersburg and Moscow by industrialization had begun to form unions. The Social Revolutionaries, a party combining the traditions of populism and

terrorism, grew more active; the Marxist Social Democrats organized in exile and strengthened their ties within Russia.

In this atmosphere liberal members of the *zemstvos* held a national congress in 1904, though forbidden to by the government, and insisted on civil liberties. Then in January 1905 striking workers in St. Petersburg marched on the Winter Palace to petition the tsar for a national constitution and the recognition of labor unions. The workers carried religious icons and sang "God save the tsar," but the army opened fire, killing scores and wounding hundreds more.

"Bloody Sunday" led to agitation so widespread that in March the tsar promised to call an assembly of notables and announced immediate reforms: religious toleration, reduced restrictions on Jews and non-Russian nationals, and cancellation of part of the payments peasants owed for their land. Agitation for a constitution only grew stronger, expressed through urban strikes, peasant riots, and mutinies in both the army and navy. In August the tsar conceded more, declaring he would consult a national assembly, the Imperial Duma. A dissatisfied public responded with a wave of strikes.

On Bloody Sunday in January 1905, protesters, led by a priest and carrying a petition to the tsar, marched on the Winter Palace, where they were fired on by Russian soldiers. That bloodshed, following rising demands for a representative assembly, marked the beginning of the Revolution of 1905.
Sovfoto

A Russian Constitution   For the last ten days of October, Russia's economic life came to a halt in the most effective general strike Europe had ever seen. It won from the tsar the **October Manifesto,** which granted a constitution. Crowds danced in the streets, but proponents of change were divided. Those willing to work with this constitution, which guaranteed freedom of speech and assembly but was vague on much else, became known as Octobrists. Liberals who insisted on a constituent assembly and broader guarantees formed the Constitutional Democratic party, called Cadets for short. Further to the left, socialists and revolutionaries rejected compromise, and the St. Petersburg Soviet, a committee of trade union leaders and socialists, called another general strike. It was only partially successful, and an emboldened government arrested the leaders of the Soviet in December and bloodily defeated the Moscow workers who revolted in protest.

The Fundamental Laws, announced in May 1906, defined the limitations of the tsar's concessions. He would keep the power of veto, the right to name his ministers, and full command of the executive, the judiciary, and the armed forces; the national legislature would have an upper house in addition to the Duma, with half its members appointed by the tsar. Elections under this new system, however, brought the Cadets a large majority, which demanded representative government. Nicholas then disbanded the legislature and held new elections, but they produced an even more radical assembly; it, too, was disbanded. Only a new electoral law favoring the propertied classes ensured conservative majorities in subsequent legislatures.

The Revolution of 1905 had nevertheless brought important changes. Russia now had parliamentary institutions and organized parties, the power of the aristocracy had been greatly reduced, and the nation was clearly set on a modern course. The prime minister from 1906 to 1911, Peter Stolypin, reformed education and administration and strove to stimulate the economy by turning away from the *mir* system of communal lands in favor of the full private ownership of land. With the aid of foreign capital, the pace of industrialization rapidly increased. While discontent remained serious and radical movements were sternly repressed, the Cadets were finding it possible to work with the new system. Liberals throughout Europe rejoiced that the giant of the East had at last begun to follow the path of Western progress.

Austria-Hungary: The Delicate Balance

The political problems of Austria-Hungary were revealed not so much in crises as in stalemate. Creation of an autonomous regime in Hungary led to conflicts with the rest of the empire, and these political and nationalist issues were exacerbated by the divergent economic interests of the empire's industrializing and agrarian regions. The conservative instincts of the imperial court, the aristocracy, and the bureaucracy stymied further reforms.

Shifting Stalemates   Ruling elites settled on a cautious prime minister, Count Eduard von Taaffe, who held office from 1879 to 1893, but his parliamentary coalition was so divided that legislative inaction was the safest course. Social change brought further disagreements. In response to workers' agitation, Taaffe proposed welfare measures but repressed socialists, antagonizing both left and right. After his fall, governments came to rely more on decree powers and support from the crown than on parliament. After universal male suffrage was introduced in 1907, the Christian Socialists and the Social Democrats became the two largest parties, although neither was acceptable to the leaders of the empire. Kept from imperial office, they competed in the city of Vienna, where the Christian Socialists gained sway by combining social programs with demagogic anti-Semitism.

Within Hungary, Magyar notables maintained their dominance over other nationalities by requiring that the Magyar language be used in government and schools, by controlling the electoral system, and by subverting the bureaucracy through corruption. In 1903, when Hungary's leaders demanded greater autonomy for their own army, they touched on an issue about which Emperor Franz Joseph I cared too much to yield. He suspended the Hungarian constitution, ruled without parliament, and frightened the Magyars into submission by threatening to subject them, a minority in their own country, to universal male suffrage. Magyars and the empire needed each other; and Magyar politics, admired in the 1840s as a model of liberal nationalism, had turned by 1906 into the defensive strategy of a threatened aristocracy.

Spain: Instability and Loss of Empire

Spain developed a remarkable tradition of parliamentarism in which governments were careful to keep the support of the army, the Church, big business, and regional interests. By emphasizing the economy, a liberal coalition held power from 1854 to 1863, years in which Spain experienced on a smaller scale the waves of speculation, railroad building, economic growth, and ostentation associated with the Second Empire in France.

Revolution and Restoration This growth brought new demands that old alliances, palace intrigue, and electoral manipulation could not check. Rising discontent led in 1868 to the flight of the unpopular Queen Isabella II and to revolution. The leaders of the revolution were political moderates who quickly agreed on a constitutional monarchy with universal male suffrage, trial by jury, and freedom of religion and the press. It proved easier to adopt a new constitution, however, than to find a new king. The Italian prince who finally did accept the throne gave it up after three years in the face of rising opposition from left and right. The subsequent republic lasted only

two years before the military installed Isabella's son on the throne as Alfonso XII.

He began his reign in 1875 with a new constitution closer to the one in effect at midcentury than to the more democratic ones that had succeeded it. In a parliamentary system based on limited suffrage, the Conservative and Liberal parties alternated in power with little change in policy, a system that by keeping the state weak masked bitter social divisions. As in Russia and Austria, industrialization exacerbated these tensions. Unable to establish a consistent policy for its colonies, the government met unrest in Cuba with alternating policies of repression and laxity. Cuban resistance became guerrilla war, and in 1898 the United States entered the conflict with an imperialist enthusiasm of its own. As a result of the Spanish-American War, Spain was forced to withdraw from Cuba and to cede Puerto Rico, Guam, and the Philippine Islands to the United States.

Those losses led to a great deal of soul searching. A group of Spanish intellectuals known as the generation of 1898 brought new vitality to Spanish public life, but neither the caution of conservatives nor the mild reforms of liberals could stem the increasing dissension in which the Church denounced the liberals while growing anarchist and socialist movements attacked the whole establishment. In 1909 these conflicts burst forth in a week of violence in Barcelona during which churches were burned and looted and private citizens were murdered. Yet the authorities soon restored order. Spain's unadmired moderate regime remained less divisive than the alternatives.

Great Britain: Edging toward Democracy

From Russia to Spain, European nations adopted parliamentary systems, and until the end of the century, Britain provided the model of how such a system was supposed to work. In Britain, Parliament gradually reduced legal inequalities, opening the civil service to those who passed competitive examinations, removing the legal disabilities of Jews, and eliminating special taxes on behalf of the Church of England. At the same time, order was maintained through respect for law, toleration, and social deference. There were serious domestic tensions, but they were attenuated by a thriving two-party system.

The Liberal and Conservative Parties The creation of modern political parties led by two brilliant leaders facilitated Britain's adaptation to change. William Gladstone was instrumental in transforming the Whigs into the Liberal party, and Benjamin Disraeli led in making the Tories into the modern Conservative party. Gladstone was a skilled parliamentary tactician

EMMELINE PANKHURST ON WOMEN'S RIGHTS

Emmeline Pankhurst founded the Women's Social and Political Union in 1903. As the militant leader of the British suffragettes, she won headlines and eventually significant support for her cause with her disruptive tactics and powerful speeches. Her fame was international by the time she went on a speaking tour in Canada in 1912, where on January 14 she gave a long speech from which this passage is taken. Delighting her audience with stories of the resistance she had met, she focused on the right to vote but made clear that her vision of women's roles was much broader.

"There has been a great deal of talk lately of new legislation for those who are about to enter into marriage. Women should have a say as one of the contracting parties. There are the questions of divorce and of the training of children. Who knows better of these matters than do women? There are also the trades and professions which are at the present time open to women. It is only right that we should have some say in the legislation concerning us. We have heard much of the English divorce law. It is a disgrace to any civilized country. The only redeeming feature of the matter is that the bulk of men are better than the law allows. But there is the minority, and the law should be severe for them. They are as bad as the law allows them to be. If woman only had weight in politics this would be rectified soon. She will serve to call more attention to such questions of national welfare. If we are to have any divorce law at all, and that is a much-debated question, it should be a law that is equal both for man and woman. Unless women get the vote we have no guarantee that it will be so.

" . . . Men are responsible if they allow the present condition of things to continue. Women have the power to work out their own salvation. But as it is, if a woman is ruined, if a child is injured, man is responsible for it all. It is a responsibility I would not care to have, and, as things are, I would not be a man for all the world. If women fail as men have failed, then they will bear the burden with them. But since men cannot protect and shield us, let us share the duty with them, let us use our power so that woman may be a participant, not to tyrannize over man but to take a share in the responsibilities of ruling, without which there is no real representative government. What we really are interested in in this fight is the uplifting of the sex and better conditions of humanity than men can secure. In the legal home there is but the man. What we want is the combined intelligence of man and woman working for the salvation of the children of the race. This will make for the world a better time than ever before in its history. It will raise mankind to heights of which now it has little conception. We must only make this last fight for human freedom that as the class distinction disappeared so that sex distinction may pass, and then you will get better things than men can by themselves secure."

From Emmeline Pankhurst, "The Last Fight for Human Freedom," speech given in Canada in 1912, in Brian MacArthur, *Twentieth-Century Speeches*, New York: Viking, 1992.

sympathetic to liberal reformers and even radicals, for whom political liberalism was a moral cause. Somewhat hesitantly, he made increased suffrage a central plank, but his complicated bill was defeated in Parliament.

Instead, Disraeli persuaded his startled party to support a simpler, more generous reform, which passed in 1867. It doubled the electorate by extending the right to vote to all men who paid property taxes directly or indirectly through rent (about one adult male in three). Equally important, imperial policies and major programs of reform now became a regular part of the competition for popular favor.

Political Reforms   The enlarged electorate after the 1867 reform gave the Liberals a great victory, and for six years Gladstone's first ministry fundamentally altered the relations between government and society. State aid to elementary schools, both religious and secular, brought Britain closer to universal education. The Liberals also reformed the army and disestablished the Anglican Church of Ireland (so that an overwhelmingly Catholic population no longer paid taxes to support a Protestant church). Recognizing the festering poverty and discontent in Ireland, new laws restricted the abuses of absentee landlords and provided peasants some protection against eviction.

The Conservatives, returned to power in the elections of 1874, were more willing than the Liberals to expand the authority of the state. A public health act established a national code for housing and urban sanitation, and new measures allowed striking workers to picket, making unions more effective. These social concerns, which offered a British parallel to the policies of Bismarck and Napoleon III, became the cornerstone of the revived Conservative party.

Gladstone, in turn, adopted the principle of universal male suffrage, which became law in 1885. Men with an independent place of residence could now vote, but this one requirement excluded roughly one-third of all adult males. Gladstone's perpetual compromises, moreover, were losing their appeal. His renewed efforts on behalf of Irish peasants failed to satisfy Irish nationalists who wanted an independent parliament of their own, and when Gladstone acquiesced to Irish home rule in 1886, his party split. A group of Liberals led by Joseph Chamberlain allied with the Conservatives. A radical in domestic social policy, Chamberlain was also an ardent imperialist, a stance which would help the Conservatives stay in office for sixteen of the nineteen years between 1886 and 1905.

Rising Social Tensions

While projecting British power around the world, Conservative governments remained active at home. They extended the reforms of the civil service and, in an act of 1902, established a national education system that for the first time included secondary schooling. Yet these important changes did not address the needs of the working class, whose rising dissatisfaction was marked by the dramatic strikes of London match girls in 1888 and dockworkers the next year. The strikes, which won public sympathy, were part of a "new unionism" that included unskilled workers in a more militant labor movement.

In 1900 a combination of union representatives and some prominent intellectuals formed the Labour party on a platform of democratic socialism. Both the Labour and Liberal parties campaigned for social programs that the Conservatives resisted, relying instead on the popular appeal of empire to keep them in power. In 1906 the Liberals won the most one-sided electoral victory since 1832. They immediately established systems of worker's compensation, old-age pensions, and urban planning. These measures—and the expanding arms race—required new revenues, and in 1909 David Lloyd George, the Chancellor of the Exchequer, proposed a "people's budget." A skilled orator who delighted in the rhetoric of class conflict, he promised to place the costs of social welfare squarely on the rich.

Constitutional Crisis

An irate House of Lords rejected Lloyd George's budget, an unprecedented act that forced a constitutional crisis and new elections. The king's threat to appoint hundreds of additional peers finally forced the upper house to accept not only the hated budget but also a major change in the constitution. By law, the Lords could no longer veto money bills or any measure that passed the Commons in three successive sessions.

The peers' intemperate outburst, which cost them so much, was part of a general rise in social tension. From 1910 to 1914 strikes increased in frequency, size, and violence; a general strike became a real and much-talked-of threat. Women campaigning for the right to vote interrupted public meetings, invaded Parliament itself, smashed windows, and planted bombs. Arrested, they went on hunger strikes until baffled statesmen ordered their release. As the movement gained strength, recruiting women (and some men) from every social class, its outraged attack on smug male assumptions reinforced the rising challenge to a whole social order (see "Emmeline Pankhurst on Women's Rights," p. 726).

Nor was the threat of violence limited to the left. In 1914 the Commons for the third time passed a bill granting Irish home rule, which made it immune to a veto in the House of Lords. The Protestants of northern Ireland openly threatened civil war. Squads began drilling, and the British officer corps seemed ready to mutiny rather than fight to impose home rule on Protestant loyalists.

Only the outbreak of world war generated the national unity that neither imperialism nor social reform had been able to achieve.

Summary

In the period from 1870 to 1914 every European nation faced major political crises; yet as political systems worked to diminish class conflict and balance clashing interests, the trend toward greater democracy and large-scale organization seemed undeniable. There were fewer major upheavals, save in backward Russia, and no European war, facts that contemporaries often cited as proof of progress. In most countries there was greater freedom of expression, more political participation, more leisure, increased literacy and education, and better health care than in the past. In general, productivity and prosperity, already at levels never achieved before, continued to rise. Science and technology promised still greater wonders. Even in retrospect, the level of creativity in the arts and scholarship and the growth of knowledge and professional standards in every field remain impressive.

Yet the civilization that achieved all this was bitterly denounced not only for its manifest injustices, which stood out in contrast to its achievements, but more fundamentally for its lack of coherent values, for its materialism, for the ugliness of industrial society, and for the privileged position of a middle class portrayed as self-serving and philistine. Perhaps European society was evolving toward solutions of these deficiencies, as many believed. Or maybe the positive trends were less significant than the effects of imperialism, domestic social conflict, and the arms race. In 1914 the very compromises that had held society together and kept the peace exploded—not in revolution, but in total war.

QUESTIONS FOR FURTHER THOUGHT

1. How did the second industrial revolution differ from previous examples of economic growth? Was its social impact equally unprecedented?
2. In what respects did discoveries in the natural sciences influence developments in the social sciences?
3. In what ways did the nineteenth-century women's movement reflect economic and social change?
4. How could an era widely proclaimed as an age of progress produce such powerful and diverse criticism?

RECOMMENDED READING

Sources

Dangerfield, George. *The Strange Death of Liberal England.* 1935. Skillfully crafted, contentious account of a society in crisis that has influenced subsequent interpretations of the period.

Hélias, Pierre-Jackez. *The Horse of Pride: Life in a Breton Village.* June Guicharnaud (tr.). 1980. A compelling memoir of a preindustrial society about to be transformed at the turn of the century.

Snyder, Louis L. *The Dreyfus Case: A Documentary History.* 1973. These well-edited documents convey the passions that this famous affair stirred and the broad implications that all sides saw in it.

Weintraub, Stanley. *The Yellow Book: Quintessence of the Nineties.* 1964. The stories and articles in this collection are all taken from the most daring literary quarterly of the day; nearly every piece is an exercise in the rejection of Victorian properties and, in that respect, characteristic of the new movements in the arts.

Studies

Abrams, Lynn. *The Making of Modern Woman: Europe 1789–1918.* 2002. Provides a thorough and wide-ranging examination of both the changing role of women throughout the nineteenth century and the extensive historiography on this subject.

Agulhon, Maurice. *The French Republic 1879–1992.* Translated by Antonia Nevill. 1993. The first part of this comprehensive history of France discusses the Third Republic, with special emphasis paid to political developments.

Avineri, Shlomo. *The Social and Political Thought of Karl Marx.* 1971. There are dozens of excellent introductions to Marx's thought; this one stands out for its clarity and freshness.

Berghahn, Volker R. *Germany, 1871–1914: Economy, Society, Culture, and Politics.* 1993. A thematic survey unusual in its breadth, particularly attentive to public culture and social structure.

Berlanstein, Lenard R. *The Working People of Paris, 1871–1914.* 1984. Looks at the important changes in the lives of wage earners, in the nature of work, and in the workplace, as well as their impact on working-class movements.

Bowler, P. *Evolution: The History of an Idea.* 1989. Combining recent work in the history of science with more general intellectual history, this book traces the various conceptions of evolution in different fields.

Canning, Kathleen. *Languages of Labor and Gender: Female Factory Work in Germany, 1850–1914.* 1996. Connects social changes in the nature of work to changes in women's lives and to the shifting discourse on gender.

Derfler, Leslie. *Socialism since Marx: A Century of the European Left.* 1973. Thoughtful discussion of the movements that stemmed from Marx, showing their variety, creativity, and contradictions.

Evans, Richard J. (ed.). *Society and Politics in Wilhelmine Germany.* 1979. An important collection of essays applying the "history from below" approach to the study of German history and society.

Gullickson, Gay L. *Unruly Women of Paris: Images of the Commune.* 1997. A richly illustrated study of the newspaper accounts of the role of women in the Commune.

Hughes, H. Stuart. *Consciousness and Society: The Reorientation of European Social Thought, 1890–1930.* 1958. A gracefully written and indispensable analysis of the currents of modern thought in this time of transition from midcentury certitudes.

Johnson, Douglas. *France and the Dreyfus Affair.* 1966. A cogent account of the affair that explains its extraordinary impact.

Joll, James. *The Second International, 1889–1914.* 1966. A general history of the socialist movement in this period, with striking portraits of the major figures.

Kaplan, Marion. *The Making of the Jewish Middle Class: Women, Family, and Identity in Imperial Germany.* 1991. An engaging analysis of the position and priorities of Jewish women in late-nineteenth-century Germany.

Kennedy, Paul. *The Rise of the Anglo-German Antagonism, 1860–1914.* 1980. This massive study of international relations includes economic and political rivalry as well as imperialism in accounting for the rising tension between the two nations.

Kocka, Jürgen, and Allan Mitchell (eds.). *Bourgeois Society in Nineteenth-Century Europe.* 1993. A collection of essays examining and comparing the rise of the middle class in Britain, France, Germany, and Italy.

Lidtke, Vernon. *The Alternative Culture: Socialist Labor in Imperial Germany.* 1985. A significant analysis of how German socialists created Europe's best-organized working-class subculture.

Löwith, Karl. *From Hegel to Nietzsche: The Revolution in Nineteenth-Century Thought.* 1964. A sober essay on the pessimistic and irrationalist transformations in modern thought and the powerful insights that resulted.

McLellan, David. *Karl Marx: His Life and Thought.* 1977. Considers the more youthful writings as well as *Das Kapital,* bringing out their essential unity.

Milward, Alan S., and S. B. Saul. *The Development of the Economies of Continental Europe, 1850–1914.* 1977. A study of the second great wave of industrialization, which underscores the difference between this later continental experience and the earlier English one.

Moses, Claire. *French Feminism in the Nineteenth Century.* 1984. Reveals the vigor of a feminist movement quite different from its British and German counterparts.

Mosse, George L. *The Crisis of German Ideology.* 1964. Looks for the currents of Nazi ideology in the views of nation and race embodied in the popular ideas and movements of the late nineteenth century.

Nord, Philip. *Paris Shopkeepers and the Politics of Resentment.* 1986. Explores the antimodern militancy of lower-middle-class shopkeepers seen in response to the rise of mass-produced goods and the prominence of the department store.

Paret, Peter. *The Berlin Secession: Modernism and Its Enemies in Imperial Germany.* 1980. Examines the Berlin Secessionist movement, which was a major cultural force in German politics and culture between 1898 and 1918.

Pick, Daniel. *Faces of Degeneration: A European Disorder, c. 1848–1918.* 1989. Comparative study of the cultural preoccupation with "degeneration" in Great Britain, Italy, and France in the decades before the First World War.

Ralston, David B. *The Army of the Republic, 1871–1914.* 1967. Treats the role of the military in France both before and after the Dreyfus affair.

Reddy, William M. *Money and Liberty in Modern Europe: A Critique of Historical Understanding.* 1987. A critical look at the social impact of the expansion of capitalism in England, France, and Germany, probing the nature of the inequality that resulted.

Schivelbusch, Wolfgang. *The Railway Journey: The Industrialization of Time and Space in the 19th Century.* 1986. Explores the psychological and technological impact of the introduction and expansion of rail travel throughout later nineteenth-century Europe.

Schorske, Carl E. *Fin-de-Siècle Vienna: Politics and Culture.* 1980. Sensitive and imaginative assessment of one of the important moments in European cultural history.

Seton-Watson, Christopher. *Italy from Liberalism to Fascism.* 1967. A general political account of Italy in its first period of rapid industrialization.

Sheehan, James J. *German Liberalism in the Nineteenth Century.* 1978. A detailed assessment of a much disputed and critical issue, the place of liberalism in German intellectual and political life.

Showalter, Elaine. *Sexual Anarchy: Gender and Culture at the Fin de Siècle.* 1990. Analyzes the myths and images of sexual crisis that were dominant in both Europe and the United States at this time.

Smith, Helmut Walser. *The Butcher's Tale: Murder and Anti-Semitism in a German Town.* 2002. Engaging analysis of an unsolved murder, committed in 1900 in the easternmost part of the German empire, that testifies to both the strength and irrationality of European anti-Semitism at the turn of the century.

Weber, Eugen. *Peasants into Frenchmen: The Modernization of Rural France, 1880–1914.* 1976. A provocative treatment stressing how resistance in rural France to pressures for change delayed modernization efforts.

Thomas Jones Barker
THE SECRET OF ENGLAND'S GREATNESS, CA. 1863
Painted by Thomas Jones Barker in 1863, this painting, titled *The Secret of England's Greatness*, epitomizes the nineteenth-century liberal conception of empire. Prince Albert and the statesmen Lord Palmerston and Lord John Russell look on as Queen Victoria gives a Bible to a kneeling African. The queen represents empire as a benevolent, paternalist force, bestowing European civilization and Christianity on the colonies. The African symbolizes the colonial subject, who embraces his subordinate position and gratefully receives these gifts.
The National Portrait Gallery, London

Chapter Twenty-Five

NINETEENTH-CENTURY EMPIRES

THE BIRTH OF THE LIBERAL EMPIRE • EUROPEAN EXPANSION IN THE MIDCENTURY •
THE NEW IMPERIALISM, 1870–1914 • IMPERIALISM AT ITS PEAK

Since the first invasions of the Spanish conquistadors in the early sixteenth century, Europeans had amassed a vast New World empire. A flourishing plantation economy, sustained by African slave labor, formed the economic base of this world, the hub of which was the prosperous sugar colonies of the West Indies. The New World colonies served the mercantilist goal to enrich the monarchical state through the creation of advantageous trade monopolies with its colonies and found moral justification in the religious mission of saving the immortal souls of "heathens."

In the early nineteenth century, a new liberal empire supplanted this older religious-mercantilist colonial regime. Abandoning the New World, European entrepreneurs, merchants, missionaries, and explorers staked claims in Asia and Africa. European governments frequently followed in their wake, carving out spheres of influence to protect their interests and activities. Operating increasingly within the context of a market economy, nineteenth-century Europeans perceived the non-Western world as untapped markets for European manufactures and capital investment and as sources of

raw materials for Europe's burgeoning industries. Steeped in the culture of the Enlightenment and principles of liberal universalism, moreover, Europeans saw empire not just as a means of benefiting themselves, but as an opportunity to bring the fruits of European civilization to the non-Western world.

In the late nineteenth century, empire's foundations shifted once more. The "new imperialism" of this period was characterized by the aggressive expansionism of competing European nation-states. In the space of a few decades, Europeans conquered and colonized virtually all of Africa and vast regions of Asia. European attitudes toward colonial subjects changed as well, shaped by anticolonial insurgence and, after Darwin, the ascendancy of biological determinism in thinking about culture and race. These developments undermined the liberal aims of the early nineteenth century, raising new doubts about both the desirability and the feasibility of Europeanizing non-European peoples. The turn of the century was thus a moment of intense contradictions: the peak moment of Europe's global power, but also one in which Europeans began to rethink the scope and future of empire.

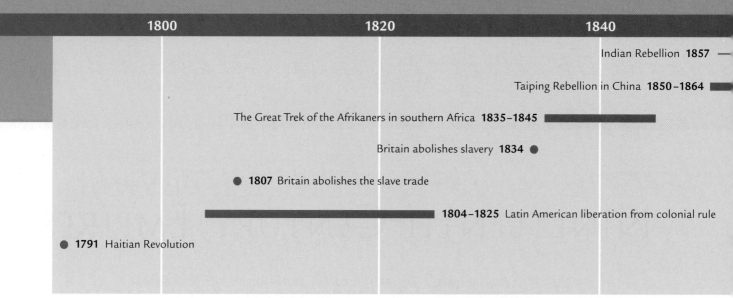

Indian Rebellion **1857** —

Taiping Rebellion in China **1850–1864** ▬

The Great Trek of the Afrikaners in southern Africa **1835–1845** ▬▬▬▬▬▬

Britain abolishes slavery **1834** ●

● **1807** Britain abolishes the slave trade

▬▬▬▬▬▬▬▬▬▬▬▬▬▬ **1804–1825** Latin American liberation from colonial rule

● **1791** Haitian Revolution

THE BIRTH OF THE LIBERAL EMPIRE

In the nineteenth century, Europeans lost their Atlantic empires and built new ones in Asia and Africa. Although the first two-thirds of the century saw little outright colonization, Europeans steadily expanded their influence overseas. As European merchants, missionaries, explorers, and settlers penetrated different parts of the world, European governments provided them with support and, in so doing, became increasingly involved in the affairs of foreign polities. The expansionism of this period had its economic foundation in the growth of a capitalist market economy and its philosophical roots in the Enlightenment culture of liberal universalism. Europeans thus saw the acquisition of overseas spheres of influence as a way to secure new sources of raw materials and new markets for their industrial manufacturers and, equally important, as an opportunity to "civilize" the non-Western world by making it over in the European image.

The Decline of the Mercantile Colonial World

The mercantile colonial world sustained an unprecedented series of external and internal challenges during the late eighteenth and early nineteenth centuries. Outside of Europe, the threat to empire came primarily in the form of independence movements and slave revolts. Simultaneously, within Europe, the gradual rise of a market economy and the cultural revolution sparked by the Enlightenment undermined the foundations of the old empire.

External Challenges Independence movements, starting with the American Revolution of 1776, drove European colonial powers from much of the New World at the turn of the nineteenth century. From 1804 to 1824, France lost control of Haiti (then known as Saint-Domingue); Portugal of Brazil; and Spain the rest of Latin America except for Cuba and Puerto Rico (see chapter 21). Led by landed Creole elites (American-born people of European descent), Latin American independence movements were influenced by Enlightenment thought and the examples of the French and American Revolutions.

Slave agitation constituted a central part of the assault on the mercantile colonial world. From the late eighteenth through the early nineteenth centuries, runaway slaves called *Maroons*, living in outlaw societies behind the lines of colonial settlement in South America, the Caribbean, and Spanish Florida, waged sporadic guerilla attacks against local plantations, a phenomenon known as the Maroon Wars. Simultaneously, a series of increasingly well-planned and militant slave revolts from Dutch Surinam to British Jamaica erupted in the second half of the eighteenth century, culminating in the Haitian Revolution in the French colony of Saint-Domingue in 1791.

The Antislavery Movement in Europe A rapidly expanding European movement to end slavery further threatened the Atlantic colonial system during the late eighteenth century. Although abolitionists organized in the Netherlands and France as well, the British campaign was by far the strongest and most effective.

Religious antislavery sentiment served as the catalyst to abolitionism. In spite of the fact that most world religions had historically sanctioned slavery, by the eighteenth century newer forms of Protestantism—Quakerism among them—condemned slavery as a sin antithetical to religious tenets of brotherly love and

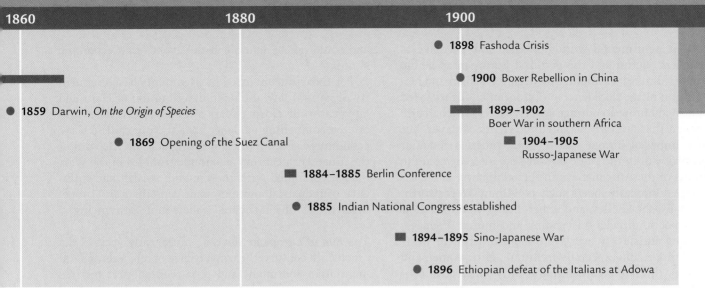

1860   1880   1900

● **1898** Fashoda Crisis

● **1900** Boxer Rebellion in China

1899–1902
Boer War in southern Africa

■ **1904–1905**
Russo-Japanese War

● **1859** Darwin, *On the Origin of Species*

● **1869** Opening of the Suez Canal

■ **1884–1885** Berlin Conference

● **1885** Indian National Congress established

■ **1894–1895** Sino-Japanese War

● **1896** Ethiopian defeat of the Italians at Adowa

spiritual equality. These religious dissenters sparked the movement and established its emotive tone and ethic of benevolence, but antislavery soon spread from there to the religious mainstream, including well-connected Evangelicals, such as the parliamentary member William Wilberforce.

The Influence of the Enlightenment Secular reformers joined forces with religious abolitionists. Although philosophers had debated the morality of slavery well before sustained Christian opposition to slavery burgeoned, most had found ways to justify slavery as a rational and efficient economic and social system. Such justifications became more difficult to make in the humanist intellectual climate of the Enlightenment. Thus, while the seventeenth-century political theorist John Locke himself condoned slavery, his ideas—in particular, his critique of arbitrary power, appeal to rule by reason, and championing of natural and universal human rights—shaped arguments mounted against slavery by Enlightenment humanists such as Baron Montesquieu and Denis Diderot a century later.

Most fundamentally, Enlightenment universalism, or belief in the basic sameness of all humans, undermined the acceptance of slavery and allowed eighteenth-century thinkers to link oppressed Africans to the disenfranchised poor of Europe. Values and principles rooted in this universalist framework, including belief in the individual's natural and inalienable right to freedom, ownership of one's self and labor, and equality before the law, also clashed deeply with the concept of human bondage. Finally, the Enlightenment's optimism and emphasis on the inner goodness and malleability of human beings made it difficult to defend slavery as a necessary evil for less "civilized" peoples. This view was perhaps best encapsulated in Rousseau's cult of the noble savage, which contrasted the natural virtues of

Illustration from a nineteenth-century British children's book of a slave being flogged. Part of the abolitionist campaign against British slavery, the image was intended to stir compassion for the slaves' suffering in young readers. The British Library, London

the so-called primitive with the moral flaws of civilized Europeans and further fostered popular sympathy for enslaved Africans. Taken together, these ideas persuaded Enlightenment thinkers across Europe to soundly reject slavery as an unreasonable, unnatural, and immoral system.

Enlightened philosophical and religious arguments also influenced a romantically oriented popular culture of feeling in the late eighteenth century. This helped make antislavery a pervasive, even fashionable, position among the European elite, especially among well-to-do women, who came to play a pivotal role in the British movement. Religious emphasis on the goodness of humans and the importance of compassion fit with a secular, sentimental worldview that cast the slave as innocent victim and the civilized European as heroic savior. Similarly, Enlightenment universalism and recognition of the decadence of European civilization fed educated European outrage against slavery as a barbaric system that not only violated the rights of slaves, but also impeded Europe's own moral progress. Popular primitivism in the wake of Rousseau also elevated the status of the African slave in the public eye, while acclaimed Romantic poets such as William Wordsworth, Percy Bysshe Shelley, and Robert Burns fashioned their own poetic attacks on tyranny and human bondage, making antislavery ever more modish. All over western Europe, and especially in Britain, elite women and men of the late eighteenth and early nineteenth century inspired by these trends joined abolitionist circles, signed antislavery petitions, and circulated tracts and images that exposed the cruelties of human bondage.

The Free-Trade Lobby By themselves these intellectual and cultural developments probably would not have had the force to abolish slavery. However, antislavery sentiment was strongly reinforced by merchants and industrialists seeking to replace the mercantile colonial system—and its system of protective tariffs intended to privilege trade between colony and mother country—with free trade. By the early nineteenth century, European manufacturers objected increasingly to the protective tariffs levied on foreign imports in the mercantile marketplace. These tariffs effectively prevented domestic manufacturers and consumers from buying cheaper foreign goods, compelling them instead to purchase goods exclusively from domestic producers, at home or in the colonies. British sugar refiners, for example, felt exploited by a system that forced them to buy high-priced raw sugar from Jamaica, while shielding Jamaican sugar producers from competition from French sugar producers in Saint-Domingue and Spanish sugar producers in Cuba.

Capitalists in favor of free trade based their arguments on both theory and real-world experience. For theoretical support, they drew on critiques of **mercantilism** and the slave economy elaborated by Enlightenment classical economists such as Adam Smith and David Ricardo. Smith and Ricardo contended that the mercantile colonial economy was an inefficient, irrational system that flouted the natural law of rational utility by preventing most people from pursuing their economic self-interest. In contrast, they argued, market competition was both natural and rational because it afforded economic liberty to individuals and benefited the majority by generating lower prices all around. Smith also censured the built-in inefficiency and inflexibility of the slave economy, pointing out that slaves, unlike wage laborers, lacked the incentive to work hard and could not be laid off in the event of an economic slump.

For those unconvinced by arguments based on utility or natural law, the rapid deterioration of Haiti and Jamaica in the closing years of the eighteenth century offered compelling evidence that the mercantile slave economy was economically retrograde. By the turn of the nineteenth century, economic troubles in the West Indies, combined with the growing wealth and influence of industrial and merchant capitalists in Europe, made the claims of the free traders more convincing.

The End of European Slavery In the early years of the nineteenth century, the convergence of religious and humanitarian sentiment and economic support for free market competition led to the abolition of the European slave trade. Denmark outlawed the Atlantic slave trade first in 1803, followed by Britain and the United States in 1807. Although Spain, Portugal, France, and the Netherlands agreed to abolish the slave trade in 1815, they did little to eliminate it. Britain, by contrast, embarked on a zealous antislaving mission, searching ships in the Atlantic suspected of carrying slave cargo and rescuing slaves along the West African coast. They provided the latter with passage to Liberia, an African settlement created for and partly by freed American slaves in 1821. By 1850 the European slave trade had essentially ended.

Britain abolished slavery itself in 1834, emancipating the remaining 780,000 British-owned slaves in the West Indies. The British government paid £20 million to slave owners to compensate them for their loss of property. While France and Denmark followed suit in 1848, slavery continued until 1863 in the Dutch New World colonies, 1865 in the United States, 1886 in Spanish Cuba, and 1888 in Brazil. These dates often mattered more to Europeans than to freed slaves, however, who in some cases continued to be treated as slaves for several decades after emancipation.

New Sources of Colonial Legitimacy

Just as the economic, religious, and intellectual forces of the Enlightenment undermined the mercantile colonial world, they also built the new liberal empire that replaced it.

The Growth of the Market Economy The continued growth of industrial capitalism and the market economy brought a new economic rationale to empire. Free-trade advocates in the business world became richer and more influential during the early nineteenth century. By the 1830s, their belief in the individual pursuit of profit in a free, self-regulating market as efficient, natural, and moral was considered common sense. Yet, while free market competition was the mantra of early-to-mid-nineteenth-century capitalists, economic practice sometimes contradicted imperial rhetoric. From 1830 to 1870—the peak era of economic liberalism—European nation-states competed with one another for spheres of economic influence abroad. Europeans were quick to abandon free trade, in other words, when they perceived their own economic interests to be threatened by indigenous and other European competitors.

Enlightenment Universalism The liberal empire's philosophical underpinnings also differed fundamentally from those of early modern empire. Liberal empire had roots in Enlightenment theories of human biological and cultural sameness and belief in human improvement through the application of reason to social reform. While pre-Enlightenment Europeans had emphasized the irreconcilable, permanent gap between themselves and others, eighteenth-century philosophers from Montesquieu to Voltaire claimed the similarities between human societies to be far more significant than the differences. Likewise, although Enlightenment natural scientists like the Swede Carolus Linnaeus or the Frenchman Georges-Louis Leclerc de Buffon sought to classify the varieties of human physical types, they assumed that the "races" of man belonged to a single species. Enlightened Europeans posited that, although different societies had attained different levels of civilization, all occupied positions along a common developmental path. This belief meant not only that change was possible, but that the process of development could be guided and accelerated through reasoned social intervention.

Cultural Relativism Europeans at the turn of the nineteenth century were also less firmly convinced of their own superiority and more critical about the colonial enterprise than their forebears. The universalist framework of the eighteenth century allowed for a new cultural relativism that recognized the value and achievements of other societies. Voltaire's respect for ancient Chinese and Islamic civilizations and the English historian Edward Gibbon's admiration for Islam exemplify this trend, as does the rhetoric of Christian brotherhood preached by evangelical missionaries. Similarly, cultural relativism permitted Rousseau and his followers to exalt New World societies as models of virtue and freedom for a decadent Europe. In the main, however, European cultural relativists still insisted on their own supremacy, even while acknowledging the achievements of other cultures.

These Enlightenment ideas had radical implications for the colonial project. During the sixteenth and seventeenth centuries, colonizers had concerned themselves primarily with the "heathen" nature of "savage" societies and the future of their immortal souls. Assimilation to a European way of life had occurred largely as an unintended consequence of missionary efforts to impart Christian faith to New World peoples. By the turn of the nineteenth century, in contrast, universalism had humanized the colonial subject, and assimilation, rather than exclusion or outright exploitation, emerged as the dominant model for confronting the difference of the non-European. The majority of Europeans, both secular and religious, saw the assimilation of other peoples to European political, economic, and cultural models as a moral imperative and colonial domination as the ideal means to achieve this end. At the same time, a powerful new sense of instrumentality—of the ability of humans to shape the world around them—lent confidence to their civilizing endeavors.

Thomas Rowlands
The Burning System, **1815**
This engraving shows an Indian woman committing sati, or burning herself on the funeral pyre of her dead husband. On one side are native musicians. On the other, Englishmen debate the pros and cons of abolishing sati, the practice of which was considered a sign of India's backwardness.
The British Library, London

MACAULAY'S MINUTE ON INDIAN EDUCATION

Thomas Macaulay (1800–1859) was the Law Member of the Governor General's Council and an important example of the British liberal voice in India. He believed that "backward" societies like India's could be transformed through the introduction of law, free trade, and education. In the early part of the nineteenth century, Orientalist scholars and administrators felt that India should be ruled through its own laws and through indigenous institutions and languages. British liberals like Macaulay thought otherwise. In 1835 a major debate took place as to what kind of education the British should promote and finance. Macaulay argued that Indians should be taught Western subjects and the English language instead of Arabic and Sanskrit. This was seen as imperative to disseminate moral values as well as maintain and strengthen British rule in India. On Macaulay's advice, English was made the medium of education in secondary schools established in major cities across India.

"How, then, stands the case? We have to educate a people who cannot at present be educated by means of their mother-tongue. We must teach them some foreign language. The claims of our own language it is hardly necessary to recapitulate. It stands pre-eminent even among the languages of the west. It abounds with works of imagination not inferior to the noblest which Greece has bequeathed to us; with models of every species of eloquence; with historical compositions, which, considered merely as narratives, have seldom been surpassed, and which, considered as vehicles of ethical and political instruction, have never been equalled; with just and lively representations of human life and human nature; with the most profound speculations on metaphysics, morals, government, jurisprudence, and trade; with full and correct information respecting every experimental science which tends to preserve the health, to increase the comfort, or to expand the intellect of man. Whoever knows that language has ready access to all the vast intellectual wealth, which all the wisest nations of the earth have created and hoarded in the course of ninety generations. It may safely be said, that the literature now extant in that language is of far greater value than all the literature which three hundred years ago was extant in all the languages of the world together. Nor is this all. In India, English is the language spoken by the ruling class. It is spoken by the higher class of natives at the seats of Government. It is likely to become the language of commerce throughout the seas of the East. It is the language of two great European communities which are rising, the one in the south of Africa, the other in Australasia; communities which are every year becoming more important, and more closely connected with our Indian empire. Whether we look at the intrinsic value of our

literature, or at the particular situation of this country, we shall see the strongest reason to think that, of all foreign tongues, the English tongue is, that which would be the most useful to our native subjects. . . .

"To sum up what I have said, I think it clear that we are not fettered by the Act of Parliament of 1813; that we are not fettered by any pledge expressed or implied; that we are free to employ our funds as we choose; that we ought to employ them in teaching what is best worth knowing; that English is better worth knowing than Sanscrit or Arabic; that the natives are desirous to be taught English, and are not desirous to be taught Sanscrit or Arabic; that neither as the languages of law, nor as the languages of religion, have the Sanscrit and Arabic any peculiar claim to our engagement; that it is possible to make natives of this country thoroughly good English scholars, and that to this end our efforts ought to be directed.

"In one point I fully agree with the gentlemen to whose general views I am opposed. I feel with them, that it is impossible for us, with our limited means, to attempt to educate the body of the people. We must at present do our best to form a class who may be interpreters between us and the millions whom we govern; a class of persons, Indian in blood and colour, but English in taste, in opinions, in morals, and in intellect. To that class we may leave it to refine the vernacular dialects of the country, to enrich those dialects with terms of science borrowed from the Western nomenclature, and to render them by degrees fit vehicles for conveying knowledge to the great mass of the population."

G. M. Young (ed.), Speeches by Lord Macaulay with His Minute on Indian Education, Oxford University Press, 1935.

The Case of Captain Cook The new ideological underpinnings of the emergent liberal empire were exemplified by Captain James Cook's expeditions to the South Pacific. The prototypical colonialist of the Enlightenment, Cook's explicit goals were not merely commercial but also scientific: his voyage was part of a series of eighteenth-century expeditions to explore this region, the last maritime frontier for Europeans, and, in

particular, to locate the missing continent, known as *Terra Australis*. Toward this end, a team of more than twenty ethnographers, geographers, botanists, and other scientific experts, accompanied Cook on his South Seas voyages.

Cook's voyages to the South Pacific also bore traces of Europeans' new moral scruples in their interactions with non-Europeans. Unlike earlier generations of colonizers,

Cook and his contemporaries were self-conscious about the delicate nature of their enterprise and sought to justify their intrusion with the lofty goals of advancing science and spreading civilization. As universalists, they accorded rights to non-Europeans; as cultural relativists, they ascribed value to cultural difference. In practical terms, this meant that King George III authorized Cook to establish British authority in Hawaii in 1779, for example, but cautioned him to do so only with the express consent of the natives; similarly, the Royal Scientific Society, one of the chief backers of the voyage, instructed Cook to treat the local customs and culture with the utmost respect. In ways such as these, late-eighteenth-century colonizers sought not only to legitimize their role as civilizers in the eyes of the colonized but to reinforce their own identities as the civilized by divorcing themselves from the brutality of their imperial precursors.

The Civilizing Mission in India   In the early nineteenth century, India was the laboratory in which Britain conducted its most ambitious civilizing experiments. While evangelical missionaries such as Charles Grant and William Wilberforce sought to bring religious enlightenment and to stamp out Indian "superstition," secular liberal reformers like Jeremy Bentham, James Mill, his son, John Stuart Mill, and Thomas Macaulay determined to rid India of "Oriental despotism" by eradicating "barbaric" Indian laws and customs and introducing a British-style educational system (see "Macaulay's Minute on Indian Education," p. 736). Macaulay claimed that the "entire native literature of India and Arabia" was not worth "a single shelf of a good European library," asserting that a British model of education was needed to produce "a class of persons Indian in blood and color, but English in taste, in opinions, in morals and intellect." The potent triad of law, education, and free trade, British reformers believed, would bring the hopelessly backward Indians into the modern world.

Liberal reformers sought to apply liberal ideas to eliminate the barriers of custom and tradition and managed to bring about several important policy changes in India. One of the controversial reforms was to prohibit *sati*, the practice of the widow burning herself to death on the funeral pyre of her dead husband.

For the British, *sati* epitomized both the moral weakness of Indian men, who degraded rather than protected their women, and the general backwardness of Indian civilization as a whole. Although *sati* became a key public symbol of the liberal reform agenda, it was not, in fact, a widespread practice, but was actually limited only to certain groups of upper-caste Hindus.

British civilizing efforts came to an abrupt halt, however, with the Indian Rebellion of 1857 (see "The Indian Rebellion of 1857," pp. 758–760). Hereafter, British officials ceded issues of Indian reform to Indian social reformers, because they saw their interference in Indian religion and ritual as one of the key causes of the discontent that had sparked the rebellion.

EUROPEAN EXPANSION IN THE MIDCENTURY

During the first two-thirds of the nineteenth century, European commercial involvements in Africa and Asia intensified, and Europeans acted to protect their economic interests in new, more assertive ways. This intensification was driven primarily by industrialization in Britain and, with that, the rise of British economic, military, and technological might. Although other western European nations behaved similarly, it was the British who took the initiative in aggressively developing and safeguarding overseas commercial contacts during this period.

India and the Rise of British Sovereignty

The economic penetration of Asia in the nineteenth century exploited commercial ties between Europe and the East cultivated over the course of several centuries. From the seventeenth century on, joint stock companies—the Dutch, the French, and the English East India companies—were the chief players in a European-Asian trade based on the exchange of Asian spices, silks, and other luxury goods for European specie. By the early eighteenth century, Europeans, including the representatives of the East India Companies, clustered in what were known as "factories"—trading posts—along the coasts from India to Java, the Philippines, and China, in ports such as Bombay, Batavia, and Canton. Although traders and trading companies of several nationalities could be found in any of these locations, different nations dominated the Asian trade in periods. The Portuguese were leaders in the sixteenth- and seventeenth-century trade with Asia, superseded by the Dutch in the late seventeenth century and by the French and British in the early eighteenth century.

The British East India Company   Until the middle of the eighteenth century, nothing distinguished the British East India Company from the other companies in Asia. This state of affairs changed dramatically in 1757, when the decisive victory over the nawab of Bengal in the Battle of Plassey catapulted the British to ascendancy in Asia and, indeed, the world (see chapter 18). Plassey's significance was both economic and symbolic: it dealt a crushing blow to the already weak Mughal Empire, fortified the British East India Company as a political power within the subcontinent, and gave Britain access to enormous Indian wealth. The capture of Bengal thus gave the

British East India Company a firm base for territorial expansion in India over the course of the next century.

The conquest brought economic disaster to Bengal, until then a flourishing center of Indian commerce and industry (and the source of 75 percent of the British East India Company's trade). Before 1757, the British had paid for Bengali textiles, metal goods, and spices in silver bullion from the New World. With the conquest secured, the British used Bengali land revenues to pay for Bengali goods and assumed direct control of Bengal's external trade. As the British expanded out of Bengal, this same pattern repeated itself all over India. The British conquest thus transformed the Indian economy into a closed system, forcing India through taxation to effectively give away its exports to Britain and severing its independent trade connections with the outside world.

British rule in India also irrevocably altered the structure and orientation of the Indian economy. As it industrialized at the turn of nineteenth century, Britain stopped importing Indian calicoes and other textiles, transforming India into a supplier of raw materials (especially cotton and indigo) for British textile mills as well as a major market for British manufactures. As a consequence, Indian manufacturing went into decline, with British imports accounting for more than half of India's textile consumption by the 1840s. In addition, the commercialization of Indian agriculture led to the abandonment of subsistence farming, leaving the Indian peasantry more vulnerable than ever to famine.

Further British Expansion in Asia

The British East India Company's conquest of India also promoted British expansionism elsewhere in central Asia, as the company sought to extend its power and influence in neighboring territories to protect its Indian empire. Their chief adversary was Russia, which harbored imperial ambitions in the region. In the 1840s Britain annexed Punjab and Sind, to the west of India, as buffer zones against the Russians. When the British tried to do the same to Afghanistan, they met with stubborn resistance in the Afghan Wars of 1839–1842 and 1878–1880. Although the British never formally colonized Afghanistan, it became, for all practical purposes, a client state by the 1880s. Simultaneously, the fiercely independent kingdom of Burma (Myanmar) harassed the British on the northeastern frontier of the Indian Empire. After a series of Anglo-Burmese wars fought in 1826, 1852, and 1886, the British annexed Burma.

The "Sick Men": The Ottoman Empire and China

While the British tightened their territorial stranglehold over Mughal India, Europeans took a fundamentally different approach to the other two major non-Western empires, that of the Ottomans and Qing China. Labeled respectively the "Sick Man of Europe" and the "Sick Man of the East," the Ottoman Empire and Qing China were perceived as ailing polities. But in contrast to the military conquest and direct rule of Mughal India, Europeans exploited the Chinese and Ottoman empires through financial subjugation and political maneuvering. This strategy avoided the costs of direct rule, which promised to be especially high because the Qing and the Ottomans were relatively successful at holding their empires together. It also allowed Europeans to use the empires as buffers against Russian and Japanese expansionism.

The Ottoman Empire

The Ottoman Empire was ripe for this kind of infiltration by the nineteenth century. The empire was still vast, stretching from Algeria in the west to the borders of Persia and Arabia in the east and from the Balkans in the north to Egypt and Sudan in the south, but its power had declined sharply from its peak point in the sixteenth century. While the predominantly Muslim identity of Ottoman subjects gave the empire some political and cultural cohesion, the ambitions of provincial governors were challenging the authority of the Sultan, Mahmud II.

Hoping to rejuvenate the empire, the sultan himself attempted to initiate a program of administrative, legal, and technological Westernization known as the *Tanzimat* (reorganization) reforms in the 1830s. Although he faced strong resistance to his efforts on the part of the Muslim military and clerics who feared the pollution of Islamic culture by the West, the European powers, especially the British, supported his efforts for their own diplomatic and political reasons. This support turned into Ottoman dependency on Britain in 1838, when the sultan asked the British to intervene militarily to restore Ottoman control in Syria, which had been seized by the breakaway Ottoman province of Egypt in 1831. In return for military assistance, the British and French demanded the full implementation of Tanzimat, along with trade privileges and extraterritorial judicial rights for themselves.

By the early 1840s, the sultan's efforts to check the burgeoning power of the Europeans faltered and the Ottoman Empire became a de facto economic colony of the British, forced to export raw materials (cotton, cereals, opium) to Britain and to import British manufactures (textiles, machinery) in large quantities. These new arrangements dealt a near-fatal blow to local Ottoman handicraft industries, especially textile production. Economic dependence turned into subjugation during the Crimean War (1852–1854) (see chapter 23), when the Ottoman government borrowed money on extremely unfavorable terms from the French and the British to subsidize its military mobilization. The formation of the Ottoman Public Debt Commission in 1881 formalized British and French control of the bankrupt Ottoman economy, including taxation, tariffs, and the provincial tribute system.

European financial involvement was not without social and cultural repercussions. The once culturally cohesive Ottoman Empire fragmented across ethnic and religious lines as the British and the French sought to align themselves with non-Muslim Ottoman minorities. Local Christian and Jewish intermediaries who facilitated the economic transactions of British and French merchants were permitted to buy European passports, which qualified them for the same judicial immunity granted to Europeans. Economic considerations only partially motivated the Europeans, who also saw themselves as the civilizers of a degenerate "Oriental" empire, shoring up Christianity and rooting out all traces of "despotism." Overall, internal discord within the empire grew as privileged groups profited from a European presence that brought extensive suffering to peasants and artisans.

China The narrative of imperial domination was roughly similar in China. At the turn of the nineteenth century, the ruling Qing Dynasty, members of the foreign Manchu minority who had ruled China since the mid-seventeenth century, enjoyed considerable economic prosperity and sought to extend the boundaries of the empire in Asia. However, they remained resolutely isolated from and indifferent to Europe. Not only did the Chinese remain unaware of the culture of Enlightenment influencing elites in Europe, North America, and South America, but they also exhibited no interest in European manufactures. By contrast, Europeans long had been eager consumers of Chinese tea, silk, porcelain, and paper, among other goods.

This imbalance was dramatically reversed in the late eighteenth century, when opium smoking became an entrenched practice at all levels of Chinese society. Despite an official ban on opium imports, the Chinese demand for opium skyrocketed as the British East India Company, followed by other European merchants, flooded the Chinese market with cheap Indian-produced opium, which they used to pay for Chinese goods, especially tea. By the turn of the nineteenth century, this situation had wreaked economic and social havoc. Not only did the Chinese experience huge silver shortages as Europeans stopped paying for Chinese imports with metal specie, but opium addiction was debilitating large segments of Chinese society. In 1840, when the emperor tried to gain control of the situation by blockading the port of Canton and seizing the opium supplies of foreign merchants, the British sent a naval force to defy him. The Opium War of 1840–1842 ended in Chinese defeat. The Treaty of Nanjing ceded Hong

In this American newspaper cartoon of 1864, England, personified by John Bull, forces China to accept opium at gunpoint. The Opium Wars, which erupted when the Chinese attempted to restrict the opium trade in the midcentury, ended in Chinese defeat and in treaties conferring extraordinary economic and legal privileges on the European victors. How did European encroachment in China differ from the European conquest of India?
The Granger Collection, NY

Kong to Britain, gave the British trading rights in five ports, and forced the Chinese to pay an indemnity for the war. A second Opium War (1856–1858), fought over the same issues, also ended in Chinese defeat and the ceding of extraterritorial rights, trading privileges, and missionary protection to Britain, France, the United States, and Russia. When the Qing emperor refused to ratify the peace treaties, British and French forces occupied Peking in 1860 and burned the emperor's imperial gardens at the Summer Palace, while Russia obtained Vladivostock.

Fomented by the economic hardships and political humiliation brought by the Opium War, the bloody Taiping Rebellion of 1850–1864 further destabilized Chinese politics and society. A millenarian peasant movement to overthrow the European-dominated Qing regime and establish a harmonious, egalitarian society, the rebellion ravaged the Chinese countryside, with a staggering death toll of twenty million. In the mid-1850s, the European powers intervened militarily in the conflict, acting to safeguard their trading privileges. By 1864, the Western-trained "Ever-Victorious Army," under the leadership of General Charles "Chinese" Gordon, definitively quashed the rebellion, although sporadic resistance continued in parts of the country until 1868. The European role in rescuing the floundering Qing Dynasty greatly strengthened European commercial interests in China.

Although the British constructed an economically exploitative relationship with China during the nineteenth century, they never formally colonized it (except for Hong Kong). Moreover, because European traders remained clustered in port cites, foreigners did not penetrate Chinese society to the extent that they did elsewhere. Even so, British-Chinese relations had deeply colonial overtones. From the British point of view, China's economic subjugation was part of a larger plan to make empire self-financing. India was at the center of this system, both as a model of economic exploitation and as a source of cheaply obtained goods that the British used to trade with others. By the turn of the nineteenth century, the British had incorporated the Chinese into this arrangement; since the British bought opium at a mere pittance from Indian producers, they effectively forced India to finance Britain's trade with China. Like India, China lost access to the silver bullion that the British formerly had used to buy its goods, but China also squandered its metal reserves to sustain its debilitating opium habit. In both cases, overtaxed peasants bore the brunt of lost government revenues, fomenting political unrest in the countryside.

Expansion in Southeast Asia and the Pacific Rim

European engagement in India and China led to further expansion in Southeast Asia. In Australia and New Zealand, Europeans established settler colonies in this period, while in Japan, their attempts to exert influence met with failure for the first time.

Southeast Asia　To safeguard the critical trade route between India and China, the British East India Company sought to establish fortified settlements in Southeast Asia from the 1780s on. They seized the opportunity to consolidate their position when the Dutch—the most important European power in the area—asked the British to oversee their Southeast Asian holdings during the French revolutionary occupation of the Netherlands starting in 1795. Although the Dutch resumed control of these holdings in 1808, the episode provided the British with additional territory and whetted their appetite for greater involvement in the region. By the 1820s, they had emerged as the preeminent European commercial presence in Southeast Asia, in possession of the valuable ports of Penang, Malacca, and Singapore (known collectively as the Straits Settlements).

This flourishing British-dominated trade economy, however, soon came to an abrupt halt. With the passage of the Charter Act of 1833, the British East India Company lost its monopoly of the China trade and the company's interest in the India-China trade route waned sharply. While the British no longer valued Southeast Asia as a trade depot, they did develop an interest in the region as a source of raw materials, investing in tin mining and rubber production. In this way, Southeast Asia entered into the classic colonial economic arrangement, producing raw materials for industrial production in Europe.

Meanwhile, kingdoms and chiefdoms outside of the British sphere of interest were also being gradually drawn into the European orbit. Even Siam (Thailand), often touted as the exception to the rule, ultimately lost its political and cultural sovereignty, if not its formal political independence, to the British. The process began in the 1820s and 1830s, when the Siamese monarch abandoned a century-long isolationist policy and resumed relations with Europe, negotiating trade treaties and relinquishing some of Siam's border territories in the interests of maintaining the kingdom's political independence. While he managed to fend off direct conquest, he did so in part by launching an ambitious program of Westernization, including the implementation of a European-style educational system and the appointment of foreign advisors to the government. While the fiction of independence was maintained, Siamese policy decisions were essentially dictated by foreign advisors or made within the context of the competing European interests in the region. Following a pattern emerging in many parts of the world, the Siamese king's decision to modernize along Western lines constituted a form of implicit colonization.

The Pacific Rim　There were a few notable exceptions to the European pattern of implicit colonization in the Pacific Rim. The conquest of Australia and New Zealand and establishment of settler colonies there deviated sharply from the ideology of liberal paternalism and practices of economic imperialism that characterized European ventures abroad during the early nineteenth century. The narrative of settlement in Australasia instead mirrored the conquest of the Americas in the seventeenth and eighteenth centuries in its strident frontier mentality, thirst for land, and unapologetic decimation of indigenous populations.

Although the British government claimed Australia as a penal colony—and a humane alternative to capital punishment—in 1788, the government nonetheless opposed the emigration of free labor there as a drain on British manpower. Land-hungry settlers came anyway, in pursuit of economic opportunity. British settlement in Australia increased in the 1840s as the first generations of free settlers offered cash incentives to try to induce more and more affluent Britons to emigrate.

Emigration soared after the Australian Gold Rush of 1851. New Zealand followed a similar path. British settlers began to arrive in 1839, enticed by the foundation of the New Zealand Trading Company, even though the British government actively discouraged emigration.

As increasing numbers of settlers poured in—over a million British citizens emigrated in the 1850s alone, most of them to Australia—the British government grew more psychologically invested in its settler colonies and came to perceive emigration as a demographic and economic necessity. The preponderance of British-descended settlers in these colonies, known as "the White Dominions," naturally afforded them a uniquely privileged position in the colonial hierarchy. Over time British settlers began to self-identify as natives of the region and, as that happened, to press for self-government. They achieved that status incrementally. In the 1850s, Britain granted New Zealand and Australia limited autonomy. It conferred Dominion status—a classification that offered domestic autonomy to the settler colonies but retained British control over foreign policy and trade—first on Canada in 1867, then on Australia and New Zealand in 1907, and South Africa in 1910.

White settlement in Australasia devastated indigenous populations and destroyed existing economies, just as it had in North and South America. European diseases killed most of the local inhabitants. Of those who survived, most were forced off their land by expropriating settlers. They also lost major food sources as entire ecosystems were destroyed by settlers seeking to turn forest and prairie into farmland. The British government offered crucial military support for settlers and made the displacement of local peoples a violent affair. In New Zealand, for example, both the settlers and the British government signed the Waitangi Treaty in 1840 promising indigenous Maoris protection of their land rights, but the settlers quickly reneged on their promises. When the Maoris fought back and the settlers were drawn into armed conflict with them, the British government ultimately intervened to savagely crush Maori resistance during the 1860s.

Japan   Only Japan managed to escape European rule, implicit or explicit, in nineteenth-century Asia. Nonetheless, during the first two-thirds of the century, it appeared that Japan would follow in China's footsteps. Starting with Russian interference in the late eighteenth century, Europeans and Americans tried to end Japanese isolationism and foster trading contacts. Once the American naval commander Commodore Matthew Perry induced the Japanese Tokugawa government to sign a treaty opening some of its ports to Western trade in 1854, other major European nations soon followed suit. By midcentury, the European penetration of Japan was under way, although on a considerably smaller scale than in China.

But Japan was to radically shift course with the downfall of the Tokugawa regime and the advent of the revolutionary Meiji Restoration in 1868. Meiji leaders dismantled an essentially feudal system that had lasted

At the turn of the nineteenth century, the Scottish explorer Mungo Park led two ill-fated expeditions to west Africa to explore the course of the Niger River. This drawing, the frontispiece of his book, *Travels in the Interior of Africa*, shows him, assisted by local guides, as he locates the Niger for the first time. Explorers' accounts such as Park's were enormously popular reading and helped stoke public interest in Africa.

for seven centuries by promoting rapid-fire industrialization of the economy and Westernizing key aspects of the government and educational system. Industrialization rapidly catapulted Japan to the status of a global economic competitor. It also made Japan strong enough to retain control of the Westernization process, thus preempting the kind of covert European colonialism experienced elsewhere in Asia. Instead, Japan was able not only to revise the unequal trade treaties it had signed with the West at midcentury, but to emerge as a world political player and an imperialist nation in its own right, forcing trade concessions from Korea and extending its influence there starting in 1873.

The European Awakening to Africa

Perhaps the greatest imperial shift of the nineteenth century was in the European stance toward Africa. Before the late eighteenth century, the vast majority of Europeans had paltry knowledge of Africa and, in marked contrast to the New World and the South Seas, scant interest in it. In maps, writings, and visual imagery, Europeans tended to imagine Africa as outside the bounds of civilization: a hostile natural terrain whose few human inhabitants were savage brutes bereft of civilization. The fact that Africans had constituted the primary labor source for the Atlantic slave economy for four centuries only reinforced this notion of Africa as beyond the human pale.

New Interest in Africa In large measure, European ignorance and indifference stemmed from a lack of contact with Africa. Apart from Portuguese slave traders, who settled along the west African coast (Angola), French traders in the Senegambia region (Senegal), and Dutch and English settlers on the Cape of Good Hope at the southern tip of Africa, Europeans had little experience of Africa.

This pattern of negligible contact changed at the turn of the nineteenth century. As a capitalist economy based on free enterprise took shape in western Europe, Africa came into focus as a potential marketplace. For the first time, Europeans perceived Africa both as a source of raw materials to feed its industrial economy (peanut and palm oil from West Africa, for example, were used to lubricate industrial machinery) and as an outlet for its new manufactures. Thinking about Africa's economic potential in this way meant imagining it as a site of civilization in a way Europeans had never before done: an Africa that could be a European trading partner was an Africa that had states, cities, and markets of its own. The late-eighteenth-century formation of the African Association, dedicated to British commercial expansion in Africa, reflected this sudden surge of awareness of Africa's commercial potential. The best known of the

Association's agents was the explorer Mungo Park, whose expeditions up the Niger River in West Central Africa in 1795 and 1805 brought him into contact with the sophisticated Fulani and Bambara states, confirming hopes that Africa possessed the commercial infrastructure to become a significant British trading partner.

But if Park's expeditions exemplified the new interest in Africa, they also demonstrated the obstacles to European penetration in the early nineteenth century. The devastation of both his expeditions by illness curbed the enthusiasm of would-be explorers. Disease posed a formidable barrier to the European pursuit of African commercial ties until the middle of the nineteenth century. Unlike the New World, where European strains of disease virtually obliterated indigenous peoples, in Africa it was the local inhabitants who had the advantage. Dysentery, yellow fever, typhoid, and, above all, malaria decimated European visitors so predictably that nineteenth-century Africa became widely known by the epithet "The White Man's Grave." Standard remedies for malaria were either ineffective or—as in the case of dosing with mercury—lethal. Not until the 1820s did European chemists discover that quinine, a substance from the bark of the South American cinchona tree, could treat malaria. By the 1850s, Europeans realized that the prophylactic use of quinine prevented the contraction of the disease. Yet, even though improvements in the treatment and prevention of malaria and other tropical diseases by midcentury made European infiltration of Africa possible, death rates from disease remained so high that, as late as the 1870s, more European soldiers involved in African military campaigns died from disease than from warfare.

Africa's topography, with its jungles, deserts, and complex river systems, also impeded European access to the continent. The early-nineteenth-century advent of the steamboat, which applied James Watt's steam engine to boat travel, greatly facilitated the exploration of continental interiors by river in Africa, as well as in Asia and Australia. Not only could steamboats navigate independent of wind conditions, but the power of the steam engine allowed them to travel against the current at high speeds. After steamboats were in use, Europeans were able to gain access to virtually every region in Africa, with the notable exception of areas lacking navigable waterways such as the Horn of Africa (these areas, not incidentally, were among the last to be colonized). Even so, steamboat exploration in Africa remained difficult for some time, in part because steamboats had to be dismantled, carried in sections around rapids, and then reassembled.

Missionaries and Explorers By the middle of the nineteenth century, many of the obstacles preventing European expansion into Africa thus had been removed.

Missionaries, many of them abolitionist evangelicals seeking to end slavery in Africa, often ventured first into the African interior. They strove not merely to save souls, as their early modern predecessors had, but to Europeanize native subjects whom they now saw as more primitive brethren. Likewise, they saw the cultivation of commerce and the conversion to Christianity as mutually reinforcing goals, since both were part of the overall civilizing process that would ultimately elevate non-Europeans to the level of Europeans. Mission stations in the African interior quickly attracted other Europeans, in particular traders, who made use of missionary expertise and contacts with the local population for commercial ends. In seeking government backing and protection, moreover, missionaries also promoted European political involvement in Africa.

Following in the footsteps of missionaries, explorers raised public interest in Africa to a fever pitch by midcentury. Most explorers were unknown adventurers who publicized their exploits in book form and on lecture tours in the hope of raising money for their expeditions from the government, scientific authorities, and the general public. The most successful were often the most skilled speakers and rhetoricians, able to dramatize their experiences and aggrandize their contributions. Many of these became national icons. Among the best known was David Livingstone, a missionary-explorer who described his dual quest to open central Africa to commerce and religion in his book *Missionary Travels* (1857). A distinctly different model of the explorer as adventurer and entrepreneur was represented by Henry Stanley, an Anglo-American hired by the *New York Herald* to find Livingstone when the latter was thought to be missing in the Central Congo. Stanley became an overnight celebrity with the publication of his great scoop, *How I Found Livingstone*, in 1872.

While explorers' encounters brought Africa to life for European audiences, they also provided Europeans with

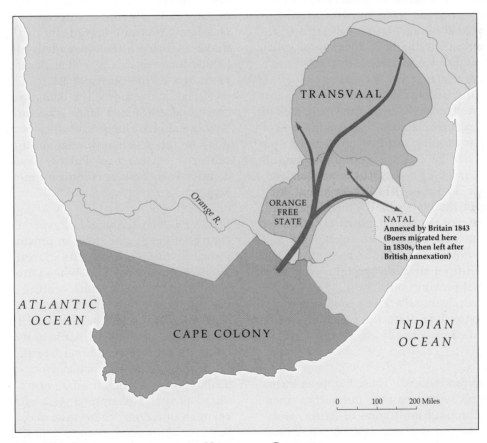

MAP 25.1 SOUTHERN AFRICA IN THE NINETEENTH CENTURY
Friction between Afrikaner and British settlers in southern Africa sparked Afrikaner emigration from the Cape Colony during the 1830s and 1840s (the Great Trek) and led to the establishment of independent Afrikaner republics. British expansionist aspirations, intensified by the discovery of diamonds and gold in Afrikaner territory in the late nineteenth century, threatened the long-term survival of the republics. They were absorbed into British South Africa after the Boer War of 1889–1902. How did conflict between Europeans and Africans in the region affect the intra-European conflict?

extensive misinformation and helped to fashion an increasingly negative portrait of African cultures and societies. Henry Stanley's writings, for example, influenced Europeans in their association of darkness—defined variously as savagery, irrationality, and immorality—with Africa. Stanley's exploits captured the imagination of writers and intellectuals, including the American novelist Edgar Rice Burroughs (*Tarzan of the Apes*, [1912]) and the Polish-English novelist Joseph Conrad (*Heart of Darkness* [1902]).

Expansion into the Interior European traders and settlers on the African coast also began to spread out of established enclaves into new areas in the interior during this period. In the southwest, the Portuguese extended their holdings in present-day Angola. In the northwest, the French moved inland from the coastal city of Saint Louis into modern-day Senegal. They also expanded from Algiers—conquered in a military invasion in 1830—into the Algerian interior. French troops spent the better part of the 1840s and 1850s trying to consolidate their holdings in Algeria, fighting a costly and difficult war with well-armed Algerian guerrillas under the leadership of Abdelkader. By 1869 France claimed Algeria as a colony.

In southern Africa, fifteen thousand Afrikaners migrated north of the Orange River in the Great Trek of 1835–1845, fleeing British control and seeking land of their own. Despite ongoing battles over territory with Bantus, in particular the Zulus (a southern Bantu people), the Afrikaners flourished as cattle ranchers and, by the late 1830s, had established independent Afrikaner republics in the Natal, the Orange Free State, and the Transvaal. For the British, however, Afrikaner expansionism threatened their own sovereignty and plans for further expansion in southern Africa. To cut the Afrikaners off from strategic coastal access, they annexed the Natal province outright in 1843 and, although the British eventually recognized the sovereignty of the Orange Free State and the Transvaal in 1854, they meddled continually in Bantu-Afrikaner conflicts.

Clashes with African Powers These European incursions did not meet with a passive, quiescent Africa. Parallel to the European infiltration of Africa, widespread internal war and conquest destabilized African politics and economic life in large parts of the continent during the early to mid-nineteenth century. In particular, Zulu political ambitions in southern Africa and the theocratic aims of Islamic jihad states in West Africa during this period created political and economic upheaval across broad swathes of Africa. In many cases, African polities on the move collided with expansionist Europeans, often ending in violent confrontation.

The sudden ascendancy of the Zulus in South Africa in the early nineteenth century was a case in point. In the 1820s, the military genius Shaka Zulu built a powerful and extensive Zulu empire in the Natal region, sparking major disturbances in southern Africa. Although many inhabitants of the area capitulated outright to Shaka's dominion, his raiding armies also drove many other Bantu peoples, including the Ndebele, to seek refuge elsewhere. As huge numbers of Bantus fled the Zulus south into British territory and north into the Afrikaner republics, Bantus and Afrikaners warred continually over land. The Zulus themselves also battled Afrikaners who migrated north into Zulu dominions in 1837–1838, as well as the British, most notably in the Anglo-Zulu War of 1878–1879. Although the latter marked the first defeat of a European power by an African force in the Battle of Isandhlwana, the British ultimately crushed the Zulus.

The expansion of Islam in Africa during this period also triggered great turmoil. In the late eighteenth century and early nineteenth century, a fundamentalist Islamic revival emerged among the Fulani people in West Africa. The Fulani reviled indigenous religious beliefs and practices as well as European Christianity as threats to the purity of Islam. Overthrowing the local Hausa chieftains, the Fulani established an enduring decentralized state structure known as the Sokoto caliphate in 1809, which waged *jihad*—holy war—to impose Islam throughout the region. By midcentury, expansionist Fulani jihadists came into conflict with French colonizers moving east out of Senegal.

European Encroachment in Egypt Europeans sought control of Egypt, an Ottoman province since the sixteenth century, because of its strategic location on the Red Sea en route to India. When Ottoman control wavered in the late eighteenth century, Napoleon seized the opportunity to invade Egypt in 1798, although British forces, backed by Ottoman Turks, ultimately destroyed his fleet in the Battle of the Nile. Although the Ottomans regained nominal rule of the province, the Sultan lost control when Mohammed Ali, an Albanian officer in the Ottoman army of reoccupation, seized power. Mohammed Ali's efforts to establish Egyptian autonomy were thwarted, however, by the Sultan's continued resistance and British and French commercial interests in Egypt. By midcentury, Europeans controlled a large portion of Egypt's trade and European bankers were financing modernization projects. These included constructing an Egyptian railway system from Alexandria to Cairo and building the Suez Canal connecting the Red Sea to the Mediterranean Sea under Ferdinand Lesseps's direction from 1859 to 1869.

THE NEW IMPERIALISM, 1870–1914

In the closing decades of the nineteenth century, Europeans remapped the contours of empire. By the 1870s, the piecemeal expansionism of the earlier part of the century gave way to a systematic campaign of explicit conquest and occupation of much of Africa and Asia. This global conquest is often described as the "new imperialism" to differentiate it from earlier forms of empire. Indeed, while late-nineteenth-century imperialism was built on many of the same ideological foundations as the midcentury empire and endorsed the liberal civilizing mission at the outset, it soon metamorphosed into a distinctive intellectual and material enterprise.

Four features of the new imperialism stand out as novel. First, late-nineteenth-century European nations adopted imperialism as an official policy for the first time, replacing empires governed largely by traders with those ruled by expansionist states. Although European nation-states had sponsored imperial expansion earlier in the century, they had most often done so after the fact, in an effort to protect and promote the activities of their missionaries and merchants overseas; now it was the state that took the imperial initiative. Second, the entrance of a new group of nations into the race for territory during this period changed the rules of the imperial game. In Europe, Germany, Belgium, and Italy appeared on the imperial scene, while outside Europe, the United States and Japan emerged as major imperial powers. As multiple players competed aggressively for territory and power, Britain's longstanding global sovereignty began to fade. Third, the more competitive imperial climate changed the political objectives of imperial nations. No longer content with informal influence, they now sought explicit territorial occupation and political conquest. Finally, the new imperialism defined its own distinctive ideological mission, gradually abandoning the universalist premise of the liberal empire for a belief in the unbreachable gap between Europe and its colonial subjects. As that happened, Europeans began to retreat from the civilizing goals of the early to midcentury and to seek increasingly to secure and consolidate imperial rule through force. Unfettered by the moral constraints of early nineteenth-century colonizers, the new imperialism brought Europe to the peak of its power.

Europe Transformed: Explaining the New Imperialism

No single factor can explain the new imperialism. Rather, it emerged out of a number of significant changes that occurred in Europe during the second half of the nineteenth century.

Technology By the late nineteenth century, Europeans had access to new and astonishingly efficient technologies that would change the course of colonial conquest and domination. To be sure, technology

In 1897, the British troops attacked and looted the Edo capital of Benin, in present-day southern Nigeria. The Benin expedition was a punitive one, responding to the ambush of a British military party sent to force trade concessions from the Edo king a year earlier. This photograph shows British officers of the expedition surrounded by booty, including the famed Benin bronzes, seized from the royal compound. The plundered objects ended up in European and American art museums.
Courtesy of the Trustees of The British Museum

had played a major role in spreading European influence abroad throughout the nineteenth century and earlier; steamships, industrial weaponry, and the use of quinine to treat malaria had allowed Europeans to penetrate continental Africa, and the arrival of gunboats—armed steamboats—had played decisive roles, for example, in the conquest of Burma and the opening of China. Nevertheless, the advent of the second industrial revolution (see chapter 24) in the late nineteenth century made technology an even more important factor in the speed, extent, and vigor of the conquests. Ironclad warships with steam turbines now spread the power of far more advanced and deadly European weaponry overseas, while the invention of the telegraph radically simplified the logistics of military mobilization from afar. After conquest, dynamite lessened the difficulty of building roads, and modern medicine significantly reduced the dangers of fighting and living in the tropics.

Nationalism　While turn-of-the-century technologies made possible conquest on a global scale, they did not create new incentives to conquer. Most historians would agree that it was nationalism—understood in the broadest sense of the term—that propelled the new imperialism forward. Although nationalism was hardly new, it developed in strikingly new ways during this period. The ideological tenor of nationalism changed, moving away from its early-nineteenth-century romantic and liberal origins and tilting toward a more strident, aggressive, and exclusionary variant. Nationalism was transformed, in other words, from a phenomenon associated with the democratic and liberal left to one linked to the emergence of a new mass politics on the right. Based on emotional appeals to community and history, the new nationalism challenged the liberal politics of the midcentury based on the rational individual and the possibilities of societal progress. Imperial domination, in this context, was seen as a sign of national vigor and a marker of prestige.

Nationalism also played an integral role in the rise of a new political and economic order of nation-states in this period. Germany's national unification transformed it overnight into one of the foremost continental powers. Its meteoric economic and political ascent, along with the emergence of Japan and the United States as industrial giants, fundamentally reconfigured the global balance of power and in so doing changed the stakes of empire. The new order sharply challenged British global sovereignty, unrivaled since the late eighteenth century, and demoted Britain's lagging rival, France, to a third-rate power. On the economic and political defensive, Britain and France sought to expand their empires to compensate for their loss of economic primacy and political prestige. Germany, Japan, and the United States responded in turn by carving out their own colonial empires.

Economic Factors　Within this charged nationalist framework, economic, political, and cultural forces each played their role in promoting the imperial scramble. Economic factors were critical. As they had done earlier in the century, turn-of-the-century imperial nations viewed their colonies as vital markets for selling European industrial goods, buying raw materials and cash crops, and investing surplus capital. But now the economic context had changed. One new factor was the presence of Germany and the United States as leading industrial powers. By 1890 both Germany and the United States had surpassed British steel and iron production and Germany was outselling the British in certain overseas markets (Latin America, China, and the Ottoman Empire). A lengthy industrial depression from 1873 to the early 1890s played a significant role as well. This unstable economic context promoted the view that colonial markets could act as buffers against the fluctuations of global commerce. As a consequence, the western European nations started to abandon the rhetoric of free trade in the 1880s and 1890s, once again endorsing mercantilist policies that—in addition to raising trade barriers in the domestic market—explicitly demarcated the colonies as protected economic spheres. Finally, the advent of a new, more advanced phase of industrial capitalism in the late nineteenth century brought with it fears of saturation of the domestic market and, with that, industrial overproduction. In this context, many Europeans came to view empire as an essential outlet for surpluses of goods and capital.

As scholars of empire have pointed out, however, economic incentives alone cannot account for the new imperialism, and nation-states often pursued imperial objectives even when their economic costs appeared to outweigh their benefits. Undoubtedly, the colonies furnished attractive markets for Europe's industrial manufactures in the late nineteenth century; in 1890 Britain exported one-third of its industrial goods and one-quarter of its investment capital to India. However, strictly in terms of trade volume, European nations traded far more with other independent countries, including their European neighbors, than they did with their colonies. Britain, the largest overseas investor and trader, traded more with Latin America and the United States, for example, than with its African or even its Asian colonies. Moreover, it was not always the most industrialized, economically powerful nations that took the imperial initiative. Although France lagged far behind Germany as an industrial producer, for example, it was the French who amassed the world's second largest empire.

Political Motives   The primacy of the nation-state during this period also put strategic and territorial ambitions at center stage. The actions of European nations within the imperial arena were taken as much to jockey for political power and to preempt the territorial claims of other nations as they were to pursue economic gain. For Kaiser Wilhelm II, the German ruler from 1888 to 1918, for example, a central motivation for building up a strong German navy was to contest Britain's global power, so dependent on its naval strength, in North Africa, China, and the Ottoman Empire. The new nation of Italy likewise sought a colonial empire in North and East Africa as part of its quest to achieve great-power status.

Cultural Incentives   In the cultural realm, too, late-nineteenth-century nation-states mobilized imperialism to assist with internal processes of state-building. Newly unified nation-states, in particular, but older and established ones as well, actively sought to fully unify their citizens, in large part by inducing them to transfer their primary loyalties from their local community to the far more abstract, "imagined" community of the nation.

This process met with significant resistance, particularly since it entailed a loss of regional identity, and national leaders used the attractions of empire as one means of appealing to its citizens. Empire was presented as the shared symbolic property of the nation, an asset that in theory (but not in practice) transcended social class and allowed peasants and workers—as much as members of the upper classes—to cast themselves as superior to the nation's colonial subjects. Governments also encouraged their citizens to conceive of empire as a measure of the nation's virile masculinity, seen in favorable contrast to the supposedly weak, "effeminate" colony. Imperialism and, more specifically, imperial racism helped to consolidate the nation-state, in other words, by substituting race hierarchies for the hierarchies of class.

The Scramble for Africa

The scramble for Africa constituted by far the most remarkable chapter of the European expansion of the late nineteenth century. Between 1880 and 1912, seven European states partitioned most of the African

This is an image of a popular French children's board game from the late nineteenth century, the objective of which was to conquer Africa. Popular culture proved a powerful tool for propagating ideas about the "natural inferiority" of Africans and the legitimacy of the European conquest.

continent, leaving only Abyssinia (Ethiopia) and Liberia independent.

The Berlin Conference   By the mid-1880s, a number of European governments had begun to object to the haphazardness with which conflicts over African territory were being settled. The Berlin Conference of 1884–1885, presided over by the German Prime Minister Otto von Bismarck, was convened to sort out the conflict between the Portuguese and the Belgians over control of the Congo River in particular and, more generally, to lay the ground rules for colonization. A watershed in European diplomacy, the conference brokered conflicting claims without recourse to intra-European violence, even as it came to inflict bloodshed and suffering on Africa. European cooperation at Berlin owed a great deal to Bismarck's diplomatic shrewdness. Seeking to compensate France and Britain for their loss of power in the European arena and, at the same time, to fuel Franco-British imperial rivalry, he conceded the bulk of African territories to Britain and France. Despite its small number of African colonies, Germany's foreign policy thus decisively influenced the scramble.

Since the lines of partition had been drawn long before the Berlin Conference, its main role was to formally ratify the principle that coastal settlement by a European nation also gave it claim to the hinterlands beyond as long as it could establish authority in the region. Although the Berlin participants legitimized some new claims in central Africa—such as those of Belgium's King Leopold II in the Congo—in the main, the African partition extended European control from older coastal enclaves into the interior of the continent.

For Africans, the carving up of the continent redrew the African map in ways that consolidated previously separate polities and ethnic groups in new, European-made units—a single new colony, for example, could comprise three hundred smaller political units. The Berlin Conference thus centralized power in a previously decentralized political landscape. In addition, by using the artificial entity of the "tribe" to designate previously distinct groups of the same region, it permanently reconfigured ethnic and cultural identities in African society. While colonial rule and the work of Christian missionaries in standardizing related language dialects ultimately strengthened the cultural bonds between disparate groups, many of the African "tribes" of the present day are at least partial inventions of the Berlin Conference.

The Berlin Conference also extended the European abolition of slavery and the slave trade to Africa. Missionaries such as David Livingstone had campaigned ardently against the slave trade in East Africa since mid-century without making much headway. As formal colonizers, however, Europeans could enforce abolitionism

As African guides clear their path through thick vegetation, French and German negotiators consult their maps and renegotiate the boundaries of French Equatorial Africa and German Cameroon. European powers frequently came into conflict with one another on African soil, but for the most part were able to resolve their differences peacefully.

to a much greater extent than before. Their desire to abolish African slavery emerged both from a genuine humanitarianism and from the understanding that it was politically expedient as a justification for conquest. In spite of partial successes, clandestine slavery and slave trading in Africa continued into the early twentieth century and new forms of forced labor, heavily relied upon by European colonizers themselves, also replaced slavery in many regions.

The Wars of Conquest   In the aftermath of the Berlin Conference, the conquest of Africa unfolded in a series of bloody wars that took place between the 1880s and the first decade of the twentieth century. Although European powers faced fierce African resistance, they enjoyed several advantages in these conflicts. Their footholds on the African coast and, in many cases, long-standing commercial connections with coastal communities provided them with a base of operations and a ready source of supplies. Europeans also benefited from, and sometimes ruthlessly exploited, the divisions between local communities. In their expansion into West Africa (Nigeria) in the 1890s, for example, the British profited from local enmity by mobilizing the subjugated Nupe against their Fulani overlords, only to conquer the Nupe soon afterward.

Most important in facilitating the conquest was the immense and growing technological advantage enjoyed by the Europeans, especially in weaponry. To be sure, the weapons gap was nothing new. But the new military equipment produced by the second industrial revolution magnified the inequality between African and European forces. By the time Africans acquired rifles in the late nineteenth century, Europeans were deploying, first, rapid-firing breechloaders (repeating rifles) and, later, machine guns. In fact, most of the new weaponry of the First World War was first tested in the laboratory of late-nineteenth-century colonial warfare. One example of the devastation wrought by these new technologies was in the Battle of Omdurman in Sudan in 1898, where field artillery and hand-driven Gatling machine guns allowed Anglo-Egyptian forces to kill 11,000 and wound 16,000 Sudanese soldiers, with only 49 dead and 382 wounded among their own ranks. In the few cases where Africans had access to equally advanced technology, they were often able to thwart conquest. In part of French West Africa (Mali), for example, the troops of Islamic Malinké ruler Samori Touré, armed with up-to-date European weaponry, staved off French conquest from the mid-1880s to the late 1890s. These exceptions further underscore how critical advanced weaponry was to the European conquest.

New Imperial Nations While France and Britain dominated the conquest, other European nations carved out significant African territories as well. After the Berlin Conference had recognized King Leopold II's claims in the Congo in exchange for free trading and shipping rights in the region for other European states, Belgium emerged as a major African power. The full-scale subjugation of the massive Congo Free State (Democratic Republic of the Congo)—76 times as large as Belgium—took over ten years and met with continued insurgence, particularly from Arab slave traders of the Lualaba River region.

Germany also played a central role in the scramble. At Berlin, Bismarck had ceded dominance in Africa to Britain and France, claiming a few protectorates in the areas where German traders and missionaries were most active, such as Togoland (Togo), Cameroon, South West Africa (Namibia), and East Africa (Tanzania). In 1888, however, the accession of Wilhelm II to the German throne and the subsequent dismissal of Bismarck ushered in a new era of aggression in German foreign

CHRONOLOGY
Scramble for Africa

1881	French occupy Tunisia.
1882	Revolt in Egypt (against British and French financial influence by Arabi Pasha) prompts occupation by British.
1883	Start of French conquest of Madagascar.
1884	Germany acquires South West Africa, Togo, Cameroon. Berlin Conference.
1885	King Leopold II of Belgium acquires Congo.
1886	Germany and Britain divide East Africa.
	Discovery of gold in South Africa.
1889	Italy establishes colonies in Eritrea and Somaliland.
	Cecil Rhodes's British South Africa Company begins colonization of Rhodesia.
1894	Britain occupies Uganda.
1896	Abyssinian (Ethiopian) army defeats invading Italian army.
1898	Fashoda Crisis.
1899–1902	Boer War.
1905–1906; 1911	Morocco Crises

policy. Thereafter, Germany posed an active threat to France and Britain in the imperial arena. The Moroccan Crisis of 1905–1906 developed, for example, when Germany protested against the Franco-Spanish division of power in the region and demanded a sphere of its own. A second crisis, the Agadir Incident of 1911, erupted when the Kaiser sent a gunboat to the Moroccan port of Agadir in a display of German power meant to intimidate the French. Although both crises were resolved diplomatically, with France retaining effective control of Morocco, episodes like these signal the belligerent diplomatic stance of post-Bismarckian Germany and the consequent heightening of imperial competition.

Worried about Belgian and German encroachment on its colonial borders, Portugal managed to enlarge its Angolan holdings on the West African coast and to establish Portuguese East Africa (Mozambique) on the southeastern coast of Africa. These incursions sparked extended wars of resistance, especially in the Zambezi Valley. Meanwhile, the new nation-state of Italy, seeking to enhance its international standing by staking out terrain in East Africa, faced the unique humiliation of being defeated by an African polity. On the Horn of Africa, Italy seized Eritrea and Somaliland (Somalia) as colonies in 1889, but failed to conquer Abyssinia (Ethiopia), when King Menelik II's troops—about 100,000 soldiers armed with European breechloaders, a few machine guns, and field artillery—soundly defeated an Italian force of 14,500, equipped with inaccurate maps, at the Battle of Adowa in 1896. Italy fared better in Tripoli (Libya), declaring a protectorate there in 1912.

France   French and British expansion in Africa overshadowed that of all other powers. Although the British denigrated the French Empire as a large "sandbox," France clearly dominated West Africa and North Africa. From Algeria, where they had been entrenched since 1830, France expanded in virtually every direction. To the east, it squeezed out Italian and British interests, using the growing indebtedness of the ruling bey as the pretext for making Tunisia a French protectorate in

1881. To the west, France moved on Morocco, thwarting German interests and appeasing Spain with a small zone of control. By 1895 they dominated an enormous swath of sub-Saharan territories known as French West Africa (Ivory Coast, Senegal, Guinea, Mali). In 1897, France seized the French Congo in central Africa (Republic of the Congo) and, three years later, invaded the Lake Chad region, thereby linking up its possessions in the west and the north with those in central Africa. In 1911 it combined Chad and French Congo to form French Equatorial Africa. On the east coast, the French also claimed part of Somaliland and, in 1896, conquered the island of Madagascar, where they established a prosperous sugar plantation economy based on the forced labor of the local population.

Britain and the Boer War   British imperialists envisioned a railway from Capetown to Cairo that would span their African Empire. Starting in the 1880s, Britain moved to consolidate its hold on Egypt and Sudan. Although Britain had shared financial control with France

Image of the Battle of Adowa of 1896, in which the troops of Menelik II, armed with European weaponry, routed the Italian army and effectively saved Abyssinia (Ethiopia) from colonial conquest.
The Mary Evans Picture Libary

THE EARL OF CROMER: WHY BRITAIN ACQUIRED EGYPT

Evelyn Baring (1871–1917), First Earl of Cromer, was the first British Commissioner of the Egyptian Public Debt Office and then British Agent and Consul General after Egypt became a British colony in 1882. Ruling Egypt with an iron hand, Cromer reorganized its financial, judicial, and administrative system as well as defended it from the incursions of other European powers. Although he brought about important changes in Egypt and virtually rescued it from bankruptcy, the Egyptians disliked his autocratic ways and his willingness to subordinate the interests of Egypt to those of Britain. He ignored demands by middle-class Egyptians for higher education, for instance, for fear that it would lead to the emergence of nationalist sentiment, as it had in India. Likewise, the primary objective of his successful agricultural experiments to promote the growth of Egyptian cotton was to provide British industries with raw materials. Still, Cromer was greatly admired in the West. When he died in 1917, the London Times *called him the "Maker of Modern Egypt." In this excerpt, Cromer explains why the British and not any other European power could—and did—take over Egypt.*

"History, indeed, records some very radical changes in the forms of government to which a state has been subjected without its interests being absolutely and permanently shipwrecked. But it may be doubted whether any instance can be quoted of a sudden transfer of power in any civilized or semi-civilized community to a class so ignorant as the pure Egyptians, such as they were in the year 1882. These latter have, for centuries past, been a subject race. Persians, Greeks, Romans, Arabs from Arabia and Baghdad, Circassians, and finally, Ottoman Turks, have successively ruled over Egypt, but we have to go back to the doubtful and obscure precedents of Pharaonic times to find an epoch when, possibly, Egypt was ruled by Egyptians. Neither, for the present, do they appear to possess the qualities which would render it desirable, either in their own interests, or in those of the civilized world in general, to raise them at a bound to the category of autonomous rulers with full rights of internal sovereignty.

"If, however, a foreign occupation was inevitable or nearly inevitable, it remains to be considered whether a British occupation was preferable to any other. From the purely Egyptian point of view, the answer to this question cannot be doubtful. The intervention of any European power was preferable to that of Turkey. The intervention of one European power was preferable to international intervention. The special aptitude shown by Englishmen in the government of Oriental races pointed to England as the most effective and beneficent instrument for the gradual introduction of European civilization into Egypt. An Anglo-French, or an Anglo-Italian occupation, from both of which we narrowly and also accidentally escaped, would have been detrimental to Egyptian interests and would

ultimately have caused friction, if not serious dissension, between England on the one side and France or Italy on the other. The only thing to be said in favor of Turkish intervention is that it would have relieved England from the responsibility of intervening.

"By the process of exhausting all other expedients, we arrive at the conclusion that armed British intervention was, under the special circumstances of the case, the only possible solution of the difficulties, which existed in 1882. Probably also it was the best solution. The arguments against British intervention, indeed, were sufficiently obvious. It was easy to foresee that, with a British garrison in Egypt, it would be difficult that the relations of England either with France or Turkey should be cordial. With France, especially, there would be a danger that our relations might become seriously strained. Moreover, we lost the advantages of our insular position. The occupation of Egypt necessarily dragged England to a certain extent within the arena of Continental politics. In the event of war, the presence of a British garrison in Egypt would possibly be a source of weakness rather than of strength. Our position in Egypt placed us in a disadvantageous diplomatic position, for any power, with whom we had a difference of opinion about some non-Egyptian question, was at one time able to retaliate by opposing our Egyptian policy. The complicated rights and privileges possessed by the various powers of Europe in Egypt facilitated action of this nature."

From The Earl of Cromer, *Modern Egypt*, vol. 1, New York: Macmillan, 1908, pp. xvii–xviii.

over an increasingly bankrupted Egypt during the late nineteenth century and the French had financed the construction of the Suez Canal, the British finally edged the French out of Egypt in the 1870s and 1880s, claiming it as a protectorate in 1882 (see "The Earl of Cromer: Why Britain Acquired Egypt," above).

Once entrenched in Egypt, the British moved to extend their power south into Turco-Egyptian-controlled Sudan. There they clashed with the millenarian jihadist Mahdist state, which had sought repeatedly to overthrow Egyptian rule during the 1880s. In 1885, the armies of the Mahdi (the Guided One) attacked Khartoum, the

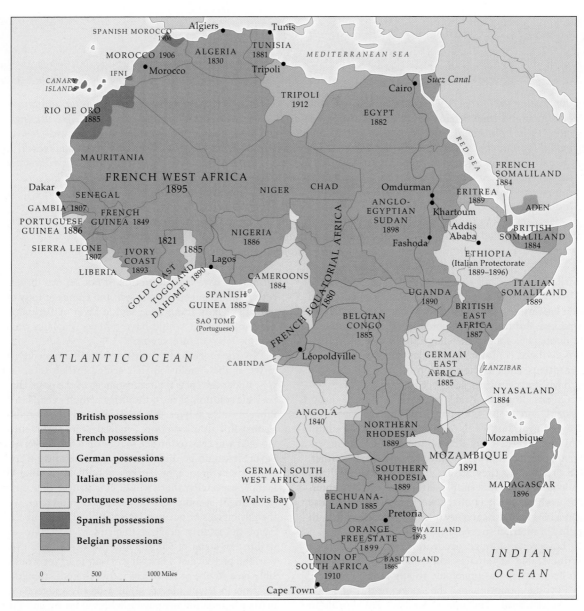

MAP 25.2 AFRICA, 1914
This map shows the European partition of Africa. Only Liberia and Ethiopia were independent after the turn of the century. Notice how the west-east axis of French territories runs into the north-south axis of British holdings. How were the European powers able to overrun an entire continent in such a short period of time?

Egyptian capital of Sudan and, after a ten-month siege, annihilated Anglo-Egyptian troops led by General Charles Gordon (known as "Chinese" Gordon because of his role in suppressing the Taiping Rebellion). At nearby Omdurman, the Mahdi established an Islamic state, which thrived for the next twelve years. But the British did not forget the defeat at Khartoum and in 1896 launched a new campaign to take the Sudan. In 1898 British troops led by Lord Kitchener handed the Mahdist State a fatal defeat at the battle of Omdurman.

The expansion into Sudan allowed Britain to link up Egypt with its territories to the southeast, British East

Africa (Kenya) and Buganda (Uganda), seized in 1888 and 1894, respectively. At the same time, in West Africa, the British expanded from trading forts along the Gold Coast, purchased earlier from the Dutch and the Danes, and defeated the Asante to colonize Ghana. In an effort to protect the commercial interests of British palm oil merchants in the Niger River delta, the British-chartered Royal Niger Company, under the leadership of George Goldie, also expanded into Nigeria between 1886 and 1899.

Pressing north from the British Cape Colony, the British fought the Zulus in the Anglo-Zulu War of

1878–1879. Led by the archetypal expansionist Cecil Rhodes, they took Bechuanaland (Botswana) in 1885, Rhodesia (Zimbabwe) in 1889, and Nyasaland (Malawi) in 1893. In so doing, the British managed to create a wedge separating German South West Africa (Namibia) and German East Africa (Rwanda, Burundi, continental Tanzania, part of Mozambique) and to approach the southern border of the Congo Free State. More importantly, this expansion threatened the independent Afrikaner republics north of the Cape Colony, a conflict that ultimately led to the Boer War of 1899–1902, in which approximately 75,000 lives were lost.

The British encroachment on the Afrikaner republics had been fueled by the discovery there of diamonds in the 1860s and gold in the 1880s. By 1890 the Afrikaner republics were overrun by British citizens and surrounded by British colonies. Conflicts between the two groups grew more heated, and in 1899 the Afrikaners declared war. British forces rapidly occupied the major cities of the Afrikaner republics, but it took two years to subdue the Afrikaners' skillful guerrilla resistance. The rest of Europe watched Britain's slow progress with surprise and then shock as farmhouses were destroyed and homeless Afrikaners herded together in guarded areas called concentration camps, where disease and starvation killed at least 20,000 of them. In Great Britain, the Boer War initially produced patriotic fervor, but politicians and the public alike grew disillusioned as the war dragged on. British victory allowed the establishment in 1910 of the Union of South Africa, a partial fulfillment of Rhodes's ambitions. To appease the disaffected Afrikaner minorities, British leaders implemented Afrikaner policies of *apartheid*, and the legal segregation of white and black Africans became the law of the land.

Intra-European Conflict in Africa

By the turn of the century, the extent of European expansion, compounded by the heightened tension within Europe, led to a growing number of intra-European imperial clashes. The Boer War, in which Afrikaners were armed with German weapons, was one of these. Another important confrontation occurred between Britain and France at Fashoda, on the Nile, in 1898. With the French driving inland across Africa from west to east and the British expanding south from Egypt and north from the Cape Colony, such conflict was inevitable. At Fashoda, British troops marching south from Omdurman met French expeditionary forces advancing east from the Congo. Both sides declared that their national honor was at stake, but after several weeks of threats the French government backed down, distracted by the Dreyfus affair at home. After the French retreat from Fashoda, the French agreed to recognize British control of the Nile in return for British recognition of French West Africa.

Conquest in Asia

While Africa was the main theater of late-nineteenth-century imperial expansion, Asia was the second key site of aggressive expansionism at the turn of the twentieth century.

The Middle East

In the late nineteenth century, the British began to withdraw their support from the Ottoman Empire. Although the empire had been strategically and commercially important to the British as the gateway to Asia, it no longer played that role after the opening of the Suez Canal in 1869. Bankrupted, in commercial decline, and riven by internal dissent, the empire ceased to be the attractive ally the British had made use of earlier in the century.

South and Central Asia

India, ruled directly by the British crown after 1857, remained the jewel of the British Empire. It continued to be invaluable, in terms of both trade and capital investment. During the last quarter of the nineteenth century, London financiers invested more than £2.5 million in India, most of it in railways. By the eve of the First World War, India also had emerged as the chief export market for British industrial goods.

The security of India continued to obsess British politicians, who sought to protect her borders from other expansionist powers, in particular Russia. The British, allied with the French and the Ottoman Turks, had fought the Russians directly in the Crimean War (1854–1856) but otherwise grappled with the Russian threat through a combination of formal and informal diplomacy known as the "Great Game." The political maneuverings of the Great Game finally ended with

Russian postcard (ca. 1902), showing the United States and Britain pushing Japan, the only imperial Asian state, into a confrontation with Russia. Japan would defeat Russia shortly thereafter in the Russo-Japanese War of 1904–1905.

the Anglo-Russian Entente of 1907, which resolved British and Russian differences over Persia, Tibet, and Afghanistan, dividing Persia into British and Russian spheres of influence and effectively consolidating Russian power in Central Asia.

Southeast Asia and the South Pacific In Southeast Asia, the Dutch strengthened their hold over the Dutch East Indies (Indonesia), including Sumatra, Java, Borneo, and the western half of New Guinea, and continued to prosper from a colonial plantation economy based largely on rubber and coffee. The British, meanwhile, expanded their territories in Southeast Asia, annexing upper Burma in 1886 and a part of Malaya (Malaysia) in 1896. The French, who had established commercial interests in Indochina at the turn of the nineteenth century, steadily increased their holdings there in the late nineteenth century, taking Tonkin and Annam (Vietnam) in 1883 and Cambodia and Laos in 1893. Although a militant and well-organized Vietnamese resistance movement, known as the "Black Flags," fought French infiltration (even appealing for help from the Chinese, their former colonial masters)

the French prevailed. Following a series of protracted military campaigns, France formed the French Indochina Union in 1894.

From the mid-nineteenth century on, the South Pacific also emerged as an arena for competition among the colonial powers. Europeans perceived South Pacific Islanders, like Africans, to be childlike "primitives" in need of European protection and divided the many islands of the region among themselves. While Britain and Germany split the western half of New Guinea, France seized New Caledonia and Tahiti. Germany also acquired the Marshall Islands, and the British took Fiji and Tonga. The Germans, British, and Americans fought for dominance in Samoa, resulting in a split between German and American Samoa, while the Germans and the British divided up the Solomon Islands. In addition to a highly prosperous sugar economy centered in Fiji, the region also provided cheap labor for Australian sugar plantations.

As the European powers snatched up Pacific islands, the generally isolationist United States became involved in the imperial politics of the region. In 1898 it annexed Hawaii, a strategic Pacific naval base and a

Chinese woodblock print showing Western soldiers being humiliated in a battle during the Boxer Rebellion of 1900 directed against Western exploitation of China. Although China was battered by the Rebellion and the Western powers emerged with still more influence over Chinese affairs, the Rebellion influenced the establishment of the first Chinese nationalist movement, led by Sun Yat-sen.
The British Library, London

profitable sugar cane and pineapple producer. After defeating Spain in the Spanish-American War, ignited by conflict over the control of Cuba, the United States received a number of Spanish territories, including the Philippines, Cuba, Puerto Rico, and Guam. In the Philippines, the Americans faced a fierce indigenous resistance movement that sought Filipino independence, but after three years of fighting and the capture of the insurrection leader, Emilio Aguinaldo, the United States declared the Philippines its territory. These conquests, combined with growing American influence and economic power in Latin America during this period, transformed the United States into a formidable global power.

East Asia   The continued decline of China and rise of Japan were the central developments in East Asia during the late nineteenth century. Although some Chinese reformers favored economic and technological modernization, including the building of railways, as a way to strengthen the nation, considerable conservative opposition to the process existed. The pattern of the midcentury thus continued unabated, with the European powers and the United States forcing trade concessions, annexing territory, and lending money to the Chinese government on disadvantageous terms. In the aftermath of the Sino-Japanese War of 1894–1895, fought over control of Korea, the Chinese were forced to borrow money from Europe to pay a war indemnity to Japan and, in return, the Europeans exacted more trade privileges and concessions to build railways. The 1897 murder of two German missionaries in China led to further concessions. The Germans received a lease of the port of Quingdao and the right to build railways in Shandong Province, the Russians took Port Arthur, and the French acquired a lease on Canton Bay and a sphere of influence in southern China. To prevent the further partitioning of China, the United States initiated the Open Door policy in 1898, agreed upon by all colonizing nations with the exception of Japan. Allowing all nations equal trading rights in all parts of China, the Open Door policy also protected China's territorial integrity.

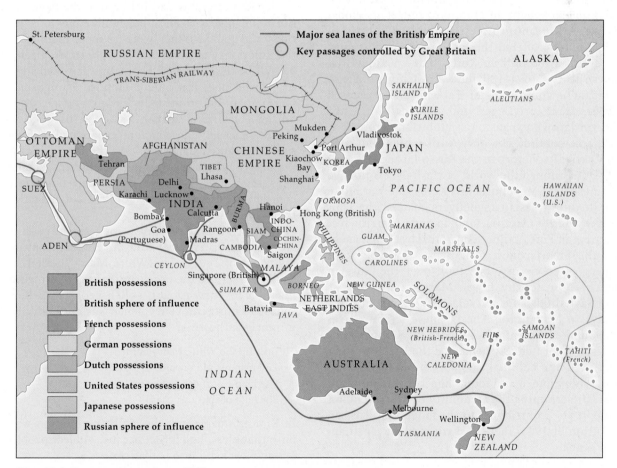

MAP 25.3 IMPERIALISM IN ASIA, 1900
This map shows the European colonies in Asia. Notice British dominance in this part of the world, centered largely on India. How did the entry of Japan and the United States into the Asian imperial arena change the power balance in the region?

Foreign encroachment and exploitation sparked the Boxer Rebellion in 1900. A clandestine society called the "Patriotic Harmonious Fists"—known as Boxers because of the martial arts training of its members—organized to protest the corrupting influence of "foreign devils," including missionaries, traders, and soldiers. The Boxer Rebellion erupted in northern China, where Boxers attacked European, American, and Chinese Christians in Shandong Province, sabotaged rail lines, and besieged foreign embassies in Beijing for almost two months. A force of twenty thousand British, French, German, Russian, Italian, American, and Japanese troops viciously suppressed the Boxer Rebellion and imposed a huge indemnity on the Qing regime. Continued degradation and economic exploitation at the hands of the Europeans, Americans, and Japanese (often in the form of disadvantageous railway leases) fueled the Chinese nationalist movement led by Sun Yat-sen, which finally overthrew the beleaguered Qing Dynasty in 1911.

Japan's fate differed dramatically from that of China. An industrial giant after the Meiji Restoration of 1868, Japan sought an empire to reflect its global standing. A Korean insurrection against Chinese influence in 1894 offered the Japanese an opportunity to establish a foothold in Korea. The ensuing Sino-Japanese War of 1894–1895 ended in Chinese defeat, the Japanese annexation of Taiwan, and increased Japanese trade privileges and political influence in Korea. Japan's expansionist ambitions brought it into direct conflict not only with China, but also with Russia. Its victory in the Russo-Japanese War of 1904–1905 stunned the world. A clash over influence in Chinese-held Manchuria and Korea, the war broke out following Russian maneuvers to take the Chinese province of Liaotung (and, in particular, the ice-free harbor of Port Arthur), controlled by the Japanese since the Sino-Japanese War. Japan not only kept Liaotung after victory, but took over the Russian sphere of influence in Chinese Manchuria, as well as half of Sakhalin Island, and seized Russian-controlled railways in Manchuria. The Japanese triumph over Russia marked a turning point both for European imperialists, who suddenly perceived the limits to their power, and for colonial subjects from Bombay to Cairo, who rejoiced and found hope in the European defeat. Undermining the credibility of Tsar Nicholas' regime, it also contributed to the failed first Russian Revolution of 1905. In 1910 a triumphant Japan annexed Korea.

The New Imperial Mission

New ideological foundations also distinguished the new imperialism from the liberal empire. Responding to anticolonial insurgency in India and to the Darwinian revolution at home, Europeans reconsidered the nature of their political, cultural, and biological relationship to subject peoples.

The Failure of the Liberal Vision Europeans at the end of the nineteenth century confronted their vast global empire with a transformed sense of mission. Gradually abandoning the liberal conceit of Europeanizing the non-Western world for the more modest goal of improving the "natives" within their own cultural context, Europeans increasingly replaced paternalist justifications of empire with the unabashed consolidation of imperial rule by force. The new mission did not appear overnight. In fact, the self-critical attitude and eagerness to legitimize Europe's imperial presence characteristic of colonial encounters of the late eighteenth and early nineteenth centuries were already fading by midcentury, supplanted by a growing intolerance of cultural difference.

By the late nineteenth century, attitudes had further hardened. Europeans still believed in the flagrant inferiority of subject peoples, but, unlike previous generations of colonizers, they were far more inclined to see this inferiority as biological and, therefore, irremediable. While they continued to vaunt their own superiority as the justification for empire, Europeans thus increasingly questioned the extent of their responsibilities as civilizers and the likelihood that such efforts would succeed. The concrete experience of imperial rule contributed significantly to the new cynicism. In the case of Britain, for example, the Indian Rebellion of 1857 (see p. 758–760) irrevocably changed not only the conception of imperial duty but British expectations of their colonial subjects.

By the end of the century, many took the pessimistic view of the British poet Rudyard Kipling, captured in his poem of 1898, "The White Man's Burden." In it Kipling described the unrewarding task of bringing civilization to "new-caught, sullen peoples," whose response to European benevolence was not gratitude but intransigent hostility:

Take up the White Man's burden—
And reap his old reward:
The blame of those ye better,
The hate of those ye guard—

In Kipling's depiction, the civilizing mission was not only thankless, but futile, because subject peoples inevitably backslid into barbarism:

And when your goal is nearest
The end for others sought,
Watch sloth and heathen Folly
Bring all your hopes to nought

Darwinian Challenges to the Enlightenment   Even more than the politics of imperial rule, ideological developments within Europe profoundly influenced the civilizing mission. The Darwinian revolution of the late nineteenth century irrevocably changed what it meant to be human and, therefore, to be European. Although decades of nineteenth-century scientific research on race difference and racial development had seriously weakened the Enlightenment conception of a single human species developing largely through environmental influence, it was Darwin's particular formulation of the theory of evolution—and its distortion by social Darwinists (see chapter 24) to explain cultural difference—that most affected late-nineteenth-century European views about the capacity of "primitives" to become civilized.

Darwinian theory undermined several key tenets of liberal Enlightenment thought. First, in linking humans to a common ape ancestor, Darwin raised the specter of the animal nature—and thus, the fundamental primitivity—of all humans. Scandalized Europeans responded by accentuating the gap between their own civilized nature and the primitive nature of other "races." Although they disagreed intensely as to whether the gap was wide enough to warrant the classification of other races as separate species (and Darwin himself favored the idea of a single species), most came to view the differences between the races as more significant than the similarities. As a consequence, some abandoned the Enlightenment notion of a single human trajectory along which all cultures developed at varied paces and came to believe in the separate and incommensurable developmental paths of different cultures. Social Darwinian thought thus dealt the liberal universalism of the Enlightenment a serious blow.

Second, Darwin's theory of **natural selection,** which held that the natural selection of traits best adapted to survival served as the prime motor of human development, also challenged European understandings of human agency. In contrast to Europeans of the Enlightenment, who believed that environment—both natural and social—shaped culture, their late-nineteenth-century counterparts took Darwin's theory to mean that biology determined culture. Darwin's influence thus undercut the liberal Enlightenment belief in the human mastery of nature and the possibility of socially engineered progress.

Finally, whereas Enlightenment thinkers stressed the mutability of human beings, Darwin's theory of race differentiation lent itself to belief in the permanence of racial traits. Unlike all other human traits, which evolved continually under the pressures of natural selection, Darwin argued, the superficial physical distinctions between the races emerged early in human history through the process of **sexual selection,** prefer-

ences marked out in the sexual competition for mates. Because these sexually selected traits—such as hair texture or skin color—provided no benefit for survival, moreover, they tended either not to change or to evolve much more slowly than other traits. While Darwin himself never said that racial traits were fixed, many race scientists of the late nineteenth century made that mental leap themselves and erroneously used Darwin to assert that racial difference was permanent. Social Darwinian misinterpretations of Darwin in this way eroded the liberal Enlightenment belief in mutability and progress.

Popular Views of Race   Darwinian and social Darwinian ideas had an astonishingly broad impact on European conceptions of race and empire. Racist tracts influenced by Darwin, in tandem with newspapers, periodicals, and imperial adventure novels, shaped popular conceptions of the colonial "native," inculcating the widespread belief that non-Western peoples were biologically—and not simply culturally—retrograde and lacked the capacity to improve. Although racist propagandists had been disseminating their ideas for decades (two of the most influential racist writers of the nineteenth century, Count Gobineau and Robert Knox, published their works almost ten years before Darwin), Darwinian theory seemed to many to grant them new legitimacy and authority.

Africa and black Africans occupied a special place in post-Darwinian racist hierarchies because of their presumed proximity to apes. While these links had been made much earlier, they were now widely regarded as having been verified by scientific inquiry and therefore to constitute a sound basis for imperial policy. Some of the most extreme arguments—like those made by social Darwinist imperialist propagandists such as Benjamin Kidd, author of *Social Evolution* (1894)—cast Africans as biologically defective and asserted the inevitability of black extinction and white rule in Africa. While Europeans had viewed African blacks as lesser beings for centuries, for many blackness now became the mark of innate and unchanging biological inferiority.

Race Science and Eugenics   Darwin's work decisively influenced scholarly views of the "native" as well. Race scientists, for example, used—and distorted—his ideas to support theories of race hierarchy. Like Darwin, the race scientists of the late nineteenth century believed in the animal nature of humans and the biological, rather than social, determinants of civilization. Unlike Darwin, however, they believed in the permanent character of race traits and in the unbreachable gap between different race-culture groups. These theories were far from new. Polygenism, or the belief in many human species, had been on the rise in the scientific

THE INDIAN REBELLION OF 1857

The Rebellion of 1857 was an event of immense significance, not just for modern South Asia but also for British colonialism in general. Sparked off by a military mutiny, the rebellion spread through North India, nearly overthrowing the rule of the British East India Company. Although distinctly local in character, the Rebellion of 1857 had dramatic global repercussions, fundamentally shaping the ways in which British colonies were henceforth viewed and governed by their colonial masters.

In the summer of 1857, rumors spread in the military camps in the town of Meerut that the cartridges for the new English rifles used by Indian soldiers or "sepoys" were greased with cow and pig fat. This practice offended the religious sensibilities of both Hindus and Muslims, and on May 9, the sepoys violently revolted against their British officers, who were caught unawares. Many officers were killed in the fracas that followed.

While the issue of the greased cartridges triggered the rebellion, the causes for dissatisfaction with British rule went far deeper. The rebel sepoys were largely recruited from the peasantry in the princely state of Awadh in Northwestern India. Under the British, peasants in places such as Awadh were forced to pay exorbitant taxes. In addition, the British Governor-General Lord Dalhousie had recently conquered Awadh, disregarding his treaty obligations to its ruler, Nawab Wajid Ali Shah. The peasants of Awadh now faced both financial hardship and the humiliation of having their king treated with indignity. Led by the former elites of the Awadh court, the peasantry joined the sepoys and rose in protest against their colonial masters, attacking institutions representative of British rule, such as courts, police stations, and revenue offices. They marched on the capital, Delhi, to reinstate the old and decrepit Mughal emperor, Bahadur Shah Zafar, as their rightful and legitimate ruler. Many similar rebellions in support of local rulers occurred in other parts of India, such as Jhansi and Gwalior in Northern India and the territories ruled by the Maratha chieftains of Central India.

Although the rebels of 1857 toppled British administration in many towns, the British army ultimately suppressed the uprising with great brutality. Despite widespread support for the rebellion among the peasantry and the artisanal classes, it was limited to northern and central India alone. Furthermore, the middle-class intelligentsia as well as many Indian princes loyal to the British refused to participate in the movement, seriously weakening its potency. Both factors contributed to British success in regaining control over the rebellious regions.

The East India Company refused to acknowledge that the rebellion was in any way a result of its own conduct, casting it instead as an unprovoked betrayal on the part of ungrateful subjects. Determined to teach the rebelling Indians a lesson and to inspire enough fear to prevent another rebellion, it torched villages, capturing and executing rebels, some of whom were blown to bits from the mouths of cannons. It also exiled the Mughal emperor, Bahadur Shah Zafar, to Burma and killed his sons.

The British Parliament was less than convinced that mistakes on the part of the East India Company had not contributed to sparking the rebellion. As a result, Parliament transferred the right to rule India from the Company to the Crown on August 2, 1858. The supreme authority in India was to be the "Viceroy"; Queen Victoria became the empress of India and, instead of the board of governors of the East India Company in London, a secretary of state for India who belonged to the British cabinet exercised decision-making and control over Indian affairs.

The British government was now determined that none of the administrative errors of the past would ever be repeated. Since many commentators perceived that British interference in Indian religion and customs had fostered the widespread resentment that had led to the uprising, British rule after the rebellion claimed

When the Indian rebellion erupted in 1857, the rebels besieged the city of Lucknow, the capital of Oudh (in northwestern India), for two months. British troops rescued the British inhabitants of the city and took revenge on the local population. This photograph, taken a few months after the British attack, shows the courtyard of the Sikander Bagh, the royal garden and summer estate of the Nawab of Oudh, littered with the skulls and bones (only one skeleton is complete) of about two thousand Indian insurgents killed there.
Hulton Archive/Getty Images

explicitly to avoid involvement in the religious and customary practices of Indians. In this context, Queen Victoria's Proclamation in 1858 proclaimed grandly that the government would respect the "ancient rites, usages and customs of India."

Postrebellion British rule in India therefore moved away from the liberal civilizing mission of the early nineteenth century to the idea that India could be efficiently ruled only through its own institutions. This shift, however, often had unfortunate repercussions since the government's identification of certain practices and ideas as "customary" was often flawed and inaccurate, in part because it relied on the advice of upper-caste elites who propagated their own biased views. As a result, the British codified, systematized, and made

rigid everyday practices that had been flexible for centuries. This change in ruling ideology and practice affected not just India, but other colonies as well, in particular those in Africa, which were colonized in the late nineteenth century and governed on the Indian model.

Racism also increased alarmingly in the years after the rebellion as the British grappled with feelings of outrage and fear of their subject population. More and more, British and Indians began to live and socialize separately. Furthermore, as social Darwinism became influential in Europe, the British began to see Indians in increasingly racialized ways, often stereotyping groups of people. The British also conferred special privileges on certain segments of the population, such

continued

as rulers who had remained loyal to them during the revolt, while treating those who had been active in the rebellion as traitors, including many Muslims. By deepening the divisions in Indian society, these policies helped the British maintain control over Indian subjects and prevent future uprisings.

Antagonistic feelings toward Indians ran high not just among the British in India, but in Britain itself. In spite of the extreme brutality with which the rebellion had been suppressed, the popular press and literature depicted British rule as a noble and benign one that had been attacked by savages. Particularly offensive to the British imagination was the idea that Englishwomen had been "defiled" by the rebels, and Victorian paintings and mass market novels were filled with lurid accounts and images of white women being raped and mutilated by Indians. Such images contributed to an enduring British view of the Indian as barbaric and uncivilized.

In the final analysis, how does one judge the Rebellion of 1857? Depending on the perspective, the Rebellion of 1857 has been regarded as a "Mutiny" or the "First War of Indian Independence." As we have seen, British colonial officials perceived the uprising as mindless violence by an ungrateful native population. Indian nationalist leaders and historians have glorified the rebellion as representing the first stirrings of nationalist sentiment in India. Most modern historians, however, emphasize that it is somewhat anachronistic to see the Rebellion of 1857 in terms of the emergence of Indian nationalism. No sense of a shared mission united the

local rulers who rose up in rebellion against the British. The loyalty of these rulers was to their own kingdoms, not to the Indian nation. Even the Mughal emperor was seen as the supreme head of a feudal system, not as a representative of a modern state. In their turn, peasants did not always understand that many of their difficulties emerged out of colonial exploitation and attacked the most visible manifestations of oppression such as local landlords and moneylenders. In fact, peasant nationalism was not to emerge in India until the twentieth century.

In spite of its ultimate failure, however, the Rebellion of 1857 remains extremely important for many reasons. It was certainly the largest anticolonial movement that had taken place so far in British India. Moreover, its emphasis on Hindu-Muslim unity made it a powerful symbol for later nationalist leaders. Although many Muslims felt the end of Mughal rule meant that their fortunes and prestige would be under threat, there was also a real recognition that Muslims and Hindus suffered together under British oppression, and in many places they fought side by side against what they perceived as a common foreign enemy. In addition, although led by the landed elite and feudal chieftains, the rebellion saw the participation of different classes, including tribal peoples and low castes. In many ways, therefore, the rebellion marked a crucial turning point in the history of colonial India. Perhaps its greatest legacy is that it served as an inspiration to anticolonial movements, not just in India, but also in Asia and Africa in the late nineteenth and twentieth centuries.

community since 1800 and dominant since 1850. But Darwin's work lent new conviction and credibility to this theoretical foundation for race science.

The new field of **eugenics** was also an outgrowth of Darwin's influence. Both a science of human heredity and a social program of selective breeding, eugenics was founded in 1883 by Darwin's cousin, Francis Galton, and Galton's colleague, Karl Pearson. Believing that biological differences between races and individuals

determined the social order, eugenicists sought to control the process of natural selection and, thereby, to engineer the production of a fitter race. Using the techniques of **biometry,** early eugenicists such as Pearson and Galton tried to apply statistical analysis to identify the salient traits of the races. But Galton soon realized that the eugenicist project required more research into the laws of heredity. That recognition led to the acceptance of the new science of genetics, which identified century were a motley political group. While Galton himself was a Victorian liberal committed to human progress, for example, Pearson embraced social Darwinist views and argued in his work *National Life from the Standpoint of Science* (1901) that Africans must be eliminated from British South Africa for the biological and moral purification of the colony (see "Karl Pearson on National Life from the Standpoint of Science," p. 763).

The Rise of Anthropology   Darwinian theory also had a formative impact on the view of the "native" adopted by the new field of anthropology, which emerged as a formal academic discipline in the late nineteenth century to chart the stages of human cultural evolution and to identify the universal cultural traits of humankind through the comparative study of cultures. Anthropologists and archaeologists of the period fiercely debated whether contemporary "savages" were remnants of the European past, whether they had degenerated from a higher level of civilization, and whether they had the capacity to improve. A dominant model was expounded by the social evolutionary anthropologist Edward Burnett Tylor. His **doctrine of survivals** argued that contemporary "savages" were evolutionary atavisms whose cultural life provided a window onto the European past. A liberal universalist and relativist himself, Tylor admired many of the moral traits he observed in "savage" culture and acknowledged certain defects in European society. Nevertheless, his social evolutionary paradigm reinforced the view that contemporary "savage" culture—especially that of black Africans—had developed outside of the evolutionary mainstream and, therefore, would always remain inferior to European civilization.

If nineteenth-century anthropology created images of innate or cultural primitivity that seemed to invite European domination, European colonizers also made use of anthropological study to implement imperial rule. Believing that knowledge of "primitive culture" was the key to the consolidation of colonial rule, European governments were frequently the sponsors of ethnographic research in the late nineteenth century. They had also done this earlier, of course, and the late-nineteenth-century application of scientific study to political control was in a sense merely a continuation of the Enlightenment project of systematically studying the world in order to master it; Captain James Cook's scientific voyages to the Pacific had embodied this project, as had Mungo Park's African expeditions. Two key ideas, however, frequently distinguished the project in the late nineteenth century: first, the conviction that European cultural superiority stemmed from biological roots and, second, that this superiority—and with it the mandate to rule the world—was a permanent feature of the global order.

This photograph was taken around the turn of the twentieth century by Harry Hamilton Johnston (1858–1927), a colonial administrator, geographer, and naturalist. Like many contemporaries, Johnston was preoccupied with the "racial" classification of colonial subjects and used anthropometry, the measurement of differences in the body types of the human "races," as a tool toward this end.
Royal Geographical Society, London

the gene as the unit of inheritance. Although the Austrian scientist Gregor Mendel had first elaborated the gene-based theory of heredity in the 1860s, it was not until Galton and Pearson made use of Mendelian genetics around 1900 that genetic theory gained scientific respectability.

By the turn of the century, the eugenics movement was a highly prestigious scientific movement in Europe, the United States, and Japan. As such, it influenced public policy, including the forced sterilization of "unfit" groups (people with mental impairment, for example) and the introduction of immigration quotas limiting the influx of "racial undesirables." Despite the nefarious connotations of the movement, especially in the aftermath of Hitler, the eugenicists of the early twentieth

IMPERIALISM AT ITS PEAK

By the turn of the century, Europeans had transformed the constructed environment, the economic life, the social order, and the cultural practices of their colonial subjects. The emergence of the first anticolonial nationalist movements in this period responded to this upheaval. At the same time, ordinary Europeans were becoming more aware of the empire. By the eve of the First World War, the colonies permeated European consciousness and culture as never before. Just as empire imposed European culture on the non-Western world, it brought that world into the heart of Europe.

The Reordering of Colonial Life

Once Europeans had secured control over their colonies, they moved to consolidate and exploit that power to its fullest. In so doing, they transformed every aspect of colonial life, from building colonial cities and establishing a cash crop economy to introducing Western education and remapping indigenous social hierarchies.

Building Colonial Infrastructure With the global conquest completed by the turn of the twentieth century, European colonizers embarked on the massive enterprise of building colonial infrastructure and implementing colonial administration. In less urbanized parts of the empire they erected colonial cities, towns, and ports, and in them schools, hospitals, clock towers, and ceremonial gateways. In places where cities and ports existed, such as Cairo, Lagos, Singapore, and Bombay, Europeans undertook ambitious modernization projects, including clearing slums and constructing new housing and roadways. They also brought new modes of transportation to their empires, in the form of highway systems, bridges, canals, and railway networks, as well as new systems of communication, notably the telegraph. By 1865 telegraph lines connected India to Europe; by 1871 a cable ran from Vladivostok to Shanghai, Hong Kong, and Singapore. In addition to constructing a new built environment, colonial rulers imposed European models of administration in many spheres of colonial life. Colonial administrators reorganized the police, army, judiciary, and postal service along European lines and, to varying degrees, introduced European models of education—including European language instruction—and Western-style medicine.

Europeans regarded these projects as central to the task of colonial rule. The use of grid layouts in colonial cities and ports and the laying of railway lines were intended to efficiently transport goods to both domestic and metropolitan markets and thus to facilitate European commercial exploitation of the colonies. This infrastructure also had military and strategic importance. Railways and telegraphs allowed for the rapid mobilization of European troops, while urban street grids permitted the policing and surveillance of local populations. The construction of colonial cities and towns also revealed the European agenda to regulate

With the conquest of much of the world complete by the turn of the twentieth century, Europeans turned their attention to the introduction of European technologies and communications in their colonies. Using local and imported colonial labor, they built extensive road and rail networks in many parts of Africa and Asia. This photograph of 1891 shows workers clearing the ground for a railway in rural Kenya. What strategic and economic objectives motivated European colonizers to undertake these projects?
Hulton Archive/Getty Images

KARL PEARSON ON NATIONAL LIFE FROM THE STANDPOINT OF SCIENCE

Karl Pearson (1857–1936) was an English, Cambridge-educated mathematician who also studied law and social and political philosophy. He held the first chair of eugenics at University College, London, and became the director of the eugenics laboratory there. He was a disciple of Francis Galton, the founder of eugenics, which sought to improve the human race through selective breeding. Pearson, in his turn, applied statistical methods to the study of biological problems, especially evolution and heredity, a science he called biometrics. Pearson's views on eugenics are seen as deeply problematic and racist today. He claimed that he was a socialist, committed to uplifting the masses, but in fact, his "scientific" view of a nation, as presented in National Life from the Standpoint of Science, *claimed that a country's progress and well-being depended on constantly replenishing its "better" stock at the expense of its "inferior races." The twentieth century was to see many undesirable applications of the principles of eugenics in the Western world, including the mass exterminations carried out by Nazi Germany.*

"History shows me one way, and one way only, in which a high state of civilization has been produced, namely, the struggle of race with race, and the survival of the physically and mentally fitter race.... The struggle means suffering, intense suffering, while it is in progress; but that struggle and that suffering have been the stages by which the white man has reached his present stage of development, and they account for the fact that he no longer lives in caves and feeds on roots and nuts. This dependence of progress on the survival of the fitter race, terribly black as it may seem to some of you, gives the struggle for existence its redeeming features; it is the fiery crucible out of which comes the finer metal. You may hope for a time when the sword shall be turned into the plowshare, when American and German and English traders shall no longer compete in the markets of the world for their raw material and for their food supply, when the white man and the dark shall share the soil between them, and each till it as he lists. But, believe me, when that day comes mankind will no longer progress; there will be nothing to check the fertility of inferior stock; the relentless law of heredity will not be controlled and guided by natural selection. Man will stagnate; and unless he ceases to multiply, the catastrophe will come again; famine and pestilence, as we see them in the East, physical selection instead of the struggle of race against race, will do the work more relentlessly, and, to judge from India and China, far less efficiently than of old....

"There is a struggle of race against race and of nation against nation. In the early days of that struggle it was a blind, unconscious struggle of barbaric tribes. At the present day, in the case of the civilized white man, it has become more and more the conscious, carefully directed attempt of the nation to fit itself to a continuously changing environment. The nation has to foresee how and where the struggle will be carried on; the maintenance of national position is becoming more and more a conscious preparation for changing conditions, an insight into the needs of coming environments.

"We have to remember that man is subject to the universal law of inheritance, and that a dearth of capacity may arise if we recruit our society from the inferior and not the better stock. If any social opinions or class prejudices tamper with the fertility of the better stocks, then the national character will take but a few generations to be seriously modified.... You will see that my view—and I think it may be called the scientific view of a nation—is that of an organized whole, kept up to a high pitch of internal efficiency by insuring that its numbers are substantially recruited from the better stocks, and kept up to a high pitch of external efficiency by contest, chiefly by way of war with inferior races, and with equal races by the struggle for trade-routes and for the sources of raw material and of food supply. This is the natural history view of mankind, and I do not think you can in its main features subvert it."

From Karl Pearson, *National Life from the Standpoint of Science*, 1900, available at housatonic.net/Documents/333.htm.

race relations in this period through the spatial separation of "natives" and Europeans. Colonizers built better ventilated, more sanitary residential areas for themselves—for security reasons, often near military cantonments—where they re-created European-style institutions, including clubs, polo fields, and churches, leaving "natives" to cluster in what they saw as crowded and unhealthy urban spaces. The British, for example, successfully segregated colonial Madras into European and Indian quarters and labeled them, respectively, "White Town" and "Black Town."

The New Colonial Economy Explicit colonial rule also triggered major economic transformations. Although the global terms of trade had long worked against Asia and Africa, the European conquest, along with increased industrial development in Europe, further widened the gap between **metropole** and colony in the late century. As they had done earlier, the industrial economies of Europe exported manufactured goods to their colonies and imported raw materials, especially cash crops, from them. By the late nineteenth century, however, more countries were flooding colonial markets with industrial goods, while the European adoption of neomercantilist trade policies from the 1880s on prevented the colonies from pursuing trade relationships outside the metropole.

Above all, the conquests of the late nineteenth century ensured that European colonists could use coercion to install and support new agricultural and labor regimes. The advent of a cash-based agricultural economy meant that many peasants no longer primarily relied on subsistence farming, turning instead to the production of crops required as raw materials to feed industrial production in Europe or to wage labor, both on small farms and big European-run plantations. British India, for instance, became a major producer of opium, rice, indigo, tea, and, above all, cotton during this period. While some peasants prospered from cash-crop production, many paid an exorbitant price for the abrupt transition to a new agricultural economy. Their abandonment of subsistence farming based on food grain production made them much more vulnerable to famine and also exposed them to the fluctuations of international commerce. Thus, for example, the invention of synthetic dyes in the early twentieth century rendered Indian indigo, long a staple of the British textile industry, obsolete, leaving thousands of Indian indigo farmers bankrupted. Despite the weakened economic position of peasants, taxes remained high, thus forcing rural populations to migrate to cities and towns in search of work as urban laborers.

Another distinctive feature of the late-nineteenth-century colonial economy was the global migration of labor. The advent of modern transportation allowed Europeans to dispatch millions of indentured laborers to build irrigation systems and railroads and to work on plantations and in mines in regions far from their homes. This diaspora of migrant labor divided families and created local demographic imbalances. Cochin-Chinese (Vietnamese) laborers worked the plantations of French Cambodia, for example, while tens of thousands of Indian and Chinese laborers, known as "coolies," migrated to work in British possessions, including South Africa, East Africa, Ceylon (Sri Lanka), the West Indies, Burma, Malaya, Fiji, and Australia. In certain cases, indentured labor from existing colonies facilitated the colonization of other regions. The construction of a vast railway network by indentured laborers from India, for example, made possible the British settlement of East Africa.

The Cultural Dimensions of Colonial Rule Europeans conquered the globe not merely by military, diplomatic, and economic means, but by cultural domination as well. This Western cultural influence reached far and wide—including education, the maintenance of law and order, relations between different groups in society, language use, and dress codes—and often fundamentally transformed and restructured the existing social fabric. In fact, few aspects of everyday life in postcolonial societies are untouched by the colonial encounter, from the architecture in towns like Dakar and Delhi and the vast networks of railroads across Asia and Africa to the immense popularity of cricket in the West Indies and South Asia and the addition of the blouse to the sari at the behest of prudish missionaries in India.

One important effect of European dominance was to create new hierarchies and divisions within colonial society. The establishment of Western-style schools and universities throughout the European empires, for example, served the purpose of producing a Western-educated colonial elite. European colonizers hoped in this way to create loyal subjects who would serve their imperial rulers in the lower levels of the local colonial administration and, to some extent, bridge the gap between colonizers and colonized. However, this vision was only partially fulfilled. In many situations, European colonizers favored traditional elites at the expense of the newly educated professional classes, believing the former to be more reliable supporters of colonial rule. Indeed, Western-educated colonial subjects found themselves doubly marginalized, by Europeans who continued to condescend to them and to exclude them from positions of power, and by their own alienation from the indigenous masses. As one example of this kind of cultural displacement, educated Algerians refused to speak Arabic, favoring French, the language of their colonial masters, instead.

As they sought to understand and classify native societies, European colonial rulers also emphasized particular social identities of the colonized, thus fueling social conflict between different indigenous groups. In late-nineteenth-century British India, for example, colonial administrators and politicians reinforced divisions of caste (the hierarchical division of society based on birth). Following the questionable advice of upper-caste Indian scholars, the British declared caste to be the foundation of traditional Indian society, even though it had been only one of several such social markers in precolonial India. British authorities relied increasingly on caste stereotypes. They labeled the Gurkhas and the Sikhs, for example, as "martial" and considered them to be good recruits for the British army, while they classified others, such as the Kallars, as intrinsically "criminal" and treated them with deep disdain and suspicion. With time, these classifications became increasingly fixed, leading to the hardening of social boundaries within Indian society.

Methods of Governance

How did Europeans govern the vast empire of the late nineteenth and early twentieth centuries? Virtually everywhere, the new imperial mission of the period translated into transformed models of colonial governance, although these models—and their implementation—varied widely from empire to empire and, within each empire, from colony to colony.

Brute Force: Exploitation in the Belgian Congo In some places, Europeans ruled by brute force. Perhaps the most egregious example of domination through ruthless violence was the Belgian King Leopold II's Congo Free State. There, the increasingly cynical and racist European view of the colonial "native" was taken to its logical conclusion. Between 1898 and 1905, Leopold's troops impressed Congolese men into hard labor at gunpoint. Some were used to build roads, while others served long periods in the army and, after discharge, in the rural police. This indigenous police force, in turn, compelled the rest of the population to abandon subsistence farming and instead produce rubber for the state. When the police encountered resistance to these arrangements, they responded by shooting recalcitrants, turning over baskets of severed hands from the corpses—as well as from the living—to the Belgian authorities as proof that punishment had been carried out.

Although Leopold's methods saved him from bankruptcy, other European powers condemned his de facto enslavement, murder, and maiming of his subjects as a moral outrage. In 1908 the Belgian Parliament assumed control of the colony as a direct consequence of this international outcry. An official inquiry mounted by a Belgian commission reported in 1919 that Leopold's methods had reduced the population of the Congo by half. Most recent scholarly assessments have been even grimmer, estimating that the population of the Congo Free State shrank from between 20 and 30 million to 8 million during Leopold's rule.

Indirect Rule in the British Empire More than any other ruling power, Britain took the lessons of empire to heart in elaborating a new system of "indirect rule." Interpreting the Indian Rebellion as evidence of the futility and folly of direct colonial involvement, British administrators devised a relatively hands-off policy that largely delegated power to traditional chiefs, kings, and princes. These traditional leaders, in turn, were expected to carry out the dictates of colonial officials. The system was implemented in its fullest form in colonial Africa.

Photograph of mutilated workers from the Belgian Congo from the late nineteenth century. Under the rule of King Leopold II, Africans were forced into rubber cultivation at gunpoint. Those that did not meet their production quotas were either killed or had their hands cut off. The forced labor regime of rubber production in Leopold's Congo was one of the most atrocious chapters in the history of the European colonization of Africa.
Courtesy of Anti-Slavery International

The British favored indirect rule for a variety of reasons. Because it relied largely on local people, it was far less expensive than other methods of rule. Furthermore, by using indigenous leaders and thus attaching themselves to "tradition," the British sought to gain legitimacy among subject peoples. This legitimacy, it was hoped, would make British colonial administration more stable and better able to withstand colonial insurgence.

Indirect rule had several negative consequences for the colonies. First, although the British made much of the fact that indirect rule left indigenous cultures essentially intact, this was not the case. In the African context, for example, indirect rule removed traditional limitations on the power of the local chieftain. Required to obey the British authorities alone, he was no longer accountable to his subjects or to other political leaders in the community. By thus granting unfettered power to traditional leaders, the British cleared the way for the establishment of despotic regimes. The Fulani Emirs who acted as British agents in Nigeria, for example, were effectively dictators. Second, by casting themselves as the benevolent guardians of African "custom" and "tribal" practice, the British promoted the tribal identity at the expense of other social affiliations and loyalties in colonial society. Indirect rule thus fomented division and conflict along "tribal" or ethnic lines. Finally, in emphasizing African "tradition," indirect rule tended to neglect the higher education of colonial subjects, at the same time marginalizing Western-educated Africans perceived as threatening to British rule.

Sustaining the Civilizing Mission in the French Empire

While the Germans and Dutch adopted some variant of the British model of indirect rule and the Portuguese and the Belgians ruled by unadorned coercion and violence, the French developed an alternative model of governance. In many (although not all) parts of the French Empire, they implemented a system of "direct rule" that unequivocally repudiated the authority of existing leaders and political institutions in favor of that of French officials, laws, and codes. The method of direct colonial rule reflected the French *mission civilisatrice*, its civilizing mission to assimilate the "native" to French culture. The French thus retained the ideal of assimilationism even after other nations had begun to move away from it.

In part, this can be explained as an outgrowth of French chauvinism and the sense that France had been the guardian of "civilization" in Europe for centuries. But there were other reasons as well. Although the *mission civilisatrice* was simply a variant of the liberal civilizing mission, with its origins in Enlightenment universalism and principles of universal equality and rationality, the French tradition of republicanism made these beliefs more central to French political identity and culture than they were elsewhere in Europe. Also, because French philosophical and scientific tradition tended to emphasize the importance of environment in determining human development, Darwin's influence and that of biological determinism came later to France and carried less weight there than in other European nations.

The French method of governance had contradictory effects. On the one hand, the French policy destroyed indigenous political and cultural institutions even more than the British policy did. On the other hand, "natives" were in principle seen as potential Frenchmen, with the implication that, once civilized, they could be granted the rights of French citizens. In some instances, France conferred citizenship rights on colonial subjects. For example, in 1848 African males from the coastal region of Senegal were granted voting rights and sent a Senegalese representative, Durand Valentin, to the French legislature. However, even the promise of French citizenship was double-edged, connoting greater dependence on and integration with colonial masters, rather than greater self-determination and autonomy. In practice, moreover, intense racism and violent subjugation undermined lofty French ideals of republicanism and democracy. In places like West Africa, for example, the exclusion of Africans from administrative posts and the denial of their right to elect their own representatives tarnished the rhetoric of full citizenship.

Comparing French and British Rule

Despite these important ideological distinctions, the difference between French and British forms of governance should not be exaggerated. In practice, both Britain and France relied on a combination of direct rule through a European official and indirect rule through local collaborators and paid agents. The French also focused their assimilationist efforts on those colonies—like Algeria—which they felt had the greatest potential for Europeanization. Elsewhere—as in Indochina, Madagascar, and Morocco—they settled for improving "natives" within the context of their own cultures. Moreover, as Darwinian ideas grew stronger in France, the debate over whether the cultural assimilation of colonial subjects was possible or even desirable intensified, leading to the abandonment of the *mission civilisatrice* as official policy after the First World War. French and British rule thus differed more in theory than they did in practice.

Non-Western Nationalisms

The mid-to-late nineteenth century witnessed the emergence and growth of nationalist sentiments not only in Europe, but in its colonies in Asia and Africa as well.

Characteristics of Colonial Nationalism

In the late nineteenth century, notions of the nation and nationhood in the colonial world shared important features with their European counterparts. Nationalisms in Asia and Africa thus typically centered on the belief in a shared—sometimes fabricated—history and culture. For Chinese nationalists like Sun Yat-sen, the splendors of the Chinese past rendered the present-day subjugation of the Chinese under the Qing and the European powers unnatural and unacceptable. Likewise, the Pan African movement appealed to an imagined precolonial past in which harmony between African polities and ethnicities prevailed.

Like late-nineteenth-century European nationalism, non-Western nationalisms also frequently defined themselves in racial, ethnic, and religious terms. Chinese nationalists, for example, privileged the majority Han as the "true" Chinese and denied equal status to other

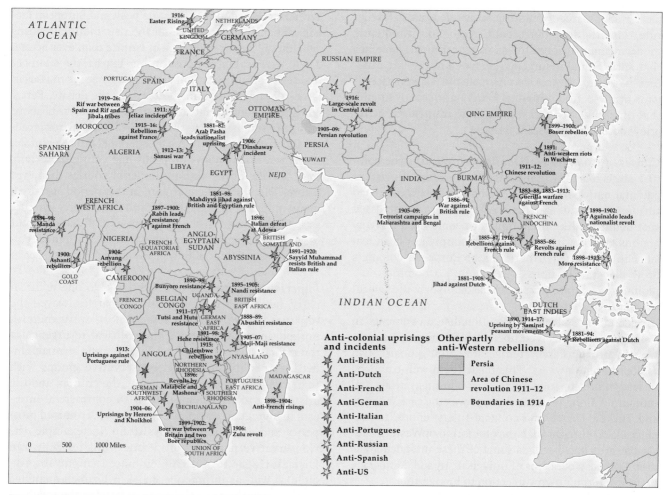

MAP 25.4 RESISTANCE TO IMPERIALISM, 1880–1920
This map reveals widespread opposition to colonial rule at the turn of the twentieth century. Although strategic and technological advantages allowed the European nations to conquer much of Africa and Asia in this period, indigenous resistance made the full-scale pacification of the colonies a longer, more difficult process. How did European methods of colonial governance attempt to thwart rebellion?

ethnic groups, such as the Tibetans and Mongols. Exclusion along religious or cultural lines was also common. In India, a Hindu branch of nationalism claimed Indian history as Hindu history, labeling the long periods of Muslim rule in India as the dark years of foreign invasion. With the substantial Muslim population in India thus excluded from Indian nationalism, some Muslim leaders pledged loyalty to the British while others demanded a separate Muslim nation.

Some nationalist movements, notably those in China and the Ottoman Empire, saw the indigenous regime that had allowed European encroachment as the primary enemy. Under the leadership of Sun Yat-sen, Chinese nationalists attacked and, in 1911, ultimately overthrew the declining Qing Dynasty, which they condemned as both inefficient and illegitimate. Likewise, a group of nationalist reformers known as the Young Turks revolted against Ottoman rule in 1908, blaming both Sultan Abdul Hamid's authoritarian

regime and European intervention for the decline of Ottoman power. Seeking to introduce Western-style political and administrative reforms independent of European interference, the Young Turks succeeded, for a brief period, in establishing a constitutional government with secular institutions.

Non-Western nationalist movements at the turn of the century differed sharply from other forms of anticolonial insurgence. The latter tended to be local in character and aimed against the direct oppressor, rather than at colonial rule. The Indian Rebellion of 1857, for example, targeted local Indian landholders and moneylenders and local colonial magistrates and police, rather than the British government in India. Similarly, in the Maji Maji Rebellion of 1906–1907 in German East Africa, traditional religious leaders led angry peasants in fighting the imposition of cotton cultivation by the Germans, targeting African as well as German overseers. Non-Western nationalist movements, by contrast, clearly articulated their struggle as one against foreign rule, with the long-range political goal of introducing modern constitutional forms of government. The fact that anticolonial insurgence persisted in the late nineteenth century reveals that African and Asian nationalisms of the period remained largely elitist movements that often failed to address the more immediate, acute grievances of the colonial masses.

Causes of Colonial Nationalism   Ironically, the colonial state itself in many ways facilitated the rise of colonial nationalism. First, colonial educational institutions, courts of law, and railways that crisscrossed vast countries like India brought people from faraway regions together in ways that had simply not been feasible in the past. Furthermore, as European colonists drew disparate regions together into a common, exploitative economic system, nationalists could appeal to a sense of shared fate.

Second, most leaders of nationalist movements in Asia and Africa received liberal educations in Western-style institutions and often became professionals, such as doctors and lawyers. This made them well-equipped to lead efforts to modernize their administrations and economies along Western lines, as was the case in Egypt and Turkey. Hence, the colonial rulers' efforts to produce a local elite through the promotion of Western education often backfired, as some of these intended allies used European concepts of universalism and democracy to question their own subjection to foreign rule.

The emergence of the mass press and, with that, the growth of a politically informed civic public also contributed to the growth of colonial nationalisms. Print media, including newspapers, journals, books, and pamphlets, that addressed nationalist issues now circulated among a much larger literate audience. This literature appeared not just in the languages of the colonizer but in local languages that had become systematized and standardized with their own formal grammars in this period, both by educated natives and by colonial administrators and missionaries seeking to modernize and master languages unfamiliar to them. The formation of a broad range of indigenous voluntary associations also created a new arena in which the educated public came together to discuss the pertinent issues of the day. Nationalist organizations, such as the Indian National Congress (founded in 1885), often took shape in this setting.

Debating Empire: Imperial Politics in the Metropole

While a common cultural framework informed European attitudes toward empire in the nineteenth century, a range of different views and voices nevertheless existed. In fact, in the late nineteenth century, with Western global domination at its peak and European racism and cultural arrogance on the rise, more Europeans debated the nature and scope of empire than ever before. There were several reasons for this. In part, the efforts of nineteenth-century nation-states to engage the masses in issues of empire explain the reach of the debate. Better educated, more literate Europeans now learned about empire in state-supported primary schools and from reading the mass press. With the broadening of the electorate, moreover, many more Europeans had voting rights and, thus, a stake in the nation's imperial politics than ever before. The vast scale of empire in this period also drew many more Europeans directly into the empire, whether as soldiers fighting in colonial wars, as civil servants sent to govern the empire, as emigrants to the settlement colonies, or as relatives of Europeans abroad.

Imperialist Politicians and Parties   No one political party, but rather groups within all parties, waved the imperial banner. Nonetheless, almost everywhere in Europe, imperialism aided the political resurgence of the right, especially in Great Britain and Germany. Indeed, imperialism allowed conservative groups with their traditional base in the army, the church, and the aristocracy to ally themselves with commercial interests in a program of popular appeal that promised prosperity and national glory. In Britain, for example, the Conservative party, led by Prime Minister Benjamin Disraeli (1868; 1874–1880), embraced empire in principle as well as in practice. In 1875 Disraeli snatched up shares in the Suez Canal in 1875 from the indebted Khedive in a successful attempt to outmaneuver the French and secure British control over Egypt. In 1876 he conferred the title Empress of India on Queen Victoria, a gesture that captured the popular imagination.

Liberals and centrists took the imperial initiative elsewhere. In France, republicans like Jules Ferry and Leon Gambetta, backed by a group of former colonial administrators and military men in the parliament, promoted expansionism in an effort to bolster national prestige after the demoralizing defeat in the Franco-Prussian War of 1870–1871. Likewise, Italian liberals such as Francesco Crispi and Giovanni Giolitti pursued imperial ventures in the hope of fostering Italian nationalist sentiment.

Critics of Empire   Outspoken critics of empire could be found, however, in almost all political camps. In Belgium, the king's sponsorship of empire met with political opposition from the entire Belgian parliament. Some on the political right also disapproved of empire as a dangerous distraction from domestic issues. According to French rightists, for example, empire diverted attention from the nation's mission to take back Alsace-Lorraine, seized by the Germans in 1871. In

HOBSON'S INTERPRETATION OF IMPERIALISM

Debate on the interpretation of imperialism has not ceased since the publication of J. A. Hobson's Imperialism: A Study *in 1902. The work went through many editions and remains worth reading today. Hobson was a highly respected British economist and social scientist, and his study is filled with statistics and careful argument. His conclusions capture some of the essence and polemic tone of the case he made.*

"If Imperialism may no longer be regarded as a blind inevitable destiny, is it certain that imperial expansion as a deliberately chosen line of public policy can be stopped?

"We have seen that it is motivated, not by the interests of the nation as a whole, but by those of certain classes, who impose the policy upon the nation for their own advantage.... The essentially illicit nature of this use of the public resources of the nation to safeguard and improve private investments should be clearly recognized.

"... Analysis of Imperialism, with its nature supports, militarism, oligarchy, bureaucracy, protection, concentration of capital and violent trade fluctuations, has marked it out as the supreme danger of modern national States. The power of the imperialist forces within the nation to use the national resources for their private gain, by operating the instrument of the States, can only be overthrown by the establishment of a genuine democracy."

Britain, the liberals largely opposed further imperial expansion, particularly after the Indian Rebellion of 1857. Liberals also rejected many of the techniques of imperial expansion, including the use of ambiguous treaties and the hasty reliance on force. The liberal leader William Gladstone (1868–1874; 1880–1885; 1886; 1892–1894) won the election of 1880 after campaigning against the immoral and un-Christian imperialist policies of the Conservatives and only supported imperial rule in the most lukewarm fashion. Even so, many liberal imperialists joined the conservative Tories because of Gladstone's "betrayal" and, ultimately, the Liberal party hatched its own imperial wing.

Across Europe, the radical left, especially socialists, presented the most consistent and vocal opposition to imperialism. Anatole France, one of France's most popular authors, told a protest meeting in 1906, "Whites do not communicate with blacks or yellow people except to enserf or massacre them. The people whom we call barbarians know us only through our own crimes." Socialists, radicals, and labor leaders likened the suppression of strikers and radical agitators to the brutality of imperial repression and protested the living conditions of European workers and peasants by comparing their subordination to that of colonial subjects.

The opposition of leftists to empire emerged not only out of feelings of solidarity with oppressed peoples but also out of their fundamental ideological antagonism toward capitalism, which they saw as inextricably entwined with imperialism. Leftist thinkers, in fact, wrote some of the first and most influential (if inaccurate) analyses of the causes and consequences of empire at the turn of the nineteenth century. In *Imperialism: A Study* (1902), the British left liberal economist J. A. Hobson argued that imperialism emerged out of the inherent logic of industrial capitalism and its fundamentally unequal distribution of wealth (see "Hobson's Interpretation of Imperialism," above). Underconsumption caused by the low wages of industrial workers and the excess savings of the wealthy created insufficient aggregate demand in the domestic economy, and profit-seeking capitalists therefore turned to new markets overseas as a more profitable setting in which to invest their surplus capital. Imperialism thus stemmed from capitalist exploitation of the European working classes and fostered still greater injustice in its exploitation of the colonial masses.

Hobson inspired the even more scathing critique of imperialism's exploitation of the global masses of the Russian Marxist leader V. I. Lenin. In *Imperialism: The Last Stage of Capitalism* (1916), Lenin elaborated on Hobson's analysis, linking imperialism specifically to the advent of monopoly capitalism, a new and more advanced phase of capitalist development in which financial, rather than industrial, capital propelled the European economy. In his view, the new imperialism was fomented by competition between an ever-smaller number of monopoly capitalists—large firms—for domination of global investment and raw material markets. For Lenin, imperialism represented capitalism in its highest and most parasitic stage.

Popular Attitudes toward Imperialism While imperial support cut across class divisions, certain social groups nevertheless tended to identify more with the imperial mission than others.

Imperial rule had particular meaning, for example, for members of the aristocracy, especially in Britain

Although missionaries confronted great obstacles—including little success in converting Africans and colonial administrators who regarded Christian conversion as a potential threat to the status quo—they continued to come to Africa in large numbers. In this photograph, from late-nineteenth-century French Equatorial Africa, the missionary's evident satisfaction in his paternalistic role provides a stark contrast to the sullenness of his flock.

and France. Aristocrats, after all, expected to feel distant from the people they ruled and were comfortable with a language of subordination applicable to both European and colonial societies. In Britain, the younger sons of aristocratic families had a long tradition of government and military service. With democratization and the rise of a civil service, their best chances for the experience of governing or of military command were in the empire. In France, where the Republic turned anticlerical after 1875, Catholic and monarchist nobles were largely excluded from public positions at home but could still find them in the colonies.

The European working classes were divided on the issue. In Britain and Germany, they tended to support empire more often than not. In Britain, the popularity of proimperialists skits and songs in music halls and pubs attests to the **jingoism** of working-class audiences. In Germany, the government's dedication to militarism and nationalism promoted popular support of the German Empire. By contrast, large segments of the French and Italian masses opposed colonialism, even during the zenith of expansion in the late nineteenth century, and protested conscription to fight in colonial wars. Ill-fated imperial ventures, in fact, swept both the French leader Jules Ferry (1885) and the Italian leader Francesco Crispi (1896) from office.

The Effects of Imperialism on European Society

Although empire did not necessarily constitute the central political or social issue of the late nineteenth century, it nevertheless touched the lives of ordinary Europeans more than ever before. This new reach reflected the scope of empire itself, which attracted increasing numbers of Europeans overseas. Growing awareness of and involvement in empire may also be traced to the rise of a new commercial culture, exposing Europeans to a flood of imperial imagery and goods. Finally, as empire became closely identified with new European gender roles, it became further integrated into the mainstream of European culture.

Europeans in the Empire Although European manpower was scarce almost everywhere outside the few colonies where Europeans had settled, European soldiers, administrators, and missionaries came to the empire in growing numbers. European conscripts fought not only in wars of conquest but in the ongoing repression of anticolonial insurgence as well. For officials at every level of the expanding colonial administration, employment in the colonial service conferred a degree of prestige and power that an analogous position in Europe simply could not bring. Peasants and villagers revered the District Collector (tax collector) in India, for example, as a minor *raja* or deity. Missionaries also continued to flock to the empire, where they confronted new challenges, including the advance of Islam and the erosion of their authority in the form of breakaway "Africanized" Christian churches. They also faced the obstructionism of colonial administrators who feared that conversion efforts would spark indigenous unrest.

With the opening of the Suez Canal (which cut the distance by boat from England to India almost in half), the introduction of faster steamships, and the expansion of colonial railway networks, European women also appeared on the imperial scene in new numbers. In addition to married women who joined their husbands in the army or the colonial administration, a substantial number of single women emigrated to the colonies during the late nineteenth century in search of employment or marriage opportunities unavailable at home. Many of them failed to find suitable jobs, suffering downward economic mobility and a loss of social status.

In addition, European migration to the settlement colonies peaked in this period, although it never approached the numbers of Europeans emigrating to the United States. The French emigrated primarily to Algeria in the late nineteenth century, where they ultimately constituted 10 percent of the Algerian population. British emigration to Canada, Australia, and New Zealand also increased substantially. Between 1896 and 1914, for example, 150,000 British citizens resettled in Canada. By the end of the century, many French and British citizens had friends or relatives who lived in or had completed a stint in the colonies.

Representing the Empire In the late nineteenth century, Europeans absorbed information about and images of the empire in myriad new ways. To begin with, a more literate European public, educated in state-supported primary schools, now could read about empire in a variety of print venues. The most important of these was the mass press. European governments were quick to recognize the political potential of the press and to use it to mobilize public opinion in favor of empire at key moments. When British metropolitan support for the Boer War was at low ebb, for example, the *London Times* played a critical role in drumming up anti-Afrikaner sentiment. Europeans also avidly read the memoirs of explorers and missionaries and devoured imperial adventure novels during this period. H. Rider Haggard's best-selling novel, *King Solomon's Mines* (1885), detailing the exploits of British heroes as they penetrate a remote African region, encounter savages, and discover the riches of a vanished civilization, exemplifies the genre.

Beyond the world of print media, the empire was on visual display, often in spectacular form, at the turn of the century. Unlike earlier periods, when elite boutiques sold luxury goods from the empire to the rich, the emergence of the department store meant that middle-class consumers could purchase an array of moderately priced imperial exotica, ranging from Persian rugs to shawls from India. From the 1880s on, department stores catered to the middle-class European taste for Japanese and Chinese ornaments—screens, fans, and porcelain, for example—in household decor. By the 1890s, some department stores featured fashions designated specifically for the colonies, often with a rugged or military look, to outfit the fashionable European elite overseas.

PEARS' SOAP IN THE SOUDAN.

"Even if our invasion of the Soudan has done nothing else it has at any rate left the Arab something to puzzle his fuzzy head over, for the legend PEARS' SOAP IS THE BEST, inscribed in hugh white characters on the rock which marks the farthest point of our advance towards Berber, will tax all the wits of the Dervishes of the Desert to translate."—Phil Robinson, *War Correspondent (in the Soudan) of the Daily Telegraph in London,* 1884.

This advertisement from the *Illustrated London News* in 1897 depicts a group of Sudanese warriors dumbfounded at the sight of the Pears' soap slogan carved into a cliff-side. Pears had no intention of selling soap to the Sudanese. Instead, its product was being presented to British consumers as a symbol of the superiority of British civilization and its imperative to dominate others.
The Mary Evans Picture Libarary

The budding advertising industry also exploited imperial imagery in magazines, on city billboards and posters, and in product brochures. Advertisers exploited the appeal of empire to market products with no imperial connection, plastering likenesses of the popular explorer of Africa, Henry Stanley, for example, on advertisements for Bovril bouillon and Congo Soap. Some advertisements seemed to serve as much as imperial propaganda as they did marketing tools. In a striking example, an advertisement for Pears' Soap linked themes of cleanliness, civilization, and hygiene by depicting awed Sudanese "savages" genuflecting before a cliff etched with the words "PEARS' SOAP IS THE BEST" (see above).

From the 1860s on, Europeans began to exhibit their empires in the setting of world's fairs. Mounted in different European and American cities about once every decade, the fairs displayed the industrial prowess of participating nations to vast audiences. By the 1890s, no world's fair was complete without its own ethnographic displays of colonial peoples, often located, significantly, next to the animal displays. Grouped in reconstructed colonial villages, between fifty and two hundred men, women, and children lived for months at a time on the fairgrounds. There they carried out "exotic" rituals, such as indigenous dancing, along with the mundane activities of daily life, in effect performing the role of "primitive" before rapt European audiences. The most popular exhibits were often those of peoples deemed to be most "savage," such as villagers from Dahomey (Benin).

In addition to the imaginary travel enabled by the world's fairs, middle- and upper-class Europeans began to visit parts of the empire as tourists in the late nineteenth century. While the tourist industry itself was new and still developing largely around seaside and spa resorts within Europe, improved steamships and the development of railway networks in many parts of the world made it possible to travel farther afield. Starting in the 1850s, the British entrepreneur Thomas Cook organized the first commercial tours to North Africa and the Middle East. Algeria and Egypt quickly emerged as popular destinations. Relying on Baedeker and other guidebooks to provide insight into the exotic, British, German, French, and American tourists admired indigenous architecture, purchased "native" handicrafts, and gawked at the local populations.

Empire also influenced the development of high art in the late nineteenth century, in particular the birth of artistic modernism. Imperial expansion fueled new interest in the "primitive" as a subject of art, as in the case of the French artist Paul Gauguin, who left Europe to relocate to Oceania, where he took a series of indigenous wives and embarked on a career of painting unspoiled and sensual "noble savages." By the turn of the century, "primitive" art itself soon came to influence the artistic vanguard in Europe. As invading Europeans conquered new terrain, plundered art and artifacts from Africa and Oceania began to surface as curios in European flea markets and as parts of ethnographic exhibits in natural history museums. Avant-garde artists in Dresden, Berlin, and Paris (including Wassily Kandinsky, Henri Matisse, and Pablo Picasso) quickly "discovered" them and sought to incorporate "primitive" elements into their own art. For Picasso, for example, the simple geometric abstractions of African masks could convey powerful emotions with an immediacy and directness lacking in European representational art. His efforts to reproduce this effect by fusing features of African art with elements of ancient Iberian

This illustration of 1900 shows French tourists in Biskra, Algeria, visiting the Ouled Nails, a nomadic tribe well known for its dancing women. The man consults his Baedeker guide while the woman inspects the Ouled Nails women through her lorgnette, almost as if the women were animals or inanimate objects.

sculpture gave rise to **Cubism,** one of the first European forays into abstraction.

Gender and Empire With a European population comprising mainly male colonial administrators, soldiers, and missionaries, empire emerged as a male-dominated sphere early in the nineteenth century. This male ethos became even more pronounced in the latter part of the century, as the empire became closely associated with a new model of masculinity. Under the influence of Darwinian theory, a substantial number of Europeans came to fear that "overcivilization"—the loss of instinct and physical fitness due to urbanization and industrialization—was promoting the "degeneration" of the white race. They targeted modern men, in particular, as the passive, enfeebled, unmanly products of the machine age, urging participation in the competitive arenas of nature, war, and empire as the cure. In effect, the new masculinity cast off what were seen as the "soft" female characteristics of midcentury manhood, such as sensitivity and dependency, and embraced "hard" masculine values of instinct, aggression, virility, and self-reliance. In European primary schools, in popular books and magazines, and in a slew of new scouting, hiking, gymnastics, and hunting organizations designed to toughen boys and young men, a whole generation learned to celebrate empire as a proving ground for masculinity. Enthusiasts applied the same formula to the nation: Just as competition and the struggle for domination could make men out of boys, so would imperial conquest empower weak and degenerate nations.

The imperial experience also shaped feminine gender ideals, both in the metropole and abroad. Earlier in the century, Victorian domestic ideology had established women's special mission to be that of safeguarding civilized values and morally and spiritually elevating those around them. For British women, this mission found particular expression in their intense involvement in the antislavery movement. Europeans still assigned this moralizing role to women in the late nineteenth century but imbued it, in the aftermath of Darwin, with new racial significance. As women took their place in the empire, their charge was not merely to protect European standards of morality but to defend the biological purity of the white race.

European women were to fulfill these responsibilities in several ways. They were expected both to produce white offspring and to deter European men from having sexual relations with indigenous women, thereby preventing interbreeding between "natives" and Europeans, said to contaminate whiteness and lead to the degeneration of the race. They were also intended to police the cultural and social boundaries between Europeans and subject peoples, in large part by implementing the rules of European etiquette. By insisting that Indian subjects appear before the British without shoes, for example, British women clearly demarcated the social distance between ruler and ruled. After the arrival of women, the British club also became a much more exclusive institution, where the social rituals of British life—dances, card-playing, teas—were meticulously reproduced. Because women's presence in the empire exposed them to the supposed lechery of barbarous natives, moreover, the lines between white and nonwhite societies furthered hardened, as European males felt that the virtue of their women had to be protected at all costs. Acting out of those beliefs, colonial administrators subjected colonized men to new surveillance and, if suspected of any infraction, to draconian punishments.

The presence of women in the colonies thus tended to exacerbate tensions between Europeans and indigenous populations. The most extreme example of this was the role played by the British woman in India, the detested **memsahib**, in part a caricature, in part a real social type. Pampered and spoiled, blatantly racist and contemptuous of all things Indian, the *memsahib* quickly earned the hatred of her colonial subjects. British men, as well, often blamed her for deteriorating relations between Indians and British, conveniently ignoring the fact that economic changes—including the intensified expropriation of peasant lands, political mobilization by Indian nationalists, and the more general rise in European racism—were clearly at fault. Moreover, while the *memsahib* did indeed accentuate the boundaries between the colonizer and the colonized, in doing so she merely carried out the imperial duty that had been assigned to her.

Summary

Europeans conquered much of the world during the nineteenth century. During the first two-thirds of the century, Europeans built their empire gradually and implicitly, as governments intervened politically and militarily to protect commercial interests overseas. They legitimized their growing global presence through the liberal mission of "civilizing" the non-European world. In the last quarter of the century, all this changed. European nation-states now took the imperial lead, competing with one another in an intense race for colonial territory. Influenced by Darwinian biological determinism and disillusioned by anticolonial insurgency, moreover, Europeans increasingly scaled back their civilizing ambitions, often exchanging the exercise of paternalistic authority for that of unapologetic domination.

The European conquest fundamentally altered life both in the colonies and in Europe itself. For colonial subjects, European intervention meant the destruction of indigenous economic, political, and cultural arrangements. The fierce resentment provoked by European rule manifested itself in anticolonial violence and in nationalist movements to end colonial rule. European colonial domination also profoundly influenced European society and culture in this period, affecting everything from gender roles and national identity to popular culture and art.

QUESTIONS FOR FURTHER THOUGHT

1. European colonial rule changed the face of much of the non-Western world during the nineteenth century. How did the imperial experience affect European identity?

2. European colonialism caused immense suffering among subject peoples. Did any segments of colonized societies benefit from colonial rule?

3. In what ways did Europeans themselves contribute to the eventual downfall of their empires?

RECOMMENDED READING

Studies

Adas, Michael. *Machines as a Measure of Man: Science, Technology, and the Ideology of Western Dominance.* 1989. Argues that the formation of imperial ideology in Africa and Asia was linked to notions of scientific progress prevalent in Europe.

Anderson, Benedict. *Imagined Communities: Reflections on the Origin and Spread of Nationalism.* 1983. Classic on the creation and global spread of national identity in the nineteenth century.

Bayly, C. A. *Imperial Meridian: The British Empire and the World, 1780–1830.* 1989. Comprehensive analysis of the expansion of the British Empire in the late eighteenth and early nineteenth century.

Betts, Raymond, ed. *Scramble for Africa: Causes and Dimensions of Empire.* 1966. Early, seminal work on European expansion in Africa.

———. *Assimilation and Integration in French Colonial Theory.* 1961. The now classic study of the shift in the governing ideology of French colonialism from the conversion of the colonized into French citizens to a rejection of this universalism in the years after the First World War.

Boahen, Adu. *African Perspectives on Colonialism.* 1989. Views on the colonial encounter in Africa by a well-known historian from Ghana.

Brantlinger, Patrick. *Rule of Darkness: British Literature and Imperialism, 1830–1914.* 1988. Important exploration of the ways in which imperialist assumptions pervaded Victorian literature.

Brion Davis, David. *The Problem of Slavery in the Age of Revolution.* 1999. A classic on the different factors that influenced opinions on slavery in late-eighteenth- and early-nineteenth-century England and America.

Burton, Antoinette. *Burdens of History: British Feminists, Indian Women, and Imperial Culture, 1865–1915.* 1994. Analysis of the role of imperial ideology in shaping British feminism in the late nineteenth century.

Chaudhuri, Nupur, and Margaret Strobel (eds.). *Western Women and Imperialism: Complicity and Resistance.* 1992. Important collection of essays that analyzes the complex and sometimes contradictory relationship between European women in the colonies and imperial ideology and practice.

Cohn, Bernard. *Colonialism and Its Forms of Knowledge: The British in India.* 1996. Landmark book that argues that imperialism was a project of cultural and not merely military or diplomatic control.

Conklin, Alice. *A Mission to Civilize: The Republican Idea of Empire in France and West Africa, 1895–1930.* 1997. Argues that the democratic assimilationist ideology of the French Third Republic in its colonies was deeply hierarchical and racist.

Coombs, Annie. *Reinventing Africa: Museums, Material Culture, and Popular Culture in Late Victorian and Edwardian England.* 1994. Discusses how the representation of Africa in exhibits and displays in nineteenth-century Europe served to shape notions of African "otherness" and European superiority.

Cooper, Frederick. *Africa since 1940: The Past of the Present.* 2002. History of decolonization and independence in Africa that links developments in the processes of nation and state building by contemporary African leaders to its colonial history.

Cooper, Frederick, and Ann Laura Stoler. *Tensions of Empire: Colonial Cultures in a Bourgeois World.* 1997. Important collection of essays on the ways in which imperialism shaped both metropolitan and colonial cultures.

Curtin, Philip D. *The World and the West: The European Challenge and the Overseas Response in the Age of Empire.* 2000. An overview of the response of the colonized parts of the world to European expansion.

Duus, Peter. *The Abacus and the Sword: The Japanese Penetration of Korea, 1895–1910.* 1995. Discusses the Japanese expansion into Korea in the heyday of Meiji-era imperialism.

Fieldhouse, David Kenneth. *The Colonial Empires: A Comparative Survey from the Eighteenth Century.* 1982. Classic on the subject from a comparative perspective.

Hall, Catherine. *Civilising Subjects: Colony and Metropole in the English Imagination, 1830–1867.* 1992. Using the example of Jamaica, this seminal work argues that the idea of empire was at the heart of the self-imagining of Britain by the middle of the nineteenth century.

Headrick, Daniel R. *The Tools of Empire: Technology and European Imperialism in the Nineteenth Century.*

1981. Argues convincingly for the importance of technology for various aspects of European imperialism.

Hobsbawm, E. J. *Age of Empire: 1875–1914.* 1987. Discusses the role of imperialism in shaping political and social life in the metropole.

Hochschild, Adam. *King Leopold's Ghost: A Story of Greed, Terror, and Heroism in Colonial Africa.* 1998. The story of the ruthless plundering of the Belgian Congo by King Leopold II of Belgium in the early nineteenth century and the battles against him both by African rebel leaders and by other Europeans.

Mamdani, Mahmood. *Citizen and Subject: Contemporary Africa and the Legacy of Late Colonialism.* 1996. Bold, insightful analysis of how British indirect rule in colonial Africa reproduced racial and ethnic divisions that have stood in the way of democratic reforms in contemporary times.

Metcalf, Thomas. *Ideologies of the Raj.* 1995. Examines the transformation in British rule in India after the Rebellion of 1857.

Owen, Roger, and Bob Sutcliffe. (eds.). *Studies in the Theory of Imperialism.* 1972. Seminal collection of Marxist and non-Marxist essays on theories of imperialism.

Pitts, Jennifer. *A Turn to Empire: The Rise of Imperial Liberalism in Britain and France.* 2005. Looks at the changes in nineteenth-century liberal thought from a critique of empire to its justification by men like John Stuart Mill and Alexis de Tocqueville.

Richards, Thomas. *The Commodity Culture of Victorian England: Advertising Spectacle 1851–1914.* 1990. Examines how capitalism and empire influenced consumerism in Victorian England.

Said, Edward. *Culture and Imperialism.* 1993. This landmark books draws connections between imperialism and Western literature in the nineteenth and twentieth centuries.

Stocking, George. *Race, Culture, and Evolution: Essays on the History of Anthropology.* 1968. Classic on the history of the discipline of anthropology, focusing on the shifts in the approach to the issue of race.

Stokes, Eric. *English Utilitarians in India.* 1959. Classic study of liberal thinkers and British administrators in India.

Henry Tonks
AN ADVANCED DRESSING STATION IN FRANCE, 1917
A British surgeon and painter, Henry Tonks, was sent to the front in 1917 to paint this scene
of a dressing station at the Somme, where officers classify the wounded while the artillery
barrages go on.
Imperial War Museum, London

Chapter Twenty-Six

WORLD WAR I AND THE WORLD IT CREATED

THE COMING OF WORLD WAR • THE COURSE OF THE WAR
• THE PEACE • POSTWAR DEMOCRACY

In 1914 Germany, Russia, Austria-Hungary, France, and Great Britain were suddenly at war—a war different from any that had gone before, a war that permanently altered society and politics, and a war that even in retrospect stands as the dividing point between two eras. Interpreting its origins is thus crucial to any understanding of modern history and is still the subject of controversy. Historians have given few subjects closer study than the system of alliances and the diplomatic moves that led to World War I. We understand the role of events, the arms race, and strident nationalism in leading to catastrophe.

The larger question is whether these fatal steps were themselves a result of long-term trends—economic expansion, imperialism, social divisions, ideological conflicts, and democratic politics. Once it came, the war strained every resource of the belligerents and mobilized civilian life as never before. As it ended, the victors were shaken, their societies and politics different. The losing states crumbled, opening the way to still more dramatic political changes. The complicated peace settlement, which changed the map of Europe and tried to make democracy universal, was meant above all to ensure that there would not be another world war.

● **1890** French-Russian Alliance

● **1882** Triple Alliance between Germany, Austria-Hungary, and Italy

● **1878** Berlin Congress awards Bosnia-Herzogovina to Austria-Hungary

● **1871** German Empire founded under Emperor William I and Chancellor Bismarck

THE COMING OF WORLD WAR

International relations held center stage in the period from 1870 to World War I for a variety of reasons. The balance of power established at the Congress of Vienna in 1815 had been overturned by the unification of Italy and Germany and by Prussia's defeat of Austria in 1866 and of France in 1870. The heightened sense of insecurity that followed led to an intricate web of alliances requiring constant attention. At the same time, imperialism, economic competition, and an escalating arms race multiplied the arenas in which national interests might clash. In addition, every threat, insult, or setback was magnified in daily journalism and domestic politics, for nationalism sold newspapers and made political careers. Foreign ministries worked to keep these conflicting pressures under control through diplomacy conducted by gentlemen, largely in secret and according to elaborate rules.

Bismarck dominated the Congress of Berlin in 1878 much as he dominates this portrait, which shows him being congratulated by the Russian delegate, with Count Andrassy of Austria-Hungary on the left.
AKG London

Bismarck's System of Alliances

From the 1860s to 1890, Bismarck dominated international relations. His diplomacy was essential to the creation of the Second Reich, and he led Europe's major nations in addressing a series of long-term issues, particularly the decline of Ottoman power, the resulting power vacuum in the Balkans, and competing Russian and Austrian ambitions there. His first concern was to make the new German nation secure from any potential foreign threat. Although intended to increase security, the treaties Bismarck fostered ultimately stimulated a dangerous arms race.

The Congress of Berlin, 1878 Bismarck established his mastery at the Congress of Berlin in 1878. Again, as at the time of the Crimean War twenty years earlier,

Russia had expanded its influence in the Balkans by defeating Turkey in war and by forcing the sultan to cede territory across the Caucasus Mountains to Russia, to allow creation of an enlarged Montenegro and Serbia, and to grant full independence to a large and autonomous Bulgaria, which everyone believed would be a Russian puppet. This was more than the other European powers would allow. The aim of the Congress was to restrain Russian ambitions while finding a response to Balkan nationalism and Ottoman weakness that avoided further war.

With few German interests directly involved, Bismarck presented himself as an "honest broker" and skillfully orchestrated agreements in which everyone got something. The settlement granted autonomy to a

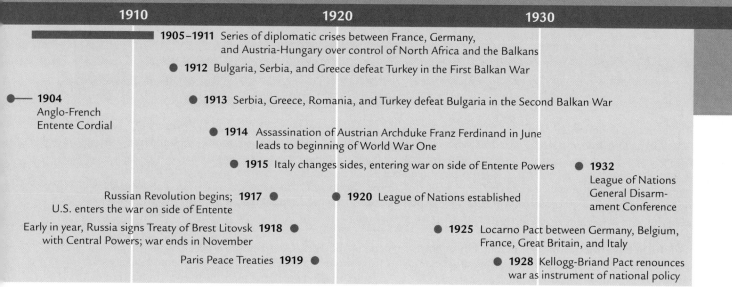

| 1910 | 1920 | 1930 |

1905–1911 Series of diplomatic crises between France, Germany, and Austria-Hungary over control of North Africa and the Balkans

1912 Bulgaria, Serbia, and Greece defeat Turkey in the First Balkan War

1904 Anglo-French Entente Cordial

1913 Serbia, Greece, Romania, and Turkey defeat Bulgaria in the Second Balkan War

1914 Assassination of Austrian Archduke Franz Ferdinand in June leads to beginning of World War One

1915 Italy changes sides, entering war on side of Entente Powers

1932 League of Nations General Disarmament Conference

Russian Revolution begins; **1917** U.S. enters the war on side of Entente

1920 League of Nations established

Early in year, Russia signs Treaty of Brest Litovsk **1918** with Central Powers; war ends in November

1925 Locarno Pact between Germany, Belgium, France, Great Britain, and Italy

Paris Peace Treaties **1919**

1928 Kellogg-Briand Pact renounces war as instrument of national policy

greatly reduced Bulgaria (thus lessening Russia's gains) and recognized the independence of Serbia, Romania, and Montenegro (acknowledging rising nationalism).[1] Austria-Hungary, nervous about a challenge from new and nationalist Balkan states, was authorized in compensation to occupy Bosnia and Herzegovina, which nevertheless remained formally under Ottoman rule. In addition Britain's occupation of Cyprus was confirmed, and Tunis was in effect promised to France. The balance the Congress of Berlin achieved among competing nations had come at the expense of a weakening Ottoman Empire and by extending the dominion of the major powers—a pattern characteristic of imperialism.

Germany's Alliances Fresh from this triumph, Bismarck persuaded Austria-Hungary to a mutual defense pact. Austria was worried by Russia's ambitions and grateful for Germany's support at the Congress, and the secret pact became the foundation of German foreign policy. The two nations promised that should either be attacked by Russia the other would come to its defense. But Bismarck sought further insurance, and so in 1881 he audaciously persuaded Russia (eager to escape diplomatic isolation) to join Germany and Austria-Hungary in promising to remain neutral in the event of war between any of them and a fourth power. To these understandings, Bismarck then added a third, the Triple Alliance of Italy, Germany, and Austria-Hungary. This renewable, five-year pact was first signed in 1882. In creating this treaty, Bismarck took advantage of Italy's resentment of France for occupying Tunis in 1881.

[1] The tsar's nephew was elected to the Bulgarian throne. Rumelia, the southern part of Bulgaria, remained under Turkish rule as a separate province. The provinces of Wallachia and Moldavia had been joined in 1862 to form Romania and received their own prince two years later. A Hohenzollern, he became King Carol in 1881.

While imperial competition worked in his favor, Bismarck's goal was the diplomatic isolation of France, for he feared the continuing bitterness in France over the loss of Alsace-Lorraine to Germany in 1870.

Formally, these treaties were defensive, although the secrecy surrounding them fostered a sense of insecurity (see "The Terms of the Triple Alliance," p. 780). They gave Germany an international influence rare in peacetime, but holding them together took great skill. Italy and Russia had more reasons for conflict with Austria-Hungary than with any other nation, and it was hard to keep them tied to Germany. In fact, Russia and Austria-Hungary let their alliance lapse in 1887 because of their disagreements in the Balkans, and Bismarck could only partially repair the damage through a separate Reinsurance Treaty in which Germany and Russia promised to remain neutral toward each other if one of them was at war. For Italy, Austria-Hungary was not only the traditional enemy Italy had fought to achieve unification but the occupier of Italian-speaking lands in the region of Trieste. To persuade Italy to renew the Triple Alliance in 1887, Bismarck had to recognize a range of Italian ambitions in the Balkans, Africa, and elsewhere.

The Shifting Balance

Germany's system of alliances was already showing strains when the Kaiser dismissed Bismarck from office in 1890. Without him, that system disintegrated and German diplomacy became erratic and even abrasive.

German Diplomacy after Bismarck Bismarck's successors understood the importance of Germany's alliances but tended to overlook the new factor that could draw other nations together: common fear of Germany. When Germany's new leaders let the Reinsurance

THE TERMS OF THE TRIPLE ALLIANCE

These articles are from the treaty of 1912 in which Austria-Hungary, Germany, and Italy renewed the Triple Alliance for the fifth time since 1882. This version essentially continued earlier ones, except for articles VI through XI, not printed here, which dealt rather vaguely with the Balkans, Ottoman territories, Egypt, and North Africa. With respect to those regions, the signatories reassured each other that they preferred to maintain the status quo but promised mutual understanding and even support if Austria-Hungary or Italy found it necessary temporarily to occupy territory in the Balkans or if Italy had to take measures against French expansion in North Africa. The promises of support to Italy indicated the higher price now required to keep Italy in the Alliance.

"Article I. The High Contracting Parties mutually promise peace and friendship, and will enter into no alliance or engagement directed against any one of their States.

"They engage to proceed to an exchange of ideas on political and economic questions of a general nature which may arise, and they further promise one another mutual support within the limits of their own interests.

"Article II. In case Italy, without direct provocation on her part, should be attacked by France for any reason whatsoever, the two other Contracting Parties shall be bound to lend help and assistance with all their forces to the Party attacked.

"This same obligation shall devolve upon Italy in case of any aggression without direct provocation by France against Germany.

"Article III. If one, or two, of the High Contracting Parties, without direct provocation on their part, should chance to be attacked and to be engaged in a war with two or more Great Powers nonsignatory to the present Treaty, the *casus foederis* will arise simultaneously for all the High Contracting Parties.

"Article IV. In case a Great Power nonsignatory to the present Treaty should threaten the security of the states of one of the High Contracting Parties, and the threatened Party should find itself forced on that account to make war against it, the two others bind themselves to observe towards their Ally a benevolent neutrality. Each of them reserves to itself, in this case, the right to take part in the war, if it should see fit, to make common cause with its Ally.

"Article V. If the peace of one of the High Contracting Parties should chance to be threatened under the circumstances foreseen by the preceding Articles, the High Contracting Parties shall take counsel together in ample time as to the military measures to be taken with a view to eventual cooperation.

"They engage, henceforth, in all cases of common participation in a war, to conclude neither armistice, nor peace, nor treaty, except by common agreement among themselves.

"Article XII. The High Contracting Parties mutually promise secrecy as to the contents of the present Treaty."

From Sidney Bradshaw Fay, *The Origins of the World War*, Macmillan, 1930.

Treaty with Russia lapse, France pressed Russia for an understanding. By 1894 that became a full alliance. France and Russia promised that each would support the other if either were attacked by Germany or by another member of the Triple Alliance that was aided by Germany. Such an accord between the Russian autocracy and the French Republic had seemed politically impossible, despite Russia's having already turned to France for loans and arms purchases. Now the tsar greeted French delegates while a band played the "Marseillaise," previously outlawed in Russia as a song of revolution.

In response, German diplomats were determined to reassert Germany's importance in world affairs. They did so in inconsistent, even contradictory, ways. On the one hand, the Kaiser attempted to reach some understanding with Great Britain and spoke of a "natural" alliance between the Teutonic and Anglo-Saxon races.

On the other hand, the Germans antagonized and alienated the British. When, in 1896, the South African Boers foiled an attack on the republic of the Transvaal mounted by the British Cape Colony (the Jameson Raid), Kaiser William II sent a telegram congratulating the president of the Boer republic (the Kruger telegram). The British public responded with anger. The Kaiser also explored the possibility of organizing a continental coalition against Great Britain. Above all, the massive expansion of the German navy, vigorously lobbied for by the German Navy League, roused the hostility of the British.

Anglo-French Understanding Relations between Great Britain and France had centered on their colonial competition, in which they had seemed ready to risk war. Instead, they settled for defined spheres of influence. Following the confrontation at Fashoda in 1898, the French set about turning humiliation into good relations. They accepted British domination in Egypt in return for Britain's recognition of French interests in North Africa, particularly Morocco. Further understandings followed, culminating in the Anglo-French Entente Cordiale of 1904, in which France and Great Britain eliminated their major issues of imperial conflict. Those issues stretched from Asia to the Atlantic (from Siam to Newfoundland) and across the African continent (from the Niger River to North Africa). Formally a mere understanding, the Entente implied much more, as the exchange of public visits between Edward VII and the president of France was meant to demonstrate.

Germany's diplomatic position remained strong, and German leaders reasoned that an assertive foreign policy would demonstrate that strength. But the tenor of international relations was changing. As armaments increased and treaties proliferated, each power became more obsessed with its own security, and public opinion grew more sensitive to questions of national honor.

Testing Alliances: Three International Crises From 1905 to 1911 three diplomatic crises—each of which initially seemed a German victory—in fact drew Germany's opponents closer together. The first of these crises arose over Morocco. France, with well-known designs on Morocco, had carefully won acquiescence from the powers except for Germany. The German chancellor, Bernhard von Blow, demanded that an international conference settle Morocco's future. He aimed to demonstrate that France was isolated, and in fact his warnings forced the resignation of Théophile Delcassé, France's foreign minister and the architect of French policy. When in 1906 the conference met at Algeciras, it confirmed that Morocco had special international status but recognized the primacy of French interests. The crisis was a disaster for German diplomacy. Only Austria-Hungary loyally voted with its ally. Italy, Russia, Great Britain, and the United States (now a regular participant in such international agreements) supported France, and Germany's threatening tactics led French and British officials to begin talks about their mutual military interests.

The second crisis arose over the Balkans. Austria was concerned that Serbia, led by a new king and a radical nationalist government, had become a dangerous antagonist. Austria also feared that Turkey's influence in the Balkans would grow following the 1908 revolution in Turkey—led by a group known as the Young Turks, who were determined to modernize their nation. In response, Austria-Hungary decided to annex Bosnia and Herzegovina. That move, which threatened Serbia, in turn outraged Russian Slavophiles. They were nationalists who believed that Russia should defend the interests of Slavs everywhere, and they demanded an international conference. Britain and France agreed. Germany supported Austria-Hungary, although angered by the sudden annexation.

Diplomatic crises were becoming tests of alliances (and significantly, Italy expressed resentment at not being consulted by Austria-Hungary rather than loyalty to the Triple Alliance). There had been earlier signs that Italy might drift away. In 1902 France recognized Italian ambitions in Libya, and France and Italy pledged neutrality if either was attacked by a third power (i.e., Germany). Although the Triple Alliance was renewed in the same year, Italy now sat on the fence between the Franco-Russian and the Austro-German alliances. Only time would tell on which side Italy might end up.

The third major crisis once again involved Morocco, which France now wanted to annex. It had consulted all the European powers, and talks with Germany seemed to be going well when suddenly in 1911 the Germans sent the gunboat *Panther* to the Moroccan port of Agadir (a show of power and a classic imperialist gesture) and then asked for all of the French Congo as the price for accepting France's annexation of Morocco. Both the demands and the method seemed excessive, and in Great Britain David Lloyd George publicly denounced them. Once again, eventual compromise (France would cede parts of its Congo lands and bits of its other African territories adjacent to German colonies) counted for less than the rising tension and growing international distrust of the Germans.

The Arms Race The standing armies of France and Germany doubled between 1870 and 1914, and all able-bodied men had some military responsibilities from the age of twenty to their late fifties. In 1889 Great Britain adopted the principle that its navy must equal in size the two next-largest fleets combined, and in 1906 it had launched the *Dreadnought*, the first battleship armed entirely with big guns. By 1914 Britain had twenty-nine ships of this class afloat and thirteen under construction. The German navy had eighteen, with nine being built. With the dangers of a European arms race ever more apparent, especially the growing naval competition between Britain and Germany, the major powers agreed to two great conferences on disarmament and compulsory arbitration. The conferences met at The Hague in 1899 and again in 1907, but no country was willing to sacrifice any of its strength. At the second conference German delegates bluntly rejected any limitation on their sovereign right to make war, while at that very moment Kaiser William complained to the British press that England should be grateful to Germany for having remained neutral in the Boer War. This time, British recriminations against the outspoken Kaiser reflected an important shift in policy as well as anger.

MAP 26.1 THE BALKANS, 1878–1914

These two maps of southeastern Europe show the new nations created in the period between the Congress of Berlin in 1878 and the beginning of the First World War. Notice which of these nations had gained considerable territory by the end of this period. What developments and events led to such geographical changes in the region, and which of these new countries do you suppose were most aggrieved by these various settlements?

The Triple Entente   In 1902 Britain ended its long tradition of refusing peacetime alliances and did so by signing a treaty with Japan, the rising power in the East. It was a first step toward reducing conflicts over imperial claims. That agreement was followed in 1907 by an accord among France, Russia, and Japan. It delimited each nation's areas of interest and, by guaranteeing the integrity of China, sought to reduce their competition there. Such understandings opened the way for further agreement between Great Britain and Russia, old imperial antagonists. They resolved points of contention reaching from the Black Sea to Persia, Afghanistan, and Tibet. The treaty between Britain and Russia, each already allied with France, brought into being the Triple Entente as an informal coalition of France, Russia, and Britain. It was clearly intended to counterbalance the Triple Alliance of Germany, Austria, and Italy, and its implications became clear when Britain decided in 1912 to withdraw its battleships from the Mediterranean, leaving the French navy to defend Britain's interests

there while the British fleet concentrated on the German threat in the North Sea.

The Outbreak of World War

The Triple Alliance and the Triple Entente glared menacingly at each other, increasing their armament and measuring every international event as a gain or loss for their side.

The Balkan Threat   Turmoil in the Balkans became a test of strength for the two sides. The ferment there of nationalism, modernization, militarism, and shaky parliamentarism echoed Europe-wide trends, but it was complicated by centuries of oppression, by disputed boundaries (most of recent invention), and by social, ethnic, and religious rivalries. The privileged role of Hungarians in Austria-Hungary and the Hungarian policy of enforced "Magyarization"—both consequences of the Compromise of 1867 (see chapter 23) fostered resentment and stoked nationalist aspirations among other ethnic groups living in the Habsburg Empire. The competition between Russia and Austria-Hungary quickly became enmeshed in these conflicts, and so did the Balkan ambitions of Germany (with railway and economic interests in the peninsula) and of Italy.

Italy's defeat of Turkey in 1912, when Italy gained Libya and important Mediterranean islands, triggered what came to be known as the first Balkan War. In the fall of that year Bulgaria, Serbia, and Greece also declared war on Turkey. In a few months they drove the Ottomans from all their remaining holdings in Europe except Constantinople. After a partial truce and months of border skirmishes, the great powers hammered out the terms of peace at the end of May 1913.

One month later Serbia and Greece, quickly joined by Romania and Turkey, declared war on Bulgaria, the big winner in the previous war. This conflict ended in a few weeks, but local anger and international concern did not. The great powers pressured the belligerents to accept peace, but they were watching each other more closely still.

The Assassination of an Austrian Archduke
In this atmosphere of growing distrust, tension between Austria-Hungary and Serbia increased. Groups of Serbian nationalists scattered throughout the Balkan region agitated on behalf of their fellow Slavs living under Austrian rule in Bosnia and Herzegovina, and Austria threatened to use force against Serbia if it did not abandon some of its nationalist claims. Against this background, Archduke Francis Ferdinand, the heir to the Austrian and Hungarian thrones, chose to parade in Sarajevo, the capital of Bosnia, on June 28, 1914. If the archduke wished to display Habsburg authority, others were eager to demonstrate against Austria. As the archduke's car moved down the street, a bomb just missed him. Then other conspirators lost their courage and failed to fire as his car passed by. At that point his driver made a wrong turn, started to back up, and yet another young Bosnian revolutionary fired point-blank, killing both the archduke and his wife.

The leaders of Austria-Hungary, convinced that the Serbian government was involved, believed it essential to respond strongly. They dispatched a special emissary to Berlin, where he was promised Germany's full support, and on July 23 Austria sent an ultimatum to Serbia. Meant to be unacceptable, it gave Serbia forty-eight hours in which to apologize, ban all anti-Austrian propaganda, and accept Austria-Hungary's participation in investigations of the plot against Francis Ferdinand.

Serbia replied with great tact, accepting all terms except those that diminished its sovereignty and offering to submit even these to arbitration. Great Britain proposed an international conference, to which France

I. B. HAZELTON
The assassination of Archduke Francis Ferdinand and his wife in Sarajevo, painted as a dramatic moment when a single act affected the course of history.
Bettmann/Corbis

and Russia reluctantly agreed, and Germany hinted that Serbia and Austria-Hungary alone should settle the matter. Another crisis seemed about to pass when, on July 28, Austria-Hungary declared war on Serbia.

Stumbling into War
The system of alliances, increasing armament, bluster, and compromise had become a trap. Austria-Hungary was in reality not yet ready to fight. Germany and Great Britain still hoped the Austrians would limit themselves to occupying Belgrade, the Serbian capital, and then agree to an international conference. But Russia could not appear to abandon its role as protector of the Slavs nor let Austria-Hungary unilaterally extend its sway in the Balkans.

On July 29 Russia ordered partial mobilization, making clear that its move was aimed at Austria-Hungary only. The following day, however, the Russians discovered they lacked the organization for a partial call-up

By 1912 this Krupp factory at Essen was devoted to the arms race that was consuming an increasing proportion of Europe's energy and wealth.
AKG London

and so announced a general mobilization instead. On July 31 Germany proclaimed a state of readiness, sent Russia an ultimatum demanding demobilization within twelve hours, and requested France to declare what it would do in case of a Russo-German war.

France answered that it would act in its own interests and then mobilized but held its troops ten kilometers (about six miles) from the German frontier to prevent any incidents. The Germans, who had planned next to demand that France guarantee its neutrality by surrendering its border fortresses, were unsatisfied.

On August 1 Germany mobilized and declared war on Russia. Convinced this step meant war on the Western front as well, Germany also invaded Luxembourg and sent an ultimatum to the Belgians demanding the unobstructed passage of German troops. On August 3 Germany declared war on France and invaded Belgium. The following day Great Britain declared war on Germany. Of Europe's six major powers, only Italy remained neutral. Within forty-eight hours, each belligerent had two million soldiers under orders. World War I had begun.

The Origins of World War

The question of what caused the Great War—or, more simply, who was to blame—would become an important issue in European affairs. Four years later the victors in that war blamed Germany so insistently that they would write its guilt into the peace treaty. Most historians have considered that assessment to be one-sided. German scholars rejected it with special force,

which explains the furor some forty years later (after another world war) that greeted the research of the German historian Fritz Fischer. He found evidence that Germany's leaders had, in fact, looked forward to war and nurtured almost boundless ambitions for military dominance. But the question remains without a final answer, for the causes adduced depend very much on how long-range a view one takes.

The Response to an Assassination The immediate cause, the assassination of the archduke, almost did not happen. The tensions that made it so significant had deeper roots, however: in Balkan struggles for independence, in Austria-Hungary's declining power, and in each nation's fears for its safety. Human judgment was also involved, and individual leaders and governments can be blamed for Austria-Hungary's untoward haste in attacking Serbia, Germany's irresponsible support of Austria-Hungary, Russia's clumsy and confused diplomacy, and France's eagerness to prove loyalty to the Russians. British leaders were at fault as well. Not wanting to admit that they were already attached to one side, they failed to warn the Germans that an attack on France meant war with Britain.

The Limits of Diplomacy Such an analysis, however, may make statesmen seem to have been more autonomous and therefore more to blame than they were. The system of alliances that was intended to achieve security had been hardened by habit, military imperatives, and domestic politics. The fears that cemented these commitments were reflected in Britain's conviction

Summer hats in the air, an August crowd in London's Trafalgar Square cheers the declaration of war on Austria, as it had a week earlier the announcement of war with Germany. Similar scenes occurred throughout that week of 1914 in France and Germany. Bettmann/Corbis

In Berlin during August 1914, German volunteers march down the street hailing their good fortune; they will soon fight for their country. Ullstein Bilderdienst/The Granger Collection, New York

that empire required supremacy at sea; France's eagerness to revenge the defeat of 1870 and regain Alsace-Lorraine; Russia's 150 years of territorial expansion; Italy's need to show itself a great power; Austria's dependence, since Metternich, on foreign policy to sustain a shaky regime; and Germany's fear of encirclement and use of prestige abroad to reduce conflict at home.

The arms race itself contributed to the outbreak of war. Strategy was a factor, too. Germany's victory over France in 1870 had been understood to prove the superiority of the Prussian system of universal conscription, large reserves, and detailed military planning.

Military mobilization, which in the eyes of some diplomats was a cumbersome but effective show of resolve, was considered by military men in each country to be an essential act of self-defense. Even slight disadvantages in numbers, weapons, speed, or tactics might prove fatal. Thus, each increase in personnel and weapons was quickly matched, often with enormous effort; France, for example, had only 60 percent of Germany's potential manpower and yet equaled its

Newly mobilized French recruits pose in front of the flower decked train that will carry them off to military duty.
Editions Tallandier

rival through more burdensome conscription. The arms race, justified by the fear that it was meant to allay, fed on itself.

Public Opinion Because such large military expenditures had to be justified to parliaments and the public, there was a heavy political investment in the build-up to war. In every country, those who feared socialism or had military and imperial interests at stake used flag-waving to win votes and nationalism to overcome domestic divisions. This push by conservative forces was especially strong in Germany, where economic growth and social change threatened Prussian dominance and the Junker ruling elite and where militaristic interests groups such as the Pan-German League had been manipulating public opinion since the 1890s.

Throughout Europe, the press added its voice to other pro-war forces. Warmongering appealed most to upper- and middle-class young men who were imbued with the "manly virtues" of perseverance and heroic sacrifice in public schools and universities—but others were not so quick to celebrate. Although many in the working class ended strikes and antiwar protests when war was declared, their response was hardly enthusiastic. For farmers, the coming conflict meant the requisition of their horses and wagons and the drafting of their farmhands. Some historians assert that even among the cheering crowds in the capitals of Europe, exuberance

was short-lived and that most people exhibited solemn resignation at the prospect of war.

THE COURSE OF THE WAR

For decades European military staffs had prepared detailed plans for the situation they now faced. The French intended to drive into Alsace and Lorraine in coordinated dashes that reflected their almost mystic belief in the spirit of a patriotic offensive. German strategy began from the desire to avoid fighting on two fronts simultaneously: A detailed plan adopted years earlier called for assigning minimal forces to hold the Russians in the East and to slow the expected French attack in Alsace. Then Germany's main armies would pour through Belgium and on to Paris. The German aim was to knock France out of the war before Russia could bring its massive armies into play and before British aid could make a difference. That strategy envisioned the German army as a coiled spring to be released the moment war began, and it required the invasion of neutral Belgium, further labeled Germany as the aggressor, and determined Britain's entry into the war. Both sides believed they were ready. The Triple Alliance was reduced to two, Germany and Austria-Hungary, referred to as the **Central Powers.** Italy announced its neutrality when war broke out, declaring the attack on Serbia an offensive action that did not meet the terms of the Triple Alliance. Against the Central Powers stood Britain, France, and Russia, referred to as the **Entente Powers** or the Allies.

The Surprises of the First Two Years

In 1914 the belligerents all assumed the war could not last long. It was thought that modern economies, intricately connected by trade, would be unable to sustain a long conflict and that modern weapons would make for brief wars of rapid movement (as in 1870). But in a few months it began to be clear that the war being fought was not the one planned, though commanders were slow to admit it. Increased firepower gave defensive forces unexpected strength. Cavalry was ineffectual, for rifles could now hit horses from great distances; infantry, loaded down with equipment, could not go far very rapidly; and the common soldier proved able to absorb more punishment than anyone had thought possible.

The German Offensive In their western advance, German commanders had originally sought to implement a set of elaborate plans, first drawn up by Count Alfred von Schlieffen in 1891 and regularly modified thereafter. The plan called for the German armies to advance in a northern arc through France, capture Paris, and thus definitively defeat France. For such a victory, the general staff was willing to violate Belgian and Dutch neutrality and leave the Eastern Front largely to Austrian forces, for which they had little respect. The **Schlieffen Plan** was based on a series of assumptions: that there was no decisive strategic objective on the Eastern Front (which proved true), that Russia would be slow to mobilize (less true than expected), and that modest German forces therefore would be sufficient to hold off the Russians while Germany, employing two-thirds of its forces against the French, would gain an overwhelming advantage on the Western Front.

Despite initial successes, the Germans did not achieve the great victory they had hoped for. Belgium offered unexpected resistance, thus delaying the German advance through the formerly neutral country (Germany ultimately did not invade the Netherlands, which remained neutral for the duration of the war). Then, when a small British force arrived sooner than expected and Russian armies made unexpected advances on the Eastern front, the indecisive if not unstable German chief of staff, Helmuth von Moltke (nephew of the field marshal who had led the Prussians to victory in 1866 and 1870 over France and Austria), modified the Schlieffen Plan. He ordered troops intended for the Western Front to the east and sent extra forces to Alsace in hope of a breakthrough there. The

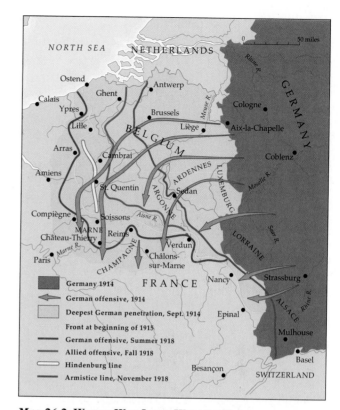

MAP 26.2 WORLD WAR I, THE WESTERN FRONT
This map illustrates both the initial German assault on France and Belgium and subsequent Allied offensives. For the remainder of the war, the battle lines on the Western Front would be drawn around these areas. How did this German assault of the first few months of the war differ from the original Schlieffen Plan?

French, for their part, saw their offensive halted in Alsace, where both German and French forces suffered heavy losses. The French command had underestimated by half the forces they would face at the outbreak of war, and in the first weeks the Germans drove to within thirty miles of Paris. However, with von Moltke's change in plans, the Germans halted their advance east of Paris. The German army soon found itself as battered as its opponents, its casualties as high, and its lines of communication and supply dangerously stretched. After each bloody encounter, the enemies retreated but were not routed, and German officers were surprised they took so few prisoners. This pattern of small initial advances followed by long periods of attrition would remain in place on the Western Front for the duration of the war.

French and Russian Offensives On the other side, the French commander in chief, Joseph Joffre, remained imperturbably confident of the ultimate success of a

CHRONOLOGY
The Western Front

August 1914	Germany invades Belgium.
September 1914	Battle of the Marne ends in stalemate.
December 1914	Battle lines for rest of the war established.
April–May 1915	Germans introduce chlorine gas during Second Battle of Ypres and make slight gains.
May–June 1915	Second Battle of Artois, with some gains for French.
February–July 1916	Battle of Verdun results in nearly 350,000 casualties for each side.
July–November 1916	Battle of the Somme: British lose 400,000 men; French lose 200,000; Germans lose nearly 500,000.
April 1917	United States declares war on Germany and enters the war.
May 1917	Mutinies in the French Army.
July–November 1917	British-led offensive in Flanders; Battle of Passchendaele results in 300,000 dead or wounded British soldiers.
March–June 1918	German offensive makes major gains but is then checked.
May 1918	First major engagement of American troops at the Third Battle of the Aisne.
July–August 1918	Second Battle of the Marne; Germans forced back over Marne.
September 1918	Battle of Argonne and Fourth Battle of Ypres, with slow Allied advance.
November 11, 1918	Armistice.

the Western Front for the next four years. France had not been knocked out of the war, but Germany held the important industrial and agricultural area of northeastern France, a tenth of its territory, and nearly all of Belgium.

On the Eastern Front, Russian armies scored important gains in early August, taking eastern Galicia from Austria-Hungary and beginning an invasion of eastern Prussia in the north. Moltke talked in panic of a general retreat until the battle of Tannenberg late in August. There generals Paul von Hindenburg and Erich Ludendorff, who became Germany's greatest war heroes, surrounded and destroyed a Russian army and then pushed on almost to Warsaw before being stopped.

In the south, Austria-Hungary halted the Russian advance with German aid and took Belgrade despite the strong resistance of the Serbian army. By the end of 1914, Germany and Austria-Hungary had made impressive gains at every hand. They had also gained from Turkey's entry into the war in late October on the side of the Central Powers (and against its old enemy, Russia), which threatened Britain and France through the eastern Mediterranean all the way to Suez.

Trench Warfare   After the first month, it became clear that new military technology and mass transport had changed the manner in which war would be conducted, with terrifying results. The Eastern Front experienced the traditional warfare of mobile armies and shifting battlefields, but the great armies on the Western Front soon found themselves bogged down in siege conditions. Transport by trains allowed for a nearly endless supply of soldiers and material to a front in which the new machine guns, mass shelling by artillery, and fields of barbed wire made advance practically impossible. Both sides dug trenches stretching thousands of miles across France, dotted with concrete huts called pillboxes and lined with communication cables. From these trenches, the Allied armies repeatedly mounted offensives, only to be stopped when German reinforcements arrived. Battles were now numbered—the Second Battle of Ypres (April–May 1915), the Second Battle of Artois (May–June), the Second Battle of Champagne (September–November), the Third Battle of Artois (September–October)—and after a year's bloodshed, the Western Front remained essentially the same, though hundreds of thousands of men had lost their lives.

Within the trenches, morale declined as the soldiers waited for months, suffering through ice, wind, rain, mud, lice, and vermin, while facing interminable boredom and the threat of death. Attempts by the British and the Germans to break the stalemate by using poison gas added to the horror, but neither side was able to capitalize on the momentary gains this new weapon

great French drive. In September the French launched a counteroffensive along the Marne River that saved Paris and hurled the Germans back to the natural defenses of the Aisne River. There, despite repeated Allied attacks, the Germans held. In the next few months the armies tried to outflank each other but succeeded only in extending the front northward to the sea. With changes of only a few miles, the battle lines that were established at the end of 1914 would remain those of

The ruins of Verdun stood like a broken tombstone after the siege that bled both armies.
AP Images

provided. Among many on the front lines, the constant shelling and specter of death led to psychic distress called **shell shock.** Its widespread diagnosis was a testament to the enormous strain **trench warfare** placed on soldiers, many of whom had envisioned a quick and heroic war.

Italy Joins the Allies Nothing broke the stalemate, neither desperate new offensives nor Italy's entry into the war. Both sides had been negotiating with Italy; Britain and France could make the better offer. In April 1915 Italy signed a secret agreement, the Treaty of London, and committed itself to the Allies. In return Italy was promised considerable territory along its border with Austria-Hungary, important Dalmatian islands, and expansion of its colonial holdings. Italy declared war in May and soon advanced to a line along the Isonzo River. Eleven battles would be fought along that line in the next two years.

Costly Offensives Early in 1916 the Germans launched another all-out offensive to knock France out of the war. They stormed the fortifications at Verdun. Their aim, knowing the French would be determined to hold, was more to bleed the enemy than to take territory. For days shells poured down, and then the Germans attacked in overwhelming numbers. From February to July 1916 the fighting continued at full pitch. German forces captured two outlying forts, but the French managed a brief counterattack. Verdun held; and though the French losses, more than 300,000 men, weakened

the subsequent Allied offensive, Germany casualties were only slightly less.

The Allied attack in the Battle of the Somme, from July to November, brought still heavier casualties and a maximum advance of seven miles. The doctrine of the offensive, like general morale, was sinking in mud and gore. If tactics could not guarantee victory, then attrition, systematically exhausting men and resources, was the alternative.

There was more movement on the Eastern Front but no decisive result. The Central Powers (Germany, Austria-Hungary, and the countries on their side) launched an offensive through Galicia in May 1915, drove forward a hundred miles, and followed that with a general offensive in July. By late September—while their new ally, Bulgaria, pushed into Serbia—the Central Powers were massed on a line from Riga in the north to the easternmost part of Hungary. Russia lost Poland and Lithuania.

The following year, however, in one of the few really well-conducted Russian campaigns, General Alexis Brusilov regained a large part of those losses. The effort cost Russia a million men and used up the capacity to do more. Although the Russian offensive brought Romania into the war on the Allied side, Austria-Hungary took Bucharest at the end of the year.

The Naval War Naval strength, so significant to the arms race, proved more important in terms of supply lines than combat. The single large-scale attack by sea, the dramatic landing of Allied forces on the Gallipoli peninsula in April 1915, was a failure. The Allies were grateful to withdraw in December without having either opened the Dardanelles as a pipeline to Russia or forced the Ottomans out of the war.

Britain's naval blockade of Germany was more effective. As the blockade began to hurt, Germany countered in 1915 by announcing a submarine blockade of Britain; but the angry reaction of neutrals, led by the United States, forced Germany to abandon the tactic. The sinking of passenger ships—most sensationally the *Lusitania*, killing more than a thousand civilians—gave way in 1916 to attacks on armed merchant ships and then, in the face of American warnings, to the renunciation of "unlimited" submarine warfare. The one great naval battle of the war, at Jutland in May 1916, was indecisive. British and German fleets lost the same number of ships, though three British battle cruisers were sunk to only one German capital ship. The British retained a two-to-one naval superiority, however, and after Jutland the feared German fleet stayed in its harbors.

Adjustment to Total War

In contrast to nineteenth-century conflicts, the First World War was conducted on a massive scale, not only affecting soldiers in the battlefield, but also radically disrupting the lives of civilians at home.

Domestic Mobilization Across Europe, the first domestic response to the war was national unity. The German public was convinced that theirs was a just and defensive war, and the parliament unanimously approved funding for the war. The French hailed their "sacred union," and a leading socialist joined the cabinet. In Great Britain the Liberal government soon gave way to a coalition that included Conservatives, and in Russia the czar's government seemed almost popular. In the warring countries of western Europe, military leaders assumed a leading if not dominant role within society, particularly for the first year of the war. French General Joseph Joffre exercised virtually dictatorial powers and censorship was severe. Nevertheless, in France and Great Britain, civilian authority began to reassert itself by 1915.

Despite the initial surge of patriotism, Europeans soon began to feel the effects of the war at home. At first, factories closed and unemployment rose despite conscription; a labor shortage followed as war production became crucial. Everywhere, agricultural output dropped, contributing to the food shortages of subsequent years. Prices rose rapidly, and consumer hoarding further strained faltering systems of distribution. Just as the rules of warfare were bent or shattered by unlimited submarine warfare, poison gas, and a block-

ade that included consumer goods, so governments expanded their powers to move workers, censor the press, control railroads and shipping, and direct the economy.

CHRONOLOGY
The Eastern Front

August 1914	German victory over Russia at the Battle of Tannenberg; General von Hindenberg is proclaimed the "Hero of Tannenberg."
October 1914	Turkey enters war on the side of the Central Powers.
January 1915	German and Austrian forces launch attack in Galicia; they break through Russian lines in May.
May 1915	Italian forces tie down Austrian and German troops in the Tyrol.
September 1915	Bulgaria joins war on side of Central Powers.
October 1915	Austro-Hungarian army, with Bulgarian support, defeats and occupies Serbia.
August 1916	Romania enters the war on the side of the Entente and declares war on Austria.
February–March 1917	Russian Czar Nicholas II abdicates; Russian Revolution begins.
October–November 1917	Bolshevik regime created.
February 1918	Russians sign Treaty of Brest-Litovsk with Central Powers, although treaty is then annulled in November; Russians withdraw from the war.
September 1918	Bulgaria surrenders and signs armistice.
October 1918	Austro-Hungarian armies defeated in Italy; other Southern fronts of the Central Powers collapse; Czechoslovakia and Yugoslavia declare their independence from the Austro-Hungarian Empire.
November 3, 1918	Austria signs armistice.
November 11, 1918	German armistice.

Unprepared for the ever greater amounts of ammunition and supplies required by the war, governments quickly learned to use paper money, rationing, and central planning.

In the first weeks of German advances, France lost half of its iron ore and coal fields and more than half its heavy industry; yet as commissions established quotas and allocated supplies, production steadily increased. Similarly, in Great Britain the government requisitioned supplies and forced industry to new efficiency. Despite voluntary enlistments that raised the largest army in British history, it had to adopt conscription in 1916, a step Winston Churchill would call "the greatest revolution in our system since the institution of feudalism under William the Conqueror." Rebellion in Ireland that Easter was quickly put down; yet it was a serious diversion for British troops and a disturbing reminder of how cruelly war tested every weakness in the social structure.

Germany, deprived of critical raw materials, developed the most fully controlled economy of any of the combatants, under the brilliant direction of Walther Rathenau. Private firms were organized into sectors of production so that the most important could be favored, inefficient firms closed, and national planning enforced. The chemical industry created rubber substitutes, culled aluminum from local clays, manufactured fertilizers from nitrates in the air, and made textiles from wood pulp. Substitutes, which made *ersatz* an international word, included chestnut flour and clover meal used in the "war bread" that, like meatless days and conscription, soon made civilians feel the burden of all-out war. German officials were less sensitive to civilian needs, and far less efficient in meeting them, than Allied leaders.

Great Britain, France, and Germany adjusted effectively to the new challenge of fielding vast armies while increasing industrial production and maintaining intricate logistical networks. The Austro-Hungarian and Russian empires could not match these feats. Their industries were less well developed; supplies and trained personnel were often lacking. Equally important, neither government knew how nor dared try to squeeze from the economy the quantities of food, ammunition, and clothing that war required. Russian armies increasingly showed the effects of fighting ill-fed and ill-shod, with inadequate weapons and ammunition, and without good communication. (Orders to Russian troops were broadcast uncoded, and the German ability to intercept them contributed to Ludendorff's reputation as a great tactician.) In adversity, Austria-Hungary could not rely on the continued loyalty of subject peoples, and soldiers were carefully dispatched to zones far from their native lands so as not to be fighting against people who spoke their own language. Poles, for example, found themselves fighting for both sides, as they served in the respective armies of the Austro-Hungarians, the Germans, and the Russians.

Social Effects By the winter of 1916–1917, the strains were visible to all. Everywhere on the bloodied continent, Europeans were thinner, more shabbily dressed, overworked, and grieved by the endless losses of husbands, sons, and homes. Poor crops and overloaded transportation systems further reduced the diet; this winter was Germany's "turnip winter," when the best prepared of the domestic war economies could barely keep its people healthy. Society itself was subtly altered from the first month, when Belgian refugees poured into France, until years after the war. The strains of war were changing society. As the queue became a kind of public rite and rationing a way of life, distinctions of social class blurred. Each government awkwardly tried to restrict the consumption of alcohol and worried about rising rates of illegitimacy.

Women on the Home Front While men fought on the battlefront, women were essential in sustaining what was now called the **home front,** and even most feminists—at odds with their governments over the issue of female suffrage—rallied to support the war effort. In every country, women left home and domestic service to work in industry, transportation, and business. Such employment was often divided by class. In Great Britain, two million upper- and middle-class women worked without pay in medical, paramilitary, and aid organizations, while their working-class compatriots often found employment in army auxiliary corps or in industry. In the latter area especially, women's involvement represented a dramatic shift in employment. Many found jobs in the new munitions factories and other war-related industries that previously had employed only men. In Great Britain's munitions industries, the number of women workers rose steadily to become one-third or more of the total. Women also ran farms, became firefighters and bus conductors, and worked in offices. On the front, they served as nurses.

The feminization of the workforce, however, was not accompanied by new enlightened attitudes toward women. War propaganda reinforced traditional gender stereotypes by emphasizing the enemy's brutality toward women and the maternal care that nurses provided the wounded. In Britain the first women who volunteered for the war effort were rejected, and only the pressures of war pushed the government to encourage women to go to work with the Munitions Act of 1915. Such employment was supposed to be temporary: Women first entered the workforce to replace conscripted male relatives until their return from the

At a Vickers factory in England, women labored with patriotic seriousness at the task of preparing artillery shells.
© Hulton-Deutsch Collection/Corbis

front. In France women were not allowed to provide military support services at all for two years. However, the need for their contribution overrode qualms about allowing the "weaker sex" to hold jobs previously reserved for men. By 1917 the British government denied contracts to employers unwilling to hire women (see "Meet the 'Khaki Girls,'" p. 793). The French government forbade hiring men for jobs that women could do; and in Germany the Krupp steelworks, which had no women employees in 1914, counted twelve thousand by 1917.

Women's contributions outside the home were publicly acknowledged as loyal service to the nation, and for some women wartime activities brought increased independence. They were more likely to live on their own and go out in public alone. For most women, however, income provided the greatest compensation for the danger and drudgery of the work. Lower-class women often worked 60 to 70 hours a week and still endured poor living conditions outside the factory. Inevitably, questions arose about unequal pay and whether men might be permanently displaced, and there was debate over the proper role of women, echoing the issues raised by the suffrage movement before the war.

As a result, women's roles in the workplace created as much criticism as praise, especially among the men on the front lines. Women were attacked for spending money, or even for benefiting from the war as their husbands, sons, and brothers paid the ultimate sacrifice. Women in Britain and France also had to defend themselves from accusations that their work outside the home was motivated by their desire to win the right to vote rather than by patriotism.

Nevertheless, women in the workforce stood to benefit from a general wartime trend toward a more democratic, inclusive conception of national politics. Trade unions were treated with new respect, and officials began to talk of the benefits to be granted after the war. Even the Kaiser spoke of ending the three-class voting system in Prussia and hinted at a government that would be responsible to parliament, while the House of Commons, in a notable reversal, declared its support in principle for women's suffrage.

Changes on the Battlefield While economic pressures brought rapid social change at home, the men on the front felt increasingly cut off from their families and countries. The reality of the trenches led many to express contempt for and alienation from what the poet Siegfried Sassoon described as the "callous complacency" of the civilian view of the war.[2] Mired in the trenches, facing death every day, soldiers soon relinquished their ideas of war as a heroic or patriotic duty and instead sustained themselves through close relationships with those who shared their battlefield experiences and the memories of dead comrades.

Meanwhile, the continuation of the war brought changes in the high command. In France Joffre's intolerance of civilian leaders brought his downfall in December 1916; he was replaced by the tactful and dashing General Robert Georges Nivelle, who planned a

[2] Robert Giddings, *The War Poets* (Bloomsbury, 1990), p. 111.

Meet the "Khaki Girls"

The two women who wrote this brief article, published in June 1917 in The Englishwoman, *a women's magazine, present it as an upbeat account of the dedication of women workers, but it is also a document about class distinctions.*

"We got out of the tram and walked up the short, muddy path, past the sentry, who with fixed bayonet guards the entrance to A₃, the 'shop' in which we work. It was twenty minutes past two—ten minutes before the hour for the shift to begin—so there were plenty of our fellow-workers passing through the door. Among the three hundred girls employed on this shift there are not more than four or five lady-workers, so the crowd was made up of 'khaki girls,' the colloquial name given to the industrial hands, originating from the fact that when women were admitted last July to the munition shops they wore khaki overalls, which since have been replaced for economical reasons by those made of black material.

"We had grown accustomed to the sight of the endless procession of girls pouring into the factory . . . all of the same type, rather wild, yet in their quieter moods giving an impression of sullen defiance, ready to answer you back if you should happen to tread on their very tender corns. So long, though, as you keep off those corns, and do not let these wayward creatures feel you are intruding nor provide yourself with anything which they have not, even though it be merely a newspaper to sit upon in preference to a dusty board, they will show their good nature to you—and they have plenty. Then there is their good humour and their gay spirits. No matter how strenuous the work, nor how wearing the hardships, they will always give out from this wonderful gaiety of spirits, and keep the ball rolling with their sense of humour—obvious and childlike—running as it does mostly to nicknaming, pelting the mechanics with orange peel, or skipping with a rope of steel shavings cut from the shell on the lathe.

"Every one of them carries a brown or green despatch-case. Most of them are flashily dressed: a cherry-coloured coat, a black-and-white check skirt, a satin blouse trimmed with swansdown, a hat, small in shape but too large to fit, so it drops over one eye, and down-trodden boots, is typical of what they wear. Some of them are exceedingly pretty; they are all heavily powdered, and in some cases rouged. Their hair is dressed with great care, and even if it does fall about their eyes it is not untidiness, but an effect purposely arranged by the aid of the small mirror—often a beautiful thing to look upon, either encrusted with shells or mounted on scarlet plush—carried in that despatch-case which is the essential part of a khaki girl's equipment, since it contains the food with which she is obliged to provide herself.

"We stood in the doorway a moment looking at the sun shining down upon the river. 'Do you think the Zeppelins will come tonight?' one of us said to the other. 'It will be a good night for them.' 'There's no moon.' 'Nor wind—and they were at Paris last night.'

"Then we went to our work, and the absorption of screwing plugs into shells, turning them on the lathe, taking them out and gauging them, working to exceed the standard number, swallowed up every other thought."

From Brenda Girvin and Monica Coxens, "Meet the 'Khaki Girls,'" *The Englishwoman*, 1917.

---

massive new offensive. This one, he promised, would break through German defenses.

In Germany two heroes of the Eastern Front had been promoted. Hindenburg received overall command and with Ludendorff took charge of campaigns in the West in the fall of 1916. To destroy the shipping on which Britain depended, Germany returned to unlimited submarine warfare in January 1917. Aware that such a step might bring the United States into the war, the Germans calculated that Britain would have to sue for peace before American power could make a difference.

Political Changes   In Great Britain, Lloyd George, made minister of war in June 1916, became prime minister in December. Eloquent and energetic, once a radical orator who had terrified the upper classes, he now seemed the kind of popular and decisive leader who could galvanize the British war effort. After French morale hit a dangerous low, that country made the fiery Clemenceau premier again in November 1917.

Change came to Russia too—through revolution. In March 1917 popular protest forced the tsar to abdicate (see "Revolution in Russia," p. 816), and a new provisional government proclaimed sweeping democratic reforms while promising to continue the war. At the same time, however, physical conditions on the Russian military and home fronts were rapidly deteriorating. For the Allies these changes in Russia gave the war itself new meaning. Now democracies, led by politicians with ties to the left, were fighting together against authoritarian governments. A war that involved the people more fully than any before took on

Illustration of Indian soldiers, supported by a British grenade thrower, engaged in hand-to-hand combat with Germans on the Western Front, from the *Illustrated London News*, March 27, 1915. Such images were used to demonstrate to the British public the bravery and devotion of the imperial troops.
Illustrated London News Picture Library

an ideological meaning. The Allies' sense of democratic purpose was strengthened in April when the United States—resentful that Germany was sinking its ships and making overtures to Mexico that included promises of the return of former Mexican lands now part of the United States—declared war on Germany.

The Armenian Genocide   The most extreme example of civilian involvement in the First World War was the Armenian Massacre of 1915, in which civilians themselves became the targets of violence. For decades before the outbreak of the First World War, the large Armenian minority living in the Ottoman Empire had been subject to repression and violence. In the late nineteenth century, about 200,000 Armenians living in eastern Anatolia were killed, with government authorities citing their nationalist ambitions and cooperation with Russia. The position of the Armenians further deteriorated after they refused to support the Ottoman Empire during the Balkan Wars. In February 1914, as a result of international and especially Russian pressure, the Ottoman government

agreed to allow international monitors into the empire, who were to ensure that Armenian minority rights would be protected. With the outbreak of war, however, the Ottoman government renounced this agreement and instead formulated a plan for the forced relocation of Armenians, ostensibly to protect them from the Russians. Beginning in March 1915, the Ottoman government deported 1,750,000 Armenians to the deserts of Syria and Mesopotamia. At least 800,000 Armenians died during this expulsion from their homes, and thousands more were killed before reaching the desert. This calculated large-scale massacre both demonstrates the nature of **total war** and its effects upon civilians and foreshadows the kind of mass murder later seen during the Second World War.

The Empire at War   World War One was a total war in yet another crucial sense. Although fought mainly in Europe, imperialism transformed the conflict into a global one. All the major European powers saw the war as an opportunity to gain more territory overseas. Britain and France both hoped to gain dominance over the

In March 1917 women demonstrated in Petrograd, demanding that the rations for soldiers' families be increased. Sovfoto

weakening Ottoman Empire, and Germany drew up plans for imperial control of parts of eastern Europe as well as most of Southern Africa.

As a result, the war spread to colonial areas and involved peoples from countries where Europe had imperial aspirations. Battles between the Allies and German-led forces took place throughout the Ottoman Empire, most notably in Gallipoli, Baghdad, Jerusalem, Syria, and Beirut. Fighting also spread to West Africa and German-held areas of southwest Africa. Thousands of individuals from European colonies were recruited or conscripted to fight in Europe itself: 62,000 Indian soldiers died fighting alongside the British; 30,000 Senegalese lost their lives for France; and over 400,000 Africans served the Allies by transporting supplies and the wounded. On the home front, colonial recruits manned factories necessary for war production; in France alone, 250,000 workers were from its overseas colonies. Many of those who came voluntarily to assist the war effort expected new rights or even full independence for their home countries and would assert their claims at the end of the war. Instead of reinforcing imperialism, the involvement of the colonies threatened to undermine Europe's global power.

The Great Trials of 1917–1918

In the fighting itself, neither new leaders nor shared ideals seemed to make much difference (see "Wilfred Owen Describes Trench Warfare," p. 796). Relentlessly, the war went on. Russia's collapse aided the Central Powers; American entry into the war was a gain for the Allies. Not until late in the summer of 1918 did the outcome begin to be clear.

Fighting in the West On the Western Front, French general Robert Georges Nivelle launched his great offensive in April and May 1917 despite multiple handicaps. The Germans had strengthened their defenses; disagreements arose between the British and French commands; and some French troops, dispirited by two years of endless death on the same desolate terrain, mutinied, refusing to fight. The Second Battle of the Aisne and the Third Battle of Champagne took a toll as great as their predecessors and made even slighter gains. Nivelle was replaced by General Henri Philippe Pétain, the hero of Verdun, who began a concerted effort to raise morale, but it would be months before France dared another offensive.

The British went ahead with plans for an attack in the north, spurred by the desperate need to knock out at least some of the submarine bases from which German U-boats were sinking such enormous tonnages that the Admiralty openly wondered how many months Great Britain could last. The noise of battle could be heard in England, and hundreds of thousands of men fell, but the British fared no better in the Third Battle of Ypres (July–November) than the French had in their spring offensive. British morale, too, was shaken; yet stalemate continued. Germany's submarine warfare

WILFRED OWEN DESCRIBES TRENCH WARFARE

Wilfred Owen's moving poems about World War I were published after he was killed in action in 1918, and they continue to be widely read. His first tour of duty had ended when he was sent home suffering from "shell shock." Some months later, he was back in France. On January 4, 1917, he wrote his mother that "on all the officers' faces there is a harassed look that I have never seen before," adding, "I censored hundreds of letters yesterday, and the hope of peace was in every one of them." He was back in the fighting a few days later, when he wrote her this letter.

Tuesday, 16 January 1917
[2nd Manchester Regt, B.E.F.]

"My own sweet Mother,

" . . . I can see no excuse for deceiving you about these last 4 days. I have suffered seventh hell.

"I have not been at the front.

"I have been in front of it.

"I held an advanced post, that is, a 'dug-out' in the middle of No Man's Land.

"We had a march of 3 miles over shelled road then nearly 3 along a flooded trench. After that we came to where the trenches had been blown flat out and had to go over the top. It was of course dark, too dark, and the ground was not mud, not sloppy mud; but an octopus of sucking clay, 3, 4, and 5 feet deep, relieved only by craters full of water. Men have been known to drown in them. Many stuck in the mud & only got on by leaving their waders, equipment, and in some cases their clothes.

"High explosives were dropping all around us, and machine-guns spluttered every few minutes. But it was so dark that even the German flares did not reveal us.

"Three quarters dead, I mean each of us 3/4 dead, we reached the dug-out, and relieved the wretches therein. I then had to go forth and find another dug-out for a still more advanced post where I left 18 bombers. I was responsible for other posts on the left but there was a junior officer in charge.

"My dug-out held 25 men tight packed. Water filled it to a depth of 1 or 2 feet, leaving say 4 feet of air.

"One entrance had been blown in & blocked.

"So far, the other remained.

"The Germans knew we were staying there and decided we shouldn't.

"Those fifty hours were the agony of my happy life.

"Every ten minutes on Sunday afternoon seemed an hour.

"I nearly broke down and let myself drown in the water that was now slowly rising over my knees.

"Towards 6 o'clock, when, I suppose, you would be going to church, the shelling grew less intense and less accurate: so that I was mercifully helped to do my duty and crawl, wade, climb and flounder over No Man's Land to visit my other post. It took me half an hour to move about 150 yards.

"I was chiefly annoyed by our own machine-guns from behind. The seeng-seeng-seeng of the bullets reminded me of Mary's canary. On the whole I can support the canary better.

"In the Platoon on my left the sentries over the dug-out were blown to nothing. One of these poor fellows was my first servant whom I rejected. If I had kept him he would have lived, for servants don't do Sentry Duty."

From Harold Owen and John Bell (eds.), *Wilfred Owen: The Collected Letters*, Oxford University Press, 1967.

---

had come close to its goal, but Allied losses dropped to a tolerable level in mid-1917 with the development of the convoy, in which fleets of armed ships accompanied merchant vessels across the ocean. With America's entry into the war, the tonnage those convoys delivered grew still greater.

Allied Defeats: Russia and Italy   Elsewhere, the picture was different. On the Eastern Front, Russian advances in July soon turned into almost constant retreat, and Russian troops suffered from shortages in essential supplies and equipment. In November, the communists gained control of the government. They invited all nations to join in peace without annexations or indemnities, then entered into independent negotiations with the Central Powers. The most populous of the Allies had been defeated.

Able now to engage more troops on the Italian front, Germany and Austria-Hungary launched a concentrated attack there in October, scoring an overwhelming victory at the Battle of Caporetto. Italy's armies collapsed as tens of thousands died, surrendered, or deserted. But the Italians regrouped along the Piave River; Britain and France rushed in reinforcements, and the Austro-German onslaught was slowed and then stopped.

Desolation surrounded weary Allied soldiers as they made their way across the mud on the battlefield at Ypres.
Imperial War Museum, London

The Last Year Although the Russians stopped fighting in February 1918, the Central Powers did not. They continued their eastward march until Russia signed the Treaty of Brest Litovsk in March. Russia surrendered Russian Poland, the Baltic provinces, the Ukraine, and Transcaucasia. Germany had acquired invaluable wheat and oil when it most needed them and a respite on one front. But merely safeguarding such immense gains required substantial numbers of troops badly needed elsewhere, especially since the incredibly harsh terms of the Brest Litovsk Treaty intensified the Allies' determination to win the war.

On the Western Front, the Germans, their reserves of personnel and resources nearing exhaustion, opened a great offensive. Attacking sector after sector from March through June, they made the greatest advances seen there in four years. It was a triumph of careful strategy, improved tactics, heavy artillery, and gas. To correct the weakness of divided command, the Allies named General Ferdinand Foch supreme commander of all their forces; and they retained their reserves while the Germans exhausted theirs. Enemy guns once more bombarded Paris before the Allied counteroffensive began in July. Slowly, then faster, the Germans were driven back over the familiar and devastated landscape. By the end of August, German armies had retreated to the Hindenburg line, a defensive position established at the beginning of 1917. The Allies continued their push in battles of the Argonne and Ypres in September and October, gaining inexorably—even if less rapidly than hoped or expected.

The Collapse of the Central Powers On other fronts the Central Powers collapsed dramatically. In the Middle East, Turkish and German troops were defeated by British and Arab forces led by T. E. Lawrence, whose exploits in mobilizing Arab opposition to Turkey became part of the romantic lore in which this war was poorer than most. In October the sultan was deposed, and a new government sued for peace. Combined Serbian, French, British, and Greek forces under French leadership drove up the Balkan Peninsula. Bulgaria surrendered at the end of September, and the Allies moved toward Romania.

The Austro-Hungarian Empire was disintegrating. Czech, Yugoslav, Romanian, and Polish movements for independence, encouraged by the Allies, gained strength throughout 1918. Austria-Hungary attacked once more on the Italian front but withdrew after heavy losses. Its armies, defeated at Vittorio Veneto at the end of October, began simply to dissolve as the various nationalities left for home and revolution. Czechoslovakia and the kingdom later called Yugoslavia both declared their independence. In November Austria-Hungary surrendered unconditionally to the Italians.

At the end of September, Ludendorff had demanded that Germany seek an armistice, but that required political changes as well. Twice in 1917 Kaiser William II had promised to make his cabinet subject to a majority in the Reichstag; and in October 1918 he appointed Prince Max of Baden as chancellor to begin this transformation from above. Ludendorff resigned his command at the end of October, and Germany asked for peace on the general terms set forth by President Woodrow Wilson. But Wilson now insisted on the evacuation of occupied territories and a democratic German government with which to negotiate.

The German Republic Accepts an Armistice While German leaders hesitated, they faced the threat of revolution at home. A liberal believer in parliamentary government, Prince Max represented a compromise that might have worked earlier but now could not in the face of uprisings in the name of peace, democracy, and socialism. Germany threatened to break apart. Prince Max pleaded with William to abdicate and, when revolt spread to Berlin, simply announced that the kaiser had done so. William II abdicated on November 9 after a mutiny in the German fleet and revolution in Munich. The government was handed over to Friedrich Ebert, the leader of the Social Democrats; a German Republic was proclaimed and an armistice commission sent to meet with Foch. The commission agreed to terms on November 11. By then Allied troops were approaching German borders in the west and had crossed the Danube in the east, taken Trieste on the Adriatic, and sailed through the Dardanelles. In the meantime, revolution was sweeping across central Europe.

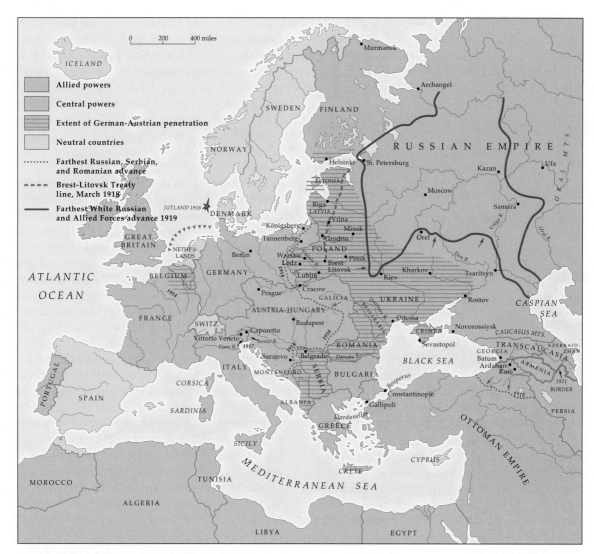

MAP 26.3 TERRITORIAL GAINS, 1914–1919
This map illustrates the vast expanses of territory held by the Allied powers during the war, as well as the considerable part of eastern Europe occupied by the Central Powers. At what point in the war were these Central Power advances repelled by the Allied powers?

THE PEACE

From the Rhine to Russia so many governments were new and so many boundaries undecided that, by default as well as victory, the Allies seemed free to construct the new Europe of peaceful democracies their wartime statements had foreshadowed. Instead, the diplomats assembled at the Peace Conference in Paris found their task complicated by the very extent of victory and beset by more interests than they could satisfy. So great an opportunity and so grand an undertaking fed the extremes, first of hope, then of disillusionment. Meanwhile, away from Paris, more direct means were being used to shape the postwar world.

The Effects of World War I

The war itself had some of the effects of revolution. Among the defeated nations, governments were overturned and shaky new ones established. Even among the Allies, war had created so much that no one could be sure what the postwar world would be like. Society had to be put together again.

The New State of Affairs   Throughout central Europe, political conflict adopted the techniques of force. In Germany radical groups staged a number of local revolts, creating an air of instability sustained by ***Freikorps*** ("free corps"), mercenary squads made up of former soldiers available to any movement that could pay them for street fighting and marauding. To the east of Germany, new regimes and sometimes whole new nations replaced the defeated states.

The victorious governments, having shown the capacity to mobilize society for war, would now be held more responsible than in the past for society's peacetime needs, as evidenced in a spate of postwar legislation on housing, education, and pensions. Clemenceau, Lloyd George, and Wilson, the spokesmen of victory, had all been vigorous reformers, but now they watched with apprehension the revival of the radical left.

Life in wartime had affected social classes differently. Even where there was no open revolution, the aristocracy and other traditional elites had been weakened by the general democratization of political life and by the decline in purchasing power that resulted from inflation, reduction in the value of land, and increased taxes (especially in England). A middle class confident in 1914 found itself exposed and vulnerable after the war, its savings threatened, its possibilities limited, its values challenged. Those on salary or fixed income suffered more from inflation than those on workers' wages; middle-class life became less lavish, and there were fewer servants (some 400,000 English women left domestic service in the course of the war). Workers, particularly the skilled, were on the whole relatively well off. Although rates of pay usually lagged behind inflation, the years of full employment and more jobs for women had increased family income; and trade unions used their greater influence to maintain shorter hours and higher pay. Peasants, though declining in number, were also often better off, helped by the demand for food and by inflation, which made it easier to pay off their debts.

The Change in Social Mores Even ordinary manners and dress were different. Gentlemen, forced to use public transportation, had abandoned their top hats; women's clothes grew simpler and their skirts shorter. Women of the working class took to wearing cosmetics and high-heeled shoes and smoking and drinking in public, as did their middle-class sisters. Such changes in customs, even more than the increase in violent crime and juvenile delinquency, shocked moralists, who associated them with casual encounters between the sexes, increased illegitimacy, and the popularity of dance halls.

Public appearance thus added to the economic and political disruptions of wartime in suggesting a new openness and uncertainty, a more fluid society in which old standards could not be recaptured. Millions of refugees constituted more tangible displacement, and millions of other Europeans (especially peasants and women) were not eager to return to their old way of life. Of course

It would take years to recover from the damage to roads and bridges and private housing in Belgium and northeastern France. The French village of Craonne, where Napoleon once won a battle and which was the scene of fighting in 1917 and 1918, looked like this in 1919.
Roger-Viollet/Getty Images

most people more or less did, and by the 1920s prewar constraints of class and gender were largely back in place, despite some relaxation.

The psychological impact of war, harder to demonstrate than the social changes, may have been just as important. Throughout society, there was a tendency following the war to expect instability. Intellectuals suffered what one historian has called "minds scorched by war"; and among the populace, a cynical distrust of leaders and institutions seems to have spread after years of wartime promises. There was a cleavage, too, between those who had fought and those who stayed home, those whose lives were transformed and those who had more nearly maintained business as usual. Bitterness about these inequalities of sacrifice surfaced in public denunciations of war profiteers and in a more inflammatory political rhetoric. At the same time, with a kind of selective nostalgia, many regretted the loss of that sense of common purpose and national unity that war had brought, and some even yearned again for the thrill of combat.

Economic Effects Military needs had stimulated the rapid development of certain technologies. When World War I began, the cavalry was a major element of every army, pack horses and horse-drawn wagons the principal form of transport from rail lines to the front. By war's end, the practical importance of automobiles and airplanes, radio, and the chemical industry had become clear to all. In many factories the effort to speed up industrial production altered the nature of work as tasks were reorganized in ways thought to be more rational and efficient but that workers found increasingly impersonal and demanding.

Although some sectors of the economy gained from their wartime importance, the overall losses were dramatic. World trade had been disrupted and Europe's place in it transformed. In 1914 Europe was the world's greatest lender of money; in 1918 its nations were debtors. The physical destruction of property, aside from the billions lost in war matériel, was greatest in Belgium and France. In France alone, thousands of bridges and factories as well as a million buildings were destroyed. Total European production in the 1920s would fall below the level of 1913.

The Dead and the Culture of Mourning The greatest change in postwar Europe resulted directly from the war: the deaths of 10 to 13 million people, perhaps one-third of them civilians. Among the armed forces, casualties ran about 50 percent for the major combatants except France, which suffered higher losses. In each country whole classes from the elite schools were virtually wiped out. For France, with its older population and low birthrate, the war was a demographic catastro-

MILITARY FATALITIES IN WORLD WAR I (MAJOR POWERS)	
Germany	1,900,000
Russia	1,700,000
France	1,400,000
Austria-Hungary	1,200,000
British Empire	900,000
Ottoman Empire	700,000
Italy	600,000
United States	100,000

phe in which 10 percent of the adult population—one out of every two Frenchmen between the ages of 20 and 32—disappeared on the Western Front. Moreover, for every soldier who died, two or three were wounded, and millions were maimed for life.

The stupefying death toll not only affected the economy through manpower losses, but placed a heavy burden on European governments. Throughout Europe, the one-armed, the one-legged, and the blind would live on, supported by pensions and performing menial tasks, in silent testimony to the cost of total war. Millions of widows with young children also relied on the state, though often the income was meager, especially as inflation increased in the postwar years.

As divided as Europe had been in war, it was now united in grieving and remembrance. Associations such as the Red Cross and informal groups offered consolation for those most directly affected and helped to mend social dislocation by creating bonds between widows, former soldiers, and others whose lives were disrupted. Memorials sprang up throughout Europe, especially on sites that witnessed the most carnage in Belgium and France. These often became the focus of pilgrimages through which the public could express its collective grief. Publicly commemorating the dead took perhaps its most concrete form in tombs of "unknown soldiers" erected in Europe's capitals, and the ceremonies surrounding Armistice Day became a central experience of interwar life.

Faced with such loss, the leaders of exhausted nations sat down to make a lasting peace, one that would end the secret diplomacy that juggled spheres of influence and national interests without regard for public opinion. With Wilson as its greatest advocate, democracy—meaning popular participation in public life—seemed to the Allies the best guarantee against future conflict.

The Revolutionary Situation

The Russian Revolution, while clearly the most dramatic, was not the only political upheaval conceived in war. Disruptions of normal life, including mass migrations, military desertions, and mutinies, posed acute threats to the established authorities. The war weakened many European states, giving radicals on the left and right new opportunities to claim power.

New Nations in Eastern Europe The peoples suddenly released from Habsburg and Russian rule fought to define the boundaries of their new nations. In the Baltic lands, Lithuanian, Estonian, and Latvian republics marked their independence by war with Russia. Lithuania was also at odds with the new republic of Poland; and Poland faced conflict on all its other borders—against Russians, Ukranians, Czechs, and Germans. The creation of Czechoslovakia and the new kingdom of Yugoslavia led to renewed warfare as Hungary attacked Czechoslovakia, while in the Balkans Romania attacked both Hungary and Yugoslavia—just the kind of hostility that had preceded World War I.

Leftist Militancy Russia's communists had good reason to hope that revolution would sweep from east to west, and Marxists throughout Europe looked to the miraculous events in Russia as the beginning of the socialist future they had so long imagined. In March 1919 delegates from a score of countries met in Moscow to establish the Third International. Communists were active in the Baltic states, and in 1919 Lenin's friend Béla Kun led a communist government in Hungary until Romanian armies ended his brief reign. There was also communist agitation in Vienna, where the provisional government of truncated Austria, all that was left of the Habsburg Empire, looked forward to union with the new German republic. Such an alliance, however, was forbidden by the Allies and embodied in the Paris Peace Treaty Austria was made to sign.

Marxists, however, had long set their eyes on highly industrialized Germany, finding revolutionary promise in its class tensions and strong socialist movement. Germany's defeat and a shaky new German republic appeared to fulfill old portents. In January 1919 a communist revolt broke out in Berlin, and the following spring another uprising managed for a few weeks to make Bavaria a Soviet republic. Both were quickly defeated by remnants of the German army. Russia remained the center of the communist world.

The Peace Treaties

President Wilson's Fourteen Points had won acceptance as a basis for defining a new European order. The points dealt mainly with territorial adjustments but idealistically proclaimed the self-determination of peoples to be the governing principle of the peace. Wilson's call for free trade and open seas had long been part of the liberal canon. His attention to the dangers of colonial warfare, the need for disarmament, and the benefits of open diplomacy was more radical but echoed the common belief that such policies would have averted world war. Wilson's final point, and the one closest to his heart, called for a **League of Nations** to guarantee the safety of all. The American president's talk of "impartial justice," a "peace that will be permanent," and covenants that will be "sacredly observed" caught the imagination of the world.

When Woodrow Wilson paraded through the streets, Parisians cheered the representative of a new democratic era as well as an ally in victory. The Granger Collection, New York

The Paris Conference At the Paris Peace Conference, which opened in January 1919, all parties agreed not to repeat the mistakes of the Congress of Vienna a century earlier. No defeated nations would take part in the early discussions; no German Talleyrand would divide the Allies. The atmosphere was one of sober business, organized around commissions of expert advisers. Thirty nations had joined the Allies, at least formally,[3] but the major decisions would be taken by the five big powers: France, the United Kingdom, Italy, Japan, and the United States.

Although Japan was a colonial power in its own right, primary authority resided in four men: Clemenceau, Lloyd George, Premier Vittorio Orlando, and Wilson. Disagreements among the Big Four soon became the center around which the negotiations turned. All were elected leaders, sensitive to public opinion, faced with grave domestic problems, and worried by the turmoil in central and eastern Europe. Experienced politicians, they knew they had to hurry.

The Treaty with Germany To settle by May the complicated terms for peace with Germany was a remarkable achievement. Haste itself probably made the treaty more severe than it might otherwise have been. Commissions, assuming their proposals would be subject to later bargaining, tended to begin with maximum terms, but these were often simply written into the treaty itself.

Germany lost its overseas territories in Africa and the Pacific, which were assigned by the League of Nations to the various Allied powers to be administered as mandates. It also lost territory much closer to home, such as Alsace-Lorraine, but was still able to remain a powerful state. Germany's new boundaries in Europe continued to be a source of problems. France was satisfied with the return of Alsace-Lorraine, but it did not receive the left bank of the Rhine, as it had wanted. Instead, the Allies were to occupy the Rhineland for fifteen years; and the coal-producing regions along the Saar River, while remaining under German sovereignty, would be supervised by France until a later plebiscite by universal suffrage determined the final disposition. Plebiscites would also decide whether Germany surrendered part of Schleswig to Denmark and part of upper Silesia to Poland.

The Polish provinces of eastern Prussia, where Germans formed about 40 percent of the population, were immediately ceded to Poland. That created the controversial Polish corridor to the sea, which awkwardly separated eastern Prussia from the rest of Germany.

Although a majority of the population within the corridor was Polish, its outlet was the German port city of Danzig, restored to its ancient status as a free city. Poland would always feel insecure with an arrangement the Germans never accepted.

Germany was to have no large artillery, submarines, or military air force, and no more than 100,000 men under arms—requirements that were intended to lead to a general disarmament. The lists of items Germany had to deliver to the Allies were more punitive: horses and railway carriages, quantities of coal, most of its present ships, and some new vessels to be specially built.

Reparations The required reparations were more burdensome still. Despite fine talk of not requiring an indemnity, the Allies decided that Germany should pay for civilian damages. The claims of Belgium, a neutral attacked without warning, were easily justified; and Clemenceau could argue that the most destructive fighting had occurred in Belgium and France. But Lloyd George had campaigned on a platform of making Germany pay. He insisted, over American objections, on including Allied military pensions as civilian costs—a demand that made Germany liable for sums unspecified and without foreseeable end. Germany was required to accept Article 231 of the Versailles Treaty, which was known as the **war guilt clause.** This clause required Germany to accept "responsibility" for losses from a war "imposed . . . by the aggression of Germany and her allies." The war guilt clause became a subject of controversy in every country and a source of bitter resentment, official and private, in every part of Germany.

In German eyes, the treaty was an intolerable *Diktat* that German delegates had no chance to discuss until it was already drafted, when only minor revisions could be made. Faced with these terms, the German government resigned, and the parliament at first rejected the treaty's stipulation of German guilt. But when the Allies held firm, parliament angrily acquiesced. The treaty was signed on June 28, 1919, the fifth anniversary of the assassination at Sarajevo, in the Hall of Mirrors at Versailles, where Bismarck and Kaiser Wilhelm I had announced the founding of the German Empire forty-eight years before. The symbolism was complete.

Italian Aims For the Big Four, Italy's expectations were especially difficult, and Italian insistence on them particularly irksome. The Treaty of London of 1915 had promised Italy much of the Slavic-speaking lands of the Dalmatian coast, and the Italian delegates expected to get them. Wilson was determined to prevent further violations of the principle of nationality beyond

---

[3] The newly created nations of Yugoslavia, Czechoslovakia, and Poland were treated as Allies; the new republics of Austria, Hungary, and Germany as the defeated Central Powers.

allowing Italy, for strategic reasons, to have the Tyrol south of the Brenner Pass through the Alps, although that former Austrian land was German-speaking.

Using a press interview, Wilson in effect spoke directly to the Italian people, asking them to reject the position taken by their representatives at the conference. The Italian delegation withdrew in protest, to a great outpouring of nationalist feeling at home. Eventually, Italy was given the Istrian Peninsula and some islands but not Dalmatia. For years to come, resentment over the promises not kept at Paris would be a disruptive issue in Italian domestic politics.

The Other Treaties   With the signing of the Treaty of Versailles, the Big Four dispersed, leaving the details of the remaining settlements to their foreign offices. The treaty with Austria in September was closely modeled on the treaty with Germany, but reparations and demilitarization, including naval restrictions, hardly seemed appropriate for the shaky little landlocked Austrian republic. Boundaries for the other new states were settled on the basis of nationality in some cases and strategic needs in others.

Treaties with Bulgaria in November and with Hungary in June 1920 gave Bohemia to Czechoslovakia on historical grounds, while Hungarian claims to a larger historical kingdom were largely ignored. Hungary lost almost three-quarters of its former lands. Although Bulgaria surrendered relatively little territory to Greece, Romania, and Yugoslavia, it greatly resented its new borders. Romania, by contrast, emerged as the territorial winner, gaining land not only from Bulgaria, but from Austria, Hungary, and the Soviet Union. Every state in eastern Europe, it seemed, lay claim to territory based on history, culture, or religion, so that existing railways, economic ties, and more "natural" boundaries such as rivers and mountain ranges simply did not coincide with the borders established at Paris. It would fall to the new League of Nations to make these arrangements work.

Much remained to negotiate. The fate of many territories was determined later, sometimes by plebiscite. Moreover, some peace arrangements engendered great hostility or were simply untenable. One example was the Minorities Protection Treaty, promising just treatment for minorities such as Jews and other ethnic and national minorities, which the nations of eastern Europe took as an affront to their new-found sovereignty. One of the great tensions created by the peace treaty—although the European powers did not realize it at the time—was over the scope of self-determination. African and Asian colonial subjects interpreted the Wilsonian principle of national sovereignty as applicable to their own situations, particularly in light of the massive colonial contribution to the war effort. Yet European leaders had no intention of extending self-determination to their colonies, and their failure to recognize the rights of colonial subjects fostered great bitterness, spurring the growth of colonial nationalism.

The Unstable Settlement in the Middle East   The final treaty, with Turkey, was not signed until August 1920, and much of it never went into effect. The Allies' aims had been contradictory all along, and the postwar situation spawned indigenous movements in the former Ottoman Empire as complex and uncontrollable as those in eastern Europe. The Russian and Habsburg empires no longer competed for influence there, and the Soviet government's release of earlier secret Allied plans for partitioning the Ottoman Empire reinforced suspicions that Britain and France were more committed to an old imperialism than to any new arrangements.

A nationalist revolt in Turkey had brought the reforming Mustafa Kemal (Atatürk) to power, and he succeeded in ensuring Turkey's territorial integrity. Arabia's independence was also recognized, although internal conflict there created further opportunities for European influence. The pressing need to create political order on the eastern shores of the Mediterranean was met by a solution defined as temporary. France was to have a supervisory authority in Syria, and a vaguely defined area—carved from Palestine, Trans-Jordan, and Iraq—would be subject to British authority. Aside from recognizing the presence of Britain and France in the Middle East, the treaty settled little, and lasting boundaries would be determined only through the conflicts and diplomacy of the next few years.

British intentions in separating Palestine from Trans-Jordan were especially confusing. Anti-imperialist sentiment was strong in the Middle East, where it was often connected to Islam. During the war, the European powers had competed with each other in showing sympathy for the region's nationalist movements; and the Allies had encouraged Arab nationalism. In 1917 the British foreign secretary, Arthur Balfour, had also promised that a "national home" for Jews would be created in Palestine. In accord with the propaganda and humanitarian concern of that difficult year, the Balfour Declaration also guaranteed the rights of Muslims. In short, British intentions for Palestine remained uncertain, and their subsequent statements provided little clarification.

Colonial Mandates   The peace settlements also saw an important innovation, established in part to safeguard British and French imperial interests. Under the new arrangements, German and Ottoman colonial territories were declared "mandates" of the League of

MAP 26.4 TERRITORIAL SETTLEMENTS, 1919–1926
This map shows the national boundaries of Europe as they were decided upon after the First World War; they would remain in existence for nearly thirty years. Note the new nations that emerged out of the former Russian, Austro-Hungarian, and Ottoman Empires. Notice, too, the areas where national affiliations were to be decided by local plebiscites. Why do you suppose the representatives at Paris decided to hold these plebiscites?

Nations and assigned to "classes." Under the auspices of the League, Britain, France, South Africa, Australia, and New Zealand all served as administrators for these **colonial mandates.** The parts of the Ottoman Empire newly placed under British or French rule were Class A mandates, states considered on the verge of self-government. Most of the reassigned African territories were Class B mandates. The League of Nations restricted European authority in these mandates in ways intended to protect the rights of the indigenous population. For example, Europeans were prohibited from subjecting mandate subjects to military training and were forced to grant them religious freedom. Class C mandates were primarily Pacific islands, to be ruled essentially as colonies.

In every case, the mandate power had to submit annual reports to the League of Nations for review. Like much else in the treaties, the system of mandates can be seen both as an expression of conscience toward the rest of the world and as a device for absorbing former German colonies while legitimating continued European dominance.

Europe's Diminished Position Taken together, all these arrangements confirmed Europe's importance in world affairs and the dominance of Britain and France among the European powers. Yet these provisions also reflected changes in Europe's position. The French and British could take pride in the contributions of wealth and people they had received from their empires, but imperialism was weakened by the war. Its assumptions and ideals were challenged around the world; in fact, the mandate system itself was a response to widespread criticism of European rule. During the war, China and Siam (Thailand) eliminated many of the treaties that granted special rights to European states. In India, South Africa, Madagascar, and Egypt, powerful new nationalist groups began to demand self-government, and the African and African-American leaders meetings at the Pan-African Congress in February 1919 launched claims for better treatment from the colonial powers. Yet Europe was still reeling from the effects of war, and those within the imperial nations who might support colonial reforms were distracted by domestic and economic issues. When European nations did not respond to colonial concerns after the war, many nationalist movements began to abandon their moderate plans for the more militant objective of complete independence from the European powers.

Economically, while Europe had been enormously weakened, its suppliers (including countries with a single valuable crop, like Chile or Cuba) had prospered. The two that benefited most were Japan and the United States. Japan sold munitions and weapons to the belligerents, especially Russia, and quickly replaced German traders throughout East Asia. American production reached new heights in sector after sector (steel production doubled), and by war's end the United States had a huge new merchant fleet. The United States, increasingly willing to intervene in South America, economically, politically, and militarily, now dominated that continent, while its financiers directed the flow of world capital.

In the conflict everyone called "The Great War," the battles that mattered most had all taken place in Europe, but it had been a world war in the sense that its effects were felt around a globe that was getting smaller. The improved communications that carried supplies more rapidly across the seas (the Panama Canal opened in 1914) and on railroads from Japan to Russia and across Africa (the railroad from the Cape of Good Hope to Cairo was completed in 1918) also opened the possibility of communications and trade independent of Europe.

Disillusionment Not since 1848 had liberal conceptions so thoroughly dominated European politics. There was much to hope for in the call for self-determination and plebiscites, the League of Nations, the system of colonial mandates, and the establishment of representative regimes throughout central Europe. By 1920, however, the limitations of what had been accomplished at Paris were all too apparent. Although the Allies had endorsed high principles in Paris, many of the agreements reached there actually reflected a cold assertion of national interest and a realistic appraisal of power.

Living in a time of revolutionary changes that they themselves had advocated, the leaders who forged the peace were not revolutionaries. They never managed to find a place for Russia at the conference. They took little account of the social and economic complexities of eastern Europe. Believers in democracy, they were baffled by the turmoil it created. They stimulated nationalist movements but recognized the dangers of nationalism. Slogans that sounded radical in November 1918 gave way to frightened insistence on order a few months later. None of the leaders of democracy yet fully understood how much had changed.

Disillusionment came quickly. Having claimed moral leadership, America would in the end fail to assume the role. In March 1920 the United States Congress, again adopting an isolationist stance, refused to approve American membership in the League of Nations. This alienated the French, who had dropped demands to weaken Germany in return for the promise of American and British protection from future German aggression. Meanwhile, China refused to sign the treaties because of terms that gave Japan, in addition to other gains, extensive rights in China. Japan was offended by the conference's rejection of a formal declaration that all races are equal.

The reparations were denounced in a brilliant and influential pamphlet in which the English economist John Maynard Keynes castigated the Carthaginian peace the victors had exacted.[4] He argued that the Allies owed one another more money than Germany could

---

[4] John Maynard Keynes, *The Economic Consequences of the Peace*, 1920; and the famous rebuttal, Etienne Mantoux, *The Carthaginian Peace: Or the Economic Consequences of Mr. Keynes*, 1946. The reference is to the harsh peace terms that Roman senators demanded upon the defeat of Carthage in the Third Punic War, 149–146 B.C.

pay and that reparations would merely slow Europe's economic recovery. His analysis helped undermine confidence in the terms of peace, but his prescriptions—cancellation of international war debts and recognition that the international economic system was essentially artificial—were as utopian in their way as any of Woodrow Wilson's points. Keynes's criticisms, like those that for decades would ring from party platforms in every country, tended to exaggerate how much of the postwar world could be shaped by worried statesmen quarreling in Paris.

Postwar Democracy

From Finland to the Balkans, most of the states of eastern Europe were new, and most of them had democratic constitutions. The disappearance of the Russian, Austrian, and Ottoman empires opened the way for systematic modernization using the administrative institutions and practices they left behind. There were some hopeful signs. Schools, for example, were built by the thousands and functioned fairly effectively despite issues of language and nationality. But stability was threatened by economic, social, and ethnic conflict.

The New Governments

Economic Underdevelopment and Ethnic Conflict   The newly independent states of Central and eastern Europe had to construct a reliable administrative system while dealing with the destruction and dislocation left by war. In addition, their economies were hampered by national tariffs intended to protect local producers but that made conditions worse by impeding the prewar flow of goods.

Extensive help from the new League of Nations proved essential as growing populations, widespread illiteracy, and lack of capital plagued economic development. Only Austria and Czechoslovakia had advanced industries that could compete in European markets. Elsewhere, land remained the central economic issue, as many countries remained primarily agricultural.

Independence brought the eviction of "foreign" landlords, the breakup of large estates in the Baltic countries, and land reform in Bulgaria, Romania, and Czechoslovakia. These measures, less effective than expected, fostered accusations in each region of special treatment for favored nationalities. In Poland and still more in Hungary, the great estate owners of the aristocracy succeeded in protecting their interests.

These resentments favored peasant parties, which combined agrarian radicalism with more modern populism; these parties soon dominated most of eastern Europe. In this environment, economic and social conflicts were reinforced by ethnic and religious differences. German minorities in Poland, Czechoslovakia, Hungary, and Bulgaria were resented; the rural Slovaks were at odds with the Czechs of industrialized western Czechoslovakia; and anti-Semitism was especially virulent in Poland and Romania, where it was partly an expression of rural hostility toward village moneylenders and urban values. In Yugoslavia the claims of Greek Orthodox Serbians to be the "national" people angered the Roman Catholic Croatians and Slovenes. Macedonians—their homeland divided among Yugoslavia, Greece, and Bulgaria—agitated in all three countries and staged an insurrection in Bulgaria from 1923 to 1925.

Such circumstances encouraged military intervention in politics, as in the new Greek republic and in

Friedrich Ebert took the oath of office as provisional president of Germany in February 1919; note the absence of men in uniform.
Ullstein Bilderdienst

Hungary. But most of the governments of eastern Europe worked more or less within their constitutions; Czechoslovakia, under President Tomáš Masaryk and Foreign Minister Edvard Beneš, became a model of the order, freedom, and prosperity that democracy was supposed to bring.

The Weimar Republic   The German provisional government was established just in time to sign the armistice. Its officials referred proudly to the German "revolution" and promulgated decrees promising democracy, freedom of speech, a return to the eight-hour workday, and improvements in social security. Frightened of a communist revolution, the government quickly reached an accommodation with the army, which was already encouraging the legend that it had not lost the war but had been stabbed in the back by politicians and radicals at home. General Wilhelm Groener, who replaced Ludendorff as Hindenburg's principal aide, promised to assist the government provided it would not meddle in the army's affairs.

President Ebert accepted those terms, and when the Spartacists, a group of left-wing Marxists, gained control of most of Berlin in January 1919, the army, supported by the paramilitary Freikorps, crushed the revolt and shot its leaders. Lenin's best hope for a communist revolution in Germany died with them. One of those murdered was Rosa Luxemburg, who had drafted the Spartacist platform calling for a proletarian revolution. An effective leader and impressive intellectual, she had urged the Spartacists to avoid useless violence and had recognized that most workers remained loyal to Ebert's Social Democratic government. But she would not abandon her party when hotter heads chose armed conflict. Her death was a lasting blow to the radical left, the government's reliance on the army a blow to Germany's new democracy.

Nevertheless, Germany's new leaders held elections in January 1919 for a constituent assembly. It met in Weimar, with nearly three-quarters of the delegates intent on installing a republic. They wrote a thoroughly democratic constitution that joined proportional representation to universal suffrage. The president, directly elected for a seven-year term, would nominate the chancellor, or prime minister, who would have to be approved by the Reichstag. The Reichsrat, the upper house, would still represent the individual states but with reduced powers. In the new Germany, government would be responsible to parliament, minorities would be fairly represented, the aristocracy would hold no political privilege, and civil rights and private property would be guaranteed. With women voting, the Social Democrats in power, and a broad spectrum of parties, German politics was launched on a new course.

By November 1923 German children could play with their nation's worthless paper money.
AKG London

German Inflation   The gravest problem of these years was inflation. Early in 1923 French and Belgian forces occupied the Ruhr district of Germany, after it failed to make the coal deliveries required as reparations. The local population, encouraged by the German government, responded with passive resistance, a kind of general strike that made the occupation fruitless. The resulting dislocation and scarcity drastically accelerated the already serious inflation. The German government, which from 1920 on found it easier to print more money than to raise taxes, continued that practice in 1923 as its expenses rose and its revenues declined.

The German mark, valued at 4 marks to 1 U.S. dollar in 1914 and 9 to 1 in 1919, was exchanged at 500 to 1 by 1922. Its subsequent fall was cataclysmic. One dollar was worth 18,000 marks in January 1923, 350,000 marks in July, and nearly 5,000,000 in August. New money was run off the presses at top speed, and old notes with additional zeros printed on them were rushed to the banks before they, too, became valueless. Prices changed within hours, always upward. By

November a newspaper could sell for nearly 100 billion marks (see "German Inflation," p. 809).

By the end of the year a restructuring was begun. The government imposed stringent new financial measures, a moratorium on reparations, and subsequently a new schedule of payments. Some fortunes had been made during the inflation, especially by speculators and financiers; many large industries and property owners had fared quite well. Small businesses were more often hurt, as were nearly all wage earners. Savings held in cash had been wiped out. Although a slow recovery began, it did not last very long and the same pattern emerged once again in the late 1920s.

Domestic Conflict At the height of the Ruhr crisis, a little-known man named Adolf Hitler led a nationalist *putsch*, or coup, in Munich. Notable for Ludendorff's participation, it was quickly defeated, and the plotters' punishment was ludicrously light. Ludendorff was acquitted, and Hitler was given a five-year sentence in comfortable prison quarters, where he composed *Mein Kampf (My Struggle)* during the thirteen months he actually served. Such attacks on the new government were becoming less frequent, however. Its moderate policies and general prosperity brought relief from the assassinations and revolts of the earlier years, and it was reasonable to believe in 1924 that Germany was on the road to stability.

But the divisions in German society were sharpening, and there was no significant group with primary loyalty to the existing regime. The leading statesman was Gustav Stresemann, who sat in every cabinet, usually as foreign minister, from 1923 to his death in 1929. A nationalist of the center-right, he acquiesced in the army's violations of the disarmament clauses, but the right denounced him for his conciliatory tone toward former enemies and for bringing Germany into the League of Nations. German workers felt little was being done for them. The middle class could not forgive the inflation. The political extremes were growing at the expense of the center. When President Ebert died in 1925, a rightist coalition elected General von Hindenburg as his successor, defeating the candidate supported by both the Center and the Social Democratic parties.

The Established Democracies

Except for Italy, where Fascism came to power in 1922, democracy at first fared rather well in the postwar years. Belgium recaptured its place among Europe's most prosperous and freest countries. The Netherlands faced nationalist unrest in its colony of the Dutch East Indies, but such problems hardly threatened democratic institutions at home. The Scandinavian countries, while often at odds among themselves, sustained effective democracies.

Social Changes In every country the most militant Marxists felt strengthened by the presence of the Soviet Union as an international homeland for the proletariat. Nevertheless, the founding of Communist parties and allegiance to the Soviet Union split and weakened the left in domestic affairs. Economic recovery, though slower than expected, brought a general prosperity by the mid-1920s that contributed to the electoral victories of moderate and conservative parties. Constitutional democracy was the European norm, and many were convinced that even the Soviet Union and Italy would in time return to that standard.

Generally, the central government now spent a higher proportion of national wealth; although most of that went to the military, the national debt, and to pensions, some of it was used to lay the basis for broader measures of social security for all. Politically, both business interests and labor unions exercised a more direct influence, supporting efforts to achieve economic stability. Yet despite periods of prosperity and a genuine boom in certain industries, the 1920s did not provide the steady growth of the prewar decade. Economic uncertainty, increased by inflation and unemployment, tended, like the disillusionment over reparations or the specter of Bolshevism, to favor caution.

Changes in Women's Lives Women's suffrage, once hotly debated, had been adopted in the Scandinavian countries (Finland, 1906; Norway, 1907; Denmark, 1917; Sweden, 1919) and in Great Britain (1918) and was part of the new constitutions of Austria and Germany. The effects on public life were less dramatic than either advocates or opponents had predicted, but there was significance in the growing sense that for women to vote was a natural extension of democracy.

The most fundamental social changes of the period were usually not the result of deliberate policy. Employment in services such as sales and office work increased more rapidly than in industry, and the number of domestic servants continued to decline. These changes affected unmarried women especially. In most countries more women were gainfully employed than before the war despite a sharp decline from the wartime peak and despite the strong tendency for women to leave work upon marriage. Everywhere, women received more years of schooling than before, and the number of middle-class male youths enrolled in universities increased sharply. A rising standard of living and the automobile began to alter middle-class life.

Limited Recovery in France Life in France quickly returned to prewar patterns. The nation had become par excellence the land of the middle class, the artisan, and the peasant proprietor fiercely attached to a tiny plot of

GERMAN INFLATION

The German statistical office published this description of the effects of inflation in 1923. Obviously concerned that foreigners did not understand how bad the effects of inflation were, the account also expresses the rising insecurity of the middle class.

"The greater part of the population has been forced down far below their old standard of living, even with regard to the most important necessities of life.

"Consequently the foreigner, for example, who has visited Germany since the war, would do well to ask himself whether, in the overcrowded first-class railway carriages, he has found many Germans, or whether in the best seats at the theatre Germans are in the majority. He would do well to inquire whether in fashionable places of entertainment the German or the foreign public predominates, and if he does see Germans present spending their money for light entertainment, let him consider whether these are the majority of the German people. He must not forget either that many people today are influenced by the psychological fact that saving is no longer of any use: 100 marks today will perhaps be only 50 marks tomorrow. He who before the war, for example, had saved 5,500 marks could purchase for that amount furniture for a middle-class flat of three rooms as well as clothing, for a married couple with two children. In the middle of February 1923 (with an average dollar rate of 27,819 for February) the same person, for the same articles, would have had to spend 26.3 million marks in paper money. The man who did not spend the 5,500 marks, but preferred to save it together with the interest thereon might have over 7,000 marks today, with which, however, he cannot even buy a shirt! Who would care to 'save' under such conditions? Does the stranger realize, moreover, that such violent changes in the valuation of German money have meant for many thousands of German savers the annihilation of their savings? Does the stranger see the formerly well-to-do men and women of the middle class who today with a heavy heart carry their old family jewellery to the dealer, in order to prolong their physical existence a little longer? He who before the war could spend the interest on 1 million marks was a rich man, even up to 1919 he could still live upon it with reasonable comfort; today he is poor, for with his 50,000 marks interest he can today barely provide his own person with the necessities of life for a week! Does the stranger see the women and girls from the higher circles, even up to the highest, who are compelled to take up some occupation or who help to eke out the family income by working in their homes for a miserable wage? Does the stranger see the 1½ millions of war cripples, who are struggling desperately to earn their living, because the pensions that the State can afford to pay them are utterly inadequate?"

From Sidney Pollard and Colin Holmes (eds.), *Documents of European Economic History*, Vol. 3: *The End of Old Europe, 1914–1939*, St. Martin's Press, 1972.

land. Though the expected cornucopia of reparations never materialized, ordinary people accomplished miracles of reconstruction, carefully making their new buildings look as much as possible like those destroyed. The Chamber of Deputies elected in 1919 at the height of patriotic pride in victory was the most conservative since the founding of the Third Republic; and politics, too, focused on restoration.

The depreciation of the franc, for a century one of the world's most stable currencies, was the principal concern of President Raymond Poincaré's conservative program. Inadequate taxation during the war lay at the root of the problem, and budgetary contraction was the preferred solution. The rigid focus on a stable franc and military security reflected the psychological as well as the economic and demographic costs of war.

In the subsequent prosperity, competent leaders presided over governments content with policies that permitted domestic stagnation and encouraged inflexibility in foreign affairs. Poincaré's concern for national honor and a stable currency appealed to a cautious middle class but avoided more difficult long-term issues of working conditions, social inequality, cultural change, or international peace.

The Altered Circumstances of the United Kingdom

In the United Kingdom, also, the elections of 1919—the first in which women were allowed to vote—produced an overwhelming victory for leaders who promised to extract enough from Germany to make winning the war worthwhile. Lloyd George remained prime minister, but his government was essentially conservative. The breakup of the wartime coalition exposed the Liberal party's decline, and in 1924 new elections brought the Labour party briefly to power. Except for recognizing the Soviet Union, Labour did little to recall its leftist origins. For most of that decade, Britain was led with dull caution by the Conservatives and Stanley Baldwin,

Demonstrations and parades were banned in Dublin and Belfast, where an armored car stands ready to put down any trouble; violence had become an expected part of political struggle in Ireland.
Bettmann/Corbis

who inherited problems of unemployment, Irish nationalism, and a changing empire.

A crisis in the coal industry led to a ten-day general strike in 1926 that became a lightning rod for social division. Frightened by the bitter class conflict, many of the well-to-do volunteered in maintaining essential services, thus helping to break the strike. That response and the antilabor legislation that followed did much to deepen the resentments of British workers and heighten the angry rhetoric of public life.

Irish Independence The Irish question was equally explosive. The promise of home rule had been suspended during the war, and the Easter Rebellion of 1916 had been firmly suppressed. In 1919, however, the most militant Irish nationalists, led by the Sinn Fein (meaning "We Ourselves") party, refused to take their seats in the House of Commons and met instead at Dublin in a parliament of their own, the Dail Eireann. There, they declared Ireland an independent nation.

To this defiance the London government responded slowly and ineptly, finally choosing to suppress the Sinn Fein party and with it Irish independence. The government then sent armed reinforcements in numbers sufficient to spread the fighting without ending it, troops that soon became the most hated symbol of British repression. Violent civilian resisters called themselves the Irish Republican Army. By the 1920s the two sides were fighting a bloody war.

With pressure mounting at home and abroad for some settlement, the British government in 1920 passed the Ireland Act, creating two Irish parliaments, one in the predominantly Catholic areas of the south

and west, and the other in the predominantly Protestant counties of the northeast. Sinn Fein warred against this division of the island during almost two more years of fighting. Nevertheless, in December 1922 the Irish parliament sitting in Dublin in the Catholic south proclaimed, with British acquiescence, the existence of the Irish Free State, which included all Ireland except the six northern counties of Ulster. As Northern Ireland, these counties maintained the traditional union with Great Britain in an uneasy peace.

The British Commonwealth Only in imperial affairs did flexible compromise still seem to work. Canadian complaints led the Imperial Conference of 1926 to a significant new definition of all dominions as "autonomous communities . . . equal in status . . . united by a common allegiance to the crown and freely associated as members of the British Commonwealth of Nations." Autonomous in all domestic and foreign affairs, dominions accepted ties to the British crown as the expression of their common traditions and loyalties. Given legal sanction by the Statute of Westminster in 1931, this conception of empire proved a skillful adaptation to new conditions crowned by the stability, prosperity, and loyalty of dominions such as Canada, New Zealand, and Australia.

International Relations

From 1924 to 1930 the conduct of international relations reflected some of the idealism of the Paris Peace Conference. The League of Nations, formally established in 1920, successfully resolved a number of disputes, despite the absence of the United States, Britain's greater concern for its empire, and France's tendency to use the League for its own security. The League's special commissions helped restructure the disjointed economies of new states, aided refugees, and set international standards for public health and working conditions. To further the rule of law, the League also established the Permanent Court of International Justice in The Hague, and in the late 1920s its decisions were treated with great respect.

Debt Payments Crises over debt payments were dealt with directly by the major powers. As Germany fell behind in its payments, the Allies took the position that they, in turn, could not pay their war debts to the United States. Some compromise was essential, and in 1924 the nations involved accepted the proposals of an international commission of financial experts, headed by the American banker Charles G. Dawes. The Dawes Plan fixed Germany's reparations payments on a regular scale, established an orderly mode of collection, and provided loans to Germany equal to 80 percent of the reparations payment Germany owed in the first year of the plan.

The Dawes Plan did not admit any connection between Allied debts to the United States and German reparations to the European victors, but it did end the worst of the chaos. For the next six years, Germany, fed by loans largely from the United States, made its reparations payments on schedule. The issue seemed forever resolved with the adoption of the Young Plan in 1929, which finally set a limit to Germany's obligations, reduced annual payments, and ended foreign occupation of the Rhineland. Under the leadership of American bankers, the interests of international capital had come to shape policy.

The Locarno Era International efforts to outlaw war led to a series of treaties in 1925 known as the Locarno Pact. In the major agreement—entered into by Germany, Belgium, France, Great Britain, and Italy—all parties accepted Germany's western frontier as defined by the Versailles Treaty and promised to arbitrate their disagreements. In addition, France pursued a more traditional diplomacy, signing a mutual-defense alliance with Poland and Czechoslovakia. A continental war caused by German aggression now seemed impossible.

The optimism of the Locarno era was capped by the Kellogg-Briand pact of 1928. The French had suggested that the American entry into World War I be commemorated by a friendship pact, and the Americans proposed to include others as well. More than a score of nations signed the pact, which, though unenforceable, renounced war "as an instrument of national policy."

Disarmament From 1921 on, some League commission was always studying the problem of disarmament. Given the enormous cost of capital ships, naval disarmament seemed especially promising. At the Washington Conference of 1921–1922, the United States, Great Britain, Japan, France, and Italy agreed after some difficulty to fix their relative strength in capital ships at current levels,[5] not to expand their naval bases, and even to scrap some of their larger vessels. Never again did discussions of naval disarmament prove so fruitful. At Geneva in 1927 and London in 1930, Italy and France refused to accept a treaty. By 1935 Japan would reject even the Washington accord.

Attempts to limit land and air arms were even less successful. League commissions could not agree on

the definition of offensive weapons, whether a professional army was comparable to a reserve force, and on whether limitations should be expressed in terms of budgets, weapons, or personnel. German and Russian proposals that their own military weakness be made the standard for other nations only aroused suspicion. After much preparation, these League commissions called a conference on general disarmament in 1932. Before agreements could be reached, however, Hitler had come to power in Germany, and a new arms race ensued.

The Beginning of a New Era To contemporaries, and for historians since, World War I was the beginning of a new era. The war itself was understood to have resulted from a dangerous system of alliances, secret diplomacy, and the arms race. Creation of the League of Nations, agreements like the Locarno treaties, and conferences on disarmament were unusual examples of an extensive effort to learn from history and to correct the errors of the past. Postwar international relations differed in other respects, too; the nations of Europe were now deeply in debt, and their hold on empire was weakened.

Multiple new states with contested boundaries, in which nationalism was often the strongest communal bond, wrestled with the unfamiliar complications of democracy. In those countries and in the established democracies, the relationship between politics and the general public had changed. Old elites were less trusted, the techniques of mass mobilization now more familiar and available to every party, and groups once treated as peripheral (such as workers, farmers, women, and veterans) were more assertive. Disillusionment with politics was deep after years of propaganda; yet more was expected of government. Revolutionary new political movements on both the right and the left threatened to change the rules of politics altogether.

Economic conditions were different, too. The war and the terms of peace left enormous problems of physical destruction, burdens of debt, and broken trade patterns. The flood of former soldiers seeking jobs while war industries shrank was followed by long-term changes involving new technologies and the reorganization of production to incorporate American techniques of mass production for mass markets.

In these circumstances the radical ideas and shocking cultural movements of the 1890s had new relevance. Nearly all Europeans had personal experience of lives disrupted—families broken up, women adding new roles to demanding old ones, jobs gained and suddenly lost, savings wiped out, property destroyed, invading armies, civil war, or sickness and death. All these changes at once, from the international to the personal, marked the advent of a new era.

---

[5] The current level was defined as parity between the United States and Great Britain at 525,000 tons apiece in capital ships, 315,000 tons for Japan, and 175,000 tons each for France and Italy.

Summary

In 1914 the nations of Europe stumbled into the most destructive war in their history. Machine guns and poison gas created unforeseen carnage on the battlefield. The subsequent drain on each nation's resources disrupted civilian life; eliminated the German, Austro-Hungarian, and Russian empires; and left the victors only marginally better off than the losers. Countries were forced to change their political systems or face dangerous political unrest and to rely on new segments of the population, especially women and colonial peoples, for economic and military support. After the war, the Allies promulgated democratic values and created, through the League of Nations and diplomatic agreements, a short-lived era of international cooperation. While these values never overcame national rivalries, the war gave rise to more democratic social structures and greater gender equality. The response of this reconstructed Europe to the new challenges arising in the postwar world would determine the chances for domestic and international peace.

QUESTIONS FOR FURTHER THOUGHT

1. What factors led to the outbreak of World War I?
2. The First World War is often referred to as the "first modern war." What made this war particularly modern, and did new technology alone win the war for the Allies?

3. How did the war disrupt and permanently change life on the home front? What tensions arose from such changes?

RECOMMENDED READING

Sources

Brittain, Vera. *Testament of Youth: An Autobiographical Study of the Years 1900–1925.* 1933. Memoir written by a young upper-middle-class British woman containing reflections on her wartime work as a nurse and her return to a changed Europe.

Junger, Ernst. *Storm of Steel.* 1920. Details the author's wartime experiences as a company commander in the German army; glorifies the behavior of soldiers and the significance of war in modern life.

Nicholson, Harold. *Peacemaking, 1919.* 1965. The retrospective analysis of an experienced diplomat who was a disillusioned participant at the Versailles Conference.

Remarque, Erich Maria. *All Quiet on the Western Front.* First published in Germany in 1928, this novel with its realistic (and antinationalist) depiction of the war became the subject of great controversy there. Its moving rejection of modern warfare made it a best seller throughout Europe and in the United States.

Sassoon, Siegfried. *Memoirs of a Fox-Hunting Man; Memoirs of an Infantry Officer; Sherston's Progress.* Series of pseudo-autobiographical works written by the British poet, novelist, and former trench soldier, which were collected and published in the 1930s.

Studies

Becker, Jean-Jacques. *The Great War and the French People.* 1985. Shows the multiple ways in which the war was a turning point in French life.

Culleton, Claire A. *Working-Class Culture, Women, and Britain, 1914–1921.* 1999. Uses oral history collections to demonstrate that, despite their wartime contributions, the position of women workers within British society remained largely the same after the war.

Feldman, Gerald D. *Army, Industry, and Labor in Germany, 1914–1918.* 1966. A fundamental analysis of the war's effects on institutions and power in Germany.

Ferguson, Niall. *The Pity of War: Explaining World War One.* 1999. A controversial work. The author refutes conventional explanations for the origins, events, and aftermath of the First World War and argues that Britain's involvement created a world war out of a localized conflict.

Fischer, Fritz. *Germany's Aims in the First World War.* 1967. The reassessment that became a center of controversy among German historians.

Fussell, Paul. *The Great War and Modern Memory.* 1975. An important study of the cultural impact of the war, as seen by soldier poets and writers.

Grayzel, Susan. *Women's Identities at War: Gender, Motherhood, and Politics in Britain and France during the First World War.* 1999. Shows how the war challenged conventional views of women and describes the backlash against those challenges in the postwar period.

Hermann, David G. *The Arming of Europe and the Making of the First World War.* 1997. Uses new archival evidence to show the importance of military considerations in the diplomacy that led to world war.

Horne, John N., and Alan Kramer. *German Atrocities, 1914: A History of Denial.* 2001. The authors recount the atrocities committed by German troops as they advanced through Belgium and France and explore how the stories of these atrocities became national, if often fabricated, legends in Belgium.

Joll, James. *The Origins of the First World War.* 1987. A synthesis of the vast literature on this controversial topic that takes a balanced perspective on the question.

Keegan, John. *The First World War.* 1998. Standard and comprehensive account of the war's military developments, concentrating on the Western Front.

Kennedy, Paul (ed.). *The War Plans of the Great Powers, 1880–1914.* 1979. Places the arms race in the context of imperialist and political rivalries in the prewar era.

Kocka, Jürgen. *Facing Total War: German Society, 1914–1918.* Translated by Barbara Weinberger. 1984. A leading social historian's assessment of the impact of the war on the German home front.

Marwick, Arthur. *War and Social Change in the Twentieth Century: A Comparative Study of Britain, France, Germany, Russia, and the United States.* 1975. Develops the case for the revolutionary effects of World War I and World War II on the domestic economies of modern Western society.

Miller, S. (ed.). *Military Strategy and the Origins of the First World War.* 1985. Collection of essays assessing the role of the military in the decisions that led to war.

Smith, Leonard V., Stéphane Audoin-Rouzeau, and Annette Becker. *France and the Great War, 1914–1918.* Synthesizes decades of scholarship examining France's wartime experiences on the battlefront and the home front, as well as postwar issues facing the French national community.

Stone, Norman. *Eastern Front, 1914–1917.* 1975. The leading account of the war's other military theater, concluding with the Russian Revolution and the Treaty of Brest Litovsk.

Verhey, Jeffrey. *The Spirit of 1914: Militarism, Myth, and Mobilization in Germany.* 2000. Uses an array of contemporary sources to refute "The Myth of 1914," which proclaimed that the German public responded to the outbreak of war with unqualified enthusiasm.

Williamson, Samuel R. *Austria-Hungary and the Origins of the First World War.* 1991. Examines how Austria-Hungary's involvement in the war was motivated by its leaders' fears of domestic disorder and willingness to risk a general war to settle a local conflict.

Winter, J. M., and R. M. Wall, eds. *The Upheaval of War: Family, Work, and Welfare in Europe, 1914–1918.* 1988. An insightful assessment of the effects of the war on domestic society.

Winter, Jay. *Sites of Memory, Sites of Mourning.* 1996. A powerful study of the impact of the war on European culture.

This idealized image of Lenin addressing the people conveys the power of Lenin's oratory skills and the sense that his leadership began a new era. The portrait of impassioned workers, soldiers and sailors, men and women—all inspired by their leader—and the careful placement of Stalin just behind Lenin reveal the painting as the subsequent official view of the Soviet government. One of the marks of the new era in Europe was, in fact, the effective propaganda of single-party states.
Sovfoto

Chapter Twenty-Seven

THE GREAT TWENTIETH-CENTURY CRISIS

TWO SUCCESSFUL REVOLUTIONS • THE DISTINCTIVE CULTURE OF THE TWENTIETH CENTURY • THE GREAT DEPRESSION AND THE RETREAT FROM DEMOCRACY • NAZI GERMANY AND THE USSR • THE DEMOCRACIES' WEAK RESPONSE

The 1920s and 1930s opened an era of intense hope and great fear. As the prosperity and consumerism of the 1920s gave way to economic depression, Europe's liberal governments had difficulty responding. Domestic divisions grew sharper, reinforced by the example of radical alternatives; for, although most of the revolutions in the aftermath of World War I had failed, new political systems emerged in Communist Russia and Fascist Italy. Relatively isolated at first, these new regimes became influential models. The possibility of communist revolution and the potential of fascist nationalism reshaped political life throughout Europe.

Cultural life was unsettling, too. A flourishing popular culture, flippant and commercial, undermined nineteenth-century standards of propriety (and the confidence that went with them). Europe's most interesting artists and intellectuals disdained the prosperity of the 1920s, and provocative theories, in both the physical and social sciences, invited skepticism about absolute truths and traditional values. Politics and culture both struggled with questions about the nature of modern mass society.

There were also immediate reasons for discontent among workers who had expected the postwar world to bring greater improvements in their way of life, among peasants who found it hard to make a living from small but often inefficient holdings, among ethnic groups resentful of sudden minority status as a result of the boundary changes in eastern Europe, among nationalists angry that their new states had not gained more territory, and among all those who disliked the altered lifestyle of the postwar era. Then economic depression drove home the failures of capitalism, the limitations of liberalism, and the weaknesses of democracy.

Two nations seemed to rise above the economic crisis: Communist Russia under Stalin and Nazi Germany under Hitler. Their apparent escape from the Great Depression, their capacity to mobilize popular support, and their brutal use of force contrasted with the hesitant compromises of more democratic governments. In the 1930s, that contrast sharpened as they began asserting their authority in international relations.

1929 ●
Lateran Agreements between the Vatican and Mussolini's government;
Virginia Woolf, *A Room of One's Own*; stock market crash leads to Great Depression

First Five-Year Plan in Soviet Union **1928–1932** ▬

Penicillin discovered in England **1928** ●

● **1922**
James Joyce, *Ulysses*;
Benito Mussolini appointed prime minister of Italy

● **1921** Lenin launches New Economic Policy

● **1918** Oswald Spengler, *Decline of the West*; Treaty of Brest Litovsk

● **1917** Russian Revolution

TWO SUCCESSFUL REVOLUTIONS

In Russia and in Italy the aftermath of war was revolution. Both nations had begun rapid industrialization in the 1890s, and both were sorely tested in the world war that followed. Revolution in Russia began while the war was still going on, and it continued for several years before the outcome was certain. Revolution in Italy occurred quickly a few years after the war. Each resulted in a new kind of political regime, and only gradually did it become clear that Russian communism and Italian fascism might change the face of Europe.

Revolution in Russia

When world war broke out in 1914, Russia's parliament (the Duma) and local councils (or *zemstvos*) helped coordinate the war effort. But when the Cadet party maintained its insistence on further liberal reforms, the tsar suspended the Duma. Resentful that political aims should be pursued in wartime—they still did not see that a more representative government could strengthen the war effort—the tsar and his officials grew increasingly isolated from the country. More comfortable as a military strategist than as a head of state, Tsar Nicholas II grandly departed to command his army, leaving Tsarina Alexandra and those closest to her to oppose any program for reform. Her chief confidant was Grigori Rasputin, an ignorant and corrupt mystic whose influence symbolized the decadence of this regime.

The February Revolution   Throughout 1916 signs of Russia's failures accumulated. Production and transportation were undependable, war refugees filled the roads, inflation soared, and food shortages became critical. All this came on top of years of rising anger among peasants eager for land and workers determined to change their lot. Without realizing the depth of this social strife, officials were well aware of how serious the situation was. Even in the highest circles, there was talk of deposing the tsar. In November in the reconvened Duma, Pavel Milyukov, a noted historian and the leader of the liberal Cadets, courageously delivered a biting attack on the government. In December a group of nobles murdered Rasputin. Strikes spread, and in March 1917, when strikers filled the streets of Petrograd,[1] their economic demands quickly broadened to include political issues. The army could not be relied on to oppose them. Again, much as in 1905, a soviet of workers (now called the Soviet of Workers' and Soldiers' Deputies) became the voice of revolution, and they joined with a Duma committee in seeking a provisional government. They prepared to resist any tsarist force that might be sent against them. None came. The military situation was desperate, the government in disarray, and the tsar unpopular. With nowhere to turn, Nicholas II abdicated, and the February Revolution[2] was hailed with joy and relief throughout the country.

The provisional government's central figure was Milyukov; its only socialist was Aleksandr Kerensky, a member of the Social Revolutionary party and vice-chairman of the Petrograd soviet. The new government

---

[1] St. Petersburg was a Germanic name, and in 1914 Nicholas had changed it to the Russian *Petrograd*. The capital until 1918, the city would become Leningrad in 1924 and St. Petersburg again in 1991.

[2] These events occurred on March 8–12 according to the Gregorian calendar used throughout the West. Russia, however, had never abandoned the older Julian calendar (which continues to be the calendar of the Orthodox Church). The revolutions of March 8–12 and November 7, 1917, according to the Gregorian system, were dated thirteen days earlier according to the Julian, and they continue to be called the February and October revolutions.

● **1933** Adolf Hitler becomes chancellor of Germany; Reichstag fire in Berlin; World Economic Conference meets in London

1933–1937 Second Five-Year Plan

● **1934** Austrian Chancellor Engelbert Dollfuss assassinated; Politburo member Sergei Kirov assassinated

● **1935** Italy invades Ethiopia

● **1936** John Maynard Keynes, *The General Theory of Employment, Interest, and Money;* German troops enter the Rhineland; Rome-Berlin Axis; Anti-Comintern Pact; King Edward VIII of England abdicates

● **1937** Pablo Picasso produces *Guernica* for the World's Fair in Paris

● **1938** *Kristallnacht* in Nazi Germany

Third Five-Year Plan **1938–1942**

quickly established broad civil liberties, an amnesty for political prisoners, and the end of religious persecution. It also proposed granting a constitution to Finland, which Russia ruled, and independence to Russian Poland. Declaring its support for an eight-hour workday and for the abolition of class privileges, it left most other social issues to a constituent assembly, which it promised to call soon.

In fact, the parties of revolution sharply disagreed on these issues. The Cadets, who dominated the provisional government, came to accept the idea of a republic, political democracy, and distribution of land with compensation to former owners. To their left, the Social Revolutionary party and the Menshevik wing of the Social Democratic party, which was especially strong in the soviets forming across the nation, demanded more drastic reforms. These parties were divided, too, however. Some of their members were willing to postpone these further reforms until after the war, which, like the Cadets, they still meant to win. The more radical of them stressed an early end to the war, without yet advocating an immediate armistice. For the time being, the soviets, watching from the outside and ever ready to criticize, allowed the provisional government its chance. To the left of all these factions stood a small group known as the Bolsheviks.

The Bolsheviks In 1898 Russian Marxists had secretly formed the Social Democratic party, which functioned mainly in the conspiratorial world of exile. At the party's second congress, held in Brussels and London in 1903, it had split into two groups, called the **Bolsheviks** (majority) and Mensheviks (minority); in fact, the Bolsheviks rarely had a majority, but these nicknames stuck. Their differences were theoretical, organizational, and personal. The theoretical issues, which

engaged Marxists everywhere, were fought with the special intensity of revolutionaries far from home and power. On the whole, the Mensheviks placed greater emphasis on popular support and parliamentary institutions, which implied cooperation with other parties. The Bolsheviks stressed instead the need for a disciplined revolutionary party to instruct and lead the masses, which might otherwise be likely to settle for immediate gains rather than the European revolution that would bring about socialism. Led by Georgi Plekhanov and V. I. Lenin, the Bolsheviks denounced as enemies all who did not join them. Only later would these party battles waged in foreign cities prove significant for Russian history.

The ideas of socialism that spread in Russia after 1905 were not so much those of the Bolsheviks as those of the Mensheviks and the Social Revolutionaries, who were less consistently Marxist and were closer to the peasants. Although Plekhanov tried on his own to heal the breach in the Social Democratic party, Lenin's conception of iron discipline allowed little room for compromise; and he soon consigned Plekhanov to the Mensheviks.

Lenin's Tactics Removed from events in Russia, Lenin continued from Switzerland to organize selected followers, denounce the heresies of others, and develop his theoretical view of the special role a militant party should play in a country that, like Russia, was just achieving modern capitalism. The party could achieve its aims, he argued, only by recognizing the revolutionary potential in the peasants' hunger for land (most Marxists considered the peasantry a socially backward class and believed land ownership was opposed to socialism). Thus, the Bolsheviks, although they lacked a large following in Russia, had a theory of how to make a revolution.

The armed civilians in the foreground are Red Guards, demonstrating their might and protecting the Bolshevik leaders addressing a large crowd of workers.
Sovfoto

Lenin considered World War I a civil war among capitalists, and in a sense that theoretical stand gave Lenin his chance, for it suggested to the Germans that his presence in Russia as an agitator might be useful in undermining the Russian war effort. In April 1917 the Germans arranged to send Lenin by sealed train through Germany and Scandinavia to Russia. Lenin, however, had something grander than mere agitation in mind.

Marxists were ambivalent in their attitude toward the February Revolution, which they welcomed as progressive but tended to disdain as a bourgeois revolution and not a victory of the proletariat. Lenin offered another interpretation: Revolution in Russia was part of a larger revolution about to sweep all of Europe. Socialists had no interest in the capitalist war, which Russia's provisional government continued to support, but Bolsheviks could seize the chance to push the revolution beyond its bourgeois phase to a "second stage" in which the soviets would be the true representatives of the proletariat. That in turn dictated the tactics the Bolsheviks should follow: They must gain the leadership of the soviets, and then Russia could join in the international revolution that was imminent. Historians have emphasized Lenin's tactical flexibility, but in

April his views seemed impossibly dogmatic even to radicals. It was the force of his personality, his political skill, and his oratory that kept him leader of the Bolsheviks.

Summer Crisis While the soviets were building a national organization that claimed authority over railroads, telegraph lines, and troops, the provisional government was falling apart. Its members disagreed over war policy and land reform; its police and officials were abandoning their posts. Workers continued to strike, and nationalist movements erupted in Latvia, Georgia, and the Ukraine. Milyukov resigned, four more socialists joined the cabinet, and Kerensky, an energetic leader and effective orator, became the cabinet's leading figure.

The Kerensky government was quickly attacked from left and right. The Bolsheviks criticized Kerensky at the first all-Russian Congress of Soviets in June but gained support from just over 100 of the 800 plus delegates. In July they attempted a coup in Petrograd. That was decisively defeated, and many of the coup leaders were arrested. Lenin fled to Finland. Meanwhile, cities were torn by strikes and demonstrations as the situation at the front grew more perilous. In the countryside, rioting peasants demanding land burned manor houses and murdered landlords.

Convinced that a strong military hand was what the nation needed, the army's commander in chief, General Lavr Kornilov, led an attack on Petrograd in September. Kerensky asked the soviets (and thus the Bolsheviks as well) to defend the government. Most of Kornilov's men had refused to follow his orders, and the threat passed quickly. But in the meantime Bolshevik leaders had been released from prison, and Bolshevist propaganda was gaining ground with simple slogans promising peace, land, and bread—issues at the heart of daily life and ones for which the provisional government had no clear solutions.

The Bolsheviks won control of the soviets in Moscow and Petrograd, electing Leon Trotsky chairman of the latter. Trotsky, who had worked with Lenin in exile, had until recently stood somewhat aloof from party conflicts. Now firmly in Lenin's camp, he proceeded to organize the armed forces in Petrograd. With the Social Revolutionaries supporting peasant expropriation of land, the provisional government was left politically alone in a city it could not control, trying to rule a nation in chaos and still at war.

The October Revolution To the dismay of many in his party, Lenin, who had reentered Russia, boldly decided to seize power. When the second all-Russian Congress of Soviets met on November 7, he confronted it with a new government. Kerensky began countermeasures a few days before that date, but it was too late. On November 6, Red Guards (squads of armed workers), sailors, and soldiers captured the Winter Palace and strategic points throughout the city. A simultaneous movement in Moscow won control of the city in a week. Lenin announced to the Congress that the Bolsheviks held power and sent out a young officer to take command of the armies. At each stop along his route, the troops enthusiastically cheered his announcement of the Bolshevik coup. Their commanders could only acquiesce. Kerensky, who had escaped from the capital, tried to muster support, but the one group of Cossacks who moved on Petrograd was soundly defeated. The world's first communist government had taken office (see "Two Accounts of Revolution in Russia," p. 820).

"All power to the soviets!" had been one of the Bolsheviks' most effective slogans, and the Congress readily approved the one-party cabinet Lenin presented it. The rudiments of a new form of government emerged: The Congress of Soviets replaced parliament and elected a Central Executive committee to advise the Council of People's Commissars, or cabinet. From the very first, Bolshevik rule did not depend on any elected body. Elections for the promised constituent assembly, held at the end of November, would be the last open competition among parties for more than seventy years. The Bolsheviks won a quarter of the seats, other socialist parties more than 60 percent, conservatives and liberals the rest. As the assembly met on its second day, the military guards told it to adjourn.

Lenin provided a basis for such ruthlessness in his pamphlet "The State and Revolution," written in Finland in the summer of 1917. It used the Marxist conception that the state is the coercive organ of the ruling class to argue that, once the Bolsheviks held power, the proletariat would be that ruling class. The dictatorship of the proletariat, Lenin reasoned, was the only way to lead backward Russia through the transition to that higher historical stage that Marxists envisioned in which a state would no longer be necessary. The nationalization of land and factories would achieve socialism. Communism would follow once everyone learned to work for the good of society and once production met the needs of all. Until then, the single party, the "vanguard of the proletariat," would be model and guide.

Toward a Communist Society

Millions of workers, soldiers, and peasants had joined in pulling down the old system, and the Bolshevik leaders were determined to snatch their historical moment. The day after taking the Winter Palace, the new government decreed that land, livestock, and farm equipment belonged to the state but could be "temporarily" held by peasant committees, thereby legitimizing the rural revolution that was taking place anyway.

Initial Policies No peasant was to work for hire, and committees of the poor would supervise the allocation of land and produce. Workers' committees would share in factory management, and everyone would be paid according to the work done (the state's new leaders assigned themselves laborers' salaries). All social titles and military ranks were abolished. "People's tribunals" and workers' militias replaced tsarist courts and police. Church and state were separated; the equality of the sexes was decreed and followed by regulations allowing divorce by mutual consent, measures that enhanced the reputation of Russian communism among progressives in western Europe. Even the alphabet was reformed and the Gregorian calendar adopted.

In the next few months, railroads, banks, and shipping concerns were nationalized, foreign trade became a state monopoly, and Russia's debts were repudiated. The various nationalities of Russia were declared equal and granted the right of secession; Finland took advantage of that decree to separate from Russia in December 1917, while the Bolsheviks struggled to prevent the

TWO ACCOUNTS OF REVOLUTION IN RUSSIA

The culmination of the Russian Revolution came on November 7, 1917, when the Communists captured the Winter Palace, which was then the seat of the Kerensky government. Eyewitnesses saw the event very differently. The first account is by Pitirim Sorokin, a young member of the Social Revolutionary party, who would soon go into exile and have a distinguished career as a professor of sociology at Harvard. In his memoir, Leaves from a Russian Diary, *he recalled that day. The second description is from* Ten Days That Shook the World, *the famous book by John Reed, an American journalist who admired the Bolsheviks.*

"Lying ill all day on my bed, I listened to the steady booming of the cannon and the spatter of machine-guns and crack of rifles. Over the telephone I learned that the Bolsheviki had brought up from Kronstadt the warship *Aurora* and had opened fire on the Winter Palace, demanding the surrender of members of the Provisional Government, still barricaded there. At seven in the evening I went to the Municipal Duma. With many matters before us, the immediate horror that faced us was this situation at the Winter Palace. There was a regiment of women and the military cadets were bravely resisting an overwhelming force of Bolshevist troops, and over the telephone Minister Konovalov was appealing for aid. Poor women, poor lads, their situation was desperate, for we knew that the wild sailors, after taking the Palace, would probably tear them to pieces. What could we do? After breathless council it was decided that all of us, the Soviets, Municipalities, Committees of Socialist Parties, members of the Council of the Republic, should go in procession to the Winter Palace and do our utmost to rescue the Ministers, the women soldiers, and the cadets. Even as we prepared to go, over the telephone came the despairing shout: 'The gates of the Palace have been forced. The massacre has begun. . . . Hurry! The mob has reached the first floor. All is over. Goodbye. . . . They break in. They are. . . .' The last word . . . from the Winter Palace was a broken cry."

From Pitirim Alexandrovitch Sorokin, *Leaves from a Russian Diary*, exp. ed., 1920; Beacon Press, 1950.

"Carried along by the eager wave of men we were swept into the right-hand entrance, opening into a great bare vaulted room, the cellar of the east wing, from which issued a maze of corridors and staircases. A number of huge packing cases stood about, and upon these the Red Guards and soldiers fell furiously, battering them open with the butts of their rifles, and pulling out carpets, curtains, linen, porcelain plates, glassware. . . . One man went strutting around with a bronze clock perched on his shoulder; another found a plume of ostrich feathers, which he stuck in his hat. The looting was just beginning when somebody cried, 'Comrades! Don't touch anything! Don't take anything! This is the property of the People!' Immediately twenty voices were crying, 'Stop! Put everything back! Don't take anything! Property of the People!' Many hands dragged the spoilers down. Damask and tapestry were snatched from the arms of those who had them; two men took away the bronze clock. Roughly and hastily the things were crammed back in their cases, and self-appointed sentinels stood guard. It was all utterly spontaneous. Through corridors and up staircases the cry could be heard growing fainter and fainter in the distance, 'Revolutionary discipline! Property of the People'"

From John Reed, *Ten Days That Shook the World*, 1919.

Ukraine and the ethnic groups of the Baltic regions from following suit.

Revolutionary measures also made way for a reign of terror. A new secret police, the Cheka, differed from tsarist police in determination more than method. The citizens who sat on the new committees and tribunals often combined revolutionary enthusiasm with personal vengeance, and tens of thousands lost their property, their rights, and their lives for "mistaken" alliances, "false" ideas, or "suspect" gestures. Such practices, which helped the regime solidify support, also threatened to undermine the regular procedures of government.

Ending the War with Germany The most pressing issue was to find a way out of the war. In February 1918 a delegation headed by Trotsky, having failed to arrange terms of peace with Germany, proposed a policy of no peace, no war: Russia would just stop fighting. The following month, with the Germans just 100 miles from Petrograd, the Russians accepted the Treaty of Brest Litovsk. Russia surrendered more than 1 million square miles of territory to Germany, including a third of its arable land, a third of its factories, and three-quarters of its deposits of iron and coal. It granted the independence of Finland, Georgia, and the Ukraine; left to Germany the disposition of Russian Poland, Lithuania,

CHRONOLOGY

The Conflicts That Resulted in Communist Victory

March 1917	February Revolution.
March 1917	February Revolution.
November 1917	October Revolution.
March 1918	Peace of Brest Litovsk.
1918–1920	Civil war.
1920–1921	War with Poland.
1921	Kronstadt mutiny.
1922	Japanese troops leave Russian territory.

Latvia, and Estonia; and ceded parts of Transcaucasia to the Ottoman Empire. The Communists paid this high price for peace, confident that revolution in Germany would soon nullify the kaiser's gains.

The peace treaty, like the course of the revolution itself, exposed the discontent among non-Russian nationalities, and in July a new constitution tried to meet that problem by declaring Russia a federation—the Russian Soviet Federated Socialist Republic (R.S.F.S.R.). Great Russia, extending through Siberia, was the largest member. Ostensibly, political power rested with the local soviets, organized by occupation and elected by the votes of all men and women except for members of the clergy, former high officials, and those classified as bourgeois "nontoilers." These soviets elected delegates to the congress of soviets of their canton, the smallest administrative unit, and each of these congresses in turn sent delegates to a congress at the next administrative level. The system, which continued by steps up to the all-Russia Congress, allowed considerable control from the top. The constitution did not mention the Russian Communist party, as it was now named, although it was the real center of political authority. Its Central Committee elected the smaller **Politburo,** which shared ruling power with the governing Council of People's Commissars. Lenin was the dominant figure in both.

Civil War   The Bolsheviks were still surrounded by enemies. In March Allied troops in small numbers had landed in Murmansk, Archangel, and Vladivostok to prevent the supplies they had shipped to Russia from falling into German hands, but those detachments might also be used to support a change of regime (a move some Allied officials favored). At the same time, a number of tsarist generals, among them the army's former commander-in-chief, Kornilov, were preparing to lead a small but excellent army of Cossacks against the Bolsheviks. It was the beginning of a civil war that would last for two terrible years.

While Trotsky undertook to organize the new regime's army, anti-Bolsheviks of every stripe, including the Social Revolutionaries, organized in hundreds of villages and towns. Across Russia, food riots, battles over land, skirmishes between workers and bourgeois, and ethnic hatred added to the violence. With the economy near collapse, the Bolsheviks adopted "War Communism," a program to extract from a country in chaos just enough men and supplies to fight a civil war through propaganda, requisitioning, police repression, and terror. With the firm leadership of Lenin, the military talent of Trotsky, and above all the mistakes of their enemies, they would eventually win.

By mid-1919 the major remaining threat came from armies under the command of former tsarist officers. One army pushed from the Urals toward Moscow but was stopped before it got there. Another took Kiev in August and reached within 300 miles of Moscow by October, while a third stood only 30 miles from Petrograd. These armies were weakened, however, by their conflicting ambitions; and they did little to win popular support. The areas under their control experienced a terror less efficient but at least as brutal as that conducted by the revolutionaries. With each defeat, more of the anticommunist soldiers melted away until hardly more than marauding bands were left. By the end of 1919, however, they were in general retreat. Their most important group withdrew to the Crimea early in 1920 and stubbornly fought on before finally heeding Allied advice and evacuating their remaining soldiers in November 1920.

The Last of the Fighting   The Communists had to fight against Poland as well. As provided by the Versailles treaty, an Allied commission had determined the Russo-Polish border, placing it along a line that assigned to Poland most areas in which Poles were a clear majority. Poland wanted more and insisted on its boundary of 1772, well to the east, citing cultural and historical arguments. Rejecting Russian offers of compromise, Poland sent an army into the Ukraine in March 1920. Within a month it took Kiev, but the Ukrainian nationalists who had fought the Russians were unwilling to fight for the Poles. In August the Red army, by now a relatively efficient military machine, launched an assault that soon threatened Warsaw. An effective Polish counterattack led in 1921 to a compromise settlement after all, one by which Poland gained considerable non-Polish territory in the Ukraine and in the adjacent region of White Russia. Once Russia's western border was settled, it was possible to agree on a boundary with Turkey as well. It ignored local independence movements and assigned Armenia and Georgia to the Soviet federation, Kars and Ardahan to Turkey. Fighting continued in Asia until 1922, when Japan withdrew from eastern Siberia. By then, the Soviet Union was firmly in Communist hands.

Continuing Turmoil Under War Communism, regimentation and bloodshed were the means of survival, and by using them, the Communist party had become increasingly powerful; yet most of the countryside was still subject to the whims of local party officials and roving bands of armed men. Cities were partially empty, a million Russians had gone into exile, tens of millions more had died, manufacturing produced less in 1920 than in 1913, foreign trade had almost ceased, and poor harvests raised the specter of famine. Requisitions spurred resistance, and black markets flourished. Thus, the mutiny of sailors at the Kronstadt naval base in March 1921 was an ominous sign.[3] These sailors were the sort of men who had made the October Revolution possible; though their revolt was soon quelled and their demands for political liberty rejected, Lenin recognized the need for change.

The New Economic Policy Lenin announced the **New Economic Policy (NEP)**, a major turning point in the development of Communist Russia. To many, the NEP seemed a departure from Marxism, but Lenin saw Russia's problems as the result not of flaws in Marxist theory but of having stormed the "citadel of capitalism" too fast. Russia suffered from old habits hard to uproot and from a lack of the technical experts and managers that a modern economy required. With noteworthy pragmatism, Lenin proposed a moderate course that earlier the Bolsheviks would have opposed.

Under the NEP, peasants were no longer subject to requisitions but rather to a tax in kind. Businesses employing fewer than twenty workers could be run as private enterprises, and nationalized industries could be leased to foreigners as a way of training Russians in efficient methods. Fiscal reforms guaranteed a stable currency, helping Russia's external trade to emerge from the pattern of barter into which it had fallen. Recovery was slow. Millions died in the famine of 1920–1921 despite the extensive aid of the American Relief Administration, and not for another six years would production reach prewar levels.

Communist Rule Abandoning the hope of creating communism all at once, the NEP was nevertheless the reaffirmation of Communist determination. Every social institution was recruited to help create a stable new society. Cooperatives and trade unions, newspapers and public meetings taught efficiency and pride in class and nation, as did the school system, which was improved and extended. Its curriculum stressed official doctrines; workers' children were favored for admission to selective schools, and teachers were urged to abandon old-fashioned rote learning. Women were encouraged to work outside the home and were provided a whole series of programs aimed at their special needs as mothers. The problems of ruling over multiple nationalities had eased somewhat with the cession of so much territory in the Treaty of Brest Litovsk, and three-quarters of the remaining population could be called Russian. Officially non-Russian nationalities were given more recognition than ever before, as the Communist government reassembled much of the Russian Empire, and the Orthodox Church, while kept under tight supervision, was permitted to function.

In practice, the Communist party, which remained a restricted elite, was the most important instrument of rule. Organized in a hierarchy that paralleled the bureaucracy, it reached into every aspect of public life—factories, hundreds of new centers for adult education, and youth associations—propagandizing and encouraging, pressuring and explaining. In 1922 cultural activities were placed directly under the Ministry of Education, and the Western artistic movements recently welcomed were discouraged in favor of books and art that met the current definition of communist aesthetics: realistic in style, popular in appeal, and useful to the new order. Issues of practical policy were thrashed out within the government and the party, but to be on the losing side could be politically and sometimes personally fatal. Although the Communist government would never abandon the fear of foreign attack established during the civil war, it gave signs of seeking normal diplomatic relations; by 1924, the year of Lenin's death, every major power except the United States had recognized the new regime. An object of fear to liberals and conservatives, the new communist state became a source of inspiration and hope for the far left throughout the world.

Italian Fascism

Italy, too, experimented with a new form of government. Economically the least developed of the major Western powers, Italy and Russia had begun extensive industrialization at about the same time in the late nineteenth century, and there were many parallels between the two countries, despite Italy's more urban society, greater freedom, stronger constitutional tradition, and more

---

[3] Denounced as part of an international counterrevolutionary conspiracy, the members of the Kronstadt base who were captured after the mutiny was crushed were subject to executions and deportations, and for seventy years the event was cited in Soviet histories as an example of the kinds of forces arrayed against the revolution. In 1994 Boris Yeltsin announced the rehabilitation of these rebels, and the event was used as evidence that the brutality of Communist rule had begun with Lenin's ruthlessness.

responsive governments. With the end of the war, Italy was racked by inflation, unemployment, and talk of revolution. In many places peasants simply confiscated the land they had long been promised; when industrialists met a series of strikes with lockouts in 1920, workers answered by occupying factories, and many in the upper classes feared a communist revolution. Social conflicts that the state had largely ignored for twenty years now challenged the established system. The peace treaty, too, was disillusioning. Although granted considerable territory, Italy got less than expected, and its treatment by the other Allies was often humiliating. Disposition of the Dalmatian port of Fiume was still being argued in 1919 when a private expedition led by Gabriele d'Annunzio dramatically captured it for Italy. The nation's most famous living poet, d'Annunzio ruled Fiume for more than a year at the head of an "army" of the unemployed, whose nationalist frenzy and vulgar slogans were for many a welcome contrast to the wordy frustration of diplomacy. Eventually, the Italian government evicted him, but he had shown the effectiveness of direct action in a nationalist cause.

The Victory of Fascism **Fascism** was born amid these crises. The term *fascio*, meaning "bundle," comes from an ancient Roman symbol of authority—a bundle of sticks, individually weak but strong in unity. Echoes of imperial Rome were part of the Fascist mystique. The movement centered around Benito Mussolini, whose polemical skills won him promotion to the editorship of the Socialist party newspaper until he was expelled in 1915 for favoring Italy's entry into the war. Mussolini, who established another paper, became one of Italy's noisiest nationalists, using the rhetoric of the left to denounce liberalism and parliamentary indecision and the slogans of nationalism to castigate Marxists. Fascism grew from this diverse heritage. Both a movement and a party, it employed propaganda, symbols, and activism in new ways, making party militants in their black shirts seem a civilian army.

At first the Fascists had little electoral success, but the changes in Italian politics offered them multiple opportunities. The elections of 1921 were the first in Italy with universal male suffrage, and two newer, well-organized mass parties overshadowed traditional leaders and groups. The Catholic Popular party demanded major reforms, but much of its real strength came from rural and conservative groups. The Socialists, for all their increased strength, were weakened by the split with their left wing, which formed a Communist party, inspired by the Bolsheviks' success in Russia.

The Fascists, who had won no seats in 1919, gained thirty-five in the new Chamber; and the aging Giolitti, who had been a dominating prime minister in the

Italian fascists frequently invoked the heritage of the Roman Empire as part of their intensely nationalist rhetoric. This photograph shows Mussolini commemorating the 2,698th anniversary of the city of Rome on April 21, 1936. How did this kind of public ritual help to consolidate fascist power? AP Images

prewar era, tried to patch together a personal coalition that included the Fascists in a "national bloc" of candidates. Giolitti thought the Fascists could thus be domesticated to parliamentary ways. Instead, they used the electoral campaign to demonstrate their style. Fascist squads in black shirts planted bombs, beat up opponents, and disrupted meetings, employing violence and intimidation while denouncing Marxists as a threat to order. And they benefited from the sympathy of many in the police and administration as well as the support of many property owners.

The Weakness of Opposition When left-wing unions called a general strike in 1922, raising fears of revolution, Mussolini's Black Shirts grew more threatening and started taking over town councils by force. While politicians struggled to find a parliamentary majority, the Fascists staged a march on Rome in October. Motley squads of party militants moved on the capital in a grand gesture of revolt while Mussolini cautiously waited in Milan. Belatedly, parliamentary leaders called for martial law, but King Victor Emmanuel III refused. Mussolini dashed to Rome, where the king invited him to form a cabinet; the largely symbolic revolt had been enough to capture power. Claiming the office both as a matter of perfect legality and by right of conquest, Mussolini at age thirty-nine became prime minister of a coalition government. In the elections of 1924, Fascists won a massive victory. Intimidation and fraud contributed to this success, but most Italians were willing to give the new party a chance.

It soon became clearer what a Fascist regime would mean. Giacomo Matteotti, a Socialist who bravely stood before the entire Chamber to enumerate Fascist crimes, was subsequently murdered in gangland style. As public condemnation mounted, Mussolini's government seemed about to topple, but the opponents of fascism were no more able to unite now than when they had been stronger. The Fascists gradually isolated first the Socialist and then the Popular party, which was weakened by the Vatican's distaste for its program of social reform. By 1925 all the opponents of fascism had been expelled from the legislature, and newspapers either printed what they were told or risked suppression. The Fascist period had begun.

To many in and out of Italy, it seemed merely that the nation at last had a strong, antisocialist leader. Some distinguished Italians were associated with the regime in various ways, men such as d'Annunzio, the sociologist Vilfredo Pareto, the composer Giacomo Puccini, the playwright Luigi Pirandello, and some of the avant-garde Futurist artists. Even moderates found it hard to believe that a party whose program contained so many contradictions—Fascists praised revolution and promised a strong state, defended property and called for social change, advocated order and used violence—could be dangerous for long.

Fascist Rule Mussolini moved slowly to institutionalize his power. A series of special laws passed by 1926 declared the Duce (leader) of Fascism the head of state with the right to set the Chamber's agenda and to govern by decree. For twenty years, nearly all the laws of Italy would be issued in that way. Opposition parties were outlawed, scores of potential opponents arrested, and the civil service and judiciary purged of anyone thought too independent. Italy's newspapers were filled with pictures of Mussolini overawing visitors, captivating vast throngs, leaping hurdles on horseback, flying airplanes, harvesting grain. No story was too silly: The Duce recited the cantos of Dante from memory, he worked all night (the light in his office was carefully left on), he inspired philosophers and instructed economists, American razor blades were inadequate to the toughness of his beard, and his speed in race cars frightened experts.

These ten-year-old boys were not, official propaganda declared, just playing at being soldiers but were ready with half-size rifles and lunch kits to defend their country. Millions of Italian children were enrolled in five organizations: one for boys and girls 6 and 7 years old, two separate ones for boys and girls from the ages of 8 to 13, and two more for those from 14 to 17. For the four years after that, they could belong to the Young Fascists.
Bettmann/Corbis

Slogans such as "The Duce is always right" and "Believe, Obey, Fight" soon covered walls throughout Italy. The victory of an Italian athlete or the birth of a child to a prolific mother became an occasion for hailing the new order as Mussolini's propaganda pumped pride and confidence into a troubled nation.

Despite considerable skepticism, the good news and sense of energy were welcome. Mussolini's sensitivity to the masses brought to Italian government a popular touch that it had lacked. By 1931 when the government demanded that all professors sign a loyalty oath, only eleven refused. With most people frightened into silence and organized resistance shattered, the regime had little to fear from some secret Communist groups and an underground centered in France.

The authoritarian single party, completely subordinate to the Duce, reached into every city and town with its own militia, secret police, and tribunals. Recruited

FASCIST DOCTRINE

The most carefully constructed single statement of Fascist doctrine was the article "Fascism: Doctrine and Institutions," written in 1932 for the Enciclopedia Italiana, *one of the most impressive intellectual works accomplished under the Fascist regime. Although the article was officially listed as by Mussolini himself, most of it was written by Giovanni Gentile, a noted philosopher who was an early supporter of Fascism.*

"It [Fascism] is opposed to classical liberalism which arose as a reaction to absolutism and exhausted its historical function when the State became the expression of the conscience and will of the people. Liberalism denied the State in the name of the individual; Fascism reasserts the rights of the State as expressing the real essence of the individual.... The Fascist conception of the State is all-embracing; outside of it no human or spiritual values can exist, much less have value. Thus understood, Fascism is totalitarian, and the Fascist State—a synthesis and a unit inclusive of all values—interprets, develops, and potentiates the whole life of a people.

" ... First of all, as regards the future development of mankind—and quite apart from present political considerations—Fascism does not, generally speaking, believe in the possibility or utility of perpetual peace. It therefore discards pacifism as a cloak for cowardly supine renunciation in contradistinction to self-sacrifice. War alone keys up all human energies to their maximum tension and sets the seal of nobility on those peoples who have the courage to face it. ...

"Fascism denies the materialistic conception of happiness. ... This means that Fascism denies the equation: well-being = happiness, which sees in men mere animals, content when they can feed and fatten, thus reducing them to a vegetative existence pure and simple.

"After socialism, Fascism trains its guns on the whole block of democratic ideologies, and rejects both their premises and their practical applications and implements. Fascism denies that numbers, as such, can be the determining factor in human society; it denies the right of numbers to govern by means of periodic consultations; it asserts the irremediable and fertile and beneficent inequality of men who cannot be leveled by any such mechanical and extrinsic device as universal suffrage.

" ... The State, as conceived and realized by Fascism, is a spiritual and ethical entity for securing the political, juridical, and economic organization of the nation, an organization which in its origin and growth is a manifestation of the spirit. The State guarantees the internal and external safety of the country, but it also safeguards and transmits the spirit of the people, elaborated down the ages in its language, its customs, its faith. The State is not only the present, it is also the past and above all the future. Transcending the individual's brief spell of life, the State stands for the immanent conscience of the nation."

From S. William Halperin (ed.), Mussolini and Italian Fascism, *Van Nostrand, 1964.*

---

in its early years mainly from among the unemployed and alienated, the Fascist party soon won hundreds of thousands of new members eager for the advantages it offered, until by the 1930s the party decided to accept members more selectively in an effort to achieve internal discipline. There were associations for Fascist teachers, workers, and university students. In youth organizations for every age group over four years old, the next generation wore black shirts, marched, and recited official slogans. Citizens were to replace the handshake with the extended right arm of the Fascist salute,[4] and regulations established the Fascist names to give one's children and the form of address to use with one's friends.

[4] The salute was a stylized form of the greeting used in ancient Rome and portrayed in the statue of Marcus Aurelius that since the Renaissance had stood on the Capitoline Hill in Rome, where Michelangelo designed a piazza to frame it. The salute quickly became an international symbol.

Fascist doctrine, never wholly consistent, denounced the principles of the French Revolution and of majority rule but hailed "the people." The much-advertised principle of authority was reduced to simple obedience to the Duce. Authority itself was deemed purer when arbitrary. There was said to be a Fascist style in art and philosophy, sport and war. A candid irrationalism suspicious of intellectuals and traditional culture stressed the virtues of intuitive "thinking with the blood" and joy in war. As the antithesis of the decadent materialism of the democracies, Italy would influence the world and reclaim the heritage of imperial Rome (see "Fascist Doctrine," above).

The Corporate State The most discussed element of Fascism, the corporate state, was partly facade, partly an institutional expression of ideology. The intent was to organize each sector of production into a huge confederation, or corporation. Each corporation encompassed a syndicate of employers and one of workers, each headed by party members appointed by the government. Corporations were to establish industrywide policies and wage scales, and by 1926 the system was sufficiently in place to outlaw strikes, lockouts, and independent unions. In 1934 the number of corporations was set at twenty-two.[5] The Duce, as president of each corporation, appointed its council of delegates, which then also sat in the National Council of Corporations. These institutions, which never attained real autonomy, were further undercut by the strength of established interests and by Mussolini's habit of legislating by decree. They were presented, however, as the Fascist alternative to liberal forms of representation, replacing conflict with coordination and eliminating class conflict.

Domestic Policies   Fascist economic policy sought *autarchy*, a self-sufficient national economy, and emphasized industrialization and technology. Initial distrust of big business soon lessened, but the government remained active in economic affairs and often favored nationalization. For reasons of prestige, the value of the lira was set to equal the French franc, which hurt Italian exports and required restrictions that led to a painful devaluation. In the interest of self-sufficiency, the government launched its famous battle of grain in 1926, which succeeded (with enormous hoopla) in doubling grain production at great cost in efficiency.

Output per capita declined in the Fascist era. Generally, the industrial giants in steel, automobiles, rubber, and chemicals found it easy to deal with (and often to manipulate) Fascist bureaucracy. At the same time, the Institute for Industrial Reconstruction (IRI) established in 1933 provided subsidies to weak industries and often ended up owning them, a significant extension of government ownership. By 1940 real wages were down in both industry and agriculture.

Efforts to keep peasants on the land and to increase the birthrate at most merely slowed the contrary trends. But the regime did score some notable achievements, which it vigorously advertised. It suppressed the activities in Sicily of criminal groups called *mafia*, drained the malaria-infested marshes near Rome, built new railroads, and launched some superhighways. Enormous building projects contributed to employment.

Workers benefited from the creation of centers with recreation halls, meeting rooms, and libraries in most towns and programs for vacations at seaside or mountain resorts. Family bonuses gave the poor an increased sense of security, and educational reforms put more people in school for longer periods.

The Lateran Agreements   Fascism's most publicized accomplishment was its accommodation with the Vatican. Although Mussolini and most of his early followers were thoroughly anticlerical, the Fascist government adopted many measures the Church would welcome, putting crucifixes in classrooms and raising the budget for clerical salaries and church repairs. The Lateran treaties of 1929 ended sixty years of conflict between Italy and the Church. They recognized the tiny area of Vatican City as an independent state, and related agreements established religious teaching in public schools, guaranteed that marriage laws would conform to Catholic doctrine, promised to restrict Protestant activities, and determined the indemnity the Church should be paid for its losses during Italian unification. A dispute that had seared the consciences of millions of Italians was at last resolved.

Within the country, potential opponents of Fascism were baffled by Mussolini's apparent successes and, surrounded by propaganda, felt isolated and uncertain of what to believe. Indeed, most Italians probably shared some pride in their nation's heightened prestige. Outside Italy, important groups in all European and many South American nations sang the praises of Fascism's "bold experiment" that ended petty squabbling, ran the trains on time, kept order, and eliminated the threat of communism.

THE DISTINCTIVE CULTURE OF THE TWENTIETH CENTURY

The exciting intellectual and cultural movements of the 1920s built on those of the prewar period. Many of the works that marked new directions in science, philosophy, and the arts had appeared in the decades just before and after the turn of the century. These new trends, disquieting then, gained the momentum to become dominant in many fields after the war. Psychology, literature, and art explored the irrational and surreal. The sciences uncovered complexities in nature that made uncertainty a theoretical principle, and theories of society adopted a tough-minded "realism" that spoke of power and interest more than values. Norms of behavior that had been considered the essence of civilization just a generation earlier were now called into question.

---

[5] A corporation covered an entire sphere of production, from raw materials to manufacture and distribution, and the corporations were divided into three groups: (1) grains, fruits and vegetables, wines, edible oils, beets and sugar, livestock, forestry and lumber, and textiles; (2) metals, chemicals, clothing, paper and printing, construction, utilities, mining, and glass and pottery; (3) insurance and banking, fine arts and liberal professions, sea and air transportation, land transportation, public entertainment, and public lodging.

Freudian Psychology

No one disturbed accepted views more deeply than Sigmund Freud, a Viennese physician whose clinical studies had taken him gradually from an interest in neurology to the study of psychiatry. Freud followed the method—close and detailed observation—of medical science, and his writings were as careful in their logic as in their literary elegance. Freud had done his most important work before 1914, and in many ways he was old-fashioned. For the most part, he accepted as socially necessary the norms of respectable behavior promulgated by the nineteenth-century middle class. He was deeply influenced by ideas of evolution, and his metaphors and assumptions betray the liberal economist's appreciation of self-discipline and calculated self-interest. His attention to the phenomenon of hysteria and his use of hypnosis built on the work of others to create a startling view of the human mind, which he insisted could be universally applied. His great impact, however, came in the twentieth century.

The Unconscious   In treating neurotics, Freud found that they often experienced relief of their symptoms by recalling forgotten events under hypnosis. He concluded that the recollection itself was crucial, not for its accuracy, but as an expression of the psychic reality with which the patient had been unconsciously struggling. Within the unconscious, conflicting urges contended in what Freud labeled the *id*. Here universal basic desires (similar to instincts) seek satisfaction, and Freud found the most troublesome and psychologically significant desires to be sexual. The *ego* tries to channel and control these desires, directed to do so by the *superego*, which (rather like the conscience in more traditional conceptions) imposes a socially conditioned sense of what is acceptable behavior. Thus, mental life is marked by perpetual tension between the id and the superego.

This conflict, uncomfortably mediated by the ego, is unconscious, for one of the mind's responses is to repress from consciousness the id's desires. Most people remain unaware of their own deepest motivations. Repression, however, causes an enormous mental strain that often finds an outlet in neurotic behavior. As the patient comes to face and understand what is being repressed, neurosis is relieved.

Psychoanalysis   From this conception of the human psyche, Freud developed an elaborate, subtle, and shocking theory that ascribed sexual lusts to every person at every age. The idea of infant sexuality was especially offensive to contemporaries, but so was the notion of the Oedipus or Electra complex, through which the boy's angry competition with his father (or the daughter's with her mother) could produce a child's unconscious guilt-ridden wish for the death of one parent in order to possess the other. Few in Freud's time could tolerate this ascription of base desires to decent people. Freudian theory proclaimed that such decent people were merely the most repressed. Similarly, religion provided satisfaction for infantile and obsessive needs. Even the greatest human achievements in art and science were the result of sublimation, by which Freud meant the diversion of the id's primitive demands to other, higher purposes.

Psychoanalysis, the name Freud gave his body of theory and his therapeutic technique, calls on the analyst not to pass judgments but rather to help the patient discover aspects of self that proper society held to be quite simply unmentionable. By implication, these ideas and therapeutic techniques called for a shift in aesthetic and intellectual standards. Freud considered whatever seemed real to the psyche to be important; dreams and slips of the tongue were serious expressions of psychic conflict. Hypnosis and free association (in which patients are encouraged to let their thoughts ramble) were valued as modes of expression in which hidden connections emerged without the intervention of narrative or logic. Freud pioneered new ways of comprehending life and literature on several levels at once and provided the model for doing so.

Wider Implications   In the 1920s the broad implications of Freud's discoveries gained wider public recognition despite continued hostility. If repression leads to neuroses, one extrapolation went, then greater sexual freedom and, above all, greater candor will produce healthier people. This inference remains perhaps the most widespread popular notion drawn from Freudian teaching, though it was not a view he held. Related to this view is the belief that guilt is evil, a kind of Christian perversion of human nature. Freudian insights encouraged literary and personal introspection and supported the view that childhood is the most important phase of life. Although his theories stimulated new visions of a freer and happier life, Freud's dark conclusion was that "the price of progress in civilization is paid in forfeiting happiness." Civilization, then, is based on the repression of primitive and still very powerful drives, which may burst forth at any moment. Freud, who feared the explosion he foresaw, died in 1939, driven into exile by the anti-Semitism of the Nazis.

Freudians strove to maintain these doctrines whole as science and therapy, treating deviations as heresies; but there would be many deviations. The best known came from the Swiss psychologist Carl G. Jung, who soon broke from Freud and developed his theory of the collective unconscious, the common psychic inheritance of whole peoples, which they most commonly expressed in the symbols and rituals of religion. Jung's somewhat looser and more mystical perspectives have fascinated religious thinkers, attracted theorists of nation and race, and influenced philosophers and artists. More generally, the concepts and vocabulary of psychoanalysis penetrated much of Western culture, apparent in art and literature, journalism, and advertising.

The Humanities

Art and Literature   Some artists in the postwar period—the Surrealists, with their dreamlike canvases, are an example—applied Freudian ideas directly, and in his manifesto of Surrealism (1924), the writer André Breton proclaimed that art must liberate the subconscious. Quite independent of Freud, explorations of human irrationality fairly exploded in prose and poetry. The novels of Marcel Proust, Franz Kafka, and James Joyce most clearly mark the change in style and content.

Marcel Proust died in 1922, soon to be hailed as one of the great stylists of the French language. His long novel, *Remembrance of Things Past*, built an introverted and delicately detailed picture of upper-class Parisian life into a monumental and sensitive study of one man's quiet suffering, which became a model of interior monologue, of the novel in which the subject is not action seen from the outside but feelings observed from within.

Franz Kafka, who wrote in German though born in Prague, died in 1924, leaving instructions for his manuscripts to be burned. They were not, and they came to be accepted as quintessentially modern, with their realistic and reasonable descriptions of fantasies that convey the torture of anxiety. In *The Trial* the narrator tells of his arrest, conviction, and execution on charges he can never discover, an exploration of the psychology of guilt that foreshadows the totalitarian state.

James Joyce's international fame came with the publication of his novel *Ulysses* (1922), the presentation on a mythic scale of a single day in the life of a modest Dubliner, written in an exuberant, endlessly inventive game of words in which puns, cliché, parody, and poetry swirl in a dizzying stream of consciousness.

Virginia Woolf, who used related devices in her novels, was less widely read at the time, but her work would become very influential a generation later. A political activist and feminist who was prominent in England's intellectual circles, her book *A Room of One's Own* (1929) subtly explored the value of a female perspective and the ways in which women were discouraged from intellectual independence. Not all of the most important writers turned away from the objective tone and chronological clarity of traditional narrative.

But even those who made use of more familiar techniques—like Thomas Mann in Germany, André Gide in France, and D. H. Lawrence in England—tended to explore topics and attitudes offensive to convention.

The Other Arts   In all the arts, shock became one of the points of creative expression. Dada, a movement that originated during World War I, put on displays, part theater and part art exhibition, of noisy nonsense and absurd juxtapositions that were intended to infuriate the Parisian bourgeoisie. Italian Futurists, poets and playwrights as well as artists, promised to build a new art for a technological age—"The world has been enriched by a new beauty: the beauty of speed"—and in their manifesto of 1909 had issued a call to "burn the libraries . . . demolish the venerated cities." The Fauves in France and the Expressionists in Germany and Scandinavia gloried in their reputation for wild and often brutal candor in the style and content of their paintings as well as in their conduct.

Works of art became more difficult to comprehend. Cubist and Expressionist painters, like composers using the twelve-tone scale and dissonance, deliberately eschewed the merely decorative or pleasant and seemed eager to incorporate violence and amorality. Even when more sober traditions prevailed—as in the carefully constructed, cerebral poetry of William Butler Yeats and of the younger Ezra Pound and T. S. Eliot—foreboding and obscurity intertwined. Today the richness and profundity of the greatest of these works are readily apparent. To contemporaries, however, they were more threatening than attractive, dangerously widening the chasm between "serious" art and the popular culture most intellectuals disdained.

Philosophy   The philosophical work most widely read in the 1920s was Oswald Spengler's *Decline of the West*, which had appeared in 1918. Spengler treated whole civilizations as biological organisms, each with a life cycle of its own, and presented his study of Western culture as an achievement of German philosophy. But his fame rested on the dire prediction of his title: World War I had begun the final act of Western civilization. José Ortega y Gasset's *The Revolt of the Masses*, published in 1930, was hardly more optimistic. The masses, he warned, were destined to use their rising power to destroy civilization's highest achievements. Scores of other writers joined in scorn for modern culture as vapid and directionless.

The most striking innovation in philosophy, however, came from another tradition entirely and was monumentally set forth in *Principia Mathematica* (1910) by Bertrand Russell and Alfred North Whitehead. It became the cornerstone of analytic philosophy, which holds that philosophers should concern themselves

Otto Dix
GROSSTADT, **1927–1928**
Like many German Expressionists, Otto Dix challenged the public with a series of paintings that simultaneously lampooned and celebrated the decadence of life in Berlin in the Weimar era. Kunstmuseum, Stuttgart, Germany. © 2010 Artists Rights Society (ARS), New York/VG Bild-Kunst, Bonn/Erich Lessing/Art Resource, NY

only with what is precise and empirically demonstrable. On the Continent a group known as the Vienna Circle developed a related system, logical positivism. The work of Ludwig Wittgenstein, especially his *Tractatus Logico-Philosophicus* (1921), influenced both schools of thought. According to Wittgenstein, the philosopher's task was to analyze every statement, stripping away those connotations and values, however appealing, that do not convey precise meaning.

The Sciences

Science had also moved beyond the layperson's comprehension since the late nineteenth century. Even when the achievements of science were apparent to everyone, they often rested on theoretical advances that overturned established certainties. And the fields in which scientists worked became ever more highly specialized.

The Nature of Matter   One line of scientific investigation stemmed from an experiment by two Americans, Albert A. Michelson and Edward W. Morley, in 1887. By demonstrating that the speed of light leaving earth was the same whether the light traveled in the direction of the earth's movement or against it, they challenged the established theory that the universe was filled with a motionless substance called "ether," which was thought necessary because waves could not function in empty space. The implications were fundamental, and exploring them led Albert Einstein to his theory of **relativity,** which he set forth in two brief papers published in 1905 and 1915. They were of the highest philosophical as well as scientific interest: Space and time are not absolute, he said, but must be measured in relation to the observer and on the most fundamental levels are aspects of a single continuum.

As Einstein developed his theory of relativity, physicists were also achieving a new understanding of matter. Wilhelm Roentgen's discovery of x-rays in 1895 had given the first important insight into the world of subatomic particles. Within two years the English physicist J. J. Thomson showed the existence of the electron, the subatomic particle that carries a negative electrical charge. The atom was not the basic unit of matter. By the turn of the century, Pierre and Marie Curie, among others, had found radium and other materials to be radioactive; that is, they emitted both subatomic particles and a form of electromagnetic radiation. Soon, largely through the work of the English physicist Ernest Rutherford, radioactivity was identified with the breakdown of heavy and unstable atoms.

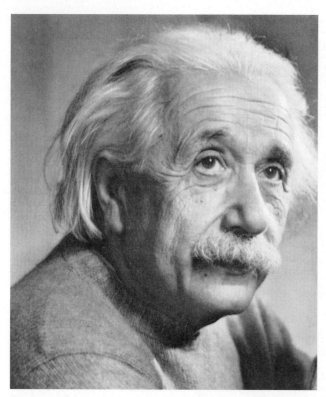

Einstein's face remains one of the best-known icons of the twentieth century, a symbol of humanity, universal genius, and Jewish exile.
Library of Congress

These discoveries made it possible to link the structure of atoms with Dmitri Mendeleev's periodic table of elements. Elements with similar chemical properties were also similar in their atomic structures. A simpler and clear understanding of matter seemed in the offing.

Quantum Physics But continuing research soon revealed phenomena that Newtonian physics could not explain. In 1902 the German physicist Max Planck challenged Newtonian assumptions by announcing that energy in the subatomic world was released or absorbed not in a continuous stream but in discrete, measurable, and apparently irreducible units, which Planck called quanta. Energy, in effect, possessed many of the properties of matter.

This finding implied that matter and energy might be interchangeable, and Einstein incorporated the insight into his theory of relativity in the famous equation $E = mc^2$. Energy (E) is equivalent to mass (m) times the square of the speed of light, a constant (c), which means that, at least in theory, small quantities of matter could be turned into enormous amounts of energy. In this respect Newtonian physics was wrong; matter could be transformed after all. In 1919 Rutherford produced changes in the structure of the nitrogen atom by bombarding it with subatomic particles, and other atomic changes were soon produced in the laboratory.

Uncertainty Principle By the mid-1920s, however, physicists had to face troubling anomalies. Planck's quantum theory, though verified in numerous experiments, considered particles to behave in probabilistic rather than absolutely regular patterns—a concept Einstein himself could never wholly accept. Furthermore, electromagnetic radiation, including visible light, seemed to behave like a flow of particles in some circumstances and in others as a wave—a regular disturbance of particles in which the particles themselves do not advance. Nor, the German physicist Werner Heisenberg argued, was it possible at the same time to determine a particle's position and its momentum, for at the subatomic level measurement interfered with the variables measured—a disturbing effect that Heisenberg appropriately named "the uncertainty principle." Conceptions of matter had been transformed in just a few years. Inside atoms there was mostly empty space and particles that did not behave with absolute regularity; and in both the subatomic world and the stellar universe, the position and purpose of the observer fundamentally affected what was observed.

The new theories proved powerful tools, but physicists who chose to philosophize about such matters now spoke in humbler and more tentative tones. Physics became one of the most prestigious, highly organized, and expensive of human activities, recognized rather than understood by the public through its applications: x-ray technology, the electron microscope, and eventually the controlled fission of atomic energy. Newtonian principles, physicists insisted, still obtained in most cases, as solid and predictable as ever. But there was a loss. The Western world had long looked to the sciences for confirmation of its philosophy and even its theology. In the twentieth century no popularizer would build a general outlook on society from the latest scientific discoveries as Voltaire had once done from the ideas of Newton.

The Biological and Social Sciences Although the new work in other fields of science was less revolutionary, it often had immediate impact. Knowledge of the mechanisms of heredity furthered scientific breeding of animals and the creation of plant hybrids that would greatly increase the productivity of agriculture. The isolation of viruses opened a new field of study, and the discovery of penicillin in 1928 by Englishmen Sir Alexander Fleming and Sir Howard Florey brought medicine a new armory of invaluable drugs.

The understanding of society was deeply affected by two giants of modern sociology, the Frenchman Émile Durkheim and the German Max Weber, whose work is central to modern social science. Durkheim's use of statistical tools and Weber's use of the "ideal type" to analyze how societies function remain influential, as does their concern with the customs and beliefs that hold society together. Both, for example, emphasized the importance of religion, although they were concerned not with its metaphysical truth but with its contribution to the development of the state and of capitalism. Both stressed the threat to society when group norms broke down, and both saw a danger of that breakdown in modern trends. Through this emphasis on the function of communal values rather than their validity and on the role of myth and ritual in all societies including our own, anthropology, sociology, and history have tended to share psychology's insistent relativism.

Public Culture

To the public at large, developments in science and the arts were associated with the prosperity and brash excitement of the twenties. Science meant the spread of automobiles, radios, and airplanes; new trends were known through colorful stylish advertising, risqué literature, and vibrant theater. The surprising crisp architecture and applied design of Walter Gropius' Bauhaus school in Germany, with its emphasis on relating form to function, began to win a following, and there was curiosity about the still more daring endeavors in France of Le Corbusier to envision a wholly modern city as a machine for living.

Cinema During the 1920s, motion pictures became more popular and more profitable than any form of entertainment had ever been. Germany, Britain, France, and Italy each built thousands of theaters, often on the most elegant streets of major cities. Many of these theaters gaudily combined the exoticism of a world's fair with reassuring luxury. Egyptian and Greek motifs, marble columns, fountains, and statues reinforced the fantasies on the screen.

People from every stratum of society attended the same films, and women often attended without male escorts. Influenced by the movies, middle-class and working-class families increasingly discussed the same topics and began to imagine different and better lives for themselves. Reviews and movie magazines helped to provide the publicity essential to success in a business that relied on stars and vast distribution networks. American companies did all this very effectively, filling screens around the world. The United States made the most films, followed by Japan and Germany.

The rapid transition to talking pictures between 1929 and 1930 underscored national differences, and every country had some ministry empowered to restrain

Gaudy movie palaces like this Parisian theater, one of the first, became prominent monuments in every city, offering the masses an exotic luxury previously associated with the great opera houses.
Editions Tallandier

the presentation on the screen of sex and violence. In 1919 an English Watch committee condemned a film of the Johnson-Jeffries fight, fearing it could "demoralize and brutalize the minds of young persons." Sunday showings were an issue for years. Politics was present, too. Many countries restricted or banned German films in the 1920s; France, generally the most tolerant, in effect proscribed films made in the Soviet Union where, with Lenin's encouragement, the director Sergei Eisenstein brilliantly showed how well suited the medium was to depicting official views of the revolutionary power of the masses.

Consumerism While moralists worried about the cynicism of mass entertainment and the amoral excess of nightlife in cabarets and theaters, millions joined a kind of dizzying celebration. Middle-class families bought their first car; millions from every class, their first radio. Sophistication was a kind of shibboleth,

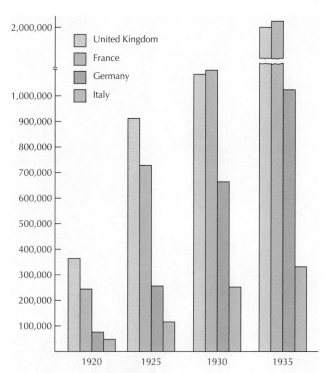

NUMBER OF MOTOR VEHICLES
The number of automobiles in a society reflects its general wealth, adaptation to a consumer economy, and changing patterns of communication. (Note that the United Kingdom, France, and Italy each had about 40 million people; Germany had 65 million.) This graph gives evidence of impressive prosperity and change; by 1935 France and the United Kingdom had one vehicle for every 20 people.

used to justify lipstick, short skirts, alcohol, and one brash fad after another but also to underscore the cosmopolitanism that valued American jazz, openly learned from African art, and welcomed the new. For perhaps the only time, Berlin rivaled Paris as a European artistic center, more famous as the home of acid satire in art and theater than for its thriving cultural institutions of a more traditional sort. Modernism turned its back on gentility.

THE GREAT DEPRESSION AND THE RETREAT FROM DEMOCRACY

Within less than a decade after the Paris Peace Conference, democracy was in retreat across Europe. By 1929 authoritarian regimes had violated or eliminated the liberal constitutions of Hungary, Spain, Albania, Portugal, Lithuania, Poland, and Yugoslavia as well as Italy. By 1936 political liberty had also been suppressed in Romania, Austria, Bulgaria, Estonia, Latvia, and Greece as well as Germany. Most of these countries were among the poorest in Europe, but their political difficulties

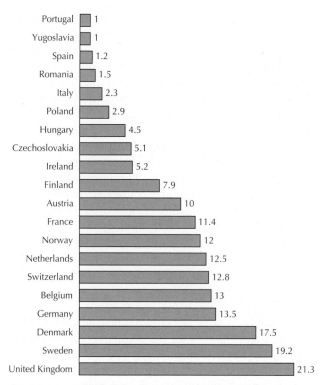

APPROXIMATE NUMBER OF RADIOS LICENSED FOR EVERY 100 PEOPLE IN 20 SELECTED COUNTRIES (1938)
Radio was an important new instrument of communication and propaganda. These statistics suggest that most families in the United Kingdom had a radio, that nearly everyone could sometimes listen to the radio in Finland and Austria, and that from Italy to Portugal millions of people heard the radio only on special occasions when speakers blared in public places.

illustrate the broader trend. Divided over issues of social reform, nationality, and religion—differences amplified by new and angry socialist and peasant parties—they suffered increased disruption with each economic crisis and foreign threat.

Authoritarian Regimes

Authoritarian leaders often flirted with fascism on the Italian model, only to find it dangerously uncontrollable. They sought through decisiveness and force to achieve stability in societies riven by social conflict and where religious and ethnic loyalties could be readily fanned into anger and hatred by ambitious politicians.

The Monarchies of Central and Eastern Europe   During the 1920s and 1930s, many eastern European nations experimented with fascist policies and tactics. In Hungary, for example, a series of anti-Semitic governments, beginning with the regime of Admiral Miklos Horthy in 1920, discouraged democracy and introduced

Police in Vienna prepare to confront socialists in 1927. The socialists were protesting the release of men believed to have murdered a socialist. In the ensuing riots, the palace of justice was burned and a hundred people were killed, part of the cycle of violence shaking the Austrian republic.
Bettmann/Corbis

many fascist trappings. In Romania the government of King Carol II—an admirer of Mussolini—stripped most Jews of land and citizenship, tightened censorship, and imposed martial law. A 1934 coup by the military in Bulgaria abolished parliamentary government and free speech in that country. Similarly, in 1929 King Alexander I of Yugoslavia assumed dictatorial powers in an effort to tame the divisive forces of Serbian, Croatian, and Slovenian nationalism.

By the end of the 1930s, however, all of these countries had taken major steps to limit or suppress fascist activities. One reason for these policy shifts was opposition from France, on whose support these countries depended. In addition, the eastern European authoritarian leaders found themselves threatened by both the ambitions of the fascists themselves and popular backlashes against fascism. Although these governments moved away from fascism, however, most of them remained authoritarian.

The Republics of Poland and Austria   Events in Poland followed a somewhat different course. Like other European nations, Poland was wracked by internal conflicts: Catholics versus socialists, conservative landowners versus radical peasants. In 1926 Marshall Jozef Pilsudski assumed power in a military revolt. Once his followers attained a majority in parliament, Pilsudski resigned. However, men from the military continued to run the country.

In Austria the republic was undermined by the sharp division between a Catholic German countryside and a cosmopolitan imperial Vienna. The left-wing Social Democrats had little strength beyond Vienna. Meanwhile, the conservative Christian Socialists—whose nineteenth-century programs of welfare, nationalism, and anti-Semitism had influenced the young Hitler—moved steadily toward fascism. As violent clashes between the parties intensified, Chancellor Engelbert Dollfuss, a Christian Socialist, responded by suspending parliament, outlawing communists, and eventually banning all parties except his own Fatherland Front, a coalition of conservative groups. In 1934 he used military force to crush the Social Democrats. That same year, however, a group of Austrian Nazis assassinated Dollfuss, an act they hoped would lead to *Anschluss,* or union with Germany. Although the *Anschluss* did not take place until 1938, Austria's authoritarian government, having repressed the left, found if difficult to mobilize opposition to growing Nazi pressure.

International Fascism Whether they won power or not, Europe's fascist movements had much in common. Generally influenced by Italian Fascism, they looked and sounded similar. They liked uniforms, starting with a shirt of one color. Cheap to buy and easy to adopt, it made a group of supporters (however few or poor) look like a movement, a historical force. They used paramilitary organization that promised decisive action to remake society through discipline and force. They created drama in the streets—noise, marches, colorful demonstrations, symbolic acts, and real violence—that undermined conventional standards of public behavior while advertising fascism as something new and powerful. They borrowed heavily from working-class movements and used all the devices of democratic politics, while seeming to stand outside the corrupting process of compromise and responsibility. Populist tactics were thus attached to the promise of order.

Fascists nostalgically evoked the enthusiastic patriotism of World War I to offer simple solutions to real problems. The disruption and inequity of capitalism, class conflict, a faltering economy, and aimless governments were the fault of enemies—liberal politicians, Marxist revolutionaries, Jews, and foreigners. Those enemies, although ridiculed and denounced in fascist propaganda, were credited with hidden powers that only the force of fascism could overcome. Fascism promised to create a united, orderly, prosperous community.

There was more to these movements than their simple myths, camaraderie, and sinister attraction to violence. Fascists addressed real fears. They spoke to a rural society that felt threatened by urbanization, to small-business people threatened by the competition of large corporations and to all business people threatened by workers' demands and government intervention, to a middle class threatened by socialism, to the privileged threatened by democracy, to the unemployed threatened by continuing economic depression, to the religious threatened by a secular society. Everywhere, they played on fear of a communist revolution.

The Appeal of Fascism Fascists could do all this by borrowing freely from ideas current throughout Europe.

They used socialist criticisms of liberalism and capitalism, conservative values of hierarchy and order, and intellectual denunciations of modern culture. They amplified a widespread contempt for parliamentary ineffectiveness, used doctrines of race made familiar by war and imperialism, and laid claim to the nationalism that every government liked to invoke. At the same time, as admirers of technology and organization, fascists promised to create more modern societies. And they laid claim to corporatism, which Mussolini's Italy advertised as the wave of the future.

Corporatist thought had a long and respectable history. Organizing society as well as parliament according to occupation promised to do away with the selfish competition of interests and parties characteristic of liberalism, to preserve social hierarchy, and to eliminate class conflict. The idea of so integrated a society gained attractiveness in the years of economic depression and prestige with Pope Pius XI's encyclical *Quadragesimo Anno* ("In the Fortieth Year") issued in 1931 on the fortieth anniversary of Leo XIII's *Rerum Novarum.* The new encyclical went further in rejecting the injustices of capitalism and the solutions of Marxism, and it called instead for harmony based on religion and cooperation through corporative organization. Many anxious people found in that papal pronouncement a sympathy for fascism that seemed to justify overlooking its deeply antireligious qualities.

The appeal of fascism was not limited to poor nations. Its ambiguities made it applicable everywhere. In Britain Sir Oswald Mosley, once considered a likely Labour prime minister, founded the British Union of Fascists. In Belgium fascism benefited from the antagonism between Catholics and anticlericals and between French-speaking Walloons and Dutch-speaking Flemings, who were increasingly sympathetic to fascism and to the Nazis. In the Netherlands a National Socialist movement rose to prominence in the 1930s, and there were a number of fascist and protofascist movements in France, including *Action Française,* which had become prominent in the furor of the Dreyfus case.

The Great Depression

Above all, fascist and Marxist movements benefited from a worldwide economic depression that undermined social and political stability and seemed to many the death knell of capitalism.

The Stock Market Crash On October 24, 1929, the price of stocks on the New York Exchange began to plummet. Suspecting that speculation had pushed stock prices too high, nervous investors sold their shares. Day after day tens of millions of dollars in paper assets disappeared. Such panics were not new, and they had spread from New York to Europe in the previous century. Now, however, the United States was the world's wealthiest nation and greatest creditor, and this panic settled into full-scale depression as banks failed, businesses cut back, consumption declined, factories closed, and unemployment rose. Its banks and exchanges shaken, the European economy suffered further from the decline in world trade and the withdrawal of American investments and loans. Financial panic hit Europe in May 1931 when Austria's largest bank nearly went under. The panic started a run on Austrian and German banks and then spread, as it had in the United States, to other sectors of the economy and to other nations.

The late 1920s had been years of boom in the United States and of general prosperity in much of Europe, but the Great Depression exposed deep-seated problems. Not all industries had recovered after the war. Coal and textile industries had long been sliding toward chronic depression. Former trade patterns had not revived, especially among the underdeveloped new countries of Eastern Europe, and economic difficulties were increased by Germany's inflation and Russia's withdrawal from commerce. Europe, which lost huge amounts of foreign investments during the war, had not regained its prewar percentage of world trade (about half), and American investments in Europe increased dramatically throughout the 1920s. Too much of the international economy rested on the unproductive passing of paper from the United States to Germany as loans, from Germany to the Allies as reparations, and from the Allies to the United States as payment of war debts; and the United States raised tariffs in 1922 and again in 1930 to levels that made it nearly impossible for Europeans to earn dollars by selling to Americans. Much of the prosperity of the 1920s rested on new processes and on new products, such as automobiles and synthetic fabrics, which proved vulnerable to the withdrawal of American investment and the decline in consumer confidence. The Great Depression underscored how uneven and artificial much of the preceding prosperity had been and showed that, for Europe, a decade had not been long enough to overcome the effects of World War I.

The Repercussions By 1932 the world's industrial production was two-thirds of what it had been in 1929. Unemployment climbed to more than 13 million in the United States, 6 million in Germany, and nearly 3 million in Great Britain. Among leading industrial nations, only France, with its balanced economy and lower fertility rate, escaped a crisis of unemployment. Since the war, and especially in democracies, governments were expected to provide solutions to economic problems. They looked first for international help. Because the reparations system had broken down amid the world economic crisis, European nations declared that they could no longer make debt payments to the United States. The United States refused to acknowledge the connection. Instead, President Hoover proposed that all intergovernment payments be suspended; his proposal, quickly accepted in 1932, was supposed to be temporary but in fact marked the end of both kinds of payments.

Other crises loomed. Austria's banking system had been saved from bankruptcy with British loans; but the deepening depression and other financial burdens forced Great Britain to abandon the gold standard, which meant it no longer guaranteed the value of the pound sterling. The important bloc of countries that traded in sterling followed suit. Tantamount to devaluation, these moves threatened chaos for international monetary exchanges and trade; and so the League of Nations sponsored a World Economic Conference that met in London in 1933. Begun with visions of high statesmanship, it ended in failure. When the United States also went off the gold standard, the structure of credit and exchange that had been one of the signal achievements of liberal finance fell apart. For a century, nations, like so many bankers, had supported international financial stability by honoring these rules of liberal economics, and that historic era had ended.[6]

National Responses In this crisis democracies responded first to domestic pressures. Austria and Germany sought a customs union, which was opposed by France and rejected by the World Court. Nearly everyone raised tariffs and import quotas, further reducing trade, while domestic programs protected political interests. Liberals were at a loss as to what else to do, and socialists were no better prepared to solve the problems of declining commerce, insufficient capital, and—most pressing of all—unemployment. Socialists could find some vindication in the evident weakness of capitalism, but their favorite nostrum, the nationalization of industry, was barely relevant. In practice, they adopted rather orthodox measures of budget reduction while supporting whatever palliatives for unemployment could be suggested, though the dole, the most common one, strained the budgets they wanted to balance.

Most government policies, then, did little to help and may have made the situation worse; bankers and financiers, desperate to stem their losses, gave little attention to the international or social effects of their actions. And the millions of unemployed were more

---

[6] Karl Polanyi elaborated on the significance of abandoning the gold standard in a famous essay, *The Great Transformation: The Political and Economic Origins of Our Time.*

Unemployed workers from Glasgow set out for London on a "famine march" in 1934. The Mary Evans Picture Library

helpless still, standing in line for the dole, eating whatever they could get, taking any bits of work available. Growing communist parties let no one forget that while a whole international system had been collapsing, Soviet production advanced at a steady pace.

Gradually, economic conditions did improve; and by 1937 production in Germany, Britain, and Sweden was well above the 1929 level, though it remained below the 1929 level in the United States, Italy, Belgium, and France. Subsequent government intervention to shore up industries and provide employment did alleviate distress and improve morale. It also changed economic and political life and, at least in democracies, was often as socially divisive as the Depression itself. Democracies faced the dual threat of communism and fascism with a heavy burden of economic and social failure.

NAZI GERMANY AND THE USSR

In the 1930s Nazi Germany and the Soviet Union acquired unprecedented power over their own populations and used it in ways that changed the world. Understanding how these regimes evolved, their techniques of rule, and the policies they pursued remains a central challenge of twentieth-century history. Dictatorship has been recognized since ancient times as a specific political form. The most important dictatorships of this century, however, were different enough from previous examples to merit a separate term. They relied on a single political party, absolute devotion to a leader, domination of mass communications, direction of the economy, and the ruthless use of force—all in the name of an explicit, official ideology. The term **totalitarianism** refers to the combination of these characteristics and describes a system of rule more than specific policies, a system inclined to use oppression and terror to force citizens to participate in the regime's activities and belief system. In principle, totalitarianism seeks to shape every aspect of life and to crush "enemies" identified by their race, occupation, region, or religion. Such a vision and the institutions that would attempt to carry it out did not develop all at once but evolved, primarily in Communist Russia, Fascist Italy, and Nazi Germany.

Useful as the concept of totalitarianism is, it has also come under heavy criticism for a number of reasons. In practice, none of the totalitarian regimes achieved total control. They often gave way before customs and institutions they could not afford to offend and negotiated with entrenched interests. Inefficiency and duplication were characteristic, even endemic, for these regimes were not monolithic. Officials and party members often bickered among themselves. No totalitarian ideology was entirely coherent or unanimously embraced, and there were important differences among totalitarian systems. The values promulgated and policies pursued in Soviet Russia were not at all the same as those of Nazi Germany. Italy's claim to be totalitarian was largely propaganda, and that is the point. *Totalitarianism* is a useful term not for describing how these regimes actually functioned but rather for describing the ambitions and techniques that made Europe's leading twentieth-century tyrannies a fundamentally new political form.

Hitler's Germany

The Nazi regime won power in a democracy with an advanced economy and a strong administrative tradition. It played upon selected elements of German history, from militarism and nationalism to the weakness of the Weimar Republic, and it took advantage of the social shocks Germany had recently suffered: defeat in war, failed revolutions, inflation, clashing ideologies, and a Depression that brought the most extensive unemployment in Europe.

The Rise of Hitler   As a young man, Adolf Hitler was undistinguished, his ambition to be an artist thwarted when the Academy in Vienna rejected his application. Service in World War I had been a kind of salvation, providing comradeship and some accomplishment: He was promoted in the field. In Munich after the war, he found brief employment spying on the small German Worker's party, which the army considered dangerous. He also took to addressing political rallies in the beer halls, where he learned the potential of a movement that combined the personal loyalty of a paramilitary corps with mass appeal and where he molded the speaking style that would make him the most powerful figure in Germany.

His speeches combined crude accusations, a messianic tone, and simple themes repeated in a spiraling frenzy. Race and universal struggle were the core of his message. Germans were victims of vast conspiracies mounted by foreign powers, capitalists, Marxists, Freemasons, and (above all) Jews—the gutter anti-Semitism that Hitler had absorbed in Vienna. Jews were behind war profits, reparations, inflation, and depression; but Marxism was also Jewish, and communists were agents of the Jewish conspiracy. Internationalism and pacifism were Jewish ideas intended to destroy Germany as the bastion of Western civilization.

To Hitler, Western civilization was Aryan, an old term for the prehistoric peoples of Eurasia that he used to describe race. Germans and Nordic peoples were the purest Aryans, Jews their enemy. Life was a desperate struggle won by the ruthless, and Germany's destiny was victory over enemies who threatened the nation by means of the Versailles Treaty, economic disasters, communists, Jews, moral decay, and abstract art. All attacked the Germanic *Volk*, the German people whose primitive virtues must be welded into an irresistible force.

The Growth of the Nazi Party   Hitler named his party the National Socialist German Workers' party. *Nazi* was its acronym. The party was one of many such nationalist movements when in 1923 Hitler led them in the Munich *Putsch*, or rising. After it failed and Hitler was sent to prison, the book he wrote there, *Mein Kampf*, won little notice, for it was a turbulent, repetitious outpouring of his political views interlarded with demoniac statements about how human beings are manipulated by fear, big lies, and simplistic explanations. In prison and after his release in 1925, Hitler worked to reorganize and strengthen the party. To the SA, his street army of brown-shirted storm troopers, he added the SS, an elite corps in black uniforms who served as his bodyguards and special police.

Hitler's intensity and bad manners offended many, but others felt the fascination of a personality that radiated power. He soon gathered a group of absolutely loyal men: Hermann Göring, an air ace; Joseph Goebbels, journalist and party propagandist; and Heinrich Himmler. They worked ceaselessly to enlarge the party, orchestrate impressive rallies, and terrorize their opponents. The Nazis were gaining attention and support. In 1930 they became the second-largest party in the Reichstag, and the following year a group of Rhineland industrialists promised the Nazis financial support.

By the 1930s, the party was broadly based, and the issue of what social groups were first drawn to the Nazis has been the subject of historical controversy, because different interpretations of **Nazism** follow from the answer. Workers were probably the biggest single group of members, but most workers continued to favor socialists and communists. Disproportionately large numbers of Nazi supporters were small-business people and tradespeople, civil service employees, and (to a lesser extent) farmers—all groups fearful of losing income and status.

In the Depression, promises of recovery, higher agricultural prices, and more employment (tens of thousands found jobs in the SA and SS) had concrete appeal.

Many people were drawn to the call to rebuild the army and to save society from socialism. In 1931 an array of right-wing nationalists joined the Nazis in a manifesto denouncing the "cultural Bolshevism" of the Weimar Republic and hinting that, once they seized power, the Nazis would protect only those who had joined them now. The Nazis spoke simultaneously like a government in office and like an underworld gang, and they demonstrated their seriousness by beating up Jews and socialists.

Collapse of the Weimar Republic

The Social Democrats led the government that faced the Great Depression and did the best they could with a shaky parliamentary majority and an uncooperative president. In 1930 the government resigned, to be replaced by the Center party and Heinrich Brüning, a cautious man with little popular appeal.

The elections of 1930 gave Nazis more than a hundred new seats, from which they contemptuously disrupted parliamentary proceedings. His confidence growing, Hitler became a candidate for president in 1932, when Hindenburg's term expired. Worried politicians persuaded the nearly senile field marshal to run for reelection. Ludicrously cast as the defender of the constitution, the eighty-four-year-old Hindenburg won handily, but Hitler got more than 13 million votes. When Brüning proposed a financial reform that included expropriation of some East Prussian estates, Hindenburg dismissed him and turned to Franz von Papen, a friend of important army officers and Junkers.

Hoping to create a right-wing coalition, von Papen lifted Brüning's ban on the SA and SS, named four barons and a count to his cabinet, and declared martial law in Prussia so he could unseat the socialist government there. The outcry led Hindenburg to call another election. This one resulted in a Nazi landslide. With 40 percent of the Reichstag's seats, the Nazis were by far its largest party. Hindenburg avoided naming Hitler chancellor by refusing to grant him the full decree powers he insisted on. The nation was sent to the polls again, and although the Nazis lost a little, they remained the largest party.

Hitler Takes Office

Hindenburg then named another chancellor, General Kurt von Schleicher, a conventional army officer. He made an easy target for the Communists, the disgruntled von Papen (who thought he saw his chance to regain power), and the Nazis. Von Papen, confident he could use Hitler but contain him, persuaded the men around Hindenburg to appoint Hitler the head of a coalition government. In fact Hitler was the only leader acceptable to the right who could also command a popular following. He took office in January 1933.

Hitler almost immediately called another election. Previous campaigns had been ugly, but this one was marked by systematic terror, especially in Prussia, where Hermann Göring was now minister-president and the police acted like electoral agents. The climax came with the burning of parliament, the Reichstag fire that the Nazis loudly blamed on the Communists. Hindenburg agreed to issue special laws—Ordinances for the Protection of the German State and Nation—that ended most civil liberties, including freedom of the press and assembly. The voters gave the Nazis 44 percent of the seats, enough, with the Nazis' nationalist allies, for a bare majority. Hitler pressed on. Communists were expelled from the Reichstag, conservatives wooed with calls to nationalism, and the Center party enticed with promises to respect the privileges of the Catholic Church. By March Hitler dared demand a special enabling act that gave him, as chancellor, the right to enact all laws and treaties independent of constitutional restraints for four years. Of the 566 deputies left in the Reichstag, only 94 Social Democrats (out of 121) voted no. Blandishment and terror had done their work, but the tragedy went deeper: German politics offered no clear alternative to Hitler.

Consolidating Nazi Rule

Hitler's regime moved quickly to destroy the potential for opposition. It established concentration camps, first on private estates and then in larger and more permanent institutions. The new order appeared to enjoy all but unanimous support. A campaign to boycott Jewish businesses was followed in April by laws eliminating most Jews from public service and limiting Jews to 1.5 percent and women to 10 percent of university enrollment. On May Day 1933, workers arrayed by occupation marched beside Nazi banners and slogans. By July all parties except the National Socialist had been outlawed, and soon all competing political organizations disappeared.

In the elections of November 1933, the Nazis won more than 90 percent of the vote. They restructured government, purged the civil service and judiciary, outlawed strikes, and clamped stricter controls on the press. In a few months Hitler had achieved fuller power than Mussolini had managed in years, and in the next few years Nazi policies on racial purity would be extended step by step throughout public life by ordinances, official policies, and police brutality.

Hitler's most serious potential rivals were within his own party, and his solution was barbarically simple. On a long weekend in June 1934, leaders of the Nazi left wing were shot or stabbed. Among hundreds of others, so were General von Schleicher and his wife, some Catholic leaders, some socialists, and some taken by mistake. Hitler admitted to seventy-four deaths;

Nazi party troops march out of the rally on Nuremberg Party Day, 1933, carrying victory banners proclaiming "Germany Awake."
AKG London

subsequent estimates raise the figure to as many as a thousand. The Night of the Long Knives proved that any horror was possible; and the purge, like the noisy accusations of homosexuality that accompanied it, established the tone of Germany's new order. When Hindenburg died in August, Germans voted overwhelmingly to unite presidency and chancellorship in the person of Adolf Hitler, who took the official title of *Führer* ("Leader").

Administrative and Economic Policies   The federal states lost their autonomy through a policy of *Gleichschaltung,* or coordination, and all government employees were made appointees of the Führer. New people's courts heard secret trials for treason, now very broadly defined, and rewritten statutes allowed prosecution for intent as well as for overt acts. Arrest and detention without charge or trial became a regular practice. At the same time, the Nazi party was restructured to parallel the state, with administrative *Gaue* ("regions") headed by a party *Gauleiter.* The party also had its own office of foreign affairs and its own secret police, the Gestapo, which infiltrated both the bureaucracy and the army.

Economic policies scored impressive successes. Unemployment dropped steadily thanks to great public works projects—government offices, highways, public housing, reclamation, and reforestation. Many of these projects used special labor battalions, in which one year's service was soon compulsory. Later the burgeoning armaments industry and growing armed forces eliminated the problem of joblessness entirely. By spending money when more traditional governments thought it essential to balance their budgets, the Nazis reduced unemployment more effectively than any other Western nation.

Paying the Cost   Such programs were expensive, and they were paid for in several ways. A currency scheme largely designed by Hjalmar Schacht, a brilliant economist, required that payments for foreign trade be made with special marks whose value changed according to the products and the nations involved. Goods that Germany bought were paid for in marks redeemable only through purchases in Germany. Tantamount to barter, this system increased Germany's self-sufficiency and its influence in countries that depended on German markets. Additional revenues came from property confiscated from Jews, high taxes, forced loans, and carefully staged campaigns urging patriotic Germans to contribute their personal jewelry to the state. Ultimately, costs would be covered by printing paper currency, with effects long hidden by a war economy and the exploitation of conquered lands. By 1945 the mark had fallen to about 1 percent of its 1933 value.

Labor policies met related goals. Strikes were outlawed and the mobility of workers regulated. The National Labor Front, which represented all workers and management, froze wages and directed personnel in the interests of business and government. Industrialists were relieved of the uncertainties of the Weimar years.

Winning Approval   Meanwhile, the regime advertised the new benefits provided workers, including the summer camps and special cruises that were part of the

Nazi program of Strength Through Joy. Nazi propaganda also reassured those ordinary people fearful of contemporary trends by denouncing modern art, the decadence of Berlin nightlife (and especially of homosexuality), and new roles for women. Special benefits to new families aided young couples in a depressed economy. Along with improved prenatal care and special honors for the most prolific mothers, such measures were part of the Nazi obsession with biology.

Initially, women were discouraged from working outside the home as a way to reduce unemployment among men, but the concern with women went far deeper. Wifely subordination was presented as a principle of social order and the foundation of the family. Women could not be lawyers or judges and could not constitute more than 10 percent of the learned professions. Social policies, schools, and clinics reinforced propaganda praising the role of Aryan women as breeders of a pure race. Severe penalties for performing abortions on healthy Aryans were accompanied by forced sterilization of the "unfit." Boys and girls were required to join the Hitler Youth.

The military had clear reasons for gratitude. Disregarding the disarmament clauses of the Treaty of Versailles (which Germany formally repudiated in 1935), Hitler pushed rearmament from the first. With the return of universal compulsory service in 1935 and the creation of an air force, Germany was soon spending several times as much on arms as Britain and France combined. All military officers were required to take an oath of personal loyalty to Hitler. By 1938 Hitler had removed the minister of war, chief of staff, and more than a dozen generals, thereby consolidating his control over the military and the foreign service.

The Nazis and the Churches

The churches presented a different challenge. A concordat with the Vatican in 1933 gave the state some voice in the appointment of bishops while assuring the Church of its authority over Catholic orders and schools. Protestant denominations agreed to form a new body, the Evangelical Church, under a national bishop whom Hitler named; but when the bishop declared a need to "Aryanize" the church, dissidents formed the separate Confessional Church. The Minister for Church Affairs was authorized to confiscate ecclesiastical property, withhold funds, and have pastors arrested; but in practice the state kept religion in line more through the local harassment of individual clergy. Some priests and ministers cooperated with the regime—enthusiastically supporting war, race, and Reich. Most resisted at least the more outrageous demands made of them, and some individuals spoke out courageously. In 1937 Martin Niemoeller, the leader of the Confessional Church, was arrested for his opposition to Nazism; and Pope Pius XI condemned both the deification of the state and Nazi racial doctrine. In the following years some Catholic churches were burned, and members of religious orders were frequently tried on morals charges.

Anti-Semitism

Anti-Semitism was central to Nazi ideology and practice, and the Nuremberg laws of 1935 codified and extended previous regulations. Jews (anyone with one or more Jewish grandparents was considered a Jew) were declared to be mere subjects but no longer citizens. The Law for the Protection of German Blood and Honor prohibited marriage or sexual intercourse between Aryans and Jews, "Gypsies, negroes or their bastards." Subsequently, Jews were expelled from one activity after another, required to register with the state, and ordered to give their children identifiably Jewish names.

In 1938 the murder of a German diplomat by a young Jewish boy touched off a new round of terror. Many Jews were arrested, and the SS led an orgy of violence (named *Kristallnacht*, the "night of broken glass") in which Jews were beaten and murdered, their homes and businesses smashed, and synagogues burned. A fine of 1 billion marks was levied on the Jews of Germany, and they were barred from the theater and concerts, forbidden to buy jewelry, forced to sell their businesses or property, denied access to certain streets, and made to wear a yellow star. Worse would come.

For most Germans, life went on much as before but a little better, and there was a new excitement in the air. From the beginning, the Nazis' publicity had been flamboyant, their posters striking, and their rallies well staged; after the movement came to power, propaganda became a way of life. Torchlight parades, chorused shouts of *Sieg Heil!* ("Hail to victory!"), book burnings, the evocation of Norse gods, schoolyard calisthenics, the return to Gothic script—a thousand occasions offered Germans a feeling of participating, of being swept up and implicated in some great historical transformation. At the Reich Chamber of Culture, Joseph Goebbels saw to it that cinema, theater, literature, art, and music all promoted Nazism (see "Goebbels' Populist View of German Culture," p. 841). Things primitive and brutal were praised as Aryan; any who opposed or even doubted the Führer ceased to be German. For this new regime, warfare was its natural condition.

Stalin's Soviet Union

Communists held that dictatorship in the Soviet Union was incidental and supposedly temporary. The reality proved different. Communist rule became more systematically brutal and bloody after Lenin's death, but in the last decade historians have uncovered substantial evidence in newly opened Russian archives

GOEBBELS' POPULIST VIEW OF GERMAN CULTURE

As minister of propaganda in the German government, Joseph Goebbels was also president of the Reich Chamber of Culture, an organization divided into separate sections for the various arts and for film, radio, and the press. Artists had to belong in order to exhibit, perform, or be published. The speech quoted here was an address given by Goebbels to the annual Congress of the Chamber and of the Strength Through Joy organization held in Berlin in November 1937. Goebbels' efforts were at their peak, and he reported proudly on the campaign against decadent art (which included much of the modern art most admired today), on the abolition of art criticism, and on the new recreation homes for veterans and the elderly, saying, "Nothing similar has even been tried ever or anywhere else in the world."

"My Führer! Your excellencies!

"My racial comrades!

"Organization plays a decisive role in the lives of people. . . . For every organization must demand that its members surrender certain individual private rights for the benefit of a greater and more comprehensive law of life. . . .

"The purging of the cultural field has been accomplished with the least amount of legislation. The social estate of creative artists took this cleansing into its own hands. Nowhere did any serious obstructions emerge. Today we can assert with joy and satisfaction that the great development is once again set in motion. Everywhere people are painting, building, writing poetry, singing, and acting. The German artist has his feet on the ground. Art, taken out of its narrow and isolated circle, again stands in the midst of the people and from there exerts its strong influences on the whole nation.

". . . True culture is not bound up with wealth. On the contrary, wealth often makes one bored and decadent. It is frequently the cause of uncertainty in matters of the mind and of taste. Only in this way can we explain the terrible devastations of the degeneration of German art in the past. Had the representatives of decadence and decline turned their attention to the masses of the people, they would have come up against icy contempt and cold mockery. For the people have no fear of being scorned as out of step with the times and as reactionary by enraged Jewish literati. Only the wealthy classes have this fear. . . . These defects are familiar to us under the label 'snobbism.' The snob is an empty and hollow culture lackey. . . . He goes in black tie and tails to the theater in order to breathe the fragrance of poor people. He must see suffering, which he shudderingly and shiveringly enjoys. This is the final degeneration of the rabble-like amusement industry. . . . The Volk visits the theater, concerts, museums, and galleries for other reasons. It wants to see and enjoy the beautiful and the lofty. That which life so often and stubbornly withholds from the people . . . here ought to unfold before their eyes gleaming with astonishment. The people approach the illusions of art with a naïve and unbroken joyousness and imagine themselves to be in an enchanted world of the Ideal. . . . The people seek joy. They have a right to it.

". . . 'Hence bread and circuses!' croak the wiseacres. No: 'Strength Through Joy!' we reply to them.

"This is why we have thus named the movement for the organization of optimism. It has led all strata of the people by the million to the beauties of our country, to the treasures of our culture, our art, and our life. . . . The German artist of today feels himself freer and more untrammeled than ever before. With joy he serves the people and the state. . . . National Socialism has wholly won over German creative artists. They belong to us and we to them.

". . . In this hour, we all look reverently upon you, Führer, you who do not regard art as a ceremonial duty but as a sacred mission and a lofty task, the ultimate and mightiest documentation of human life."

From Salvator Attanasio et al. (trs.), "Speech of Goebbels," in George L. Mosse, *Nazi Culture: Intellectual, Cultural, and Social Life in the Third Reich*, Grosset & Dunlap, 1966.

---

that Lenin had already laid the groundwork for such policies.

The Succession to Lenin   No one knew who Lenin's successors would be when he died in 1924 or even how the succession would be determined. For more than a year, Lenin had been ill and nearly incapacitated, but his prestige had precluded any public scramble for power, and many expected a more relaxed government by committee to follow. In a famous letter, Lenin had assessed two likely successors: Trotsky, whom he called overconfident but the best man in the Politburo, and Stalin, whom Lenin found "too rude" though an able organizer.

Over the next three years, Russia's leaders publicly debated complex issues of Communist theory and practical policy. Trotsky led those who clung to the traditional vision that revolution would spread across Europe, and he favored an uncompromisingly radical program at home and abroad. Stalin declared that the

Soviet Revolution must survive alone, a "revolution in one country." No theoretician, and little informed about the world outside Russia, Stalin was not wholly at ease in these debates with more intellectual and experienced opponents. But they, in turn, underestimated his single-minded determination. When the Politburo formally adopted his position in December 1925, his victory rested on more than ideas.

The Rise of Stalin As general secretary of the party's Central Committee, Stalin was the link between the Politburo and the party organization below it, and he could count on the loyalty of party officials, many of whom he had appointed. He played effectively on personal antagonisms and on resentment of Trotsky's tactless arrogance. When the Politburo elected three new members at that December meeting, all were Stalin's associates. He then effectively eliminated his opponents. When leading figures publicly sided with Trotsky, Stalin labeled the break in party solidarity a threat to communism. Trotsky and Grigori Zinoviev—the head of the Comintern, the organization of the Third International intended to lead communists around the world, whose prominence made him dangerous—were expelled from the Politburo in 1926 and from the party in 1927.

The left was broken, and the following year Zinoviev recanted his "mistake" in having supported Trotsky. Nikolai Bukharin, perhaps the party's subtlest theoretician and a leader of the right, recanted too. Trotsky, who refused to change his mind, was deported, continuing from abroad his criticism of Stalin's growing dictatorship. None of these veterans of the October Revolution had attempted to oust Stalin; even Trotsky, who built the Red Army, never tried to use it against him. Old Bolsheviks fervently accepted the need for party loyalty, and Stalin made sure that the open debates of those early years would not recur.

The First Five-Year Plan: Agriculture In aims and enforcement, the First **Five-Year Plan** reflected some of the qualities that had brought Stalin to the top. It shamelessly incorporated ideas Stalin had denounced just months before, but it was thoroughly his in the bold assumption that Russia could be transformed into an industrial power by mobilizing every resource. By 1928, when the plan was launched, Russian production had regained prewar levels in most sectors. Lenin's New Economic Policy had depended heavily on private entrepreneurs in commerce and peasant owners in agriculture. The task now was to create a socialist economy, and the first step was to collectivize agriculture.

Using the improved techniques and the mechanization that peasants had on the whole resisted, Soviet agriculture could produce enough both to feed industrial workers and to export grain that in turn would pay for importing the machinery that industrialization required. The problem was that Russian peasants continued to withhold their goods from market when agricultural prices fell. Some 4 or 5 percent of them had the means to hire labor and lend money within their villages, which gave them a further hold over the local economy.

As famine threatened, the government mounted a sweeping campaign of propaganda and police action against these wealthier peasants, calling them *kulaks*—the old, pejorative term for grasping merchants and usurers. Their grain was seized (informers were given a quarter of any hoard uncovered), hundreds of thousands of people killed, and untold numbers deported to till the unbroken soil of Siberia. Peasants destroyed crops and animals rather than let the government have them.

The explosive antagonisms of rural society raged out of control, and Stalin had to intervene in 1930 to halt a virtual civil war. By then, more than half the peasants belonged to collective farms, but the strife had badly hurt production, which contributed to serious famine in 1932–1933. A kind of compromise followed. Even on collective farms peasants were permitted individual plots and privately owned tools. Larger machinery was concentrated at Machine Tractor Stations, which became the rural base for agricultural agents and party officials. By 1933 output was sufficiently reliable to permit the state to concentrate on the most massive and rapid industrialization in history.

The First Five-Year Plan: Industry According to the five-year forecast, industrial production was to double in less than five years, and in some critical areas, such as electrical power, it was to increase sixfold. More than 1,500 new factories were to be put into operation, including large automobile and tractor plants. Projects on a still grander scale included a Dnieper River power station and a great coal and iron complex in a whole new city, Magnitogorsk. These goals were met somewhat ahead of schedule, and there was only slight exaggeration in the government's proud claim to have made Russia an industrial nation almost overnight.

To pay for that achievement, indirect taxes were levied, wages allowed to increase only slightly, planned improvements postponed, peasants displaced, and peasant land collectivized. Food and most consumer items were rationed, with allotments varying according to one's contribution to the plan. Success required much more than money. Unskilled or poorly trained, laborers were unaccustomed to the pace now required: Turnover was high; output and quality, low. The state resorted to a continuous work week and moved special "shock brigades" of abler workers from plant to plant.

Women and young people were urged into industrial jobs. "Socialist competition" pitted groups of workers and whole factories against each other for bonuses and prizes; piecework payment, once a hated symbol of capitalism, became increasingly common. Violators of shop rules were fined; malingering, pilfering, and sabotage (often loosely defined) became crimes against the state. "Corrective" labor camps, initially a mode of prison reform, became another way to get more work done. Special courses within factories and enlarged technical schools trained new managers and engineers to replace the foreigners who were still essential to efficient industrial production.

In effect, an entire nation was mobilized, and the need for social discipline replaced an earlier emphasis on revolutionary enthusiasm. In schools, the formal examinations, homework, and academic degrees, recently abolished, began to return; classroom democracy gave way to greater authority for the teacher. The state stressed the importance of the family and praised the virtues of marriage, and the earlier emphasis on freedom for women gradually gave way to an emphasis on their contribution to Soviet productivity. Divorce was discouraged, and regulations on abortion, which had been legalized in 1920, became increasingly restrictive. Associations of writers, musicians, and artists worked on propaganda for the plan. Mass organizations of youth and workers met for indoctrination. Within the party, criticism or even skepticism was akin to treason. Hundreds of thousands of party members were expelled, and new recruits were carefully screened. "Overfulfillment" was triumphantly announced in 1932; the miracle of industrialization came with creation of a Russian totalitarianism.

Growth in the 1930s The Second (1933–1937) and Third (1938–1942) Five-Year Plans continued the push for industrialization at somewhat lower pressure. Consumer goods were more available, and rationing was eliminated by 1936. Standards of quality rose, and dramatic improvement in transportation, especially domestic aviation, made previously remote territories accessible. By 1939 Soviet Russia ranked third among the world's industrial producers behind only the United States and Germany, producing twenty-four times more electrical power and five times more coal and steel than in 1913. Literacy among people older than school age rose from below 50 percent in 1926 to more than 80 percent in 1939. As millions moved to cities, the number of higher schools, libraries, and hospitals doubled or tripled. In these years one-seventh of the population moved to the cities, making the country more urban than ever before. More than 90 percent of peasant households were on collective farms serviced by the Machine Tractor Stations.

Villagers watch with anticipation for the first light bulb in Bryansk Province to be switched on, an achievement of the First Five-Year Plan.
Novosti/Sovfoto

Announcing that the stage of socialism had been reached, the Soviet Union adopted a new constitution in 1936. The changes it made were mainly formal. Direct voting by secret ballot replaced the cumbersome indirect elections for the Soviet of the Union. The other house, the Soviet of the Nationalities, represented the republics, which on paper had considerable autonomy. The two houses together elected the Council of Ministers (the term *Commissars* thus passed away) as well as the Presidium, which legislated and whose chairman was head of state. The constitution recognized the Communist party as "the vanguard of the working people" and provided social and political guarantees that Communists hailed as the most democratic in the world. Ninety-six percent of the population voted in the next elections, 98 percent of them for the list the party presented.

Stalinism A more confident government showed signs of relaxing its campaigns against potential enemies. Some political prisoners were amnestied in 1935, and a more controlled political police, the NKVD, replaced the sinister secret police. The campaign against religion abated. Opportunities for advancement in this

This Soviet poster of 1930 hails the International Day of Women Workers, part of the government's extended campaign to encourage women to work in factories.
Edimedia

expanding economy were great. White-collar classes got more respect, officers were restored to the army and navy, and supervisors were reinstalled in factories. Expression of opinion remained tightly controlled, however. Writers, Stalin commented ominously, were "engineers of human souls." Although harassed less than during the First Five-Year Plan, intellectuals had long since learned the necessity of caution. The Russian Academy of Science, an important source of money and prestige, was never far from politics.

At the center of Soviet society stood Stalin, adulated as leader in every activity. Works of art were dedicated to him, factories named after him. His picture was everywhere. Patriotism overshadowed the socialist internationalism of an earlier generation, and Stalin was placed with Ivan the Terrible and Peter the Great as one of the molders of Russia. Although he held no official position other than party secretary, he demonstrated his awful power in the great purges of the late 1930s. Directed against engineers, Ukrainian separatists,

former Mensheviks, and party members accused of being counterrevolutionaries, the purges were touched off by the assassination in 1934 of Sergei Kirov, a member of the Politburo who had been a close associate of Stalin's (in fact, Stalin himself was probably behind the assassination). Party and state mobilized to root out a great conspiracy. Zinoviev and members of the "left opposition" were twice tried for treason and were executed in 1937.

Other public trials followed: party leaders and army officers in 1937, members of the "right opposition," Nikolai Bukharin and other old Bolsheviks, in 1939. To the outside world, the indictments seemed vague and the evidence unconvincing. Yet the accused consistently confessed—the effect of torture perhaps, or the wish to protect their families, or maybe the final act of faith by men who were convinced of the inevitable course of history and believed that anyone resisting it was "objectively" a traitor. A reign of terror swept the country, feeding local vendettas until Stalin called a halt in 1939. The dead were countless; jails and labor camps were bursting with prisoners, perhaps 10 million. More than twice that many had gone into exile. Soviet totalitarianism had grown to be ominously like that of Germany and Italy, except for the values it professed.

THE DEMOCRACIES' WEAK RESPONSE

Confident Communist, Fascist, and Nazi regimes had moved dramatically to meet the challenge of the Depression and to forge social unity while tightening their hold on power. Europe's democracies responded more uncertainly, forever compromising and unable to disguise the social and ideological dissension that politics could not overcome.

Divisive Social Change

The Economy Economic recovery by the mid-1930s did not lessen these divisions, even though standards of living were rising again. Agriculture became more productive by becoming more mechanized and scientific, but those changes required increased capital (thus favoring larger holdings) and employed fewer laborers. Workers benefited from better transportation, mechanical refrigeration, cheaper clothes, and more leisure; but it took organized conflict for them to pry better wages from employers.

Many employees now enjoyed a shorter work week, but work itself was more subject to "American" efficiency on speeded-up assembly lines, forcing workers to repeat the same tasks at a pace set by factory managers (and known as Fordism, after the production methods of Henry Ford in Detroit). This form of production and the use of elaborate time and motion studies intended to reorganize work in ways that would further increase productivity (called Taylorism, after studies by the American efficiency expert, Frederick W. Taylor) seemed to suggest that efficiency meant treating human beings like machines.

The middle classes recouped much that inflation and Depression had undermined, but not their former confidence. While small businesses and craft industries remained insecure, larger corporations benefited first from the economic upturn and tended to form more powerful cartels, combining many firms within a single field so as to gain control of the entire production process from raw materials to marketing. And businesses large and small feared labor unions and socialist parties that were sounding increasingly militant.

Cultural Life   Even cultural life lacked the healing qualities once expected of it. The scholars, scientists, and artists exiled from the new regimes in Russia, Italy, and Germany went to London, Paris, and especially the United States. They brought knowledge, methods, and artistic achievements that stimulated an explosion of creativity, and they brought their fears and disillusionment. Cultural movements seemed all the more foreign, politicized, and ideological. The new media did

much to bridge the chasm between rural and urban life, but mass entertainment was not given to thoughtful discourse and moral uplift. The distinction between high and popular culture sharpened, and to many intellectuals culture itself was threatened as never before by the frothy commercialism of talking motion pictures and radio. Social scientists, poets, and novelists probed the theme of alienation, denounced faceless mass society, and engaged in radical politics.

In Paris, the Spanish painter Pablo Picasso became the dominant figure of twentieth-century art, restlessly experimenting with one new style after another. His most political work, *Guernica*, was a searing comment on war prepared for the Spanish pavilion at the Paris World's Fair of 1937 (see below). Some artists defended the "experiments" of Hitler and Mussolini; far more joined Marxist groups, convinced that only socialism could create an acceptable society and preserve culture. The energy of the propaganda that advertised the transformation of Soviet society or the happy order, well-lit factories, and vacation resorts of Germany and Italy underscored the contrast between the ideologically coherent and purposeful societies of a single party and the aimless dislocation and dissension in the democracies.

The Argument for Liberty

Against the strident claims of radicals and fascists, four major groups of intellectuals—Marxists, Christian

Pablo Picasso
***Guernica*, 1937**
Pablo Picasso used the still-new stylistic techniques he had mastered to protest the bombing of the Spanish town of Guernica by German planes in 1937. The huge, dark canvas, a political act in opposition to Franco and the Spanish Nationalists, foreshadowed modern warfare's brutal impact on civilian life. Kept in the United States for nearly fifty years, the painting can now be exhibited in a democratic Spain.
© 2010 The Estate of Pablo Picasso/Artists Rights Society (ARS), New York/Art Resource, NY

thinkers, liberals, and economists—expressed a revived commitment to freedom. The most prominent of these thinkers were the Marxists. The Russian Revolution had enthralled millions of Europeans with visions of economic progress in a backward nation and of social equality and high culture in a mass society. This appeal grew as capitalist economies staggered, and it reached a peak with the promulgation of the Soviet constitution of 1936. At the same time, socialists and even communists insisted on the importance of justice, equality, and liberty, asserting that dictatorship in the Soviet Union was a special case.

Christians and Liberals

In Christian thought, traditional arguments against the idolatry of the state gained new meaning. The Protestant Karl Barth and the Catholic Jacques Maritain built on firm theological orthodoxy to stress the importance of individual freedom and social justice. Similar concerns emerged in the influential work of the Russian Orthodox Nikolai Berdyaev and the Jewish scholar Martin Buber.

From a more secular perspective, noted poets and novelists such as W. H. Auden, Thomas Mann, and André Malraux wrote powerfully in behalf of human dignity and social justice, warning of the dangers of power and the evils of war. Most vigorous in the politics and universities of Britain and France, liberals were also heard even in Fascist Italy. In his important *History of European Liberalism*, Guido de Ruggiero argued that liberal values, modified yet again, offered a practical path to stability and progress; and Benedetto Croce made liberty the central theme of his historical and philosophical writings.

Keynesian Economics

Economic theory also contributed to the argument for political freedom through the work of John Maynard Keynes, whose book *The General Theory of Employment, Interest, and Money* appeared in 1936. Keynes rejected classical views of economic man and the self-regulating economy. Few people, he argued, consistently act in their own financial interest, for no one is free of ideas, values, and tastes that shape actions. Nor do iron economic laws inexorably dictate a pattern of booms and busts. To Keynes, massive unemployment was not only intolerable but proof that capitalism must not be left to its own devices.

At the same time, he dismissed Marxism as outmoded. Instead, he offered a sophisticated theory that called on governments to smooth out the economic cycle. When the economy lagged, the government should lower interest rates to encourage production and should finance public works and social welfare to stimulate consumption. As the economy expanded, the opposite policies should check inflation and excessive speculation. Keynes advocated granting government a more active role while preserving free markets. In effect, he gave a theoretical foundation for practices already partially adopted under Swedish socialism, the French Popular Front (see later in this chapter), and the American New Deal, President Franklin D. Roosevelt's program of social and economic reform inaugurated in 1933. An advocate of capitalism, Keynes defended it by denying that its social evils were inevitable; most capitalists denounced him as a socialist.

Few thinkers were neutral. With socialist anger, Auden, the British poet who chose to live in America, warned capitalists that "the game is up for you and for the others."[7] T. S. Eliot, the American poet who chose to live in Britain, proposed still tougher choices in a voice of Christian outrage: "The term 'democracy' . . . does not contain enough positive content to stand alone. . . . If you will not have God (and He is a jealous God) you should pay your respects to Hitler or Stalin."[8]

Domestic Politics

The Great Depression and rising international dangers undermined the traditional programs of democratic parties, left and right. Conservative parties pursued balanced budgets with results that embittered the unemployed. Liberals reluctantly accepted tariffs and subsidies that had few positive results. Socialists, weakened by competition from communists, antagonized workers by accepting weak welfare measures in the interest of better-balanced budgets. Issues of foreign policy had an even more paradoxical effect. Conservatives, historically supporters of military strength, were now inclined to downplay the dangers arising from Italy and Germany. Parties of the left, arguing that fascism must be resisted, tended to abandon their antimilitary rhetoric. As Finland and Czechoslovakia, whose economic growth and political freedom had made them models of the new postwar nations, felt the pressure from their stronger neighbors, the cause of democracy increasingly depended on Britain and France.

Cautious Compromise in Great Britain

Ramsay MacDonald became the British prime minister after a Labour victory in 1929. Following the advice of experts, he made drastic cuts in welfare and unemployment payments, measures that divided his own party. He then formed a national government with members from all three parties, in effect a conservative government in

[7] W. H. Auden, "Consider This" and "In Our Time," in *A Little Treasury of Great Poetry*, Oscar Williams (ed.), New York: Charles Scribner's Sons, 1947, p. 689.

[8] T. S. Eliot, *The Idea of a Christian Society*, New York: Harcourt Brace, 1960.

disguise, and was expelled from the Labour party amid bitter recriminations. His government adopted controls on foreign exchange and increased tariffs, policies that split the Liberals. When MacDonald resigned in 1935, tired and unloved, his coalition government had overseen a slow recovery of the British economy, redefined imperial relations, and initiated some cautious steps toward government planning. But it had done so by pursuing conservative policies, and it had devastated the proletarian movement to which MacDonald had devoted his life.

He was succeeded by Stanley Baldwin's Conservative government, his third time as prime minister. Baldwin campaigned as a strong supporter of the League of Nations, in which he actually had little interest; and, with a complacency that masked indecision, he steered clear of political extremes. The parliament elected with him, which would continue to sit through 1945 as the longest-lived in modern history, would later reveal a wealth of talent, testimony to the continued vitality of British political life.

In retrospect, even the crisis of 1936 could be seen as a comforting assertion of tradition. King Edward VIII, who had acceded to the throne, insisted on marrying an American divorcée. He was forced to abdicate, and the transition to George VI went smoothly, quelling talk of the end of the monarchy. At the time, however, British institutions appeared weak. As international affairs grew more ominous, Britain's uncertain foreign policy further undermined the capacity of continental states to resist the expansionist policies of Germany and Italy. Doubts about Britain's role increased in 1937 when Baldwin turned the prime ministership over to his earnest Chancellor of the Exchequer, Neville Chamberlain, who was convinced he could avoid the danger of war through caution and compromise.

Weak Government in France   France experienced the Depression later and less severely than other highly industrialized countries, but when the decline came, it lasted. The left won the legislative elections of 1932, as the economic slump began to be felt, but found it difficult to construct a reliable majority, for the Socialists refused to participate in bourgeois governments. The result was unstable governments committed to reducing expenditures and protecting established interests. Outside parliament, rightist factions, including the fascist Croix de Feu (Cross of Fire), grew increasingly noisy. On February 6, 1934, their uniformed militants led demonstrations against parliament that resulted in more bloodshed than Paris had seen since the Commune of 1871; many believe that the Third Republic nearly died that day. France seemed more bitterly divided than at any time since the Dreyfus affair at the turn of the century.

The exposure of a gigantic investment swindle perpetrated by one Serge Stavisky, who had important political connections, became the basis for a strident campaign against the republic by protofascist groups using the now familiar devices of uniforms, anti-Semitism, propaganda, and demonstrations. To meet the emergency, a former president of the republic, Gaston Doumergue, was recalled from retirement to take the premiership and empowered to govern by decree. The sober old man, supported by every party except the royalists and the Marxists, held office for nine calming months before giving way to a parliament that insisted on its prerogatives but little else.

The elections of 1936 brought a dramatic change. Moderate republicans, Socialists, and Communists formed an antifascist Popular Front (cooperation made possible by the decision of the Comintern directed from the Soviet Union to permit Communist alliances with other parties). Such rare solidarity brought the three parties a resounding victory and France its first Socialist premier, Léon Blum. He was a learned, humane intellectual and a Jew—attributes his enemies distrusted. Even as it took office, the new government faced a wave of strikes by workers determined to collect the fruits of their victory. They occupied factories, and many conservatives took that to be the revolution they dreaded. Eventually the strikes ended as the government pushed through legislation that provided for a general 12 percent increase in wages, two-week paid vacations, a forty-hour work week, and compulsory arbitration. Other reforms were soon added. Public works were launched, the Bank of France (long distrusted by the left) restructured, the arms industry nationalized, veterans given increased pensions, and small businesses offered subsidies. Each of these measures, like the devaluation of the franc, which in 1937 could no longer be avoided, frightened the business classes. New programs were hard to finance, and the economy proved more accessible to regulation than to stimulation. Blum's government—one of the Third Republic's most admired and most hated—had hardly begun the tax reforms its plans required when, after a year in office, it was defeated in the conservative senate. The Popular Front itself soon broke up. Subsequent governments were less daring amidst political feuds and public slander. Meanwhile, France's carefully constructed international position was collapsing.

The Failures of Diplomacy

The internationalism of the twenties had faded, and the sense of unreality in international affairs was underscored by the absence of the Soviet Union, which was effectively ostracized, and by the limited participation of the United States, which was absorbed in domestic affairs.

Italy and Germany Test Their Strength   In October 1935 Italy invaded Ethiopia, seemingly an old-fashioned imperialistic venture preceded by carefully arranged understandings with Britain and France. But the racist propaganda and enthusiastic bombing of defenseless populations signaled something new. Europeans were shocked, and the League of Nations labeled Italy an aggressor and banned the sale to Italy of essential war materials. Most of Europe seemed united in this crucial test of the League's peacekeeping powers. Although the embargo angered Italy and caused some hardship, it did not stop the war, partly because the most important commodity of all, oil, was not included.

More important, some leaders in France and Britain considered Italy's friendship more important than the League, including the two foreign ministers: Pierre Laval, a slippery politician who had drifted steadily to the right, and Sir Samuel Hoare, an experienced conservative diplomat. Secretly, they arranged a settlement that would, in effect, give Italy most of Ethiopia. When the plan leaked to the press, public outrage forced both men to resign; but they had delayed efforts to add oil to the list of sanctions and undermined confidence in the two democracies. By May 1936, Ethiopia had capitulated, Italy could celebrate the lifting of the embargo, and all could see the ineffectiveness of the League of Nations.

Germany then began to exploit its opportunities. Everyone knew that Germany was rebuilding its fighting forces, and when German troops marched into the demilitarized Rhineland in 1936, there was no compelling international response. Italy this time did nothing. France, unwilling to act alone as it had in 1923, consulted the British, who urged acquiescence. The German troops were cheered by their countrymen in the Rhineland just as they had been the year before when France had turned over the Saar following a plebiscite overwhelmingly in favor of German rule. The fascist powers wanted radical changes in the international balance, and they had the initiative. Britain and France were internally divided, their leaders kept off balance by Germany's protests against the Versailles Treaty, by exuberant propaganda, and by shifting demands. Eastern European nations were torn between fear of the Soviet Union and fear of Germany.

The Spanish Civil War   Civil war in Spain drove home the sense that all of Europe was divided between the fascist right and the Marxist left, destined for a life-and-death struggle. Spain had been a strifetorn nation since the end of World War I. In 1923 General Miguel Primo de Rivera assumed office as a de facto dictator and implemented a series of policies similar to the corporatist program of Mussolini. However, popular discontent, coupled with economic depression, forced Primo de Rivera into exile in 1930. In municipal elections held the following year, republicans and socialists triumphed, ushering in the second Spanish republic. Meanwhile, political turmoil and violence continued as power shifted between leftist and conservative governments. The political climate became increasingly polarized, especially following the formation of the Falange—a movement modeled after Italian fascism—by José Antonio Primo de Rivera, the dictator's son. Finally, in July 1936, Spanish army officers stationed in Morocco rose up against the republic. The Spanish Civil War had begun.

General Francisco Franco soon emerged as their leader of the military revolt. The insurgent officers counted on support from Italy, Germany, and Portugal, where Antonio de Oliveira Salazar had already established his dominance over a single-party, corporative, conservative, and Catholic state. Little interested in doctrines or ideologies, Franco recognized the utility of a modern mass appeal and a disciplined movement. His supporters were called the Nationalists. Dominated by the army, they appealed to the monarchists and fascistic Falangists, to most of the clergy, and to all who favored desperate measures to escape from anarchy and communism. Italy and Germany quickly proffered their support and formed the Rome-Berlin Axis. Germany and Japan asserted their mutual sympathy and opposition to communism in the Anti-Comintern Pact. In addition to signing treaties, the fascist powers provided military support in the form of advisors, planes, tanks, and ammunition, as well as significant numbers of Italian troops. Mussolini welcomed the chance to enhance Italian prestige, and Hitler used the opportunity to test new German military technology. The Nationalist cause had become ideological and international.

The Spanish government's supporters included republicans, socialists, communists, anarchists, labor groups, and Catalan and Basque nationalists, a loose and badly split coalition. Known as the Loyalists, they saw themselves as the defenders of democracy against fascist aggression and of social justice against reaction; and they looked to the democracies for support. They received little except from the thousands of idealistic young men who went to Spain to fight as volunteers in national units like the Lincoln Brigade and the Garibaldi Brigade (which had its greatest moment when it defeated troops of the regular Italian army sent by Mussolini).

The Course of the Conflict   Among foreign nations, only the Soviet Union provided reliable, if limited, assistance to the Loyalists. Even this aid terminated in 1938, when Stalin decided to cut his losses. France, Britain, and the United States all adopted official policies of neutrality, even as aid to the Nationalists flowed in from Germany and Italy.

Foreign aid, trained troops, better military organization, and modern weapons made the victory of Franco's forces almost inevitable. They nearly won Madrid and the war itself in the summer of 1936, but the Loyalists held on and in a last-minute counterattack broke the Nationalists' assault. For more than two years, despite poor equipment and internal conflict, the republicans fought on, heartened by occasional victories. As the war progressed, the Loyalists became increasingly dependent on the Soviet Union for supplies, and that dependency plus the communists' organizational skills made them increasingly influential.

To the disgust of his Axis supporters, Franco conducted a war of attrition. Not until the spring of 1939, when Soviet supplies had ceased to come and Britain had signed special treaties of friendship with Italy, did the Spanish republic finally fall. Thousands of refugees wearily crossed into France while Franco filled Spain's capacious prisons with potential enemies, undid the republic's social measures, and restored the power of the Church over education. Franco then joined the Anti-Comintern Pact and took Spain out of the League of Nations. The civil war had taken more than a million Spanish lives, many at the hands of firing squads and mobs. The bombing of the town of Guernica by German aircraft in 1937 made people shudder before the vision of what war now meant for civilians, and the tales of atrocities on both sides fed the angry arguments between left and right throughout Europe and the United States. The one clear lesson was that the Western democracies, fearful and divided, had accepted defeat while the Axis acted.

Summary

For European societies the 1920s and 1930s were a period of innovation in cultural expression, social organization, and political mobilization. Where economic disaster, social failure, and political conflict were greatest, the response brought official ideologies, systematically enforced and apparently deeply believed. Using skillful mass propaganda disseminated on an unprecedented scale, governments found new ways to organize whole societies in the name of unanimity and efficiency, exercising powers rarely equaled even in wartime. That organization of society made the vague decencies of democracy with its social and ideological conflicts and the hypothetical opportunities of free markets seem limp in comparison. The anger, intolerance, and raw violence in European domestic life soon extended to international relations, creating a situation that clearly could not last. Optimists hoped that these crises might dissipate; pessimists could only wait for them to explode as states increased their military strength.

QUESTIONS FOR FURTHER THOUGHT

1. What are the significant similarities and differences between the revolutions in Russia and Italy, in the tactics that brought communists and fascists to power, and in the regimes they created?
2. On almost every front, cultural developments appeared to undermine established beliefs and values, but, looking back from today's perspective, is that a correct assessment?
3. Did the 1930s reveal inherent, and maybe universal, weaknesses in democracy and free markets or were those weaknesses the result of specific, and unusual, circumstances and the inadequacies of particular leaders?
4. Soviet Russia and Nazi Germany each set out to transform society and won fervent support at home and abroad. As models, each is now largely discredited, but are there aspects of their appeal and their policies that remain influential?

RECOMMENDED READING

Sources

Adamthwaite, Anthony P. (ed.). *The Making of the Second World War.* 1979. A valuable collection of documents on the events and policies leading to war, with a useful introductory essay.

Ciano, Count Galiazzo. *Diary, 1937–1938.* 1952. *Diary, 1939–1943.* 1947. The diaries of Mussolini's son-in-law and, eventually, foreign minister are often self-serving, but they give a vivid picture of the intrigue and confusion at the center of the Fascist regime.

Engel, Barbara Alpern, and Anastasia Posadskaya-Vanderbeck (eds.). *A Revolution of Their Own: Voices of Soviet Women in Soviet History.* 1997. Interviews with eight women born before the Russian Revolution reveal the difficulties and gains experienced by women from different backgrounds under Russian communism.

Ortega y Gasset, José. *The Revolt of the Masses.* 1957. First published in 1932, this essay by one of Spain's leading philosophers and historians, an important work in its own right, is also a significant document of the disquiet that intellectual elites felt over the effects that increased specialization and mass society were having on the traditional culture of the West.

Reed, John. *Ten Days That Shook the World.* Available in many editions, this classic account of the Russian revolution was first published in 1922. John Reed went to Russia as a journalist and radical. His enthusiastic and perceptive report on the revolution captures both the excitement of the moment and the communist revolution's dramatic and international appeal.

Studies

Adamson, Walter. *Avant-Garde Florence: From Modernism to Fascism.* 1993. An insightful and provocative assessment of the links between prewar avant-garde literary movements and fascism.

Allen, William S. *The Nazi Seizure of Power: The Experience of a Single German Town, 1930–1935.* 1965. A much-used microcosmic study.

Arendt, Hannah. *The Origins of Totalitarianism.* 1958. This important study begins with a profoundly pessimistic application of hindsight to the imperialism and anti-Semitism of the late nineteenth century to make the case for Nazi totalitarianism as a phenomenon rooted in Western history.

Bracher, Karl D. *The German Dictatorship.* Translated by Jean Steinberg. 1970. A major synthesis of work on the origins, structure, and impact of the Nazi movement.

Bullock, Alan. *Hitler: A Study in Tyranny.* 1971. The best biography of Hitler and one that gives an effective picture of Nazi society.

Carr, Raymond. *The Civil War in Spain.* 1986. An unusually balanced study that puts the events of the war in the context of Spanish history and international relations.

Carsten, F. L. *The Rise of Fascism.* 1967. The careful synthesis of a distinguished scholar that looks at the varieties of fascist regimes.

Colton, Joel C. *Léon Blum: Humanist in Politics.* 1966. The biography of this appealing figure is particularly useful for the period of the Popular Front.

Fitzpatrick, Sheila. *The Russian Revolution, 1917–1932.* 1982. A valuable, fresh overview that emphasizes social conditions.

Kershaw, Ian. *The Nazi Dictatorship: Problems and Perspectives of Interpretation.* 2000. A significant assessment that provides an excellent introduction to and interpretation of a vast literature.

Kershaw, Ian, and Moshe Lewin (eds.). *Stalinism and Nazism: Dictatorships in Comparison.* 1997.

Kindleberger, Charles P. *The World in Depression, 1929–1939.* 1973. A study of the origins of the Depression and of responses to it in different countries.

Kolb, Eberhard. *The Weimar Republic.* Translated by P. S. Falla. 1988. A comprehensive account of the difficulties and failures of Germany's experiment with democracy.

Koonz, Claudia. *Mothers in the Fatherland: Women, the Family, and Nazi Politics.* 1987. Shows the importance of gender policies to Nazi ideology and rule.

Lee, Stephen J. *The European Dictatorships: 1918–1945.* 1987. A comprehensive and systematic comparison of Communist Russia, Fascist Italy, and Nazi Germany.

Mack Smith, Denis. *Mussolini.* 1981. An informed, skeptical account by the leading English scholar of modern Italy.

Nolte, Ernst. *Three Faces of Fascism.* Leila Vennewitz (tr.). 1965. A learned effort to place the intellectual history of fascism in France, Germany, and Italy in the mainstream of European thought.

Peukert, Detlev J. K. *Inside Nazi Germany: Conformity, Opposition, and Racism in Everyday Life.* 1987. Makes use of a great deal of recent research to explore the effects of Nazi tyranny on ordinary life and the difficulties of opposition to it.

Pipes, Richard. *The Formation of the Soviet Union.* 1964. A clear, comprehensive, and very critical treatment of Soviet rule.

Tannenbaum, Edward R. *The Fascist Experience: Italian Society and Culture, 1922–1945.* 1972. A wide-ranging effort to recapture the meaning in practice of Fascist rule.

Thompson, John M. *Revolutionary Russia, 1917.* 1989. A good overview of what the revolution meant for ordinary life throughout the country.

Ulam, Adam B. *Lenin and the Bolsheviks.* 1969. Combines the study of ideas and of policy to explain Lenin's triumph.

Weinberg, Gerhard L. *The Foreign Policy of Hitler's Germany.* 1970. A major study by a leading American diplomatic historian that helps explain Hitler's early successes.

Leonard Henry Rosoman
A House Collapsing on Two Firemen, Shoe Lane London EC4
This painting of a collapsing building captures the frightful devastation of aerial bombardment during World War II. The scene could have occurred in dozens of cities across Europe, such as Warsaw, Rotterdam, Liverpool, Hamburg, Dresden, or (in this case) London.

Chapter Twenty-Eight

THE NIGHTMARE: WORLD WAR II

THE YEARS OF AXIS VICTORY • THE GLOBAL WAR, 1942–1945 • BUILDING ON THE RUINS

World War II was a long ordeal for European civilization. The outbreak of war followed a series of international crises, but in a larger sense it resulted from the kinds of governments that came to power and from the social tensions of the era. For more than a decade, a kind of ideological civil war exposed every weakness in Europe's social and political fabric. New communist, fascist, and Nazi regimes carried those conflicts into international affairs, challenging the status quo and the democracies that defended it. When war erupted it would prove more total and more worldwide than its horrendous predecessor. World War II required massive mobilization of manpower and national economies. At first Germany gained everywhere, its preparations farther along, its tactics more ruthless. The balance shifted, however, after the Soviet Union halted the German advance and the United States joined in the battle against Nazi Germany and Japanese militarism. Slowly the Allies gained the upper hand militarily, even as the Nazis intensified the systematic horrors of torture, concentration camps, and genocide. Allied victory in 1945 left Europe a devastated continent where tens of millions had perished and millions of survivors had lost homes, family, health, and hope. It would be a struggle just to make society function again.

Nuremberg trials of Nazi war criminals; fourth French Republic launched **1946**

Yalta Conference; Germany surrenders; socialist government elected in Britain; atomic bombing of Japan **1945** ●

Allied invasion of Normandy **1944** ●

Germans defeated at Stalingrad **1943** ●

Sieges of Moscow, Leningrad, Stalingrad; Allies land in North Africa **1942** ●

Hitler invades USSR; Pearl Harbor **1941** ●

Fall of France **1940** ●

1939 ●
Hitler-Stalin Pact; outbreak of World War II

● **1938** Munich Agreement (height of appeasement)

THE YEARS OF AXIS VICTORY

The civil war in Spain had made the international situation frighteningly clear. Germany and Italy were allied, rearming, and aggressive. France and Britain, reluctantly rearming, still hoped to avoid war. The countries of eastern Europe were effectively paralyzed, and the Soviet Union was an enigma, for no one knew whether it would eventually take sides or could fight effectively if it did. Once war began, German forces went from victory to victory.

The Path to War

For eighteen months Hitler orchestrated a series of escalating demands that culminated in the outbreak of World War II in September 1939.

The Anschluss In February 1938, with the outcome of civil war in Spain still uncertain, Hitler began to pressure Austria. He summoned the Austrian chancellor, Kurt von Schuschnigg, to the Führer's secluded mountain retreat at Berchtesgaden and subjected him to a humiliating harangue. Schuschnigg promised to include Austrian Nazis in his cabinet. On returning home, he felt braver and decided to hold a plebiscite in the hope that public opinion would rally to save Austria's independence. Hitler, furious, massed the German army on the Austrian border, and Schuschnigg realized his position was hopeless. He had previously disbanded the Socialist party, the strongest opponent of union with Germany, and Italy warned that this time it would not oppose the German moves as it had a few years earlier. The friendless Austrian chancellor was replaced by a Nazi, who invited German troops to restore order. They did so on March 13, and Nazis indulged in the brutal public humiliation of Viennese

Jews and intellectuals. Within a month Austria's annexation to Germany was almost unanimously approved in a plebiscite run by the Nazis. The dream of union with Germany, *Anschluss*, had been fulfilled. Hitler's popularity at home rose still higher, and German influence spread more deeply into the Balkans. Britain and France merely protested.

Czechoslovakia Two weeks after the Austrian plebiscite, Hitler demanded autonomy for the Sudetenland, an overwhelmingly German-speaking section of Czechoslovakia (see map 29.1). Again, the claims that the Versailles settlement had been unfair and that Germans were being abused rallied support at home and weakened opposition abroad. Although this challenge to the Czech republic was far more daring—Czechoslovakia was a prosperous industrial state protected by a respectable army, well-fortified frontiers, and mutual-aid treaties with both France and Russia—the parallel with Austria was lost on no one. Supported by its allies, Czechoslovakia mobilized, and Hitler ordered the Sudeten Nazis to quiet down. But Czechoslovakia was vulnerable, and Hitler was adept at fanning ethnic resentments. The republic, dominated by the more prosperous Czech region, was barely able to maintain the loyalty of the Slovaks; a pro-Nazi party had won more votes than any other in the 1935 elections, and the great powers remained divided. Britain's prime minister, Neville Chamberlain, wanted to parlay directly with Germany, believing that no nonnegotiable British interest was at stake in the Sudetenland. Many in France and England, deeply alarmed at how close to war they were, doubted that fighting for Czechoslovakia's sovereignty over a German population was worth the risk. Throughout the summer, Sudeten Nazi leaders negotiated with the Czech state in an atmosphere heated by demonstrations there and in Germany.

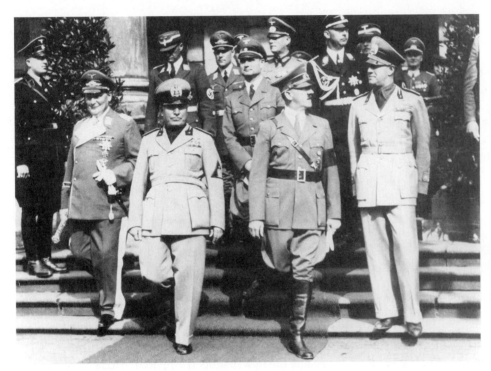

Hitler and Mussolini on the way to the train station after the Munich conference. Count Galeazzo Ciano, the Italian foreign minister, is on Hitler's left; Hermann Göring is on Mussolini's right; General William Keitel, Rudolf Hess, and Heinrich Himmler are among those behind them.
Ullstein Bilderdienst

In August, Chamberlain, with French concurrence, sent his own emissary to mediate while German troops held maneuvers on the Czech border, and Hitler pointedly toured Germany's fortifications in the west. Hitler's speeches became more bellicose, and Chamberlain decided, once again with French support, to visit the Führer at Berchtesgaden. When they met on September 15, Hitler raised the stakes, demanding that Germany annex the Sudetenland. Britain and France advised Czechoslovakia to submit. Desperately, the Czechs sought some escape, but only the Soviet Union was ready to support Czech resistance. In a week Chamberlain flew back to Germany with the good news that

Czechoslovakia had agreed to Hitler's terms, only to find them changed again: German troops must occupy the ceded territory immediately. The Czechs would have no time to move factories and military supplies or provide for citizens who wished to evacuate. A shocked Chamberlain said no, and for five days the world listened for war.

The Munich Agreement Then Mussolini persuaded Hitler to meet with the Duce and the prime ministers of Britain and France. They met on September 29, 1938, in Munich, where just fifteen years earlier Hitler had failed to capture the town hall. Now he dealt in terms

MAP 28.1 EUROPE ON THE EVE OF WORLD WAR II

of nations. During an afternoon and evening of discussions, Hitler was granted all he asked. Neither the Soviet Union nor Czechoslovakia was consulted. The next day Czechoslovakia submitted to Hitler's terms and accepted last-minute demands from Poland and Hungary for additional pieces of Czechoslovak territory that they had long coveted. At a single stroke, Czechoslovakia surrendered one-third of its population, its best military defenses, and much of its economic strength. Central Europe's strongest democracy was reduced to a German dependency, and a keystone of France's continental security was shattered. As the French prime minister's plane circled the Paris airport on his return from Munich, he watched the crowd below with dread. But it cheered him, and in Britain, Chamberlain became a hero.

Peace, the newspapers trumpeted, had been preserved. A minority of dissenters warned that such craven **appeasement** of Hitler would lead only to new threats and demands by the Führer.

Poland and the Hitler-Stalin Pact German might, Hitler's speeches, virulent anti-Semitism, goose-stepping troops marching through central Europe, and news of what life was like in the newly annexed lands and in Germany itself—all gave Jews, ethnic groups the Nazis labeled inferior, peoples living along the German borders, and whole nations reason to be terrified. Early in 1939 German troops occupied all of Czechoslovakia and annexed the seaport of Memel from a frightened Lithuania. The pretext of absorbing only German peoples had now been abandoned.

Well-coordinated armored and
mechanized infantry units
spearheaded Germany's
blitzkrieg (lightning war)
against Poland.
AP Images

Chamberlain, believing that not even Nazis could want world war, was one of many in Europe who hoped concessions would appease Hitler; but most people in England and France had finally become resigned to the fact that Germany could only be stopped by force. Italy, inspired by Hitler's success, began a noisy campaign to get Nice and Corsica from France and in the summer of 1939 invaded and annexed Albania. The Rome-Berlin Axis was formally tightened into the "Pact of Steel." Late in August the leader of the Nazi party in German-speaking Danzig declared that his city, which the Versailles treaties had assigned to Poland, must be returned to the fatherland. The denunciations of the Versailles boundaries that poured from Germany, along with claims that Germans living within the Polish corridor were being persecuted, made it clear that Poland was next. As they had all summer, Britain and France renewed their pledges to protect Poland.

The summer's most important contest was for some alliance with the Soviet Union, and Hitler won that, too. Germany and the Soviet Union announced a non-aggression pact. The USSR had made overtures to Britain and France, suggesting that the territorial integrity of all the states between the Baltic and Black seas be guaranteed. The Western powers, reluctant to grant a communist nation such extensive influence, had responded weakly. Since 1935 the Soviet Union had advocated disarmament, supported the League of Nations, supplied Loyalist Spain, and offered support to Czechoslovakia, but Stalin feared that the democracies would welcome

a war between Germany and the Soviet Union. In May 1939 he replaced his foreign minister, Maxim Litvinov, the eloquent spokesman for a pro-Western policy, with Vyacheslav Molotov, a tougher old ally. Hitler offered the Soviet Union a free hand in Finland, Estonia, Latvia, eastern Poland, and part of Romania should Germany seek any changes in its own eastern border. That became the basis for a nonaggression pact between the international sponsor of antifascist fronts and the creators of the Anti-Comintern Pact, a masterpiece of cynicism (and very old-fashioned diplomacy) that shocked a world still unaccustomed to totalitarian opportunism.

The last days of August resounded with formal warnings and clarifications from the major powers. On September 1, Germany invaded Poland. Britain and France mobilized, sent Germany an ultimatum, and declared war on September 3, 1939. One year after surrendering democratic Czechoslovakia, they would fight, at least in principle, for authoritarian Poland.

The Last European War, 1939–1941

One argument for the policy of appeasement was that it had enabled Britain and France to buy time. They had been strengthening their armed forces, and the domestic consensus that war required was slowly taking shape. But much remained to be done; Germany had gained, too, in territory and power, and now there was no time left.

Blitzkrieg and Phony War   For two years the Axis scored one victory after another. Having carefully prepared the invasion, Germany attacked Poland with overwhelming force in September 1939, the first **blitzkrieg,** or "lightning war." Poland fell in less than a month, and Hitler suggested that the war could now end. Few were tempted by his hints of peace. Concerned to strengthen its frontiers against Germany, the Soviet Union attacked Finland in November and met such fierce resistance that the war lasted until the following spring. Having regained boundaries close to those of the last tsars, Russia could afford to wait. The Western powers had been waiting, too. Hitler refrained from attacking along the French border, and the Allied commanders resolved not to risk precious planes too soon or to repeat the pointless assaults of World War I. This was the period of the so-called phony war, during which arms production and mobilization speeded up, the world waited, and little happened. The strain was bad for morale.

With the Soviet Union standing aside from the conflict, French communists now attacked the war as a pointless imperialist conflict; their party was suppressed. Paul Reynaud, energetic and determined, replaced Daladier as premier, and the Allies prepared to defend Norway, an obvious German target. But on April 9, 1940, Germany attacked Denmark, taking it in a day, and captured Norway's most important strategic points in short order, giving Germany bases for numerous assaults on British ships. In Britain, Chamberlain resigned after a wide-ranging and often angry parliamentary debate, and Winston Churchill became prime minister of an all-party government on the day that the Germans attacked on the Western front. A Conservative who believed in empire and an opponent of appeasement, Churchill was a political maverick given his chance in the face of disaster. His decisiveness and eloquence made him one of England's greatest leaders.

The Fall of France   On May 10, and without warning, German troops flooded the Netherlands and Belgium. The Dutch, who had expected to escape this war as they had all others since the Napoleonic wars, surrendered in five days. The better-prepared and larger Belgian army held out for eighteen days. On May 14 a skillfully executed German offensive broke through the Ardennes forest, thought to be impervious to tanks, reached Sedan, and drove to the English Channel, trapping the British forces fighting there along with much of the French army. The German air force, the Luftwaffe, controlled the skies, and the Allies' proudest achievement in the battle for France was the evacuation from the port town of Dunkirk of 340,000 troops pinned against the sea. They left for Britain in a motley flotilla of naval vessels, commercial ferries, and private craft. With deft propaganda the British government

French refugees with all the possessions they can carry clog the roads, expecting to be able to escape the German armies in 1940 as their parents had twenty-five years before.
Roger-Viollet/Getty Images

turned this military debacle into a symbol of grit and heroism.

With the British evacuation the Allied defense of France collapsed. German forces renewed the attack on June 5 and took Paris in a week. Anxious lest he miss the war entirely, Mussolini attacked France on June 10. France surrendered on June 16, 1940. The armistice was signed in the railway car used for Germany's surrender in 1918. More ironic still, the man who chose to sign for France was the World War I hero of Verdun, Marshal Henri Philippe Pétain.

Germany's Victory over France   Hitler seemed invincible and the blitzkrieg some terrible new Teutonic force, a totalitarian achievement other societies could not hope to equal. In fact, however, many of the tactical ideas on which it rested were first put forward by British and French experts, including a French officer, Charles de Gaulle. The blitzkrieg was the result not so much of new technology as new strategy. It combined air attacks with rapid movements of motorized columns to overcome the advantages that defensive positions had previously enjoyed. Massed tanks roared through and behind enemy lines, a maneuver requiring speed and precision that were alien to older theories. In the flat terrain of Poland, Germany's panzer tank divisions quickly encircled the enemy; in France, they often assaulted troops so far in the rear that they were not yet prepared for battle. The aim was less to capture ground than to break up communications. Then the Germans used air power to disorient and terrify the retreating army. The strafing of French roads clogged with civilian refugees and the bombing of Rotterdam had their place in the campaign to demoralize.

French strategy had relied too much on the defensive strength of the Maginot Line, a system of fortifications extending from the Belgian border to Switzerland, and on the assumption that Germany would respect the neutrality of Belgium and the Netherlands. The French had numerous tanks of their own but had been slow to deploy them; their air force was momentarily weakened because it was changing models. During the phony war, morale sagged with memories of the previous war and policy was undermined by politics rife with suspicion of the British, of the army, of the politicians, and of the left. Pétain, who believed France must now make its way in Hitler's Europe, blamed the Third Republic, and for a moment the nation turned to the octogenarian marshal with stunned accord.

He accepted terms of surrender that put three-fifths of the country under Nazi occupation and allowed 1.5 million French prisoners of war to be kept in Germany. The unoccupied southeastern part of France could have its own government, and that was established at Vichy. There, a reconvened parliament maneuvered by Pierre Laval named Pétain chief of state. The new regime, known as Vichy France, relied on a confused coalition of militant fascists and the traditional right and would never really be independent of Germany. After adopting bits of corporatism and some fascist trappings, it settled into a lethargy of its own, an often willing collaborator in Hitler's new order, ruling a truncated state as rife with intrigue and personal ambition as the Third Republic it so heartily denounced.

The Battle of Britain Great Britain now stood alone. Unprepared for such enormous victories so soon, German officers planned their invasion of Britain while, beginning in June 1940, their bombers roared over England in sustained attacks that many believed would be enough to force surrender. Instead, in September the projected invasion was postponed, while the air attacks continued. The German navy had suffered enough damage in encounters with the British to favor caution, and by the next spring even the air raids were letting up.

Londoners sheltering in an underground subway station from the lethal destruction and sleep-destroying din of the German "Blitz" in 1940–1941.
© Corbis

The waves of German planes flying across the channel sustained losses far greater than those of Britain's Royal Air Force. British fighter planes, particularly the newer spitfires, proved at least the equal of the German; and they were aided by new techniques of antiaircraft defense, including radar, an English development that was the most critical addition to military technology in these years. At first the air raids concentrated on ports and on airfields, their aim being to destroy the fighter planes that could deter any invasion force. In September Hitler unwisely changed tactics and directed his bombers to British cities in the hope of wrecking industrial production and demoralizing the population. This left great burning holes in London and completely destroyed the industrial city of Coventry. But the diversity of targets dissipated the economic and military effects of the bombing, and the terror from the skies seemed to raise morale in a nation ever better organized and more fiercely determined to carry on. Merely to survive from June 1940 to June 1941 was a kind of victory in what Churchill memorably called Britain's "finest hour."

The Balkans With all the Continent from Norway to Sicily and the Atlantic in their own hands or under

The invading Germans laid siege to Moscow and Leningrad but finally met unyielding resistance. Soviet troops often engaged the enemy in ferocious close-quarter combat.
The Art Archive

friendly dictators in Spain and Portugal, the Axis powers looked eastward. In October 1940 Italian forces moved from Albania into Greece only to be pushed back, and Hitler had to bail out Mussolini by sending in German troops and further squeezing the Balkan states, which were rapidly losing their independence. In June 1940 the Soviet Union, stretching the terms of its pact with Germany, took Bessarabia from Romania. Hungary and Bulgaria then took some of Romania for themselves, and Hitler announced that he would protect the rest of the country. In fact, all three eastern European nations, already implicated in Hitler's mapmaking, were closely tied to Germany. It was no great step for them to join the Axis, welcome German troops in March 1941, and cooperate with Germany in invading Yugoslavia (which had hesitated too long over whether to join the Axis) and in attacking Greece.

The invasion was launched in April 1941 and swept through both countries within the month. Some Greek and British forces pulled back to Crete, only to be forced out almost immediately by German gliders and paratroops. The Allies retreated to Egypt, where British forces had held off an attack from Italy's neighboring colony of Libya. The Axis now threatened to dominate the Mediterranean, too.

The Invasion of the Soviet Union   Having conquered so much, Hitler decided to complete his domination of the Continent. On June 22 German forces attacked the Soviet Union. The Soviets had long feared such a move, yet they appeared genuinely surprised, at least by the timing and the size of the German invasion. The assault, in three broad sectors, was the largest concentration of military power that had ever been assembled, and once more the blitzkrieg began. Germany's armored divisions ripped through Russian lines and encircled astonishing numbers of troops. It looked to many observers as if the Soviet Union might collapse. Stalin, apparently in a state of shock, was silent for the first week after German forces invaded the Soviet Union. Finally, on July 3, 1941, he spoke by radio to the Soviet people. His address acknowledged initial defeats, invoked the example of Russian victories over invaders in the past, and emphasized that the Allies were fighting together against Nazi tyranny. He also called for ordinary citizens to continue the fight by destroying anything that might be helpful to the invaders (known as the "scorched earth" policy) and by constant sabotage.

German armies crossed the lands Russia had acquired since 1939, taking Riga and Smolensk in July, reaching the Dnieper in August, claiming Kiev and the whole Ukraine in September. Then the pace slowed, but while one German force lay siege to Leningrad in the north, a second hit Sevastopol in the south and moved into the Crimea. By December still another had penetrated to the suburbs of Moscow. There the German advance stopped temporarily, halted by an early and severe winter, by strained supply lines, and (at last) by sharp Russian counterattacks. The territory now held by Germany had accounted for nearly two-thirds of Russia's production of coal, iron, steel, and aluminum, as well as 40 percent of its grain and hogs.

MAP 28.2 THE HEIGHT OF AXIS POWER, 1942
After the sweeping Axis conquests depicted in this map, the Battle of Britain (the struggle for supremacy in the air) thwarted Hitler's next invasion plan. But in actually turning the tide, how crucial do you suppose were the battles of El Alamein in North Africa and Stalingrad in Russia?

As the war engulfed all of Europe,[1] German power at the end of 1941 was at its height, encompassing between 7 and 10 million soldiers, a superb air force, and a navy that included more than 150 submarines, which would sink nearly 400 Allied ships in the summer of 1942. Italy added sizable forces that were especially important in Africa. And yet Axis dominance proved short-lived.

[1] Only Sweden, Spain, Portugal, Switzerland, and Eire remained even technically neutral by grace of geography.

THE GLOBAL WAR, 1942–1945

From the 1930s on, the fascist powers had held the initiative in politics, international relations, and war. Germany's invasion of the Soviet Union extended the war across Europe and the British retreat carried it to North Africa. Japan's attack on the United States in 1941 continued the pattern of Axis surprises, but it also marked the beginning of a significant change. War in the Pacific made this a truly global war—involving Asia, the Middle East, and North Africa—and the addition of American power helped tip the balance toward the Allies, whose industrial capacity was far greater than their enemies'. Axis propaganda was losing effect in the face of the brutal realities of German rule, which gave weight to Allied claims that they were fighting for civilization as Russia, America, and the British Empire set out to liberate Europe.

The Turn of the Tide

The United States Enters the War Despite its deep partisanship for France and Britain, the United States remained technically at peace, even as the American government sold weapons to private firms for transfer to Great Britain and traded fifty old American destroyers for the lease of British bases in the western Atlantic. The United States, which Roosevelt called "the arsenal of democracy," extended loans to Britain and then the Soviet Union, budgeted billions for its own rearmament, and introduced its first peace-time draft. But isolationist sentiment prevented Roosevelt from going any further with direct military intervention against the Nazis. In August, Churchill and Roosevelt met at sea to draft the Atlantic Charter, which envisioned a world "after the destruction of the Nazi tyranny" that included collective security and self-determination for all nations, a world in which "all the men of all the lands may live out their lives in freedom from fear and want."

Ideological commitment, however, did not bring the United States into the war. Japan did that. Its attack on Manchuria in 1931 had been followed by a series of aggressive actions, from war with China starting in 1937 to the conquest of French Indochina in 1941. Tension between the United States and Japan increased with each new act of Japanese aggression, and America replied to the assault on Indochina with sanctions. Anticipating more, Japan gambled that the United States could be rendered nearly harmless in one blow, an attack on the American Pacific fleet at Pearl Harbor. The raid, on December 7, was devastating, and the United States declared it an act of war. All sides immediately recognized that the wars in Asia, Europe, and North Africa were one. Germany and Italy declared war on the United States three days later. Unless the Allies were driven from the seas, the industrial and military power of the United States might make a decisive difference in a war fought around the world.

Stalingrad Winter snows raised the specter of a continuing two-front war for Germany, which Hitler had sworn to avoid. For all its losses, Russia's Red Army was intact, and its scorched-earth policy in retreat left the German army little to live on. To secure its massive victories, Germany had to knock Russia out of the

CHRONOLOGY
Major Moments of World War II

March 1938	*Anschluss:* Germany annexes Austria.
September 1938	Munich Agreement, Germany takes Sudetenland.
August 1939	Hitler-Stalin Pact.
September 1939	Germany invades Poland; beginning of World War II.
April 1940	Germany invades Denmark, Norway.
May 1940	Germany invades Belgium, Netherlands, France.
June 1940	France surrenders.
October 1940	Italy invades Albania and Greece.
April 1941	Romania, Bulgaria, Hungary, and Germany invade Yugoslavia.
June 1941	Germany invades the USSR.
August 1941	Atlantic Charter.
December 1941	Japan attacks Pearl Harbor.
August 1942– February 1943	Battle of Stalingrad.
November 1942	Allies land in North Africa.
July 1943	Allies land in Sicily; Mussolini ousted.
November– December 1943	Teheran Conference.
June 1944	Allies land in Normandy.
February 1945	Yalta Conference.
May 1945	Germany surrenders.
July–August 1945	Potsdam Conference.
August 1945	U.S. drops atomic bombs and Japan surrenders.

war. But the siege of Leningrad, the attacks on Moscow, and even a drive into southern Russia in the summer of 1942 that took Sevastopol (and desperately needed grain) did not accomplish that goal. The crucial battle of the eastern front began around **Stalingrad** (now Volgograd) in August 1942. A breakthrough for the Germans at that strategic center would open the way to the oilfields of southern Russia.

By September the Germans had penetrated the city and fighting continued from building to building. The heroic defense gave Russia time to amass more troops than the Germans thought were available, and in the meantime Germany's supplies dwindled. A Russian counterattack encircled the German army, which Hitler frantically ordered to stand its ground. When it finally surrendered, in February 1943, fewer than one-third of its 300,000 men were left. The giant Russian pincers had cost the Germans more than half a million casualties. Stalingrad was the turning point of the war on the eastern front.

Strategic Bombing and the Invasion of North Africa

In the West, too, the Axis position was eroding. The losses that German submarines inflicted were less crippling after 1942, and Allied air supremacy extended to the Continent, where thousands of tons of explosives were dropped on Germany each month in 1942, a rate that would increase fivefold in 1943. The Americans bombed strategic targets during the day; the British preferred nighttime area bombing, with a city itself as the target. The inferno created by the firebombing of Hamburg in 1943 was a horror to be exceeded two years later in a yet more massive raid that leveled Dresden, a cultural center without important industry. Meanwhile, the Germans were unaware that the secret codes they believed unbreakable had been cracked in London as early as 1940, giving the Allies an advantage that would grow as the war progressed.[2]

The Allies also regained control of the Mediterranean. Fighting had spread to Libya as soon as Italy entered the war, and battle lines then ebbed and flowed as each side balanced military needs elsewhere against the chance for victory in North Africa. In April 1941 Germany sent significant reinforcements, and General Erwin Rommel, the German "desert fox," began a drive toward the Egyptian border. In October 1942 his *Afrikakorps* reached El Alamein but was defeated there, allowing Britain's General Bernard Montgomery to launch a counteroffensive as British and American forces landed in Morocco and Algeria. That November invasion, the largest amphibious action yet attempted, and the campaign that followed was an important test of green American troops and of Allied coordination under an American commander, General Dwight D. Eisenhower. It succeeded. By May 1943, after heavy losses, the Axis powers had been pushed out of Africa.

---

[2] The code was cracked in a project named Ultra, using devices that foreshadowed the computer. The secret of Ultra was not revealed until long after the war, and historians are still assessing its impact. The information that the Allies gained through Ultra appears to have been especially important in the Battle of Britain, the protection of Atlantic shipping, later in the war in Egypt, and in the Normandy landing.

Halting the Japanese Advance in the Pacific

After costly stands at Bataan and Corregidor, the United States lost the Philippine Islands early in 1942. By March, the Japanese had conquered Malaya and the Dutch East Indies (today's Indonesia), defeating the British and the Dutch in costly naval and land battles. The fall of Singapore, Britain's Pacific naval bastion, was a crippling blow and a momentous symbolic marker in the fading of British imperial power. The rest of the war against Japan would be fought primarily by Australia and the United States. Stopping further Japanese expansion in the summer of 1942 was thus an important turning point. Although a naval engagement in the Coral Sea in May brought no clear-cut victory to either side, the United States was better able than Japan to replace its losses. A month later the Japanese suffered heavy losses of aircraft carriers at Midway in a naval battle they had sought.

In August American forces launched a relatively small invasion of their own in the Solomon Islands. Each side poured in reinforcements, and the ferocious fighting on Guadalcanal continued for six months before the Japanese were defeated. The war was far from won, but these victories ended the threat that Japan might invade Australia or cut off supply lines from India to the Middle East. The Allies could feel comfortable with their agreement that the war in Europe should have priority—an acknowledgement of fear that the Soviet Union might not survive without massive help, of the importance of European industrial power, and of the bonds of Western culture.

Competing Political Systems

War on this scale required the coordination of entire economies and cooperation from every sector of society. After their slow start, Britain and the United States achieved that with impressive effect. The Soviet Union proved far stronger than expected, and Germany, the state that in theory was most devoted to militarism, managed in practice less well than its enemies.

The Allied Effort at Home

As bombs rained down on Britain, support for the war effort was nearly unanimous. Civilians accepted sacrifice and welcomed the end of unemployment. One-third of all males between 14 and 64 were in uniform, and unmarried women were mobilized. More women were employed in industry than ever before in both Britain and the United States. Labor unions signed a no-strike pledge, as they did in the United States. With tight rationing and government control of the economy, no society mobilized more thoroughly. Civilians accepted blackouts and suffered air raids and the temporary evacuation of 3.5 million women and children to the safer countryside. Even with that effort and that bravery, Britain increasingly depended on American aid. With its economic resources fully mobilized, the United States by the end of 1942 produced more war matériel than all its enemies combined. Ships, planes, tanks, arms, and munitions from American factories and food from American farms flowed across the oceans to Britain and the Soviet Union.

Even before 1939 Stalin had adopted the policy of industrializing the more backward regions east of the Urals, a safe distance from Russia's western border, and in the months preceding Hitler's attack in 1941 hundreds of factories were moved there piece by piece. Despite its enormous losses of productive capacity, the Soviet Union throughout the war produced most of the military supplies it needed. Central planning, rationing, military discipline, and the employment of women were not such a dramatic change in this communist regime, but the increased hours of labor, the destruction of homes, the death of loved ones, and the loss of

men and territory required patriotism of a rather old-fashioned sort. Patriotism became the dominant theme of Soviet public life.

Nazi Rule Until 1943 German civilians did not experience hardships comparable to the sacrifices of the Soviets or the lowered standard of living of the British. Nor was German output much greater than at the war's outset. The illusion, fed by military success and propaganda, that the war would soon be over encouraged interim measures. Competing elements of the Nazi party worked at cross purposes with each other and the government. Mutual distrust made it difficult for the Nazis to cooperate consistently with science and industry. Only when Albert Speer was given increased powers over the economy did coordination improve. In mid-July 1943 German production doubled from what it had been in 1939, despite Allied bombing. A year later it was three times the prewar level.

The laborers' barracks at Buchenwald at the end of the war.
Bettmann/Corbis

A Gas Chamber

At a meeting of high Nazi officials on January 20, 1942, Reinard Heydrich, Plenipotentiary for the Preparation of the Final Solution of the European Jewish Question, spoke proudly of the liquidation of the Jews already accomplished and of the concentration camps already established but called for a further step. "We have the means, the methods, the organization, experience, and people. And we have the will. This is a historic moment in the struggle against Jewry. The Führer has declared his determination. . . [and sees destruction of the Jews] as exterminating fatal bacteria to save the organism. . . . We will work effectively but silently." (Heydrich was later assassinated by the Czech resistance in Prague.) Nazi extermination camps indeed followed strikingly similar procedures, and the following description of the Birkenau camp is typical of hundreds of survivors' testimonies. It was written by a French doctor, André Lettich, who was a member of the "special commando" squad, whose job it was to empty the crematoria of corpses and make them ready for the next round.

"Until the end of January 1943, there were no crematoria in Birkenau. In the middle of a small birch forest, about two kilometres from the camp, was a peaceful looking house, where a Polish family had once lived before it had been either murdered or expelled. This cottage had been equipped as a gas chamber for a long time.

"More than five hundred metres further on were two barracks: the men stood on one side, the women on the other. They were addressed in a very polite and friendly way: 'You have been on a journey. You are dirty. You will take a bath. Get undressed quickly.' Towels and soap were handed out, and then suddenly the brutes woke up and showed their true faces: this horde of people, these men and women were driven outside with hard blows and forced both summer and winter to go the few hundred metres to the 'Shower Room.' Above the entry door was the word 'Shower.' One could even see shower heads on the ceiling which were cemented in but never had water flowing through them.

"These poor innocents were crammed together, pressed against each other. Then panic broke out, for at last they realised the fate in store for them. But blows with rifle butts and revolver shots soon restored order and finally they all entered the death chamber. The doors were shut and, ten minutes later, the temperature was high enough to facilitate the condensation of the hydrogen cyanide, for the condemned were gassed with hydrogen cyanide. This was the so-called 'Zyklon B,' gravel pellets saturated with twenty per cent of hydrogen cyanide which was used by the German barbarians.

"Then, *SS Unterscharführer* Moll threw the gas in through a little vent. One could hear fearful screams, but a few moments later there was complete silence. Twenty to twenty-five minutes later, the doors and windows were opened to ventilate the rooms and the corpses were thrown at once into pits to be burnt. But, beforehand the dentists had searched every mouth to pull out the gold teeth. The women were also searched to see if they had not hidden jewelry in the intimate parts of their bodies, and their hair was cut off and methodically placed in sacks for industrial purposes."

From J. Noakes and G. Pridham (eds.), *Nazism, 1919–1945: A Documentary Reader*, Vol. 3: *Foreign Policy, War, and Racial Extermination*, University of Exeter Press.

Germany certainly benefited from its vast gains of territory rich in resources, industry, and personnel, but the Nazis alienated those they conquered with their labor conscription, racial policies, and oppressive brutality. A high percentage of Ukrainians, for example, had welcomed liberation from Russian rule, but brief acquaintance with Nazi treatment of the "racially inferior" Slavs discouraged their cooperation. Nazi rule was most severe and most destructive in eastern Europe and less harsh among the "Aryan" populations of the Nordic lands. But even in France, food rations provided only about half the minimum that decent health requires. Germany's most crucial need was for workers, and slave labor was an answer in accord with Nazi racial theory. Eventually some 5 million Slavs were shipped like cattle to labor in Germany. By 1944 the 8 million foreign workers in Germany constituted one-fifth of the workforce.

Genocide   The hysteria of racial hatred got the better of rational planning. Brutalized and starving workers could hardly be efficient. Transporting and guarding slave laborers became an enormous, corrupting, and expensive enterprise. Many millions of people died in forced labor, and perhaps 3 million Soviet prisoners of war were massacred or starved to death. These deaths, evidence of massive brutality and consonant with Nazi ideas about inferior races, were echoed in the German practice of killing large numbers of civilian hostages in occupied lands as a means of demoralizing resistance. Hounding Jews, cramming them into concentration camps, and killing them had less to do with the brutality of war than with the implementation of Nazi racial theory. Throughout the fall of 1941, mobile SS squads executed Jews who had been rounded up on the eastern front. Men and women, old and young, were lined up, made to undress, and marched toward ditches to be shot by the SS (one squad reported having killed more than 200,000 people). The orders, equipment, and reports this slaughter required establish that many people had to have known about it.

The Holocaust In January 1942, at a secret meeting of high officials held just outside Berlin, it was agreed that the systematic and efficient extermination of Jews should be made a general policy, "the **final solution** of the Jewish question" (see "A Gas Chamber," p. 865). By 1945, nearly 6 million Jews and as many other people (Poles, Roma, and Magyars especially) had died in

concentration camps like Buchenwald and Dachau and the more recently constructed death camps like Auschwitz and Treblinka. Some of these camps were also supposed to be centers of production: A Krupp arms factory, an I. G. Farben chemical plant, and a coal mine were part of the Auschwitz complex. But the chief product of Auschwitz was corpses, at a rate that reached twelve thousand a day.

The extermination camps remain the ultimate nightmare of modern history. Beating and torturing prisoners of war was not new, though rarely so common as under the Nazis, but the industrial organization of death in Nazi camps raises terrifying questions about modern civilization. Hundreds of thousands of people were involved in operating those camps and in rounding up men, women, and children to be shipped to them. At first, the victims were primarily Slavs and

The scene that greeted the Allies on entering Lansberg concentration camp. American forces required several hundred German civilians in the area to come look at it as well.
Bettmann/Corbis

HISTORICAL ISSUES: THE HISTORIANS' DEBATE ON GERMAN GENOCIDE

Over the past decades historians of Germany, particularly in Germany itself, have sustained a heated debate about the ways of understanding Nazi genocide. Among the issues in this debate, are the role of racial theories, the example of the Soviet Union, and whether genocide had distinctly German roots. The citations here, from three well-known scholars, illustrate these positions.

HENRY FRIEDLANDER

"Historians investigating Nazi genocide have long debated who gave the order to commit mass murder, when it was issued, and how it was transmitted. Although the specific mechanism has been a matter of contention between rival groups of historians . . . , there now appears to be a general agreement that Hitler had a deciding voice, although no one has ever discovered, or is likely to discover, a smoking gun. Recently historians have focused on the specific dates when the idea to launch the physical annihilation of the European Jews was first advanced and when the decision to do so became irrevocable. . . . My own approach is somewhat different. I am not particularly interested in exact dates. Instead, I want to trace the sequential development of mass murder.

"I define Nazi genocide, what is now commonly called the Holocaust, as the mass murder of human beings because they belonged to a biologically defined group. Heredity determined the selection of victims. Although the regime persecuted and often killed men and women for their politics, nationality, religion, behavior, or activities, the Nazis applied a consistent and inclusive policy of extermination only against three groups of human beings: the handicapped, Jews, and Gypsies (Roma).

"The attack on these targeted groups drew on more than fifty years of political and scientific arguments hostile to the belief in the equality of man. Since the turn of the century, the German elite, that is the members of the educated professional classes, had increasingly accepted an ideology based on human inequality. Geneticists, anthropologists, and psychiatrists had advanced a theory of human heredity that had merged with the racist doctrine of *völkisch* nationalists to form a political ideology of a nation based on race. The Nazi movement both absorbed and advanced this ideology. After 1933 they created the political framework that made it possible to translate this ideology of inequality into a policy of exclusion, while the German bureaucratic, professional, and scientific elite provided the legitimacy the regime needed for the smooth implementation of this policy."

From Henry Friedlander, "Step by Step: The Expansion of Murder, 1939–1941," *German Studies Review* 17, October 1994.

ERNST NOLTE

"Auschwitz is not primarily a result of traditional anti-Semitism and was not, in its essential core, mere 'genocide';

rather, it was, above all, a reaction—born out of anxiety—to the annihilations which occurred during the Russian Revolution. This copy was far more irrational than the earlier original (because it was simply an absurd notion to imagine that 'the Jews' had ever wished to annihilate the German bourgeoisie or even the German people), and it is difficult to attribute to it even a perverted ethos. It was more horrifying than the original because it carried out the annihilation of human beings in a quasi-industrial manner. It was more repulsive than the original because it was based on mere suppositions, and was almost completely free of that mass hatred which, within the midst of horror, remains nonetheless an understandable—and thus, to a limited extent, reconciling—element. All this supports the notion of singularity, yet does not alter the fact that the so-called annihilation of the Jews during the Third Reich was a reaction or a distorted copy—and not a first act, not the original."

From Ernst Nolte, "Between Historical Myth and Revisionism," *Yad Vashem Studies* 19, 1988.

HANS-ULRICH WEHLER

"Nolte's thesis concerning the fatal consequences of the Bolsheviks' anxiety-producing class warfare is directed above all against a well-grounded interpretation: that Hitler and National Socialism were products of German and Austrian history. Only after factors rooted in that past have been assessed should the broader European context be considered. Nolte has sought to undermine this hard-won insight by displacing the 'primary historical guilt' onto Marx, the Russian Revolution, and the extermination policy of the Bolsheviks. I shall emphasize below the main points of the opposing view—a view that is better grounded empirically and more convincing in its interpretive approach than Nolte's theory:

"—Hitler and countless other National Socialists had internalized a fanatical anti-Marxism long before the First World War: that is, before the Russian Revolution, the civil war, and class warfare in the new Soviet Union could confirm and strengthen their hatred of the 'Reds.'

"—Social Darwinism in its vulgar (racist) form was one of the strongest forces driving the highly ideological 'worldview' of Hitler and many other Nazis well before 1917. Contemporary developments thereafter only served as confirmation to these confused minds.

continued

"—The poisonous morass of German and Austrian anti-Semitism was the source of the crazed ideas associated with the Nazi hatred of the Jews. The new racist, political anti-Semitism that flourished in the late 1870s quickly led to the explicit idea of extermination. For example, in its Hamburg resolutions of September 1899, the German Social Reform Party claimed publicly and without any embarrassment that 'in the course of the twentieth century, the Jewish question must be solved . . . once and for all by the complete separation and (if necessary for defensive purposes) the definitive extermination of the Jewish people.' What was new in the 1930s was 'only' that Hitler and his cohorts took this program literally—and brought with them the will to carry out the deed itself.

"—The Nazis effortlessly adopted the widespread, fully developed antidemocratic, antiliberal, and antiparliamentary political ideology that had already been fully developed by the German Right before 1917/18.

"—The Nazis were able to exploit the deeply corrosive anticapitalist resentments of the Protestant, provincial bourgeoisie and of peasant society. They were also able to counter the difficult conflicts of a modern class society with the hypertrophied idealization of an oft-evoked *Volksgemeinschaft* (national community).

"—National Socialism benefitted from long-term conditions in Germany: the antagonisms of Germany's social structure, an authoritarian mentality, the peculiarities of Prussian militarism, the Protestant subservience to the state, the national susceptibility to charismatic leaders, a particular kind of political philosophy, etc. Hitler's regime also profited from more recent conditions that stemmed from the experiences of the period 1914–33. Among these were 'the experience of war,' 'the nation in arms,' the 'total war' of 1916–18, the beginning of the defeat, the renunciation of all war aims, the stab-in-the-back myth, the 'disgraceful peace' at Versailles, the war reparations and postwar hyperinflation, and the destructive force of the Depression. These events belong to a long list of favorable factors with fatal consequences.

"Above all, the traditions and burdens of Germany's past influenced the course of National Socialism. Only after these have been identified should historians proceed to analyze the influence of the wider European and world-historical context."

From Hans-Ulrich Wehler, "Unburdening the German Past? A Preliminary Assessment," in Peter Baldwin (ed.), *Reworking the Past: Hitler, the Holocaust, and the Historians' Debate,* Beacon Press, 1990.

Jews from the conquered lands of eastern Europe; then Jews from western Europe were hunted down and added to the flow. They came by trainload, crammed into boxcars, hungry, thirsty, frightened, and confused. Upon arrival at the camps, the weakest and least "useful" (the ill, the elderly, children, and often women) were sent immediately to showers that proved to be gas chambers. The others were given uniforms, often with patches that distinguished into neat categories the common criminals, political prisoners, homosexuals, communists, Jehovah's Witnesses, Slavs, and Jews, their identities transformed into serial numbers tattooed on their arms. Many were literally worked to death or were killed when they could work no longer. The prisoners themselves, reduced to blind survival, were caught up in this dehumanized world of beatings, limited rations, constant abuse, and contempt. Neither submission nor animal cunning guaranteed another day of life. Many inmates nevertheless managed haunting gestures of human feeling through a story told, a song sung, a bit of food shared.

German clerks and bureaucrats kept elaborate records of names, stolen possessions, and corpses, which were efficiently stripped of gold fillings and useful hair before being turned to ashes in crematoria. Doctors invented new tortures under the guise of medical experiments to benefit the Aryan race. The sadistic pseudoscience

of these doctors elaborated on the paranoid dream of purifying the Aryan race. Forced sterilization and euthanasia of the chronically ill, the physically handicapped, and the mentally retarded had been advocated and practiced by Nazis since they first came to power in Germany. In *Mein Kampf* Hitler had referred to Jews as a plague and like a bacillus weakening the Aryan race. Racial laws had extended that point to all aspects of social life, and brutal treatment helped to make prisoners seem inferior, even subhuman. Organized killing carried this denial of humanity one step further.

Yet even the SS guards—like the camp commandants, the people who arranged for trains, and the business people who bid for contracts to build gas chambers—employed euphemisms rather than acknowledge what was really happening. The residents of nearby towns rarely discussed what was carried in the trains rumbling by or asked about the odor that settled over the countryside from crematoria smokestacks. Nor did the Allies quite believe or choose to act on the stories that filtered out of occupied Europe about atrocities on a scale too terrible to comprehend.

Resistance Movements   Millions of Europeans came to rely on the British Broadcasting Corporation for news and for encouragement in occupied lands, where every act of opposition—a speech not applauded, a whispered joke—took on symbolic significance. Gradually, against great odds, organized resistance movements formed. Some developed around neighborhood groups; some were connected to prewar political parties. Always composed of a small minority, these partisan movements achieved particular strength in Denmark and Norway, the Netherlands, France, and Yugoslavia. Many of them received material aid and guidance from exiles operating from London, the most notable being the Free French, headed by General de Gaulle.

Nazi reprisals for acts of resistance were meant to be horrible. When Czechs assassinated their new Nazi governor, Reinard Heydrich, in June 1942, the Germans retaliated by wiping out the village of Lidice, which they suspected of hiding the murderers: Every man was killed; every woman and child deported. On a single day in 1943, the Germans put 1,400 men to death in a Greek village. Hundreds of towns across occupied Europe have their memorials, a burned-out building or a ditch where clusters of civilians were massacred.

Yet the underground movements continued to grow, and their actions became a barometer of the course of the war. In France, partisan activities expanded from single exploits—smuggling Allied airmen out of the country, dynamiting a bridge, or attacking individual German officers—to large-scale intelligence and propaganda operations coordinated from London. Norway's resistance helped force the Germans to keep 300,000 troops there and away from more active fronts. In Yugoslavia, two groups of partisans maintained an active guerrilla war, although the British decision to support the group led by the communist Tito all but ensured his control of the country at the end of the war. After the Allied invasion of Italy, partisan groups there maintained an unnerving harassment of Fascist and Nazi forces. Even in Germany itself, a group of army officers began to plot against Hitler. In July 1944 a group of conspirators planted a bomb under the table as the Führer conducted a conference with his staff. Hitler escaped serious injury, but the sense that he was doomed had spread to the heart of Germany.

These partisan movements were important for more than their immediate contribution to the war. The memory of their bravery partially eased the painful reality of defeat, and in countries like France, Italy, and Norway, where many had acquiesced in fascist regimes, the militant opposition of the resistance could be taken to express the real will of the people. In fact, many of the major political parties of the postwar era were formed in the resistance, and the ideas of democracy, freedom, and equality that circulated so passionately then would be repeated in constitutions and party platforms later. Most resistance fighters were young men, but many women, too, experienced the camaraderie of activism as secret couriers, provisioners, and occasionally group commanders. By joining in the resistance, women were being drawn into the rudimentary renewal of national political life.

Allied Strategy

By 1943 the Axis was on the defensive although it had the advantage of shorter, direct lines of supply. While Hitler continued to imagine that some daring thrust or miracle weapon would bring him victory, the Allies continued to disagree as to how they should attack Hitler's "fortress Europe."

A Second Front The Soviet Union had repeatedly urged opening a **second front** on the Continent, and most of the American military command favored an immediate invasion. The British warned against the high cost of such an expedition, and, with Roosevelt's support, Churchill prevailed. The Allies invaded North Africa instead, ending the threat to Egypt. When that was not followed by landings on the Continent, the Soviets suspected that they and the Germans were being left to annihilate each other. The Americans continued to favor an invasion of occupied France, but the British argued for tightening the blockade of Germany and for making more limited assaults in the eastern Mediterranean and southern Europe, on what Churchill called the "soft underbelly."

More than military strategy was at stake. The Allies had not been specific about their long-range goals, and were divided. Stalin looked forward to regaining the Polish territory lost in 1939 (Poland could be compensated with territory taken from a defeated Germany). The British recalled the earlier communist aim of revolution across the Continent. The British hoped to place Anglo-American troops in such a way that, after the war, they could have a voice in the disposition of eastern Europe. In London the exiled leaders of the eastern European countries agitated for their own nationalist goals, alarmed by Stalin's references to the need for "friendly" governments along Russia's borders.

With such issues before them, Roosevelt and Churchill met at Casablanca in January 1943. There they decided (to the Soviets' disgust) to invade Sicily and agreed to demand the unconditional surrender of Italy, Germany, and Japan, an expression of moral outrage against fascism that was also meant to prevent the Soviet Union and the Western Allies from making any separate deals with the enemy. Welcomed by Allied public opinion at the time, the refusal to negotiate with the Axis was subsequently criticized for strengthening their desperate defense after defeat was inevitable.

The Invasion of Italy In July a mammoth amphibious assault carried Anglo-American forces into Sicily. A victim of his own propaganda, Mussolini had consistently overestimated Italian strength. As the invaders advanced, the Fascist Grand Council in a secret session voted Mussolini out of office. The Duce was arrested, and Marshal Pietro Badoglio was named prime minister. A coalition of monarchists and moderate Fascists then sought an armistice. But Committees of National Liberation had sprung up throughout Italy. Composed of anti-Fascists from liberals to communists, these Committees wanted nothing to do with Badoglio, a Fascist hero of the campaign in Ethiopia, or with the king, who had bowed to Mussolini for twenty years.

In September Allied forces in Sicily invaded southern Italy, where they were well dug in by the end of the month. The German army, however, had snatched control of the rest of the peninsula. Although the Allies captured Naples in October, their campaign in Italy soon bogged down in difficult terrain and in the face of fierce German resistance. In a daring rescue, German paratroops snatched Mussolini from his mountaintop prison and took him to northern Italy, where he proclaimed a Fascist republic that was blatantly a German puppet. At the same time, Italy's anti-Fascist partisans were becoming increasingly effective. Italians, their country a battleground for foreign armies, were caught in civil war.

The Free French Italy was not the first place in which the Allies indicated they might compromise with tainted regimes. At the moment of the North African invasion (November 1942), Admiral Jean François Darlan, a former vice premier of Vichy France and commander of its armed forces, happened to be in Algiers. Eisenhower's staff quickly agreed to make him governor-general of French Africa provided his forces would not resist the Allied invasion. De Gaulle was outraged. He had claimed to represent a Free France since his first call for continued resistance in 1940 when, from London, he organized French forces fighting with the Allies. His outsized ego, his insistence on a voice in Allied policy, and his success in winning support in the French colonies had made his relations with Britain and the United States difficult at best. The assassination of Darlan in December 1942 eased the situation, and Germany's decision to occupy all of France in response to the Allied invasion of North Africa reduced de Gaulle's fears that the Allies might choose to deal with the Vichy regime.

The Teheran Conference Finally, at the end of November 1943, Roosevelt, Churchill, and Stalin met for the first time, at Teheran. The conversations were not easy. Previously, the British had mediated between the United States and the Soviet Union, but now the Americans took a middle position. The Allies reached a tentative understanding that the Soviet Union would accept a border with Poland similar to the one proposed in 1919, and they left open the question of what kind of government a liberated Poland might have. Their unity thus preserved by postponing the most difficult issues, the Allies could plan vigorous prosecution of the war. Stalin promised to declare war on Japan as soon as

Stalin, Roosevelt, and Churchill, meeting for the first time at Teheran, reached an understanding that laid the groundwork for Allied cooperation in pursuing the war.
Bettmann/Corbis

Germany surrendered, and Churchill's proposal for an invasion of the Dardanelles was rejected. The British and Americans agreed instead to land in France in the following year to open a true second front.

The Road to Victory

The Italian Front   The Allies progressed slowly in Italy, taking five months to fight their way past a costly new beachhead at Anzio. In December 1943, King Victor Emmanuel III announced that he would abdicate in favor of his son, and Badoglio gave way to a cabinet drawn from members of the Committees of National Liberation. Italy then officially joined the Allies. The Germans, however, held the advantage of entrenched positions on one mountain ridge after another. Northern Italy became another German-occupied country in which Jews were rounded up for death camps, and captured Italian soldiers were sent to slave labor in Germany. The Allies slowly pushed northward, aided by partisan risings, while the main forces were held aside for the invasion of France. Only in May 1944 did Anglo-American armies finally seize the old Benedictine abbey of Monte Cassino, north of Naples, after a destructive bombardment. Rome, the first European capital to be liberated, was taken in June.

The Soviet Union   Soviet successes were more spectacular. In the spring of 1943 the Germans could still launch an offensive of their own, but it slowed within weeks. In July the Soviet army began a relentless advance that continued, with few setbacks, for almost two years. With armies now superior in numbers and matériel, Soviet forces reached the Dnieper and Kiev by November. In February 1944 they were at the Polish border. They retook the Crimea in the spring, Romania surrendered in August, and Finland and Bulgaria fell a few weeks later. Soviet power loomed over eastern Europe.

The Western Front   For months Germany absorbed constant pounding from the air, and the Germans knew an invasion across the English Channel was imminent. They believed it would come in the area around Calais, the shore closest to England, as a series of calculated feints seemed to indicate. Instead, on June 6, 1944, the Allies landed in Normandy. The largest amphibious landing in history, it put 150,000 men ashore within two days, supported by 5,000 ships and 1,500 tanks. In a complex series of landings, Eisenhower's Allied force poured onto the French beaches. Made possible by overwhelming control of the air and helped by a poorly coordinated German defense, the landings nevertheless suffered heavy losses. Within a few months, more than

This photo conveys a key problem for allied success in the Normandy invasion of June 1944: the need rapidly to deploy huge numbers of men and vast amounts of equipment after the first waves of troops secured the beachhead.
History101.com

a million men disembarked. In July they broke through the German defense and began a series of rapid drives through France. A second amphibious attack, in southern France in mid-August, led to swift advances inland that were greatly aided by well-organized French resistance groups. On August 24 the Parisian underground rose against the Germans, and Free French forces from the Normandy invasion were diverted to Paris to assist the uprising. Brussels fell a week later, and ten days after that, American troops crossed the German frontier.

Germany had launched its "miracle" weapon in June, the relatively ineffective V-1 pilotless plane, which was followed in September by the far more dangerous V-2 rocket. Had the Nazis recognized its potential earlier, the effects might have been devastating. The V-2 flew faster than the speed of sound and was almost impossible to intercept; but these rockets were hard to aim, and too few and too late to be decisive. More threatening was a counterstroke through the Ardennes in December that rocked the Allied line back. The Battle of the Bulge, the last offensive the Germans would mount, cost about 70,000 men on each side before the Allies regained the initiative in January 1945.

The Yalta Conference

When Allied leaders held their last wartime meeting, at Yalta in February 1945, Russian troops occupied part of Czechoslovakia and stood on the German frontier of Poland. The decisions of the Big Three at Yalta, which were widely hailed at the time, later became the most controversial of World War II. The hurried meeting dealt with four broad issues,

each a measure of the Allies' mutual distrust. They agreed to create a United Nations Organization. The Soviet Union asked for sixteen votes, one for each of its republics, to counterbalance the votes of the British Commonwealth and of Latin America, which the United States was expected to dominate. That request was reduced to three, and the Soviet Union got the veto it demanded but with some slight restrictions on its use. The USSR promised to declare war against Japan within ninety days of Germany's defeat in return for the territories Russia had surrendered to Japan in 1905 and for a sphere of influence in Manchuria.

A more contentious issue was the treatment of Germany. Each of the Big Three was assigned a zone of occupation, and Russia reluctantly agreed to the American and British plan to carve a zone for France from the areas under their control. Russia's demands for huge reparations and "labor services" were so troubling that specific terms had to be postponed. The form of Italy's government was in fact now largely set, as was de Gaulle's ascendance in an independent France. The main issue was Soviet dominance in Eastern Europe. The creation of new governments for the liberated nations, the most difficult issue of all, could not be postponed much longer, yet every proposal exposed fundamental differences between the Soviet Union and the Western powers.

In most of the countries they occupied, the Soviets were tolerating broad coalitions that included all the old antifascist parties, but they would not allow a role for the Western powers. When Churchill visited Moscow four months earlier, he had proposed a division of

General de Gaulle leading an informal victory parade down the Champs Elysées right after the liberation of Paris from the Nazis in August 1944. Towering over his compatriots from the resistance, the general was not hard to spot by the enthusiastic crowds.
AP Images

interests: The Soviet Union would have predominance in Romania and the largest influence in Bulgaria, Britain would have a free hand in Greece, and the two powers would recognize their equal interests in Yugoslavia and Hungary. Such crude understandings offered few guarantees, however, though Stalin remained silent when Britain intervened in the civil war raging in Greece in order to rout the leftists.

Stalin in turn exercised a free hand in Poland after the Polish underground rose against the Germans in August 1944. As Soviet troops approached Warsaw, the Russians simply halted their advance until the Germans had wiped out the resistance fighters, who were closely tied to the anticommunist Polish government in London. The Yalta Conference did not in fact adopt cynically drawn spheres of influence, but the conference's formulas, with their vague references to democratic governments and free elections, would in the end be interpreted by those who held the guns.

The Final Months   As the Allies pushed into Germany from all sides, it became clear that Berlin would be the final battleground. Fearing that Hitler planned a last desperate stand at his retreat at Berchtesgaden in the southern German mountains, Eisenhower halted the eastward advance of American and British armies at the Elbe River. The Russians took Berlin, where Hitler had ensured the maximum destruction by ordering a

MAP 28.3 THE ALLIED VICTORY IN WORLD WAR II
Armies of the Western allies converged with the forces of the Soviet Union at the Elbe River in Germany. How does this map help explain the postwar Soviet domination of Eastern Europe?

defense to the death. The Führer committed suicide on April 30, 1945, and his aides burned his body, which has never been found. Four days later a group of German officers signed the final unconditional surrender. The war in Europe was over.

World conflict continued in Asia for four months more. It was expected to last much longer, even with the Russian help that had seemed so necessary when promised at Yalta. Despite massive bombing and repeated naval victories, Allied progress through the islands and jungles of the Pacific toward Japan had been laborious and bloody. Americans conquered Guam, landed in the Philippines, and took Iwo Jima but at great cost. The tactic of landing on some islands while skipping others, often leaving Japanese forces isolated and useless, created bases from which Allied planes threatened the Japanese fleet and the mainland itself. Eventual victory was no longer in doubt. During the three months following Germany's surrender, strategic bombing obliterated Japan's navy, industrial plants, and large parts of its cities. Firebombing killed nearly

200,000 people in Tokyo in just one week. But still the Japanese would not surrender, and estimates of Allied casualties from any invasion of Japan's home islands reached into the hundreds of thousands.

On August 6 the new president of the United States, Harry Truman (Roosevelt had died in April), authorized the use of a new weapon that had been developed after years of secret research, the atomic bomb. In one blow, half of the city of Hiroshima disappeared from the face of the earth. A quarter of its 320,000 inhabitants were killed. On August 9 the Americans dropped an even more powerful atomic bomb on the city of Nagasaki. On August 15 Emperor Hirohito announced that Japan now faced the unthinkable humiliation of defeat, and on September 2, 1945, Japan formally surrendered unconditionally. The atomic bomb, an extraordinary achievement of science and technology made possible by great wealth and scores of European scientists driven to sanctuary in the United States, permitted a great democracy to end World War II by unleashing a new order of terror upon humanity. Later, many people

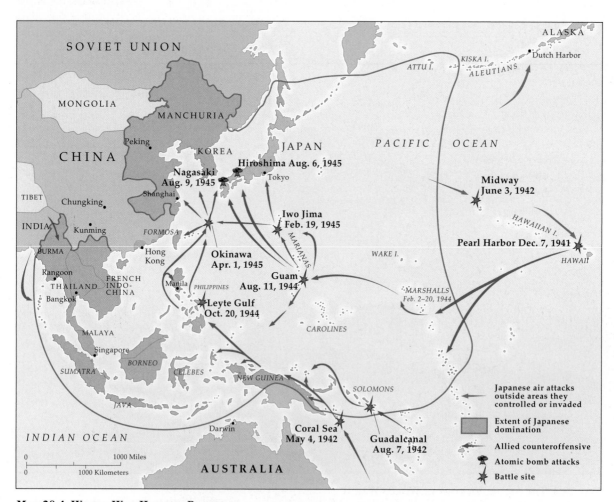

MAP 28.4 WORLD WAR II IN THE PACIFIC
As depicted in this map, what are the stories behind the incredible advance of Japanese power in the Pacific, its subsequent retreat under Allied pressure, and its eventual demise?

would question the morality of using so terrible a weapon. Even in the jubilation of victory, leaders reordering a shattered world now knew that another war might bring the end of civilization.

BUILDING ON THE RUINS

For most Europeans the immediate postwar period brought little improvement in their living conditions, and for years individuals, institutions, and governments struggled with the effects of death, destruction, and the displacement of millions of people. Overcoming such fundamental problems on so vast a scale was the central achievement of the next decade. Euphoria was brief even among the victors and the newly liberated, as people set about their daily tasks in an uncertain world of economic hardship, social dislocation, and political division. As European nations gained in political stability and economic strength, they remained distinctly subordinate to the United States and the Soviet Union in a world divided by the Cold War.

Immediate Crises

The Devastation   In contrast to World War I, a majority of the fatalities in World War II were civilian. About 4 million men died on battlefields; and for every soldier killed, two more were either wounded or taken captive. Civilian losses are harder to categorize, and often there was no one to do the counting. The Germans killed between 12 and 20 million people in occupied countries and concentration camps. Across Europe millions more civilians died just for being where armies chose to bomb or shell or shoot. In all, the European casualties in World War II were five or six times greater than in World War I (only for Britain and France were they lower). The Soviet Union lost some 27 million people; Poland, about 6 million (including 3 million Jews); Germany, nearly 5 million. So the total European casualties of World War II—dead, wounded, or crippled by inhumane treatment—remain an estimate, a number hard to comprehend in its gruesome total or ghostly imprecision: some 45 to 55 million people.

Europe's industrial capability in 1945 was perhaps half what it had been in 1939, and only parts of such major cities as Frankfurt, Dresden, Brest, and Toulon were still standing. The Continent's most important ports, bridges, and rail lines had been all but destroyed. Agriculture was also hard hit. Large areas of farmland in France, Italy, and Germany could not be cultivated; the number of cattle in France had been reduced by half. In the winter of 1945–1946, starvation was a threat in many places, and in some, such as Vienna, thousands died of famine. Disease was an ever-present danger, too, although penicillin helped limit the epidemics that erupted. The rationing of food and clothes (and illegal black markets) continued in many countries into the 1950s, and Europeans looked to the United States and the Soviet Union for relief as Allied troops occupied the Continent.

Refugees   In addition to the millions without jobs or housing, there were more refugees in Europe than ever before in history. Some 8 million slave laborers in the Third Reich and survivors in its concentration camps

Hiroshima, the victim of one of science's great achievements. The world had entered a new era of warfare, and for a generation the Japanese would suffer from the environmental destruction and the effects of radiation.
AP Images

were put on trains headed back to where their homes had been. There were German prisoners of war and Allied prisoners in Germany. More than 7 million Soviet citizens in Germany, including defectors, had no place to go. Some 2 million Poles and Czechs returning from prison in the Soviet Union joined millions of Ukrainians and Poles who moved west to stay on the other side of the shifting border with the USSR. Romanians drove out Hungarians; Czechs expelled Hungarians and Germans. Millions of Germans whom the Nazis had transplanted to Poland in the interests of Germanization were forced to leave, and many of the 1.5 million Poles the Nazis had evicted wanted to go back home. The question of where national boundaries should be drawn, which had so troubled the peacemakers of Versailles, was settled now by first drawing the lines and then pushing inconvenient nationalities across them.

Most of the refugees who carried their few belongings along unfamiliar roads were civilians, perhaps 60 million in all, a majority of them women and children who had lost their homes and livelihood. Separated from kin and possessions, they struggled to survive in strange lands that were impoverished by war. We will never know how many died or were abused or robbed. Governments tried to make nice distinctions between the homeless (those in or near their own country) and displaced persons (who were mostly stateless—some 12 million were so registered in 1945). Abandoned factories and warehouses, even former concentration camps, were used to house refugees, along with specially built crude barracks meant to be temporary. Bit by bit the fortunate were assigned a destination, but "unaccompanied children," the disabled, and the aged were harder to place.

The Terms of Peace: Potsdam No great peace conference took place after World War II. When the leaders of the Soviet Union, Great Britain, and the United States

Citizens of Dresden, nearly a year after the war ended, making their way through the rubble from Allied saturation bombing.
Bettmann/Corbis

met at Potsdam for two weeks in July 1945, they hardly knew each other. President Harry Truman had been in office only three months following the death of Roosevelt, and in the midst of the meeting Clement Attlee replaced Churchill, who had been defeated in the British elections.

The Potsdam meeting outlined the future of Germany but left details for the future. The Allies readily agreed that all Nazi institutions must be abolished, German arms production prohibited, and German industry controlled. Democracy and free speech were to be restored. In the meantime Germany was divided into four zones of occupation, and so was Berlin, isolated in the Soviet zone. Germany's eastern border was moved westward to the Oder and Neisse rivers, enlarging Poland. During the next year, the foreign ministers of the four principal Allies (now including France) drafted treaties for the other defeated states, but their meetings soon became a forum for quarrels between the Soviets and the other three. Italy, Romania, Hungary, Bulgaria, and Finland each ceded minor territories to its neighbors. Austria,

like Germany, remained divided into four occupied zones and without a formal treaty.

The Potsdam Conference had also laid down the terms for peace with Japan. The Soviet Union would get some territory, and the European nations would regain their Asian colonies. But the prime beneficiaries were China and, above all, the United States, whose troops already held most of the strategic islands in the Pacific and were to occupy Japan.

War Crimes Trials   Within Europe, rooting out fascism was a major concern. In countries the Nazis had occupied, there were summary executions of collaborators and some public prosecutions, notably in France, where Pierre Laval and Marshal Pétain were tried. In Germany itself, however, the numbers involved made denazification difficult. Millions of forms were filled out and hundreds of trials held, but the drive against former Nazis soon waned. Determined to establish some lasting standard, the Allies created an international tribunal to try Hitler's closest associates for

Göring, Hess, and von Ribbentrop (the first three on the left in the prison's dock) listen to the proceedings at the beginning of the Nuremberg trial for war crimes.
Bettmann/Corbis

crimes against humanity. The trials, held in Nuremberg in 1945 and 1946, were also intended to inform the German people of the full horror of Nazi rule. The appalling revelations of those solemn hearings were followed by restrained judgments—only twelve of the twenty-two prime defendants were condemned to death, and three were acquitted.

International Agencies The belief in international law that underlay the Nuremberg trials and the United Nations Organization was tempered by a determination to learn from the past. This peace would not be punitive; devastated nations, defeated enemies as well as those liberated from German rule, must be helped. Even before the UN had its charter, its first agency, the United Nations Relief and Rehabilitation Administration (UNRRA), was created, late in 1943. UNRRA played a major role in reconstructing postwar Europe, organizing relief of food and medical supplies, and coordinating international loans. To avoid the dangerous inflation that had followed World War I, a conference at Bretton Woods, New Hampshire, in 1944 created the International Monetary Fund and an International Bank for Reconstruction and Development (later the World Bank). Those institutions, with nearly $20 billion in assets, furthered reconstruction and capital investment by supporting stable currencies. They would become influential mechanisms for shaping the international capitalist economy.

But the main instrument of peace was to be the United Nations, and a few months after the Yalta meeting, fifty-one countries approved the United Nations Charter at a special conference held in San Francisco. The charter established a General Assembly of all members to determine policy, a decision-making Security Council of eleven nations to supervise "the maintenance of international peace," and various economic, social, and legal agencies. The United States, the Soviet Union, China, Great Britain, and France each received a permanent seat on the Security Council along with a right to veto any council action; the remaining six seats were filled by election from among the other member states. The fact that the United States and the Soviet Union belonged to the UN was a promising contrast to the League of Nations, but the conflict between them dominated international relations even within the UN, where the superpowers competed for the support of Asian, African, and Latin American nations.

The Divide in Postwar Europe

The conflict between communists and anticommunists divided Europe, domestically between the national parties of left and right, then more deeply between two sets of values and ideology, and ultimately between Eastern European nations dominated by the USSR and Western ones allied with the United States. With the fall of fascism, communists enjoyed the prestige of having played a central part in most resistance movements, and communist calls for social justice and greater democracy resonated with postwar idealism. Quickly, however, nearly every disagreement between communists and anticommunists became part of a larger power struggle.

Eastern Europe: New Communist Regimes At war's end, Soviet troops occupied Eastern Europe from the Adriatic to the Baltic. The three formerly independent states of Estonia, Latvia, and Lithuania became Soviet republics, and Russia annexed territory from East Prussia, Poland, Hungary, and Romania. In the ostensibly autonomous nations of Eastern Europe, the Soviets discouraged independent revolutions like those that had followed World War I but skillfully used social issues and crude coercion to establish governments friendly to them. Communist parties had considerable support throughout the region, and the common pattern was to build on that base, excluding prominent anticommunists from the governing coalition, then using propaganda campaigns and sudden arrests to drive noncommunists from a share of power. The result was a series of single-party dictatorships on the Soviet model that consolidated their position through purge trials and use of the secret police (see "Churchill Sees an Iron Curtain," p. 879).

The USSR had an economic as well as a political purpose. Its production had sunk to less than two-thirds of prewar levels, and the new Five-Year Plan of 1946 openly depended on ransacking occupied areas, especially in the eastern zone of Germany. Early in 1946 the Russians forced a merger of East Germany's Social Democratic party with the smaller Communist party, and Soviet control was soon complete. After expropriating much of German industry and restricting trade with the West, the Russians gradually allowed increased industrial activity in the eastern zone and in 1949 gave it independent status as the German Democratic Republic. Germany had been divided in two.

Poland, where the communists were weakest, had been promised free elections, but repressive measures weakened the Peasant Party in the elections of 1947. It was soon purged, and the largest party of Independent Socialists subordinated itself to the communist Workers' party. The government could then put a Russian in command of the army and attack the Catholic Church. The president and the foreign minister of Czechoslovakia, Eduard Beneš and Jan Masaryk, were the heirs of a notable democratic tradition. But the Communists were the largest party, and when in 1948 they threatened to take over the country, Beneš gave

CHURCHILL SEES AN IRON CURTAIN

On March 5, 1946, Winston Churchill gave a speech at Westminster College in Fulton, Missouri, that immediately received worldwide attention. After years of official emphasis on the cooperation among the wartime Allies, its directness was shocking. In effect, it announced the Cold War.

"A shadow has fallen upon the scenes so lately lighted by the Allied victory. Nobody knows what Soviet Russia and its Communist international organization intends to do in the immediate future, or what are the limits, if any, to their expansive and proselytizing tendencies. I have a strong admiration and regard for the valiant Russian people and for my wartime comrade, Marshal Stalin. There is deep sympathy and goodwill in Britain—and I doubt not here also—towards the peoples of all the Russias and a resolve to persevere through many differences and rebuffs in establishing lasting friendships. We understand the Russian need to be secure on her western frontiers by the removal of all possibility of German aggression. We welcome Russia to her rightful place among the leading nations of the world. We welcome her flag upon the seas. Above all, we welcome constant, frequent and growing contacts between the Russian people and our own people on both sides of the Atlantic. It is my duty, however, for I am sure you would wish me to state the facts as I see them to you, to place before you certain facts about the present position in Europe.

"From Stettin in the Baltic to Trieste in the Adriatic, an iron curtain has descended across the Continent. Behind that line lie all the capitals of the ancient states of Central and Eastern Europe. Warsaw, Berlin, Prague, Vienna, Budapest, Belgrade, Bucharest and Sofia, all these famous cities and the populations around them lie in what I must call the Soviet sphere, and all are subject in one form or another, not only to Soviet influence but to a very high and, in many cases, increasing measure of control from Moscow.

". . . An attempt is being made by the Russians in Berlin to build up a quasi-Communist party in their zone of Occupied Germany by showing special favours to groups of left-wing German leaders. At the end of the fighting last June, the American and British Armies withdrew westwards, in accordance with an earlier agreement, to a depth at some points of one hundred and fifty miles upon a front of nearly four hundred miles, in order to allow our Russian allies to occupy this vast expanse of territory which the Western Democracies had conquered.

"If now the Soviet Government tries, by separate action, to build up a pro-Communist Germany in their areas, this will cause new serious difficulties in the British and American zones, and will give the defeated Germans the power of putting themselves up to auction between the Soviets and the Western Democracies. Whatever conclusions may be drawn from these facts—and facts they are—this is certainly not the Liberated Europe we fought to build up. Nor is it one which contains the essentials of permanent peace."

Reprinted in Brian MacArthur, *The Penguin Book of Twentieth-Century Speeches,* New York: Viking, 1992, and available in many other places.

way and Masaryk died in a mysterious fall from a window. Hungary's coalition government, which had an anti-Communist majority, lost to the Communists in a dubious election in 1949. In each of these cases Britain and the United States protested, with little effect, and the new regimes established close links with the Soviet Union. By 1950 Romania, Albania, and Bulgaria were also solid members of the communist bloc.

Only Yugoslavia followed a different course. Marshal Tito easily won the 1945 national election, and communists dominated the government, but Tito resisted Soviet efforts to influence his foreign and domestic policies. After having joined the Cominform, which had replaced the Comintern and was similarly designed to coordinate international communist activity, Yugoslavia broke with its neighbors in 1948, using ties with the West to resist economic and political pressure from the East—an example to others of how small states could use the tense balance between the superpowers.

Western Europe: Postwar Politics Although Spain and Portugal remained defiant dictatorships, the other countries of Western Europe returned to democratic political life and projects of social reform. The new constitutions of France and Italy spoke of the right to work, guaranteed social as well as civil rights, and at last gave women the vote. West Germany's federal structure and its two dominant parties, the Christian Democrats and the Social Democrats, recalled the pre-Nazi Weimar Republic. Everywhere social programs received much attention, but reconstruction took precedence over reform.

Ironically, at war's end Germany's industry was in better shape than that of any other continental nation, and the Allies soon relaxed restrictions on its economic activity. Early in 1949 they acknowledged the division of Germany and recognized the western sectors that Britain, France, and the United States had occupied as the Federal Republic of Germany. For the next fourteen years, Konrad Adenauer, the head of the Christian Democrats, served as chancellor. Mayor of Cologne from 1917 to 1933, he was seventy-three years old in 1949, a firm and conservative leader closely allied with the United States, who promoted an atmosphere of efficient calm.

Italy, too, became a republic when a majority of the electorate voted in 1946 to replace a monarchy tainted by Fascism. As the largest party, the Christian Democrats gave Alcide De Gasperi, prime minister from 1945 to 1953, a solid basis from which to govern. A wily politician, he successfully ostracized the Communists—the largest Communist party in the West—and took advantage of a split among Socialists to bring Italy into close alliance with the United States. Winning the crucial elections of 1948, with the help of heavy American pressure, he launched a program of moderate reform intended to lessen poverty in southern Italy and to stimulate industry in the north. Italian politics had returned to the unheroic tradition of parliamentary maneuver the Fascists had overturned.

Before the liberation of France, an umbrella group of Resistance organizations including the communists had pledged to restore democracy, to provide economic security to all French citizens, and to modernize production through government regulation. As Albert Camus wrote in the resistance newspaper *Combat:* "The goal we must pursue is to make life free for the individual but just for all. Our plan is to make justice reign through the economy and to guarantee freedom through politics." Initially General de Gaulle headed a provisional unity government drawing on all elements of the Resistance, but that interregnum began to wind down in October 1945 when Frenchmen and (for the first time) women voted for a Constituent Assembly that would draft a new republican constitution. Unable to abide criticism from that body, de Gaulle abruptly resigned as acting president in January 1946 and retreated for the time being into retirement.

A political alliance of the three dominant political parties (the Communists, the Socialists, and a new social-Catholic or Christian Democratic party) filled the vacuum, thrashed out a new constitution after prolonged debate, and oversaw major steps toward recovery from the devastation of war and occupation. The communist party and trade unions cooperated fully in the "battle for production" by working tirelessly in the coal mines and other sectors, and by

forgoing steep wage increases despite rising prices. The tripartite alliance proved fragile, however; by mid-1947 the communists were out of the government and in fierce opposition over labor and foreign policy issues, while de Gaulle's followers launched a challenge to the Fourth Republic from the right. By 1948 the consensus of the Resistance had given way in France to political instability, class conflict, and cold war polarization.

Britain did not require constitutional change after the war; instead, the end of the wartime electoral truce brought the first general election since 1935. While the people revered Churchill as a war leader, they looked to the socialist Labour Party for the postwar future. With its platform pledging far-reaching social and economic reform, Labour won the election of July 1945 in a landslide. Under prime minister Clement Attlee the new government nationalized the Bank of England, air and rail transport, the coal mines, electricity, and iron and steel. In the face of severe shortages and the need to damp down consumption in favor of exports, Labour continued the rigors of wartime rationing. But the socialists offset this austerity with laws that bolstered trade unions, established new social insurance for the unemployed and the elderly, family allowances, public housing programs, and above all a new National Health Service that provided free hospital, medical, and dental care for all. True to its principles, the Labour government also began Britain's withdrawal from the empire to which Churchill had been so attached.

Family allowance payments for children of the working class began to arrive at local post offices in August 1946—a first installment on Britain's postwar "cradle to grave" welfare state.
Hulton Archive/Getty Images

Summary

Europe's war, like its ideological divisions, had spread around the world, and it had taken a worldwide mobilization to defeat the Axis. The exhausting victory over Fascism, Nazism, and Japanese militarism took an immense toll in lives and resources. Yet European nations rebounded with remarkable speed after 1945, and the dominant states on the whole adjusted realistically to the loss of their empires and of their former international preeminence. The Cold War's ideological and geographical division of Europe became a basic fact of life. But disillusionment could be found on both sides of the divide. The new welfare states of the democracies scarcely solved all their problems, and in the Communist block, one-party dictatorship and repression continued long after Stalin's demise. Europe had recovered from the nightmare of World War II, but its economic, social, and cultural place in the modern world remained unclear.

QUESTIONS FOR FURTHER THOUGHT

1. What were the possible arguments for and against appeasement of Hitler in the 1930s? Is "appeasement" a useful category of analysis in international relations in recent times?
2. Initially, in 1939–41, new military technology and tactics made a crucial difference in the course of the war, but was the later phase of World War II reminiscent of, even a continuation of, the Great War?
3. How did the Holocaust develop? On what grounds should the Holocaust be considered a singular event and on whom should the onus be placed? What ideological, moral, and political conclusions might be drawn in looking back at that event?

RECOMMENDED READING

Sources

Camus at COMBAT:. Writing 1944–1947 (ed.) J. Lévi-Valensi. 2006. Documents the sprit of the Resistance and its tribulations in postwar France.

Churchill, Sir Winston S. *The Second World War.* 6 vols. 1948–1954. Each volume of Churchill's detailed account can be read singly. His masterly prose recaptures the drama and meaning of the century's greatest war.

Frank, Anne. *Diary of a Young Girl.* 1947. The unvarnished thoughts of a doomed Jewish girl hiding in Amsterdam during the Nazi occupation.

Hitler's *Table-Talk.* Hugh Trevor-Roper (ed.). 1988. Recorded by his aides, Hitler's opinionated ramblings and reminiscences have a chilling fascination.

Studies

Calder, Angus. *The People's War: Britain 1939–1945.* 1969. A spirited account of the British home front.

Chambers, John Whiteclay II, and David Culbert (eds.). *World War II, Film and History.* 1996. A study of the formation of popular images.

Clendinnen, Inga. *Reading the Holocaust.* 1999. A discussion of what the Holocaust meant to perpetrators and victims, as reflected in memoirs and fiction.

Crossman, Richard H. (ed.). *The God That Failed.* 1950. The moving testimony of former Marxists about their lost faith during the era of Stalin.

Dawidowicz, Lucy S. *The War against the Jews, 1933–1945.* 1976. An extensive consideration of the twentieth century's greatest horror.

Déak, Istvan et al. (eds.). *The Politics of Retribution in Europe: World War II and Its Aftermath.* 2000. Case studies of collaboration, resistance, and retribution in Western and Eastern Europe after the Nazi occupation.

Friedlander, Saul. *Years of Extermination: Nazi Germany and the Jews, 1939–45.* 2007. A compelling overview and interpretation by an expert in German and Jewish history.

Gildea, Robert. *Marianne in Chains: Daily Life in the Heart of France during the German Occupation.* 2002. A case study of one region that brings to life the varied responses of ordinary French people to the Nazi occupation and the Vichy regime.

Gross, Jan. *Neighbors: The Destruction of the Jewish Community in Jedwabne, Poland.* 2001. A case study of murderous anti-Semitism and its appalling results.

Hennessy, Peter. *Never Again: Britain, 1945–1951.* 1993. A balanced narrative of the triumphs and failures of Britain's postwar socialist government.

Jackson, Julian. *France: The Dark Years, 1940–1944.* 2001. A comprehensive and balanced account of collaboration and resistance.

———. *The Fall of France: The Nazi Invasion of 1940.* 2003. A persuasive recounting and explanation of the astonishing collapse of British and French forces in 1940 and the triumph of the invading Germans.

Keegan, John. *The Second World War.* 1989. A highly readable synthesis by a leading military historian.

Kershaw, Ian. *Hitler, the Germans, and the Final Solution.* 2008. The foremost biographer of Hitler considers the Nazi extermination of the Jews.

Lagrou, Pieter. *The Legacy of Nazi Occupation: Patriotic Memory and National Recovery in Western Europe, 1945–1965.* 1999. A comparative study of how France, Belgium, and the Netherlands dealt with the impact of Nazi occupation as they undertook postwar reconstruction.

Laqueur, Walter. *Europe since Hitler.* 1982. One of the ablest surveys of the foundations of contemporary Europe that sees Europe as a whole.

Liddell-Hart, Basil H. *History of the Second World War.* 1980. The crowning work of this renowned strategist and military historian.

Mason, Tim, and Jane Caplan (eds.). *Nazism, Fascism, and the Working Class.* 1995. Ten essays engage leading historical interpretations on fascism and social class.

Mazower, Mark. *Dark Continent: Europe's Twentieth Century.* 1999. An original and critical interpretation.

———. *Hitler's Empire: How the Nazis Ruled Europe.* 2008. This important study emphasizes the lack of coherence in Nazi policy toward occupied territories and its extreme and counterproductive brutality.

Milward, Alan S. *The Reconstruction of Western Europe, 1945–1951.* 1984. Concludes that the economic boom of the 1950s and 1960s began as early as 1945, when government policy established international economic interdependence.

Rioux, Jean-Pierre. *The Fourth Republic, 1945–1958.* 1987. A close look at and a critical assessment of the period before de Gaulle's reemergence.

Sherwin, M. J. A. *A World Destroyed: The Atomic Bomb and the Grand Alliance.* 1975. A scholarly and balanced account of this controversial subject.

Ulam, Adam B. *Expansion and Coexistence: The History of Soviet Foreign Policy, 1917–1973.* 1974. An expert appraisal of the consistent patterns and political pressures underlying Soviet policy.

Weinberg, Gerhard. *A World at Arms: A Global History of World War II.* 1994. Remarkably balanced synthesis, attentive to political and economic as well as military aspects of the war.

Wilkinson, James D. *The Intellectual Resistance in Europe.* 1981. A wide-ranging assessment of the content and legacy of the antifascist resistance and its place in contemporary thought.

Winter, Jay, and Emmanuel Sivan. *War and Remembrance in the Twentieth Century.* 2000. Essays on the cultural and psychological impact of war as a major element of modern history.

Ziegler, Philip. *London at War, 1939–1945.* 1995. Focuses primarily but not exclusively on how Londoners responded to the "blitz" of massive German bombing.

In the first decade of the twenty-first century, soaring gas prices and shortages are not unfamiliar sights. But those who endured the oil crisis of the 1970s and 80s have seen this before, as evidenced by this "No Petrol" sign from Britain in 1973. Getty Images

Chapter Twenty-Nine

EUROPE IN THE POSTWAR ERA

THE POSTWAR LANDSCAPE • THE END OF EMPIRE • POLITICAL TENSIONS IN THE
BIPOLAR WORLD • 1968 AND ITS AFTERMATH

World War II, a war more total and more worldwide than its predecessor, required massive organization, challenged national economies, and altered social relations. When peace finally came, Europe was a continent devastated; millions had lost homes, family, health, and hope. Although the years immediately following the war were ones of political turbulence and economic privation, by the 1950s Europeans not only had managed to overcome most of the acute problems created by war and its aftermath, but had entered a period of unprecedented economic growth. Even as European nations gained in wealth and stability, however, they were dominated by the two new superpowers, the United States and the Soviet Union, in a world split in half by the Cold War. At the same time, colonial na-

tionalist movements, which had been gathering steam since the interwar period, expelled European rulers from their colonies once and for all, further diminishing European power and changing the face of global politics. Cultural rebellion added to the atmosphere of insecurity in the late 1960s and early 70s as a new generation of European youth raised in the postwar period fundamentally challenged the social order and the values of their parents. When the economic boom of the postwar era came to a sudden and shocking halt with the oil crisis in the early 1970s, Europeans were forced to face the limitations of both capitalism and communism without resort to colonial exploitation and without the sense of conviction that European civilization could provide the answers to all problems.

1947 Berlin Blockade; Marshall Plan; Indian independence

1947–1949 Communist governments in Yugoslavia, Poland, Czechoslovakia, Hungary, Romania

1949 East and West German states established; NATO founded; establishment of People's Republic of China; Simone de Beauvoir, *The Second Sex*

Death of Stalin **1953**

Algerian War for independence from France begins **1954**

Hungarian uprising put down by Soviet troops; Suez Crisis **1956**

Treaty of Rome establishes European Economic Community **1957**

THE POSTWAR LANDSCAPE

The central reality confronting postwar Europe was the emergence of the Cold War between the U.S. and the USSR. Not only had the war depleted the European nations, but they now faced two superpowers that dwarfed them in economic strength and political power. Yet, while bipolar politics shackled the European nations, by the 1950s they had entered a period of extraordinary economic growth.

From Hot to Cold War

The wartime alliance between the Soviet Union and the United States began to fray almost immediately after the war. A turning point came in 1947, when distrust between the two powers hardened into a worldwide military, political, and ideological conflict quickly dubbed the Cold War.

The Emergence of Hostilities As Russia moved to assert its authority in Eastern Europe, the American president announced the Truman Doctrine, promising military and economic aid to nations in danger of communist takeover. His immediate concern was the civil war in Greece, where local communists were aided by neighboring Yugoslavia. The United States also sought bases in Turkey, for Britain could no longer sustain its power and influence in the eastern Mediterranean, and the United States replaced Britain as the leading anticommunist force there. American money and supplies poured into Greece, and this, combined with Yugoslavia's break with Russia, enabled the Greek government to crush the opposition by 1949. Turkey, slowly moving toward democracy, received similar assistance. If opposing communism and Soviet influence had become the focus of American policy,

the rise of the United States to superpower status made that policy of signal importance to the rest of the world, not least the European nations.

The Cold War colored every aspect of postwar politics, including aid to the devastated nations of Europe. A few months after the announcement of the Truman Doctrine, Secretary of State George Marshall unveiled a bold plan to stimulate European recovery and overcome the postwar economic crisis in which communism was likely to prosper. The United States would offer massive economic aid to all nations still recovering from the war. Remarkably, communist governments were eligible, too, but the USSR forbade their participation and instead established its own program, the Council of Mutual Economic Assistance (Comecon). In the West, communist parties feared the Marshall Plan came with political strings attached and opposed it despite its obvious benefits; in response, the United States used its growing influence to see that communists were excluded from coalition governments in France and Italy in 1947 (West Germany banned the party itself in 1956). The two halves of Europe followed the lead of their powerful patrons.

Escalating Confrontation Worried that Marshall Plan money would lead to the resurgence of a strong Germany and fearful of American support for anticommunist movements everywhere, the Soviet Union tightened its grip over the states of Eastern Europe. Suddenly, in June 1948, the Soviets closed off overland access to Berlin, which they saw as a dangerous outpost of Western power. War seemed imminent. The United States responded with the extraordinary Berlin airlift: for nearly a year, until the Soviets backed down, a steady stream of flights brought in all of West Berlin's supplies.

When the Soviet Union tested its own atomic bomb in 1949, the United States announced that work had

● **1961** Berlin Wall

● **1962** Algerian independence; Pope John XXIII convenes Vatican II

● **1964** Khrushchev removed from power in the USSR

● **1968** Student revolts in Paris and Prague; Soviet-led invasion
of Czechoslovakia

● **1969** De Gaulle resigns as president of France

● **1972** Palestinian terrorists kill Israeli athletes at
Munich Olympic Games

● **1973** Energy crisis begins

Death of Spanish dictator Franco **1975** ●

Thatcher elected British prime minister **1979** ●

The world was as impressed as
the children of Berlin by the
airlift that carried supplies to the
city and completed 277, 264
flights in a year.
Fenno Jacobs/Black Star/
StockPhoto

begun on the even more devastating hydrogen bomb. But
the U.S.'s loss of a monopoly on atomic weapons made
ground forces that did not depend on them an essential
deterrent to Soviet aggression. Consequently, in 1949 the
North Atlantic Treaty Organization (NATO) was created
to coordinate the military planning of the United States,
Canada, and ten Western European nations,[1] which now

received U.S. military aid. The Soviets replied with the
Warsaw Pact of communist states in 1955.

At first, the Cold War was primarily a conflict over
Europe, waged as a competition for public opinion as
well as international power. But with Eastern Europe
isolated behind what Churchill called an "iron curtain" (See "Churchill Sees an Iron Curtain," p. 879)
and communists excluded from political power in the
West, the focus of the Cold War shifted. When the
communist North Koreans invaded South Korea in
1950, the United States asked the United Nations to
intervene, and the UN (with the USSR temporarily

[1] Great Britain, France, Belgium, the Netherlands, Luxemburg,
Italy, Portugal, Denmark, Norway, and Iceland were the Euro-
pean members. Greece and Turkey would be added in 1952;
West Germany, in 1955.

absent) called for an international army to stop the North Koreans. The Cold War was now worldwide, as it spread to colonial issues and conflicts in the Middle East and Asia (see "The Soviet Union Denounces the United States While Calling for Arms Reduction," p. 889).

The Postwar Boom

By the early 1950s, a remarkable economic recovery was under way, and international tensions eased somewhat. In 1955, the wartime Allies—including the USSR—came to an agreement granting Austria independence and withdrawing occupation forces. The same year, the USSR also granted diplomatic recognition to West Germany despite its having joined NATO. Reinvigorated economies, however, depended heavily on old industries, new state programs, and the policies of the two superpowers. Political stability remained vulnerable to ideological divisions.

Economic Resurgence Across Europe, extraordinary economic growth from 1947 to 1957 was connected to a distinctive European emphasis on the role of the state. National governments not only played a central economic role but developed social policies that set new standards for equity and well-being.

Despite the shortages of capital and supplies, the postwar situation had provided some opportunities. European nations had access to a backlog of unexploited technology, including atomic power, the jet engine, television, antibiotics, and frozen foods. The very need to rebuild factories and transportation networks made it easier to adopt the most efficient methods and newest machinery. Similarly, the tragic displacement of millions of people increased the availability of skilled labor. Demographic developments also reflected Europe's remarkable resilience. A European "baby boom," though not so large as the one in the United States, lasted until 1963, helping to replace some of the losses of war.

Stimulus from the Soviet Union and the United States The recovery of Eastern Europe depended heavily on the Soviet Union. A strenuous effort enabled it to exceed prewar industrial output by 1953, and its leaders confidently predicted that the USSR would surpass the United States. As the economy expanded, however, the costs of administration increased disproportionately, and the inefficiencies of centralized management became more pronounced. Without a free market, government planners had difficulty judging costs and performance. Agriculture was a major disappointment: the grain harvest in 1953 was only slightly larger than in 1913.

The Soviet Union nevertheless provided an important market and economic stimulus for the countries of the Communist bloc, which organized their economies along the Soviet model. All but Poland collectivized farmlands, and all instituted five-year plans to achieve rapid industrialization. In varying degrees, these governments adopted some elements of a mixed economic system—"goulash socialism," as Hungary's compromise came to be called. The state retained ownership of most means of production, but managers operated within the structure of a largely free market and increased the production of consumer goods. Initially most successful in the already advanced economies of Czechoslovakia and East Germany, the model was generally adopted throughout Eastern Europe, which, although dramatically less prosperous than the West, experienced the highest economic growth rate in its history by the 1950s.

The Western European nations looked to the United States for help. In 1946 the United States extended $4.4 billion in long-term credit to Great Britain and, subsequently, $1.2 billion to France. A year later the United States acknowledged that Europe's economic problems existed on a scale that threatened to undermine recovery and announced the Marshall Plan. Over the next four years, more than $15 billion was channeled into Europe under the direction of the Organization for European Economic Cooperation (OEEC), which eighteen Western states established for this purpose. That was followed by the European Payments Union, which regulated currency exchanges from 1950 to 1958. Europe's rapid recovery was made possible by this financial stability, by the planning the Marshall Plan required, and by the importation of goods from the United States the plan provided for (which also benefited the American economy). In the three years from 1948 to 1950, the combined gross national product of the OEEC participants increased at an astonishing annual rate of 25 percent. By 1952 the gross product was approximately 50 percent higher than it had been in 1938, and per capita income was a third higher. Western Europe had never been wealthier.

The Economic Role of the State The increased economic importance of the public sector resulted in part from the extension of wartime measures and from immediate social needs after the war. It also reflected a changed attitude toward government's role. Britain and France nationalized utilities, transport, coal, and some of their heavy industry and banking systems after the war, and in Italy the new state inherited from Fascism the ownership of huge conglomerates that directed hundreds of firms in some of the critical industrial sectors. West Germany alone made no effort to expand

THE SOVIET UNION DENOUNCES THE UNITED STATES WHILE CALLING FOR ARMS REDUCTION

Andrei Vishinsky, the Russian delegate to the United Nations, spoke to the General Assembly on November 1, 1948, proposing steps toward arms reduction and control of atomic weapons. The address was testimony, however, to the global range of the Cold War. Most of it consisted of a lengthy denunciation of the policies of the United States, which was accused of undermining the United Nations; of intervening against democracy and peace in Korea, Greece, Indonesia, and Palestine; and of harming Europe's economy with the Marshall Plan while forming a military alliance with the nations of Western Europe aimed at the "freedom-loving" states of Eastern Europe.

"The policy of the USSR is a consistent and constant policy of expanding and strengthening international cooperation. This follows from the very nature of the Soviet State. A socialist State of workers and peasants deeply interested—a State, I repeat, which is deeply interested in the establishment of the most favorable conditions for peaceful creative work in the building of a socialist society. The foreign policy of the Soviet Union pursues the course of cooperation among all countries prepared for peaceful cooperation. The USSR consistently fights against any plan and measures and designs intended to create a gap, a cleavage, among peoples. It fights for the realization and implementation of democratic principles which were born out of the war.

"Such is not the case with the present foreign policy of the United States. After the termination of the recent war, the Government of the United States has changed its foreign policy: from a policy of fighting against aggressive forces, the United States has passed over to a policy of expansion. It is now attempting to realize plans for world domination. It is in open support in various countries of the most reactionary and monarchofascist regimes and groups and rendering to them systematic aid with money and armaments for the suppression of democratic national liberation movements in these countries; organization of military alliances or blocs, the construction of new military air and naval bases as well as the expansion and reconstruction in accordance with the newest military technical requirements of old bases established during the war with Germany, Japan, and Italy; furthermore, unchecked propaganda of a new war against the Soviet Union and the new democracies of Eastern Europe; a wild race of armaments; a true worship of the cult of the atomic bomb and allegedly a means of escape from all the dangers and misfortunes threatening the capitalistic world: these are the principal aspects, the characteristic features, of the foreign policy of the United States of America at present.

"Such a policy is inciting the psychosis of war, sowing restlessness and fear among the broad masses which strive for peace and peaceful creative labor. Such a policy has nothing in common whatsoever with a policy of peace.

"[A] . . . map by the ESSO Company of New York is of the same insolently arrogant and war-inciting nature. This map is published by the Standard Oil Company of New Jersey. It is called, quite provocatively, 'The Map of the Third World War.' That is what they are publishing in the United States—the Map of the Third World War! They are handing them out to motorists. This map, with provocatively militant appeals, carries the heading: 'Pacific Theatre of Military Operations.' The map is an example of the malicious war propaganda against the Soviet Union and the new democracies of East Europe.

". . . The reactionary circles of the United States and the United Kingdom as well as of countries such as France, Belgium, and others, do not confine themselves to slander and abuse alone. This campaign is now being headed not only by amateurs from the family of retired politicians, statesmen, Senators and Members of Parliament, but also by persons now holding high official posts in the Governments of the United States, the United Kingdom, France and some other countries.

". . . On the instructions of the Soviet Union Government the delegation of the USSR proposes to the General Assembly, for the purpose of strengthening the cause of peace and removing the menace of a new war which is being fomented by expansionists and other reactionary elements, the adoption of the following resolution:

". . . as the first step in the reduction of armaments and armed forces to reduce by one-third during one year all present land, naval, and air forces. . . .

". . . to prohibit atomic weapons as weapons intended for aims of aggression and not for those of defense;

". . . to establish within the framework of the Security Council an international control body for the purpose of the supervision and control of the implementation of . . . these measures. . . ."

Speech by Andrei Y. Vishinsky to the United Nations, November 1, 1948, from *Vital Speeches of the Day*, Vol. 15, No. 2, New York: City News Pub. Co., 1949.

the number of state-owned industries, but there, too, the government had an important role (as it had during the war) in coordinating economic growth. State ownership gave no assurance of efficient management, good labor relations, or a high return on capital, but it encouraged governments to develop economic policies to guide both public and private enterprises in the interests of overall growth.

Nearly all European governments established programs to protect ordinary citizens and their families against sickness, impoverished old age, and unemployment. Great Britain provided one of the earliest and most complete examples of what has come to be called the welfare state. Its cornerstone was the National Health Service, inaugurated in 1948, which assumed nearly the total cost of medical, dental, and hospital care for every citizen. Such programs were themselves an outcome of the war effort, which had lessened inequality in Britain (the diet of the very poor had actually improved). Continental governments also provided universal health care, family allowances with payments for minor children, housing programs, and a growing array of social services. By reducing insecurity, these measures also stimulated consumption. To meet their cost, states raised taxes and became more efficient in collecting them, in the process accumulating reserves that they used for investment according to their economic plans.

Postwar Culture

The burst of artistic creativity that followed World War II embraced new trends and styles in all the arts. At the same time, the global expansion of a dynamic popular culture is one of the hallmarks of the second half of the twentieth century. Gradually interwoven into modern social thought, these developments have contributed to new ideas about culture that have spread through the humanities and social sciences and influenced modern social movements.

Postwar Creativity With the end of the war, European artists were free to take part in artistic movements banned under fascism and to incorporate new ideas and styles coming from America. Authors wanting to show how ordinary people had experienced dictatorship, war, and postwar dislocation favored a style noted for its directness and telling detail. Called neorealism, this style flourished especially in Italy. The novels of Ignazio Silone and Alberto Moravia gave incisive, often bitter, yet affectionate accounts of the daily struggles of people buffeted by movements and events beyond their control, and the films of Roberto Rossellini and Vittorio de Sica combined the harsh eye of the candid camera with sympathy for society's victims.

These forms gradually gave way to ones that built on more radical prewar art and presented several points of view simultaneously, challenging any assumption of a single reality. In Germany, the Marxist writer Bertolt Brecht crafted plays in this vein (and in 1949 left the West to live in East Berlin), and the savagely satirical

novels of Heinrich Böll extended the once-shocking surrealism of Franz Kafka to convey Central Europe's experience of the twentieth century. Stimulus from outside Europe was also important. African art influenced the English sculptor Henry Moore in his design of huge reclining figures that combined clean lines, solid masses, and provocative empty spaces.

Adapting Traditional Values The arguments for human decency needed restatement following the horrors of genocide, totalitarianism, and war. **Existentialism,** one of the most influential movements of the postwar period, offered a radical solution to the problem of ethics. Life may be absurd and meaningless, the French philosopher Jean-Paul Sartre reasoned, but to take any action is to make a decision, and doing so is to make a personal moral choice. Building on the prewar work of Karl Jaspers and Martin Heidegger in Germany, Sartre constructed a radical individualist philosophy that centered on moral responsibility. Even in the worst of circumstances, the sum of the choices made give each life its moral meaning. The soldier could refuse to torture; the civilian could choose to resist custom or authority. Underneath its relentless pessimism, Sartre's existentialism—set forth in essays, dramas, and criticism—held out the possibility of moral heroism.

Christian voices shared in the postwar anguish over values. Leading theologians like Jaspers, Karl Barth, and Jacques Maritain were studied with renewed interest. The Protestant Paul Tillich and the Catholic Pierre Teilhard de Chardin achieved a large following with their systematic claims for Christianity's relevance to modern life. This confidence, reflected in the postwar vigor of Christian political parties, illuminated the papacy (1958–1963) of Pope John XXIII. He was extraordinarily popular, admired by Protestants as well as Catholics, and by peasants and workers as well as intellectuals. Determined to recast the Church's position in the modern world, he called the Vatican Council known as **Vatican II,** which opened in 1962. The Council sought to bring the Catholic Church up to date not just organizationally but in social policy as well. It made the leadership of the Church far more international, directed attention to the concerns of developing nations, made respect for Jews a formal policy, and expressed belief in religious liberty. Putting more emphasis on individual understanding than institutional uniformity, it ordered that Masses be conducted in the vernacular instead of Latin. These changes encountered resistance, and with Pope John's death before the Council was completed, the Church turned to more cautious consolidation of doctrine and structure.

After Pope John XXIII died on June 3, 1963, the Council continued to meet under his successor, Paul

John Paul II made several visits to the United States, drawing huge crowds each time.
Historicus, Inc.

VI, until 1965. Although many Catholics embraced the changes encouraged by the Council, others became concerned that the Church had deviated too far from its traditional teachings. In 1978 Karol Wojtyla of Poland became Pope John Paul II. John Paul became a strong critic of Western materialism and a proponent of global social justice. At the same time, he staunchly defended Catholic orthodoxy and papal authority. He alienated many liberal Catholics with his continued opposition to homosexuality, abortion and birth control, and the ordination of female priests.

The Influence of American Popular Culture   One of the major trends in the cultural life of postwar Europe was the ever-increasing influence of American popular culture. American dominance in the motion picture industry, for example, first became apparent in the 1930s but had grown enormously since the war. While Europeans flocked to cinemas to see American movies, however, European businesses and governments saw American movies as a threat to the national economy and identity. They tried a variety of measures intended to reduce the proportion of American productions in their movie theaters and on television, but these by and large failed. In the 1950s over half of the movies that Europeans attended were from the United States, and by the 1990s the figure was more than 80 percent.

American productions had similar success on European television, as privately owned television networks competed with government-run networks by filling a majority of their airtime with inexpensive American reruns. In fact, American television productions dem-

onstrated remarkably wide appeal. The television series *Dallas* was as popular and well-known in Europe as in the United States, and Italian judges found themselves explaining to defendants more familiar with *Perry Mason* than with their own justice system that "your honor" is not a term used in Italian courts. By the 1990s, soap operas from Brazil (especially popular in Portugal and Spain) and Australia (especially popular in Great Britain) appeared alongside American shows as regular fare on European television networks owned by Italian, French, and German media tycoons. Theme parks, too, spread from the United States to Europe.

This photo of a nuclear family gathered around the television set is an iconic image of the postwar world.
Archive Photos/Getty Images

Denmark built Legoland, and the French opened Parc Asterix, based on a comic book series, on the outskirts of Paris, not far from the Disneyland Resort Paris.

American influences also reshaped the European music scene. American jazz had been popular in Europe since the 1920s, especially in France, and after the war, the presence of American troops and the programs of Armed Forces Radio did much to disseminate American popular music. The new musical culture did not come exclusively from the United States, however. The Beatles, who combined American influences with those of the British music hall, were by far the most influential popular music group of the 1960s and, along with the Rolling Stones, helped to create a transatlantic culture of rock and roll as popular on the Continent and in Latin America as in Britain and the United States. By the 1980s an international tour was a standard feature of the popular music scene. In each country, performances were usually preceded by local groups, adding to the sense of single culture with national variants.

Much criticized on both sides of the Atlantic, such commercial entertainment had been especially troubling to many European intellectuals who feared that their societies would follow the American example. Conservatives worried that American-style democracy undermined the values that supported high culture; Marxists believed that ruthless capitalism made culture a commodity, mass-produced, cheap, and aimed at the lowest taste.

New Directions in Art and Architecture   The arts had never been more international than after World War II, and they were necessarily affected by the energy of new

Inspired by American musicians such as Chuck Berry, Little Richard, and Elvis Presely, the Beatles took the United States by storm in the 1960s.
© Hulton-Deutsch Collection/Corbis

forms of popular culture. French filmmakers like Jean-Luc Godard and François Truffaut led the way in the *nouvelle vague* of the 1960s, which rejected much of cinematic convention while paying tribute to Hollywood moviemaking. Another response was to turn away from the fast-paced plots of American cinema in favor of a more reflective mood. The films of Ingmar Bergman were contemplative personal essays, rich in images simultaneously surreal and real.

Overall, the arts tended to become less austere and less concerned with formal principles. Nowhere was this shift more apparent than in architecture. Modern architecture, influenced by the Bauhaus school, had developed an international style that favored the pure and simple, geometric forms, and unadorned walls of glass. By the 1970s, however, newer styles rejected that aesthetic, instead featuring unexpected shapes, pitched roofs with gables, echoes of many older styles, and whimsical ornamentation. Because the element that this eclectic architecture most obviously shared was its rejection of modernism, it came to be called *post-modern*, a term soon applied to many other fields as well. A preference for playful attitudes and individualistic innovation more than a formal school of thought, postmodernism reflected important cultural tendencies. Labeling regularity, rigid logic, and the control of nature or human beings as modern made postmodernism a convenient way to describe a new direction in the arts and social sciences.

THE END OF EMPIRE

In 1945, European empires spanned more than 40 countries, containing over one-quarter of the world's population; two decades later, almost all of them had become independent states. Although the European powers remained unaware to the very end of the degree to which colonial nationalism threatened their empires, the first nationalist movements appeared as early as the late nineteenth century. During the interwar period, colonial nationalist movements became well organized, widespread, and more militant than ever before. The defeats and disruptions of the Second World War thus hastened an imperial collapse that was long in the making.

Colonial Nationalism in the Early Twentieth Century

The fact that the colonies had fought on behalf of the European powers in the First World War, combined with the principles of the postwar political reconstruction, created expectations of colonial reform. When these hopes were dashed, colonial nationalist movements took up more radical agendas and a more belligerent tone.

The First World War and Its Aftermath

A truly global war, the First World War saw the European powers deploy colonial soldiers to fight on their behalf both on the Western Front and in colonial theaters of war in Africa, the Middle East, and Asia. Nearly 200,000 soldiers from French West Africa, almost 300,000 North Africans, 50,000 Indochinese, 40,000 soldiers from Madagascar, and 60,000 from other colonies were among the more than 600,000 colonial subjects who fought for France, of whom about 200,000 died; close to a million and a half Indian soldiers did combat for Britain, with over 60,000 killed. African soldiers also fought for Germany on the African front, but racism prevented the German military command from shipping Africans to Europe. They saw the use of French *tirailleurs sénégalais* (Senegalese soldiers) in the trenches of the Western Front, in fact, as proof of French degeneracy.

In the aftermath of the war, the principles of the peace settlement raised hopes of colonial reform. American anticolonialism and, especially, Woodrow Wilson's cherished ideal of the nation's right to self-determination led colonial leaders to believe that greater local autonomy and constitutional equality would be extended to them. These expectations were encouraged by the League of Nation's development of the mandate system for the distribution of the dominions of the defeated Ottoman Empire and Germany to the Allied powers. The League devised three categories of mandates, based on their degree of political and economic development. The former Ottoman provinces of Syria, Lebanon, Iraq, and Palestine received a Class A designation, which defined them as almost ready for independence, and therefore subject only to provisional European administrative control. Although the European powers effectively ruled Class B mandates (most of the German colonies in Africa) and Class C mandates (the remaining German African colonies and German possessions in the South Pacific) as they did ordinary colonies, the very notion of a progressive path to independence introduced the idea that Europe viewed imperial rule as transient, a form of temporary guardianship rather than a permanent state. The fact that the "white dominions"—the former colonies of European settlement such as Canada and Australia—successfully asserted their autonomy to become self-governing during this period also added to the belief that the empire gradually was being phased out. Finally, promises to increase certain aspects of self-government in the colonies (tariff autonomy, for example) made by the European powers, especially Britain, reinforced the mood of anticipation.

The Growth of the Nationalist Movements

The colonies earned little by way of reward for their contribution to the war effort, however, and bitterness about the postwar settlement soon fueled the growth of colonial nationalism. Although nationalist movements had been developing since before World War I, especially in Algeria, India, Indonesia, and Vietnam, the war and its aftermath transformed them. Before the war, colonial nationalism had been a largely elite affair, primarily aimed at colonial reform; now nationalist sentiment began to spread among the colonial masses and to adopt a more aggressive tone and far-reaching political agenda. In some parts of the world, movements called for greater autonomy; in others (India, for example) they demanded outright independence.

The turn to militancy gave rise to nationalist unrest in several parts of the world, including a 1925 uprising in Syria against French mandate rule, an insurrection in the Dutch East Indies in 1926, a series of peasant rebellions in Indochina in the early 1930s, and an Arab revolt against the British mandate in Palestine from 1936–39. In India, the passage of the Rowlatt Acts of 1919, extending wartime restrictions on the civil liberties of Indians, spurred a major demonstration of 10,000 people in Amritsar in the Punjab region. After British troops fired on the unarmed crowd, killing nearly 400 and wounding about 1,200, the demonstrations became known as the Amritsar Massacre, an event that converted millions of Indians to the nationalist cause. Capitalizing on the widespread mood of disaffection, Gandhi launched the noncooperation movement of 1920–22, which boycotted British goods and institutions in favor of local alternatives. Insurgencies and revolutions in parts of the world where ruling regimes were seen as corrupted by Western influence echoed these developments: examples include Sun Yat-Sen's ousting of the Qing dynasty and establishment of a Chinese republic in 1911 and Mustapha Kemal's creation of the Turkish Republic out of the crumbling Ottoman Empire in 1922.

In addition to the intensification of nationalist activism, opponents of colonialism mounted important theoretical critiques in this period. In *Imperialism: The Highest Stage of Capitalism*, Vladimir Lenin denounced colonialism as the inevitable last stage of the capitalist exploitation of the masses; first published in 1917, it became widely influential in the 1920s. At the same time, under the influence of the cultural anthropologist Franz Boas, European and American anthropology overturned the racist typologies of the late nineteenth century to embrace a new cultural relativism.

Other criticism of colonialism emerged from within the colonial world. In addition to older movements such as Pan-Africanism (which had formed around the turn of the twentieth century to express the sense of a shared cultural identity among Africans), the cultural movement of *Négritude* emerged among French colonial subjects in the 1930s, influenced by the American Harlem Renaissance of the 1920s. Led by Léopold Senghor of Senegal (later its first president), Aimé Césaire of Martinique, and Léon Damas of French Guiana, the movement asserted pride in African values of community and solidarity while condemning the barbarism of European colonialism.

The European powers did not entirely ignore nationalist calls for change. The colonial powers shifted their position after the First World War, abandoning the unapologetic domination of the "new imperialism" of the turn of the century for policies designed to be more humane and to recognize the legitimacy of local cultures. In the French case, this meant a turn to a policy of "associationism" that sought to disseminate French culture to the colonies, but that also acknowledged the value of indigenous culture. Likewise, the Dutch spoke of developing an "ethical" colonial approach.

In economic terms, the postwar effort to legitimize the empire translated into policies designed to promote "colonial development." This included the building of infrastructure, including railroad and harbor expansion, but it also encompassed policies that fostered the economic integration of colony and metropole and tightened the regulation of colonial economies, including the use of labor and the extraction of resources. The British called this approach "constructive imperialism," and while the name suggested benefit to the colonies, the policy was intended to preserve the empire through the close regulation of imperial trade and to develop the empire into a self-sufficient market. For France as well, the economic interdependence of metropole and colonies offered a means of overcoming the French trade deficit and recovering from the economic turmoil created by the war. During the 1930s, moreover, these policies made it possible for the European states to use the colonies to mitigate some of the effects of the depression.

The tightening of colonial control, in combination with the increased economic burdens imposed on the colonies, spurred the further growth of colonial nationalism. Alienated colonial elites, in particular, did not see colonial development policy as beneficial to the colonies, while the growing economic marginalization of the masses did a great deal to win them over to the nationalist cause. Although a range of nationalist groups existed, each with different goals, almost everywhere a radical strand of nationalism appeared, one that sought not merely to reform colonial rule and attain a measure of autonomy from the metropole, but rather to expel the European colonizing state.

The Postwar Disintegration of the Empire

If the First World War intensified and spread anticolonial nationalism, the disruptions and defeats of the Second World War precipitated the final collapse of the European empires.

The Impact of the Second World War and the Cold War Although many Allied leaders believed that with some concessions they could restore their empires after World War II, pressures to the contrary soon proved to be too strong. During the war, Japan had seized the East Indies from the Netherlands, Indochina from France, and Malaya from Britain, while the Vichy government had lost touch with much of France's empire. The wartime loss of control over the colonies made it extremely difficult to reestablish authority after the war.

Nationalist movements also had grown much stronger during the war, not least because of its devastating effects on colonial economic life. This was particularly true in Asia, which had been a major theater of war. In the short term, the war generated intense economic activity: wartime shutdowns of supplies in Europe increased the demand for food, raw materials, and manufactures from the colonies, promoting high employment. But the war also led to steep price increases, especially for agricultural products such as grain, creating major economic hardship for large segments of the population, including the colonial middle classes and peasantry. Their grievances turned these groups into new converts to colonial nationalism.

At the same time, a pervasive anticolonialism in the international arena made it more difficult than ever to assert the legitimacy of the European empires. The establishment of the United Nations in 1945 created a prestigious international forum that stood resolutely against colonial rule. Just as important, the United States staunchly opposed colonialism, and the USSR not only denounced it but frequently aided colonial uprisings. In Europe, too, opposition to imperialism (primarily from parties on the left) grew stronger, inspired, in part, by colonial nationalist leaders and intellectuals and reinforced by the public's greater interest in having money spent on reconstruction at home.

All that changed, however, with the outbreak of the Cold War. Campaigns for colonial independence now became entangled with revolutionary movements and Cold War interests. The United States, in particular, did an about-face on the issue of empire; where Roosevelt had pressured Europe to withdraw from its colonies, Truman urged the colonial powers to hold the line in order to thwart the spread of communist revolution. Mao Zedong's establishment of a communist regime in China in 1949 acutely heightened these concerns. As a counterweight, the United States promoted the economic revival of a now democratic Japan and gave strong economic and military support to Taiwan (a large island off China held by the Chinese nationalists).

Things Fall Apart Despite clear signs of their empires' imminent collapse, the European powers remained determined to hold on to or reconquer their colonies after the war. The British struggled to prevent India from achieving immediate and complete independence. Failing that, they set their sights on preserving the rest of their empire, and Conservatives like Winston Churchill even envisioned colonial expansion. Believing that it would take at least twenty-five years for the Dutch East Indies to become independent, the Dutch sent their army to try to reconquer the colony, while the French embarked on long and bitter wars in both Indochina and Algeria.

But the independence movements began to prevail. Where imperial rule was direct and of long standing, colonial officials offered concessions that somehow always came a little too late or led to demands for more. When they used force, opposition tended to increase, not only on the scene but around the world. News of effective resistance in one colony stimulated new protests and uprisings in others around the world. Efforts to censor the news and renewed campaigns against subversive agitators only increased their following and cost the support of native local elites. Wherever large settler communities were present (as, for example, in Algeria, Kenya, and Rhodesia) independence struggles generally were much more violent. Bloody conflict within colonized populations also accompanied several independence struggles, most notably during the Mau Mau rebellion in Kenya from 1952 to 1956 and the partition of India and Pakistan in 1947.

One after another, the colonies emancipated themselves. Gandhi had gained worldwide admiration for his credo of nonviolent resistance, which contributed greatly to the movement that forced Britain to grant independence to India in 1947. Neither Gandhi nor the British, however, could prevent the violent conflict between Hindus and Muslims that led to partition, an independent Pakistan, and Gandhi's assassination in 1948. Ceylon (Sri Lanka) and Burma (Myanmar) gained their independence from Great Britain in 1948. In Malaya, conflict lasted from 1947 until complete British withdrawal in 1960. Indonesia similarly won freedom in 1949 only after years of combat, although the Dutch clung to West Papua for another fifteen years. In Vietnam, the French-educated communist leader Ho Chi Minh organized a brilliant guerrilla campaign to unify the nation. With the Vietnamese communists receiving strong support from the USSR and China, the United States encouraged France to engage them in what turned out to be a costly and futile war. After a decisive defeat in the battle of Dien Bien Phu, the French finally withdrew in 1954.

In the Middle East, France relinquished its mandates in Lebanon and Syria by 1946. Foreign troops left Iraq and Iran, and negotiations began for British forces to depart from Egypt and the Sudan. Great Britain also sought to create separate Jewish and Arab states in Palestine, despite Arab opposition. Britain removed its troops in May 1948, amid mounting terror campaigns from both sides. Arab forces invaded the day the British left but were driven back. The United Nations, eager to provide Jews a refuge following Nazi persecution, endorsed the creation of an Israeli state,

Lord Mountbatten, war hero and England's last Viceroy of India, speaks to India's Constituent Assembly on the day India became independent, August 18, 1947.
Hulton Archive/Getty Images

In January 1957 French paratroopers, searching for terrorists on the outskirts of Algiers, frisk a civilian in Arab clothing.
Bettmann/Corbis

and UN mediators brought about a shaky truce that confirmed Israel's existence.

In Africa, European officials, business people, and residents did what they could to prolong European rule with grants of autonomy and promises of aid, but they could only delay the inevitable. Britain acceded to Ghana's independence in 1957. Kenya won independence from Britain in 1963, after years of brutal warfare and the systematic use of torture by the British to suppress the Mau Mau insurgency. By the mid-60s, most African states had won formal independence, although Portugal held on to its colonies until the overthrow of its own military dictatorship in 1974. The two biggest colonies, Angola and Mozambique, were almost immediately caught up in a civil war in which the United States supported one side and the Soviet Union the other.

The Algerian War　The fight for Algerian independence, waged by the FLN (National Liberation Front), unfolded in one of the longest and bloodiest of the colonial wars starting in 1954. A French colony since 1830, Algeria had a sizable French population, known as *pieds noirs*, which had lived there for generations. Their insistence that Algeria should remain French had patriotic appeal to metropolitan France, which supported the war enthusiastically. By 1958, however, the French public had tired of the war and the government, a center-left coalition, was moving toward negotiations with the FLN. Determined to prevent Algerian independence at all costs, a group of right-wing French army officers seized political control in Algeria in 1958 and

threatened to move against the French government. At the same time, the *pieds noirs* built barricades in the streets of Algiers and swore to prevent Algerian independence. Faced with the specter of civil war and a right-wing coup, the French legislature turned to World War II hero Charles de Gaulle, who replaced the shaky Fourth Republic with the Fifth. Although de Gaulle promised to keep Algeria French, as president he opened secret negotiations with the FLN. News of this led outraged right-wing officers to form a secret army, the OAS, which for the next eighteen months employed terrorist tactics in both Algeria and France. Nevertheless, by the end of 1962, Algeria gained its independence. A million *pieds noirs* (along with the *harkis*, Algerians who had fought for the French) were forcibly repatriated to France, where they experienced a difficult adjustment.

After Empire

Decolonization posed new challenges for both the former colonies and the European colonial powers. Postcolonial nations sought to define a new global position for themselves and, for a time, found strength in solidarity. Europeans had to come to terms with their diminished power and grapple with their responsibility for the negative legacies of colonial rule.

The Birth of the "Third World"　One challenge facing the postcolonial nations was to carve out an independent role for themselves in the bipolar politics of the Cold War era. Postcolonial leaders first formulated the idea of a "Third World" political coalition in 1955 at the Bandung Conference in Indonesia, organized by twenty-nine African and Asian nations in support of the anticolonial wars in Algeria and Vietnam. Attended by, among others, Jawaharlal Nehru of India, Kwame Nkrumah of the Gold Coast (soon to be Ghana), Gamal Abdel Nasser of Egypt, Chou En Lai of China, Ho Chi Minh of Vietnam, Sukarno of Indonesia, and Congressman Adam Clayton Powell of Harlem in the United States, the conference debated strategies to strengthen independence from the superpowers, but also to overcome the economic and social legacies of colonialism. The "Third World" thus emerged in part as a political concept. Despite their often leftist, and even socialist, orientation, Third World countries rejected any notion of Soviet domination, seeking instead to act as a united, "nonaligned" bloc in the Cold War. At the same time, the "Third World" was an economic concept, evoking the longterm structural inequalities faced by the ex-colonial nations and the ways in which Western domination persisted in the aftermath of empire.

One of the foremost theoreticians of the "Third World" was Frantz Fanon, a Martinican-born psychiatrist and political philosopher who attended medical school in France. Fanon's experiences of alienation from both French and Martinican society inspired him to write his first book, *Black Skin, White Masks* (1952), in which he explored the ways in which colonial domination psychologically damaged colonial subjects who were educated by the colonial power to believe in their own inferiority. Appointed to work as a child psychiatrist in Algeria in 1953, Fanon became caught up in the Algerian nationalist movement. His best-known work, *The Wretched of the Earth* (1961), called for the violent overthrow of European imperialism and became the leading colonial nationalist manifesto of its day. In contrast to Pan-Africanism, *Négritude*, or any of the other anticolonial critiques that sought to preserve and protect a particular cultural identity, Fanon's conception of the Third World was universalist, in which solidarity between the former colonies emerged not from a common culture, but rather from their shared experience of subordination.

During the 1960s and 70s, scholars and political figures debated the long-term effects of colonialism on the politics and economies of the "Third World." Underdevelopment theorists, for example, tried to explain the economic dependency of former colonies on the West as the result of structural disadvantages inherited from the colonial era; they asserted that the European extraction of raw materials from their colonies had introduced the latter into the international economy in a subordinate position that, in the postcolonial era, left them unable to industrialize and effectively locked into an economically dependent role. Other theorists

wrote about the crisis of the postcolonial state, tracing its roots back to the colonial period as well. Contemporary Africa in particular, it was argued, faced problems dating back to the colonial era. The European powers had largely invented the African colonies at the Berlin Conference of 1884–1885, without regard to local political, ethnic, or cultural boundaries. As a result, African nationalists faced a double challenge after decolonization: they had to struggle not merely to oust the colonial power, but to find ways, sometimes in the face of ethnic enmity, to forge a sense of national unity where none existed. In some cases, that pursuit of unity failed, defeated by ethnic conflict (such as that between the Tutsis and Hutus of Rwanda). Moreover, the fact that African independence was not achieved through a mobilization of the African masses, but rather through negotiations between nationalist leaders and colonial powers, has favored the development of postcolonial states modeled after their authoritarian colonial predecessors.

The "Third World" has all but disappeared since the 1990s. In many ways, the collapse of communism in Europe and the end of the era of bipolar politics rendered the idea of the "Third World" obsolete. At the same time, critics of the "Third World" concept took issue with its portrayal of postcolonial nations as the passive victims of the West, suggesting instead that a more complex interplay took place between the West and non-West, the global and the local. More broadly, it was felt that the "Third World" no longer adequately captured either the material or the psychic condition of the postcolonial world. By the 1990s, some "Third World" nations had achieved a measure of material well-being and most of them could no longer be described as revolutionary or socialist. For the most part, postcolonial nations seek to become integrated into the global economy as consumers; for better or worse, they seem to be coming to terms with transnational capitalism.

The Persistence of European Involvement   The crumbling of empire did not always end Europe's involvements in its colonial possessions. Conflicts within postcolonial states tended to draw the European powers back into the political life of former colonies as local leaders appealed to old interests. Some African nations preferred to work with the European country from which they had gained independence rather than embrace the Cold War alignment that tended to come with American or Soviet aid. Thus, Britain and France continued to influence affairs in their former colonies, especially in Africa, by taking advantage of diplomacy, economic interests, common languages, and similar educational, legal, and administrative institutions. Through the Commonwealth of Nations, Great Britain gathered its former colonies in an often influential international club, even if it could not always resolve conflicts between its own members. In the former French colonies in Africa, it was not uncommon for former colonial administrators to become diplomatic officials to the post-independence states. Cold War competition, which increased the amount of economic and military aid available, also helped keep corrupt and dictatorial regimes in power by playing the superpowers against each other. Foreign intervention did not end with the passing of European empires.

European Memories of Empire   European states have only begun to confront their colonial pasts, prompted, in part, by the growing importance attached to group and individual rights in the world community. Until 1999, the French state refused to call the Algerian War a "war," referring to it instead as a "public order operation." Then, in 2000, after forty years of denial, the French government was forced to acknowledge the systematic torture of Algerians during the war after revelations made by Paul Aussaresses, a high-ranking general who served in Algeria. The French government also returned the remains of Saartje Baartman in 2002, known in the nineteenth century as "the Hottentot Venus," to the Khoisan people of South Africa. A Khoisan slave near Capetown, Baartman was sold in 1810 to an Englishman, who exhibited her across Britain for her unusual anatomy, in particular her oversized buttocks; for decades after her death, her skeleton, brain, and genitals were displayed in the Musée de l'Homme in Paris.

Other colonial powers also sought to address wrongdoings of the past. In an interview in 2002, the British

Foreign Secretary Jack Straw attributed many of the world's current problems, including the conflicts in Kashmir and the Middle East, to British colonialism. In 2005, forty-five years after the Belgian Congo won its independence, the Belgian Royal Museum for Central Africa mounted the first-ever exhibition of the Congo under King Leopold II (1885-1908). His brutal forced-labor regime used mutilation and murder to terrorize colonial subjects into meeting production quotas, making his reign one of the most notorious chapters of European colonial history. Australia designated May 26 "National Sorry Day" in 1998, an acknowledgment of the harm done to the so-called Stolen Generations, aboriginal children forcibly removed from their families by the Australian state from 1869 through the 1970s; in February 2008 Australian Prime Minister Kevin Rudd also issued an official apology to the Stolen Generations. Various groups also have claimed—and in some cases received—political recognition and rights as so-called "First Nations," including the Sami of northern Scandinavia, Aboriginal Australians, and the Maori of New Zealand. The Sami have organized their own parliaments in Norway in 1989, in Sweden in 1993, and in Finland in 1996.

Despite this trend, the European states have a distance to go before coming to terms with colonialism. Former French colonial subjects were outraged, for example, by the passing of a French law in 2005 requiring schools and history textbooks to portray the French role in its colonies in a positive light. Although the controversial clause of the law was repealed in 2006, France's current president Nicolas Sarkozy has gained

The Maori are one indigenous group that has gained political recognition and rights in the postcolonial era.
Alamy Images

notoriety for his lack of contrition for France's colonial past. Speaking about the role of the *pieds noirs*, he said in March 2007, "I want us to stop this systematic repentance [about]. . . . the colonial system."[2]

POLITICAL TENSIONS IN THE BIPOLAR WORLD

The Cold War continued to dominate the domestic and international politics in Europe of the 1950s and 60s. Politics in the West turned more conservative, while in the Soviet Union, the death of Stalin eased some of the more repressive aspects of the communist regime. In Eastern Europe, however, efforts to achieve a measure of autonomy from the Soviet Union were harshly quelled. In the international arena, Cold War tensions of the 1950s and early 60s gave way to a more stable bipolar balance of power.

New Political Directions

The stability and prosperity of the 1950s tended, in many cases, to favor more conservative policies. Only in Scandinavia did socialists continue in office. In Britain the Conservatives regained power in 1951 and kept it for the next thirteen years, ending rationing and lowering taxes but not undoing most of Labour's social program. Italy's Christian Democrats turned more to the right while keeping Communists isolated, and West Germany under Konrad Adenauer became a model of stable affluence. More dramatic political changes took place in France and the Soviet Union.

The Crisis of France's Fourth Republic France's multiparty system tended not to produce strong governments; yet in many respects the Fourth Republic performed very well. In 1954 an able prime minister of the center-left, Pierre Mendès-France, announced a dynamic program of political reform and social modernization and at the same time set about extricating France from Indochina. Some on the right saw this as dangerous weakness, and the reform measures further antagonized an angry movement of small shopkeepers and farmers—people bypassed by the benefits of modernization. The electorate shifted away from the center toward Charles de Gaulle, the very symbol of strength and order, and to the communist left.

The Fifth Republic and the Return of De Gaulle Given these social strains, it is not surprising that the colonial crisis in Algeria proved fatal to the Fourth Republic. In 1958, the legislature turned to de Gaulle to diffuse that crisis and to stave off the threat of civil war and a right-wing coup. At his behest, a new constitution, overwhelmingly approved by popular referendum in September 1958, established the Fifth Republic as a presidential regime with a chief executive elected for a seven-year term. De Gaulle was chosen president two months later, and Gaullists became by far the largest party in parliament, where the Communists were reduced to a handful.

De-Stalinization in the Soviet Union After thirty years of dictatorship, Joseph Stalin died of a stroke in 1953. The shock and sense of loss in the Soviet Union was compounded by the problem of succession, something its communist government had faced only once before. It went surprisingly smoothly, and a form of collective leadership emerged. Only in 1956–1957 did it become clear that Nikita Khrushchev was the dominant figure. The competition for leadership involved two principal issues. Stalin's last years had brought heavy repression (with terror), ugly anti-Semitism, and a party line enforced on everything from socialist realism in the arts to the fallacious genetic theories of Trofim Lysenko. Many Russians wanted an end to such policies. The second issue was the standard of living, which had been sacrificed to the demanding goals of the latest five-year plan. Even Stalin had hinted that it might be time to increase consumption as well as build industry. Khrushchev had seemed conservative on the need for change, and his triumph showed again that control of the Communist party remained the key to power. Still, the infighting that brought him to the top, which included sudden dismissals and even executions, was followed not by purges but by the reassignment of his opponents to less prominent positions.

With a speech to the Twentieth Party Congress in 1956, Khrushchev established his surprising new direction. He attacked the "cult of personality" under Stalin, naming many of Stalin's excesses, his paranoid distrust, his interference in the conduct of war, and his responsibility for the purge trials of the 1930s. Nothing like it had occurred before. Myths that for a generation had been central to the nation's enormous sacrifices were suddenly unmasked. Khrushchev's charges circulated widely in secret and then more openly, with unsettling effects in the Soviet Union, Eastern Europe, and communist movements everywhere. Streets and squares were renamed; statues and pictures disappeared. With the thaw following Stalin's death, a freer and more open society appeared in prospect. Although Khrushchev quickly clamped down on criticism amid rising complaints about domestic problems and rumblings from within the Soviet bloc, restraints were never again so

---

[2] Elaine Sciolino, "The Sarkozy of the Future Jousts with the Chirac of the Past," *The New York Times*, May 11, 2007.

rigid or arbitrary as they had been under Stalin. When the Soviet Union celebrated the fortieth anniversary of the Russian Revolution in 1957 by launching the world's first space satellite, *Sputnik*, the USSR's status as a state both powerful and stable seemed confirmed.

Khrushchev's Effort The Soviet Union's most impressive achievement, admired throughout the world, had been its industrial growth. By the 1960s its economy was second in overall production and wealth only to that of the United States. It sent the first person into orbit around the earth in 1961; and as the world's largest producer of steel, iron, and, more recently, oil, the USSR was apparently gaining in the economic competition with the West. Brashly confident, Khrushchev declared that the Soviet Union "would bury" the United States and promised that his government was now able to give more attention to consumer products and adequate housing. Like his campaign of de-Stalinization, such policies opened the possibility of a new evolution in Soviet rule, but real change proved difficult.

Khrushchev's plans to increase agricultural production failed, and the issue of whether to invest in consumer goods or heavy industry reopened long-standing conflicts within the highest circles. Many Kremlin leaders worried as well about the growing restiveness in Eastern Europe and the rift with China, which since 1956 had consistently denounced the Soviet Union's international policies as a betrayal of communism. When, in the process of solidifying his authority, Khrushchev antagonized the military, they and his opponents in the Politburo and the Central Committee felt strong enough to speak against him. In 1964 they voted him out of office and sent him into quiet retirement.

The International Context

Although Britain and France were on the Security Council and Scandinavians served as the UN's general secretaries until 1961, the United Nations reflected a redistribution of international power in which Europe no longer dominated. Economic strength made Western European nations prominent in such international economic organizations as the International Monetary Fund and in arms sales but did not lessen their subordination to the superpowers. Often restive individual nations sought to follow distinctive paths.

The Suez Crisis Great Britain asserted its independence during a crisis in relations with Egypt, once a part of their empire. Gamal Abdel Nasser's government was distrusted in the West for its nationalism, its radical domestic program, and its willingness to accept aid from nations in the Communist bloc. When the Western

MAP 29.1 THE ARAB-ISRAELI CONFLICT, 1947–1982
This map includes the boundaries of Israel after UN partition in 1947 as well as conflicts and changing boundaries until 1982. Which surrounding states have been most involved in this ongoing conflict?

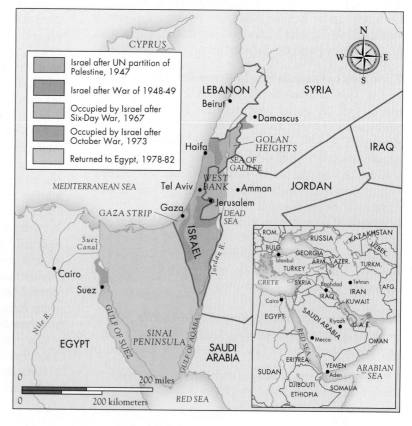

powers, following the United States, refused aid for the construction of a high dam across the Nile at Aswan, Nasser nationalized the Suez Canal, still owned by a British-controlled company. Britain responded strongly and, after efforts at compromise broke down, conspired with Israel and France to take military action. Israel attacked Egypt in October 1956 and occupied the banks of the canal, aided by an Anglo-French bombardment. Because both the Soviet Union and the United States opposed the entire venture, the United Nations was able to force a cease-fire within a week and the withdrawal of foreign troops shortly afterward. This return to old imperialist tactics merely demonstrated that their time had passed and that British and French action required American acquiescence. That remained true even though Britain soon became the third nation to possess a hydrogen bomb, and France would later be the fourth.

The Soviet Bloc

The Communist governments of Eastern Europe had closely mimicked Soviet rule in the ruthless use of secret police and internment camps, in the idolization of Stalin, and in general policy. But resentment of the USSR's exploitation became more public after Stalin's death. Within three months, the workers of East Berlin took to the streets in a general strike, protesting the increased production quotas they blamed on the Soviet Union. Russian tanks rushed in to put down the revolt, but it had long-lasting effects. Walter Ulbricht became the new leader of East Germany and offered a program of higher wages and better living conditions even while strengthening the dictatorship. Although still tightly tied to the Soviet Union, East Germany expanded its trade with West Germany and developed a voice of its own in the councils of communist countries.

A workers' protest in Poland in 1956 even won support from nationalists within the Communist party. Again Soviet forces intervened, this time to public jeers. The Polish Communist party then elected its secretary, Wladyslaw Gomulka, in preference to the pro-Russian candidate. Gomulka retained power until 1970 by convincing the Soviets of his loyalty while arguing that socialist states needed to follow distinctive national paths. Poland demanded and received a share of the war reparations that Germany paid, negotiated economic aid from the United States, and mitigated its repression of the Catholic Church and of Polish intellectuals. Risings in Hungary ended more tragically. Riots in October 1956 were fiercely anti-Russian, and the Soviet troops at first withdrew from Budapest, seemingly disposed to accept Hungary's increased autonomy. Then Imre Nagy, who had been arrested the year before for "right-wing deviationism," became premier. Bowing to popular pressure, he agreed to replace the alliance with Russia with a policy of neutrality. The Soviet leaders pressured,

threatened, and finally sent their army to crush the revolution. It did so in ten days of bitter fighting while rebel radio stations pleaded for the Western aid that many Hungarians expected. None came. Hungary suffered a heavy-handed, repressive Soviet occupation, and a new wave of refugees left the country. Nagy himself was eventually executed, yet his successor, Janos Kadar, slowly led the country on a more independent course.

Washington denounced Russian imperialism but remained preoccupied with the crisis over the Suez Canal within its own alliance, in effect acknowledging a Soviet sphere of influence. The USSR would not allow satellite regimes to defy Soviet policy. Under Tito, the former leader of the Yugoslav antifascist resistance, Yugoslavia remained the great exception, and improved relations with Khrushchev did not affect Yugoslavia's trade with the West or its experiments at decentralization. Albania, isolated from the Soviet sphere by geography, and the most backward country on the Continent, formed closer ties to communist China as a kind of challenge to the USSR. Romania, like Bulgaria among the most Stalinist of the satellite regimes, distanced itself slightly by seeking better relations with the West. Little more was possible.

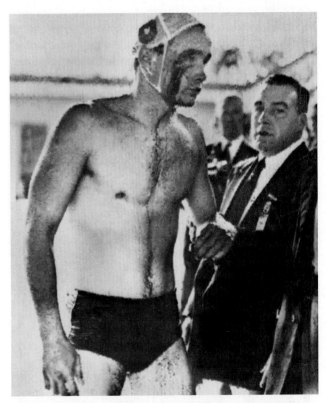

At the 1956 Olympic Games in Melbourne, Australia, as the Red Army crushed the Hungarian uprising, a water polo match between Hungary and the USSR deteriorated into a violent brawl.
Getty Images

The stark concrete wall, topped with barbed wire, became a symbol of the Cold War.
AGE Fotostock

Bipolar Stability

Bipolar Stability The Warsaw Pact and the NATO alliance institutionalized the armed confrontation between the superpowers in Europe. For some thirty years their competition shaped international relations, at times becoming a rigid opposition and at others allowing some flexibility. In 1961 East-West tension was literally cast in stone when East Germany built a long gray wall across the center of Berlin, eventually extending it along East Germany's entire western border. As a symbol and as a device to keep East Germans from leaving, the wall fostered international distrust. There was a still more ominous crisis in 1961, when the United States sponsored an invasion of Cuba aimed at the overthrow of Fidel Castro. It failed, and in the following year the Soviet Union began to base missiles in Cuba. War seemed imminent until, as the Americans massed their fleet, the Soviets withdrew their missiles. There was, after all, a mutual interest in not disturbing the balance of power, and the Soviet Union was facing a growing rift with China that made diplomatic exchanges with the United States more attractive.

Literally in the middle, European governments used their influence to favor East-West negotiations at summit conferences and on specific issues. They promoted agreements on space exploration in 1967, the opening of the Strategic Arms Limitation Talks in 1969, and accord on the principles of human rights at the Helsinki Conference in 1975. Through trade, loans, and technical agreements, the governments of Western Europe encouraged those of Eastern Europe toward whatever autonomy from the Soviet Union they were willing to attempt.

National Interests Individual states continued to probe ways to serve their interests. West Germany gradually asserted some of the political weight that its wealth implied. Less committed to the Cold War than Adenauer had been, Willy Brandt skillfully negotiated a new opening to the East. The resulting treaty between West Germany and the Soviet Union, signed in 1970,

A group of strikers from Women Strike for Peace demonstrate at the UN.
Historicus, Inc.

was a milestone that earned Brandt the Nobel Peace Prize. While allowing for a peaceful reunification of Germany as a possibility, it accepted West Germany's eastern boundary, pointed to a normalization of the status of Berlin (still divided between Soviet and Western occupation), and paved the way for extensive relations between West Germany and the governments of Eastern Europe.

Great Britain emphasized its close ties to the United States rather than to Europe, and the Scandinavian countries tended to position themselves as friends of nonaligned countries and mediators between the superpowers. The most flamboyant search for an independent policy was de Gaulle's. Resentful of American policy toward France, he set upon a course that by 1966 led to the withdrawal of French forces from NATO command (and of NATO forces from French soil), although France remained a member of the alliance. France also strengthened its relations with Eastern Europe and increased its aid to developing nations. Greater independence from American policy appealed to many others in the West, especially on the left, and in 1981 nearly half a million young people in Bonn and perhaps another million in other capitals marched to demand that Europe be freed of the nuclear weapons of both sides.

1968 and Its Aftermath

In retrospect, the basis for Europe's greater integration and economic transformation was established by 1957, but that prospect was often called into question between then and 1989. At the time, the tensions of the Cold War in a divided continent and domestic social and political conflicts were more obvious. Two periods of crisis stand out, one culminating in 1968 and the other beginning in 1973; both challenged established economic and political systems.

Waves of Protest

Greater well being seemed to fuel moral outrage. Many Western Europeans were appalled by the rising commercialism and inequality that accompanied prosperity. Many Eastern Europeans were determined to win some of the advantages that their Western neighbors enjoyed. A number of otherwise very different movements sought alternatives to the status quo.

The Revolutions of 1968   For a few weeks in May 1968, the students of Paris seemed to recapture the revolutionary spirit of 1848, with their barricades of paving stones and trees, imaginative posters, and mocking slogans. In Germany, Italy, Great Britain, and the United States as well, students briefly acted as an independent political force in 1968 and 1969. Inspired by the movements of national liberation in Africa and Asia and outraged by the war in Vietnam, they denounced imperialism as a product of capitalist societies that used consumer goods to mask inequality and injustice.

More specifically, they excoriated the rigidities and inadequacies of the educational system to which they were subject. Their elders noted with surprise that these angry protesters were in fact the beneficiaries of expanded educational opportunities and increased prosperity. As revolutions, these movements failed. Labor unions and the traditional left were suspicious of privileged college students; liberals and conservatives were

University of Paris students riot in the streets May 14, 1968, to protest police brutality. Within days, the unrest spread throughout France, sparking off strikes and riots among students and dissatisfied workers.
Hulton Archive/Getty Images

As Soviet tanks rolled into Prague, the hope ignited by Dubcek's rise to power was extinguished.
Josef Koudelka/Magnum Photos, Inc.

offended by rudeness and violence. In elections following these upheavals, the majority of voters turned to parties that emphasized order. These protest movements nevertheless stimulated important reforms, especially of education; and their style of protest, their challenges to middle-class values, and their questioning of authority have remained important elements in public discourse and in a distinctive youth culture. Ever since, movements of social criticism have used the organizing skills and tactics of satire and street theater that worked so well in 1968 to win the attention of a complacent society. The Greens are very much the heirs of those student activists.

In Czechoslovakia, the optimism of 1968, when Alexander Dubcek came to power, was short lived. As Communist party secretary, he was able to adopt a program of liberalization including greater autonomy for Slovakia and freedom of speech, assembly, and religion. Students were noisily enthusiastic for this "communism with a human face," but Moscow saw it as an intolerable danger. In the largest military operation in Europe since World War II, troops from the Soviet Union, East Germany, Hungary, and Poland invaded Czechoslovakia in August. Dubcek was soon ousted; of his springtime program, only Slovakian autonomy was allowed to stand.

The Women's Movement Women were prominent in the student demonstrations across Europe and the United States, but many discovered that male radicals, despite their rhetoric of equality in matters of race and class, tended to allocate subordinate roles to women. Simone de Beauvoir's *The Second Sex* and Betty Friedan's *The Feminine Mystique* helped women identify the problem.

When her book first appeared in 1949, Beauvoir was well established in French intellectual circles but best

Women's marches such as this one in France took place in both Europe and the United States.
© G. Pierre/Corbis

Simone de Beauvoir's relationship with Jean-Paul Sartre was well-known, but her publication of *The Second Sex* brought her international fame as a leader of the feminist movement.
© Gianni Giansanti/Corbis

known as the intimate friend of Jean-Paul Sartre, the most admired intellectual of the day. *The Second Sex*, a memoir of her own experiences, made her famous. The book gained power in the context of the 1960s, for it reflected on the ways in which society tends to make women ancillary to others (institutions, families, husbands). Beauvoir wondered whether equality for women, even if possible, would be enough to overcome this subordination to other interests or whether women did not need to establish their own distinctive voice. Her questions and her candor pushed the women's movement in new directions.

The Feminine Mystique appeared in 1963. Betty Friedan, an experienced American journalist and mother of three, wrote about what she saw as the split between the idealized vision of the perfect homemaker and the reality of women's lives. In the years after World War II, women were expected to find personal fulfillment as wives and mothers. Instead, Friedan identified women as suffering from "the problem that has no name" and a profound crisis in identity. Along with *The Second Sex*, *The Feminine Mystique* became a handbook of the women's movement in the 1960s and 1970s. The new politics centering on women's needs and women's rights became one of the important developments of the latter half of the twentieth century.

Terrorism Rather than abandon fading hope for revolution, some radical groups turned to terrorism. The skills and equipment necessary for a terrorist campaign were not hard to come by in the semisecret world of international crime, espionage, and arms deals that flourished during the Cold War. Although terrorists were few in number, modern urban society is vulnerable to their anonymity and surprise tactics. These small groups did not aim to capture power but rather to provoke the authorities into repressive acts that would alienate the public. German terrorists shot at business leaders as well as politicians until caught by severely efficient police. Basque terrorists shook several Spanish governments with their bombs and murders but accomplished little more.

In Italy, Marxist and neo-Fascist underground bands competed in kidnappings and bombings accompanied by revolutionary proclamations. In 1978 the best known of the radical groups, the Red Brigades, climaxed a series of attention-getting exploits by kidnapping Aldo Moro, a prominent politician. Police searched for him in vain as the nation held its breath until his bullet-riddled body was found in an abandoned car. Across the political spectrum, the public responded with outrage against terrorism rather than anger at the state. Although the Red Brigades remained active, they were on the wane by the time their leaders were arrested a few years later. Such incidents, like the shooting of Pope John Paul II

by a Turkish terrorist in 1981, provoked outcries about the alienation and violence of modern society but did little to change it.

Terrorism was more effective where local hatreds gave it a popular base. Irish Protestants, determined to maintain British rule in Northern Ireland, had long clashed with their Catholic neighbors who wanted Northern Ireland to be part of the Irish Republic. Neither side had much faith in the British government's proposed compromises permitting local rule, proposals never tested because terrorism reached the level of continuous war. Underground organizations on each side killed hundreds of innocent people. Although a majority of people said they favored some workable solution, loyalty to neighbors, nationalism, and recollections of past injustice, discrimination, and repression sustained the violence and prevented a resolution.

More distant religious strife brought terrorists to the Continent, too. Supporters of the Palestine Liberation Organization, seeking a Palestinian state, killed Israeli athletes at the Munich Olympic Games in 1972, and in the 1980s Paris was the site of sporadic attacks by anti-Israel terrorists. Terrorists gained little for their various causes, but heightened urban fear and made tough security measures and heavily armed police a prominent part of European city life.

Eurocommunism By the 1980s, communist parties in Western Europe realized that they had to broaden their appeal. Throughout Western Europe, years of electoral and union activity had led communist parties to form coalitions and take positions on scores of practical issues. Arguing for social justice and political freedom invited commitment to pluralism and democracy. The French and Italian parties had objected to the Soviet invasion of Czechoslovakia in 1968, and the Italian party even accepted NATO. Criticizing Soviet policies in Eastern Europe opened prospects for an alternative program.

That alternative came to be known as **Eurocommunism,** and Italy's Communist party was its model and major proponent.[3] It proclaimed its commitment to civil rights, multiple parties, and free elections, and its increased electoral successes stimulated a trend toward Eurocommunism on the left. The French Communist party, traditionally among Europe's most rigid, and a

---

[3] Communist parties had traditionally attracted nearly one-third of the electorate in Italy, one-fifth in France and Finland, one-eighth in Spain, and much less elsewhere: about 5 percent in Sweden, 4 percent in Denmark, 3 percent in Belgium, 2 percent in Greece and the Netherlands, and less than 1 percent in West Germany and Great Britain. The parties in Portugal, briefly powerful after the revolution there, and in Finland were the two least inclined to Eurocommunism.

newly revived Spanish Communist party adopted Eurocommunist positions despite pressure from the Soviet Union to preserve the unity of communism and remain loyal to Soviet leadership. By the sixtieth anniversary of the Russian Revolution in 1977, Eurocommunism represented a schism within the communist movement. But suspicion of communist parties ran deep, and even limited electoral success stimulated opposition on the right.

The End of Dictatorship in Greece, Portugal, and Spain While the Western European Left was moderating its goals, opposition to anti-Communist dictatorships grew stronger. In Greece, army officers had overthrown the unstable parliamentary system in 1967. A countercoup removed them from power in 1973, and a new democratic constitution was adopted in 1975. That Greece was clearly on a course toward a stable democracy and economic growth was confirmed by its acceptance as a member of the European Community in 1981.

Despite a stroke suffered by the Portuguese dictator António de Oliveira Salazar in 1968, his beleaguered regime clung to power until 1974, when it was overthrown by a group of army officers. This "Carnation Revolution" restored political democracy and civil rights and granted Portugal's colonies independence. The election of a socialist government in 1976 ended the post-revolution economic and political turmoil, and a decade later Portugal was able to join the European Community.

The political transformation in Spain was more gradual. Franco retired in 1973 but skillfully maintained his influence until his death two years later. In 1969 he had called on Juan Carlos, the grandson of Spain's last king, to take the empty throne, in effect as Franco's heir. Juan Carlos, however, proved himself more committed to democracy. In 1978 Spanish voters approved a new constitution and an attempted military coup was foiled. Greater regional autonomy reduced agitation from separatists and a stagnant economy rebounded under the socialist government of Felipe González. In 1986, Spain definitively ended a half-century of isolation when it joined the European Community.

Capitalist Countries: The Challenge of Recession

When economic growth slowed, political conflict sharpened. Traditional political programs lost relevance, and weakened governments struggled with problems deeply embedded in their social and economic systems. Nearly everywhere the crisis brought a change of government as opposition parties gained power.

The Energy Crisis European economies were instantly vulnerable when, in October 1973, the oil-exporting nations (mainly in the Middle East) banded together in a cartel to raise international prices. Europe imported nearly two-thirds of its energy in the form of petroleum, and only the Soviet Union could meet its own energy needs through domestic production. In response to higher prices, Western nations redoubled efforts to develop domestic sources of energy. Over the next decade the exploitation of North Sea oilfields made Norway self-sufficient and Britain nearly so, and

Gasoline lines, such as this one in Britain, were common sights during the energy crisis of 1973. Getty Images

France invested more heavily in nuclear energy than did any other country. Well run and efficient, the French plants provoked little public opposition, but nothing could make the giant stacks seem to belong in their bucolic surroundings.
Getty Images

the Netherlands developed Europe's largest fields of natural gas. But Europe's energy consumption continued to rise, and greater self-sufficiency depended heavily on nuclear energy. By 1976 more than half the world's nuclear power plants operating or under construction were in Europe, where France became the world leader. These measures and the collapse of oil prices in 1986 eased the immediate economic crisis, but its effects remained.

Opposition to reliance on nuclear power, long led by the Greens, increased after the meltdown of a nuclear reactor at Chernobyl in the Soviet Union in 1986. Radioactive clouds swept over much of Central Europe, creating concern for safety that increased in the following years as the full extent of the casualties within the Soviet Union came to be known.

Stagflation The high cost of energy added to inflationary pressures. Among major capitalist nations, only West Germany consistently managed to hold the rate of inflation below 5 percent a year. It rose to more than 20 percent in Britain and Italy in 1975–1976 (30 percent in Portugal) and undermined planning, savings, and trade while squeezing salaried employees and many workers. This widespread inflation called into question practices on which prosperity had seemed to rest: deficit financing by governments, increased imports, and business reliance on raising prices to maintain profits. Efforts to change these policies initiated conflicts over social programs, especially in Britain and Italy. Economists identified a new condition, stagflation, the paradoxical combination of economic stagnation—or recession—and rising prices.

Where strong anti-inflationary measures were imposed, as in Britain, unemployment rose, and in Europe generally became higher in the 1980s than at any time since World War II (although it would rise higher still a decade later). Europe was undergoing a major and painful economic transition. Its now-aging industries faced increased competition from the Japanese and from new plants in other parts of the world, and the state's capacity to respond was limited. The public supported social programs but opposed still higher taxes, leaving little room for maneuver, and an unexpected rise in regionalism brought new accusations that central governments disadvantaged local interests. Thus, long-accepted national policies were called into question amid new divisions. Although each country developed its own response, the central issues were similar.

Opening to the Left: France The student revolt in May 1968 shook de Gaulle's government. It weathered the storm through firmness and promises of reform because student radicals had frightened French voters, but the Fifth Republic was never the same. The government passed education reforms, broadened social programs, and made the civil service more responsive; but when a referendum on de Gaulle's vague but far-reaching plans for decentralizing the state was defeated in 1969, he resigned. The next two presidents from the center-right differed from him more in style than policy, winning close elections with promises of stability and moderation, while the opposition criticized the political system as isolated from public opinion in its reliance on highly trained experts, however brilliant.

Although most French voters were centrist, the division between a more or less Marxist left and a technocratic right dominated politics.

In 1981 the socialist leader of that opposition, François Mitterrand, won the presidential election by attempting to bridge that divide. He promised a new emphasis on issues of culture, leisure, and urban life but maintained his alliance with the Communists and supported the traditional demands of the left for the nationalization of many industries and for a more equitable distribution of income. On election night there was dancing in the streets and optimistic talk of a post-Gaullist era. The new government began with dramatic measures, nationalizing many heavy industries and most banks, raising wages and benefits, and increasing social expenditures. The daring gamble failed to stimulate an economy hurt by business distrust, the fall of the franc, and an unfavorable international economy. Within a few years, separated from the Communists, Mitterrand adopted policies of austerity, deflation, and investment in high technology that were more like those of his predecessors than his own platform. As the right gained in elections, France found a socialist president leading a government of the center that was concerned with economic modernization, military strength, and support of the European Community. As to the new social problems—large pockets of endemic unemployment, drug addiction, and racial conflict—politicians had few solutions.

Opening to the Left: Italy

In 1983 Bettino Craxi became Italy's first Socialist prime minister. A wily politician who had rebuilt the Socialist party, his arrival in power was the culmination of two long-term political trends. The Christian Democrats had dominated Italian politics since the founding of the republic in 1946, relying on a system of semisecret negotiations and labyrinthine deals. The Communists continued to be excluded from these coalitions, as were the Socialists until 1963. While the economy boomed—Italy had enjoyed the longest period of economic growth of any European nation—this domination was acceptable. In the face of recession, however, restiveness with this closed and often corrupt system surfaced. Meanwhile, the growing respectability of the Communist party helped it win local offices in much of the north, especially in the newly established regional administrations and in most of Italy's largest cities. Having gained a reputation for probity and efficiency, they argued for a "historic compromise," in which Communists and Christian Democrats would govern together in the interests of stability and reform.

Some such compromise seemed all but inevitable until Craxi sought to distance the Socialists from the Communists and build a Socialist-Christian Democrat coalition. He became prime minister and brought a new decisiveness to government, but the hoped-for reforms gave way to more immediate economic issues. His government brought stability, an impressive achievement in a tension-filled nation undergoing rapid social change, but one that fell far short of the significant changes promised.

Shift to the Right: West Germany

In West Germany, political issues tended to be overshadowed by the satisfying fact of prosperity as the Federal Republic surpassed the United States in world trade. Even the significant shift in 1969 to a government led by the Social Democrats did not lessen the commitment to encouraging investment, expanding trade, and preventing inflation. Often surprisingly conservative in their economic policies, the Social Democrats pursued democratization in other ways, carrying through educational reforms, expanding social services, and requiring large firms to have elected labor representatives on a central board of directors. Then in 1982 an unfavorable economic climate helped the Christian Democrats to regain office under Helmut Kohl, who would remain prime minister for longer than anyone since Bismarck. Kohl's government was more closely tied to the United States and friendlier to business but almost as eager as its predecessors to maintain good relations with the East. Like France and Italy, Germany looked more and more to the European Community to provide a program for the future and to shape its international role.

Shift to the Right: Great Britain

Continuity had characterized British policy for thirty years until Margaret Thatcher became prime minister in 1979. When the Conservatives were in power, they favored the private sector but largely accepted the extensive welfare programs and mixed economy they inherited. Constrained by the plight of the British economy, Labour governments in their turn reduced public expenditures and pressured trade unions to accept wage limits, while improving transport and expanding higher education.

Britain's overwhelming problem was the economy, and neither North Sea oil nor membership in the European Community solved it. Businesses failed to modernize plants or raise productivity at the pace of other industrial nations. Inflation depressed the rate of investment. Analysts found it easier to lay blame—on the enormous cost to Britain of World War II, unimaginative and weak business managers, an inadequate educational system, the selfish conservatism of labor unions, and the high costs of welfare and defense—than to prescribe remedies. In office as the recession got worse, the Labour party lost the 1979 election.

Margaret Thatcher

A doctrinaire advocate of free enterprise, Thatcher reversed the course of British domestic

Margaret Thatcher was Britain's first female prime minister and the first to serve three consecutive terms in office. She was a dominant figure in European politics throughout the 1980s.
Historicus, Inc.

policy, and the two major parties became more ideological. Out of power, Labour was dominated by its left wing, a fact that divided the opposition and helped the Conservatives stay in office. The results of Thatcher's decisive policies were impressive. The British economy restructured, and productivity rose in the late 1980s, increasing prosperity and reducing still-high unemployment. That restructuring, combined with reductions in social services, including education, also increased social inequality.

Even her opponents—and she was widely disliked—grudgingly admired Thatcher's outspokenness and fearless consistency, and there was no arguing with economic growth. She strengthened her position by appealing to nationalist fervor in 1982 when Argentina suddenly attacked the Falkland Islands (which Britain had held and Argentina had claimed for more than a century), and she took much of the credit for Britain's victory. In 1990 she won her third consecutive election, something no prime minister had done in 160 years. But her unbending defense of unrestrained capitalism and her view of Britain's national interest made for abrasive relations with many leaders at home and with the European Community. A revolt in her own party forced her to resign soon after her last electoral victory. Her less divisive successor, John Major, kept his party in power until Labour's overwhelming victory in the elections of 1997, but the Thatcher years remain a turning point in modern British history.

Summary

Although World War II took an immense toll in lives and resources, the European nations rebounded with remarkable speed after 1945. In fact, Western Europe enjoyed sustained, rapid economic growth up until the recession following the oil crisis of 1973. The dominant states on the whole adjusted realistically to the sudden collapse of their empires and, with that, of their former international preeminence. The Cold War's ideological and geographical division of Europe became a basic fact of life. But disillusionment could be found on both sides of the divide. The new welfare states of the democracies scarcely solved all their problems, as the protests of 1968 revealed, and in the Communist bloc, one-party dictatorship and repression continued long after Stalin's demise. Moreover, the economic setbacks of the 1970s proved fundamental, marking the end of the postwar prosperity and security. Europe had recovered from the nightmare of World War II, but its economic, social, and cultural place in the modern world remained unclear.

QUESTIONS FOR FURTHER THOUGHT

1. To what extent were American and Western European policies partly responsible for the Cold War? To what extent did the actions of the Soviet Union precipitate the Cold War?

2. Why were the European powers unable to maintain their empires after the Second World War?

3. Why did the student protests of 1968 erupt during a period of unprecedented prosperity in Europe? What was the nature of their grievances?

RECOMMENDED READING

Sources

De Beauvoir, Simone. *Memoirs of a Dutiful Daughter*. Translated by James Kickup. 1959. *All Said and Done*. Translated by Patrick O'Brian. 1974. Important to the history of contemporary feminism, Beauvoir's memoirs also give a sense of the intellectual life of the times.

Monnet, Jean. *Mémoires*. 1978. The chief architect of the European Community here reveals the roots of his vision and the personal style that made him so effective.

Studies

Albertini, Rudolf von. *Decolonization: The Administration and Future of the Colonies, 1919–1960*. Translated by Francisca Garvie. 1982. A solid account that focuses on Britain and France and is especially valuable for its historical depth.

Ansprenger, Frank. *The Dissolution of the Colonial Empires*.1989. An excellent study that explores the collapse of empire from the point of view of both colonial subjects and colonial powers.

Aron, Raymond. *The Imperial Republic: The United States and the World, 1945–1973*. 1974. A leading French thinker of the time analyzes the period of American dominance.

Betts, Raymond. *Uncertain Dimensions: Western Overseas Empires in the Twentieth Century*. 1985. A classic account of the impact of two World Wars on the colonial empires.

Brown, Colin, and Peter J. Mooney. *Cold War to Détente, 1945–1980*. 1981. A largely narrative account of relations between the superpowers.

Cooper, Frederick. *Africa since 1940: The Past of the Present*. 2002. Explores the roots of Africa's current situation in the colonial period.

Crossman, Richard H. (ed.). *The God That Failed*. 1950. The moving testimony of former Marxists about their lost faith during the era of Stalin.

Crouzet, Maurice. *The European Renaissance since 1945*. 1971. An optimistic essay on postwar Europe and the growth of the European Community.

DePorte, A. W. *Europe between the Superpowers*. 1979. An assessment of Europe's place in the postwar bipolar system.

Elkins, Caroline. *Imperial Reckoning. The Untold Story of Britain's Gulag in Kenya*. 2004. Documents the brutal British campaign of torture and forced removal against the independence revolt in Kenya in the 1950s.

Fejto, François. *A History of the People's Democracies: Eastern Europe since Stalin*. 1971. The conflicts and variety among Eastern European states under Soviet dominance.

Fink, Carole, Philipp Gassert, and Detlef Junker (eds.). *1968: The World Transformed*. 1998. Essays on the worldwide phenomenon of the protest movements from China and the United States to Eastern Europe, attentive not only to global influences and their use of common themes but to the variety of specific issues, including race, women, and consumerism.

Grosser, Alfred. *The Western Alliance: European-American Relations since 1945*. 1983. A clear-headed account of how international relations have worked in practice.

Hennessy, Peter. *Never Again: Britain, 1945–1951*. 1993. A balanced narrative of the triumphs and failures of Britain's postwar socialist government.

———, and Anthony Seldons. *Ruling Performance: British Governments from Attlee to Thatcher*. 1987. Contrasting perspectives on British politics in radically different governments.

Hoffmann, Stanley et al. *In Search of France*. 1965. A group of scholars attempt to define the unique patterns of French political and social life.

Hoffmann, Stanley, and Paschalis Kitromilides. *Culture and Society in Contemporary Europe*. 1981. An anthology of essays by leading intellectuals attempting to evaluate the interplay of tradition and modernity in Europe.

Katzenstein, Mary F., and Carol M. Mueller (eds.). *The Women's Movements of the United States and Western Europe*. 1987. These collected essays make for a book with wide coverage that underscores some striking national differences.

Kavanagh, Dennis, and Anthony Seldon (eds.). *The Thatcher Effect*. 1989. A variety of critical appraisals of Thatcher's policies.

La Feber, Walter. *America, Russia, and the Cold War*. 1967. Argues for the responsibility of the United States in creating the Cold War.

Levine, Philippe. *The British Empire: Sunrise to Sunset*. 2007. A synthetic treatment that considers the global impact of the Empire.

Maier, Charles S. (ed.). *The Origins of the Cold War and Contemporary Europe*. 1978. Essays seeking not so much to lay blame for the Cold War but to study its connection to domestic societies.

Mazower, Mark. *Dark Continent: Europe's Twentieth Century*. 1999. An original and critical interpretation.

Milward, Alan S. *The Reconstruction of Western Europe, 1945–1951*. 1984. Concludes that the economic boom of the 1950s and 1960s began as early as 1945, when government policy established international economic interdependence.

Neff, Donal. *Warriors at Suez*. 1981. This dramatic account by a journalist focuses on the political leaders of the nations involved in the crisis of 1956.

Rioux, Jean-Pierre. *The Fourth Republic, 1945–1958.* 1987. A close look at and a critical assessment of the period before de Gaulle's reemergence.

Shipway, Martin. *Decolonization and its Impact: A Comparative Approach to the End of the Colonial Empires.* 2008. A comparative study of decolonization from the end of the Second World War through the early 1960s.

Talbott, John E. *The War without a Name: France in Algeria, 1954–1962.* A compelling account of the Algerian conflict.

Thomas, Martin. *Empires of Intelligence: Security Services and Colonial Disorder after 1914.* 2008. Looks at British and French efforts to maintain control of their empires in the Middle East and Africa in the face of growing anticolonial nationalism.

Ulam, Adam B. *Expansion and Coexistence: The History of Soviet Foreign Policy, 1917–1973.* 1974. An expert appraisal of the consistent patterns and political pressures underlying Soviet policy.

In November 1989 the East German government suddenly granted free access to West Berlin; the spontaneous celebrations that followed became the symbol of one of history's great turning points.
© Robert Maass/Corbis

EUROPE IN THE GLOBAL ERA

In the 1990s, a series of profound political, economic, and cultural changes set Europe on a new course. With the overthrow of communism in Eastern Europe in 1989 and the collapse of the Soviet Union in 1991, the Cold War came to a sudden end, and with it the bipolar world it had created. The reverberations of this change were incalculable. It sparked a deadly upsurge of nationalism that led to war in the Balkans and the former Soviet Union and prompted Europe to rethink its relationship to America and the rest of the world. Economically, the decisive failure of communism opened the way for a free-market dominance not seen since the middle of the nineteenth century.

Other, less dramatic but equally critical, political changes also took place in the 1990s. With the 1992 signing of the Maastricht Treaty, the European Community transformed itself from a small group of nations adhering to a set of international agreements into the European Union (EU), a new political community that has steadily expanded in membership, authority, and ambition. The institutions of the EU have posed challenges to the sovereignty of the traditional nation-state and afforded Europe a new identity in the wider world.

Economic, social, and cultural transformations also have played a critical role in reshaping Europe in the last quarter century. The gradual decline of a manufacturing-based economy and its replacement by a service economy, along with the globalization of the economy, marked by the flow of money, goods, services, people, and ideas across borders, have benefited some Europeans and harmed others. These developments have brought issues of the environment, persistent unemployment, and postcolonial immigration to center stage.

Immigration has become an especially charged issue in European politics over the past twenty years. Postcolonial immigrants have altered the demographic and cultural profile of major European cities, eliciting new and intense forms of racism. European nations—along with the EU—have sought to stem the flow of immigration, while each has grappled differently with the integration of immigrant communities.

Far from the locus of world power it was at the turn of the twentieth century, Europe in the twenty-first century is on its way toward staking out a new role for itself in the global order. Part of that process has involved claiming greater independence from the United States, above all in the political arena. Another part centers on Europe's engagement in a host of transnational humanitarian organizations and its endorsement of international laws supporting global human rights. The process of redefinition is far from completed, however, and Europe has much work to do to meet increasing demands for democracy and social justice.

Dayton Agreement ends war in Bosnia and Herzegovina **1995** ———●

Czechoslovakia divides into the Czech Republic and Slovakia **1993** ●

Maastricht Treaty, converting the EC to the European Union (EU), is signed **1992** ●

USSR officially dissolves **1991** ●

East and West Germany reunited; breakup of Yugoslavia begins **1990** ●

Communist regimes fall in Poland, Hungary, Czechoslovakia, East Germany, Bulgaria, Romania **1989** ●

Soviet troops begin to withdraw from Afghanistan **1987** ●

Gorbachev becomes leader of the Soviet Union **1985** ●

● **1980** Tito dies, leading to destabilization in Yugoslavia

THE FALL OF THE SOVIET UNION AND THE EASTERN BLOC

The Cold War had shaped Europe's international relations, domestic politics, culture, and trade for forty years. Then, in one of history's sudden great turns, communist governments fell across Europe, bringing new regimes in the East and easing domestic divisions in the West by undermining ideologies of the left and the right. Market economies and parliamentary democracies were the order of the day.

The Failure of the Soviet Model

The economic crisis of the 1970s posed grave challenges to the Soviet economy, while political repression intensified. By the 1980s, the Soviet Union was ripe for the wholesale reforms promoted by Mikhail Gorbachev. Yet no one, not even Gorbachev himself, realized that his reforms had set in motion processes that would obliterate the entire Soviet system.

Signs of Failure: The 1970s Khrushchev's successors, led by Leonid Brezhnev, were tough party technicians who held a firm grip on power and offered no fresh solutions. The cold-blooded invasion of Czechoslovakia, the continuing agricultural crisis (which required the purchase of American grain in 1972 and 1975), and the need to import industrial technology, particularly from Italy and France, were all signs of a system failing to adapt to change.

Evidence of arbitrary repression continued to tarnish the country's international image. Throughout the West the press revealed the plight of Soviet Jews, who were subject to discrimination and attack. When Boris Pasternak's novel *Doctor Zhivago* exposed the seamy aspects of Soviet life and earned him the Nobel Prize for Literature in 1958, Pasternak was not permitted to go to Stockholm to receive it. The case of Alexander Solzhenitsyn caused still greater international furor. He, too, was prevented from receiving the Nobel Prize that he won in 1970 for his story of the Gulag Archipelago, a haunting account of the terrors of Soviet labor camps. Four years later he was arrested and deported, joining a chorus of Russian writers and scientists whose criticisms were widely published outside the USSR and increasingly well known at home.

Gorbachev's Gamble When Brezhnev died in 1982, he was succeeded by elderly and ailing party figures who exemplified the bureaucratic grayness of Soviet rule. Thus, the appointment in 1985 of Mikhail Gorbachev to be general secretary of the Communist party marked a new era. At fifty-four, the youngest man to lead the Soviet Union since Stalin, Gorbachev gradually revealed a personality and daring that led him in startling new directions. He spoke openly about problems of inefficiency and alienation (absenteeism and alcoholism among the workforce had reached alarming levels), and he recognized the importance of radical reform in order to meet the growing demand for consumer goods and to sustain the arms race with the United States. The cost, and risk, of that competition rose as the president of the United States, Ronald Reagan, poured more money into new weapons. Meanwhile, the contrast between East and West in both agricultural and industrial production had grown more striking, and the USSR's earlier achievements in heavy industry were now economically less important than its underperformance in new technologies and in services.

Gorbachev confronted these problems on three fronts. He set about restructuring Soviet society by decentralizing decision making, which required more

914

- **1997** Tony Blair becomes British Prime Minister

- **1999** Euro is introduced as a common currency in the EU

- **2000** Putin elected president of Russia

- **2001** September 11 terrorist attacks in the United States

- **2003** Invasion of Iraq divides the United States from many European allies

- **2004** Terrorist bombings in Madrid; EU incorporates ten new countries

- **2005** Terrorist bombings in London; Pope John Paul II dies; Benedict XVI selected; France and the Netherlands rejected the EU constitution

- **2008** Global financial crisis

For years Gorbachev was mobbed by enthusiastic well-wishers whenever he visited Western Europe and the United States; his trip to West Germany in 1990, where he was accompanied by Chancellor Kohl, was one of his last triumphal tours.
R. Bossu/Corbis Sygma

open communication, greater authority for local managers, and a reduction in the role of the Communist party. Gorbachev had to overcome entrenched resistance at all levels, but his efforts made **perestroika** (political and economic restructuring) and **glasnost** (greater openness) international buzzwords and won him admirers around the world. Internationally, his foreign policy made him the most popular figure in Soviet history. He campaigned against the threat of nuclear war and, at a summit meeting with Reagan in 1986, Gorbachev suddenly proposed breathtaking reductions in nuclear arms that nearly won Reagan's acquiescence before aides hurriedly dissuaded him. Gorbachev also knew that he must end the war in Afghanistan. Soviet troops first invaded in 1979 to sup-

port a Communist government entangled in a bloody guerrilla war against rebels heavily supported by the United States. The war was a dangerous drain on Soviet lives, wealth, and morale, and in 1987 Gorbachev began a staged withdrawal.

Remarkably, he also extended *glasnost* to Eastern Europe. Gorbachev realized that those governments, too, needed to restructure; and he was glad to end costly barter arrangements with the Comecon nations, which permitted them to buy Soviet oil at below-world-market prices in exchange for Eastern European products that the Soviet Union did not want. But once launched, *glasnost* was hard to contain. When some of the East European nations began to request that Soviet troops leave their territory and to replace their Communist

A Lithuanian crowd holds up a banner that says "Ivan Go Home" and cheers as a Soviet soldier is burned in effigy. This demonstration in April 1990 followed two years of similar agitation.
Bettmann/Corbis

regimes, Gorbachev accepted those changes, too. However necessary, such concessions troubled hostile hardliners at home, and each step toward reform revealed the need for more.

Ethnic Conflict in the USSR

A still greater danger to Soviet stability arose from the explosion of nationalist unrest in 1988. Demonstrations and violent clashes occurred around the perimeter: on the western frontier (in Georgia, Moldavia, and the Ukraine), among the Baltic republics (Latvia, Lithuania, and Estonia), and in the southern republics (Armenia and Azerbaijan). The Baltic states created at the end of World War I had lost their independence in World War II, becoming part of the Soviet Union by war's end. Demonstrations there now revived passionate memories of independence, and formerly rubber-stamp representative bodies began to act like parliaments. While they wrote new laws and constitutions, Gorbachev offered general promises, argued for the benefits of membership in the USSR, restrained his own army, and delayed any final stand on their status.

In the southern republics, Azerbaijanis and Armenians engaged in open war, inflamed by conflicts that were ethnic (Azeri and Armenians had fought for centuries), religious (between Shia Muslims and Armenian Orthodox Christians), social (the Armenians had generally been wealthier and better educated), political (involving territorial claims and relations with Moscow), and economic (Azerbaijan's oil industry, its principal source of wealth, was declining). Soviet troops attempted to separate the combatants but did not try to exercise sovereign authority over them.

Russians constituted the largest ethnic group in the multinational USSR, and theirs was the largest republic. They had long enjoyed privileged status throughout the federation. Now, Russian nationalists fanned the fears of losing that status with a campaign in the name of culture (with appeals to the Orthodox Church), order (attractive to the military and some party members), and race (including virulent anti-Semitism). Nationalism was as grave a challenge to Gorbachev as bloated bureaucracy and stores with empty shelves. The bonds of ideology, institutions, and custom that had held a great state together were beginning to look weak.

Pressure for Change in Eastern Europe

In 1968 the "Brezhnev doctrine" had declared that a "threat to socialism" in one country was a threat to all. He had followed the invasion of Czechoslovakia with efforts to strengthen the economic ties binding the Comecon countries, but the nations of Eastern Europe were looking

Lech Walesa addressed workers outside a factory in Zyrardow, not far from Warsaw, in October 1981. The scene, reminiscent of the long history of labor movements except for the television cameras, marked the rising power of the Solidarity movement.
Giansanti/Corbis Sygma

westward for increased trade and badly needed loans. Romania, not content with its allotted role as a Soviet granary, had charted its own course of industrialization and an independent foreign policy that made its brutal dictator, Nicolae Ceausescu, welcome in the West. East Germany, the second industrial power among communist states (and the seventh in Europe), oscillated between friendly overtures toward and suspicious rejection of West Germany much as it alternated between concessions and repression at home, where there were riots against the government in the early 1970s.

The pressures for change were stronger still in Czechoslovakia, Hungary, and Poland, where cultural ties to Western Europe remained strong and the Catholic Church became an outlet for growing restiveness. Violent protests against the police took place in Hungary, which had one of the strongest and most consumer-oriented economies of Eastern Europe. Riots in Poland in 1976 forced postponement of a projected rise in food prices, and four years later strikes led to the recognition of Solidarity, an organization of independent trade unions, whose leader, Lech Walesa, became a national hero. With support from the Catholic Church, the Solidarity movement grew strong enough to prompt a change of government. This was an amazing feat in a world in which public protest was dangerous and rare. But there was no telling where it would lead. The new head of the Polish Communist party, General Wojciech Jaruzelski, resorted to martial law and clamped down on Solidarity. East European governments continued to rely on force in the face of rising public resentment.

Yugoslavia was the maverick among communist states. Its limited market economy and its independence from the Soviet Union had once suggested another kind of communism. Weakened by the death of its longstanding leader Tito in 1980 and by contention among its member republics, Yugoslavia could not manage the reforms necessary to shake its economy out of a prolonged downturn. There was, in fact, no model of how to make desired changes and preserve communist rule. Soviet presence remained the central fact of life in Eastern Europe.

The Miracles of 1989

Although the contradictions had become obvious, no one expected communist rule to collapse completely. Eastern European governments had for years eased up on controls and repression when greater efficiency or popular anger seemed to require it. When, however, those steps exposed institutional blockage and touched off open dissent, communist governments had usually moved to stifle reform and silence opposition. In 1989 they did not, and one by one communist regimes were swept away.

Poland   In Poland, despite martial law, Solidarity continued its underground propaganda with wit and daring. It turned the 1987 visit of the pope, who was Polish, into an occasion for more demonstrations. Placards and pamphlets, rumors and clandestine radio broadcasts nourished rising agitation. This time the government did not call out the army. Gorbachev had told the

United Nations in 1988 that the Soviet Union would allow its allies to go their own way. Now that policy was tested. Sensing Walesa's popularity and the power of Solidarity, Jaruzelski relaxed martial law and released some political prisoners. But public anger and frustration increased, and the economy worsened. In February 1989, the government, in a major concession, acknowledged Solidarity's legitimacy, but Solidarity demanded free elections. The government hesitated, and Gorbachev signaled that Poland was on its own. In April, when elections took place, Solidarity won almost all the seats in the parliament. Stunned and frightened, Communist party members did not know what to do. After various formulas for compromise failed, Solidarity took over the cabinet in August, the first noncommunist government in the Soviet bloc.

Hungary Hungarians were well aware of events in Poland, for the irrepressible flow of information was an important factor in the events of 1989. Political discussion, like economic activity, was already freer in Hungary than other Eastern European countries, and by April even some party officials joined in public discussions of the need for free speech, civil rights, and the protection of private property. At the annual May Day celebrations, international communism's grandest occasion, opponents dwarfed the official celebration, and a huge demonstration in June dared to honor the uprising of 1956. Even some members of the government chose to attend. In October the Hungarian Communist party flexibly changed its name to the Socialist party and promised free elections for the following year. The power of people aroused seemed irresistible.

East Germany Many old-line Communist leaders remained convinced that a good show of force would restore order and keep the party in power. In October, Erich Honecker, the head of East Germany's Communist party and its prime minister, took that tack. His soldiers beat and arrested demonstrators in East Berlin. A week later, however, he resigned, for Gorbachev announced that he disapproved such use of force; worse, the East German republic was literally walking away. Every day hundreds of people, especially the young and those with marketable skills, abandoned their country. Most went to Hungary, where they mobbed the West German embassy, seeking visas. Embarrassed Hungarian and West German governments arranged for special trains to carry them west, and more people came, pushing and shouting and climbing over embassy walls.

On November 9, 1989, Honecker's successor, Egon Krenz, announced that East Germany's border with West Berlin would be opened that very day. The guards could not believe their orders. Late that night they stepped aside as hordes of people pushed through the gates of the Berlin Wall. Hundreds, then thousands, cheered and waved from atop that symbol of oppression before strolling past the well-stocked shops of West Berlin. The celebrations continued in front of the television cameras for days, even after work crews began dismantling the wall. Thousands continued to come each day, some just testing what it felt like to move freely, others seeking a different life in West Germany. Throughout East Germany, meetings that would have been illegal a few weeks earlier took place in churches and public squares as the police watched and then withdrew. The government's promises for reform and official pleas for order were drowned in revelations of past corruption and talk of uniting the two Germanies.

The Final Round in Eastern Europe For a while the harsher East European governments—in Czechoslovakia, Bulgaria, and Romania—remained unscathed by the changes around them, but that isolation did not last. Crowds of protesters were filling Wenceslas Square in Prague, 40,000 people in October, then 200,000 after a riot in which police beat up demonstrating students. A few days later 300,000 came to shout, sing, and jingle keys as a good-humored suggestion that it was time for the Communists to leave. In now familiar rites, slogans were scrawled everywhere, posters covered the walls, and new political groups formed. By December 1989 the best organized of these, Civic Forum, had won power and elected as president of Czechoslovakia its leader, Václav Havel, the popular playwright whose

In 1989, Václav Havel went from a prison cell to leadership of the opposition movement in Czechoslovakia to president. In this photo, he addresses a crowd in December of that year. AP Images

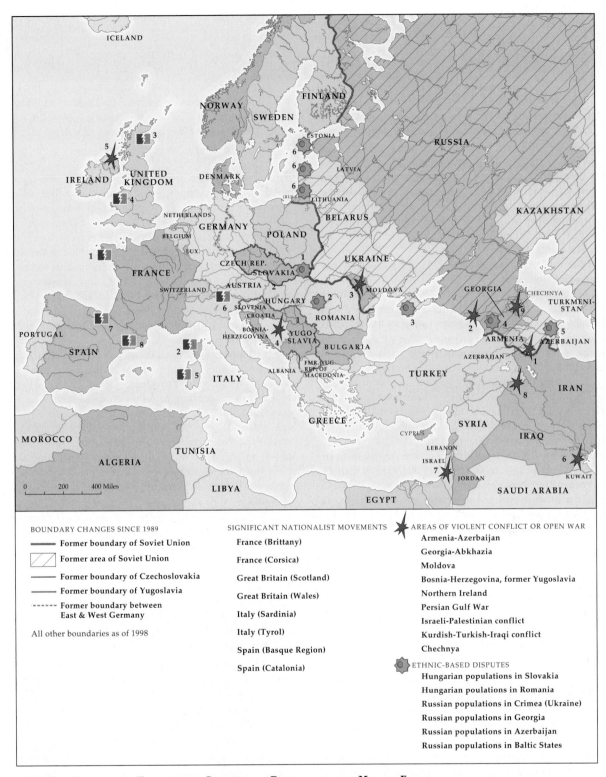

MAP 30.1 ETHNIC AND TERRITORIAL CONFLICT IN EUROPE AND THE MIDDLE EAST

Examine the movements, conflicts, and disputes illustrated on this map within the context of political developments, changing borders, and ongoing strife. Have any of these conflicts been resolved or do they continue still?

HAVEL'S INAUGURAL ADDRESS

Václav Havel was perhaps the most widely admired of the new leaders of Eastern Europe, and his literary skill and philosophic bent made him a particularly effective spokesperson. In his inaugural address on January 1, 1990, as president of the Czech Republic, he commented on the historical meaning of the dramatic changes that brought him to office.

"My dear fellow citizens, for forty years you heard from my predecessors on this day different variations of the same theme: how our country flourished, how many million tons of steel we produced, how happy we all were, how we trusted our government, and what bright perspectives were unfolding in front of us.

"I assume you did not propose me for this office so that I, too, would lie to you.

"Our country is not flourishing. The enormous creative and spiritual potential of our nation is not being used sensibly. Entire branches of industry are producing goods which are of no interest to anyone, while we are lacking the things we need. A state which calls itself a workers' state humiliates and exploits workers. Our obsolete economy is wasting the little energy we have available. A country that once could be proud of the educational level of its citizens spends so little on education that it ranks today as seventy-second in the world. We have polluted our soil, our rivers and forests, bequeathed to us by our ancestors, and we have today the most contaminated environment in Europe. Adult people in our country die earlier than in most other European countries. . . .

"But all this is still not the main problem. The worst thing is that we live in a contaminated moral environment. We fell morally ill because we became used to saying something different from what we thought. We learned not to believe in anything, to ignore each other, to care only about ourselves. Concepts such as love, friendship, compassion, humility, or forgiveness lost their depth and dimensions, and for many of us they represented only psychological peculiarities, or they resembled gone-astray greetings from ancient times, a little ridiculous in the era of computers and spaceships. Only a few of us were able to cry out loud that the powers that be should not be all-powerful, and that special farms, which produce ecologically pure and top-quality food just for them, should send their produce to schools, children's homes, and hospitals if our agriculture was unable to offer them to all. The previous regime—armed with its arrogant and intolerant ideology—reduced man to a force of production and nature to a tool of production. In this it attacked both their very substance and their mutual relationship. It reduced gifted and autonomous people, skillfully working in their own country, to nuts and bolts of some monstrously huge, noisy, and stinking machine, whose real meaning is not clear to anyone. It cannot do more than slowly but inexorably wear down itself and all its nuts and bolts."

From Brian MacArthur (ed.), *The Penguin Book of Twentieth-Century Speeches*, New York: Viking, 1992.

---

works had long been banned (see "Havel's Inaugural Address," above).

Even Bulgaria and Romania, with less-developed economies and weaker traditions of political participation, could not escape the historic pressure. Bulgaria's Communist party took its cues from the Soviet Union and in November forced from office Todor Zhivkov, party secretary for thirty-five years and head of state for twenty-seven. He was jailed and plans for free elections were announced. Romania, in contrast, suffered weeks of bloodshed. When, in December, crowds gathered in Bucharest, the government gave the order to shoot. Still the crowds formed, and violence increased. Romania's dictator, Ceausescu, tried to make his escape but was caught and executed by firing squad on Christmas Day. Fighting continued for a week between the army and special police loyal to Ceausescu. Everywhere Romanians waved flags with a conspicuous hole in the center where the Communist hammer and sickle had been.

Rarely has there been so sudden a political collapse and on such a scale. Economic failure and resentment of Soviet dominance explain a good deal. Workers and Catholics in Poland, party members and entrepreneurs in Hungary, and students and intellectuals in Czechoslovakia mobilized their fellow citizens with surprising speed and skill. For years, despite all the efforts at censorship, radio and television had conveyed the knowledge that life was better in the West, and in the fall of 1989, images of cheering or rioting crowds spread the contagion of revolt. In the face of such diffuse anger, officials remarkably ready to quit and citizens determined to push revealed shockingly widespread cynicism about these regimes. The frequent comparisons to the revolutions across Europe in 1848 made sense.

May 1990: Having pulled a statue of Lenin to the ground, Romanian workers remove the cable from his neck.
Bettmann/Corbis

Young men and women, especially students, echoed the events of 1968 and revealed the impact of an international youth culture in their clothes and music, their sense of theater and use of mockery, and their slogans. As crowds lost their fear, contempt for the communist regimes and hunger for freedom swept aside the authority of officialdom, party ideology, and the police.

The fall of the communist regimes illuminated not only their appalling failures and corruption but also the problems still to be faced. Within months, unaccustomed freedoms resurrected old divisions—ethnic, social, and ideological. All at once, the Eastern Europe of 1990 looked much like that of the 1920s. Moderate conservatives gained the lead among Hungary's multiple parties and expressed nationalist resentment at the treatment Romania accorded Hungarians living in its territory. Czechoslovakia was soon debating yet again the relations of Czechs and Slovaks. As Poland risked the drastic medicine of sudden conversion to a market economy, rifts appeared within Solidarity. In Bulgaria, Communist party members won most of the seats in free elections, and in

Romania leaders who claimed no longer to be Communists showed little willingness to allow real democracy. East Germans voted for those who promised the most rapid assimilation into the German Federal Republic.

The Disintegration of the USSR

A hero in Western Europe and the United States, Gorbachev was never so popular at home. Efforts to create more of a market economy threatened jobs. Attempts to make one sector more efficient were stymied by related sectors that operated in the old ways. The new price structure increased inflation, uncertainty, and hoarding. Many party members and the army resented the erosion of their own authority and the weakening of the Soviet Union's international position.

The Opposition to Gorbachev   Seeking a strong political base, Gorbachev called for a huge Congress of People's Deputies as a step toward greater democracy. It met in 1989 and elected Gorbachev president of the Soviet Union. It also rejected the constitution's assertion that the Communist party must be preeminent (like all Soviet leaders since Stalin, Gorbachev's power had previously come from his position as party secretary). Discussions were more open than ever before. Deputies attacked old abuses, denounced the KGB, and gave vent to a rising chorus of competing ethnic demands. Solzhenitsyn warned against allowing Western decadence to infiltrate Russian society. Caught in the middle, Gorbachev clamped down on the media and allowed the army to threaten that it might restore order in the Baltic republics.

Among the opponents of this authoritarian turn, Boris Yeltsin, the head of the Communist party in Moscow, stood out. An outspoken populist, he reached ordinary people as Gorbachev never had, and in 1991 he was elected president of the Russian Republic, the largest in the Soviet Union. Other enemies of Gorbachev were active, too. When Gorbachev took his August vacation in the Crimea, hard-liners in his own government, in the military, and in the KGB staged a coup. Tanks filled the streets, and the coup leaders announced that Gorbachev had been replaced. Beyond that, they seemed to have no plan. Yeltsin held firm against the coup with remarkable support from public opinion. Crowds pleaded with the soldiers not to act, miners in Siberia went on a strike, demonstrators marched in city after city, and some army officers declared their support of Yeltsin.

Within two days, the leaders of the coup were in prison and Gorbachev was back in Moscow, but he was now overshadowed by Yeltsin. Gorbachev had no party, for across the nation, people pulled down the symbols of communism and closed and sometimes looted Communist party offices. Only eight of the fifteen Soviet republics responded to his call for a meeting. In October 1991 Russia, Ukraine, Belarus, and Kazakhstan declared that the Soviet Union had ceased to exist. No significant group fought to save it, and it was replaced by the looser Confederation of Independent States. Gorbachev resigned, a victim of the revolution he had unleashed.

Europe without Cold War

The fall of communism and the collapse of the Soviet Union meant the end of the Cold War. The policies of fifty years had to be rethought, along with the hardheaded assumptions on which they had rested. No one could know the implications of such fundamental changes, but it was clear that domestic politics, economic policies, and international relations would all now be different.

German Unification The fall of communism affected Germany right away. Chancellor Kohl pushed for the immediate unification of East and West Germany, moving faster than many Germans thought wise, outmaneuvering the opposition parties, and capturing popular enthusiasm. By the end of 1989, he had gained the support of the United States and then of France, in effect forcing a reluctant Britain to join in negotiations aimed at winning Soviet acceptance of German unification. Many were frightened at the prospect, but Kohl reassured the West with the promise that an enlarged Germany would be fully integrated into the European Community. The Soviet Union feared the increase in NATO's strength, but such concerns were rooted in an era quickly passing. In August 1990 the victors of World War II—the Soviet Union, the United States, Britain, and France—signed a treaty with the two Germanies. In return for the promise to respect its boundary with Poland and to limit the size of its combined army, Germany could unify and remain in NATO as Europe's richest and most powerful state.

For Germans, however, the benefits were not immediate. The East German economy, which had been the most productive in Eastern Europe, revealed enormous weakness. Its outmoded and inefficient industry could not compete in the dynamic economy of the West, and unemployment rose. East Germans, who suffered through these conditions, resented what felt like subordinate status, and West Germans struggled with the unexpectedly high cost of unification as well as a flood of German immigrants. Confidently, parliament voted to make Berlin once again the capital of a united Germany, launching a building boom there that has made it one of Europe's most exciting and dynamic cities.

Nevertheless, by 1998 German unemployment hit a postwar high at 12.6 percent, and in the election of that year the Christian Democrats lost to the Social Democrats. Shortly after that Helmut Kohl, the hero of unification, was disgraced by revelations of corrupt practices in party finance, and the Christian Democrats chose Angela Merkel to lead them in opposition. She was the first woman to head a major German party.

New Political Alignments The collapse of communist regimes had important repercussions elsewhere, too. Italian politics since World War II had been shaped by the presence of a powerful Communist party that was excluded from power. Increasingly moderate, it responded to the events of 1989 by making a final break with old-line communism and changing its name. The Christian Democrats, however, lost their principal reason for being, which had been to keep the Communists out of power. When charges of corruption uncovered a vast network of graft, the Christian Democratic party and their Socialist allies both simply disintegrated. In the next parliament, two-thirds of the deputies had never held any elective office and most belonged to new parties with new leaders. Public contempt for the old political class and a new electoral system (reducing the effects of proportional representation) opened the way for a restructuring of the political system.

The enfeeblement of the Marxist left, the weakening of the anticommunist right, and resentment of foreigners affected politics throughout Europe. The result was a shift toward the political center during the 1990s and early 2000s. For example, in France, Jacques Chirac, the head of a conservative coalition, defeated the Socialist Lionel Jospin in 1995 to become president. In Italy, media mogul Silvio Berlusconi defeated Romano Prodi of the center-left "Olive Tree Coalition" to become prime minister in 2001. In Great Britain, Tony Blair was elected to three consecutive terms as prime minister as the leader of the "New Labour" party. Under Blair's leadership the party moved toward the center and embraced the basic principles of free enterprise.

Perhaps the dominant political development during these years was a widespread movement to cut back the large-scale social welfare states that had evolved over the course of the twentieth century. One major impetus for this policy was the Maastricht Treaty of 1992, which required all EU members to agree to restrictions on inflation rates, budget deficits, and public debt. Significantly, governments undertook these efforts regardless of which party was in power. For example, in France, the conservative Chirac government reduced taxes and sought to privatize the state pension system. At the same time, in Germany, the Social Democratic government of Gerhard Schröder attempted to reduce spending by cutting unemployment benefits and government pensions. Similarly, while serving as prime minister of Italy during the 1990s, Prodi introduced an austerity budget and trimmed social welfare spending. These policies frequently generated opposition from labor unions and other groups. The role of the government in promoting social welfare loomed as a major issue in the opening years of the twenty-first century.

The Transition from Communism

The governments of Eastern Europe turned out to have heavier debts and more outmoded industries than even the critics of communism had suspected, and industrial pollution on an enormous, sometimes life-threatening, scale was a difficult problem for new governments in strapped economies. Unsure of the loyalty or competence of their own administrations, they attempted painful reforms while subject to unfamiliar public criticism. The capitalism suddenly unleashed was often socially disruptive, and the search for a new sense of community encouraged appeals to ethnic identity.

Poland undertook the most radical shift to a market economy, and economic indicators showed dramatic improvement. Ordinary citizens often suffered, however, and former Communists gained in the elections of 1993 by promising to slow the transition. Russia, Hungary, Poland, and the Czech Republic pleaded for more foreign aid and foreign investment. The relentless drive to capitalism in prosperous Czech regions and the cynical ambitions of Slovak politicians forced the breakup of Czechoslovakia in 1993, creating the Czech Republic and Slovakia, although opinion polls indicated a majority in each country would have preferred to stay together. Elsewhere, too, economic strains reinforced ethnic and religious conflict, something nationalist parties were quick to use, especially in Romania.

The Breakup of Yugoslavia

Former Communists, in fact, proved particularly adept at stirring ethnic resentments, especially in the former Soviet Union and, most tragically of all, in Yugoslavia. Ethnic differences had not prevented Yugoslavia's six republics from effectively functioning together even after the death of Tito. By the 1980s, Croatia and Slovenia, economically the most developed Yugoslav republics, openly objected to the economic and political policies of the Serbian-dominated government of Yugoslavia. As demands for reform grew stronger with the fall of communism elsewhere, Serbian communists resisted by raising support at home through appeals to Serbian nationalism. In 1990–1991, Slovenia and Macedonia joined Croatia and Bosnia-Herzegovina in declaring their independence. But large numbers of Serbs lived in parts of the latter two lands. Efforts to expel the Serbs and their

UN soldiers, in their blue helmets, distribute aid to civilians during the civil war in Bosnia-Herzegovina in 1995. Note the anguished woman in the foreground, the barbed wire, and the fact that the civilians are almost entirely women and children.
J. Jones/Corbis

own armed resistance, supported by the Yugoslav government under Slobodan Milosevic, created civil war. Regional, economic, and ideological differences fanned ethnic hatred as each side, recalling past injustices, committed new atrocities. Truces were signed and broken. Uncontrolled local units could count on support no matter what horrors they committed. Slaughter and rape destroyed whole villages. By 1993 Serb forces had recaptured about one-third of Croatia and nearly two-thirds of Bosnia-Herzegovina, a republic in which Serbs, Croatians, and Muslims had once been proud of living peacefully together.

Despite these horrors and the risk that war could spread, NATO and the EU responded weakly, denouncing ethnic violence but not wanting to be drawn into a Balkan war. Slowly, the United States assumed a cautious leadership, pressuring the contending parties to accept a truce signed in 1995 in Dayton, Ohio. American and even some Russian troops then joined European and UN forces as peacekeepers with limited roles. Although Milosevic faced opposition at home, militant nationalism and alert police squelched voices of moderation. Meanwhile, ethnic Albanians grew increasingly restive in Kosovo, a Serbian province historically tied to Serb identity. Milosevic responded with a familiar pattern, tightening control, using nationalist rhetoric, and in 1998 launching an assault to drive more than 600,000 Albanians out of the country. NATO forces, led by the United States, responded in March 1999 with an air assault on Serbia (including the capital, Belgrade) that lasted three months before the Serbs withdrew from Kosovo. Yugoslavia, its infrastructure badly damaged, was reduced to Serbia and a discontented Montenegro. The uneasy peace in the Balkans depended on

Former border of Yugoslavia

Border of Bosnia-Herzegovina

Dayton Agreement inter-entity boundary (November 1995)

Bosnian Serb territory, after Dayton

Croat-Muslim Federation portion of Bosnia, after Dayton

MAP 30.2 FORMER YUGOSLAVIA
In 1990 and 1991, Slovenia, Croatia, Bosnia-Herzegovina, and Macedonia declared their independence from Slobodan Miloševic's Yugoslavian government, sparking a brutal civil war. The country of Yugoslavia was created in 1919 as a result of World War I peace treaties. How do you suppose this history contributed to the bloody policies of ethnic cleansing?

the presence of foreign troops keeping ethnic groups apart, while most of those accused of war crimes remained out of reach.

Hope for a more principled outcome revived in the fall of 2000, however, when Miloševic was forced from power. His efforts to manipulate elections had brought the opposition parties, students, and farmers together in demonstrations reminiscent of those in Warsaw and Prague a decade earlier. Police and propaganda lost effectiveness, and Europe's last communist government fell. Its shaky replacement looked to the EU for economic and political support. Yugoslavia had to deal with a devastated economy and do so—like much of Eastern Europe—with ramshackle institutions, administrators and police from the previous regime, and a populace in poverty, harboring tragic memories and bitter resentments only partially repressed. Tensions eased, however, in a more open regime. It allowed

Miloševic to be tried for war crimes in The Hague (although he died before the verdict) and in 2002 Serbia and Montenegro agreed to split while keeping their diplomatic and military services in common. Yugoslavia was no more.

The New Russia   Only Yugoslavia faced more serious ethnic conflicts than Russia, and no former communist country found the transition to free markets more difficult. As president, Yeltsin tried to moderate disputes within the new Confederation of Independent States while pushing drastic economic reform. The effects, though limited, were painful. Unemployment rose, the ruble all but collapsed, and production fell to about half of what it had been a few years before. The rapid privatization of formerly state-owned businesses created economic equality and, in many cases, the process degenerated into lawlessness, with the government essentially giving away its companies to a "kleptocracy" of well-connected insiders. Managers did not know how to adjust to a market economy; many officials resisted change altogether. As repression eased, corruption spread, criminal gangs flourished, and ugly groups of nationalists grew louder.

Free elections in 1991 produced a Congress of People's Deputies in which Yeltsin's opponents—communists, nationalists, members of the military, and representatives of regional movements—outnumbered his supporters. Yeltsin compromised when possible and ignored the Congress when he could. As parliamentary resistance stiffened and his own popularity declined, Yeltsin risked a national presidential election in the spring of 1993 and won. A few months later Yeltsin declared the parliament dissolved. Several hundred delegates refused to obey. Holed up in their offices, they collected arms and called on the people and the army for support. The army remained silent, but the delegates were heartened when groups of Yeltsin's opponents gathered outside the parliament building. Amid calls to bring the government down, shots were fired from within. Finally, the army bombarded and then stormed the building. A hundred or more people died—more domestic bloodshed than Moscow had seen since 1917.

Reliance on the military, like Yeltsin's measures against parliament and his indifference to the rulings of the supreme court, was troubling proof that Russia had not achieved a constitutional system or the rule of law. Although seemingly rather indifferent, the public supported Yeltsin when forced to choose, and he surprised pollsters by winning reelection in 1996. By then the economy was improving slightly, and Russia could take its place in meetings of the nations with the largest economies. Ill and exhausted, Yeltsin named Vladimir Putin his successor and stepped down on December 31, 1999.

Members of the cabinet and presidential staff applaud as Prime Minister Vladimir Putin, front left, shakes hands with President Boris Yeltsin in Moscow's Kremlin on Friday December 31, 1999. In a television speech that stunned Russia, Yeltsin announced he was stepping down six months before his term was supposed to finish.
AP Images

Putin, a relatively unknown former KGB officer, won the presidential election in 2000 and then again in a landslide in 2004. With the Russian economy on the rebound during his eight-year term, thanks primarily to oil revenues, Putin quickly emerged as an enormously popular domestic leader; his approval ratings soared further when he crushed a decade-long separatist insurgency in the oil-rich Muslim republic of Chechnya in the Caucasus. Yet Putin was harshly criticized by political leaders and human rights advocates for his authoritarian politics at home and abroad. Critics condemned his perpetration of atrocities in Chechnya, in particular, as well as his censorship of the Russian media and repression of political opponents of his regime.

When Dmitry Medvedev, Putin's hand-picked successor and acolyte, took office in 2008, one of his first moves was to nominate Putin as prime minister, a post the latter assumed in May 2008. As a consequence, Medvedev's regime does not differ substantially in style from Putin's "managed democracy," with its combination of relatively free markets but tight control over civil liberties (and its political corruption). In the international arena, too, Russia continues to project a tough, uncompromising stance, exemplified by its incursion into Georgia in the summer of 2008. The new Russia supposedly has moved closer to Western models of economics and politics, but a huge gulf—and tense relations—continues to separate it from Europe and the United States. And while Russia has restored its primacy on the political scene, it is still regarded as an implacable and untrustworthy state by other Western powers.

TRANSNATIONAL EUROPE

While the Cold War divided Europe for decades, other forces were at work forging a united Europe in the West. Postwar recovery in Western Europe, grounded in transnational programs like the Bretton Woods system (see p. 878), created economic unity, while the Cold War itself produced political cooperation, as in NATO. Economic and political needs cohered in the creation of new European institutions that paved the way toward the European Union. The transnational Europe that emerged is better suited to the mobile and borderless global economy of the twenty-first century, one in which flows of goods, services, capital, information, images, and people are more independent of national economies and state imperatives than ever before.

The Formation of the European Union

Movements calling for some kind of European integration sprang up in many parts of Europe in the postwar period, and deliberations to consider the possibilities began almost immediately. Among a variety of integrative initiatives, three alliances stand out as being of signal importance: the European Coal and Steel Community of 1951, the European Economic Community of 1957, and the European Union in 1992.

The Council of Europe In 1948, a conference met in The Hague to discuss European integration. A thousand delegates from twenty countries gathered for the meeting. It was chaired by Winston Churchill, who had spoken a few years earlier about the need for a United States of Europe. Divisions that persist to this day appeared from the outset. Some countries (initially led by France and Belgium) wanted to create a European body with real political power, whereas others (primarily Great Britain and the Scandinavian countries) favored a kind of continuing conference.

The Council of Europe founded in the following year was a compromise. The foreign ministers of the member states would constitute the Council. There would also be a merely consultative assembly, whose delegates eventually came to be selected by their national parliaments. Headquarters were established in Strasbourg; ten Western European nations joined. A declaration of human rights, drawn up in 1950, went into effect in 1953 to safeguard "the ideals and principles of . . . [the members'] common heritage," and a European Court of Human Rights held its first hearing in 1960. Maintaining individual freedom and the rule of law was a requirement that excluded all the nations of Eastern Europe as well as Spain, Portugal, and Greece while they were ruled by dictators. Remarkably, the decisions of the Council and its Court of Justice have been obeyed by member states. By 1970 eight more nations had joined. The Council has gained authority over the years and today, some forty-one nations, from Russia to the Atlantic, including all the smallest ones, belong to the Council.

The Coal and Steel Community Stronger transnational institutions proved hard to establish, however, and so two leaders who envisioned a more integrated Europe decided to begin with small steps. Jean Monnet, a leading French economist, and Robert Schuman, France's foreign minister, proposed creating the French-German Coal and Steel Authority, which was established in 1950. A year later, propelled by the euphoria of recovery, Italy and the three Benelux countries (Belgium, Netherlands, and Luxemburg) joined to establish the European Coal and Steel Community (ECSC), which was given the power to coordinate the production and distribution of the coal and steel critical to industrial growth. That became the kernel of a common market.

As the ECSC demonstrated its economic value and as its authority increased, further steps became possible, just as Monnet and Schuman had hoped. In the Treaty of Rome, signed in 1957, the six members of the ECSC created a new agency to coordinate the development of atomic energy (EURATOM) and agreed to gradually eliminate tariffs between each other and to establish a common tariff toward goods from other nations. This was the European Economic Community (EEC), also known as the Common Market. Its prospects were anything but certain. Britain refused to take part, and the new French leader Charles de Gaulle was less internationalist than his predecessors. Nevertheless, the six original member nations declared that they were "determined to lay the foundations of ever-closer union among the peoples of Europe . . . and to ensure economic and social progress by common action."

EEC vs. EFTA Reluctant to accept permanent political ties to the Continent or to loosen its Commonwealth connections, Great Britain fostered the creation of the European Free Trade Association (EFTA) in 1960. This looser association, which set more limited goals (free trade among its members, for example, but not a common external tariff) and had very limited powers of enforcement, was joined by Sweden, Norway, Denmark, Austria, Switzerland, and Portugal. In the ensuing years the states of the EEC enjoyed the highest increases in per capita productivity, more than 4 percent a year. By

CHRONOLOGY
The Making of the European Union

1950	Germany and France form the Coal and Steel Authority.
1951	Italy and the Benelux nations join.
1957	The Treaty of Rome creates the European Economic Community of six nations.
1965	The EEC becomes the European Community.
1973	Great Britain, Ireland, and Denmark join the EC.
1979	Citizens elect the EC parliament.
1981	Greece joins the EC.
1986	Spain and Portugal join the EC.
1987	The Single Europe Act.
1992	Maastricht Treaty calls for European Union, common currency.
1995	Austria, Finland, and Sweden join the EU.
1999	Common currency, central bank take effect.
2004	The EU adds ten new members, primarily from Eastern Europe.
2005	Voters in France and the Netherlands reject the European constitution.
2007	Bulgaria and Romania join the EU

1968 all tariffs among the member states had been abolished. Continued economic growth among its members made the organization ever more attractive.

The European Community In 1967 the EEC's three organizations—the EEC, the ECSC, and EURATOM—were folded into a single entity, the European Community (EC). Its name, like its goals, now explicitly reached beyond the merely economic. After extended negotiations, Great Britain, Ireland, and Denmark joined the EC in 1973. Together, the nine members of the European Community surpassed the United States in the production of automobiles and steel, and by 1979 in total gross national product (GNP) as well.

The executive of the EC (and its successor, the EU) is the Commission, to which each member nation appoints at least one member and the larger countries more. Members of the Commission are independent of any national government. The programs adopted by the Commission often have set new precedents and have led to a large bureaucracy at its headquarters in Brussels. New legislation proposed by the Commission must be approved by a Council of Ministers, specialists in the relevant fields, such as agriculture or finance, appointed by and responsible to the member governments. Clearly intended as a check on the EC's autonomy, the Council of Ministers was nevertheless empowered in the 1980s to set some policies by majority vote rather than unanimity.

The heads of government of the EC countries began in 1972 to hold meetings several times a year as the European Council, in itself an important step toward more coordinated policies. Every six months the head of a different government serves as president, and a tendency developed for presidents of the European Council to seek some new accomplishment to mark their term, another stimulus to expanded activity.

The European Parliament is another cornerstone EC/EU institution. Despite its very limited powers, the creation of an elected parliament was hailed as "the birth of the European citizen." In 1979 the citizens of each member nation began voting directly for delegates to the Community's parliament, where the representatives sit according to political party rather than nationality. Over the years the European Parliament has increasingly asserted its authority and supervised the Commission more closely.

With the main institutions in place, the process of integration continued, with the creation of a mechanism for regulating currency exchange rates and through the rulings of the EC's court. Thus, uniform regulations spread to many fields (on standards of product quality, insurance, and environmental issues, for instance) and common legal rights (in the case, for example, of migrant workers) were put in place. Agricultural policy was especially contentious. The EC's subsidies, which had strong domestic support from farmers, resulted in costly stockpiles of unsold produce. Because Britain imports most of its food and has a smaller farm population, it contributed far more toward these costs than the EC spent in Britain. Its vigorous protests forced adjustments and then some reform of agricultural policies in 1981; but the issue was further complicated by the enlargement of the Community to include Greece in 1981 and Spain and Portugal in 1986, all countries with competing agricultural interests. Special grants to poorer regions—including the northwestern part of the British Isles, southern Italy, and the poorer members generally (Ireland, Portugal, Spain, and Greece)—helped to bring those regions closer to the EC's general level of prosperity.

The Single European Act In 1986 Jacques Delors, the president of the Commission, succeeded in winning support for the Single European Act, an agreement to create a single market. The act declared that by the end of 1992 there would no longer be any restrictions within the Community on the movement of goods, services, labor, or capital. These terms were met, with minor exceptions, and they have brought striking changes to the lives of ordinary people. Most of the border checkpoints between member states on the continent have disappeared. All citizens of the member states carry a community passport, crossing national boundaries without restriction. Any of them can open a bank account, take out a mortgage, receive medical care, or practice a profession anywhere in the EC because, in principle at least, the licenses and university degrees of one country are recognized in all the others.

The Single European Act required that vast arrays of national regulations be made uniform. Anticipating European integration, businesses, government agencies, and schools set about on their own to bring their practices in line with those of the EC, forming ties with colleagues in other countries. Organizations and individuals began to think and operate in terms of the Community as a whole; and sensing this momentum, the leaders of the EC pressed for more.

The European Union and the Euro The **Maastricht Treaty** of 1992 changed the name of the EC to the European Union (EU) to indicate its greater integration. The treaty also enlarged the powers of its parliament and called for a coordinated foreign policy and the adoption of a common European currency by 1999.

Though the introduction of the euro has facilitated EU integration, it has also brought its own set of challenges. Getty Images

Apart from Great Britain, Denmark, and Sweden who opted not to join the common currency, in the rest of the EU, banks, businesses, and governments began in 1999 to keep accounts in euros, and in 2002 the traditional coins and bills emblazoned with national symbols gave way to currency in euros (only the coins have national emblems, on one side).

Intended to facilitate EU integration and to strengthen its economy, the euro brought with it a host of new difficulties. To prevent weaker economies from

MAP 30.3 GROWTH OF THE EUROPEAN UNION TO 2007
Established in 1967 as the European Economic Community (or Common Market), the European Union was originally composed of six nations and by 2007 had grown to twenty-seven. Why did some of these nations choose to adopt a common currency? What other nations do you suppose may join?

burdening stronger ones, "euro zone" members agreed to standardize economic policy. The agreement required members to limit budget deficits to 3 percent of their GDP (gross domestic product) and to restrict public debt to 60 percent of it; failure to meet these regulations incurred a major fine. But the differences between the various euro zone economies made adherence to these rules problematic, particularly since the new Frankfurt-based European Central Bank established high rates of interest to support the currency and prevent inflation. In nations with relatively sluggish economies (Portugal, for example), the government could no longer cut interest rates to stimulate economic activity. Despite these problems, the euro has had an overall positive impact on the EU economy, increasing the stability of prices and promoting trade within the euro zone by eliminating exchange-rate risks. The use of a single currency also simplifies many aspects of banking and finance and removes numerous transaction costs.

The Expansion of the EU   In 2004, the EU significantly expanded its domain by incorporating ten new states: Poland, the Czech Republic, Slovakia, Slovenia, Hungary, Estonia, Latvia, Lithuania, Cyprus, and Malta. Romania and Bulgaria followed in 2007. Most of the new member states either were located in Eastern Europe or were former Soviet republics and they tended to be smaller and poorer than the original member states. With the addition of these new countries, the EU expanded its boundaries far to the east and became a massive organization. Its twenty-seven member states have a total population of close to half a billion and an aggregate economy roughly equal in size to that of the United States.

To help manage the organization's expanded size and to promote greater unity, European leaders initiated a convention in 2002 to draft a European constitution. After two years of deliberation, the convention finalized the document. The constitution was designed to streamline the decision-making process while encouraging members to adopt common policies regarding defense, immigration, and foreign affairs. Its provisions included a longer term for its president, a written bill of rights, and new laws to deal with terrorism.

But implementing the constitution proved problematic. To become law, the constitution had to be ratified by all members within two years, but in the spring of 2005, voters in France and the Netherlands, respectively, rejected it by large margins. They voted "no" in protest of high unemployment and weak job growth, but also out of fear that the constitution would jeopardize national autonomy and the welfare state, and lead to increased immigration. European leaders are currently working to make the constitution palatable to all member states, but a similar situation arose once again in June of 2008, when Ireland rejected the Lisbon Treaty, an agreement intended to consolidate power and simplify EU governance. These divisions within the EU highlight the extent to which it remains a controversial entity: nations continue to see it as a threat to their sovereignty, while many groups within member states see the EU as an undemocratic institution, governed by "Eurocrats"—elite-oriented bureaucrats—indifferent to their needs.

The European Economy in the Global Age

In Europe, as in many parts of the world, ways of creating wealth have changed and so have lifestyles in the past half century. The emergence of postindustrial economies in many parts of Europe has created new wealth and new dislocations, while intensified global integration has increased economic competition. Despite major recessions in the 1970s and the 1990s, the European nations today are all richer and boast standards of living higher than ever before. They play a vital role in the global economy, one partly made possible by the emergence of a new transnational European community.

Europe's Economic Resources and Infrastructure
Newly discovered oil and natural gas in the North Sea now supplement the coal and iron ore deposits once so important to European industrialization. Except for Russia, however, much of Europe has historically been disadvantaged by its limited natural resources. That deficit is now less crucial. Economies today create wealth primarily through capital-intensive production of goods and services; Europe, like the United States, possesses abundant capital, well-developed economic institutions, advanced technology, experienced managers, skilled workers, efficient marketing, rapid communication, high levels of education, and high consumption.

During the 1960s every European nation launched new road-building projects, and by 1980 the most important of them had been completed. Superhighways now run from Stockholm to south of Valencia and from Naples to Hamburg. Railroads, valued for passenger travel as well as for transportation of goods (and usually considered a service to be provided by the state), have been extensively modernized. In 1981 French high-speed trains began to carry passengers from Paris to Lyons at 165 miles per hour. A tunnel under the English Channel, a project considered for centuries, opened in 1994 to provide direct automobile and rail links between Britain and the Continent. Water transport along Europe's coasts, rivers, and canals

Flags of the member states fly outside the Brussels headquarters of the European Union.
Steve Vidler/eStock Photo

DOCUMENTARY AND STATISTICAL SOURCES

European Monitoring Centre on Racism and Xenophobia, *Muslims in the European Union: Discrimination and Islamophobia* (2006).

European Union Agency for Fundamental Rights, *Report on Racism and Xenophobia in the Member States of the EU 2007* (2008).

European Union Agency for Fundamental Rights, *Trends and Developments 1997–2005: Combating Ethnic and Racial Discrimination and Promoting Equality in the European Union* (2007).

Organisation for Economic Cooperation and Development, *Where Immigrant Students Succeed: A Comparative Review of Performance and Engagement in PISA 2003* (2006).

Organisation for Economic Cooperation and Development: *OECD Observer:* http://www.oecdobserver.org/

Pew Research Center, *The Pew Global Attitudes Project* http://pewglobal.org/

The European Commission: Eurostat http://epp.eurostat.ec.europa.eu

The European Union Monitory and Advocacy Program: *Equal Access to Quality Education for Roma,* Vols. 1–2 (2007).

The European Union On-Line: http://europa.eu/

United Nations High Commissioner for Refugees http://www.unhcr.org/

is relatively inexpensive, and air travel is dense throughout the Continent.

European agricultural productivity has increased in recent years while the number of people who work on the land has continued to decline. With only about 3 percent of the world's farmland, Western Europe produces nearly one-third of the world's dairy products and 15 percent of the world's eggs, potatoes, and wheat.

In the face of American and Japanese competition, Western European nations remain among the technological leaders in electronic communication, especially wireless telephones and satellite communication. Fifty-four percent of EU households are connected to the Internet, ranging from 20 percent in Bulgaria, Romania, and Greece to 80 percent in Sweden, Denmark, and the Netherlands. Europe's banks and stock markets began in the 1980s to become more flexible and in the 1990s to join international and global mergers. In 2000 the Frankfurt and London stock markets joined forces. Until the 1980s, in much of Western Europe as well as the communist nations outside the USSR, economic growth rested on mixed economies, with an important role for state planning in the West and some room for private enterprise in Eastern Europe. Since then, a strong trend toward privatization has brought more rapid growth but also painful social adjustments

High-speed electric trains poised for their dash from Paris to Lyons.
Getty Images

from cost cutting, rising unemployment, and international competition. The emphasis on productive efficiency, new products, marketing, and personal consumption that once seemed characteristically American now pervades Europe as well.

Europe's Position in the Global Economy   It is not only the United States and Japan that compete with Europe in today's economy. Although the United States decisively ended the era of European economic primacy after the Second World War, East Asia emerged as a new epicenter of industrial dynamism and wealth in the last quarter of the twentieth century. Modeling themselves after the region's economic giant, Japan, the "Asian Tigers," Hong Kong, South Korea, Singapore, and Taiwan, underwent rapid, export-driven industrialization and technological growth under the auspices of state-regulated capitalism. By the 1990s, other parts of Asia, including Vietnam, Thailand, Malaysia, Indonesia, China, and India, also experienced industrial booms and rapid market growth.

Not only did these developments create a new international division of labor—shifting much industrial production to the non-Western world—but the success of the Asian model of capitalism (and, in particular, the Japanese model emphasizing corporate loyalty over competition) seemed to challenge the Western conception of a single path to economic modernity. Although the Asian boom was followed by a bust in 1997, Asia now plays a central role in the global industrial and trade economy. The old economic map, divided between "North"—the developed economies of the north-ern hemisphere—and "South"—the less-developed economies of the southern hemisphere—is too simplistic to accurately describe the world as it is today.

The Advent of a Postindustrial Economy   As other parts of the world industrialize, European economies have been moving in other directions. By the end of the twentieth century, neither industrial production nor agriculture dominated in many parts of Europe. This happened as the service sector expanded dramatically, employing growing numbers of people in retail, recreation, banking and financial services, communication, health services, education, and other social services. Economies and societies so structured are often called *postindustrial* to indicate the importance of these changes and, in particular, their emphasis on new technologies. Some commentators prefer the term "information society" and, more recently, the "digital economy," centered on the Internet and dominated by e-business. These terms underscore the importance of information in the postindustrial economy, along with the ways in which digital media have revolutionized economic activity in terms of speed and distance.

The postindustrial shift has been uneven across Europe. Most advanced in Western Europe, postindustrial economies developed more slowly and encountered more obstacles in Eastern Europe. Even in Western Europe, however, the transformation has not been complete: a service economy prevails in many parts of Germany, for example, whereas an industrial economy persists in certain regions. In a few nations, such as Spain and Greece, the term "postindustrial" does not

Singapore, one of the four "Asian Tigers" that patterned their 1990s economic growth on the Japanese model, endured the later economic bust and now plays a central role in the global industrial and trade economy. Corbis

remotely describe economic life in most regions, which were still making the transition from an agricultural to an industrial economy during the same decades that postindustrial economies took shape elsewhere. Yet wherever and whenever the transformation to a postindustrial economy did occur, it enriched elites and brought painful dislocation, unemployment, and greater inequality to many Europeans.

The postindustrial economy differs from the industrial economy in the economic and social organization of production. Industrial production relies on unskilled and semiskilled assembly line production; in contrast, postindustrial manufacturing tends to be decentralized, broken up into smaller units, and geared toward "flexible specialization," or small-scale, specialized production aimed at particular, often high-end, consumer markets. A good deal of production (along with services) is also outsourced or subcontracted to overseas manufacturers by the multinational corporations that increasingly dominate the postindustrial economy.

These trends have altered the lives of European workers. The outsourcing practices of multinational corporations, the service sector's eclipse of industry, and the growth of newer, technology-intensive industries requiring smaller labor forces have cost many European workers their jobs. Among the hardest hit have been workers in industries associated with nineteenth-century industrialization (steel, textiles, and shipbuilding, for example) because these industries have declined not only in relative but in absolute terms, a process known as "deindustrialization." The net effect of these developments has been to marginalize the traditional blue-collar work-

ing classes. Yet, although the typical postindustrial worker is now white collar, a huge rift still divides the elite, composed of finance experts, professionals, government officials, scientists, technology workers, education workers, and researchers, from a new, poorly paid white-collar underclass, made up of low-level sales personnel, health care workers, leisure industry workers, and personal fitness and grooming workers.

Globalization Starting in the mid-1970s and accelerating in the 1990s, the European economies have been drawn into the global economy at an increasing rate. This trend is part of a larger pattern known as globalization, in which communications, economic activity, and cultural exchanges increasingly take place on a worldwide scale.

In some sense, globalization has been going on for centuries. In the thirteenth century, the Mongol empire fostered extensive trade between East Asia, Central Asia, and Europe; from the sixteenth century on, the growth of the European colonial empires intensified and expanded global trade, incorporating the Americas and Africa into world trade circuits. By the late nineteenth century, the "new imperialism" of the European nation-states further expanded international trade, organizing it into a much more elaborate system. At the same time, the adoption of the gold standard integrated world financial markets more tightly than ever. The postwar period through the 1970s saw increased global integration, the result in large measure of the GATT (General Agreement on Tariffs and Trade) of 1947, which lowered trade barriers, and the Bretton Woods

Once the imperial palace to Ming and Qing Dynasty emperors, the Forbidden City now hosts a Starbucks coffee shop.
© Macduff Everton/Corbis

system of fixed exchange rates (which valued all currencies in relation to the dollar and thus, in effect, to the gold standard) of 1944, which minimized exchange rate risk. These developments facilitated the movement of goods and money and massively increased international trade flows.

Few would disagree, however, that we have recently entered into a new phase of the globalization process. One of the most important catalysts of this new phase has been the global revolution in communications and information technology witnessed in the last decades of the twentieth century. New inventions such as desktop and laptop computers, the Internet, e-mail, cellular telephones, personal digital assistants (PDAs), CD and DVD players, portable media players (such as the iPod), digital photography, and satellite-based communication systems have dramatically accelerated and extended the transfer of information, making text, image, and audio data available instantaneously across the globe. This development has definitively reshaped the worlds of business and entertainment.

Capital, jobs, goods, and services are also more mobile than ever before. Much of this movement occurs inside multinational corporations, which are based in one country but have operations in many countries. Significantly, more than 90 percent of the largest mul-

tinational corporations are based in Western Europe, the United States, or Japan. Among the most prominent European-based multinationals are the oil giant BP (Great Britain), the food manufacturer Nestlé (Switzerland), the electronics firm of Siemens (Germany), the consumer staples producer Unilever (Holland), the sporting goods company Adidas (Germany), the furniture retailer IKEA (Sweden), and the telecommunications corporation Nokia (Finland). In the 1950s and 60s, multinationals established themselves abroad primarily to connect with foreign consumer markets. More recently, they have also increasingly moved production, jobs, and capital to developing countries in the non-Western world to cut labor costs and avoid regulation. Much of this subcontracting of the production process is to East Asia and, since the early 1990s, to China, where labor costs are even lower.

Two developments have enabled multinationals to move production and jobs more easily. First, a new era of deregulated capitalism began in the early 1970s, when the United States abandoned the gold standard, ending the Bretton Woods system. Whereas the old regime had been based on the collective coordination of currency and banking, the new system of floating exchange rates eliminated the need to control capital flows. This enabled the deregulation of financial markets in the 1980s, making it easier to move money across national borders. Second, the information technology revolution has made it possible to better control and coordinate manufacturing across great geographical distances.

The Globalization of Culture Globalization has had some of its most dramatic effects in the cultural arena. With its lightning-fast flow of images and entertainments across national borders, globalization has made Western, especially American, culture readily accessible to people on every continent. American television series like "24," "Prison Break," "Oprah," "Friends," "Desperate Housewives," and "Sex in the City" are watched in the Gaza Strip, the United Arab Emirates, Bangladesh, and Indonesia; Hollywood movies are hugely popular the world over.

Although American entertainments and media have dominated the globe since at least the end of the Second World War, the core distinction between the world then and now is in the reach and the speed of transmission of images and entertainments. In addition, culture flows are far less unidirectional than they once were, and images and entertainments from other parts of the world play an increasingly important role in European and American cultures. This is exemplified by the ability of satellite television to broadcast to immigrant communities in Europe (Al-Jazeera, the Arab-language news network, is one example).

Debating Globalization The impact of globalization has been much scrutinized and discussed. One key issue in the debate is its effect on the distribution of European and world wealth. Within Europe, the clear beneficiaries of globalization include economic elites and formerly economically disadvantaged Europeans (Eastern Europeans, the Irish) who recently have entered the ranks of consumers. At the same time, many European workers have lost their jobs to cheaper foreign labor as the result of intensified global competition.

Outside of Europe, the impacts are still more ambiguous and uneven. Everyone would agree that immense gaps in wealth and economic growth currently divide different regions of the world, but experts take different views as to the long-term effects of globalizing processes on these divisions. Its defenders assert that globalization ultimately benefits everyone, from the richest to the poorest nations. In particular they see globalization as a tool for developing less-developed economies, spreading capital and technological knowledge, fostering market growth, and gradually integrating less-developed nations into a global network of goods and services. Moreover, many take the view that globalization not only improves the economic

In many European cities, immigrant suburbs, such as this one in Berlin, are readily recognizable by the ubiquity of satellite dishes used to watch television broadcasts from abroad.
Getty Images

well-being of less-developed nations, but will actually allow them to "catch up" with the developed world. By democratizing world resources, some even say, globalization will foster the dissemination of shared values and global human rights, alleviating conflict and promoting peace.

But critics argue that globalization does not necessarily set societies on the same developmental path. One school of thought suggests that globalization hinges on the circulation of goods and images, but that it fails to disseminate the necessary technological knowledge or capital needed for economic development and therefore does not lead to either economic or cultural convergence. Globalization is thus widening the gap between the developed and less-developed world. Another point of view asserts that globalization has the potential to redistribute world economic resources, but that in current-day practice it tends to harm poorer nations with weaker market economies, largely by promoting the opening of less-developed economies to free trade too quickly. This has frequently necessitated the imposition of economic austerity measures by the World Bank (see p. 878) and the International Monetary Fund (IMF) (see p. 878) on these nations to enable them to pay their debt.

Globalization has come under the harshest criticism from activists and theorists on the left, who see it as a process strengthening the rights of capital at the expense of nations and individuals. Antiglobalization activists target multinational corporations—whom they see as backed by transnational agencies such as the World Trade Organization (WTO; the successor to the GATT), the World Bank, and the IMF—as the foremost practitioners of unregulated, socially irresponsible capitalism. According to them, multinationals not only rob Western workers of their jobs, but exploit foreign laborers, paying them meager wages and depriving them of basic rights and job security. In addition, they accuse Western multinationals of outsourcing to despotic regimes. For example, although the Tiananmen Square crackdown on political protest of 1989 slowed outsourcing to China, President Clinton allowed China to be granted a Most Favored Nation trading status on the condition that it improve its human rights record. In fact, however, little pressure was placed on China to make concrete reforms and it was able to join the WTO in 2001.

Scholars also disagree about the effects of globalization on culture. Critics warn that globalization is obliterating local cultures and identities, producing a bland, homogenized—and largely Americanized—global culture. But many theorists argue that globalization produces both uniformity and diversity. They insist on the capacity of local cultures to "indigenize" or incorporate outside cultural elements in ways that effectively sever them from their original context. This perspective also emphasizes the multidirectional nature of cultural traffic and, in particular, the widespread dissemination of many non-American cultural products and influences (India's Bollywood film industry offers one example). On balance, then, a mutually enriching process of cultural cross-fertilization defines the global cultural economy.

From Postindustrial to Globalized Society

While poverty and exclusion still exist in European societies, they have nonetheless made great leaps forward with respect to the equalization of social opportunity since the end of the Second World War. The tremendous economic growth of the postwar era played an important role in making these developments possible. So did the new social contract of the postwar era, one embodied in the welfare state's notion of social citizenship—the state's responsibility to care for its citizens from cradle to grave. European social norms and cultural expectations have also undergone significant change in the last half century, especially since the student movements of 1968, affecting ideas about social class, gender roles, the place of religion, and environmental politics.

The Spread of Education   Education has been one of the chief channels of social mobility in late twentieth-century Europe. Traditionally, secondary education was the great mark of social difference and only a small fraction of students went to secondary schools noted for their demanding and usually classical curriculums. These schools were the gateway to a university education. A larger proportion of students went to vocational secondary schools, and half or more of the youths beyond the ages of twelve to fourteen went directly to work. Despite efforts to make this segregation an effect of academic performance, in practice social class made a critical difference.

The fact that modern societies require citizens to be more highly educated than ever before led to extensive and controversial reforms intended to make the system more democratic in the late 1960s and early 1970s. These reforms offended defenders of the older curriculum while they did not go far enough to satisfy student radicals. Nevertheless, they instituted important changes. In the West, enrollments in the more prestigious forms of secondary education doubled and trebled, and a trend toward "comprehensive" schools more like the American high school allowed many of the graduates of those schools to go on to higher education. The number of university students has increased enormously, and more women than men now receive postsecondary education in most Western countries. In communist societies, the children of workers and party members had priority for admission to such schools, although before 1989 total enrollments increased more slowly than in the West. This increase in schooling and access to it has required increased state expenditure and that families support children for a longer period before they begin to work. It has made social mobility a more universal goal and turned education into the subject of intense debate about fairness, culture, and employment.

Educational systems also have tended to become more similar across Western Europe, although important differences in national tradition remain. Despite the creation of hundreds of new institutions of higher education, often with American-style campuses, enrollments in many countries swelled beyond capacity. Among European nations, the Scandinavian countries, France, Italy, Belgium, and the Netherlands have the highest proportion of young adults in some form of postsecondary education, with the proportion somewhat lower in Great Britain and Germany.

Social Welfare Although the gap between the wealthiest and poorest segments of society is much narrower in Europe than in the United States, large pockets of unemployment and poverty remain. In communist Europe, professionals and officials lived at a much higher standard and with far greater freedom of choice than workers or peasants, an important element in the unpopularity and ultimate downfall of those governments. The full impact of social inequality in both Eastern and Western Europe is softened by complex provisions for social security, minimal fees for education, universal medical care, many provisions for the elderly, and a wide variety of family benefits and services. Not surprisingly, rates of infant mortality have declined and longevity rates have improved; those in Western Europe are among the most favorable in the world. Because birthrates in Europe are now generally the lowest in the world (with the lowest rates in the Catholic countries) and the elderly constitute an ever-increasing proportion of the population as people live longer, social expenditures by necessity have increased. In Eastern Europe since 1991, privatization has led to huge gaps in the social safety net.

In the 1970s unemployment began to rise, depressing regions dependent on declining industries as well as those that had never enjoyed industrial prosperity. By the 1990s, endemic unemployment, generally averaging more than 10 percent and hitting young people and immigrants the hardest, had become one of Europe's most pressing social problems. On the whole, programs of special subsidies and tax incentives have had disappointing results. With taxation already relatively high, governments have had little new to offer, while demands for lower taxes became a mainstay of the political center and right. Subsidized housing had mixed results. Although relatively cheap in communist Europe, good housing remained scarce, leading to long waiting lists for cramped apartments. In the West, where much new housing was subsidized by governments (in the 1980s about one-third of new housing in Germany, one-half in Great Britain, two-thirds in Sweden and France), the result was the segregation of less-affluent people in isolated and dismal surroundings.

The Changing Roles of Women Across Europe, one of the most important developments of the last half century has been the arrival of greater gender equality than ever before, in both ideological and practical terms. The birth of second-wave feminism (the first wave being the suffrage movements of the late nineteenth through the mid-twentieth centuries) as an outgrowth of the student movements of 1968 brought the issue of gender equality to the center of public debates. While

institutional, legal, and interpersonal sexism certainly remain prominent features of European society—with significant variation across countries—the status and opportunities of European women in the past thirty years simply cannot be compared with those of women of earlier generations. Women have become more prominent in all the professions and in politics. Most European women over the age of fifteen are part of the labor force (the proportion ranges from about half in Italy, Spain, and Ireland to more than 80 percent in the Czech Republic, Poland, and the Scandinavian countries). Women make up from one-fifth to half of all managers in most countries, especially in smaller enterprises, although they rarely occupy top positions. They also constitute from one-half to nearly two-thirds of professional and technical workers. European governments and employers have made child care available to most women, in effect, encouraging mothers to have careers. Nevertheless, on average, women workers continue to earn less than men (between two-thirds as much in Britain and four-fifths as much in France).

Young women expect to have a freedom of movement that their mothers did not as they train, travel, work, and socialize outside their families. The availability of contraception and, by the 1970s, abortion (changes more accepted in Europe than in the United States) has added to the sense that women have the right to plan their life course. State-supported child care and generous maternity leave policies in many parts of Europe have also gone some way toward easing the burden of working mothers. The change in social norms is further reflected in strong statements adopted by the EU and many governments in favor of gender equality and against sexual harassment. Gender discrimination, however, remains a serious problem, and European women continue to wrestle with the challenge of multiple responsibilities.

The Environment Economic growth also brought pollution that contaminated the air, waterways, and countryside as it poured from factories and automobiles and littered the landscape. Monuments and scenic places revered for centuries came to be seriously threatened. Western Europe was slow to respond, and in Eastern Europe the problem was ruthlessly ignored. The Rhine became one of the most polluted international waterways, and high concentrations of mercury were recorded in Geneva's Lac Leman. Escaped industrial gases caused illness and death in the outskirts of Milan, and the magnificent palaces of Venice were discovered to be slowly sinking, apparently because the earth beneath their pilings gives way as underground water is pumped up on the mainland for industrial use. Acid rain is destroying Germany's Black Forest, and it is now dangerous to bathe in or eat fish from parts of the Baltic and Mediterranean seas. The remaining monuments of ancient Greece and Rome and the ornate facades of Gothic churches in city after city crumble and crack from the vibrations and fumes of modern traffic.

Governments intent upon stimulating growth were reluctant to impose the restrictions and to undertake the expense that protecting the environment required, until strong ecology movements in Germany, Britain, the Low Countries, and France forced their hand. Political parties, known everywhere as the Greens, focused on these environmental issues, and several international agencies now enforce European standards against pollution. Although much more remains to be done, the gains have been impressive. Stern regulations eliminated the smog that had plagued London since the sixteenth century (and that killed thousands in the Great Smog of 1952). The Thames has become a clean river for the first time in centuries. In the 1960s and 1970s, nearly every building in Paris was stripped of the somber, dark patina of soot accumulated through 150 years of industrialization (only to begin darkening anew from automotive exhaust). By the 1980s, citizens' movements, well-organized programs for recycling, and strict regulations were changing the landscape across Europe, and European states had become leaders in international measures to protect the environment. Green parties have remained small, even in Germany, where the movement is strongest, but in the early 1990s, they formed the European Federation of Green Parties and, in 2004, the Federation then became a transnational European Green party. In addition, larger, more conventional parties have adopted much of the Green's program. In 1999, EU member states joined eighty-four countries from around the world (with the notable exception of the United States) in signing the Kyoto Protocol, an environmental treaty intended to reduce the greenhouse gas emissions that cause global warming.

Religious Life Contemporary European societies are far more secular than the United States, although religious pockets (particularly in Eastern Europe) remain. At the same time—and perhaps in response to the tide of secularism—religious communities both in Eastern and Western Europe have become increasingly conservative. The Catholic Church exemplifies this trend. After John Paul II died on April 2, 2005, Benedict XVI was chosen as his successor. Formerly the Cardinal Joseph Ratzinger, he had been appointed prefect of the Congregation for the Doctrine of the Faith in 1981. In this position Ratzinger moved to enforce orthodoxy within the Church while denouncing the "dictatorship of relativism." Many people have interpreted his elevation to the papacy as a sign that the Church will continue to move in a conservative direction.

These developments within the Catholic Church have coincided with a global movement toward religious fundamentalism. In the United States, the growing numbers of evangelical Protestants emerged as a major political force. George Bush's reelection in 2004 was due in part to his ability to appeal to both Protestant fundamentalists and conservative Catholics. At the same time, a worldwide Islamic revival has played a vital role in shaping political and social life in the Middle East. In a world in which religion has assumed an increasingly important place not only in private but in public life, Europe's secularism and laicism—the separation of religious institutions from the state—stands out starkly.

POSTCOLONIAL EUROPE

From the 1950s on, massive migrations from other parts of the world, especially former colonies, have reshaped European society. As sizable immigrant populations emerged, European nations faced a host of new issues concerning the accommodation of cultural difference: should immigrant groups be integrated into mainstream society? If so, to what extent should they be asked to give up their own cultural identities and practices? What should be the criteria for citizenship? While nations implemented widely differing policies in answer to these questions, all across Europe the immigrant presence evoked a new xenophobia, manipulated and fanned by far-right political parties. Immigrants themselves thus confronted a daunting set of problems: economic marginalization, racist attitudes, and state policies that at times clashed with immigrant cultures.

Postcolonial Migration

The nations of Western Europe actively recruited immigrants as laborers during the postwar economic boom. By the 1970s, however, economic downturn transformed migration from a boon into a problem and European nations began increasingly to close their doors to immigrants. Despite these obstacles, a new stream of migrants, including refugees from the former Soviet bloc and from war-torn regions of Africa and Asia, poured into Europe in the 1990s.

Labor Migration in the Postwar Period Two factors drove immigration to Europe during the period of economic recovery after the Second World War. First, an acute labor shortage created a demand for migrant labor as the Western European economies underwent rapid expansion in the 1950s and 60s. Second, decolonization provided a ready supply of ex-colonial subjects eager to seek economic opportunity in Europe. In the UK, the first dramatic wave of postcolonial immigration in the 1950s brought migrants from India, Pakistan,

Bangladesh, Africa, and the Caribbean. Migrants from North Africa flocked to France, and those from Indonesia and Surinam went to the Netherlands. Alongside the flow of postcolonial immigrants, labor migrants also circulated within Europe: Southern Italians went to northern Italy, Switzerland, and Germany; Spaniards and Portuguese to France; and Yugoslavs, Turks, and Greeks to northern Europe.

This first generation of labor migrants was composed predominantly of men who left families behind in their countries of origin (although their families often followed later on). Because many of them migrated not only to a new nation, but from the countryside to the city, their immigration entailed a double dislocation. The majority found full-time jobs in industry, mining, and construction, while others worked as domestic servants, street sweepers, and menial laborers of all kinds. By the 1970s foreign immigrants made up 17 percent of the workforce in Switzerland, some 8 percent in Germany, and slightly less in France.

Global Migration in the 1990s   The era of relatively open immigration came to an abrupt end during the 1970s and 1980s, when economic recession and rising unemployment led to European-wide restrictions on labor immigration. But a new wave of migration surged in the 1990s. This one differed substantially from the first wave of postwar labor migration. Although the majority came, as they did in the age of labor migration, from Africa and Asia, the collapse of the Soviet bloc in the 1990s triggered a massive movement of migrants from eastern and southeastern Europe. Five million migrants from eastern Europe went to Germany alone in the early 1990s. A million-and-a-half Russians of German descent went to Germany, while close to half a million Russian Jews left Russia, most for Israel, some to the United States. Russians living outside of Russia proper—who had lived a privileged life under the Soviet regime—also left their homes in droves. Approximately 350,000 ethnic Turks emigrated from an unstable Bulgaria. Five million refugees fled the former Yugoslavia to go to east central and western Europe before violence in Kosovo sparked still more migration.

Recent migration also differs from postwar migration in other important ways. In addition to migrating to traditional countries of immigration such as France, Great Britain, and Germany, immigrants now also seek entry into former nations of emigration, such as Spain, Italy, Greece, Cyprus, and Ireland. Some come in search of economic opportunity, whereas others seek return to ethnic homelands, and still others migrate to flee political instability and ethnic conflicts. Contemporary migrants also occupy a much more precarious economic position than postwar labor migrants. Apart from a minority of educated professionals, most are unskilled labor. Many end up unemployed, and those who do work often can find only part-time jobs without security or benefits. Finally, since the 1980s, women constitute almost half of the migrants to Europe, many of whom work as domestic laborers. Female migrants include a substantial number of young girls, Eastern European and Romani girls in particular, involved in the sex trafficking industry. The typical pattern is that young girls and women are lured to Western Europe with the promise of jobs and citizenship, only to be violently coerced into prostitution and sexual slavery.

After European countries closed the channels of economic migration in the early 1970s, most migration to Europe became that of political asylum seekers, with between half a million and two million refugees entering EU countries each year. In the early 1990s, most came from Eastern Europe, but migration from other parts of the world has since eclipsed intra-European migration. The vast majority of these seek refuge from intrastate conflicts or political oppression in, among other places, Afghanistan, Iraq, the former Yugoslavia, Somalia, Rwanda, China, and Turkey. In the early 1990s, most sought access to Germany, but today's most popular migrant destination in Europe is the UK. Immigration to southern Europe is also at an all-time high. All in all, net migration into the EU increased by 200 percent, from 600,000 to 1.8 million per year, between 1994 and 2004. These numbers are all the more surprising given the extraordinary risks many refugees take to get into Europe and the difficulties that await them if they are allowed to enter. A frequent pattern is for migrants to be smuggled in via Mediterranean ports. Some die in the process, drowning when their typically decrepit, overloaded boats capsize. Those who make it in are frequently held for long periods in unsanitary, overcrowded detention centers, where some have been subjected to extreme ill-treatment. The majority are ultimately deported.

The Politics of Immigration

As immigration to Europe has increased over the years, immigrant populations have become increasingly noticeable in many European cities. European nations have dealt differently with these communities, implementing policies that range from full-scale assimilation to laissez-faire multiculturalism. At the same time, the immigrant presence has evoked widespread hostility in many quarters, especially in times of economic decline. For the immigrants themselves, conditions have gotten progressively worse. Segregated into urban ghettos with high rates of unemployment, immigrants have had to contend not only with economic and social marginalization, but with growing racism.

European Immigration Policy By the mid-1950s, the Western European economies were booming and could no longer meet the demand for labor. To fill the gap, European nations turned first to southern Europe, and then to their former colonies to recruit male laborers. They thus welcomed immigrants as a temporary workforce, needed to sustain economic recovery. Germany and Switzerland explicitly labeled these labor migrants "guest workers," the very term revealing the temporary nature of their welcome. Across Europe, governments thus paid little attention to the "political" status of these migrants. In 1973, the oil crisis and the subsequent economic downturn prompted governments to stop labor recruitment and to implement new laws limiting immigration. With the exception of family reunion immigration permitting male migrant laborers to bring in their families, entry to Europe thus became difficult during the 1970s and 1980s. In the 1990s, the implementation of further restrictions, along with efforts to coordinate policy within the EU, led to the image of a barricaded "Fortress Europe," sparking criticism from human rights organizations such as Amnesty International. By 2000, unskilled Asians and Africans had very little chance of getting into Europe, although a number of countries—including France, Germany, and Denmark—sought to facilitate the immigration of the more educated and skilled.

While a similar pattern thus emerged across Europe with respect to entry policy, the European nations took different approaches to managing their immigrant communities. The British government passed laws stemming the flow of migrants even in the heyday of labor migration, but once in Britain, immigrants have been able to become naturalized citizens through a relatively straightforward process. However, the government has not viewed the social incorporation of immigrants as its responsibility. In terms of attitudes toward diversity, the British endorse a kind of laissez-faire multiculturalism, emphasizing respect for different cultural and ethnic communities and noninterference on the part of the state. For example, the government does not impose any restrictions on the wearing of head scarves by Muslim schoolgirls, instead leaving that decision to particular schools.

More than any other European nation, France has sought to incorporate its immigrants into French culture. Although citizenship has traditionally been easy for non-nationals to attain, in return the state seeks their full assimilation into French culture and asks them to avoid displays of their cultural or ethnic difference in civic spaces. This policy comes out of the French Republic's universalist ideals, which see the interests and identities of groups as a threat to the good of the nation. Put differently, the French state recognizes immigrants as individuals, but refuses to grant them rights on the basis of group identification. So much is this the case that the French census does not collect data on the ethnicity, religion, or racial background of French citizens (it is illegal for employers to request such information) and the government has long eschewed affirmative action for minorities.

German immigrants faced the most restrictive citizenship laws in Europe, based on the longstanding concept of Germanness as a non-transferable ethnic or descent-based trait. This meant that not only first-generation German immigrants, but even their German-born offspring, could not ever become citizens. During the 1990s, Germans became more receptive to a pluralistic notion of German society and in 2000, under Gerhard Schröder's Socialist government, Germany fundamentally liberalized its citizenship laws, deeming birthplace, rather than ethnicity, the central criterion of citizenship. This made second-generation immigrants whose parents were legal residents eligible for citizenship. With respect to cultural diversity, Germany occupies a middle ground between France and Britain, supporting but also seeking to regulate expressions of cultural difference; thus, for example, the government has introduced Islamic religious instruction into some public schools as means of promoting a form of Islam compatible with German values.

Elsewhere, a range of immigration and integration policies pertain. Spanish immigration policy is among the most relaxed in the EU, and Spain still recruits workers (for example, from Senegal) and offers special treatment to members of former Spanish colonies. Sweden also has had relatively liberal immigration law and favors multiculturalist policies—for example, offering instruction in immigrant languages in public schools. The Netherlands has had a fairly restrictive citizenship policy but promoted multiculturalism, providing public funding for separate schools for immigrant groups and actively encouraging them to maintain their native languages and to develop organizations to sustain their cultural practices. By the late 1990s, however, the Dutch government began to reconsider its position, leading to a greater emphasis on assimilation. In 2002, Denmark turned some of the most liberal immigration laws in Europe into some of the most restrictive. Since 2005, moreover, the government mandates that immigrants assimilate to Danish culture, including learning to speak Danish and understanding the "fundamental norms and values of Danish society."

Political asylum remains one of the only channels of legal immigration to Europe, and the growing number of asylum-seekers has become both a cause of popular concern and a policy issue in the EU. Many Europeans suspect migrants of making spurious claims to refugee status as a means of gaining entry into Europe; they resent the influx of "freeloaders" and claim that foreigners want to exploit the privileges of citizenship in modern welfare states without having earned them. Governments have responded to these concerns by introducing legislation narrowing the grounds for asylum, despite the fact that Western European nations signed the UN Refugee Convention in 1951, obligating them to grant entry to those defined as refugees (people unable to return to their place of origin because of fear of persecution).

The New Racism   From the 1970s on, economic downturn and the steady growth of postcolonial immigrant communities have stoked xenophobia and racism in many parts of Europe. Some sociologists consider this upsurge of racism to be of a distinctive type, different from the "scientific" racism that predominated from the late nineteenth century to the end of the Second World War. Instead of emphasizing the biological inferiority of non-Europeans, the new racism is primarily cultural or ethnic in nature, based on the assumption that people ought to live alongside those who share their culture. Right-wing political slogans advocating the repatriation of outsiders—"Holland is full" and "France is for the French"—exemplify the shift, as does widespread European hostility toward Muslim immigrants.

Racist sentiment surfaced in some places with the arrival of the first labor immigrants. In Britain, violent race riots broke out as early as 1958 and then again in the early 1980s. Opportunist politicians capitalized on the growing mood of intolerance. In 1968, Enoch Powell, a highly respected Conservative MP, refashioned himself as a right-wing leader with a strong anti-immigrant platform; his famous "Rivers of Blood" speech repelled the political establishment but inspired thousands of British workers to take to the streets in his support. By the 1970s, the extreme-right National Front movement, once a political sideshow, was drawing more supporters than ever, and mainstream parties had begun to pander to popular xenophobia as well. In 1978, the Conservative politician Margaret Thatcher successfully won her campaign for prime minister partly by promising that she would protect Britain from being "swamped by people with a different culture."[1]

Both the French and the Germans initially believed that most labor migrants would eventually return home, but race politics began to heat up in the 1980s as migrant laborers began bringing in their families and developing permanent communities. In Germany, a spike in applications for asylum in the mid-1980s—encouraged by Germany's generous Basic Law of 1949, which established the fundamental right to asylum—further politicized the immigration issue. In France,

Jean Marie Le Pen's anti-immigration National Front party made newspaper headlines and grew popular enough to win 10 percent of the vote, gaining 35 seats in the legislature in the 1986 election. Despite these victories, the fact that Le Pen's votes came overwhelmingly from the south of France shows that race politics by and large remained a regional issue during this period.

In the 1990s, however, popular racism metamorphosed from a local to a national issue across Europe. Heightened by a new influx of migrants and growing unemployment, anti-immigrant feeling fed on the competition for ill-paying jobs. Shrill right-wing political parties, often with neo-fascist tendencies, gained public attention and electoral support by playing on the growing fear of foreigners. In Italy a new party, the Northern League, gained ground in the prosperous north by combining in one program opposition to immigration and denunciation of the central government's corruption and high taxes. In France unemployed industrial workers who had voted communist in the past became sympathetic to the xenophobic platform of Le Pen's National Front. And in post-reunification Germany, where hundreds of thousands of people had fled the faltering economies of Eastern Europe, incidents in which gangs of skinheads and neo-Nazis burned immigrant housing ominously evoked Germany's past. Denounced by most political leaders, these movements also inspired the formation of a host of antiracist organizations, including the French group SOS Racisme, its Spanish counterpart SOS Racismo, and the Anti-Nazi League in the UK.

Anti-immigrant movements and parties attracted new followers following the September 11, 2001, terrorist attacks against the United States by Islamic militants. In Denmark, a country with a historical reputation for tolerance, an anti-immigrant party known as the Danish People's party won 12 percent of the vote in the parliamentary elections of November 2001. In the Netherlands, another traditional bastion of tolerance, the right-wing politician Pim Fortuyn denounced Islam as a "backward culture" and called for immigration restrictions in the election campaign of 2002. Fortuyn was assassinated (by an opponent of the xenophobic right) shortly before the election, but his party captured the second-highest number of seats in the Dutch parliament. The most dramatic and widely publicized illustration of the growing prominence of the far right occurred during the first round of the French presidential election of 2002, when Jean Marie Le Pen finished second to President Chirac. But Le Pen's electoral success shocked observers and galvanized French voters, many of whom took to the streets in protest. On May Day 2002, almost 1.5 million people throughout France demonstrated against the National

---

[1] Jonathan Kandell, "French Act to Curb Flow of Immigrants," *The New York Times*, May 31, 1979.

Front. Determined to prevent Le Pen from achieving a respectable showing in the election, the French left joined with the moderate right to support Chirac. As a result, Chirac won the election with an overwhelming 82 percent of the vote.

Overall, anti-immigrant parties on the far right have achieved only limited success, and some experts claim that their threat to European politics has been exaggerated. Nevertheless, the xenophobic right did make significant electoral gains in a few countries, including Austria, Denmark, France, and the Netherlands. In Austria, for example, the Freedom party led by Joerg Haider, who has expressed admiration for Hitler, gained a share in the ruling coalition in 2000 (prompting other EU nations to refuse formal cooperation with the Austrian government). Their most important impact, however, has been to influence mainstream party politics and state policy: the popularity of these parties has both forced established ones to take a harder line on immigrants and pressured governments to further limit immigration and reduce benefits to immigrant populations.

The Immigrant Experience Resented by native workers competing for jobs and higher pay, despised as sources of crime and heavy welfare costs, postcolonial immigrants have faced a rising tide of racism since arriving in Europe. Often lacking the protections of citizenship, they are the targets of verbal harassment, physical violence, and widespread discrimination, yet racism casts them as a fundamentally delinquent class. As a consequence, they are subjected to excessive police harassment and surveillance as well as discrimination in the criminal courts.

Immigrants also constitute an economic and social underclass in many parts of Europe. Rates of unemployment among them are extremely high—in some parts of Europe roughly twice that of native Europeans. Those who work, moreover, tend to have poorly paid, menial jobs at the bottom of the social hierarchy, often as part-time laborers without benefits or job security. Most such jobs are not unionized and many are illegal. Female immigrants are particularly heavily concentrated at the low end of the service sector, working as child-care providers, domestics, or in the sex trade.

Clustered in low-income housing, often in segregated, crime-ridden neighborhoods, immigrants tend to be spatially separated from native Europeans. The trend toward segregation began during the early years of labor migration, when migrant workers often lived in squalid, makeshift accommodations. As immigrants put down permanent roots, Western European states built public housing projects on the outskirts of cities and began to provide some social services for them. Yet, even though these projects were intended to benefit immigrants, poverty and isolation from other communities have created ghettos both resistant to and rejected by the larger society. In many respects these immigrant suburbs are like separate cities, where young people are unemployed and without hope of entry into the social mainstream.

Within immigrant neighborhoods, living conditions are typically substandard. Overcrowding is rampant. In Spain in 2006, almost 20 percent of migrants lived in less than ten square meters and more than 60 percent have less than one room per person. Some migrant groups, in particular asylum seekers and undocumented migrants, suffer high rates of homelessness or live in conditions of extreme destitution, lacking basic facilities such as running water, toilets, and electricity. In 2006, the NGO Doctors Without Borders reported that asylum-seekers in Syracuse, Italy, were living in huts without running water. Similarly, an EU report of that year found Ukrainian and other Eastern European migrants to Portugal living in dwellings lacking in sanitation, running water, heat, and electricity, and 3 percent of them residing at their place of work.

Unequal education tends to keep many immigrants locked into this separate world. Although performance levels vary widely across immigrant subgroups and between European nations, many immigrants have less access to education and function less well as students (in part because many lack proficiency in the language of instruction). While the irregular legal situation of illegal immigrants and asylum seekers either prevents them from enrolling in school or leads to sporadic attendance, regularized first- and second-generation immigrants also under-perform in school, drop out at much higher rates, and attain lower overall levels of education than native Europeans, with the most extreme lags found in Western Europe. In a number of countries, a quarter of all second-generation immigrant students, schooled entirely in Europe, do not attain basic mathematical or reading proficiency, putting them at a serious disadvantage in the labor market.

The Roma deserve special mention as Europe's most discriminated-against minority, going back to efforts by the Nazis to exterminate them altogether. They are also Europe's largest ethnic minority, with 8 to 10 million Roma in the twenty-seven EU countries alone. The vast majority live in Eastern Europe, particularly Bulgaria and Romania, where one in ten people are Roma. Between half and three-quarters of all Roma are unemployed, and in some parts of Eastern Europe 90 to 100 percent of Roma are jobless. They also experience the worst housing conditions in Europe. According to a recent EU study, 80 percent of Roma in Spain live in shantytowns; in Galicia, Poland, 10 Roma families squatted in an abandoned factory for over twenty years;

and in Slovakia, 8,000 Roma live in municipal housing intended for 4,000 tenants. Landlords often refuse Roma as tenants; in a 2007 court case in Sweden, the Swedish Discrimination Ombudsman charged a landlord with changing the locks to an apartment after discovering that the family living there was not Thai but Roma. In education, too, Roma fare worse then other groups by every measure. In Romania and Bulgaria, 15 percent of Roma children never enroll in school. Those in school drop out at rates four to six times higher than others. In Serbia, the drop-out rate among Roma is fifteen times higher than that of non-Roma.

Since the late 1990s, the EU has sought to establish more stringent laws against ethnic discrimination and to create institutions to monitor racism as well as agencies and organizations to support victims of attacks. The results have been uneven across the member states. By 2000, most EU states had laws on the books addressing racial and ethnic discrimination. However, these laws were typically either weak and ineffective, for example, in the Czech Republic, Germany, and Spain, or not consistently applied, for example, in Austria, Denmark, France, and Italy. In Germany and Denmark, the framework exists for mounting discrimination cases in court, but the burden of proof remains largely on the victim. Elsewhere, such as in Sweden, a significant spike in discrimination cases over the past decade suggests more effective legal and civil society protections for immigrants.

Immigrant Culture For most immigrants, material disadvantage and social exclusion go hand in hand with cultural dislocation. This is true even in northwest Europe, where approximately half of those considered immigrants are actually of immigrant descent, born in Europe, and citizens in their countries of birth. Widespread feelings of marginalization show that, while citizenship is necessary for the protection of minority rights, it cannot by itself create a sense of belonging. Germany, for example, systematically denied immigrants and their German-born children citizenship until 2000, but the granting of citizenship did not change the fact that most Germans still refused to recognize immigrants and their descendents as full-fledged Germans.

Nevertheless, the current situation of second- and third-generation immigrants differs substantially from that of early labor migrants. While first-generation migrants remained attached to their countries of origin, their European-born children and grandchildren do not necessarily share those ties. Growing up in Europe, they are educated in European schools, speak the language of their European country, and are savvy about European culture in ways unimaginable to the older generation. This very familiarity, however, often sharpens their bitterness at being socially and economically excluded from the mainstream. At the same time, it can also accentuate the foreignness of their family's culture of origin. Postcolonial literature frequently takes up this theme of the cultural rootlessness of immigrant youth; one of the earliest examples is Mehdi Charef's novel *Tea in the Harem* (1983), in which the French-born son of Algerian immigrants describes himself as "lost between two cultures, two histories, two languages"[2] (see "A Turkish Girl Arrives in Germany," p. 943).

One symptom of widespread disaffection among young immigrants was widespread rioting in France in the fall of 2005. Outraged by the death of two immigrant teenagers fleeing the police, mobs of angry young men, largely Muslims of North African descent, from the immigrant-dominated suburbs of Paris and other French cities looted stores, burned cars, and engaged in street violence for over three weeks. The riots vented the profound alienation and anger at discrimination felt by many immigrants in French society, and the response of then-Interior Minister Nicholas Sarkozy, who called the rioters "scum" whose neighborhoods should be "cleansed with a power hose," only intensified these emotions.

Postcolonial Youth Culture The alienation of second- and third-generation immigrants has also produced a vibrant, creative youth culture. Since the 1990s, much of this culture has centered on hip-hop music. Some European hip-hop is angry and violent in the style of American gangsta rap, but another branch is deliberately cosmopolitan, celebrating cultural diversity and condemning racism and xenophobia. In response to rising racism in Germany in the early 1990s, for example, a vibrant hip-hop culture blossomed among young German Turks in Berlin. A key band in this subculture was the German-Turkish group Kanaks With Attitude, who appropriated the German pejorative term for a Turk—"Kanak"—as a badge of ethnic pride, but at the same time rejected a narrow identity politics, rapping in Turkish, but also in German and English. The Danish hip-hop group Outlandish is another example of this kind of multicultural politics: influenced by Moroccan, Pakistani, and Latin American music, the band's lyrics are in English, Spanish, Urdu, Danish, and Arabic. More than anywhere else in Europe, hip-hop has thrived in France, which now boasts the second biggest market in the world. Among the most popular groups is the Marseille-based Muslim group IAM (Imperial Asiatic Man), which seeks to fight racism by disseminating positive messages of religious and racial tolerance.

[2] Mehdi Charef, *Le thé au harem d'Archi Ahmed* (Paris: Gallimard, 1983) 17.

A Turkish Girl Arrives in Germany

Aynur, a young Turkish girl, published in a Turkish newspaper a very personal and frank account of her life in Germany. She had gone to Germany with her mother to live with her father, who had worked there several years. Leaving her village elementary school behind, she went to a Turkish school in Germany and lived there into her teens. As she adopted new ways, she became alienated from her family, found German friends only among groups of homosexuals and drug addicts, and eventually made several visits to Turkey in search of old ties to her extended family and native culture. She ends her account with the comment, "On my birth certificate it is written that I am a 'Turk.' But in the full sense, more correctly, with my thinking, I am not completely a Turk. I do not want to be a German either." In the passage quoted here, she describes her first days in Germany.

"A bustle of activity commenced as soon as the plane landed in Berlin. Everyone wanted to disembark. I looked for the sun as soon as we went out, but it wasn't to be seen. I thought I was before a gray wall. The weather was cloudy and rainy. Later on I started looking for blond people. I always thought that all Germans were blond.

"We took a taxi. I was watching out of the window. I was trying to see the white houses which I had dreamed about. All around were large brick buildings. There were no people in sight on the wide boulevards. I was constantly asking my father, 'Which one looks like our house?'

"Finally we got out of the taxi. I was looking around to find the house that they lived in. My father, pointing to a somewhat larger door, said, 'You enter here.' An old door, all the edges of which were broken, and a somewhat large building from which the plaster was falling. After we entered through the large door and went through the small concrete courtyard, we started climbing the stairs. The holding-on places were broken.

"Suddenly all of my illusions were shattered. Pessimism and dejection overcame me. We climbed until the fourth floor. My father opened the door. A small hallway, a living room, and a kitchen. That was all there was to the home. The toilet was outside, they said.

"I asked myself, 'Is this our house?' I withdrew to a corner and started to investigate the living room. In the middle a faded rug was laid. Around it stood a few old armchairs. The only new thing was a fairly large television that stood in the corner. Forgetting everything, we started playing with the television. At each press of a button, a different film appeared.

"Six of us started to live together in the one-room house. This situation did not strike me as odd. In our village, too, we used to live all together. Since I had not had any different living experience, this did not seem unusual.

"My older sister and I did not get out of the room for a period of three months. We were afraid, and moreover, our father was not giving us permission. Our only tie to the outside was a window facing the courtyard. Children were playing in the courtyard. My only wish was to play with them. From time to time I was able to talk through the kitchen window with our neighbor's daughter, who was a year older than I. I was impatiently waiting for her return from school. My first friend in Germany was this girl.

"Her hair was cut very short. She looked like a very modern girl. We went down together to the courtyard entrance to play. I gained a little courage. After that I started going to their home.

"We used to wear skirts over pajamas in our village. My father had bought slacks for us in Istanbul. From then on we wore slacks under our skirts instead of pajamas. Slowly I began to imitate my friend. When no one was at home, I would take off my skirt and walk around in my slacks. At other times, I would take off my slacks and walk around in just my skirt. My older sister was not able to dare to do this. She would sit at the window as my look-out.

"For a long time when we went outside, we wore slacks under our skirts."

From Akural Aynur (tr.), in Ilhan Basgöz and Norman Furniss (eds.), *Turkish Workers in Europe*, Turkish Studies Publications, 1985. Reprinted by permission.

The broad popularity of these musical forms reflects two important developments. It relies on the widespread use of new information technologies—the Internet and streaming video, cell phones, iPods, and satellite dishes—that enable the wide diffusion of cultural products at lightning speed between otherwise disconnected communities. Equally important is the fact that postcolonial exotica has become big business. The music industry (along with other culture industries) has become increasingly adept at capitalizing on the novelty and difference of ethnic cultural forms, and growing numbers of mainstream European artists routinely borrow from postcolonial cultural repertories, going back to the incorporation of Caribbean reggae and ska by British punk and New Wave bands like The Clash and The Police and the use of African musical motifs by the British rock star Peter Gabriel and including the recent influence of North African music on the Irish band U2. Yet, while market forces have intensified the cross-pollination of culture, they also commercialize cultural forms, simplifying them and divesting them of political content to make them palatable and nonthreatening to a broad audience. Some observers see this as a process that enriches all parties, but many paint it in a negative light, as a form of European "musical tourism" based on the exploitation of non-European culture.

Europe's Encounter with Islam Apart from the Roma, in recent years no immigrant group has been more marginalized than Europe's Muslims. But while the Roma are a forgotten community whose plight is of little interest to most Europeans, Muslims are the most high-profile immigrant group, at the very center of public debate about immigration. Since the 9/11 attacks on the United States, moreover, Europe's tense encounter with Islam has become increasingly charged.

Muslim populations have lived in the Balkans and in Spain, Portugal, Cyprus, and Sicily for many centuries, but their numbers increased and they appeared in other parts of Europe starting in the late 1950s and 60s; a new, much smaller influx arrived as refugees in the 1990s. The total European Muslim population is 13 to 14 million, constituting 3.5 percent of the total population of Europe. In relative terms, France has the largest Muslim population in Western Europe (close to 10 percent), followed by the Netherlands (over 5 percent), Switzerland, Germany, Austria, Belgium, Sweden, Denmark, (3 to 4 percent), and Britain (2.5 percent); the Muslim population hovers around 1 percent or lower in the rest of Western Europe. Muslims make up a much higher percentage of the population in parts of Eastern Europe, including 12 percent in Bulgaria, 19 percent in Russia as well as Serbia, 40 percent in Bosnia and Herzegovina, and a full 70 percent in Albania. European Muslims are of diverse ethnic, linguistic, and national origins. Most are Sunni, although a Shiite minority does exist. Approximately one-half are European born and almost all are urban. The Muslim population is very young compared to the rest of the European population and has a substantially higher birthrate.

Like the Roma, European Muslims form a socioeconomic underclass in every European nation. An EU report of 2006 documented that Europe's Muslims tend to live in segregated neighborhoods with poor quality housing, are less educated than other Europeans, have higher rates of unemployment than average, and work in low-paying, low-skill jobs. In Great Britain, the unemployment rate among Muslims is three times greater than in the rest of the population; 40 percent of British Muslims who are employed are in low-skill occupations and over 70 percent of Muslim children live in poverty. Almost one-quarter of German Turks are jobless, while in some Muslim neighborhoods in France, 50 percent of young people are unemployed. Because jobs are a critical means of integrating populations, the situation of Muslims in the European labor market is especially worrisome.

In addition to material deprivation and social exclusion, Muslim Europeans live in an atmosphere of mutual mistrust with non-Muslim Europeans. In some places, culture clashes have precipitated major public controversies. In France, efforts to induce French Muslims to conform to French culture sparked the notorious *affaire du foulard* (the headscarf affair), concerning the right of Muslim girls to wear headscarves in French schools. The headscarf affair first erupted following the 1989 expulsion of three girls wearing headscarves from high school and again in 2004, when the government legally banned headscarves in schools, branding them as religious symbols (along with large Christian crosses, Jewish skullcaps, and Sikh turbans) inimical to the republic's commitment to secular education. Opponents also argued that the headscarf symbolized the patriarchal oppression of Muslim women and therefore contradicted republican ideals of gender equality. In July of 2008, a French court went still further, denying citizenship to a Moroccan-born Muslim woman on the grounds that her wearing of the burka, a head-to-toe covering, showed a commitment to "radical" Islam incompatible with French culture.

Tensions between Muslim and non-Muslim Europeans have reached the flash point in other nations, too. In 2004, the issue of Muslim intolerance to criticism and the right of non-Muslims to criticize Islam made headlines in the Netherlands. As retribution for a short film condemning Islam's treatment of women, a Dutch Muslim murdered the filmmaker Theo Van Gogh (grandnephew of the painter Vincent Van Gogh). In spite of the fact that Dutch Muslims demonstrated en masse against Van Gogh's murder, the assassination sparked an upsurge in anti-Muslim sentiment. Similar issues surfaced in Denmark in 2006 with the publication of a series of cartoons lampooning the Muslim prophet Muhammad. Responding to outrage from the Muslim communities around the world, the Danish Prime Minister and the newspaper that first published the cartoons issued official apologies; but the republication of the cartoons in other European newspapers prompted protests on an even wider scale. For many people, this episode recalled the Iranian leader Khomeini's 1989 issue of a *fatwa* (death sentence) against the novelist Salman Rushdie, a Muslim immigrant to Britain, for having blasphemed Islam in his novel *The Satanic Verses*. Both the Rushdie affair and the cartoon controversy have been seen by some as proof of Islam's irreconcilability with secular European modernity.

The causes of these conflicts are complex, but several can be singled out. First, there are genuine conflicts of culture. A religious revival among European Muslims in the past two decades has accentuated these

Outside the headquarters of the school authorities in Strasbourg, France, a French Muslim girl demonstrates against the ban on headscarves in schools in 2004. The sign behind her reads "School is my right; the headscarf is my choice." Getty Images

differences, slowing the assimilation of Muslim communities to secular European culture. A major point of contention for the secular European nation-states is the central role many Muslims assign to religion in civic and political life. At one end of the spectrum, Islamic radicals believe that religion and politics cannot be separated and reject the very notion of the secular state in favor of theocracy; but there are also many moderate Muslims who equate secularization with Westernization and want to make religion more important to social, if not political, life. They see the Qur'an not only as a spiritual guide, but as a kind of constitution prescribing behavior in daily life.

Real differences aside, debates about cultural conciliation are clouded by European misconceptions of Muslim culture. In particular, they fail to differentiate between different kinds of European Muslims, an extremely heterogeneous group with respect to origins, language, cultural identity, and religious belief and practice. Defenders of the headscarf, for example, argue that non-Muslims who interpret the headscarf as a reflection of gender oppression or religious fanaticism do not understand its varied meanings. While some Muslim women certainly don the headscarf as a sign of piety, they say, others wear it as a cultural—rather than religious—assertion of feminine modesty and still others as a badge of cultural identity. Commentators have also emphasized how the media's focus on cases of forced marriage and so-called honor killings in Muslim communities creates a skewed image of Muslim gen-

der relations and family life. Deplorable as such incidents are, it is argued, the media's fascination with them has the effect of casting all Muslim women as passive victims of an oppressive Islam, ignoring the many for whom Islamic cultural and religious practices are a positive source of identity and empowerment.

Further complicating the discussion is anti-Muslim racism—sometimes labeled "Islamophobia"—fomented by the anti-immigrant right and by simplistic stereotyping in the European media depicting Islam as a threat to European society. Islamophobes portray Muslims as a monolithic and unchanging group of fanatical fundamentalists who despise European society. At best, they portray Muslims as disloyal to Europe; at worst, as sympathetic to terrorism. Another claim of the Islamophobes is that Muslim immigration, combined with the population's high birthrate—the highest in Europe—spells the future "Islamicization" of Europe. In the words of the Italian journalist Oriana Fallaci, Muslims are demographically and culturally conquering Europe, making it only a matter of time before Europeans "end up with minarets in place of. . . belltowers, with the burka in place of the mini-skirt."[3]

Such attitudes can no longer be pinned on the political right alone as mainstream Europeans have become increasingly susceptible to racist and xenophobic ideas. Anti-Muslim racism has been fanned by the rise of Islamic fundamentalism worldwide in the past thirty

[3] Margaret Talbot, "The Agitator," *The New Yorker*, June 5, 2006.

The wreckage of the World Trade Center in New York City. Searing images of airplanes slamming into the twin towers and of the resulting destruction burned into the American consciousness.
Sipa Press

years and its links to a host of terrorist episodes, from the 9/11 destruction of the World Trade Center in New York City to the lethal bombings of public transportation systems by Islamic extremists in Madrid in 2004 and in London in 2005. An EU-sponsored report of 2006 monitoring European "Islamophobia" finds that nearly half of all Europeans—and substantially higher numbers in Germany, Spain, and the Netherlands—take a largely negative view of Muslims and that, since 9/11, it has become far more acceptable to make openly anti-Muslim statements in politics.

But how widespread is fundamentalist Islam in Europe? In the past decade, Islamic extremism has indeed been on the rise among young European Muslim men, sparked by a wide range of events, including the recent wars in Afghanistan, Bosnia, and Iraq, and the long-standing Israeli conflict with Palestinians. But the attraction of young alienated men living in poor urban enclaves to radical Islam—also known as "garage Islam" and "basement Islam"—is only one part of the story. The majority of European Muslims are best described as moderates who themselves have expressed deep concern over this trend. Muslim feminists have been particularly outspoken critics of the sexism they

see as part of radical Islam, among them the French feminist—and urban affairs minister—Fadela Amara, the daughter of Algerian immigrants. As a young girl growing up in the immigrant suburbs, Amara took issue with fundamentalist views of women and began a movement to reform Islam, *Ni Putains, Ni Soumises* (Neither Whores Nor Doormats), that has since attracted many supporters. Another well-known liberal Muslim who has harshly censured the fundamentalist oppression of women is the Somali-born Dutch politician Ayaan Hirsi Ali, best known for collaborating with Theo Van Gogh on the film that led to his murder. Others subscribe to a distinctively European form of Islam that seeks to unite Western values with those of the Qur'an. On balance, European Muslims are more moderate and take a more positive perspective on Western culture than Muslims elsewhere in the world.

It is also worth noting that each terrorist attack linked to Islam generated many counterattacks; the 2004 murder of Theo Van Gogh in the Netherlands, for example, sparked hundreds of violent incidents, including the burning and defacing of Muslim mosques and schools and the beating of Muslims. Moreover, most European Muslims describe themselves as largely unsympathetic to terrorism. In short, far-right parties and media hysteria greatly sensationalize the growth of Islamic extremism and create a distorted portrait of Europe's Muslims, one that ignores liberal strands of Islam and the views of the moderate majority.

For Muslims, rising racism and cultural misunderstanding have deepened their alienation from and anger at non-Muslim Europeans. Many complain that their sense of belonging within Europe is threatened not only by the rising tide of bigotry, but by the failure of European states to counter that prejudice by promoting the social integration of Muslim communities. The rise of radical Islam among angry third-generation European Muslims, they say, is the direct consequence of this failure. Muslim leaders thus counter charges of separatism with the claim that European society excludes them, rather than the other way around, and argue that their acceptance into that society is made contingent on their renunciation of Islamic culture.

EUROPE IN THE GLOBAL ERA

In the last quarter century, Europe's identity and role in the world have been transformed. Major shifts in global politics, from the rise of Islamic fundamentalist terrorism to the perceived unilateralism of U.S. foreign policy under George W. Bush, have prompted Europe to rethink its foreign policy. Although relations between Europe and the United States remain close, Europe has tried to assert its political independence in the past decade; on the domestic front, Europeans continue to prefer a European way of life quite different from that of Americans. That way of life, however, is now being tested by heightened international economic competition as well as the challenge of integrating Europe's growing immigration population.

Europe in the Post 9/11 World

While domestic terrorism has long been a feature of European life, terrorist acts by radical Islamists belonging to global networks have captured public attention in recent years, provoking fear as well as creating a backlash against European Muslims.

Terrorism in the Contemporary World Although terrorism broadly defined as extralegal violence can be used to describe most insurgencies in history, the notion of terrorism as a new form of warfare is essentially a postwar phenomenon. Without the means to wage traditional or full-scale war, terrorists use targeted, localized violence against civilians in the hope of inciting widespread panic and creating pressure that will,

indirectly, facilitate the achievement of their social or political goals. In the 1970s and 80s, terrorism in Europe was associated with marginal groups on the extreme left and extreme right that often attacked well-known individuals. The extremist left-wing Red Brigades in Italy, for example, kidnapped and murdered the former Italian Prime Minister Aldo Moro in 1978; in Germany, the Baader-Meinhof gang, a self-described Marxist "urban guerilla" group, abducted and killed prominent members of society, including bankers, businessmen, and judges. Other well-known terrorist movements of the period had their roots in long-standing domestic political conflicts, such as the Irish Republican Army's thirty-six-year fight to end British rule in Northern Ireland, which took a toll of 3,500 lives on both sides until the declaration of a ceasefire in 2005. Similarly, the separatist group ETA's campaign to gain autonomy from Spain for the Basque region has spawned countless terrorist acts since its formation in 1959.

Since the 1980s and especially the 1990s, new forms of terrorism, linked to a global revival of radical Islam, increasingly have taken center stage. This brand of terrorism is a far-flung transnational movement with epicenters not only in Europe but in many other regions, one which has also garnered growing support in the Arab world. Moreover, instead of specific, local goals (such as the overthrow of a particular government or the attainment of national sovereignty), its objectives tend to be global, diffuse, even apocalyptic, associated with radical Islam's cultural attack on the secular West. Radical Islamic terrorist groups began to make headlines increasingly in the 1990s, with bombings, hijackings, and other violent episodes, widely publicizing the idea of terrorism as a *jihad*—holy war against the enemies of Islam. While radical Islamist terrorism has not wholly supplanted other forms—the violence of ETA in Spain, for example, has become rarer but persists—it is at the forefront of the public imagination, so much so that for many Europeans, Islam has become synonymous with terrorism.

Without question, the most notorious of recent terrorist acts were the 9/11 attacks against the United States, when nineteen men hijacked four domestic flights. One flew into the Pentagon, and two others deliberately smashed into the twin towers of the World Trade Center in New York City. The planes, loaded with fuel for transcontinental flights, were incendiary bombs, setting fires that blasted people out of the buildings and melted steel girders, unexpectedly causing the towers to crumble completely into a fountain of debris. Some three thousand people died from these assaults on symbols of American economic and military strength. Television carried live images around the world of the largely futile rescue efforts in an inferno of flames and smoke that lasted for days. Expressions of sympathy and outrage poured in from nearly every nation, and the public learned that this devastating act of terrorism had apparently been the work of a network of Muslim extremists known as al Qaeda. Their headquarters were in Afghanistan, where they were led by Osama bin Laden, a wealthy Saudi opposed to the Saudi Arabian government, which he denounced as a repressive agent of the American infidel. In Afghanistan he cooperated with the fanatically intolerant Taliban regime that gained control of most of the country in the aftermath of the Afghan war against the Soviet Union.

Religion, geopolitics, a global economy, and global communications came together in the training camps Osama bin Laden maintained. His group was responsible for at least three major attacks on American forces and embassies in the Middle East and Africa starting in 1993. While he escaped American efforts to hunt him down, he gained sympathy in the Muslim world by fanning resentment of American policy in the Middle East, especially its support for Israel, and by denouncing America's "immoral" culture and selfish economic power. With a network of agents and funds scattered across Europe and into Asia, he had accomplished the first important attack on American soil since the War of 1812.

Europe has had its share of terrorist attacks associated with radical Islam as well. In 2004, bombs exploded in commuter trains during the morning rush hour in Madrid, killing 191 and wounding over 1,800. In the summer of 2005, two separate attacks were mounted on London's subways and buses. More than 50 people died and 700 were wounded.

Responses to Terrorism   Americans responded to 9/11 with patriotic fervor, and President Bush declared the focus of his administration to be the war against terrorism around the world. NATO, for the first time in its history, invoked a treaty clause that considered an attack on one member an attack on all. Britain and France offered their armed forces, as did other members of NATO. Russia announced its willingness to join (noting that it considered the Chechen rebels to be terrorists, too). The United Nations unanimously supported the United States, while Muslim nations and leaders cautiously distanced themselves from the Afghan government and the terrorists it harbored. As the United States assembled its military force, governments everywhere began to freeze bank accounts the terrorists might use and to round up Middle Easterners suspected of ties to terrorists. Amid remarkable international cooperation and many hopeful signs, people everywhere wondered what else they had to fear. No one knew quite how this new kind of war would be fought, how extensive it might become, or how long it would last.

Under U.S. leadership, the response to terrorism quickly assumed the form of conventional warfare. Shortly after 9/11, the U.S. government demanded that the Taliban turn over bin Laden and shut down all al Qaeda operations in Afghanistan. When the Taliban

Red Cross helpers lift a body bag containing the victim of a bomb blast from a train about one kilometer outside the main train station in Madrid, March 11, 2004. Ten simultaneous explosions killed 182 people on packed Madrid commuter trains in Europe's bloodiest attack in more than 15 years.
© Kali Pfaffenbach/Reuters/Corbis

refused, the United States and Great Britain began a massive and sustained air bombardment that supported a ground offensive by anti-Taliban forces. By the end of the year the Taliban had been overthrown, a new and more moderate government had been established in Kabul, and the UN had authorized a multinational peacekeeping force for the country. A presidential election finally was held in October 2004, with Hamid Karzai winning an overwhelming victory. The Taliban, however, began to regroup almost immediately after their defeat in 2001. In the past few years, they have waged an intense military campaign, threatening the stability of the Karzai government and miring 50,000 U.S. and NATO soldiers in Afghanistan for the foreseeable future.

The European response to terrorism was not unlike that of the United States', and a number of nations have enacted a host of laws designed as antiterrorist measures. Although none of these is as stringent as the American Patriot Act, they are of similar design. After the London bombings of 2005, the British government passed a law limiting free speech in situations that might involve provocations to terrorism and another permitting indefinite detention of individuals deemed too dangerous to deport. The German state also tightened asylum laws and enacted legislation making deportation much easier, and in Italy the government expanded police power. Far more than in the United States, however, radical Islamic terrorism has produced a racist backlash against Muslims in many parts of Europe. According to an EU report of 2006 monitoring violence against European Muslims, attacks against them have been sharply on the rise in the last few years, ranging from verbal abuse and physical violence against individuals to attacks on property, including the desecration of mosques.

Europe's Contradictory Relationship with the United States

Since the end of the Second World War, the power of the United States has been a central fact of European life. By the 1990s, however, the configuration of power in the West had changed. While the downfall of the Soviet bloc deprived Europe of a strong counterweight to American influence, the political integration of the Continent, fostered by the end of Cold War hostilities and the growth of the EU, offered Europe a chance to chart a new course in its relationship with the United States.

European Responses to American Global Politics After the fall of communism, the overarching international reality was that the United States had become the world's only superpower. Issues were thus often defined as reactions to U.S. policy. America's hesitant

interventions to end civil wars and foster democracy in Africa, the Caribbean, and the Balkans had mixed results and garnered criticism. But if the "Vietnam syndrome" made the United States cautious about direct military intervention, America's influence and power were felt everywhere.

In 2001, the accession of George W. Bush to the presidency set the United States on a new divisive course. In short order, the United States rejected a number of international agreements, including those on the environment and nuclear arms and announced that it would not undertake "nation building" in unstable societies. This shift brought denunciations from Russia and cries of protest from Europe against American "unilateralism."

Iraq also became a central preoccupation of U.S. foreign policy. In 1991, in response to Iraq's invasion of neighboring Kuwait, the United States had led an international coalition in a war that defeated Iraq, but left the brutal dictatorial regime of Saddam Hussein in place. Then, in 2002, the United States accused Iraq of stockpiling weapons of mass destruction (WMDs) and cooperating with al Qaeda and other terrorist groups. Under pressure from the United States and Great Britain, the UN Security Council declared Iraq to be in violation of numerous UN rulings, insisting that it permit UN inspectors to search the country for WMDs. In March 2003, the United States and Britain asserted that Saddam Hussein continued to defy UN demands. Coalition forces from the United States and other countries invaded Iraq, ousting Hussein's regime. But this turned out to be not the end, but the beginning, of the war. Despite the election of a new Iraqi government in 2005, violent resistance to it and to the presence of occupation forces remained widespread. At the end of Bush's presidency in 2009, the war still engages well over 100,000 American soldiers in Iraq.

Its aggressive policies in Iraq created a fissure between the United States and many of its traditional European allies. The tensions surrounding U.S. policy in Iraq contrast with the cooperation and consensus over Kuwait a decade earlier. Whereas the First Gulf War was unequivocally sanctioned by a UN Security Council newly freed from the paralysis of the Cold War, this time war had to be waged despite the objections of several UN Security Council members. Many European countries, particularly France, Germany, and Russia, felt strongly that the UN weapons inspectors led by Hans Blix should have been given more time to complete their mission and that the willingness of the United States to invade without a clear UN mandate reflected growing American unilateralism and militarism. Continued violence in Iraq and the inability of the coalition forces to find any WMDs reinforced these sentiments.

The ongoing war in Iraq has damaged infrastructure, such as water supplies, as evidenced by these two young Iraqi girls filling a plastic bottle from a damaged water outlet.

The European response to the war in Iraq was not monolithic, and initial British, Italian, and Spanish support of the war countered French, German, and Russian opposition. But even in countries whose governments supported the war, public opinion against it was strong, and it quickly became a serious political liability for the governments of Britain and Italy, while in Spain, these sentiments actually drove the government out of power. In the wake of a terrorist bombing in Madrid linked to Spain's involvement in the war, the governing Conservative party lost the 2004 elections, and the newly elected Socialist Prime Minister Luis Rodriguez Zapatero promptly withdrew the Spanish troops from Iraq.

Differences over Iraq also have heightened tensions over long-standing political conflict between the United States and Europe concerning the Middle East. Although many European nations supported Israel (and some, including France, supplied it with arms) from independence through the late 1960s, attitudes shifted after the 1967 and 1973 wars, as the Israeli occupation of the West Bank, Gaza, and Sinai transformed European views of Israel from underdog to the dominant power in the region. Since the 1990s, Europeans have been increasingly vocal about their criticisms of Israeli policy as well as of American support of Israel's incursions into Lebanon and settlement-building in the occupied West Bank.

Further complicating the relationship between the United States and Europe is the revival of Russia as a great power since Vladimir Putin's accession to power in 1999. Its military engagement in Georgia in the summer of 2008 is the latest example of Russia's more aggressive stance. With the United States tied up in wars in Iraq and Afghanistan, Russia seized the opportunity to assert itself, backing rebels in South Ossetia and Abkhazian seeking independence from the republic of Georgia. The invasion was intended to reestablish Russian military credibility and to challenge America as the guarantor of European security, thereby creating divisions in NATO. More broadly, this served Russia's objective of thwarting NATO's expansion into Eastern Europe and the Baltic states and limiting American military power in Europe. Whereas some European nations—France, Germany, and Italy among them—are keen to offset American military might by developing a strategic pact with Russia, others, particularly in Central and Eastern Europe, fear Russian bellicosity and seek to keep NATO strong.

The European Social Contract Despite Western Europe's alliance with the United States during the Cold War, European and American society remain quite different. Many Europeans take their distance from American religiosity (particularly from groups that wish to assign religion a central role in political life). They object to America's use of the death penalty (abolition of the death penalty is a condition for EU membership), the ease with which American citizens can buy guns, and the bloated American criminal justice system, which incarcerates people at a much higher rate than any European system. Europeans frequently voice criticism of the United States' large military budget, favoring multilateral negotiation over military action as a response to international conflict and social over military spending at home. Finally, despite the fact that Europeans watch American films and television shows and buy American clothes, some of them disapprove of American materialism and consider American culture to be vulgar and commercial.

Perhaps the most important European divergence from the United States concerns attitudes toward market society. Since the nineteenth century, European models of capitalism have differed from American ones in valuing social solidarity alongside economic self-interest. These priorities gave rise to state efforts to mitigate the effects of capitalism as early as the late nineteenth century (the introduction of worker's sickness insurance in Germany in the 1880s is one example). In the twentieth century, it shaped the construction of welfare states that offered broad social support and protections to its citizenry, including universal state-supported health care, education, child care, and old age pensions. At the same time, a combination of labor legislation and collective agreements brokered by European unions created generous employment policies. Whereas Europeans are legally guaranteed between four and six weeks of paid annual vacation, Americans on average receive less than two weeks (and because no minimum legal requirement exists and American labor unions are weak, employers largely determine workers' vacation entitlements). Europeans also work a significantly shorter workweek than Americans. The average American works a 46-hour week; the average French worker works 35 hours a week, and the average worker in the Netherlands, Norway, Sweden, and Denmark works even fewer hours. Compared to Americans, European workers can also retire early (many at 55) and receive liberal parental leaves and sick-day entitlements.

When the European states attempted to pare down these generous provisions in response to economic contraction in the 1990s, citizens protested en masse. In France, proposed benefit cutbacks in 1995 generated a massive wave of strikes, demonstrating huge public support for the welfare state, while in May 1997, members of trade unions from across Europe demonstrated in Brussels in defense of workers' rights. Likewise, government efforts to slash Austrian pensions in 2003 gave rise to the biggest national strike in 50 years, and attempts to reduce expenditures on benefits in Germany that same year also produced widespread resistance. In Italy, too, millions of workers staged national walkouts four times between 2001 and 2004 in response to Prime Minister Silvio Berlusconi's plans to drastically cut public spending. While economic pressures since the 1990s have caused welfare provisions to become more restrictive, creating more poverty and exclusions, Europeans continue to believe in social citizenship: the state's obligation to guarantee not only the political rights, but the social and economic well-being of its citizens.

These traditions of social solidarity and the continued importance of the welfare state are among the most important components of a European way of life. The United States continues to spend massively on defense (in absolute terms, ten times more than France and Britain), while Europe devotes significant amounts of its resources to public services. Income inequality is also far less extreme in Europe than it is in the United States. Where American society is notorious for huge gaps between its richest and poorest citizens, the European income spectrum is far narrower: 20 percent of Americans are classified as poor, as compared to 8 percent in Europe. More telling than the distribution of wealth, however, are attitudes toward it. To underwrite the welfare state, European citizens pay much higher payroll and income taxes than do Americans. Whereas Americans hold fast to the ethos of self-help and individualism, Europeans on balance thus still favor the values of collective welfare and social equality. Although they want economic growth and see the United States as a role model in some ways, they are unwilling by and large to sacrifice the European way of life to get it.

Yet there are also points of convergence between Europe and the United States. Europe has borrowed from American models of production and consumption throughout the twentieth century, even as it sustained its commitment to social democracy. During the 1980s, scholars spoke of the further Americanization of Europe, pointing to the declining power of European unions and deregulation of the market. And they did so again in the 1990s, when economic recession and rising unemployment made the more market-oriented American economy more of a model for Europeans.

Rather than marking a shift in sensibility and values, however, European convergences with the United States from the 1980s on tend to reflect changing global circumstances, above all, rising economic competition. When the Great Depression hit Europe in the early 1930s, labor unions in France staged successful strikes demanding that governments combat unemployment, guarantee vacations, and shorten the workweek. During the financial crisis of 2008, European workers had no such response. Some commentators point to the success of leaders like the French President Nicolas Sarkozy in thwarting the power of unions. But the truth is more complicated. European workers and their unions are nowhere near as powerful today. While workers still protest layoffs and factory shutdowns, European unions have far fewer members than they traditionally have had, and the bigger unions have fragmented into several smaller ones. Most important, unions have less leverage in today's economic climate, when multinational corporations are choosing increasingly to outsource production to countries with cheaper labor costs. As the head of the largest French union recently put it, "Striking is hardly a threat when management doesn't want you to work."[4] The point is not that Europeans have abandoned their values of social solidarity for American individualism, but rather that the global

---

[4] Katrin Bennhold, "French Unions Losing Influence in Downturn," *The New York Times*, December 26, 2008.

economy is changing in ways that weaken the position of European workers. Yet, even as globalization poses new challenges to the European model of managed capitalism, it is challenging the American model as well.

Europe's Changing Identity

From both an internal and an external perspective, Europe's identity has changed dramatically over the course of the past twenty years. Despite its precipitous fall from global primacy in the aftermath of the Second World War, Europe in the post-1989 era has taken on a new and significant international role. At the same time, dramatic changes in its demography, culture, and political configuration have transformed Europe from within and confronted twenty-first-century Europeans with a host of new challenges.

Europe in the Global Arena With the European empires in collapse and the European states held hostage to the bipolar politics of the Cold War superpowers, the postwar period saw the decisive end to a centuries-long era of European dominance. By the 1990s, however, new developments were again remaking the world order and Europe's place in it. In some ways, these changes reinforced the loss of primacy of Europe's Great Powers. The fall of the Soviet Union deprived Europe of a counterbalance to American influence, while the growth of the EU in some ways has threatened the political sovereignty of the European states. Yet in other ways, these same developments have increased Europe's influence as a whole. The end of the Cold War and the creation of the EU swept away long-standing divisions and forged intra-European unity and cooperation on an unprecedented scale; the EU has also brought economic prosperity to much of the continent and restored some of Europe's political authority.

While European global power has declined irreversibly in absolute terms, Europe has managed to stake out a new role for itself in the post-Cold War world order. American military power remains supreme in the world, but the EU has begun to pose a genuine challenge to the United States with respect to economic power and authority. Over the past two decades, Europe has matched the United States in terms of labor productivity, exports, and the adoption of new telecommunications technology and has outpaced the United States when it comes to protecting the environment.

Politically, Europe still seeks to project its internal values globally. One way is through involvement with its former colonies. Europeans played an important role, for example, in pressuring South Africa to dismantle its apartheid state in the early 1990s. More often than not, however, such exercises have failed. In 1994, for example, ethnically motivated conflict broke out

between Hutus and Tutsis in Rwanda, a former Belgian colony, leading to the genocidal massacre of almost a million Tutsis (about 10 percent of the entire Rwandan population). France, which exercised significant influence in the region, sent troops to Rwanda, although too late and in numbers insufficient to stop the mass killings. Some commentators have laid blame for the genocide on France and the UN, arguing that the French knew that this kind of violence was in the making for years and that, after it did break out, they remained largely passive. But others take the view that French President François Mitterand was unaware of the depths of ethnic hatred or, later, of the staggering scale of the massacres.

There is also a more unequivocally positive side of European global involvements. In 2003, the EU provided more than half of the world's development aid and two thirds of grant-in-aid to poor nations. U.S. foreign aid as a fraction of GNP, by contrast, is less than one-third of the European average. The EU has a far better record than the United States, as well, with respect to environmental causes. While the Bush administration refused to sign the Kyoto Protocol limiting greenhouse gas emissions, the EU states have been leaders in their reduction. The EU also has the greatest number of peacekeepers—ten times that of the United States—in the world. In addition, Europeans have been deeply involved in the promotion of global human rights. In part, they have done so through their involvements in NGOS: Europeans founded Amnesty International, a watchdog organization that monitors rights abuses in countries around the world, as well as Doctors Without Borders (Médecins Sans Frontières), a group of doctors devoted to providing health care to war-torn regions and developing countries. Finally, they have been at the forefront in the development of international human rights law.

Redefining Citizenship The definition of Europe—and the identities and allegiances of Europeans—has also undergone critical transformations since 1989. The downfall of the Soviet bloc erased decades-old lines of political and ideological conflict, creating new possibilities for European political and economic integration. The growth of the EU has exploited these new possibilities, forging unprecedented unity across Europe and producing a new transnational European identity. These developments, however, have called into question the power and scope of the traditional nation-state, and other trends have reinforced that challenge: globalization has diminished the hold of national governments on their economies, while the information technology revolution has created a transnational civil society further limiting the nation's purview. At the same time, decades of migration to

Europe has produced a community of immigrants who define themselves as outsiders with respect to European culture. They have forced Europeans to begin to rethink the connections between ethnicity, culture, and citizenship.

Yet, for all these changes, it would be a mistake to see the European nation-state as in serious decline. On the contrary, national borders and cultures remain enormously important. Transnational organizations such as the UN and the Council of Europe may play a more important role than they did before, but their significance should not be exaggerated. The power of individuals and global networks has grown but, in many ways, they are no match for state power. In short, while its boundaries are more porous, its authority more circumscribed, and its culture more diverse, the European nation-state continues to exercise enormous power and, moreover, to occupy a role of central importance in the governance and identification of most of its citizens. By the same token, although the EU has introduced the concept of a transnational European identity, it has failed to generate the kind of mass loyalty and emotional attachment that the European nation-states still command. It is a paradox, but a historical reality nonetheless, that national identities and nationalist sentiment have undergone a revival at a time of unprecedented transnational cooperation and of the proliferation of social identities that are more deterritorialized—without ties to a particular place—than ever before.

While the nation-state is in no danger of disappearing, the transformations of the past twenty years have certainly posed serious, unresolved challenges to traditional European notions of national identity and citizenship. First, the highly visible presence of immigrant communities has tested definitions of nationality and national culture from below. Although the European states have grappled with their immigrants in a variety of ways, they have tended to use traditional concepts of nationality to exclude more than they have expanded these concepts to incorporate outsiders. At the same time, the development of a transnational European identity and form of citizenship has challenged national identities and legal status from above. Here, however, the effects on national identity and citizenship have varied for different groups. For European elites, it has been a largely positive development. The EU has created not only a unified market but a new kind of cosmopolitan political public. For these groups, EU citizenship complements rather than supplants national citizenship, offering them new kinds of political capital and authority.

But that is not the case for poorer Europeans in general and immigrants in particular. The EU is unique as a transnational political community that confers citizenship, but at the moment it does not offer a form of citizenship that addresses most of the problems faced by immigrants. From a legal standpoint, EU citizenship is a derivative and therefore vulnerable status: one becomes an EU citizen by virtue of being a citizen of an EU member state and, like national citizenship, EU citizenship can be denied by that state. More important, new conceptions of a unified Europe have fostered new modes of exclusion. In Italy, for example, the term "extracommunitario" became a widely used—and pejorative—label for immigrants from outside the EU in the 90s. Like the individual European nation-states, the EU has also tightened its asylum laws, cracked down on illegal immigration, and failed to protect the rights and dignity of immigrant communities. Rather than presenting an alternative, more inclusive political space, the EU, at least for now, is only as inclusive as its nation-states.

Europe thus faces serious challenges in the coming decades. Both the European states and the EU need to rethink policy toward immigrants and their descendents. That policy must protect immigrants' rights—including illegal immigrants—since the exploitation of illegal aliens implicitly puts the rights and protections of all workers at risk. It must also find ways to socially integrate immigrant communities and to address the issue of European racism. Furthermore, national and EU policy must develop different strategies to regulate immigration flows, including revising asylum rules to take greater responsibility for refugees who enter Europe illegally. In addition to incorporating immigrants who already live in Europe, the EU must decide whether to admit Turkey—long seen as a Muslim outsider to Europe—and, if so, on what terms.

But policy change is not enough. Europe must also formulate a new conception of citizenship that takes account of immigrants in a meaningful way. Some theorists argue that the traditional nation-state, which ties citizenship to shared culture, no longer offers a viable model of citizenship in an era characterized by global migration and increasingly diverse societies. They assert that national citizenship by necessity excludes those who do not belong to the national community in both political and cultural terms; they therefore advocate replacing national citizenship with transnational citizenship, which would by definition separate political belonging from nationality and cultural identity. This separation then could be institutionalized in multiple ways: in the laws and political bodies of nations; in policies that foster social inclusion regardless of cultural identity; and through more fluid boundaries between nation-states. As articulated by, among others, the German political philosopher Jürgen Habermas, this ideal bases European citizenship in shared civil rights rather than common culture, envisioning a Europe that is politically homogeneous but culturally diverse as the best protection for the rights of immigrants.

Some scholars, however, take issue with the idea that European democracy and social justice are best served through the strengthening and broadening of transnational citizenship. They emphasize the fact that it is European nation-states—not the EU or NGOs—which control education, social welfare, public health, and the social distribution of resources. They argue further that, while universal human rights are increasingly widely recognized and morally bolstered by the emergence of a transnational civil society devoted to their promotion, it is nevertheless nation-states that have to put these rights into practice; by extension, it is within the framework of the nation-state that rights must be claimed. For these reasons, they contend, the development of a more robust and inclusive model of national citizenship remains the best guarantor of human rights.

Other commentators hedge their bets, urging that rights be strengthened and criteria for citizenship expanded within both national and transnational contexts. They also point to the longer-term ways in which the development of a transnational, multicultural Europe is itself enlarging and revising definitions of citizenship in positive ways. According to this view, the EU is not superseding the European nation-states, and immigrant communities are not destroying national cultures; on the contrary, their coexistence has granted greater legitimacy to multiple identities, making it possible for an individual to see him or herself, for example, as European, French, and Algerian at the same time.

While theorists and politicians disagree about which of these models of citizenship offers the most compelling vision of a future Europe, one thing is clear: the forces that have eroded the old Europe of nation-states and created a new transnational and multicultural model have compelled Europeans to begin to think about how to build a community out of difference. While they have far to go before this community has incorporated its disenfranchised immigrants, they have embarked on the project. Europe is, in the words of the political philosopher Étienne Balibar, "a democracy under construction."[5]

[5] Étienne Balibar, *We, The People of Europe? Reflections on Transnational Citizenship* (Princeton: Princeton University Press, 155).

Summary

In the past twenty years, a host of developments have fundamentally altered European identity. The end of the Cold War and demise of the Soviet Union reconfigured the ideological and political boundaries of Europe, ending fifty years of bipolar politics. The coming of capitalism to Eastern Europe also brought dangerous dislocation, and political freedom allowed ethnic conflicts to erupt. The development of the EU has integrated Europe politically and economically, and strengthened its global political position. Globalization has transformed Europe's economic landscape, further integrating the European economies into the world economy and facilitating the flow of capital, goods, ideas, and images across borders, while confronting Europe with increased international competition. New information technologies, so central to global economic integration, have also altered the content of national cultures, allowing Europeans to forge transnational connections and build global cultural identities. Meanwhile, decades of postcolonial immigration have created a genuinely multicultural Europe, but also a racialized and stratified one, forcing European nations to rethink their definitions of citizenship. Europe is in the process of redefining its place in the international order, particularly as the power of the United States seems in some ways to be waning. While it is likely to be China or India that will usurp its position in the future, if Europe can address its most pressing problems at home, it can continue to be a key protagonist in the global arena, one that plays a role in formulating the agenda of world politics.

QUESTIONS FOR FURTHER THOUGHT

1. How do you explain the growth of the European Union despite hesitant beginnings, frequent disagreements, and continual setbacks that all along the way have led most commentators to predict its failure?

2. Why did the Communist regimes in Eastern Europe fail?

3. How has immigration in the postwar period changed Europe politically and culturally?

RECOMMENDED READING

Sources

Ash, Timothy Garton. *The Magic Lantern: The Revolution of '89 Witnessed in Warsaw, Budapest, Berlin, and Prague.* 1990. An eyewitness account by a particularly keen and informed observer.

Gorbachev, Mikhail. *Perestroika: New Thinking for Our Country and the World.* 1989. This presentation of Gorbachev's vision of the future is as revealing for the issues it does not address as for its specific recommendations.

Studies

Ash, Timothy Garton. *The Polish Revolution: Solidarity.* 1984. Rich in insights into the social roots, techniques, ideas, and effectiveness of a moment that captured worldwide attention.

Balibar, Etienne. *We, the People of Europe? Reflections on Transnational Citizenship.* 2004. Essays by a well-known French political philosopher on a range of topics, including the impact of globalization and the EU on concepts of citizenship.

Berezin, Mabel and Martin Schain, eds. *Europe without Borders: Remapping Territory, Citizenship, and Identity in a Transnational Age.* 2003. An interdisciplinary exploration of the transformation of European political and cultural identity since the formation of the EU.

Burgess, Michael. *Federalism and the European Union.* 2000. Reviews the history of the European Union to make the case for the continuing importance of the national states within it.

Caplan, Richard, and John Feffer. *Europe's New Nationalism: States and Minorities in Conflict.* 1996. Essays on regions from Scotland to Eastern Europe that discuss the important historical issues raised by some of the less-familiar outbursts of nationalism since the end of the Cold War.

Gaspard, Françoise. *A Small City in France.* 1995. An account of the 1983 rise to power of the right-wing National Front party in Dreux in northern France by a historian and former mayor of the city.

Göktürk, Deniz, David Gramling, and Anton Kaes, eds. *Germany in Transit: Nation and Migration 1995–2005.* 2007. An excellent sourcebook of documents charting Germany's development into a multi-ethnic society.

Hoskins, Geoffrey. *The Awakening of the Soviet Union.* 1990. An excellent overview of how change came to a society that had resisted it for so long.

Hughes, H. Stuart. *Sophisticated Rebels.* 1990. An intellectual historian considers the nature of dissent in the West as well as in Eastern Europe during the critical years of 1988 and 1989.

Hulsberg, Werner. *The German Greens: A Social and Political Profile.* 1988. A systematic treatment of the strongest of the European environmental movements.

Janssens, Ruud, and Rob Kroes, eds. *Post-Cold War Europe, Post-Cold War America.* 2004. Examines Europe's changing relationship to the United States in the aftermath of the Cold War.

Jarausch, Konrad H. *The Rush to German Unity.* 1994. Uses recently opened archives to provide a historian's assessment of the complicated events that united the two Germanies.

Kennedy, Paul. *Preparing for the Twenty-First Century.* 1993. A historian's skeptical look at power relations in the near future.

Laurence, Jonathan, and Justin Vaisse. *Integrating Islam: Political and Religious Challenges in Contemporary France.* 2006. A well-documented study of the interaction between French Muslims and the state.

Lewin, Moshe. *The Gorbachev Phenomenon.* 1988. A brilliant analysis written as the phenomenon was unfolding that relates current events to the developments in Soviet society over the previous fifty years.

Maier, Charles S. *Dissolution: The Crisis of Communism and the End of East Germany.* 1997. Connects domestic and international politics to ideology and social conditions to explain the collapse of communism and the German unification.

Modood, Tariq, and Pnina Werbner, eds. *The Politics of Multiculturalism in the New Europe: Racism, Identity, and Community.* 1997. Essays present multicultural policies as the outcome of negotiations between European governments and ethnic minorities.

Pagden, Anthony, ed. *The Idea of Europe: From Antiquity to the European Union.* 2002. A set of essays charting how the conception of Europe has evolved over the centuries.

Panayi, Panikos. *An Ethnic History of Europe since 1945.* 2000. Compares the experience of ethnic minorities across Europe.

Parker, Geoffrey. *The Logic of Unity.* 1975. Usefully analyzes the forces for European unity from a geographer's perspective.

Reid, T.R., *The United States of Europe: The New Superpower and the End of American Supremacy.* 2004. Argues that American individualism is a thing of the past and that European cooperation represents the future.

Sheehan, James. *Where Have All the Soldiers Gone: The Transformation of Modern Europe.* 2008. A compelling analysis of Europe's turn away from war and armed conflict in the postwar era.

Silber, Laura, and Allan Little. *The Death of Yugoslavia.* 1995. A moving, penetrating, and unusually balanced account.

Stiglitz, Joseph. *Making Globalization Work.* 2006. An economist and Nobel Laureate examines the failure of globalization to benefit many and proposes ways to reform the process.

Glossary

absolutism Political doctrine that the monarch is the source of all authority and government in a kingdom.

Academy Quarter of Athens in which Plato established a school.

Aeneid Epic poem by Roman poet Virgil about the founding of Rome.

agora Central market of a polis.

Allah Islamic term for God that derives from the Arabic word *al ilah*, meaning "The God."

Amon-Re "Hidden"; an unseen, universal god of Egypt.

Anabaptists Individuals who, pointing out that the Bible nowhere mentions infant baptism, argued that the sacrament was effective only if the believer understood what was happening and that therefore adults ought to be rebaptized. Opponents argued that infant baptism was necessary so that a baby would not be denied salvation if it died young.

anarchists Radical activists who called for the abolition of the state, sometimes by violent means.

anti-Semitism Anti-Jewish sentiment used to reinforce conservative, antiliberal and nationalist politics.

appeasement The policy by antiwar governments in Britain and France to placate Nazi Germany. Culminated in the Munich conference giving Germany control of Czechoslovakia in 1938; encouraged further German aggression.

apprenticeship Method by which young candidates, or apprentices, studied a particular trade under a master of that skill before admittance into the guild.

Areopagus Rock in central Athens that gave its name to a powerful governing council.

Arianism Heresy based on the teaching of Arius, an Alexandrian priest, which denied that Jesus was coequal with God the Father.

assignats Paper money issued by the French revolutionary governments, whose value was backed by nationalized church lands.

aton Disk of the sun, worshiped by Akhnaton, an Egyptian pharaoh.

Augustus "Most honored"; name conferred on the first emperor of Rome.

balance of power The belief that no one state should be permitted a dominant role in international affairs, and that alliances among their neighbors ought to restrain ambitious rulers.

Baroque Ornate style of art, music, literature, and architecture that emerged in the seventeenth century, characterized by an emphasis on grandeur, power, drama, and rich color.

Bastille A fortress prison seized on July 14, 1789, by Parisians looking for munitions to repulse the royal army; the event symbolized the Revolution's popular support.

Beguines Pious laywomen who lived in communities outside of convents.

Beowulf Anglo-Saxon epic that illustrates the weakness of tribal kingship.

Bill of Rights Document (usually only in a constitutional system) listing the protections from government oppression enjoyed by individual citizens.

billeting Providing board and lodging for troops by making ordinary citizens house and feed soldiers in their homes.

biometry The application of statistical methods to the analysis of biology and medicine.

Bismarck, Otto von The chief minister of Prussia's king, he masterminded the unification of Germany through military aggression and nationalist appeals.

Black Death Great plague of the fourteenth century that spread throughout Europe and resulted in huge loss of human life.

blitzkrieg "Lightning war"; German military tactic in which enemies were overrun with lightning speed using tanks and air power; led to the quick defeat of Poland in 1939 and France in 1940.

Bolsheviks "Majority faction"; the Leninist wing of the Russian Marxist party; after 1917, the Communist party.

broadsides Brief pamphlets or leaflets, often satiric, making sharp comments about a major issue of the day.

Brumaire The coup d'état in 1799 that overthrew the Directory and led to the dictatorship of Napoleon Bonaparte.

cahiers Grievance petitions written by local electoral assemblies, to be presented to the king by the deputies attending the Estates General in France.

Caliph In the Middle Ages, he was the religious and civil ruler of the Muslim empires, as in the Abbasid Caliphate.

Carolingian minuscule New form of formal, literary writing that used capital letters for the beginning of sentences and lowercase letters for the text.

cartel An informal association of manufacturers or suppliers who maintain prices at a high level and set production limits to control market demand.

Central Powers Name given to the coalition including Germany, Austria-Hungary, Turkey (the Ottoman Empire), and Bulgaria in World War I.

Chartism A mass working-class movement in Britain between 1837 and 1848 that derived its name from the People's Charter, a document calling for universal male suffrage, frequent elections by secret ballot, and other democratic reforms.

chivalry A new code of behavior that refined the manners of knights and nobles and adapted them to life in a noble household.

Cistercians Monastic order founded in 1098; they emphasized the emotional devotion to Christ's and Mary's humility.

Civil Code (Napoleonic Code) A grand codification of French law under Napoleon, which preserved certain gains of the Revolution such as legal equality and the abolition of seigneurial property, while clarifying contract and family law.

Civil Constitution of the Clergy The French Revolution's 1790 reform of the Catholic Church under which priests and bishops were elected by the laity, and parishes and dioceses were redrawn; created opposition to the Revolution and a schism within French Catholicism.

Classicism A movement in the arts that seeks to recapture the style and the subjects associated with ancient Greece and Rome.

Colonial Mandate Designation for the former colonial possessions of Germany and the Ottoman Empire, which the League of Nations placed under the control of the various Allied nations after World War I.

colonus In the Roman Empire, a free man who was settled as a worker on the land of another.

comitatus A Germanic warrior band organized under the leadership of an established chief.

Committee of Public Safety A committee of deputies to the National Convention that set political and military strategy and formed the hub of the revolutionary dictatorship of 1793–1794.

common law Laws that applied to the entire kingdom and were thus distinct from local customs, especially associated with England.

commune In medieval and Renaissance Europe, a self-governing association created by townsmen and headed by elected officials.

Concert of Europe A loose agreement by the major European powers to act together to maintain the conservative order in Europe and repress liberal and nationalistic uprisings after 1815.

Conciliar Movement Advocates of the authority of General Councils, rather than the papacy, in the Roman Church, especially active in the 1400s.

Concordat (of 1801) The religious settlement with Pope Pius VII that made Catholicism the "preferred" religion in France but protected religious freedom for non-Catholics.

confraternity A voluntary association of people; in earlier times, usually associations of laymen who wanted to intensify their religious piety.

Congress of Vienna An international congress that met from 1814 to 1815 to set peace terms for continental Europe after the Napoleonic Wars; notable for its creation of a European balance of power and the restoration of old dynasties.

conquistador A Spanish minor nobleman who led his country's expeditions of conquest into Central and South America in the sixteenth century.

conscription Policy of requiring all males of a certain age to sign up for a nation's army.

Constitutionalism The political doctrine that authority in a state depends on consent by the governed, or at least by the leaders of the society.

consuls Supreme magistrates in the Roman Republic, always holding office in pairs.

Continental System Economic sanctions established by Napoleon under which all ships carrying British goods or trading with Britain, even those from neutral countries, were banned from European ports and subject to seizure.

Corn Laws British grain tariffs seen as benefiting the landed gentry at the expense of higher bread prices for urban consumers; an opposition movement by middle-class reformers led to the repeal of nearly all duties in 1846.

Cortes The legislatures of the Spanish kingdoms—Aragon, Castile, and Navarre—which were made up of representatives of the Church, the aristocracy, and towns.

Counter-Reformation Refers to those who see the Catholic revival of the sixteenth century as a response to the Reformation. Those who consider it a natural development within the Church refer to the revival as the Catholic Reformation.

courtly love The polite relations between men and women.

crusades In the eleventh through thirteenth centuries, a series of armed expeditions of Christians to the East to overturn Islamic rule of the Holy Land.

Cubism Art form pioneered by Pablo Picasso and Georges Braque in the early twentieth century that rejected the artistic conventions of three-dimensional perspective and naturalistic representation for a flat, two-dimensional perspective and an abstract style.

Cuneiform System of writing by pressing wedge (Lat. *cuneus*) into clay.

curia regis An assembly of men who advised the king and acted as his principal court.

curiales Councilors in the Roman Empire.

curia Town council in the Roman Empire; later means royal court and central directing body of the Roman Catholic Church.

Cyrillic alphabet Developed by Cyril, a Slavonic script based on Greek letters.

danse macabre "Dance of death"; popular artist motif that depicted people from all different walks of life dancing with a skeleton as a foretaste of their deaths.

decolonization The gradual postwar withdrawal of European nations from colonial empires and the rise of national self-determination in former colonies; initiated a new era of global politics that intersected with the Cold War.

deism Belief in the existence of a supreme being but arising from reason rather than revelation.

Delian League Alliance of Greek states headed by Athens; became the Athenian Empire.

demesne land Land, worked by serfs, that the lord held for his own crops and profit.

demographic transition A pattern of declining birth rate accompanied by a more rapidly falling mortality rate that is characteristic of modern societies.

dialectic The art of analyzing logical relationships among propositions in a dialogue or discourse. Later, a philosophical term for Hegel, who applies the term simultaneously to both world history and ideas. It describes the development from one stage of consciousness to a superior one through a dynamic process of the fusion of contradictions into a higher truth.

dictator In the Roman Republic, a supreme officer whose term was limited to six months; this limit was broken by Sulla and Julius Caesar.

Diet The legislature of the Holy Roman Empire and many German states, bringing together representatives of princes, cities, and the Church.

Directory The centrist republican regime in France between 1795 and 1799; characterized by a weak executive, political polarization, and instability.

Divine Comedy Written by Dante, a medieval poem of personal spiritual exploration.

divine right of kings The belief that a monarch's powers derived directly from God, and thus that treason was a kind of blasphemy.

Doctrine of Petrine Succession The traditional Catholic (and medieval) view that Jesus himself endowed the apostle Peter with supreme responsibility for his church.

doctrine of survivals A term first employed by the anthropologist Edward Tyler (1832–1917) to refer to vertigial cultural phenomena from the past that continue to survive even though they have lost their utility.

Dorian Greeks Last wave of Greeks to immigrate, speaking the Doric dialect.

dynasty A family, usually of rulers, that maintains its authority from generation to generation.

East India Co. (British) A corporation that initially traded with native groups in India but eventually exercised an oppressive colonial dominance over Indian affairs.

enclosure The act of consolidating and fencing in land used in open-field agriculture or village common land.

Entente Powers Name of the members of the Triple Entente of 1907—Britain, France, and Russia—which expanded during World War I to include Belgium, Serbia, Greece, Italy, Romania, the Soviet Union, and the United States.

entrepreneur A person who organizes and assumes risk in a business venture in hopes of making a profit.

Epicureans Followers of the philosopher Epicurus who taught that everything is made of atoms (*a-toma* in Greek) and recommended a quiet life free of powerful emotional attachments.

epicycles In traditional astronomy, small circular orbits, revolving around the main circular orbit, that planets follow as they move through the sky.

epistemology Theory of how one obtains and verifies knowledge or truth.

equestrians Originally the Roman cavalry; became the business class of Rome.

Estates In a number of countries in Europe, representative assemblies that were composed of three houses of representatives: the clergy, the nobility, and townsmen.

Estates General An assembly convened by Louis XVI in 1789 that represented the clergy, the nobility, and the Third Estate; once used to win support for royal policy, it had not met since 1614.

ethnic cleansing A coordinated assault to drive members of a specific ethnicity out of a particular region.

Eucharist Also known as communion; Christian sacrament offered during a religious service in which consecrated bread and wine are consumed in celebration of the Lord's Last Supper.

eugenics The study of the improvement of the human race through selective breeding to eradicate less desirable traits in society. An extrapolation from the work of Charles Darwin, it was popularized by his cousin Francis Galton (1821–1911), in the nineteenth century.

Eurocommunism An alternative program for Western Europeans who disagreed with Soviet policies (particularly the invasion of Czechoslovakia) in Eastern Europe.

evolution The process by which species develop through the natural selection of traits best adapted to the environment.

existentialism A twentieth-century philosophy asserting that individuals are responsible for their own values and meanings in an indifferent universe.

famine Period of severe food scarcity due to too much or too little rainfall.

fascism A philosophy or system of government that advocates a dictatorship of the extreme right together with an ideology of belligerent nationalism.

fealty An oath, often accompanying the oath of homage, in which the vassal swears to uphold his homage.

feudalism An economic, political, and social organization of medieval Europe. Land was held by vassals from more powerful overlords in exchange for military and other services.

fief Land given to a vassal from his lord in exchange for specified terms of service; sometimes called benefice.

"Final Solution" Based on Nazi theories of racial inferiority, the systematic extermination of Jews in German-occupied Europe in massacres and death camps like Auschwitz from 1941 to 1945. Also known as the Holocaust or the Shoah.

Five-Year Plans Plans for the rapid, massive industrialization of the nation under the direction of the state initiated by the Soviet Union in the late 1920s.

forms In the thought of Plato, perfect models of all things; any object we see in life is only an imperfect imitation of the object's form (in Greek, *idea*, meaning something that can be seen).

Franco-Prussian War The conflict from 1870 to 1871 that led to the unification of Germany and (indirectly) to the creation of the French Third Republic; signaled the rise of Germany as a military power.

Frankfurt Parliament The assembly elected in 1848 to unify the various states of Germany under a new liberal constitution and a single monarch; it was dissolved in 1849 when Prussia spurned its projects.

Freikorps German postwar paramilitary groups, consisting mainly of war veterans, employed by both the new republican government and especially by far-right political movements such as the Nazis; literally "volunteer troops."

"general will" Rousseau's idealized concept of popular consensus, under which individual interests are subordinated to the public good.

gentry Owners of significant country estates in England, forming a distinct social group immediately below the nobility.

glasnost A Soviet policy under Mikhail Gorbachev permitting a more open discussion of political and social issues and freer dissemination of news and information.

Golden Horde The capital of a division of the Mongol Empire at Sarai, on the lower Volga River.

Gothic Style of Western European architecture and art that developed in the twelfth century; the style is characterized by vaulting and pointed arches.

Great Schism Major split of the Church in the period of 1378–1417, in which two, and later three, popes fought over the rule of the Church.

Greek Orthodox Church Modern term for the Eastern Orthodox Church, whose main departure from Catholicism is their belief that, in the Holy Trinity, the Holy Spirit proceeds only from the father.

guerillas In Spain during the Napoleonic occupation, groups of irregular fighters who harassed French troops, restricted access to supplies, and punished collaborators; a pioneering model for modern guerrilla warfare.

guilds Associations formed by merchants and master artisans to defend and promote their interests and to regulate the quality of the goods they produced and sold.

Hanseatic League Association of northern European trading cities that by the fourteenth century had imposed a monopoly over cities trading in the Baltic and North Seas.

heavy-wheeled plow A heavy, powerful plow that cut more deeply into the ground, forming furrows that drained excess water. It permitted cultivation of heavier river valley soils.

Hellenistic Age In Greek history, the period 323–330 B.C.

helots Publicly owned slaves in Sparta.

heresy Any belief contrary to church dogma; from Greek *hairesis*, "choice."

hieroglyphs "Sacred carvings"; Egyptian style of writing using pictures.

hijra Muhammad's migration from Mecca to Medina in 622; it marks the beginning of the Islamic calendar.

homage An oath of allegiance sworn by a vassal to his lord.

home front In the new time of total war during World War I, civilians—mostly women and men ineligible for military duty—remaining at home assumed a primary role in the national economy; their continued efforts were held up as indispensable to the war being fought on the military front.

Homo erectus "Erect human being"; predecessor of the modern human species *Homo sapiens*.

Humanism An intellectual movement of the Renaissance that emphasized the importance of having the ability to read, understand, and appreciate the writings of the ancient world.

Hundred Years' War War between France and England fought in the fourteenth and fifteenth centuries. Allegedly sparked by a dispute over French royal succession.

Hussites Followers of Hus, the Bohemian priest whose practices attempted to reduce the distinction between priest and worshippers.

iconoclasm In the Byzantine Empire, a rejection of religious icons or pictures of Jesus, Mary, and the saints that led to the destruction of a number of these religious images.

imperium Power of command held by Roman officers.

Impressionists A group of artists who conveyed subjective experiences by capturing the effects of light and color on canvas.

induction Starting with observation, the logical process by which one moves to general principles.

indulgences Grants to sinners by the Roman Catholic Church that reduce time for their souls in purgatory before they can ascend to heaven.

Inquisition A special papal court instituted by Pope Gregory IX for the purpose of rooting out heresy.

intendants French officials who ruled the country's provinces as direct representatives of the king.

Investiture Controversy Conflict between the German emperor and the pope over who had the authority to appoint bishops and "invest" them with their spiritual symbols of office, the ring and the staff.

Islam Strong monotheistic religion founded by Muhammad.

itinerant justices English justices who traveled and heard both criminal and civil pleas. In both cases, they relied on the testimony of a jury.

iurisprudentes **or** *iurisconsulti* Jurists or advisers in the Roman legal system whose opinions shaped laws.

ius civile "Civil law," or law relating to Roman citizens.

ius gentium "Law of the nations"; Roman law as applied to noncitizens or to all cultures.

Jacobin Club An influential political club whose leaders propelled the French Revolution toward a democratic republic and supported the use of severe repression against the Revolution's enemies.

Jacquerie French peasant revolt in 1358.

jingoism Attitude of extreme and belligerent patriotism often used to gain popular support for war and other political causes.

Julio-Claudians Dynasty of related rulers from 27 B.C. to A.D. 68 in Rome.

July Monarchy The liberal constitutional monarchy established in France from 1830 to 1848, in which the House of Orléans replaced the Bourbons; its modest reforms benefited most the wealthy middle class.

June Days An uprising in Paris in 1848 by radicals and workers that was brutally suppressed by government forces of France's new republic; the event symbolized the conflict between liberal democracy and working-class militancy.

Junkers Prussian aristocrats whose large estates and tradition of military and bureaucratic service ensured their dominance within the Prussian state.

justification by faith A central tenet of Luther's theology: belief that one is saved through the grace of God rather than good deeds.

Justinian's Code Known as the *Corpus Iuris Civilis*, this was the codification of Roman law undertaken by the Byzantine Emperor Justinian in 528.

Keynesian economics Economic theories and programs ascribed to John M. Keynes and his followers. Keynes argued against a totally laissez-faire economy, urging governments to minimize the effects of boom-and-bust economic cycles by manipulating interest rates and employment (through public works projects).

Koran The Muslim holy book that contains the prophecies Allah revealed to Muhammad; it was written between 651 and 652.

kyrios Greek, roughly "master"—for example, head of a family; used for Christian God.

laissez-faire The theory in which individual self-interest and free markets, rather than state regulation or guild protection, stimulate economic progress.

"last decree" *Senatus consultum ultimum*, "final resolution of the Senate"; an instruction to a consul to "see that the state suffers no harm"; a declaration of martial law, first used in 121 B.C. in Rome.

latifundia Large plantations in the Roman world, worked mainly by slaves.

League of Nations International organization created in the wake of the end of World War I and located in Geneva; the forerunner to the modern-day United Nations.

legion Main unit of the Roman army, in principle 6,000 men.

levée en masse A military draft by the French National Convention in August 1793 of unmarried men between the ages of eighteen and twenty-five that recruited about 300,000 new soldiers.

Linear B Script used on Crete, as well as in Greece, to write the early form of Greek.

Lollards Followers of Wycliffe, a vocal dissenter of the church's leadership. This group became an underground rural movement.

Lyceum School established by Aristotle, meeting in and taking its name from a grove in Athens.

Maastricht Treaty Changed the name of the European Community (EC) to the European Union (EU) in 1992. It also enlarged the powers of its parliament and called for a coordinated foreign policy and a common European currency by 1999.

maat Egyptian concept of right order.

Magna Carta "The Great Charter"; English royal charter of liberties granted by King John in 1215. Intended to settle disputes over the rights and privileges of England's nobility.

Magyars The Hungarian-speaking population of the Hapsburg Empire who began to push for Hungary's independence in the 1840s.

Mannerism Art style that emerged in the sixteenth century in response to the serenity and idealization of the High Renaissance. Mannerism is characterized by distorted, esoteric imagery and a sense of artificiality.

manor An estate held by the lord that included land, the people on the land, and a village, usually with a mill. A fief might contain a number of manors or sometimes just part of one.

manorialism An agricultural, legal, and social organization of land, including a nucleated village, large fields for agriculture, and serfs to work the land.

Marxism The political philosophy of Karl Marx, based on the premise that economic conditions determine the nature of society. Marxists advocate the overthrow of capitalism, which they believe will lead to the establishment of a classless society.

memsahib A term of respect used by Indians to address female social superiors. Used in the nineteenth century to refer to British women in colonial India, the term came to connote the blatant ethnocentrism and spoiled behavior associated with these women.

mendicant Orders of religious men, followers of Sts. Dominic and Francis of Assisi, who preached among the poor townsmen and lived a life of begging.

mercantilism The belief that the amount of wealth in the world was fixed, and that a nation should try to gain as much as it could at the expense of other nations, either by accumulating more gold or, in a more sophisticated version, by improving its balance of trade—that is, by exporting more than it imported. This doctrine led to some governmental regulation of commerce in a number of countries in the seventeenth and eighteenth centuries.

Mesopotamia "Land between the [Tigris and Euphrates] rivers," home of early civilizations.

Messiah In Hebrew, *mashiah:* one anointed by God to rule; title given by Christians to Jesus.

metropole Term used to describe European countries in the context of the dominant economic and cultural relationships they had with their colonies.

Middle Passage The harsh voyage of slaving ships from Africa to the Americas during which an average of 10 percent of the slaves perished.

Minoan Name for civilization on Crete, derived from legendary King Minos.

monasticism Practice of withdrawing from daily life to devote oneself to prayer in isolated communities.

Muslims Those who submit to the will of Allah. In Western Europe, often referred to as Saracens.

nationalism A social and political outlook insisting that the state should embody a national community united by some or all of the following: history, ethnicity, religion, common culture, and language.

nationalization State takeover of privately owned businesses; used in fascist Italy and the Soviet Union, but also in postwar Britain and France, to promote greater economic efficiency and social justice.

natural history The science of the earth's development accomplished through the study of geology, zoology, and botany.

natural rights Liberties that should be common to all people by virtue of their nature as human beings; one basis for the French Declaration of the Rights of Man and Citizen of 1789.

natural selection A central feature of Charles Darwin's (1809–1882) theory of evolution that suggests that only organisms best adapted to their environment survive and transmit their genes to succeeding generations, whereas those less adapted are eliminated.

Nazism The body of political and economic doctrines put into effect by the National Socialist German Workers' party in the Third German Reich. A fascist form of government based on state control of all industry, predominance of groups assumed to be racially superior, and supremacy of the Führer.

Neoclassicism A style of art and poetry inspired by themes from antiquity and its conceptions of form and beauty.

Neolithic Age New Stone Age; date of beginning of agriculture, about 11,000 B.C.

Neoplatonism Influential school of thought during the Renaissance, based on Plato's belief that truth lay in essential but hidden forms.

Neostoicism A sixteenth- and seventeenth-century school of philosophy dedicated to the revival of moral values, such as calmness, self-discipline, and steadfastness, first advanced by the Stoics in ancient Greece and Rome.

New Economic Policy (NEP) Lenin's compromise on economic and social policy for the USSR during the 1920s.

New World Name given to the Americas by sixteenth-century explorers and settlers.

Nicene Creed Declaration made at Nicaea in 325 that Jesus was coeternal with God.

Nominalists Indviduals who subscribed to a school of thought in medieval Europe that rejected abstractions as the subject matter of philosophy and focused instead on one's experience of individual, distinct beings and objects.

North Atlantic Treaty Organization (NATO) Created in 1949 to coordinate military forces from the United States, Canada, and ten Western European nations in response to perceived Soviet threats in Europe.

notables Locally prominent and wealthy individuals whose support for Napoleon and subsequent French governments was encouraged by state recognition and honors.

novus homo A "new man"; in Roman politics, a man elected consul with no ancestor who had held this office.

October Manifesto Declaration by the tsar of Russia in 1905 that provided Russia with a written constitution and guaranteed freedom of speech and assembly.

oligarchy The rule of a state by a small number, often the Wealthy citizens.

open-field system The division of agricultural land on a manor into three large fields. The lord held land for his direct profit in these, and his serfs also had strips of land in all three fields. The land farmed by each individual was therefore mixed in with, and open to, neighboring plots. The medieval system lasted long after serfdom ended in England and France.

oral tradition Tales, songs, and adages passed on orally that were the core of traditional popular culture.

Osiris Egyptian god of fertility.

ostracism Procedure in ancient Athens by which men could be banished from the city; voting was done by scratching names on *ostraka* (potsherds).

Ottoman Empire Powerful and much feared empire of the Ottoman Turks, whose holdings stretched across the Middle East and Europe; began as a small state in the fourteenth century but soon took over Asia Minor and surrounded Byzantine territory, resulting in the fall of Constantinople in 1453.

Paleolithic Age Old Stone Age; age of stone tools, ending about 11,000 B.C.

papal bulls Papal letters, closed with a lead seal, or *bulla*.

papal *curia* The central bureaucracy of the pope; it served as the central financial and judicial administration and selected the new pope.

parlements The chief law courts in the regions of France; the members, who owned their offices, claimed the right to approve royal legislation for their regions, and sometimes clashed with the king.

Parliament English legislature, consisting of a House of Lords whose members were nobles and bishops, and a House of Commons whose members were elected gentry and townsmen.

patricians Upper class, a small minority, in Rome; the status was heredity.

perestroika A policy of economic and governmental reform instituted by Mikhail Gorbachev in the Soviet Union during the mid-1980s.

pharaoh Title of Egyptian kings from the New Kingdom onward.

Pharisees Jewish sect that believed in resurrection and accepted non-Jewish converts.

Philippics Orations by the Athenian politician, Demosthenes, attacking King Philip II of Macedonia; used also to refer to speeches of Cicero against Mark Antony.

philosophes A group of French intellectuals who used rational inquiry to advocate intellectual and religious freedom and a variety of practical reforms.

plebeians The great mass of Roman citizens; they were not blocked from holding office.

polis Especially in classical Greece, a city that was also an independent state, not sharing citizenship with any other state.

Politburo The principal policy-making and executive committee of the Russian Communist party.

postmodernism A later twentieth-century approach to the arts stressing relativism and multiple interpretations.

predestination The belief that God has preordained whether a person will be saved or damned, and nothing can be done to reverse this fate.

prefect The chief administrator in each French department appointed by the central government; a hallmark of centralization established by Napoleon but lasting into the twentieth century.

Principate The Roman Empire from Augustus down to Diocletian, so named from the republican term *princeps*, roughly "first citizen."

protoindustrialization Heavy concentrations of pre-factory manufacturing, in which urban merchants employed rural households to produce goods, especially textiles.

psychoanalysis A method of analyzing psychic phenomena and treating emotional disorders that involves treatment sessions during which the patient is encouraged to talk freely about personal experiences and especially about early childhood and dreams.

public sphere Forums outside the royal court, such as newspapers, salons, and academies, in which the educated public could participate in debate on the issues of the day.

Puritans Devout Protestants who believed in a stern moral code and rejected all hints of Catholic ritual or organization.

raj British rule in India, which had spread through most of the subcontinent by the mid-nineteenth century.

realism The depiction of ordinary, everyday subjects in art and literature as part of a broader social commentary; a reaction against the themes and styles typical of Romanticism or of academic painting.

reasons of state Often known by its French name, *raison d'état*, the doctrine that, especially in foreign affairs, a state is bound by no restraint when pursuing its interests.

Reformation The period of major change and variance in the fundamental beliefs of Christianity. The demands of the faithful varied and intensified throughout Western Europe, making it difficult for the Roman Catholic Church alone to accommodate all of them.

relativity Einstein's theory that all aspects of the physical universe must be defined in relative terms.

Renaissance Rebirth of classical culture that occurred in Italy after 1350.

Restorations Attempts by the powers in Europe to restore the dynasties and monarchical institutions (including the Bourbons in France) disrupted by the revolutionary and Napoleonic upheavals.

risorgimento A term meaning "resurgence," used to describe the liberal nationalist movement that led to the unification of Italy by 1870.

Roman Catholic "Universal" church; Christian church headed by a pope.

Romanesque Style of Western European architecture and art developed after 1000; the style is characterized by rounded arches, massive walls, and relatively simple ornamentation.

Romanticism An artistic movement that rejected classical aesthetic forms and norms, and which emphasized personal experience, emotion, or spirituality.

sacrament Means by which God distributes grace. Luther retained only baptism and the Eucharist.

Sadducees Conservative Jewish sect that did not believe in angels or resurrection because such teachings were not found in the five books of the Old Testament, known as the Pentateuch.

sagas Adventure stories told in prose that cover the Viking period to about 1000, when Iceland converted to Christianity.

Saint-Simonians A nineteenth-century movement that called for the reorganization of society by scientists and industrialists to achieve planned progress and prosperity.

salons Social gatherings, usually organized by elite women, that sought to promote discussion of Enlightenment ideas.

sans-culottes Parisian militants, mainly artisans and shopkeepers, who called for repression of counter-revolutionaries, price controls, and direct democracy; helped bring the Jacobins to power in 1793.

satyr play Comic, often vulgar, play performed after an ancient Greek tragedy.

Schlieffen Plan In World War I, the German military plan specifying how the army would fight a two-front war: Germany would invade Belgium and the Netherlands on its way to France, score a quick defeat in the west, and then concentrate its forces against Russia in the east.

Scholasticism A form of argument, or dialectic, developed in the Middle Ages, particularly with Abelard and Thomas Aquinas.

Scientific Revolution The succession of discoveries and the transformation of the investigation of nature that was brought about in the fields of astronomy, physics, and anatomy during the sixteenth and seventeenth centuries.

Second Empire The reign of Napoleon III in France from 1852 to 1870; while authoritarian in nature, the regime fostered popular support through social programs and nationalist sentiment.

second front In World War II, the establishment of an Allied front in Western Europe to match the Russians battling the Nazis in the East; after several delays, the Allies launched the second front with the Normandy invasion in June 1944.

seigneurialism A system prevalent in Western Europe by which peasants owed various fees and dues to the local lord even if the peasants owned their land.

serf or villein Peasant who was personally free, but bound to the lord of a manor and worked the land on the manor.

serfdom A feudal system of agricultural exploitation in which peasants were bound to their lord's estate and owed him forced labor.

sexagesimal System of mathematics based on the number 60.

sexual selection The theory that the traits that increase an organism's (typically male's) success in mating and transmitting its genes are selected and perpetuated. Differs from natural selection, which focuses only on traits that influence survival.

shell shock New psychological diagnosis applied to those soldiers exhibiting signs of psychic distress during the First World War, thought to be caused by the near-constant shelling experienced in the trenches.

sister republics States and territories that fell under French control during the Directory and were reconstituted as republics in collaboration with native revolutionaries.

Skepticism Philosophy that questions whether human beings can ever achieve certain knowledge.

Slavophiles Russian intellectuals who opposed Westernization and saw Russia's unique institutions and culture as superior; some supported autocracy but also favored emancipation of the serfs.

social Darwinism The application of Darwin's scientific theory of evolution to society, often in the service of reactionary and even racist ideas.

social welfare State-run programs for social security, education, medical care, and family benefits.

Sophists Teachers of rhetoric in classical Greece, especially in Athens.

Stalingrad The place where Russians fought ferociously, street by street, to halt the German advance in 1942; marked the turning point of the war on the Eastern front.

state of nature Description in political theory of the condition of humanity before the creation of governments.

steam engine A machine patented in 1782 that converted steam into mechanical energy; provided a cheap and flexible source of power critical for early industrialization.

Stoics Followers, in Greece and Rome, of thought of Zeno, who taught that the wise man leads a life of moderation, unmoved by joy or grief, and stands by his duty according to natural law.

strategic bombing A military doctrine of aerial bombardment of populated and industrial areas; intended to destroy morale and the industrial capacity to fight. Initiated by the Germans on Britain, but most fully used by the British and U.S. air forces.

Sturm und Drang A literary and artistic movement in Germany that emphasized strong artistic emotion; a precursor of the Romantic movement.

subinfeudation The grant of a fief by a vassal to a subordinate who becomes his vassal.

Sunni-Shiite schism Division within the Islamic religion over who should rule after Mohammad's death.

syndicalism A movement in which worker's organizations attempted to destroy bourgeois capitalism and gain control of industry by general strikes.

Talmud General body of Jewish tradition.

tariff A duty or custom fee imposed on imports, often to protect local agriculture or industry from competition.

Tetrarchy Rule of four co-emperors of Rome under Diocletian.

Thermidorian reaction The period between the fall of Robespierre and the establishment of the Directory during which the Convention dismantled the Terror and attacked egalitarian politics.

thermodynamics The study of the relationships between heat and other forms of energy; becomes one of the bases of nineteenth-century physics.

three-field system Agricultural system in which two-thirds of the land was cultivated on a rotating basis; it replaced the two-field system and resulted in increased productivity.

Tory English political party committed to a strong monarch and a strong Anglican Church.

total war Unprecedented type of warfare in which all segments of society, civilians and soldiers, men and women, were mobilized in the hope of ensuring victory.

totalitarianism A twentieth-century form of authoritarian government using force, technology, and bureaucracy to effect rule by a single party and controlling most aspects of the lives of the population.

tragedy The supreme dramatic form in ancient Greece, usually treating a mythological theme and leading to catastrophe for some of the characters.

transubstantiation Belief that bread and wine are transformed into the body and blood of Christ during the Eucharist.

Treaty of Paris (1763) Peace treaty ending the British and French war for empire in which France surrendered Canada to the British and lost its foothold in India.

Treaty of Tordesillas Signed in 1494, the treaty confirmed the pope's division of the world between the Portuguese and Spanish for exploration and conquest. Under its terms, a line was drawn some 1,200 miles west of the Cape Verde Islands, with Portugal granted all lands to the west and Spain granted all lands to the east.

trench warfare Static, defensive type of combat seen mostly on the Western front of World War I, where a war of attrition was fought in a complex system of underground trenches and supply lines.

triangular trade A complex pattern of colonial commerce between the home country (Britain or France) and its colonies in which refined or manufactured goods were exchanged for raw materials or slaves from West Africa.

tribunes Ten Roman plebeians, elected to protect the common people; some of them became powerful political activists.

triremes Greek warship, powered by three banks of oars.

triumvirate "Body of three men," a term applied to two such cabals in the Roman Republic.

trivium and quadrivium School curriculum that became the standard program of study in universities. The trivium comprised the verbal arts (grammar, rhetoric, and logic), while the quadrivium comprised the mathematical arts (arithmetic, astronomy, geometry, and music).

troubadour A writer of vernacular romantic lyrics or tales who enjoyed the patronage of nobles around Europe in the twelfth through fifteenth centuries.

tsar Title adopted by the Russian king; the term was the Slavic equivalent of the Latin term *caesar*.

tyrant In ancient Greek states, a powerful man who ruled in a polis without legal sanction, not necessarily a cruel despot.

ultraroyalists French reactionaries who not only supported divine-right monarchy but called for the return of lands taken from the émigrés during the Revolution.

usury Interest of profit on a loan; it was prohibited by the Church.

Utilitarianism British reform movement that believed that society should be based on "the greatest happiness for the greatest number," and that sound governments could make such calculations.

utopian Having to do with an ideal society, as presented in Sir Thomas More's book *Utopia*, which means "nowhere" in Greek.

vassal A free warrior who places himself under a lord, accepting the terms of loyal service, fighting in times of war, and counseling in times of peace.

Vatican II Vatican council called by Pope John XXIII in 1962. Vatican II made the leadership of the Church more international, directed attention to the concerns of developing nations, and ordered that Masses be conducted in the vernacular instead of Latin.

Vulgate The Latin translation of the Bible in the fourth century, identified with St. Jerome, which became the medieval Church's standard text and was deemed holy in the sixteenth century.

war guilt clause Article 231 of the Treaty of Versailles, specifying that Germany alone was responsible for causing the First World War.

Warsaw Pact The Russian response to NATO; an international military organization established in 1955 that included the Soviet Union and Eastern European communist states.

Weimar Republic Left-liberal German government established after the war, named for the city where German politicians formed the republic; instituted universal suffrage, and wrote a new democratic constitution.

Wergeld Literally, "man-payment"; in Germanic tribes, as a means to prevent feuds, payments given in compensation for crimes committed; the amount of compensation depended on the social rank of the individual.

Whig English political party committed to a strong Parliament and religious toleration.

Yalta Conference In February 1945, the meeting between Roosevelt, Churchill, and Stalin to set the postwar order in Europe. The conference agreed on the creation of the United Nations but was unable to counter future Soviet dominance in Eastern Europe.

Zeus Sky god; the chief god in Greek myth.

ziggurat Terraced tower built of baked brick in Mesopotamia.

Zollverein A customs union established by Prussia among most states in the German Confederation that allowed for free movement of goods; promoted the economic unification of Germany.

Text Credits

Chapter 15

Page 423 Walter Scott (ed.), A Collection of Scarce and Valuable Tracts, on the Most Interesting and Entertaining Subjects: But Chiefly Such as Relate to the History and Constitution of These Kingdoms, Vol. 1, London, 1809, pp. 429–430. **Page 437** From Thomas Carlyle (ed.), Oliver Cromwell's Letters and Speeches, Vol. 3, London, 1908, pp. 230, 231 and 235. **Page 439** From Louis Andre (ed.), Testament politique (Editions Robert Laffont, 1947), pp. 347–348 and 352, translated by Theodore K. Rabb. **Page 441** Adapted from J. H. Elliott, Imperial Spain, 1469–1716. Edward Arnold, The Hodder Neadling PLC Group, 1964, p. 175.

Chapter 16

Page 454 From Giorgio de Santillana, "Galileo and Kepler on Copernicus", from The Crime of Galileo. Chicago: University of Chicago Press, 1955, pp. 11 and 14–15. Reprinted by permission of University of Chicago Press. **Page 469** From Jan de Vries, The Economy of Europe in an Age of Crisis, 1600–1750. Cambridge University Press, 1976, p. 5. Reprinted by permission of Cambridge University Press. **Page 476** From George L. Burr (ed.), "The Witch Persecutions," Translations and Reprints from the Original Sources of European History, Vol. 3, Philadelphia: University of Pennsylvania, 1902, pp. 13–14.

Chapter 17

Page 483 From J. M. Thompson, Lectures on Foreign History, 1494–1789, Oxford: Blackwell, 1956, pp. 172–174. **Page 488** From Church. PEURCIV LOUIS SIV, 1E. © 1959 Wadsworth, a part of Cengage Learning, Inc. Reproduced by permission. www.cengage.com/permissions. **Page 488** From John C. Rule, "Louis SIV, Roi-Bureaucrate," in Rule (ed.), Louis SIV and the Craft of Kingship, Columbus: Ohio State University Press, 1969, pp. 91–92. **Page 506** From John Locke, The Second Treatise of Civil Government, Thomas P. Peardon (ed.), Indianapolis: Bobbs-Merrill, 1952, chapter 9, pp. 70–73.

Chapter 18

Page 521 A. Smith, an Inquiry into the Nature and Causes of the Wealth of Nations, 1776, Book 4, ch. 2. **Page 523** Andrew Ure, The Philosophy of Manufactures, 1835. **Page 527** Alexander Radischev, A Journey from St. Petersburg to Moscow, 1790. **Page 531** Adapted from Phyllis Dean and W. A. Cole, British Economic Growth, 1688–1959, Cambridge University Press, 1964, p. 49. Reprinted by permission. **Page 532** From Philip D. Curtin, The Atlantic Slave Trade. © 1969. Reprinted by permission of The University of Wisconsin Press. **Page 533** Malachy Postlethwayt, The National and Private Advantages of the African Trade Considered, London 1746.

Chapter 19

Page 545 From C.A. Macartney (ed.), The Habsburg and Hohenzollern Dynasties in the 17th and 18th Centuries, pp. 151 and 155–157. Copyright © 1970 by C. A. Macartney. Reprinted by permission of HarperCollins Publishers. **Page 551** From A Vindication of the Rights of Woman, Norton Critical Edition, Second Edition by Mary Wollstonecraft, edited by Carol H. Poston. Copyright © 1988, 1975 by W. W. Norton & Company, Inc. Used by permission of W. W. Norton & Company, Inc. **Page 552** From Jean-Jacques Rousseau, The Social Contract, Book 1, David Campbell Publishers. **Page 574** Georges Lefebvre, The Coming of the French Revolution. © 1947 Princeton University Press, 1975 renewed PUP. Reprinted by permission of Princeton University Press.

Chapter 20

Page 574 From William Doyle, Origins of the French Revolution, 1988. Reprinted by permission of Oxford University Press. **Page 580** R. R. Palmer, The Age of Democratic Revolution. © 1959 Princeton University Press, 1987 renewed PUP. Reprinted by permission of Princeton University Press. **Page 591** From Robespierre's speech to the convention on "The Moral and Political Principles of Domestic Policy," February 1794.

Chapter 21

Page 617 From Political Constitution of the Spanish Monarchy, proclaimed in Cadiz, March 19, 1812, (trans. James B. Tueller). **Page 621** From B. Las Cases (ed.), Memorial de Sainte-Helene.

Chapter 22

Page 630 From Prince Richard Metternich (ed.), Memoirs of Prince Metternich 1815–1829, Mrs. Alexander Napier (tr.), Scribner's Sons Publishers, 1970. **Page 632** From Louis L. Snyder (ed.), Documents of German History. Rutgers University Press, 1958, pp. 158–159. **Page 636** From B. R. Mitchel, European Historical Staitistics, 1750–1970, 1975, Columbia University Press. Reproduced with permission of Palgrave Macmillan. **Page 647** From Sidney Pollard and Colin Holmes (eds.), Documents of Euopean Economic History, Vol. 1, St. Martin's Press. Rerpinted by permission of Palgrave Macmillan. **Page 648** From John L. and Barbara Hammond, The Rise of Modern Industry, M. S. G. Haskell House, 1925. **Page 648** From Thomas S. Ashton, "The Standard of Life of the Workers in England, 1970–1830," Journal of Economic History, Vol. 9, 1949. Reprinted by permission of Cambridge University Press. **Page 648** From Eric J. Hobsbawm, "The British Standard of Living, 1970–1850," Economic history Review, 1957. Reprinted by permission of John Wiley & Sons, Ltd. **Page 649** From Ronald M. Hartwell, "The Rising Standard of Living in England, 1800–1850," Economic History Review, 1961. **Page 649** From Theodore S. Hamerow, The Birth of a New

Europe: State and Society in the Nineteenth Century, University of North Carolina Press, 1983, pp. 140–141. **Page 652** From William Wordsworth, Preface to the Second Edition of Lyrical Ballads in William Wordsworth: Selected Poems and Prefaces, Jack Stillinger (ed.), Houghton Mifflin, 1965. **Page 655** From John Stuart Mill, "The Subjection of Women," Three Essays. Oxford: Oxford University Press, 1975.

Chapter 23

Page 674 From Louis L. Snyder (ed.), The Documents of German History, New Brunswick: Rutgers University Press, 1958. **Page 681** From Giuseppe Massini, On the Duties of Man. Greenwood Publishing Group. **Page 687** From Louis L. Snyder (ed.), The Documents of German History, New Brunswick: Rutgers University Press, 1958.

Chapter 24

Page 700 From Karl Wittgensteing, "Kartelle in Osterreich," in Gustav Schmoller (ed.), Uber wirtschaftliche Kartelle in Deutschland und im Auslande (Leipzig, 1894); as quoted in Carroll and Embree, Readings in European History since 1814 (1930). **Page 707** From Thomas H. Huxley, Evolution and Ethics and Other Essays, New York: D. Appleton and Company, 1916. **Page 716** From Richard Levy, Antisemitism in the Modern World. Copyright © 1991 by D. C. Heath and Company. Used with permission of Houghton Mifflin Company. **Page 726** From Emmeline Pankhurst, "The Last Fight for Human Freedom," speech given in Canada in 1912 in Brian MacArthur, Twentieth-Century Speeches, New York: Viking, 1992.

Chapter 25

Page 736 G. M. Young (ed.), Speeches by Lord Macauley with his Minute on Indian Education, Oxford University Press, 1935. **Page 751** From the Earl of Cromer, Modern Egypt, vol. I, New York: Macmillan, 1908, pp. xvii–xviii. **Page 763** From Karl Pearson, National Life from the Standpoint of Science, 1900.

Chapter 26

Page 780 Reprinted with the permission of Scribner, a Division of Simon & Schuster Adult Publishing Group from Origins of the World War, Volume II, Revised Edition by Sidney B. Fay. Copyright © 1930 by The Macmillan Company; copyright © 1958 by Sidney Bradshaw Fay. All rights reserved. **Page 793** From Brenda Girvin and Monica Coxens, "Meet the 'Khaki Girls'," The Englishwoman, 1917. **Page 796** From Harold Owen and John Bell (eds.), Wilfred Owen: The Collected Letters, Oxford University Press, 1967. Reprinted by permission. **Page 809** From Sidney Pollard and Colin Holmes (eds.), Documents of European

Economic History, Vol. 3: The End of Old Europe, 1914–1939 (St. Martin's Press, 1972). Reprinted by permission of Palgrave Macmillan.

Chapter 27

Page 820 From Pitirim Alexandrovitch Sorokin, Leaves from a Russian Diary, exp. Ed. 1920; Beacon Press, 1950. **Page 820** From John Reed, Ten Days That Shook the World, 1919. **Page 825** From S. William Halperin (ed.), Mussolini and Italian Fascism (Van Nostrand, 1964). **Page 841** From Salvator Attanasio et al. (trs.), "Speech of Goebbels," in George L. Mosse, Nazi Culture: Intellectual Cultural, and Social Life in the Third Reich, Grosset & Dunlap, 1966. **Page 841** From Salvator Attaasio et al (trs.), Speech of Goebbels, in George L. Mosse, Nazi Culture: Intellectual, Cultural, and Social Life in the Third Reich, University of Wisconsin Press, 1966. Reprinted by permission.

Chapter 28

Page 865 From J. Noakes and G. Pridham (eds.), Nazism 1919–1945 Volume Two, State Economy and Society 1933–1939; A Documentary Reader. ISBN: 0859895998. Reprinted by permission of the University of Exeter Press. **Page 867** From Henry Friedlander, "Step by Step: The Expansion of Murder, 1939–1941," German Studies Review 17, October 1994. Reprinted by permission. **Page 867** From Ernst Nolte, "Between Historical Myth and Revisionism," Yad Vashem Studies 19, 1988. Reprinted by permission. **Page 868** From Peter Baldwin, Reworking the Past. Copyright © 1990 by Peter Baldwin. Reprinted by permission of Beacon Press, Boston. **Page 879** From Winston Churchill speech at Westminster College, Fulton, MO, March 5, 1946. Reproduced with permission from Curtis Brown Ltd., London on behalf of Winston S. Churchill. Copyright Winston S. Churchill.

Chapter 29

Page 888 From Winston Churchill speech at Westminster College, Fulton, MO, March 5, 1946. Reproduced with permission from Curtis Brown Ltd., London on behalf of Winston S. Churchill. Copyright Winston S. Churchill. **Page 889** Speech by Andrei Y. Vishinsky to the United Nations, "November 1, 1948, from Vital Speeches of the Day, Vol. 15, No. 2 (New York: City News Publishing Co., 1949). Reprinted by permission.

Chapter 30

Page 943 From Akural Aynur (tr.), in Ilhan Basgoz and Norman Furniss (eds.), Turkish Workers in Europe, Turkish Studies Publications, 1985. Reprinted by permission.

Index